Writing Arguments

Writing Arguments
A Rhetoric with Readings

Sixth Edition

John D. Ramage
Arizona State University

John C. Bean
Seattle University

June Johnson
Seattle University

PEARSON
Longman

New York   San Francisco   Boston
London   Toronto   Sydney   Tokyo   Singapore   Madrid
Mexico City   Munich   Paris   Cape Town   Hong Kong   Montreal

Senior Vice President and Publisher: Joseph Opiela
Vice President and Publisher: Eben W. Ludlow
Development Manager: Janet Lanphier
Development Editor: Marion B. Castellucci
Executive Marketing Manager: Ann Stypuloski
Senior Supplements Editor: Donna Campion
Media Supplements Editor: Nancy Garcia
Production Manager: Donna DeBenedictis
Project Coordination, Text Design, and Electronic Page Makeup: Elm Street Publishing
     Services, Inc.
Cover Design/Manager: Wendy Ann Fredericks
Cover Art: "Motherhood and Social Housekeeping": Poster emphasizing the maternal role of women
     as a basis for the right to vote. National Museum of American History, Smithsonian Institution,
     Behring Center.
Photo Researcher: Photosearch, Inc.
Manufacturing Buyer: Alfred C. Dorsey
Printer and Binder: R.R. Donnelley & Sons Company, Harrisonburg
Cover Printer: Phoenix Color Corporation

For permission to use copyrighted material, grateful acknowledgment is made to the copyright
holders on pp. 759 to 765, which are hereby made part of this copyright page.

Library of Congress Cataloging-in-Publication Data
Ramage, John D.
          Writing arguments: A rhetoric with readings/John D. Ramage, John C. Bean, June
          Johnson—6th ed.
               p.   cm.
          Includes index.
          ISBN 0-321-16337-0

1. English language—Rhetoric.   2. Persuasion (Rhetoric)
3. College reader's.   4. Report writing.   I. Bean, John C.
II. Johnson, June.   III. Title.
PE1431.R33   2003
808'.0427—dc21

Please visit our website at http://www.ablongman.com/ramage

ISBN 0-321-16337-0 (Complete Edition)
ISBN 0-321-16341-9 (Brief Edition)
ISBN 0-321-16338-9 (Concise Edition)

1 2 3 4 5 6 7 8 9 10—DOH—06 05 04 03

Brief Contents

Detailed Contents   *vii*

Color Plates   *xxxiv*

Preface   *xxxv*

Acknowledgments   *xlv*

Part One   **Overview of Argument**   **1**

1   Argument: An Introduction   3
2   Reading Arguments   22
3   Writing Arguments   49

Part Two   **Principles of Argument**   **73**

4   The Core of an Argument: A Claim with Reasons   75
5   The Logical Structure of Arguments   87
6   Using Evidence Effectively   109
7   Moving Your Audience: *Ethos* and *Pathos*   129
8   Accommodating Your Audience: Treating Differing Views   140
9   Conducting Visual Arguments   165

Part Three   **Arguments in Depth: Six Types of Claims**   **197**

10   An Introduction to the Types of Claims   199
11   Categorical and Definitional Arguments: X Is (Is Not) a Y   208
12   Causal Arguments: X Causes (Does Not Cause) Y   241
13   Resemblance Arguments: X Is (Is Not) Like Y   269
14   Evaluation and Ethical Arguments: X Is (Is Not) a Good Y; X Is Right (Wrong)   289
15   Proposal Arguments: We Should (Should Not) Do X   319

Part Four   The Researched Argument   355

16   Finding and Evaluating Sources   357

17   Using, Citing, and Documenting Sources   384

Appendixes   424

Appendix One   Informal Fallacies   424

Appendix Two   The Writing Community:
                  Working in Groups   438

Part Five   An Anthology of Arguments   457

An Overview of the Anthology   458

Guide Questions for the Analysis and Evaluation of
    Arguments   459

Environmental Friendliness Versus Market Freedom:
    The Case of the Sport-Utility Vehicle   462

Biotechnology, Organic Food, and the Ethics of Food
    Production   486

Responses to Terrorism: Public Safety, Civil Liberties,
    and War   524

Hip-Hop, Film, and Racial Identity   550

Gender and Technology in Advertising   568

Marriage and Family in the New Millennium   576

Globalization, World Markets, and the Carnival Against
    Capitalism   607

Internet Censorship: Hate Sites, Pornography, and Spam   638

Troubled Teens and Violence   657

The Cultural Debate on Stem Cell Research and Cloning   675

Criminal Justice and Postpartum Psychosis: The Case of
    Andrea Yates   705

The United States as Superpower   725

Credits   759

Index   767

Detailed Contents

Color Plates   *xxxiv*

Preface   *xxxv*

Acknowledgments   *xlv*

Part One   Overview of Argument   1

1   Argument: An Introduction   3

What Do We Mean by Argument?   3
    Argument Is Not a Fight or a Quarrel   3
    Argument Is Not Pro-Con Debate   4
    Arguments Can Be Explicit or Implicit   4

"Dulce et Decorum Est" —Wilfred Owen   5
    A World War I poet, describing a gas attack, argues implicitly that it is not sweet and fitting to die for one's country.

The Defining Features of Argument   7
    Argument Requires Justification of Its Claims   7
    Argument Is Both a Process and a Product   9
    Argument Combines Truth Seeking and Persuasion   10

Argument and the Problem of Truth   12

A Successful Process of Argumentation: The Well-Functioning Committee   15

"Petition to Waive the University Mathematics Requirement" —Gordon Adams (student)   17
    A student accepted to law school but delayed by a remaining math requirement argues to be exempted.

Conclusion   21

2   Reading Arguments   22

Why Reading Arguments Is Important for Writers   22

Strategy 1: Reading as a Believer   23

"Playing with Our Food" —Lisa Turner   24

> A health food advocate with training in naturopathy argues against genetic modification of food and the use of irradiation.

Summary Writing as a Way of Reading to Believe   27

Suspending Doubt: Willing Your Own Belief in the Writer's Views   30

Strategy 2: Reading as a Doubter   31

Strategy 3: Exploring How Rhetorical Context and Genre Shape the Argument   33

Understanding the Genres of Argument   33

Analyzing Rhetorical Context and Genre   36

Strategy 4: Seeking Out Alternative Views and Analyzing Sources of Disagreement   37

Disagreement about Facts or Their Relevance   38

Disagreement about Values, Beliefs, or Assumptions   38

"Why Biotech Labeling Can Confuse Consumers" —Council for Biotechnology Information   40

> An organization promoting the value of biotechnology in agriculture argues that biotech foods are safe and that labeling them would confuse consumers and increase food costs.

Writing an Analysis of a Disagreement   43

"An Analysis of the Sources of Disagreement between Lisa Turner and the Council for Biotechnology Information"   43

> In this example essay, we analyze the disagreements of fact and value between two opposing viewpoints on genetically modified food.

Strategy 5: Using Disagreement Productively to Prompt Further Investigation   45

Accepting Ambiguity and Uncertainty   45

Seeking Sources of Facts and More Complete Versions of Alternative Views   46

Determining What Values Are at Stake for You and Articulating Your Own Values   47

Considering Ways to Synthesize Alternative Views   47

Conclusion   48

3   Writing Arguments   49

Who Writes Arguments and Why?   49

Tips for Improving Your Writing Process   52

Starting Point   52

Exploring, Researching, and Rehearsing   53

Writing a First Draft   53
Revising through Multiple Drafts   54
Editing for Style, Impact, and Correctness   55

Using Exploratory Writing to Discover Ideas and Deepen
    Thinking   56
Freewriting or Blind Writing   56
Idea Mapping   57
Playing the Believing and Doubting Game   58
Brainstorming for Pro and Con *Because* Clauses   60
Brainstorming a Network of Related Issues   61

Shaping Your Argument: Classical Argument as a Planning Tool   62
The Structure of Classical Argument   62
An Illustration of Classical Argument as a Planning Guide   65

Discovering Ideas: Two Sets of Exploratory Writing Tasks   67
Set 1: Starting Points   67
Set 2: Exploration and Rehearsal   69

Writing Assignments for Chapters 1–3   70

Part Two   Principles of Argument   73

4   The Core of an Argument: A Claim with Reasons   75

The Rhetorical Triangle   75

Issue Questions as the Origins of Argument   76
Difference between an Issue Question and an Information
    Question   77

Difference between a Genuine Argument and a
    Pseudo-Argument   79
Pseudo-Arguments: Fanatical Believers and Fanatical Skeptics   79
Another Source of Pseudo-Arguments: Lack of Shared
    Assumptions   79

Frame of an Argument: A Claim Supported by Reasons   81
What Is a Reason?   81
Advantages of Expressing Reasons in *Because* Clauses   82

Application of this Chapter's Principles to Your Own Writing   84

Application of this Chapter's Principles to the Reading
    of Arguments   86

Conclusion   86

5   The Logical Structure of Arguments   87

An Overview of *Logos*: What Do We Mean by the "Logical Structure" of an Argument?   87

Adopting a Language for Describing Arguments: The Toulmin System   91

Using Toulmin's Schema to Determine a Strategy of Support   98

The Power of Audience-Based Reasons   101
Difference between Writer-Based and Audience-Based Reasons   102
Finding Audience-Based Reasons: Asking Questions about Your Audience   104

Conclusion   108

6   Using Evidence Effectively   109

General Principles for the Persuasive Use of Data   109
Apply the STAR Criteria to Data   110
Use Sources That Your Reader Trusts   111

Rhetorical Understanding of Evidence   111
Kinds of Evidence   112
Angle of Vision and the Selection and Framing of Evidence   116
Rhetorical Strategies for Framing Evidence   119
Special Strategies for Framing Statistical Evidence   121

Gathering Evidence   122
Creating a Plan for Gathering Evidence   122
Gathering Data from Interviews   123
Gathering Data from Surveys or Questionnaires   124

Conclusion   125
Writing Assignments for Chapters 4–6   125

" 'Half-Criminals' or Urban Athletes? A Plea for Fair Treatment of Skateboarders" —David Langley (student)   126
An avid skateboarder argues that he and his skateboarding friends are treated unfairly by police, civic officials, and the general public.

7   Moving Your Audience: *Ethos* and *Pathos*   129

Ethos and *Pathos* as Persuasive Appeals: An Overview   129

How to Create an Effective *Ethos:* The Appeal to Credibility   131
Be Knowledgeable about Your Issue   131

Be Fair   131

Build a Bridge to Your Audience   132

How to Create *Pathos:* The Appeal to Belief and Emotions   132

Use Concrete Language   133

Use Specific Examples and Illustrations   133

Use Narratives   134

Choose Words, Metaphors, and Analogies with Appropriate
    Connotations   136

Using Images for Emotional Appeal   137

Conclusion   139

**8   Accommodating Your Audience:
    Treating Differing Views   140**

One-Sided versus Multisided Arguments   140

Determining Your Audience's Resistance to Your Views   141

Appealing to a Supportive Audience: One-Sided Argument   143

Appealing to a Neutral or Undecided Audience: Classical
    Argument   144

Summarizing Opposing Views   144

Refuting Opposing Views   145

Strategies for Rebutting Evidence   148

Example of a Student Essay Using Refutation Strategy   149

From *First Place: A Healing School for Homeless Children*
    —Marybeth Hamilton (student)   150

A student who does volunteer work in an alternative school for homeless children refutes the arguments of those who want to shut off the school's funding.

Conceding to Opposing Views   152

Appealing to a Resistant Audience: Delayed Thesis or Rogerian
    Argument   152

Delayed-Thesis Argument   153

"Minneapolis Pornography Ordinance" —Ellen Goodman   153

Rogerian Argument   156

A nationally syndicated columnist reluctantly disagrees with an antipornography ordinance proposed by feminists.

"Letter to Jim" —Rebekah Taylor (student)   158

Using the strategies of Rogerian argument, a vegan and animal rights activist
suggests a small step her meat-eating friend might take toward fair treatment of
animals.

Appealing to a Resistant Audience: Using Humor   160

Conclusion   163

Writing Assignments for Chapters 7 and 8   164

9 Conducting Visual Arguments   165

Understanding Design Elements in Visual Argument   166
Use of Type   166
Use of Space or Layout   168
An Analysis of a Visual Argument Using Type and Spatial
Elements   169

"A Single Hit of Ecstasy . . ." (advocacy advertisement)
—Drug Enforcement Administration   170
Use of Color   172
Use of Images and Graphics   172
An Analysis of a Visual Argument Using All the Design
Components   173

The Compositional Features of Photographs and Drawings   174
An Analysis of a Visual Argument Using Images   176

The Genres of Visual Argument   179
Posters and Fliers   180
Public Affairs Advocacy Advertisements   180
Cartoons   183
Web Pages   186

Constructing Your Own Visual Argument   186

"Drink and Then Drive? Jeopardize My Future?" (poster)
—Leah Johnson (student)   188

Using Graphics as Visual Arguments   189
How Tables Contain a Variety of Stories   189
Using a Graph to Tell a Story   191
Bar Graphs   191
Pie Charts   192
Line Graphs   193

Incorporating Graphics into Your Argument 194
Designing the Graphic   194
Numbering, Labeling, and Titling the Graphic   194
Referencing the Graphic in Your Text   195

Conclusion   196

Writing Assignments for Chapter 9   196

Part Three   **Arguments in Depth:**
Six Types of Claims   197

10   An Introduction to the Types of Claims   199

An Overview of the Types of Claims   199

Type 1: Simple Categorical Arguments (Is X a Y?, Where You and Your
Audience Agree on the Meaning of Y)   200

Type 2: Definitional Arguments (Is X a Y?, Where the Definition of
Y Is Contested)   201

Type 3: Cause/Consequence Arguments (Does X Cause Y? Is Y a
Consequence of X?)   201

Type 4: Resemblance Arguments (Is X like Y?)   202

Type 5: Evaluation Arguments (Is X Good or Bad? Is X a Good or
Bad Y?)   202

Type 6: Proposal Arguments (Should We Do X?)   203

What Is the Value of Studying Claim Types?   204

Help in Focusing an Argument and Generating Ideas   204

Help in Organizing and Developing an Argument   207

11   Categorical and Definitional Arguments:
X Is (Is Not) a Y   208

An Overview of the Categorical Arguments   209

Simple Categorical Arguments   210

Difference between Facts and Simple Categorical Claims   210

Variations in the Wording of Simple Categorical Claims   211

Supporting Simple Categorical Claims: Supply Examples   212

Refuting Simple Categorical Claims   213

An Overview of Definitional Arguments   214

The Criteria-Match Structure of Definitional Arguments   214

Conceptual Problems of Definition   217

Why Can't We Just Look in the Dictionary?   217

Definitions and the Rule of Justice: At What Point Does
X Quit Being a Y?   217

Kinds of Definitions   219

Aristotelian Definition   219

Effect of Rhetorical Context on Aristotelian Definition   221

Operational Definitions   222

Strategies for Defining the Contested Term in a Definitional
    Argument   222
    Reportive Approach: Research How Others Have Used the Term   223
    Stipulative Approach: Create Your Own Definition   224

Conducting the Match Part of a Definitional Argument   226

Writing a Definitional Argument   227

Writing Assignment for Chapter 11   227
    Exploring Ideas   227
    Organizing a Definitional Argument   228
    Revising Your Draft   229

Questioning and Critiquing a Definitional Argument   230
    Questioning the Criteria   230
    Questioning the Match   231

Readings   231

"Why Not Taiwan?" —Jack K. C. Chiang   231
    In this letter to the editor, the Director General of the Taipei Economic and
    Cultural Office argues that Taiwan meets all the criteria for entrance into the
    United Nations.
    Critiquing "Why Not Taiwan?"   232

"Oncore, Obscenity, and the Liquor Control Board"
    —Kathy Sullivan (student)   233
    A student investigating a public controversy over photographs in a gay bar ar-
    gues that they are not pornographic.
    Critiquing "Oncore, Obscenity, and the Liquor Control Board"   235

"This Isn't a 'Legal' Matter, This Is War"
    —Charles Krauthammer   235
    Two days after the September 11, 2001, attacks on the World Trade Center and
    Pentagon, a conservative columnist argues that the terrorist acts are not a
    "crime" but an "act of war."
    Critiquing "This Isn't a 'Legal' Matter, This Is War"   237

"Court Win for Martin Not a Defeat for Pro Sports"
    —Blaine Newnham   238
    A sports columnist creates definitional criteria to argue that golfer Casey Martin, dis-
    abled by a leg disease, should be allowed to ride a cart in professional tournaments.
    Critiquing "Court Win for Martin Not a Defeat for Pro Sports"   239

12   Causal Arguments:
       X Causes (Does Not Cause) Y   241

An Overview of Causal Arguments   242
The Nature of Causal Arguing   242

Describing a Causal Argument in Toulmin Terms   244

Three Methods for Arguing That One Event Causes Another   246
   First Method: Explain the Causal Mechanism Directly   246
   Second Method: Use Various Inductive Methods to Establish a
      High Probability of a Causal Link   248
   Third Method: Argue by Analogy or Precedent   251

Glossary of Terms Encountered in Causal Arguments   252

Writing Your Causal Argument   254

Writing Assignment for Chapter 12   254
   Exploring Ideas   255
   Organizing a Causal Argument   256

Questioning and Critiquing a Causal Argument   257

Readings   259
   "The Monster That Is High School" —Daeha Ko (student)   259
      An op-ed writer for a university newspaper argues that the Columbine massacres
      were caused, at least partially, by the cliquish social structure of high school.
   Critiquing *"The Monster That Is High School"*   261
   "Kids Who Do Not Participate..." (advocacy advertisement)
      —United Way   262
   Critiquing the United Way advocacy ad   262
   "When Mothers on Welfare Go to Work"—Richard Rothstein   263
      An educational consultant uses statistical data to argue that when mothers on
      welfare go to work teenagers are harmed more than younger children.
   Critiquing *"When Mothers on Welfare Go to Work"*   264
   "The Causes of Teen Sexual Behavior"—Holly Miller (student)   265
      A student researching the cultural causes of teen sexuality finds that differences in
      parental styles may be an important factor in determining teens' sexual behavior.
   Critiquing *"The Causes of Teen Sexual Behavior"*   268

13   Resemblance Arguments: X Is (Is Not) like Y   269

An Overview of Resemblance Arguments   270

Arguments by Analogy   272
   Using Undeveloped Analogies   273
   Using Extended Analogies   273

Arguments by Precedent   275

Writing a Resemblance Argument   278

Writing Assignment for Chapter 13   278
   Exploring Ideas   278
   Organizing a Resemblance Argument   278

Questioning and Critiquing a Resemblance Argument   279

Readings   280

"Whales Need Silence" —Megan Matthews (student)   280

> In this letter to the editor, a student uses an opening analogy to motivate concern for whales harmed by Navy sonar.

Critiquing *"Whales Need Silence"*   281

"Iraq War Plans" —Jean Arbeiter   281

> A letter writer to the *New York Times* uses an analogy to Winston Churchill's actions prior to World War II to argue for going to war against Iraq.

Critiquing *"Iraq War Plans"*   282

"The Long Haul" —Paul Klugman   282

> A liberal columnist opposes the metaphor of "war" in the "war on terrorism" by arguing that terrorist attacks are more like natural disasters than like conventional wars.

Critiquing *"The Long Haul"*   284

"Knock! Knock!" (political cartoon) —Sven Van Assche   285

> Critiquing the Internet Chat Room Cartoon   285

From *Against Our Will: Men, Women, and Rape* —Susan Brownmiller   285

> A feminist writer argues that pornography is "anti-female propaganda" analogous to Nazi propaganda against Jews or Blacks.

Critiquing the Passage from *Against Our Will: Men, Women, and Rape*   288

14   Evaluation and Ethical Arguments: X Is (Is Not) a Good Y; X Is Right (Wrong)   289

An Overview of Evaluation Arguments   289

Criteria-Match Structure of Categorical Evaluations   290

Conducting a Categorical Evaluation Argument   291

Determining Criteria for a Categorical Evaluation Argument   292

Determining Whether X Meets the Criteria   294

An Overview of Ethical Arguments   296

Two Major Ethical Systems   297

Consequences as the Base of Ethics   297

Principles as the Base of Ethics   298

Conducting an Ethical Argument   298

Constructing a Principles-Based Argument   298

Constructing a Consequences-Based Argument   299

Common Problems in Making Evaluation Arguments   300

Writing an Evaluation Argument   302

Writing Assignment for Chapter 14   302
    Exploring Ideas   302
    Organizing an Evaluation Argument   303
    Revising Your Draft   304

Questioning and Critiquing an Evaluation Argument   305
    Critiquing a Categorical Evaluation Argument   305
    Critiquing an Ethical Argument   306

Readings   307
"Would Legalization of Gay Marriage Be Good for the Gay Community?" —Sam Isaacson (student)   307
    Writing to a gay audience rather than the general public, this student evaluates the potential impact upon the gay community of legalizing same sex marriages.
    Critiquing "Would Legalization of Gay Marriage Be Good for the Gay Community?"   310
"A Woman's View of Hip-Hop" —Tiffany Anderson (student)   310
    A young middle-class white woman, initially repelled by hip-hop, explains her growing attraction to hip-hop music produced by female artists such as Lauryn Hill and Eve.
    Critiquing "A Woman's View of Hip-Hop"   313
"Public Schools, U.S.A. 2001" (political cartoon) —Ann Cleaves   314
    Critiquing the Education/Testing Cartoon   314
"Eight Is Too Many: The Case against Octuplets" —Dr. Ezekiel J. Emanuel   315
    A noted bioethicist argues that multiple births caused by fertility drugs should be a cause for alarm rather than public celebration.
    Critiquing "Eight Is Too Many: The Case against Octuplets"   318

15 Proposal Arguments: We Should (Should Not) Do X   319

An Overview of Proposal Arguments   320

The Structure of Proposal Arguments   320

Special Concerns for Proposal Arguments   321
    The Need for Presence   321
    The Need to Overcome People's Natural Conservatism   322
    The Difficulty of Predicting Future Consequences   322
    The Problem of Evaluating Consequences   322

Developing a Proposal Argument   323
Convincing Your Readers That a Problem Exists   323
Showing the Specifics of Your Proposal   324
The Justification: Convincing Your Readers That Your Proposal
Should Be Enacted   324

Proposal Arguments as Advocacy Posters or Advertisements   325

Using the Claim-Type Strategy to Develop a Proposal Argument   327

Using the "Stock Issues" Strategy to Develop a Proposal
Argument   330

Writing a Proposal Argument   332

Writing Assignment for Chapter 15   332
Exploring Ideas   334
Organizing a Proposal Argument   335
Revising Your Draft   335
Designing a One-Page Advocacy Advertisement   337

Questioning and Critiquing a Proposal Argument   337

Readings   339

"A Proposal to Provide Tips for Hosts at Stone's End"
—Laurel Wilson (student)   340
A former hostess at a popular brewpub details the unfair pay received by hosts
in comparison with servers and proposes a more just way to handle tips.
Critiquing *"A Proposal to Provide Tips for Hosts at Stone's End"*   343

"A Proposal for Universal Health Insurance in the United States"
(MLA-style research paper) —Mark Bonicillo (student)   344
Concerned with the growing problem of Americans who don't have health in-
surance, a student examines alternative approaches and proposes a solution.
Critiquing *"A Proposal for Universal Health Insurance in the United
States"*   351

"The Supreme Court's Unfree Speech" —Akhil Reed Amar and
Steven G. Calabresi   351
Two law professors, arguing for the public's right to know the processes by
which government decisions are made, propose live broadcasts of Supreme
Court deliberations.
Critiquing *"The Supreme Court's Unfree Speech"*   352

*"She's the Test Subject for Thousands of Toxic Chemicals.
Why?"* (advocacy advertisement)
—Center for Children's Health and the Environment   354
Critiquing the Advocacy Ad from the Center for Children's Health
and the Environment   354

Part Four   The Researched Argument   355

16   Finding and Evaluating Sources   357

Formulating a Research Question   358

Understanding Differences in the Kinds of Sources   360
Books Versus Periodicals Versus Web Sites   360
Scholarly Books Versus Trade Books   363
Scholarly Journals Versus Magazines   364
Print Sources Versus Cyberspace Sources   364

Finding Books: Searching Your Library's Online Catalog   365

Finding Print Articles: Searching a Licensed Database   365
What Is a Licensed Database?   365
Keyword Searching   367
Illustration of a Database Search   368

Finding Cyberspace Sources: Searching the World Wide Web   369
The Logic of the Internet   370
Using Web Search Engines   371
Determining Where You Are on the Web   372

Reading Your Sources Rhetorically   373
Reading with Your Own Goals in Mind   373
Reading with Rhetorical Awareness   373

Taking Effective Notes   374

Evaluating Sources   376
Angle of Vision   376
Degree of Advocacy   377
Reliability   378
Credibility   378

Understanding the Rhetoric of Web Sites   378
The Web as a Unique Rhetorical Environment   378
Analyzing the Purpose of a Site and Your Own Research Purpose   378
Sorting Sites by Domain Type   379
Evaluating a Web Site   380

"Spread of Active Sonar Threatens Whales" (web page)
—National Resources Defense Council   382

Conclusion   383

17   Using, Citing, and Documenting Sources   384

Using Sources for Your Own Purposes   384

Creating Rhetorically Effective Attributive Tags   387
    Using Attributive Tags to Separate Your Ideas from
        Your Source's   387
    Creating Attributive Tags to Shape Reader Response   387

Working Sources into Your Own Prose   388
    Summarizing   388
    Paraphrasing   389
    Quoting   389

Avoiding Plagiarism   392

Understanding Parenthetical Citation Systems with
    Bibliographies   393

Understanding MLA Style   394
    The MLA Method of In-Text Citation   394
    MLA Format for the "Works Cited" List   395
    MLA Quick Reference Guide for the Most Common Citations   395
    MLA Citations   397
    Formatting an Academic Paper in MLA Style   405
    Student Example of an MLA-Style Research Paper   405

Understanding APA Style   406
    APA Method of In-Text Citation   406
    APA Format for the "References" List   407
    APA Quick Reference Guide for the Most Common Citations   407
    APA Citations   409

Conclusion   415
    Student Example of an APA-Style Research Paper   415

"Sounding the Alarm: Navy Sonar and the Survival of Whales"
    —Megan Matthews (student)   416
        Detailing the potential damage to whales from the Navy's new sonar systems, a
        student argues that preserving marine mammals and ocean ecology outweighs
        the Navy's need for new sonar.

Appendixes   424

One   Informal Fallacies   424

The Problem of Conclusiveness in an Argument   424

An Overview of Informal Fallacies   425
    Fallacies of *Pathos*   426
    Fallacies of *Ethos*   427
    Fallacies of *Logos*   430

Two   The Writing Community: Working in Groups   **438**

From Conflict to Consensus: How to Get the Most Out of the
    Writing Community   438
    Avoiding Bad Habits of Group Behavior   439
    The Value of Group Work for Writers   439

Forming Writing Communities: Skills and Roles   440
    Working in Groups of Five to Seven People   441
    Working in Pairs   443

A Several-Day's Group Project: Defining "Good Argumentative
    Writing"   445

*"Good Writing and Computers for Today's Modern American
    Youth of America"*   446

"Bloody Ice"   448

"RSS Should Not Provide Dorm Room Carpets"   449

"Sterling Hall Dorm Food"   451

"ROTC Courses Should Not Get College Credit"   451

"Legalization of Prostitution"   453

A Classroom Debate   454

Part Five   **An Anthology of Arguments**   **457**

An Overview of the Anthology   458

Guide Questions for the Analysis and Evaluation of
    Arguments   459
    List 1: Questions for Analyzing and Evaluating a
        Conversation   459
    List 2: Questions for Analyzing and Evaluating an Individual
        Argument   460
    List 3: Questions for Responding to a Reading and Forming Your
        Own Views   461

Environmental Friendliness Versus Market Freedom: The Case of the Sport-Utility Vehicle 462

"Driving Global Warming"
—Bill McKibben   462

A journalist argues that SUVs' contribution to global warming and other environmental problems particularly affecting third world countries raises serious moral issues.

"The American Dream: Why Environmentalists Attack the SUV"
—John Bragg   465

A policy analyst claims that cars and SUVs symbolize American freedom and argues that opposition to SUVs stems from environmentalists' fundamental hostility to technology.

"Better Gas Mileage, Greater Security"
—Robert F. Kennedy, Jr.   467

A lawyer and environmentalist argues that we should return to the fuel conservation strategies of the 1970s to pursue "a sound national energy policy, economic policy, and foreign policy."

"Gas and Gasbags. . . or, the Open Road and Its Enemies"
—Henry Payne and Diane Katz   468

A cartoonist and a policy analyst argue against using gas taxes or fuel-cell vehicles to reduce U.S. dependence on foreign oil, suggesting instead diesel-powered vehicles.

"Gimme an SUV—ASAP: Teenagers Are the Next Big Market for Sport-Utility Vehicles—and the Consequences Could Be Deadly" —Keith Bradsher   471

This writer warns against the dangers of inexperienced teen drivers driving powerful SUVs and against the automobile industry's campaign to capture teen consumers.

"CAFE Belongs in the Graveyard with Its Victims: We Can Increase Fuel Economy without Costing Lives"
—Tom Randall   477

In this researched proposal, a policy analyst exposes the political motives in proposals to improve fuel economy by increasing CAFE standards and speaks out in favor of diesel engines.

"Floor Statement on Boehlert-Markey CAFE Amendment"
—Congressman Sherwood Boehlert   479

In this speech to Congress, Representative Boehlert argues that the auto industry can raise the fuel economy of new vehicles without sacrificing safety, jeopardizing auto workers' jobs, or hurting the industry.

"Notice of Violation: Mock Ticket"
—StayFreeMagazine.org   481

An advocacy organization uses humor in its campaign against SUVs.

"Cancelled" (political cartoon)
  —Henry Payne   482
  A cartoonist argues that producing fuel-efficient, environmentally friendly vehicles creates economic problems.

"Ford on Risk" (political cartoon)
  —Bill Wasserman   483
  A cartoonist satirizes the Ford Motor Company's response to criticisms of SUVs.

"SUV and Miata" (political cartoon)
  —Horsey   484
  A cartoonist depicts one of the main objections opponents have to SUVs.

For Class Discussion   **485**

Biotechnology, Organic Food, and the Ethics of Food Production   486

"Organic Food Seasoned with Fear"
  —Steven Milloy   486
  A Cato Institute scholar claims that the organic food market is profiting from unfounded consumer fears about pesticides, irradiation, and genetic engineering of food.

"Ten Reasons Why Biotechnology Will Not Ensure Food Security, Protect the Environment, and Reduce Poverty in the Developing World"
  —Miguel A. Altieri and Peter Rosset   488
  Two scholars assert that there are better ways to "increase world agricultural productivity" than with bioengineered crops, which pose serious environmental risks without helping poor farmers.

"Executive Summary: Biotechnology and Food"
  —American Council on Science and Health   496
  An advocacy organization provides an overview of its complete publication supporting bioengineered foods.

"Why Voluntary Labeling of Genetically Engineered Foods Won't Help Consumers" —Center for Food Safety   498
  An advocacy organization argues that labeling genetically engineered foods is a complex problem that calls for strict guidelines and regulations.

"Invoking the Lessons of Edison in the Great 'Frankenfoods' Dispute" —John Bissell   502
  A public relations strategist advises biotechnology advocates to promote genetically engineered foods by using Thomas Edison's "direct benefit statements and powerful emotional appeals."

"Science Good, Nature Bad: The Biotech Dogma"
—Kristina Canizares   506

A writer argues that the public needs to know that there is disagreement within the scientific community about the benefits and safety of genetically modified foods and that scientific experiments can be biased.

"Lessen the Fear of Genetically Engineered Crops"
—Gregory A. Jaffe   510

A policy analyst proposes to make the public more accepting of genetically engineered foods by improving the testing process and government regulations and by showing consumers how they will benefit.

"Food Industry Should Modify Its Stance on Altered Food"
—Froma Harrop   511

A nationally syndicated columnist explains her reasons for supporting the labeling of genetically modified foods.

"What Is the FDA Trying to Feed Us?" (poster)
—Sustainusa.org   513

An advocacy organization uses the "Piranhaberry" image as part of its "Keep Nature Natural" campaign against genetically modified foods.

"The Ethics of Eating" —Rich Heffern   514

The opinion editor of the *National Catholic Reporter* criticizes current food production and marketing, finding problems with social justice, safety, and effects on the environment.

For Class Discussion 522

Responses to Terrorism: Public Safety, Civil Liberties, and War   524

"Testimony to the Senate Committee on the Judiciary"
—John Ashcroft   524

Attorney General John Ashcroft praises and justifies federal policing powers legalized by the USA PATRIOT Act.

"The Ashcroft Raids" —David Cole   529

A law school professor, writing for Amnesty International, criticizes human rights violations resulting from the U.S. war on terrorism.

"Legally, What Are the Detainees?" —Mary Jacoby   533

A journalist explores the legal status of Taliban and Al-Qaeda "detainees" at Guantánamo Bay Naval Base in Cuba.

"Guantánamo Prisoners Getting What They Deserve"
—Charles Krauthammer   535

A conservative journalist argues that Guantánamo prisoners should not be considered "prisoners of war" protected by the Geneva Conventions.

"The New Face of Racial Profiling: How Terrorism Affects the Debate" —Sherry F. Colb   537

A law professor explores how the war on terrorism might alter civic debates about racial profiling.

"Profiling Terrorists" —Roger Clegg   541

A contributing editor to *National Review Online* argues that racial profiling is justified in the search for suspected terrorists.

"Racial Profiling and the War on Terrorism" —American Civil Liberties Union   543

In this one-page poster argument, the ACLU expresses its opposition to racial profiling as a means of fighting terrorism.

"What Would Mohammed [Atta] Do? An Interview with Michelle Malkin" —Kathryn Jean Lopez   544

Conservative columnist and Fox News analyst Michelle Malkin argues for extensive "immigration reform" to reduce the number of foreigners entering the United States.

"All-American Osamas" —Nicholas D. Kristof   547

A *New York Times* columnist reminds readers that many terrorists are not foreign-born Muslims but white, ultra-right-wing American extremists.

For Class Discussion   548

Hip-Hop, Film, and Racial Identity   550

"Money, Power, Elect: Where's the Hip-Hop Agenda?" —Raquel Cepeda   550

The editor in chief of sayshe.com, a Web site focused on urban culture and women, assesses hip-hop culture's influence on her generation of African Americans and speculates about hip-hop's political potential.

"The White Boy Shuffle" —Yvonne Bynoe   557

A cultural commentator and the founder of Urban Think Tank, Inc. challenges the motives and racism behind white appropriation of rap music and hip-hop culture.

"Denzel Washington Plays a Bad Guy, and That's Good" —Leonard Pitts, Jr.   561

While agreeing that actors always represent their race, a syndicated columnist argues that actors should also be free to explore their range as actors.

"The False Promise of Being First" —Ellis Cose   563

A well-known author, editor, and columnist argues that truly breaking down racial and group barriers is more important than the first awards given to members of these races and groups.

"Save the Labels for the Category of Achievement" —Ron Aiken   564

In a letter to the editor, a newspaper reader protests the media's emphasis on race over merit.

"Monster's Mask" —Steven Mitchell   565

> In a letter to the editor, a newspaper reader argues that the Oscar-winning roles played by Halle Berry and Denzel Washington were racially demeaning.

For Class Discussion   566

Gender and Technology in Advertising   568

"This Is Automatic Xerography"
—Haloid Xerox   569

> Praising the latest advances in duplicating technology, this ad also depicts the business world and gender roles of the 1960s.

"Like Magellan, Grady Has Pioneered a Global Network" and
"Maria Hates Computers"
—FedEx Express   570

> Promoting FedEx Express efficient transmission of information and materials and its contribution to global business, these ads focus on diverse, satisfied customers.

"Try MIT's Magazine of Innovation . . ."
—Technology Review   572

> This ad for a digital subscription to *Technology Review* shows a man away from his office engrossed in reading this publication online using his laptop computer.

"Spacious Corner Office, Redefined"
—Siemens Corporation   573

> Claiming to equip people to access and exchange information anywhere, this Seimens ad shows a casually dressed woman working outside on her laptop.

For Class Discussion   574

Marriage and Family in the New Millennium   576

*"Restoring a Culture of Marriage: Good News for Policymakers
from the Fragile Families Survey"* —Patrick Fagan and
Jennifer Garrett   576

> In this white paper, the Heritage Foundation argues that "the most effective way to reduce child poverty and increase child well-being is to increase the number of stable two-parent married families."

"Statement Regarding Hearing on Welfare and Marriage Issues"
—Alternatives to Marriage Project   584

> In this white paper, the Alternatives to Marriage Project opposes the Bush administration's proposal to use welfare funds to promote marriage and discourage illegitimacy.

"Here Comes the Groom: A (Conservative) Case for Gay Marriage"
—Andrew Sullivan   586

> A former *New Republic* editor argues that legalizing gay marriage is not a radical step but a conservative one that will promote the social value of marriage.

"Gay Marriage, an Oxymoron" —Lisa Schiffren   590
A former speechwriter for Vice President Dan Quayle argues that one may feel affection for one's gay friends and share happiness in their relationships while "opposing gay marriage for principled reasons."

"Affidavit of Steven K. Lofton" —Steven K. Lofton   591
A plaintiff in an ACLU class action lawsuit to overturn Florida's ban on gay adoptions explains how he and his gay partner have raised three HIV-positive children since infancy.

"Technical Report: Coparent or Second-Parent Adoption by Same-Sex Parents" —Ellen C. Perrin   594
Based on a study of the scientific literature, a professor of pediatrics argues that children who grow up with one or two gay or lesbian parents fare as well as children growing up in a heterosexual household.

"Egg Heads" —Kathryn Jean Lopez   601
An editor for *National Review Online* argues that the expanding market for egg donors is disrupting traditional ideas of family, motherhood, and child.

"Who Needs a Husband?" —Hila Colman   604
A widow after forty happy years of marriage explains why elderly widows don't need new husbands, but elderly widowers want new wives to "take care of them."

For Class Discussion   605

Globalization, World Markets, and the Carnival Against Capitalism   607

"I'd Like a Tall Decaf Non-Fat Mocha Latte. . . " (political cartoon)
—Gary Clement   608
A well-known political cartoonist catches the irony of middle-class youth protesting globalization.

"Carnival Against Capitalism" (poster)   609
This poster uses visual argument to recruit activists in protest against multinational corporations and global markets.

"Evolutionaries" —Thomas L. Friedman   610
The foreign affairs columnist for the *New York Times* argues that "globalization, properly managed, can be the poor's best ladder out of misery."

"The End of Globalization? Multinational Corporations Are More Vulnerable Than You Think" —Michael Shuman   611
An attorney focusing on creating local markets to fight globalization gives five reasons why "multinational corporations are more vulnerable than you think."

"Open Societies Do Better" —Mike Moore   614
This speech by the Director General of the World Trade Organization defends globalization and open markets as the best way to improve the conditions of the poor and promote world peace.

"The Neoliberal World Order: The View from the Highlands of Guatemala" —John D. Abell   619

An economist traces the economic realities of impoverished coffee pickers whose wages of less than three dollars per day (when work is available) help sustain corporate profits.

"Let Them Sweat" —Nicholas D. Kristof   626

A liberal columnist for the *New York Times* surprises fellow liberals by arguing in favor of sweatshops.

"Nicholas D. Kristof: Columnist Endorses Slave Labor for Children" —Chris Anderson   627

In this letter to the editor, Anderson responds angrily to Kristof's argument supporting sweatshops.

"Pennies an Hour, and No Way Up" —Tom Hayden and Charles Kernaghan   628

Two workers' rights activists argue that sweatshops will not be a first step out of poverty unless governments pressure corporations to help workers "elbow and push their way up from squalor."

"From Cherry Garcia to Sweatshop Reform" —Danielle Stein (student)   630

In this op-ed piece in a major college newspaper, a student praises a new clothing company dedicated to paying living wages to its workers.

"Heart of Cheapness" —Paul Krugman   631

Commenting on a tour of Africa by Paul O'Neill, then Secretary of the Treasury, and Bono, lead singer for U2, a columnist explains that the Bush administration would rather end the estate tax to benefit America's wealthiest families than address global poverty.

"Aldo Leopold's Land Ethic: Is It Only Half a Loaf?" —Douglas W. MacCleery   633

A professional forester writing for a scholarly journal argues that globalization will harm the environment unless a "land use ethic" helps constrain consumer choices.

For Class Discussion   636

Internet Censorship: Hate Sites, Pornography, and Spam   638

"Cracking Down on E-Mail Harassment" —Brooke A. Masters   638

In this news analysis piece, staff writer Brooke A. Masters cites recent examples of e-mail harassment and asks whether they should be regarded as protected free speech or criminal stalking in cyberspace.

"Hate Speech Conviction Outlaws Email" —Kenneth Lake   641

British journalist Kenneth Lake outlines the dangers to free speech posed by the Machado decision in the United States.

"Internet's Hate Sites Can Be Hidden, but They Can't Be Ignored"
—Lawrence J. Magid   643

A syndicated columnist and expert on online safety argues for "a massive education campaign" to teach children and teenagers how to respond to hate sites.

"It's Time to Tackle Cyberporn" —John Carr   645

An Internet consultant and advocate for children argues that some level of Internet censorship is necessary to protect consumers, especially children, from unwanted hate and porn sites.

"Anti-Censorship Advocate Locks Horns with Anti-Pornography Filterers" —Associated Press   648

An AP news story recounts the crusade of Internet activist Bennett Haselton, who developed free downloads to help minors unlock the filtering programs installed on their computers by their parents.

"Taking On Junk E-Mail" —New York Times   650

A *New York Times* editorial argues that junk e-mail—often called SPAM— overloads e-mail servers and reduces worker productivity.

"An Approach to Spam" —Jim Conway   651

A lobbyist for the Direct Marketing Association explains his organization's preference for spamming laws that distinguish legitimate e-mail advertising from "truly junk e-mail."

"The Constitution Does Not Protect Spamming"
—Adam Cohen   652

An editorial writer for the *New York Times* challenges the contention that the First Amendment protects commercial speech and thus makes unconstitutional any attempts to censor or restrict spam.

"China's Cyberspace Censorship" —New York Times   654

The editors of the *New York Times* argue against political censorship of the Internet in China.

For Class Discussion   655

Troubled Teens and Violence   657

"Teenage Terrorism" —Riki Anne Wilchins   657

In this editorial, a leading speaker and writer in the gay community underscores the seriousness of gender violence and bullying in American schools.

"Supremacy Crimes" —Gloria Steinem   659

A feminist writer and editor theorizes that the drive for dominance and superiority causes white middle-class males to commit "virtually all of the serial, sexually motivated, sadistic killings."

"Sex, Drugs, Rock 'n' Roll Revisited"
—Victor C. Strasburger   662

A professor of pediatrics faults his own generation for having knowledge and yet not using it responsibly "to protect [kids] from violence, from drugs, from early sexual activity."

"Debunking the 10 Worst Myths about America's Teens"
—Mike Males   664

A sociology instructor, senior researcher, and columnist argues that teen violence and teen problems are reflections of adult problems and behaviors.

"Children in a Violent World: A Metaphysical Perspective"
—James Garbarino   667

A professor of human development and family studies and author of numerous books on children, class, and poverty explains how exposure to violence psychically wounds children and suggests how these children can find spiritual healing.

For Class Discussion   673

The Cultural Debate on Stem Cell Research and Cloning   675

"It's Worth Copying Canada's Model for Cloning Legislation"
—Richard Hayes   676

In this op-ed piece, the director of a nonprofit genetics organization explains the many advocacy groups invested in the cloning controversy and argues in favor of Canada's middle course.

"Of Clones and Clowns" —Robert A. Weinberg   678

A biology professor clarifies the difference between the goals and achievements of serious scientific research, the biotech industry, and sensational science, claiming that the media play a big role in confusing the public about scientific issues.

"What Human Genetic Modification Means for Women"
—Judith Levine   686

A journalist points out how experimentation with human genetic material endangers women and children and how this issue intersects with controversies over abortion and eugenics.

"Human Cloning" —Senator Sam Brownback   690

On his Web site, a U.S. Senator presents a policy statement against all cloning research.

"Open Letter to U.S. Senators on Human Cloning and Eugenic Engineering"—Center for Genetics and Society   691

This letter, addressed to the U.S. Senate and signed by over fifty members of the Center for Genetics and Society, calls for a moratorium on therapeutic cloning.

"Letter to Senator Tom Daschle Opposing a Moratorium on Nuclear Transplantation"
—American Society for Cell Biology   693

This letter from an organization representing ten thousand international biomedical researchers objects to a moratorium, proposing instead legalization and regulation of therapeutic cloning.

"The President's Narrow Morality" —New York Times   694

The editors of the New York Times challenge what the newspaper calls President Bush's simplistic, poorly reasoned rejection of all cloning research.

"Hatch Makes the Case for Regenerative Medicine"
—Senator Orrin G. Hatch   695
In this speech, Republican Senator Orrin Hatch presents his pro-life, pro-family, religious case for therapeutic cloning.

"Stem Cell Simplicities" —Mona Charen   699
A syndicated columnist argues against therapeutic stem cell research on the grounds that an embryo is an entity that deserves special respect.

"A New Look, an Old Battle" —Anna Quindlen   701
Taking a liberal view on embryonic stem cell research, a contributing editor to *Newsweek* argues that the suffering of "real live loved ones" takes precedence over the imagined future life of the unborn.

For Class Discussion   703

Criminal Justice and Postpartum Psychosis: The Case of Andrea Yates   705

"Media Photographs of Andrea Yates" (photographs)   705
These widely published photographs of Andrea Yates with her family and then after her arrest helped shape public reaction to her case.

"Mommy Undearest" —Sally Satel   706
A practicing psychiatrist writing for the Web magazine *Slate* provides medical background on postpartum psychosis.

"Maternal Madness. . . or Sheer Iniquity? Mothers Who Kill"
—John Derbyshire   709
Asking the question "Was the lady sick, or just very wicked?", a conservative writer makes the case that Andrea Yates deserves the death penalty.

"Andrea Yates Wasn't Responsible for Her Crime"
—Charles Krauthammer   712
A conservative op-ed writer makes the opposing case that Andrea Yates had a diseased mind that prevented her from acting freely and responsibly.

"Punishment That Fits" —Michelle Cottle   713
Writing for the centrist *New Republic Online,* Cottle positions herself against the liberal views of Yates's defenders and yet resists advocating either the death penalty or lifelong imprisonment.

"Playing God on No Sleep" —Anna Quindlen   717
A Pulitzer prize-winning journalist examines the cultural pressures on young mothers, distinguishes the real version of motherhood from the "Hallmark-card version," and explores her sympathetic understanding of Andrea Yates.

"Yates Should Be Treated Like Any Other Murderer"
—Peter Renn (student)   719
In an op-ed piece for a university student newspaper, Renn argues that sympathy for Andrea Yates shows the enduring sexism of American society: "When a man commits murder, he is a criminal; when a woman commits murder, she is a victim."

"Questioning the Motives of Home-Schooling Parents"
—Froma Harrop   720

An op-ed columnist looks at a different aspect of the Andrea Yates case and raises disturbing questions about the home-schooling movement.

"Andrea Yates: New Moms and Our Misplaced Priorities"
—Lynne K. Varner   722

An editorial writer for a major city newspaper examines her state's social supports for mothers, including mental health services, and shows how young mothers often feel isolated and helpless when problems arise.

For Class Discussion   724

The United States as Superpower   725

"President Bush Delivers Graduation Speech at West Point"
—George W. Bush   726

In this graduation speech at West Point, the President of the United States explains his administration's policy of unilateral preemptive first strikes in the war against terrorism.

"The New Bush Doctrine" —Richard Falk   730

A writer for the liberal magazine *Nation* critiques "the new strategic doctrine of preemption" set forth in Bush's graduation speech.

"Our 'Next Manifest Destiny'" —John J. Miller   735

A prominent conservative writer argues for American military control of space—"to use space for projecting American power around the globe."

"I Want You to Invade Iraq" (poster) —TomPaine.com   741

A liberal web magazine uses irony to oppose a war with Iraq.

"Briefing #2: Preemptive Strikes and International Law"
—Jeff Guntzel   742

This position paper for an advocacy Web site promoting world peace asks the United States to heed international opinion and abide by international law.

"The Moral Authority of the UN" —Mona Charen   743

A conservative op-ed writer dismisses the moral authority of the UN, arguing that "the world does not and probably never will run on cooperation, peaceful dispute resolution, and friendship."

"A Statement of Conscience" (advocacy advertisement)
—Not in Our Name Project   745

In a full-page advertisement published in papers across the United States, prominent left-wing intellectuals explain their opposition to Bush's superpower foreign policy.

"The Progressive Interview: Edward W. Said"
—David Barsamian   747

A well-known literary critic and advocate for the Palestinian cause in the Middle East provides his insights into the Bush administration's foreign policy.

"Terrorism and the Intellectuals" —Donald Kagan   751

A professor of classics and history at Yale, writing for a conservative scholarly journal, critiques left-wing intellectuals and calls for a revival of patriotism that will make us "powerfully armed, morally as well as materially."

For Class Discussion 757

Credits 759

Index 767

Color Plates

(Insert following page 176)

A. Sustain, "What If Everything Was Labeled Like Genetically Engineered Foods?" (advocacy advertisement)

B. Council for Biotechnology Information, "Would You Be Surprised to Know That Growing Soybeans Can Help the Environment?" (advocacy advertisement)

C. Tom Reese/*The Seattle Times,* Mosh Pit Crowd Surfer (news photo)

D. Alex Quesada/Matrix, Woman Crossing Bridge in Haitian Slum (news photo)

E. Save the Children, "She's the Best Qualified Teacher for Her Children" (advocacy advertisement)

F. EarthJustice, "It's Just Not the Same without Bears" (advocacy advertisement)

G. General Motors, "Creatures of the Evergreen Forest" (product advertisement)

H. Center for Consumer Freedom, "PETA: Not as Warm and Cuddly as You Thought" (advocacy advertisement)

I. U.S. Network for Global Economic Justice, "Welcome to 50 Years Is Enough" (Web site)

Preface

Through its first five editions, *Writing Arguments* has established itself as the leading college textbook in argumentation. By treating argument as a means of discovery as well as persuasion, *Writing Arguments* introduces students to the role of argument in professional and civic life. It shows students how argument entails productive dialogue in search of the best solutions to problems rather than pro-con debate with winners and losers. Users and reviewers have consistently praised the book for its teaching of the critical thinking that helps students *write* arguments: how to analyze the occasion for an argument; how to ground an argument in the values and beliefs of the targeted audience; how to develop and elaborate an argument; and how to respond sensitively to objections and alternative views. Available in three versions—a regular edition, which includes an anthology of readings; a brief edition, which offers the complete rhetoric without the anthology; and a concise edition with fewer readings and examples—*Writing Arguments* has been used successfully at every level, from first-year composition to advanced argumentation courses.

In this sixth edition, we have maintained the signature strengths of *Writing Arguments* while making important changes that reflect our own evolving understanding of the theory and practice of argumentation. As in previous editions, our aim is to integrate a comprehensive study of argument with an effective pedagogy that engages students' interest, builds their confidence as writers and critical thinkers, and gives them tools for effective problem solving and advocacy in civic life. In both its treatment of argumentation and its approach to teaching writing, the text is rooted in current research and theory. Our emphasis throughout is on providing a student-friendly text that really works in the classroom.

What's New in the Sixth Edition?

The sixth edition retains all the features that have made earlier editions successful. In addition, the sixth edition has been improved in the following ways:

- An attractive new design, including eight pages of color plates, enhances the book's visual appeal and supports an increased emphasis on visual rhetoric throughout the text. The color plates, along with other images and graphics interspersed throughout the text, highlight the function of political cartoons, advocacy ads, photographs, fliers, posters, and quantitative graphics as important genres of argument in contemporary culture.
- A new Chapter 9, "Conducting Visual Arguments," provides an overview of visual arguments to help students create and incorporate effective

images and graphics into their own arguments. It teaches students how to analyze visual arguments, giving them the skills they need to produce their own advocacy advertisements, posters, or fliers. It shows students how to use type, layout, color, and images to construct their own advocacy advertisements and posters. The chapter also helps writers interpret tables of numeric data and select and display numbers in rhetorically effective bar graphs, line graphs, or pie charts.

- A reconceptualized anthology more effectively introduces students to the social and rhetorical context of arguments as they are actually encountered in civic and professional life. The anthology now contains nine new topic areas—selected for their high student interest and cultural importance—and includes twice the number of readings as the fifth edition across a wider range of genres. Concise introductions to each unit provide background and context for the arguments, including brief explanations of the multiple ways that arguers frame a contested issue. The anthology now contains more than one hundred essays across a wide range of argument genres such as organizational white papers, op-ed pieces, congressional speeches, and articles in scholarly journals, and more than forty visual arguments such as advocacy advertisements, posters, news photographs, and political cartoons. (For a table of contents organized by genre, see inside the back cover.) In many cases, the anthology units build on issues first introduced in the rhetoric portion of the text. For example, the Frankenfood debate examined in Chapter 2 and the SUV controversy introduced in Chapter 9 are developed in detail in the anthology units "Biotechnology, Organic Food, and the Ethics of Food Production" and "Environmental Friendliness Versus Market Freedom: The Case of the Sport Utility Vehicle."

- A completely revised Part Four ("The Researched Argument") uses an improved pedagogy for teaching research writing derived from our classroom research on students' difficulties in negotiating print and cyberspace sources. Chapters 16 and 17 now emphasize strategies for evaluative interaction with sources—including an awareness of a source's rhetorical context and bias, particularly with regard to Web sites. Chapter 16 explains the purposeful nature of research, differences between print and Web-based sources, strategies for reading and evaluating sources rhetorically, the primacy of the writer's own voice, and strategies for positioning oneself inside an argumentative conversation. Chapter 17 provides an improved explanation of MLA and APA styles, with special attention given to the latest MLA and APA guidelines for citing electronic sources. An engaging new student APA-style research paper, on the danger to whales posed by the Navy's use of sonar, replaces the policewoman argument used in the fifth edition.

- A substantial revision of Chapter 2, "Reading Arguments," includes new material on the multiple genres of contemporary argument aimed at helping students understand how arguments are positioned in a rhetorical context and shaped by the constraints and purposes of a genre. The chapter teaches strategies for summarizing and interrogating texts, showing students how to analyze disagreements, cope with ambiguity, and produce questions for further research. In this edition, the controversy over genetic engineering of food replaces the articles on gender pay equity in the fifth edition; this issue, which holds high interest for today's students, integrates questions from science, agriculture, world trade, and the ethics of food production.

- Chapter 5, "The Logical Structure of Arguments," has been reorganized to integrate the treatment of audience-based reasons (formerly in Chapter 7) with the discussion of the enthymeme and the Toulmin system. Foregrounding audience-based reasons in Chapter 5 helps students understand Toulmin's concepts not as inert terms but as generative tools for creating successful arguments for particular audiences in particular contexts.

- A substantially revised Chapter 6 ("Using Evidence Effectively") presents helpful charts to explain the kinds of evidence available for arguments and to help students evaluate each kind's potential strengths and limitations for a given audience, purpose, or genre. This chapter also explains strategies for finding, evaluating, and selecting evidence and for framing it to anticipate an audience's queries and increase its rhetorical effectiveness.

- Throughout the text, shorter revisions improve the clarity, interest level, and effectiveness of instruction. For example, the revised section on Socrates and the Sophists in Chapter 1 explains more clearly philosophic disagreements about the meaning of "truth." In Chapter 3, new examples on hate speech show how the structure of classical argument can be used as a heuristic to help students generate ideas. Throughout the claim-type chapters (Chapters 11–15), updated examples and new readings explore recent controversies in a range of areas from national and international affairs to popular culture. In Chapter 14, the treatment of ethical arguments is now integrated with evaluation arguments to provide a more economical introduction to ethical arguing and to show how ethical claims are a subtype of evaluation claims.

- Eight new student essays or visual arguments have been selected for the quality of their arguments and the appeal of their subject matter. Drawn from popular culture issues and other contemporary concerns, these arguments connect effectively to the interests of today's students. For example, Tiffany Anderson's "A Woman's View of Hip-Hop" (Chapter 14) updates the fifth edition's evaluation of the Spice Girls, and Laurel Wilson's practical proposal on providing tips for hosts at a local brewpub (Chapter 15) replaces the fifth edition's proposal about saving Bernie's Blintzes Restaurant. Other new student arguments focus on becoming a vegetarian, saving whales from Navy sonar, providing medical insurance for the uninsured, and protesting a local dance ordinance (poster argument).

- The rhetoric portion of the text includes nine new professional essays chosen for the appeal of their subject matter and for the range of genres they represent. The new professional essays address such issues as the legal status of Guantánamo Bay "detainees" (Charles Krauthammer's "This Isn't a 'Legal' Matter, This Is War," Chapter 11), the unanticipated consequences of welfare reform (Richard Rothstein's "When Mothers on Welfare Go to Work," Chapter 12), and a proposal to televise Supreme Court deliberations (Akhil Reed Amar and Steven G. Calabresi's "The Supreme Court's Unfree Speech," Chapter 15). In addition to new professional essays, the rhetoric portion of the text also includes many new examples of visual arguments including advocacy ads for and against biotech food, a political cartoon about pressures on teenagers, and news photographs of President George W. Bush.

What Hasn't Changed? The Distinguishing Features of *Writing Arguments*

Building on earlier success, we have preserved the signature features of earlier editions praised by students, instructors, and reviewers:

- Focus throughout on writing arguments. Grounded in composition theory, this text combines explanations of argument with class-tested discussion tasks, exploratory writing tasks, and sequenced writing assignments aimed at developing skills of writing and critical thinking. This text builds students' confidence in their ability to enter the argumentative conversations of our culture, understand diverse points of view, synthesize ideas, and create their own persuasive texts.

- Equal focus on the rhetoric of argument, particularly on analyzing audience, on understanding the real-world occasions for argument, and on appreciating the rhetorical context and genre of arguments. Throughout the text, we have infused a philosophical view of argument with pedagogical concern for helping students think reflectively and critically at every stage of the construction of an argument.

- Focus on both the reading and the writing of arguments with emphasis on argument as inquiry and discovery as well as persuasion. The text emphasizes the critical thinking that underlies effective arguments, particularly the skills of critical reading, of believing and doubting, of empathic listening, of active questioning, and of negotiating ambiguity and seeking synthesis.

- Integration of four different approaches to argument: The Toulmin system as a means of invention and analysis of arguments; the enthymeme as a logical structure rooted in the beliefs and values of the audience; the classical concepts of *logos, pathos,* and *ethos* as persuasive appeals; and stasis theory (called claim types) as an aid to inventing and structuring arguments through understanding of generic argumentative moves associated with different categories of claims.

- Copious treatment of the research process, including two student examples of documented research papers—one using the MLA system and one using the APA system.

- Numerous "For Class Discussion" exercises and sequenced Writing Assignments and Microthemes designed to teach critical thinking and build argumentative skills. All "For Class Discussion" exercises can be used either for whole class discussions or for collaborative group tasks.

- Numerous student and professional arguments used to illustrate argumentative strategies and stimulate discussion, analysis, and debate. Altogether the sixth edition contains more than one hundred essays and more than forty visual arguments drawn from the public arena as well as fifteen student essays and two student visual arguments.

Our Approaches to Argumentation

Our interest in argumentation grows out of our interest in the relationship between writing and thinking. When writing arguments, writers are forced to lay bare their thinking processes in an unparalleled way, grappling with the complex interplay between inquiry and persuasion, between issue and audience. In an effort to engage students in the kinds of critical thinking that argument demands, we draw on four major approaches to argumentation:

- *The enthymeme as a rhetorical and logical structure.* This concept, especially useful for beginning writers, helps students "nutshell" an argument as a claim with one or more supporting *because* clauses. It also helps them see how real-world arguments are rooted in assumptions granted by the audience rather than in universal and unchanging principles.

- *The three classical types of appeal*—logos, ethos, *and* pathos. These concepts help students place their arguments in a rhetorical context focusing on audience-based appeals; they also help students create an effective voice and style.

- *Toulmin's system of analyzing arguments.* Toulmin's system helps students see the complete, implicit structure that underlies an enthymeme and develop appropriate grounds and backing to support an argument's reasons and warrants. It also highlights the rhetorical, social, and dialectical nature of argument.

- *Stasis theory concerning types of claims.* This approach stresses the heuristic value of learning different patterns of support for different types of claims and often leads students to make surprisingly rich and full arguments.

Throughout the text these approaches are integrated and synthesized into generative tools for both producing and analyzing arguments.

Structure of the Text

The text has five main parts plus two appendixes. Part One gives an overview of argumentation. These first three chapters present our philosophy of argument, showing how argument helps writers clarify their own thinking and connect with the values and beliefs of a questioning audience. Throughout we link the process of arguing—articulating issue questions, formulating propositions, examining alternative points of view, and creating structures of supporting reasons and evidence—with the processes of reading and writing.

Part Two examines the principles of argument. Chapters 4 through 6 show that the core of an effective argument is a claim with reasons. These reasons are often stated as enthymemes, the unstated premise of which must sometimes be brought to the surface and supported. In effective arguments, the reasons are audience-based so that the argument proceeds from underlying beliefs, values, or assumptions held by the intended audience. Discussion of Toulmin logic shows students how to discover both the stated and unstated premises of their arguments and how to provide audience-based structures of reasons and evidence to support them. Chapter 7 focuses on *ethos* and *pathos* as means of persuasion, while Chapter 8 focuses on strategies for accommodating arguments to different kinds of audiences from sympathetic to neutral to hostile. Finally, Chapter 9 focuses on the theory and practice of visual arguments—both images and quantitative graphics—giving students the tools for analyzing visual arguments and for creating their own.

Part Three discusses six different types of argument: simple categorical arguments, definitional arguments, causal arguments, resemblance arguments, evaluation arguments including ethics, and proposal arguments. These chapters introduce students to two recurring strategies of argument that cut across the different category types: Criteria-match arguing in which the writer establishes criteria for making a judgment and argues whether a specific case does or does not meet those criteria, and causal arguing in which the writer shows that one event or phenomenon can be linked to others in a causal chain.

Part Four (Chapters 16 and 17) shows students how to incorporate research into their arguments, including the skills of formulating a research question; understanding differences in the kinds of sources; conducting effective searches of online catalogs, electronic databases, and the Web; reading sources rhetorically to understand context and bias; evaluating sources according to one's purpose, audience, and genre; understanding the rhetoric of Web sites; incorporating sources into the writer's own argument using summary, paraphrase, and judicious quotation; and documenting sources according to MLA or APA conventions. Unlike standard treatments of the research paper, our discussion explains to students how the writer's meaning and purpose control the selection and shaping of source materials.

The appendixes provide important supplemental information useful for courses in argument. Appendix One gives an overview of informal fallacies while Appendix Two shows students how to get the most out of collaborative groups in an argument class. Appendix Two also provides a sequence of collaborative tasks that will help students learn to peer-critique their classmates' arguments in progress. The numerous "For Class Discussion" exercises within the text provide additional tasks for group collaboration.

Finally, Part Five, the anthology, provides a rich and varied selection of professional arguments arranged into twelve high-interest units including responses to terrorism, the image of women in technology advertisements, the ethics of stem cell research and cloning, and the role of the United States as the sole superpower. The anthology selections are grouped by topic rather than by issue question to encourage students to see that any conversation of alternative views gives rise to numerous embedded and intertwined issues. Formulating the issue question, targeting an audience, framing the issue as a claim, and determining the depth and complexity of the argument are all part of the writer's task. Many of the issues raised in the anthology are first raised in the rhetoric (Parts One through Four). For example, numerous issues related to the war on terrorism or the United States as superpower are first raised in the rhetoric, as are issues related to genetic modification of food, marriage and family in the new millennium, the politics of hip-hop, and troubled teens and violence.

Writing Assignments

The text provides a variety of sequenced writing assignments. Parts One and Two include exploratory tasks for discovering and generating arguments, "microthemes" for practicing basic argumentative moves (for example, supporting a reason with evidence), and assignments calling for complete arguments (a classical argument for neutral audiences, a delayed thesis or Rogerian argument for resistant audiences, and an advocacy ad or poster). Each chapter in Part Three on claim types includes a writing assignment based on the claim type covered in the chapter. (Chapter 15 includes both a practical proposal assignment and a researched policy proposal assignment.) Finally, Part Five, the anthology, provides case assignments focusing on problems related to each anthology unit. Instructors can also design anthology assignments requiring argument analysis. Thus, the text provides instructors with a wealth of options for writing assignments on which to build a coherent course.

The Instructor's Manual

The Instructor's Manual has been revised to make it more useful for teachers and writing program administrators. Written by coauthor June Johnson, the revised Instructor's Manual has the following features:

- Discussion of planning decisions an instructor must make in designing an argument course: for example, how to use readings; how much to emphasize Toulmin or claim-type theory; how much time to build into the course for invention, peer review of drafts, and other writing instruction; and how to select and sequence assignments.

- Three detailed syllabi showing how *Writing Arguments* can support a variety of course structures and emphases:

  Syllabus #1: This course emphasizes argumentative skills and strategies, uses readings for rhetorical analysis, and asks students to write on issues drawn from their own interests and experiences.

  Syllabus #2: This more rigorous course works intensely with the logical structure of argument, the classical appeals, the Toulmin schema, and claim-type theory. It uses readings for rhetorical analysis and for an introduction to the argumentative controversies that students will address in their papers.

  Syllabus #3: This course asks students to experiment with genres of argument (for example, op-ed pieces, visual arguments, white papers, and researched freelance or scholarly arguments) and focuses on students' choice of issues and claim-types.

- For instructors who include Toulmin, an independent, highly teachable introductory lesson on the Toulmin schema, and an additional exercise giving students practice using Toulmin to generate argument frames.

- For new instructors, a helpful discussion of how to sequence writing assignments and how to use a variety of collaborative tasks in the classroom to promote active learning and critical thinking.

- Chapter-by-chapter responses to the For Class Discussion exercises.

- Numerous teaching tips and suggestions placed strategically throughout the chapter material, including several sample quizzes asking students to explain and apply argumentative concepts.

- For instructors who teach visual arguments, suggestions for encouraging students to explore how visual arguments have molded public thinking in historical controversies, as in the poster argument on the cover of this text.

- For instructors who like to use student essays in class exercises and discussions, a number of new student essays showing how students responded to assignments in the text. Several of these student pieces exemplify stages of revision.

- Helpful suggestions for using the exercises on critiquing readings in Part Three, "Arguments in Depth: Six Types of Claims." By focusing on rhetorical context as well as the strengths and weaknesses of these arguments, our suggestions will help students connect their reading of arguments to their writing of arguments.

- At the end of each claim-type chapter in Part Three, a list of anthology readings that employ the same claim type, either as a major claim or as a substantial portion of the argument.

■ A substantially revised approach to our analysis of anthology readings that better connects the anthology to the rhetoric portion of the text. Using a bulleted, quick-reference format, each analysis briefly discusses (1) the core of the argument, (2) the major or dominant claims of the argument, (3) the argument's use of evidence and argumentative strategies, (4) the appeals to *ethos* and *pathos* in the argument, and (5) the argument's genre. This easy-to-scan format helps instructors select readings and provides good starting points for class discussion. Our analyses also point out striking connections among readings, suggesting how the readings participate in larger societal argumentative conversations.

Companion Website

The Companion Website to accompany the *Writing Arguments* series (http://www.ablongman.com/ramage), written by Laurie Cubbison of Radford University and Jonathan Sabol of Fordham University, offers a wealth of resources for both students and instructors. Students will have access to reviews of the concepts in each chapter of their book, exploratory writing exercises, online activities, and Web resources to help them develop their skills of argumentation. In addition, instructors will find Web resources and the Instructor's Manual available for download.

John D. Ramage
John C. Bean
June Johnson

Acknowledgments

We are happy for this opportunity to give public thanks to the scholars, teachers, and students who have influenced our approach to composition and argument. We would like to thank our student researchers who helped us explore current civic controversies: LeaEllen Ren, for her excellent library skills; Chris Ronk, for his witty, novel views of contemporary culture; and Megan Matthews, for the complexity and keenness of her assessment of environmental issues. We would especially like to thank Megan, as well as Tiffany Anderson and Mark Bonicillo, for contributing their writing to this text and for their enthusiasm and professionalism. We are also grateful to all our students whom we have been privileged to teach in our writing classes; a number of their arguments from these classes appear in this text. They have inspired us and have profoundly affected how we understand and teach argumentation. We thank too the many users of our texts who have given us encouragement about our successes and offered helpful suggestions for improvements. Particularly we thank the following scholars and teachers who reviewed *Writing Arguments*, sixth edition, in its various stages:

Janet Eldred, University of Kentucky; Judy Gardner, University of Texas at San Antonio; Gregory R. Glau, Arizona State University; Tammy D. Harvey, State University of West Georgia; Heidi A. Huse, The University of Tennessee at Martin; Karen Kornweibel, Stephen F. Austin State University; Dixie Lee Larson, North Carolina State University; Mary Massier, Baylor University; Linda Moore, University of West Florida; Gary L. Myers, Mississippi State University; Roy Stamper, North Carolina State University; Abby Wallace, Owensboro Community College; and Rebecca M. Whitten, Mississippi State University.

Our deep thanks also to our editor, Eben Ludlow, whose unflagging good humor and faith in our approach to both composition and argument have kept us writing and revising for the better part of eighteen years. We especially want to express our gratitude to Marion Castellucci, our development editor, for her indispensable teamwork, for the brilliance and organizational wizardry with which she has managed both the big picture and the myriad of details of this project, and for her expert candid advice. She has been a model of patience, professionalism, and good humor.

Finally, we would like to thank our families. John Bean thanks his wife, Kit, also a professional composition teacher and director of a writing center, and his children, Matthew, Andrew, Stephen, and Sarah, who have grown to adulthood since he first began writing textbooks. June Johnson thanks her husband, Kenneth Bube, a mathematics professor and researcher, who has been an invaluable supporter of this intellectual endeavor, offering astute insights into civic arguments, knowledge of teaching and scientific writing, and Internet expertise. She also thanks her daughter, Jane Ellen, who knows well how much time and work textbook writing takes and who has contributed her own wisdom and delightful humor.

J. D. R.

J. C. B.

J. J.

Writing Arguments

Part One

Overview of Argument

1 Argument: An Introduction

2 Reading Arguments

3 Writing Arguments

This political cartoon presents one of the major perspectives in the public controversy over genetically modified foods, an issue discussed in Chapter 2, pp. 24–26 and 43–44. Source: Steve Breen and Copley News Service.

1 Argument

An Introduction

At the outset of a book on argument, we ought to explain what an argument is. Instead, we're going to explain why no simple definition is possible. Philosophers and rhetoricians have disagreed over the centuries about the meaning of the term and about the goals that arguers should set for themselves. This opening chapter introduces you to some of these controversies. Our goal is to introduce you to various ways of thinking about argument as a way of helping you become a more powerful arguer yourself.

We begin by asking what we mean by argument and then proceed to three defining features: *Argument* requires justification of its claims, it is both a product and a process, and it combines elements of truth seeking and persuasion. We then explore more deeply the relationship between truth seeking and persuasion by asking questions about the nature of "truth" that arguments seek. Finally, we give you an example of a successful arguing process.

What Do We Mean by Argument?

Let's begin by examining the inadequacies of two popular images of argument—fight and debate.

Argument Is Not a Fight or a Quarrel

To many, the word *argument* connotes anger and hostility, as when we say, "I just got in a huge argument with my roommate," or "My mother and I argue all the time." What we picture here is heated disagreement, rising pulse rates, and an urge to slam doors. Argument imagined as fight conjures images of shouting talk-show guests, name-calling letter writers, or fist-banging speakers.

But to our way of thinking, argument doesn't imply anger. In fact, arguing is often pleasurable. It is a creative and productive activity that engages us at high levels of inquiry and critical thinking, often in conversation with persons we like and respect. For your primary image of argument, we invite you to think not of a fist-banging speaker but of a small group of reasonable persons seeking the best solution to a problem. We will return to this image throughout the chapter.

Argument Is Not Pro-Con Debate

Another popular image of argument is debate—a presidential debate, perhaps, or a high school or college debate tournament. According to one popular dictionary, *debate* is "a formal contest of argumentation in which two opposing teams defend and attack a given proposition." While formal debate can develop critical thinking, its weakness is that it can turn argument into a game of winners and losers rather than a process of cooperative inquiry.

For an illustration of this weakness, consider one of our former students, a champion high school debater who spent his senior year debating the issue of prison reform. Throughout the year he argued for and against propositions such as "The United States should build more prisons" and "Innovative alternatives to prison should replace prison sentences for most crimes." We asked him, "What do you personally think is the best way to reform prisons?" He replied, "I don't know. I haven't thought about what I would actually choose."

Here was a bright, articulate student who had studied prisons extensively for a year. Yet nothing in the atmosphere of pro-con debate had engaged him in truth-seeking inquiry. He could argue for and against a proposition, but he hadn't experienced the wrenching process of clarifying his own values and taking a personal stand. As we explain throughout this text, argument entails a desire for truth; it aims to find the best solutions to complex problems. We don't mean that arguers don't passionately support their own points of view or expose weaknesses in views they find faulty. Instead, we mean that their goal isn't to win a game but to find and promote the best belief or course of action.

Arguments Can Be Explicit or Implicit

Before proceeding to some defining features of argument, we should note also that arguments can be either explicit or implicit. An *explicit* argument states directly a controversial claim and supports it with reasons and evidence. An *implicit* argument, in contrast, doesn't look like an argument. It may be a poem or short story, a photograph or cartoon, a personal essay or an autobiographical narrative. But like an explicit argument, it persuades its audience toward a certain point of view. John Steinbeck's *Grapes of Wrath* is an implicit argument for the unionization of farm workers, just as the following poem is an implicit argument against the premise that it is sweet and fitting to die for one's country.

Dulce et Decorum Est
Wilfred Owen

Bent double, like old beggars under sacks,
Knock-kneed, coughing like hags, we cursed through sludge
Till on the haunting flares we turned our backs,
And towards our distant rest began to trudge.
Men marched asleep. Many had lost their boots,
But limped on, blood-shod. All went lame, all blind;
Drunk with fatigue; deaf even to the hoots
Of gas-shells dropping softly behind.

Gas! Gas! Quick, boys—An ecstasy of fumbling,
Fitting the clumsy helmets just in time,
But someone still was yelling out and stumbling
And flound'ring like a man in fire or lime.
Dim through the misty panes and thick green light,
As under a green sea, I saw him drowning.

In all my dreams before my helpless sight
He plunges at me, guttering, choking, drowning.

If in some smothering dreams, you too could pace
Behind the wagon that we flung him in,
And watch the white eyes writhing in his face,
His hanging face, like a devil's sick of sin,
If you could hear, at every jolt, the blood
Come gargling from the froth-corrupted lungs
Bitter as the cud
Of vile, incurable sores on innocent tongues,—
My friend, you would not tell with such high zest
To children ardent for some desperate glory,
The old lie: *Dulce et decorum est
Pro patria mori.**

Here Wilfred Owen makes a powerful case against the "old lie"—that war is honorable, that dying for one's country is sweet and fitting. But the argument is implicit: It is carried in the horrible image of a soldier drowning in his own fluids from a mustard gas attack rather than through an ordered structure

---

*"How sweet and fitting it is to die for one's country." Wilfred Owen (1893–1918) was killed in World War I and wrote many of his poems while in the trenches.

FIGURE 1.1 *Albanian refugees during the Kosovo War*

of thesis, reasons, and evidence. Visual images can also make implicit arguments, often by evoking powerful emotions in audiences. The perspective photos take, the stories they tell, or the vivid details of place and time they display compel viewers literally to see the issue from a particular angle. Take, for instance, the photo (Figure 1.1) of Albanian refugees during the Kosovo War. The photographer conveys the nightmare of this war by foregrounding the old woman, probably a grandmother, perched precariously atop a heavily loaded wheelbarrow, her canes or crutches sticking out from the pile, and the five other persons in the scene hastening down a stark road against an ominous gray background. Here *showing* the urgency of the Albanians' flight for their lives and the helplessness of the two who can't walk is an effective strategy to arouse sympathy for the Albanians. Photographs of this kind regularly appeared in American newspapers during the war, serving to heighten U.S. support of NATO bombing. Meanwhile, Serbs complained that no American newspapers showed photographs of KLA (Kosovo Liberation Army) atrocities against Serbs.

1. In your own words, how do explicit and implicit arguments differ?

2. Imagine that you wanted to take a photograph that creates an implicit argument persuading (1) teenagers against smoking; (2) teenagers against becoming sexually active; (3) the general public toward banning handguns; (4) the general public against banning handguns; (5) the general public toward saving endangered species; (6) the general public toward supporting timber companies' desire to harvest old-growth forests. Working individually or in small groups, describe a photograph you might take that would create an appropriate implicit argument.

EXAMPLE: To create an implicit argument against legalizing hard drugs, you might photograph a blank-eyed, cadaverous teenager plunging a needle into her arm.

Although implicit arguments can be powerful, the predominant focus of this text is on explicit argument. We don't leave implicit arguments entirely, however, because their strategies—especially the persuasive power of stories and narratives—can often be incorporated into explicit arguments, as we discuss more fully in Chapter 7.

The Defining Features of Argument

We turn now to examine argument in more detail. (From here on, when we say "argument," we mean "explicit argument.") This section examines three defining features.

Argument Requires Justification of Its Claims

To begin defining argument, let's turn to a humble but universal site of disagreement: the conflict between a parent and a teenager over rules. In what way and in what circumstances do such conflicts constitute arguments?

Consider the following dialogue:

YOUNG PERSON (*racing for the front door while putting coat on*):　Bye. See you later.

PARENT:　Whoa! What time are you planning on coming home?

YOUNG PERSON (*coolly, hand still on doorknob*):　I'm sure we discussed this earlier. I'll be home around 2 A.M. (*The second sentence, spoken very rapidly, is barely audible.*)

PARENT (*mouth tightening*):　We did *not* discuss this earlier and you're *not* staying out till two in the morning. You'll be home at twelve.

At this point in the exchange, we have a quarrel, not an argument. Quarrelers exchange antagonistic assertions without any attempt to support them rationally. If the dialogue never gets past the "Yes-you-will/No-I-won't" stage, it either remains a quarrel or degenerates into a fight.

Let us say, however, that the dialogue takes the following turn:

YOUNG PERSON (*tragically*):   But I'm *sixteen years old*!

Now we're moving toward argument. Not, to be sure, a particularly well-developed or cogent one, but an argument all the same. It's now an argument because one of the quarrelers has offered a reason for her assertion. Her choice of curfew is satisfactory, she says, *because* she is sixteen years old, an argument that depends on the unstated assumption that sixteen-year-olds are old enough to make decisions about such matters.

The parent can now respond in one of several ways that will either advance the argument or turn it back into a quarrel. The parent can simply invoke parental authority ("I don't care—you're still coming home at twelve"), in which case argument ceases. Or the parent can provide a reason for his or her view ("You will be home at twelve because your dad and I pay the bills around here!"), in which case the argument takes a new turn.

So far we've established two necessary conditions that must be met before we're willing to call something an argument: (1) a set of two or more conflicting assertions and (2) the attempt to resolve the conflict through an appeal to reason.

But good argument demands more than meeting these two formal requirements. For the argument to be effective, an arguer is obligated to clarify and support the reasons presented. For example, "But I'm sixteen years old!" is not yet a clear support for the assertion "I should be allowed to set my own curfew." On the surface, Young Person's argument seems absurd. Her parent, of all people, knows precisely how old she is. What makes it an argument is that behind her claim lies an unstated assumption—all sixteen-year-olds are old enough to set their own curfews. What Young Person needs to do now is to support that assumption.* In doing so, she must anticipate the sorts of questions the assumption will raise in the minds of her parent: What is the legal status of sixteen-year-olds? How psychologically mature, as opposed to chronologically mature, is Young Person? What is the actual track record of Young Person in being responsible? and so forth. Each of these questions will force Young Person to reexamine and clarify her assumptions about the proper degree of autonomy for sixteen-year-olds. And her response to those questions should in turn force the parents to reexamine their assumptions about the dependence of sixteen-year-olds on parental guidance and wisdom. (Likewise, the parents will need to show why "paying the bills around here" automatically gives them the right to set Young Person's curfew.)

---

*Later in this text we will call the assumption underlying a line of reasoning its *warrant* (see Chapter 5).

As the argument continues, Young Person and Parent may shift to a different line of reasoning. For example, Young Person might say: "I should be allowed to stay out until 2 A.M. because all my friends get to stay out that late." (Here the unstated assumption is that the rules in this family ought to be based on the rules in other families.) The parent might in turn respond, "But I certainly never stayed out that late when I was your age"—an argument assuming that the rules in this family should follow the rules of an earlier generation.

As Young Person and Parent listen to each other's points of view (and begin realizing why their initial arguments have not persuaded their intended audience), both parties find themselves in the uncomfortable position of having to examine their own beliefs and to justify assumptions that they have taken for granted. Here we encounter one of the earliest senses of the term *to argue*, which is "to clarify." As an arguer begins to clarify her own position on an issue, she also begins to clarify her audience's position. Such clarification helps the arguer see how she might accommodate her audience's views, perhaps by adjusting her own position or by developing reasons that appeal to her audience's values. Thus Young Person might suggest an argument like this:

> I should be allowed to stay out until 2 on a trial basis because I need enough space to demonstrate my maturity and show you I won't get into trouble.

The assumption underlying this argument is that it is good to give teenagers freedom to demonstrate their maturity. Because this reason is likely to appeal to her parent's own values (the parent wants to see his or her daughter grow in maturity) and because it is tempered by the qualifier "on a trial basis" (which reduces some of the threat of Young Person's initial demands), it may prompt productive discussion.

Whether or not Young Person and Parent can work out a best solution, the preceding scenario illustrates how argument leads persons to clarify their reasons and provide justifications that can be examined rationally. The scenario also illustrates two specific aspects of argument that we will explore in detail in the next sections: (1) Argument is both a process and a product. (2) Argument combines truth seeking and persuasion.

Argument Is Both a Process and a Product

As the preceding scenario revealed, argument can be viewed as a *process* in which two or more parties seek the best solution to a question or problem. Argument can also be viewed as a *product*, each product being any person's contribution to the conversation at a given moment. In an informal discussion, the products are usually short, whatever time a person uses during his or her turns in the conversation. Under more formal settings, an orally delivered product might be a short impromptu speech (say, during an open-mike discussion of a campus issue) or a longer, carefully prepared formal speech (as in a PowerPoint presentation at a business meeting or an argument at a public hearing for or against a proposed city project).

Similar conversations occur in writing. Roughly analogous to a small-group discussion is an e-mail discussion of the kind that occurs regularly through informal chat groups or professional listservs. In an online discussion, participants have more thinking time to shape their messages than they do in a real-time oral discussion. Nevertheless, messages are usually short and informal, making it possible over the course of several days to see participants' ideas shift and evolve as conversants modify their initial views in response to others' views.

Roughly equivalent to a formal speech would be a formal written argument, which may take the form of an academic argument for a college course; a grant proposal; a guest column for the op-ed* section of a newspaper, a legal brief, a letter to a member of congress; or an article for an organizational newsletter, popular magazine, or professional journal. In each of these instances, the written argument (a product) enters a conversation (a process)—in this case, a conversation of readers, many of whom will carry on the conversation by writing their own responses or by discussing the writer's views with others. The goal of the community of writers and readers is to find the best solution to the problem or issue under discussion.

Argument Combines Truth Seeking and Persuasion

In thinking about argument as a product, the writer will find herself continually moving back and forth between truth seeking and persuasion—that is, between questions about the subject matter (What is the best solution to this problem?) and about audience (What do my readers already believe or value? What reasons and evidence will most persuade them?). Back and forth she'll weave, alternately absorbed in the subject of her argument and in the audience for that argument.

Neither of the two focuses is ever completely out of mind, but their relative importance shifts during different phases of the development of a paper. Moreover, different rhetorical situations place different emphases on truth seeking versus persuasion. We could thus place arguments on a kind of continuum that measures the degree of attention a writer gives to subject matter versus audience. At the far truth-seeking end of the continuum might be an exploratory piece that lays out several alternative approaches to a problem and weighs the strengths and weaknesses of each with no concern for persuasion. At the other end of the continuum would be outright propaganda, such as a political campaign advertisement that reduces a complex issue to sound bites and distorts an opponent's position through out-of-context quotations or misleading use of data. (At its most blatant, propaganda obliterates truth seeking; it will do anything,

---

Op-ed stands for "opposite-editorial." It is the generic name in journalism for a signed argument that voices the writer's opinion on an issue, as opposed to a news story that is supposed to report events objectively, uncolored by the writer's personal views. Op-ed pieces appear in the editorial-opinion section of newspapers, which generally feature editorials by the resident staff, opinion pieces by syndicated columnists, and letters to the editor from readers. The term *op-ed* is often extended to syndicated columns appearing in newsmagazines, advocacy websites, and on-line news services.

including the knowing use of bogus evidence, distorted assertions, and outright lies, to win over an audience.) In the middle ranges of the continuum, writers shift their focuses back and forth between truth seeking and persuasion but with varying degrees of emphasis.

As an example of a writer focusing primarily on truth seeking, consider the case of Kathleen, who, in her college argument course, addressed the definitional question "Is American Sign Language (ASL) a 'foreign language' for purposes of meeting the university's foreign language requirement?" Kathleen had taken two years of ASL at a community college. When she transferred to a four-year college, the chair of the foreign languages department at her new college would not allow her ASL proficiency to count for the foreign language requirement. ASL isn't a "language," the chair said summarily. "It's not equivalent to learning French, German, or Japanese."

Kathleen disagreed, so she immersed herself in developing her argument. While doing research, she focused almost entirely on subject matter, searching for what linguists, neurologists, cognitive psychologists, and sociologists had said about the language of deaf people. Immersed in her subject matter, she was only tacitly concerned with her audience, whom she thought of primarily as her classmates and the professor of her argument class—persons who were friendly to her views and interested in her experiences with the deaf community. She wrote a well-documented paper, citing several scholarly articles, that made a good case to her classmates (and the professor) that ASL was indeed a distinct language.

Proud of the big red A the professor had placed on her paper, Kathleen returned to the chair of the foreign languages department with a new request to count ASL for her language requirement. The chair read her paper, congratulated her on her good writing, but said her argument was not persuasive. He disagreed with several of the linguists she cited and with the general definition of *language* that her paper assumed. He then gave her some additional (and to her, fuzzy) reasons why the college would not accept ASL as a foreign language.

Spurred by what she considered the chair's too-easy dismissal of her argument, Kathleen decided, for a subsequent assignment in her argument class, to write a second paper on ASL—but this time aiming it directly at the chair of foreign languages. Now her writing task falls closer to the persuasive end of our continuum. Kathleen once again immersed herself in research, but this time it focused not on subject matter (whether ASL is a distinct language) but on audience. She researched the history of the foreign language requirement at her college and discovered some of the politics behind it (an old foreign language requirement had been dropped in the 1970s and reinstituted in the 1990s, partly—a math professor told her—to boost enrollments in foreign language courses). She also interviewed foreign language teachers to find out what they knew and didn't know about ASL. She discovered that many teachers thought ASL was "easy to learn," so that accepting ASL would allow students a Mickey Mouse way to avoid the rigors of a "real" foreign language class. Additionally, she learned that foreign language teachers valued immersing students in a foreign culture; in fact, the foreign language requirement was part of her college's effort to create a multicultural curriculum.

This new understanding of her target audience helped Kathleen totally reconceptualize her argument. She condensed and abridged her original paper down to one line of reasoning in her new argument. She added sections showing the difficulty of learning ASL (to counter her audience's belief that learning ASL was easy), showing how the deaf community formed a distinct culture with its own customs and literature (to show how ASL met the goals of multiculturalism), and showing that the number of transfer students with ASL credits would be negligibly small (to allay fears that accepting ASL would threaten enrollments in language classes). She ended her argument with an appeal to her college's public emphasis (declared boldly in its mission statement) on eradicating social injustice and reaching out to the oppressed. She described the isolation of deaf people in a world where almost no hearing people learn ASL, and she argued that the deaf community on her campus could be integrated more fully into campus life if more students could "talk" with them. Thus the ideas included in her new argument—the reasons selected, the evidence used, the arrangement and tone—all were determined by her primary focus on persuasion.

Our point, then, is that all along the continuum writers are concerned both to seek truth and to persuade, but not necessarily with equal balance. Kathleen could not have written her second paper, aimed specifically at persuading the chair of foreign languages, if she hadn't first immersed herself in truth-seeking research that convinced her that ASL was indeed a distinct language. Nor are we saying that her second argument was better than her first. Both fulfilled their purposes and met the needs of their intended audiences. Both involved truth seeking and persuasion, but the first focused primarily on subject matter whereas the second focused primarily on audience.

Argument and the Problem of Truth

The tension that we have just examined between truth seeking and persuasion raises an ancient issue in the field of argument: Is the arguer's first obligation to truth or to winning the argument? And just what is the nature of the truth to which arguers are supposed to be obligated?

In Plato's famous dialogues from ancient Greek philosophy, these questions were at the heart of Socrates' disagreement with the Sophists. The Sophists were professional rhetoricians who specialized in training orators to win arguments. Socrates, who valued truth seeking over persuasion and believed that truth could be discovered through philosophic inquiry, opposed the Sophists. For Socrates, Truth resided in the ideal world of forms, and through philosophic rigor humans could transcend the changing, shadowlike world of everyday reality to perceive the world of universals where Truth, Beauty, and Goodness resided. Through his method of questioning his interlocutors, Socrates would gradually peel away layer after layer of false views until Truth was revealed. The good person's duty, Socrates believed, was not to win an argument but to pursue this higher Truth. Socrates distrusted rhetoricians because they were interested only in the temporal power and wealth that came from persuading audiences to the orator's views.

Let's apply Socrates' disagreement with the Sophists to a modern instance. Suppose your community is divided over the issue of raising environmental standards versus keeping open a job-producing factory that doesn't meet new guidelines for waste discharge. The Sophists would train you to argue any side of this issue on behalf of any lobbying group willing to pay for your services. If, however, you followed the spirit of Socrates, you would be inspired to listen to all sides of the dispute, peel away false arguments, discover the Truth through reasonable inquiry, and commit yourself to a Right Course of Action.

But what is the nature of Truth or Right Action in a dispute between jobs and the environment? The Sophists believed that truth was determined by those in power; thus they could enter an argument unconstrained by any transcendent beliefs or assumptions. When Socrates talked about justice and virtue, the Sophists could reply contemptuously that these were fictitious concepts invented by the weak to protect themselves from the strong. Over the years, the Sophists' relativist beliefs were so repugnant to people that the term *sophistry* became synonymous with trickery in argument.

However, in recent years the Sophists' critique of a transcendent Universal Truth has been taken seriously by many philosophers, sociologists, and other thinkers who doubt Socrates' confident belief that arguments, properly conducted, necessarily arrive at a single Truth. For these thinkers, as for the Sophists, there are often different degrees of truth and different kinds of truths for different situations or cultures. From this perspective, when we consider questions of interpretation or value, we can never demonstrate that a belief or assumption is true— not through scientific observation, not through reason, and not through religious revelation. We get our beliefs, according to these contemporary thinkers, from the shared assumptions of our particular cultures. We are condemned (or liberated) to live in a pluralistic, multicultural world with competing visions of truth.

If we accept this pluralistic view of the world, do we then endorse the Sophists' radical relativism, freeing us to argue any side of any issue? Or do we doggedly pursue some modern equivalent of Socrates' truth?

Our own sympathies are with Socrates, but we admit to a view of truth that is more tentative, cautious, and conflicted than his. For us, truth seeking does not mean finding the "Right Answer" to a disputed question, but neither does it mean a valueless relativism in which all answers are equally good. For us, truth seeking means taking responsibility for determining the "best answer" or "best solution" to the question for the good of the whole community when taking into consideration the interests of all stakeholders. It means making hard decisions in the face of uncertainty. This more tentative view of truth means that you cannot use argument to "prove" your claim, but only to make a reasonable case for your claim. One contemporary philosopher says that argument can hope only to "increase adherence" to ideas, not absolutely convince an audience of the necessary truth of ideas. Even though you can't be certain, in a Socratic sense, that your solution to the problem is the best one available, you must ethically take responsibility for the consequences of your claim and you must seek justice for stakeholders beyond yourself. You must, in other words, forge a personal stance based on your examination of all the evidence and your articulation of values that you can make public and defend.

To seek truth, then, means to seek the best or most just solution to a problem while observing all available evidence, listening with an open mind to the views of all stakeholders, clarifying and attempting to justify your own values and assumptions, and taking responsibility for your argument. It follows that truth seeking often means delaying closure on an issue, acknowledging the pressure of alternative views, and being willing to change one's mind. Seen in this way, learning to argue effectively has the deepest sort of social value: It helps communities settle conflicts in a rational and humane way by finding, through the dialectic exchange of ideas, the best solutions to problems without resorting to violence or to other assertions of raw power.

For Class Discussion

On any given day, newspapers provide evidence of the complexity of living in a pluralistic culture. Issues that could be readily decided in a completely homogeneous culture raise questions in a society that has fewer shared assumptions. Choose one of the following cases as the subject for a "simulation game" in which class members present the points of view of the persons involved.

CASE 1: MOSH PITS: IT'S NOT ALL FUN AND MUSIC

This news story begins with the case of a fourteen-year-old boy who suffered brain damage when he was dropped while crowd surfing at a Rage Against the Machine concert in Seattle. The article then discusses the controversy over crowd safety at grunge concerts:

> Most concerts do not result in injuries and deaths. But the increasing frequency of serious injuries—including broken bones, brain damage and paralysis—is shining a spotlight on what some critics see as fun and freedom pushed to irresponsible limits.
>
> The injuries have prompted a handful of U.S. cities and some bands to ban crowd surfing and stage diving, but there are no national standards for concert safety, and no one has exact numbers on how many people are injured in mosh pits every year. One survey cites at least 10 deaths and more than 1,000 injuries resulting from just 15 U.S. concerts last year.

Your task: Imagine a public hearing in which city officials are trying to develop a city policy on mosh pits at concerts. Should they be banned altogether? If not, how might they be regulated and who is responsible for injuries? Hold a mock hearing in which classmates present the views of the following: (a) a rock band that values crowd surfing and stage diving; (b) several concert fans who love mosh pits; (c) parents of a teenager seriously injured in a mosh pit accident; (d) a woman who was groped while crowd surfing; (e) local police; (f) concert promoters; (g) a venue owner fearing a liability lawsuit; (h) a city attorney fearing a liability lawsuit.

CASE 2: HOMELESS HIT THE STREETS TO PROTEST PROPOSED BAN

The homeless stood up for themselves by sitting down in a peaceful but vocal protest yesterday in [name of city].

About 50 people met at noon to criticize a proposed set of city ordinances that would ban panhandlers from sitting on sidewalks, put them in jail for repeatedly urinating in public, and crack down on "intimidating" street behavior.

"Sitting is not a crime," read poster boards that feature mug shots of [the city attorney] who is pushing for the new laws. [. . .] "This is city property; the police want to tell us we can't sit here," yelled one man named R. C. as he sat cross-legged outside a pizza establishment.

Your task: Imagine a public hearing seeking reactions to the proposed city ordinance. Hold a mock hearing in which classmates play the following roles: (a) a homeless person; (b) an annoyed merchant; (c) a shopper who avoids places with homeless people; (d) a citizen advocate for the homeless; (e) the city attorney.

A Successful Process of Argumentation: The Well-Functioning Committee

We have said that neither the fist-banging speaker nor the college debate team represents our ideal image of argument. The best image for us, as we have implied, is a well-functioning small group seeking a solution to a problem. In professional life such small groups usually take the form of committees.

We use the word *committee* in its broadest sense to indicate all sorts of important work that grows out of group conversation and debate. The Declaration of Independence is essentially a committee document with Thomas Jefferson as the chair. Similarly, the U.S. Supreme Court is in effect a committee of nine judges who rely heavily, as numerous books and articles have demonstrated, on small-group decision-making processes to reach their judgments and formulate their legal briefs.

To illustrate our committee or small-group model for argument, let's briefly consider the workings of a university committee on which coauthor John Ramage once served, the University Standards Committee. The Arizona State University (ASU) Standards Committee plays a role in university life analogous to that of the Supreme Court in civic life. It's the final court of appeal for ASU students seeking exceptions to various rules that govern their academic lives (such as registering under a different catalog, waiving a required course, or being allowed to retake a course for the third time).

The issues that regularly come before the committee draw forth all the argumentative strategies discussed in detail throughout this text. For example, all of the argument types discussed in Part Three regularly surface during committee deliberations. The committee deals with definition issues ("Is math anxiety a 'learning disability' for purposes of exempting a student from a math requirement? If so, what criteria can we establish for math anxiety?"); cause/consequence issues ("What were the causes of this student's sudden poor performance during spring semester?" "What will be the consequences of approving or denying her appeal?"); resemblance issues ("How is this case similar to an earlier case that we considered?"); evaluation issues ("Which criteria should take precedence in assessing this sort of appeal?"); and proposal issues ("Should we make it a policy to allow course X to substitute for course Y in the General Studies requirements?").

On any given day, the committee's deliberations showed how dialogue can lead to clarification of thinking. On many occasions, committee members' initial views shifted as they listened to opposing arguments. In one case, for example, a student petitioned to change the catalog under which she was supposed to graduate because the difference in requirements would let her graduate a half-year sooner. Initially, most committee members opposed the petition. They reminded the committee that in several earlier cases it had denied petitions to change catalogs if the petitioner's intent was to evade the more rigorous graduation requirements imposed by a new General Studies curriculum. Moreover, the committee was reminded that letting one student change catalogs was unfair to other students who had to meet the more rigorous graduation standards.

However, after emphatic negative arguments had been presented, a few committee members began to voice support for the student's case. While acknowledging the truth of what other committee members had said, they pointed out reasons to support the petition. The young woman in question had taken most of the required General Studies courses; it was mostly changes in the requirements for her major that delayed her graduation. Moreover, she had performed quite well in what everyone acknowledged to be a demanding course of study. Although the committee had indeed turned down previous petitions of this nature, in none of those cases had the consequences of denial been so dire for the student.

After extended negotiations between the two sides on this issue, the student was allowed to change catalogs. Although the committee was reluctant to set a bad precedent (those who resisted the petition foresaw a deluge of similar petitions from less worthy candidates), it recognized unique circumstances that legitimately made this petitioner's case different. Moreover, the rigor of the student's curriculum, the primary concern of those who opposed the change, was shown to be greater than the rigor of many who graduated under the newer catalog.

As this illustration suggests, what allowed the committee to function as well as it did was the fundamental civility of its members and their collective concern that their decisions be just. Unlike some committees, this committee made many decisions, the consequences of which were not trivial for the people involved. Because of the significance of these outcomes, committee members were more willing than they otherwise might have been to concede a point to another member in the name of reaching a better decision and to view their deliberations as an ongoing process of negotiation rather than a series of win-lose debates.

To give you firsthand experience at using argument as a process of clarification, we conclude this chapter with an actual case that came before the University Standards Committee. We invite you to read the following letter, pretending that you are a member of the University Standards Committee, and then proceed to the exercises that follow.

Petition to Waive the University Mathematics Requirement

Standards Committee Members,

I am a 43-year-old member of the Pawnee Tribe of Oklahoma and a very nontraditional student currently pursuing Justice Studies at the Arizona State University (ASU) College of Public Programs. I entered college as the first step toward completion of my goal—becoming legal counsel for my tribe, and statesman.   1

I come before this committee in good faith to request that ASU suspend, in my special case, its mathematics requirement for undergraduate degree completion so I may enter the ASU college of Law during Fall 1993. The point I wish to make to this committee is this: I do not need algebraic skills; I will never use algebra in my intended profession; and, if forced to comply with ASU's algebra requirement, I will be needlessly prevented from graduating in time to enter law school next fall and face an idle academic year before my next opportunity in 1994. I will address each of these points in turn, but a few words concerning my academic credentials are in order first.   2

Two years ago, I made a vow of moral commitment to seek out and confront injustice. In September of 1990, I enrolled in college. Although I had only the benefit of a ninth grade education, I took the General Equivalency Diploma (GED) examination and placed in the top ten percent of those, nationwide, who took the test. On the basis of this score I was accepted into Scottsdale Community College (SCC). This step made me the first in my entire family, and practically in my tribe, to enter college. During my first year at SCC I maintained a 4.0 GPA, I was placed on the President's list twice, was active in the Honors Program, received the Honors Award of Merit in English Humanities, and was conferred an Honors Scholarship (see attached) for the Academic year of 1991–1992 which I declined, opting to enroll in ASU instead.   3

At the beginning of the 1991 summer semester, I transferred to ASU. I chose to graduate from ASU because of the courses offered in American Indian studies, an important field ignored by most other Universities but necessary to my commitment. At ASU I currently maintain a 3.6 GPA, although my cumulative GPA is closer to 3.9, I am a member of the Honors and Justice Colleges, was appointed to the Dean's List, and awarded ASU's prestigious Maroon and Gold Scholarship twice. My academic   4 standing is impeccable. I will enter the ASU College of Law to study Indian and criminal law during the Fall of 1993—if this petition is approved. Upon successful completion of my juris doctorate I will return to Oklahoma to become active in the administration of Pawnee tribal affairs as tribal attorney and advisor, and vigorously prosecute our right to sovereignty before the Congress of the United States.

5   When I began my "college experience," I set a rigid time schedule for the completion of my goal. By the terms of that self-imposed schedule, founded in my belief that I have already wasted many productive years, I allowed myself thirty-five months in which to achieve my Bachelor of Science degree in Justice Studies, for indeed justice is my concern, and another thirty-six months in which to earn my juris doctorate—summa cum laude. Consistent with my approach to all endeavors, I fell upon this task with zeal. I have willingly assumed the burden of carrying substantial academic loads during fall, spring and summer semesters. My problem now lies in the fact that in order to satisfy the University's math requirement to graduate I must still take MAT-106 and MAT-117. I submit that these mathematics courses are irrelevant to my goals, and present a barrier to my fall matriculation into law school.

6   Upon consideration of my dilemma, the questions emerged: Why do I need college algebra (MAT-117)? Is college algebra necessary for studying American Indian law? Will I use college algebra in my chosen field? What will the University gain or lose, from my taking college algebra—or not? I decided I should resolve these questions.

7   I began my inquiry with the question: "Why do I need college algebra (MAT-117)?" I consulted Mr. Jim _____ of the Justice College and presented this question to him. He referred to the current ASU catalog and delineated the following answer: I need college algebra (1) for a minimum level of math competency in my chosen field, and (2) to satisfy the university math requirement in order to graduate. My reply to the first answer is this: I already possess ample math skills, both practical and academic; and, I have no need for algebra in my chosen field. How do I know this? During the spring 1992 semester at ASU I successfully completed introductory algebra (MAT-077), scoring the highest class grade on one test (see attached transcript and test). More noteworthy is the fact that I was a machine and welding contractor for fifteen years. I used geometry and algebra commonly in the design of many welded structures. I am proficient in the use of Computer Assisted Design (CAD) programs, designing and drawing all my own blueprints for jobs. My blueprints and designs are always approved by city planning departments. For example, my most recent job consisted of the manufacture, transportation and installation of one linear mile of anodized, aluminum handrailing at a luxury resort condo on Maui, Hawaii. I applied extensive use of math to calculate the amount of raw materials to order, the logistics of mass production and transportation for both men and materials from Mesa to Maui, the job site installation itself, and cash flow. I have successfully completed many jobs of this nature—all without a mathematical hitch. As to the application of math competency in my chosen field, I can guarantee this committee that there will not be a time in my practice of Indian law that I will need algebra. If an occasion ever occurs that I need algebra, I will hire a mathematician, just as I would an engineer if I need engineering, or a surgeon if I need an operation.

I then contacted Dr. _____ of the ASU Mathematics Department and presented   8
him with the same question: "Why do I need college algebra?" He replied: (1) for a
well rounded education; (2) to develop creative thinking; and (3) to satisfy the university math requirement in order to graduate. Responding to the first answer, I
have a "well rounded education." My need is for a specific education in justice and
American Indian law. In fact, I do not really need the degree to practice Indian law
as representative of my tribe, just the knowledge. Regarding the second, I do not
need to develop my creative thinking. It has been honed to a keen edge for many
years. For example, as a steel contractor, I commonly create huge, beautiful and in-
tricate structures from raw materials. Contracting is not my only experience in creative thinking. For twenty-five years I have also enjoyed the status of being one of
this country's foremost designers and builders of racebikes. Machines I have designed and brought into existence from my imagination have topped some of Japan
and Europe's best engineering efforts. To illustrate this point, in 1984 I rode a bike
of my own design to an international victory over Honda, Suzuki, Laverda, BMW and
Yamaha. I have excelled at creative thinking my entire life—I called it survival.

Expanding on the question of why I need college algebra, I contacted a few   9
friends who are practicing attorneys. All responded to my question in similar manner. One, Mr. Billy _____, Esq., whose law firm is in Tempe, answered my two
questions as follows: "When you attended law school, were there any courses you
took which required algebra?" His response was "no." "Have you ever needed algebra during the many years of your practice?" Again, his response was "no." All
agreed there was not a single occasion when they had need for algebra in their professional careers.

Just to make sure of my position, I contacted the ASU College of Law, and   10
among others, spoke to Ms. Sierra _____. I submitted the question "What law
school courses will I encounter in which I will need algebra?" The unanimous reply
was, they knew of none.

I am not proposing that the number of credit hours I need for graduation be   11
lowered. In fact, I am more than willing to substitute another course or two in its
place. I am not trying to get out of anything hard or distasteful, for that is certainly
not my style. I am seeking only to dispose of an unnecessary item in my studies,
one which will prevent me from entering law school this fall—breaking my stride.
So little holds up so much.

I agree that a young adult directly out of high school may not know that he   12
needs algebraic skills. Understandably, he does not know what his future holds—
but I am not that young adult. I claim the advantage. I know precisely what my future holds and that future holds no possibility of my needing college algebra.

Physically confronting injustice is my end. On reservations where government   13
apathy allows rapacious pedophiles to pose as teachers; in a country where a million and a half American Indians are held hostage as second rate human beings
whose despair results in a suicide, alcohol and drug abuse rate second to no other
people; in prisons where helpless inmates are beaten like dogs by sadistic guards
who should be the inmates—this is the realm of my chosen field—the disenfranchised. In this netherworld, algebra and justice exist independently of one another.

14   In summary, I am convinced that I do not need college algebra for a minimum level of math competency in my chosen field. I do not need college algebra for a well rounded education, nor to develop my creative thinking. I do not need algebra to take the LSAT. I do not need algebra for any courses in law school, nor will I for any purpose in the practice of American Indian law. It remains only that I need college algebra in order to graduate.

15   I promise this committee that ASU's integrity will not be compromised in any way by approving this waiver. Moreover, I assure this committee that despite not having a formal accreditation in algebra, I will prove to be nothing less than an asset to this University and its Indian community, both to which I belong, and I will continue to set a standard for integrity, excellence and perseverance for all who follow. Therefore, I ask this committee, for all the reasons described above, to approve and initiate the waiver of my University mathematics requirement.

[Signed: Gordon Adams]

For Class Discussion

1. Before class discussion, decide how you would vote on this issue. Should this student be exempted from the math requirement? Write out the reasons for your decision.

2. Working in small groups or as a whole class, pretend that you are the University Standards Committee, and arrive at a group decision on whether to exempt this student from the math requirement.

3. After the discussion, write for five to ten minutes in a journal or notebook describing how your thinking evolved during the discussion. Did any of your classmates' views cause you to rethink your own? Class members should share with each other their descriptions of how the process of argument led to clarification of their own thinking.

We designed this exercise to help you experience argument as a clarifying process. But we had another purpose. We also designed the exercise to stimulate thinking about a problem we introduced at the beginning of this chapter: the difference between argument as clarification and argument as persuasion. Is a good argument necessarily a persuasive argument? In our opinion, this student's letter to the committee is a *good* argument. The student writes well, takes a clear stand, offers good reasons for his position, and supports his reasons with effective evidence. To what extent, however, is the letter a *persuasive* argument? Did it win its case? You know how you and your classmates stand on this issue. But what do you think the University Standards Committee at ASU actually decided during its deliberations?

We will return to this case again in Chapter 5.

Conclusion

In this chapter we have explored some of the complexities of argument, showing you why we believe that argument is a matter not of fist banging or of win-lose debate but of finding, through a process of rational inquiry, the best solution to a problem or issue. What is our advice for you at the close of this introductory chapter? Briefly, to see the purpose of argument as truth seeking as well as persuasion. We suggest that throughout the process of argument you seek out a wide range of views, that you especially welcome views different from your own, that you treat these views respectfully, and that you see them as intelligent and rationally defensible. (Hence you must look carefully at the reasons and evidence on which they are based.)

Our goal in this text is to help you learn skills of argument. If you choose, you can use these skills, like the Sophists, to argue any side of any issue. Yet we hope you won't. We hope that, like Socrates, you will use argument for truth seeking and that you will consequently find yourselves, on at least some occasions, changing your position on an issue while writing a rough draft (a sure sign that the process of arguing has complicated your views). We believe that the skills of reason and inquiry developed through the writing of arguments can help you get a clearer sense of who you are. If our culture sets you adrift in pluralism, argument can help you take a stand, to say, "These things I believe." In this text we will not pretend to tell you what position to take on any given issue. But as a responsible being, you will often need to take a stand, to define yourself, to say, "Here are the reasons that choice A is better than choice B, not just for me but for you also." If this text helps you base your commitments and actions on reasonable grounds, then it will have been successful.

2   Reading Arguments

Why Reading Arguments Is Important for Writers

In the previous chapter we explained how argument is a social phenomenon in which communities search for the best answers to disputed questions. As you'll see in this chapter, we live in an environment saturated with oral, visual, print, and hypertext arguments. When we enter an argumentative conversation, we need to position ourselves as inquirers as well as persuaders, listening attentively to alternative points of view. Doing so, we will often be compelled not only to protest an injustice or work for change but also to reexamine our values, assumptions, and behaviors, perhaps even to change our views. Rhetorician Wayne Booth proposes that when we enter an argumentative conversation we should first ask, "When should I change my mind?" rather than "How can I change your mind?"* In this chapter, we focus on reading arguments as a process of inquiry. We present five strategies that will help you listen to the arguments you encounter, resist simplistic answers, delve into multiple views, and emerge from your intellectual wrestling with informed, deepened, and supportable solutions to problems.

Because argument begins in disagreements within a social community, you should examine any argument as if it were only one voice in a larger conversation. We therefore recommend the following sequence of strategies:

1. Read as a believer.
2. Read as a doubter.
3. Explore how the rhetorical context and genre are shaping the argument.
4. Consider alternative views and analyze sources of disagreement.
5. Use disagreement productively to prompt further investigation.

Let's now examine each of these strategies in turn.

---

*Wayne Booth raised these questions in a featured session with Peter Elbow entitled "Blind Skepticism vs. the Rhetoric of Assent: Implications for Rhetoric, Argument, and Teaching" at CCCC Convention, Chicago, Illinois, March 2002.

Strategy 1: Reading as a Believer

When you read an argument as a believer, you practice what psychologist Carl Rogers calls *empathic listening*. Empathic listening requires that you see the world through the author's eyes, adopt temporarily the author's beliefs and values, and suspend your skepticism and biases long enough to hear what the author is saying.

Because empathic listening is such a vital skill, we soon will invite you to practice it on a brief argument opposing the genetic engineering of food. Before we ask you to read the argument, however, we want to introduce you to this issue. Since 1994, when genetically modified foods first appeared in supermarkets, they have become increasingly more prevalent, but not without resistance from some consumers. Antibiotechnology groups have labeled genetically modified foods "Frankenfoods" after the power-seeking scientist who created the monster in Mary Shelley's novel *Frankenstein*. This catchy and shrewd word "Frankenfoods" connotes God-playing scientists whose work backfires into an uncontrollable destructive force. The proponents of biotechnology, in contrast, see genetic engineering as beneficial and progressive, offering ways to create disease-resistant plants, more environmentally friendly agricultural methods, and more promising ways to feed the world. With this background, you are now ready to examine for yourself some of the controversies surrounding genetic engineering of food.

For Class Discussion

1. Suppose you are thumbing through a magazine and come across the advocacy advertisement shown in Color Plate A. The ad is sponsored by three groups called "Citizens for Health," the "Center for Food Safety," and "Sustain." Working as a whole class or in small groups, respond to the following questions:

   a. What is the claim of this ad? Whom or what is it arguing against?

   b. Does this ad make you nervous about eating genetically modified foods? What aspects of the ad are most effective in influencing your response? (Consider both the text of the ad and its visual elements.)

2. Now suppose you saw in the op-ed section of your local newspaper the political cartoon shown at the beginning of Part One of this text (p. 1).

   a. What is the claim of this cartoon? Whom or what is it arguing against?

   b. How does this cartoon speak back to the "Keep Nature Natural" ad in Color Plate A?

3. What is your current view of genetically modified foods? (If you buy your food from supermarkets, you are probably eating some genetically modified ingredients. According to some sources, 33 percent of corn, 50 percent of soy, and 50 percent of cotton crops are genetically modified.)

4. Based on the "Keep Nature Natural" ad and the political cartoon, what do you think are the major arguments for and against genetically modified foods?

Now that you have done some thinking about genetic modification of food, read carefully the following article, which appeared in a health food magazine called *Better Nutrition* in June 2000.

Playing with Our Food
Genetic Engineering and Irradiation
Lisa Turner

1   It used to be that getting clean food wasn't so hard. A trip to the local health food store and a quick scan of food labels, and you could fill your 'fridge with whole, healthy foods. Now, even tofu is likely to be tainted with genetically modified organisms, and your favorite natural tabouli mix may contain irradiated herbs and spices. Is nothing sacred? Not in the brave new world of "biotech" foods.

GENETIC ENGINEERING WEIRD SCIENCE

2   Flounder genes in your pasta sauce? Insect genes in your mashed potatoes? Welcome to the high-tech process of artificially shuffling genes from one organism to another. Proponents of *genetic engineering* say it's a sure way to boost food supply, reduce pesticide use and possibly breed super-foods with extraordinary nutritional profiles. The problem is, no one really knows the long-term effects of such complex *genetic* manipulation—and the potential *dangers* to humans and the environment are substantial.

3   Don't think that *genetic engineering* is merely a stepped-up version of traditional cross-breeding techniques. It's a new, weird science that allows the insertion of genes from any plant or animal into any other organism. One example: an "anti-freeze" gene that allows flounder to survive in very cold water is inserted into tomatoes to boost their tolerance to frost. Or insect-killing genes from bacteria may be inserted into corn or potatoes to up their defenses against pests.

4   Shuffling genes between species raises plenty of scary possibilities. The technology is new enough to be frighteningly imprecise, with generally uncertain outcomes. And because no long-term safety tests have been conducted, no one really knows the full scope of potential health risks. According to an editorial in a 1996 issue of the *New England Journal of Medicine*, "Questions of safety vex federal regulators and industry as well as the public. The transfer of genes from microbes, plants

or animals into foods raises issues about the unintended consequences of such manipulations."

Some of these consequences include the production of new allergens in foods 5 and unexpected mutations in an organism, which can create new and higher levels of toxins. One example: in 1993, 37 people died and more than 1,500 people suffered partial paralysis from a disease called eosinophilia-myalgia, which was eventually linked to a tryptophan supplement made with genetically engineered bacteria.

Another worrisome possibility is that insects, birds and the wind can carry genet- 6 ically altered seeds into neighboring fields and beyond, where they can cross-polli- nate, threatening the future of wild crops, genetically natural crops and organic foods.

And once genetically modified organisms are introduced into the food supply, 7 they can't be recalled. "Unlike pesticide use, *genetic engineering* introduces living organisms that will be replicated in other living organisms," says Susan Haeger, president/CEO of Citizens for Health, a non-profit consumer advocacy group based in Boulder, Colorado. "Once they're in the environment, there's no way to bring them back."

IRRADIATION: ZAPPING OUR FOOD

What happens when you cross a potato with 10,000 rads of ionizing radiation— 8 more than 2,500,000 times the dose of a chest X-ray? Better find out before you eat your next order of french fries. Irradiation, used to extend shelf life and kill mi- croorganisms in food, can also lower nutritional value, create environmental haz- ards, promote the growth of toxins and produce compounds called unique radiolytic products, which have been associated with a variety of biological abnormalities.

Food irradiation was proposed by the Atomic Energy Commission in the early 9 1950s as a way of dealing with a formidable nuclear waste problem from the manu- facture of nuclear weapons, according to Michael Colby, editor of the *Food & Water Journal.* In the mid-1980s, the FDA began to approve a huge range of foodstuffs for irradiation, including meat, poultry, produce, herbs and spices. Since then, permis- sible levels of radiation have been dramatically increased, and the amount now al- lowed is substantial.

Proponents say irradiation destroys harmful microorganisms and may reduce 10 outbreaks of salmonella and trichinosis from meat. It is also said that irradiation in- creases shelf life of various foods and can reduce the use of toxic chemicals as post- harvest fumigants. Absurd, say irradiation opponents. "Irradiation is destroying our food supply," says Gary Gibbs, D.O., author of *The Food That Would Last Forever.* "It is nothing more than a toxic band-aid approach to the problems."

Adequate cooking, sanitary handling and preparation and hygienic processing 11 methods are better ways to reduce illness from microorganisms in meat. Shelf life is an unfounded concern in the United States, and the cost of irradiation in less- developed countries would usually offset savings from extended shelf life. As for the argument that irradiation would reduce the need for post-harvest chemical fu- migants, some say that irradiated foods are more prone to infection by certain fungi.

12   The FDA and irradiation proponents claim the process is safe, but compelling evidence to the contrary says otherwise. Meanwhile, considerable controversy exists regarding safety studies. Although 441 studies have been conducted on food irradiation, the FDA based their toxicity evaluation on only five animal studies, according to Gibbs. Of these five studies, two were found to be methodologically flawed, one suggested that irradiated food could have adverse effects on older animals and two investigated foods irradiated at doses well below FDA-approved levels.

13   Few human trials exist, because of obvious ethical considerations, but some small studies have raised concerns, suggesting that food irradiation can cause chromosomal abnormalities.

14   Irradiation of food can lead to cardiac disease, cancer, kindney disease, fetal malformations and a dramatic shortening of the life span, according to Gibbs. "A lot of studies have shown problems with the heart, specifically that irradiation causes bleeding in the heart," he says. "Also, when food is irradiated, it creates benzene and formaldehyde, which are known mutagens and suspected carcinogens."

15   Irradiation also apears to cause significant nutrient loss in foods, especially of vitamins A, B, C and E. Generally, the higher the amount of radiation, the greater the nutrient loss. Add to that environmental concerns, including hazards in transporting and handling radioactive isotopes, danger of exposure to workers and possible security problems at irradiation facilities. Right now, there are about 50 irradiation facilities in the United States, says Colby, but a huge increase is expected if irradiation is embraced in the marketplace. The result: a substantial increase in potential environmental disasters.

WHAT TO DO

16   Because biotech foods are still new, the core issues are safety testing and consumer awareness. "It may be that there are some positive aspects to biotech food," says Haeger. "We don't know. Our concern is that the commercialization of biotech foods and their integration in the food system is outpacing the science and is being promoted without the awareness of the public."

17   More stringent safety testing is critical, as are more comprehensive labeling requirements. Under current laws, irradiated foods must be labeled as such, with a written notice and a "radura"—the international irradiation symbol—but processed foods and foods prepared for restaurants, hospitals or school cafeterias are exempt from such labeling. Additionally, no labeling requirements exist for genetically engineered foods.

18   Some say *genetic engineering* and food irradiation should be banned. "This is beyond labeling considerations," says Gibbs. "It should be completely outlawed. We shouldn't even have to have conversations about labeling." It the meantime, the primary thrust is toward public awareness.

19   "Our main concern is for consumers to be aware of food manipulation," says Haeger. "We want to ensure that they are informed and have adequate information on what they're purchasing, so they can make their own choices."

References

Belongia, F.A., et al. "The eosinophilia-myalgia syndrome and tryptophan," *Annu Rev Nutr* 12: 235–56, 1992.

Bhaskaram, C., Sadasivan, G. "Effects of feeding irradiated wheat to malnourished children," *American Journal of Clinical Nutrition* 28(2): 130–35, 1975.

Hickman, J.R., McLean, L.A., Ley, F.J. "Rat feeding studies on wheat treated with gamma radiation," *Food and Cosmetic Toxicology* 2(2): 175–180, 1964.

Khattak, A.B., Klopfenstein, C.F. "Effects of gamma irradiation on the nutritional quality of grains and legumes," *Cereal Chemistry* 66(3): 171–72, 1989.

McGivney, W.T. "Preservation of food products by irradiation," *Seminars in Nuclear Medicine* 18: 36, 1998.

Nyhan, W.L., et al. "New approaches to understanding Lesch-Nyhan disease," *New England Journal of Medicine* 334(24): 1602–4, 1996.

Piccioni, R. "Food irradiation: Contaminating our food," *The Ecologist* 18(2): 48, 1988.

Radomski, J.L., et al. "Chronic toxicity studies in irradiated beef stew and evaporated milk," *Toxicology and Applied Pharmacology* 7(1): 113–21, 1965.

Raica, N., Scott, J., Nielson, N. "Nutritional quality of irradiated foods," *Radiation Research Review* 3(4): 447–57, 1972.

Shanghai Institute of Radiation Medicine and Shanghai Institute of Nuclear Research. "Safety evaluation of 35 kinds of irradiated human foods," *Chinese Medical Journal* 100(9): 715–18, 1987.

Summary Writing as a Way of Reading to Believe

Now that you have finished the article, ask yourself how well you "listened" to it. If you listened well, you should be able to write a summary of Turner's argument in your own words. A *summary* (also called an *abstract*, a *précis*, or a *synopsis*) presents only a text's major points and eliminates supporting details. Writers often incorporate summaries of other writers' views into their own arguments, either to support their own claims or to represent alternative views that they intend to address. Summaries can be any length, depending on the writer's purposes, but usually they range from several sentences to one or two paragraphs.

Practicing the following steps should help you be a better summary writer:

Step 1: Read the argument first for general meaning. Don't judge it; put your objections aside; just follow the writer's meaning, trying to see the issue from the writer's perspective. Try to adopt the writer's values and belief system. Walk in the writer's shoes.

Step 2: Read the argument slowly a second and a third time, writing in the margins brief *does* and *says* statements for each paragraph (or group of closely connected paragraphs). A *does* statement identifies a paragraph's function, such as "summarizes an opposing view," "introduces a supporting reason," "gives an example," or "uses statistics to support the previous point." A *says* statement summarizes a paragraph's content.

Your challenge in writing *says statements* is to identify the main point in each paragraph. This process may actually be easier with an academic article that uses long block paragraphs headed by topic sentences than it is for more informal journalistic articles like Turner's that use a string of shorter, less developed paragraphs. What follows are the *does* and *says* statements for the first six paragraphs of Turner's article.

DOES/SAYS ANALYSIS OF TURNER'S ARTICLE

Paragraph 1:   *Does*: Introduces the problem of "the brave new world of 'biotech' foods." *Says*: It is becoming difficult today to find foods that have not been irradiated or genetically modified.

Paragraph 2:   *Does*: Briefly sketches the benefits of genetic engineering and shifts to the potential dangers. *Says*: Advocates claim that biotechnology can increase the food supply, reduce the use of pesticides, and increase the nutritional value of foods, but no one knows the long-term effects of genetic engineering on humans or the environment.

Paragraph 3:   *Does*: Elaborates on how genetic engineering works with some specific examples. *Says*: Genetic engineering alters plants and animals far beyond crossbreeding.

Paragraph 4:   *Does:* Elaborates on the potential dangers of genetic engineering. *Says*: Imprecision and unpredictable long-term consequences make this biotechnology frightening.

Paragraph 5:   *Does*: Offers examples of some of the dangerous consequences so far. *Says*: Genetic engineering created toxins that caused deaths and partial paralysis in 1993.

Paragraph 6:   *Does*: States another problem of genetic engineering. *Says*: Cross-pollination can contaminate wild or organic plants.

For Class Discussion

Working individually or in groups, write *does* and *says* statements for the remaining paragraphs of Turner's article.

Step 3:   Examine your *does* and *says* statements to determine the major sections of the argument, and create a list of major points and subpoints. If you are visually oriented, you may prefer to make a diagram, flowchart, or scratch outline of the sections of Turner's argument.

Step 4:   Turn your list, outline, flowchart, or diagram into a prose summary. Typically, writers do this in one of two ways. Some start by joining all their *says* statements into a lengthy paragraph-by-paragraph summary and then prune it and streamline. They combine ideas into sentences and then revise those sentences to make them clearer and more tightly structured. Others start with a one-sentence summary of the argument's thesis and major supporting reasons and then flesh it out with more supporting ideas. Your

goal is to be as neutral and as objective as possible by keeping your own responses to the writer's ideas out of your summary. To be fair to the writer,
you also need to cover all the writer's main points and give them the same
emphasis as in the original article.

Step 5:   Revise your summary until it is the desired length and is sufficiently clear, concise, and complete. When you incorporate a summary of
someone else's argument into your own essay, you must distinguish that
author's words and ideas from your own by using *attributive tags*
(expressions like "Turner says," "according to Turner," or "Turner further
explains"), by putting any directly borrowed language in quotation marks,
and by citing the original author using appropriate conventions for documenting sources.

As illustration, we will show our summaries of Turner's article—a one-paragraph version and a single-sentence version. In the one-paragraph version, we illustrate the MLA documentation system in which page numbers for direct quotations are placed in parentheses after the quotation and complete bibliographic
information is placed in a Works Cited list at the end of the paper. See Chapter 17
for a complete explanation of the MLA and APA documentation systems.

ONE PARAGRAPH SUMMARY OF TURNER'S ARGUMENT

Identification of
author and source

Insertion of short
quotation; MLA
documentation
shows page
numbers in
parentheses

Attributive tags

Continued use of
attributive tags

In an article entitled "Playing with Our Food" from the magazine
Better Nutrition, health food advocate Lisa Turner warns readers
that much of our food today is genetically modified or irradiated.
She describes genetic engineering as artificial gene shuffling that
differs completely from "traditional cross-breeding" (24). She argues that the potential, unforeseen, harmful consequences of this
"new, weird science" (24) offset the possible benefits of increasing
the food supply, reducing the use of pesticides, and boosting the
nutritional value of foods. Turner asserts that genetic engineering
is imprecise, untested, unpredictable, irreversible, and also uncontrollable due to animals, insects, and winds. She also objects to the
use of irradiation to enable foods to stay fresh longer and to kill
harmful microorganisms. Claiming that the FDA has not tested irradiation at the levels that it allows, she suggests that irradiation
has many harmful effects: depleting vitamins in foods, causing
cancer and cardiac problems, and increasing amounts of radioactive material in the environment. Turner concludes by saying that
the marketing of these products has proceeded much more quickly
than scientific knowledge about them warrants. If we don't ban
genetic engineering and irradiation completely (a course that some
people propose), Turner argues that at the very least more safety
testing and labeling are needed. We consumers must know how
our food has been manipulated. (220 words)

Works Cited

Correct citation of article in MLA format. (In a formal paper the "Works Cited" list begins a new page.)

> Turner, Lisa. "Playing with Our Food." *Better Nutrition* June 2000: 56–59. Rpt. in *Writing Arguments: A Rhetoric with Readings.* John D. Ramage, John C. Bean, and June Johnson. 6th ed. New York: Longman, 2004.

ONE-SENTENCE SUMMARY OF TURNER'S ARGUMENT

In her article in *Better Nutrition,* health food writer Lisa Turner warns readers of the prevalence, risk, and potential health and environmental dangers of genetic modification and irradiation of food, arguing that these products should undergo more stringent testing for safety and should be labeled for consumer protection.

Whether you write a very short summary or a more detailed one, your goal should be to come as close as possible to a fair, accurate, and balanced condensation of the author's argument and to represent the relationships among the parts fairly and accurately. We don't want to pretend that summary writing is easy; often it's not, especially if the argument is complex and if the author doesn't explicitly highlight his or her thesis and main supporting reasons. Nonetheless, being able to summarize the arguments of others in your own words is an important skill for arguers.

Suspending Doubt: Willing Your Own Belief in the Writer's Views

Summarizing an argument is only the first step in your effort to believe it. You must also suspend doubt and will yourself to adopt the writer's view. Suspending doubt is easy if you already agree with the author. But if an author's views affront your own values, then "believing" can be a hard but valuable exercise. By struggling to believe strange, threatening, or unfamiliar views, we can grow as learners and thinkers.

To believe an author, search your mind for personal experiences, values, and beliefs that affirm his or her argument. Here is how one student wrote a journal entry trying to believe Turner's article.

JOURNAL ENTRY SHOWING STUDENT'S ATTEMPT TO BELIEVE TURNER

Although I had heard of genetic modification of plants and of hormones given to cows to produce more milk, I never thought about how I might be affected. Turner's article made me worry about how many of the things I eat have been produced by artificial genetic processes and how many have been treated with radiation. How much do scientists actually know about long-term effects of growing and eating biotech food? I know of lots of cases where scientists have tried to fix environmental problems, and their intervention has had disastrous results. My biology teacher told us about a failed scientific intervention involving cane toads brought into Australia to eat the beetles and grubs plaguing the sugar cane. The natural cycles of the grubs, beetles, and toads didn't match. Now the cane toads have proliferated out of control because they have no native predators. What's worse, they are poisonous! Ten years from now will genetic engineering be failed science in the category of "it seemed like a great idea at the time"? As it is, every year we read studies that say vitamin C or some food that we thought was good for us is actually harmful. Turner's article has made me want to know how the government is regulating what biotech foods are sold. Maybe I should spend more time reading the labels on all the food I buy. How much more will I have to pay to avoid foods that have been genetically modified or treated with radiation?

Strategy 2: Reading as a Doubter

Reading as a believer is an important part of being a powerful reader, but you must also learn to read as a doubter by raising objections, asking questions, expressing skepticism, and withholding your assent. When you read as a doubter, you also question what is *not* in the argument. What is glossed over, unexplained, or left out? In the margins of the text you add a new layer of notes demanding proof, doubting evidence, challenging the author's assumptions and values, and so forth. Because writing marginal notes helps you read a text actively—to follow the author's argument and speak back to it in your own voice—we show you an example of one reader's marginal notes for a section of Turner's text (Figure 2.1). Note how it is a mixture of believing and doubting commentary.

Some of these consequences include the production of new allergens in foods and unexpected mutations in an organism, which can create new and higher levels of toxins. One example: in 1993, 37 people died and more than 1,500 people suffered partial paralysis from a disease called eosinophilia-myalgia, which was eventually linked to a tryptophan supplement made with genetically engineered bacteria. [5]	This "eventual link" sounds weak. I need more explanation. Where did this case occur? What food was involved? What is a "tryptophan supplement"?
Another worrisome possibility is that insects, birds and the wind carry genetically altered seeds into neighboring fields and beyond, where they can cross-pollinate, threatening the future of wild crops, genetically natural crops and organic foods. [6]	Seems like a strong point. Supports what I've read about cross-pollination and organic forms.
And once genetically modified organisms are introduced into the food supply, they can't be recalled. "Unlike pesticide use, genetic engineering introduces living organisms that will be replicated in other living organisms," says Susan Haeger, president/CEO of Citizens for Health, a non-profit consumer advocacy group based in Boulder, Colorado. "Once they're in the environment, there's no way to bring them back." [7]	This quote not from scientist. Would scientists agree about dangers to the environment?

FIGURE 2.1   *Believing and doubting notes for Turner article*

For Class Discussion

Return now to Turner's article, reading skeptically. Raise questions, offer objections, and express doubts. Then, working as a class or in small groups, list all the doubts you have about Turner's argument.

Now that you have doubted Turner's article, compare your doubts to some raised by our students.

- In the third sentence of her article, Turner says that tofu is "likely to be tainted with genetically modified organisms." Her word "taint" suggests a strong bias against technology right from the start.

- She mentions the possible advantages of genetic engineering in only one sentence—boosting food supply, reducing needs for pesticides, and so forth. These seem like major advantages that should be investigated. How successful has biotechnology been at achieving its stated goals? What scientific breakthroughs has genetic engineering made? What good has it done so far?

- She gives no sources for her claim that an antifreeze gene from flounders is inserted into tomatoes. We would like to learn if this claim is true and see how scientists describe the purpose and results. There may be another side to this story.

- She doesn't claim that biotech foods are not safe. She just claims that they haven't been tested enough. The only negative evidence she provides is the 37 persons killed by a disease that was "linked" to genetically engineered bacteria. Why the weak word "linked"? Did scientists prove that the disease was caused by genetic engineering? Is this case exceptional? Is it good evidence to show that all genetically engineered foods are potentially harmful?

- The case against irradiation is not supported by evidence but by testimony from Gary Gibbs and Susan Haeger, whose scientific credentials aren't clearly stated. Turner claims that "compelling evidence" refutes the claim of the FDA that irradiation is safe. She doesn't provide or document this compelling evidence. She makes numerous frightening claims about irradiation without any evidence that the claims are true.

These are only some of the objections that might be raised against Turner's argument. Perhaps you and your classmates have other objections that are equally important. Our point is that you should practice "doubting" an argument as well as "believing" it. Both skills are essential. *Believing* helps you expand your view of the world or modify your arguments and beliefs in response to others. *Doubting* helps protect you from becoming overpowered by others' arguments and teaches you to stand back, consider, and weigh points carefully.

Strategy 3: Exploring How Rhetorical Context and Genre Shape the Argument

The strategies of believing and doubting an argument urge you toward further exploration and inquiry. In the next stage of analysis, you should consider the rhetorical context of the argument as well as its genre. In this section we'll explain these concepts and show you why they are important.

Understanding the Genres of Argument

Knowing the genre of an argument helps you understand how the writer's purpose, intended audience, and angle of vision or bias have shaped the argument. A "genre" is a recurring type or pattern of argument such as a letter to the editor, a scholarly journal article, or the home page of an advocacy Web site. Genres are often categorized by format, purpose, or type of publication; as we'll see, they place on writers certain demands (such as the need for a particular tone or kind of evidence) and constraints (such as limits on length).

When you read arguments anthologized in a textbook such as this one, you lose clues about the argument's original genre. (You should therefore note the information about genre provided in our introductions to readings.) You can also lose clues about genre when you download articles from the Internet or from licensed databases such as LexisNexis or ProQuest. (See Chapter 16 for explanations of these research tools.) When you do your own research, you therefore need to be aware of the original genre of what you are reading: Is this piece a newspaper editorial, an article from a magazine, an organizational white paper, an academic argument in a peer-reviewed journal, a student paper posted to a Web site, or something else?

In the following list, we identify most of the genres of argument through which readers and writers carry on the conversations of a democracy.

- *Personal correspondence.*   This category includes letters or e-mail messages sent to specific decision makers in order to achieve the writer's purpose (complaint letter, request for a certain action). The style can range from a formal business letter to an informal note. The tone depends on purpose and audience.

- *Letters to the editor.*   Letters to the editor provide an excellent forum for ordinary citizens to voice their views on public issues. Published in newspapers and some public affairs magazines, letters are aimed at the readers of the publication to influence opinion on recently discussed issues. They are very short (fewer than three hundred words) and time sensitive. They can sometimes be summaries of longer arguments, but often focus in "sound bite" style on one point. Their perspective or bias can vary widely since editors seek a wide range of opinions.

- *Newspaper editorials and op-ed columns.* Often written in response to a recent occurrence, political event, or social problem in the news, editorials and op-ed pieces are widely read, influential types of arguments. Editorials, which appear on the editorial page of a newspaper and promote the views of the editors, are short (usually fewer than five hundred words), and are written in a journalistic style, often without detailed evidence. They can range from conservative to liberal, depending on the political bias of the editors (see p. 377 in Chapter 16). Op-ed columns appear "opposite the editorial page" (hence the abbreviation "op-ed") and are usually written by syndicated columnists who are professional writers ranging in bias from ultraconservative to socialist (see p. 377 in Chapter 16). Op-ed columns typically average 500–1000 words and can vary from explicit thesis-driven arguments to implicit arguments with stylistic flair. Newspapers also publish "guest op-ed pieces" by local writers on a one-time or occasional basis when a person has particular expertise on an issue. Sometimes an especially good but overly long letter to the editor is published as an op-ed piece.

- *Public affairs or niche magazine articles.* Public affairs magazines such as *National Review, New Republic, Atlantic Monthly,* or *The Progressive* are outlets for in-depth studies of current issues. Written by staff writers or freelancers, articles in public affairs magazines usually reflect the political bias of the magazine (see p. 361 in Chapter 16). The articles often have a journalistic style with informal documentation, and they frequently include narrative elements rather than explicit thesis-and-reasons organization. Many of the best articles give well-researched coverage of various perspectives on a public issue. In contrast to public affairs magazines, niche magazines advocate for the interests of a particular profession or target audience. Niche magazines include trade publications such as *Automotive Week* or *Construction Marketing Today,* arts and entertainment magazines such as *Rolling Stone* or *Cinema,* and culture and society magazines aimed at particular audiences, such as *The Advocate* (gay and lesbian issues) or *Minority Business Entrepreneur.*

- *Scholarly journals.* Scholarly journals are nonprofit magazines subsidized by universities or scholarly societies. They publish academic articles that have been reviewed by scholars in the field. Although scholars try scrupulously to collect evidence in an unbiased way and analyze it objectively, their work necessarily reflects the biases, methods, and strategies associated with a specific school of thought or theory within a discipline. Scholarly articles usually employ a formal academic style and include academic documentation and bibliographies. When scholars write to influence public opinion on the basis of their research, they often use a more popular style and may seek outlets other than scholarly journals, such as a public affairs magazine or an academic Web site. (Student papers in an argument class often fit this genre—academic argument aimed at a popular audience on a public issue.)

- *Organizational white papers.* This is perhaps the most common genre of argument in an organizational or professional setting. White papers are in-house documents written by individuals or committees to influence organization de-cisions or policies or to give informed advice to clients. Sometimes they are written for external audiences to influence public opinion favorable to the or-ganization, in which case they reflect the organization's bias and perspective (external white papers are often posted on Web sites or sent to legislators). They are usually desktop published for use within an organization and written in a utilitarian style with thesis-and-reasons organization and formal docu-mentation. They often include graphics and other visuals. They can vary in style from the dully bureaucratic (satirized in *Dilbert* cartoons) to the cogent and persuasive.

- *Proposals.* Typed or desktop published, proposals identify a problem, propose a specific solution, and support the solution with a justifying argument. Proposals focus on the needs of the targeted audience, using the audience's values and desires to justify the writer's proposed solution. They are often used to seek grant funding or secure contracts with clients. Proposals are the lifeblood of organizations that depend on meeting the needs of clients for their livelihood.

- *Legal briefs and court decisions.* Legal briefs are written by attorneys to support the position of one of the parties in a trial or judicial review. "Friends of the court" briefs are written by stakeholders in a case to influence appeals courts such as the U.S. Supreme Court. Briefs are usually written in legalese, but use a logical, well-organized reasons-and-evidence structure. Friends of the court briefs are se-rious reasons-and-evidence position papers reflecting the bias or perspective of the writer. Once a judge or court makes a decision, the "court decision" is often published to explain the judge's reasoning. Court decisions—particularly those of the U.S. Supreme Court—make fascinating reading; they reveal the complexities of the issue and the intricacies of the judges' thinking. They also include minority arguments if the decision was not unanimous.

- *Public affairs advocacy advertisements.* Published as posters, fliers, Web pages, or paid advertisements, these condensed arguments try to influence public opinion on civic issues. Using a succinct "sound bite" style, these ads often em-ploy document design, bulleted lists, and visual elements such as graphics, photographs, or drawings for rhetorical effect. They have an explicit bias and often ignore the complexities of an issue by focusing strongly on one view. During periods of civic debate, advocacy groups often purchase full-page newspaper ads to influence public opinion.

- *Advocacy Web sites.* Often identified by the extension ".org" in the Web site ad-dress, advocacy Web sites support the views of the site owner on civic issues. Web sites by well-financed advocacy groups such as the NRA (National Rifle Association) or PETA (People for the Ethical Treatment of Animals) are profes-sionally designed with extensive links to other sites supporting the same views. Well-designed sites use visuals and hyperlinked texts aimed at creating an im-mediate visceral response favorable to the site owner's views. Advocacy sites reflect the bias of the site owner; ethically responsible sites explicitly announce their bias and purpose in an "about us" link on the home page. (For further discussion of reading and evaluating Web sites, see Chapter 16, pp. 378–381.)

- *Posting to chat rooms, MOOs, electronic bulletin boards.* These postings are written in truncated, informal style often using the jargon and code words of a particular audience. They are posted by individuals to influence opinions of other participants in an online discussion. They usually reflect a wide range of perspectives and are excellent places to try out ideas-in-progress.

- *Visual arguments.* Although seldom appearing by themselves without some accompanying text, photographs, drawings, political cartoons, and graphics can have an intense rhetorical impact (see Chapter 9). Visuals make strong emotional appeals, often reducing complex issues to one powerful perspective.

- *Speeches.* Many of the important arguments in our culture, including those in print, begin initially as speeches—either formal speeches such as a presidential address or a keynote speech at a professional meeting, or more informal speeches such as presentations at hearings or interviews on talk shows. Often transcriptions of speeches are printed in newspapers or made available on the Web.

Now that you have a brief overview of the genres of argument, we can apply this knowledge to the issue we have been examining—the genetic engineering of food. As we did our own research on this issue, we found letters to editors, newspaper editorials, op-ed pieces, magazine articles in public affairs and niche magazines, scholarly academic articles, professional and scientific proposals, political speeches, advocacy ads and posters, and white papers presenting the views of organizations, advocacy groups, and governmental agencies. The public debate about genetic engineering of foods is thus being carried on across the total spectrum of argument genres.

Analyzing Rhetorical Context and Genre

Besides understanding an argument's genre, you need to reconstruct its rhetorical context—that is, learn more about the conversation the writer is joining and about the writer's credentials, purpose, audience, and motivation. Awareness of genre and rhetorical context can help you determine how much influence an argument should have on your own thinking about an issue. To explore the rhetorical context of an argument, you can use the following guide questions:

Questions about Rhetorical Context and Genre

1. Who is the author? What are the author's credentials and what is his/her investment in the issue?

2. What audience is he or she writing for?

3. What motivating occasion prompted this writing? What is the author's purpose?

4. What genre of argument is this? How do the conventions of that genre help determine the depth, complexity, and even appearance of the argument?

5. What information about the publication or source (magazine, newspaper, advocacy Web site) explains the angle of vision that shapes the argument?

Consider how we applied these questions to Lisa Turner's article "Playing with Our Food." We began by investigating the identity of the author and the kind of publication. Checking on Lisa Turner's background (by keyboarding her name into a Web search engine), we discovered that she specializes in alternative health therapies and has training in naturopathy, Chinese herbal medicine, yoga, and meditation techniques. She has written five books on nutrition and health published by presses associated with alternative medicine, regularly appears on talk shows to promote natural health, teaches cooking classes at Whole Foods Market (one of the biggest organic food chains), and owns a catering company called "The Healthy Gourmet." We learned that *Better Nutrition* is a niche magazine about consumer health and alternative therapies distributed primarily at health food stores. It is indexed in CINAHL, the main nursing index, but not in MEDLINE, one of the main medical indexes. (Its absence from MEDLINE means that mainstream medical researchers, who value the scientific method, don't regard the magazine as an outlet for serious scholarship.)

When we returned to the article "Playing with Our Food" and analyzed it rhetorically, we saw more clearly how Turner's background, the type of magazine, and her sense of audience shaped her argument. She is strongly biased toward organic foods and alternative approaches to medicine and health. Because *Better Nutrition* is a natural health magazine, Turner assumes that her audience will share her opposition to scientific intervention in farming and food processing. Although this article does include references, they are not the most current or the most exact. The two sources that she quotes directly—the CEO of the advocacy group Citizens for Health and the author of the book *The Food That Would Last Forever*—do not appear in her list of references. Her alarmist tone and vehement language as well as the scarcity of specific examples suggest that she is writing to an audience who may be uninformed but who nevertheless share her bias. We decided that this article represents a "health foods" point of view in the biotech foods controversy but provides only a starting point for inquiry into this complex issue.

Strategy 4: Seeking out Alternative Views and Analyzing Sources of Disagreement

When you analyze an argument, you shouldn't isolate it from the general conversation of differing views that form its context. If you were an arbitrator, you wouldn't think of settling a dispute between A and B on the basis of A's testimony only. You would also insist on hearing B's side of the story (and perhaps also C's and D's if they are stakeholders in the dispute). In analyzing an argument, therefore, you should try to seek out the views of those who disagree with the author to appreciate the full context of the issue.

As you listen to differing views, try to identify sources of disagreement, which often fall into two categories: (1) disagreement about the facts or reality of the case and (2) disagreement about underlying beliefs, values, or assumptions, including assumptions about definitions or appropriate analogies. Let's look at each in turn.

Disagreement about Facts or Their Relevance

Often disputants in an argument disagree about facts in a case or about the relevance of certain facts. Consider the controversies over global warming. Although the majority of scientists believe that the earth is getting hotter and that at least some portion of this increase is caused by the emission of greenhouse gases, scientists have factual disputes about the rate of global warming, about its causes (How much is natural? How much is human-caused?), and about its environmental effects. Additionally, disputants can disagree on the significance or relevance of a fact. For example, global warming activists often cite the dramatic shrinking of the glacial ice cap on Africa's Mount Kilimanjaro as evidence of human-caused global warming. But some climatologists, who agree that Kilimanjaro's ice cap is shrinking, argue that nonhuman causes such as changes in solar output or natural climate variability may be the primary factors. In this case, a fact that urges one person to propose political action to combat global warming leaves another person unmoved. Other examples of disagreements about facts or reality include the following:

- In arguing whether silver-mercury amalgam tooth fillings should be banned, dental researchers disagree on the amount of mercury vapor released by older fillings; they also disagree on how much mercury vapor has to be present before it is harmful.

- In arguing about the legalization of drugs, writers disagree about the degree to which Prohibition reduced alcohol consumption; they also disagree on whether crack cocaine is "crimogenic" (has chemical properties that induce violent behavior).

Disagreement about Values, Beliefs, or Assumptions

A second source of disagreement concerns differences in values, beliefs, or assumptions. Here are some examples:

- Persons A and B might agree that a huge tax on gasoline would cut down on the consumption of petroleum. They might agree further that the world's supply of petroleum will eventually run out. Thus Persons A and B agree at the level of facts. But they might disagree about whether the United States should enact a huge gas tax. Person A might support the law in order to conserve oil. Person B might oppose it, perhaps because B believes that scientists will find alternative energy sources before the petroleum runs out or because B believes the short-term harm of such a tax outweighs distant benefits.

■ Person A and Person B might agree that capital punishment deters potential murderers (an agreement on facts). Person A supports capital punishment for this reason, but Person B opposes it, believing that the taking of a human life is always wrong in principle even if the state does it legally (a disagreement about basic beliefs).

Sometimes differing beliefs or values present themselves as disagreements about definitions or appropriate analogies.

■ Social Theorist A and Social Theorist B disagree about whether the covers of some women's magazines like *Cosmopolitan* are pornographic. This disagreement turns on the definition of *pornography*, with different definitions reflecting different underlying values and beliefs.

■ In supporting a Texas law forbidding flag burning, Chief Justice William Rehnquist argued that desecration of a flag in the name of free speech is similar to desecrating the Washington Monument. He thus makes this analogy: Just as we would forbid desecration of a national monument, so should we forbid desecration of the flag. Opposing justices did not think the analogy was valid.

■ Person A and Person B disagree on whether it is ethically acceptable to have Down's syndrome children undergo plastic surgery to correct some of the facial abnormalities associated with this genetic condition. Person A supports the surgery, arguing that it is analogous to any other cosmetic surgeries done to improve appearance. Person B argues against such surgery, saying it is analogous to the racial self-hatred of some minority persons who have tried to change their ethnic appearance and become lily white. (The latter analogy argues that Down's syndrome is nothing to be ashamed of and that persons should take pride in their difference.)

We now invite you to consider a different view of biotechnology. Examine Color Plate B, which is an advocacy advertisement sponsored by the Council for Biotechnology Information. This ad, promoting biotech soybeans, appeared in a July 2002 issue of *Time* magazine. A similar ad, also by the Council for Biotechnology Information, appeared in an April 2002 issue of *Atlantic Monthly*. Then read this same organization's argument opposing consumer labels for genetically engineered foods. (We found the argument on the Council's Web site.) These pro-biotech arguments—in conversation with Turner's article and the "Keep Nature Natural" ad (Color Plate A)—vividly exemplify the differing values and beliefs that compete for our allegiance in a pluralistic world.

Why Biotech Labeling Can Confuse Consumers

Council for Biotechnology Information

1 Consumers want food product labels with clear, meaningful information.

2 A grocery shopper, for example, finds a wealth of factual information on labels, whether it's about nutrient and caloric content or specific health aspects of a food product.

3 Should that same shopper also be able to read on the label whether those corn chips or that bottle of cooking oil contains biotech ingredients? Some say yes. Given the concerns raised by a few about biotech safety, there's an important "right to know," they contend.

4 Others say there's no need to label foods with biotech ingredients that are the same as foods with ingredients from conventional crops. Requiring a label for biotech ingredients, they say, would confuse consumers, not inform them.

5 The U.S. Food and Drug Administration (FDA), which oversees food safety issues in the United States, takes the second view. The agency performs exhaustive safety tests on every biotech food entering the marketplace, and requires special labeling only when the new food product is significantly different from its conventional counterpart.

TESTED FOR SAFETY

6 Before they reach a farmer's field, biotech corn, soybeans and other genetically enhanced foods undergo years of review by researchers, university scientists, farmers and other government agencies in addition to the FDA.

7 The results are unambiguous. Biotech crops are safe to eat. No studies or test results have said otherwise. There hasn't been a single documented case of an illness caused by biotech foods.[1] A report issued in 2000 by the National Academy of Sciences, an independent group of scientists and scholars, confirmed that all approved biotech products are as safe as their conventional counterparts.[2]

8 So safety is not at issue in labeling biotech food. Instead, the FDA considers whether a biotech orange, for example, is "substantially equivalent" to a traditional orange. Does it produce the same nutrients? If it does, there's no need for a label. If it doesn't—if the orange has a higher or lower level of vitamin C—then the FDA requires a label.

9 Under this line of thinking, labeling *all* biotech foods would make a distinction without a difference. Rather than communicating relevant health or safety information, it would merely explain the *process* by which the food was developed. And in so doing it could sow confusion among consumers. Ninety-two percent of food industry leaders, for example, believe that mandatory biotech food labeling—which proponents often position simply as an informational tool—will instead be perceived as a "warning" by at least some consumers.[3]

The American Medical Association (AMA) has stated that "there is no scientific   10
justification for special labeling of genetically modified foods, as a class."[4]

Statistics show that the current FDA policy—labeling biotech foods when   11
there's a meaningful reason to do so—is what consumers want. When surveyed for
their opinions, two-thirds to three-quarters consistently approve of the existing system once it's explained that biotech foods have been reviewed and found safe by experts, and would be specially labeled if the nutritional content has been significantly changed.[5]

When asked in an open-ended way what information they'd like more of on   12
product labels, only 1 percent of consumers mentioned biotechnology. Three percent said ingredients, four percent nutrition and 75 percent said they wanted no
additional information.[6]

COSTLY AND CONFUSING

Countries and trading blocs that want to require labels have had to develop a   13
long list of exemptions and loopholes.[7] That's the case in Europe, which enacted labeling requirements and other restrictions. An article in the *Wall Street Journal*
pointed out that the European system has "confused consumers" and "spawned a
bewildering array of marketing claims, counterclaims and outright contradictions
that only a food scientist possibly could unravel."[8]

Labeling requirements also increase costs. Keeping biotech commodity crops   14
separate from traditional ones requires new expenses in the agricultural supply
chain—in added handling measures, testing requirements, and so on—that inevitably will be passed on to consumers.

A Canadian study estimated that mandatory labeling would cost that country's   15
consumers $700 million to $950 million annually[9]—arguably, a food tax on the majority to pay for the labeling demands of a few.[10]

An alternative is the voluntary labeling guidelines for biotech and nonbiotech   16
products currently being developed by the FDA. Under this system, manufacturers
can let consumers know if a food was developed using biotechnology to have a beneficial trait such as reduced saturated fat—or, conversely, if biotech ingredients
were not used in making a food.[11]

Professor Thomas Hoban, director of the Center for Biotechnology in Global   17
Society at North Carolina State University, points out that voluntary labeling can
provide choice "without imposing costs on . . . the majority of consumers who support or have no objection to biotechnology."[12]

FOCUSING DEBATE

Biotechnology is a fast-changing science that's raising environmental, eco-   18
nomic and ethical issues. Given the importance of food in a fast-growing world
where about 840 million people go hungry, those issues deserve to be considered on
their merits.

19   By raising questionable concerns in the minds of consumers, and introducing unnecessary costs, mandatory labeling requirements may only distract from what's truly important: a rational, fact-informed debate about the risks of biotechnology, balanced against the benefits it offers.

Notes

[1] Aaron, David L., U.S. Undersecretary of Commerce for Trade, Reuters, September 16, 1999; also, "In Support of Biotechnology (Expert Views)" The Alliance for Better Foods, <www.betterfoods.org/Expert/Expert.htm>.

[2] Woo, Robin Y., "No Room for Politics on Food Labels, "*Des Moines Register*, May 11, 2000, reprinted at <index.asp?id=1226&redirect=con508mid17%2Ehtml>.

[3] Hoban, Thomas J., "Market Acceptance of Agricultural Biotechnology," North Carolina State University, electronic multimedia presentation.

[4] "Genetically Modified Crops and Foods," American Medical Association (AMA), <www.ama-assn.org/ama/pub/article/2036-3604.html>.

[5] Hoban, Thomas J., "Biotechnology," *Forum*, Fourth Quarter 2000, p. 102.

[6] Hoban, Thomas J., "Biotechnology," *Forum*, Fourth Quarter 2000, p. 95.

[7] Chin, Mary Lee, "Confusing Customers," *Denver Post*, June 17, 2001.

[8] Stecklow, Steve, "Genetically Modified Label Confuses U.K. Shoppers," *The Wall Street Journal*, October 27, 1999.

[9] "Economic Impact Study: Potential Costs of Mandatory Labeling of Food Products Derived from Biotechnology in Canada," KPMG Consulting, December 1, 2000.

[10] "Labeling Biotechnology Foods and the Organic Lobby," Economic & Agricultural Trade 2000, <www.eat2k.org/issues/laveling_backgrounder.html>.

[11] "Guidance for Industry: Voluntary Labeling Indicating Whether Foods Have or Have Not Been Developed Using Bioengineering," U.S. Food and Drug Administration, January 2001, <www.cfsan.fda.gov/dms/biolabgu.html>.

[12] Hoban, Thomas J., "Biotechnology," *Forum*, Fourth Quarter 2000, p. 103.

For Class Discussion

Working as a whole class or in small groups, respond to the following questions about the readings and visual arguments you have just considered.

1. What claims about biotech foods does the soybean ad (Color Plate B) make?

2. Consider this ad in dialogue with Turner and the "Keep Nature Natural" ad (Color Plate A). How does this ad try to allay the fears and answer the objections of the opponents of genetically engineered foods?

3. The genre of the advocacy ad requires brevity and strong, clear, audience-based appeals to a target audience. Why did the Council for Biotechnology Information choose to publish its ads in *Time* and *Atlantic Monthly*? What audiences is it trying to reach?

4. What does this advocacy ad do to establish its authority and credibility?

5. Now consider the Council's policy argument on biotech labeling. To what extent do Lisa Turner and the Council disagree about the basic facts concerning genetically engineered foods?

6. To what extent do Turner and the Council disagree about values, beliefs, and underlying assumptions?

Writing an Analysis of a Disagreement

A common writing assignment in argument courses asks students to analyze the sources of disagreement between two or more writers who take different positions on an issue. In writing such an analysis, you need to determine whether the writers disagree primarily about facts/reality or values (or both). Specifically, you should pose the following questions:

1. Where do the writers disagree about facts and/or the interpretation of facts?

2. Where do the writers disagree about underlying beliefs, values, or assumptions?

3. Where do the writers disagree about key definitions or about appropriate analogies? How do these differences imply differences in values, beliefs, or assumptions?

To illustrate how these three questions can help you write an analysis, we've constructed the following model: our own brief analysis of the disagreement between Turner and the Council for Biotechnology Information written as a short formal essay.

An Analysis of the Sources of Disagreement between Lisa Turner and the Council for Biotechnology Information

Lisa Turner and the Council for Biotechnology Information clash about facts and values in their arguments over the genetic engineering of food. Turner stresses the dangers of biotechnology while the Council stresses the value of scientific advancement

At the heart of their controversy is disagreement about facts. Have genetically engineered foods been appropriately tested for safety? "No," says Turner; "yes," says the Council. These antithetical views determine the stand each source takes on the need for biotech labeling. Turner argues that biotech foods are risky. Her strategy is to raise doubts about the safety of genetically engineered food, mainly by suggesting frightening hypothetical scenarios. She emphasizes the experimental quality of these modifications, arguing that they are imprecise, uncontrollable, and irreversible because they alter living things that pass on genetic modifications when they propagate and affect natural cycles that involve other plants and animals. She mentions the creation of new allergens that could provoke dangerous allergic reactions. She cites one example of deaths and paralysis in 1993, but she does not explain what food product caused this response. (The Council states that no death or disease has ever resulted from biotech foods.) Her main point is that scientists, farmers, and marketers are foisting these entirely experimental foods on an uninformed public.

3   In contrast, the Council for Biotechnology Information assumes the safety of genetically engineered foods. It has confidence in the U.S. Food and Drug Administration's declaration that biotech foods are safe and agrees with the FDA rule that labels are needed only when a biotech food substantially differs from its natural counterpart. The Council asserts that these biotech foods have undergone rigorous tests "by researchers, university scientists, farmers, and other government agencies in addition to the FDA" (paragraph 6). However, in the conclusion of the article, the Council does mention that "[b]iotechnology is a fast-changing science" (paragraph 18) and there is a need for "a rational, fact-informed debate about the risks of biotechnology" (paragraph 19).

4   The "facts" in these two arguments derive from the authors' dramatically different values and assumptions. Turner's article appeared in a health food magazine, and she writes to an audience who shares her distrust of technology. Turner reveals her angle of vision as a health and natural foods practitioner in her strong alarmist tone and her antagonism to genetic engineering, which come through her choice of language. Words such as "nothing sacred," "brave new world of 'biotech foods,'" "artificially shuffling genes," and "new, weird science" express her antitechnology bias (paragraphs 1–3). Clearly, she believes that plants, animals, and foods in their natural state are superior to anything that is artificially created.

5   In contrast, the Council for Biotechnology Information makes an effort to sound balanced, rational, and knowledgeable, but this article also reveals its underlying values. The Council, which is an advocacy organization for the biotechnology industry, believes that biotechnology is a beneficent force that uses human ingenuity to improve nature. Its slogan "Good ideas are growing" (found on its Web site home page) encodes the idea that progress results when humans can manipulate natural processes. This article enhances its credibility by citing the American Medical Association's endorsement of the safety of genetically engineered foods and documenting its reputable sources. However, under the guise of concern for cost to consumers, the Council hides its pro-big business and pro-government bias. The hidden reality here is that the creation and marketing of genetically modified foods are highly profitable enterprises. It also assumes that the FDA and other government regulatory agencies are completely neutral and have consumers' well-being foremost in mind. Thus while Turner sees the labeling of biotech ingredients as a needed warning to consumers, the Council sees its costs as a tax on food brought about by a small minority.

6   These arguments sketch out in bold strokes two alternative views of genetically engineered foods, demonstrating how different values cause persons to perceive different realities and construct different facts.

Works Cited

Council for Biotechnology Information. "Biotech Labeling." 2002. 11 July 2002. <http://whybiotech.com/index.asp?id=1812>. Rpt. in *Writing Arguments: A Rhetoric with Readings*. John D. Ramage, John C. Bean, and June Johnson. 6th ed. New York: Longman, 2004.

Turner, Lisa. "Playing with Our Food." *Better Nutrition* June 2000: 56–59. Rpt. in *Writing Arguments: A Rhetoric with Readings*. John D. Ramage, John C. Bean, and June Johnson. 6th ed. New York: Longman, 2004.

Strategy 5: Using Disagreement Productively to Prompt Further Investigation

Our fifth strategy—using disagreement productively to prompt further investigation—is both a powerful strategy for reading arguments and a bridge toward constructing your own arguments. Our goal is to suggest ways to help you proceed when the experts disagree. Encountering divergent points of view, such as the disagreement between Turner and the Council, can create intense intellectual pressure. Inexperienced arguers sometimes opt for easy escape routes. Either they throw up their hands, claim that "everyone has a right to his own opinion," and leave the argumentative arena, or they latch on to one of the competing claims, defend it against all comers, and shut off opportunity for growth and change. What our fifth strategy invites you to do is stay in the argumentative arena. It urges you to become an active questioner and thinker—to seek answers where possible to disputed questions of fact and value and to articulate and justify your own beliefs and assumptions, which will ultimately inform the positions you take on issues.

As you sort through conflicting viewpoints, your goal is not to identify one of them as "correct" but to ask what is the best solution to the problems being debated here. You may eventually decide that one of the current viewpoints is indeed the best solution. Or you may develop a synthesis that combines strengths from several divergent viewpoints. In either case, you will emerge from the process with an enlarged, informed understanding. You will have developed the ability to remain intellectually flexible while listening to alternative viewpoints. Most important, you will have learned how to avoid falling into a valueless relativism. Responding productively to disagreement thus becomes part of your preparation for writing ethically responsible arguments.

To illustrate the process of responding to disagreements, we now show you how we responded to the disagreement between Turner and the Council for Biotechnology Information over genetically engineered food.

Accepting Ambiguity and Uncertainty

When confronted with conflicting positions, you must learn to cope with ambiguity. If there were no disagreements, of course, there would be no need for argument. It is important to realize that experts can look at the same data, can analyze the same arguments, can listen to the same authorities, and still reach different conclusions. Seldom will one expert's argument triumph over another's in a field of dissenting claims. More often, one expert's argument will modify another's and in turn will be modified by yet another. Accepting ambiguity is a way of suspending judgment as you enter the complexity of an issue. A willingness to live with ambiguity enables you to delve deeply into an issue and to resist easy answers.

Seeking Sources of Facts and More Complete Versions of Alternative Views

After analyzing the sources of disagreement between Turner and the Council for Biotechnology Information (see our essay on pp. 43–45), we pondered how we would continue our search for personal clarity on the issue. We decided to seek out alternative views through library and online research (see Part Four for instruction on research strategies), particularly exploring these questions:

- Are genetically engineered foods safe? What kinds of tests are currently used to verify short-term and long-term safety? How rigorous are they? How accurate are Turner's claims that these foods are potentially dangerous?

- What are the current regulations on the sale and labeling of genetically engineered crops and food? What legislation is being proposed?

- Among disinterested scientists who don't have contracts with the biotech industry, what is the view of the potential benefits and dangers of genetically modified foods? What is the view of the dangers and benefits to the environment?

- What are the achievements of genetic engineering of food so far? How extensive is genetic engineering? Have there been any catastrophes or near catastrophes?

- What is the feasibility and practicality of labeling foods with biotech ingredients?

- What are alternatives to using biotechnology?

When we began our research, we found major disagreement among scientists. For example, the Union of Concerned Scientists (www.ucsusa.org) gives a detailed list of the specific crops that have been modified, the corporations or companies that control the modification, and the traits that genetic engineers are trying to create. This organization raises questions about the safety of these food products, proposing a slower investigative process—basically calling for more science and less business in the whole biotech movement. On the other hand, the American Council on Science and Health (www.asch.org), consisting of physicians, scientists, and policy advisers, actively campaigns for further implementation of what it considers to be highly advantageous and beneficial scientific processes. We discovered that other scientific groups such as the American Medical Association (www.ama-assn.org) take a middle position, praising current advances in genetic engineering of foods but recommending closer monitoring of these crops and more scientifically sound criteria for testing them.

The range of views on testing and labeling of genetically modified foods revealed to us the complexity of this issue. The arguments we found most useful acknowledged the potential value of genetic engineering of foods while realistically confronting the risks and calling for more pre-market testing. We were also drawn to arguments that exposed the profit-making motives driving much of the experimentation with biotech foods. Finally, we welcomed discussions of the real challenges of accurately and helpfully labeling these food products.

Determining What Values Are at Stake for You and Articulating Your Own Values

In responding to disagreement, you need to articulate your own values and try to justify them by explaining the reasons you hold them. The authors of this text, for instance, support the pursuit of scientific knowledge but often question the motives and actions of big business. We believe in the value of strong oversight of scientific experimentation—both from peer review by disinterested scientists and from government regulatory agencies that represent the common good. We like the idea of health food stores, of organic farming, of small family farms, and of less commercialism, but we also appreciate inexpensive food and the convenience of supermarkets. Additionally, we are drawn to technologies that might help feed the world's poor. Therefore, we are trying to stake out our own positions within the complex middle ground on genetic engineering.

Considering Ways to Synthesize Alternative Views

As a final step in your evaluation of conflicting sources, you should consider what you have gained from the different perspectives. How do alternative views modify each other or otherwise "speak to each other"? How might we synthesize the apparently polarized views on genetic engineering of food?

Environmentalists and organic food supporters like Lisa Turner teach us the need for long-range thinking. They prompt us to be more active in exploring alternative solutions to agricultural problems. They advise society to weigh human health and well-being against profits, and they exhort us to be responsible, pro-active citizens and knowledgeable, assertive consumers. At the same time, the Council for Biotechnology Information shows us that the "science as bad guy" view is much too simplistic and that science and technology may help us solve otherwise intractable problems. In trying to synthesize these divergent perspectives, we would look for ways to combine sensible caution and rigorous science.

When you try to synthesize points from conflicting views, as we begin to do here, you tap into the dialectical nature of argument, carefully reflecting when you should change your mind, questioning and modifying positions in response to new perspectives. Your ultimate goal is to find a position that is reasonable and responsible in light of the available facts and your own values.

Conclusion

This chapter has explained why reading arguments is crucially important to writers of arguments and has offered five main strategies for deep reading: (1) Read as a believer. (2) Read as a doubter. (3) Explore how rhetorical context and genre shape an argument. (4) Consider alternative views and analyze sources of disagreement. (5) Use disagreement productively to prompt further investigation. This chapter has also shown you how to summarize an article and incorporate summaries into your own writing through the use of attributive tags. It has explained who writes arguments and how writer, purpose, audience, and the genre of the argument are closely connected and must be considered in any thoughtful response to an argument.

In the next chapter we turn from the reading of arguments to the writing of arguments, suggesting ways that you can generate ideas for arguments, structure your arguments, and improve your own writing processes.

3 Writing Arguments

As the opening chapters suggest, when you write an argument, you try to achieve two goals: (1) to see your issue complexly enough so that your stance reflects an ethical consideration of conflicting views and (2) to persuade your audience toward your stance on the issue. Because managing these tasks takes time, the quality of any argument depends on the quality of the thinking and writing processes that produced it. In this chapter, we suggest ways that you can improve these processes. We begin by looking at the social contexts that produce arguments, asking who writes arguments and why. We then present some writing tips based on the composing practices of experienced writers. Finally, we describe nuts-and-bolts strategies for generating ideas and organizing an argument for an intended audience, concluding with two sets of exploratory exercises that can be adapted to any kind of argumentative task.

Who Writes Arguments and Why?

In the previous chapter we described the genres of arguments ranging from letters to the editor to advocacy Web sites. To help you see further how writers operate in a social context—how they are spurred to write by a motivating occasion and by a desire to change the views of particular audiences—we begin this chapter by asking you to consider more fully why someone would produce an argument.

To illustrate the multiple contexts for persuasion, let's return to the issue of biotech foods that we used in Chapter 2. Who in our culture actually writes arguments on this issue? To whom are they writing and why? Here is a partial list of these writers and their contexts:

- *Lobbyists and advocacy groups.* Advocacy groups commit themselves to a cause, often with passion, and produce avidly partisan arguments aimed at persuading voters, legislators, or other targeted decision makers. We have seen how both proponents and opponents of biotechnology have formed well-established advocacy groups that buy advertisement space in magazines, maintain professional Web sites, and exert lobbying pressure on political candidates and elected officials. Opponents of biotech foods advocate for labeling of biotech ingredients in food, for family farms and local production of food, and for stricter, long-term safety testing of biotech products. Proponents lobby for research grants and for agricultural and world trade legislation conducive to the biotech industry.

■ *Legislators, political candidates, and government officials.*   Whenever new laws, regulations, or government policies are proposed, staffers do research and write white papers recommending positions on an issue. Because the production of biotech food is a highly contested national and world issue—along with related issues involving organic farming, pesticides, agribusiness, third-world development, and agricultural production in general—numerous staff researchers for legislators, political candidates, or government officials have produced white papers on food and agricultural issues. Often these white papers are available on the Web.

■ *Business professionals.*   Businesses devoted to organic foods, holistic medicine, family farming, and "natural" substances in diets and nutrition tend to oppose biotech foods, while those devoted to factory farming, scientific methods in agriculture, and biotech research support biotech foods. Executives and staff writers in all these organizations regularly produce arguments supporting their views for a variety of different audiences.

■ *Lawyers and judges.*   Many biotech issues have legal dimensions ranging from patent disputes to class action lawsuits. Lawyers write briefs supporting their clients' cases. Sometimes lawyers or legal experts not directly connected to a case, particularly law professors, file "friends of the court" briefs aimed at influencing the decision of judges. Finally, judges write court opinions explaining their decisions on a case.

■ *Media commentators.*   Whenever biotech issues get in the news, media commentators (journalists, editorial writers, syndicated columnists) write on the issue, filtering it through the perspective of their own political views.

■ *Professional freelance or staff writers.*   Some of the most thoughtful analyses of public issues are composed by freelance or staff writers for public forum magazines such as *Atlantic Monthly, The Nation, Ms., The National Review, Utne Reader,* and many others. Arguments on biotechnology surface whenever the topic seems timely to magazine editors.

■ *Scholars and academics.*   A key public role played by college professors comes from their scholarly research. Almost all public debates on science, technology, and social policy derive at least some data and analysis from the scholarship of college professors. Although no research can be purely objective—unshaped by the biases of the researcher—scholarly research differs substantially from advocacy argument in its systematic attempt to arrive at the best answers to questions based on the full examination of all relevant data. Much scholarship has been devoted to the biotechnology issue—primarily by agricultural scientists, nutritionists, economists, political scientists, and sociologists. Scholarly research is usually published in refereed academic journals rather than popular magazines. (Of course, scholars can also take personal positions on social issues and use their research for advocacy arguments.)

■ *Citizens.* Average citizens influence social policy through letters, contributions to advocacy Web sites, guest editorials for newspapers, speeches at public forums, or pieces in professional newsletters or other media. Biotech issues reach national consciousness when enough individuals make their views heard. The movement to label biotech ingredients on food products arose through grassroots efforts promoted by ordinary citizens.

   Where do student writers fit on this list? As a student you are already a member of both the "citizen" group and the "scholars and academics" group. Moreover, you may often be given opportunities to role-play membership in other groups as well. As a professional-in-training, you can practice both advocacy arguments and inquiry-based research pieces. Some students taking argument courses in college publish their work as letters to the editor or guest editorials (in the case of advocacy pieces) or present their work at undergraduate research conferences (in the case of scholarly pieces). Others try to influence public opinion by writing persuasive letters to legislators, submitting proposals to decision makers in the workplace, or posting their arguments on Web sites.

   What all these writers have in common is a deep engagement with their issues. They share a strong belief that an issue matters, that decisions have consequences, and that the stakes are often high. You can engage an issue either by having a strong position to advocate or by seeking to clarify your stand on a complex problem. What is important to note is how fluid a writer's position can be along this continuum from advocate to inquirer (analogous to the continuum between "persuasion" and "truth seeking" discussed in Chapter 1, pp. 10–12). An advocate, while writing an argument, might discover an issue's complexity and be drawn into inquiry. Likewise, an inquirer, in the course of studying an issue, might clarify her thinking, establish a strong claim, and become an advocate. It is also possible to write arguments from any position on the continuum: You can be a tentative advocate as well as an avidly committed one, or you can be a cautious skeptic. You can even remain an inquirer by arguing that no proposed solution to a problem is yet adequate.

   So how do you become engaged? We suggest that you immerse yourself in the arguments of the communities to which you belong—your classroom community, your dorm or apartment community, your work community, your civic community—and look for points of entry into these conversations: either places where you can take a stand or places where you are puzzled and uncertain. By opening yourself to the conversations of your culture, and by initiating these conversations when you encounter situations you would like to change, you will be ready to write arguments.

Tips for Improving Your Writing Process

Once you are motivated to write, you can improve your arguing ability if you know something about the writing processes of experienced writers. Too often inexperienced writers cut this process short, producing undeveloped arguments that don't speak effectively to the needs of the intended audience. Although no two writers follow the same process, we can describe the evolution of an argument in a loose way and offer tips for making your writing processes more effective. You should regard the writing process we are about to describe as *recursive*, meaning that writers often loop back to earlier phases by changing their minds on an issue, by throwing out a draft and starting over, or by going back to do more research late in the process.

Starting Point

Most writers of arguments start with an issue about which they are undecided or a claim they want to assert. At the outset, they may pose questions such as these: Who are the interested parties in this conversation? What are the causes of disagreement? What is the best way to solve the problem being debated? Who is the audience that must be persuaded? What is the best means of persuading members of that audience? What are the subtleties and complexities of this issue? Often a specific occasion spurs them to write. They feel hooked.

Tips for Starting the Process

- In many cases arguers are motivated to write because they find situations in their lives that they want to change. You can often focus on argument by asking yourself who has the power to make the changes you desire. How can you craft an argument that connects your desired changes to this audience's beliefs and values? What obstacles in your audience's environment might constrain individuals in that audience from action? How can these obstacles be overcome? This rhetorical focus—identifying the decision makers who have the power to change a situation and looking at the constraints that keep them from action— can give you a concrete sense of audience and clarify how your argument might proceed.

- In a college context you sometimes may have only a secondary occasion for writing—an assignment due date rather than an issue that hooks you. In such cases you can use some of the exploratory exercises described later in this chapter. These exercises help you inventory issues within the communities to which you belong, find points of engagement, and articulate the values and consequences that are at stake for you. Knowing why an issue matters to you can help you make it matter to others.

- Discuss issues with friends and classmates. Talking about ideas in small groups may help you discover claims that you want to make or issues that you find significant yet perplexing. By questioning claims and presenting multiple points of view, groups can help you understand points of disagreement on an issue.

Exploring, Researching, and Rehearsing

To discover, refine, and support their claims, writers typically research their issues carefully, trying to understand arguments on all sides, to resolve disagreements about facts or reality, to clarify their own values, and to identify the beliefs and values of their audience. While researching their issues, writers often discover that their own views evolve. During research, writers often do exploratory writing in online chat rooms, e-mail exchanges, or a writer's journal, sometimes drafting whole pieces of an argument.

Tips for Exploring, Researching, and Rehearsing

- When you research an issue, focus on your rhetorical context. You need to research not only the issue itself, but also the values and beliefs of your targeted audience, and obstacles in your audience's social environment that might prevent individuals from acting on your claim or adopting your beliefs. The exploratory writing strategies and idea-generating procedures described later in this chapter will help you establish and maintain this focus.

- As you explore divergent views on your issue through library or Internet research or through interviews and field research, pay particular attention to why your views may be threatening to others. Later chapters in this text explain strategies for overcoming audience resistance.

- Stay in conversation with others. Active discussion of your issue—especially with persons who don't agree with you—is a powerful way to explore an argument and find the best means of persuasion. As you talk through your argument, note where listeners look confused or skeptical and where they question your points. Skeptics may find holes in your reasoning, argue from different values, surprise you by conceding points you thought had to be developed at length, and challenge you by demanding more justification of your claim.

Writing a First Draft

At some point in the process, a writer's attention begins to shift away from gathering data and probing an issue to composing a first draft. The act of writing a draft forces deep and focused thinking, which may then send the writer back to do more research and exploration. Effective first drafts are likely to be jumbled, messy, and full of gaps. Ideas appear at the point the writer thought of them rather than where readers need them. The writer's tone and style may be inappropriate, needed evidence may be entirely missing, the audience's beliefs and values may not be adequately addressed, and the whole draft may be confusing to an outside reader. Moreover, writers may discover that their own views are still shifting and unstable. Nevertheless, such drafts are a crucial first step. They get your ideas onto paper and give you material to work with.

Tips for Writing a First Draft

- Try lowering your expectations. Writers can quickly create writer's block if they aim for perfection on the first draft. If you get blocked, keep writing. Don't worry about grammar, correctness, or polish. Just get ideas on paper.

- Rehearse your ideas orally. Working in pairs with another student, talk through your argument orally before you write it down. Make a scratch outline first to prompt you as you talk. Then let your partner question you to help you flesh out your argument with more details.

- For a first draft, try following the template for a "classical argument" described on pages 62–65. This strategy will help you consider and respond to opposing views as well as clarify the reasons and evidence that support your own claim.

- Do the exploration tasks entitled "Set 2: Exploration and Rehearsal" (pp. 69–70) prior to writing a first draft. These exercises will help you brainstorm most of the ideas you'll need for an initial draft.

Revising through Multiple Drafts

After completing a first draft, you have materials out on the table to work with. Most writers need multiple drafts to convert an early draft into a persuasive finished product. Sometimes writers revise their claims significantly during revision, having discovered hidden complexities in the issue while composing the first draft.

Tips for Revising

- Don't manicure your drafts; rebuild them. Cross out whole paragraphs and rewrite them from scratch. Move blocks of text to new locations. Make a mess. Inexperienced writers often think of revision as polishing and correcting rather than as making substantial changes (what writing teachers call "global revision"). Revising means to rethink your whole argument. Some writers even throw away the first draft and start fresh.

- Improve your mechanical procedures. We recommend that you revise off double-spaced hard copy rather than off the computer screen. Leave lots of space between lines and in the margins on your drafts so that you have room to draw arrows and make pencil or pen deletions and inserts. When your draft becomes too messy, keyboard your changes back into the computer. If you manage all your drafts on computer, you may find that copying to a new file for each new draft gives you more freedom to experiment with changes (since you can always recover an earlier draft).

- As you revise, think of your audience. Many first drafts show why the writer believes the claim but not why the intended audience should believe it or act on it. As we explain later in this text (especially Chapters 5, 6, and 8), first drafts often contain "writer-based reasons" rather than "audience-based reasons." How can you hook into your audience's beliefs and values? Look also at the obstacles or constraints that keep your audience from adopting your beliefs or acting on your claim. How can you address those constraints in your revision?

■ As you revise, also consider the image of yourself conveyed in your tone and style. Do you want to come across as angry? As sarcastic? As conciliatory and sympathetic? Also, to what extent do you want to appeal to readers' emotions and imagination as well as to their logical intellects? These concerns are discussed in Chapter 7 under the headings *ethos* and *pathos.*

■ Exchange drafts with classmates. Ask classmates where your argument is not persuasive, where your tone is offensive, where they have doubts, where your writing is unclear or undeveloped. Ask your classmates to role-play your intended audience. Explain the values and beliefs of this audience and the constraints members face. Let them give you their reactions and advice. Classmates can also help you meet your readers' needs for effective organization, development, and style.

■ Loop back to do more exploration and research. Revising your first draft may involve considerably more research and exploration.

Editing for Style, Impact, and Correctness

Writers now polish their drafts, rephrasing sentences, finding the precise word, and establishing links between sentences. At this point, you should turn to surface features such as spelling, punctuation, and grammar as well as to the appearance and form of the final manuscript.

Tips for Editing

■ Read your draft out loud. Your ear can often pick up problems missed by the eye.

■ Use your computer's spell check program. Remember, however, that spell checkers won't pick up mistakes with homonyms like *to/two/too, here/hear,* or *affect/effect.* Be skeptical of computerized grammar checkers, which cannot "read" with human intelligence but can only mechanically count, sort, and match. Your instructor can guide you on what grammar checkers can and cannot do.

■ Use a good handbook for up-to-date advice on usage, punctuation, style, and manuscript form.

■ Ask a classmate or friend to proofread your paper.

■ Be prepared to loop back again to earlier stages. Sometimes thinking of a better way to word a sentence uncovers larger problems of clarity and meaning requiring you to rewrite a whole section of your argument.

Using Exploratory Writing to Discover Ideas and Deepen Thinking

What follows is a compendium of strategies to help you discover and explore ideas. None of these strategies works for every writer. But all of them are worth trying. Each requires practice, so don't give up on the strategy if it doesn't work at first. We recommend that you keep your exploratory writing in a journal or in easily identified files in your word processor so you can review it later and test the "staying power" of ideas produced by the different strategies.

Freewriting or Blind Writing

Freewriting is useful at any stage of the writing process. When you freewrite, you put pen to paper and write rapidly *nonstop,* usually ten to fifteen minutes at a stretch. The object is to think of as many ideas as possible without stopping to edit your work. On a computer, freewriters often turn off the monitor so that they can't see the text being produced. Such "blind writing" frees the writer from the urge to edit or correct the text and simply to let ideas roll forth. Some freewriters or blind writers achieve a stream-of-consciousness style, recording their ideas at the very moment they bubble into consciousness, stutters and stammers and all. Others produce more focused chunks, though without clear connections among them. You will probably find your initial reservoir of ideas running out in three to five minutes. If so, force yourself to keep writing or typing. If you can't think of anything to say, write "relax" or "I'm stuck" over and over until new ideas emerge.

Here is an example of a freewrite from a student named Jean, exploring her thoughts about hate speech following a class discussion of the "Machado Case" in which a Los Angeles man, Richard Machado, was convicted in 1998 for sending e-mail death threats to fifty nine Asian students at the University of California, Irvine. He sent the e-mails from a campus computer and signed them "Asian hater."

> I was really disturbed in class today when we talked about the Machado case of the man who made e-mail death threats to Asians saying that he would hunt them down and kill them if they did not leave the campus—I think it was in California somewhere—anyway I just shivered and shuddered to think about this creepy guy. I haven't heard anything like this on our campus but after 9/11 a lot of discussions have gotten really heated with people saying hateful things about Arabs and also about Jews. The whole Israeli/Palestinian conflict divides people and creates stereotypes that get really close to hate speech. Do I think hate speech ought to be banned? I don't know it is such a hard question because I can see both sides of this issue. I don't think people should be allowed to use hateful words for races or sexes in class discussions but just banning the words doesn't mean that people still don't feel the same hate. I wish people could just be nicer to each other, but that's relax relax relax what do I think about hate speech? A lot of hate speech can lead to violence it has the effect of making people want to fight and shout rather than conduct real conversations. Hate speech is like the Jerry Springer show instead of an intelligent discussion. But does that mean it should be banned? I don't know. I hope we get to discuss this more in class.

For Class Discussion

Individual task: Choose one of the following controversial claims (or another chosen by your instructor) and freewrite your response to it for five or ten minutes. **Group task:** Working in pairs, in small groups, or as a whole class, share your freewrite with classmates. Don't feel embarrassed if your freewrite is fragmentary or disjointed. Freewrites are not supposed to be finished products; their sole purpose is to generate a flow of thought. The more you practice the technique, the better you will become.

1. A student should report a fellow student who is cheating on an exam or plagiarizing an essay.
2. States should legalize marriages between homosexuals.
3. Companies should not be allowed to enforce English-only policies in the workplace.
4. Spanking children should be considered child abuse.
5. State and federal governments should legalize hard drugs.
6. For grades 1 through 12, the school year should be extended to eleven months.
7. It is permissible to use racial profiling for airport screening.
8. Violent video games such as Soldier of Fortune should be made illegal.
9. Rich people are morally obligated to give part of their wealth to the poor.
10. Women should be assigned to combat duty equally with men.

Idea Mapping

Another good technique for exploring ideas is *idea mapping*. When you make an idea map, draw a circle in the center of the page and write some trigger idea (a broad topic, a question, or working thesis statement) in the center of the circle. Then record your ideas on branches and subbranches extending from the center circle. As long as you pursue one train of thought, keep recording your ideas on the branch. But when that line of thinking gives out, start a new branch. Often your thoughts jump back and forth between branches. That's a major advantage of "picturing" your thoughts; you can see them as part of an emerging design rather than as strings of unrelated ideas.

Idea maps usually generate more ideas, though less well-developed ones, than freewrites. Writers who practice both techniques report that each strategy causes them to think about their ideas very differently. When Jean, the student who produced the freewrite on hate speech (p. 56), decided to explore this issue further, she created the idea map shown in Figure 3.1.

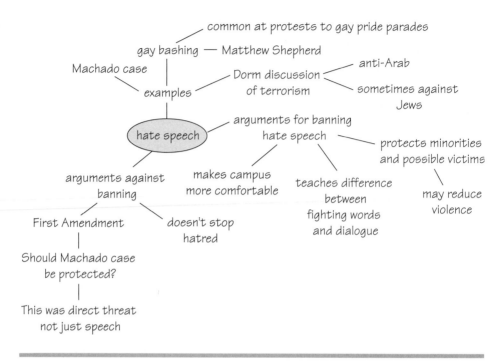

FIGURE 3.1   *Jean's Idea Map on Hate Speech*

For Class Discussion

Choose a controversial issue—national, local, or campus—that's interesting to the class. The instructor will lead a class discussion on the issue, recording ideas on an idea map as they emerge. Your goal is to appreciate the fluidity of idea maps as a visual form of idea generation halfway between an outline and a list.

Playing the Believing and Doubting Game

The believing/doubting game* is an excellent way to imagine views different from your own and to anticipate responses to those views.

As a believer, your role is to be wholly sympathetic to an idea, to listen carefully to it, and to suspend all disbelief. You must identify all the ways in which the idea might appeal to different audiences and all the reasons for believing the idea. The believing game is easy so long as you already accept an idea. But in dealing with ideas that strike you as shaky, false, or threatening, you will find that the believing game can be difficult, even frightening.

---

*A term coined by Peter Elbow, *Writing without Teachers* (New York: Oxford UP, 1973), 147–90.

The doubting game is the opposite of the believing game. As a doubter, your role is to be judgmental and critical, to find faults with an idea. You do your best to find counterexamples and inconsistencies that undermine it. Again, it is easy to play the doubting game with ideas you reject, but doubting those you've invested in can be threatening.

When you play the believing and doubting game with an assertion, simply write two different chunks, one chunk arguing for the assertion (the believing game) and one chunk opposing it (the doubting game). Freewrite both chunks, letting your ideas flow without censoring. Or, alternatively, make an idea map with believing and doubting branches.

To illustrate the believing and doubting game, we ask you to consider the following classified ad seeking young college women to be egg donors for an infertile couple.

> Infertile professional couple seeks egg donor for artificial insemination. Donor should be slim, athletic, blue-eyed with 1400 SAT's or better. $50,000 and all medical expenses. Must be discrete and willing to sign documents giving up all legal rights to a baby that might be produced.

Here is how one student played the believing and doubting game in response to the assertion "Recent advances in reproductive technology, including the use of egg donors, are good for society."

BELIEVING EXAMPLE

The latest advances in reproductive technology are good for society. Up until now, infertile couples had only adoption to turn to if they wanted a child. Using egg donation enables the parents to feel like real parents because the mother does carry the child. The parents can be a bit more selective about the child they get because egg donors are carefully screened. I think egg donors are more stable and safe than women who carelessly or accidentally get pregnant and give up their babies for adoption. Egg donors can be smart, healthy young women, such as college students. These young women also get an opportunity to make some money. Another point is that women can preserve some of their own eggs from their youth and actually have a child much later in life when they are ready for such a commitment. I can see how egg donation can help infertile couples, young women, and older women.

DOUBTING EXAMPLE

While egg donation sounds promising, I think the supporters of it often leave out the dark side and the moral implications. The process is changing having babies from a natural experience to a completely commercial one. Eggs are bought and judged like any other product. The high prices reaching even tens of thousands of dollars mean that only rich couples will be able to afford the process. The fact that the preferred egg donors have common traits (are Ivy League students, are tall, blonde, and blue eyed) only serves to increase a certain elitism. The donor part has pitfalls too. I can understand the attraction of the large sums of money, but the medical process is not easy.

The young women must take fertility drugs and injections to boost their egg production. These drugs may have side effects and long-term complications. I wouldn't want my girlfriend to undergo this process.

Although this writer condemns these medical advances in reproductive technology, he does a good job of trying to sympathize with women who are involved in them. Playing the believing and doubting game has helped him see the issue more complexly.

For Class Discussion

Return to the ten controversial claims in the For Class Discussion on page 57. **Individual task:** Choose one of the claims and play the believing and doubting game with it by freewriting for five minutes trying to believe the claim and then for five minutes trying to doubt the claim. Or, if you prefer, make an idea map by creating a believing spoke and a doubting spoke off the main hub. Instead of freewriting, enter ideas onto your idea map, moving back and forth between believing and doubting. **Group task:** Share what you produced with members of your group or with the class as a whole.

Repeat the exercise with another claim.

Brainstorming for Pro and Con *Because* Clauses

This activity is similar to the believing and doubting game in that it asks you to brainstorm ideas for and against a controversial assertion. In the believing and doubting game, however, you simply freewrite or make an idea map on both sides of the issue. In this activity, you try to state your reasons for and against the proposition as *because* clauses. The value of doing so is discussed in depth in Chapter 4, which shows how a claim with *because* clauses can form the core of an argument.

Here is an example of how you might create *because* clauses for and against the claim "The recent advances in reproductive technology, including the use of egg donors, are good for society."

PRO

The recent advances in reproductive technology, including the use of egg donors, are good for society.

- because children born using this technology are really wanted and will be given loving homes
- because infertility is a medical disorder that can destroy marriages
- because curing this disorder will support marriages and create loving families
- because this technology restores to parents some measure of control over their reproductive capabilities

CON

The recent advances in reproductive technology, including the use of egg donors, are dangerous to society.

- because this technology could lead to situations in which persons have no idea to whom they are genetically related
- because the technology might harm persons such as the egg donors who do not know what the long-term consequences of tampering with their reproductive systems through the use of fertility drugs might be
- because using donor eggs is equivalent to "special ordering" children who may not live up to the parents' expectations (to be smart, tall)
- because the expense of reproductive technology (especially when it results in multiple births) is too large for individuals, insurance companies, or the state to bear

For Class Discussion

Generating *because* clauses like these is an especially productive discussion activity for groups. Once again return to the ten controversial claims in the For Class Discussion exercise on page 57. Select one or more of these claims (or others provided by your instructor) and, working in small groups, generate pro and con *because* clauses supporting and attacking the claim. Share your group's *because* clauses with those of other groups.

Brainstorming a Network of Related Issues

The previous exercise helps you see how certain issues can provoke strong pro-con stances. Occasionally in civic life, an issue is presented to the public in such a pro-con form, as when voters are asked to approve or disapprove a referendum or when a jury must decide the guilt or innocence of a defendant.

But in most contexts, the argumentative situation is more open-ended and fluid. You can easily oversimplify an issue by reducing it to two opposing sides. Because most issues are embedded in a network of subissues, side issues, and larger issues, seeing an issue in pro-con terms can often blind you to other ways to join a conversation. For example, a writer might propose a middle ground between adversarial positions, examine a subissue in more depth, connect an issue to a related side issue, or redefine an issue to place it in a new context.

Consider, for example, the assertion about reproductive technology. Rather than arguing for or against this claim, a writer might focus on reproductive technology in a variety of other ways:

- Who should determine the ethics of reproductive technology? Families? Doctors? Government?
- How can risky physical outcomes such as multiple births (mothers carrying seven and eight babies) be avoided?

- What effect will the new reproductive technologies have on our concepts of motherhood and family?
- In case of divorce, who has legal rights to frozen embryos and other genetic material?
- Will reproductive technology lead to control over the sex and genetic makeup of children? Should it?
- What is the difference between paying someone to donate a kidney (which is illegal) and paying a woman to donate her eggs (which is currently legal)?
- Currently many adopted children want to seek out their birth mothers. Would children born from donated eggs want to seek out their genetic mothers?
- Who should pay for reproductive technology?

For Class Discussion

Working as a whole class or in small groups, choose one or more of the controversial assertions on page 57. Instead of arguing for or against them, brainstorm a number of related issues (subissues, side issues, or larger issues) on the same general subject. For example, brainstorm a number of issues related to the general topics of cheating, gay marriage, women in combat, and so forth.

Shaping Your Argument: Classical Argument as a Planning Tool

We turn now from discovery strategies to organizing strategies. As you begin drafting, you need some sort of plan. How elaborate that plan is varies considerably from writer to writer. Some writers plan extensively before writing; others write extensively before planning. But somewhere along the way, all writers must decide on a structure. This section gives you an overview of a powerful template for initial planning—a structure often called "classical argument" because it follows the conventions of persuasive speeches as taught by ancient rhetoricians.

The Structure of Classical Argument

In traditional Latin terminology, classical argument has the following parts:

- the *exordium,* which gets the audience's attention
- the *narratio,* which provides needed background
- the *propositio,* which introduces the speaker's proposition or thesis
- the *partitio,* which forecasts the main parts of the speech

- the *confirmatio,* which presents arguments supporting the proposition
- the *confutatio,* which refutes opposing views
- the *peroratio,* which sums up the argument, calls for action, and leaves a strong last impression

In slightly homelier terms (see Figure 3.2), writers of classical argument typically begin with a dramatic story or a startling statistic that commands attention. Then they focus the issue, often by stating it directly as a question and perhaps by briefly summarizing opposing views. Next, they contextualize the issue by providing needed background, explaining the immediate context, or defining key terms. They conclude the introduction by presenting the thesis and forecasting the argument's structure.

The body of a classical argument has two major sections—one presenting the writer's own position and the other summarizing and critiquing alternative views. Figure 3.2 shows that the writer's own position comes first. But writers have the option of reversing that order. Where you place the opposing arguments depends on whether you picture an undecided audience who will listen openmindedly to your argument or a resistant audience initially hostile to your views. The more resistant your audience, the more it is advantageous to summarize and respond to opposing views before you present your own argument. Doing so reassures skeptics that you have thoughtfully considered alternative positions, thus reducing their initial hostility to your own argument. In contrast, undecided audiences often benefit from hearing your argument first, before you summarize and respond to alternative views. In Chapter 8, we explain these considerations in more detail and give you additional options for addressing resistant audiences.

Whether you place your own argument before or after your summary and critique of opposing views, this section is usually the longest part of a classical argument. Here writers present the reasons and evidence supporting their claims, typically choosing reasons that tie into their audience's values, beliefs, and assumptions (see the discussion of "warrants" and of "audience-based reasons" in Chapter 5, pp. 91–97, 101–107). Usually each reason is developed in its own paragraph or sequence of paragraphs. When a paragraph introduces a new reason, writers state the reason directly and then proceed to support it with evidence or a chain of ideas. Along the way, writers guide their readers with appropriate transitions.

When summarizing and responding to opposing views, writers have several options. If there are several opposing arguments, writers may summarize all of them together and then compose a single response, or they may summarize and respond to each argument in turn. As we will explain in Chapter 8, writers may respond to opposing views either by refuting them or by conceding to their strengths and shifting to a different field of values where these strengths seem less decisive.

Finally, in their conclusion, writers sum up their argument, often calling for some kind of action, thereby creating a sense of closure and leaving a strong final impression.

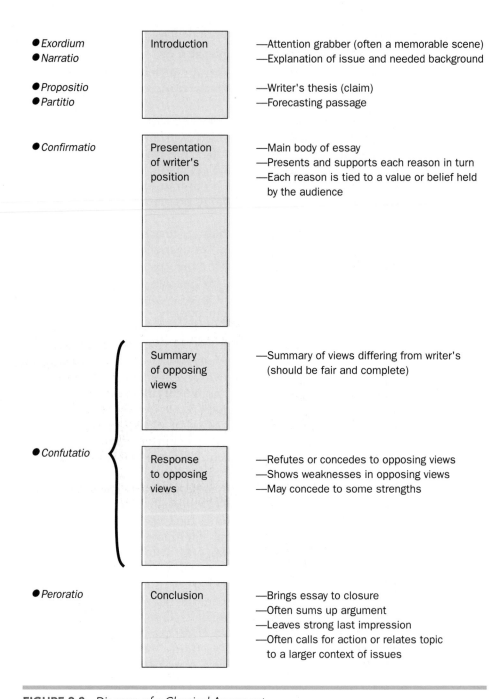

FIGURE 3.2 *Diagram of a Classical Argument*

For all its strengths, the classical argument may not always be your best model. In some cases, for example, delaying your thesis or ignoring alternative views may be justified (see Chapter 8). Even in these cases, however, the classical argument is a useful planning tool. Its call for a thesis statement and a forecasting statement in the introduction helps you see the whole of your argument in miniature. And by requiring you to summarize and consider opposing views, classical argument alerts you to the limits of your position and to the need for further reasons and evidence. Moreover, the classical argument is a particularly persuasive mode of argument when you address a neutral or undecided audience.

An Illustration of Classical Argument as a Planning Guide

Here is how Jean, the student whose freewrite and idea map on hate speech you have already read, used the structure of classical argument to plan an initial draft of her paper. Note how the classical argument template helps her create a flow-chart for her initial ideas.

Jean's Planning Notes Based on Classical Argument
INTRODUCTION

Attention grabber	I'll think of a good opening story about hate speech—maybe the Machado example or an antigay example (Matthew Shepard case) or something from my own campus about hateful slurs against Arabs.
Explanation of issue	I'll give some background on the controversy—how college campuses are trying to figure out ways to ban hate speech without infringing on free speech.
My claim	"Colleges should *not* try to ban hate speech."
Forecasting of structure	I don't know yet the exact structure, but when I do I may need to forecast the structure (I'll come back to this problem).

SUMMARY AND RESPONSE TO OPPOSING VIEWS

Summary of opposing views	I want to put the opposing views first because I picture an audience quite resistant to my views. I'll need to summarize the following arguments that support a ban on hate speech:

- Banning hate speech will lead to a safer environment (show how hate speech promotes violence, etc.).
- Banning hate speech raises consciousness about importance of manners, politeness, and civility in public dialogue.

- Banning hate speech will make life more comfortable for minorities and other potential victims.

- Banning hate speech shows importance of intelligent, reasoned argument, rather than ignorant name-calling, as central to the marketplace of ideas on a college campus.

- Anything else?

Response to opposing views

I'm not sure how I am going to refute these. I actually agree with these arguments. Maybe I can say that I concede to these arguments, but they have one serious flaw: banning hate speech doesn't ban hate. It just drives hate underground. (I'll have to ask my peer response group if readers need more rebuttal.)

PRESENTATION OF MY OWN ARGUMENT

Development of my own reasons and evidence in support of my claim

So far I have two major reasons why I think campuses should not ban hate speech.

- Reason 1: Hate speech is protected by the First Amendment. (First Amendment protects all sorts of things we don't like such as Nazi marches. Banning hate speech could lead to more and more censorship based on views of those in power.)

- Reason 2: It doesn't help overcome hate (doesn't let people understand each other's anger; doesn't promote dialogue; doesn't help people learn to listen to each other; it's like putting your head in the sand instead of dealing with a problem).

Conclusion

There are better ways to deal with prejudice and hatred.

- Let the ugly incidents happen.
- Create discussions around the ugly incidents.

Once again it is important to understand that classical argument doesn't provide a rigid template for all arguments. Many times you will want to vary substantially from this kind of top-down, thesis-first structure. In some cases, for example, you might want to create a more implicit argument based on stories and personal narrative. In other cases, you might want to omit references to opposing views, or to blend rebuttals into your own argument, or to delay your thesis until the end. But as Jean discovered, the template of classical argument can guide you through the process of producing an argument—hooking your readers' initial interest, focusing your issue and presenting your claim, summarizing and responding to views different from your own, and presenting your own argument.

Discovering Ideas: Two Sets of Exploratory Writing Tasks

The following tasks use exploratory writing to help you generate ideas. The first set of tasks helps you gather ideas early in a writing project either by helping you think of issues to write about or by deepening and complicating your response to readings. The second set of tasks helps you think about your ideas systematically before you compose a first draft.

Set 1: Starting Points

Task 1: Make an Inventory of the Communities to Which You Belong and the Issues That Arise   All of us belong to a variety of communities. For example, you have a classroom community for each course you are taking. Each club or organization has its own community, as does the community where you live (dorm, apartment, your family). Beyond these small communities, you have your campus community and beyond that your city, state, region, nation, and world communities. You may also belong to a work or job community, to a church/mosque/synagogue community, or to communities related to your hobbies or avocations.

The occasion for argument grows out of your life in these communities—your desire to make a difference on some issue that divides or troubles the community. As an arguer, you might tackle a big issue in your world community (What is the best way to prevent destruction of rain forests?) or a small issue in your dorm (Should quiet hours be enforced?). In your classroom community, you might tackle a practical problem (What should the instructor do about persons coming in late?) or intellectual issues in the discipline itself (Is Frankenstein's monster good or evil? Is gender socially constructed?).

For this task make a list of the communities to which you belong. Then brainstorm controversies in these communities—issues that are being debated or that you would like to see debated. You might find one or more of the following "trigger questions" helpful:

- Persons in my dorm (at work, in the state legislature, at the United Nations) disagree about. . . .
- Our campus (this dorm, my hometown, my worksite, our state, our country) would be a better place if. . . .
- Something that really makes me mad about this campus (my apartment life, city government, our society) is. . . .
- In the career I hope to pursue, X is a serious problem that needs to be addressed.
- Person X believes . . . ; however, I believe. . . .

Task 2: Make an Inventory of Issues That Interest You   The previous task can overwhelm students with the sheer number of issues that surround them. Once you broaden out to the large communities of city, state, nation, and world, the numbers of issues multiply rapidly. Moreover, each large issue has numerous subissues. For this task make an inventory of ten to fifteen possible issues that you would like to explore more deeply and possibly write about. Share your list with classmates, adding their ideas to yours.

Task 3: Choose Several Areas of Controversy for Exploration   For this task choose two or three possible controversies from the list above and explore them through freewriting or idea mapping. Try responding to the following questions: (a) What is my position on this issue and why? (b) What are opposing or alternative positions on this issue? (c) Why do people disagree about this issue? (Do they disagree about the facts of the case? About underlying values, assumptions, and beliefs?) (d) To argue a position on this issue, what evidence do I need to find and what further research will be required?

Task 4: Choose a Local Issue and Explore Its Rhetorical Context   For this task choose a local issue (some situation that you would like to see changed on your campus, in your place of work, or in your town or city) and explore its rhetorical context: (a) What is the situation you would like to change? (b) Who has the power to change that situation? (c) What are the values and beliefs of these decision makers? (d) What obstacles or constraints may prevent these decision makers from acting on your desires? (e) What reasons and evidence would exert the most pressure on these decision makers? (How can you make acting on your proposal a good thing for them?)

Task 5: Identify and Explore Issues That Are Problematic for You   A major assignment often given in argument courses is to write a research-based argument on an issue or problem initially puzzling to you. Perhaps you don't know enough about the issue (for example, establishing international controls on pesticides), or perhaps the issue draws you into an uncomfortable conflict of values (for example, assisted suicide, legalization of drugs, noncriminal incarceration of sexual predators). Your goal for this task is to identify several issues about which you are undecided, to choose one, and to explore your current uncertainty. Why can't you make up your mind on this issue?

Task 6: Deepen Your Response to Readings   This task requires you to read a collection of arguments on an issue and to explore them thoughtfully. As you read the arguments assigned by your instructor, annotate the margins with believing and doubting notes as explained in Chapter 2. Then respond to one or more of the following prompts, using freewriting or idea mapping:

- Why do the writers disagree? Are there disagreements about facts? About underlying values, beliefs, and assumptions?
- Identify "hot spots" in the readings—passages that evoke strong agreement or disagreement, anger, confusion, or any other memorable response—and explore your reaction to these passages.

- Explore the evolution of your thinking as you read and later review the essays. What new questions have they raised? How did your thinking change? Where do you stand now and why?
- If you were to meet one of the authors on a plane or at a ball game, what would you say to him or her?

Set 2: Exploration and Rehearsal

The following tasks are designed to help you once you have chosen a topic and begun to clarify your thesis. While these tasks may take two or more hours to complete, the effort pays off by helping you produce a full set of ideas for your rough draft. We recommend using these tasks each time you write an argument for this course.

Task 1   What issue do you plan to address in this argument? Try wording the issue as a one-sentence question. Reword your question in several different ways because each version will frame the issue somewhat differently. Then put a box around your best version of the question.

Task 2   Now write out your tentative answer to the question. This will be your beginning thesis statement or claim. Put a box around this answer. Next write out one or more different answers to your question. These will be alternative claims that a neutral audience might consider.

Task 3   Why is this a controversial issue? Is there insufficient evidence to resolve the issue, or is the evidence ambiguous or contradictory? Are definitions in dispute? Do the parties disagree about basic values, assumptions, or beliefs?

Task 4   What personal interest do you have in this issue? What are the consequences for you if your argument succeeds or doesn't succeed? How does the issue affect you? Why do you care about it? (Knowing why you care about it might help you get your audience to care about it.)

Task 5   Who is the audience that you need to persuade? If your argument calls for an action, who has the power to act on your claim? Can you address these persons of power directly? Or do you need to sway others (such as voters) to exert pressure on persons in power? With regard to your issue, what are the values and beliefs of the audience you are trying to sway?

Task 6   What obstacles or constraints in the social or physical environment prevent your audience from acting on your claim or accepting your beliefs? What are some ways these obstacles can be overcome? If these obstacles cannot be overcome, should you change your claim?

Task 7   In this task you will rehearse the main body of your paper. Using freewriting or idea mapping, think of the main reasons and evidence you could use to sway your intended audience. Brainstorm everything that comes to mind that might help you support your case. Because this section will eventually provide the bulk of your argument, proceed rapidly without worrying whether your argument makes sense. Just get ideas on paper. As you generate reasons and evidence, you are likely to discover gaps in your knowledge. Where could your argument be bolstered by additional data such as statistics, examples, and expert testimony? Where and how will you do the research to fill these gaps?

Task 8   Now reread what you wrote for Tasks 5 and 6, in which you examined your audience's perspective. Role-playing that audience, imagine all the counterarguments members might make. Where does your claim threaten them or oppose their values? What obstacles or constraints in their environment are individuals likely to point to? ("I'd love to act on your claim, but we just don't have the money" or "If we grant your request, it will set a bad precedent.") Brainstorm all the objections your audience might raise to your argument.

Task 9   How can you respond to those objections? Take them one by one and brainstorm possible responses.

Task 10   Finally, explore again why this issue is important. What are its broader implications and consequences? What other issues does it relate to? Thinking of possible answers to these questions may prove useful when you write your introduction or conclusion.

WRITING ASSIGNMENTS
FOR CHAPTERS 1–3

OPTION 1: *An Argument Summary*   Write a 250-word summary of an argument selected by your instructor. Then write a one-sentence summary of the same argument. Use as models the summaries of Lisa Turner's argument on biotech foods in Chapter 2.

OPTION 2: *An Analysis of Sources of Disagreement in a Controversy*   Using as a model the analysis of the controversy between Turner and the Council for Biotechnology Information in Chapter 2, write an analysis of the sources of disagreement in any two arguments that take differing views on the same issue.

OPTION 3: *Evaluating Your Use of Exploratory Writing*   For this option your instructor will assign one or more of the exploratory exercises in Chapter 3 for you to do as homework. Do the tasks as well as you can, submitting your exploratory writing as an exhibit for evidence. Then write a reflective evaluation of how well the assignment worked for you. In your evaluation address questions such as these:

a. Did the exercise help you develop ideas? (Why or Why not?)

b. What are examples of some of the ideas you developed?

c. What did the exercise teach you about the demands of good arguments?

d. What did the exercise teach you about your own writing and thinking process?

OPTION 4: *Propose a Problem for a Major Course Project* An excellent major project for an argument course is to research an issue about which you are initially undecided. Your final essay for the course could be an argument in which you take a stand on this issue. Choose one of the issues you listed in "Set 1: Starting Points," Task 5—"I am unable to take a stand on the issue of . . ."—and make this issue a major research project for the course. During the term keep a log of your research activities and be ready, in class discussion or in writing, to explain what kinds of arguments or evidence turned out to be most persuasive in helping you take a stand.

For this assignment, write a short letter to your instructor identifying the issue you have chosen, and explain why you are interested in it and why you can't make up your mind at this time.

Part Two

Principles of Argument

4 The Core of an Argument: A Claim with Reasons

5 The Logical Structure of Arguments

6 Using Evidence Effectively

7 Moving Your Audience: *Ethos* and *Pathos*

8 Accommodating Your Audience: Treating Differing Views

9 Conducting Visual Arguments

This poster voices a protest against the pollution and stress of our car-based lifestyle and proposes an alternative.
Courtesy of Doug Minkler, San Francisco Bay area poster maker.

Part Two

Principles of Argument

4 The Core of an Argument

A Claim with Reasons

The Rhetorical Triangle

Before we examine the structure of arguments, we should explain briefly their social context, which can be visualized as a triangle with interrelated points labeled *message, writer/speaker,* and *audience* (see Figure 4.1). Effective arguments consider all three points on this *rhetorical triangle*. As we will see in later chapters, when you alter one point of the triangle (for example, when you change the audience for whom you are writing), you often need to alter the other points (by restructuring the message itself and perhaps by changing the tone or image you project as writer/speaker). We have created a series of questions based on the "rhetorical triangle" to help you plan, draft, and revise your argument.

Each point on the triangle in turn corresponds to one of the three kinds of persuasive appeals that ancient rhetoricians named *logos, ethos,* and *pathos. Logos* (Greek for "word") refers primarily to the internal consistency and clarity of the message and to the logic of its reasons and support. The impact of *logos* on an audience is referred to as its *logical appeal.*

Ethos (Greek for "character") refers to the credibility of the writer/speaker. *Ethos* is often conveyed through the tone and style of the message, through the care with which the writer considers alternative views, and through the writer's investment in his or her claim. In some cases, it's also a function of the writer's reputation for honesty and expertise independent of the message. The impact of *ethos* on an audience is referred to as its *ethical appeal* or *appeal from credibility.*

Our third term, *pathos* (Greek for "suffering" or "experience"), is often associated with emotional appeal. But *pathos* appeals more specifically to an audience's imaginative sympathies—their capacity to feel and see what the writer feels and sees. Thus, when we turn the abstractions of logical discourse into a palpable and immediate story, we are making a pathetic appeal. While appeals to *logos* and *ethos* can further an audience's intellectual assent to our claim, appeals to *pathos* engage the imagination and feelings, moving the audience to deeper appreciation of the argument's significance.

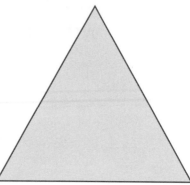

Message
(LOGOS: *How can I make the argument internally consistent and logical? How can I find the best reasons and support them with the best evidence?*)

Audience
(PATHOS: *How can I make the reader open to my message? How can I best appeal to my reader's values and interests? How can I engage my reader emotionally and imaginatively?*)

Writer or Speaker
(ETHOS: *How can I present myself effectively? How can I enhance my credibility and trustworthiness?*)

FIGURE 4.1 *The rhetorical triangle*

Given this background on the rhetorical triangle, let's turn now to *logos*—the logic and structure of arguments.

Issue Questions as the Origins of Argument

At the heart of any argument is an issue, which we can define as a controversial topic area such as "the labeling of biotech foods" or "racial profiling," that gives rise to differing points of view and conflicting claims. A writer can usually focus an issue by asking an issue question that invites at least two alternative answers. Within any complex issue—for example, the issue of abortion—there are usually a number of separate issue questions: Should abortions be legal? Should the federal government authorize Medicaid payments for abortions? When does a fetus become a human being (at conception? at three months? at quickening? at birth?)? What are the effects of legalizing abortion? (One person might stress that legalized abortion leads to greater freedom for women. Another person might respond that it lessens a society's respect for human life.)

Difference between an Issue Question and an Information Question

Of course, not all questions are issue questions that can be answered reasonably in two or more differing ways; thus not all questions can lead to effective argument essays. Rhetoricians have traditionally distinguished between *explication,* which is writing that sets out to inform or explain, and *argumentation,* which sets out to change a reader's mind. On the surface, at least, this seems like a useful distinction. If a reader is interested in a writer's question mainly to gain new knowledge about a subject, then the writer's essay could be considered explication rather than argument. According to this view, the following questions about teenage pregnancy might be called information questions rather than issue questions:

> How does the teenage pregnancy rate in the United States compare with the rate in Sweden? If the rates are different, why?

Although both questions seem to call for information rather than for argument, we believe that the second one would be an issue question if reasonable people disagreed on the answer. Thus, different writers might agree that the teenage pregnancy rate in the United States is four times higher than the rate in Sweden. But they might disagree about why. One writer might emphasize Sweden's practical, secularized sex-education courses in the schools, leading to more consistent use of contraceptives among Swedish teenagers. Another writer might point to the higher use of oral contraceptives among teenage girls in Sweden (partly a result of Sweden's generous national health program) and to less reliance on condoms for preventing pregnancy. Another might argue that moral decay in the United States is at fault. Still another might argue that the American welfare system helps promote teenage pregnancy (a popular conservative argument in the late 1990s). Thus, underneath the surface of what looks like a simple explication of the "truth" is really a controversy.

You can generally tell whether a question is an issue question or an information question by examining your purpose in relationship to your audience. If your relationship to your audience is that of teacher to learner, so that your audience hopes to gain new information, knowledge, or understanding that you possess, then your question is probably an information question. But if your relationship to your audience is that of advocate to decision maker or jury, so that your audience needs to make up its mind on something and is weighing different points of view, then the question you address is an issue question.

Often the same question can be an information question in one context and an issue question in another. Let's look at the following examples:

- How does a diesel engine work? (This is probably an information question since reasonable people who know about diesel engines will probably agree on how they work. This question would be posed by an audience of new learners.)

- Why is a diesel engine more fuel-efficient than a gasoline engine? (This also seems to be an information question since all experts will probably agree on the answer. Once again, the audience seems to be new learners, perhaps students in an automotive class.)

- What is the most cost-effective way to produce diesel fuel from crude oil? (This could be an information question if experts agree and you are addressing new learners. But if you are addressing engineers and one engineer says process X is the most cost-effective and another argues for process Y, then the question is an issue question.)

- Should the present highway tax on diesel fuel be increased? (This is certainly an issue question. One person says yes; another says no; another offers a compromise.)

For Class Discussion

Working as a class or in small groups, try to decide which of the following questions are information questions and which are issue questions. Many of them could be either, depending on the rhetorical context. For such questions, create hypothetical contexts to show your reasoning.

1. What percentage of public schools in the United States are failing?
2. What is the cause of failing public schools in the United States?
3. Should states use high-stakes testing of students to motivate improvement of public schools?
4. What percentage of TV shows during prime-time hours depict violence?
5. What is the effect of violent TV shows on children?
6. Are chiropractors legitimate health professionals?
7. How does chiropractic treatment of illness differ from a medical doctor's treatment?
8. Are caffeinated sodas harmful to children?
9. Should a woman with a newly detected breast cancer opt for a radical mastectomy (complete removal of the breast and surrounding lymph tissue) or a lumpectomy (removal of the malignant lump without removal of the whole breast)?
10. Is Simone de Beauvoir correct in calling marriage an outdated, oppressive, capitalist institution?

Difference between a Genuine Argument and a Pseudo-Argument

While every argument features an issue question with alternative answers, not every dispute over answers is a rational argument. Rational arguments require two additional factors: (1) reasonable participants who operate within the conventions of reasonable behavior and (2) potentially sharable assumptions that can serve as a starting place or foundation for the argument. Lacking one or both of these conditions, disagreements remain stalled at the level of pseudo-arguments.

Pseudo-Arguments: Fanatical Believers and Fanatical Skeptics

A reasonable argument assumes the possibility of growth and change; disputants may modify their views as they acknowledge strengths in an alternative view or weaknesses in their own. Such growth becomes impossible—and argument degenerates to pseudo-argument—when disputants are fanatically committed to their positions. Consider the case of the fanatical believer or the fanatical skeptic.

Fanatical believers believe their claims are true because they say so, period. They may cite some authoritative text—the Bible, the *Communist Manifesto*, or *The Road Less Traveled*—but in the end it's their narrow and quirky reading of the text or their faith in the author (which others might not share) that underlies their argument. Disagreeing with a fanatical believer is like ordering the surf to quiet down. The only response is another crashing wave.

The fanatical skeptic, in contrast, dismisses the possibility of proving anything. So what if the sun has risen every day of recorded history? That's no proof that it will rise tomorrow. Short of absolute proof, which never exists, fanatical skeptics accept nothing. In a world where the most we can hope for is increased audience adherence to our ideas, the fanatical skeptic demands an ironclad, logical demonstration of our claim's rightness. In the presence of fanatical believers or skeptics, then, genuine argument is impossible.

Another Source of Pseudo-Arguments: Lack of Shared Assumptions

A reasonable argument is difficult to conduct unless the participants share common assumptions on which the argument can be grounded. Like axioms in geometry, these shared assumptions serve as the starting point for the argument. Consider the following conversation, in which Randall refuses to accept Rhonda's assumptions:

RHONDA: Smoking should be banned because it causes cancer.

RANDALL: So it causes cancer. What's so bad about that?

RHONDA: Don't be perverse, Randy. Cancer causes suffering and death.

RANDALL: Rhonda, my dear girl, don't be such a twinkie. Suffering and death are just part of the human condition.

RHONDA: But that doesn't make them desirable, especially when they can be avoided.

RANDALL: Perhaps in particular cases they're avoidable for a while, but in the long run, we all suffer and we all die, so who cares if smoking causes what's inevitable anyway?

This, we would suggest, is a doomed argument. Without any shared assumptions (for example, that cancer is bad, that suffering should be minimized and death delayed), there's no "bottom" to this argument, just an endless regress of reasons based on more reasons. While calling assumptions into question is a legitimate way to deepen and complicate our understanding of an issue, the unwillingness to accept any assumption makes argument impossible.

Our smoking example may be a bit heavy handed, but less obvious variants of this debate happen all the time. Whenever we argue about purely personal opinions—opera is boring, soccer is better than baseball, pizza is tastier than nachos—we're condemned to a bottomless dispute. Because there are no common criteria for "boring" or "better" or "tastier," we can't put our claims to any common test. We can only reassert them.

Of course, reasonable arguments about these disputes become possible once common assumptions are established. For example, a nutritionist could argue that pizza is better than nachos because it provides a better balance of nutrients per calorie. Such an argument can succeed if the disputants accept the nutritionist's assumption that "a better balance of nutrients per calorie" is a criterion for "better." But if one of the disputants responds, "Nah, nachos are better than pizza because nachos taste better," then he makes a different assumption—"My sense of taste is better than your sense of taste." This is a wholly personal standard, an assumption that others are unable to share.

For Class Discussion

The following questions can all be answered in alternative ways. However, not all of them will lead to reasonable arguments. Try to decide which questions will lead to reasonable arguments and which will lead only to pseudo-arguments.

1. Is Spike Lee a good film director?
2. Is postmodern architecture beautiful?
3. Should cities subsidize professional sports venues?
4. Is this abstract oil painting by a monkey smearing paint on a canvas a true work of art?
5. Are nose rings and tongue studs attractive?

Frame of an Argument:
A Claim Supported by Reasons

We said earlier that an argument originates in an *issue question*, which by definition is any question that provokes disagreement about the best answer. When you write an argument, your task is to take a position on the issue and to support it with reasons and evidence. The *claim* of your essay is the position you want your audience to accept. To put it another way, your claim is your essay's thesis statement, a one-sentence summary answer to your issue question. Your task, then, is to make a claim and support it with reasons.

What Is a Reason?

A *reason* (also called a *premise*) is a claim used to support another claim. In speaking or writing, a reason is usually linked to the claim with connecting words such as *because, since, for, so, thus, consequently,* and *therefore,* indicating that the claim follows logically from the reason.

Let's take an example. In one of our recent classes a woman naval ROTC student surprised her classmates by remarking that women should not be allowed to serve on submarines. A heated discussion quickly followed, expanding into the more general issue of whether women should be allowed to join military combat units. Here are frameworks the class developed for two alternative positions on that issue:

One View

CLAIM: Women should be barred from joining military combat units.

REASON 1:   Women for the most part don't have the strength or endurance for combat roles.

REASON 2:   Serving in combat isn't necessary for women's career advancement in the military.

REASON 3:   Women in close-knit combat units would hurt unit morale by introducing sexual jealousies.

REASON 4:   Pregnancy or need to care for infants and small children would make women less reliable to a unit.

REASON 5:   Women haven't been socialized into fighters and wouldn't have the "Kill them with a bayonet!" spirit that men can get.

Alternative View

CLAIM: Women should be allowed to join combat units in the military.

REASON 1:   Millions of women are stronger and more physically fit than most men; women selected for combat duty would have the strength and endurance to do the job.

REASON 2:   The image of women as combat soldiers would help society overcome harmful gender stereotyping.

REASON 3:   Serving in combat units would open up many more opportunities for women's career advancement in the military.

REASON 4:   The justice of equal rights for women demands that women be allowed to serve in combat units.

Formulating a list of reasons in this way breaks your argumentative task into a series of subtasks. It gives you a frame for building your argument in parts. In the previous example, the frame for the argument opposing women in combat suggests five different lines of reasoning a writer might pursue. A writer might use all five reasons or select only two or three, depending on which reasons would most persuade the intended audience. Each line of reasoning would be developed in its own separate section of the argument.

For example, one section of an argument opposing women in combat might open with the following sentence: "Women shouldn't be allowed to join combat units because they don't have the strength or endurance for combat roles." In this section, the writer would describe the levels of strength and endurance currently required for combat service and provide evidence that these requirements would have to be lowered if women were to join combat units. In this section the writer might also need to support the unstated assumption that underlies this reason—that a high level of physical strength and endurance is a necessary criterion for combat effectiveness. (How one articulates and supports the underlying assumptions of an argument will be developed in Chapter 5 in our discussion of warrants and backing.)

The writer would proceed the same way for each separate section of the argument. Each section would open with a clear statement of the reason to be developed. The writer would then support each reason with evidence or chains of other reasons. In addition, if needed for the intended audience, the writer would support any underlying assumptions on which the reason depends.

To summarize our point in this section, the frame of an argument consists of a claim (the thesis statement of the essay), which is supported by one or more reasons, which are in turn supported by evidence or sequences of further reasons.

Advantages of Expressing Reasons in *Because* Clauses

Chances are that when you were a child the word *because* contained magical explanatory powers:

DOROTHY: I want to go home now.

TOMMY: Why?

DOROTHY: Because.

TOMMY: Because why?

DOROTHY: Just because.

Somehow *because* seemed decisive. It persuaded people to accept your view of the world; it changed people's minds. Later, as you got older, you discovered that *because* only introduced your arguments and that it was the reasons following *because* that made the difference. Still, *because* introduced you to the powers potentially residing in the adult world of logic.

Of course, there are many other ways to express the logical connection between a reason and a claim. Our language is rich in ways of stating *because* relationships:

- Women shouldn't be allowed to join combat units because they don't have the strength or endurance for combat roles.

- Women don't have the strength or endurance for combat roles. Therefore women should not be allowed to join combat units.

- Women don't have the strength or endurance for combat roles, so they should not be allowed to join combat units.

- One reason why women should not be allowed to join combat units is that they don't have the strength or endurance for combat roles.

- My argument that women should not be allowed to join combat units is based mainly on evidence that women don't have the strength or endurance for combat roles.

Even though logical relationships can be stated in various ways, writing out one or more *because* clauses seems to be the most succinct and manageable way to clarify an argument for oneself. We therefore suggest that sometime in the writing process you create a *working thesis statement* that summarizes your main reasons as *because* clauses attached to your claim.* Just when you compose your own working thesis statement depends largely on your writing process. Some writers like to plan out their whole argument from the start and often compose their working thesis statements with *because* clauses before they write their rough drafts. Others discover their arguments as they write. And sometimes it is a combination of both. For these writers, an extended working thesis statement is something they might write halfway

---

*A working thesis statement for an argument opposing women in combat units might look like this: *Women should not be allowed to join combat units because they lack the strength, endurance, and "fighting spirit" needed in combat; because being pregnant or having small children would make them unreliable for combat at a moment's notice; and because women's presence would hurt morale of tight-knit combat units.* (A working thesis statement for an argument supporting women in combat is found on page 85.)

You might not put a bulky thesis statement like this into your essay itself; rather, a working thesis statement is a behind-the-scenes way of summarizing your argument for yourself so that you can see it whole and clear.

through the composing process as a way of ordering their argument when various branches seem to be growing out of control. Or they might compose a working thesis statement at the very end as a way of checking the unity of the final product.

Whenever you write your extended thesis statement, the act of doing so can be simultaneously frustrating and thought provoking. Composing *because* clauses can be a powerful discovery tool, causing you to think of many different kinds of arguments to support your claim. But it is often difficult to wrestle your ideas into the *because* clause shape, which sometimes seems to be overly tidy for the complex network of ideas you are trying to work with. Nevertheless, trying to summarize your argument as a single claim with reasons should help you see more clearly what you have to do.

For Class Discussion

Try this group exercise to help you see how writing *because* clauses can be a discovery procedure. Divide into small groups. Each group member should contribute an issue that he or she might like to explore. Discussing one person's issue at a time, help each member develop a claim supported by several reasons. Express each reason as a *because* clause. Then write out the working thesis statement for each person's argument by attaching the *because* clauses to the claim. Finally, try to create *because* clauses in support of an alternative claim for each issue. Recorders should select two or three working thesis statements from the group to present to the class as a whole.

Application of This Chapter's Principles to Your Own Writing

In Chapter 2 we discussed the difficulties of summarizing various types of arguments. Generally, an argument is easiest to summarize when the writer places her thesis in the introduction and uses explicit transitions to highlight the argument's reasons and structural frame. Such arguments are said to have a *self-announcing structure* because they announce their thesis (and sometimes supporting reasons) and forecast their shape at the outset. Such self-announcing arguments typically follow the conventional format of classical argument discussed in Chapter 3. The invention strategies set forth in this chapter—generating parallel *because* clauses and nutshelling them in a working thesis statement—lead naturally to a classical argument with a self-announcing structure. Each *because* clause, together with its supporting evidence, becomes a separate section of the argument.

An argument with an *unfolding structure,* in contrast, is considerably harder to summarize. In an unfolding structure, the thesis is delayed until the end or is unstated and left to be inferred by the reader from a narrative that may be both complex and subtle. As we explain in Chapter 8, unfolding structures can be especially effective for dealing with hostile audiences or with troubling or tangled issues. In contrast, classical arguments are often more effective for neutral or undecided audiences weighing alternative views on a clear-cut issue.*

In our own classes, we ask students initially to write arguments with self-announcing structures, thereby forcing them to articulate their arguments clearly to themselves and helping them to master the art of organizing complex ideas. Later on in the course, we invite students to experiment with structures that unfold their meanings in subtler, more flexible ways.

In writing classical arguments, students often ask how much of the argument to summarize in the introduction. Consider the following options. You might announce only your claim:

> Women should be allowed to join combat units.

Or you could also forecast a series of parallel reasons:

> Women should be allowed to join combat units for several reasons.

Or you could forecast the actual number of reasons:

> Women should be allowed to join combat units for four reasons.

Or you could forecast the whole argument:

> Women should be allowed to join combat units because they are physically capable of doing the job; because the presence of women in combat units would weaken gender stereotypes; because opening combat units to women would expand their military career opportunities; and because it would advance the cause of civil rights.

Those, of course, are not your only options. If you choose to delay your thesis until the end (a typical kind of unfolding argument), you might place the issue question in the introduction without giving away your own position:

> Is the nation well served by allowing women to join combat units?

No formula can tell you how much of your argument to forecast in the introduction. In Chapters 7 and 8 we discuss how forecasting or withholding your thesis affects your *ethos*. We also show how a delayed thesis argument may be a better option for hostile audiences. It is clear at this point, though, that the more you forecast, the

---

*Instead of the terms *self-announcing* and *unfolding*, rhetoricians sometimes use the terms *closed form* and *open form*. *Closed-form* structures tell the reader in advance where the argument is headed. In choosing to use a closed form, which forecasts the structure in the introduction, the writer also chooses to follow through with that structure in a straightforward, undeviating way. In contrast, *open-form* structures are like stories or narratives, keeping the reader in suspense about the argument's final destination.

clearer your argument is to your reader, whereas the less you forecast, the more surprising your argument will be. The only general rule is this: Readers sometimes feel insulted by too much forecasting. In writing a self-announcing argument, forecast only what is needed for clarity. In short arguments readers often need only your claim. In longer arguments, however, or in especially complex ones, readers appreciate your forecasting the complete structure of the argument (claim with reasons).

Application of This Chapter's Principles to the Reading of Arguments

When you read a complex argument that lacks explicit forecasting, it is often hard to discern its structural core, to identify its claim, and to sort out its reasons and evidence. The more "unfolding" its structure, the harder it is to see exactly how the writer makes his or her case. Moreover, extended arguments often contain digressions and subarguments. Thus there may be dozens of small interlinked arguments going on inside a slowly unfolding main argument.

When you feel yourself getting lost in an unfolding structure, try converting it to a self-announcing structure. (It might help to imagine that the argument's author must state the argument as a claim with *because* clauses. What working thesis statement might the writer construct?) Begin by identifying the writer's claim. Then ask yourself: What are the one, two, three, or four main lines of argument this writer puts forward to support that claim? State those arguments as *because* clauses attached to the claim. Then compare your *because* clauses with your classmates'. You can expect disagreement—indeed, disagreement can enrich your understanding of a text—because the writer has left it to you to infer her intent. You should, however, find considerable overlap in your responses.

Once you have converted the support for the claim to *because* clauses and reached consensus on them, you will find it much easier to analyze the writer's reasoning, underlying assumptions, and use of evidence.

Conclusion

This chapter has introduced you to the rhetorical triangle with its key concepts of *logos, ethos,* and *pathos.* It has also shown how arguments originate in issue questions, how issue questions differ from information questions, and how arguments differ from pseudo-arguments. At the heart of this chapter we explained that the frame of an argument is a claim supported by reasons. As you generate reasons to support your own arguments, it is often helpful to articulate them as *because* clauses attached to the claim. Finally, we explained how you can apply the principles of this chapter to your own writing and reading of arguments.

In the next chapter we will see how to support a reason by examining its logical structure, uncovering its unstated assumptions, and planning a strategy of development.

5 The Logical Structure of Arguments

In Chapter 4 you learned that the core of an argument is a claim supported by reasons and that these reasons can often be stated as *because* clauses attached to a claim. In the present chapter we examine the logical structure of arguments in more depth.

An Overview of *Logos:* What Do We Mean by the "Logical Structure" of an Argument?

As you will recall from our discussion of the rhetorical triangle, *logos* refers to the strength of an argument's support and its internal consistency. *Logos* is the argument's logical structure. But what do we mean by "logical structure"?

First of all, what we *don't* mean by logical structure is the kind of precise certainty you get in a philosophy class in formal logic. Logic classes deal with symbolic assertions that are universal and unchanging, such as "If all ps are qs and if r is a p, then r is a q." This statement is logically certain so long as p, q, and r are pure abstractions. But in the real world, p, q, and r turn into actual things, and the relationships among them suddenly become fuzzy. For example, p might be a class of actions called "Sexual Harassment," while q could be the class called "Actions That Justify Dismissal from a Job." If r is the class "Telling Off-Color Stories," then the logic of our p–q–r statement suggests that telling off-color stories (r) is an instance of sexual harassment (p), which in turn is an action justifying dismissal from one's job (q).

Now, most of us would agree that sexual harassment is a serious offense that might well justify dismissal from a job. In turn, we might agree that telling off-color stories, if the jokes are sufficiently raunchy and are inflicted on an unwilling audience, constitutes sexual harassment. But few of us would want to say categorically that all people who tell off-color stories are harassing their listeners and ought to be fired. Most of us would want to know the particulars of the case before making a final judgment.

In the real world, then, it is difficult to say that *rs* are always *ps* or that every instance of a *p* results in *q*. That is why we discourage students from using the word *prove* in claims they write for arguments (as in "This paper will prove that euthanasia is wrong"). Real-world arguments seldom *prove* anything. They can only make a good case for something, a case that is more or less strong, more or less probable. Often the best you can hope for is to strengthen the resolve of those who agree with you or weaken the resistance of those who oppose you.

A key difference, then, between formal logic and real-world argument is that real-world arguments are not grounded in abstract, universal statements. Rather, as we shall see, they must be grounded in beliefs, assumptions, or values granted by the audience. A second important difference is that in real-world arguments these beliefs, assumptions, or values are often unstated. So long as writer and audience share the same assumptions, it's fine to leave them unstated. But if these underlying assumptions aren't shared, the writer has a problem.

To illustrate the nature of this problem, consider one of the arguments we introduced in the last chapter.

> Women should be allowed to join combat units because the image of women in combat would help eliminate gender stereotypes.

On the face of it, this is a plausible argument. But the argument is persuasive only if the audience agrees with the writer's assumption that it is a good thing to eliminate gender stereotyping. The writer assumes that gender stereotyping (for example, seeing men as the fighters who are protecting the women and children back home) is harmful and that society would be better off without such fixed gender roles. But what if you believed that some gender roles are biologically based, divinely intended, or otherwise culturally essential and that society should strive to maintain these gender roles rather than dismiss them as "stereotypes"? If such were the case, you might believe as a consequence that our culture should socialize women to be nurturers, not fighters, and that some essential trait of "womanhood" would be at risk if women served in combat. If these were your beliefs, the argument wouldn't work for you because you would reject its underlying assumption. To persuade you with this line of reasoning, the writer would have to show not only how women in combat would help eliminate gender stereotypes but also why these stereotypes are harmful and why society would be better off without them.

The previous core argument ("Women should be allowed to join combat units because the image of women in combat would help eliminate gender stereotypes") is an incomplete logical structure called an *enthymeme*. Its persuasiveness depends on an unstated assumption or belief that the audience must accept. To complete the enthymeme and make it effective, the audience must willingly supply a missing premise—in this case, that gender stereotypes are harmful and should be eliminated. The Greek philosopher Aristotle showed how successful enthymemes, which he considered the main underlying structure of argument, root the speaker's argument in assumptions, beliefs, or values held by the audience. The word *enthymeme* comes from the Greek *en* (meaning "in") and *thumos* (meaning "mind"). Listeners or readers must have "in mind" an assumption, belief, or value that lets them willingly supply the missing premise. If the audience is unwilling to supply the missing premise, then the argument fails. Our point is that successful arguments depend both on what the arguer says and on what the audience already has "in mind."

To clarify the concept of "enthymeme," let's go over this same territory again more slowly, examining what we mean by "incomplete logical structure." The sentence "Women should be allowed to join combat units because the image of women in combat would help eliminate gender stereotypes" is an enthymeme. It combines a claim (women should be allowed to join combat units) with a reason expressed as a *because* clause (because the image of women in combat would help eliminate gender stereotypes). To render this enthymeme logically complete, the audience must willingly supply an unstated assumption—that gender stereotypes are harmful and should be eliminated. If your audience accepts this assumption, then you have a starting place on which to build an effective argument. If your audience doesn't accept this assumption, then you must supply another argument to support it, and so on until you find common ground with your audience.

To sum up:

1. Claims are supported with reasons. You can usually state a reason as a *because* clause attached to a claim (see Chapter 4).

2. A *because* clause attached to a claim is an incomplete logical structure called an enthymeme. To create a complete logical structure from an enthymeme, the unstated assumption (or assumptions) must be articulated.

3. To serve as an effective starting point for the argument, this unstated assumption should be a belief, value, or principle that the audience grants.

Let's illustrate this structure by putting the previous example—plus a new one—into schematic form.

INITIAL ENTHYMEME: Women should be allowed to join combat units because the image of women in combat would help eliminate gender stereotypes.

CLAIM: Women should be allowed to join combat units.

STATED REASON: because the image of women in combat would help eliminate gender stereotypes

UNSTATED ASSUMPTION: Gender stereotypes are harmful and should be eliminated.

INITIAL ENTHYMEME: Cocaine and heroin should be legalized because legalization would eliminate the black market in drugs.

CLAIM: Cocaine and heroin should be legalized.

STATED REASON: because legalization would eliminate the black market in drugs

UNSTATED ASSUMPTION: An action that eliminates the black market in drugs is good.

For Class Discussion

Working individually or in small groups, identify the claim, stated reason, and unstated assumption that completes each of the following enthymemic arguments.

EXAMPLE:

Rabbits make good pets because they are gentle.

CLAIM: Rabbits make good pets.

STATED REASON: because they are gentle

UNSTATED ASSUMPTION: Gentle animals make good pets.

1. We shouldn't elect Joe as committee chair because he is too bossy.
2. Buy this stereo system because it has a powerful amplifier.
3. Drugs should not be legalized because legalization would greatly increase the number of drug addicts.
4. Practicing the piano is good for kids because it teaches discipline.
5. Airport screeners should use racial profiling because doing so will increase the odds of stopping terrorists.
6. Racial profiling should not be used by airport screeners because it violates a person's civil rights.
7. We should strengthen the Endangered Species Act because doing so will preserve genetic diversity on the planet.
8. The Endangered Species Act is too stringent because it severely damages the economy.
9. The doctor should not perform an abortion in this case because the mother's life is not in danger.
10. Abortion should be legal because a woman has the right to control her own body. (This enthymeme has several unstated assumptions behind it; see if you can re-create all the missing premises.)

Adopting a Language for Describing Arguments: The Toulmin System

Understanding a new field usually requires us to learn a new vocabulary. For example, if you were taking biology for the first time, you'd have to memorize dozens and dozens of new terms. Luckily, the field of argument requires us to learn a mere handful of new terms. A particularly useful set of argument terms, one we'll be using occasionally throughout the rest of this text, comes from philosopher Stephen Toulmin. In the 1950s, Toulmin rejected the prevailing models of argument based on formal logic in favor of a very audience-based courtroom model.

Toulmin's courtroom model differs from formal logic in that it assumes that (1) all assertions and assumptions are contestable by "opposing counsel" and that (2) all final "verdicts" about the persuasiveness of the opposing arguments will be rendered by a neutral third party, a judge or jury. Keeping in mind the "opposing counsel" forces us to anticipate counterarguments and to question our assumptions. Keeping in mind the judge and jury reminds us to answer opposing arguments fully, without rancor, and to present positive reasons for supporting our case as well as negative reasons for disbelieving the opposing case. Above all else, Toulmin's model reminds us not to construct an argument that appeals only to those who already agree with us. In short, it helps arguers tailor arguments to their audiences.

The system we use for analyzing arguments combines Toulmin's language with Aristotle's concept of the enthymeme. It builds on the system you have already been practicing. We simply need to add a few key terms from Toulmin. The first term is Toulmin's *warrant,* the name we will now use for the unstated assumption that turns an enthymeme into a complete logical structure. For example:

INITIAL ENTHYMEME: Women should be allowed to join combat units because the image of women in combat would help eliminate gender stereotypes.

CLAIM: Women should be allowed to join combat units.

STATED REASON: because the image of women in combat would help eliminate gender stereotypes

WARRANT: Gender stereotypes are harmful and should be eliminated.

INITIAL ENTHYMEME: Cocaine and heroin should be legalized because legalization would eliminate the black market in drugs.

CLAIM: Cocaine and heroin should be legalized.

STATED REASON: because legalization would eliminate the black market in drugs

WARRANT: An action that eliminates the black market in drugs is good.

Toulmin derives his term *warrant* from the concept of "warranty" or "guarantee." The warrant is the value, belief, or principle that the audience has to hold if the soundness of the argument is to be guaranteed or warranted. We sometimes make similar use of this word in ordinary language when we say, "That is an unwarranted conclusion," meaning one has leapt from information about a situation to a conclusion about that situation without any sort of general principle to justify or "warrant" that move. Thus if we claim that cocaine and heroin ought to be legalized because legalization would end the black market, we must be able to cite a general principle or belief that links our prediction that legalization would end the black market to our claim that legalization ought to occur. In this case the warrant is the statement "An action that eliminates the black market for drugs is good." It is this underlying belief that warrants or guarantees the argument. Just as automobile manufacturers must provide warranties for their cars if they want skeptical customers to buy them, we must provide warrants linking our reasons to our claims if we expect skeptical audiences to "buy" our arguments.

But arguments need more than claims, reasons, and warrants. These are simply one-sentence statements—the frame of an argument, not a developed argument. To flesh out our arguments and make them convincing, we need what Toulmin calls *grounds* and *backing*. Grounds are the supporting evidence—facts, data, statistics, testimony, or examples—that cause you to make a claim in the first place or that you produce to justify a claim in response to audience skepticism. Toulmin suggests that grounds are "what you have to go on" in an argument. In short, they are collectively all the evidence you use to support a reason. It sometimes helps to think of grounds as the answer to a "How do you know that . . . ?" question preceding a reason. (How do you know that letting women into combat units would help eliminate gender stereotypes? How do you know that legalizing drugs will end the black market?) Here is how grounds fit into our emerging argument schema.

CLAIM: Women should be allowed to join combat units.

STATED REASON: because the image of women in combat would help eliminate gender stereotypes

GROUNDS: data and evidence showing that a chief stereotype of women is that they are soft and nurturing whereas men are tough and aggressive. The image of women in combat gear packing a rifle, driving a tank, firing a machine gun from a foxhole, or radioing for artillery support would shock people into seeing women not as "soft and nurturing" but as equal to men.

CLAIM: Cocaine and heroin should be legalized.

STATED REASON: because legalization would eliminate the black market in drugs

GROUNDS: data and evidence showing how legalizing cocaine and heroin would eliminate the black market (statistics, data, and examples describing the size and effect of the current black market, followed by arguments showing how selling cocaine and heroin legally in state-controlled stores would lower the price and eliminate the need to buy them from drug dealers)

In many cases, successful arguments require just these three components: a claim, a reason, and grounds. If the audience already accepts the unstated assumption behind the reason (the warrant), then the warrant can safely remain in the background unstated and unexamined. But if there is a chance that the audience will question or doubt the warrant, then the writer needs to back it up by providing an argument in its support. *Backing* is the argument that supports the warrant. Backing answers the question "How do you know that . . . ?" or "Why do you believe that . . . ?" prefixed to the warrant. (Why do you believe that gender stereotyping is harmful? Why do you believe that the benefits of ending the black market outweigh the costs of legalizing cocaine and heroin?) Here is how *backing* is added to our schema:

WARRANT: Gender stereotypes are harmful and should be eliminated.

BACKING: arguments showing how the existing stereotype of soft and nurturing women and tough and aggressive men is harmful to both men and women (examples of how the stereotype keeps men from developing their nurturing sides and women from developing autonomy and power; examples of other benefits that come from eliminating gender stereotypes include more egalitarian society, no limits on what persons can pursue, deeper respect for both sexes)

WARRANT: An action that eliminates the black market in drugs is good.

BACKING: an argument supporting the warrant by showing why eliminating the black market in drugs is good (statistics and examples about the ill effects of the black market, data on crime and profiteering, evidence that huge profits make drug dealing more attractive than ordinary jobs, the high cost of crime created by the black market, the cost to taxpayers of waging the war against drugs, the high cost of prisons to house incarcerated drug dealers)

Toulmin's system next asks us to imagine how a resistant audience would try to refute our argument. Specifically, the adversarial audience might challenge our reason and grounds by showing how letting women become combat soldiers wouldn't do much to end gender stereotyping or how legalizing drugs would *not* end the black market. Or the adversary might attack our warrant and backing by showing how some gender stereotypes are worth keeping, or how the negative consequences of legalizing drugs might outweigh the benefit of ending the black market.

In the case of the argument supporting women in combat or of legalizing heroin and cocaine, an adversary might offer one or more of the following rebuttals:

CONDITIONS OF REBUTTAL

Rebutting the reasons and grounds: Evidence that letting women join combat units wouldn't overcome gender stereotyping (very few women would want to join combat units; those who did would be considered freaks; most girls would still identify with Barbie doll models, not with female infantry)

Rebutting the warrant and backing: Arguments showing that it is important to maintain gender role differences because they are biologically based, divinely inspired, or otherwise important culturally; women should be nurturers and mothers, not fighters; essential nature of "womanhood" sullied by putting women in combat.

Rebutting the reasons and grounds: Arguments showing that legalizing cocaine and heroin would not eliminate that black market in drugs (perhaps taxes on the drugs would keep the costs above black market prices; perhaps new kinds of illegal designer drugs would be developed and sold on the black market).

Rebutting the warrant and backing: Arguments showing that the costs of eliminating the black market outweigh the benefits: the number of new drug users and addicts would be unacceptably high; our social structure would have too many harmful changes; the health and economic costs of treating drug addiction would be too high; the consequences to families and communities resulting from addiction or erratic behavior during drug-induced "highs" would be too great.

As these examples show, adversaries can question an argument's reasons and grounds or its warrant and backing or sometimes both. Conditions of rebuttal remind writers to look at their arguments from the perspective of skeptical readers.

Toulmin's final term, used to limit the force of a claim and indicate the degree of its probable truth, is *qualifier.* The qualifier reminds us that real-world arguments almost never prove a claim. We may say things like "very likely," "probably," or "maybe" to indicate the strength of the claim we are willing to draw from our grounds and warrant. Thus if there are exceptions to your warrant or if your grounds are not very strong, you will have to qualify your claim. For example, you might say, "Except in rare cases, women should not be allowed in combat units," or "With full awareness of the potential dangers, I suggest we consider the option of legalizing drugs as a way of ending the ill effects of the black market."

Although the system just described might at first seem complicated, it is actually fairly easy to use after you've had some opportunity to practice. The following chart will help you review the terms:

ORIGINAL ENTHYMEME: your claim with *because* clause

CLAIM: the point or position you are trying to get your audience to accept

STATED REASON: your *because* clause;* your reasons are the subordinate claims you make in support of your main claim

GROUNDS: the evidence (data, facts, testimony, statistics, examples) supporting your stated reason

WARRANT: the unstated assumption behind your enthymeme, the statement of belief, value, principle, and so on, that, when accepted by an audience, warrants or underwrites your argument

BACKING: evidence or other argumentation supporting the warrant (if the audience already accepts the warrant, then backing is usually not needed, but if the audience doubts the warrant, then backing is essential)

CONDITIONS OF REBUTTAL: your acknowledgment of the ways that skeptics might challenge your argument, show its weaknesses, or identify conditions under which it does not hold; adversaries can question either your reason and grounds or your warrant and backing

QUALIFIER: words or phrases limiting the force of your claim

To help you practice using these terms, here are two more examples, displayed this time so that the conditions of rebuttal are set in an opposing column next to the reason/grounds and the warrant/backing.

INITIAL ENTHYMEME: Women should be barred from combat duty because the presence of women would harm unit morale.

CLAIM: Women should be barred from combat duty.

STATED REASON: because the presence of women would harm unit morale

CONDITIONS OF REBUTTAL:

Rebutting the reason and grounds: arguments that letting women join combat units would *not* harm unit morale (times are changing rapidly; men are used to working professionally

---

*Most arguments have more than one *because* clause or reason in support of a claim. Each enthymeme thus develops only one line of reasoning, one piece of your whole argument.

GROUNDS: evidence and examples of how the presence of women would lead to romantic or sexual relationships and create sexual competition and jealousy; evidence that male bonding is difficult when women are present; fear that a woman wouldn't be strong enough to carry a wounded buddy off a battlefield, etc.; fear that men couldn't endure watching a woman with her legs blown off in a minefield with women; examples of successful mixed-gender sports teams and mountain-climbing teams; example of women astronauts working in close quarters with men; arguments that sexual and romantic liaisons would be forbidden and sexual activity punished; after a period of initial discomfort, men and women would overcome modesty about personal hygiene, etc.)

WARRANT: Combat units need high morale to function effectively.

Rebutting the warrant and backing: arguments that unit morale is not as important for combat efficiency as are training and discipline; unit morale is not as important as promoting women's rights; men will have to learn to deal with the presence of women and treat them as fellow soldiers; men can learn to act professionally even if their morale is lower

BACKING: arguments supporting the warrant by showing that combat soldiers have to have an utmost faith in buddies to do their job; anything that disrupts male bonding will make the unit less likely to stick together in extreme danger or endure being prisoners of war; examples of how unit cohesion is what makes a fighting unit able to withstand battle

QUALIFIER: In many cases the presence of women would hurt morale.

ORIGINAL ENTHYMEME: The exclusionary rule is a bad law because it allows drug dealers to escape prosecution.*

CLAIM: The exclusionary rule is a bad law.

CONDITIONS OF REBUTTAL:

Rebuttal of reason and grounds: evidence that the exclusionary rule does not allow many drug dealers to escape prosecution (counterevidence showing numerous times when police and prosecutors followed the exclusionary rule and still obtained convictions; statistical analysis showing that the percentage of cases in which the exclusionary rule threw evidence out of court is very low)

STATED REASON: because it allows drug dealers to escape prosecution

GROUNDS: numerous cases wherein the exclusionary rule prevented police from presenting evidence in court; examples of nitpicking rules and regulations that allowed drug dealers to go

---

*The exclusionary rule is a court-mandated set of regulations specifying when evidence can and cannot be introduced into a trial. It excludes all evidence that police obtain through irregular means. In actual practice, it demands that police follow strict procedures. Opponents of the exclusionary rule claim that its "narrow technicalities" handcuff police.

free; testimony from prosecutors and police about how the exclusionary rule hampers their effectiveness

WARRANT: It is beneficial to our country to prosecute drug dealers.

BACKING: arguments showing the extent and danger of the drug problem; arguments showing that prosecuting and imprisoning drug dealers will reduce the drug problem

Rebuttal of warrant and backing: arguments that reversing the exclusionary rule would have serious costs that outweigh benefits; arguments that softening the exclusionary rule would undermine civil liberties (arguments showing that the value of protecting individual liberties outweighs the value of prosecuting drug dealers)

QUALIFIER: perhaps, tentatively

For Class Discussion

Working individually or in small groups, imagine that you have to write arguments developing the ten enthymemes listed in the For Class Discussion exercise on page 90. Use the Toulmin schema to help you determine what you need to consider when developing each enthymeme. As an example, we have applied the Toulmin schema to the first enthymeme.

ORIGINAL ENTHYMEME: We shouldn't elect Joe as committee chair because he is too bossy.

CLAIM: We shouldn't elect Joe as committee chair.

STATED REASON: because he is too bossy

GROUNDS: various examples of Joe's bossiness; testimony about his bossiness from people who have worked with him

WARRANT: Bossy people make bad committee chairs.

BACKING: arguments showing that other things being equal, bossy people tend to bring out the worst rather than the best in those around them; bossy people tend not to ask advice, make bad decisions; etc.

CONDITIONS OF REBUTTAL: *Rebuttal of reason and grounds:* perhaps Joe isn't really bossy (counterevidence of Joe's cooperativeness and kindness; testimony that Joe is easy to work with; etc.)

Rebuttal of the warrant and backing: perhaps bossy people sometimes make good chairpersons (arguments showing that at times a group needs a bossy person who can make decisions and get things done); perhaps Joe has other traits of good leadership that outweigh his bossiness (evidence that, despite his bossiness, Joe has many other good leadership traits such as high energy, intelligence, charisma, etc.)

QUALIFIER: In most circumstances, bossy people make bad committee chairs.

Using Toulmin's Schema to Determine a Strategy of Support

Having introduced you to Toulmin's terminology for describing the logical structure of arguments, we can turn directly to a discussion of how to use these concepts for developing your own arguments. As we have seen, the claim, supporting reasons, and warrant form the frame for a line of reasoning. The majority of words in an argument, however, are devoted to grounds and backing—the supporting sections that develop the argument frame.

For an illustration of how a writer can use the Toulmin schema to generate ideas for an argument, consider the following hypothetical case. A student, Ramona, wants to write a complaint letter to the head of the philosophy department about a philosophy professor, Dr. Choplogic, whom Ramona considers incompetent. Ramona plans to develop two different lines of reasoning: (1) Choplogic's courses are disorganized. (2) Choplogic is unconcerned about students. Let's look briefly at how she can develop her first main line of reasoning, which is based on the following enthymeme:

Dr. Choplogic is an ineffective teacher because his courses are disorganized.

The grounds for this argument will be all the evidence Ramona can muster showing that Choplogic's courses are disorganized. Figure 5.1 shows her initial brainstorming notes based on the Toulmin schema. The information Ramona lists under "grounds" is what she sees as the facts of the case—the hard data she will use as evidence to support her reason. The top of page 99 shows how this argument might look when placed into written form.

Claim: Dr. Choplogic is an ineffective teacher.
Stated reason: because his courses are disorganized
Grounds: What evidence is there that his courses are disorganized?
—no syllabus in either Intro or Ethics
—never announced how many papers we would have
—didn't know what would be on tests
—didn't like the textbook he had chosen; gave us different terms
—didn't follow any logical sequence in his lectures

FIGURE 5.1   *Ramona's initial planning notes*

FIRST PART OF RAMONA'S ARGUMENT

Claim and reason

One reason that Dr. Choplogic is ineffective is that his courses are poorly organized. I have had him for two courses—Introduction to Philosophy and Ethics—and both were disorganized. He never gave us a syllabus or explained his grading system. At the begin-

Grounds (evidence in support of reason)

ning of the course he wouldn't tell us how many papers he would require, and he never seemed to know how much of the textbook material he planned to cover. For Intro he told us to read the whole text, but he covered only half of it in class. A week before the final I asked him how much of the text would be on the exam and he said he hadn't decided. The Ethics class was even more disorganized. Dr. Choplogic told us to read the text, which provided one set of terms for ethical arguments, and then he told us he didn't like the text and presented us in lecture with a wholly different set of terms. The result was a whole class of confused, angry students.

As you can see, Ramona has plenty of evidence to support her contention that Choplogic is disorganized. But how effective is this argument as it stands? Is this all she needs? The Toulmin schema also encourages Ramona to examine the warrant, backing, and conditions of rebuttal for this argument. Figure 5.2 shows how her planning notes continue.

This section of her planning notes helps her see her argument more fully from the audience's perspective. She believes that no one can challenge her reason and grounds—Choplogic is indeed a disorganized teacher. But she recognizes that some people might challenge her warrant ("Disorganized teachers are ineffective"). A supporter of Dr. Choplogic might say that some teachers, even though they are hopelessly disorganized, might nevertheless do an excellent job of stimulating thought and discussion. Moreover, such teachers might possess other valuable traits that outweigh their disorganization. Ramona therefore decides to address these concerns by adding another section to this portion of her argument.

CONTINUATION OF RAMONA'S ARGUMENT

Backing for warrant (shows why disorganization is bad)

Dr. Choplogic's lack of organization makes it difficult for students to take notes, to know what to study, or to relate one part of the course to another. Moreover, students lose confidence in the teacher because he doesn't seem to care enough to prepare for class.

Response to conditions of rebuttal

In Dr. Choplogic's defense, it might be thought that his primary concern is involving students in class discussions or other activities to teach us thinking skills or get us involved in philosophical discussions. But this isn't the case. Students rarely get a chance to speak in class. We just sit there listening to rambling, disorganized lectures.

Claim: Dr. Choplogic is an ineffective teacher.

Stated reason: because his courses are disorganized

Grounds: What evidence is there that his courses are disorganized?
—no syllabus in either Intro or Ethics
—never announced how many papers we would have
—didn't know what would be on tests
—didn't like the textbook he had chosen; gave us different terms
—didn't follow any logical sequence in his lectures

Warrant: Disorganized teachers are ineffective.

Backing:
—organization helps you learn
—gets material organized in a logical way
—helps you know what to study
—helps you take notes and relate one part of course to another
—when teacher is disorganized, you think he hasn't prepared for class; makes you lose confidence

Conditions of rebuttal: Would anybody doubt my reasons and grounds?
—No. Every student I have ever talked to agrees that these are the facts about Choplogic's courses. Everyone agrees that he is disorganized. Of course, the department chair might not know this, so I will have to provide evidence.

Would anybody doubt my warrant and backing? Maybe they would.
—Is it possible that in some cases disorganized teachers are good teachers? Have I ever had a disorganized teacher who was good? My freshman sociology teacher was disorganized, but she really made you think. You never knew where the course was going but we had some great discussions. Choplogic isn't like that. He isn't using classtime to get us involved in philosophical thinking or discussions.
—Is it possible that Choplogic has other good traits that outweigh his disorganization? I don't think he does, but I will have to make a case for this.

FIGURE 5.2   *Ramona's planning notes, continued*

As the marginal notations show, this section of her argument backs the warrant that disorganized teachers are ineffective and anticipates some of the conditions for rebuttal that an audience might raise to defend Dr. Choplogic. Throughout her draft, Ramona has supported her argument with effective use of evidence. The Toulmin schema has shown her that she needed evidence primarily to support her stated reason ("Choplogic is disorganized"). But she also needed some evidence to support her warrant ("Disorganization is bad") and to respond to possible conditions of rebuttal ("Perhaps Choplogic is teaching thinking skills").

In general, the evidence you use for support can come from your own personal experiences and observations, from field research such as interviews or questionnaires, or from reading and library or Internet research. Although many arguments depend on your skill at research, many can be supported wholly or in part from your own personal experiences, so don't neglect the wealth of evidence from your own life when searching for data. Chapter 6 is devoted to a more detailed discussion of evidence in arguments.

For Class Discussion

1. Working individually or in small groups, consider ways you could use evidence to support the stated reason in each of these following partial arguments.

   a. Another reason to oppose a state sales tax is that it is so annoying.

   b. Rap music has a bad influence on teenagers because it promotes disrespect for women.

   c. Professor X is an outstanding teacher because he (she) generously spends so much time outside of class counseling students with personal problems.

2. Now create arguments to support the warrants in each of the partial arguments in exercise 1. The warrants for each of the arguments are stated below.

   a. Support this warrant: We should oppose taxes that are annoying.

   b. Support this warrant: It is bad to promote disrespect for women.

   c. Support this warrant: Time spent counseling students with personal problems is an important criterion for identifying outstanding teachers.

3. Using Toulmin's conditions of rebuttal, work out a strategy for refuting either the stated reasons or the warrants or both in each of the arguments above.

The Power of Audience-Based Reasons

As we have seen, both Aristotle's concept of the enthymeme and Toulmin's concept of the warrant focus on the arguer's need to create what we will now call "audience-based reasons." Whenever you ask whether a given piece of writing is persuasive, the immediate rejoinder should always be "Persuasive to whom?" What seems like a good reason to you may not be a good reason to others. Finding audience-based reasons means finding arguments whose warrants the audience will accept—that is, arguments effectively rooted in your audience's beliefs and values.

Difference between Writer-Based and Audience-Based Reasons

To illustrate the difference between writer-based and audience-based reasons, consider the following hypothetical case. Suppose you believed that the government should build a dam on the nearby Rapid River—a project bitterly opposed by several environmental groups. Which of the following two arguments might you use to address environmentalists?

1. The government should build a dam on the Rapid River because the only alternative power sources are coal-fired or nuclear plants, both of which pose greater risk to the environment than a hydroelectric dam.
2. The government should build a hydroelectric dam on the Rapid River because this area needs cheap power to attract heavy industry.

Clearly, the warrant of Argument 1 ("Choose the source of power that poses least risk to the environment") is rooted in the values and beliefs of environmentalists, whereas the warrant of Argument 2 ("Growth of industry is good") is likely to make them wince. To environmentalists, new industry means more congestion, more smokestacks, and more pollution. However, Argument 2 may appeal to out-of-work laborers or to the business community, to whom new industry means more jobs and a booming economy.

From the perspective of logic alone, Arguments 1 and 2 are both sound. They are internally consistent and proceed from reasonable premises. But they will affect different audiences very differently. Neither argument proves that the government should build the dam; both are open to objection. Passionate environmentalists, for example, might counter Argument 1 by asking why the government needs to build any power plant at all. They could argue that energy conservation would obviate the need for a new power plant. Or they might argue that building a dam hurts the environment in ways unforeseen by dam supporters. Our point, then, isn't that Argument 1 will persuade environmentalists. Rather, our point is that Argument 1 will be more persuasive than Argument 2 because it is rooted in beliefs and values that the intended audience shares.

Let's consider a second example by returning to Chapter 1 and student Gordon Adams's petition to waive his math requirement. Gordon's central argument, as you will recall, was that as a lawyer he would have no need for algebra. In Toulmin's terms, Gordon's argument looks like this:

CLAIM: I should be exempted from the algebra requirement.

STATED REASON: because in my chosen field of law I will have no need for algebra

GROUNDS: testimony from lawyers and others that lawyers never use algebra

WARRANT: (largely implicit in Gordon's argument) General education requirements should be based on career utility (that is, if a course isn't needed for a particular student's career, it shouldn't be required).

BACKING: (not provided) arguments that career utility should be the chief criterion for requiring general education courses

In our discussions of this case with students and faculty, students generally vote to support Gordon's request, whereas faculty generally vote against it. And in fact, the University Standards Committee rejected Gordon's petition, thus delaying his entry into law school.

Why do faculty and students differ on this issue? Mainly they differ because faculty reject Gordon's warrant that general education requirements should serve students' individual career interests. Most faculty believe that general education courses, including math, provide a base of common learning that links us to the past and teaches us modes of understanding useful throughout life.

Gordon's argument thus challenges one of college professors' most cherished beliefs—that the liberal arts are innately valuable. Further, it threatens his immediate audience, the committee, with a possible flood of student requests to waive other general education requirements on the grounds of their irrelevance to a particular career choice.

How might Gordon have created a more persuasive argument? In our view, Gordon might have prevailed had he accepted the faculty's belief in the value of the math requirement and argued that he had fulfilled the "spirit" of that requirement through alternative means. He could have based his argument on an enthymeme like this:

> I should be exempted from the algebra requirement because my experience as a contractor and inventor has already provided me with equivalent mathematical knowledge.

Following this audience-based approach, he would drop all references to algebra's uselessness for lawyers and expand his discussion of the mathematical savvy he acquired on the job. This argument would honor faculty values and reduce the faculty's fear of setting a bad precedent. Few students are likely to have Gordon's background, and those who do could apply for a similar exemption without threatening the system. Again, this argument might not have won, but it would have gotten a more sympathetic hearing.

For Class Discussion

Working in groups, decide which of the two reasons offered in each instance would be more persuasive to the specified audience. Be prepared to explain your reasoning to the class. Write out the implied warrant for each *because* clause and decide whether the specific audience would likely grant it.

1. Audience: a beleaguered parent
   a. I should be allowed to stay out until 2 A.M. because all my friends do.
   b. I should be allowed to stay out until 2 A.M. because only if I'm free to make my own decisions will I mature.

2. Audience: a prospective employer
   a. I would be a good candidate for a summer job at the Happy Trails Dude Ranch because I have always wanted to spend a summer in the mountains and because I like to ride horses.
   b. I would be a good candidate for a summer job at the Happy Trails Dude Ranch because I am a hard worker, because I have had considerable experience serving others in my volunteer work, and because I know how to make guests feel welcome and relaxed.

3. Audience: people who oppose the present grading system on the grounds that it is too competitive
   a. We should keep the present grading system because it prepares people for the dog-eat-dog pressures of the business world.
   b. We should keep the present grading system because it tells students that certain standards of excellence must be met if individuals are to reach their full potential.

4. Audience: young people ages fifteen to twenty-five
   a. You should become a vegetarian because an all-vegetable diet is better for your heart than a meaty diet.
   b. You should become a vegetarian because that will help eliminate the suffering of animals raised in factory farms.

5. Audience: conservative proponents of "family values"
   a. Same-sex marriages should be legalized because doing so will promote public acceptance of homosexuality.
   b. Same-sex marriages should be legalized because doing so will make it easier for gay people to establish and sustain long-term, stable relationships.

Finding Audience-Based Reasons: Asking Questions about Your Audience

As the preceding exercise makes clear, reasons are most persuasive when linked to your audience's values. This principle seems simple enough, yet it is easy to forget. For example, employers frequently complain about job interviewees whose first concern is what the company will do for them, not what they might do for the company. Conversely, job search experts agree that most successful job candidates do extensive background research on a prospective company so that in an interview they can relate their own skills to the company's problems and needs. Successful arguments typically grow out of similar attention to audience needs.

To find out all you can about an audience, we recommend that you explore the following questions:

1. *Who is your audience?*   Your audience might be a single, identifiable person. For example, you might write a letter to your student body president arguing for a change in intramural policies or to a vice president for research proposing a new research and development project for your company. Or your audience might be a decision-making body such as the University Standards Committee or a philanthropic organization to which you're writing a grant proposal. At other times your audience might be the general readership of a newspaper, church bulletin, magazine, or journal, or you might produce a flier to be handed out on street corners.

2. *How much does your audience know or care about your issue?*   Are members of this audience currently part of the conversation on this issue, or do they need considerable background information? If you are writing to specific decision makers (for example, the administration at your college about restructuring the student orientation program), are they currently aware of the problem or issue you are addressing, and do they care about it? If not, how can you get their attention? Your answers to these questions will especially affect your introduction and conclusion.

3. *What is your audience's current attitude toward your issue?*   Are members of this audience supportive of your position on the issue? Neutral or undecided? Skeptical? Strongly opposed? What other points of view besides your own will your audience be weighing? In Chapter 8, we will explain how your answers to these questions can help you decide the structure and tone of your argument.

4. *What will be your audience's likely objections to your argument?*   What weaknesses will audience members find? What aspects of your position will be most threatening to them and why? How are your basic assumptions, values, or beliefs different from your audience's? Your answers here will help determine the content of your argument and will alert you to extra research you may need to do to bolster your response to audience objections.

5. *Finally, what values, beliefs, or assumptions about the world do you and your audience share?*   Despite differences of view on this issue, where can you find common links with your audience? How might you use these links to build bridges to your audience?

Suppose, for example, that you support racial profiling (rather than random selection) for determining persons to receive intensive screening at airports. It's important from the start that you understand and acknowledge the interests of those opposed to your position. Middle Eastern men, the most likely candidates for racial profiling, will object to your racial stereotyping, which lumps all persons of Arabic or Semitic appearance into the category "potential terrorists." African Americans and Hispanics, frequent victims of racial profiling by police in U.S.

cities, may object to further extension of this hated practice. Also, most political liberals, as well as many moderates and conservatives, may object to the racism inherent in selecting persons for airport screening on the basis of ethnicity.

What shared values might you use to build bridges to those opposed to racial profiling at airports? Suppose that you are writing a guest op-ed column for a liberal campus newspaper and imagine readers repulsed by the notion of racial profiling. (Indeed you too feel repulsed by racial profiling.) You need to develop a strategy to reduce your audience's fears and to link your reasons to their values. Your thinking might go something like this:

Problem: How can I create an argument rooted in shared values? How can I reduce fear that racial profiling in this situation endorses racism or will lead to further erosion of civil liberties?

Bridge-building goals: I must try to show that my argument's goal is to increase airline safety by preventing terrorism like that of 9/11/01. My argument must show my respect for Islam and for Arabic and Semitic peoples. I must also show my rejection of racial profiling as normal police practice.

Possible strategies:
- Stress the shared value of protecting innocent people from terrorism.
- Show how racial profiling significantly increases the efficiency of secondary searches. (If searches are performed at random, then we waste time and resources searching the elderly, women, children, and others who are statistically unlikely to be terrorists.)
- Argue that airport screeners must also use indicators other than race to select persons for searches (for example, traits that might indicate a domestic terrorist like Timothy McVeigh).
- Show my respect for Islam.
- Show sympathy for persons selected for searching via racial profiling and acknowledge that this practice would normally be despicable except for the extreme importance of airline security, which overrides personal liberties in this case.
- Show my rejection of racial profiling in situations other than airport screening—for example, stopping African Americans for traffic violations more often than whites and then searching their cars for drugs or stolen goods.
- Perhaps show my support of affirmative action, which is a kind of racial profiling in reverse.

These thinking notes allow you to develop the following plan for your argument.

Airport screeners should use racial profiling rather than random selection to determine which persons undergo intensive screening.

- because doing so will make more efficient use of airport screener's time, increase the odds of finding terrorists, and thus lead to greater airline safety (*WARRANT: increased airline safety is good;* or, at a deeper level: *The positive consequences of increasing airline safety through racial profiling outweigh the negative consequences*)
- because allowing racial profiling in this specific case does not mean allowing it in everyday police practices (*WARRANT: Racial profiling is unacceptable in everyday police practices*) nor does it imply disrespect for Islam or for Middle Eastern males (*WARRANT: It is wrong to show disrespect for Islam or Middle Eastern males*)

As this plan shows, your strategy is to seek reasons whose warrants your audience will accept. First, you will argue that racial profiling will lead to greater airline safety, allowing you to stress that safe airlines benefit all passengers. Your concern is the lives of hundreds of passengers as well as others who might be killed in a terrorist attack. Second, you plan to reduce adversaries' resistance to your proposal by showing that the consequences aren't as severe as they might fear. Using racial profiling in airports would not justify using it in urban police work (a practice you find despicable) and it would not imply disrespect for Islam or Middle Eastern males. As this example shows, your focus on audience—on the search for audience-based reasons—shapes the actual invention of your argument from the start.

For Class Discussion

Working individually or in small groups, plan an audience-based argumentative strategy for one or more of the following cases. Follow the thinking process used by the writer of the racial profiling argument: (1) State several problems that the writer must solve to reach the audience, and (2) develop possible solutions to those problems.

1. An argument for the right of software companies to continue making and selling violent video games: Aim the argument at parents who oppose their children's playing these games.
2. An argument to reverse grade inflation by limiting the number of A's and B's a professor can give in a course: Aim the argument at students who fear the results of getting lower grades.

3. An argument supporting a $1-per-gallon increase in gasoline taxes as an energy conservation measure: Aim your argument at business leaders who oppose the tax for fear it will raise the cost of consumer goods.

4. An argument supporting the legalization of cocaine: Aim your argument at readers of *Reader's Digest*, a conservative magazine that supports the current war on drugs.

Conclusion

Chapters 4 and 5 have provided an anatomy of argument. They have shown that the core of an argument is a claim with reasons that usually can be summarized in one or more *because* clauses attached to the claim. Often, it is as important to support the unstated assumptions in your argument as it is to support the stated reasons because a successful argument must eventually be rooted in beliefs and values held by your audience. In order to plan an audience-based argument strategy, arguers can use the Toulmin schema, which helps writers discover grounds, warrants, and backing for their arguments and to test them through conditions of rebuttal. Finally we showed how a search for audience-based reasons helps you keep your audience in mind from the start whenever you design a plan for an argument.

6 Using Evidence Effectively

In Chapters 4 and 5 we introduced you to the concept of *logos*—the logical structure of reasons and evidence in an argument—and showed you how an effective argument advances the writer's claim by linking its supporting reasons to one or more assumptions, beliefs, or values held by the intended audience. In this chapter, we turn to the uses of evidence in argument. By "evidence," we mean all the verifiable information a writer might use as support for an argument, such as facts, observations, examples, cases, testimony, experimental findings, survey data, statistics, and so forth. In Toulmin's terms, evidence is part of the "grounds" or "backing" of an argument in support of reasons or warrants.

In this chapter, we show you how to use evidence effectively. We begin by explaining some general principles for the persuasive use of evidence. Next we describe and illustrate various kinds of evidence and then present a rhetorical way to think about evidence, particularly the way writers select and frame evidence to support the writer's reasons while simultaneously guiding and limiting what the reader sees. By understanding the rhetorical use of evidence, you will better understand how to use evidence ethically, responsibly, and persuasively in your own arguments. We conclude the chapter by suggesting strategies to help you gather evidence for your arguments, including advice on conducting interviews and using questionnaires.

General Principles for the Persuasive Use of Data

Consider a target audience of educated, reasonable, and careful readers who approach an issue with healthy skepticism, open-minded but cautious. What demands would such readers make upon a writer's use of evidence? To begin to answer that question, let's look at some general principles for using evidence persuasively.

Apply the STAR Criteria to Data

Our open-minded but skeptical audience would first of all expect the evidence to meet what rhetorician Richard Fulkerson calls the STAR criteria:*

Sufficiency: Is there enough evidence?

Typicality: Are the chosen data representative and typical?

Accuracy: Are the data accurate and up-to-date?

Relevance: Are the data relevant to the claim?

Let's examine each in turn.

Sufficiency of Evidence How much evidence you need is a function of your rhetorical context. In a court trial, opposing attorneys often agree to waive evidence for points that aren't in doubt in order to concentrate on contested points. The more a claim is contested or the more your audience is skeptical, the more evidence you may need to present. If you provide too little evidence, you may be accused of *hasty generalization* (see Appendix 1), a reasoning fallacy in which a person makes a sweeping conclusion based on only one or two instances. On the other hand, if you provide too much evidence your argument may become overly long and tedious. You can guard against having too little or too much evidence by appropriately qualifying the claim your evidence supports.

Strong claim: Working full time seriously harms a student's grade point average. (much data needed—probably a combination of examples and statistical studies)

Qualified claim: Working full time often harms a student's grade point average. (a few representative examples may be enough)

Typicality of Evidence Whenever you select data, readers need to believe the data are typical and representative rather than extreme instances. Suppose that you want to argue that students can combine full-time work with full-time college and cite the case of your friend Pam who pulled a straight-A grade average while working forty hours per week as a night receptionist in a small hotel. Your audience might doubt the typicality of Pam's case since a night receptionist can often use work hours for studying. What about more typical jobs, they'll ask, where you can't study while you work?

Accuracy of Evidence Data can't be used ethically unless they are accurate and up-to-date, and they can't be persuasive unless the audience believes in the

---

*Richard Fulkerson, *Teaching the Argument in Writing* (Urbana, IL: National Council of Teachers of English, 1996), 44–53. In this section, we are indebted to Fulkerson's discussion.

writer's credibility. As a writer, you must be scrupulous in using the most recent and accurate data you can find. We have already encountered a case of doubtful data in the two articles on biotech food in Chapter 2. Lisa Turner cites a 1993 case in which thirty-seven people died from a rare disease allegedly linked to bioengineered food (see Chapter 2, p. 25), yet the Council for Biotechnology Information states, "There hasn't been a single documented case of an illness caused by biotech foods" (p. 40). One of these writers must be using inaccurate data—a problem the reader can unravel only through additional research. Faith in the accuracy of a writer's data is one function of *ethos*—the audience's confidence in the writer's credibility and trustworthiness (see Chapter 7, p. 131).

Relevance of Evidence Finally, data will be persuasive only if the reader considers them relevant to the contested issue. Consider the following student argument: "I deserve an A in this course because I worked exceptionally hard." The student then cites substantial evidence of how hard he worked—a log of study hours, copies of multiple drafts of papers, testimony from friends, and so forth. Such evidence is ample support for the claim "I worked very hard" but is irrelevant to the claim "I deserve an A." Although some instructors may give partial credit for effort, the criteria for grades usually focus on the quality of the student's performance, not the student's time spent studying.

Use Sources That Your Reader Trusts

Another way to enhance the persuasiveness of your evidence is to choose data, whenever possible, from sources you think your readers will trust. Because questions of fact are often at issue in arguments, readers may be skeptical of certain sources. When you research an issue, you soon get a sense of who the participants in the conversation are and what their reputations tend to be. Knowing the political biases of sources and the extent to which a source has financial or personal investment in the outcome of a controversy will also help you locate data sources that both you and your readers can trust. Citing a peer-reviewed scholarly journal is often more persuasive than citing an advocacy Web site. Similarly, citing a conservative magazine such as the *National Review* may be unpersuasive to liberal audiences, just as citing a Sierra Club publication may be unpersuasive to conservatives. (See Chapter 16 for further discussion of how to evaluate research sources from a rhetorical perspective.)

Rhetorical Understanding of Evidence

In the previous section we presented some general principles for the effective use of evidence. We now want to deepen your understanding of how evidence persuades by asking you to consider more closely the rhetorical context in which evidence operates. We'll look first at the kinds of evidence used in arguments and then show you how writers select and frame evidence for persuasive effect.

Kinds of Evidence

Writers have numerous options for the kinds of evidence they can use in an argument, ranging from personal experience data to research findings to hypothetical examples. To explain these options, we present a series of charts that categorize different kinds of evidence, illustrate how each kind might be worked into an argument, and comment on the strengths and limitations of each.

Data from Personal Experience   One powerful kind of evidence comes from personal experience:

CATEGORY	EXAMPLE	STRENGTHS AND LIMITATIONS
Examples from personal experience or knowledge	Despite recent criticism that Ritalin is overprescribed for hyperactivity and attention deficit disorder, it can often seem like a miracle drug. My little brother is a perfect example. Before he was given Ritalin he was a terror in school. . . . (Tell the "before" and "after" story of your little brother.)	▪ Personal experience examples help readers identify with the writer; they show the writer's personal connection to the issue. ▪ Vivid stories capture the imagination. ▪ Skeptics may sometimes argue that personal experience examples are insufficient (writer is guilty of hasty generalization), not typical, or not adequately scientific or verifiable.
Personal observation or field research	The intersection at Fifth and Montgomery is particularly dangerous because pedestrians almost never find a comfortable break in the heavy flow of cars. On April 29, I watched fifty-seven pedestrians cross the street. Not once did cars stop in both directions before the pedestrian stepped off the sidewalk onto the street. (Continue with observed data about danger.)	▪ Field research gives the feeling of scientific credibility. ▪ It increases typicality by expanding the database beyond the example of one person. ▪ It enhances the *ethos* of the writer as personally invested and reasonable. ▪ Skeptics may point to flaws in how observations were conducted, showing how data are insufficient, inaccurate, or nontypical.

Data from Interviews, Questionnaires, Surveys You can also gather data by interviewing stakeholders in a controversy, creating questionnaires, or doing surveys. (See pp. 122–124 for advice on how to conduct this kind of field research.)

EXAMPLE	STRENGTHS AND LIMITATIONS
In the first two months after the terrorist attacks on September 11, 2001, Muslim students on our campus suffered from anxiety at an especially severe rate. In a survey I conducted through the Student Affairs Office, 87 percent of Muslim students reported (give details of survey). Additionally, in my interviews with three Muslim students—two international students from Saudi Arabia and one American student born and raised in Chicago—I discovered that (report interview data).	■ Interviews, questionnaires, and surveys enhance the sufficiency and typicality of evidence by expanding the database beyond the experiences of one person. ■ Quantitative data from questionnaires and surveys often increase the scientific feel of the argument. ■ Surveys and questionnaires often uncover local or recent data not available in published research. ■ Interviews can provide engaging personal stories enhancing *pathos.* ■ Skeptics can raise doubts about research methodology, questionnaire design, or typicality of interview subjects.

Data from Reading and Research For many arguments, evidence is derived from reading, particularly through library or Internet research. Part Four of this text offers detailed advice on conducting research.

CATEGORY	EXAMPLE	STRENGTHS AND LIMITATIONS
Facts, examples, illustrative cases drawn from reading	Although reproductive technology cannot solve all infertility problems, breakthroughs continue. In addition to fertilizing eggs in petri dishes, reproductive technology can detect abnormalities in embryos before they are implanted. To combat male infertility, which makes up nearly half the infertility problems, reproductive technology can concentrate sperm for artificial insemination and inject a sperm directly into an egg. Since 1970, the number of	■ Researched evidence is often powerful, especially when sources are respected. ■ Skeptics might doubt the accuracy of facts or credentials of a source. ■ Skeptics might raise doubts about sufficiency, typicality, or relevance of data.

CATEGORY	EXAMPLE	STRENGTHS AND LIMITATIONS
	women in their thirties and forties having their first child has quadrupled, partly as a result of these scientific advances (Kalb 40–43).*	
Findings from experimental reports; summaries of research studies	The belief that a high-carbohydrate–low-fat diet is the best way to lose weight has been challenged by research conducted by Walter Willett and his colleagues in the department of nutrition in the Harvard School of Public Health. Willett's research suggests that complex carbohydrates such as pasta and potatoes spike glucose levels, increasing the risk of diabetes. Additionally, some fats can be good for you—especially monounsaturated and polyunsaturated fats found in nuts, fish, and most vegetable oils—which help lower "bad" cholesterol levels (45).	■ Reports and studies are an excellent source of persuasive data, especially if the studies are peer reviewed in respected journals. ■ These enhance the writer's *ethos* if the writer composes clear summaries in the writer's own voice without insider jargon. ■ Skeptics might doubt the research design of the study or cite other studies with different results.
Testimony	Although the Swedish economist Bjorn Lomborg claims that acid rain is not a significant problem, many environmentalists disagree. According to David Bellamany, president of the Conservation Foundation, "Acid rain does kill forests and people around the world, and it's still doing so in the most polluted places, such as Russia" (qtd. in BBC News).	■ Testimony is frequently used when data are too technical or complex for lay audiences to understand; it can also supplement the use of actual data. ■ By itself, it is generally less persuasive than direct data. ■ Persuasiveness can be increased if the source has impressive credentials, which the writer must state. ■ Skeptics might undermine testimonial evidence by questioning the credentials of a source, showing the source's bias, or quoting a countersource.

*Examples of parenthetical citations in this section follow the MLA documentation system. See Chapter 17 for a full discussion of how to cite and document sources.

Statistical Data   Many contemporary arguments rely heavily on statistical data, often supplemented by graphics such as tables, pie charts, and graphs. (See Chapter 9 for a discussion of the use of graphics in argument.)

EXAMPLE	STRENGTHS AND LIMITATIONS
Americans are delaying marriage at a surprising rate. In 1970, 85 percent of Americans between the ages of fifteen and twenty-nine were married. In 2000, however, only 54 percent were married (U.S. Census Bureau).	■ Statistics can give powerful snapshots of aggregate data from a wide database. ■ They are often used in conjunction with graphics (see pp. 189–196). ■ They can be calculated and displayed in different ways to achieve different rhetorical effects, so the reader must be wary (see pp. 191–194). ■ Skeptics might question statistical methods, research design, and interpretation of data.

Hypothetical Examples, Cases, and Scenarios   Arguments occasionally use hypothetical examples, cases, or scenarios, particularly to illustrate conjectured consequences of an event or to test philosophical hypotheses.

EXAMPLE	STRENGTHS AND LIMITATIONS
Consider what might happen if we continue to use biotech soybeans that are resistant to herbicides. The resistant gene, through cross-pollination, might be transferred to an ordinary weed, creating an out-of-control superweed that herbicides couldn't kill. Such a superweed could be an ecological disaster.	■ Scenarios have strong imaginative appeal. ■ They are persuasive only if they seem plausible. ■ A scenario narrative often conveys a sense of "inevitability," even if the actual scenario is unlikely; hence rhetorical effect may be illogical. ■ Skeptics might show the implausibility of the scenario or offer an alternative scenario.

Reasoned Sequence of Ideas   Sometimes arguments are supported with a reasoned sequence of ideas rather than with concrete facts or other forms of empirical evidence. The writer's concern is to support a point through a logical progression of ideas. Such arguments are conceptual, supported by linked ideas, rather than evidential. This kind of support occurs frequently in arguments and is often intermingled with evidentiary support.

EXAMPLE	STRENGTHS AND LIMITATIONS
Embryonic stem cell research, despite its promise in fighting diseases, may have negative social consequences.	■ These sequences are often used in causal arguments to show how causes are linked to effects or in

EXAMPLE	STRENGTHS AND LIMITATIONS
This research encourages us to place embryos in the category of mere cellular matter that can be manipulated at will. Currently we reduce animals to this category when we genetically alter them for human purposes, such as engineering pigs to grow more human-like heart valves for use in transplants. Using human embryos in the same way—as material that can be altered and destroyed at will—may benefit society materially, but this quest for greater knowledge and control involves a reclassifying of embryos that could potentially lead to a devaluing of human life.	definitional or values arguments to show links among ideas. ■ They have great power to clarify values and show the belief structure upon which a claim is founded. ■ They can sketch out ideas and connections that would otherwise remain latent. ■ Their effectiveness depends on the audience's acceptance of each link in the sequence of ideas. ■ Skeptics might raise objections at any link in the sequence, often by pointing to different values or outlining different consequences.

Angle of Vision and the Selection and Framing of Evidence

You can increase your ability to use evidence effectively—and to analyze how other arguers use evidence—by becoming more aware of a writer's rhetorical choices when using evidence to support a claim. Where each of us stands on an issue is partly a function of our own critical thinking, inquiry, and research—our search for the best solution to a problem. But it is also partly a function of who we are as persons—our values and beliefs as formed by the particulars of our existence such as our family history, our education, our gender and sexual orientation, our age, class, and ethnicity, and so forth. In other words, we don't enter the argumentative arena like disembodied computers arriving at our claims through a value-free calculus. We enter with our own ideologies, beliefs, values, and guiding assumptions.

These guiding assumptions, beliefs, and values work together to create a writer's "angle of vision." (Instead of "angle of vision," we could also use other words or metaphors such as *perspective, bias, lens,* or *filter*—all terms that suggest that our way of seeing the world is shaped by our values and beliefs.) A writer's angle of vision, like a lens or filter, helps determine what stands out for that writer in a field of data—that is, what data are important or trivial, significant or irrelevant, worth focusing on or worth ignoring.

To illustrate this concept of selective seeing, we ask you to consider the selection of evidence in two arguments presented to a city council on how to spend city funds. Consider how their differing angles of vision cause the two speakers presenting the arguments to see homeless persons in different ways. The first speaker argues that the city should provide more services to the homeless. The second speaker argues that the city should encourage more tourism. Both arguers include data about the homeless, but they select different data for their overall arguments and frame these data in different ways. (Our use of the word "frame" derives metaphorically from a window frame or the frame of a camera's viewfinder. When you look through a frame, some part of your field of vision is blocked off, while the material appearing in the frame is emphasized. Through framing, a writer maximizes the reader's focus on some data, minimizes the reader's focus on other data, and otherwise guides the reader's vision and response.)

The first speaker wants to increase the council members' sympathy for the homeless. He needs to frame homeless persons positively, perhaps by telling the story of one homeless man's struggle to find shelter and nutritious food. The second speaker, who focuses on shopkeepers' loss of revenues, wants to focus the audience's attention on economic data concerning lost tourist dollars. His argument includes data about the homeless (perhaps using some of the same numerical data used by the first speaker), but treats the homeless in a different way by framing them as "panhandlers" who need to be removed from picturesque downtown tourist areas. As arguers, both speakers want their audience to see the homeless from their own angles of vision. Consequently, lost tourist dollars don't show up at all in the first speaker's argument, while the story of a homeless man's night in the cold doesn't show up in the second speaker's argument. As this example shows, one goal writers have in selecting and framing evidence is to bring the reader's view of the subject into alignment with the writer's angle of vision. The writer selects and frames evidence to limit and control what the reader sees.

To help you better understand the concepts of selection and framing, we offer the following class discussion exercise to give you practice in a kind of controlled laboratory setting. As you do this exercise, we invite you to observe your own processes for selecting and framing evidence.

For Class Discussion

Suppose that your city has scheduled a public hearing on a proposed city ordinance to ban mosh pits at rock concerts. (See p. 14, where we introduced this issue.) Among the factual data available to various speakers for evidence are the following:

Possible Data for Mosh Pit Argument

- Some bands, like Nine Inch Nails, specify festival seating that allows a mosh pit area.
- A female mosher writing on the Internet says: "I experience a shared energy that is like no other when I am in the pit with the crowd. It is like we are all a bunch of atoms bouncing off of each other. It's great. Hey, some people get that feeling from basketball games. I get mine from the mosh pit."
- A student conducted a survey of fifty students on her campus who had attended rock concerts in the last six months. Of the respondents, 80 percent thought that mosh pits should be allowed at concerts.
- Narrative comments on these questionnaires included the following:
- Mosh pits are a passion for me. I get an amazing rush when crowd surfing.

- I don't like to be in a mosh pit or do crowd surfing. But I love festival seating and like to watch the mosh pits. For me, mosh pits are part of the ambience of a concert.

- I know a girl who was groped in a mosh pit, and she'll never do one again. But I have never had any problems.

- Mosh pits are dangerous and stupid. I think they should be outlawed.

- If you are afraid of mosh pits just stay away. Nobody forces you to go into a mosh pit! It is ridiculous to ban them because they are totally voluntary. They should just post big signs saying "City assumes no responsibility for accidents occurring in mosh pit area."

- A 14-year-old boy suffered permanent brain damage from a mosh pit accident when he went to hear Rage Against the Machine in Seattle in 1996.

- A teenage girl suffered brain damage and memory loss at a 1998 Pearl Jam concert in Rapid City, South Dakota. According to her attorney, she hadn't intended to body surf or enter the mosh pit but "got sucked in while she was standing at its fringe."

- There were twenty-four concert deaths recorded in 2001, most of them in the area closest to the stage where people are packed in.

- A 21-year-old man suffered cardiac arrest at a Metallica concert in Indiana and is now in a permanent vegetative state. Because he was jammed into the mosh pit area, nobody noticed he was in distress.

Tasks: Working individually or in small groups, complete the following tasks:

1. Compose two short speeches, one supporting the proposed city ordinance to ban mosh pits and one opposing it. How you use these data is up to you, but be able to explain your reasoning in the way you select and frame them. Share your speeches with classmates.

2. After you have shared examples of different speeches, explain the approaches that different classmates employed. What principle of selection was used? If arguers included evidence contrary to their positions, how did they handle it, respond to it, minimize its importance, or otherwise channel its rhetorical effect?

3. In the preceding task, we assigned you two different angles of vision— one supporting the ordinance and one opposing it. If you had to create your own argument on a proposal to ban mosh pits and if you set for yourself a truth-seeking goal—that is, finding the best solution for the problem of mosh pit danger, one for which you would take ethical responsibility—what would you argue? How would your argument use the list of data we provided? What else might you add?

Rhetorical Strategies for Framing Evidence

What we hope you learned from the preceding exercise is that an arguer consciously selects evidence from a wide field of data and then frames these data through rhetorical strategies that emphasize some data, minimize others, and guide the reader's response. Now that you have a basic idea of what we mean by framing of evidence, here are some strategies writers can use to guide what the reader sees and feels.

Strategies for Framing Evidence

- *Controlling the space given to supporting versus contrary evidence:* Depending on their audience and purpose, writers can devote most of their space to supporting evidence and minimal space to contrary evidence (or omit it entirely). Thus persons arguing in favor of mosh pits may have used lots of evidence supporting mosh pits, including enthusiastic quotations from concertgoers, while omitting (or summarizing very rapidly) the data about the dangers of mosh pits.

- *Emphasizing a detailed story versus presenting lots of facts and statistics:* Often, writers can choose to support a point with a memorable individual case or with aggregate data such as statistics or lists of facts. A memorable story can have a strongly persuasive effect. For example, to create a negative view of mosh pits, a writer might tell the heartrending story of a teenager suffering permanent brain damage from being dropped on a mosh pit floor. In contrast, a supporter of mosh pits might tell the story of a happy music lover turned on to the concert scene by the rush of crowd surfing. A different strategy is to use facts and statistics rather than case narratives—for example, data about the frequency of mosh pit accidents, financial consequences of lawsuits, and so forth. The single narrative case often has a more powerful rhetorical effect, but it is always open to the charge that it is an insufficient or nonrepresentative example. Vivid anecdotes make for interesting reading, but by themselves they may not be compelling logically. In contrast, aggregate data, often used in scholarly studies, can provide more compelling, logical evidence but sometimes make the prose wonkish and dense.

- *Providing contextual and interpretive comments when presenting data:* When citing data, writers can add brief contextual or interpretive comments that act like lenses over the readers' eyes to help them see the data from the writer's perspective. Suppose you want to support mosh pits, but want to admit that mosh pits are dangerous. You could make that danger seem irrelevant or inconsequential by saying: "It is true that occasional mosh pit accidents happen, just as accidents happen in any kind of recreational activity from swimming to weekend softball games." The concluding phrase frames the danger of mosh pits by comparing them to other recreational accidents that don't require special laws or regulations. The implied argument is this: banning mosh pits because of an occasional accident would be as silly as banning recreational swimming because of occasional accidents.

- *Putting contrary evidence in subordinate positions:*   Just as a photographer can place a flower at the center of a photograph or in the background, a writer can place a piece of data in a subordinate or main clause of a sentence. Note how the structure of the following sentence minimizes emphasis on the rarity of mosh pit accidents: "Although mosh pit accidents are rare, the danger to the city of multimillion-dollar liability lawsuits means that the city should nevertheless ban them for reasons of fiscal prudence." The factual data that mosh pit accidents are rare is summarized briefly and tucked away in a subordinate *"although* clause," while the writer's own position is elaborated in the main clause where it receives grammatical emphasis. A writer with a different angle of vision might say, "Although some cities may occasionally be threatened with a lawsuit, serious accidents resulting from mosh pits are so rare that cities shouldn't interfere with the desires of music fans to conduct concerts as they please."

- *Choosing labels and names that guide the reader's response to data:*   One of the most subtle ways to control your reader's response to data is to choose labels and names that prompt them to see the issue as you do. If you like mosh pits, you might refer to the seating arrangements in a concert venue as "festival seating, where concertgoers have the opportunity to create a free-flowing mosh pit." If you don't like mosh pits, you might refer to the seating arrangements as "an accident-inviting use of empty space where rowdies can crowd together, slam into each other, and occasionally punch and kick." The labels you choose, along with the connotations of the words you select, urge your reader to share your angle of vision.

- *Using images (photographs, drawings) to guide the reader's response to data:* Another strategy for moving your audience toward your angle of vision is to include a photograph or drawing that portrays a contested issue from your perspective. (See Chapter 9 for a complete discussion of the use of visuals in argument.) Consider the photograph of crowd surfing shown in Color Plate C. This photograph supports a positive view of mosh pits. The crowd looks happy and relaxed (rather than rowdy or out of control) and the young woman lifted above the crowd smiles broadly, her body relaxed, her arms extended.

- *Revealing the value system that determines the writer's selection and framing of data:* Ultimately, how a writer selects and frames evidence is linked to the system of values that organize his or her argument. If you favor mosh pits, you probably favor maximizing the pleasure of concertgoers, promoting individual choice, and letting moshers assume the risk of their own behavior. If you want to forbid mosh pits, you probably favor minimizing risks, protecting the city from lawsuits, and protecting individuals from the danger of their own out-of-control actions. Sometimes you can foster connections with your audience by openly addressing the underlying values that you hope your audience shares with you. You can often frame your selected data by stating explicitly the values that guide your argument.

Special Strategies for Framing Statistical Evidence

Numbers and statistical data can be framed in so many ways that this category of evidence deserves its own separate treatment. By recognizing how writers frame numbers to support the story they want to tell, you will always be aware that other stories are also possible. Ethical use of numbers means that you use reputable sources for your basic data, that you don't invent or intentionally distort numbers for your own purposes, and that you don't ignore alternative points of view. Here are some of the choices writers make when framing statistical data:

- *Raw numbers versus percentages.* You can alter the rhetorical effect of a statistic by choosing between raw numbers or percentages. In the summer of 2002, many American parents panicked over what seemed like an epidemic of child abductions. If you cited the raw number of these abductions reported in the national news, this number, although small, could seem scary. But if you computed the actual percentage of American children who were abducted, that percentage was so infinitesimally small as to seem insignificant. You can apply this framing option directly to the mosh pit case. To emphasize the danger of mosh pits, you can say that twenty-four deaths occurred at rock concerts in the year 2001. To minimize this statistic, you could compute the percentage of deaths by dividing this number by the total number of persons who attended rock concerts during the year, certainly a number in the several millions. From the perspective of percentages, the death rate at concerts is extremely low.

- *Median versus mean.* Another way to alter the rhetorical effect of numbers is to choose between the median and the mean. The mean is the average of all numbers on a list. The median is the middle number when all the numbers are arranged sequentially from high to low. In 1998 the mean annual income for retired families in the United States was $32,600—not a wealthy amount but enough to live on comfortably if you owned your own home. However, the median income was only $19,300, a figure that gives a much more striking picture of income distribution among older Americans. This median figure means that half of all retired families in the United States had annual incomes of $19,300 or less. The much higher mean income indicates that many retired Americans are extremely wealthy. This wealth raises the average of all incomes (the mean) but doesn't effect the median.

- *Unadjusted versus adjusted numbers.* Suppose your boss told you that you were getting a 5 percent raise. You might be happy—unless inflation rates were running at 6 percent. Economic data can be hard to interpret across time unless the dollar amounts are adjusted for inflation. This same problem occurs in other areas. For example, comparing grade point averages of college graduates in 1970 versus 2002 means little unless one can somehow compensate for grade inflation.

- *Base point for statistical comparisons.* In the summer of 2002, the stock market was in precipitous decline if one compared 2002 prices with 2000 prices. However, the market still seemed vigorous and healthy if one compared 2002 with 1990. One's choice of the base point for a comparison often makes a significant rhetorical difference.

For Class Discussion

A proposal to build a new ballpark in Seattle, Washington, yielded a wide range of statistical arguments. All of the following statements are reasonably faithful to the same facts:

- The ballpark would be paid for by raising the sales tax from 8.2 percent to 8.3 percent during a twenty-year period.
- The sales tax increase is one-tenth of 1 percent.
- This increase represents an average of $7.50 per person per year—about the price of a movie ticket.
- This increase represents $750 per five-person family over the twenty-year period of the tax.
- For a family building a new home in the Seattle area, this tax will increase building costs by $200.
- This is a $250 million tax increase for the residents of the Seattle area.

How would you describe the costs of the proposed ballpark if you opposed the proposal? How would you describe the costs if you supported the proposal?

Gathering Evidence

We conclude this chapter with some brief advice on ways to gather evidence for your arguments. We begin with a list of brainstorming questions that may help you think of possible sources for evidence. We then provide suggestions for conducting interviews and creating surveys and questionnaires, since these powerful sources are often overlooked by students. For help in conducting library and Internet research—the most common sources of evidence in arguments—see Part Four: "The Researched Argument."

Creating a Plan for Gathering Evidence

As you begin contemplating an argument, you can use the following checklist to help you think of possible sources for evidence.

A Checklist for Brainstorming Sources of Evidence

- What personal experiences have you had with this issue? What details from your life or the lives of your friends, acquaintances, or relatives might serve as examples or other kinds of evidence?

- What observational studies would be relevant to this issue?

- What persons could you interview to provide insights or expert knowledge on this issue?

- What questions about your issue could be addressed in a survey or questionnaire?

- What useful information on this issue might encyclopedias, specialized reference books, or the regular book collection in your university library provide? (See Chapter 16.)

- What evidence might you seek on this issue using licensed database indexing sources in magazines, newspapers, and scholarly journals? (See Chapter 16.)

- How might an Internet search engine help you research this issue? (See Chapter 16.)

- What evidence might you find on this issue from reliable statistical resources such as U.S. Census data, the Centers for Disease Control, or *Statistical Abstracts of the United States?* (See Chapter 16.)

Gathering Data from Interviews

Conducting interviews is a useful way not only to gather expert testimony and important data but also to learn about alternative views. To make interviews as productive as possible, we offer these suggestions.

- *Determine your purpose.* Think out why you are interviewing the person and what information he or she is uniquely able to provide.

- *Do background reading.* Find out as much as possible about the interviewee before the interview. Your knowledge of his or her background will help establish your credibility and build a bridge between you and your source. Also, equip yourself with a good foundational understanding of the issue so that you will sound informed and truly interested in the issue.

- *Formulate well-thought-out questions but also be flexible.* Write out beforehand the questions you intend to ask, making sure that every question is related to the purpose of your interview. However, be prepared to move in unexpected directions if the interview opens up new territory. Sometimes unplanned topics can end up being the most illuminating and useful.

- *Come well prepared for the interview.* As part of your professional demeanor, be sure to have all the necessary supplies (notepaper, pens, pencils, perhaps a tape recorder, if your interviewee is willing) with you.

- *Be prompt and courteous.* It is important to be punctual and respectful of your interviewee's time. In most cases, it is best to present yourself as a listener seeking clarity on an issue rather than an advocate of a particular position or an opponent.

During the interview, play the believing role. Save the doubting role for later, when you are looking over your notes.

- *Take brief but clear notes.*   Try to record the main ideas and be accurate with quotations. Ask for clarification of any points you don't understand.

- *Transcribe your notes soon after the interview.*   Immediately after the interview, while your memory is still fresh, rewrite your notes more fully and completely.

When you use interview data in your writing, put quotation marks around any direct quotations. In most cases, you should also identify your source by name and indicate his or her title or credentials—whatever will convince the reader that this person's remarks are to be taken seriously.

Gathering Data from Surveys or Questionnaires

A well-constructed survey or questionnaire can provide lively, current data that give your audience a sense of the popularity and importance of your views. To be effective and responsible, however, a survey or questionnaire needs to be carefully prepared and administered, as we suggest in the following guidelines.

- *Include both closed-response questions and open-response questions.*   To give you useful information and avoid charges of bias, you will want to include a range of questions. Closed-response questions ask participants to check a box or number on a scale and yield quantitative data that you can report statistically, perhaps in tables or graphs. Open-response questions elicit varied responses and often short narratives that allow participants to offer their own input. These may contribute new insights to your perspective on the issue.

- *Make your survey or questionnaire clear and easy to complete.*   Think out the number, order, wording, and layout of the questions in your questionnaire. Your questions should be clear and easy to answer. The neatness and overall formal appearance of the questionnaire will also invite serious responses from your participants.

- *Explain the purpose of the questionnaire.*   Respondents are usually more willing to participate if they know how the information gained from the questionnaire will benefit others. Therefore, it is a good idea to state at the beginning of the questionnaire how it will be used.

- *Seek a random sample of respondents in your distribution of the questionnaire.*   Think out where and how you will distribute and collect your questionnaire to ensure a random sampling of respondents. For example, if a questionnaire about the university library went only to dorm residents, then you wouldn't learn how commuting students felt.

- *Convert questionnaires into usable data by tallying and summarizing responses.*   Tallying the results and formulating summary statements of the information you gathered will yield material that might be used as evidence.

Conclusion

Effective use of evidence is an essential skill for arguers. In this chapter we introduced you to the STAR criteria and other strategies for making your data persuasive. We showed you various kinds of evidence and then examined how a writer's angle of vision influences the selection and framing of evidence. We also described framing strategies for emphasizing evidence, de-emphasizing it, and guiding your reader's response to it. Finally we concluded with advice on how to gather evidence, including the use of interviews, surveys, and questionnaires.

WRITING ASSIGNMENTS
FOR CHAPTERS 4–6

OPTION 1: A Microtheme   Write a one- or two-paragraph argument in which you support one of the following enthymemes, using evidence from personal experience, field observation, interviews, or data from a brief questionnaire or survey. Most of your microtheme should support the stated reason with evidence. However, also include a brief passage supporting the implied warrant. The opening sentence of your microtheme should be the enthymeme itself, which serves as the thesis statement for your argument. (Note: If you disagree with the enthymeme's argument, recast the claim or the reason to assert what you want to argue.)

1. Reading fashion magazines can be detrimental to teenage girls because such magazines can produce an unhealthy focus on beauty.
2. Surfing the Web might harm your studying because it causes you to waste time.
3. Service-learning courses are valuable because they allow you to test course concepts within real-world contexts.
4. Summer internships in your field of interest, even without pay, are the best use of your summer time because they speed up your education and training for a career.
5. Any enthymeme (a claim with a *because* clause) of your choice that can be supported without library or Internet research. (The goal of this microtheme is to give you practice using data from personal experience or from brief field research.) You may want to have your instructor approve your enthymeme in advance.

OPTION 2: A Classical Argument   Write a classical argument that uses at least two reasons to support your claim. Classical argument is explained in detail in

Chapter 3. As we explain further in Chapter 8, classical argument is particularly effective when you are addressing neutral or undecided audiences. It has a self-announcing or closed-form structure in which you state your claim at the end of the introduction, begin body paragraphs with clearly stated reasons, and use effective transitions throughout to keep your reader on track. In developing your own argument, place your most important reason last, where it will have the greatest impact on your readers. Typically, a classical argument also summarizes anticipated objections to the writer's argument and responds to them briefly. You can place this section either before or after you develop your main argument. (Chapter 8, pp. 145–150, gives a detailed explanation of how to respond to objections and alternative views.) See Chapter 3, pages 62–66, for further description of a classical argument, including a diagram of its typical structure.

The student essay that follows illustrates a classical argument. This essay grew out of a class discussion about alternative sports, conflicts between traditional sports and newer sports (downhill skiing and snowboarding), and middle-age prejudices against groups of young people.

"Half-Criminals" or Urban Athletes? A Plea for Fair Treatment of Skateboarders

David Langley (Student)

1   For skateboarders, the campus of the University of California at San Diego is a wide-open, huge, geometric, obstacle-filled, stair-scattered cement paradise. The signs posted all over campus read, "No skateboarding, biking, or rollerblading on campus except on Saturday, Sunday, and Holidays." I have always respected these signs at my local skateboarding spot. On the first day of 1999, I was skateboarding here with my hometown skate buddies and had just landed a trick when a police officer rushed out from behind a pillar, grabbed me, and yanked me off my board. Because I didn't have my I.D. (I had emptied my pockets so I wouldn't bruise my legs if I fell—a little trick of the trade), the officer started treating me like a criminal. She told me to spread my legs and put my hands on my head. She frisked me and then called in my name to police headquarters.

2   "What's the deal?" I asked. "The sign said skateboarding was legal on holidays."

3   "The sign means that you can only *roll* on campus," she said.

4   But that's *not* what the sign said. The police officer gave one friend and me a warning. Our third friend received a fifty-dollar ticket because it was his second citation in the last twelve months.

5   Like other skateboarders throughout cities, we have been bombarded with unfair treatment. We have been forced out of known skate spots in the city by store-owners and police, kicked out of every parking garage in downtown, compelled to

skate at strange times of day and night, and herded into crowded skateboard parks. However, after I was searched by the police and detained for over twenty minutes in my own skating sanctuary, the unreasonableness of the treatment of skateboarders struck me. Where are skateboarders supposed to go? Cities need to change their unfair treatment of skateboarders because skateboarders are not antisocial misfits as popularly believed, because the laws regulating skateboarding are ambiguous, and because skateboarders are not given enough legitimate space to practice their sport.

Possibly because to the average eye most skateboarders look like misfits or delinquents, adults think of us as criminal types and associate our skateboards with antisocial behavior. But this view is unfair. City dwellers should recognize that skateboards are a natural reaction to the urban environment. If people are surrounded by cement, they are going to figure out a way to ride it. People's different environments have always produced transportation and sports to suit the conditions: bikes, cars, skis, ice skates, boats, canoes, surfboards. If we live on snow, we are going to develop skis or snowshoes to move around. If we live in an environment that has flat panels of cement for ground with lots of curbs and stairs, we are going to invent an ingeniously designed flat board with wheels. Skateboards are as natural to cement as surfboards are to water or skis to snow. Moreover, the resulting sport is as healthful, graceful, and athletic. A fair assessment of skateboarders should respect our elegant, nonpolluting means of transportation and sport, and not consider us hoodlums.

A second way that skateboarders are treated unfairly is that the laws that regulate skateboarding in public places are highly restrictive, ambiguous, and open to abusive application by police officers. My being frisked on the UCSD campus is just one example. When I moved to Seattle to go to college, I found the laws in Washington to be equally unclear. When a sign says "No Skateboarding," that generally means you will get ticketed if you are caught skateboarding in the area. But most areas aren't posted. The general rule then is that you can skateboard so long as you do so safely without being reckless. But the definition of "reckless" is up to the whim of the police officer. I visited the front desk of the Seattle East Precinct and asked them exactly what the laws against reckless skateboarding meant. They said that skaters are allowed on the sidewalk as long as they travel at reasonable speed and the sidewalks aren't crowded. One of the officers explained that if he saw a skater sliding down a handrail with people all around, he would definitely arrest the skater. What if there were no people around, I asked? The officer admitted that he might arrest the lone skater anyway and not be questioned by his superiors. No wonder skateboarders feel unfairly treated.

One way that cities have tried to treat skateboarders fairly is to build skateboard parks. Unfortunately, for the most part these parks are no solution at all. Most parks were designed by nonskaters who don't understand the momentum or gravity pull associated with the movement of skateboards. For example, City Skate, a park below the Space Needle in Seattle, is very appealing to the eye, but once you start to ride it you realize that the transitions and the verticals are all off, making it unpleasant and even dangerous to skate there. The Skate Park in Issaquah, Washington, hosts about thirty to fifty skaters at a time. Collisions are frequent and close calls, many. There are simply too many people in a small area. The people who built the park in Redmond, Washington, decided to make a huge wall in it for graffiti artists "to tag on" legally. They apparently thought they ought to throw all us teenage "half criminals" in together. At this park, young teens are nervous about skating near a gangster "throwing up his piece," and skaters become dizzy as they take deep breaths from their workouts right next to four or five cans of spray paint expelling toxins in the air.

9   Of course, many adults probably don't think skateboarders deserve to be treated fairly. I have heard the arguments against skateboarders for years from parents, storeowners, friends, police officers, and security guards. For one thing, skateboarding tears up public and private property, people say. I can't deny that skating leaves marks on handrails and benches, and it does chip cement and granite. But in general skateboarders help the environment more than they hurt it. Skateboarding places are not littered or tagged up by skaters. Because skaters need smooth surfaces and because any small object of litter can lead to painful accidents, skaters actually keep the environment cleaner than the average citizen does. As for the population as a whole, skateboarders are keeping the air a lot cleaner than many other commuters and athletes such as boat drivers, car drivers, and skiers on ski lifts. In the bigger picture, infrequent repair of curbs and benches is cheaper than attempts to heal the ozone.

10   We skateboarders aren't going away, so cities are going to have to make room for us somewhere. Here is how cities can treat us fairly. We should be allowed to skate when others are present as long as we skate safely on the sidewalks. The rules and laws should be clearer so that skaters don't get put into vulnerable positions that make them easy targets for tickets. I do support the opening of skate parks, but cities need to build more of them, need to situate them closer to where skateboarders live, and need to make them relatively wholesome environments. They should also be designed by skateboarders so that they are skater-friendly and safe to ride. Instead of being treated as "half criminals," skaters should be accepted as urban citizens and admired as athletes; we are a clean population, and we are executing a challenging and graceful sport. As human beings grow, we go from crawling to walking; some of us grow from strollers to skateboards.

7 Moving Your Audience
Ethos and *Pathos*

In Chapters 5 and 6 we focused primarily on *logos*—the logical structure of reasons and evidence in an argument. When writers initially concentrate on *logos*, they are often trying to clarify their own thinking as much as to persuade. However, as they start to focus on the discovery of audience-based reasons—so that they link their own arguments to the assumptions, values, and beliefs of their audience—they automatically appeal also to *ethos* and *pathos* by enhancing the reader's trust in the writer and by triggering the reader's sympathies and imagination. In this chapter, we turn our attention away from *logos* to the other two points on the rhetorical triangle introduced in Chapter 4 (pp. 75–76): *ethos* and *pathos*. We hope to show you how knowledge of these classical appeals can increase the persuasiveness of your arguments.

Ethos and *Pathos* as Persuasive Appeals: An Overview

At first, one may be tempted to think of *logos, ethos*, and *pathos* as "ingredients" in an essay, like spices you add to a casserole. Succumbing to this metaphor, you might say to yourself something like this: "Just enough *logos* to give the dish body; but for more piquancy it needs a pinch of *pathos*. And for the back of the palate, a tad more *ethos*."

But this metaphor is misleading because *logos, ethos*, and *pathos* are not substances; they are ways of seeing rather than objects of sight. A better metaphor might be that of different lamps and filters used on theater spotlights to vary lighting effects on a stage. Thus, if you switch on a *pathos* lamp (possibly through using more concrete language or vivid examples), the resulting image will engage the audience's sympathy and emotions more deeply. If you overlay an *ethos* filter (perhaps by adopting a different tone toward your audience), the projected image of the writer as a person will be subtly altered. If you switch on a *logos* lamp (by adding, say, more data for evidence), you will draw the reader's attention to the logical appeal of the argument. Depending on how you modulate the lamps and filters, you shape and color your readers' perception of the issue.

Our metaphor is imperfect, of course, but our point is that *logos, ethos,* and *pathos* work together to create an impact on the reader. Consider, for example, the different impacts of the following arguments, all having roughly the same logical appeal:

1. People should adopt a vegetarian diet because only through vegetarianism can we prevent the cruelty to animals that results from factory farming.

2. I hope you enjoyed your fried chicken this evening. You know, of course, how much that chicken suffered just so you could have a tender and juicy meal. Commercial growers cram the chickens so tightly together into cages that their beaks must be cut off to keep them from pecking each other's eyes out. The only way to end the torture is to adopt a vegetarian diet.

3. People who eat meat are no better than sadists who torture other sentient creatures to enhance their own pleasure. Unless you enjoy sadistic tyranny over others, you have only one choice: Become a vegetarian.

4. People committed to justice might consider the extent to which our love of eating meat requires the agony of animals. A visit to a modern chicken factory—where chickens live their entire lives in tiny, darkened coops without room to spread their wings—might raise doubts about our right to inflict such suffering on sentient creatures. Indeed, such a visit might persuade us that vegetarianism is a more just alternative.

Each argument has roughly the same logical core:

CLAIM: People should adopt a vegetarian diet.

STATED REASON: because only vegetarianism will end the suffering of animals subjected to factory farming

GROUNDS: the evidence of suffering in commercial chicken farms, where chickens are crammed together, and lash out at each other; evidence that only widespread adoption of vegetarianism will end factory farming

WARRANT: If we have an alternative to making animals suffer, we should adopt it.

But the impact of each argument varies. The difference between Arguments 1 and 2, most of our students report, is the greater emotional power of Argument 2. Whereas Argument 1 refers only to the abstraction "cruelty to animals," Argument 2 paints a vivid picture of chickens with their beaks cut off to prevent their pecking each other blind. Argument 2 makes a stronger appeal to *pathos* (not necessarily a stronger argument), stirring feelings by appealing simultaneously to the heart and to the head.

The difference between Arguments 1 and 3 concerns both *ethos* and *pathos.* Argument 3 appeals to the emotions through highly charged words like *torture, sadist,* and *tyranny.* But Argument 3 also draws attention to its writer, and most of our students report not liking that writer very much. His stance is self-righteous and insulting. In contrast, Argument 4's author establishes a more positive *ethos.* He establishes rapport by assuming his audience is committed to justice and by qualifying his argument with conditional terms such as *might* and *perhaps.* He also invites sympathy for his problem—an appeal to *pathos*—by offering a specific description of chickens crammed into tiny coops.

Which of these arguments is best? They all have appropriate uses. Arguments 1 and 4 seem aimed at receptive audiences reasonably open to exploration of the issue, whereas Arguments 2 and 3 seem designed to shock complacent audiences or to rally a group of True Believers. Even Argument 3, which is too abusive to be effective in most instances, might work as a rallying speech at a convention of animal liberation activists.

Our point thus far is that *logos, ethos,* and *pathos* are different aspects of the same whole, different lenses for intensifying or softening the light beam you project onto the screen. Every choice you make as a writer affects in some way each of the three appeals. The rest of this chapter examines these choices in more detail.

How to Create an Effective *Ethos:* The Appeal to Credibility

The ancient Greek and Roman rhetoricians recognized that an argument would be more persuasive if the audience trusted the speaker. Aristotle argued that such trust resides within the speech itself, not in the prior reputation of the speaker. In the speaker's manner and delivery, in the speaker's tone, word choice, and arrangement of reasons, in the sympathy with which he or she treats alternative views, the speaker creates a trustworthy persona. Aristotle called the impact of the speaker's credibility the appeal from *ethos.* How does a writer create credibility? We suggest three ways.

Be Knowledgeable about Your Issue

The first way to gain credibility is to *be* credible—that is, to argue from a strong base of knowledge, to have at hand the examples, personal experiences, statistics, and other empirical data needed to make a sound case. If you have done your homework, you will command the attention of most audiences.

Be Fair

Besides being knowledgeable about your issue, you need to demonstrate fairness and courtesy to alternative views. Because true argument can occur only where persons may reasonably disagree with one another, your *ethos* will be strengthened if you demonstrate that you understand and empathize with other points of view. There are times, of course, when you may appropriately scorn an opposing view. But these times are rare, and they mostly occur when you address audiences pre-disposed to your view. Demonstrating empathy to alternative views is generally the best strategy.

Build a Bridge to Your Audience

A third means of establishing credibility—building a bridge to your audience—has been treated at length in our earlier discussions of audience-based reasons. By grounding your argument in shared values and assumptions, you demonstrate your goodwill and enhance your image as a trustworthy person respectful of your audience's views. We mention audience-based reasons here to show how this aspect of *logos*—finding the reasons that are most rooted in the audience's values—also affects your *ethos* as a person respectful of your readers' views.

How to Create *Pathos:* The Appeal to Beliefs and Emotions

At the height of the Vietnam protest movement, a group of demonstrators "napalmed" a puppy by dousing it with gasoline and setting it on fire, thereby outraging people all across the country. Many sent indignant letters to their local newspapers, provoking the following response from the demonstrators: "Why are you outraged by the napalming of a single puppy when you are not outraged by the daily napalming of human babies in Vietnam?"

From the demonstrators' view, napalming the puppy constituted an appeal from *pathos. Logos*-centered arguments, the protesters felt, numbed the mind to human suffering; in napalming the puppy, they intended to reawaken in their audience a capacity for gut-level revulsion that had been dulled by too many statistics, too many abstract moral appeals, and too much superficial TV coverage of the war.

Of course, the napalmed puppy was a real-life event, a street theater protest, not a written argument. But writers often use a similar strategy. Anti-abortion proponents use it whenever they graphically describe the dismemberment of a fetus during abortion; euthanasia proponents use it when they describe the prolonged suffering of a terminally ill patient hooked hopelessly to machines. And a student uses it when he argues that a professor ought to raise his grade from a C to a B, lest he lose his scholarship and leave college, shattering the dreams of his dear old grandmother.

Are such appeals legitimate? Our answer is yes, if they intensify our response to an issue rather than divert our attention from it. Because understanding is a matter of feeling as well as perceiving, *pathos* can give access to non-logical, but not necessarily nonrational, ways of knowing. Used effectively, pathetic appeals reveal the fullest human meaning of an issue, helping us walk in the writer's shoes. That is why arguments are often improved through the use of sensory details that allow us to see the reality of a problem or through stories that make specific cases and instances come alive.

Appeals to *pathos* become illegitimate, we believe, when they confuse an issue rather than clarify it. To the extent that students' grades should be based on performance or effort, the student's image of the dear old grandmother is an illegitimate appeal to *pathos* because it diverts the reader from rational to irrational criteria. The weeping grandmother may provide a legitimate motive for the student to study harder but not for the professor to change a grade.

Although it is difficult to classify all the ways that writers can create appeals from *pathos*, we will focus on four strategies: concrete language; specific examples and illustrations; narratives; and connotations of words, metaphors, and analogies. Each of these strategies lends "presence" to an argument by creating immediacy and emotional impact.

Use Concrete Language

Concrete language—one of the chief ways that writers achieve voice—can increase the liveliness, interest level, and personality of a writer's prose. When used in argument, concrete language typically heightens *pathos*. For example, consider the differences between the first and second drafts of the following student argument:

> *First draft:* People who prefer driving a car to taking a bus think that taking the bus will increase the stress of the daily commute. Just the opposite is true. Not being able to find a parking spot when in a hurry to work or school can cause a person stress. Taking the bus gives a person time to read or sleep, etc. It could be used as a mental break.
>
> *Second draft:* Taking the bus can be more relaxing than driving a car. Having someone else behind the wheel gives people time to chat with friends or cram for an exam. They can balance their checkbooks, do homework, doze off, read the daily newspaper, or get lost in a novel rather than foaming at the mouth looking for a parking space.

In this revision, specific details enliven the prose by creating images that trigger positive feelings. Who wouldn't want some free time to doze off or to get lost in a novel?

Use Specific Examples and Illustrations

Specific examples and illustrations serve two purposes in an argument: They provide evidence that supports your reasons; simultaneously, they give your argument presence and emotional resonance. Note the flatness of the following draft arguing for the value of multicultural studies in a university core curriculum:

> *Early draft:* Another advantage of a multicultural education is that it will help us see our own culture in a broader perspective. If all we know is our own

heritage, we might not be inclined to see anything bad about this heritage because we won't know anything else. But if we study other heritages, we can see the costs and benefits of our own heritage.

Now note the increase in "presence" when the writer adds a specific example:

> *Revised draft:* Another advantage of multicultural education is that it raises questions about traditional Western values. For example, owning private property (such as buying your own home) is part of the American dream and is a basic right guaranteed in our Constitution. However, in studying the beliefs of American Indians, students are confronted with a very different view of private property. When the U.S. government sought to buy land in the Pacific Northwest from Chief Sealth, he is alleged to have replied:
>
> > The president in Washington sends words that he wishes to buy our land. But how can you buy or sell the sky? The land? The idea is strange to us. If we do not own the freshness of the air and the sparkle of the water, how can you buy them? [. . .] We are part of the earth and it is part of us. [. . .] This we know: The earth does not belong to man, man belongs to the earth.
>
> Our class was shocked by the contrast between traditional Western views of property and Chief Sealth's views. One of our best class discussions was initiated by this quotation from Chief Sealth. Had we not been exposed to a view from another culture, we would have never been led to question the "rightness" of Western values.

The writer begins his revision by evoking a traditional Western view of private property, which he then questions by shifting to Chief Sealth's vision of land as open, endless, and unobtainable as the sky. Through the use of a specific example, the writer brings to life his previously abstract point about the benefit of multicultural education.

Use Narratives

A particularly powerful way to evoke *pathos* is to tell a story that either leads into your claim or embodies it implicitly and that appeals to your readers' feelings and imagination. Brief narratives—whether true or hypothetical—are particularly effective as opening attention grabbers for an argument. To illustrate how an introductory narrative (either a story or a brief scene) can create pathetic appeals, consider the following first paragraph to an argument opposing jet skis:

> I dove off the dock into the lake, and as I approached the surface I could see the sun shining through the water. As my head popped out, I located my cousin a few feet away in a rowboat waiting to escort me as I, a twelve-year-old girl, attempted to swim across the mile-wide, pristine lake and back to our dock. I made it, and that glorious summer day is one of my most precious memories. Today, however, no one would

dare attempt that swim. Jet skis have taken over this small lake where I spent many summers with my grandparents. Dozens of whining jet skis crisscross the lake, ruining it for swimming, fishing, canoeing, row-boating, and even water-skiing. More stringent state laws are needed to control jet-skiing because it interferes with other uses of lakes and is currently very dangerous.

This narrative makes a case for a particular point of view toward jet skis by winning our identification with the writer's experience. She invites us to relive that experience with her while she also taps into our own treasured memories of summer experiences that have been destroyed by change.

Opening narratives to evoke *pathos* can be powerfully effective, but they are also risky. If they are too private, too self-indulgent, too sentimental, or even too dramatic and forceful, they can backfire on you. If you have doubts about an opening narrative, read it to a sample audience before using it in your final draft.

For Class Discussion

Suppose that you want to write arguments on the following issues. Working individually or in groups, think of an introductory scene or brief story that would create a pathetic appeal favorable to your argument.

1. a. an argument supporting the use of animals for biomedical research
   b. an argument opposing the use of animals for biomedical research (Note that the purpose of the first narrative is to create sympathy for the use of animals in medical research; perhaps you could describe the happy homecoming of a child cured by a medical procedure developed through testing on animals. The second narrative, aimed at evoking sympathy for abolishing animal research, might describe a lab rabbit's suffering.)

2. a. an argument for a program to restore a national park to its natural condition
   b. an argument for creating more camping places and overnight sites for recreational vehicles in national parks

3. a. an argument favoring legalization of drugs
   b. an argument opposing legalization of drugs

In addition to their use as opening scenes or as examples and illustrations, narratives can sometimes inform a whole argument. If the argument is conveyed entirely through narrative, then it is an *implicit* rather than *explicit* argument (see Chapter 1, pp. 4–6). But explicit arguments can sometimes contain an extensive narrative component. One source of the powerful appeal of Gordon Adams's petition to waive his math requirement (Chapter 1, pp. 17–20) is that the argument embodies aspects of his personal story.

In his appeal to the Standards Committee, Gordon Adams uses numerous standard argument devices (for example, testimony from legal practitioners that knowledge of algebra is not required in the study or practice of law). But he also makes a strong pathetic appeal by narrating the story of how he assembled his case. By foregrounding his encounters with all the people from whom he seeks information, he makes himself an actor in a story that might be called "Gordon's Quest for Truth."

The story of Gordon's construction of his argument, meanwhile, is situated inside a larger story that lends weight to the points he makes in the smaller story. The larger story, the story of Gordon's "awakening" to injustice and his fierce commitment to overcoming injustice for his people, links Gordon's desire to waive his algebra requirement to a larger, more significant story about overcoming oppression. And beyond Gordon's story lies an even larger, richer story, the history of Native American peoples in the United States over the past century, which lends an even greater resonance and clarity to his personal story. By telling his story, Gordon makes himself more human and familiar, more understandable and less threatening. This is why whenever we want to break down difference, overcome estrangement, grow closer to people we don't know well, we tell them our stories. Telling his story allowed Gordon to negotiate some considerable differences between himself and his audience of mostly white, middle-class faculty members. Even though he lost his case, he made a powerful argument that was taken seriously.

Choose Words, Metaphors, and Analogies with Appropriate Connotations

Another way of appealing to *pathos* is to select words, metaphors, or analogies with connotations that match your aim. We have already described this strategy in our discussion of the "framing" of evidence (Chapter 6, pp. 119–120). By using words with particular connotations, a writer guides readers to see the issue through the writer's angle of vision. Thus if you want to create positive feelings about a recent city council decision, you can call it "bold and decisive"; if you want to create negative feelings, you can call it "haughty and autocratic." Similarly, writers can use favorable or unfavorable metaphors and analogies to evoke different imaginative or emotional responses. A tax bill might be viewed as a "potentially fatal poison pill" or as "unpleasant but necessary economic medicine." In each of these cases, the words create an emotional as well as intellectual response.

For Class Discussion

Outside class, rewrite the introduction to one of your previous papers (or a current draft) to include more appeals to *pathos*. Use any of the strategies for giving your argument presence: concrete language, specific examples, narratives, metaphors, analogies, and connotative words. Bring both your original and your rewritten introductions to class. In pairs or in groups, discuss the comparative effectiveness of these introductions in trying to reach your intended audience.

Using Images for Emotional Appeal

One of the most powerful ways to engage an audience emotionally is to use photos or other images. If you think of any news event that has captured wide media attention, you will probably recall memorable photos. Many of us are shaken to the core simply by recalling a still photograph of the hijacked airliner about to crash into the second tower of the World Trade Center, or subsequent photos of heroic firefighters, of posters from loved ones attached to the fence around St. Paul's Chapel, of mayor Rudy Giuliani wearing a NYFD hat (or a Yankees hat), or of Osama bin Laden.

Sometimes photographs create more than an emotional response to an event; they shape our perception of the event in subtle ways. Consider the image most frequently used to accompany stories of the U.S. women's soccer team winning the world championship in 1999—not the great goal-keeping photo of African American Briana Scurry blocking the last penalty kick, but of Brandi Chastain removing her jersey to reveal a black sports bra. Many analysts observed that the famous Brandi Chastain photograph shaped the public's emotional memory of that game by linking it with stereotypical views of women as sex objects rather than with women's athletic prowess. Sometimes we are only partially aware of how the specific subject matter selected for a photo, its angle and cropping, the arrangement and posing of figures, and other details can encode an argument. Chapter 9 deals extensively with these aspects of visual arguments.

Because of the power of images, professional writers often use photographs or drawings to enhance their arguments. Images accompanying an argument can be particularly effective at grabbing viewers' attention, conveying the seriousness of an issue, and evoking strong emotions ranging from compassion to revulsion. While many written arguments do not lend themselves to visual illustrations, we suggest that when you construct arguments you consider the potential of visual support. Imagine that your argument were to appear in a newspaper or magazine where space would be provided for one or two visuals. What photographs or drawings might help persuade your audience toward your perspective?

When images work well, they are analogous to the verbal strategies of concrete language, specific illustrations, narratives, and connotative words. The challenge in using visuals is to find material that is straightforward enough not to require elaborate explanations, that is timely and relevant, and that clearly adds impact to a specific part of your argument. As an example, suppose you are writing an argument supporting fund-raising efforts to help third-world countries. To add a powerful appeal to *pathos*, you might consider incorporating into your argument the photograph shown in Color Plate D—a photograph of a Haitian woman walking on a rickety bridge over a vast garbage heap in a Haitian slum. This photograph, which appeared in the *New York Times* in the summer of 2002, creates an almost immediate emotional and imaginative response.

For Class Discussion

Working in small groups or as a whole class, share your responses to the following questions:

1. How would you describe the emotional/imaginative impact of Color Plate D (the photograph of a Haitian slum)?

2. Many appeals for helping third-world countries show pictures of big-bellied, starving children during a famine, often in Africa. How is your response to Color Plate D similar or different from the commonly encountered pictures of starving children? How is Color Plate D's story about the ravages of poverty different from the stories of starving children?

3. Figures 7.1 and 7.2 show two photographs of John Walker Lindh, the "American Taliban" captured in Afghanistan as part of the U.S. military's response to the September 11 terrorist attacks in 2001. Figure 7.1 shows the photograph of Lindh taken by the Alexandria, Virginia, Sheriff's Department after Lindh was incarcerated in the United States, shaved, and placed in a prison uniform. This photograph was widely reproduced in arguments calling for Lindh's prosecution as a traitor. In late March 2002, the

FIGURE 7.1   *Sheriff's office photograph of John Walker Lindh*

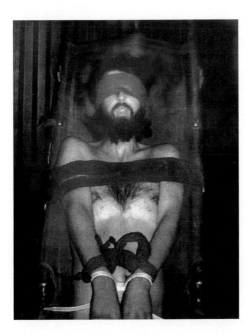

FIGURE 7.2   *Photograph of Lindh during incarceration in Afghanistan*

U.S. government was forced to release a photograph of Lindh (Figure 7.2) taken while he was held captive in Afghanistan before being transferred to the United States. This photograph was immediately used by Lindh's defense attorneys and by groups seeking Lindh's release.

   a. How would you describe the emotional and intellectual impact of Figure 7.2? As a visual argument, what claim does it make?

   b. Why would prosecuting attorneys favor Figure 7.1 while defense attorneys favor Figure 7.2?

4. Sometimes drawings as well as photographs can enhance an argument's emotional appeal. Consider the poster argument advocating bicycle riding as an alternative to cars (the opening of Part Two, p. 73). How do the features of the drawing, working in conjunction with the verbal text, create an appeal to *pathos*?

Conclusion

In this chapter, we have explored ways that writers can strengthen the persuasiveness of their arguments by creating appeals to *ethos* and *pathos*. Arguments are more persuasive if readers trust the credibility of the writer and if the argument appeals to readers' hearts and imaginations as well as their intellects. Sometimes images such as drawings or photographs may reinforce the argument by evoking strong emotional responses, thus enhancing *pathos*.

8 Accommodating Your Audience

Treating Differing Views

In the previous chapter we discussed the appeals of *ethos* and *pathos* as means of persuasion. In this chapter we focus on strategies for accommodating different kinds of audiences. Particularly, we discuss the problem of addressing opposing or alternative views—whether to omit them, refute them, concede to them, or incorporate them through compromise and conciliation. We show you how your choices about structure, content, and tone may differ depending on whether your audience is sympathetic, neutral, or strongly resistant to your views. The strategies explained in this chapter will increase your flexibility as an arguer and enhance your chance of persuading a wide variety of audiences.

One-Sided versus Multisided Arguments

Arguments are sometimes said to be one-sided or multisided. A *one-sided* argument presents only the writer's position on the issue without summarizing and responding to alternative viewpoints. A *multisided* argument presents the writer's position but also summarizes and responds to possible objections that an audience might raise. Which kind of argument is more persuasive to an audience?

According to some researchers, if people already agree with a writer's thesis, they usually find one-sided arguments more persuasive. A multisided argument appears wishy-washy, making the writer seem less decisive. But if people initially disagree with a writer's thesis, a multisided argument often seems more persuasive because it shows that the writer has listened to other views and thus seems more open-minded and fair. An especially interesting effect has been documented for neutral audiences. In the short run, one-sided arguments seem more persuasive to neutral audiences, but in the long run multisided arguments seem to have more staying power. Neutral audiences who've heard only one side of an issue tend to change their minds when they hear alternative arguments. By anticipating and in some cases refuting opposing views, the multisided argument diminishes the surprise and force of subsequent counterarguments and also exposes their weaknesses.

In the rest of this chapter we will show you how your choice of writing one-sided or multisided arguments is a function of how you perceive your audience's resistance to your views.

Determining Your Audience's Resistance to Your Views

When you write an argument, you must always consider your audience's point of view. One way to imagine your relationship to your audience is to place it on a scale of resistance ranging from strong support of your position to strong opposition (see Figure 8.1). At the "Accord" end of this scale are like-minded people who basically agree with your position on the issue. At the "Resistance" end are those who strongly disagree with you, perhaps unconditionally, because their values, beliefs, or assumptions sharply differ from your own. Between "Accord" and "Resistance" lies a range of opinions. Close to your position will be those leaning in your direction but with less conviction than you have. Close to the resistance position will be those basically opposed to your view but willing to listen to your argument and perhaps willing to acknowledge some of its strengths. In the middle are those undecided people who are still sorting out their feelings, seeking additional information, and weighing the strengths and weaknesses of alternative views.

Seldom, however, will you encounter an issue in which the range of disagreement follows a simple line from accord to resistance. Often resistant views fall into different categories so that no single line of argument appeals to all those whose views are different from your own. You have to identify not only your audience's resistance to your ideas but also the causes of that resistance.

Consider, for example, an issue that divided the state of Washington when the Seattle Mariners baseball team demanded a new stadium. A ballot initiative asked citizens to approve an increase in taxes to build a new retractable-roof stadium for the Mariners. Supporters of the initiative faced a complex array of resisting views (see Figure 8.2). Opponents of the initiative could be placed into four categories. Some simply had no interest in sports, cared nothing about baseball, and saw no benefit in building a huge sports facility in downtown Seattle. Another group loved baseball, perhaps followed the Mariners passionately, but was philosophically opposed to subsidizing rich players and owners with taxpayer money. This

FIGURE 8.1   *Scale of resistance*

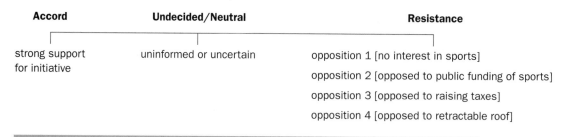

FIGURE 8.2   *Scale of resistance, baseball stadium issue*

group argued that the whole sports industry needed to be restructured so that stadiums were paid for out of sports revenues. Still another group was opposed to tax hikes in general. It focused on the principle of reducing the size of government and of using tax revenues only for essential services. Finally, another powerful group supported baseball and supported the notion of public funding of a new stadium but opposed the kind of retractable-roof stadium specified in the initiative. This group wanted an old-fashioned, open-air stadium like Baltimore's Camden Yards or Cleveland's Jacobs Field.

Writers supporting the initiative found it impossible to address all these resisting audiences at once. If a supporter of the initiative wanted to aim an argument at sports haters, he or she could stress the spinoff benefits of a new ballpark (for example, the new ballpark would attract tourist revenue, renovate the deteriorating Pioneer Square neighborhood, create jobs, make sports lovers more likely to vote for public subsidies of the arts, and so forth). But these arguments were irrelevant to those who wanted an open-air stadium, who opposed tax hikes categorically, or who objected to public subsidy of millionaires.

Another kind of complexity occurs when a writer is positioned between two kinds of resisting views. Consider the position of student writer Sam, a gay man who wished to argue that gay and lesbian people should actively support legislation to legalize same-sex marriage (see Figure 8.3). Most arguments that support same-sex marriage are aimed at conservative heterosexual audiences who tend to

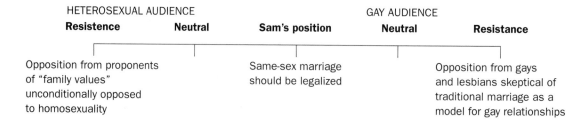

FIGURE 8.3   *Scale of resistance for same-sex marriage issue*

disapprove of homosexuality and stress traditional family values. But Sam imagined writing for a gay magazine such as the *Harvard Gay and Lesbian Review* or *The Advocate,* and he wished to aim his argument at liberal gay and lesbian activists who opposed traditional marriage on different grounds. These thinkers, critiquing traditional marriage for the way it stereotypes gender roles and limits the freedom of partners, argued that heterosexual marriage wasn't a good model for relationships in the gay community. These persons constituted an audience 180 degrees removed from the conservative proponents of family values who oppose same-sex marriage on moral and religious grounds.

In writing his early drafts, Sam was stymied by his attempt to address both audiences at once. Only after he blocked out the conservative "family values" audience and imagined an audience of what he called "liberationist" gays and lesbians was he able to develop a consistent argument. (You can read Sam's essay on pp. 307–310.)

The Mariners example and the same-sex marriage example illustrate the difficulty of adapting your argument to your audience's position on the scale of resistance. Yet doing so is important because you need a stable vision of your audience before you can determine an effective content, structure, and tone for your argument. As we showed in Chapter 5, an effective content derives from choosing audience-based reasons that appeal to your audience's values, assumptions, and beliefs. As we show in the rest of this chapter, an effective structure and tone are often a function of where your audience falls on the scale of resistance. The next sections show how you can adjust your arguing strategy depending on whether your audience is supportive, neutral, or hostile.

Appealing to a Supportive Audience: One-Sided Argument

Although arguing to a supportive audience might seem like preaching to the choir, such arguments are common. Usually, the arguer's goal is to convert belief into action—to inspire a party member to contribute to a senator's campaign or a bored office worker to sign up for a change-your-life weekend seminar.

Typically, appeals to a supportive audience are structured as one-sided arguments that either ignore opposing views or reduce them to "enemy" stereotypes. Filled with motivational language, these arguments list the benefits that will ensue from your donations to the cause and the horrors just around the corner if the other side wins. One of the authors of this text recently received a fund-raising letter from an environmental lobbying group declaring, "It's crunch time for the polluters and their pals on Capitol Hill." The "corporate polluters" and "anti-environment politicians," the letter continues, have "stepped up efforts to roll back our environmental protections—relying on large campaign contributions, slick PR firms and well-heeled lobbyists to get the job done before November's election." This letter makes the reader feel part of an in-group of good guys fighting the big business "polluters." Nothing in the letter examines environmental issues from business's perspective or attempts to examine alternative views fairly. Since the intended audience already believes in the cause, nothing in the letter invites readers to consider the issues more complexly. Rather, the goal is to solidify support, increase the fervor of belief, and inspire action. Most appeal arguments make it easy to act, ending with an 800 phone number to call, a tear-out postcard to send in, or a congressperson's address to write to.

Appealing to a Neutral or Undecided Audience: Classical Argument

The in-group appeals that motivate an already supportive audience can repel a neutral or undecided audience. Because undecided audiences are like jurors weighing all sides of an issue, they distrust one-sided arguments that caricature other views. Generally the best strategy for appealing to undecided audiences is the classical argument described in Chapter 3 (pp. 62–66).

What characterizes the classical argument is the writer's willingness to summarize opposing views fairly and to respond to them openly—either by trying to refute them or by conceding to their strengths and then shifting to a different field of values. Let's look at these strategies in more depth.

Summarizing Opposing Views

The first step toward responding to opposing views in a classical argument is to summarize them fairly. Follow the *principle of charity,* which obliges you to avoid loaded, biased, or "straw man" summaries that oversimplify or distort opposing arguments, making them easy to knock over.

Consider the difference between an unfair and a fair summary of Lisa Turner's "Playing with Our Food" (pp. 24–26), which we examined in Chapter 2.

UNFAIR SUMMARY

In a biased article totally lacking in scientific understanding of biotechnology, natural foods huckster Lisa Turner parrots the health food industry's party line that genetically altered crops are Frankenstein's monsters run amuck. She ignorantly claims that consumption of biotech foods will lead to worldwide destruction, disease, and death ignoring the wealth of scientific literature showing that genetically modified foods are safe. Her misinformed attacks are scare tactics aimed at selling consumers on overpriced "health food" products to be purchased at boutique organic food stores.

This summary distorts and oversimplifies Turner's argument while continually interjecting the writer's own views rather than fairly summarizing Turner's views. It uses loaded phrases ("huckster," "parrots the health food industry's party line," "ignorantly," "scare tactics") and creates an *ad hominem* attack (see pages 428–430 for a definition of this reasoning fallacy) by implying that Turner is motivated by health food industry profits rather than genuine concern. The writer thus sets up a straw man that is easier to knock over than is Turner's original argument.

In contrast, consider the following more fair summary, which follows the principle of charity and tries to represent Turner's views as justly and accurately as possible. (For a longer summary of Turner's article, see Chapter 2, p. 29.)

FAIR SUMMARY

In an article appearing in a nutrition magazine, health food advocate Lisa Turner warns readers that much of our food today is genetically modified using gene-level techniques that differ completely from ordinary cross-breeding. She argues that the potential, unforeseen, harmful consequences of genetic engineering offset the possible benefits of increasing the food supply, reducing the use of pesticides, and boosting the nutritional value of foods. Turner asserts that genetic engineering is imprecise, untested, unpredictable, irreversible, and also uncontrollable due to animals, insects, and winds.

For Class Discussion

Suppose that you believe that ROTC courses ought to receive academic credit and thus you oppose the views of the student writer of "ROTC Courses Should Not Get College Credit" on pp. 451–453. Working individually or in groups, prepare two different summaries of this writer's views, as follows:

1. Unfair summary using loaded language or straw man oversimplification or distortion
2. Fair summary following the principle of charity

When you are finished, be prepared to read your summaries aloud to the class.

Refuting Opposing Views

Once you have summarized opposing views, you can either refute them or concede to their strengths. In refuting an opposing view, you attempt to convince readers that its argument is logically flawed, inadequately supported, or based on erroneous assumptions. In refuting an argument, you can rebut (1) the writer's stated reason and grounds, (2) the writer's warrant and backing, or (3) both. Put in less specialized language and you can rebut a writer's reasons and evidence or the writer's underlying assumptions. Let's begin with a simple example. Suppose you wanted to refute this argument:

We shouldn't elect Joe as committee chair because he is too bossy.

Displayed in Toulmin's terms, the argument looks like this:

CLAIM: We shouldn't elect Joe as committee chair.

STATED REASON: because he is too bossy

GROUNDS: evidence that Joe is bossy

WARRANT: Bossy people make bad committee chairs.

One way to refute this argument is to rebut the stated reason and grounds:

REBUTTAL OF REASON AND GROUNDS

I disagree with you that Joe is bossy. In fact, Joe is very unbossy. He's a good listener who's willing to compromise, and he involves others in decisions. The example you cite for his being bossy wasn't typical. It was a one-time circumstance that doesn't represent his normal behavior. [The writer could then provide examples of Joe's cooperative nature.]

Or you could concede that Joe is bossy but rebut the argument's warrant that bossiness is a bad trait:

REBUTTAL OF WARRANT

I agree that Joe is bossy, but in this circumstance bossiness is just the trait we need. This committee hasn't gotten anything done for six months and time is running out. We need a decisive person who can come in, get the committee organized, assign tasks, and get the job done.

Let's now illustrate these strategies in a more complex situation. For an example, we'll look at the issue of whether recycling is an effective strategy for saving the environment. A controversial subissue of recycling is whether the United States is running out of space for sanitary landfills. Here is how environmental writers George C. Lodge and Jeffrey F. Rayport argue that there are no places left to dump our garbage:

Because the United States is running out of landfill space, Americans will simply not be able to put the 180 million tons of solid waste they generate each year into landfills, where 70 percent of it now goes. Since 1979, the United States has exhausted more than two-thirds of its landfills; projections indicate that another one-fifth will close over the next five years. Between 1983 and 1987, for example, New York closed 200 of its 500 landfills; this year Connecticut will exhaust its landfill capacity. If the problem seemed abstract to Americans, it became odiously real in the summer of 1989 as most of the nation watched the notorious garbage barge from Islip, New York, wander 6,000 miles, searching for a place to dump its rancid 3,100-ton load.

This passage tries to persuade us that the United States is running out of landfill space. Now watch how writer John Tierney attempts to refute this argument in an influential 1996 *New York Times Magazine* article entitled "Recycling Is Garbage":

REBUTTAL OF ARGUMENT THAT AMERICA
IS RUNNING OUT OF LANDFILL SPACE

[Proponents of recycling believe that] our garbage will bury us. The *Mobro's** saga was presented as a grim harbinger of future landfill scarcity, but it actually represented a short-lived scare caused by new environmental regulations. As old municipal dumps were forced to close in the 1980's, towns had to send their garbage elsewhere and pay higher prices for scarce landfill space. But the higher prices predictably encouraged companies to open huge new landfills, in some regions creating a glut that set off price-cutting wars. Over the past few years, landfills in the South and Middle West have been vying for garbage from the New York area, and it has become cheaper to ship garbage there than to bury it locally.*

America has a good deal more landfill space available than it did 10 years ago. [. . .] A. Clark Wiseman, an economist at Gonzaga University in Spokane, Wash., has calculated that if Americans keep generating garbage at current rates for 1,000 years, and if all their garbage is put in a landfill 100 yards deep, by the year 3000 this national garbage heap will fill a square piece of land 35 miles on each side.

This doesn't seem a huge imposition in a country the size of America. The garbage would occupy only 5 percent of the area needed for the national array of solar panels proposed by environmentalists. The millennial landfill would fit on one-tenth of 1 percent of the range land now available for grazing in the continental United States.

In this case, Tierney uses counterevidence to rebut the reason and grounds of the original enthymeme: "Recycling is needed because the United States is running out of landfill space." Tierney attacks this argument by disagreeing with the stated reason that the United States is running out of landfill space.

Writers are also likely to question the underlying assumptions (warrants) of an opposing view. For an example, consider another recycling controversy: From an economic perspective, is recycling cost-effective? In criticizing recycling, Tierney argues that recycling wastes money; he provides evidence that "every time a sanitation department crew picks up a load of bottles and cans from the curb, New York City loses money." In Toulmin's terms, Tierney's line of reasoning is structured as follows:

TIERNEY'S ENTHYMEME: Promoting recycling is bad policy because it costs more to recycle material than to bury the same material in a landfill.

CLAIM: Promoting recycling is bad policy.

STATED REASON: because it costs more to recycle material than to bury the same material in a landfill

GROUNDS: evidence of the high cost of recycling [Tierney cites evidence that it costs New York City $200 more per ton to collect and dispose of recyclables than to bury them]

WARRANT: We should dispose of garbage in the least expensive way.

Mobro is the name of the notorious garbage barge from Islip, New York, referred to at the end of the previous quotation.

In rebutting Tierney's argument, proponents of recycling typically accepted Tierney's figures on recycling costs in New York City (that is, they agreed that in New York City recycling was more expensive than burying garbage). But in various ways they attacked his warrant. Typically, proponents of recycling said that even if the costs of recycling were higher than burying wastes in a landfill, recycling still benefited the environment by reducing the amount of virgin materials taken from nature. This argument says, in effect, that saving virgin resources takes precedence over economic costs.

These examples show how a refutation can focus either on the stated reasons and grounds of an argument or on the warrants and backing.

For Class Discussion

Imagine how each of the following arguments might be fleshed out with grounds and backing. Then attempt to refute each argument by suggesting ways to rebut the reason and grounds, or the warrant and backing, or both.

1. Writing courses should be pass/fail because the pass/fail system would encourage more creativity.
2. The government should make cigarettes illegal because cigarettes cause cancer and heart disease.
3. Majoring in engineering is better than majoring in music because engineers make more money than musicians.
4. People should not eat meat because doing so causes needless pain and suffering to animals.
5. The endangered species law is too stringent because it seriously hampers the economy.

Strategies for Rebutting Evidence

Whether you are rebutting an argument's reasons and grounds or its warrant and backing, you will frequently need to question a writer's use of evidence. Here are some strategies that you can use.

Deny the Truth of the Data   What one writer considers a fact another may consider a case of wrong information. If you have reason to doubt a writer's facts, then call them into question.

Cite Counterexamples or Countertestimony   One of the most effective ways to counter an argument based on examples is to cite a counterexample. The effect of counterexamples is to deny the conclusiveness of the original data. Similarly, citing an authority whose testimony counters other expert testimony is a good way to begin refuting an argument based on testimony.

Cast Doubt on the Representativeness or Sufficiency of Examples Examples are powerful only if the audience feels them to be representative and sufficient. Many environmentalists complained that John Tierney's attack on recycling was based too largely on data from New York City and that it didn't accurately take into account the more positive experiences of other cities and states. When data from outside New York City were examined, the cost-effectiveness and positive environmental impact of recycling seemed more apparent.

Cast Doubt on the Relevance or Recency of the Examples, Statistics, or Testimony The best evidence is up-to-date. In a rapidly changing universe, data that are even a few years out-of-date are often ineffective. For example, as the demand for recycled goods increases, the cost of recycling will be reduced. Out-of-date statistics will skew any argument about the cost of recycling. Another problem with data is their occasional lack of relevance. For example, in arguing that an adequate ozone layer is necessary for preventing skin cancers, it is not relevant to cite statistics on the alarming rise of lung cancers.

Call into Question the Credibility of an Authority If an opposing argument is based on testimony, you can undermine its persuasiveness if you show that a person being cited lacks up-to-date or relevant expertise in the field. (This procedure is different from the *ad hominem* fallacy discussed in Appendix 1 because it doesn't attack the personal character of the authority but only the authority's expertise on a specific matter.)

Question the Accuracy or Context of Quotations Evidence based on testimony is frequently distorted by being either misquoted or taken out of context. Often scientists qualify their findings heavily, but these qualifications are omitted by the popular media. You can thus attack the use of a quotation by putting it in its original context or by restoring the qualifications accompanying the quotation in its original source.

Question the Way Statistical Data Were Produced or Interpreted Chapter 6 provides fuller treatment of how to question statistics. In general, you can rebut statistical evidence by calling into account how the data were gathered, treated mathematically, or interpreted. It can make a big difference, for example, whether you cite raw numbers or percentages or whether you choose large or small increments for the axes of graphs.

Example of a Student Essay Using Refutation Strategy

The following extract from a student essay is the refutation section of a classical argument appealing to a neutral or undecided audience. In this essay, student writer Marybeth Hamilton argues the claim that First Place, an alternative public school for homeless children that also provides support services for their families, should continue to be publicly funded because it provides the emotional and educational support homeless children need to become mainstreamed. In the beginning of her essay, Marybeth explains that First Place provides not only a nurturing, supportive educational environment for its homeless students but also services such as counseling and therapy for the students' families. At least 80 percent of the children at First Place have witnessed domestic violence or have experienced physical, sexual, or emotional abuse. Lacking permanent housing, many of these children have moved from school to school. Because running First Place is costly and can accommodate only 4 percent of her city's homeless children who need help, Marybeth recognizes that her audience may object to First Place. Consequently, to reach the neutral and resistant members of her audience, she devotes the following portion of her argument to summarizing and refuting opposing views.

From "First Place: A Healing School for Homeless Children"

Marybeth Hamilton (Student)

1   . . . As stated earlier, the goal of First Place is to prepare students for returning to mainstream public schools. Although there are many reasons to continue operating an agency like First Place, there are some who would argue against it. One argument is that the school is too expensive, costing many more taxpayer dollars per child than a mainstream school. I can understand this objection to cost, but one way to look at First Place is as a preventative action by the city to reduce the future costs of crime and welfare. Because all the students at First Place are at-risk for educational failure, drug and alcohol abuse, or numerous other long-term problems, a program like First Place attempts to stop the problems before they start. In the long run, the city could be saving money in areas such as drug rehabilitation, welfare payments, or jail costs.

2   Others might criticize First Place for spending some of its funding on social services for the students and their families instead of spending it all on educational needs. When the city is already making welfare payments and providing a shelter for the families, why do they deserve anything more? Basically, the job of any school is to help a child become educated and have social skills. At First Place, students' needs run deep, and their entire families are in crisis. What good is it to help just the child when the rest of the family is still suffering? The education of only the child will not help the family out of poverty. Therefore, First Place helps parents look for jobs by providing job search help including assistance with résumés. They even supply clothes to wear to an interview. First Place also provides a parent

support group for expressing anxieties and learning coping skills. This therapy helps parents deal with their struggles in a productive way, reducing the chance that they will take out their frustration on their child. All these "extras" are an attempt to help the family get back on its feet and become self-supporting.

Another objection to an agency like First Place is that the short-term stay at First Place does no long-term good for the student. However, in talking with Michael Siptroth, a teacher at First Place, I learned that the individual attention the students receive helps many of them catch up in school quite quickly. He reported that some students actually made a three-grade-level improvement in one year. This improvement definitely contributes to the long-term good of the student, especially in the area of self-esteem. Also, the students at First Place are in desperate situations. For most, any help is better than no help. Thus First Place provides extended day care for the children so they won't have to be unsupervised at home while their parents are working or looking for work. For example, some homeless children live in motels on Aurora Avenue, a major highway that is overrun with fast cars, prostitutes, and drugs. Aurora Avenue is not a safe place for children to play, so the extended day care is important for many of First Place's students.

Finally, opponents might question the value of removing students from mainstream classrooms. Some might argue that separating children from regular classrooms is not good because it further highlights their differences from the mainstream children. Also, the separation period might cause additional alienation when the First Place child does return to a mainstream school. In reality, though, the effects are quite different. Children at First Place are sympathetic to each other. Perhaps for the first time in their lives, they do not have to be on the defensive because no one is going to make fun of them for being homeless; they are all homeless. The time spent at First Place is usually a time for catching up to the students in mainstream schools. When students catch up, they have one fewer reason to be seen as different from mainstream students. If the students stayed in the mainstream school and continued to fall behind, they would only get teased more.

First Place is a program that merits the community's ongoing moral and financial support. With more funding, First Place could help many more homeless children and their families along the path toward self-sufficiency. While this school is not the ultimate answer to the problem of homelessness, it is a beginning. These children deserve a chance to build their own lives, free from the stigma of homelessness, and I, as a responsible citizen, feel a civic and moral duty to do all I can to help them.

For Class Discussion

Having worked as a teacher's aide at First Place school, Marybeth Hamilton is familiar with the public criticism that the school receives. Individually or in groups, analyze the refutation strategies she employs in her argument.

1. Summarize each of the opposing reasons that Marybeth anticipates from her audience.

2. How does she attempt to refute each line of reasoning in the opposing argument? In each case does she refute her audience's reason and grounds, the warrant, or both?

3. Which of her counterexamples and counter-reasons do you think is her strongest? After reading her argument, would you as a city resident vote for the allotment of more public money for this school? Why or why not?

Conceding to Opposing Views

In writing a classical argument, a writer must sometimes concede to an opposing argument rather than refute it. Sometimes you encounter portions of an argument that you simply can't refute. For example, suppose you support the legalization of hard drugs such as cocaine and heroin. Adversaries argue that legalizing hard drugs will increase the number of drug users and addicts. You might dispute the size of their numbers, but you reluctantly agree that they are right. Your strategy in this case is not to refute the opposing argument but to concede to it by admitting that legalization of hard drugs will promote heroin and cocaine addiction. Having made that concession, your task is then to show that the benefits of drug legalization still outweigh the costs you've just conceded.

As this example shows, the strategy of a concession argument is to switch from the field of values employed by the writer you disagree with to a different field of values more favorable to your position. You don't try to refute the writer's stated reason and grounds (by arguing that legalization will *not* lead to increased drug usage and addiction) or the writer's warrant (by arguing that increased drug use and addiction is not a problem). Rather, you shift the argument to a new field of values by introducing a new warrant, one that you think your audience can share (that the benefits of legalization—eliminating the black market and ending the crime, violence, and prison costs associated with procurement of drugs—outweigh the costs of increased addiction). To the extent that opponents of legalization share your desire to stop drug-related crime, shifting to this new field of values is a good strategy. Although it may seem that you weaken your own position by conceding to an opposing argument, you may actually strengthen it by increasing your credibility and gaining your audience's goodwill. Moreover, conceding to one part of an opposing argument doesn't mean that you won't refute other parts of that argument.

Appealing to a Resistant Audience: Delayed Thesis or Rogerian Argument

Whereas classical argument is effective for neutral or undecided audiences, it is often less effective for audiences strongly opposed to the writer's position. Because resisting audiences often hold values, assumptions, or beliefs widely different from the writer's, they are unswayed by classical argument, which attacks their worldview too directly. On many values-laden issues such as abortion, gun control, gay rights, and welfare reform, the distance between a writer and a resisting audience can be so great that dialogue hardly seems possible.

Because of these wide differences in basic beliefs and values, a writer's goal is seldom to convert resistant readers to the writer's position. The best that the writer can hope for is to reduce somewhat the level of resistance, perhaps by opening a channel of conversation, increasing the reader's willingness to listen, and preparing the way for future dialogue. If you can get a resistant audience to say, "Well, I still don't agree with you, but I now understand you better and respect your views more," you will have been highly successful.

Delayed-Thesis Argument

In many cases you can reach a resistant audience by using a *delayed-thesis* structure in which you wait until the end of your argument to reveal your thesis. Classical argument asks you to state your thesis in the introduction, support it with reasons and evidence, and then summarize and refute opposing views. Rhetorically, however, it is not always advantageous to tell your readers where you stand at the start of your argument or to separate yourself so definitively from alternative views. For resistant audiences, it may be better to keep the issue open, delaying the revelation of your own position until the end of the essay.

To illustrate the different effects of classical versus delayed-thesis arguments, we invite you to read a delayed-thesis argument by nationally syndicated columnist Ellen Goodman. The article appeared shortly after the nation was shocked by a brutal gang rape in New Bedford, Massachusetts, in which a woman was raped on a pool table by patrons of a local bar.*

Minneapolis Pornography Ordinance
Ellen Goodman

Just a couple of months before the pool-table gang rape in New Bedford, Mass.,   1
Hustler magazine printed a photo feature that reads like a blueprint for the actual crime. There were just two differences between *Hustler* and real life. In *Hustler,* the woman enjoyed it. In real life, the woman charged rape.

There is no evidence that the four men charged with this crime had actually   2
read the magazine. Nor is there evidence that the spectators who yelled encouragement for two hours had held previous ringside seats at pornographic events. But there is a growing sense that the violent pornography being peddled in this country helps to create an atmosphere in which such events occur.

---

*The rape occurred in 1985 and was later made the subject of an Academy Award–winning movie, *The Accused,* starring Jodie Foster.

3   As recently as last month, a study done by two University of Wisconsin researchers suggested that even "normal" men, prescreened college students, were changed by their exposure to violent pornography. After just ten hours of viewing, reported researcher Edward Donnerstein, "the men were less likely to convict in a rape trial, less likely to see injury to a victim, more likely to see the victim as responsible." Pornography may not cause rape directly, he said, "but it maintains a lot of very callous attitudes. It justifies aggression. It even says you are doing a favor to the victim."

4   If we can prove that pornography is harmful, then shouldn't the victims have legal rights? This, in any case, is the theory behind a city ordinance that recently passed the Minneapolis City Council. Vetoed by the mayor last week, it is likely to be back before the Council for an overriding vote, likely to appear in other cities, other towns. What is unique about the Minneapolis approach is that for the first time it attacks pornography, not because of nudity or sexual explicitness, but because it degrades and harms women. It opposes pornography on the basis of sex discrimination.

5   University of Minnesota Law Professor Catherine MacKinnon, who co-authored the ordinance with feminist writer Andrea Dworkin, says that they chose this tactic because they believe that pornography is central to "creating and maintaining the inequality of the sexes. . . . Just being a woman means you are injured by pornography."

6   They defined pornography carefully as, "the sexually explicit subordination of women, graphically depicted, whether in pictures or in words." To fit their legal definition it must also include one of nine conditions that show this subordination, like presenting women who "experience sexual pleasure in being raped or . . . mutilated. . . ." Under this law, it would be possible for a pool-table rape victim to sue *Hustler.* It would be possible for a woman to sue if she were forced to act in a pornographic movie. Indeed, since the law describes pornography as oppressive to all women, it would be possible for any woman to sue those who traffic in the stuff for violating her civil rights.

7   In many ways, the Minneapolis ordinance is an appealing attack on an appalling problem. The authors have tried to resolve a long and bubbling conflict among those who have both a deep aversion to pornography and a deep loyalty to the value of free speech. "To date," says Professor MacKinnon, "people have identified the pornographer's freedom with everybody's freedom. But we're saying that the freedom of the pornographer is the subordination of women. It means one has to take a side."

8   But the sides are not quite as clear as Professor MacKinnon describes them. Nor is the ordinance.

9   Even if we accept the argument that pornography is harmful to women—and I do—then we must also recognize that anti-Semitic literature is harmful to Jews and racist literature is harmful to blacks. For that matter, Marxist literature may be harmful to government policy. It isn't just women versus pornographers. If women win the right to sue publishers and producers, then so could Jews, blacks, and a long list of people who may be able to prove they have been harmed by books, movies, speeches or even records. The Manson murders, you may recall, were reportedly inspired by the Beatles.

We might prefer a library or book store or lecture hall without *Mein Kampf* or the Grand Whoever of the Ku Klux Klan. But a growing list of harmful expressions would inevitably strangle freedom of speech. 10

This ordinance was carefully written to avoid problems of banning and prior restraint, but the right of any woman to claim damages from pornography is just too broad. It seems destined to lead to censorship. 11

What the Minneapolis City Council has before it is a very attractive theory. What MacKinnon and Dworkin have written is a very persuasive and useful definition of pornography. But they haven't yet resolved the conflict between the harm of pornography and the value of free speech. In its present form, this is still a shaky piece of law. 12

Consider now how this argument's rhetorical effect would be different if Ellen Goodman had revealed her thesis in the introduction using the classical argument form. Here is how this introduction might have looked:

GOODMAN'S INTRODUCTION REWRITTEN IN CLASSICAL FORM

Just a couple of months before the pool-table gang rape in New Bedford, Mass., *Hustler* magazine printed a photo feature that reads like a blueprint for the actual crime. There were just two differences between *Hustler* and real life. In *Hustler,* the woman enjoyed it. In real life, the woman charged rape. Of course, there is no evidence that the four men charged with this crime had actually read the magazine. Nor is there evidence that the spectators who yelled encouragement for two hours had held previous ringside seats at pornographic events.

But there is a growing sense that the violent pornography being peddled in this country helps to create an atmosphere in which such events occur. One city is taking a unique approach to attack this problem. An ordinance recently passed by the Minneapolis City Council outlaws pornography not because it contains nudity or sexually explicit acts, but because it degrades and harms women. Unfortunately, despite the proponents' good intentions, the Minneapolis ordinance is a bad law because it has potentially dangerous consequences.

Even though Goodman's position can be grasped more quickly in this classical form, our students generally find the original delayed-thesis version more effective. Why is this?

Most people point to the greater sense of complexity and surprise in the delayed-thesis version, a sense that comes largely from the delayed discovery of the writer's position. Whereas the classical version immediately labels the ordinance a "bad law," the original version withholds judgment, inviting the reader to examine the law more sympathetically and to identify with the position of those who drafted it. Rather than distancing herself from those who see pornography as a violation of women's rights, Goodman shares with her readers her own struggles to think through these issues, thereby persuading us of her genuine sympathy for the ordinance and for its feminist proponents. In the end, her delayed thesis renders her final rejection of the ordinance not only more surprising but more convincing.

Clearly, then, a writer's decision about when to reveal her thesis is critical. Revealing the thesis early makes the writer seem more hardnosed, more sure of her position, more confident about how to divide the ground into friendly and hostile camps, more in control. Delaying the thesis, in contrast, complicates the issues, increases reader sympathy for more than one view, and heightens interest in the tension among alternative views and in the writer's struggle for clarity.

Rogerian Argument

An even more powerful strategy for addressing resistant audiences is a conciliatory strategy often called *Rogerian argument*, named after psychologist Carl Rogers, who used this strategy to help people resolve differences.* Rogerian argument emphasizes "empathic listening," which Rogers defined as the ability to see an issue sympathetically from another person's perspective. He trained people to withhold judgment of another person's ideas until after they listened attentively to the other person, understood that person's reasoning, appreciated that person's values, respected that person's humanity—in short, walked in that person's shoes. Before disagreeing with another person, Rogers would tell his clients, you must be able to summarize that person's argument so accurately that he or she will say, "Yes, you understand my position."

What Carl Rogers understood is that traditional methods of argumentation are threatening. When you try to persuade people to change their minds on an issue, Rogers claimed, you are actually demanding a change in their worldview—to get other people, in a sense, to quit being their kind of person and start being your kind of person. Research psychologists have shown that persons are often not swayed by a logical argument if it somehow threatens their own view of the world. Carl Rogers was therefore interested in finding ways to make arguments less threatening. In Rogerian argument the writer typically waits until the end of the essay to present his position, and that position is often a compromise between the writer's original views and those of the resisting audience. Because Rogerian argument stresses the psychological as well as logical dimensions of argument, and because it emphasizes reducing threat and building bridges rather than winning an argument, it is particularly effective when dealing with emotionally laden issues.

Under Rogerian strategy, the writer reduces the sense of threat in her argument by showing that *both writer and resistant audience share many basic values.* Instead of attacking the audience as wrongheaded, the Rogerian writer respects the audience's intelligence and humanity and demonstrates an understanding of the audience's position before presenting her own position. Finally, the Rogerian writer never asks the audience to capitulate entirely to the writer's side—just to shift somewhat toward the writer's views. By acknowledging that she has already

---

*See Carl Rogers's essay "Communication: Its Blocking and Its Facilitation" in his book *On Becoming a Person* (Boston: Houghton Mifflin, 1961), 329–37. For a fuller discussion of Rogerian argument, see Richard Young, Alton Becker, and Kenneth Pike, *Rhetoric: Discovery and Change* (New York: Harcourt Brace, 1972).

shifted toward the audience's views, the writer makes it easier for the audience to accept compromise. All of this negotiation ideally leads to a compromise between—or better, a synthesis of—the opposing positions.

The key to successful Rogerian argument, besides the art of listening, is the ability to point out areas of agreement between the writer's and reader's positions. For example, if you support a woman's right to choose abortion and you are arguing with someone completely opposed to abortion, you're unlikely to convert your reader, but you might reduce the level of resistance. You begin this process by summarizing your reader's position sympathetically, stressing your shared values. You might say, for example, that you also value babies; that you also are appalled by people who treat abortion as a form of birth control; that you also worry that the easy acceptance of abortion diminishes the value society places on human life; and that you also agree that accepting abortion lightly can lead to lack of sexual responsibility. Building bridges like these between you and your readers makes it more likely that they will listen to you when you present your own position.

In its emphasis on establishing common ground, Rogerian argument has much in common with recent feminist theories of argument. Many feminists criticize classical argument as rooted in a male value system and tainted by metaphors of war and combat. Thus, classical arguments, with their emphasis on assertion and refutation, are typically praised for being "powerful" or "forceful." The writer "defends" his position and "attacks" his "opponent's" position using facts and data as "ammunition" and reasons as "big guns" to "blow away" his opponent's claim. According to some theorists, viewing argument as war can lead to inauthenticity, posturing, and game playing. The traditional pro-con debate—defined in one of our desk dictionaries as "a formal contest of argumentation in which two opposing teams defend and attack a given proposition"—treats argument as verbal jousting, more concerned to determine a winner than to clarify an issue.

One of our female students, who excelled as a debater in high school and received straight A's in argument classes, recently explained in an essay her growing alienation from male rhetoric: "Although women students are just as likely to excel in 'male' writing [. . .] we are less likely to feel as if we were saying something authentic and true." Later the student elaborated on her distrust of "persuasion":

> What many writing teachers have told me is that "the most important writing/speaking you will ever do will be to persuade someone." My experience as a person who has great difficulty naming and expressing emotions is that the most important communication in my life is far more likely to be simply telling someone how I feel. To say "I love you," or "I'm angry with you," will be far more valuable in most relationship contexts than to say "These are the three reasons why you shouldn't have done what you did [. . .] ."*

Writers who share this woman's distrust of classical argumentation often find Rogerian argument appealing because it stresses self-examination, clarification,

---

*Our thanks to Catherine Brown for this paragraph from an unpublished paper written at Seattle University.

and accommodation rather than refutation. Rogerian argument is more in tune with win-win negotiation than with win-lose debate.

To illustrate a conciliatory or Rogerian approach to an issue, we show you student writer Rebekah Taylor's argument written in response to the assignment on page 164. Rebekah chose to write a Rogerian argument in the form of a letter. An outspoken advocate for animal rights on her campus, Rebekah addressed her letter to an actual friend, Jim, with whom she had had many long philosophical conversations when she attended a different college. Note how Rebekah "listens" empathically to her friend's position on eating meat and proposes a compromise action.

A Letter to Jim
Rebekah Taylor (Student)

Dear Jim,

1   I decided to write you a letter today because I miss our long talks. Now that I have transferred colleges, we haven't had nearly enough heated discussions to satisfy either of us. I am writing now to again take up one of the issues we vehemently disagreed on in the past—meat-based diets.

2   First, I must express to you that I have listened to and understood your opposition to my argument in the past. For you, eating meat has been a normal, unquestioned part of life. Through observation of your parents, you came to understand and accept that humans eat animals just as humans drink water, sleep, and defecate. This view was reinforced at school. All of the children around you ate meat; your school did not offer—and probably had never heard of—any vegetarian options. The image of a "food pyramid" based on meat protein was burned into your mind. Also, having been raised in a conservative Christian household, you were taught that God intended for humans to have ultimate dominion over all creatures of the earth, sea, and sky. You were taught that God made us fleshly creatures who feed off other living organisms just as do bears, cats, and birds. For humans, eating meat is part of the cycle of nature.

3   I understand, then, that our life histories have created for us very different views about eating meat. You were raised in a family and community that accepted meat-based diets as normal, healthy, and ethically justifiable. I was raised in a family that cared very deeply for animals and attended a church that frequently entertained a vegan as a guest speaker. The conditions in which we were raised allowed us to become the people we are today and to shape the beliefs that we hold.

4   Let me now briefly reiterate for you my own basic beliefs about eating animals. As I have shared with you, my personal health is important to me, and I, along with other vegetarians and vegans, believe that a vegetarian diet is much more healthy than a meat diet. But my primary motivation is my deep respect for animals. I have

always felt an overpowering sense of compassion for animals and forceful sorrow and regret for the injuries that humans inflict upon them. I detest suffering, especially when it is forced upon creatures that cannot speak out against it. These deep feelings led me to become a vegetarian at the age of 5. While lying in bed one night, I looked up at the poster of a silky-white harbor seal that had always hung on my wall. As I looked at the face of that seal, I made a connection between that precious animal on my wall and the animals that had been killed for the food I ate every day. In the dim glow of my Strawberry Shortcake night-light, I promised those large, dark seal eyes that I would never eat animals again. Seventeen years have passed now and that promise still holds true. Every day I feel more dedicated to the cause of animal rights around the world.

I know very well that my personal convictions are not the same as yours. However, I believe that we might possibly agree on more aspects of this issue than we realize. Although we would not be considered by others as allies on the issue of eating meat, we do share a common enemy—factory farms. Although you eat animal products and I do not, we both share basic common values that are threatened by today's factory farms. We both want the food we eat to be healthy, we both care about people, and we both disapprove of the unnecessary suffering of animals.

Let me briefly relate to you the ways in which factory farms threaten our common values. Widespread global implementation of factory farming has made food more dangerous for humans to eat. At factory farms, pigs, cows, and chickens eat foods laden with pesticides, receive injections of dangerous hormones, and are raised in unsanitary, crowded, and stressful conditions. All of these elements of life at a factory farm combine to make many of the food products that humans eat extremely unhealthy. In fact, most instances of meat-borne illnesses in humans, such as e-coli, salmonella, and mad cow disease, come about because of the horrible conditions at factory farms.

Also, factory farms cause the needless suffering of animals. Though we might disagree on the morality of using animals for food at all, we do agree that such animals should not be made to suffer. Yet at factory farms, billions of animals across the world are born, live, and die in horribly cramped, dark, and foul-smelling barns. Most receive only about five hours of human contact in their entire lives, and those that receive more are often brutally abused. None of these animals know the feeling of fresh air, or of warm, blessed sunlight on their backs. Most do not move out of their tight, uncomfortable pens until the day that they are to be slaughtered. At these factory farms, animals are processed as if they were inanimate objects, with no regard for the fact that they do feel fear and pain.

I hope it is evident now that although we may disagree on whether or not humans should eat meat and other animal products, we do agree that the way these products are derived at factory farms is unnecessarily unhealthy, potentially destructive to humans, and cruel to animals. I am optimistic that our shared dislike of factory farms will help us take a crucial first step towards recognizing and understanding each other's views. This common ground shows me that though we will always disagree about many things, we are not that different, you and I.

It is because of our shared values that I ask you to consider making an effort to buy meat from small, independent local farmers. I am told by friends that all supermarkets offer such meat options. This would be an easy and effective way to fight factory farms. I know that I could never convince you to stop eating meat, and I will never try to force my beliefs on you. As your friend, I am grateful simply to be able to write to you so candidly about my beliefs. I trust that regardless of what your ultimate reaction is to this letter, you will thoughtfully consider what I have written, as I will thoughtfully consider what you write in return.

Sincerely,

Rebekah

For Class Discussion

1. In this letter, what shared values between writer and reader does the writer stress?

2. How is Rebekah's proposal—the action she asks of Jim—a compromise? How does this compromise show respect for Jim's values?

3. Imagine this letter rewritten as a classical argument. How would it be different?

Appealing to a Resistant Audience: Using Humor

Another strategy that can sometimes appeal to a resistant audience is humor. Anyone who has experienced moments of hilarity with others—friends, a lover, family members, coworkers—knows how powerful laughing together can be in building relationships. Humor can also relieve stress and open up fresh perspectives, even momentarily turn the world upside down to show us what we couldn't see before. In arguments, humor can strengthen the bonds among people who already agree by solidifying their common ground. It can also be used in arguments to win over resistant audiences, often by neutralizing their objections through entertaining amusement. Humor, especially when it evokes laughter, is disarming; it melts opposition, sometimes winning our assent to ideas we might reject if they were presented seriously. Humor can also be a way for you, the arguer, to express your concern, exasperation, or anger about an issue more productively than through direct or serious confrontation with your audience. When and how you use humor in your arguments has to be your call, based on context. Despite our fondness for humorous writing, we have to offer this caveat: Using humor in arguments is risky business that may backfire on you, especially if a resistant audience feels ridiculed. But humor may be powerfully persuasive.

Although we can't give you simple rules to determine when to use humor in your arguments, we can briefly explain some of the tools you can employ to construct an argument using humor. Some of the humorist's main tools are these imaginative uses of language: hyperbole (or exaggeration), understatement, repetition, and witty, memorable lines. *Hyperbole* refers to a writer's exaggeration of an idea. Often, inflating or blowing up an idea to enormous proportions compels an audience to see that idea as ridiculous and to laugh with you about it. *Understatement* works in an opposite manner: A writer leaves unsaid, but strongly implies, an idea, drawing the audience into a "shared" joke by asking the audience to see beyond the words. When you use understatement, you express an idea so far below the intensity it deserves that you push readers to supply the unsaid meaning in their own minds. *Repetition* of an idea builds up momentum (that "on a roll now" feeling) and collaborates with exaggeration by piling up details or ideas to ridiculous levels, conveying an idea through the sheer weight and rhythm of the language. *Witty, memorable lines* are funny flashes of insight expressed in well-placed colorful images or surprisingly suitable words; they can be those zingers or punch lines that drive home a point and leave the audience amazed and amused.

To show you how these tools of humor can operate in argument, we present below excerpts from the transcript of a public hearing in New York City on the possible relocation of Richard Serra's *Tilted Arc,* a sculpture placed in the plaza of the Jacob Javits Federal Building in lower Manhattan.* Some members of the community found this gigantic piece of metal offensive. In this hearing, the artist and his sympathizers argued that art should resist easy comprehension and challenge, even disturb, our perceptions. Other people at the hearing condemned and rejected this notion of art.

In the following passage, Phil La Basi, a federal employee who worked in a building on the plaza, protests the artist's definition of art and uses hyperbole, repetition, and witty lines to try to make the audience see his vision of this sculpture.

USING HYPERBOLE, WIT, AND REPETITION
TO ARGUE A POSITION

Hyperbole	What I see there is something that looks like a tank trap to prevent an armed attack from Chinatown in case of a Soviet invasion. In my mind it probably wouldn't even do that well, because one good Russian tank could probably take it out.
Witty lines playing on "tilted arc"	To be very serious, I wouldn't call it *Tilted Arc.* To me it looks like crooked metal or bent metal. I think we can call anything art if we call that art. I think any one of those people here could come
Hyperbole Repetition	along with an old broken bicycle that perhaps got run over by a car, or some other piece of material, and put it up and call it art and name it something. I think that is what was done here. [. . .]

*A more complete version of the transcripts of the public hearing in New York City on *Tilted Arc* is printed in Margaret P. Battin, John Fisher, Ronald Moore, and Anita Silvers, *Puzzles about Art* (New York: St. Martin's Press, 1989). Phil La Basi's remarks appear on pages 186–87; Peter Hirsh's testimony is on pages 183–84.

Another speaker at the hearing, Peter Hirsh, the research director and legal counsel for the Association of Immigration Attorneys, used understatement to denounce the sculpture. Notice the low-key way in which Hirsh basically says he thinks the sculpture is garbage.

USING UNDERSTATEMENT TO MAKE A POINT

Understatement leaving unsaid the writer's full dislike and disgust

My membership has authorized me to say that we are entirely opposed to *Tilted Arc*. My own personal view is that a good place to put *Tilted Arc* would be in the Hudson River. [. . .] I am told that they are going to have to put artificial things in the river to provide shelter for the striped bass. I think *Tilted Arc* would make a very fine shelter.

Humorous arguments can often take the form of satire or parody. In *satire*, a writer adopts an ironic point of view and appears to praise the very thing he or she is holding up for criticism. Often by exaggerating the weaknesses, foolishness, wrongness, or evils of some issue while seeming to support the issue (saying the opposite of what is really thought or meant), the writer can expose those weaknesses to ridicule. In this indirect and disruptive way, satire seeks to win the audience's acceptance of the writer's perspective. On a continuum ranging from "playfully critical and funny" to "harshly condemning and biting," satire often leans toward the latter.

Humorous argument can also be written as parody. A *parody* imitates a serious piece of work or even an event but seeks to ridicule it. It takes the familiar but changes it into something new that reminds readers of the original, plays off it, and in some way criticizes the original.

As a reaction to the recent volatile discussions of government regulation of guns in the House of Representatives, an article entitled "The Gun Commandments" appeared in the magazine *The Economist*.* In the passages from this article that follow, you can see that the piece employs both satire and parody. The article satirizes the House's ineffective approach to gun control by appearing to side with the anti–gun control position and by exaggerating that position to absurd proportions. It also parodies the House's stance toward gun control and its decision to post the Ten Commandments in schools by rewriting the Ten Commandments as Gun Commandments.

USING SATIRE AND PARODY TO ARGUE A POSITION

Satire

It is in the spirit of Mr. DeLay that the House decided, rather than controlling guns, to allow the Ten Commandments to be posted on the walls of every public school in America. That will teach them.

Satire

It is, of course, possible that the Supreme Court (a Godless institution) will decide that this offends against the separation of church and state. If this happens, Congress has an alternative set of commandments ready. They will do just as well.

Parody {

1. Honour the National Rifle Association, and remember that it doth contribute $4m to congressional campaigns. [. . .]

3. Honour the Sabbath day and keep it holy. Six days shalt thou labour and do all thy work, and on the seventh thou shalt do target practice. [. . .]

5. Thou shalt not kill, except when provoked. But if thou dost, remember that thy *gun* had nothing to do with it. [. . .]

In this example of satire and parody, the writer manages to express harsh criticism of and anger at Congress and the anti–gun control faction but does so in a clever, surprising way that makes even a resistant audience listen before turning off. The piece lures readers into its perspective, couching its real view of gun control in irony. If nothing else, the writer makes the audience think of the gun control issue in a wacky, distorted way that exposes the flaws in the anti–gun control position and the weaknesses in Congress's response.

As you contemplate both your investment in your claim and the level of resistance of your intended audience, determine whether humor as a main approach or as a way to make a point here and there might be an effective means to diminish your audience's resistance and perhaps even warm the audience up to your argument.

Conclusion

This chapter has shown you the difference between one-sided and multisided arguments and explained why multisided arguments are likely to be more persuasive to neutral or resisting audiences. A multisided argument generally includes a fair summary of differing views, followed by either refutation, concession, or Rogerian synthesis. The strategies you use for treating resistant views depend on the audience you are trying to reach and your purpose. We explained how audiences can be placed on a scale of resistance ranging from "strongly supportive" to "strongly resistant." In addressing supportive audiences, writers typically compose one-sided arguments with strong motivational appeals to action. Neutral or undecided audiences generally respond most favorably to classical arguments that set out strong reasons in support of the writer's position yet openly address alternative views, which are first summarized and then either rebutted or conceded to. When the audience is strongly resistant, a delayed thesis or Rogerian strategy is most effective at reducing resistance and helping move the audience slightly toward the writer's views. Sometimes humor is also effective at winning consideration from a resistant audience.

WRITING ASSIGNMENT
FOR CHAPTERS 7 AND 8

The assignment for Chapters 7 and 8 has two parts. Part One is an actual argument you will write. Part Two is your own self-reflective analysis on how you chose to appeal to and accommodate your audience.

PART ONE: For this assignment, argue against a popular cultural practice or belief that you think is wrong, or argue for an action or belief that you think is right even though it will be highly unpopular. Your claim, in other words, must be controversial—going against the grain of popular actions, values, and beliefs—so that you can anticipate considerable resistance to your views. This essay invites you to stand up for something you believe in even though your view will be highly contested. Your goal is to persuade your audience toward your position.

In writing and revising your argument, draw upon appropriate strategies from Chapters 7 and 8. From Chapter 7 consider strategies for increasing your appeals to *ethos* and *pathos*. From Chapter 8 consider strategies for appealing to audiences according to their level of resistance. Choose the most resistant audience that you think you can sway to your point of view. Whether you use a refutation strategy, a delayed-thesis strategy, a Rogerian strategy, a humorous strategy, or some combination of these approaches is up to you.

PART TWO: Attach to your argument a self-reflective letter to your instructor and classmates explaining and justifying the choices you made for appealing to your audience and accommodating their views. In your letter address questions such as the following:

1. At the most resistant end of the spectrum, why are people opposed to your claim? How does your claim challenge their views and perhaps threaten their own value system?

2. Whom did you picture as the audience you were trying to sway? Where on the spectrum from "accord" to "resistance" did you address your argument? Why?

3. What strategies did you use for appealing to that audience?

4. What choices did you make in trying to accommodate differing views?

5. What challenges did this assignment present for you? How successful do you think you were in meeting those challenges?

9 Conducting Visual Arguments

In today's visually oriented culture, arguments increasingly use photographs, drawings, graphics, and innovative page and text design for persuasive effect. As we shall see, visuals can enhance the *logos*, *pathos*, and *ethos* of an argument by supporting or clarifying an argument's logical core, moving audiences imaginatively and emotionally, or enhancing the writer's credibility and authority. They can also substantially enliven a writer's argument, keeping readers hooked and engaged. In this chapter, we ask you to explore with us the enormous rhetorical potential of visual elements in arguments, particularly the way that visual and verbal elements can collaborate to achieve persuasive effects.

Using visuals in arguments also poses challenges. It places on arguers an even greater burden to understand their audience, to think through the effect visuals will have on that audience, and to make sure that the verbal and visual parts of an argument work together. Before we examine visual design, we want to describe three recent examples of both the power and challenge of using visuals.

- In May 1999, the Makah, a Native American tribe in western Washington state, reinstated its cultural practice of hunting whales. Although guaranteed the right by treaty and by a permit from the International Whaling Commission to hunt and kill four gray whales a year, the Makah encountered vehement protests from environmental groups and whale lovers. This hostility was further inflamed by the media coverage that showed the hunting and killing of a whale in detail on national television. To manage angry public response to the footage of this killing, the Makah called in David Margulies, president of a Dallas-based public relations firm. In a newspaper article, Margulies, while commenting on this crisis, described the impact of visuals: "The picture is always the most powerful element of the story," and "One of the first things you want to do in public relations is control the picture. Whichever side has the better picture very often controls the argument."

- In an article entitled "Sending the Right Message in Art Form," posted on the Web site of the Humane Society of the United States, the author warns local

Humane Society chapters against the careless use in their newsletters of drawings and photos that can undermine the organization's goals. To motivate people to care for their animals responsibly, the article proposes these guidelines: avoid showing any unneutered males or females with litters, dogs with prong collars or choke chains unless they are in training sessions, unsupervised dogs outside or cats outdoors, or dogs tied to trees, doghouses, or fences. Photos and drawings should show all dogs and cats with visible collars and ID tags and should depict mixed breeds as well as purebreds and mature animals as well as adorable puppies and kittens.

■ In July 2002, Fox News and MSNBC evoked angry responses from the White House when they used a split screen to televise President Bush's speech on the economy, expanding their stock market tickers to take up most of the screen and reducing the president to a small box. As Bush talked about improvement in the economy, the larger portion of the screen showed stock market numbers falling. White House spokesman Ari Fleischer called the split-screen approach "a troubling new development that sensationalizes and distorts what makes markets go up and down. It suggests to viewers that there's a causal connection between a president's speech and minute-by-minute market shifts, which is a misleading representation. . . . It's economic nonsense."

Each of these instances demonstrates the suggestive power of visual elements and the challenge of planning exactly how visuals should function in your argument.

With this background in mind, we turn now to explaining some basic components of visual design. We then examine several genres of visual argument such as posters and fliers, public affairs advocacy ads, political cartoons, and Web pages. The third section of the chapter explains how you can use visual elements in your own arguments and invites you to create your own poster or advocacy advertisement. In the final section, we explain how you can display numerical data graphically for rhetorical effect.

Understanding Design Elements in Visual Argument

To understand how visual images can produce an argument, you need to understand the design elements that work together to create a visual text. In this section we'll explain and illustrate the four basic components of visual design: use of type, use of space and layout, use of color, and use of images.

Use of Type

Type is an important visual element of written arguments. Variations in type, such as size, boldface, italics, or all caps, can direct a reader's attention to an argument's structure and highlight main points. In arguments designed specifically for visual impact, such as posters or advocacy advertisements, type is often used

TABLE 9.1   *Examples and uses of type fonts*

Font Style	Font Name	Example	Use
Serif fonts	Times New Roman Courier New Bookman Old Style	Use type wisely. Use type wisely. Use type wisely.	Easy to read; good for long documents, good for *body type*, or the main verbal parts of a document
Sans serif fonts	Arial Century Gothic	Use type wisely. Use type wisely.	Tiring to read for long stretches; good for *display type* such as headings, titles, slogans
Specialty fonts	Dauphin Broadway	Use type wisely. Use type wisely.	Difficult to read for long stretches; effective when used sparingly for playful or decorative effect

in eye-catching and meaningful ways. In choosing type, you need to consider the typeface or font style, the size of the type, and formatting options. The main type-faces or fonts are classified as serif, sans serif, and specialty type. Serif type has lit-tle extensions on the letters. (This text is set in serif type.) Sans serif type lacks these extensions. Specialty type includes script fonts and special symbols. In addi-tion to font style, type comes in different sizes. It is measured in points, with one point equal to 1/72 of an inch. Most text-based arguments consisting mainly of body text are written in ten- to twelve-point type whereas more image-based argu-ments may use a mixture of type sizes that interact with the images for persuasive effect. Type can also be formatted using bold, italics, underlining, or shading for emphasis. Table 9.1 shows examples of type styles, as well as their typical uses.

The following basic principles for choosing type for visual arguments can help you achieve your overall goals of readability, visual appeal, and suitability.

Principles for Choosing Type for Visual Arguments

1. If you are creating a poster or advocacy advertisement, you will need to decide how much of your argument will be displayed in words and how much in images. For the text portions, choose *display type* (sans serif) or specialty fonts for titles, headings, and slogans and *body or text type* (serif) for longer passages of text.

2. Make type functional and appealing by using only two or three font styles per document.

3. Use consistent patterns of type (similar type styles, sizes, and formats) to in-dicate relationships among similar items or different levels of importance.

4. Choose type to project a specific impression (a structured combination of serif and sans serif type to create a formal, serious, or businesslike impres-sion; sans serif and specialty type to create a casual, informal, or playful impression, and so forth).

Besides these general principles, rhetorical considerations of genre and audience expectations should govern decisions about type. Text-based arguments in scholarly publications generally use plain, conservative fonts with little variation whereas text-based arguments in popular magazines may use more variations in font style and size, especially in headings and opening leads. Visual arguments such as posters, fliers, and advocacy ads exploit the aesthetic potential of type.

Use of Space or Layout

A second component of visual design is layout, which is critical for creating the visual appeal of an argument and for conveying meaning. Even visual arguments that are mainly textual should use space very purposefully. By spacing and layout we mean all of the following points:

- Page size and type of paper
- Proportion of text to white space
- Proportion of text to image(s) and graphics
- Arrangement of text on page (space, margins, columns, size of paragraphs, spaces between paragraphs, justification of margins)
- Use of highlighting elements such as bulleted lists, tables, sidebars, boxes
- Use of headings and other means of breaking text into visual elements

In arguments that don't use visuals directly, the writer's primary visual concern is document design, where the writer tries to meet the conventions of a genre and the expectations of the intended audience. For example, Megan Matthews' researched argument on pages 416–423 is designed to meet the document conventions of the American Psychological Association (APA). Note the use of a plain, conventional typeface (for easy reading), double-spacing, and one-inch margins (to leave room for editorial marking and notations), and special title page, headers, and page number locations (to meet expectations of readers familiar with APA documents—which all look exactly the same).

But in moving from verbal-only arguments to visual arguments that use visual elements for direct persuasive effect—for example, posters, fliers, or advocacy ads—creative use of layout is vital. Here are some ideas to help you think about the layout of a visual argument.

Principles for Laying Out Parts of a Visual Text

1. Choose a layout that avoids clutter and confusion by limiting how much text and how many visual items you put on a page.
2. Focus on creating coherence and meaning with layout.
3. Develop an ordering or structuring principle that clarifies the relationships among the parts.

4. Use layout and spacing to indicate the importance of items and to empha-size key ideas. Because Western readers read from left to right and top to bottom, top and center are positions that readily draw readers' eyes.

An Analysis of a Visual Argument Using Type and Spatial Elements

To illustrate the persuasive power of type and layout, we ask you to consider Figure 9.1, which shows an advocacy ad sponsored by a coalition of organizations aimed at fighting illegal drugs.

This ad, warning about the dangers of the drug Ecstasy, uses different sizes of type and layout to present its argument. The huge word "Ecstasy" first catches the reader's attention. The first few words at the top of the ad, exuding pleasure, lull the reader with the congruence between the pleasurable message and the playful type. Soon, however, the reader encounters a dissonance between the playful type and the meaning of the words: "dehydrate," "hallucinate," "paranoid," and "dead" name unpleasant ideas. By the end of the ad, readers realize they have been led through a downward progression of ideas beginning with the youth cul-ture's belief that Ecstasy creates wonderfully positive feelings and ending with the ad's thesis that Ecstasy leads to paranoia, depression, and death. The playful infor-mality of the font styles and the unevenly scattered layout of the type convey the seductiveness and unpredictability of the drug. The ad concedes that the first ef-fects are "falling in love with the world" but implies that what comes next is in-creasingly dark and dangerous. At the end of the ad, in the lines of type near the bottom, the message and typestyle are congruent again. The question "Does that sound harmless to you?" marks a shift in type design and layout. The designer composed this section of the ad in conventional fonts centered on the page in a ra-tional, businesslike fashion. This type design signals a metaphoric move from the euphoria of Ecstasy to the ordered structure of everyday reality, where the reader can now consider rationally the drug's harm. The information at the bottom of the ad identifies the ad's sponsors and gives both a Web address and a telephone num-ber to call for more information about Ecstasy and other illegal drugs.

For Class Discussion

This exercise asks you to examine Figure 9.2, an advocacy ad sponsored by Common Sense for Drug Policy. This ad also focuses on the drug Ecstasy and also uses type and layout to convey its points. (This ad appeared in the liberal maga-zine *The Progressive* in October 2000.) Individually or in groups, study this advo-cacy ad and then answer the following questions.

1. What is the core argument of this ad? What view of drug use and what course of action is this ad promoting? What similarities and differences do you see between the argument about Ecstasy in this ad and the ad in Figure 9.1?

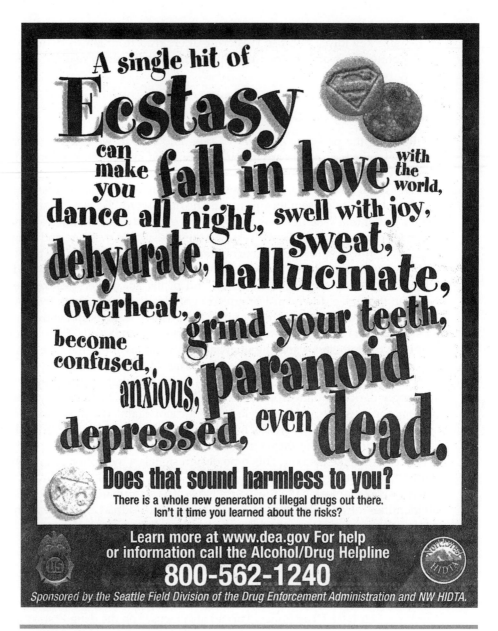

FIGURE 9.1   *Advocacy advertisement warning against ecstasy*

2. What are the main differences in the type and layout of the two ads in Figure 9.1 and 9.2? To what extent do the ad makers' choices about type and layout match the arguments made in each ad?

What We Know About Ecstasy

What is Ecstasy?

Ecstasy, MDMA,[1] is a semi-synthetic drug patented by Merck Pharmaceutical Company in 1914 and abandoned for 60 years. In the late 1970s and early 1980s psychiatrists and psychotherapists in the US used it to facilitate psychotherapy.[2] In 1985 its growing recreational use caused the DEA to criminalize it.

Ecstasy's effects last 3 to 6 hours. It is a mood elevator that produces feelings of empathy, openness and well-being. People who take it at all night "rave" dances say they enjoy dancing and feeling close to others. It does not produce violence or physical addiction.[3]

What are the greatest risks from Ecstasy?

Death is a possibility when using MDMA. According to coroner reports, there were nine Ecstasy-related deaths (three of these involved Ecstasy alone) in 1998.[4] Some of these deaths are related to overheating. MDMA slightly raises body temperature. This is potentially lethal in hot environments where there is vigorous dancing and the lack of adequate fluid replacement.[5] Many of these tragic deaths were preventable with simple harm reduction techniques such as having free water available and rooms where people can rest and relax.

One of the recent risks associated with Ecstasy is the possibility of obtaining adulterated drugs that may be more toxic than MDMA. Some of the reported deaths attributed to Ecstasy are likely caused by other, more dangerous drugs.[6] Deaths from adulterated drugs are another consequence of a zero tolerance approach. While we do not encourage Ecstasy use, we recommend that the drug be tested for purity to minimize the risk from adulterated drugs by those who consume it.[7] However, MDMA itself has risks. For example, it raises blood pressure and heart rate. Persons with known cardiovascular or heart disease should not take MDMA.

Recent studies have indicated that individuals who have used MDMA may have decreased performance in memory tests compared to nonusers. These studies are presently controversial because they involved people who used a variety of other drugs. Furthermore, it is difficult to rule out possible pre-existing differences between research subjects and controls.[8]

What is a rave?

Raves are all-night dance parties popular with young people that feature electronic music. A variety of drug use, from alcohol to nicotine, and including ecstasy, occurs at raves. Hysteria is leading to criminalization of raves, thus pushing them underground and into less safe and responsible settings.

Let's deal with legal and illegal drugs knowledgeably, understand their relative dangers, act prudently and avoid hysteria.

Kevin B. Zeese, President, Common Sense for Drug Policy, 3220 N Street, NW #141, Washington, DC 20007
www.csdp.org * www.DrugWarFacts.org * www.AddictintheFamily.org * info@csdp.org
202-299-9780 * 202-518-4028 (fax)

1, 3 & 4 - methylenedioxymethamphetamine. 2 - Greer G. and Tolbert R., A Method of Conducting Therapeutic Sessions with MDMA. In Journal of Psychoactive Drugs 30 (1998) 4:371.379. For research on the therapeutic use of MDMA see: www.maps.org. 3 - Beck J. and Rosenbaum M., Pursuit of Ecstasy: The MDMA Experience. Albany: State University of New York Press, 1994. 4 - Drug Abuse Warning Network, Office of Applied Studies, Substance Abuse and Mental Health Services Administration, Report of March 21, 2000. (This was a special report because the published report only includes drugs where there were over 10 deaths.) 5 - C.M. Milroy; J.C. Clark; A.R.W. Forrest, Pathology of deaths associated with "ecstasy" and "eve" misuse, Journal of Clinical Pathology Vol 49 (1996) 149-153. 6 - Laboratory Pill Analysis Program, DanceSafe. For results visit www.DanceSafe.org. See also, Byard RW et al., Amphetamine derivative fatalities in South Australia—is "Ecstasy" the culprit?, American Journal of Forensic Medical Pathology, 998 (Sep) 19(3): 261-5. 7 - DanceSafe provides testing equipment and a testing service which can be used to determine what a substance is. See www.DanceSafe.org. 8 - E. Gouzoulis-Mayfrank; J. Daumann; F. Tuchtenhagen; S. Pelz; S. Becker; H.J. Kunert; B. Fimm; H. Sass; Impaired cognitive performance in drug-free users of recreational ecstasy (MDMA), by Journal Neurol Neurosurg Psychiatry Vol 68, June 2000, 719-725; K.I.Bolla; U.D.; McCann; G.A. Ricaurte; Memory impairment in abstinent MDMA ('Ecstasy') users, by Neurology Vol 51, Dec 1998, 1532-1537.

FIGURE 9.2 *Common Sense for Drug Policy advocacy ad*

3. How would you analyze the use of type and layout in Figure 9.2? How does this ad use typestyles to convey its argument? How does it use layout and spacing?

4. The ad in Figure 9.1 appeared in the weekly entertainment section of *The Seattle Times*, a newspaper with a large general readership, whereas the ad in Figure 9.2 appeared in a liberal news commentary magazine. In what ways is each ad designed to reach its audience?

Use of Color

A third important element of visual design is use of color, which can contribute significantly to the visual appeal of an argument and move readers emotionally and imaginatively. In considering color in visual arguments, writers are especially controlled by genre conventions. For example, academic arguments use color minimally whereas popular magazines often use color lavishly. The appeal of colors to an audience and the associations that colors have for an audience are also important. For instance, the psychedelic colors of 1960s rock concert posters would probably not be effective in poster arguments directed toward conservative voters. Color choices in visual arguments often have crucial importance, including the choice of making an image black and white when color is possible. As you will see in our discussions of color throughout this chapter, makers of visual arguments need to decide whether color will be primarily decorative (using colors to create visual appeal), functional (for example, using colors to indicate relationships), realistic (using colors like a documentary photo), aesthetic (for example, using colors that are soothing, exciting, or disturbing), or some intentional combination of these.

Use of Images and Graphics

The fourth design element includes images and graphics, which can powerfully condense information into striking and memorable visuals, clarify ideas, and add depth, liveliness, and emotion to your arguments. A major point to keep in mind when using images is that a few simple images may be more powerful than complicated and numerous images. Other key considerations are (1) how you intend an image to work in your argument (for example, convey an idea, illustrate a point, evoke an emotional response) and (2) how you will establish the relationship between the image or graphic and the verbal text. Because using images and graphics effectively is especially challenging, we devote the rest of this chapter to explaining how images and graphics can be incorporated into visual arguments. We treat the use of photographs and drawings in the next main section and the use of quantitative graphics in the final section.

An Analysis of a Visual Argument Using All the Design Components

Before we discuss the use of images and graphics in detail, we would like to illustrate how all four of the design components—use of type, layout, color, and image—can reinforce and support each other to achieve a rhetorical effect. Consider the "Save the Children" advocacy ad appearing as Color Plate E. This advocacy ad combines type, layout, color, and image skillfully and harmoniously through its dominant image complemented by verbal text that interprets and applies the ideas conveyed by the image. The layout of the ad divides the page into three main parts, giving central focus to the image of the mother standing and looking into the eyes of the child she is holding in her arms. The blank top panel leads readers to look at the image. Two color panels, mauve behind the child and rose behind the mother, also highlight the two figures, isolate them in time and space, and concentrate the readers' attention on them. The large type in the black borders ("SHE'S THE BEST QUALIFIED TEACHER FOR HER CHILDREN." "IMAGINE IF SHE HAD AN EDUCATION.") frames the image, attracts readers' eyes, and plants the main idea in readers' minds: mothers should be equipped to teach their children.

This advocacy ad, which appeared in *Newsweek*, skillfully blends familiar, universal ideas—a mother's love for her child and the tenderness and strength of this bond—with unfamiliar, foreign associations—a mother and child from a third-world country, wearing the traditional clothing of their country depicted by the head scarf the mother is wearing and the elaborate design on her sleeve. In addition to the familiar-unfamiliar dynamic, a universal-particular dynamic also operates in this ad. This woman and baby are *every* mother and child (after all, we don't know exactly where she is from), but they are also from some specific third-world country. The two figures have been posed to conjure up Western paintings and statues of the Madonna and Christ child. With this pose, the ad intends that readers will connect with this image of motherly love and devotion and respond by supporting the "Every Mother/Every Child" campaign. Color in this ad also accents the warm, cozy, hopeful impression of the image; pink in Western culture is a feminine color often associated with women and babies. In analyzing the photographic image, you should note what is *not* shown: any surroundings, any indication of housing or scenery, any concrete sense of place or culture. The text of the ad interprets the image, provides background information, and seeks to apply the ideas and feelings evoked by the image to urging readers to action. The image, without either the large type or the smaller type, does convey an idea as well as elicit sympathy from readers, but the text adds meaning to the image and builds on those impressions and applies them.

The ad designer could have focused on poverty, illiteracy, hunger, disease, and high mortality rates but instead has chosen to evoke positive feelings of identification and to convey hopeful ideas. While acknowledging their cultural difference from this mother and child, readers recognize their common humanity and are moved to "give mothers and children the best chance to survive and thrive."

The large amounts of blank space in this ad help to convey that the main points here are important, serious, elemental, but also simple—as if the ad has gotten to the heart of the matter. The bottom panel of the ad gives readers the logo and name of the organization "Save the Children" and a phone number and Web address to use to show their support.

The Compositional Features of Photographs and Drawings

Now that we have introduced you to the four major elements of visual design—type, layout, color, and images—we turn to an in-depth discussion of photographic images and drawings. Used with great shrewdness in product advertisements, photos and drawings can be used with equal shrewdness in posters, fliers, advocacy ads, and Web sites. When an image is created specifically for an argument, almost nothing is left to chance. Although such images are often made to seem spontaneous and "natural," they are almost always composed: Designers consciously select the details of staging and composition as well as manipulate camera techniques (filters, camera angle, lighting), and digital or chemical development techniques (airbrushing, merging of images). Even news photography can have a composed feel. For example, public officials often try to control the effect of photographs by creating "photo-ops" (photographing opportunities), wherein reporters are allowed to photograph an event only during certain times and from certain angles. Political photographs appearing in newspapers are often press releases officially approved by the politician's staff. (See the photographs of President Bush later in this chapter on p. 178.)

To analyze a photograph or drawing, or to create visual images for your own arguments, you need to think both about the composition of the image and about the camera's relationship to the subject. Since drawings produce a perspective on a scene analogous to that of a camera, design considerations for photographs can be applied to drawings as well. The following list of questions can guide your analysis of any persuasive image.

- *Type of photograph or drawing:* Is the image documentary-like (representing a real event), fictionlike (intended to tell a story or dramatize a scene), or conceptual (illustrating or symbolizing an idea or theme)? The photo of a girl crowd-surfing in a mosh pit in Color Plate C, is a documentary photo capturing a real event in action. The drawing of the lizards in Color Plate F, is both a fictional narrative telling a story and a conceptual drawing illustrating a theme.

- *Distance from the subject:* Is the image a close-up, medium shot, or long shot? Close-ups tend to increase the intensity of the image and suggest the importance of the subject; long shots tend to blend the subject into the background. The photograph of the girl with a kitten in Color Plate H, is an extreme close-up. In contrast, the photograph of the young woman crossing the bridge in the

Haiti photograph (Color Plate D) is a long-range shot showing her blending into the poverty-stricken background, suggesting the devastating effect of poverty.

- *Orientation of the image and camera angle:* Is the camera (or artist) positioned in front of or behind the subject? Is it positioned below the subject, looking up (a low-angle shot)? Or is it above the subject, looking down (a high-angle shot)? Front-view shots, such as the one of Albanian refugees in Figure 1. 1 (p. 6), tend to emphasize the persons being photographed. In contrast, rear-view shots often emphasize the scene or setting. A low-angle perspective tends to make the subject look superior and powerful, whereas a high-angle perspective can reduce the size—and by implication—the importance of the subject. A level angle tends to imply equality. The high-angle shot of the "American Taliban" John Lindh strapped naked to a stretcher (Figure 7.2, p. 139) emphasizes the superiority of the camera and the helplessness of Lindh. In contrast the low-angle perspective of the lizards in Color Plate F, emphasizes the power of the lizards and the inferiority of the viewer.

- *Point of view:* Does the camera or artist stand outside the scene and create an objective effect as in the Haiti photograph in Color Plate D? Or is the camera or artist inside the scene as if the photographer or artist is an actor in the scene, creating a subjective effect as in the drawing of the lizards in Color Plate F.

- *Use of color:* Is the image in color or in black and white? Is this choice determined by the restrictions of the medium (the publication can't afford color, as in many newspaper photographs) or is it the conscious choice of the photographer or artist? Are the colors realistic or muted? Have special filters been used (a photo made to look old through the use of brown tints)? The bright colors in the lizard and Goldilocks drawing in Color Plate F, and in the forest scene in Color Plate G, resemble illustrations in books for children. The subdued colors in the soybean ad in Color Plate B, are intended to look realistically natural and neutral.

- *Compositional special effects:* Is the entire image clear and realistic? Is any portion of it blurred? Is it blended with other realistic or nonrealistic images (a car ad that blends a city and a desert; a body lotion ad that merges a woman and a cactus)? Is the image an imitation of some other famous image such as a classic painting (as in parodies)? Both the Earthustice ad in Color Plate F, and the Saturn VUE ad in Color Plate G, are conscious imitations of children's picture books.

- *Juxtaposition of images:* Are several different images juxtaposed, suggesting relationships between them? Juxtaposition can suggest sequential or causal relationships or can metaphorically transfer the identity of a nearby image or background to the subject (as when a bath soap is associated with a meadow). This technique is frequently used in public relations to shape viewers' perceptions of political figures as when President Bush is positioned in front of Mount Rushmore in Figure 9.5 (p. 178).

- *Manipulation of images:* Are staged images made to appear real, natural, documentary-like? Are images altered with airbrushing? Are images actually composites of a number of images (for instance, using images of different women's bodies to create one perfect model in an ad or film)? Are images cropped for emphasis? What is left out? Are images downsized or enlarged? For an example of a staged photo that is intended to look natural, see the "Save the Children" advocacy ad in Color Plate E. Note too how the figures in the "Save the Children" ad are silhouetted to remove all background.

- *Settings, furnishings, props:* Is the photo or drawing an outdoor or indoor scene? What is in the background and foreground? What furnishings and props, such as furniture, objects in a room, pets, and landscape features, help create the scene? What social associations of class, race, and gender are attached to these settings and props? The white girl holding a cat in the Center for Consumer Freedom ad in Color Plate H, is a calculated choice. The ad maker could have used an African American boy with a dog or an Asian girl with a rabbit but selected the girl-and-cat photograph for a rhetorical purpose.

- *Characters, roles, actions:* Does the photo or drawing tell a story? Are the people in the scene models? Are the models instrumental (acting out real-life roles) or are they decorative (extra and included for visual or sex appeal)? What are the facial expressions, gestures, and poses of the people? What are the spatial relationships of the figures? (Who is in the foreground, center, and background? Who is large and prominent?) What social relationships are implied by these poses and positions? In the "Save the Children" advocacy ad shown in Color Plate E, the pose of the mother and child—each completely absorbed in adoration of the other—tells the story of the bonds of love between mothers and babies.

- *Presentation of images:* Are images separated from each other in a larger composition or connected to each other? Are the images large in proportion to verbal text? How are images labeled? How does the text relate to the image(s)? Does the image illustrate the text? Does the text explain or comment on the image? For example, the image of the soybean plant in Color Plate B, dominates the right side of the advocacy ad, while attractively designed type dominates the left side of the ad. (You might consider why the ad maker places text on the left and image on the right instead of reversing the order or placing text on top and image on the bottom.) The image of the coat hanger hook dominates the advocacy ad on page 182, while the image of the can in Color Plate A, shares the page with a substantial amount of verbal text.

An Analysis of a Visual Argument Using Images

To show you how images can be analyzed, let's examine the advertisement for a Saturn VUE sport-utility vehicle (Color Plate G). At one level, the persuasive

WHAT IF EVERYTHING WAS LABELED LIKE GENETICALLY ENGINEERED FOODS?

Genetically engineered (GE) fruits, vegetables and meats are on your dinner plate. Up to 70% of processed foods now contain GE ingredients. Yet, despite the fact that most Americans have indicated in national polls that they want to be able to identify these products, there is no label for GE foods, and no way for consumers to know whether the food they eat contains them.

Because the government doesn't require rigorous independent safety testing, no one can predict the long-term effects of these foods on our health, the environment, the economy, or the future of farming.

We believe that consumers have the right to know if their food has been genetically engineered. Join with us in asking the Food and Drug Administration to better regulate GE foods by requiring mandatory labeling and safety testing.

Take Action Today!

KEEP NATURE NATURAL

Learn more! 800-357-2211
www.keepnatural.org

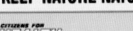 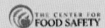 Sustain

---

COLOR PLATE A   *"Keep Nature Natural" advocacy ad. This ad ran in* Vegetarian Times *and the* Utne Reader.

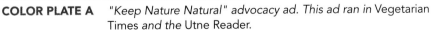

WOULD IT
SURPRISE YOU TO KNOW
THAT GROWING SOYBEANS CAN
HELP THE ENVIRONMENT?

Biotech soybeans have been widely
planted by American farmers and they
help preserve our natural resources.
Plant biotechnology makes it easier to
control weeds and plow soybean fields
less—which means less soil erosion.

But before those soybean seeds could
be planted, it took years of research and
testing to ensure that biotech crops
were safe for people and the environment. Extensive testing by scientists
shows foods derived from plant
biotechnology are as safe to eat as
traditional foods.

In fact, three government agencies
share the authority to evaluate the safety
of new biotech products from incep-
tion to approval—the U.S.
Department of Agriculture
(USDA), the Environmental Protection
Agency (EPA), and the Food and Drug
Administration (FDA). If you want to
learn more, we invite you to call or
visit our Web site.

WWW.WHYBIOTECH.COM
1-800-980-8660

Biotech
Soybean

COLOR PLATE B   *Biotechnology advocacy ad*

COLOR PLATE C   *Crowd-surfing at a rock concert* (TOM REESE/THE SEATTLE TIMES)

COLOR PLATE D   *La Saline, a slum in Port-au-Prince, Haiti* (© 2002 Alex Quesada/Matrix)

SHE'S THE BEST QUALIFIED TEACHER FOR HER CHILDREN.

In a world where almost one-third of women are illiterate, improving access to education is urgent. Studies show that an educated mother is more likely to provide her children with adequate nutrition, seek needed health care, and send her girls, as well as boys, to school. Support the Every Mother/Every Child campaign, and give mothers and children the best chance to survive and thrive.

IMAGINE IF SHE HAD AN EDUCATION.

1-800-728-3843 • savethechildren.org

plan)et

Save the Children®

COLOR PLATE E   *Save the Children advocacy ad*

Just then, the three lizards came home and found Goldilocks eating their porridge...

IT'S JUST NOT THE SAME WITHOUT BEARS.

Once upon a time there were over 100,000 grizzly bears in the lower 48 states. Now, there are less than a thousand grizzly bears left. The health of the grizzly is dependent on vast, undisturbed, wild lands. When bears disappear, other species will follow. Bears are such an important part of our wilderness, history, and culture that it's hard to imagine a world without them in the picture.

Grizzly bears are a threatened species, protected by the Endangered Species Act. But some special interests are pushing the U.S. Fish and Wildlife Service to remove Yellowstone grizzlies from the endangered species list. Why? They want to open up wild lands around Yellowstone

National Park to destructive logging, mining, off-road vehicle use, and development.

You can help protect our wilderness and grizzly bears. Please take a moment to contact Secretary Bruce Babbitt, Department of Interior, 1849 C St. NW, Washington DC 20240, or email Bruce_Babbitt@os.doi.gov – Tell him to keep grizzly bears on the Endangered Species List and that grizzly bears need more protection, not less.

Earthjustice Legal Defense Fund is working tirelessly to protect the grizzly bears and the wilderness they stand for. If we all work together, the grizzly bears will live happily ever after.

HELP KEEP BEARS IN THE PICTURE

www.earthjustice.org

EARTHJUSTICE
LEGAL DEFENSE FUND
1-800-584-6460

designed by Sustain

COLOR PLATE F *Earthjustice advocacy ad*

COLOR PLATE G *Saturn VUE ad* (Used with permission of General Motors Corp.)

COLOR PLATE H   *Center for Consumer Freedom advocacy ad*

IMF/WORLD BANK

50
YEARS IS

ENOUGH

US Network for Global Economic Justice

HOME
ABOUT US
ECONOMIC JUSTICE
NEWS
THE ISSUES
THE INSTITUTIONS
CONFERENCES
TAKE ACTION
LINKS
PHOTOS
FACTSHEETS
PRESS
UPDATES
JOBS / INTERNSHIPS
FEEDBACK
DONATE

JOIN THE 50 YEARS
LISTSERV

Search
[   ] Go

SUPPORT THE
NETWORK

WELCOME TO

50 YEARS IS ENOUGH

US Network for Global Economic Justice

WHAT'S NEW

Join the Movement Demands of IMF & World Bank

**International Day of
Action Against Military
and Economic
Intervention in Latin
America and the
Caribbean**

**Job Announcement
OFFICE
COORDINATOR**

Economic Justice
News - December 2002

Rebuttal to World
Bank Response to 4
Demands

We call for the immediate suspension of the
policies and practices of the International
Monetary Fund (IMF) and World Bank Group
which have caused widespread poverty,
inequality, and suffering among the world's
peoples and damage to the world's
environment....

**Read more from the 50 Years is Enough
Network Platform**

Debt

As an April 2002 report
prepared by the IMF
and World Bank
acknowledges, the
institutions' debt
management program
(HIPC) is failing.

**IMF/World Bank Debt
Plan: Still Failing After
All These Years**

Talk Back!

Declaration on Africa's
Development
Challenges

Responding to
"mainstream"
attitudes on the IMF &
World Bank

Tax the Bank!

COLOR PLATE I   *U.S. Network for Global Economic Justice web site* intent of this ad is to urge viewers to buy a Saturn VUE. But at a more subtle level, this advertisement participates in an international debate about SUVs and the environment. Whereas Europeans are buying smaller, more fuel-efficient cars, Americans are buying SUVs that guzzle gas like trucks. Among their opponents, SUVs—whether fairly or unfairly—have become a worldwide symbol of Americans' greed for oil and their disdain for the environment.

How do car manufacturers fight back? Clearly, they can't make a logical argument that owning an SUV is good for the environment. But they can use psychological strategies that urge consumers to associate SUVs with pro-environment sentiments. So in this ad Saturn turns to visual argument. Using a carefully designed drawing, the advertisement shows the Saturn VUE blending into an "evergreen forest" scene. Surrounded by a moose, a porcupine, a bear, a squirrel, and other forest birds and animals, the SUV seems to belong in its forest home. The brilliance of the ad is the insert legend at the bottom left, where the forest creatures are identified by name. The ad teaches city dwellers who buy SUVs the names of the forest animals—not just "bird" but "Black-Capped Chickadee," not just "rabbit" but "Snowshoe Hare." (Because the ad was designed as a two-page magazine spread, we had to reduce its size in Plate G, making the animal names tiny. They are easily readable in the original.) The ad becomes a mini-lesson in identifying and naming the "Creatures of the evergreen forest"—Creature number one, of course, being the Saturn VUE.

To make the Saturn VUE blend harmoniously with the forest, this ad cleverly de-emphasizes the size of the vehicle, even though the dominant size of SUVs is part of their appeal to urban consumers. To compensate for this choice, the typical appeals of SUVs are rendered symbolically. For example, the VUE's power and agility, hinted at in the brief copy at the bottom right of the ad, are conveyed metaphorically in the image of the puma, "poised" like the Saturn, crouching and oriented in the same direction, like the car's guiding spirit. It enters the scene from the outside, the predator, silent and powerful—the main animal to be identified with the car itself. Other animals close to the car and facing the same direction as the car each stand for one of the car's attributes so that the VUE also possesses the speed of the hare, the brute size and strength of the bear, and the soaring freedom of the goshawk.

The whole ad works by association. The slogan "At home in almost any environment" means literally that the car can go from city to country, from desert to mountains, from snow to tropic heat. But so can any car. The slogan's purpose is to associate the car with the words *home* and *environment*—words that connote all the warm, fuzzy feelings that make you feel good about owning a Saturn VUE. In addition, the use of drawings and the identification of animals by numbers conjure up the delightful, instructive innocence of children's books: this car must be a good thing. And in its own special way, this ad has skillfully shifted consumers' attention away from global warming and environmental degradation.

FIGURE 9.3   *President Bush clearing brush from Texas ranch*

FIGURE 9.4   *President Bush greeting a crowd*

FIGURE 9.5   *President Bush delivering a speech at Mount Rushmore*

For Class Discussion

1. The techniques for constructing photos come into play prominently in news photography. In this exercise, we ask you to examine three photographs of President Bush that accompanied news articles appearing in the *New York Times* in summer 2002. These photographs were taken at photo-ops carefully staged by White House staff. Working individually or in groups, study Figures 9.3, 9.4, and 9.5 and then answer the following questions:

   a. What are the most noticeable features of each photo?

   b. What do you think is the dominant impression of Bush that each photo seeks to convey? In other words, what is the implicit argument?

   c. What camera techniques and compositional features do you see in each photo?

   d. What image of President Bush do these photographs attempt to create for citizens and voters?

2. The image on the opening page of Part Three (page 197) is a photograph of the suffragettes' campaign for the vote for women in the early twentieth century. What is the rhetorical effect or impact of this photograph?

   a. What features of the composition of the photo and its type suggest that this is an old photo? What features most stand out in this photo?

   b. What is the dominant impression of this photo?

   c. What image of women does this photo project?

3. Examine carefully the advertisement sponsored by the Center for Consumer Freedom in Color Plate H, and then, working individually or in groups, answer the following questions:

   a. What camera techniques and compositional features do you see in this ad?

   b. What is the proportion of verbal text to image? How would you describe the layout of this ad? How does the text relate to the image?

   c. We think of most ads as *for* some product or organization, yet this ad focuses on what it is *against*. How does the cropping of the image and the intrusiveness of the verbal text help to convey the argument of the ad? How would you summarize the ad's argument?

   d. This ad appeared in *Newsweek*, a news commentary magazine with a general readership. How does the ad use its visual design to reach its audience?

The Genres of Visual Argument

We have already mentioned that verbal arguments today are frequently accompanied by photographs or drawings that contribute to the text's persuasive appeal.

For example, a verbal argument promoting United Nations action to help AIDS victims in Africa might be accompanied by a photograph of a dying mother and child. However, some genres of argument are dominated by visual elements. In these genres, the visual design carries most of the argumentative weight; verbal text is used primarily for labeling, for focusing the argument's claim, or for commenting on the images. In this section we describe specifically these highly visual genres of argument.

Posters and Fliers

To persuade audiences, an arguer might create a poster designed for placement on walls or kiosks or a flier to be passed out on street corners. Posters dramatically attract and direct viewers' attention toward one subject or issue. They often seek to rally supporters, promote a strong stance on an issue, and call people to action. For example, during World War II, posters asked Americans to invest in war bonds and urged women to join the workforce to free men for active combat. During the Vietnam War, famous posters used slogans such as "Make Love Not War" or "Girls say yes to boys who say no" to increase national resistance to the war.

The hallmark of an effective poster is the way it focuses and encodes a complex meaning in a verbal-visual text, often with one or more striking images. These images are often symbolic—for example, using children to symbolize family and home, a soaring bird to symbolize freedom, or three firefighters raising the American flag over the World Trade Center rubble on September 11, 2001, to symbolize American heroism, patriotism, and resistance to terrorism. These symbols derive potency from the values they share with their target audience. Posters tend to use words sparingly, either as slogans or as short, memorable directives. This terse verbal text augments the message encoded in an eye-catching, dominant image.

As an example of a classic poster, consider the Part Opener on page 73, which promotes bicycle riding as an alternative to cars. Note how the drawing of the tortured figures captures imaginatively both the physical damage of air pollution and the psychological damage of being trapped in traffic—ideas also captured in the carefully chosen words, which are charged with double meanings: "Exhausted" denotes both "exhaust" from cars and "exhaustion" from the snarled traffic and the hectic pace of an automobile-dominated life. "Get a life" alludes both to improving your health and to improving the quality of your lived experience through the exercise, simplicity, and freedom of a bicycle.

Fliers and brochures often use visual elements similar to those in posters. An image might be the top and center attraction of a flier or the main focus of the front cover of a brochure. However, unlike posters, fliers and brochures offer additional space for verbal arguments, which often present the writer's claim supported with bulleted lists of reasons. Sometimes pertinent data and statistics, along with testimony from supporters, are placed in boxes or sidebars.

Public Affairs Advocacy Advertisements

Public affairs advocacy advertisements share with posters an emphasis on visual elements, but they are designed specifically for publication in newspapers and magazines and, in their persuasive strategies, are directly analogous to product advertisements. Public affairs advocacy ads are usually sponsored by a corporation or an advocacy organization and often have a more time-sensitive message than do posters and a more immediate and defined target audience. Designed as condensed arguments aimed at influencing public opinion on civic issues, these ads are characterized by their brevity, audience-based appeals, and succinct, "sound bite" style. Often, in order to sketch out their claim and reasons clearly and concisely, they employ headings and subheadings, bulleted lists, different sizes and styles of type, and a clever, pleasing layout on the page. They usually have some attention-getting slogan or headline like "MORE KIDS ARE GETTING BRAIN CANCER. WHY?" or "STOP THE TAX REVOLT JUGGERNAUT!"

The balance between verbal and visual elements in an advocacy advertisement varies. Some advocacy ads are verbal only with visual concerns focused on document design (for example, an "open letter" from the president of a corporation appearing as a full-page newspaper ad). Other advocacy ads are primarily visual, using images and other design elements with the same shrewdness as advertisements. We looked closely at advocacy ads in Chapter 2, where we presented ads opposing and supporting genetically modified foods (Color Plate A, and Color Plate B), and in this chapter in the ads on Ecstasy and "Save the Children."

As another example of a public affairs advocacy ad, consider Figure 9.6, which attempts to counter the influence of the pro-life movement's growing campaign against abortion. Sponsored by the Planned Parenthood Responsible Choices Action Network, this ad appeared in a variety of liberal magazines in the United States. The ad seems to have two targeted audiences in mind: The first audience is persons already committed to a pro-choice stance; the ad urges them to action. The second audience is neutral persons who may support women's rights but may be wavering on their stance toward abortion. Such an audience, the ad makers believe, might be startled into support of the pro-choice position by this stark reminder of the negative consequences of unsafe abortions.

As you can see, this ad is dominated by one stark image: a question mark formed by the hook of a coat hanger. The shape of the hanger hook draws the reader's eye to the concentrated type centered below it. The hanger hook carries most of the weight of the argument. Simple, bold, and harsh, the image of the hanger, tapping readers' cultural knowledge, evokes the dangerous experience of illegal abortions performed crudely by nonmedical people in the dark backstreets of cities. The ad wants viewers to think of the dangerous last resorts that desperate women would have to turn to if they could not obtain abortions legally.

**When
your right
to an abortion
is taken away,
what are you
going to
do**

Reproductive rights are under attack. The Pro-Choice Public Education Project. It's pro-choice or no choice.
1(688) 253-CHOICE or www.protect.choice.org

FIGURE 9.6   *Advocacy advertisement supporting a pro-choice stance*

The hanger itself creates a visual pun: As a question mark, it conveys the ad's dilemma about what will happen if abortions are made illegal. As a coat hanger, it provides the ad's frightening answer to the printed question—desperate women will return to backstreet abortionists who use coat hangers as tools. The further implied question is, "Will you help us prevent this bleak outcome?" The whole purpose of the ad is to motivate people to take action by contacting this organization through the phone number or Web site provided. Note how the word "Responsible" is centered in the final block of text beneath the coat hanger question mark. This organization wants to convey that the "responsible" position on this issue is to keep abortion legal, safe, and available so that women don't have to return to the era of back-alley abortions.

For Class Discussion

Examine the public affairs advocacy ad shown in Color Plate F. This ad, sponsored by the Earthjustice, defends the presence of grizzly bears in Yellowstone National Park as well as other wilderness areas in the Rocky Mountains. In our classes, this ad has yielded rich discussion of its ingenuity and complexity.

Working individually or in groups, conduct your own examination of this ad using the following questions:

1. What visual features of this ad immediately attract your eyes? What principles for effective use of type, layout, and use of color and image does this ad exemplify?
2. What is the core argument of this ad?
3. Why did Earthjustice use the theme of Goldilocks? How do the lizards function in this ad? Why does the ad NOT have any pictures of grizzlies or bears of any kind?
4. How would you design an advocacy ad for the preservation of grizzly bears? What visuals would you use?

After discussing the Earthjustice advocacy ad, explore the rhetorical appeals of another advocacy ad such as the one that appears on the opening page of Part Four on page 355. The designers of this ad, sponsored by the drug-prevention organization Partnership for a Drug Free America®, have also made key choices in choosing the ad's one main image. How does this advocacy ad work to convey its argument? Consider questions about its use of type, layout, color, and image, about the core of its argument, and about its appeals to *ethos* and *pathos*.

Cartoons

An especially charged kind of visual argument is the political cartoon. Although you are perhaps not likely to create your own political cartoons, it is useful to understand how cartoonists use visual and verbal elements to convey their message. British cartoonist Martin Rowson calls himself "a visual journalist" who employs "humor to make a journalistic point." Political cartoons are often mini-narratives, portraying an issue dramatically, compactly, and humorously. They employ images and a few well-chosen words to dramatize conflicts and problems. Using caricature, exaggeration, and distortion, cartoonists distill an issue down to an image that boldly reveals the creator's perspective and subsequent claim on a civic issue. The purpose of political cartoons is usually satirical, or, as cartoonist Rowson says, "about afflicting the comfortable and comforting the afflicted." Because they are so condensed and often connected to current affairs, political cartoons are particularly dependent on the audience's background knowledge of cultural and political events. When political cartoons work well, through their perceptive combination of image and words, they flash a brilliant, clarifying light on a perspective or open a new lens on an issue, often giving readers a shock of insight.

As an illustration, note the Dana Summers cartoon in Figure 9.7, which first appeared in the *Orlando Sentinel* during a period of national debate on the right of music lovers to download free songs and CDs from the Internet. Media opinion often sided with the music industry, which held that free downloading of music constituted theft of intellectual property. A defense sometimes made by music lovers was that the music industry was gouging the market with overpriced CDs. Dana Summers' cartoon constitutes his needle-sharp rebuttal of this common argument.

FIGURE 9.7   *Political cartoon supporting the music industry in the dispute about downloaded music*

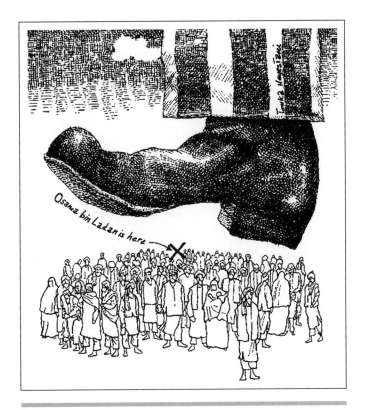

FIGURE 9.8   *Iranian cartoon showing an Iranian perspective on the U.S. war against terrorism*
Touka, CARTOONIST & WRITERS SYNDICATE/cartoonweb.com

For Class Discussion

1. Cartoons can often sum up a worldview in a single image. Figure 9.8, by an Iranian cartoonist, shows an Islamic view of the U.S. war on terrorism, particularly the search for Osama bin Laden. Working in small groups or as a whole class, explain what this cartoon is arguing. From the perspective of this cartoon, how does the Iranian "street" view the United States? How does this cartoonist's view of Osama bin Laden differ from the American view?

2. The opening page of Part One (page 1) shows a political cartoon on genetic engineering of food. What mini-narrative does it convey? What is the cartoon arguing? How does the cartoon use caricature, exaggeration, or distortion to convey its perspective?

Web Pages

So far we have only hinted at the influence of the World Wide Web in accelerating use of visual images in argument. Because reproducing high-quality images (especially color images) is expensive in a print medium, writers of argument prior to the Web often relied mainly on verbal text. But the Web has now made it possible to publish arguments incorporating powerful color images. The hypertext design of Web pages, along with its complex intermixture of text and image, has changed the way many writers think of argument. The home page of an advocacy site, for example, often has many features of a poster argument with hypertext links to galleries of images on the one hand, and to verbal arguments on the other. These verbal arguments themselves often contain photographs, drawings, and graphics. The strategies discussed in this chapter for analyzing and interpreting visual texts also apply to Web pages. Consider, for example, the home page of 50 Years Is Enough: The U.S. Network for Global and Economic Justice (Color Plate I). This organization is opposed to the economic policies of the International Monetary Fund and the World Bank Group, which, the organization claims, has caused widespread suffering and poverty over its fifty year history. The site's design uses colorful posters as "buttons" for its hyperlinks to "About Us," "Take Action," and so forth. How does the home page design and its use of images contribute to the *ethos* of the organization and the *pathos* of its appeal for grass roots action against the World Bank?

Because the Web is such an important tool in research, we have placed our main discussion of Web sites in Chapter 16, pages 369–372. On these pages you will find our explanations for reading, analyzing, and evaluating Web sites.

Constructing Your Own Visual Argument

The most common visual arguments you are likely to create are posters and fliers, public affairs advocacy ads, and possibly Web pages. You may also decide that in longer verbal arguments, the use of visuals or graphics could clarify your points while adding visual variety to your paper. The following guidelines will help you apply your understanding of visual elements in the construction of your own visual arguments.

Guidelines for Creating Visual Arguments

1. *Genre:* Determine where this visual argument is going to appear (bulletin board, passed out as a flier, imagined as a one-page magazine or newspaper spread, or as a Web page).
2. *Audience-based appeals:* Determine who your target audience is.
   - What values and background knowledge of your issue can you assume that your audience has?

- What specifically do you want your audience to think or do after read-ing your visual argument?
- If you are promoting a specific course of action (sign a petition, send money, vote for or against a bill, attend a meeting), how can you make that request clear and direct?

3. *Core of your argument:* Determine what clear claim and reasons will form the core of your argument; decide if this claim and these reasons will be ex-plicitly stated or implicit in your visuals and slogans.

- How much verbal text will you use?
- If the core of your argument will be largely implicit, how can you still make it readily apparent and clear for your audience?

4. *Visual design:* What visual design and layout will grab your audience's at-tention and be persuasive?

- How can font sizes and styles, layout, and color be used in this argu-ment to create a strong impression?
- What balance and harmony can you create between the visual and verbal elements of your argument? Will your verbal elements be a slogan, express the core of the argument, or summarize and comment on the image(s)?

5. *Use of images:* If your argument lends itself to images, what photo or draw-ing would support your claim or have emotional appeal? (If you want to use more than one image, be careful that you don't clutter your page and confuse your message. Simplicity and clarity are important.)

- What image would be memorable and meaningful to your audience? Would a photo image or a drawing be most effective?
- Will your image(s) be used to provide evidence for your claim or illustrate a main idea, evoke emotions, or enhance your credibility and authority?

As an example of a poster argument created by a student, consider Leah Johnson's poster in Figure 9.9. Intended for bulletin boards and kiosks around her college campus, Johnson's work illustrates how a writer can use minimal but well-chosen verbal text, layout, and images to convey a rhetorically effective ar-gument. (That is Leah herself in the photograph.) In this ad, Leah is joining a na-tional conversation about alcohol abuse on college campuses and is proposing a safe way of handling her university's weekly social get-together for older stu-dents, "Thirsty Thursdays." Notice how Leah in this visual argument has focused on her claim and reasons without seeing the need to supply evidence.

For Class Discussion

This exercise asks you to do the thinking and planning for a poster argument to be displayed on your college or university campus. Choose an issue that is

Drink and Then Drive?
Jeopardize My Future?

- Arrest
  - Financial Problems (fines up to $8,125)
    - Increased Insurance Rates
      - License Suspension
        - Criminal Conviction
          - Incarceration
            - Serious Injury or Death

or
Designate a Driver?

It's a no-brainer.
Join your Senior Class at Thirsty Thursday, but
designate a driver.

FIGURE 9.9   *Student advocacy ad promoting the use of designated drivers*

controversial on your campus (or in your town or city), and follow the Guidelines for Creating Visual Arguments on pages 186–187 to envision the view you want to advocate on that issue. What might the core of your argument be? Who is your target audience? Are you representing a group, club, or other organization? What image(s) might be effective in attracting and moving this audience? Possible topics for issues might be commuter parking; poor conditions in the computer lab; student reluctance to use the counseling center; problems with dorm life, financial aid programs, or intramural sports; ways to improve orientation programs for new students, work-study programs, or travel abroad opportunities; or new initiatives such as study groups for the big lecture courses or new service-learning opportunities.

Using Graphics as Visual Arguments

Besides images in the form of photographs and drawings, writers often use quantitative graphics to support arguments using numbers. In Chapter 6 we introduced you to the use of quantitative data in arguments. We discussed the persuasiveness of numbers and showed you ways to use them responsibly in your arguments. (See p. 121.) With the advent of spreadsheet and presentation programs, today's writers often create and import quantitative graphics into their documents. These visuals—such as tables, pie charts, and line or bar graphs—can have great rhetorical power by making numbers tell a story at a glance. In this section, we'll show you how quantitative graphics can make numbers speak. We'll also show you how to incorporate graphics into your text and reference them effectively.

How Tables Contain a Variety of Stories

Data used in arguments usually have their origins in raw numbers collected from surveys, questionnaires, observational studies, scientific experiments, and so forth. Through a series of calculations, the numbers are combined, sorted, and arranged in a meaningful fashion, often in detailed tables. Some of the tables published by the U.S. Census Bureau, for example, contain dozens of pages. The more dense the table, the more their use is restricted to statistical experts who pore over them to analyze their meanings. More useful to the general public are mid-level tables contained on one or two pages that report data at a higher level of abstraction.

Consider, for example, Table 9.2, published by the U.S. Census Bureau in its document "America's Families and Living Arrangements: Population Characteristics" based on the 2000 census. This table shows the marital status of people fifteen years of age and older, broken into gender and age groupings, in March 2000. It also provides comparative data on the "never married" percent of the population in March 2000 and March 1970.

Take a few moments to peruse the table and be certain you know how to read it. You read tables in two directions: from top to bottom and from left to right. Always begin with the title, which tells you what the table contains and includes elements from both the vertical and horizontal dimensions of the table. In this case the vertical dimension presents demographic categories for people "15 years and over": for both sexes, for males, and for females. Each of these gender categories is subdivided into age categories. The horizontal dimension provides information about "marital status." Seven of the columns give total numbers (reported in thousands) for March 2000. The eighth column gives the "percent never married" for March 2000, while

TABLE 9.2 Marital status of people 15 years and over: March 1970 and March 2000 (In thousands)

Characteristic	March 2000								March 1970 percent never married[a]
	Number							Percent never married	
	Total	Married spouse present	Married spouse absent	Separated	Divorced	Widowed	Never married		
Both sexes									
Total 15 years old and over..	213,773	113,002	2,730	4,479	19,881	13,665	60,016	28.1	24.9
15 to 19 years old	20,102	345	36	103	64	13	19,541	97.2	93.9
20 to 24 years old	18,440	3,362	134	234	269	11	14,430	78.3	44.5
25 to 29 years old	18,269	8,334	280	459	917	27	8,252	45.2	14.7
30 to 34 years old	19,519	11,930	278	546	1,616	78	5,071	26.0	7.8
35 to 44 years old	44,804	29,353	717	1,436	5,967	399	6,932	15.5	5.9
45 to 54 years old	36,633	25,460	492	899	5,597	882	3,303	9.0	6.1
55 to 64 years old	23,388	16,393	308	441	3,258	1,770	1,218	5.2	7.2
65 years old and over	32,620	17,827	485	361	2,193	10,484	1,270	3.9	7.6
Males									
Total 15 years old and over..	103,113	56,501	1,365	1,818	8,572	2,604	32,253	31.3	28.1
15 to 19 years old	10,295	69	3	51	29	3	10,140	98.5	97.4
20 to 24 years old	9,208	1,252	75	70	101	–	7,710	83.7	54.7
25 to 29 years old	8,943	3,658	139	170	342	9	4,625	51.7	19.1
30 to 34 years old	9,622	5,640	151	205	712	15	2,899	30.1	9.4
35 to 44 years old	22,134	14,310	387	585	2,775	96	3,981	18.0	6.7
45 to 54 years old	17,891	13,027	255	378	2,377	157	1,697	9.5	7.5
55 to 64 years old	11,137	8,463	158	188	1,387	329	612	5.5	7.8
65 years old and over	13,885	10,084	197	171	849	1,994	590	4.2	7.5
Females									
Total 15 years old and over..	110,660	56,501	1,365	2,661	11,309	11,061	27,763	25.1	22.1
15 to 19 years old	9,807	276	33	52	35	10	9,401	95.9	90.3
20 to 24 years old	9,232	2,110	59	164	168	11	6,720	72.8	35.8
25 to 29 years old	9,326	4,676	141	289	575	18	3,627	38.9	10.5
30 to 34 years old	9,897	6,290	127	341	904	63	2,172	21.9	6.2
35 to 44 years old	22,670	15,043	330	851	3,192	303	2,951	13.0	5.2
45 to 54 years old	18,742	12,433	237	521	3,220	725	1,606	8.6	4.9
55 to 64 years old	12,251	7,930	150	253	1,871	1,441	606	4.9	6.8
65 years old and over	18,735	7,743	288	190	1,344	8,490	680	3.6	7.7

[a]The 1970 percentages include 14-year-olds, and thus are for 14+ and 14–19.
Represents zero or rounds to zero.
Source: U.S. Census Bureau, Current Population Survey, March 2000.

the last column gives the "percent never married" for March 1970. To make sure you know how to read the table, pick a couple of rows at random and say to yourself what each number means. For example, the first row under "Both sexes" gives total figures for the entire population of the United States ages fifteen and older. In March 2000 there were 213,773,000 persons fifteen and older (remember that the numbers are presented in thousands). Of these, 113,002,000 were married and living with their spouses. (If you have a pocket calculator handy, you can do your own arithmetic to determine that roughly 52 percent of people over fifteen are married and living with their spouses.) As you continue across the columns, you'll see that 2,730,000 persons are married but not living with their spouses (a spouse might be stationed overseas or in prison; or a married couple might be maintaining a "commuter marriage" with separate households in different cities). Continuing across the columns, you'll see that 4,479,000 persons were separated from their spouses, 19,881,000 were divorced, and 13,665,000 were widowed, and an additional 60, 016, 000 were never married. In the next to the last column, the number of never married persons is converted to a percentage: 28.1 percent (see for yourself that 60,016 divided by 213,773 is 28.1%). Finally, the last column shows the percentage of never married persons in 1970: 24.9%. These last two columns show us that the number of unmarried persons in the United States rose 3.2 percentage points since 1970.

Now that you know how to read the table, peruse it carefully to see the kinds of stories it tells. What does the table show you, for example, about the percentage of married persons ages 25–29 in 1970 versus 2000? What does it show about different age-related patterns of marriage in males and females? By showing you that Americans are waiting much later in life to get married, a table like this initiates many causal questions for analysis and argument. What has happened in American culture between 1970 and 2000 to explain the startling difference in the percentage of married persons within, say, the 20–24 age bracket? In 2000 only 22 percent of persons in this age bracket were married (we converted "unmarried" to "married" by subtracting 78.3 from 100). However, in 1970, 55 percent of persons in this age bracket were married.

Using a Graph to Tell a Story

Table 9.2, as we have seen, tells the story of how Americans are postponing marriage until later in life. However, one has to peruse the table carefully, poring over it like a sleuth, to tease out the story from the dense columns of numbers. To focus on a key story and make it powerfully immediate, you can create a graph.

Bar Graphs

Suppose, for example, that you are writing an argument in which you want to show that the percentage of married women in age groups 20–29 has dropped significantly since 1970. You could tell this story through a simple bar graph (Figure 9.10).

Bar graphs use bars of varying length, extending either horizontally or vertically, to contrast two or more quantities. As with any graphic presentation, you

Percent

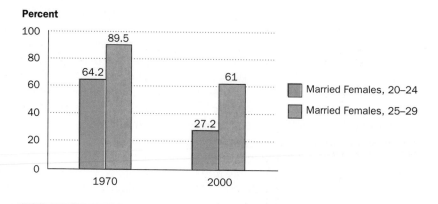

FIGURE 9.10   *Percentage of married females, ages 20–29, 1970 and 2000*
Source: U. S. Census Bureau, Current Population Survey, March 2000.

must create a comprehensive title. In the case of bar graphs, titles tell readers what is being compared to what. Most bar graphs also have "legends," which explain what the different features on the graph represent. Bars are typically distinguished from each other by use of different colors, shades, or patterns of cross-hatching. The special power of bar graphs is that they can help readers make quick comparisons between different groups across a variable such as time.

Pie Charts

Another vivid kind of graph is a pie chart, which depicts different percentages of a total (the pie) in the form of slices. Pie charts are a favorite way of depicting noteworthy patterns in the way parts of a whole are divided up. Suppose, for example,

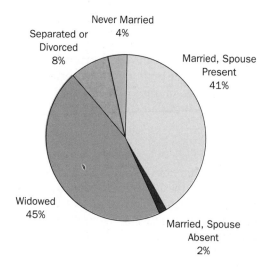

FIGURE 9.11   *Marital status of females, age 65 and older, 2000*

Source: U. S. Census Bureau, Current Population Survey, March 2000.

that you wanted your readers to notice the high percentage of widows among women 65 and older. To do so, you could create a pie chart (Figure 9.11) based on the data in the last row of Table 9.2. As you can see from Figure 9.11 a pie chart can demonstrate at a glance how the whole of something is divided into segments. The effectiveness of pie charts diminishes as you add more slices. In most cases, you'll begin to confuse readers if you include more than five or six slices.

Line Graphs

Another powerful quantitative graphic is a line graph, which converts numerical data into a series of points on a grid and connects them to create flat, rising, or falling lines. The result gives us a picture of the relationship between the variables represented on the horizontal and vertical axes.

Suppose you wanted to tell the story of the rising number of separated/divorced women in the U.S. population. Using Table 9.2, you can calculate the percent of separated/divorced females in 2000 by adding the number of separated females (2,661,000) and the number of divorced females (11,309,000) and dividing that sum by the total number of females (110,660,000). The result is 12.6 percent. You can make the same calculations for 1990, 1980, and 1970 by looking at U.S. census data from those years (available on the Web or in your library). The resulting line graph is shown in Figure 9.12.

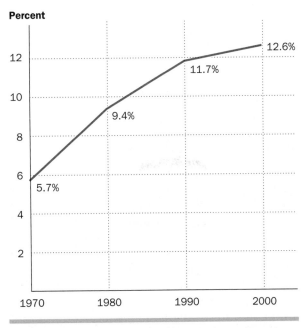

FIGURE 9.12   *Percentage of females ages 15 and older who are separated or divorced, 1970–2000*

Source: U. S. Census Bureau, Current Population Survey, March 2000.

To determine what this graph is telling you, you need to clarify what's represented on the two axes. By convention, the horizontal axis of a graph contains the predictable, known variable that has no surprises—what researchers call the "independent variable." In this case the horizontal axis represents the years 1970–2000 arranged predictably in chronological order. The vertical axis contains the unpredictable variable that forms the graph's story—what researchers call the "dependent variable"—in this case, the percentage of divorced females. The ascending curve tells the story at a glance.

Note that with line graphs the steepness of a slope (and hence the rhetorical effect) can be manipulated by the intervals chosen for the vertical axis. Figure 9.12 shows vertical intervals of 2 percent. The slope could be made less dramatic by choosing intervals of, say, 10 percent and more dramatic by choosing intervals of 1 percent.

Incorporating Graphics into Your Argument

Today writers working with quantitative data usually use graphing software that automatically creates tables, graphs, or charts from data entered into the cells of a spreadsheet. (It is beyond the scope of this textbook to explain how to use these graphing utilities.) For college papers, some instructors may allow you to make your graphs with pencil and ruler and paste them into your document.

Designing the Graphic

When you design your graphic, your goal is to have a specific rhetorical effect on your readers, not to demonstrate all the bells and whistles available on your software. Adding extraneous data in the graph or chart or using such features as a three-dimensional effect can often call attention away from the story you are trying to tell. Keep the graphic as uncluttered and simple as possible and design it so that it reinforces the point you are making in your text.

Numbering, Labeling, and Titling the Graphic

In newspapers and popular magazines, writers often include graphics in boxes or sidebars without specifically referring to them in the text itself. However, in academic or professional workplace writing, graphics are always labeled, numbered, titled, and referred to directly in the text. By convention, tables are listed as "Tables," while line graphs, bar graphs, pie charts, or any other kinds of drawings or photographs are labeled as "Figures." Suppose you create a document that includes four graphics—a table, a bar graph, a pie chart, and an imported photograph. The table would be labeled as Table 1. The rest of the graphics would be labeled as Figure 1, Figure 2, and Figure 3.

In addition to numbering and labeling, every graphic needs a comprehensive title that explains fully what information is being displayed. Look back over the tables and figures in this chapter and compare their titles to the information in the graphics. In a line graph showing changes over time, for example, a typical title will identify the information on both the horizontal and vertical axes and the years covered. Bar graphs also have a "legend" explaining how the bars are coded if necessary. When you import the graphic into your own text, be consistent in where you place the title—either above the graphic or below it.

Referencing the Graphic in Your Text

Academic and professional writers follow a referencing convention called *independent redundancy*. The general rule is this: The graphic should be understandable without the text; the text should be understandable without the graphic; the text should repeat the most important information in the graphic. Suppose, for example, that you

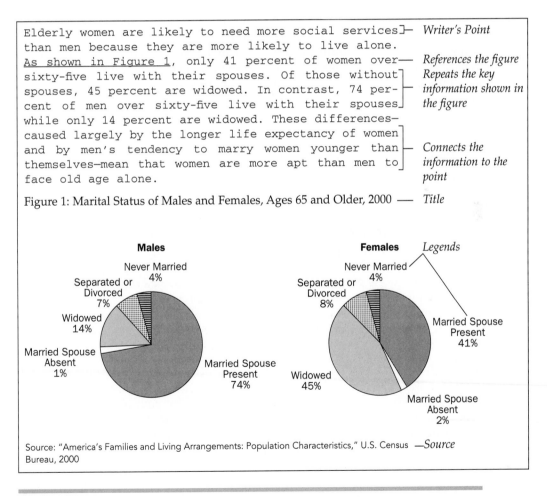

```
Elderly women are likely to need more social services⌐   Writer's Point
than men because they are more likely to live alone.
As shown in Figure 1, only 41 percent of women over──     References the figure
sixty-five live with their spouses. Of those without⌐    Repeats the key
spouses, 45 percent are widowed. In contrast, 74 per-│    information shown in
cent of men over sixty-five live with their spouses⌐    the figure
while only 14 percent are widowed. These differences─
caused largely by the longer life expectancy of women⌐
and by men's tendency to marry women younger than ├     Connects the
themselves—mean that women are more apt than men to│     information to the
face old age alone.                                 ┘    point
```

Figure 1: Marital Status of Males and Females, Ages 65 and Older, 2000 ── *Title*

Males

Never Married 4%
Separated or Divorced 7%
Widowed 14%
Married Spouse Absent 1%
Married Spouse Present 74%

Females

Never Married 4% — *Legends*
Separated or Divorced 8%
Married Spouse Present 41%
Widowed 45%
Married Spouse Absent 2%

Source: "America's Families and Living Arrangements: Population Characteristics," U.S. Census —*Source*
Bureau, 2000

FIGURE 9.13   *Example of a student text with a referenced graph*

are writing an argument saying that social services for the elderly is a women's issue as well as an age issue and you want to use a pie chart that you have constructed. In your text, you would reference this chart and then repeat its key information as shown in Figure 9.13.

Conclusion

In this chapter we have explained the challenge and power of using visuals in arguments. We have examined the components of visual design—use of type, layout, color, and images—and shown how these components can be used for persuasive effect in arguments. We have also described the argumentative genres that depend on effective use of visuals—posters and fliers, advocacy advertisements, cartoons, and Web pages—and invited you to produce your own visual argument. Finally, we showed you that graphics can tell a numeric story in a highly focused and dramatic way. Particularly we explained the functions of tables, bar graphs, pie charts, and line graphs, and showed you how to incorporate into and reference graphics in your own prose.

WRITING ASSIGNMENTS
FOR CHAPTER 9

OPTION 1: *A Poster Argument*   Working with the idea for a poster argument that you explored in the For Class Discussion on page 183, use the visual design concepts and principles presented on page 180 in this chapter, your understanding of the visual argument and the genre of poster arguments, and your own creativity to produce a poster argument that can be displayed on your campus or in your town or city. Try out the draft of your poster argument on people who are part of your target audience. Based on these individuals' suggestions for improving the clarity and impact of this visual argument, prepare a final version of your poster argument.

OPTION 2: *A Microtheme Using A Quantitative Graphic*   Write a short microtheme that tells a story based on data you select from Table 9.2 or from some other table provided by your instructor or located by you. Include in your microtheme at least one quantitative graphic (table, line graph, bar graph, pie chart), which should be labeled and referenced according to standard conventions. Use as a model the short piece shown in Figure 9.13 on page 195.

Part Three

Arguments in Depth

Six Types of Claims

10 An Introduction to the Types of Claims

11 Categorical and Definitional Arguments: X Is (Is Not) a Y

12 Causal Arguments: X Causes (Does Not Cause) Y

13 Resemblance Arguments: X Is (Is Not) like Y

14 Evaluation and Ethical Arguments: X Is (Is Not) a Good Y; X Is Right (Wrong)

15 Proposal Arguments: "We Should (Should Not) Do X"

This photograph of suffragettes in Asbury Park, New Jersey, taken some time between 1914 and 1920, depicts a major historical political issue: women campaigning for the vote.

10 An Introduction to the Types of Claims

In Part One of this text, we discussed the reading and writing of arguments, linking argument to both persuasion and inquiry. In Part Two we examined the internal structure of arguments and showed how persuasive writers link their arguments to the beliefs and values of their audience. We also showed how writers can vary their content, structure, and style to reach audiences with varying degrees of resistance to the writer's views.

Now in Part Three we examine arguments in depth by explaining six types of claims and by showing how each type has its own characteristic patterns of development and support. Because almost all arguments use one or more of these types of claims as basic argumentative "moves" or building blocks, knowing how to develop each claim type will advance your skills in argument. The types of claims to be examined in Part Three are related to an ancient rhetorical concept called *stasis* from a Greek term meaning "stand" as in "to take a *stand* on something." There are many competing theories of stasis, so no two rhetoricians discuss stasis in exactly the same way. But all the theories have valuable components in common.

In Part Three we present our own version of stasis theory, or, to use more ordinary language, our own approach to argument based on the types of claims. The payoff for you will be twofold. First, understanding the types of claims will help you focus an argument and generate ideas for it. Second, a study of claim types teaches you characteristic patterns of support for each type, thereby helping you organize and develop your arguments.

An Overview of the Types of Claims

To appreciate what a study of claim types can do, imagine one of those heated but frustrating arguments—let's suppose it's about gun control—where the question at issue keeps shifting. Everyone talks at cross-purposes, each speaker's point unconnected to the previous speaker's. The disputants start gesticulating at each other, faces contorted, voice levels rising. Sometimes you can get such a discussion back on track if one person says, "Hold it for a moment. What are we actually disagreeing about here? Are we debating whether the government should enact gun control? Whether gun ownership prevents crime? Whether getting a gun license is like getting a car license? Let's figure out what we agree on and where we disagree because we can't debate all these questions at once." Whether she recognizes it or not, this person is applying the concept of claim types to get the argument focused.

To understand how claim types work, let's return to the concept of stasis. A *stasis* is an issue or question that focuses a point of disagreement. You and your audience might agree on the answer to Question A and so have nothing to argue about. Likewise you might agree on the answer to Question B. But on Question C you disagree. Question C constitutes a *stasis* where you and your audience diverge. It is the place where disagreement begins, where as an arguer you take a *stand* against another view. Thus you and your audience might agree that handgun ownership is legal. You might agree further that widespread ownership of handguns reduces crime. But if you ask the question "Is widespread handgun ownership a good thing?" you and your audience might disagree. This last question constitutes a *stasis,* the point where you and your audience part company.

Rhetoricians have discovered that the kinds of questions that divide people have classifiable patterns. In this text we identify six broad types of claims—each type originating in a different kind of question. To emphasize the structural pattern of each type, we will first use an X and a Y to represent slots so that you can focus on the structure rather than the content of the claim type. Then we'll move quickly to actual examples. Here is a brief overview of the six claim types.

Type 1: Simple Categorical Arguments (Is X a Y?, Where You and Your Audience Agree on the Meaning of Y)

A *categorical argument* occurs when persons disagree about the category (Y) that a given thing (X) belongs to. A categorical question is said to be simple if there is no dispute about the meaning of the Y term. Examples of questions leading to simple categorical arguments are the following:

> Is *Sesame Street* a sexist program?
>
> Is surfing the Internet a new kind of addiction?
>
> Was Senator Weasel's vote for increased military spending politically motivated?

In these examples, we assume that writer and audience agree on the meaning of "sexist program," "addiction," and "politically motivated." At issue is whether *Sesame Street,* surfing the Internet, and Senator Weasel belong to these categories.

The strategy for conducting a simple categorical argument is to provide examples or other evidence to show that X does or does not belong to category Y. Yes, *Sesame Street* is sexist (provide examples). Yes, surfing the Internet is a new kind of addiction (provide examples, testimony from psychologists). No, Senator

Weasel's support for new weapons funding was not politically motivated (provide evidence that Weasel has a long record of pro-military spending). Simple categorical arguments are discussed in the first part of Chapter 11.

Type 2: Definitional Arguments
(Is X a Y?, Where the Definition of Y Is Contested)

A categorical argument becomes more complex if you and your audience disagree about the meaning of the Y term. In this second type of claim, you have to define the Y term and defend your definition against objections and alternative definitions. Suppose, for example, you want to argue that using animals for medical research constitutes cruelty to animals. Here you would have to define what you mean by "cruelty to animals" and show how using animals for medical research fits your definition. Almost all legal disputes require definitional arguing because courts must determine whether an action meets or does not meet the criteria for a crime or civil tort as defined by a law, statute, or series of previous court rulings. Examples of questions leading to definitional arguments are the following:

> Is occasional telling of off-color jokes in the workplace an instance of sexual harassment?
>
> Is e-mail spam constitutionally protected free speech?
>
> Is Pluto a planet or an asteroid?

The general strategy for conducting a definitional argument is to define the second term and then argue whether the first term meets or does not meet the definition. We call this strategy *criteria-match arguing* because to define the second term you must specify the criteria that something must meet to fit the category. Then you must argue that your first term does or does not match these criteria. Definitional arguments are treated in depth in Chapter 11.

Type 3: Cause/Consequence Arguments
(Does X Cause Y? Is Y a Consequence of X?)

Another major argument type entails cause and effect reasoning. Often such arguments arise from disagreements about the cause of an event or a trend: "What caused the stock market crash in the summer of 2002?" or "What causes teenage males to become violent?" Just as frequently, causal arguments arise from speculations about the possible consequences of an action: "What will be the consequences of a U.S. invasion of Iraq?" "Will gun control legislation reduce violence in the schools?"

The general strategy for conducting causal arguments is to describe the chain of events that lead from X to Y. If a causal chain cannot be directly established, you can argue indirectly, using inductive methods, statistical analyses, or analogies. Causal arguments are treated in detail in Chapter 12.

Type 4: Resemblance Arguments (Is X like Y?)

A fourth argument type involves disputes about appropriate analogies or precedents. Suppose you disapproved of investing in the stock market and wanted to argue that stock market investing is like gambling. In showing the similarities between investing and gambling, you would be making a resemblance argument. Examples of questions that lead to resemblance arguing are the following:

> Was Slobodan Milosevic's policy of "ethnic cleansing" in Kosovo like Hitler's "final solution" against the Jews?
>
> Is killing starlings in your attic like killing rats in your attic? (Are starlings like rats?)
>
> Does pornography disparage women the way neo-Nazi propaganda disparages people of color? (Is pornography like racist propaganda?)

The general strategy for resemblance arguments is to compare the first term to the second, pointing out similarities between them (if your goal is to make X like Y) or differences between them (if your goal is to make X unlike Y). Resemblance arguments are covered in Chapter 13.

Type 5: Evaluation Arguments
(Is X Good or Bad? Is X a Good or Bad Y?)

Categorical, causal, and resemblance arguments (types 1–4) are often called reality or truth arguments. In such arguments, people question the way things are, were, or will be; they are disagreeing about the nature of reality. In contrast, evaluation and proposal arguments (types 5 and 6) deal with values, what people consider important, good, or worth doing. Although a person's values often begin as feelings founded on personal experience, they can nevertheless form the basis of reasonable argument in the public sphere if they are articulated and justified. When you articulate your values, explain their source (if necessary), and apply them consistently to specific cases, you make your values transpersonal and shareable and can use them to build coherent and reasonable arguments.

Evaluation arguments (type 5) ask questions about whether X is good or bad. Examples of evaluation questions are the following:

> Is a European-style, single-payer health insurance system a good policy for the United States to enact?
>
> Is acquiring job experience between college and graduate school a good career plan?
>
> Is a sport-utility vehicle a good urban vehicle?

The general strategy for evaluation arguments uses criteria-match arguing similar to that used for definitional arguments: You first establish your criteria for "good" in the specific case and then show how your first term does or does not meet the criteria. A special category of evaluation arguments deals with ethical or moral issues (for example, "Is it morally justifiable to spank children?" or "Is it ethical to use human stem cells for medical research?") Evaluation arguments, including ethical evaluations, are covered in Chapter 14.

Type 6: Proposal Arguments (Should We Do X?)

Whereas argument types 1–5 all involve changing your audience's beliefs about something—whether about reality (types 1–4) or about the value of something (type 5)—proposal arguments call for action. Proposals ask your audience to *do* something, to act in some way. Typically, proposals use words like *should, ought,* or *must* followed by an action of some kind. The following questions all lead to proposal arguments:

> Should the United States provide universal health care for its citizens?
>
> Should teens who commit crimes receive the same sentences as adult criminals?
>
> Should gay marriages be legalized?

The most typical strategy for making proposal arguments is to follow a problem-solution-justification structure whereby the opening section convinces the audience that a problem exists, the second section proposes a solution to solve the problem, and the last section justifies the solution by demonstrating that the benefits of acting on the proposal outweigh the costs or that the inherent "rightness" of the solution (on moral grounds) compels action. Proposal arguments are covered in Chapter 15.

For Class Discussion

Working as a whole class or in small groups, decide which claim type is represented by each of the following questions. Sometimes the argument categories overlap or blend together. For example, the question "Is airline travel safe?" might be considered either a simple categorical question or an evaluation question.

1. Should violent video games be made illegal?
2. How effective is aspirin in reducing the risk of heart attacks and stroke?
3. Why is anorexia nervosa primarily a white, middle-class female disease?
4. Is depression in the elderly common in Asian cultures?
5. Were the terrorist attacks of September 11, 2001, like Pearl Harbor (an act of war) or like an earthquake (a natural disaster)?

6. Should professional baseball impose a salary cap on its superstar players?

7. Is this Web site racist?

8. Is tobacco a drug?

9. Are Nike's Asian shoe factories sweatshops?

10. Do American girls tend to lose self-esteem when they reach puberty, as claimed by some researchers?

What Is the Value of Studying Claim Types?

Having provided an overview of the types of claims, we conclude this chapter by showing you two substantial benefits you will derive from knowing about each type: help in focusing and generating ideas for an argument and help in organizing and developing an argument.

Help in Focusing an Argument and Generating Ideas

Knowing the different types of claims can help you focus an argument and generate ideas for it. Understanding claim types helps you focus by asking you to determine what's at stake between you and your audience. Where do you and your audience agree and disagree? What are the questions at issue? It helps you generate ideas by guiding you to pose questions that suggest lines of development.

To illustrate, let's take a hypothetical case—one Isaac Charles Little (affectionately known as I. C. Little), who desires to chuck his contact lenses and undergo the new lasik procedure to cure his nearsightedness. ("Lasik" is the common name for laser in-situ keratomileusis, a recent advance in surgical treatments for myopia. Sometimes known as "flap and zap" surgery, it involves using a laser to cut a layer of the corneal tissue thinner than a human hair and then flattening the cornea. It's usually not covered by insurance and is quite expensive.) I. C. has two different arguments he'd like to make: (1) He'd like to talk his parents into helping him pay for the procedure, and (2) he'd like to convince insurance companies that the lasik procedure should be covered under standard medical insurance policies. In the discussions that follow, note how the six types of claims can help I. C. identify points of disagreement for each audience and simultaneously suggest lines of argument for persuading each one. Note, too, how the questions at issue vary for each audience.

First imagine what might be at stake in I. C.'s discussions with his parents.

Claim Type Analysis: Parents as Audience

■ *Simple categorical argument:* I. C.'s parents will be concerned about the safety and effectiveness of this procedure. Is lasik safe? Is it effective? (These are the first questions at issue. I. C.'s mom has heard a horror story about an earlier surgical procedure for myopia, so I. C. knows he will have to persuade her that lasik is safe and effective.)

- *Definitional argument:* With parents as audience, I. C. will have to define what lasik surgery is so they won't have misconceptions about what is involved. However, he can't think of any arguments that would ensue over this definition, so he proceeds to the next claim type.

- *Causal argument:* Both parents will question I. C.'s underlying motivation for seeking this surgery. "What causes you to want this lasik procedure?" they will ask. (I. C.'s dad, who has worn eyeglasses all his adult life, will not be swayed by cosmetic desires. "If you don't like contacts," he will say, "just wear glasses.") Here I. C. needs to argue that permanently correcting his nearsightedness will improve his quality of life. I. C. decides to emphasize his desire for an active, outdoor life, and especially his passion for water sports including swimming and scuba diving, where his need for contacts or glasses is a serious handicap. Also, I. C. says that if he doesn't have to wear contacts he can get a summer job as a lifeguard.

- *Resemblance argument:* I. C. can't think of any resemblance questions at issue.

- *Evaluation argument:* When the pluses and minuses are weighed, is lasik a good thing? Would the results of the surgery be beneficial enough to justify the cost and the risks? In terms of costs, I. C. might argue that even though the procedure is initially expensive (from $1,000 to $4,000), over the years he will save money by not needing contacts or glasses. The pleasure of seeing well in the water and not being bothered by contacts or glasses while hiking and camping constitutes a major psychological benefit. (The cosmetic benefits—I. C. thinks he'll look cooler without glasses—he decides to leave out, since his dad thinks wearing glasses is fine.)

- *Proposal:* Should I. C. (or a person in general) get this operation for treatment of myopia? (All the previous points of disagreement are subissues related to this overarching proposal issue.)

What this example should help you see is that the values arguments in the last two claim types (evaluation and proposal) depend on the writer's resolving related reality/truth questions in one or more of the first four types (simple categorical, definition, cause, resemblance). In this particular case, before convincing his parents that they should help him pay for the lasik procedure (I. C.'s proposal claim), I. C. would need to convince them that the procedure is safe and effective (simple categorical arguments), that there are significant recreational and professional benefits that would result from this surgery (causal argument), and that the benefits outweigh the costs (evaluation argument). Almost all arguments combine subarguments in this way so that lower-order claims provide supporting materials for addressing higher-order claims.

The previous illustration focused on parents as audience. If we now switch audiences, we can use our theory of claim types to identify different questions at issue. Let's suppose I. C. wants to persuade insurance companies to cover the lasik procedure. He imagines insurance company decision makers as his primary audience, along with the general public and state legislators who may be able to influence them.

Claim Type Analysis: Insurance Decision Makers as Audience

- *Simple categorical argument:* No disagreements come immediately to mind (This audience shares I. C.'s belief that lasik is safe and effective.)
- *Definitional argument:* Should lasik be considered "cosmetic surgery" (as insurance companies contend) or as "medically justifiable surgery" (as I. C. contends)? This definitional question constitutes a major stasis. I. C. wants to convince his audience that lasik belongs in the category of "medically justifiable surgery" rather than "cosmetic surgery." He will need to define "medically justifiable surgery" in such a way that lasik can be included.
- *Causal argument:* What will be the consequences to insurance companies and to the general public of making insurance companies pay for lasik? For this audience, consequence issues are crucial. Will insurance companies be overloaded with claims? What will happen to insurance rates? Will optometrists and eyeglass manufacturers go out of business?
- *Resemblance argument:* Does lasik more resemble a facelift (not covered by insurance) or plastic surgery to repair a cleft palate (covered by insurance)?
- *Evaluation argument:* Would it be good for society as a whole if insurance companies had to pay for lasik?
- *Proposal argument:* Should insurance companies be required to cover lasik?

As this analysis shows, the questions at issue change when you consider a different audience. Now the chief question at issue is definition: Is lasik cosmetic surgery or medically justifiable surgery? I. C. needs to spend no time arguing that the surgery is safe and effective (major concerns for his parents); instead he must establish criteria for "medically justifiable surgery" and then argue that lasik meets these criteria. Again note how the higher-order issues of value depend on resolving one or more lower-order issues of truth/reality.

So what can a study of claim types teach you about focusing an argument and generating ideas? First, it teaches you to analyze what's at stake between you and your audience by determining major points of disagreement. Second, it shows that you can make any of the claim types your argument's major focus. Rather than tackle a values issue, you might tackle only a reality/truth issue. You could, for example, focus an entire argument on the simple categorical question "Is lasik safe?" (an argument requiring you to research the medical literature). Likewise you could write a causal argument focusing on what might happen to optometrists and eyeglass manufacturers if the insurance industry decided to cover lasik. Often arguers jump too quickly to issues of value without first resolving issues of reality/truth. Finally, a study of claim types helps you pose questions that generate ideas and suggest lines of reasoning. Later in Part Three, we will show you a particularly powerful way of using lower-order questions about reality/truth to generate supporting ideas for a proposal argument (see Chapter 15, pp. 330–331).

For Class Discussion

Select an issue familiar to most members of the class—perhaps a current campus issue, an issue prominent in the local or national news, or an issue that the class has recently discussed—and analyze it using our sequence of claim types. Consider how a writer or speaker might address two different audiences on this issue. Hypothesizing the writer/speaker's perspective and claim, make a list of points of agreement and disagreement for both audiences, using as a pattern our claim types analyses for lasik.

Help in Organizing and Developing an Argument

The second main benefit of studying claim types will become clearer as you read the chapters in Part Three. Because each type of claim has its own characteristic pattern of development, learning these patterns will help you organize and develop your arguments. Studying claim types shows you how different arguments are typically structured, teaching you generic moves needed in many different kinds of argumentative situations. If, for example, you make a proposal claim, a study of claim types will show you the generic moves typically needed in proposal arguments. If one of your supporting reasons is a definition claim or an evaluation claim, study of claim types will show you how to do the criteria-match arguing typical of such claims. Likewise such a study shows you how to develop each of the other claim types to help you construct arguments that tap into your audience's values and that include strong support to overcome your audience's resistance.

In the following chapters in Part Three, we discuss each of the claim types in depth.

11 Categorical and Definitional Arguments

X Is (Is Not) a Y

CASE 1

Following the terrorist attacks of September 11, 2001, the capture of Taliban and Al Qaeda fighters in Afghanistan gave rise to wrenching definitional questions. Was a captured Afghani fighter a "prisoner of war," in which case he was guaranteed certain rights by the Geneva Convention, including a right to a standard of food, health care, and shelter equivalent to that of U.S. troops and the right to be released and returned to his native country when the war was over? Or was a captured fighter an "unlawful combatant" still guaranteed humane treatment under the Geneva Convention but with fewer rights than a POW? Or was a captured fighter a "suspected terrorist" not entitled to any protection under the Geneva Convention? The U.S. executive branch argued that the Geneva Convention does not apply to a war against terrorism. The Human Rights Watch, an organization that opposed the U.S. treatment of prisoners in Guantanamo Bay, argued that the prisoners were captured in a war against Afghanistan (rather than against "terrorism" in general) and that most of the detainees met the four criteria for POW status: (1) be under the control of a responsible commander; (2) carry arms openly; (3) wear uniforms with distinct insignia; and (4) conduct their operations in accordance with the laws and customs of war. These definitional issues were bitterly debated in the media.

CASE 2

Recent developments in reproductive technology are creating complex definitional questions. For example, suppose an infertile couple conceives several embryos in a test tube and then freezes the fertilized embryos for future use. What category do those frozen embryos belong to when the couple divorces and disagrees about the disposition of the embryos? (In one actual case, the woman wanted to use the frozen embryos to try to get pregnant, and the man wanted to destroy the embryos.) What should be done with the embryos and who decides? Should frozen embryos be categorized as "persons," thus becoming analogous to children in custody arguments? Or should they be divided up as "property" with the man getting one half of the frozen embryos and the woman getting the other half? Or should a new legal category be created for them that regards them as more than property but less than actual persons? In one court case, the judge decided that frozen embryos "are not, strictly speaking, either 'persons' or 'property,' but occupy an interim category that entitles them to special respect because of their potential for human life."*

An Overview of Categorical Arguments

Categorical arguments are among the most common argument types you will encounter. They occur whenever you claim that any given X belongs in category Y. Does skateboarding belong in the category "true sport"? Should this forthcoming movie be placed in the category PG-13 or the category R? Is graffiti "art" or "vandalism"? Does my swerving across the center lane while trying to slap a bee on my windshield belong in the category "reckless driving"?

We place items in categories all the time, and the categories we choose can have subtle but powerful rhetorical effects, creating implicit mini-arguments. For example, if you don't like unsolicited e-mail, you might place it in the category "spam" and support legislation to make spam illegal. But people who make their livings through e-mail advertising place the same messages in the category "constitutionally protected free speech." If you favor biotech corn, you want to place it in the broad category "corn" and keep the term "biotech" off labels on cans. If you oppose it, you want to classify it as "frankenfood." Or consider the competing categories proposed for whales in an international whaling controversy accelerated by the recent desires of whaling nations such as Japan to resume commercial whaling. What category does a whale belong to? Some arguers place whales in the category "sacred animals" that should never be killed because of their intelligence, beauty, grace, and power. Others categorize whales as a "renewable food resource" like tuna, crabs, cattle, and chickens. Others worry whether the specific kinds of whales being hunted are an "endangered species"—a concept that argues for the preservation of whale stocks but not necessarily for a ban on controlled hunting of individual whales once population numbers rise sufficiently. Each of these whaling arguments places whales within a different category that implicitly urges the reader to adopt that category's perspective on whaling.

Categorical claims shift from implicit to explicit arguments whenever the arguer supplies reasons and evidence to persuade us that X does (or does not) belong in category Y. In the rest of this chapter we discuss two kinds of categorical arguments: (1) simple categorical arguments in which the writer and an audience agree on the meaning of the Y term and (2) definitional arguments in which the meaning of the Y term is itself controversial.

---

*See Vincent F. Stempel, "Procreative Rights in Assisted Reproductive Technology: Why the Angst?" *Albany Law Review 62* (1999), 1187.

Simple Categorical Arguments

A categorical argument can be said to be "simple" if there is no disagreement about the meaning of the Y term. For example, suppose you are discussing with fellow committee members whom to select as committee chairperson. You want to make the case that "David won't make a good committee chair because he is too bossy." Your supporting reason ("David is too bossy") is a simple categorical claim. You assume that everyone agrees what *bossy* means; the point of contention is whether David is or is not bossy. To support your claim, you would supply examples of David's bossiness. To refute it, someone else might supply counterexamples of David's cooperative and kind nature. As this example suggests, the basic procedural rule for developing a simple categorical claim is to supply examples and other data that show how X is (or is not) a member of category Y.

Difference between Facts and Simple Categorical Claims

Simple categorical claims are interpretive statements about reality. They claim that something does (or does not) exist or that something does (or does not) possess the qualities of a certain category. Often simple categorical claims look like facts, so it is important to distinguish between a fact and a simple categorical claim.

A *fact* is a statement that can be verified in some way, either by empirical observation or by reference to a reliable source (say, an encyclopedia) trusted by you and your audience. Here are some facts: Water freezes at 32 degrees. Boise is in Idaho, not Montana. The bald eagle is no longer on the EPA's endangered species list. These are all facts because they can be verified; no supporting arguments are needed or called for.

In contrast, a *simple categorical claim* is a contestable interpretation of facts. Consider the difference between these two sentences:

> *Fact:* The bald eagle is no longer on the EPA's endangered species list.
>
> *Simple categorical claim:* The bald eagle is no longer an endangered species.

The factual statement can be verified by looking at the list of endangered species published by the Environmental Protection Agency. We can see the date the bald eagle was placed on the list (1973) and the date it was removed (1995). The second statement is a claim. Imagine all the debates and arguments the EPA must have had as it pored over statistical data about eagle population numbers and over field reports from observers of eagles before deciding to remove the bald eagle from the list.

Often, it is difficult to draw the line between a fact and a claim. The acceptance or skepticism of a given audience can determine what passes as a fact or what becomes a claim that the arguer needs to support. Consider the statement "John F. Kennedy was killed by Lee Harvey Oswald." Most people call this statement a fact; to them, the report of the Warren Commission appointed to investigate the assassination is a reliable document that settles the issue. But conspiracy theorists, many of whom regard the Warren report as an unreliable rush to judgment, consider the statement above a highly contestable claim.

For Class Discussion

Working individually or in small groups, determine which of the following statements are facts and which are categorical claims. If you think a statement could be a "fact" for some audiences and a "claim" for others, explain your reasoning.

1. State sales taxes are not deductible on your federal income tax form.
2. State sales taxes are annoying to both buyers and sellers.
3. State sales taxes are a hardship on low-income families.
4. Nelly is a recording artist.
5. Nelly is a rapper.
6. Nelly is a gangsta rapper.
7. Eleanor Roosevelt was a very unconventional woman.
8. Eleanor Roosevelt was the most influential first lady ever to inhabit the White House.
9. Eleanor Roosevelt sometimes seemed anti-Semitic.
10. Eleanor Roosevelt was one of the drafters of the United Nations' Universal Declaration of Human Rights.

Variations in the Wording of Simple Categorical Claims

Simple categorical claims typically take the grammatical structure "X is a Y." Grammarians describe this structure as a subject followed by a linking verb (such as *to be* or *to seem*) followed by a predicate noun or adjective:

David is bossy.

State sales taxes are annoying.

Eleanor Roosevelt sometimes seemed anti-Semitic.

But other grammatical constructions can be used to make the same categorical claims:

David frequently bosses people around. (He belongs to the category "people who are bossy.")

Sales taxes really annoy people. (Sales taxes belong to the category "things that are annoying.")

On occasion, Eleanor Roosevelt made anti-Semitic remarks. (Eleanor Roosevelt belongs to the category "people who occasionally seem anti-Semitic.")

Almost any kind of interpretive statement about reality (other than causal statements, which are covered in Chapter 12) is a categorical claim of some kind. Here are a couple more examples of different kinds of categorical claims that can be translated into an "X is Y" format:

The Kosovo Liberation Army waged terrorism against the Serbs. (The Kosovo Liberation Army was in part an anti-Serb terrorist organization.)

Corporations often exaggerate the money they give to charities. (Corporate claims about their charitable giving are often exaggerated.)

Our point is to demonstrate that categorical claims are very common. Whether they are worded directly as "X is Y" statements or disguised in different grammatical structures, they assert that item X belongs in category Y or possesses the features of category Y.

Supporting Simple Categorical Claims: Supply Examples

The basic strategy for supporting a simple categorical claim is to give examples or other data showing how X belongs in category Y. If you want to argue that Sam is a party animal, provide examples of his partying behavior. If you want to argue that Eleanor Roosevelt sometimes seemed anti-Semitic, quote excerpts of anti-Semitic statements from her personal correspondence.* Because simple categorical arguments are common building blocks for longer, more complex arguments, they often take no more than one or two paragraphs inside a longer piece.

For an example of a simple categorical argument, consider the following paragraph from an article supporting regulated hunting of whales. In this article, the writer explains that many countries oppose whaling because they are no longer dependent on whale oil, having found synthetic substitutes. Whaling was never a deep part of the culture of these industrialized countries. As part of his argument, the writer wants to contrast these countries with traditional whaling countries. He makes the categorical claim that in Norway and Japan whaling was an "ancient occupation" worthy of respect. The following paragraph supports that categorical claim:

Things were different in other nations, especially Norway and Japan, where whaling is an ancient occupation worthy of the respect and support that Americans award to, say, the running of a farm. Norwegians view whaling as part of the hard, honorable life of a fisherman—a reliable slow-season activity that helps fishing communities to make it through the year. The Japanese who come from a long line of whalers have deeply

---

*Roosevelt's biographer Blanche Wiesen Cook deals sensitively with this complex issue, largely exonerating Roosevelt from the charge of anti-Semitism. See *Eleanor Roosevelt*, vol. 2, *1933–38* (New York: Viking, 1999).

held moral beliefs about maintaining their family tradition. To be prevented from honoring their ancestors in this manner is a source of shame. After the 1982 moratorium [on whaling] some Norwegian fishers went bankrupt. The same thing happened in Iceland. Given the abundance of the whale stocks, these nations ask, why can't such people be free to practice their traditional livelihood? Anthropologists have long observed the primary role played by traditional foods in the social structure and moral norms of a community—a role that is captured in the widely repeated aphorism "you are what you eat." Asking people to give up their customary diet is in many ways like asking them to give up part of their identity.*

Of course, a simple categorical claim can also be the thesis for a whole argument. We provide such an example in the letter to the editor (pp. 231–232) by the director general of the Taipei Economic and Cultural Office, arguing that Taiwan meets the criteria for admission to the United Nations.

Refuting Simple Categorical Claims

If you wish to challenge or question someone else's simple categorical claim, you have three common strategies at your disposal:

- *Deny the accuracy or truth of the examples and data.* "You say that David is bossy. But you are remembering incorrectly. That wasn't David who did those bossy things; that was Paul."

- *Provide counterexamples that place X in a different category.* "Well, maybe David acted bossy on a few occasions. But more often he is kind and highly cooperative. For example . . ."

- *Raise definitional questions about the Y term.* "Well, that depends on what you mean by 'bossy.' What you call bossiness, I call decisiveness."

The last of these strategies shows how easily a simple categorical claim can slip into a definitional dispute. In the rest of this chapter we turn our attention to definitional arguments.

For Class Discussion

Working as a whole class or in small groups, prepare brief arguments in support of each of the following categorical claims. Then discuss ways that you might call these claims into question.

1. Americans today are obsessed with their appearance.
2. Professional athletes are overpaid.
3. The video games most enjoyed by children are extremely violent.

---

*William Aron, William Burke, and Milton Freeman. "Flouting the Convention." *Atlantic* May 1999, 26.

An Overview of Definitional Arguments

As we turn now to definitional arguments, it is important to distinguish between cases where definitions are *needed* and cases where definitions are *disputed*. Many arguments require a definition of key terms. If you are arguing, for example, that after-school jobs are harmful to teenagers because they promote materialism, you will probably need to define *materialism* somewhere in your argument. Writers regularly define key words for their readers by providing synonyms, by citing a dictionary definition, by stipulating a definition, or by some other means. In the rest of this chapter, we focus on arguments in which the meaning of a key term is disputed. Consider, for example, the environmental controversy over the definition of *wetlands*. Section 404 of the federal Clean Water Act provides for federal protection of wetlands, but it leaves the task of defining wetlands to administrative agencies and the courts. Currently about 5 percent of the land surface of the contiguous forty-eight states is potentially affected by the wetlands provision, and 75 percent of this land is privately owned. Efforts to define wetlands have created a battleground between pro-environment and pro-development (or pro–private property rights) groups. Farmers, homeowners, and developers often want a narrow definition of wetlands so that more property is available for commercial or private use. Environmentalists favor a broad definition in order to protect different habitat types and maintain the environmental safeguards that wetlands provide (control of water pollution, spawning grounds for aquatic species, floodwater containment, and so forth). The problem is that defining wetlands is tricky. For example, one federal regulation defines a wetland as any area that has a saturated ground surface for twenty-one consecutive days during the year. But how would you apply this law to a pine flatwood ecosystem that was wet for ten days this year but thirty days last year? And how should the courts react to lawsuits claiming that the regulation itself is either too broad or too narrow? One can see why the wetlands controversy provides hefty incomes for lawyers and congressional lobbyists.

The Criteria-Match Structure of Definitional Arguments

As the wetlands example suggests, definitional arguments usually have a two-part structure—a definition part that tries to establish the meaning of the Y term (What do we mean by *wetland?*) and a match part that argues whether a given X meets that definition (Does this 30-acre parcel of land near Swan Lake meet the criteria for a wetland?). We use the term *criteria-match* to describe this structure, which occurs regularly not only in definitional arguments but also, as we shall see in Chapter 14, in evaluation arguments of the type "X is (is not) a good Y." The *criteria* part of the structure defines the Y term by setting forth the criteria that must be met for something to be considered a Y. The *match* part examines whether the X term meets these criteria. Here are some examples:

- *Definitional issue:* In a divorce proceeding, is a frozen embryo a "person" rather than "property"?

  Criteria part: What criteria must be met for something to be a "person"?

  Match part: Does a frozen embryo meet these criteria?

- *Definitional issue:* For purposes of my feeling good about buying my next pair of running shoes, is the Hercules Shoe Company a socially responsible company?

  Criteria part: What criteria must be met for a company to be deemed "socially responsible"?

  Match part: Does the Hercules Shoe Company meet these criteria?

To show how a definitional issue can be developed into a claim with supporting reasons, let's look more closely at this second example. Let's suppose you work for a consumer information group that wishes to encourage patronage of socially responsible companies while boycotting irresponsible ones. Your group's first task is to define *socially responsible company.* After much discussion and research, your group establishes three criteria that a company must meet to be considered socially responsible:

> *Your definition:* A company is socially responsible if it (1) avoids polluting the environment, (2) sells goods or services that contribute to the well-being of the community, and (3) treats its workers justly.

The criteria section of your argument would explain and illustrate these criteria.

The match part of the argument would then try to persuade readers that a specific company does or does not meet the criteria. A typical thesis statement might be as follows:

> *Your thesis statement:* Although the Hercules Shoe Company is nonpolluting and provides a socially useful product, it is *not* a socially responsible company because it treats workers unjustly.

Here is how the core of the argument could be displayed in Toulmin terms (note how the criteria established in your definition serve as warrants for your argument):

INITIAL ENTHYMEME: The Hercules Shoe Company is not a socially responsible company because it treats workers unjustly.

CLAIM: The Hercules Shoe Company is *not* a socially responsible company.

STATED REASON: because it treats workers unjustly

GROUNDS: evidence that the company manufactures its shoes in East Asian sweatshops; evidence of the inhumane conditions in these shops; evidence of hardships imposed on displaced American workers

WARRANT: Socially responsible companies treat workers justly.

BACKING: arguments showing that just treatment of workers is right in principle and also benefits society; arguments that capitalism helps society as a whole only if workers achieve a reasonable standard of living, have time for leisure, and are not exploited

POSSIBLE CONDITIONS OF REBUTTAL Opponents of this thesis might argue that justice needs to be considered from an emerging nation's standpoint: The wages paid workers are low by American standards but are above average by East Asian standards. Displacement of American workers is part of the necessary adjustment of adapting to a global economy and does not mean that a company is unjust.

As this Toulmin frame illustrates, the writer's argument needs to contain a criteria section (warrant and backing) showing that just treatment of workers is a criterion for social responsibility and a match section (stated reason and grounds) showing that the Hercules Shoe Company does not treat its workers justly. Your audience's initial beliefs determine how much emphasis you need to place on justifying each criterion and supporting each match. The conditions of rebuttal help the writer imagine alternative views and see places where opposing views need to be acknowledged and rebutted.

For Class Discussion

Consider the following definitional claims. Working as individuals or in small groups, identify the criteria issue and the match issue for each of the following claims.

EXAMPLE: A Honda assembled in Ohio is (is not) an American-made car.

CRITERIA PART: What criteria have to be met before a car can be called "American made"?

MATCH PART: Does a Honda assembled in Ohio meet these criteria?

1. Enron's accounting practices did (did not) constitute an illegal pyramid scheme.
2. Writing graffiti on subways is (is not) vandalism.
3. American Sign Language is (is not) a "foreign language" for purposes of a college graduation requirement.
4. Beauty contests are (are not) sexist events.
5. Bungee jumping from a crane is (is not) a "carnival amusement ride" subject to state safety inspections.

Conceptual Problems of Definition

Before moving on to discuss ways of defining the Y term in a definitional argument, we should explore briefly some of the conceptual difficulties of definition. Language, for all its wonderful powers, is an arbitrary system that requires agreement among its users before it can work. And it's not always easy to get that agreement. In fact, the task of defining something can be devilishly complex.

Why Can't We Just Look in the Dictionary?

What's so hard about defining? you might ask. Why not just look in a dictionary? To get a sense of the complexity of defining something, consider again the word *wetland*. A dictionary can tell us the ordinary meaning of a word (the way it is commonly used), but it can't resolve a debate between competing definitions when different parties have interests in defining the word in different ways. For example, the *Webster's Seventh New Collegiate Dictionary* defines *wetland* as "land containing much soil moisture"—a definition that is hardly helpful in determining whether the federal government can prevent the development of a beach resort on some landowner's private property. Moreover, dictionary definitions rarely tell us such things as *to what degree* a given condition must be met before it qualifies for class membership. How wet does a wetland have to be before it is *legally* a wetland? How long does this wetness have to last? When is a wetland a mere swamp that ought to be drained rather than protected?

Definitions and the Rule of Justice: At What Point Does X Quit Being a Y?

For some people, all this concern about definition may seem misplaced. How often, after all, have you heard people accuse each other of getting bogged down in "mere semantics"? But how we define a given word can have significant implications for people who must either use the word or have the word used on them. Take, for example, what some philosophers refer to as the *rule of justice*. According to this rule, "Beings in the same essential category should be treated in the same way." Should an insurance company, for example, treat anorexia nervosa as a physical illness like diabetes (in which case treatment is paid for by the insurance company) or as a mental illness like paranoia (in which case insurance payments are minimal)? Or, to take another example, if a company gives "new baby" leave to a mother, should it also give "new baby" leave to a father? In other words, is this kind of leave "new mother" leave, or is it "new parent" leave? And what if a couple adopts an infant? Should "new mother" or "new parent" leave be available to adoptive parents also? These questions are all definitional issues involving arguments about what class of beings an individual belongs to and about what actions to take to comply with the rule of justice, which demands that all members of that class be treated equally.

The rule of justice becomes even harder to apply when we consider Xs that grow, evolve, or otherwise change through time. When Young Person back in Chapter 1 argued that she could set her own curfew because she was mature, she raised the question "What are the attributes or criteria of a 'mature' person?" In this case, a categorical distinction between two separate kinds of things ("mature" versus "not mature") evolves into a distinction of degree ("mature enough"). So perhaps we should ask not whether Young Person is mature but whether she is "mature enough." At what point does a child become an adult? (When does a fetus become a human person? When does a social drinker become an alcoholic?)

Although we may be able arbitrarily to choose a particular point and declare, through stipulation, that "mature" means eighteen years old or that "human person" includes a fetus at conception, or at three months, or at birth, in the everyday world the distinction between child and adult, between egg and person, between social drinking and alcoholism seems an evolution, not a sudden and definitive step. Nevertheless, our language requires an abrupt shift between classes. In short, applying the rule of justice often requires us to adopt a digital approach to reality (switches are either on or off, either a fetus is a human person or it is not), whereas our sense of life is more analogical (there are numerous gradations between on and off, there are countless shades of gray between black and white).

As we can see by the preceding examples, the promise of language to fix what psychologist William James called "the buzz and confusion of the world" into an orderly set of categories turns out to be elusive. In most definitional debates, an argument, not a quick trip to the dictionary, is required to settle the matter.

For Class Discussion

Suppose your landlord decides to institute a "no pets" rule. The rule of justice requires that all pets have to go—not just your neighbor's barking dog, but also Mrs. Brown's cat, the kids' hamster downstairs, and your own pet tarantula. That is, all these animals have to go unless you can argue that some of them are not "pets" for purposes of a landlord's "no pets" rule.

1. Working in small groups or as a whole class, define *pets* by establishing the criteria an animal would have to meet to be included in the category "pets." Consider your landlord's "no pets" rule as the rhetorical context for your definition.

2. Based on your criteria, which of the following animals is definitely a pet that would have to be removed from the apartment? Based on your criteria, which animals could you exclude from the "no pets" rule? How would you make your argument to your landlord?

   - a German shepherd dog
   - a small housecat
   - a tiny, well-trained lapdog

- a gerbil in a cage
- a canary
- a tank of tropical fish
- a tarantula

Kinds of Definitions

In this section we discuss two methods of definition commonly used in definitional arguments: Aristotelian and operational.

Aristotelian Definition

Aristotelian definitions, regularly used in dictionaries, define a term by placing it within the next larger class or category and then showing the specific attributes that distinguish the term from other terms within the same category. For example, a *pencil* is a "writing implement" (next larger category) that differs from other writing implements in that it makes marks with lead or graphite rather than ink. You could elaborate this definition by saying, "Usually the lead or graphite is a long, thin column embedded in a slightly thicker column of wood with an eraser on one end and a sharpened point, exposing the graphite, on the other." You could even distinguish a wooden pencil from a mechanical pencil, thereby indicating again that the crucial identifying attribute is the graphite, not the wooden column.

As you can see, an Aristotelian definition of a term identifies specific attributes or criteria that enable you to distinguish it from other members of the next larger class. We created an Aristotelian definition in our example about socially responsible companies. A socially responsible company, we said, is any company (next larger class) that meets three criteria: (1) It doesn't pollute the environment; (2) it creates goods or services that promote the well-being of the community; and (3) it treats its workers justly.

In constructing Aristotelian definitions, you may find it useful to employ the concepts of accidental, necessary, and sufficient criteria. An *accidental criterion* is a usual but not essential feature of a concept. For example, "made out of wood" is an accidental feature of a pencil. Most pencils are made out of wood, but something can still be a pencil even if it isn't made out of wood (a mechanical pencil). In our example about socially responsible companies, "makes regular contributions to charities" might be an accidental criterion; most socially responsible companies contribute to charities, but some do not. And many socially irresponsible companies also contribute to charities—often as a public relations ploy.

A *necessary criterion* is an attribute that *must* be present for something to belong to the category being defined. For example, the property of "being a writing implement" is a necessary criterion for an object to be a pencil. The property of "marking with graphite or lead" is also a necessary criterion. However, neither of these criteria is a sufficient criterion for an object to be a pencil because many writing implements are not pencils (for example, pens), and many things that mark with graphite or lead aren't pencils (for example, a lead paperweight can make lead marks). Because an object that possesses both of these criteria together must be a pencil, we say that these two qualities together form a *sufficient criterion* for an object to be a pencil.

To show you how these concepts can help you carry on a definitional argument with more precision, let's apply them to a few examples. Suppose Felix Ungar and Oscar Madison are arguing whether an original Dodge Stealth is a true sports car. At issue are the criteria for "true sports car." Felix might argue that a Stealth is not a true sports car because it has rear seats. (To Felix, having seating for only two people is thus a necessary criterion for a true sports car.) Oscar Madison might argue, however, that having two seats is only an accidental feature of sports cars and that a Stealth is indeed a true sports car because it has a racy appearance and is designed to handle superbly on narrow, curving roads. (For Oscar, racy appearance and superb handling are together sufficient criteria for a true sports car.)

As another example, consider again our defining criteria for a "socially responsible" company: (1) The company must avoid polluting the environment; (2) the company must create goods or services that contribute to the well-being of the community; and (3) the company must treat its workers justly. In this definition, each criterion is necessary, but none of the criteria alone is sufficient. In other words, to be defined as socially responsible, a company must meet all three criteria at once. It is not enough for a company to be nonpolluting (a necessary but not sufficient criterion); if that company makes a shoddy product or treats its workers unjustly, it fails to meet the other necessary criteria and can't be deemed socially responsible. Because no one criterion by itself is sufficient, all three criteria together must be met before a company can be deemed socially responsible.

In contrast, consider the following definition of *sexual harassment* as established by the U.S. Equal Employment Opportunity Commission in its 1980 guidelines:

> Unwelcome sexual advances, requests for sexual favors, and other verbal or physical conduct of a sexual nature constitute sexual harassment when (1) submission to such conduct is made either explicitly or implicitly a term or condition of an individual's employment, (2) submission to or rejection of such conduct by an individual is used as the basis for employment decisions affecting such individual, or (3) such conduct has the purpose or effect of unreasonably interfering with an individual's work performance or creating an intimidating, hostile, or offensive working environment.*

Here each of these criteria is sufficient but none is necessary. In other words, an act constitutes sexual harassment if any one of the three criteria is satisfied.

---

*Quoted by Stephanie Riger, "Gender Dilemmas in Sexual Harassment Policies and Procedures," *American Psychologist 46* May 1991, 497–505.

For Class Discussion

Working individually or in small groups, try to determine whether each of the following is a necessary criterion, a sufficient criterion, an accidental criterion, or no criterion for defining the indicated concept. Be prepared to explain your reasoning and to account for differences in points of view.

CRITERION	CONCEPT TO BE DEFINED
presence of gills	fish
profane and obscene language	R-rated movie
birthplace inside the United States	American citizen
age of 65 or older	senior citizen
line endings that form a rhyming pattern	poem
spanking a child for discipline	child abuse
diet that excludes meat	vegetarian
killing another human being	murder
good sex life	happy marriage

Effect of Rhetorical Context on Aristotelian Definitions

It is important to appreciate how the context of a given argument can affect your definition of a term. The question "Is a tarantula kept in the house a pet?" may actually have opposing answers, depending on the rhetorical situation. You may argue that your tarantula is or is not a pet, depending on whether you are trying to exclude it from your landlord's "no pet" rule or include it in your local talk show's "weird pet contest." Within one context you will want to argue that what your landlord really means by *pet* is an animal (next larger class) capable of disturbing neighbors or harming the landlord's property (criteria that distinguish it from other members of the class). Thus you could argue that your tarantula isn't a pet in your landlord's sense because it is incapable of harming property or disturbing the peace (assuming you don't let it loose!). In the other context you would argue that a pet is "any living thing" (note that in this context the "next larger class" is much larger) with which a human being forms a caring attachment and which shares its owner's domicile. In this case you might say, "Tommy Tarantula here is one of my dearest friends and if you don't think Tommy is weird enough, wait 'til I show you Vanessa, my pet Venus's-flytrap."

To apply the same principle to a different field of debate, consider whether obscene language in a student newspaper should be protected by the First Amendment. The purpose of school officials' suspending editors responsible for such language is to maintain order and decency in the school. The school officials thus hope to narrow the category of acts that are protected under the free-speech amendment in order to meet their purposes. In contrast, the American Civil Liberties Union (which has long defended student newspaper editors) is intent on avoiding any precedent that will restrict freedom of speech any more than is absolutely necessary. The different definitions of *free speech* that are likely to emerge thus reflect the different purposes of the disputants.

The problem of purpose shows why it is so hard to define a word out of context. Some people try to escape this dilemma by returning to the "original intent" of the authors of precedent-setting documents such as the Constitution. But if we try to determine the original intent of the writers of the Constitution on such matters as "free speech," "cruel and unusual punishment," or the "right to bear arms," we must still ask what their original purposes were in framing the constitutional language. If we can show that those original purposes are no longer relevant to present concerns, we have begun to undermine what would otherwise appear to be a static and universal definition to which we could turn.

Operational Definitions

In some rhetorical situations, particularly those arising in the physical and social sciences, writers need precise definitions that can be measured empirically and are not subject to problems of context and disputed criteria. Consider, for example, an argument involving the concept "aggression": "Do violent television programs increase the incidence of aggression in children?" To do research on this issue, a scientist needs a precise, measurable definition of *aggression.* Typically, a scientist might measure "aggression" by counting the number of blows or kicks a child gives to an inflatable bozo doll over a fifteen-minute period when other play options are available. The scientist might then define *aggressive behavior* as six or more blows to the bozo doll. In our wetlands example, a federal authority created an operational definition of *wetland:* A wetland is a parcel of land that has a saturated ground surface for twenty-one consecutive days during the year. Such definitions are useful because they are precisely measurable, but they are also limited because they omit criteria that may be unmeasurable but important. Many scientists, for example, object to definitions of *wetland* based on consecutive days of wetness. What is more relevant, they argue, is not the duration of wetness in any parcel of land but the kind of plants and animals that depend on the wetland as a habitat. As another example, we might ask whether it is adequate to define a *superior student* as someone with a 3.5 GPA or higher or a *successful sex-education program* as one that results in a 25 percent reduction in teenage pregnancies. What important aspects of a superior student or a successful sex-education program are not considered in these operational definitions?

Strategies for Defining the Contested Term in a Definitional Argument

In constructing criteria to define your contested term, you can take two basic approaches—what rhetoricians call reportive and stipulative definitions. A *reportive definition* cites how others have used the term. A *stipulative definition* cites how you define the term. To put it another way, you can take a reportive approach by turning to standard or specialized dictionaries, judicial opinions, or expert testimony to establish a definition based on the authority of others. A lawyer defining a wetland based on twenty-one consecutive days of saturated ground surface would be using a reportive definition with a federal regulation as her source. The other approach is to use your own critical thinking to stipulate a definition, thereby defining the contested term yourself. Our definition of a socially responsible company, specifying three criteria, is an example of a stipulative definition. This section explains these approaches in more detail.

Reportive Approach: Research How Others Have Used the Term

When you take a reportive approach, you research how others have used the term, searching for authoritative definitions acceptable to your audience yet favorable to your case. Student writer Kathy Sullivan uses this approach in her argument that photographs displayed at the Oncore Bar are not obscene (see pp. 233–234). To define *obscenity,* she turns to *Black's Law Dictionary* and Pember's *Mass Media Laws.* (Specialized dictionaries are a standard part of the reference section of any library. See your reference librarian for assistance.) Other sources of specialized definitions are state and federal appellate court decisions, legislative and administrative statutes, and scholarly articles examining a given definitional conflict. Lawyers use this research strategy exhaustively in preparing court briefs. They begin by looking at the actual text of laws as passed by legislatures or written by administrative authorities. Then they look at all the court cases in which the laws have been tested and examine the ways courts have refined legal definitions and applied them to specific cases. Using these refined and elaborated definitions, lawyers then apply them to their own case at hand.

When research fails to uncover a definition favorable to the arguer's case, the arguer can sometimes adopt an *original intentions strategy.* For example, if a scientist is dissatisfied with definitions of *wetland* based on consecutive days of saturated ground surface, she might proceed as follows: "The original intention of the Congress in passing the Clean Water Act was to preserve the environment." What Congress intended, she could then claim, was to prevent development of those wetland areas that provide crucial habitat for wildlife or that inhibit water pollution. She could then propose an alternative definition (either a stipulative one that she develops herself or a reportive one that she uncovers in research) based on criteria other than consecutive days of ground saturation. (Of course, original intentions arguments can often be refuted by a "times have changed" strategy or by a "we can't know what they originally intended; we can only know what they wrote" strategy.)

Another way to make a reportive definition is to employ a strategy based on etymology, or *earlier meaning strategy.* Using an etymological dictionary or the *Oxford English Dictionary* (which traces the historical evolution of a word's meaning), an arguer can often unveil insights favorable to the writer's case. For example, if you wanted to argue that portrayal of violence in films is *obscene,* you could point to the etymology of the word, which literally means "offstage." The word derives from the practice of classical Greek tragedy, where violent acts occurred offstage and were only reported by a messenger. This strategy allows you to show how the word originally applied to violence rather than to sexual explicitness.

Stipulative Approach: Create Your Own Definition*

Often, however, you need to create your own definition of the contested term. An effective strategy is to establish initial criteria for your contested term by thinking of hypothetical cases that obviously fit the category you are trying to define and then thinking of hypothetical cases that obviously don't fit the category. You can then test and refine your criteria by applying them to borderline cases. For example, suppose you work at a homeless agency where you overhear street people discuss an incident that strikes you potentially as "police brutality." You wonder whether you should write to your local paper to bring attention to the incident.

CONTESTED CASE REGARDING POLICE BRUTALITY

Two police officers confront an inebriated homeless man who is shouting obscenities on a street corner. The officers tell the man to quiet down and move on, but he keeps shouting obscenities. When the officers attempt to put the man into the police car, he resists and takes a wild swing at one of the officers. As eyewitnesses later testified, this officer shouted obscenities back at the drunk man, pinned his arms behind his back in order to handcuff him, and lifted him forcefully by the arms. The man screamed in pain and was later discovered to have a dislocated shoulder. Is this officer guilty of police brutality?

To your way of thinking, this officer seems guilty: An inebriated man is too uncoordinated to be a threat in a fight, and two police officers ought to be able to arrest him without dislocating his shoulder. But a friend argues that because the man took a swing at the officer the police were justified in using force. The dislocated shoulder was simply an accidental result of using justified force.

To make your case, you need to develop a definition of "police brutality." You can begin by creating a hypothetical case that is obviously an instance of "police brutality":

CLEAR CASE OF POLICE BRUTALITY

A police officer confronts a drunk man shouting obscenities and begins hitting him in the face with his police baton. *[This is an obvious incidence of police brutality because the officer intentionally tries to hurt the drunk man without justification; hitting him with the baton is not necessary for making an arrest or getting the man into a police car.]*

---

*The defining strategies and collaborative exercises in this section are based on the work of George Hillocks and his research associates at the University of Chicago. See George Hillocks Jr., Elizabeth A. Kahn, and Larry R. Johannessen, "Teaching Defining Strategies as a Mode of Inquiry: Some Effects on Student Writing," *Research in the Teaching of English* 17 October 1983, 275–84. See also Larry R. Johannessen, Elizabeth A. Kahn, and Carolyn Calhoun Walter, *Designing and Sequencing Prewriting Activities* (Urbana, IL: NCTE, 1982).

You could then vary the hypothetical case until it is clearly *not* an instance of police brutality.

Cases That Are Clearly Not Police Brutality

Case 1: The police officer handcuffs the drunk man, who, in being helped into the police car, accidentally slips on the curb and dislocates his arm while falling. *[Here the injury occurs accidentally; the police officer does not act intentionally and is not negligent.]*

Case 2: The police officer confronts an armed robber fleeing from a scene and tackles him from behind, wrestling the gun away from him. In this struggle, the officer pins the robber's arm behind his back with such force that the robber's shoulder is dislocated. *[Here aggressive use of force is justified because the robber was armed, dangerous, and resisting arrest.]*

Using these hypothetical cases, you decide that the defining criteria for police brutality are (1) *intention* and (2) use of *excessive force*—that is, force beyond what was required by the immediate situation. After more contemplation, you are convinced that the officer was guilty of police brutality and have a clearer idea of how to make your argument. Here is how you might write the "match" part of your argument.

MATCH ARGUMENT USING YOUR STIPULATED DEFINITION

If we define police brutality as the *intentional* use of *excessive* force, then the police officer is guilty. His action was intentional because he was purposefully responding to the homeless man's drunken swing and was angry enough to be shouting obscenities back at the drunk (according to an eyewitness). Second, he used excessive force in applying the handcuffs. A drunk man taking a wild swing hardly poses a serious danger to two police officers. Putting handcuffs on the drunk may have been justified, but lifting the man's arm violently enough to dislocate a shoulder indicates excessive force. The officer lifted the man's arms violently not because he needed to but because he was angry, and acting out of anger is no justification for that violence. In fact, we can charge police officers with "police brutality" precisely to protect us from being victims of police anger. It is the job of the court system to punish us, not the police's job. Because this officer acted intentionally and applied excessive force out of anger, he should be charged with police brutality.

The strategy we have demonstrated—developing criteria by imagining hypothetical cases that clearly do and do not belong to the contested category—gives you a systematic procedure for developing a stipulated definition for your argument.

For Class Discussion

1. Suppose you wanted to define the concept "courage." Working in groups, try to decide whether each of the following cases is an example of courage:

   a. A neighbor rushes into a burning house to rescue a child from certain death and emerges, coughing and choking, with the child in his arms. Is the neighbor courageous?

b. A firefighter rushes into a burning house to rescue a child from certain death and emerges with the child in her arms. The firefighter is wearing protective clothing and a gas mask. When a newspaper reporter calls her courageous, she says, "Hey, this is my job." Is the firefighter courageous?

c. A teenager rushes into a burning house to recover a memento given to him by his girlfriend, the first love of his life. Is the teenager courageous?

d. A parent rushes into a burning house to save a trapped child. The fire marshal tells the parent to wait because there is no chance that the child can be reached from the first floor. The fire marshal wants to try cutting a hole in the roof to reach the child. The parent rushes into the house anyway and is burned to death. Was the parent courageous?

2. As you make your decisions on each of these cases, create and refine the criteria you use.

3. Make up your own series of controversial cases, like those above for "courage," for one or more of the following concepts:

a. cruelty to animals

b. child abuse

c. true athlete

d. sexual harassment

e. free speech protected by the First Amendment

Then, using the strategy of positive, contrastive, and borderline cases, construct a definition of your chosen concept.

Conducting the Match Part of a Definitional Argument

In conducting a match argument, you need to supply examples and other evidence showing that your contested case does (does not) meet the criteria you established in your definition. In essence, you support the match part of your argument in much the same way you would support a simple categorical claim.

For example, if you were developing the argument that the Hercules Shoe Company is not socially responsible because it treats its workers unjustly, your match section would provide evidence of this injustice. You might supply data about the percentage of shoes produced in East Asia, about the low wages paid these workers, and about the working conditions in these factories. You might also describe the suffering of displaced American workers when Hercules closed its American factories and moved operations to Asia, where the labor was non-union and cheap. The match section should also summarize and respond to opposing views.

Writing a Definitional Argument

WRITING ASSIGNMENT
FOR CHAPTER 11

Write an argument that develops a definitional claim of the form "X is (is not) a Y," where Y is a controversial term with a disputed definition. Typically your argument will have a criteria section in which you develop an extended definition of your Y term and a match section in which you argue that your X does (does not) meet the criteria for Y.

Exploring Ideas

Ideally, in writing this argument you will join an ongoing conversation about a definitional issue that interests you. What cultural and social issues that concern you involve disputed definitions? In the public area, you are likely to find numerous examples simply by looking through a newspaper—the strategy used by student writer Kathy Sullivan, who became interested in the controversy over allegedly obscene photographs in a gay bar (see pp. 233–234). Others of our students have addressed definitional issues such as these: Is Dr. Kevorkian a murderer (because he administered a lethal dosage to a paralyzed patient on national TV)? Are skateboarders punks or athletes? Is spanking a form of child abuse? Is flag burning protected free speech? Are today's maximum security prisons "cruel and unusual punishment"? Is tobacco a drug for purposes of federal regulation? Are chiropractors "real doctors"? Is using TiVo to avoid TV commercials a form of theft?

If you have trouble discovering a local or national issue that interests you, you can create fascinating definitional controversies among your classmates by asking whether certain borderline cases are "true" examples of some category: Are highly skilled video game players (race car drivers, synchronized swimmers, marbles players) true athletes? Is a gourmet chef a true artist? Working as a whole class or in small groups inside or out of class, create an argumentative discussion on one or more of these issues. Listen to the various voices in the controversy, and then write out your own argument.

You can also stimulate definitional controversies by brainstorming borderline cases for such terms as *courage* (Is mountain climbing an act of courage?), *cruelty to animals* (Are rodeos [zoos, catch-and-release trout fishing, use of animals for medical research] cruelty to animals?), or *war crime* (Was the American firebombing of Tokyo in World War II a war crime?).

As you explore your definitional issue, try to determine how others have defined your Y term (a reportive procedure). If no stable definition emerges from your search, stipulate your own definition by deciding what criteria must be met for any X to be deemed a Y. Try using the strategy for creating criteria that we discussed on pages 224–226 with reference to police brutality. Once you have determined your criteria for your Y term, freewrite for five or ten minutes, exploring whether your X term meets each of the criteria. Before writing your first draft, you might also explore your ideas further by doing the ten freewriting tasks on page 57 in Chapter 3.

Organizing a Definitional Argument

As you compose a first draft of your essay, you may find it helpful to know a prototypical structure for definitional arguments. Here are several possible plans.

Plan 1 (Criteria and Match in Separate Sections)

- Introduce the issue by showing disagreements about the definition of a key term or about its application to a problematic case.
- State your claim.
- Present your definition of the key term.
  State and develop criterion 1.
  State and develop criterion 2.
  Continue with rest of criteria.
- Summarize and respond to possible objections to your definition.
- Restate your claim about the contested case (it does [does not] meet your definition).
  Apply criterion 1 to your case.
  Apply criterion 2 to your case.
  Continue the match argument.
- Summarize and respond to possible objections to your match argument.
- Conclude your argument.

Plan 2 (Criteria and Match Interwoven)

- Introduce the issue by showing disagreements about the definition of a key term or about its application to a problematic case.
- Present your claim.
  State criterion 1 and argue that contested case meets (does not meet) criterion.
  State criterion 2 and argue that contested case meets (does not meet) criterion.
  Continue with criteria-match sections for additional criteria.
- Summarize opposing views.
- Refute or concede to opposing views.
- Conclude your argument.

Revising Your Draft

Once you have written a discovery draft, your goal should be to make your argument more clear and persuasive to your audience. Where might your audience call your claim, reasons, or evidence into question? Reengage with your audience to better appreciate the complexity of your issue. One way to strengthen your appeal to your readers is to use a Toulmin analysis to determine where your reasoning needs to be bolstered for your particular audience. In a definitional argument, the criteria established in your definition of the Y term are the warrants for your match argument. You might find it helpful at this time to summarize your argument as a claim with *because* clauses and to test it with Toulmin's schema. Here is how student writer Kathy Sullivan used Toulmin to analyze a draft of her essay examining the possible obscenity of photographs displayed in a gay bar in Seattle. The final version of this essay is printed on pages 233–234.

ENTHYMEME: The photographs displayed in the Oncore bar are not obscene because they do not violate the community standards of the patrons of the bar, because they do not appeal to prurient interest, because children are not likely to be exposed to them, and because they promote an important social value, safe sex, in order to prevent AIDS.

CLAIM: The photographs are not obscene.

STATED REASONS: (1) They don't violate community standards. (2) They do not appeal to prurient interests. (3) Children are not exposed to them. (4) They promote an important social purpose of preventing AIDS through safe sex.

GROUNDS: (1) evidence that most Oncore patrons are homosexual and that these photographs don't offend them (no complaints, etc.); (2) purpose of photographs is not prurient sexuality, they don't depict explicit sexual acts, the only thing complained about by the liquor board is visible body parts; (3) because this is a bar, children aren't allowed; (4) evidence that the purpose of these photographs is to promote safe sex, thus they have a redeeming social value

WARRANT: Things that don't violate community standards, do not appeal to prurient interests, don't come in view of children, and promote an important purpose are not obscene.

BACKING: These criteria come from the definition of *obscenity* in *Black's Law Dictionary,* which in turn is based on recent court cases. This is a very credible source. In addition, arguments showing why the community standard here should be that of the homosexual community rather than the community at large; arguments showing that the social importance of safe sex overrides other considerations.

CONDITIONS OF REBUTTAL: An opponent might say that the community standards should be those of the Seattle community at large, not those of the gay community. An opponent might say that photographs of male genitalia in a gay bar appeal to prurient interest.

QUALIFIER: Those photographs would be obscene if displayed anywhere but in a gay bar.

As a result of this analysis, Kathy revised her final draft considerably. By imagining where her arguments were weak ("conditions of rebuttal"), she realized that she needed to include more backing by arguing that the community standards to be applied in this case should be those of the homosexual community rather than the community at large. She also added a section arguing that visible genitalia in the photographs didn't make the photos obscene. By imagining how your readers might rebut your argument, you will see ways to strengthen your draft. Consequently, we close out this chapter by looking more carefully at the ways a definitional argument can be rebutted.

Questioning and Critiquing a Definitional Argument

Another powerful way to stimulate revision of a draft is to role-play a skeptical audience. The following means of questioning a definitional argument can be applied to your own draft to help you strengthen it or to someone else's definitional argument as a means of critiquing it closely. In critiquing a definitional argument, you need to appreciate its criteria-match structure. Your critique can question the argument's criteria, the match, or both.

Questioning the Criteria

Might a skeptic claim that your criteria are not the right ones? This is the most common way to attack a definitional argument. Skeptics might say that one or more of your argument's criteria are only accidental criteria, not necessary or sufficient ones. Or they might argue for different criteria or point out crucial missing criteria.

Might a skeptic point out possible bad consequences of accepting your argument's criteria? Here a skeptic could raise doubts about your definition by showing how it would lead to unintended bad consequences.

Might a skeptic cite extraordinary circumstances that weaken your argument's criteria? Skeptics might argue that your criteria are perfectly acceptable in ordinary circumstances but are rendered unacceptable by extraordinary circumstances.

Might a skeptic point out a bias or slant in your definition? Writers create definitions favorable to their case. By making this slant visible, a skeptic may be able to weaken the persuasiveness of your definition.

Questioning the Match

A match argument usually uses examples and other evidence to show that the contested case meets (does not meet) the criteria in the definition. The standard methods of refuting evidence apply (see pp. 148–149). Thus skeptics might ask one or more of the following questions:

Are your examples out-of-date or too narrow and unrepresentative?

Are your examples inaccurate?

Are your examples too extreme?

Are there existing counterexamples that alter the case?

By using these questions to test your own argument, you can reshape and develop your argument to make it thought provoking and persuasive for your audience.

Readings

Our first reading makes a simple categorical claim that Taiwan meets the criteria for membership in the United Nations. In this letter to the editor of a major newspaper, Jack K. C. Chiang, director general of Taipei Economic and Cultural Office, cites factual evidence about Taiwan related to the United Nations' criteria for membership. What prevents membership, Chiang notes, is the veto of mainland China (the People's Republic of China), which refuses to grant recognition to Taiwan by claiming that Taiwan is disputed territory that legitimately belongs to the People's Republic.

Why Not Taiwan?

Jack K. C. Chiang

Switzerland recently voted to join the United Nations and will become the   1
U.N.'s 190th member this September ("Neutral Swiss vote to join United Nations," Times, March 4). A question raised among the people in Taiwan (The Republic of China) and all Taiwanese Americans is: If Switzerland is qualified for U.N. membership, why not Taiwan? Consider Taiwan's list of qualifications for U.N. membership:

■ A defined territory covering some 14,000 square miles.

■ A population of some 23 million people, which is the 46th largest in the world, more than the population of two-thirds of U.N. member nations.

■ A fully democratically elected government through two popular presidential elections since 1996.

■ A vibrant economy marking the world's 16th largest, and third-largest holder of foreign exchange.

2   As a sovereign state, Taiwan absolutely meets all the criteria the U.N. uses to judge a country. Unfortunately, Taiwan has failed to be accepted by the U.N. merely because the People's Republic of China (PRC) opposes it. PRC claims that Taiwan is part of its territory so that Taiwan cannot have its delegates in the U.N. But the facts are, since 1949, the government of the Republic of China has exercised effective control and jurisdiction over Taiwan, while PRC government has over the mainland during the same time. In other words, PRC has never ruled Taiwan, even for a single day.

3   U.N. Secretary-General Kofi Annan welcomed the vote in Switzerland, saying it brought the United Nations closer to universality. Mr. Annan is perfectly right. Universality is the essence of the U.N.'s goal to world peace. So, why not Taiwan? With the participation of Taiwan, the U.N. can live up to its principle of universality, achieve its goal of preventive diplomacy, and facilitate the cross-Taiwan-strait reconciliation and peace process.

4   If the United Nations accepts Switzerland, then it should also welcome Taiwan.

Critiquing "Why Not Taiwan?"

1. Based on Chiang's letter, what are the implied criteria for membership in the United Nations? What evidence does Chiang supply to show that Taiwan meets the criteria?

2. Chiang sums up his thesis this way: "As a sovereign state, Taiwan absolutely meets all the criteria the U.N. uses to judge a country." However, this sentence masks another definitional dispute: How do you define a "sovereign state"? The People's Republic of China (mainland China), for complex historical reasons, refuses to acknowledge the sovereignty of the Taiwan government. Likewise, the international community does not yet recognize "two Chinas." Currently Taiwan seems to be an international "noncountry" somewhat analogous to the way that Washington, D.C., is a "stateless" city. Chiang attempts to counter this view of Taiwan as a "noncountry" by giving two reasons why Taiwan is a "sovereign state": (1) Taiwan has a full democratic government and (2) the People's Republic of China has not ruled the island of Formosa (where Taiwan is located) since 1949 and has never ruled the country of Taiwan. How would you define a "sovereign state"? What criteria, for example, would Palestine have to meet if a Mid East peace treaty ever established an independent Palestinian state?

The second reading, by student Kathy Sullivan, was written for the definition assignment on page 227. The definitional issue that she addresses—"Are the Menasee photographs obscene?"—became a local controversy in the state of Washington when the state liquor control board threatened to revoke the liquor license of a Seattle gay bar, the Oncore, unless it removed a series of photographs that the board deemed obscene.

Oncore, Obscenity, and the Liquor Control Board

Kathy Sullivan (student)

In early May, Geoff Menasee, a Seattle artist, exhibited a series of photographs   1
with the theme of "safe sex" on the walls of an inner city, predominantly homosexual restaurant and lounge called the Oncore. Before hanging the photographs,
Menasee had to consult with the Washington State Liquor Control Board because,
under the current state law, art work containing material that may be considered indecent has to be approved by the board before it can be exhibited. Of the almost
thirty photographs, six were rejected by the board because they partially exposed
"private parts" of the male anatomy. Menasee went ahead and displayed the entire
series of photographs, placing Band-Aids over the "indecent" areas, but the customers continually removed the Band-Aids.

The liquor control board's ruling on this issue has caused controversy in the   2
Seattle community. The *Seattle Times* has provided news coverage, and a "Town
Meeting" segment was filmed at the restaurant. The central question is this: Should
an establishment that caters to a predominantly homosexual clientele be enjoined
from displaying pictures promoting "safe sex" on the grounds that the photographs
are obscene?

Before I can answer this question, I must first determine whether the art work   3
should truly be classified as obscene. To make that determination, I will use the definition of obscenity in *Black's Law Dictionary:*

> Material is "obscene" if to the average person, applying contemporary community
> standards, the dominant theme of material taken as a whole appeals to prurient inter-
> est, if it is utterly without redeeming social importance, if it goes substantially beyond
> customary limits of candor in description or representation, if it is characterized by
> patent offensiveness, and if it is hard core pornography.

An additional criterion is provided by Pember's *Mass Media Laws:* "A work is obscene if it has a tendency to deprave and corrupt those whose minds are open to
such immoral influences (children for example) and into whose hands it might happen to fall" (394). The art work in question should not be prohibited from display at
predominantly homosexual establishments like the Oncore because it does not meet
the above criteria for obscenity.

First of all, to the average person applying contemporary community stan-   4
dards, the predominant theme of Menasee's photographs is not an appeal to prurient interests. The first element in this criterion is "average person." According to
Rocky Breckner, manager of the Oncore, 90 percent of the clientele at the Oncore
is made up of young white homosexual males. This group therefore constitutes
the "average person" viewing the exhibit. "Contemporary community standards"
would ordinarily be the standards of the Seattle community. However, this art

work is aimed at a particular group of people—the homosexual community. Therefore, the "community standards" involved here are those of the gay community rather than the city at large. Since the Oncore is not an art museum or gallery, which attracts a broad spectrum of people, it is appropriate to restrict the scope of "community standards" to that group who voluntarily patronize the Oncore.

5   Second, the predominant theme of the photographs is not "prurient interest" nor do the photographs go "substantially beyond customary limits of candor." There are no explicit sexual acts found in the photographs; instead, their theme is the prevention of AIDS through the practice of safe sex. Homosexual displays of affection could be viewed as "prurient interest" by the larger community, but same-sex relationships are the norm for the group at whom the exhibit is aimed. If the exhibit were displayed at McDonald's or even the Red Robin it might go "substantially beyond customary limits of candor," but it is unlikely that the clientele of the Oncore would find the art work offensive. The manager stated that he received very few complaints about the exhibit and its contents.

6   Nor is the material pornographic. The liquor control board prohibited the six photographs based on their visible display of body parts such as pubic hair and naked buttocks, not on the basis of sexual acts or homosexual orientation. The board admitted that the photographs depicted no explicit sexual acts. Hence, it can be concluded that they did not consider the suggestion of same-sex affection to be hard-core pornography. Their sole objection was that body parts were visible. But visible genitalia in art work are not necessarily pornographic. Since other art work, such as Michelangelo's sculptures, explicitly depict both male and female genitalia, it is arguable that pubic hair and buttocks are not patently offensive.

7   It must be conceded that the art work has the potential of being viewed by children, which would violate Pember's criterion. But once again the incidence of minors frequenting this establishment is very small.

8   But the most important reason for saying these photographs are not obscene is that they serve an important social purpose. One of Black's criteria is that obscene material is "utterly without redeeming social importance." But these photographs have the explicit purpose of promoting safe sex as a defense against AIDS. Recent statistics reported in the *Seattle Times* show that AIDS is now the leading cause of death of men under forty in the Seattle area. Any methods that can promote the message of safe sex in today's society have strong redeeming social significance.

9   Those who believe that all art containing "indecent" material should be banned or covered from public view would most likely believe that Menasee's work is obscene. They would disagree that the environment and the clientele should be the major determining factor when using criteria to evaluate art. However, in the case of this exhibit I feel that the audience and the environment of the display are factors of overriding importance. Therefore, the exhibit should have been allowed to be displayed because it is not obscene.

Critiquing "Oncore, Obscenity, and the Liquor Control Board"

1. Kathy Sullivan here uses a reportive approach for defining her Y term "obscenity." Based on the definitions of *obscenity* in *Black's Law Dictionary* and Pember's *Mass Media Laws,* what criteria for obscenity does Kathy use?

2. How does she argue that the Menasee photographs do *not* meet the criteria?

3. Working as a whole class or in small groups, share your responses to the following questions: (a) If you find Kathy's argument persuasive, which parts were particularly influential or effective? (b) If you are not persuaded, which parts of her argument do you find weak or ineffective? (c) How does Kathy shape her argument to meet the concerns and objections of her audience? (d) How might a lawyer for the liquor control board rebut Kathy's argument?

Our third reading, by conservative syndicated columnist Charles Krauthammer, was published on September 13, 2001, two days after the September 11 terrorist attacks. The United States, still reeling from the attacks, was entering the first phase of a national debate on how to respond. Krauthammer's article helped shape that debate, influencing President Bush's military response that eventually came to be called the "war" against terrorism. In this op-ed piece, Krauthammer argues that the terrorist attacks belong in the category "act of war" rather than the category "crime" and that the U.S. response should be shaped appropriately.

This Isn't a "Legal" Matter, This Is War
Charles Krauthammer

This is not crime. This is war. One of the reasons there are terrorists out there   1
capable and audacious enough to carry out the deadliest attack on the United States in its history is that, while they have declared war on us, we have in the past responded (with the exception of a few useless cruise missile attacks on empty tents in the desert) by issuing subpoenas.

Secretary of State Colin Powell's first reaction to the day of infamy was to   2
pledge to "bring those responsible to justice." This is exactly wrong. Franklin Roosevelt did not respond to Pearl Harbor by pledging to bring the commander of Japanese naval aviation to justice. He pledged to bring Japan to its knees.

You bring criminals to justice; you rain destruction on combatants. This is a   3
fundamental distinction that can no longer be avoided. The bombings of Sept. 11, 2001, must mark a turning point. War was long ago declared on us. Until we declare war in return, we will have thousands of more innocent victims.

We no longer have to search for a name for the post–Cold War era. It will   4
henceforth be known as the age of terrorism. Organized terror has shown what it

can do: execute the single greatest massacre in American history, shut down the greatest power on the globe, and send its leaders into underground shelters. All this, without even resorting to chemical, biological or nuclear weapons of mass destruction.

5   This is a formidable enemy. To dismiss it as a bunch of cowards perpetrating senseless acts of violence is complacent nonsense. People willing to kill thousands of innocents while they kill themselves are not cowards. They are deadly, vicious warriors and need to be treated as such. Nor are their acts of violence senseless. They have a very specific aim. To avenge alleged historical wrongs and to bring the great American satan to its knees.

6   Nor is the enemy faceless or mysterious. We do not know for sure who gave the final order but we know what movement it comes from. The enemy has identified itself in public and openly. Our delicate sensibilities have prevented us from pronouncing its name.

7   Its name is radical Islam. Not Islam as practiced peacefully by millions of the faithful around the world. But a specific fringe political movement, dedicated to imposing its fanatical ideology on its own societies and destroying the society of its enemies, the greatest of which is the United States.

8   Israel, too, is an affront to radical Islam, and thus of course must be eradicated. But it is the smallest of fish. The heart of the beast—with its military in Saudi Arabia, Kuwait, Turkey and Persian Gulf; with a culture that "corrupts" Islamic youth; with an economy and technology that dominates the world—is the United States. That is why we were struck so savagely.

9   How do we know? Who else trains cadres of fanatical suicide murderers who go to their deaths joyfully? And the average terrorist does not coordinate four hijackings within one hour. Nor fly a plane into the tiny silhouette of a single building. For that you need skilled pilots seeking martyrdom. That is not a large pool to draw from.

10   These are the shock troops of the enemy. And the enemy has many branches. Hezbollah in Lebanon, Hamas and Islamic Jihad in Israel, the Osama bin Laden organization headquartered in Afghanistan, and various Arab "liberation fronts" based in Damascus. And then there are the governments: Iran, Iraq, Syria and Libya among them. Which one was responsible? We will find out soon enough.

11   But when we do, there should be no talk of bringing these people to "swift justice," as Karen Hughes* dismayingly promised mid-afternoon Tuesday. An open act of war demands a military response, not a judicial one.

12   Military response against whom? It is absurd to make war on the individuals who send these people. The terrorists cannot exist in a vacuum. They need a territorial base of sovereign protection. For 30 years we have avoided this truth. If bin Laden was behind this, then Afghanistan is our enemy. *Any* country that harbors and protects him is our enemy. We must carry *their* war to them.

---

*Karen Hughes was an adviser to President Bush and often a spokesperson for the administration at the time of the terrorist attacks.

We should seriously consider a congressional declaration of war. That convention seems quaint, unused since World War II. But there are two virtues to declaring war: It announces our seriousness both to our people and to the enemy, and it gives us certain rights as belligerents (of blockade, for example). 13

The "long peace" is over. We sought this war no more than we sought war with Nazi Germany and Imperial Japan or cold war with the Soviet Union. But when war was pressed upon the greatest generation, it rose to the challenge. The question is: Will we? 14

Critiquing "This Isn't a 'Legal' Matter, This Is War"

1. In your own words, why does Krauthammer consider the terrorist attacks an "act of war" rather than a "crime"?

2. What criteria about the "enemy" have to be met, according to Krauthammer, in order for the United States to declare war against that enemy? How do the terrorists meet these criteria?

3. On September 10, 2002, on the eve of the first anniversary of the terrorist attacks, *New York Times* columnist Paul Krugman says that the United States made a mistake by placing the terrorist attacks in the category "war":

   > Yet a year later there is great uneasiness in this nation. Corporate scandals, dropping stocks and rising unemployment account for much of the malaise. But part of what makes us uneasy is that we still don't know how to think about that happened to us. Our leaders and much of the media tell us that we're a nation at war. But that was a bad metaphor from the start, and looks worse as time goes by.*

   Why might Krugman object to calling the fight against terrorism a war? What makes the fight against terrorism different from World War II or other wars? What might be the bad consequences of the United States's declaring itself in a state of "war" against terrorism?

Our last reading, by sports columnist Blaine Newnham, addresses the Supreme Court decision in spring 2001 to allow professional golfer Casey Martin, disabled by a leg disease, to ride in a motorized golf cart during tournaments. The Supreme Court decision addressed several definitional disputes: What is the definition of "disabled" in light of the federal law known as the Americans with Disabilities Act, which mandates that businesses and employers make appropriate accommodations for disabled customers and employees? Other disputed definitions are of "sport" and "golf." Which criteria for any sport are necessary and which are accidental? In the following sports column, Newnham addresses opponents who believe that the Supreme Court decision in the Martin case will mean that "anyone with an owie and battery of lawyers" can change the rules for a sport.

---

*Paul Krugman, "The Long Haul," *New York Times*, 10 September 2002, 431.

Court Win for Martin Not a Defeat for Pro Sports

Blaine Newnham

1   People are acting like they gave Ichiro* a motor scooter to get to first base.

2   They didn't make the hole any bigger for Casey Martin, the fairway any wider, the sand any smoother.

3   In yesterday's enlightened decision, the Supreme Court made a ruling about the accommodation of disabilities in the sport of golf and in the person of Casey Martin.

4   Both, as history will prove, are unique in professional athletics.

5   Martin now has won three straight court decisions, starting with what was thought to be a hometown decision by a local judge in Eugene in 1997 and finishing in the highest court in the land.

6   The game is over.

7   The doomsayers will have us lowering the baskets, widening the goal posts, shortening the base paths, altering the face of professional sports for anyone with an owie and battery of lawyers.

8   It won't happen.

9   To consider accommodation, three elements must exist:

10   An athlete's condition must be so severe as to meet the standards set in the Americans with Disabilities Act.

11   The athlete must be judged to be of the caliber to compete at the professional level.

12   And any change made to accommodate the athlete's disability must not alter the nature of the sport.

13   Allowing an athlete to ride a motorized wheelchair to get to first base alters the nature of the sport. So does lowering the basket for someone so disabled he or she can't jump.

14   The Supreme Court didn't get distracted in its decision on Martin, whose degenerative circulation problem in his leg not only keeps him from walking 18 holes of golf, but also constantly threatens amputation.

15   The Supreme Court didn't get bogged down in the argument of who makes the rules for tournament golf.

16   First of all, there is no rule in golf that says you have to walk. The PGA Tour stipulates its courses have to be walked, but then in the 1950s it also said the players had to be white. For its Seniors, it allows riding. And, for the Tour regulars, it chose to shuttle them between holes in a tournament in Hawaii to "speed up play."

17   So much for endurance as part of the game.

18   The Supreme Court asked only if riding gave Martin an advantage in competition, and decided correctly that it didn't.

---

*Ichiro Suzuki is the Seattle Mariners' right fielder and one of baseball's most well-known stars.

Wisely, the court ruled that golf is about shot-making and not about walking.   19

Could you ever make the case that basketball is not about running and jumping,   20
or football about blocking and tackling, baseball about hitting and catching?

I don't think so.   21

People will hark back to Ken Venturi's collapse in the 1964 U.S. Open at   22
Congressional Country Club in Washington.

The U.S. Open played 36 holes on the final day then; it doesn't now.   23

It was touring pro Phil Mickelson who said, "I just don't think riding a cart   24
makes a big difference. I don't see how it affects ball-striking, reading the green,
hitting the putt."

Walking is part of the game. It is just not part of the competition. In college, the   25
NCAA allowed Martin to ride.

I walk because it keeps me loose, it keeps me in touch with the hole, I concen-   26
trate better, get more exercise, pay less to play, and ultimately have more fun.

The vast majority of touring pros would rather walk, too.   27

I'm nearing 60 and carry my clubs. The touring pros have caddies. The majority   28
of the courses they play are flat. Those with bad backs and sore feet might rather
ride, but they are injured, not disabled.

I've watched Martin play with the use of a cart. He must negotiate down the   29
side of the fairway, find a place to park well away from the green, and then hobble
into a bunker or onto the green the best he can.

My guess is he uses more energy doing that than his competition does walking.   30

Martin has both a rare talent for the game—he played college golf with Tiger   31
Woods and Notah Begay—and a rare condition that is clearly not an injury.

He wanted an opportunity, not an advantage. Rather than refuse him that op-   32
portunity for fear of the precedent it might set, the Supreme Court chose to look at
one man in one sport.

You appreciate that it did.   33

Critiquing "Court Win for Martin Not a Defeat for Pro Sports"

1. Opponents of the Supreme Court decision in the Casey Martin case fear
   that it will set precedents leading to the erosion of rules and competitive
   standards in other sports. How does Newnham use definitional strategies
   to argue that Martin's situation is unique and will therefore set no precedents for other sports? For example, how does Newnham argue that a professional tournament golfer with a bad back or sore feet would not be allowed to ride a golf cart under the Supreme Court decision?

2. Without using the terms, Newnham uses the concepts of "necessary"
   versus "accidental" criteria. For example, dribbling the ball is a necessary criterion for basketball. If a player were allowed to carry the ball
   without dribbling, the game would no longer be defined as basketball.
   By analogy, is walking a necessary criterion for golf? How does
   Newnham argue that it is not? How do opponents of the Supreme Court

ruling argue that walking *is* a necessary criterion for high-level professional tournament golf?

3. Do you agree with Newnham that the Martin decision will not harm tournament golf or set precedents for other sports? How might the Martin
decision lead to controversial situations in other sports?

4. Note how Newnham's article, as a sports column written rapidly for a
deadline, follows genre conventions of journalistic prose—short paragraphs, absence of transitions, and a loose rather than formal structure.
How would you reorganize Newnham's argument if you wanted to follow the thesis-governed, formal structure that often characterizes academic arguments?

12 Causal Arguments
X Causes (Does Not Cause) Y

CASE 1

A world haunted by terrorism is also haunted by outbreaks of appalling teenage violence. On April 22, 2002, a nineteen-year-old student in Erfurt, Germany, opened fire on his classmates, shooting sixteen victims at close range before he was stopped by a courageous, unarmed teacher. In trying to understand the causes of this event, German sociologists turned to the causal debate in America following the Columbine High School massacre in Littleton, Colorado, where two male students killed twelve of their classmates and wounded twenty-three before killing themselves. Among the causes of teenage violence proposed by social scientists and media commentators were the following: violent movies, violent video games, violent TV, the music of Marilyn Manson, easy access to guns, breakdown of the traditional family, absence of parental involvement in teen lives, erosion of school discipline, inadequate school counseling, Internet neo-Nazi chat rooms, Internet lessons on how to make bombs, and the irresponsible prescribing of antidepressants to teenagers (one of the Columbine assailants was taking Prozac). For each proposed cause, the arguer suggested a different approach for reducing teen violence.

CASE 2

In the early 1990s, the Fiji Islands got satellite television, and Fijians began watching such American television shows as *Beverly Hills 90210* and *Melrose Place*. In the next four years, the number of teens at risk for eating disorders doubled. According to columnist Ellen Goodman, "74 percent of the Fiji teens in a study said they felt 'too big or fat' at least some of the time and 62 percent said they had dieted in the past month." Emphasizing eating as pleasure and a rite of hospitality, Fiji culture has traditionally valued ample flesh and a robust shape for women, an image very opposite from that of thin American television stars. A Harvard anthropologist and psychiatrist has been studying this connection between television and eating disorders. Although "a direct

241

causal link" may not be easy to support, there does seem to be a connection between projected television images of women and illness. Goodman poses the question of what harm television images can cause to women.*

An Overview of Causal Arguments

We encounter causal issues all the time. What caused the massacres in Erfurt, Germany, and Littleton, Colorado? What caused young women in Fiji to start feeling fat? What is the effect of rap music on teenagers? What caused the corporate greed leading to the Enron and WorldCom scandals in 2002? What will be the consequences of curtailing human rights in the fight against terrorism? Will the opening up of national forests to more logging (the proposed federal policy under the Bush administration) help prevent forest fires?

Sometimes an argument can be devoted entirely to a causal issue. Just as frequently, causal arguments support proposal arguments in which the writer argues that we should (should not) do X *because doing X will lead to good (bad) consequences.* Convincing readers how X will lead to these consequences—a causal argument—thus bears on the success of many proposal arguments.

Because causal arguments require close analysis of phenomena, effective causal arguing is closely linked to critical thinking. Studies of critical thinking show that good problem solvers systematically explore the causes of a problem before proposing a solution. Equally important, before making a decision, good problem solvers predict and weigh the consequences of alternative solutions to a problem, trying to determine a solution that produces the greatest benefits with the least cost. Adding to the complexity of causal arguing is the way a given event can have multiple causes and multiple consequences. In an effort to save salmon, for example, environmentalists have proposed the elimination of several dams on the Snake River above Lewiston, Idaho. Will the removal of these dams save the salmon? Nobody knows for sure, but three universally agreed-upon consequences of removing the dams will be the loss of several thousand jobs in the Lewiston area, loss of some hydroelectric power, and the shift in wheat transportation from river barges to overland trucks and trains. So the initial focus on consequences to salmon soon widens to include consequences to jobs, to power generation, and to agricultural transportation.

The Nature of Causal Arguing

Typically, causal arguments try to show how one event brings about another. On the surface, causal arguments may seem a fairly straightforward matter—more concrete, to be sure, than the larger moral issues in which they are often

---

*Ellen Goodman, "The Skinny on Fiji's Loss of a Robust Cultural Identity," *Seattle Times* 28 June 1999, B3.

embedded. But consider for a moment the classic illustration of causality—one billiard ball striking another on a pool table. Surely we are safe in saying that the movement of the second ball was "caused" by a transfer of energy from the first ball at the moment of contact. Well, yes and no. British philosopher David Hume (among others) argued long ago that we don't really perceive "causality"; what we perceive is one ball moving and then another ball moving. We infer the notion of causality, which is a human construct, not a property of billiard balls.

When humans become the focus of a causal argument, the very definition of causality is immediately vexed. When we say that a given factor X "caused" a person to do Y, what do we mean? On the one hand, we might mean that X "forced her to do Y," thereby negating her free will (for example, the presence of a brain tumor caused my erratic behavior, which caused me to lose my job). On the other hand, we might simply mean that factor X "motivated" her to do Y, in such a way that doing Y is still an expression of freedom (for example, my love of the ocean caused me to give up my job as a Wal-Mart greeter and become a California surf bum).

When we argue about causality in human beings, we must guard against confusing these two senses of "cause" or assuming that human behavior can be predicted or controlled in the same way that nonhuman behavior can. A rock dropped from a roof will always fall to the ground at 32 feet per second squared, and a rat zapped for making left turns in a maze will always quit making left turns. But if we raise interest rates, will consumers save more? If so, how much? This is the sort of question we debate endlessly.

Fortunately, most causal arguments can avoid the worst of these scientific and philosophical quagmires. As human beings, we share a number of assumptions about what causes events in the observable world, and we can depend on the goodwill of our audiences to grant us most of these assumptions. Most of us, for example, would be satisfied with the following explanation for why a car went into a skid: "In a panic the driver locked the brakes of his car, causing the car to go into a skid."

panic → slamming brake pedal → locking brakes → skid

We probably do not need to defend this simple causal chain because the audience will grant the causal connections between events A, B, C, and D. The sequence seems reasonable according to our shared assumptions about psychological causality (panic leads to slamming brake pedal) and physical causality (locked brakes lead to skid).

But if you are an attorney defending a client whose skidding car caused considerable damage to an upscale boutique, you might see all sorts of additional causal factors. ("Because the stop sign at that corner was obscured by an untrimmed willow tree, my client innocently entered what he assumed was an open intersection only to find a speeding beer truck bearing down on him. When my client took immediate decelerating corrective action, the improperly maintained, oil-slicked roadway sent his car into its near-fatal skid and into the boutique's bow windows—windows that extrude into the walkway 11 full inches beyond the limit allowed by city code.") Okay, now what's the cause of the crash, and who's at fault?

As the previous example shows, explaining causality entails creating a plausible chain of events linking a cause to its effect. Let's take another example—this time a real rather than hypothetical one. Consider an argument put forward by syndicated columnist John Leo as an explanation for the Columbine High School massacre.* Leo attributes part of the cause to the desensitizing effects of violent video games. After suggesting that the Littleton killings were partly choreographed on video game models, Leo suggests the following causal chain:

> Many youngsters are left alone for long periods of time → they play violent video games obsessively → their feelings of resentment and powerlessness "pour into the killing games" → the video games break down a natural aversion to killing, analogous to psychological techniques employed by the military → realistic touches in modern video games blur the "boundary between fantasy and reality" → youngsters begin identifying not with conventional heroes but with sociopaths who get their kicks from blowing away ordinary people ("pedestrians, marching bands, an elderly woman with a walker") → having enjoyed random violence in the video games, vulnerable youngsters act out the same adrenaline rush in real life.

Describing a Causal Argument in Toulmin Terms

Because causal arguments can involve lengthy or complex causal chains, they are often harder to summarize in *because* clauses than are other kinds of arguments. Likewise, they are not as likely to yield quick analysis through the Toulmin schema. Nevertheless, a causal argument can usually be stated as a claim with *because* clauses. Typically, a *because* clause for a causal argument pinpoints one or two key elements in the causal chain rather than trying to summarize every link. Leo's argument could be summarized in the following claim with *because* clause:

> Violent video games may have been a contributing cause to the Littleton massacre because playing these games can make random, sociopathic violence seem pleasurable.

Once stated as an enthymeme, the argument can be analyzed using Toulmin's schema. (It is easiest to apply Toulmin's schema to causal arguments if you think of the grounds as the observable phenomena at any point in the causal chain and the warrants as the shareable assumptions about causality that join links together.)

CLAIM: Violent video games may have been a contributing cause to the Littleton massacre

---

*John Leo, "Kill-for-Kicks Video Games Desensitizing Our Children," *Seattle Times* 27 Apr. 1999, B4.

STATED REASON: because playing these games can make random, socio-pathic violence seem pleasurable

GROUNDS: evidence that the killers, like many young people, played violent video games; evidence that the games are violent; evidence that the games in-volve random, sociopathic violence (not heroic cops against aliens or gangsters, but a killer blowing away ordinary people—marching bands, little old ladies, and so forth); evidence that young people derive pleasure from these games

WARRANT: If youngsters derive pleasure from random, sociopathic killing in video games, then they can transfer this pleasure to real life, thus leading to the Littleton massacre.

BACKING: testimony from psychologists; evidence that violent video games desensitize persons to violence; analogy to military training where video game strategies are used to "make killing a reflex action"; evidence that the distinction between fantasy and reality becomes especially blurred for unsta-ble children.

CONDITIONS OF REBUTTAL: *Questioning the reason and grounds:* Perhaps the killers didn't play video games; perhaps the video games are no more violent than traditional kids' games (such as cops and robbers); perhaps the video games do not feature sociopathic killing.

Questioning the warrant and backing: Perhaps kids are fully capable of distin-guishing fantasy from reality; perhaps the games are just fun with no transfer-ence to real life; perhaps these video games are substantially different from military training strategies.

QUALIFIER: (Claim is already qualified by *may* and *contributing cause*)

For Class Discussion

1. Working individually or in small groups, create a causal chain to show how the item mentioned in the first column could help lead to the item mentioned in the second.

   a. invention of the automobile   redesign of cities

   b. invention of the automobile   changes in sexual mores

   c. invention of the telephone   loss of sense of community in neighborhoods

   d. origin of rap in black urban music scene   the popularity of rap spreads from urban black audiences to white middle-class youth culture

| e. development of way to prevent rejections in transplant operations | liberalization of euthanasia laws |

2. For each of your causal chains, compose a claim with an attached *because* clause summarizing one or two key links in the causal chain. For example, "The invention of the automobile helped cause the redesign of cities because automobiles made it possible for people to live farther away from their places of work."

Three Methods for Arguing That One Event Causes Another

One of the first things you need to do when preparing a causal argument is to note exactly what sort of causal relationship you are dealing with. Are you concerned with causes or consequences of a specific one-time event (such as a mysterious airplane crash, your college faculty's decision to institute a service-learning requirement, or a recent Supreme Court decision), of a recurring phenomenon (such as eating disorders, road rage, or spousal abuse), or of a puzzling trend (such as the rising popularity of extreme sports or of recent changes in women's clothes toward micro skirts, belly shirts, and low-rider pants)?

With recurring phenomena or with trends, you have the luxury of being able to study multiple cases over long periods of time and establishing correlations between suspected causal factors and effects. In some cases you can even intervene in the process and test for yourself whether diminishing a suspected causal factor results in a lessening of the effect or whether increasing the causal factor results in a corresponding increase in the effect. Additionally, you can spend a good deal of time exploring just how the mechanics of causation might work.

But with a one-time occurrence your focus is on the details of the event and specific causal chains that may have contributed to the event. Sometimes evidence has disappeared or changed its nature. You often end up in the position more of a detective than of a scientific researcher, and your conclusion will have to be more tentative as a result.

Having briefly stated these words of caution, let's turn now to the various ways you can argue that one event causes another.

First Method: Explain the Causal Mechanism Directly

The most convincing kind of causal argument identifies every link in the causal chain, showing how X causes A, which causes B, which in turn causes C, which finally causes Y. In some cases, all you have to do is fill in the missing links. In other cases—when your assumptions about causality may seem questionable to your audience—you have to argue for the causal connection with more vigor.

A careful spelling out of each step in the causal chain is the technique used by science writer Robert S. Devine in the following passage from his article "The Trouble with Dams."* Although the benefits of dams are widely understood (cheap, pollution-free electricity; flood control; irrigation; barge transportation), the negative effects are less commonly known and understood. In this article, Devine tries to persuade readers that dams have serious negative consequences. In the following passage, he explains how dams reduce salmon flows by slowing the migration of smolts (newly hatched young salmon) to the sea.

CAUSAL ARGUMENT DESCRIBING A CAUSAL CHAIN

Such transformations lie at the heart of the ongoing environmental harm done by dams. Rivers are rivers because they flow, and the nature of their flows defines much of their character. When dams alter flows, they alter the essence of rivers.

Consider the erstwhile river behind Lower Granite [a dam on Idaho's Snake River]. Although I was there in the springtime, when I looked at the water it was moving too slowly to merit the word "flow"—and Lower Granite Lake isn't even one of the region's enormous storage reservoirs, which bring currents to a virtual halt. In the past, spring snowmelt sent powerful currents down the Snake during April and May. Nowadays hydropower operators of the Columbia and Snake systems store the runoff behind the dams and release it during the winter, when demand—and the price—for electricity rises. Over the ages, however, many populations of salmon have adapted to the spring surge. The smolts used the strong flows to migrate, drifting downstream with the current. During the journey smolts' bodies undergo physiological changes that require them to reach salt water quickly. Before dams backed up the Snake, smolts coming down from Idaho got to the sea in six to twenty days; now it takes from sixty to ninety days, and few of the young salmon reach salt water in time. The emasculated current is the single largest reason that the number of wild adult salmon migrating up the Snake each year has crashed from predevelopment runs of 100,000–200,000 to what was projected to be 150–75 this year.

This tightly constructed passage connects various causal chains to explain the decline of salmon runs:

Smolts use river flow to reach the sea → dams restrict flow of river → a trip that before development took 6–20 days now takes 60–90 days → migrating smolts undergo physiological changes that demand quick access to salt water → delayed migration time kills the smolts.

Describing each link in the causal chain—and making each link seem as plausible as possible—is the most persuasive means of convincing readers that X causes Y.

---

*Robert S. Devine, "The Trouble with Dams," *Atlantic* Aug. 1995, 64–75. The example quotation is from page 70.

Second Method: Use Various Inductive Methods to Establish a High Probability of a Causal Link

If we can't explain a causal link directly, we often employ a reasoning strategy called *induction*. Through induction we infer a general conclusion based on a limited number of specific cases. For example, if on several occasions you got a headache after drinking red wine but not after drinking white wine, you would be likely to conclude inductively that red wine causes you to get headaches. However, because there are almost always numerous variables involved, because there are exceptions to most principles arrived at inductively, and because we can't be certain that the future will always be like the past, inductive reasoning gives only probable truths, not certain ones.

When your brain thinks inductively, it sorts through data looking for patterns of similarity and difference. But the inductive process does not explain the causal mechanism itself. Thus, through induction you know that red wine gives you a headache, but you don't know how the wine actually works on your nervous system—the causal chain itself.

In this section we explain three kinds of inductive reasoning: informal induction, scientific experimentation, and correlation.

Informal Induction   *Informal induction* is our term for the habitual kind of inductive reasoning we do all the time. Toddlers think inductively when they learn the connection between flipping a wall switch and watching the ceiling light come on. They hold all variables constant except the position of the switch and infer inductively a causal connection between the switch and the light. Typical ways that the mind infers causality described by the nineteeth-century philosopher John Stuart Mill include looking for a common element that can explain a repeated circumstance. For example, psychologists attempting to understand the causes of anorexia have discovered that many anorexics (but not all) come from perfectionist, highly work-oriented homes that emphasize duty and responsibility. This common element is thus a suspected causal factor leading to anorexia. Another of Mill's methods is to look for a single difference. When infant death rates in the state of Washington shot up in July and August 1986, one event stood out making these two months different: increased radioactive fallout from the Chernobyl nuclear meltdown in the Ukraine. This single difference led some researchers to suspect radiation as a possible cause of infant deaths. Informal induction typically proceeds from this kind of "common element" or "single difference" reasoning.

Largely because of its power, informal induction can often lead you to wrong conclusions. You should be aware of two common fallacies of inductive reasoning that can tempt you into erroneous assumptions about causality. (Both fallacies are treated more fully in Appendix 1.)

The *post hoc, ergo propter hoc* fallacy ("after this, therefore because of this") mistakes precedence for cause. Just because event A regularly precedes event B doesn't mean that event A causes event B. The same reasoning that tells us that flipping a switch causes the light to go on can make us believe that low levels of radioactive fallout from the Chernobyl nuclear disaster caused a sudden rise in infant death rates in the state of Washington. The nuclear disaster clearly preceded the rise in death rates. But did it clearly *cause* it? Our point is that precedence alone is no proof of causality and that we are guilty of this fallacy whenever we are swayed to believe that X causes Y primarily because X precedes Y. We can guard against this fallacy by seeking plausible link-by-link connections showing how X causes Y.

The *hasty generalization* fallacy occurs when you make a generalization based on too few cases or too little consideration of alternative explanations: You flip the switch, but the lightbulb doesn't go on. You conclude—too hastily—that the power has gone off. (Perhaps the lightbulb has burned out or the switch is broken.) How many trials does it take before you can make a justified generalization rather than a hasty generalization? It is difficult to say for sure. Both the *post hoc* fallacy and the hasty generalization fallacy remind us that induction requires a leap from individual cases to a general principle and that it is always possible to leap too soon.

Scientific Experimentation   One way to avoid inductive fallacies is to examine our causal hypotheses as carefully as possible. When we deal with a recurring phenomenon such as cancer, we can create scientific experiments that give us inductive evidence of causality with a fairly high degree of certainty. If, for example, we were concerned that a particular food source such as spinach might contain cancer-causing chemicals, we could test our hypothesis experimentally. We could take two groups of rats and control their environment carefully so that the only difference between them (in theory, anyway) was that one group ate large quantities of spinach and the other group ate none. Spinach eating, then, would be the one variable between the two groups that we are testing. After a specified period of time, we would check to see what percentage of rats in each group developed cancer. If twice as many spinach-eating rats contracted cancer, we could probably conclude that our hypothesis held up.

Correlation   Still another method of induction is *correlation*, which expresses a statistical relationship between X and Y. A correlation between X and Y means that when X occurs, Y is likely to occur also, and vice versa. To put it another way, correlation establishes a possibility that an observed link between an X and a Y is a causal one rather than a mere coincidence. The existence of a correlation, however, does not tell us whether X causes Y, whether Y causes X, or whether both are caused by some third phenomenon. For example, there is a fairly strong correlation between nearsightedness and intelligence. (That is, in a given sample of nearsighted people and people with normal eyesight, a higher percentage of the nearsighted people will be highly intelligent. Similarly, in a sample of high-intelligence people and people with normal intelligence, a higher percentage of the high-intelligence group will be nearsighted.) But the direction of causality isn't clear. It could be that high intelligence causes people to read more, thus ruining their eyes (high intelligence causes nearsightedness). Or it could be that nearsightedness causes people to read more, thus raising their intelligence (nearsightedness causes high intelligence). Or it could be that some unknown phenomenon inside the brain causes both nearsightedness and high intelligence.

In recent years, correlation studies have been made stunningly sophisticated through the power of computerized analyses. For example, we could attempt to do the spinach-cancer study without resorting to a scientific experiment. If we identified a given group that ate lots of spinach (for example, vegetarians) and another group that ate little if any spinach (Inuits) and then checked to see if their rates of cancer correlated to their rates of spinach consumption, we would have the beginnings of a correlation study. But it would have no scientific validity until we factored out all the other variables between vegetarians and Inuits that might skew the findings—variables such as lifestyle, climate, genetic inheritance, and differences in diet other than spinach. Factoring out such variables is one of the complex feats that modern statistical analyses attempt to accomplish. But the fact remains that the most sophisticated correlation studies still cannot tell us the direction of causality or even for certain that there is causality.

Conclusion about Inductive Methods   Induction, then, can tell us within varying degrees of certainty whether X causes Y. It does not, however, explain the causal mechanism itself. Typically, the *because* clause structure of an inductive argument would take one of the following three shapes: (1) "Although we cannot explain the causal mechanism directly, we believe that X and Y are very probably causally linked because we have repeatedly observed their conjunction"; (2) " . . . because we have demonstrated the linkage through controlled scientific experiments"; or (3) " . . . because we have shown that they are statistically correlated and have provided a plausible hypothesis concerning the causal direction."

For Class Discussion

Working individually or in small groups, develop plausible causal chains that might explain the correlations between the following pairs of phenomena:

a. A person who registers a low stress level on an electrochemical stress meter   Does daily meditation

b. A white female teenager   Is seven times more likely to smoke than a black female teenager

c. A person who grew up in a house with two bathrooms   Is more likely to have higher SAT scores than a person who grew up in a one-bathroom home

d. A person who is a member of the National Rifle Association   Favors tough treatment of criminals

Third Method: Argue by Analogy or Precedent

Another common method of causal arguing is through analogy or precedent. (See also Chapter 13, which deals in more depth with the strengths and weaknesses of this kind of arguing.) When you argue through resemblance, you try to find a case that is similar to the one you are arguing about but is better known and less controversial to the reader. If the reader agrees with your view of causality in the similar case, you then try to transfer this understanding to the case at issue. In the following example, the writer tries to explain the link between environmental and biological factors in the creation of teen violence. In this analogy, the biological predisposition for violent behavior is compared to some children's biological predisposition for asthma. Cultural and media violence is then compared to air pollution.

CAUSAL ARGUMENT BY ANALOGY

To deny the role of these influences [bad parenting, easy access to guns, violence in the media] is like denying that air pollution triggers childhood asthma. Yes, to develop asthma a child needs a specific, biological vulnerability. But as long as some children have this respiratory vulnerability—and some always will—then allowing pollution to fill our air will make some children wheeze, and cough, and die. And as long as some children have a neurological vulnerability [to violent behavior]—and some always will—then turning a blind eye to bad parenting, bullying, and the gun culture will make other children seethe, and withdraw, and kill.*

Causal arguments by analogy and precedent are logically weaker than arguments based on causal chains or scientific induction. Although they can be powerfully persuasive, you should be aware of their limits. If any two things are alike in some ways (analogous), they are different in others (disanalogous), and these differences shouldn't be ignored. Consider the following example:

A huckster markets a book called *30 Days to a More Powerful Brain*. The book contains logical puzzles and other brain-teasing exercises that he calls "weight training for the mind."

This argument depends on the warrant that the brain is like a muscle. Because the audience accepts the causal belief that weight training strengthens muscles, the marketers hope to transfer that same belief to the field of mental activity (mind exercises strengthen the brain). However, cognitive psychologists have shown that the brain does *not* work like a muscle, so the analogy is false. Although the argument seems powerful, you should realize that the warrant that says X is like Y is almost always vulnerable.

All resemblance arguments, therefore, are in some sense "false analogies." But some analogies are so misleading that logicians have labeled them "fallacious"—the fallacy of *false analogy*. The false analogy fallacy covers those truly blatant cases where the differences between X and Y are too great for the analogy

---

*Sharon Begley, "Why the Young Kill," *Newsweek* 3 May 1999, 35.

to hold. An example might be the following: "Putting red marks all over students' papers causes great emotional distress just as putting knife marks over their palms would cause great physical distress." It is impossible to draw a precise line, however, between an analogy that has true clarifying and persuasive power and one that is fallacious. Whether the analogy works in any situation depends on the audience's shared assumptions with the arguer.

Glossary of Terms Encountered in Causal Arguments

Because causal arguments are often easier to conduct if writer and reader share a few specialized terms, we offer the following glossary for your convenience.

Fallacy of Oversimplified Cause: One of the greatest temptations when establishing causal relationships is to fall into the habit of looking for *the* cause of something. Most phenomena, especially the ones we argue about, have multiple causes. For example, scientists know that a number of different causes must work together to create a complex disease such as cancer. But though we know all this, we still long to make the world less complex by looking for *the* cause of cancer, thus attributing a single cause to puzzling effects.

Universal/Existential Quantifiers: Closely related to the fallacy of the single clause is the tendency to confuse what logicians call the universal quantifier *(all)* with the existential quantifier *(some)*. The mixing up of universal and existential quantifiers can falsify an argument. For example, to argue that *all* the blame for recent school shootings comes from the shooters' playing violent video games is to claim that playing violent video games is the sole cause—a universal statement. An argument will be stronger and more accurate if the arguer makes an existential statement: *Some* of the blame for this violent behavior can be attributed to playing violent video games. Arguers sometimes deliberately mix up these quantifiers to misrepresent and dismiss opposing views. For example, someone might argue that because the violent video games are not totally and exclusively responsible for the students' violent behavior, they are not an influential factor at all. In this instance, arguers are attempting to dismiss potential causes by framing them as universal statements that can be rejected because they are too extreme and indefensible. Because something is not a sole or total cause does not mean that it could not be a partial cause.

Immediate/Remote Causes: Every causal chain links backward indefinitely into the past. An immediate cause is the closest in time to the event being examined. When John F. Kennedy Jr.'s plane crashed into the Atlantic Ocean south of Martha's Vineyard in July 1999, experts speculated that the *immediate cause* was Kennedy's becoming disoriented in the night haze, losing visual control of the plane, and sending the plane into a fatal dive. A slightly less immediate cause was his decision to make an overwater flight at night without being licensed for instrument flying. The cause of that decision was the need to get to Hyannis Port quickly to attend a wedding. Farther back in time were all the factors that made Kennedy the kind of risk taker who took chances with his own life. For example, several months earlier he had broken an ankle in a hang-gliding accident. Many commentators said that the numerous tragedies that befell the Kennedy family helped shape his risk-taking personality. Such causes going back into the past are considered *remote causes*. It is sometimes difficult to determine the relative significance of remote causes. Immediate causes are obviously linked to an event, but remote causes often have to be dug out or inferred. It was difficult to know, for example, just how seriously we should have taken Hillary Clinton's explanation for her husband's extramarital affairs with Monica Lewinsky and other women. Clinton's womanizing tendencies, she claimed, were caused by "a terrible conflict between his mother and grandmother" when Clinton was four years old. During this period, she said, he "was scarred by abuse."*

Precipitating/Contributing Causes: These terms are similar to *immediate* and *remote* causes but don't designate a temporal linking going into the past. Rather, they refer to a main cause emerging out of a background of subsidiary causes. The *contributing causes* are a set of conditions that give rise to the *precipitating cause,* which triggers the effect. If, for example, a husband and wife decide to separate, the precipitating cause may be a stormy fight over money, which itself is a symptom of their inability to communicate with each other any longer. All the factors that contribute to that inability to communicate—preoccupation with their respective careers, anxieties about money, in-law problems—may be considered contributing causes. Note that the contributing causes and precipitating cause all coexist simultaneously in time—none is temporally more remote than another. But the marriage might have continued had the contributing causes not finally resulted in frequent angry fighting, which doomed the marriage.

Constraints: Sometimes an effect occurs not because X happened but because another factor—a *constraint*—was removed. At other times a possible effect will not occur because a given constraint prevents it from happening. A constraint is a kind of negative cause that limits choices and possibilities. As soon as the constraint is removed, a given effect may occur. For example, in the marriage we have been discussing, the presence of children in the home might have been a constraint against divorce; as soon as the children graduate from high school and leave home, the marriage may well dissolve.

Necessary/Sufficient Causes: A *necessary cause* is one that has to be present for a given effect to occur. For example, fertility drugs are necessary to cause the conception of septuplets. Every couple who has septuplets must have used fertility drugs. In contrast, a *sufficient cause* is one that always produces or guarantees a given effect. Smoking more than a pack of cigarettes per day is sufficient to raise the cost of one's life insurance policy. This statement

---

*"First Lady's Remarks Take White House by Surprise," *Seattle Times* 2 Aug. 1999, A1.

means that if you are a smoker life insurance companies will always place you in a higher risk bracket and charge you more for life insurance. In some cases, a single cause can be both necessary and sufficient. For example, lack of ascorbic acid is both a necessary and a sufficient cause of scurvy. (Think of all those old sailors who didn't eat fruit for months.) It is a necessary cause because you can't get scurvy any other way except through absence of ascorbic acid; it is a sufficient cause because the absence of ascorbic acid always causes scurvy.

For Class Discussion

The terms in the preceding glossary can be effective brainstorming tools for thinking of possible causes of an event. For the following events, try to think of as many causes as possible by brainstorming possible *immediate causes, remote causes, precipitating causes, contributing causes,* and *constraints*:

1. Working individually, make a list of different kinds of causes/constraints for one of the following:
   a. your decision to attend your present college
   b. an important event in your life or your family (a job change, a major move, etc.)
   c. a personal opinion you hold that is not widely shared
2. Working as a group, make a list of different kinds of causes/constraints for one of the following:
   a. why women's fashion and beauty magazines are the most frequently purchased magazines in college bookstores
   b. why American students consistently score below Asian and European students in academic achievement
   c. why the number of babies born out of wedlock has increased dramatically in the last thirty years

Writing Your Causal Argument

WRITING ASSIGNMENT
FOR CHAPTER 12

Choose an issue about the causes or consequences of a trend, event, or other phenomenon. Write an argument that persuades an audience to accept your explanation of the causes or consequences of your chosen phenomenon. Within your essay you should examine alternative hypotheses or opposing views and explain your reasons for rejecting them. You can imagine your issue either as a puzzle or as a disagreement. If a puzzle, your task will be to create a convincing case for an audience that doesn't have an answer to your causal question already in mind. If a disagreement, your task will be more overtly persuasive since your goal will be to change your audience's views.

Exploring Ideas

Arguments about causes and consequences abound in public, professional, or personal life, so you shouldn't have difficulty finding a causal issue worth investigating and arguing. Angered by media explanations for the Columbine High School massacre, student writer Daeha Ko contributed his own argument to the conversation by blaming popular cliques and the school establishment that supports them (see pp. 259–261). Student writer Holly Miller, wondering about the causes of teenage promiscuity, wrote a researched argument trying to untangle the relative contributions of various contributing causes for teenage sex (see pp. 265–268). Others of our students have focused on causal issues such as these: What causes some first-year students to develop better study habits in the first few months of college than other students? Why do kids join gangs? What causes anorexia? What are the consequences of violent video games on children? What are the consequences of mandatory drug testing (written by a student who has to take amphetamines for narcolepsy)? What are the causes of different sexual orientations? Why did the university fire a favorite assistant dean in a student affairs office? What has happened since 1970 to cause young people to delay getting married? (This question was initiated by the student's interest in the statistical table in Chapter 9, p. 190.) Why did this promising football season end so miserably for the university team? What effect will the Navy's low-frequency sonar system for finding enemy submarines have on whales and other marine mammals? (The student who posed this question eventually wrote the researched proposal argument on pp. 416–423.)

If you have trouble finding a causal issue to write about, you can often create provocative controversies among your classmates through the following strategies:

- *Make a list of unusual likes and dislikes.* Think about unusual things that people like or dislike. We find it really strange, for example, that so many people like professional wrestling or dislike writing notes in margins while they read. You could summarize the conventional explanations that persons give for an unusual pleasure or aversion and then argue for a surprising or unexpected cause. Why do people like playing the lottery? What attracts people to extreme sports? What causes math phobia? How do you explain the popularity of the new VW Beetle?

- *Make a list of puzzling events or trends.*   Another strategy is to make a list of puzzling phenomena and try to explain their causes. Start with one-time events (a cheating scandal at your school; the 2001 energy crisis in California). Then list puzzling repeated events (sudden infant death syndrome; high incidence of teenage pregnancy when contraceptives are readily available). Finally, list some recent trends (growth of naturopathic medicine; teen interest in the gothic; hatred of women in much gangsta rap). Engage classmates in discussions of one or more of the items on your list. Look for places of disagreement as entry points into the conversation.

- *Brainstorm consequences of a recent or proposed action.*   Arguments about consequences are among the most interesting and important of causal disputes. If you can argue for an unanticipated consequence of a real, hypothetical, or proposed action—for example, a bad consequence of an apparently positive event or a good consequence of an apparently negative event—you can make an important contribution to the conversation. What might be the consequences, for example, of some of the following: requiring a passing grade on a high-stakes test for graduation from high school; depleting the world's oil supply; combating terrorism by asking citizens to report suspicious behaviors of neighbors or coworkers; requiring school uniforms; legalizing marijuana; invading Iraq to overthrow Saddam Hussein (a debate that gripped the United States in 2002–2003); making e-mail spam illegal; labeling genetically engineered ingredients in food products; abolishing fraternities and sororities; reclassifying SUVs as "cars" rather than "trucks" for purposes of federal fuel-efficiency regulations; building a large-scale wind farm in Nantucket Sound (another national debate in the summer of 2002); any similar recent, hypothetical, or proposed event or action?

Organizing a Causal Argument

At the outset, it is useful to know some of the standard ways that a causal argument can be organized. Later, you may decide on a different organizational pattern, but these standard ways will help you get started.

Plan 1

When your purpose is to describe and explain all the links in a causal chain:

- Introduce phenomenon to be explained and show why it is problematical.
- Present your thesis in summary form.
- Describe and explain each link in the causal chain.

Plan 2

When your purpose is to explore the relative contribution of a number of causes to a phenomenon or to explore multiple consequences of a phenomenon:

- Introduce the phenomenon to be explained and suggest how or why it is controversial.

- Devote one section to each possible cause/consequence and decide whether it is necessary, sufficient, contributory, remote, and so forth. (Arrange sections so that those causes most familiar to the audience come first and the most surprising ones come last.)

Plan 3

When your purpose is to argue for a cause or consequence that is surprising or unexpected to your audience:

- Introduce a phenomenon to be explained and show why it is controversial.
- One by one, examine and reject the causes or consequences your audience would normally assume or expect.
- Introduce your unexpected or surprising cause or consequence and argue for it.

Plans 2 and 3 are similar in that they examine numerous possible causes or consequences. Plan 2, however, tries to establish the relative importance of each cause or consequence, whereas plan 3 aims at rejecting the causes or consequences normally assumed by the audience and argues for an unexpected surprising cause or consequence.

Plan 4

When your purpose is to change your audience's mind about a cause or consequence:

- Introduce the issue and show why it is controversial.
- Summarize your opponent's causal argument and then refute it.
- Present your own causal argument.

Plan 4 is a standard structure for all kinds of arguments. This is the structure you would use if you were the attorney for the person whose car skidded into the boutique (pp. 243–244). The opposing attorney would blame your client's reckless driving. You would lay blame on a poorly signed intersection, a speeding beer truck, and violation of building codes.

Questioning and Critiquing a Causal Argument

Because of the strenuous conditions that must be met before causality can be proven, causal arguments are vulnerable at many points. The following strategies will generally be helpful.

If you described every link in a causal chain, would skeptics point out weaknesses in any of the links?   Describing a causal chain can be a complex business. A skeptic can raise doubts about an entire argument simply by questioning one of the links. Your best defense is to make a diagram of the linkages and role-play a skeptic trying to refute each link in turn. Whenever you find possible arguments against your position, see how you can strengthen your own argument at that point.

If your argument is based on a scientific experiment, could skeptics question the validity of the experiment?   The scientific method attempts to demonstrate causality experimentally. If the experiment isn't well designed, however, the demonstration is less likely to be acceptable to skeptical audiences. Here are ways to question and critique a scientific argument:

- *Question the findings.*   Skeptics may have reason to believe that the data collected were not accurate or representative. They might provide alternative data or simply point out flaws in the way the data were collected.

- *Question the interpretation of the data.*   Many research studies are divided into "findings" and "discussion" sections. In the discussion section the researcher analyzes and interprets the data. A skeptic might provide an alternative interpretation of the data or otherwise argue that the data don't support what the original writer claims.

- *Question the design of the experiment.*   A detailed explanation of research design is beyond the scope of this text, but we can give a brief example of how a typical experiment did go wrong. When home computers were first developed in the 1980s, a group of graduate students conducted an experiment to test the effect of word processors on students' writing in junior high school. They reported that students who used the word processors for revising all their essays did significantly better on a final essay than a control group of students who didn't use word processors. It turned out, however, that there were at least two major design flaws in the experiment. First, the researchers allowed students to volunteer for the experimental group. Perhaps these students were already better writers than the control group from the start. (Can you think of a causal explanation of why the better students might volunteer to use the computers?) Second, when the teachers graded essays from both the computer group and the control group, the essays were not retyped uniformly. Thus the computer group's essays were typed with "computer perfection," whereas the control group's essays were handwritten or typed on ordinary typewriters. Perhaps the readers were affected by the pleasing appearance of the computer-typed essays. More significantly, perhaps the graders were biased in favor of the computer project and unconsciously scored the computer-typed papers higher.

If you have used correlation data, could skeptics argue that the correlation is much weaker than you claim or that you haven't sufficiently demonstrated causality?   As we discussed earlier, correlation data tell us only that two or more phenomena are likely to occur together. They don't tell us that one phenomenon caused the other. Thus correlation arguments are usually accompanied by hypotheses about causal connections between the phenomena. Correlation arguments can often be refuted as follows:

- Find problems in the statistical methods used to determine the correlation.
- Weaken the correlation by pointing out exceptions.
- Provide an alternative hypothesis about causality.

If you have used an analogy argument, could skeptics point out disanalogies? Although among the most persuasive of argumentative strategies, analogy arguments are also among the easiest to refute. The standard procedure is to counter your argument that X is like Y by pointing out all the ways that X is *not* like Y. Once again, by role-playing an opposing view, you may be able to strengthen your own analogy argument.

Could a skeptic cast doubt on your argument by reordering your priority of causes? Up to this point we've focused on refuting the claim that X causes Y. However, another approach is to concede that X helps cause Y but that X is only one of several contributing causes and not the most significant one at that.

Readings

The following essay, by student writer Daeha Ko, appeared as an op-ed piece in the *University of Washington Daily* on May 9, 1999, several weeks after the Columbine High School massacre in Littleton, Colorado. Daeha's motivation for writing is his anger at media attempts to explain the massacre—none of which focuses on the cliquish social structure of high school itself.

The Monster That Is High School
Daeha Ko (student)

In the past weeks, intensive media coverage has surrounded the shooting incident in Littleton, Colorado, where 12 students and a teacher died, along with 23 wounded. Yet people forget the real victims of the Littleton massacre are Dylan Klebold and Eric Harris.   1

What they did was against the law, but let's face it—the incident was waiting to happen. And there's nothing surprising about it.   2

The social priorities of high school are to blame. In truth, high school is a place where jocks, cheerleaders and anyone associated with them can do whatever they want and get away with it. Their exploits are celebrated in pep rallies, printed in school papers and shown off in trophy cases. The popular cliques have the most clout, and are—in a sense—local celebrities. If they ever run into disciplinary problems with the school or police, they get let off the hook under the guise that they are just kids.   3

Public schools claim to support all students, but in reality choose to invest their priorities in activities associated with popular cliques. Schools are willing to go to any means necessary to support the sports teams, for example. They care less about students who don't belong to popular cliques, leaving them almost nothing. School becomes less about getting a good education, instead priding itself on the celebration of elite cliques.   4

5   The popular cliques are nice to their own but spit out extremely cruel insults to those who don't fit in. As noted in *Time,* jocks admitted they like to pick on unpopular kids "because it's just fun to do." Their insulting words create deep emotional wounds, while school authorities ignore the cruelty of the corrupt high-school social system.

6   Schools refuse to accept any accountability and point to parents instead. While it is the job of parents to condition their kids, it is impossible for them to supervise their kids 24 hours a day.

7   As an outcast, I was harassed on an everyday basis by jocks, and received no help from school authorities. It got so bad that I attempted suicide.

8   Yes, I did (and still do) wear all black, play Doom and listen to raucous heavy metal, punk and Goth music. I was into the occult and had extensive knowledge on guns and how to build bombs.

9   I got into several fights, including one where I kicked the shit out of a basketball player. The only reason why I didn't shoot him and his jock cronies is because I lacked access to guns. I would've blown every single one of them away and not cared.

10   To defend myself, I carried around a 7-inch blade. If anyone continued to mess with me, I sent them anonymous notes with a big swastika drawn on them. I responded to harassment with "Yeah, heil Hitler," while saluting.

11   They got the hint. Eventually, I found some friends who were also outcasts. We banded together and didn't judge each other by the way we looked or what we liked. But I still held contempt for jocks whom I believed should be shot and fed to the sharks.

12   Even in their deaths, Klebold and Harris are still treated like outcasts. How dare *Time* call them "The Monsters Next Door." News analysis poured over the "abnormal" world of "Goth" culture, Marilyn Manson, violent computer games and gun control. It also targeted other outcast students as trenchcoat-goth, submerged, socially challenged kids who fail to fit the "correct" image of American teens.

13   The popular cliques have their likeness reinforced through the images of trashy teen media as seen on MTV, *90210,* and *Dawson's Creek.* It's heard in the bubble-gum pop of Britney Spears and Backstreet Boys, along with their imitators. Magazines like *YM* and *Seventeen* feature pretty-looking girls, offering advice on the latest trends in dress, makeup and dating.

14   Media coverage was saturated with memorials and funeral services of the deceased. Friends and family remembered them as "good kids." Not all those killed knew or made fun of Klebold or Harris. Obviously there were members of the popular cliques who made fun of them and escaped harm. But innocent people had to die in order to bring injustices to light that exist in our society.

15   It's tragic, but perhaps that's the price that had to be paid. Perhaps they are shocked by the fact that some "nerds" have actually defeated them for once because teasing isn't fun and games anymore.

16   With the last of the coffins being laid to rest, people are looking for retribution, someone to prosecute. Why? The two kids are dead—there is no sense in pursuing this problem any further. But lawyers are trying to go after those who they believe influenced Harris and Klebold: namely their parents, gun dealers, and the Trenchcoat

Mafia. Police heavily questioned Harris' girlfriend about the guns she gave them and arrested one person.

The families of the deceased, lawyers and the police need to get a clue and   17
leave the two kids' families and friends alone. They are dealing with just as much grief and do not need to be punished for someone else's choices. Filing lawsuits will drag on for years, burdening everyone and achieving little.

It's not like you can bring your loved ones back to life after you've won your case.   18

What we need is bigger emphasis on academic discipline and more financing to-   19
ward academic programs. Counselors and psychiatrists need to be hired to attend to student needs. People need practical skills, not the pep-rally fluff of popular cliques.

The people of Littleton need to be at peace with the fate of their town and heal   20
wounds instead of prying them open with lawsuits.

Critiquing "The Monster That Is High School"

1. Summarize Daeha Ko's argument by creating a plausible causal chain leading from popular high school cliques to the Littleton massacre. How persuasive is Daeha's argument?

2. Daeha is angered at *Time* magazine for characterizing Klebold and Harris as "the monsters next door." How would you characterize Daeha's *ethos* in this piece? Do you see him as "monstrous" himself? Or does his *ethos* help create sympathy for social outcasts in high school culture?

3. Daeha presents his causal argument as a contribution to the frantic, contentious social conflict that raged among social scientists, columnists, and other media commentators after the shootings at Columbine High School in Littleton, Colorado (see a summary of this discussion in Case 1, p. 241). Which alternative explanations for the shooting does Daeha address? What strategy does he use to rebut alternative causal arguments? Do you regard Daeha's argument as a valuable contribution to the controversy? Why or why not?

Our second reading (Figure 12.1) is an advocacy advertisement seeking donations to the "Community Safety Net Fund" of the United Way organization in a major American city. It consists of an intriguing visual image accompanied by a one-sentence statistic.

Critiquing the United Way Advocacy Ad

1. What techniques of visual argument (see pp. 166–172) are used by this advocacy ad? Do you find the visual images effective? Why or why not?

2. The verbal text for this ad consists of a single statistic. The ad maker invites its target audience to fill in the gaps in order to convert this statistic into an argument. What is the argument that this ad makes?

3. What values does this ad appeal to? How does the ad use the strategy of "audience-based reasons" (see pp. 104–107)? This ad could have used either a boy or a girl of any ethnicity (white, African American, Asian) and

Kids who do not participate
in after-school activities
are 37% more likely
to become teen parents
than kids who do.

Your gift to the Community Safety Net Fund helps bring together the people
and resources to identify and address the challenges that face our community.
Call (206) 461-GIVE or log on to unitedwayofkingcounty.org.

UNITED WAY
of KING COUNTY

BE PART OF THE ANSWER.

FIGURE 12.1 *United Way advocacy ad*

appearance (hairstyle, for example, or body piercings) participating in any after-school activity (music, art, debate team). Why do you think the ad makers chose a pony-tailed white female teenager playing basketball? (Note that the statistic lumps together males and females—it talks about teen "parents" rather than teen "mothers.")

4. The statistic cited implies a cause and effect relationship between after-school activities and reduced likelihood for teenage parenthood. How might you argue that this statistic simply shows a correlation rather than a cause and effect?

Our third reading, by educational analyst Richard Rothstein, appeared in the *New York Times* on June 5, 2002. The data in this argument are based on a research report published by the Manpower Demonstration Research Corporation, a "nonprofit, nonpartisan social policy research organization [. . .] dedicated to learning what works to improve the well-being of low-income people" (from the home page of its Web site). Rothstein's article contributes to a national discussion of the effects of welfare policy on society and particularly to the 1996 changes in welfare laws mandating that welfare recipients, including single mothers, find work.

When Mothers on Welfare Go to Work
Richard Rothstein

When Congress changed welfare in 1996, critics worried that forcing mothers   1
to work might harm their children's development unless adequate and subsidized
child care was provided. Fewer worries were expressed about teenagers. Indeed, it
was thought that the changes in welfare would help adolescents because their
newly disciplined mothers would be positive role models.

As Congress debates renewal of the welfare law this year, new evidence sheds   2
light on these expectations. Surprisingly, forcing mothers to work appears to harm
adolescents rather than younger children. When welfare recipients get jobs, their
teenagers tend not to do as well in school.

The evidence is scanty but consistent, based on experiments in the United   3
States and Canada to test new welfare-to-work rules. In 11 states and provinces,
women on welfare were randomly assigned to groups where they were required or
encouraged to work or to control groups where benefits continued under the old
rules. In some cases, the control groups were temporarily exempted from work requirements so the experiment could continue. In all, 5,500 women took part and
data were gathered on their 6,500 adolescent children.

Yesterday, the Manpower Demonstration Research Corporation, which contracts   4
to conduct social science research for governmental agencies, published a statistical
synopsis of these experiments, "How Welfare and Work Policies for Parents Affect
Adolescents." The summary reported that adolescents of the working mothers did
worse in school, on average, than adolescents whose families continued to receive
aid under the old rules.

Relying mostly on surveys of mothers about their children's school performance   5
(evidence that was confirmed by test scores, when available, and by interviews of
some teenagers themselves), the researchers estimated that scores of teenagers
whose mothers worked dropped about 4 percentiles, on average, and their chances
of repeating a grade increased by about 2 percentage points.

The experiments shed little light on why performance declined, but there is   6
a likely culprit: inadequate supervision. If their mothers are at work, teenagers
are more likely to get into trouble. They are more likely to take drugs. They are
less likely to turn off the television, stop hanging out with friends and do their
homework.

Lisa A. Gennetian, an author of the Manpower report, noted that the data   7
revealed that teenagers who have younger siblings also have a greater chance of being suspended from school or dropping out before graduation. Dr. Gennetian speculated that when mothers are at work, their adolescent children may watch their
younger brothers and sisters rather than study.

Congressional debate over renewal of the welfare law centers mainly on how   8
much new money should be provided for child care. More accessible child care
could help adolescents if it relieved them of responsibility for baby-sitting.

9   But child care is unlikely to help teenagers if good after-school activities are not provided. Many women who have gone to work under the new welfare rules have taken night and evening jobs, and often more than one low-wage job to make ends meet. Too often, adolescents are left to their own devices in the afternoons and evenings when their mothers work.

10   Middle-class working mothers who have never been on welfare also leave their teenagers unsupervised. They could use after-school programs, too.

11   In April, an organization of police officers, sheriffs, district attorneys and crime victims, calling itself Fight Crime, released a survey of youths from 14 to 17 representing all social classes in New York State. Fight Crime found that 38 percent of the teenagers were not supervised after school for three or more days a week. They were twice as likely as supervised teenagers to drink alcohol, five times as likely to take drugs and four times as likely to commit crimes or misdemeanors.

12   While mothers inclined to tolerate such activities may also be those who leave teenage children unsupervised, it is more likely that the lack of supervision contributes to this harmful behavior.

13   When the welfare law was enacted in 1996, Congress relied heavily on results of an experiment in Riverside, Calif.–also reported by the Manpower research group–that showed welfare mothers could move into jobs without further education. Though this was only one study, Congress paid attention because it was scientific.

14   Congressional leaders and the Bush administration have recently insisted even more strongly that policy be based on scientific research. It would be a shame if Congress abandoned this faith and failed to ensure that every adolescent child of a working mother could enroll in after-school activities that provide the supervision mothers can no longer give.

Critiquing "When Mothers on Welfare Go to Work"

1. When the 1996 welfare reforms were enacted, critics worried about the effects on young children of single mothers being required to work. In contrast, Rothstein focuses on the effects of working mothers on teenagers. At the time of the 1996 welfare reforms, what effect of working mothers on teenagers was initially hypothesized? What effect is reported in the research study used by Rothstein? What evidence is used to support the research findings?

2. According to the research study, when mothers return to work the most noticeable negative effect is on teenagers with younger siblings. What is Rothstein's explanation for this effect? Does his explanation seem plausible to you? Can you offer any different hypotheses?

3. Rothstein uses this report to make a plea to the U.S. Congress "that every adolescent child of a working mother could enroll in after-school activities that provide the supervision mothers can no longer give." Considering all the

other demands on federal dollars (defense, fighting terrorism, Social Security, health care, highways, transportation, and so forth), how high a priority would you place on after-school programs for teenagers? How would you use Rothstein's article (or the original Manpower Demonstration Research Corporation report available on its Web site at *mdrc.org/Reports2002*) to support or oppose federal funding for after-school programs?

4. Both Rothstein's article and the United Way advocacy ad request funds for after-school activities. How would you describe the differences in the ways that visual arguments versus verbal-only arguments make their appeals to an audience? What are the strengths, weaknesses, and appropriate uses for each kind of argument?

Our final causal argument, by student writer Holly Miller, examines the causes of teen sexual behavior. It uses the documentation form of the American Psychological Association (APA).

The Causes of Teen Sexual Behavior
Holly M. Miller (student)

Teen sex, leading all too frequently to casual promiscuity, abortion, single motherhood, or STDs including AIDS, is a widely discussed problem in our culture. According to a recent survey conducted by the Kaiser Family Foundation, whereas only 35 percent of girls and 55 percent of boys had had sex by their eighteenth birthdays in the early 1970s, 56 percent of teenage girls and 73 percent of boys had had sex by age eighteen in 1996. The same study revealed that only "one in five teenagers do not have intercourse during their teenage years." Fifty-five percent of the teens cite readiness as the reason they have sex. Simply, "they think they are ready" (Survey, 1996).

However, there should be little doubt that most teens are not ready for sexual activity. High rates of pregnancy and STDs indicate that teens do not properly protect themselves, and high numbers of abortions suggest that they are not ready for parenthood. Moreover, much sexual behavior seems attributable to emotional immaturity, which may contribute to the particularly disturbing statistic that many girls are pressured to have sex or do so involuntarily. Seventy percent of the girls who had sex before age fourteen, and 60 percent of the girls who had sex prior to their fifteenth birthday claimed that the sexual intercourse was involuntary. Additionally, "six out of ten teenage girls say another reason why teen girls may have sex is because a boyfriend is pressuring them" (Survey, 1996).

There can be no question that teen sexual behavior is a growing problem, but the explanation for this increase in sexual activity is controversial. This paper's focus is on the causes of teen sexual behavior. Why are teens having sex? Who or what is the greatest influence on teen sexual behavior? How can we slow the rate of teen sexual activity?

4   Although many causes work together to influence teen sex, one of the most significant contributing causes is the media. Victor C. Strasburger (1997), an expert on adolescence, notes, "Teenagers watch an average of three hours of TV per day" (p. 18). A study cited by the Kaiser Foundation examined TV shows most popular with teenagers in 1992–1993. This study "found that one in four interactions among characters per episode conveyed a sexual message. . . . Only two of the ten shows included messages about sexual responsibility" (Entertainment, 1996). Popular shows in 1992–1993, such as *90210* and *Melrose Place,* were just the trailblazers for the prime-time dramas now aimed at teens, such as *Dawson's Creek, Party of Five,* and *Felicity.* Beyond the sexually explicit story lines of programs, commercials use sex appeal to sell everything from cars to potato chips, and teens see twenty thousand commercials per year (Strasburger, 1997, p. 18). Another multimedia influence on teens is pornography. While statistics are hard to find because selling pornography to children is illegal, it is obvious that teens have access to pornography. One fifteen-year-old boy interviewed by *Life* magazine claimed, "No one tells you how to [have sex]. You learn it from watching pornos" (Adato, 1999, p. 38).

5   The effect of the media on teenage sexuality is probably subtle rather than direct. The media don't encourage teenagers to have sex, at least explicitly. But the influence is still there. Hollywood has long been blamed for desensitizing our culture to violence; it is entirely plausible that they have also desensitized our culture, and youth, to sex. According to Drew Altman, president of the Kaiser Family Foundation, "With the problems facing adolescents today, how sex is shown on TV is just as important as how much sex is shown on TV" (Entertainment, 1996). The frequent and graphic depictions of sex normalize the behavior for teenagers. Watching stars play characters their own age—characters with whom they can identify, characters who, just like them, have part-time jobs, too much homework, and problems with their parents—encourages teens to emulate the sexual behaviors of Bailey, Sara, Dawson, or Joey.

6   Teenagers themselves, however, will usually deny that they emulate TV characters, so we need to look also at other factors. Another contributing cause of teen sexual activity is peer pressure. The problem comes from teens' willingness to say and do things to impress others. The tendency to brag about sexual exploits was egregiously illustrated by the Spur Posse scandal of 1993. A group of popular high school "jocks" from a suburban California community formed a clique with the purpose of sleeping with girls. In fact, they competed with each other to see who could sleep with the most girls, going so far as to pressure girls as young as ten to have sex. Once exposed, several members were charged with lewd conduct, felony intercourse, and rape. The Posse members themselves say they learned about sex "the old-fashioned way": from older brothers and friends (Gelman, 1993, p. 29). Few, if any, of the guys would probably have gone to such extremes to sleep with girls had their friends not been competing in the same contest.

7   Another contributing cause is schools. According to many critics, sex education programs in the schools do little to promote safe sexual behavior, and they are often criticized by conservatives as promoting the message that it is good and normal to be sexually active (so long as you use a condom). Why are sex education programs so

ineffective? One critic notes that sex education classes focus on the mechanics of sex and avoid issues of emotions, love, and morality. "They talk about zygotes," according to one fourteen-year-old boy (Adato, 1999, p. 38). Another critic, NYU psychology professor Paul C. Vitz (1999), reviewed leading high school health textbooks and is troubled by their lack of focus on "the meaning and possibility of true love and its relationship to sexual union and marriage." Vitz claims that textbooks encourage students to evaluate behavior in terms of their own needs rather than the needs of their partners or of a relationship. He claims that "[o]ur growing tolerance of the adult 'do your own thing' morality runs smack up against the need to socialize and protect the young" (p. 547). In short, Vitz desires a sex education program that emphasizes love and morality. Yet schools avoid creating such programs because while parents are generally comfortable with their kids learning about sex from school, they are not as complacent when it comes to schools teaching morality.

8   The schools are criticized from another direction by some feminist scholars who have blamed conventional schooling for the vulnerability of girls. Nancy J. Perry (1992), citing an American Association of University Women study showing that teachers pay less attention to girls than to boys, charges that "girls come out of school ill-prepared to get ahead in society" (p. 83). Though the AAUW did not address the sexual behavior of girls, their hypothesis that schools marginalize girls, making them vulnerable, may contribute to the fact that between 60 and 70 percent of teenage girls feel pressured into sex.

9   In explaining why adolescence is so difficult for girls, however, Perry puts primary responsibility not on the schools but on parents. Although she acknowledges that peer pressure and the media's portrayal of women as sex objects are contributing factors to sexual activity among teenage girls, she identifies parental involvement as the critical factor in the development of young girls.

10   In fact, differences in parenting styles might be the chief variable that influences teenage sexual behavior. Drs. Sharon D. White and Richard R. DeBlassie, writing in the journal *Adolescence,* point out that "parents are the earliest and most important influence on sexuality" (1992, p. 184). According to their research, different parenting styles have a measurable influence on teenagers' sexual behavior. The highest rates of sexual activity come from teenagers with permissive parents who set no rules. The next highest rates, ironically, come from teenagers whose parents are unduly strict and controlling, a parenting style that often fosters rebellion. The lowest rates of sexual activity come from teenagers whose parents set firm but reasonable and moderate rules. White and DeBlassie show that parents who insist on reasonable curfews, and who supervise their teens' dating by knowing whom they are with and where they are going, produce teens with the most responsible attitudes toward sex. They suggest also that parents' implicit values—for example, abstinence until marriage or at least sex linked to love and commitment—are most likely to be transmitted to teens when the teens feel connected to their parents in a safe environment with rules.

11   So what can be done to reduce the problems of teen sexuality? Research suggests that parents have the most direct and strongest influence over teens' sexual behavior, but by no means are they the only influences. Thus, television producers

ought to provide role models of teens with less promiscuous views of sex. Teachers need to pay better attention to the needs of their students, whether the teens need to hear about emotional sides of sex or the advantages of waiting until marriage to have intercourse. Parents need to turn off the TV and open dialogue with their children. Parents need to set moderate and reasonable rules for their teens and carefully supervise their behavior. Only when parents take the lead in responsibly educating their children about sex, and in pressuring the media and the schools to create a holistic view of sex in the context of love and commitment, can we curb the trend of teen sex and its unhealthy consequences.

References

Adato, A. (1999, March 1). The secret lives of teens. *Life*, 38.

Kaiser Family Foundation. (1996). *Entertainment media as "sex educators?" and other ways teens learn about sex, contraception, STDs, and AIDS.* Retrieved May 16, 1999, from http://www.kff.org

Gelman, D. (1993, April 12). Mixed messages. *Newsweek*, 29.

Perry, N. (1992, August 10). Why it's so tough to be a girl. *Fortune*, 82–84.

Strasburger, V. (1997, May 19). Tuning in to teenagers. *Newsweek*, 18–19.

Kaiser Family Foundation. (1996). *Survey on teens and sex: What they say teens today need to know, and who they listen to.* Retrieved May 16, 1999, from http://www.kff.org

Vitz, P. (1999, March). Cupid's broken arrow. *Phi Delta Kappan*, 547.

White, S., & DeBlassie, R. (1992). Adolescent sexual behavior. *Adolescence, 27*, 183–191.

Critiquing "The Causes of Teen Sexual Behavior"

1. How does Holly Miller establish the issue of teen sexuality and suggest the controversy surrounding it?

2. What kind of causal links does Holly employ to explain why teenagers have sex? What data does she use to support those links? Are these data persuasive? What would make her interpretations more persuasive?

3. What features of causal argument contribute to the strength of her argument? What insights does this argument add to the ongoing social conflict and confusion over teen sexuality?

13 Resemblance Arguments
X Is (Is Not) like Y

CASE 1

To justify a possible invasion of Iraq during the national debate in 2002, media supporters of the Bush administration called Saddam Hussein an "Arab Hitler." A similar analogy was used when NATO began bombing Serbia during the Kosovo crisis. The Clinton administration, along with the U.S. media, likened Yugoslavian president Slobodan Milosevic to Adolf Hitler and compared the "ethnic cleansing" of Kosovo to the Nazis' "final solution" against the Jews. When justifying the bombing, Clinton frequently evoked the Holocaust and the lessons of World War II. "Never again," he said. Meanwhile, the Serbian community in the United States (and many Balkan scholars) criticized the Holocaust analogy. The Serbian community likened the Kosovo crisis not to the Nazi annihilation of the Jews but to a civil war in which Serbs were protecting their homeland against Albanian terrorists. They pointed to explanatory precedents when the Serbs themselves were victims, especially the "ethnic cleansing" of Serbs from Croatia in 1995.

CASE 2

In the 1970s and 1980s it became popular in the public schools to mainstream students with developmental disabilities rather than to isolate them in special education classes. More recently, the growing trend to identify students with learning disabilities has led to special treatments and accommodations for learning disabled students. Critics say that special treatment for students with "learning disabilities" is a disruptive and expensive fad. In response, Arthur Levine, president of Teachers College, Columbia University, justifies the special treatment of persons with learning disabilities or with different learning styles by comparing changes in education to changes in industrial economies. In today's economy, says Levine, "There is less emphasis on mass production and more customization of products and services." Just as the clothing business is offering customers alternatives to mass-produced, off-the-rack clothing, so should schools offer customized services to fit the learning differences of its students.

An Overview of Resemblance Arguments

Resemblance arguments support a claim by comparing one thing to another with the intention of transferring the audience's understanding of (or feelings about) the second thing back to the first. Sometimes an entire argument can be devoted to a resemblance claim. More commonly, brief resemblance arguments are pieces of larger arguments devoted to a different stasis. Thus cultural critic Susan Sontag, in arguing that the U.S. response to terrorism following the September 11, 2001, attacks was misguided, compared the war on terrorism to wars on cancer or poverty.

> Wars on such enemies as cancer, poverty and drugs are understood to be endless wars. There will always be cancer, poverty and drugs. And there will always be despicable terrorists. . . .

Her point is that terrorism does not constitute a one-time enemy that can be defeated (as in Japan or Germany in World War II) but an endless war (as in the war against disease or poverty). Her goal is to resist the Bush administration's use of wartime rhetoric to rally Americans to military action and to the acceptance of reduced civil liberties. The strategy of resemblance arguments is to take the audience's understanding of the point made in the comparison (you shouldn't use actual wartime strategies to fight a metaphorical war like the war on poverty or drugs) and transfer it to the issue being debated (you shouldn't use actual wartime strategies to fight the war against terrorism). Those who supported the Bush administration, in contrast, often compared the terrorist attacks on the World Trade Center and the Pentagon to Japan's attack on Pearl Harbor that initiated U.S. entry into World War II.

The persuasive power of resemblance arguments comes from their ability to clarify an audience's conception of contested issues while conveying powerful emotions. Resemblance arguments typically take the form X is (is not) like Y. Resemblance arguments work best when the audience has a clear (and sometimes emotionally charged) understanding of the Y term. The writer then hopes to transfer this understanding, along with accompanying emotions, to the X term. The danger of resemblance arguments, as we shall see, is that the differences between the X and Y terms are often so significant that the resemblance argument collapses under close examination.

Like most other argument types, resemblance arguments can be analyzed using the Toulmin schema. Suppose, for example, that you want to awaken young women to the dangers of dieting by showing them how an obsession with weight is caused, at least partially, by patriarchal constructions of female beauty that keep women submissive and powerless. You decide to make the resemblance claim that women's obsessive dieting is like foot-binding in ancient China. This argument can be displayed in Toulmin terms as follows:

ENTHYMEME: Women's obsessive dieting in America serves the same harmful function as foot-binding in ancient China because both practices keep women childlike, docile, dependent, and unthreatening to men.

CLAIM: Women's obsessive dieting in America serves the same harmful function as foot-binding in ancient China

STATED REASON: because both practices keep women childlike, docile, dependent, and unthreatening to men.

GROUNDS: evidence that both obsessive dieting and foot-binding lead to childlike subordination: Both practices involve women's painful attempts to meet patriarchal standards of beauty in which men are powerful agents and women are beautiful objects; women, in attempting to imitate society's image of the "perfect woman," damage themselves (Chinese women are physically maimed; American women are psychologically maimed and often weakened by inadequate diet or constant worry about being fat); both practices make women childlike rather than grown-up (men call beautiful women "babes" or "dolls"; anorexia stops menstruation); women obsessed with beauty end up satisfied with less pay and subordinate positions in society as long as they are regarded as feminine and pretty.

WARRANT: We should reject practices that are like Chinese foot-binding.

BACKING: arguments that the subordinate position of women evidenced in both foot-binding and obsession with weight is related to patriarchal construction of women's roles; further arguments for why women should free themselves from patriarchal views.

CONDITIONS OF REBUTTAL: All the ways that dieting and concern for weight are not like Chinese foot-binding. For example, skeptics might say that women who diet are concerned with health, not pursuit of beauty; concern for healthy weight is "rational," not "obsessive"; thin women are often powerful athletes, not at all like Chinese victims of foot-binding who can hardly walk; dieting does not cause crippling deformity; a concern for beauty does not make a woman subordinate or satisfied with less pay; dieting is a woman's choice—not something forced on her as a child.

QUALIFIER: Perhaps the writer should say "*Under certain conditions* obsessive dieting can even seem like Chinese foot-binding."

For many audiences, the comparison of women's dieting to Chinese foot-binding will have an immediate and powerful emotional effect, perhaps causing them to see attitudes toward weight and food from a new, unsettling perspective. The analogy invites them to transfer their understanding of Chinese foot-binding—which seems instantly repulsive and oppressive of women—to their understanding of obsessive concern for losing weight. Whereas social controls in ancient China were overt, the modern practice uses more subtle kinds of social control, such as the influence of the fashion and beauty industry and peer pressure. But in both cases women feel forced to mold their bodies to a patriarchal standard of beauty—one that emphasizes soft curves, tiny waists, and daintiness rather than strength and power.

But this example also illustrates the dangers of resemblance arguments, which often ignore important differences or *disanalogies* between the terms of comparison. As the "conditions of rebuttal" show, there are many differences between dieting and foot-binding. For example, the practice of foot-binding was not a conscious choice of young Chinese girls, who were forced to have their feet wrapped at an early age. Dieting, on the other hand, is something one chooses, and it may reveal a healthy and rational choice rather than an obsession with appearance. When the practice degenerates to anorexia or bulimia, it becomes a mental disease, not a physical deformity forced on a girl in childhood. Thus a resemblance argument is usually open to refutation if a skeptic points out important disanalogies.

We now turn to the two types of resemblance arguments: analogy and precedent.

Arguments by Analogy

The use of *analogies* can constitute the most imaginative form of argument. If you don't like your new boss, you can say that she's like a marine drill sergeant, the cowardly captain of a sinking ship, or a mother hen. Each of these analogies suggests a different management style, clarifying the nature of your dislike while conveying an emotional charge. The ubiquity of analogies undoubtedly stems from their power to clarify the writer's understanding of an issue through comparisons that grip the audience.

Of course, this power to make things clear comes at a price. Analogies often clarify one aspect of a relationship at the expense of other aspects. Thus, for example, in nineteenth-century America many commentators were fond of justifying certain negative effects of capitalism (for example, the squalor of the poor) by comparing social and economic processes to Darwinian evolution—the survival of the fittest. In particular, they fastened on one aspect of evolution, competition, and spoke darkly of life as a cutthroat struggle for survival. Clearly the analogy clarified one aspect of human interaction: People and institutions do indeed compete for limited resources, markets, and territory. Moreover, the consequences of failure are often dire (the weak get eaten by the strong).

But competition is only one aspect of evolution—albeit a particularly dramatic one. The ability to dominate an environment is less important to long-term survival of a species than the ability to adapt to that environment. Thus the mighty dinosaur disappeared, but the lowly cockroach continues to flourish because of the latter's uncanny ability to adjust to circumstance.

The use of the evolutionary analogies to stress the competitive nature of human existence fit the worldview (and served the interests) of those who were most fond of invoking them, in particular the so-called robber barons and conservative Social Darwinists. But in overlooking other dimensions of evolution, especially the importance of adaptation and cooperation to survival, the analogy created a great deal of mischief.

So analogies have the power to get an audience's attention like virtually no other persuasive strategy. But seldom are they sufficient in themselves to provide full understanding. At some point with every analogy you need to ask yourself, "How far can I legitimately go with this? At what point are the similarities between the two things I am comparing going to be overwhelmed by their dissimilarities?" They are useful attention-getting devices; used carefully and cautiously, they can be extended to shape an audience's understanding of a complex situation. But they can conceal and distort as well as clarify.

With this caveat, let's look at the uses of both undeveloped and extended analogies.

Using Undeveloped Analogies

Typically, writers will use short, *undeveloped analogies* to drive home a point (and evoke an accompanying emotion) and then quickly abandon the analogy before the reader's awareness of disanalogies begins to set in. Thus columnist James Kilpatrick, in arguing that it is not unconstitutional to require drug testing of federal employees, compares giving a urine specimen when applying for a federal job to going through an airport metal detector when flying:

> The Constitution does not prohibit all searches and seizures. It makes the people secure in their persons only from "unreasonable" searches and seizures. [. . .] A parallel situation may be observed at every airport in the land. Individuals may have a right to fly, but they have no right to fly without having their persons and baggage inspected for weapons. By the same token, the federal worker who refuses a urine specimen [has no right to a federal job].

Kilpatrick wants to transfer his audience's general approval of weapons searches as a condition for airplane travel to drug testing as a condition for federal employment. But he doesn't want his audience to linger too long on the analogy. (Is a urine specimen for employment really analogous to a weapons search before an airplane trip?)

Using Extended Analogies

Sometimes writers elaborate an analogy so that it takes on a major role in the argument. As an example of a claim based on an *extended analogy,* consider the following excerpt from a professor's argument opposing a proposal to require a writing proficiency exam for graduation. In the following portion of his argument, the professor compares development of writing skills to the development of physical fitness.

> A writing proficiency exam gives the wrong symbolic messages about writing. It suggests that writing is simply a skill, rather than an active way of thinking and learning. It suggests that once a student demonstrates proficiency then he or she doesn't need to do any more writing.

Imagine two universities concerned with the physical fitness of their students. One university requires a junior-level physical fitness exam in which students must run a mile in less than 10 minutes, a fitness level it considers minimally competent. Students at this university see the physical fitness exam as a one-time hurdle. As many as 70 percent of them can pass the exam with no practice; another 10–20 percent need a few months' training; and a few hopeless couch potatoes must go through exhaustive remediation. After passing the exam, any student can settle back into a routine of TV and potato chips having been certified as "physically fit."

The second university, however, believing in true physical fitness for its students, is not interested in minimal competency. Consequently, it creates programs in which its students exercise 30 minutes every day for the entire four years of the undergraduate curriculum. There is little doubt which university will have the most physically fit students. At the second university, fitness becomes a way of life with everyone developing his or her full potential. Similarly, if we want to improve our students' writing abilities, we should require writing in every course throughout the curriculum.

If you choose to write an extended analogy such as this, you will focus on the points of comparison that serve your purposes. The writer's purpose in the preceding case is to support the achievement of mastery rather than minimalist standards as the goal of the university's writing program. Whatever other disanalogous elements are involved (for example, writing requires the use of intellect, which may or may not be strengthened by repetition), the comparison reveals vividly that a commitment to mastery involves more than a minimalist test. The analogy serves primarily to underscore this one crucial point. In reviewing the different groups of students as they "prepare" for the fitness exam, the author makes clear just how irrelevant such an exam is to the whole question of mastery. Typically, then, in developing your analogy, you are not developing all possible points of comparison so much as you are bringing out those similarities consistent with the point you are trying to make.

For Class Discussion

The following is a two-part exercise to help you clarify for yourself how analogies function in the context of arguments. Part 1 is to be done outside class; part 2 is to be done in class.

PART 1   Think of an analogy that expresses your point of view toward each of the following topics. Your analogy can urge your readers toward either a positive view of the topic or a negative view, depending on the rhetorical effect you seek. Write your analogy in the following one-sentence format:

X is like Y: A, B, C . . . (where X is the main topic being discussed; Y is the analogy; and A, B, and C are the points of comparison).

EXAMPLES:

Topic: Cramming for an exam

Negative analogy: Cramming for an exam is like pumping iron for ten hours straight to prepare for a weight-lifting contest: exhausting and counterproductive

Positive analogy: Cramming for an exam is like carbohydrate loading before a big race: it gives you the mental food you need for the exam, such as a full supply of concepts and details all fresh in your mind.

1. Using spanking to discipline children
2. Using racial profiling for airport security
3. Using steroids to increase athletic performance
4. Paying college athletes
5. Eating at fast-food restaurants

An effective analogy should influence both your audience's feelings toward the issue and your audience's understanding of the issue. For example, the writer of the negative analogy in the "cramming for an exam" illustration, obviously believes that pumping iron for ten hours before a weight-lifting match is stupid. This feeling of stupidity is then transferred to the original topic—cramming for an exam. But the analogy also clarifies understanding. The writer imagines the mind as a muscle (which gets exhausted after too much exercise and which is better developed through some exercise every day rather than a lot all at once) rather than as a large container (into which lots of stuff can be "crammed").

PART 2   Bring your analogies to class and compare them to those of your classmates. Select the best analogies for each of the topics and be ready to say why you think they are good.

Arguments by Precedent

Precedent arguments are like analogy arguments in that they make comparisons between an X and a Y. In precedent arguments, however, the Y term is usually a past event where some sort of decision was reached, often a moral, legal, or political decision. An argument by precedent tries to show that a similar decision should be (should not be) reached for the present issue X because the situation of X is (is not) like the situation of Y. For example, if you wanted to argue that your college or university could increase retention by offering seminars for first-year students, you could point to the good results at other colleges that have instituted first-year seminars. If you wanted to argue that antidrug laws will never eradicate drug use, you could point to the failure of alcohol prohibition in the United States in the 1920s.

A good example of a precedent argument is the following excerpt from a speech by President Lyndon Johnson in the early years of the Vietnam War:

> Nor would surrender in Vietnam bring peace because we learned from Hitler at Munich that success only feeds the appetite of aggression. The battle would be renewed in one country and then another country, bringing with it perhaps even larger and crueler conflict, as we have learned from the lessons of history.

Here the audience knows what happened at Munich: France and Britain tried to appease Hitler by yielding to his demand for a large part of Czechoslovakia, but Hitler's armies continued their aggression anyway, using Czechoslovakia as a staging area to invade Poland. By arguing that surrender in Vietnam would lead to the same consequences, Johnson brings to his argument about Vietnam the whole weight of his audience's unhappy knowledge of World War II. Administration white papers developed Johnson's precedent argument by pointing toward the similarity of Hitler's promises with those of the Viet Cong: You give us this and we will ask for no more. But Hitler didn't keep his promise. Why should the Viet Cong?

Johnson's Munich precedent persuaded many Americans during the early years of the war and helps explain U.S. involvement in Southeast Asia. Yet many scholars attacked Johnson's reasoning. Let's analyze the Munich argument, using Toulmin's schema:

ENTHYMEME: The United States should not withdraw its troops from Vietnam because conceding to the Viet Cong will have the same disastrous consequences as did conceding to Hitler in Munich.

CLAIM: The United States should not withdraw its troops from Vietnam.

STATED REASON: because conceding to the Viet Cong will have the same disastrous consequences as did conceding to Hitler in Munich

GROUNDS: evidence of the disastrous consequences of conceding to Hitler at Munich: Hitler's continued aggression; his using Czechoslovakia as a staging area to invade Poland

WARRANT: What happened in Europe will happen in Southeast Asia.

BACKING: evidence of similarities between 1939 Europe and 1965 Southeast Asia (for example, similarities in political philosophy, goals, and military strength of the enemy; similarities in the nature of the conflict between the disputants)

CONDITIONS OF REBUTTAL: acknowledged differences between 1939 Europe and 1965 Southeast Asia that might make the outcomes different

Laid out like this, we see that the persuasiveness of the comparison depends on the audience's acceptance of the warrant, which posits close similarity between

1939 Europe and 1965 Southeast Asia. But many critics of the Vietnam War attacked this warrant.

During the Vietnam era, historian Howard Zinn attacked Johnson's argument by claiming three crucial differences between Europe in 1939 and Southeast Asia in 1965: First, Zinn argued, the Czechs were being attacked from outside by an external aggressor (Germany), whereas Vietnam was being attacked from within by rebels as part of a civil war. Second, Czechoslovakia was a prosperous, effective democracy, whereas the official Vietnam government was corrupt and unpopular. Third, Hitler wanted Czechoslovakia as a base for attacking Poland, whereas the Viet Cong and North Vietnamese aimed at reunification of their country as an end in itself.*

The Munich example shows again how arguments of resemblance depend on emphasizing the similarities between X and Y and playing down the dissimilarities. One could try to refute the counterargument made by Zinn by arguing first that the Saigon government was more stable than Zinn thinks and second that the Viet Cong and North Vietnamese were driven by goals larger than reunification of Vietnam, namely, communist domination of Asia. Such an argument would once again highlight the similarities between Vietnam and prewar Europe.

For Class Discussion

1. Consider the following claims of precedent, and evaluate how effective you think each precedent might be in establishing the claim. How would you develop the argument? How would you cast doubt on it?

   a. Gays should be allowed to serve openly in the U.S. military because they are allowed to serve openly in the militaries of most other Western countries.

   b. Gun control will reduce violent crime in the United States because many countries that have strong gun control laws (such as Japan and England) have low rates of violent crime.

   c. The United States doesn't need to go to war in Iraq because it can deter Saddam Hussein's use of weapons of mass destruction the same way it deterred the Soviets during the Cold War.

2. Advocates for "right to die" legislation legalizing active euthanasia under certain conditions often point to the Netherlands as a country where acceptance of euthanasia works effectively. Assume for the moment that your state has a ballot initiative legalizing euthanasia. Assume further that you are being hired as a lobbyist for (against) the measure and have been assigned to do research on euthanasia in the Netherlands. Working in small groups, make a list of research questions you would want to ask. Your long-range rhetorical goal is to use your research to support (attack) the ballot initiative by making a precedence argument focusing on the Netherlands.

---

*Based on the summary of Zinn's argument in J. Michael Sproule, *Argument: Language and Its Influence* (New York: McGraw-Hill, 1980), 149–50.

Writing a Resemblance Argument

WRITING ASSIGNMENT
FOR CHAPTER 13

Write a letter to the editor of your campus or local newspaper or a slightly longer guest editorial in which you try to influence public opinion on some issue through the use of a persuasive analogy or precedent. Megan Matthew's argument against the Navy's use of low-frequency sonar to locate submarines is a student piece written for this assignment (see pp. 280–281).

Exploring Ideas

Because letters to the editor and guest editorials are typically short, writers often lack space to develop full arguments. Because of their clarifying and emotional power, arguments from analogy or precedent are often effective in these situations.

Newspaper editors usually print letters or guest editorials only on current issues or on some current problem to which you can draw attention. For this assignment look through the most recent back issues of your campus or local newspaper, paying particular attention to issues being debated on the op-ed pages. Join one of the ongoing conversations about an existing issue, or draw attention to a current problem or situation that annoys you. In your letter or guest editorial, air your views. As part of your argument, include a persuasive analogy or precedent.

Organizing a Resemblance Argument

The most typical way to develop a resemblance argument is as follows:

- Introduce the issue and state your claim.
- Develop your analogy or precedent.
- Draw the explicit parallels you want to highlight between your claim and the analogy or precedent.
- Anticipate and respond to objections (optional depending on space and context).

Of course, this structure can be varied in many ways, depending on your issue and rhetorical context. Sometimes writers open an argument with the analogy, which serves as an attention grabber.

Questioning and Critiquing a Resemblance Argument

Once you have written a draft of your letter or guest editorial, you can test its effectiveness by role-playing a skeptical audience. What follows are some typical questions audiences will raise about arguments of resemblance.

Will a skeptic say I am trying to prove too much with my analogy or precedent? The most common mistake people make with resemblance arguments is to ask them to prove more than they're capable of proving. Too often, an analogy is treated as if it were a syllogism or algebraic ratio wherein necessary truths are deduced (*a* is to *b* as *c* is to *d*) rather than as a useful but basically playful figure that suggests uncertain but significant insight. The best way to guard against this charge is to qualify your argument and to find other means of persuasion to supplement an analogy or precedent argument.

For a good example of an analogy that tries to do too much, consider President Ronald Reagan's attempt to prevent the United States from imposing economic sanctions on South Africa. Ronald Reagan wanted to argue that harming South Africa's economy would do as much damage to blacks as to whites. In making this argument, he compared South Africa to a zebra and concluded that one couldn't hurt the white portions of the zebra without also hurting the black.

The zebra analogy might work quite well to point out the interrelatedness of whites and blacks in South Africa. But it has no force whatsoever in supporting Reagan's assertion that economic sanctions would hurt blacks as well as whites. To refute this analogy, one need only point out the disanalogies between the zebra stripes and racial groups. (There are, for example, no differences in income, education, and employment between black and white stripes on a zebra.)

Will a skeptic point out disanalogies in my resemblance argument? Although it is easy to show that a country is not like a zebra, finding disanalogies is sometimes quite tricky. As one example, we have already shown you how Howard Zinn identified disanalogies between Europe in 1939 and Southeast Asia in 1965. To take another similar example, during the Kosovo conflict critics of NATO policy questioned the NATO claim that Milosevic's "ethnic cleansing" of ethnic Albanians in Kosovo was analogous to Hitler's extermination of the Jews (see Case 1, p. 269). Although acknowledging the horror of Serbian atrocities, critics pointed out several disanalogies between the Serbs and the Nazis: (1) Jews in Germany and Poland were not engaged in a land dispute with the Germans, unlike ethnic Albanians, who wanted political control over Kosovo. (2) There was no Jewish equivalent of the Kosovo Liberation Army, which was committing terrorist acts against Serbs in Kosovo. (3) Although Germany was traumatized by its defeat in World War I, the Germans themselves were not recent victims of "ethnic cleansing," as were the Serbs in Croatia. (4) The Serbs were not motivated by a centralized philosophy of racial superiority supposedly grounded in evolutionary theory. (5) The Serbs' goal was to drive ethnic Albanians out of Kosovo, not to systematically exterminate an "inferior" race. Critics were not denying the evil of the Serbs' actions. But they held the Holocaust as a darker and "purer" form of evil, something of unique malignance not to be lumped in the same category as the ethnic wars in the Balkans or even the horrors of Pol Pot's killing fields in Cambodia or Stalin's massacre of the Russian peasants.*

Readings

Our first reading is a letter to the editor by student Megan Matthews written for the assignment on page 278. The letter responds to a news story appearing in the *Seattle Times* on September 26, 2002, about whales damaged by Navy sonar. Notice how Megan uses an analogy to help readers imagine how the Navy's low-frequency sonar for finding submarines, along with other human-made noise in the ocean, might disturb the lives of sea mammals. Megan later wrote the researched argument shown on pages 416–423 and used this analogy for her introduction.

Whales Need Silence
Megan Matthews (student)

1   Re: "Whales beach themselves following NATO exercise" (news story, September 26). Imagine that you are forced to live in an apartment located next to Interstate 5 with its constant roar of engines and tires against concrete, its blaring horns and piercing sirens. When you open your windows in the summer, you have to shout to be heard. What if your apartment had no windows? What if your only housing alternatives were next to other freeways?

2   Seems impossible? Not for whales, dolphins, and other marine mammals. Jacques Cousteau's "world of silence" has been turned into an underwater freeway by the rumbling of cargo ships, the explosions of undersea mineral explorations, and the cacophony of the blasting devices used by fisheries. Now the Navy is adding a new and more dangerous source of sound with its sonar systems for detecting enemy submarines. The recent beaching incident in the Canary Islands reflects the danger that Navy sonar systems pose to whales. Navy sonar systems have also been linked to other beachings, including the infamous deaths several years ago of sixteen beaked whales in the Bahamas. The Navy concluded that its midrange sonar tests caused the inner ear trauma that killed these animals.

3   To supplement or replace midrange sonar, the Navy has just been given approval to deploy even more powerful low-frequency active sonar (LFA). Low-frequency waves travel farther than high-frequency waves, which is why the bumping bass of a car stereo reverberates after the car passes you. In this case, 215 dB "pings" reflect off submarines—and whales—hundreds of miles away. LFA may be

---

*NATO's comparison of Kosovo to the Holocaust came during a decade when many scholars were reexamining the historical significance of the Holocaust. For an overview of these debates, see Karen Winkler, "German Scholars Sharply Divided Over Place of Holocaust in History," *Chronicle of Higher Education* 27 May 1987, 4–5.

even more dangerous to whales than midrange sonar, and few tests have been conducted to determine the real risk.

Marine mammals depend on sound to avoid predators, to communicate across 4 great distances between pods and prospective mates, and to establish mother-calf bonds. The extreme noise of navy sonar apparently kills whales outright, while background "freeway" noise throughout the oceans may be threatening their ability to survive as communities.

Congress should not fund further implementation of LFA, which springs from 5 an outdated Cold War model of warfare; the risks to our *environmental* security are too great.

Critiquing "Whales Need Silence"

1. What is the analogy in this piece?

2. How effective is this analogy? Does the analogy succeed in moving the readers toward a positive identification with the plight of whales and a negative view of low-frequency sonar?

3. The letter to the editor genre requires very short arguments that usually focus on one main point, but sometimes include brief summaries of more developed arguments. Compare Megan's letter to the editor with her researched argument on pages 416–423. What is the main point that Megan wishes to drive home in her letter to the editor? Where in the letter does she summarize portions of her longer argument? Based on your reading of Megan's researched argument, what other strategies might Megan have used to write a letter to the editor?

Our second reading is another letter to the editor, which appeared in the *New York Times* on September 10, 2002, at the height of a national debate on whether the United States should invade Iraq to eliminate Saddam Hussein. Whereas the *New York Times* generally took a skeptical stance toward the war plans of the Bush administration, this writer uses a precedent argument to support President Bush. The writer's initial citing of "Blair" refers to a news story from September 8, 2002, reporting British Prime Minister Tony Blair's support of Bush in the face of growing British opposition.

Iraq War Plans

Jean Arbeiter

To the Editor: 1
Re "Opposition Is Growing to Blair's Stand on Iraq" (news article, Sept. 8): 2
You report that a Londoner who had to spend nights in air-raid shelters as a child 3 during World War II does not wish to be on the side of the aggressor in going to war.

4   Doesn't she realize that if anyone had listened to Winston Churchill during the 1930's, when he argued that Germany's militaristic intentions toward Britain and the rest of Europe had to be countered, rather than appeased, the need for air-raid shelters could have been avoided, along with the deaths of millions in Europe?

5   Countering an aggressor does not make one the aggressor, as Churchill well knew; it merely makes one safer.

Critiquing "Iraq War Plans"

1. Explain in your own words Arbeiter's precedent argument.

2. The effect of this precedent argument depends on its audience's familiarity with European history in the 1930s. If there are any World War II history buffs in your class, can they help the class understand how the case of European appeasement of Hitler might be parallel to U. S. appeasement of Saddam Hussein should President Bush decide to wait rather than go to war? Explore both analogies and disanalogies. How is the U. S. relationship with Saddam Hussein like and unlike Europe's relationship with Hitler?

The third reading, by *New York Times* op-ed columnist Paul Krugman, also concerns U. S. response to terrorism and the wisdom of going to war with Iraq. It appeared on September 10, 2002, the same day as the letter to the editor by Jean Arbeiter. We introduced you to Krugman's views in Case 1 at the beginning of Chapter 11 on definition arguments (p. 208). This argument speaks back to pro-war writers such as Charles Krauthammer, whose article "This Isn't a 'Legal' Matter, This Is War" is reprinted in Chapter 11, pages 235–237.

The Long Haul

Paul Krugman

1   Americans should be proud of their reaction to Sept. 11. They didn't respond to calls for sacrifice, because no such calls were made. But they did respond to horror with calm and tolerance. There was no panic; while there were a handful of hate crimes, there were no angry mobs attacking people who look different. The American people remained true to what America is all about.

2   Yet a year later there is great uneasiness in this nation. Corporate scandals, dropping stocks and rising unemployment account for much of the malaise. But part of what makes us uneasy is that we still don't know how to think about what happened to us. Our leaders and much of the media tell us that we're a nation at war. But that was a bad metaphor from the start, and looks worse as time goes by.

3   In both human and economic terms the effects of Sept. 11 itself resembled those not of a military attack but of a natural disaster. Indeed, there were almost

eerie parallels between Sept. 11 and the effects of the earthquake that struck Japan in 1995. Like the terrorist attack, the Kobe earthquake killed thousands of innocent people without warning. Like the terrorist attack, the quake left a nation afflicted by nightmares and deep feelings of insecurity. And like the terrorist attack, the quake struck a nation already struggling with the aftermath of a financial bubble.

Yet the Kobe earthquake had only fleeting effects on the Japanese economy,   4
suggesting that the effects of Sept. 11 on the U.S. economy would be equally fleeting. And so it has proved. Kobe had longer-term effects on Japan's psyche, just as Sept. 11 has had on ours. But Japan has mostly moved on, and so will we.

Of course there is a difference between an act of God and a deliberate atrocity.   5
We were angry as well as shocked, determined to pursue and punish the perpetrators. It was natural to think of Sept. 11 as the moral equivalent of Pearl Harbor, and of the struggle that began that day as this generation's equivalent of World War II.

But if this is war, it bears little resemblance to the wars America has won in the   6
past. Where is the call for sacrifice, for a great national effort? How will we know when or if we've won? One doesn't have to be a military expert to realize that the struggle ahead won't involve any D-Days, nor will there ever be a V-J day. There will never be a day when we can declare terrorism stamped out for good. It will be more like fighting crime, where success is always relative and victory is never final, than like fighting a war.

And the metaphor we use to describe our struggle matters: some things that   7
are justifiable in a temporary time of war are not justifiable during a permanent fight against crime, even if the criminals are murderous fanatics.

This is true even of how we deal with pedestrian matters like the federal bud-   8
get. Wars are traditionally a valid reason to run budget deficits, because it makes sense for the government to borrow to cover the expense of a severe but temporary emergency. But this emergency is neither severe nor temporary. Is there any reason to expect spending on homeland security and national defense to fall back to pre-Sept.-11 levels, let alone far enough to restore budget balance, anytime in the foreseeable future? No, there isn't. So we had better figure out how to pay the government's bills on a permanent basis.

Far more important, of course, is the question of law and civil liberties. Great   9
democratic leaders have broken the rules in times of war: had Abraham Lincoln not suspended the writ of habeas corpus in 1861, there would be no United States today. But the situation was extreme, and the lapse was temporary: victory in the Civil War brought a return to normal legal procedure. Can anyone think of an event that would persuade our current leaders that they no longer need extraordinary powers?

The point is that our new, threatened condition isn't temporary. We're in this for   10
the long haul, so any measures we take to fight terrorism had better be measures that we are prepared to live with indefinitely.

The real challenge now is not to stamp out terrorism; that's an unattainable   11
goal. The challenge is to find a way to cope with the threat of terrorism without losing the freedom and prosperity that make America the great nation it is.

Critiquing "The Long Haul"

1. Early in this article, Krugman says that "Our leaders and much of the media tell us that we're a nation at war." Read Charles Krauthammer's argument "This Isn't a 'Legal' Matter, This Is WAR," on pp. 235–237. Krauthammer will give you a clear sense of the view that Krugman opposes.

2. Krugman makes the resemblance claim that the terrorist acts of September 11, 2001, were more like a natural disaster than like a military attack. He draws a surprising parallel between the terrorist attacks and the Kobe earthquake that struck Japan in 1995. From your perspective what are the similarities and the differences between the World Trade Center attacks and the Kobe earthquake? Explore both analogies and disanalogies.

3. After Krugman critiques his own earthquake analogy, he then makes a precedent argument that "if this is a war, it bears little resemblance to the wars America has won in the past." What are the differences that Krugman perceives between the war on terrorism and previous wars?

4. What are at stakes in this debate? Why does it matter to Krugman (and to us) whether we think the terrorist attacks are more like a military attack or more like a natural disaster?

5. By the time you discuss Krugman's article, you will have the benefit of retrospection. How does the debate between Krauthammer and Krugman appear several years later?

The fourth reading, a political cartoon by Sven Van Assche from the *Darien Times,* jumps into the public controversy over Internet censorship and the protection of children (see Figure 13.1). It speaks to the number of cases where chat room correspondence between children and strangers has resulted in abduction, rape, and murder.

Critiquing the Internet Chat Room Cartoon

1. What is the analogy in this cartoon?

2. Consider the simplicity of the scene and the figure of the little girl in this cartoon. What is significant about the way the scene and the girl are depicted? What cultural associations do the words and the pictures in this cartoon draw on?

3. How effective do you think the analogy in this cartoon is in influencing readers' views of the problems of chat rooms?

Our last reading is from feminist writer Susan Brownmiller's *Against Our Will: Men, Women, and Rape.* First published in 1975, Brownmiller's book was chosen by the *New York Times Book Review* as one of the outstanding books of the year. In the following excerpt, Brownmiller makes an argument from resemblance, claiming that pornography is "anti-female propaganda."

FIGURE 13.1

Courtesy of Hersam Acorn Press.

From *Against Our Will: Men, Women, and Rape*

Susan Brownmiller

Pornography has been so thickly glossed over with the patina of chic these days in the name of verbal freedom and sophistication that important distinctions between freedom of political expression (a democratic necessity), honest sex education for children (a societal good) and ugly smut (the deliberate devaluation of the role of women through obscene, distorted depictions) have been hopelessly confused. Part of the problem is that those who traditionally have been the most vigorous opponents of porn are often those same people who shudder at the explicit mention of any sexual subject. Under their watchful, vigilant eyes, frank and free dissemination of educational materials relating to abortion, contraception, the act of birth, the female biology in general is also dangerous, subversive and dirty. (I am not unmindful that frank and free discussion of rape, "the unspeakable crime," might well give these righteous vigilantes further cause to shudder.) Because the battle lines were falsely drawn a long time ago, before there was a vocal women's movement, the antipornography forces appear to be, for the most part, religious, Southern, conservative and right-wing, while the pro-porn forces are identified as Eastern, atheistic and liberal.

2   But a woman's perspective demands a totally new alignment, or at least a fresh appraisal. The majority report of the President's Commission on Obscenity and Pornography (1970), a report that argued strongly for the removal of all legal restrictions on pornography, soft and hard, made plain that 90 percent of all pornographic material is geared to the male heterosexual market (the other 10 percent is geared to the male homosexual taste), that buyers of porn are "predominantly white, middle-class, middle-aged married males" and that the graphic depictions, the meat and potatoes of porn, are of the naked female body and of the multiplicity of acts done to that body.

3   Discussing the content of stag films, "a familiar and firmly established part of the American scene," the commission report dutifully, if foggily, explained, "Because pornography historically has been thought to be primarily a masculine interest, the emphasis in stag films seems to represent the preferences of the middle-class American male. Thus male homosexuality and bestiality are relatively rare, while lesbianism is rather common."

4   The commissioners in this instance had merely verified what purveyors of porn have always known: hard-core pornography is not a celebration of sexual freedom; it is a cynical exploitation of female sexual activity through the device of making all such activity, and consequently all females, "dirty." Heterosexual male consumers of pornography are frankly turned on by watching lesbians in action (although never in the final scenes, but always as a curtain raiser); they are turned off with a sudden swiftness of a water faucet by watching naked men act upon each other. One study quoted in the commission report came to the unastounding conclusion that "seeing a stag film in the presence of male peers bolsters masculine esteem." Indeed. The men in groups who watch the films, it is important to note, are *not* naked.

5   When male response to pornography is compared to female response, a pronounced difference in attitude emerges. According to the commission, "Males report being more highly aroused by depictions of nude females, and show more interest in depictions of nude females than [do] females." Quoting the figures of Alfred Kinsey, the commission noted that a majority of males (77 percent) were "aroused" by visual depictions of explicit sex while a majority of females (68 percent) were not aroused. Further, "females more often than males reported 'disgust' and 'offense.' "

6   From whence comes this female disgust and offense? Are females sexually backward or more conservative by nature? The gut distaste that a majority of women feel when we look at pornography, a distaste that, incredibly, it is no longer fashionable to admit, comes, I think, from the gut knowledge that we and our bodies are being stripped, exposed and contorted for the purpose of ridicule to bolster that "masculine esteem" which gets its kick and sense of power from viewing females as anonymous, panting playthings, adult toys, dehumanized objects to be used, abused, broken and discarded.

This, of course, is also the philosophy of rape. It is no accident (for what else   7
could be its purpose?) that females in the pornographic genre are depicted in two
cleanly delineated roles: as virgins who are caught and "banged" or as nymphoma-
niacs who are never sated. The most popular and prevalent pornographic fantasy
combines the two: an innocent, untutored female is raped and "subjected to unnatural practices" that turn her into a raving, slobbering nymphomaniac, a dependent
sexual slave who can never get enough of the big, male cock.

There can be no "equality" in porn, no female equivalent, no turning of the ta-   8
bles in the name of bawdy fun. Pornography, like rape, is a male invention, designed
to dehumanize women, to reduce the female to an object of sexual access, not to
free sensuality from moralistic or parental inhibition. The staple of porn will always
be the naked female body, breasts and genitals exposed, because as man devised it,
her naked body is the female's "shame," her private parts the private property of
man, while his are the ancient, holy, universal, patriarchal instrument of his power,
his rule by force over *her.*

Pornography is the undiluted essence of anti-female propaganda. Yet the very   9
same liberals who were so quick to understand the method and purpose behind the
mighty propaganda machine of Hitler's Third Reich, the consciously spewed-out
anti-Semitic caricatures and obscenities that gave an ideological base to the
Holocaust and the Final Solution, the very same liberals who, enlightened by
blacks, searched their own conscience and came to understand that their tolerance
of "nigger" jokes and portrayals of shuffling, rolling-eyed servants in movies perpet-
uated the degrading myths of black inferiority and gave an ideological base to the
continuation of black oppression—these very same liberals now fervidly maintain
that the hatred and contempt for women that find expression in four-letter words
used as expletives and in what are quaintly called "adult" or "erotic" books and
movies are a valid extension of freedom of speech that must be preserved as a
Constitutional right.

To defend the right of a lone, crazed American Nazi to grind out propaganda   10
calling for the extermination of all Jews, as the ACLU has done in the name of free
speech, is, after all, a self-righteous and not particularly courageous stand, for
American Jewry is not currently threatened by storm troopers, concentration camps
and imminent extermination, but I wonder if the ACLU's position might change if,
come tomorrow morning, the bookstores and movie theaters lining Forty-second
Street in New York City were devoted not to the humiliation of women by rape and
torture, as they currently are, but to a systematized commercially successful propaganda machine depicting the sadistic pleasures of gassing Jews or lynching blacks?

Is this analogy extreme? Not if you are a woman who is conscious of the ever-   11
present threat of rape and the proliferation of a cultural ideology that makes it sound
like "liberated" fun. The majority report of the President's Commission on Obscenity
and Pornography tried to pooh-pooh the opinion of law enforcement agencies around
the country that claimed their own concrete experience with offenders who were
caught with the stuff led them to conclude that pornographic material is a causative
factor in crimes of sexual violence. The commission maintained that it was not possible at this time to scientifically prove or disprove such a connection.

12   But does one need scientific methodology in order to conclude that the antife-male propaganda that permeates our nation's cultural output promotes a climate in which acts of sexual hostility directed against women are not only tolerated but ide-ologically encouraged? A similar debate has raged for many years over whether or not the extensive glorification of violence (the gangster as hero; the loving treat-ment accorded bloody shoot-'em-ups in movies, books and on TV) has a causal ef-fect, a direct relationship to the rising rate of crime, particularly among youth. Interestingly enough, in this area—nonsexual and not specifically related to abuses against women—public opinion seems to be swinging to the position that explicit violence in the entertainment media does have a deleterious effect; it makes vio-lence commonplace, numbingly routine and no longer morally shocking.

13   More to the point, those who call for a curtailment of scenes of violence in movies and on television in the name of sensitivity, good taste and what's best for our children are not accused of being pro-censorship or against freedom of speech. Similarly, minority group organizations, black, Hispanic, Japanese, Italian, Jewish, or American Indian, that campaign against ethnic slurs and de-meaning portrayals in movies, on television shows and in commercials are per-ceived as waging a just political fight, for if a minority group claims to be of-fended by a specific portrayal, be it Little Black Sambo or the Frito Bandito, and relates it to a history of ridicule and oppression, few liberals would dare to trot out a Constitutional argument in theoretical opposition, not if they wish to main-tain their liberal credentials. Yet when it comes to the treatment of women, the liberal consciousness remains fiercely obdurate, refusing to be budged, for the sin of appearing square or prissy in the age of the so-called sexual revolution has be-come the worst offense of all.

Critiquing the Passage from *Against Our Will: Men, Women, and Rape*

1. Summarize Brownmiller's argument in your own words.

2. Brownmiller states that pornography degrades and humiliates women the same way that anti-Semitic literature degrades and humiliates Jews or that myths of black inferiority degrade and humiliate blacks. According to Brownmiller, how does pornography degrade and humiliate women?

3. What disanalogies might a skeptic point out between pornography and anti-Semitic or other racist propaganda?

4. One reviewer of Brownmiller's book said, "Get into this book and hardly a single thought to do with sex will come out the way it was." How does this passage from Brownmiller contribute to a public conversation about sexu-ality? What is thought provoking about this passage? How does it cause you to view sex differently?

14 Evaluation and Ethical Arguments

X Is (Is Not) a Good Y;

X Is Right (Wrong)

> **CASE 1**
>
> A young engineer has advanced to the level of a design group leader. She is now being considered for promotion to a management position. Her present supervisor is asked to write a report evaluating her as a prospective manager. He is asked to pay particular attention to four criteria: technical competence, leadership, interpersonal skills, and communication skills.

> **CASE 2**
>
> In early fall 2002, the Federal Drug Administration seemed ready to lift the ban on selling milk from cloned cows to the general public. Milk from cloned cows raises two kinds of evaluation issues. The first is this: Is milk from cloned cows "good milk"? (Does it contain the same nutritional value as ordinary milk? Does it taste like ordinary milk? Is it safe? Particularly, does it have any protein antigens, not present in ordinary milk, that might trigger allergic reactions in some people?) The second evaluation issue is more knotty and can't be resolved through science: Is it ethical to clone cows? If we start cloning cows, will we slide down a slippery slope toward the cloning of humans? Where do we draw the line between ethical and nonethical uses of cloning?

An Overview of Evaluation Arguments

In our roles as citizens and professionals, we are continually expected to make difficult evaluations and to persuade others to accept them. In this chapter we explain strategies for conducting two different kinds of evaluation arguments. First, we examine categorical evaluations of the kind "X is (is not) a good Y"* (Is Ramon

---

* In addition to the term *good*, a number of other evaluative terms involve the same kind of thinking—*effective, successful, workable, excellent, valuable,* and so forth.

a good committee chair? Is Design Approach A or Design Approach B the better solution to this engineering problem?) In such an evaluation, the writer determines the extent to which a given X meets or fulfills the qualities or standards of category Y. As we explain, these qualities or standards are usually based on the purposes of category Y. Second, we examine ethical arguments of the kind "X is right (wrong)." (Was it a right or wrong action to drop an atomic bomb on Hiroshima and Nagasaki? On a job application is it ethical to omit a briefly held job from which I was fired?) In these arguments, the writer evaluates a given X from the perspective of some system of morality or ethics.

Criteria-Match Structure of Categorical Evaluations

A categorical evaluation follows the same criteria-match structure that we examined in definitional arguments (see Chapter 11). A typical claim for such an argument has the following structure:

X is (is not) a good Y because it meets (fails to meet) criteria A, B, and C.

The main conceptual difference between this kind of evaluation argument and a definition argument involves the Y term. In a definition argument, one argues whether a particular Y term is the correct class or category in which to place X. (Does this swampy area qualify as a *wetland*? For purposes of federal fuel-efficiency regulations, is an SUV a *truck* or a *car*?) In a categorical evaluation argument, we know the Y term—that is, what class or category to put X into. For example, we know that this 1998 Ford Escort is a *used car*. For a categorical evaluation, the question is whether this 1998 Ford Escort is a *good used car*. Or, to place the question within a rhetorical context, Is this Ford Escort a *good used car for me to buy for college?*

As an illustration of the criteria-match structure of a categorical evaluation, let's continue with the Ford Escort example. Suppose you get in a debate with Parent or Significant Other about the car you should buy for college. Let's say that Parent or Significant Other argues that the following criteria are particularly important: (1) value for the initial money, (2) dependability, (3) safety, and (4) low maintenance costs. (If you are into muscle cars, coolness, or driving excitement you might shudder at these criteria!) Here is how an argument supporting the first criterion could be analyzed using the Toulmin system. Note that in evaluation arguments, as in definition arguments, warrants are the criteria for the evaluation while the stated reasons and grounds assert that the specific case meets these criteria.

Toulmin Analysis for Criterion 1: High Value for the Initial Money

ENTHYMEME: This 1998 Ford Escort is a good used car for you at college because it provides the most value for the initial money.

CLAIM: This 1998 Ford Escort is a good used car for you at college

STATED REASON: because it provides the most value for the initial money

GROUNDS: Used Ford Escorts give high value at less cost because they are basically boring but dependable cars that don't have high demand in the used car market; this lack of demand means that you can get a 1998 Escort for $1500 less than a comparable 1998 Honda Civic with the same mileage; this particular Escort has only 65,000 miles; a 1998 Honda Civic for the same price would have 120,000 miles or more. This 1998 Ford Escort thus gives you a low mileage car at a reasonable price—high value for the initial money.

WARRANT: High value for the initial money is an important criterion for buying your college car.

BACKING: Arguments showing why it is important to get high value for the money: money saved on the car can be used for other college expenses; low initial mileage means you can get years of dependable use without having to rebuild an engine or transmission; buying in this conservative and wise way meets our family's image of being careful, utilitarian shoppers.

CONDITIONS OF REBUTTAL: *Attacking stated reason and grounds:* Perhaps this 1998 Ford Escort isn't as good a value as it seems; my research suggests it has high projected maintenance costs after 60,000 miles; initial savings may be blown on high maintenance costs.

Attacking warrant and backing: Other criteria are more important to me: I value great handling and acceleration, the fun of driving, and the status of having a cool car. The Ford Escort doesn't meet these criteria.

As this Toulmin schema shows, Parent or Significant Other needs to argue that getting high value for the initial money is an important consideration (the criterion argument) and that this 1998 Ford Escort meets this criterion better than competing choices (the match argument). If you can't see yourself driving a Ford Escort, you've either got to argue for other criteria (attack the warrant) or accept the criterion but argue that the Ford Escort's projected maintenance costs undermine its initial value (attack the reason and grounds).

Conducting a Categorical Evalution Argument

Now that you understand the basic criteria-match structure of a categorical evaluation, let's consider the thinking strategies used for determining criteria and for arguing that your given X meets or does not meet the criteria.

Determining Criteria for a Categorical Evaluation Argument

How do you develop criteria for a categorical evaluation? What distinguishes a successful manager from a poor one, a good studying place from a bad one, or a more effective treatment for obesity from a less effective treatment? In this section we turn to the practical problem of finding criteria you'll need for conducting your categorical evaluation argument.

Step 1: Determine the Category in Which the Object Being Evaluated Belongs   In determining the quality or value of any given X, you must first figure out the category in which X belongs. For example, if you asked one of your professors to write you a letter of recommendation for a summer job, what class of things should the professor put you into? Is he or she supposed to evaluate you as a student? a leader? a worker? a storyteller? a party animal? or what? This is an important question because the criteria for excellence in one class (student) may be very different from criteria for excellence in another class (party animal).

To write a useful letter, your professor should consider you first as a member of the general class "summer job holder" and base her evaluation of you on criteria relevant to that class. To write a truly effective letter, however, your professor needs to consider your qualifications in the context of the smallest applicable class of candidates: not "summer job holder," but "law office intern" or "highway department flagperson" or "golf course groundsperson." Clearly, each of these subclasses has very different criteria for excellence that your professor needs to address.

We thus recommend placing X into the smallest relevant class because of the apples-and-oranges law. That is, to avoid giving a mistaken rating to a perfectly good apple, you need to make sure you are judging an apple under the class "apple" and not under the next larger class "fruit" or a neighboring class "orange." And to be even more precise, you may wish to evaluate your apple in the class "eating apple" as opposed to "pie apple" because the latter class is supposed to be tarter and the former class juicier and sweeter.

Step 2: Determine the Purpose or Function of This Class   Once you have located X in its appropriate class, you should next determine what the purpose or function of this class is. Let's suppose that the summer job you are applying for is tour guide at the city zoo. The function of a tour guide is to make people feel welcome, to give them interesting information about the zoo, to make their visit pleasant, and so forth. Consequently, you wouldn't want your professor's evaluation to praise your term paper on Napoleon Bonaparte or your successful synthesis of some compound in your chemistry lab. Rather, the professor should highlight your dependability, your neat appearance, your good speaking skills, and your ability to work with groups. But if you were applying for graduate school, then your term paper on Bonaparte or your chem lab wizardry would be relevant. In other words, the professor has to evaluate you according to the class "tour guide," not "graduate student," and the criteria for each class derive from the purpose or function of the class.

Let's take another example. Suppose that you are the chair of a committee charged with evaluating the job performance of Lillian Jones, director of the admissions office at a small, private college. Ms. Jones has been a controversial manager because several members of her staff have filed complaints about her management style. In making your evaluation, your first step is to place Ms. Jones into an appropriate class, in this case, the general class "manager," and then the more specific class "manager of an admissions office at a small, private college." You then need to identify the purpose or function of these classes. You might say that the function of the general class "managers" is to "oversee actual operations of an organization so that the organization meets its goals as harmoniously and efficiently as possible," whereas the function of the specific class "manager of an admissions office at a small, private college" is "the successful recruitment of the best students possible."

Step 3: Determine Criteria Based on the Purposes or Function of the Class to Which X Belongs Once you've worked out the purposes of the class, you are ready to work out the criteria by which you judge all members of the class. Criteria for judgment will be based on those features of Y that help it achieve the purposes of its class. For example, once you determine the purpose and function of the position filled by Lillian Jones, you can develop a list of criteria for managerial success:

1. Criteria related to "efficient operation"
   - articulates priorities and goals for the organization
   - is aggressive in achieving goals
   - motivates fellow employees
   - is well organized, efficient, and punctual
   - is articulate and communicates well
2. Criteria related to "harmonious operation"
   - creates job satisfaction for subordinates
   - is well groomed, sets good example of professionalism
   - is honest, diplomatic in dealing with subordinates
   - is flexible in responding to problems and special concerns of staff members
3. Criteria related to meeting specific goals of a college admissions office
   - creates a comprehensive recruiting program
   - demonstrates that recruiting program works

Step 4: Give Relative Weightings to the Criteria Even though you have established criteria, you must still decide which of the criteria are most important. In the case of Lillian Jones, is it more important that she bring in lots of students or that she create a harmonious, happy office? These sorts of questions are at the heart of many evaluative controversies. Thus a justification for your weighting of criteria may well be an important part of your argument.

Determining Whether X Meets the Criteria

Once you've established your criteria, you've got to figure out how well X meets them. You proceed by gathering evidence and examples. In the Lillian Jones case, the success of the college's recruiting program can probably be measured empirically, so you gather statistics about applications to the college, SAT scores of applicants, number of acceptances, academic profiles of entering freshmen, and so forth. You might then compare those statistics to those compiled by Ms. Jones's predecessor or to her competitors at other, comparable institutions.

You can also look at what the recruiting program actually does—the number of recruiters, the number of high school visits, the quality of admissions brochures and other publications. You can also look at Ms. Jones in action, searching for specific incidents or examples that illustrate her management style. For example, you can't measure a trait such as diplomacy empirically, but you can find specific instances where the presence or absence of this trait was demonstrated. You could turn to examples where Ms. Jones may or may not have prevented a potentially divisive situation from occurring or where she offered or failed to offer encouragement at psychologically the right moment to keep someone from getting demoralized. As with criteria-match arguments in definition, one must provide examples of how the X in question meets each of the criteria that have been set up.

Your final evaluation of Ms. Jones, then, might include an overview of her strengths and weaknesses along the various criteria you have established. You might say that Ms. Jones has done an excellent job with recruitment (an assertion you can support with data on student enrollments over the last five years) but was relatively poor at keeping the office staff happy (as evidenced by employee complaints, high turnover, and your own observations of her rather abrasive management style). Nevertheless, your final recommendation might be to retain Ms. Jones for another three-year contract because you believe that an excellent recruiting record is the most important criterion for her position. You might justify this heavy weighting of recruiting on the grounds that the institution's survival depends on its ability to attract adequate numbers of good students.

For Class Discussion

The following small-group exercise can be accomplished in one or two class hours. It gives you a good model of the process you can go through in order to write your own categorical evaluation. Working in small groups, suppose that you are going to evaluate a controversial member of one of the following classes:

   a. an athlete, a coach, a component of an athletic team (for example, the offensive line of a football team) or a whole team; a politician or officeholder; a teacher or administrator

b. a proposed or current law, a government regulation, or a government policy

c. a student service provided by your school, or any school policy or regulation; a school newspaper, a radio station, an intramural program, or a student government policy or service

d. a teaching method, your school's plagiarism policy, a homework assignment, a library orientation, or some other controversial academic policy or method

e. a play, a film, a music video, or a Web site; an actor, a director, a dancer, or other performer

f. an advertising campaign or a specific advertisement, a store, or a customer service department

g. an employer, a boss, a work policy, or a particular work environment

h. a day care center or school; a physician, dentist, or health care agency or policy

i. a restaurant, a college hangout, a vacation spot, or a study place

j. any controversial X of your choice

1. Choose a controversial member within one of these classes as the specific person, thing, or event you are going to evaluate (your school's Computer Services Help Desk, the Invite-a-Professor-to-Lunch program in your dormitory, a recent controversial film, Harvey's Hamburger Haven).

2. If not already apparent, stipulate a rhetorical context that gives importance to the issue, focuses the argument, and places the controversial X within the smallest relevant class. (Do you want to evaluate Harvey's Hamburger Haven in the broad category of *restaurants,* in the narrow category of *hamburger joints,* or in a different narrow category such as *late-night study places?* If you are evaluating a recent film, are you evaluating it as an *action film for guys,* as a possible *Academy Award nominee,* or as a *political filmmaking statement against corporate greed?*)

3. Make a list of the purposes or functions of that class, and then list the criteria that a good member of that class would need to have in order to accomplish the purpose or function. (What is the purpose or function of a Computer Services Help Desk, an action film for guys, or a late-night study place? What criteria for excellence can you derive from these purposes or functions?)

4. If necessary, rank your criteria in order to show that X is superior (inferior) to a close competitor. (For a late-night study place, what is more important: good music to study by or cheap coffee? An Internet connection or wide tables where you can spread out your work?)

5. Evaluate your X by matching X to each of the criteria. (As a late-night study place, Harvey's Hamburger Haven has the best lighting, the most

space to spread out, the least expensive coffee, and the best music to study by, but it doesn't offer Internet access and sometimes has too many rowdies. Therefore it ranks second to Carol's Coffee Closet.)

An Overview of Ethical Arguments

A second kind of evaluation argument focuses on moral or ethical issues, which can often merge or overlap with categorical evaluations. For example, many apparently straightforward categorical evaluations can turn out to have an ethical dimension. Consider again the criteria for buying a car. Most people would base their evaluations on cost, safety, comfort, stylishness, and so forth. But some people might feel morally obligated to buy the most fuel-efficient car (perhaps even an electric or hybrid car despite the extra cost), or not to buy a car from a manufacturer whose investment or labor policies they find morally repugnant. Depending on how large a role ethical considerations play in the evaluation, we might choose to call this an ethical argument based on moral considerations rather than a categorical evaluation based on the purposes of a class or category.

It is uncertainty about "purpose" that makes ethical evaluations particularly complex. In making a categorical evaluation, we assume that every class or category of being has a purpose, that the purpose should be defined as narrowly as possible, and that the criteria for judgment derive directly from that purpose. For example, the purpose of a computer repairperson is to analyze the problem with my computer, to fix it, and to do so in a timely and cost-efficient manner. Once I formulate this purpose, it is easy for me to define criteria for a good computer repairperson.

In ethics, however, the place of purpose is much fuzzier. Just what is the purpose of human beings? Before I can begin to determine what ethical duties I have to myself and to others, I'm going to have to address this question. What is my purpose in life? What kind of life do I want to lead? In ethical discussions we don't ask what a "manager" or a "judge" or "point guard" is supposed to do in situations relevant to the respective classes. Who persons are or what their social function is makes no difference to our ethical assessment of their actions or traits of character. A morally bad person may be a good judge, and a morally good person may be a bad manager and a worse point guard.

As the discussion so far has suggested, disagreements about ethical issues often stem from different systems of values that make the issue irresolvable. It is precisely this problem—the lack of shared assumptions about value—that makes it so important to confront issues of ethics with rational deliberation. The arguments you produce may not persuade others to your view, but they should lay out more clearly the reasons and warrants for your own beliefs. By writing about ethical issues, you see more clearly what you believe and why you believe it. Although the arguments demanded by ethical issues require rigorous thought, they force us to articulate our most deeply held beliefs and our richest feelings.

Two Major Ethical Systems

When we are faced with an ethical issue, we must move from arguments of good or bad to arguments of right or wrong. The terms *right* and *wrong* are clearly different from the terms *good* and *bad* when the latter terms mean simply "effective" (meets purposes of class, as in "This is a good stereo system") or "ineffective" (fails to meet purposes of class, as in "This is a bad cookbook"). But *right* and *wrong* often also differ from what seems to be a moral use of the terms *good* and *bad*. We might say, for example, that sunshine is good because it brings pleasure and that cancer is bad because it brings pain and death, but that is not quite the same thing as saying that sunshine is "right" and cancer is "wrong." It is the problem of "right" and "wrong" that ethical arguments confront.

Thus it is not enough to say that terrorism is "bad"; obviously everyone, including most terrorists, would agree that terrorism is "bad" because it causes suffering and anguish. If we want to condemn terrorism on ethical grounds, we have to say that it's also "wrong" as well as "bad." From a nonethical standpoint, you could say that certain persons are "good" terrorists in that they fully realize the purposes of the class "terrorist": they cause great anguish and damage with a minimum of resources, and they bring much attention to their cause. The ethical question here is not whether a person fulfills the purposes of the class "terrorist," but whether it is wrong for such a class to exist.

There are many schools of ethical thought—too many to cover in this brief overview—so we'll limit ourselves to two major systems: arguments from consequences and arguments from principles.

Consequences as the Base of Ethics

Perhaps the best-known example of evaluating acts according to their ethical consequences is utilitarianism, a down-to-earth philosophy that grew out of nineteenth-century British philosophers' concern to demystify ethics and make it work in the practical world. Jeremy Bentham, the originator of utilitarianism, developed the goal of the greatest good for the greatest number, or "greatest happiness," by which he meant the most pleasure for the least pain. John Stuart Mill, another British philosopher, built on Bentham's utilitarianism, using predicted consequences to determine the morality of a proposed action.

Mill's consequentialist approach allows you readily to assess a wide range of acts. You can apply the principle of utility—which says that an action is morally right if it produces a greater net value (benefits minus costs) than any available alternative action—to virtually any situation, and it will help you reach a decision. Obviously, however, it's not always easy to make the calculations called for by the principle, since, like any prediction of the future, an estimate of consequences is conjectural. In particular, it's often very hard to assess the long-term consequences of any action. Too often, utilitarianism seduces us into a short-term analysis of a moral problem simply because long-term consequences are very difficult to predict.

Principles as the Base of Ethics

Any ethical system based on principles will ultimately rest on moral tenets that we are duty bound to uphold, no matter what the consequences. Sometimes the moral tenets come from religious faith—for example, the Ten Commandments. At other times, however, the principles are derived from philosophical reasoning, as in the case of German philosopher Immanuel Kant. Kant held that no one should ever use another person as a means to his own ends and that everyone should always act as if his acts were the basis of universal law. In other words, Kant held that we are duty bound to respect other people's sanctity and to act in the same way that we would want all other people to act. The great advantage of such a system is its clarity and precision. We are never overwhelmed by a multiplicity of contradictory and difficult-to-quantify consequences; we simply make sure we are not violating a principle of our ethical system and proceed accordingly.

Conducting an Ethical Argument

To show you how to conduct an ethical argument, let's now apply these two strategies to an example. In general, you can conduct an ethical evaluation by using the frame for either a principles-based argument or a consequences-based argument or a combination of both.

> *Principles-Based Frame:* X is right (wrong) because it follows (violates) principles A, B, and C.
>
> *Consequences-Based Frame:* X is right (wrong) because it will lead to consequences A, B, and C, which are good (bad).

To illustrate how these frames might help you develop an ethical argument, let's use them to develop arguments for or against capital punishment.

Constructing a Principles-Based Argument

A principles-based argument looks at capital punishment through the lens of one or more guiding principles. Kant's principle that we are duty bound not to violate the sanctity of other human lives could lead to arguments opposing capital punishment. One might argue as follows:

> *Principles-based argument opposing capital punishment:* The death penalty is wrong because it violates the principle of the sanctity of human life.

You could support this principle either by summarizing Kant's argument that one should not violate the selfhood of another person or by pointing to certain religious systems such as Judeo-Christian ethics, where one is told "Vengeance is Mine, saith the Lord" or "Thou shalt not kill." To develop this argument further, you might examine two exceptions where principles-based ethicists may allow killing—self-defense and war—and show how capital punishment does not fall in either category.

Principles-based arguments can also be developed to support capital punishment. You may be surprised to learn that Kant himself—despite his arguments for the sanctity of life—actually supported capital punishment. To make such an argument, Kant evoked a different principle about the suitability of the punishment to the crime:

> There is no sameness of kind between death and remaining alive even under the most miserable conditions, and consequently there is no equality between the crime and the retribution unless the criminal is judicially condemned and put to death.

Stated as an enthymeme, Kant's argument is as follows:

Principles-based argument supporting capital punishment: Capital punishment is right because it follows the principle that punishments should be proportionate to the crime.

In developing this argument, Kant's burden is to show why the principle of proportionate retribution outweighs the principle of the supreme worth of the individual. Our point is that a principles-based argument can be made both for or against capital punishment. The arguer's duty is to make clear what principle is being evoked and then to show why this principle is more important than opposing principles.

Constructing a Consequences-Based Argument

Unlike a principles-based argument, which appeals to certain guiding maxims or rules, a consequences-based argument looks at the consequences of a decision and measures the positive benefits against the negative costs. Here is the frame that an arguer might use to oppose capital punishment on the basis of negative consequences:

Consequences-based argument opposing capital punishment: Capital punishment is wrong because it leads to the following negative consequences:

- The possibility of executing an innocent person
- The possibility that a murderer who might repent and be redeemed is denied that chance
- The excessive legal and political costs of trials and appeals
- The unfair distribution of executions so that one's chances of being put to death are much greater if one is a minority or is poor.

To develop this argument, the reader would need to provide facts, statistics, and other evidence to support each of the stated reasons.

A different arguer might use a consequences-based approach to support capital punishment:

Consequences-based argument supporting capital punishment: Capital punishment is right because it leads to the following positive consequences:

- It may deter violent crime and slow down the rate of murder.
- It saves the cost of lifelong imprisonment.
- It stops criminals who are menaces to society from committing more murders.
- It helps grieving families reach closure and sends a message to victims' families that society recognizes their pain.

It should be evident, then, that adopting an ethical system doesn't lead to automatic answers to one's ethical dilemmas. A system offers a way of proceeding—a way of conducting an argument—but it doesn't relieve you of personal responsibility for thinking through your values and taking a stand. When you face an ethical dilemma, we encourage you to consider both the relevant principles and the possible consequences the dilemma entails. In many arguments, you can use both principles-based and consequences-based reasoning as long as irreconcilable contradictions don't present themselves.

For Class Discussion

Working as individuals or in small groups:

1. Formulate a consequences-based argument in favor of biotech agriculture (see the readings and discussion in Chapter 2, pp. 24–27 and 40–45).
2. Now formulate a consequences-based argument opposing biotech agriculture.
3. How might a principles-based argument be constructed for or against biotech agriculture? For or against therapeutic or reproductive cloning?
4. When people argue about owning SUVs, the controversies can be either categorical or ethical or both.
   a. How would you make a categorical evaluation argument that SUVs are good (bad) cars for families in urban environments?
   b. How would you make an ethical argument that it is morally right or wrong to buy an SUV?

Common Problems in Making Evaluation Arguments

When conducting evaluation arguments (whether categorical or ethical), writers can bump up against recurring problems that are unique to evaluation. In some cases these problems complicate the establishment of criteria; in other cases they complicate the match argument. Let's look briefly at some of these common problems.

- *The problem of standards—What's commonplace versus what's ideal:* To appreciate this problem, consider again Young Person's archetypal argument with Parent about her curfew (see Chapter 1, pp. 7–8). She originally argued that staying out until 2 A.M. is fair "because all the other kids' parents let their kids stay out late," to which Parent might respond: "Well, *ideally*, all the other parents should not let their kids stay out that late." Young Person based her criterion for fairness on what is *commonplace*; her standards arose from common practices of a social group. Parent, however, argued from what is *ideal*, basing her or his criterion on some external standard that transcends social groups. We experience this dilemma in various forms all the time. Is it fair to get a ticket for going 70 mph on a 65-mph freeway when most of the drivers go 70 mph or higher? (Does what is *commonplace*—going 70—override what is *ideal*—obeying the law?) Is it better for high schools to pass out free contraceptives to students because students are having sex anyway (what's *commonplace*), or is it better not to pass them out in order to support abstinence (what's *ideal*)?

- *The problem of mitigating circumstances:* This problem occurs when an arguer claims that unusual circumstances should alter our usual standards of judgment. Ordinarily, it is fair for a teacher to reduce a grade if you turn in a paper late. But what if you were up all night taking care of a crying baby? Does that count as a *mitigating circumstance* to waive the ordinary criterion? What about your annual performance evaluation during a year when you had chronic back pain or were going through a divorce? When you argue for mitigating circumstances, you will likely assume an especially heavy burden of proof. People assume the rightness of usual standards of judgment unless there are compelling arguments for abnormal circumstances.

- *The problem of choosing between two goods or two bads:* Often an evaluation issue forces us between a rock and a hard place. Should we cut pay or cut people? Put our parents in a nursing home or let them stay at home where they have become a danger to themselves? Take the road trip I had planned across the United States or take the new job offer? In such cases one has to weigh conflicting criteria, knowing that the choices are too much alike—either both bad or both good.

- *The problem of seductive empirical measures:* The need to make high-stakes evaluations has led many persons to seek quantifiable criteria that can be weighed mathematically. Thus we use grade point averages to select scholarship winners, student evaluation scores to decide merit pay for teachers, SAT scores and GPAs for college admissions, and combined scores of judges to rank figure skaters. In some cases, empirical measures can be quite acceptable, but they are often dangerous because they discount important nonquantifiable traits. The problem with empirical measures is that they seduce us into believing that complex judgments can be made mathematically, thus rescuing us from the messiness of alternative points of view and conflicting criteria. Empirical measures seem extremely persuasive next to written arguments that try to qualify and hedge and raise questions. We suggest, however, that in many cases a fair evaluation may require such hedging.

- *The problem of cost:* A final problem that can crop up in evaluations is cost. X may be the best of all possible Ys, but if X costs too much, we have to go for second or third best. We can avoid this problem somewhat by placing items into different classes on the basis of cost. For example, a Mercedes will exceed a Hyundai on almost any criterion, but if we can't afford more than a Hyundai, the comparison is pointless. It is better to compare a Mercedes to a Lexus and a Hyundai to an equivalent Ford. Whether costs are expressed in dollars, personal discomfort, moral repugnance, or some other terms, our final evaluation of X must take cost into account.

Writing an Evaluation Argument

WRITING ASSIGNMENT
FOR CHAPTER 14

Write an argument in which you try to change someone's mind about the value of X. The X you choose should be controversial or at least problematic. By *controversial* or *problematic*, we mean that people are likely to disagree with your evaluation or X, that they are surprised at your evaluation, or that you are somehow opposing the common or expected view of X. By choosing a controversial or problematic X, you will be able to focus on a clear issue. Somewhere in your essay you should summarize alternative views and either refute them or concede to them (see Chapter 8).

Note that this assignment asks you to do something different from a typical movie review, restaurant review, or product review in a consumer magazine. Many reviews are simply informational or analytical; the writer's purpose is to describe the object or event being reviewed and explain its strengths and weaknesses. In contrast, your purpose here is persuasive. You must change someone's mind about the evaluation of X.

Exploring Ideas

Evaluation issues are all around us, sometimes in subtle forms. The most frequent evaluation arguments occur when we place an X in its most common or expected class. Is *Buffy the Vampire Slayer* a good fantasy TV drama? But more interesting and provocative evaluation questions can sometimes arise if we place X in a different class. Is *Buffy the Vampire Slayer* a good feminist drama? Or is *Buffy the Vampire Slayer* a good introduction to Gothic mythology?

If no ideas come immediately to mind, try creating idea maps with spokes chosen from among the following categories: *people* (athletes, political leaders, musicians, clergy, entertainers, businesspeople); *science and technology* (weapons systems, word-processing programs, spreadsheets, automotive advancements, treatments for diseases); *media* (a newspaper, a magazine or journal, a TV program, a radio station, a Web site, an advertisement); *government and world affairs* (an economic policy, a Supreme Court decision, a law or legal practice, a government custom or practice, a foreign policy); *the arts* (a movie, a book, a building, a painting, a piece of music); *your college or university* (a course, a teacher, a textbook, a curriculum, an administrative policy, the financial aid system); *world of work* (a job, a company operation, a dress policy, a merit pay system, a hiring policy, a supervisor); or any other categories of your choice.

Then brainstorm possibilities for controversial Xs that might fit into the categories on your map. As long as you can imagine disagreement about how to evaluate X, you have a potentially good topic for this assignment.

Once you have found an issue and have taken a tentative position on it, explore your ideas by freewriting your responses to the ten guided tasks in Chapter 3 (pp. 69–70).

Organizing an Evaluation Argument

As you write a draft, you might find useful the following prototypical structures for evaluation arguments. Of course, you can always alter these plans if another structure better fits your material.

Plan 1 (Criteria and Match in Separate Sections)

- Introduce the issue by showing disagreements about how to evaluate a problematic X (Is X a good Y? Is X right or wrong?).
- State your claim.
- Present your criteria for making the evaluation.
  State and develop criterion 1.
  State and develop criterion 2.
  Continue with the rest of your criteria.
- Summarize and respond to possible objections to your criteria.
- Restate your claim, asserting that X is (is not) a good member of class Y or that X is right (wrong).
  Apply criterion 1 to your case.
  Apply criterion 2 to your case.
  Continue the match argument.
- Summarize and respond to possible objections to your match argument.
- Conclude your argument.

Plan 2 (Criteria and Match Interwoven)

- Introduce the issue by showing disagreements about how to evaluate a problematic X (Is X a good Y? Is X right or wrong?)
- Present your claim.

  State criterion 1 and argue that your X meets (does not meet) this criterion.

  State criterion 2 and argue that your X meets (does not meet) this criterion.

  Continue with criteria-match sections for additional criteria.
- Summarize opposing views.
- Refute or concede to opposing views.
- Conclude your argument.

Revising Your Draft

Once you have written a rough draft, your goal is to make it clearer and more persuasive to your audience. Where might your audience question your claim, demand more evidence, or ask for further clarification and support of your criteria? One way to evaluate your draft's persuasiveness is to analyze it using the Toulmin schema.

Imagine that you are on a committee to determine whether to retain or fire Ms. Lillian Jones, the director of admissions we examined in the example on pages 293–294. You have been asked to submit a written argument to the committee. Here is how you might use Toulmin to suggest revision strategies for making your argument more persuasive (your thinking processes are indicated in italics):

ENTHYMEME: Despite some weaknesses, Ms. Jones has been a good manager of the admissions office because her office's recruiting record is excellent.

CLAIM: Ms. Jones has been a good manager of the admissions office.

STATED REASON: Her office's recruitment record is excellent.

GROUNDS: *My draft has statistical data showing the good results of Ms. Jones's recruiting efforts. Can I get more data? Do I need more data? Would other grounds be useful such as testimony from other college officials or comparison with other schools?*

WARRANT: Successful recruitment is the most important criterion for rating job performance of the director of admissions.

BACKING: *In my draft I don't have any backing. I am just assuming that everyone will agree that recruiting is the most important factor. But a lot of people are angry at Ms. Jones for personnel problems in her office. How can I argue that her recruitment record is the most important criterion? I could mention that maintaining a happy, harmonious staff serves no purpose if we have no students. I could remind people of how much tuition dollars drive our budget; if enrollments go down, we're in big trouble.*

CONDITIONS OF REBUTTAL: *How could committee members who don't like Ms. Jones question my reason and grounds? Could they show that her recruitment record isn't that good? Might they argue that plenty of people in the office could do the same good job of recruitment—after all, this college sells itself—without stirring up any of the personnel problems that Ms. Jones has caused? Maybe I should add to the draft the specific things that Ms. Jones has done to improve recruiting.*

Will anyone attack my warrant by arguing that staff problems in Ms. Jones's office are severe enough that we ought to search for a new director? How can I counter that argument?

QUALIFIER: *I will need to qualify my general rating of an excellent record by acknowledging Ms. Jones's weaknesses in staff relations. But I want to be definite in saying that recruitment is the most important criterion and that she should definitely keep her job because she meets this criterion fully.*

Questioning and Critiquing an Evaluation Argument

To strengthen your draft, you can role-play a skeptic in order to probe weaknesses in your ideas and develop ways to overcome them.

Critiquing a Categorical Evaluation Argument

Here is a list of questions you can use to critique a categorical evaluation argument:

Will a skeptic accept my criteria? Many evaluative arguments are weak because the writers have simply assumed that readers will accept their criteria. Whenever your audience's acceptance of your criteria is in doubt, you will need to make your warrants clear and provide backing in their support.

Are my criteria based on the "smallest applicable class" for X? For example, the 1999 film *The Blair Witch Project* will certainly be a failure if you evaluate it in the general class "movies," in which it would have to compete with *Citizen Kane* and other great classics. But if you evaluated it as a "horror film" or a "low-budget film," it would have a greater chance for success and hence of yielding an arguable evaluation.

Will a skeptic accept my general weighting of criteria? Another vulnerable spot in an evaluation argument is the relative weight of the criteria. How much anyone weights a given criterion is usually a function of his or her own interests relative to the X in question. You should always ask whether some particular group affected by the quality of X might not have good reasons for weighting the criteria differently.

Will a skeptic question my standard of reference? In questioning the criteria for judging X, we can also focus on the standard of reference used—what's commonplace versus what's ideal. If you have argued that X is bad because it doesn't live up to what's ideal, you can expect some readers to defend X on the basis of what's common. Similarly, if you argue that X is good because it is better than its competitors, you can expect some readers to point out how short it falls from what is ideal.

Will a skeptic criticize my use of empirical measures? The tendency to mistake empirical measures for criteria is a common one that any critic of an argument should be aware of. As we have discussed earlier, what's most measurable isn't always significant when it comes to assessing the essential traits needed to fulfill whatever function X is supposed to fulfill. A 95-mph fastball is certainly an impressive empirical measure of a pitcher's ability—but if the pitcher doesn't get batters out, that measure is a misleading gauge of performance.

Will a skeptic accept my criteria but reject my match argument? The other major way of testing an evaluation argument is to anticipate how readers might object to your stated reasons and grounds. Will readers challenge you by finding sampling errors in your data or otherwise find that you used evidence selectively? For example, if you think your opponents will emphasize Lillian Jones's abrasive management style much more heavily than you did, you may be able to undercut their arguments by finding counterexamples that show Ms. Jones acting diplomatically. Be prepared to counter objections to your grounds.

Critiquing an Ethical Argument

Perhaps the first question you should ask in setting out to analyze your draft of an ethical argument is "To what extent is the argument based on consequences or on ethical principles?" If it's based exclusively on one of these two forms of ethical thought, then it's vulnerable to the sorts of criticism discussed here. A strictly principled argument that takes no account of the consequences of its position is vulnerable to a simple cost analysis. What are the costs in the case of adhering to this principle? There will undoubtedly be some, or else there would be no real argument. If the argument is based strictly on consequentialist grounds, we should ask if the position violates any rules or principles, particularly such commandments as the Golden Rule—"Do unto others as you would have others do unto you"—which most members of our audience adhere to. By failing to mention these alternative ways of thinking about ethical issues, we undercut not only our argument but our credibility as well.

Let's now consider a more developed examination of the two positions, starting with some of the more subtle weaknesses in a position based on principle. In practice people will sometimes take rigidly "principled" positions because they live in fear of "slippery slopes"; that is, they fear setting precedents that might lead to ever more dire consequences. Consider, for example, the slippery slope leading from birth control to euthanasia if you have an absolutist commitment to the sanctity of human life. Once we allow birth control in the form of condoms or the pill, the principled absolutist would say, then we will be forced to accept birth control "abortions" in the first hours after conception (IUDs, "morning after" pills), then abortions in the first trimester, then in the second or even the third trimester. And once we have violated the sanctity of human life by allowing abortions, it is only a short step to euthanasia and finally to killing off all undesirables.

One way to refute a slippery-slope argument of this sort is to try to dig a foothold into the side of the hill to show that you don't necessarily have to slide all the way to the bottom. You would thus have to argue that allowing birth control does not mean allowing abortions (by arguing for differences between a fetus after conception and sperm and egg before conception), or that allowing abortions does not mean allowing euthanasia (by arguing for differences between a fetus and a person already living in the world).

Consequentialist arguments have different kinds of difficulties. As discussed before, the crucial difficulty facing anyone making a consequentialist argument is to calculate the consequences in a clear and reliable way. Have you considered all significant consequences? If you project your scenario of consequences further into the future (remember, consequentialist arguments are frequently stronger over the short term than over the long term, where many unforeseen consequences can occur), can you identify possibilities that work against the argument?

As also noted, consequentialist arguments carry a heavy burden of empirical proof. What evidence can you offer that the predicted consequences will in fact come to pass? Do you offer any evidence that alternative consequences won't occur? And just how do you prove that the consequences of any given action are a net good or evil?

In addition to the problems unique to each of the two positions, ethical arguments are vulnerable to the more general sorts of criticism, including consistency, recency, and relevance of evidence. Obviously, however, consequentialist arguments will be more vulnerable to weaknesses in evidence, whereas arguments based on principle are more open to questions about consistency of application.

Readings

Our first reading, by student writer Sam Isaacson, was written for the assignment on page 302. It joins a conversation about whether the legalization of same-sex marriage would be good for our society. However, Isaacson, a gay writer, limits the question to whether legalization of same-sex marriage would be *good for the gay community*. Earlier in this text (see Chapter 8, pp. 142–143), we discussed Isaacson's rhetorical choices as he considered the audience for his essay. Isaacson's decision was to address this paper to the readers of a gay magazine such as *Harvard Gay and Lesbian Review* or *The Advocate*.

Would Legalization of Gay Marriage Be Good for the Gay Community?

Sam Isaacson (student)

For those of us who have been out for a while, nothing seems shocking about a gay pride parade. Yet at this year's parade, I was struck by the contrast between two groups—the float for the Toys in Babeland store (with swooning drag queens and leather-clad, whipwielding, topless dykes) and the Northwest chapters of Integrity and Dignity (Episcopal and Catholic organizations for lesbians and gays), whose marchers looked as conservative as the congregation of any American church.

2   These stark differences in dress are representative of larger philosophical differences in the gay community. At stake is whether or not we gays and lesbians should act "normal." Labeled as deviants by many in straight society, we're faced with various opposing methods of response. One option is to insist that we are normal and work to integrate gays into the cultural mainstream. Another response is to form an alternative gay culture with its own customs and values; this culture would honor deviancy in response to a society which seeks to label some as "normal" and some as "abnormal." For the purposes of this paper I will refer to those who favor the first response as "integrationists" and those who favor the second response as "liberationists." Politically, this ideological clash is most evident in the issue of whether legalization of same-sex marriage would be good for the gay community. Nearly all integrationists would say yes, but many liberationists would say no. My belief is that while we must take the objections of the liberationists seriously, legalization of same-sex marriage would benefit both gays and society in general.

3   Let us first look at what is so threatening about gay marriage to many liberationists. Many liberationists fear that legalizing gay marriage will reinforce current social pressures that say monogamous marriage is the normal and right way to live. In straight society, those who choose not to marry are often viewed as self-indulgent, likely promiscuous, and shallow—and it is no coincidence these are some of the same stereotypes gays struggle against. If gays begin to marry, married life will be all the more the norm and subject those outside of marriage to even greater marginalization. As homosexuals, liberationists argue, we should be particularly sensitive to the tyranny of the majority. Our sympathies should lie with the deviants—the transsexual, the fetishist, the drag queen, and the leather-dyke. By choosing marriage, gays take the easy route into "normal" society; we not only abandon the sexual minorities of our community, we strengthen society's narrow notions of what is "normal" and thereby further confine both straights and gays.

4   Additionally, liberationists worry that by winning the right to marry gays and lesbians will lose the distinctive and positive characteristics of gay culture. Many gay writers have commented on how as a marginalized group gays have been forced to create different forms of relationships that often allow for a greater and often more fulfilling range of life experiences. Writer Edmund White, for instance, has observed that there is a greater fluidity in the relationships of gays than straights. Gays, he says, are more likely than straights to stay friends with old lovers, are more likely to form close friendships outside the romantic relationship, and are generally less likely to become compartmentalized into isolated couples. It has also been noted that gay relationships are often characterized by more equality and better communication than are straight relationships. Liberationists make the reasonable assumption that if gays win the right to marry they will be subject to the same social pressure to marry that straights are subject to. As more gays are pressured into traditional life patterns, liberationists fear the gay sensibility will be swallowed up by the established attitudes of the broader culture. All of society would be the poorer if this were to happen.

I must admit that I concur with many of the arguments of the liberationists that I have outlined above. I do think if given the right, gays would feel social pressure to marry; I agree that gays should be especially sensitive to the most marginalized elements of society; and I also agree that the unique perspectives on human relationships that the gay community offers should not be sacrificed. However, despite these beliefs, I feel that legalizing gay marriage would bring valuable benefits to gays and society as a whole.

First of all, I think it is important to put the attacks the liberationists make on marriage into perspective. The liberationist critique of marriage claims that marriage in itself is a harmful institution (for straights as well as gays) because it needlessly limits and normalizes personal freedom. But it seems clear to me that marriage in some form is necessary for the well-being of society. Children need a stable environment in which to be raised. Studies have shown that children whose parents divorce often suffer long-term effects from the trauma. Studies have also shown that people tend to be happier in stable long-term relationships. We need to have someone to look over us when we're old, when we become depressed, when we fall ill. All people, gay or straight, parents or nonparents, benefit from the stabilizing force of marriage.

Second, we in the gay community should not be too quick to overlook the real benefits that legalizing gay marriage will bring. We are currently denied numerous legal rights of marriage that the straight community enjoys: tax benefits, insurance benefits, inheritance rights, and the right to have a voice in medical treatment or funeral arrangements for a dying partner.

Further, just as important as the legal impacts of being denied the right to marriage is the socially symbolic weight this denial carries. We are sent the message that while gay sex in the privacy of one's home will be tolerated, gay love will not be respected. We are told that it is not important to society whether we form long-term relationships or not. We are told that we are not worthy of forming families of our own. By gaining the same recognitions by the state of our relationships and all the legal and social weight that recognition carries, the new message will be that gay love is just as meaningful as straight love.

Finally, let me address what I think is at the heart of the liberationist argument against marriage—the fear of losing social diversity and our unique gay voice. The liberationists are wary of society's normalizing forces. They fear that if gays win the right to marry gay relationships will simply become imitations of straight relationships—the richness gained through the gay experience will be lost. I feel, however, this argument unintentionally plays into the hands of conservatives. Conservatives argue that marriage is, by definition, the union between man and woman. As a consequence, to the broad culture gay marriage can only be a mockery of marriage. As gays and lesbians we need to argue that conservatives are imposing arbitrary standards on what is normal and not normal in society. To fight the conservative agenda, we must suggest instead that marriage is, in essence, a contract of love and commitment between two people. The liberationists, I think, unwittingly feed into conservative identification and classification by pigeonholing gays as outsiders. Reacting against social norms is simply another way of being held hostage by them.

10 We need to understand that the gay experience and voice will not be lost by gaining the right to marry. Gays will always be the minority by simple biological fact and this will always color the identity of any gay person. But we can only make our voice heard if we are seen as full-fledged members of society. Otherwise we will remain an isolated and marginalized group. And only when we have the right to marry will we have any say in the nature and significance of marriage as an institution. This is not being apologetic to the straight culture, but is a demand that we not be excluded from the central institutions of Western culture. We can help merge the fluidity of gay relationships with the traditionally more compartmentalized married relationship. Further, liberationists should realize that the decision *not* to marry makes a statement only if one has the ability to choose marriage. What would be most radical, most transforming, is two women or two men joined together in the eyes of society.

Critiquing "Would Legalization of Gay Marriage Be Good for the Gay Community?"

1. Who is the audience that Sam Isaacson addresses in this argument?
2. Ordinarily when we think of persons opposing gay marriage, we imagine socially conservative heterosexuals. However, Sam spends little time addressing the antigay marriage arguments of straight society. Rather, he addresses the antimarriage arguments made by "liberationist" gay people. What are these arguments? How well does Sam respond to them?
3. What are the criteria Sam uses to argue that legalizing gay marriage would be good for the gay community?
4. How persuasive do you think Sam's argument is to the various audiences he addresses?

Our second reading, by student writer Tiffany Anderson, developed out of discussions of hip-hop music. Tiffany was torn between a general dislike of rap combined with a growing admiration for certain female rappers. This evaluation argument took shape once she formulated her issue question: What makes a good female hip-hop artist?

A Woman's View of Hip-Hop
Tiffany Anderson (student)

1 Is there anything good about hip-hop? If you had asked me this question several years ago, I would have said no. I probably disliked hip-hop as much as any typical middle-aged white suburbanite does. I found the aggressive, ego-driven, star-powered, competitive male image of hip-hop devoid of value, especially the beat

and the strong language. I also disliked many of the themes explored in gangster rap, such as the derogatory terms for blacks, the treatment of women as sex objects, and the equation of power and money. When some boys at summer camp six years ago first introduced me to hip-hop, we listened to artists like Bone Thugs-n-Harmony, Tupak Shakur, and Biggie Smalls. These boys who liked rap were also sniffing markers and gave me my first encounter with drugs. In my sheltered white world, I associated rap with drugs and gangs, and I gravitated toward the comfort of alternative rock and punk instead.

But my view of rap began to change when I started listening to the female rappers introduced to me by my friends. During my sophomore year in high school I remember going home because of a bomb threat, and we danced to *The Miseducation of Lauryn Hill* in my living room. I liked what Lauryn was saying. Women hip-hop artists have something different to offer in a male-dominated industry, and it has been women artists who have converted me into a hip-hop fan, not the men. What exactly do these women have to offer that is so compelling? What makes a good female hip-hop artist? While many female rappers merely follow in the footsteps of male rappers by rapping about money, sex, or violence, the truly great female artists provide female listeners with a sense of self-empowerment and identity, they offer a woman's perspective on many topics, and they often create a hopeful message that counters the negativity of male rap. Through their songs, good female rappers spread positive, unique messages that not only benefit African Americans, but females of every race.

Very few male artists are able to provide women with a sense of self-empowerment or identity through their music. But excellent female hip-hop artists like Lauryn Hill address women's sense of self, as Hill does in her song "Doo Wop (That Thing)." In the first verse she criticizes a woman who loses her self-respect by doing what men want her to do ("It's silly when girls sell their souls because it's in"). She encourages women who "ain't right within" to take pride in themselves, regain their self-respect, and be true to themselves. The encouragement Lauryn offers her female audience is uplifting in an industry where women are often reduced to sex objects as scantily clad dancers, back-up singers, and eye candy in music videos. Rapper Trina, in her song "Take Me," criticizes the idea that females have to be sex objects: "I wanna go to a world where I ain't gotta be a freak ho / just so I can be noticed by people." Perhaps through such urging, girls can take pride in themselves and rebel against stereotypes. Foxy Brown addresses stereotypes in an entirely different, but equally effective, way. She uses her explicitly sexual lyrics to objectify men in her songs, where her heroine is always the dominant one. Her songs help break female sexual inhibitions, reverse the typical roles of the sexes, and allow us to be proud of our sexuality. These songs can be a cathartic release in a world that is all too often dominated by men. Female artists should address the reality of derogatory stereotypes and work to foster a positive female image; if this were left to the male rappers of the industry, females would not be as positively represented in the hip-hop industry.

Another mark of a good female hip-hop artist is that she makes songs that give a woman's perspective on the world or her songs include topics not usually addressed in hip-hop songs at all. For example, my favorite song by Lauryn Hill, "To Zion," is about how her world changed after the birth of her son, Zion. When she sings, "Now the joy of my world is Zion," I am filled with pride that I am a woman and have the ability to give birth. How often do male artists, like Nelly or DMX, sing about the joys of parenthood? It is refreshing to hear songs about the miracles of life, as opposed to the death, drugs, and destruction that are often the topics in typical rap songs. On *Eve-olution*, Eve's most recent album, she criticizes our world where she "can't trust the air," an allusion to an oncoming ecological crisis. Hip-hop artists are rarely concerned with problems that affect the entire world, but focus more on their communities. Eve shows her scope as an artist in addressing ecological problems. Another topic not often explored in hip-hop songs is religion. In her song "Confessions," Lady of Rage asks for forgiveness and calls for appreciation of the Lord: "Forgive me, God, for I have forsaken thee / I'm not gonna say that it's the devil that's makin' me." Hip-hop is so often used to name all the evils in the world and lay blame, so hearing an artist take responsibility for her actions and explore a religious theme in her music is refreshing. When a female rap artist can offer her listeners something that they don't often hear, she is truly great.

5   Most importantly, the best female rappers often see some kind of hope in life. Some people might argue that the negativity so blatant in much hip-hop music actually conveys important social and political messages, addressing racial profiling, police brutality, gun control, violence, the glorification of money and sex, and problems with education and welfare reform. These people might say that this influential urban folk art exposes economic and social realities that America needs to confront. I agree that sometimes male artists will reveal a heartbreaking perspective on this empty world by communicating how urban youth struggle with self-hatred, poverty, lack of education, hopelessness, discrimination, and injustice. For example, in Outkast's song "Git Up, Git Out," the lyrics speak of never-ending cycles of drugs, negativity, and lack of education that hold African Americans back: "I don't recall, ever graduatin' at all / Sometimes I feel I'm just a disappointment to y'all . . . Every job I get is cruel and demeanin' / Sick of taking trash out and toilet bowl cleanin' / But I'm also sick and tired of strugglin' / I never ever thought I'd have resort to drug smugglin." While male hip-hop often offers a unique, chilling perspective on the problems of urban America, their music often only serves to strengthen the cycles of despair and self-hatred. Where is hope in songs that often spend verse after verse on the negative aspects of life and the forces that hold people back?

6   In contrast, female hip-hop artists do identify the problems, but sometimes suggest ways to overcome the difficulties of their lives. For example, Eve's song "Heaven Only Knows" talks about the trouble she faced until she overcame her devastating situation by finding peace through music: "Do positive and positive will happen / Stay positive and positive was rapping / It was like my brain was clouded with unnecessary shit / But I chose to see through the negative and make hits." "Heaven Only Knows" demonstrates the power of rap music to heal. Through her songs, Eve encourages her listeners in new paths and reinforces the importance of overcoming the negative aspects of being an African American. In the title track of *The Miseducation of Lauryn Hill*, Lauryn deftly addresses the problems and offers her own personal story of how she overcame life's setbacks: "I look at my environment / And

wonder where the fire went / What happened to everything we used to be / I hear so many cry for help/Searching outside themselves / Now I know His strength is within me / And deep in my heart the answer it was in me / And I made up my mind to find my own destiny." Lauryn sings about how she rejected what was expected of her from outside sources, turned to God, and found everything she needed in herself. To impoverished people of urban America, finding inner strength and self-empowerment could be encouraging. Although Lauryn and Eve usually direct their songs to an African American audience, their words of wisdom apply to all races. Every woman alive can benefit from knowing that we can find our "own destiny" within ourselves, as Lauryn raps about.

Because the lyrics of rap are its heart and soul, what a rapper says conveys a   7
powerful worldview. The worldview of male rap for me is too violent, negative, and antiwoman, but female rap often conveys the same gritty sense of urban life without succumbing to hopelessness and without reducing women to sex objects. The best female rappers are able to arouse a sense of pride and self-worth through their thoughtful lyrics, offer a woman's perspective on the world, and include hopeful messages among the harsh realities of urban life. Female artists like Lauryn Hill, Eve, or Trina have taught me that not all hip-hop is bad, and that sometimes, I can even learn a little something from a song. I found hip-hop a surprising source of feminist pride, diversity, and hope, and this discovery served as a reminder that even in a male- and African American-dominated industry, any white girl can find something to relate to and learn from.

Critiquing "A Woman's View of Hip-Hop"

1. Controversies about popular culture can sometimes become purely subjective discussions about likes and dislikes. How effective is Tiffany Anderson at moving her evaluation of hip-hop from the purely private realm into the public arena where reasoned discussion can take place? Whose views of hip-hop do you think Tiffany wants to change?

2. What criteria does she use to evaluate the music of female hip-hop artists? Do you accept these criteria? What other criteria might an arguer offer to evaluate female hip-hop music? Can you think of good hip-hop music by a female artist that doesn't meet Tiffany's criteria?

3. For her categorical evaluation, Tiffany evaluates specific female artists within the category of "women's rap" as opposed to "men's rap." (Her criteria focus primarily on differences between women's and men's rap.) Within what other categories could you evaluate female rappers?

4. Does Tiffany effectively anticipate alternative views? If so, which alternative views does she address?

5. How effective do you find her argument? Why?

Our third reading is an Ann Cleaves political cartoon that joins a public controversy about high-stakes testing (see Figure 14.1). Driven by the desire to

FIGURE 14.1   *Education / testing cartoon*

Courtesy of Ann Cleaves.

measure the effectiveness of the nation's schools through test scores, the testing movement has sparked a vigorous national debate.

Critiquing the Education/Testing Cartoon

1. Political cartoons have the power to condense an often complex argument into a brief statement that makes a claim and implies a whole supporting argument through the use of visuals and text. In your own words, what is the claim and implied supporting argument made by this cartoon?

2. How does the drawing of the teacher's face, expression, and desktop help convey the argument?

3. What are the implied criteria for "good education" in this cartoon? How does the testing movement fail to meet these criteria?

Our final reading, "Eight Is Too Many: The Case against Octuplets," is an ethical argument by Dr. Ezekiel Emanuel, the chair of the Department of Clinical Bioethics at the National Institutes of Health. He discusses the case of the McCaughey septuplets, born on November 17, 1997, and the Chukwu octuplets, one of whom was born vaginally on December 8, 1999, and the other seven born by cesarean section on December 20, 1999. In both cases, the couple had been treated with fertility drugs. This article appeared in the *New Republic* on January 25, 1999.

Eight Is Too Many: The Case against Octuplets

Dr. Ezekiel J. Emanuel

Just like the McCaughey septuplets of Iowa, whose first birthday recently made   1
headlines in *People* magazine, the Chukwu octuplets of Texas have become a media spectacle. Daily bulletins detailing each child's respiratory status, ultrasound results, and other developments fill the papers—not just the tabloids, but respectable outlets like the *New York Times* and the *Washington Post,* as well. Inevitably, writers describe the eight live births in glowing terms—amazing, wonderful, even a miracle; they describe the mother as the brave survivor of adversity; they portray the hard-battling physicians as heroes and champions.

But what are we all celebrating? Modern reproductive technologies have   2
brought the miracle of children to many infertile couples, thereby producing enormous good. The McCaughey septuplets and Chukwu octuplets, however, represent too much of that good thing. They are the product of fertility technology misused— an error, not a wonder, and one that even the few public voices of skepticism seem not fully to appreciate.

First and most obvious, large multiple births lead to all sorts of medical problems,   3
for mothers and children alike. Nkem Chukwu had to stay in the hospital for months prior to delivery, on a bed that tilted her nearly upside down. It's too early to know how well her surviving children will fare (one died seven days after birth), but the odds do not favor them. Among children born prematurely and weighing just two pounds or less—the largest of the Chukwu infants weighed one pound, eleven ounces at birth—breathing difficulties, brain damage, and fluid imbalances are not rare.

The result is a comparatively high level of infant mortality and, in the survivors,   4
long-term complications. Studies of low-birth-weight children (not from multifetal pregnancies but from premature births) have shown that approximately 20 percent have severe disabilities; among those weighing less than 750 grams (1.7 pounds) at birth, 50 percent have functional impairments. A recent study that followed these very small infants to school showed that up to 50 percent of them scored low on standardized intelligence tests, including 21 percent who were mentally retarded. In addition, nine percent had cerebral palsy, and 25 percent had severe vision problems. As a result, 45 percent ended up enrolling in special-education programs.

Equally important, but rarely articulated, are the emotional health risks   5
children in multiple births face. Loving and raising children through the normal developmental milestones is enormously wonderful and rewarding. But it is also hard

work. Raising children is not a sprint to a healthy birth but a marathon through variable terrain until the goal of independent adulthood. The real way to assess these miraculous pregnancies—indeed, any pregnancy—is whether they are ultimately good for children. Quite clearly, they are not.

6   Attending to the physical, emotional, intellectual, and social needs of children for 18 years is hard and demanding. For infants and toddlers there are the simple physical demands—feeding, changing diapers, bathing, chasing after them to prevent injuries. Then there are the emotional and intellectual demands—cuddling them, talking to them, responding meaningfully to their smiles and first words, reading books to them, playing with them and their toys, handling the tantrums, and so on. And, while the physical demands may lessen once children grow (although parents who often feel like chefs, maids, chauffeurs, and all-around gofers may disagree with that), the emotional and intellectual demands become more complex with time. Older children need help with homework, mediation of sibling rivalry, constructive discipline, support in the trials and tribulations of friendships, encouragement in their participation in sports and other activities, help in coping with losses and defeats, and guidance through the many pitfalls of adolescence.

7   It is challenging enough to balance the demands of one or two children of different ages and attend to their needs; it is simply not physically possible for two parents to do this successfully for seven children of the same age, even if one of the parents is a full-time caregiver. Regardless of the motivation, dedication, love, or stamina of these parents, the sheer limitations of time make it impossible for each of seven identically aged children to receive appropriate parental attention and affection.

8   Just ask yourself: Would you trade being born a healthy single or twin for being born one of the "miraculous" septuplets, even a healthy one? Most of us would probably say "no" because of parental attention we would have lost. And we would be right to think that way.

9   The McCaugheys' experience proves the point. They have been able to raise their septuplets for one year only because they can fall back on a veritable army of volunteers—scores of people with tightly coordinated schedules who assist in the food preparation, feeding, diapering, and care of the seven babies. Few families with quintuplets or more children can expect or rely on such community effort. (Indeed, a Washington, D.C., couple who recently bore quintuplets, had hardly any community help at all until some belated publicity highlighted the family's plight.) And, while the McCaugheys' community-wide effort appears to have worked for the first year of life, it's hardly a sure thing that the assistance will always be there. The first is the year when, despite the demands on time, parents are most interchangeable and caregiving has the greatest, most unmitigated emotional rewards. The terrible twos and threes will try the patience and dedication of volunteers.

10   What's more, having multiple caregivers cannot fully substitute for parental time. While it's true that many children do just fine spending large amounts of time in paid day care, where multiple providers care for them, these children at least have the chance to go home and have one-on-one parental time spread among just a few siblings, of different ages. (Having multiple caregivers also becomes more prob-

lematic as the children grow, because of child-rearing styles that may differ from those of the parents, particularly on issues like discipline.) This is not possible in the McCaughey or Chukwu families, and it never will be. Spending just 20 minutes a day focusing on each individual child—hardly a lavish amount—will take nearly two and a half hours each day. When competing with sleep, meals, shopping, and all the other demands of basic existence for a family with septuplets, this focused time is likely to disappear.

Remember, too, that, while the McCaughey septuplets seem to have brought together a community to support their care, such children also impose significant costs on the community. It is now estimated that the hospital costs from birth to discharge (or death) for the Chukwu infants will exceed $2 million. And the health care costs don't stop after birth. Any complications—neurological, vision, or other problems—can drive the medical care costs sky-high. Plus, no one knows how much will be required for permanent problems that require ongoing special-education and other accommodations. Yes, there's health insurance. But health insurance exists to cover ill health and problems such as cancer, genetic defects, and accidents that are the result of random chance. The birth of octuplets, by contrast, is not a chance event; it is the result of deliberate actions (or inactions) by physicians, patients, and society. Remember, too, that financial resources are limited; money spent on octuplets is money not spent on other children with special health care and educational needs.   11

For these reasons, the standard of medical care is not to proceed with such large multiple births. But this raises legitimate ethical problems for many couples. The most common method for interrupting multiple pregnancies is "selective reduction"—that is, doctors abort some of the fetuses for the sake of the mother's health. Many people believe couples who agree to infertility treatments must not only be informed about—but should consent to—the potential need for selective reduction even before beginning the treatments. Yet this is clearly not an option for families like the McCaugheys and the Chukwus, who oppose abortion on religious grounds.   12

Fortunately, this issue doesn't have to be so morally knotty. In the usual treatment for problems with egg maturation and release (this is what both the McCaughey and Chukwu families were treated for), doctors prescribe drugs such as human menopausal gonadotropin (hMG) or Clomiphene (commonly known as Clomid) to stimulate egg development. Then they administer an additional drug, human chorionic gonadatropin (hCG), to induce ovulation. Using measurements of estrogen and ultrasound monitoring, physicians can assess the number of egg follicles developing in the ovaries. If they observe too many developing follicles, making the likelihood of multiple fertilizations high, physicians can withhold the drugs necessary to stimulate ovulation and advise against intercourse or withhold sperm injection until the next cycle, when they can go through the process again. To be sure, that treatment process can be a little more frustrating for aspiring parents. And many couples are reluctant to skip a cycle because it wastes thousands of dollars on the drugs and treatments, usually out of their own pockets. But carrying septuplets to term has costs, too.   13

14   In the end, new laws or regulations won't fix this problem. The real solution is leadership by the medical profession and by the media. Reproductive specialists who care for infertile couples are not simply passive technicians following the orders of the parents. They are engaged professionals guiding important technology that can create great joy—but also great pain. Professionalism requires deliberating with the parents about the goals and purposes of the treatments; doctors should draw upon their experience to advise and strongly recommend the best course to the parents, which is to avoid large multiple pregnancies.

15   And the media must stop glorifying the septuplets and octuplets. We live in an era that measures success in terms of quantity, that thinks bigger is necessarily better, where the best is defined by size. The best movie is the one that makes the most money; the best law firm is the one with the highest billings; the best painting is auctioned for the highest price; and the best book is the best-selling book. But, in this case, bigger may not be better—indeed, it may actually be worse. The true miracle of birth is the mysterious process by which the fusing of an egg and a sperm can create in just nine months the complex organism that is an infant with the potential to become an independent, thinking, feeling, socially responsible adult. In this way, the millions of babies born each year are miraculous whether born of singleton, twin, triplet, or octuplet pregnancies. It is the wonder of each infant that we should celebrate.

Critiquing "Eight Is Too Many: The Case against Octuplets"

1. What criteria does Emanuel use in making his case against octuplets? In your own words, summarize his argument.

2. Emanuel's article raises numerous questions of value of the kind we treated in this chapter's discussion of ethical arguments. In addressing the ethical question "Is it morally justifiable to create multiple-birth pregnancies using fertility drugs?" does Emanuel primarily argue from consequences or from principles? What popular view of the McCaugheys or the Chukwus is Emanuel trying to change?

3. Emanuel argues that octuplets are an "error," not a wonder—"the product of fertility technology misused." How convincing is Emanuel's argument? At what points does Emanuel summarize and respond to opposing views? How might defenders of the McCaugheys or the Chukwus and their doctors respond?

15 Proposal Arguments
We Should (Should Not) Do X

CASE 1

Many cultural commentators are alarmed by a new social disease brought on by addictive spending. Dubbed "affluenza" and "credititis," this disease is spreading through aggressive promotion of credit cards. Economic analysts are particularly concerned at the way credit card companies are deluging teenagers with credit card offers. Some argue that encouraging credit card debt among the young is highly irresponsible corporate behavior. In order to raise public awareness of the problem, a group of legislators proposes that the following warning label be placed prominently on all credit cards: "WARNING: Failure to research interest rates and credit cards may result in personal financial loss or possible bankruptcy."

CASE 2

A pressing world problem is the need to reduce oil consumption. In the United States, numerous methods have been tried. For example, Congress mandated that auto manufacturers make their cars more fuel efficient, but the plan was thwarted by SUVs, which are classified as trucks rather than cars. Taking a different tack, some conservationists have wondered if market forces, rather than federal regulations, might be used to stimulate purchase of more fuel-efficient cars. One proposal is to institute "feebates," which is a combination of a fee and a rebate. When purchasing gas, drivers would be charged different prices depending on the type of vehicle being fueled. A computerized system would give drivers of fuel-efficient cars an immediate rebate, reducing the price per gallon of gas. In contrast, drivers of fuel-inefficient cars would be charged a fee, increasing the price per gallon of gas. This proposal would give car buyers a market incentive for buying more fuel-efficient cars.

An Overview of Proposal Arguments

Although proposal arguments are the last type we examine, they are among the most common arguments that you will encounter or be called on to write. Their essence is that they call for action. In reading a proposal, the audience is enjoined to make a decision and then to act on it—to *do* something. Proposal arguments are sometimes called *should* or *ought* arguments because those helping verbs express the obligation to act: "We *should* do X." or "We *ought* to do X."

For instructional purposes, we will distinguish between two kinds of proposal arguments, even though they are closely related and involve the same basic arguing strategies. The first kind we will call *practical proposals,* which propose an action to solve some kind of local or immediate problem. A student's proposal to change the billing procedures for scholarship students would be an example of a practical proposal, as would an engineering firm's proposal for the design of a new bridge being planned by a city government. The second kind we will call *policy proposals,* in which the writer offers a broad plan of action to solve major social, economic, or political problems affecting the common good. An argument that the United States should adopt a national health insurance plan or that the electoral college should be abolished would be examples of policy proposals.

The primary difference is the narrowness versus breadth of the concern. *Practical* proposals are narrow, local, and concrete; they focus on the nuts and bolts of getting something done in the here and now. They are often concerned with the exact size of a piece of steel, the precise duties of a new person to be hired, or a close estimate of the cost of paint or computers to be purchased. *Policy* proposals, in contrast, are concerned with the broad outline and shape of a course of action, often on a regional, national, or even international issue. What government should do about overcrowding of prisons would be a problem addressed by policy proposals. How to improve the security alarm system for the county jail would be addressed by a practical proposal.

Learning to write both kinds of proposals is valuable. Researching and writing a *policy* proposal is an excellent way to practice the responsibilities of citizenship, which require the ability to understand complex issues and to weigh positive and negative consequences of policy choices. In your professional life, writing *practical* proposals may well be among your most important duties on the job. Effective proposal writing is the lifeblood of many companies and also constitutes one of the most powerful ways you can identify and help solve problems.

The Structure of Proposal Arguments

Proposal arguments, whether practical proposals or policy proposals, generally have a three-part structure: (1) description of a problem, (2) proposed solution, and (3) justification for the proposed solution. In the justification section of your proposal argument, you develop *because* clauses of the kinds you have practiced throughout this text.

Special Concerns for Proposal Arguments

In their call for action, proposal arguments entail certain emphases and audience concerns that you don't generally face with other kinds of arguments. Let's look briefly at some of these special concerns.

The Need for Presence

Your audience might agree with your proposal on an intellectual level, but how can you move them to *act* on your proposal, especially if the personal cost of acting may be high? Urging action often requires you to engage your audience's emotions as well as their intellects. Thus proposal arguments often require more attention to *pathos* than do other kinds of arguments (see pp. 132–138).

In most cases, convincing people to act means that an argument must have presence as well as intellectual force. By *presence* we mean an argument's ability to grip the readers' hearts and imaginations as well as their intellects. You can give presence to an argument through the effective use of details, provocative statistics, dialogue, illustrative narratives, and compelling examples that show the reader the seriousness of the problem you are addressing or the consequences of not acting on your proposal. You can also use figurative language such as metaphor and analogy to make the problem being addressed more vivid or real to your audience. Here is how one student used personal experiences in the problem section of her proposal calling for redesign of the mathematics department's calculus curriculum:

> My own experience in the Calculus 134 and 135 sequence last year showed me that it was not the learning of calculus that was difficult for me. I was able to catch on to the new concepts. The problem for me was in the fast pace. Just as I was assimilating new concepts and feeling the need to reinforce them, the class was on to a new topic before I had full mastery of the old concept. [. . .] Part of the reason for the fast pace is that calculus is a feeder course for computer science and engineering. If prospective engineering students can't learn the calculus rapidly, they drop out of the program. The high dropout rate benefits the Engineering School because they use the math course to weed out an overabundance of engineering applicants. Thus the pace of the calculus course is geared to the needs of the engineering curriculum, not to the needs of someone like me who wants to be a high school mathematics teacher and who believes that my own difficulties with math—combined with my love for it—might make me an excellent math teacher.

By describing the fast pace of the math curriculum from the perspective of a future math teacher rather than an engineering student, this writer illuminates a problem invisible to others. What before didn't look like a problem (it is good to weed out weak engineering majors) suddenly became a problem (it is bad to weed out future math teachers). Establishing herself as a serious student genuinely interested in learning calculus, she gave presence to the problem by calling attention to it in a new way.

The Need to Overcome People's Natural Conservatism

Another difficulty faced by a proposal maker is the innate conservatism of all human beings, whatever their political persuasion. One philosopher refers to this conservatism as the *law of inertia,* the tendency of all things in the universe, including human beings, to remain at rest if possible. The popular adage "If it ain't broke, don't fix it" is one expression of this tendency. Proposers of change face an extraordinary burden of proof. They have to prove that something needs fixing, that it can be fixed, and that the cost of fixing it will be outweighed by the benefits of fixing it.

The difficulty of proving that something needs fixing is compounded by the fact that frequently the status quo appears to be working. So sometimes when writing a proposal, you can't argue that what we have is bad, but only that what we could have would be better. Often, then, a proposal argument will be based not on present evils but on the evils of lost potential. And getting an audience to accept lost potential may be difficult indeed, given the inherently abstract nature of potentiality.

The Difficulty of Predicting Future Consequences

Further, most proposal makers will be forced to predict consequences of a given act. As we've seen in our earlier discussions of causality, it is difficult enough to argue backward from event Y in order to establish that X caused Y. Think how much harder it is to establish that X will, in the future, cause certain things to occur. We all know enough of history to realize that few major decisions have led neatly to their anticipated results. This knowledge indeed accounts for much of our conservatism. All the things that can go wrong in a causal argument can go wrong in a proposal argument as well; the major difference is that in a proposal argument we typically have less evidence for our conjectures.

The Problem of Evaluating Consequences

A final difficulty faced by all proposal arguments concerns the difficulty of evaluating the consequences of the proposal. In government and industry, managers often turn to a tool known as *cost-benefit analysis* to calculate the potential consequences of a given proposal. As much as possible, a cost-benefit analysis tries to reduce all consequences to a single scale for purposes of comparison. Most often, the scale will be money. Although this scale may work well in some circumstances, it can lead to grotesquely inappropriate conclusions in other situations.

Just how does one balance the money saved by cutting Medicare benefits against the suffering of the people denied benefits? How does one translate the beauty of a wilderness area into a dollar amount? On this score, cost-benefit analyses often run into a problem discussed in the previous chapter: the seductiveness of empirical measures. Because something can't be readily measured doesn't mean it can be safely ignored. And finally, what will be a cost for one group will often be a benefit for others. For example, if Social Security benefits are cut, those on Social Security will suffer, but current workers who pay for it with taxes will take home a larger paycheck.

These, then, are some of the general difficulties facing someone who sets out to argue in favor of a proposal. Although not insurmountable, they are at least daunting.

Developing a Proposal Argument

Writers of proposal arguments must focus in turn on three main phases or stages of the argument: showing that a problem exists, explaining the proposed solution, and offering a justification.

Convincing Your Readers That a Problem Exists

There is one argumentative strategy generic to all proposal arguments: awakening in the reader a sense of a problem. Typically, the development of a problem occurs in one of two places in a proposal argument—either in the introduction prior to the presentation of the arguer's proposal claim or in the body of the paper as the first main reason justifying the proposal claim. In the second instance the writer's first *because* clause has the following structure: "We should do X *because* we are facing a serious problem that needs a solution."

At this stage of your argument, it's important to give your problem presence. You must get people to see how the problem affects people, perhaps through examples of suffering or other loss or through persuasive statistics and so forth. Your goal is to awaken your readers to the existence of a problem, a problem they may well not have recognized before.

Besides giving presence to the problem, a writer must also gain the readers' intellectual assent to the depth, range, and potential seriousness of the problem. Suppose, for illustration, that you wanted to propose a special tax to increase funding for higher education in your state. In trying to convince taxpayers in your state that a problem exists, what obstacles might you face? First of all, many taxpayers never went to college and feel that they get along just fine without it. They tend to worry more about the quality of roads, social services, elementary and secondary schools, police and fire protection, and so forth. They are not too convinced that they need to worry about professors' salaries or better-equipped research labs. Thus it's not enough to talk about the importance of education in general or to cite figures showing how paltry your state's funding of higher education is.

To convince your audience of the need for your proposal, you'll have to describe the consequences of low funding levels in terms they can relate to. You'll have to show them that potential benefits to the state are lost because of inadequate funding. Perhaps you can show the cost in terms of inadequately skilled graduates, disgruntled teachers, high turnover, brain drain to other states, inadequate educational services to farmers and businesspeople, lost productivity, and so forth. Or perhaps you can show your audience examples of benefits realized from better college funding in other states. Such examples give life to the abstract notion of lost potential.

All of this is not to say that you can't or shouldn't argue that higher education is inherently good. But until your reader can see low funding levels as "problematic" rather than "simply the way things are," your proposal stands little chance of being enacted.

Showing the Specifics of Your Proposal

Having decided that there is a problem to be solved, you should lay out your thesis, which is a proposal for solving the problem. Your goal now is to stress the feasibility of your solution, including costs. The art of proposal making is the art of the possible. To be sure, not all proposals require elaborate descriptions of the implementation process. If you are proposing, for example, that a local PTA chapter should buy new tumbling mats for the junior high gym classes, the procedures for buying the mats will probably be irrelevant. But in many arguments the specifics of your proposal—the actual step-by-step methods of implementing it— may be instrumental in winning your audience's support.

You will also need to show how your proposal will solve the problem either partially or wholly. Sometimes you may first need to convince your reader that the problem is solvable, not something intractably rooted in "the way things are," such as earthquakes or jealousy. In other words, expect that some members of your audience will be skeptical about the ability of any proposal to solve the problem you are addressing. You may well need, therefore, to "listen" to this point of view in your refutation section and to argue that your problem is at least partially solvable.

In order to persuade your audience that your proposal can work, you can follow any one of several approaches. A typical approach is to lay out a causal argument showing how one consequence will lead to another until your solution is effected. Another approach is to turn to resemblance arguments, either analogy or precedent. You try to show how similar proposals have been successful elsewhere. Or, if similar things have failed in the past, you try to show how the present situation is different.

The Justification: Convincing Your Readers That Your Proposal Should Be Enacted

The justification phase of a proposal argument will need extensive development in some arguments and minimal development in others, again depending on your particular problem and the rhetorical context of your proposal. If your audience already acknowledges the seriousness of the problem you are addressing and has simply been waiting for the right solution to come along, then your argument will be successful so long as you can convince your audience that your solution will work and that it won't cost too much. Such arguments depend on the clarity of your proposal and the feasibility of its being implemented.

But what if the costs are high? What if your readers don't think the problem is serious? What if they don't appreciate the benefits of solving the problem or the bad consequences of not solving it? In such cases you have to develop persuasive reasons for enacting your proposal. You may also have to determine who has the power to act on your proposal and apply arguments directly to that person's or agency's immediate interests. You need to know to whom or to what your power source is beholden or responsive and what values your power source holds that can be appealed to. You're looking, in short, for the best pressure points.

Proposal Arguments as Advocacy Posters or Advertisements

A frequently encountered kind of proposal argument is the one-page newspaper or magazine advertisement often purchased by advocacy groups to promote a cause. Such arguments also appear as Web pages or as posters or fliers. These condensed advocacy arguments are marked by their bold, abbreviated, tightly planned format. The creators of these arguments know they must work fast to capture our attention, give presence to a problem, advocate a solution, and enlist our support. Advocacy advertisements frequently use photographs, images, or icons that appeal to a reader's emotions and imagination. In addition to images, they often use different type sizes and styles. Large-type text in these documents frequently takes the form of slogans or condensed thesis statements written in an arresting style. To outline and justify their solutions, creators of advocacy ads often put main supporting reasons in bulleted lists and sometimes enclose carefully selected facts and quotations in boxed sidebars. To add an authoritative *ethos*, the arguments often include fine-print footnotes and bibliographies. (For more detailed discussion of how advocacy posters and advertisements use images and arrange text for rhetorical effect, see Chapter 9 on visual argument.)

Another prominent feature of these condensed, highly visual arguments is their appeal to the audience through a direct call for a course of action: go to an advocacy Web site to find more information on how to support a cause; cut out a postcard-like form to send to a decision maker; vote for or against the proposition or the candidate; write a letter to a political representative; or donate money to a cause.

An example of a student-produced advocacy advertisement is shown in Figure 15.1. Here student Lisa Blattner joins a heated debate in her city on whether to close down all-ages dance clubs. Frustrated because the evening dance options for under-twenty-one youth were threatened in Seattle, Lisa directed her ad toward the general readership of regional newspapers with the special intention of reaching adult voters and parents. Lisa's ad uses three documentary-like, emotionally loaded, and disturbing photographs to give immediacy and presence to the problem. The verbal text in the ad states the proposal claim and provides three reasons in support of the claim. Notice how the reasons also pick up the ideas in the three photo images. The final lines of text memorably reiterate the claim and call readers to action. The success of this ad derives from the collaboration of layout, photos, and verbal text in conveying a clear, direct argument.

What Is Left for Teenagers to Do When the Teen Ordinance Bans Them from Dance Clubs?

Take Ecstasy   Drink at Places with   Roam the Streets
at Raves   No Adult Supervision

Is There an Answer to These Problems?

Yes! Through your support of the All Ages Dance Ordinance, teens will have a safe place to go where:

- **No hard drugs, like ecstasy and cocaine, are present**
- **Responsible adults are watching over everyone**
- **All of their friends can hang out in one place indoors, instead of outside with drug dealers, criminals, and prostitutes**

Give Your Child a Safe Place to Have Fun at Night

**Let the Seattle City Committee Know
That You Support the
All Ages Dance Ordinance**

FIGURE 15.1 *Student advocacy advertisement*

Now that you have been introduced to the main elements of a proposal argument, including condensed visual arguments, we explain in the next two sections two invention strategies you can use to generate persuasive reasons for a proposal argument and to anticipate your audience's doubts and reservations. We call these the "claim-type strategy" and the "stock issues strategy."

Using the Claim-Type Strategy to Develop a Proposal Argument

In Chapter 10 we explained how claim-type theory can help you generate ideas for an argument. Specifically, we explained how values claims often depend for their supporting reasons on the reality claims of category, cause, or resemblance. This principle leads to a powerful idea-generating strategy that can be schematized as follows:

Overview of Claim-Type Strategy

We should do X (proposal claim)

- because X is a Y (categorical claim)
- because X will lead to good consequences (causal claim)
- because X is like Y (resemblance claim)

With each of those *because* clauses, the arguer's goal is to link X to one or more goods the audience already values. For a specific example, suppose that you wanted insurance companies to pay for long-term psychological counseling for anorexia. The claim-type strategy could help you develop arguments such as these:

Insurance companies should pay for long-term psychological counseling for anorexia (proposal claim)

- because paying for such counseling is a demonstration of commitment to women's health (categorical claim)
- because paying for such counseling might save insurance companies from much more extensive medical costs at a later date (causal claim)
- because paying for anorexia counseling is like paying for alcoholism or drug counseling, which is already covered by insurance (resemblance claim)

Proposal arguments using reality claims as reasons are very common. Here is another example, this time from a famous art exhibit controversy in the early 1990s when conservatives protested government funding for an exhibition of homoerotic photographs by artist Robert Mapplethorpe:

Taxpayer funding for the Mapplethorpe exhibit should be withdrawn (proposal claim)

- because the photographs are pornographic (a categorical claim linking the photographs to pornography, which the intended audience opposes)
- because the exhibit promotes community acceptance of homosexuality (a causal claim linking the exhibit to acceptance of homosexuality, which the intended audience opposes)

- because the photographs are more like political statements than art (a re-semblance claim linking the exhibit to politics rather than art, a situation that the intended audience would consider unsuitable for arts funding)

Whatever you might think of this argument, it shows how the supporting reasons for a proposal claim can be drawn from claims of category, cause, and resemblance. Each of these arguments attempts to appeal to the value system of the audience. Each tries to show how the proposed action is within the class of things that the audience already values, will lead to consequences desired by the audience, or is similar to something the audience already values. The invention procedure can be summarized in the following way.

Argument from Category

To discover reasons by using this strategy, conduct the following kind of search:

We should (should not) do X because X is _____.

Try to fill in the blank with an appropriate adjective (for example, *good, just, ethical, criminal, ugly, violent, peaceful, wrong, inflationary,* or *healing*) or noun (such as *an act of kindness, terrorism, murder, true art,* or *political suicide*). The point is to try to fill in the blank with a noun or adjective that appeals in some way to your audience's values. Your goal is to show that X belongs to the chosen class or category.

Here are examples:

Using a "Category" Search to Generate Reasons

- Our university should abolish fraternities and sororities *because they are elitist* (or "racist" or "sexist" or "an outdated institution" or whatever).
- The public should support genetically modified foods *because they are safe* (or "healthy," or "nutritious," or "improvements over current products").

Argument from Consequence

To discover reasons by using this category, conduct the following kind of search:

We should (should not) do X because X leads to these good (bad) consequences: _____, _____, _____, _____.

Then think of consequences that your audience will agree are good (bad) as your argument requires.

Here are examples, using the same claims as before:

Using a "Consequence" Search to Generate Reasons

- Our university should abolish fraternities and sororities *because eliminating the Greek system will improve our school's academic reputation* (or "fill our dormitories," "allow us to experiment with new living arrangements," "replace rush with a better first-year orientation," "reduce the campus drinking problem," and so forth).

- The public should support genetically modified foods *because these biotech crops can reduce world hunger* (or "reduce the need for pesticides" or "increase medical advancements through related genetic research").

Argument from Resemblance

To discover supporting reasons by using this strategy, conduct the following kind of search:

We should (should not) do X because doing X is like _____.

Then think of analogies or precedents that are similar to doing X but currently have greater appeal to your audience. Your task is then to transfer to X your audience's favorable (unfavorable) feelings toward the analogy/precedent.

Here are examples:

Using a "Resemblance" Search to Generate Reasons

- Our university should abolish fraternities and sororities *because other universities that have eliminated the Greek system have reported good results* (or "because eliminating the Greek system is like leveling social classes to promote more democracy and individualism," and so forth).

- The public should support genetically modified foods *because genetic modification is like natural crossbreeding* (or "because supporting biotechnology in agriculture is like supporting scientific advancements in other fields").

These three kinds of searches—supporting a proposal claim from the perspectives of category, consequence, and resemblance—are powerful means of invention. In selecting among these reasons, choose those most likely to appeal to your audience's assumptions, beliefs, and values.

For Class Discussion

1. Working individually or in small groups, use the strategies of category, consequence, and resemblance to create *because* clauses that support each of the following claims. Try to have at least one *because* clause from each of

the categories, but generate as many reasons as possible. Don't worry about whether any individual reason exactly fits the category. The purpose is to stimulate thinking, not fill in the slots.

EXAMPLE

CLAIM: People should not own pit bulls.

REASON FROM CATEGORY: because pit bulls are vicious

REASON FROM CONSEQUENCE: because owning a pit bull leads to conflicts with neighbors

REASON FROM RESEMBLANCE: because owning a pit bull is like having a shell-shocked roommate—mostly they're lovely companions but they can turn violent if startled

    a. Marijuana should be legalized.

    b. Division I college athletes should receive salaries.

    c. High schools should pass out free contraceptives.

    d. Violent video games should be made illegal.

    e. Parents should be heavily taxed for having more than two children.

2.   Repeat the first exercise, taking a different position on each issue.

Using the "Stock Issues" Strategy to Develop a Proposal Argument

An effective way to generate ideas for a proposal argument is to ask yourself a series of questions based on the "stock issues" strategy. Suppose, for example, you wanted to develop the following argument: "In order to solve the problem of students who won't take risks with their writing, the faculty should adopt a pass/fail method of grading in all writing courses." The stock issues strategy invites the writer to consider "stock" ways (that is, common, usual, frequently repeated ways) that such arguments can be conducted.

Stock issue 1: *Is there really a problem here that needs to be solved?* Is it really true that a large number of student writers won't take risks in their writing? Is this problem more serious than other writing problems such as undeveloped ideas, lack of organization, and poor sentence structure? This stock issue invites the writer to convince her audience that a true problem exists. Conversely, an opponent to the proposal might argue that a true problem does not exist.

Stock issue 2: *Will the proposed solution really solve this problem?*   Is it true that a pass/fail grading system will cause students to take more risks with their writing? Will more interesting, surprising, and creative essays result from pass/fail grading? Or will students simply put less effort into their writing? This stock issue prompts a supporter to demonstrate that the proposal will solve the problem; in contrast, it prompts the opponent to show that the proposal won't work.

Stock issue 3: *Can the problem be solved more simply without disturbing the status quo?*   An opponent of the proposal might agree that a problem exists and that the proposed solution might solve it. However, the opponent might say, "Are there not less radical ways to solve this problem? If we want more creative and risk-taking student essays, can't we just change our grading criteria so that we reward risky papers and penalize conventional ones?" This stock issue prompts supporters to show that *only* the proposed solution will solve the problem and that no minor tinkering with the status quo will be adequate. Conversely, opponents will argue that the problem can be solved without acting on the proposal.

Stock issue 4: *Is the proposed solution really practical? Does it stand a chance of actually being enacted?*   Here an opponent to the proposal might agree that the proposal would work but that it involves pie-in-the-sky idealism. Nobody will vote to change the existing system so radically; therefore, it is a waste of our time to debate it. Following this prompt, supporters would have to argue that pass/fail grading is workable and that enough faculty members are disposed to it that the proposal is worth debating. Opponents might argue that the faculty is so traditional that pass/fail has utterly no chance of being accepted, despite its merits.

Stock issue 5: *What will be the unforeseen positive and negative consequences of the proposal?*   Suppose we do adopt a pass/fail system. What positive or negative consequences might occur that are different from what we at first predicted? Using this prompt, an opponent might argue that pass/fail grading will reduce the effort put forth by students and that the long-range effect will be writing of even lower quality than we have now. Supporters would try to find positive consequences—perhaps a new love of writing for its own sake rather than the sake of a grade.

For Class Discussion

The following collaborative task takes approximately two class days to complete. The exercise takes you through the process of creating a proposal argument.

1. In small groups, identify and list several major problems facing students in your college or university.

2. Decide among yourselves which are the most important of these problems and rank them in order of importance.

3. Take your group's number one problem and explore answers to the following questions. Group recorders should be prepared to present your group's answers to the class as a whole:

   a. Why is the problem a problem?

   b. For whom is the problem a problem?

   c. How will these people suffer if the problem is not solved? (Give specific examples.)

   d. Who has the power to solve the problem?

   e. Why hasn't the problem been solved up to this point?

   f. How can the problem be solved? (That is, create a proposal.)

   g. What are the probable benefits of acting on your proposal?

   h. What costs are associated with your proposal?

   i. Who will bear those costs?

   j. Why should this proposal be enacted?

   k. Why is it better than alternative proposals?

4. As a group, draft an outline for a proposal argument in which you

   a. describe the problem and its significance.

   b. propose your solution to the problem.

   c. justify your proposal by showing how the benefits of adopting that proposal outweigh the costs.

5. Recorders for each group should write their group's outline on the board and be prepared to explain it to the class.

Writing a Proposal Argument

WRITING ASSIGNMENT
FOR CHAPTER 15

OPTION 1: *A Practical Proposal Addressing a Local Problem*   Write a practical proposal offering a solution to a local problem. Your proposal should have three main sections: (1) description of the problem, (2) proposed solution, and (3) justification. You may include additional sections or subsections as needed. Longer proposals often include an *abstract* at the beginning of the proposal to provide a summary overview of the whole argument. (Sometimes called the *executive* *summary,* this abstract may be the only portion of the proposal read by high-level managers.) Sometimes proposals are accompanied by a *letter of transmittal*—a one-page business letter that introduces the proposal to its intended audience and provides some needed background about the writer.

Document design is important in practical proposals, which are aimed at busy people who have to make many decisions under time constraints. Because the writer of a practical proposal usually produces the finished document (practical proposals are seldom submitted to newspapers or magazines for publication), the writer must pay particular attention to the attractive design of the document. An effective design helps establish the writer's *ethos* as a quality-oriented professional and helps make the reading of the proposal as easy as possible. Document design includes effective use of heading and subheadings, attractive typeface and layout, flawless editing, and other features enhancing the visual appearance of the document. For a student example of a practical proposal, see Laurel Wilson's argument on pages 339–343.

OPTION 2: *A Policy Proposal as a Guest Editorial*   Write a two- to three-page policy proposal suitable for publication as a feature editorial in a college or city newspaper or in some publication associated with a particular group or activity such as a church newsletter or employee bulletin. The voice and style of your argument should be aimed at general readers of your chosen publication. Your editorial should have the following features:

1. The identification of a problem (Persuade your audience that this is a genuine problem that needs solving; give it presence.)
2. A proposal for action that will help alleviate the problem
3. A justification of your solution (the reasons why your audience should accept your proposal and act on it)

OPTION 3: *A Researched Argument Proposing Public Policy*   Write an eight- to twelve-page proposal argument as a formal research paper, using research data for development and support. In business and professional life, this kind of research proposal is often called a "white paper," which recommends a course of action internally within an organization or externally to a client or stakeholder. An example of a researched policy proposal is student writer Mark Bonicillo's "A Proposal for Universal Health Insurance in the United States" on pages 344–350.

OPTION 4: *A One-Page Advocacy Advertisement*   Using the strategies of visual argument discussed in Chapter 9 and on pages 325–326 of this chapter, create a one-page advocacy advertisement urging action on a public issue. Your advertisement should be designed for publication in a newspaper or for distribution as a poster or flier. An example of a student-produced advocacy advertisement is shown in Figure 15.1.

Exploring Ideas

Since *should* or *ought* issues are among the most common sources of arguments, you may already have ideas for proposal issues. To think of ideas for practical proposals, try making an idea map of local problems you would like to see solved. For initial spokes, try trigger words such as the following:

- problems at my university (dorms, parking, registration system, financial aid, campus appearance, clubs, curriculum, intramural program, athletic teams)
- problems in my city or town (dangerous intersections, ugly areas, inadequate lighting, parks, police policy, public transportation, schools)
- problems at my place of work (office design, flow of customer traffic, merchandise display, company policies)
- problems related to my future career, hobbies, recreational time, life as a consumer, life as a homeowner

If you can offer a solution to the problem you identify, you may make a valuable contribution to some phase of public life.

To find a topic for policy proposals, stay in touch with the news, which will keep you aware of current debates on regional and national issues. Also, visit the Web sites of your congressional representatives to see what issues they are currently investigating and debating. You might think of your policy proposal as a white paper for one of your legislators.

Once you have decided on a proposal issue, we recommend you explore it by trying one or more of the following activities:

- *Explore ideas by using the claim-type strategy.*   Briefly this strategy invites you to find supporting reasons for your proposal by arguing that (1) X is a Y that the audience values; (2) doing X will lead to good consequences; and (3) doing X has been tried with good results elsewhere, or doing X is like doing Y, which the audience values.

- *Explore ideas by using the "stock issues" strategy.*   You will raise vital ideas for your argument by asking the stock questions: (1) Is there really a problem here that has to be solved? (2) Will the proposed solution really solve this problem? (3) Can the problem be solved in a simpler way without disturbing the status quo? (4) Is the proposed solution practical enough that it really stands a chance of being acted on? (5) What will be the positive and negative consequences of the proposal? A fuller version of the stock questions is the eleven questions (a–k) in the third For Class Discussion exercise on page 332.

- *Explore ideas for your argument by completing the ten exploratory tasks in Chapter 3 (pp. 69–70).* These tasks help you generate enough material for a rudimentary rough draft.

Organizing a Proposal Argument

When you write your draft, you may find it helpful to have at hand some plans for typical ways of organizing a proposal argument. What follows are two common methods of organization. Option 1 is the plan most typical for practical proposals. Either Option 1 or Option 2 is effective for a policy proposal.

Option 1

- Presentation of a problem that needs solving:
  Description of problem
  Background, including previous attempts to solve problem
  Argument that the problem is solvable (optional)
- Presentation of writer's proposal:
  Succinct statement of the proposed solution serves as thesis statement
  Explain specifics of proposed solution
- Summary and rebuttal of opposing views (in practical proposals, this section is often a summary and rejection of alternative ways of solving the problem)
- Justification persuading reader that proposal should be enacted:
  Reason 1 presented and developed
  Reason 2 presented and developed
  Additional reasons presented and developed
- Conclusion that exhorts audience to act:
  Give presence to final sentences.

Option 2

- Presentation of issue, including background
- Presentation of writer's proposal
- Justification
  Reason 1: Show that proposal addresses a serious problem.
  Reason 2: Show that proposal will solve problem.
  Reason 3: Give additional reasons for enacting proposal.
- Summary and refutation of opposing views
- Conclusion that exhorts audience to act

Revising Your Draft

As you revise your draft based on peer reviews and on your own assessment of its problems and strengths, consider using a Toulmin analysis to test your argument's persuasiveness. Recall that Toulmin is particularly useful for helping you link each of your reasons to your audience's beliefs, assumptions, and values.

Suppose that there is a debate at your university about whether to banish fraternities and sororities. Suppose further that you are in favor of banishing the Greek system. One of your arguments is that eliminating the Greek system will improve your college's academic reputation. Here is how you might use the Toulmin system to make this line of reasoning as persuasive as possible.

CLAIM: Our university should eliminate the Greek system.

STATED REASON: because doing so will improve our academic reputation

GROUNDS: *I've got to provide evidence that eliminating the Greek system will improve our academic reputation. I have shown that last year the GPA of students in fraternities and sororities was 20 percent lower than the GPA of non-Greek students. What else can I add? I can talk about the excessive party atmosphere of some Greek houses, about the emphasis placed on social life rather than studying, about how new pledges have so many house duties that their studies suffer, about how new students think about rush more than about the academic life.*

WARRANT: It is good for our university to achieve a better academic reputation.

BACKING: *I see that my draft doesn't have any backing for this warrant. How can I argue that it would be good to have a better academic reputation? We would attract more serious students; the university's prestige would rise; it might attract and retain better faculty; the college would be a more intellectually interesting place; the long-range careers of our students might improve with a better education.*

CONDITIONS FOR REBUTTAL: *How would skeptics doubt my reason and grounds? Might they say that I am stereotyping Greeks? Might they argue that some of the brightest and best students on campus are in fraternities and sororities? Might they argue that only a few rowdy houses are at fault? Might they point to very prestigious institutions that have fraternities and sororities? Might they say that the cause of a poor academic reputation has nothing to do with fraternities and sororities and point instead to other causes? How can I respond to these arguments?*

How could they raise doubts about my warrant and backing? They probably wouldn't argue that it is bad to have a good academic reputation. They will probably argue instead that eliminating sororities and fraternities won't improve the university's academic reputation but will hurt its social life and its wide range of living options. To respond to these arguments, maybe I should do some research into what happened at other colleges when they eliminated the Greek system.

QUALIFIER: *Should I add a "may" by saying that eliminating the Greek system* may *help improve our academic reputation?*

As this example shows, thinking systematically about the grounds, warrant, backing, and conditions of rebuttal for each of your reasons can help you generate additional ideas to strengthen your first draft.

Designing a One-Page Advocacy Advertisement

As an alternative to a traditional written argument, your instructor might ask you to create a one-page advocacy advertisement. The first stage of your invention process should be the same as for a longer proposal argument. Choose a controversial public issue that needs immediate attention or a neglected issue about which you want to arouse public passion. As with a longer proposal argument, consider your audience in order to identify the values and beliefs on which you will base your appeal.

When you construct your argument, the limited space available demands efficiency in your choice of words and in your use of document design. Your goal is to have a memorable impact on your reader in order to promote the action you advocate. The following questions may help you design and revise your advocacy ad.

1. How could photos or other graphic elements establish and give presence to the problem?

2. How can type size, style, and layout be used to present the core of your proposal, including the justifying reasons, in the most powerful way for the intended audience?

3. Can any part of this argument be presented as a slogan or memorable catchphrase? What key phrases could highlight the parts or the main points of this argument?

4. How can document design clarify the course of action and the direct demand on the audience this argument is proposing?

5. How can use of color enhance the overall impact of your advocacy argument? (Note: One-page advertisements are expensive to reproduce in color, but you might make effective use of color if your advocacy ad were to appear as a poster or Web page.)

Questioning and Critiquing a Proposal Argument

As we've suggested, proposal arguments need to overcome the innate conservatism of people, the difficulty of anticipating all the consequences of a proposal, and so forth. What questions, then, can we ask about proposal arguments to help us anticipate these problems?

Will a skeptic deny that my problem is really a problem? The first question to ask of your proposal is "What's so wrong with the status quo that change is necessary?" The second question is "Who loses if the status quo is changed?" Be certain not to overlook this second question. Most proposal makers can demonstrate that some sort of problem exists, but often it is a problem only for certain groups of people. Solving the problem will thus prove a benefit to some people but a cost to others. If audience members examine the problem from the perspective of the potential losers rather than the winners, they can often raise doubts about your proposal.

For example, one state recently held an initiative on a proposed "bottle bill" that would fight litter by permitting the sale of soda and beer only in returnable bottles. Sales outlets would be required to charge a substantial deposit on the bottles in order to encourage people to return them. Proponents of the proposal emphasized citizens as "winners" sharing in the new cleanliness of a landscape no longer littered with cans. To refute this argument, opponents showed consumers as "losers" burdened with the high cost of deposits and the hassle of collecting and returning bottles to grocery stores.

Will a skeptic doubt the effectiveness of my solution? Assuming that you've satisfied yourself that a significant problem exists for a significant number of people, a number of questions remain to be asked about the quality of the proposed solution to solve the problem. First, "Does the problem exist for the reasons cited, or might there be alternative explanations?" Here we return to the familiar ground of causal arguments. A proposal supposedly strikes at the cause of a problem. But perhaps striking at that "cause" won't solve the problem. Perhaps you've mistaken a symptom for a cause, or confused two commonly associated but essentially unlinked phenomena for a cause-effect relationship. For example, will paying teachers higher salaries improve the quality of teaching or merely attract greedier rather than brighter people? Maybe more good teachers would be attracted and retained if they were given some other benefit (fewer students? smaller classes? more sabbaticals? more autonomy? more prestige?).

Another way to test your solution is to list all the uncertainties involved. This might be referred to as "The Devil you know is better than the Devil you don't know" strategy. Remind yourself of all the unanticipated consequences of past changes. Who, for example, would have thought back in the days when aerosol shaving cans were being developed that they might lead to diminished ozone layers, which might lead to more ultraviolet rays getting through the atmosphere from the sun, which would lead to higher incidences of skin cancer? The history of technology is full of such cautionary tales that can be invoked to remind you of the uncertain course that progress can sometimes take.

Will a skeptic think my proposal costs too much? The most commonly asked question of any proposal is simply, "Do the benefits of enacting the proposal outweigh the costs?" As we saw above, you can't foresee all the consequences of any proposal. It's easy, before the fact, to exaggerate both the costs and the benefits of a proposal. So, in asking how much your proposal will cost, we urge you to make an honest estimate. Will your audience discover costs you hadn't anticipated— extra financial costs or unexpected psychological or environmental or aesthetic costs? As much as you can, anticipate these objections.

Will a skeptic suggest counterproposals? Related to all that's been said so far is the counterproposal. Can you imagine an appealing alternative to both the status quo and the proposal that you're making? The more clearly your proposal shows that a significant problem exists, the more important it is that you be able to identify possible counterproposals. Any potential critic of a proposal to remedy an acknowledged problem will either have to make such a counterproposal or have to argue that the problem is simply in the nature of things. So, given the likelihood that you'll be faced with a counterproposal, it only makes sense to anticipate it and to work out a refutation of it before you have it thrown at you. And who knows, you may end up liking the counterproposal better and changing your mind about what to propose!

Readings

Our first reading, by student writer Laurel Wilson, is a practical proposal addressing the problem of an inequitable tipping policy for hosts in a national brewpub restaurant chain. ("Hosts" are the persons who greet you when you enter a restaurant and escort you to a table.) As a practical proposal, it uses headings and other elements of document design aimed to give it a finished and professional appearance. When sent to the intended audience, it is accompanied by a single-spaced letter of transmittal following the conventional format of a business letter.

Paul Smithson
CEO, Stone's End Restaurant and Brewery
1422 Stone Avenue
Certain City, Certain State, Zip*

Dear Mr. Smithson:

Enclosed is a proposal that addresses Stone's End corporate policy forbidding hosts from receiving tips from servers. My proposal shows the problems associated with this rule and suggests a workable solution.

The enclosed proposal suggests a modest plan for tipping hosts that would make their wages more fair. Currently hosts earn only half as much as servers, and yet are expected not only to work as hard as servers, but also to wear dressy clothes that are quite expensive. Rewarding hosts for their important work in a job that is far from easy should be supported by management and servers, who benefit from hosts who go above and beyond the call of duty.

As a former host at Stone's End, I often felt unappreciated by both servers and management. I worked very hard and was not compensated for providing excellent service. I eventually found a different job because I could not afford to work there without the extra compensation of tips. I later discovered that many other restaurants not only tipped their hosts, but also gave them a clothing allowance. I hope my idea is received well and considered as a viable option. A

---

*Laurel Wilson wrote this proposal to an actual company; with the author's permission, we have changed the names of the manager and brewpub and disguised the location.

change in corporate policy regarding the tipping of hosts might make Stone's End restaurants even more successful than they are now because hosts would feel like appreciated members of the restaurant team.

Thank you for your time.

Sincerely,

Laurel Wilson

A PROPOSAL TO PROVIDE TIPS FOR HOSTS AT STONE'S END

Submitted for Consideration by the Stone's End Corporate Office

by

Laurel Wilson, former Stone's End Host in _____

(Address and Phone Number)

If this were the actual proposal, the first page would begin on a new page following the cover page.

PROBLEM

Because the "no tips" policy for hosts at Stone's End restaurants keeps their wages significantly below those of servers, hosts often feel unnoticed and unappreciated. Hosts at Stone's End currently make a flat wage of $9.00 per hour without tips. Servers make $6.25 per hour plus tips, which range between $50 and $150 per shift. On a busy night, a server can make as much as $31.25 per hour for a four-hour shift if one adds $100 of tips to four hours of wages (6.25 x 4 + 100 divided by 4). Hosts usually have a six-hour shift making $9 per hour. In a four-hour shift a server typically makes $125, while a host makes $54 for a six-hour shift.

Some people might think that hosts shouldn't be tipped because their job is less stressful than that of servers. However, the host's job entails many things that keep the restaurant running smoothly. A host organizes the dining room in a way that accommodates all parties with no customers having to wait more than fifteen minutes for their tables. The host also has to make sure that servers do not have more than one party being seated in their section at the same time. There are usually nine servers in the dining room during the evening shift, each having five tables in his or her section. A good host will clear and wipe down tables of servers who are swamped in order to give them more time and to keep the restaurant running smoothly. At any given time a host will be dealing with cranky customers, answering a four-line phone, taking "to go" orders, trying to organize a dining room that seats over 200 people, and often clearing tables for overwhelmed servers. This is a highly stressful and active job which requires hard work and is often misunderstood by those who do not know all the duties a host performs.

PROPOSAL

I propose that servers give 1 percent of their tips to the host. As it is now, servers give 2 percent of their tips to the bartenders and 1 percent to the expediters (the expo brings the food out to the tables and arranges the servers' trays). If the servers contribute another 1 percent to their host, the cost to servers would average about one dollar per shift to their host. If you add $1 from each server (usually nine) that adds $9 to the host's pay for the shift, raising it from the $54 we figured earlier (based on six hours at $9 per hour) to $63. On a busy night, the host might get $1.50 or even $2.00 from each server—an amount that would help the host immensely while being barely a dent in the server's take-home pay for the shift.

JUSTIFICATION

Some persons might have objections to this proposal. Owners, in setting corporate policy for the national chain of Stone's End restaurants, have most likely researched all aspects of the restaurant business and decided that the "no tips" rule for hosts was the best policy. They probably have reasons for the "no tips" policy that hosts don't understand. But perhaps the owners don't currently recognize the disadvantages of this policy, which leads to disgruntled hosts and a high turnover. Running a successful restaurant hinges on the happiness of all employees. The hosts' contributions are currently disregarded, even though they are a valuable asset to the restaurant. Corporate owners would be caught in a tailspin if they spent just one night doing the job of a host.

Others might point to the plight of the servers. Servers work incredibly hard for their tips and rely on those tips to pay their bills. On a slow night (which is rare), servers might make minimal tips (maybe only $40 per shift). Taking even a small percentage out of their tips might seem painful. Also servers' shifts last about four hours whereas a host usually works a six-hour shift, sometimes even eight. Servers might argue that the host's extra hours, paid at a higher hourly rate than servers receive, give the hosts an adequate income. However, even on a very slow night in which the server makes only $40 in tips, their hourly wage is still $16.25 per hour, more than $7 per hour higher than the host's wage.

Despite the objections that might be raised by owners or servers, the hosts at Stone's End perform a difficult and thankless job that deserves recognition by both servers and the corporate office. My proposal should be enacted for the following reasons:

- Paying a small tip to hosts is a fair way to reward their contributions. The hosts' job entails many tasks that make the server's job more bearable. Servers make almost twice the amount of money that hosts do, and yet the host's job—while not as hectic as the servers'—is still one of the most difficult jobs in the restaurant. Moreover, the host makes the first impression on the customer and sets the mood for the customer's experience in the restaurant. Having to wear dressy clothes—a considerable extra expense—is only one part of the host's important job of setting a good first impression for the restaurant. During busy times, a host who goes above and beyond the call of duty helps out the servers by clearing and wiping tables and ensuring the smooth operation of the dining room.

- The current "no tips" policy set by the corporate office places local managers in the unpleasant position of having to defend a corporate policy that they don't personally support. At the Stone's End where I worked (in _____), the manager agreed with the hosts' desire to receive tips as did the servers, who agreed that hosts should be rewarded for all the help they provide servers with their hectic jobs. But the manager had to back the corporate office's "no tips for hosts" rule, making it difficult for the manager to keep every employee happy. The manager thus had to bear the brunt of the hosts' complaints without having power to change the situation.

- Finally, tipping hosts would make Stone's End more competitive with other restaurants in cities such as _____, where tipping hosts is common practice. For example, in _____, restaurants such as Il Fornaio and Pallamino's pay their hosts the same wage as Stone's End, but require that servers tip the hosts. Moreover, each of these restaurants has a clothing allowance for their hosts. Not only do their hosts look nice, but they are happy with their jobs as well.

CONCLUSION

Asking servers to tip hosts at the low rate of 1 percent of tip income would show Stone's End hosts that they are respected and appreciated by their co-workers and part of the restaurant team whose livelihood depends on happy, satisfied customers. The host works hard to keep everyone happy including servers, managers, and customers. They do not make the money they deserve. In order to keep hosts happy and Stone's End competitive with surrounding restaurants, this policy would provide a satisfactory solution to a significant problem. I believe that corporate owners would be highly pleased with the all-around benefits of having happy hosts.

Critiquing "A Proposal to Provide Tips for Hosts at Stone's End"

1. In your own words, summarize briefly the problem that Laurel Wilson addresses, her proposed solution, and her justifying reasons.

2. Why does Laurel address her proposal to the CEO of Stone's End restaurants rather than to her local manager or to servers? (After all, it is the servers who stand to lose money if this proposal is enacted.) To what extent does Laurel develop audience-based reasons for this CEO audience? How effectively does she anticipate and respond to objections her audience might raise?

3. How does Laurel establish a positive *ethos* in this argument and a meaningful picture of the problem?

4. How effective is Laurel's proposal?

Our second reading, by student writer Mark Bonicillo, is a researched public policy proposal written for the "Option 3" assignment on page 333. Bonicillo's argument is based on research he conducted into the problem of Americans without health insurance. You will note that he supplemented library and Internet research with information from a personal interview he conducted with a leading local authority on health insurance issues. Bonicillo's argument is formatted as a formal research paper using the documentation style of the Modern Language Association (MLA). A full explanation of this format is given in Chapter 17.

Mark Bonicillo

Professor Scharf

Humanities Seminar 300

June 15, 2002

A Proposal for Universal Health Insurance in the United States

1   Ian, a twenty-three-year-old college graduate and the son of one of my professors, hasn't yet found a career-type job in the current slow economy. He currently works as a waiter at a downtown restaurant that offers minimum wage plus tips with no health insurance. A few weeks ago, Ian hurt his back in a recreational soccer game, and the pain is getting worse. Unfortunately, he has no doctor to go to. Like many recent college graduates, he is no longer covered by his student insurance policy, nor can he be covered on his parents' health insurance now that he has graduated from college. He can't afford to buy health insurance on his waiter's pay (the premiums would be $300 per month), and in any case his back injury wouldn't be covered because it is a "pre-existing condition." Now he is trying to pay for food and rent on his waiter's earnings, while also paying off his student loans. Meanwhile his back is killing him.

2   Ian's frightening situation is common in the United States. According to a study from the Employee Benefit Research Institute, 32.8% of Americans ages 21–24 and 22.5% of Americans ages 25–35 do not have health insurance (Fronstin 22). But it's not just young adults who don't have health insurance. The working poor and unemployed constitute the majority of the uninsured. Based on statistical research, recent estimates suggest that almost 39 million Americans do not have any form of health insurance (Kaiser Commission on Medicaid and the Uninsured).

3   These uninsured Americans lead sicker lives than insured Americans and create an unnecessary financial drain on the health care industry. If they are sick, they have to go to hospital emergency rooms, hassle with the subsequent unpaid bills, and hope that the hospital will eventually write them off as charity expense. (This is what Ian plans to do with his bad back.) According to a recent study by the Institute of Medicine, uninsured Americans are less likely than insured Americans to get regular checkups or receive preventative care. They have higher mortality rates and sickness

Bonicillo   2

rates. Moreover, treating these persons in emergency rooms is extremely
expensive. It costs more to amputate the leg of a seriously ill diabetic than it
would to diagnose the disease, prescribe insulin, and provide regular care
(Institute of Medicine 1).

Why do so many Americans lack health insurance? The answer lies in the   4
way that insurance is paid for in the United States. In most European countries
and in Canada, medicine is socialized so that the government pays for medical
care and citizens pay the government through higher taxes. In such a system,
coverage is universal. But in the United States, medical insurance is linked to
employment. Employers pay for health insurance, which they purchase from
competing insurance companies. Generally, the employer pays a significant
percentage of the insurance costs as a fringe benefit of employment. This
system works fine as long as (1) you are employed; (2) your employer is a large
enough company to be required to purchase health insurance (many small
companies don't have to provide insurance), and (3) you have a long-term, full-
time position in the company (many companies don't provide benefits for
temporary or other low-wage workers). If you don't have employer-provided
insurance, you can purchase individual policies (assuming that you aren't
already ill with disqualifying pre-existing conditions), but the premiums are
very expensive and they are rated according to your health risk. People with
illnesses such as diabetes often can't buy private insurance at any price.

For those who are retired or are low-income earners—and therefore do   5
not have access to employer-provided insurance or cannot afford individual
insurance—the federal or state governments try to help. The federal
government provides Medicare for citizens over sixty-five and Medicaid for
poor people who meet certain federal poverty guidelines. Additionally, some
states provide subsidized health care plans for certain categories of people
near the poverty line who are not covered by Medicaid. However, as shown in
Figure 1 (based on data from the Kaiser Commission on Medicaid and the
Uninsured), a significant number of Americans—16% of the adult population
under sixty-five years of age—have no insurance.

Furthermore, two additional problems are connected to this employer-   6
based system. First, insured Americans can quickly lose their insurance if they
lose their jobs. When the economy is in recession, the number of uninsured

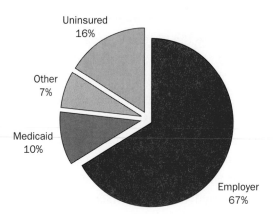

FIG. 1.   *Health Insurance Coverage in U.S., 2001, Adult Americans under 65.*

increases significantly. Diane Rowland, Executive Director of the Kaiser Commission on Medicaid and the Uninsured, estimates that "for every 100 workers added to the unemployment rolls, 85 people will join the ranks of the uninsured" (10). She cites a study that showed when unemployment rose from 4% in December 2000 to 5.8% in December 2001, the number of uninsured Americans increased by 2.2 million. As we can see, the current U.S. policy of distributing health insurance through employers leaves Americans in jeopardy of losing their health insurance at any time.

7   The second major problem with employer-provided insurance is that the attempts of the federal and state governments to create safety nets for the uninsured are underfunded and full of gaps. For example, Medicare certainly helps the elderly, but many persons fear that Medicare funding will collapse in the near future as baby boomers retire. Moreover, Medicare in some states is so poorly funded that many doctors will no longer take Medicare patients because the reimbursement payments are too low. According to a news report in the <u>Seattle Times</u>, some doctors in the state of Washington have even refused to accept new Medicare patients (Ostrom A1). In addition, the systems adopted by the states to provide insurance for persons at the poverty level are unevenly administered and burdened with red tape. In a personal interview I conducted with Randy Revelle, the director of health policy for the Washington State Hospital Association, I learned that in 1998 over fifteen thousand uninsured children in the state of Washington were

eligible for state-subsidized insurance, but they and their parents did not know it because of inadequate advertising and red tape. Similar problems occur in other states. According to Rowland, even with the knowledge that one is eligible for government-sponsored health insurance, long and burdensome application forms and language problems discourage many uninsured Americans from even applying for government health insurance (7). And so, many uninsured Americans who could have had public health insurance are still left uninsured.

Finally, we must ask why the American people haven't demanded a change from this employer-based system. Why hasn't this problem already been solved? 8

I think there are three basic reasons. First, because the majority of Americans have employer-provided insurance, they don't give this problem a high priority. Second, the general public is unwilling to support any real health care reform because they think it might lead to "socialized medicine," which raises the fearful specter of demoralized doctors, faceless patients, and long waiting lists for needed services. Finally, insurance companies, doctors, and drug companies benefit from the present system and lobby heavily to persuade politicians from adopting health care reform that might cut into their profits. 9

The solution to the problem of the uninsured is to dismantle the current employer-provided system without leading to European- or Canadian-style socialized medicine that doesn't fit American values or business structures. Based on my research, the best approach is a compromise between liberals and conservatives, evidenced in a series of interviews conducted by journalist Matthew Miller with two U.S. representatives—a liberal, Democrat Jim McDermott of Washington, who personally favors a European-style government-as-single-payer system, and a conservative, Republican Jim McCrery of Louisiana, who supports insurance companies and free markets for health care. The common ground between these two political opponents, evident in the interviews, leads to a possible solution. Based on my reading of these interviews, I offer the following three policy recommendations. 10

First, the federal government should break the linkage between health insurance and employment. Instead, according to Rep. McCrery's 11 suggestion, the government should mandate that all adult citizens purchase individual or family health insurance (Miller 84). This mandate would guarantee that all Americans would be insured. To help pay for this insurance, McCrery suggests that the insurance subsidies currently provided by employers as a fringe benefit could be passed on to employees as increased salary (Miller 86). Therefore employed persons would pay no additional costs under this system.

12   Second, McCrery and McDermott agree that the government should help unemployed or low-income people buy health insurance by providing tax subsidies on a sliding scale. The government would thus buy insurance for those at the poverty line and subsidize insurance on a sliding scale for those above it (Miller 86).

13   Third, McCrery and McDermott both agree that to make health insurance affordable for all, insurance companies must base their premiums on a community rating spread across all buyers instead of charging higher rates for persons with illnesses or identifiable risk factors. Because young, healthy Americans would be required to buy insurance, these persons would help fund the system by paying in more than they draw out and yet be fully covered if they need medical care (Miller 84).

14   These three policy recommendations would solve most of the problems with the current system and fit the American structure of business. An advantage of this proposal is that it does not eliminate insurance companies or interfere with a free-market approach to medicine. As Miller explains, insurance companies would still compete with each other for customers (85). The major change would be that health insurance companies would market to individuals rather than to employers in the same way that car and life insurance companies do. Also, drug companies would not be frightened by the prospect of the government setting prices for drugs.

15   A second advantage is that the majority of Americans would need no government subsidy because their increased insurance costs would be covered by a transfer into salary of the insurance benefit currently paid by the employer. At the same time employers would benefit by no longer having to undergo the hassles of negotiating for and providing insurance for their employees (Miller 85).

Third, this system provides a safety net for employed Americans who risk   16
losing their jobs in times of recession. The government would immediately step
in to help pay for insurance based on the sliding scale need of the unemployed
person.

Finally, this system brings health care to low-wage workers who do not   17
currently receive employer-subsidized insurance and to all currently ill or at-
risk persons whose pre-existing conditions disqualify them for self-pay
insurance. Because a community rating spreads the risk across all Americans,
the many young and healthy people paying into the system (the ones who
today are apt not to buy insurance because they aren't sick) help subsidize the
health care needed by others (Miller 84).

Undoubtedly many problems with this proposal need to be worked out—   18
including the procedures for mandating every adult to buy insurance as well as
the political battle of determining how new taxes will be assessed to pay for
the substantial costs of subsidizing insurance for the poor and the unemployed.
But this proposal attacks the problem of the uninsured and the U. S. health care
system at its core. This nation has tried many different solutions, and they
have all failed. While genuine reform is painful and politically difficult, it is the
only way to heal our sickening health care system that leaves 39 million
Americans without health insurance. Under this system, Ian would have had
government-subsidized health insurance. He could have gone to a doctor when
he first hurt his back instead of waiting a month to go to a hospital emergency
room and plead poverty.

Works Cited

Fronstin, Paul. <u>Sources of Health Insurance and Characteristics of the Uninsured: Analysis of the March 1997 Current Population Survey</u>. Employee Benefit Research Institute Issue Brief 192. Washington, D. C.: EBRI, Dec. 1997.

Institute of Medicine. <u>Care Without Coverage: Too Little, Too Late</u>. New York: Natl. Acad. P., 2002.

Kaiser Commission on Medicaid and the Uninsured. "The Uninsured and Their Access to Health Care." Feb. 2002. <u>Henry J. Kaiser Family Foundation</u>. 2 pp. 26 May 2002. <http://www.kff.org/content/ 2002/142003/142003.pdf>.

Miller, Matthew. "Health Care: A Bolt of Civic Hope." <u>Atlantic Monthly</u> Oct. 2000: 77–87.

Ostrom, Carol M. "Doctors Fleeing Medicare, Medicaid." <u>Seattle Times</u> 12 Mar. 2002: A1.

Revelle, Randy. Personal interview. 9 May 2002.

Rowland, Diane. "The New Challenge of the Uninsured: Coverage in the Current Economy." Kaiser Commission on Medicaid and the Uninsured 28 Feb. 2002. <u>Henry J. Kaiser Family Foundation</u>. 24 pp. 23 May 2002 <http://www.kff.org/content/ 2002/4042/4042.pdf>.

Critiquing "A Proposal for Universal Health Insurance in the United States"

1. In your own words, sum up the problem that Mark Bonicillo addresses and his proposed solution to the problem.

2. Although the problem of being sick and uninsured is immediately vivid, the details of the American health care system are often tedious and wonkish. When President Clinton in 1994 proposed a sweeping reform of the health care system—led by First Lady Hillary Clinton—the insurance industry defeated his proposals using the "Harry and Louise" television ad campaign, which portrayed the Clinton plan as costly, bureaucratic socialized medicine that would prevent Americans from choosing their own doctors.

   a. To what extent is Mark successful in explaining the problems of health insurance in the United States? Does his argument become too wonkish? Unclear?

   b. To what extent does his proposed solution address Americans' fear of "socialized medicine"?

3. What rhetorical strategies does Mark use to make his argument as compelling as possible? How does he try to create presence? How does he appeal to *ethos* and *pathos* as well as *logos*? How effective is his use of quantitative graphics?

4. Overall, how effective do you find Mark's argument?

The third reading is by Akhil Reed Amar, a law professor at Yale University, and Steven G. Calabresi, a law professor at Northwestern University. This short policy proposal, which appeared as an op-ed piece in the *New York Times* on October 5, 2002, joins a public debate about the extent to which certain government conversations should be made public. For example, should the executive branch of government be required to make public the behind-the-scenes conversations that lead to new government policy? In this case, Amar and Calabresi call for live public broadcasts of Supreme Court deliberations.

The Supreme Court's Unfree Speech
Akhil Reed Amar and Steven G. Calabresi

If recent history is any guide, the Supreme Court's new term, which begins   1
Monday, promises to be another good one for freedom of expression—except, that
is, within the courtroom itself. The justices support a broad view of free speech in
their rulings, but they practice something very different in their own court.

In the last eight terms, the court has invoked free-speech principles to invali-   2
date actions of other branches of government in no fewer than 25 cases. Yet it bars
television cameras and radio microphones from its own public oral arguments.

Transcripts of the dialogue between lawyers and the justices are not posted on the court's Web site until weeks later. Spectators in the gallery may not even take notes about what is being said in open court.

3   These court policies do not literally abridge free speech. But they inhibit the kind of robust and timely public discourse that, according to the court's own doctrine, lies at the very core of the First Amendment. Oral arguments take place in open court. The lawyers may take notes, as may those with official press credentials. Members of the public deserve the same right.

4   These restrictive rules are at odds with the practices of other courts. Every federal appeals court and state supreme court allows note-taking by the public. The court's approach also contrasts with the openness practiced by other branches of government. Americans can watch Congress live on C-Span and read verbatim transcripts of Congressional debate on Congress's Web site, updated daily. Presidential press conferences are customarily carried live on C-Span.

5   The Supreme Court, like other courts, has not allowed TV cameras in the court. Opponents of televised proceedings typically argue that lawyers are likely to play to the camera; that commercial news programs might broadcast short clips of trials out of context; and that witnesses would lose privacy as their faces become more publicly recognizable.

6   But these are arguments against televising ordinary civil and criminal trials. Appellate cases before the Supreme Court are different. There are no witnesses, and lawyers before the court face strict limits on their time and arguments. Granted, it can be misleading to broadcast excerpts out of context; justices sometimes ask provocative questions or make arguments merely to sharpen debate. But this is precisely why Americans should be allowed to see the entire transcript and watch the argument uncut and free of commercials. Citizens could then judge for themselves what a questioner may have meant. Even if the court continues to bar television cameras, the justices have no excuse for preventing public radio stations from broadcasting oral arguments live.

7   The First Amendment protects free expression so that the people can monitor and debate what is done by government on their behalf. The justices are public servants. Americans deserve the right to see and hear how they conduct the public's business.

Critiquing "The Supreme Court's Unfree Speech"

1. In making their case for live radio or even television broadcasts of Supreme Court deliberations, where do Amar and Calabresi use arguments from category, arguments from consequence, and arguments from resemblance?

2. Why do you suppose the Supreme Court resists live broadcasts of their deliberations? Do you think that Amar and Calabresi's summary of opposing views accurately reflects the objections the Supreme Court justices might make to their proposal?

3. This article appeared at the time of considerable national debate about whether current behind-the-scenes government deliberations should be

made open to the public. Of particular concern were the deliberations within the executive branch leading to the Bush administration's national energy policy. Administration critics claimed that the energy policy was developed and written by big oil companies. Administration supporters argued that a president could not get candid advice from stakeholders if everything said in a meeting was publicly disseminated. Where do you stand on the issue of closed-door versus open-door meetings on government policy?

Our last reading (see Figure 15.2) is a one-page paid advocacy advertisement appearing in newspapers in 2002. This is the seventh in a series of ads produced by the Center for Children's Health and the Environment located at Mount Sinai School of Medicine in New York. The ads were intended to work in concert with the organization's Web site www.childenvironment.org, which provides backup documentation including access to the scientific studies on which the ads' arguments are based. All the ads can be downloaded in pdf format from the Web site. The ads' purpose is to call public attention to environmental dangers to children and to urge public action.

Critiquing the Advocacy Ad from the Center for Children's Health and the Environment

1. A difficulty faced by many proposal writers is awakening the audience to the existence of the problem. The doctors and researchers who founded the Center for Children's Health and the Environment felt that a series of full-page newspaper ads was the best way to awaken the public to a problem that Americans either denied or didn't know existed.

   a. In your own words, what is the problem that this proposal addresses?

   b. How does the ad give presence to the problem?

2. How does this ad use the strategies of visual argument (use of images, arrangement of text, type size, and so forth) discussed in Chapter 9? The ad makers probably had available thousands of pictures of children to use in this ad. Why did they choose this photograph? Try to reconstruct the thinking of the ad makers when they decided on their use of type sizes and fonts. How is the message in different parts of the ad connected to the visual presentation of the words?

3. How effective is the actual verbal argument of this advertisement? Why does it place "Industry falsely discredits current animal testing" in bold-face type at the beginning of the text?

4. Most of this ad is devoted to presentation of the problem. What does the ad actually propose?

5. Overall, how effective do you find this advocacy advertisement? If you were thumbing through a newspaper, would you stop to read this ad? If so, what hooked you?

She's the test subject for thousands of toxic chemicals. Why?

Industry falsely discredits current animal testing.

In previous ads in this series, we physicians and scientists have presented a body of scientific evidence linking toxic chemicals to a wide range of health problems in humans, from learning disabilities and brain injury in children to certain cancers in both children and adults.

We have emphasized that these health problems are preventable. We have stressed that thorough pre-market testing of chemicals is a critical component of disease prevention.

There is a well-established and respected FDA approval process that a company must follow before it can market a chemical as a medicine. That process includes testing at various doses on animals. Only if the medicine is shown to be safe for animals is it approved for tests on humans.

America's pharmaceutical industry acknowledges, indeed embraces, these animal testing regimes for medicines. At the same time, however, certain segments of the chemical industry are making false claims about similar pre-market testing for chemicals other than medications.

They claim that testing has little value "because at a high enough dose all chemicals cause cancer." That's not true. The National Cancer Institute and the National Toxicology Program find that only 5-10% of commercial chemicals cause cancer at any dose. The industry also claims that animal testing bears little connection to human risk. That's not true either – the Human Genome Project has shown that laboratory animals and humans have very great genetic similarity and share very similar endocrine, immune and nervous systems.

The industry claims that testing has little value unless it involves tens of thousands of animals at low dose levels. Not true – the National Toxicology Program has developed sophisticated technologies for testing chemicals at a range of doses in small numbers of animals and then predicting human risk.

Inaccurate and false as all these claims are, they have found a certain audience in government and the press. These claims have paralyzed the regulatory process. They are preventing whole classes of chemicals from being properly tested. And that puts everybody's health at risk, especially the health of our children.

What We Know

– Every known human carcinogen causes cancer in animals.

– Every chemical known to cause brain damage in humans causes damage to the brain and nervous system in animals.

– Every chemical known to interfere with reproductive function in humans interferes with reproduction in animals.

– Almost every known cause of birth defects in humans also causes birth defects in animals.

– And, with few exceptions, when toxic chemicals harm animals, they almost always cause similar harm in humans.

What We Can Do

Parents should limit their children's exposure to synthetic chemicals. They should minimize use of pesticides outside and inside the house. They should choose safe cleaning products. Wherever possible, they should purchase organically produced food. Fish from contaminated waters should be avoided. There are more suggestions at www.childenvironment.org.

We must do more. The evidence is incontrovertible. We must move quickly to phase out those toxic chemicals that are known to pose a danger to human health. And we must institute a system of regulation that tests new synthetic chemicals and proves them safe before they are allowed to be sold, before our children are exposed. Isn't that the system you thought we already had?

Center for Children's Health and the Environment

MOUNT SINAI SCHOOL OF MEDICINE

Box 1043, One Gustave Levy Place, New York, NY 10029 • **www.childenvironment.org**

FIGURE 15.2 *Center for Children's Health and the Environment advocacy advertisement*

354

Part Four

The Researched Argument

16 Finding and Evaluating Sources

17 Using, Citing, and Documenting Sources

This advocacy ad, appealing to parental responsibility, is one of many ads that the Partnership for a Drug-Free America has placed in general readership news magazines.

16 Finding and Evaluating Sources

Although the "research paper" is a common writing assignment in college, students are often baffled by their professor's expectations. The problem is that students often think of research writing as presenting information rather than as creating an argument. One of our business school colleagues calls these sorts of research papers "data dumps": The student backs a truckload full of fresh data up to the professor's desk, dumps it, and says: "Here's your load of info on 'world poverty,' Prof. You make sense of it."

But a research paper shouldn't be a data dump. Like any other argument, it should use its information to support a contestable claim. Formal researched arguments have much in common with arguments that freelancers might write in a popular magazine. However, there is one major difference between a formal research paper and an informal magazine article—the presence of citations and a bibliography. In academic research, the purpose of in-text citations and a complete bibliography is to enable readers to follow the trail of the author's research. The proper formats for citations and bibliographic entries are simply conventions within an academic discipline to facilitate the reader's retrieval of the original sources.

Fortunately, you will find that writing an argument as a formal research paper draws on the same argumentation skills you have been using all along—the ability to pose a good question at issue within a community, to formulate a contestable claim, and to support your claim with audience-based reasons and evidence. What special skills are required? The main ones are these:

- The ability to use your research effectively to frame your issue and to support your claim, revealing your reputable *ethos* and knowledge of the issue. Sources should be woven seamlessly into your argument, which is written in your own voice throughout. Writers should avoid a pastiche of block quotations.

- The ability to tap the resources of libraries, online databases, and the World Wide Web.

- The ability to evaluate sources for credibility, bias, and accuracy. Special care is needed to evaluate anything retrieved from the "free access" portion of the World Wide Web.

- The ability to summarize, quote, or paraphrase sources and to avoid plagiarism through citations and attributive tags such as "according to Jones" or "Peterson says."

- The ability to cite and document sources according to appropriate conventions.

This chapter and the next should help you to develop these skills. In Chapter 16 we focus on posing a research question, on unlocking the resources of your library and the Internet, and on developing the rhetorical skills for evaluating sources effectively. In Chapter 17 we explain the more nitty-gritty details of how to incorporate that information into your writing and how to document it properly.

Formulating a Research Question

The best way to avoid writing a data dump is to begin with a good research question—the formulation of a problem or issue that your essay will address. The research question, usually in the form of an issue question, will give you a guiding purpose in doing your library research. Let's say you are interested in how toys affect the development of gender identity in children. You can see that this topic is big and unfocused. Your library research will be much easier if you give yourself a clear direction through a focused research question. For example, you might formulate a specific question like one of these:

- Why have Barbie dolls been so continuously popular?

- Does the Barbie doll reinforce traditional ideas of womanhood or challenge them?

- Is culture or biology the stronger force in making little boys interested in trucks and guns?

- Do boys' toys such as video games, complex models, electronic gadgets, and science sets develop intellectual and physical skills more than girls' toys do?

The sooner you can settle on a research question, the easier it will be to find the source materials you need in a time-saving, efficient manner. The exploration methods we suggested in Chapter 3 can help you find a research topic that interests you.

A good way to begin formulating a research question is to freewrite for ten minutes or so, reflecting on recent readings that have stimulated your interest, on recent events that have sparked arguments, or on personal experiences that might open up onto public issues. If you have no idea for a topic, try starting with the trigger question "What possible topics am I interested in?" If you already have an idea for a topic area, explore why you are interested in it. Search for the personal connections or the particular angles that most intrigue you. When student writer Megan Matthews began brainstorming possible issues for a research project, she was initially interested in the problem of storing nuclear waste, but in the middle of a freewrite she switched her focus to a newspaper article she had seen on how the hearing of whales may be threatened by the Navy's sonar technology for detecting enemy submarines. After a few hours of research, both in the library and on the Web, Megan produced the following freewrite in her research notebook:

A FREEWRITE FROM MEGAN'S RESEARCH NOTEBOOK

I'm really becoming interested in the whale issue. The Navy has its own site with a Q&A that contradicts some of its earlier findings, and NOAA [National Oceanic and Atmospheric Administration] issued approval for the military to "harass and disturb" marine mammals despite expressing earlier reservations. Hmmm. Very interesting. Is this new sonar really necessary for security? No one seems to answer that! How many whales could suffer? How dangerous to whales is this sonar? Have they really done enough testing?

Note how Megan has moved from a topic orientation (I am researching whales and Navy sonar) to a question orientation (I am doing research to find the answers to questions that I have posed). Once you get engaged with questions, then your research has a purpose guided by your own critical thinking. To emphasize the importance of questions, we'll show you one more excerpt from Megan's research notebook. Note Megan's intense desire to find answers to her questions:

ANOTHER FREEWRITE FROM MEGAN'S RESEARCH NOTEBOOK

Oh, I am so annoyed. The Navy Web site conveniently lists a lot of general information without the documents I need to evaluate their claims. For example, they justify the need for this sonar by claiming that "there are 224 non-allied subs in operation." Who falls under the category of "non-allied"? Russia? Iran? African nations with which we have no real relationships yet? Also, what's the breakdown for the 224? But when I tried to e-mail them, their mailbox was full; no phone numbers were listed anywhere on the site, nor could I find an address. . . . So, a dilemma: I want to dig deeper into this to really evaluate the argument; as it is, I have some great info from environmental organizations and some so-so stuff from the Navy. I think I'm going to have to read through all of the science and policy documents on the government sites to try getting "between the lines" to see if they've omitted anything. I'm very upset by the fact that studies were only conducted on four species of whales/dolphins, when fish, turtles, pinnapeds, and other marine/aquatic animals might be affected as well.

Megan is now caught up in the research process. We'll return to her story occasionally throughout this chapter and the next. Her final argument is reprinted in full at the end of Chapter 17.

Understanding Differences in the Kinds of Sources

Once you begin researching an issue, you will encounter many different kinds of sources ranging from articles posted on Web sites to scholarly books. To be an effective researcher, you need to understand the differences among the many kinds of books, articles, and Web sites you are apt to encounter. In this section, we explain these different kinds of resources. We summarize our points in two handy tables labeled "A rhetorical overview of print sources" (Table 16.1) and "A rhetorical overview of Web sites" (Table 16.2). By the term "rhetorical overview," we indicate a way of looking at sources that makes you fully conscious of the writer's context, bias, and intentions: For any given piece, what is the writer's purpose and who is the intended audience? What is the writer's bias, perspective, or angle of vision? What is being *left out* of this source as well as included? Once you are aware of the many kinds of sources available—and of the kinds of library or Web search strategies needed to find them—you will be a savvy and responsible researcher.

Books Versus Periodicals Versus Web Sites

When you conduct library research, you often leave the library with an armload of books and a stack of articles that you have either photocopied from journals or

TABLE 16.1   *A rhetorical overview of print sources*

Genre and Publisher	Author and Angle of Vision	How to Recognize Them
	Books	
SCHOLARLY BOOKS ■ University/academic presses ■ Nonprofit ■ Selected through peer review	**Author:** Professors, researchers **Angle of vision:** Scholarly advancement of knowledge	■ University press on title page ■ Specialized academic style ■ Documentation and bibliography
TRADE BOOKS (NONFICTION) ■ Commercial publishers (for example, Penguin Putnam) ■ Selected for profit potential	**Author:** Journalists, freelancers, scholars aiming at popular audience **Angle of vision:** Varies from informative to persuasive; often well researched and respected, but sometimes shoddy and aimed for quick sale	■ Covers designed for marketing appeal ■ Popular style ■ Usually documented in an informal rather than academic style
REFERENCE BOOKS ■ Publishers specializing in reference material ■ For-profit through library sales	**Author:** Commissioned scholars **Angle of vision:** Balanced, factual overview	■ Titles containing words such as *encyclopedia*, *dictionary*, or *guide* ■ Found in reference section of library

Genre and Publisher	Author and Angle of Vision	How to Recognize Them
	Periodicals	

SCHOLARLY JOURNALS
- University/academic presses
- Nonprofit
- Articles chosen through peer review
- Examples: *Journal of Abnormal Psychology, Review of Metaphysics*

Author: Professors, researchers, independent scholars
Angle of vision: Scholarly advancement of knowledge; presentation of research findings; development of new theories and applications

- Not sold on magazine racks
- No commercial advertising
- Specialized academic style
- Documentation and bibliography
- Cover often has table of contents

PUBLIC AFFAIRS MAGAZINES
- Commercial, "for-profit" presses
- Manuscripts reviewed by editors
- Examples: *Harper's, Commonweal, National Review*

Author: Staff writers, freelancers; scholars writing for general audiences
Angle of vision: Aims to deepen public understanding of issues; magazines often have political bias of left, center, or right

- Long, well-researched articles
- Ads aimed at upscale professionals
- Often has reviews of books, theater, film, and the arts

TRADE MAGAZINES
- Commercial, "for-profit" presses
- Focused on a profession or trade
- Examples: *Advertising Age, Automotive Rebuilder, Farm Journal*

Author: Staff writers, industry specialists
Angle of vision: Informative articles for practitioners; advocacy for the profession or trade

- Title indicating trade or profession
- Articles on practical job concerns
- Ads geared toward a particular trade or profession

NEWSMAGAZINES AND NEWSPAPERS
- Newspaper chains and publishers
- Examples: *Time, Newsweek, Washington Post*

Author: Staff writers and journalists; occasional freelance pieces
Angle of vision: News reports aimed at balance and objectivity; editorial pages reflect perspective of editors; op-ed pieces reflect different perspectives

- Readily familiar by name, distinctive cover style
- Widely available on newsstands and by subscription
- Ads aimed at broad, general audience

POPULAR NICHE MAGAZINES
- Large conglomerates or small presses with clear target audience
- Focused on special interests of target audience
- Examples: *Seventeen, People, TV Guide, Car and Driver, Golf Digest*

Author: Staff or freelance writers
Angle of vision: Varies—in some, point of view is dictated by advertisers or the politics of publisher

- Glossy paper, extensive ads, lots of visuals
- Popular, often distinctive style
- Short, undocumented articles
- Credentials of writer often not mentioned

TABLE 16.2   *A rhetorical overview of Web sites*

Type of Site	Author/Sponsor and Angle of Vision	What to Watch Out For
.COM OR .NET (A COMMERCIAL SITE CREATED BY A BUSINESS OR CORPORATION)		
■ Purpose is to enhance image, attract customers, market products and services, provide customer service ■ Creators are paid by salary or fees and often motivated by desire to design innovative sites	**Author:** Difficult to identify individual writers; sponsoring company often considered the author **Angle of vision:** Obvious bias to promote the point of view of the business; links are to sites that promote same values	■ Links are often to other products and services provided by company ■ Photographs and other visuals used to enhance corporate image
.ORG (NONPROFIT ORGANIZATIONS OR ADVOCACY GROUPS)		
■ Sometimes purpose is to provide accurate, balanced information (for example, the American Red Cross sites) ■ Frequently, purpose is to advocate the organization's political views (for example, the People for the Ethical Treatment of Animals [PETA] site)	**Author:** Often hard to identify individual writers; sponsoring organization often considered the author; some sites produced by amateurs with passionate views; others produced by professionals **Angle of vision:** Advocacy sites promote views of sponsoring organization and aim to influence public opinion and policy	■ Advocacy sites sometimes don't announce purpose on home page ■ You may enter a node of an advocacy site through a link from another site and not realize the political slant ■ Facts/data selected and filtered by site's angle of vision ■ Often uses visuals for emotional appeal
.EDU (AN EDUCATIONAL SITE ASSOCIATED WITH A COLLEGE OR UNIVERSITY)		
■ Wide range of purposes ■ Home page aimed at attracting prospective students and donors. Inside the site are numerous subsites devoted to research, pedagogy, libraries, student work, and so forth	**Author:** Professors, staff, students **Angle of vision:** Varies enormously from personal sites of professors and students to organizational sites of research centers and libraries; can vary from scholarly and objective to strong advocacy on issues	■ Often an .edu site has numerous "subsites" sponsored by the university library, art programs, research units ■ It is often difficult to determine where you are in the site—e.g., professor's course site, student site
.GOV OR .MIL (SPONSORED BY GOVERNMENT AGENCIES OR MILITARY UNITS)		
■ Provides enormous range of basic data about government policy, bills in Congress, economic forecasts, and so forth ■ Aims to create good public relations for agency or military unit	**Author:** Development teams employed by the agency; sponsoring agency is usually considered the author **Angle of vision:** varies—informational sites publish data and government documents with an objective point of view; agency sites also promote agency's point of view—e.g., Dept. of Energy, Dept. of Labor	■ Typical sites (for example, www.energy.gov, the site of the U.S. Dept. of Energy) are extremely layered and complex and provide hundreds of links to other sites ■ Valuable for research ■ Sites often promote values/assumptions of sponsoring agency

Type of Site	Author/Sponsor and Angle of Vision	What to Watch Out For
PERSONAL WEB SITES ■ An individual contracts with server to publish the site. ■ Many personal Web sites also have .edu affiliation.	**Author:** Anyone can create a personal Web site **Angle of vision:** Varies from person to person	■ Home page URL ends with initials of Web server rather than .com, .org, .mil, or .gov ■ Credentials/bias of author often hard to determine ■ Irresponsible sites might have links to excellent sites; tracing links is complicated

magazines or downloaded from a computer and printed. At home, you will have no trouble determining who wrote the books and for what purpose, but your photocopied or downloaded articles can pose problems. What is the original source of the article in your hands? If you photocopied the articles from actual journals or magazines in your library, then you can be sure that they are "periodical print sources" (*periodical* means a publication, such as a scholarly journal or magazine, issued at regular intervals—that is, periodically). If you downloaded them from a computer—which may have been connected either to a licensed database leased by the library or to the World Wide Web—they may be electronic copies of periodical print sources or they may be material posted on the Web but never published in a print periodical.

When you download a print article from a computer, you should be aware that you lose many contextual clues about the author's purpose and bias—clues that you can pick up from the original magazine or journal itself by its appearance, title, advertisements (if any), table of contents, and statement of editorial policy. When you download something from the Web that has never appeared in print, you have to be wary about its source. Because print publications are costly to produce, print articles generally go through some level of editorial review. In contrast, anyone can post almost anything on the Web. You need to become savvy at recognizing these distinctions in order to read sources rhetorically and to document them accurately in your bibliography.

Scholarly Books Versus Trade Books

Note in Table 16.1 the distinction between scholarly books, which are peer reviewed and published by nonprofit academic presses, and trade books, which are published by for-profit presses with the intention of making money. By "peer review," which is a highly prized concept in academia, we mean the selection process by which scholarly manuscripts get chosen for publication. When manuscripts are submitted to an academic publisher, the editor sends them for independent review to experienced scholars who judge the rigor and accuracy of the research and the significance and value of the argument. The process is highly competitive and weeds out much shoddy or trivial work.

In contrast, trade books are not peer reviewed by independent scholars. Instead, they are selected for publication by editors whose business is to make a profit. Fortunately, it can be profitable for popular presses to publish superbly researched and argued intellectual material because college-educated people, as lifelong learners, create a demand for intellectually satisfying trade books written for the general reader rather than for the highly specialized reader. These can be excellent sources for undergraduate research, but you need to separate the trash from the treasure. Trade books are aimed at many different audiences and market segments and can include sloppy, unreliable, and heavily biased material.

Scholarly Journals Versus Magazines

Like scholarly books, scholarly journals are academic, peer-reviewed publications. Although they may look like magazines, they almost never appear on newsstands; they are nonprofit publications subsidized by universities for disseminating high-level research and scholarship.

In contrast, magazines are intended to make a profit through sales and advertising revenues. Fortunately for researchers, a demand exists for intellectually satisfying magazines, just as for sophisticated trade books. Many for-profit magazines publish highly respectable, useful material for undergraduate or professional researchers, but many magazines publish shoddy material. As Table 16.1 shows, magazines fall in various categories aimed at different audiences.

Print Sources Versus Cyberspace Sources

Another crucial distinction exists between print sources and cyberspace sources. Much of what you can retrieve from a computer was originally published in print. What you download is simply an electronic copy of a print source, either from a library-leased database or from someone's Web site. (The next section shows you how to tell the difference.) In such cases, you often need to consider the article's original print origins for appropriate cues about its rhetorical context and purpose. But much cyberspace material, having never appeared in print, may never have undergone either peer review or editorial review. To distinguish between these two kinds of cyberspace sources, we call one kind a "print/cyberspace source" (something that has appeared in print and is made available on the Web or through library-leased databases) and the other a "cyberspace-only source." When you use a cyberspace-only source, you've got to take special care in figuring out who wrote it, why, and for what audience. Also, you document cyberspace-only material differently from print material retrieved electronically.

For Class Discussion

Your instructor will bring to class a variety of sources—different kinds of books, scholarly journals, magazines, and downloaded material. Working individually or in small groups, try to decide which category in Tables 16.1 and 16.2 each piece belongs to. Be prepared to justify your decisions on the basis of the cues you used to make your decision.

Finding Books: Searching Your Library's Online Catalog

Your library's holdings are listed in its online catalog. Most of the entries are for books, but an academic library also has a wealth of other resources such as periodical collections, government records and reports, newspapers, videos and cassettes, maps, encyclopedias, and hundreds of specialized reference works that your reference librarian can help you use.

Indexed by subject, title, and author, the online catalog gives you titles of books and other library-owned resources relevant to your research area. Note that the catalog lists the titles of journals and magazines in the library's periodical collection (for example, *Journal of Abnormal Psychology, Atlantic Monthly*), but does *not* list the titles of individual articles within these periodicals. As we explain later in this section, you can search the contents of periodicals by using a licensed database. Methods of accessing and using online catalogs vary from institution to institution, so you'll need to learn the specifics of your library's catalog through direct experience.

Finding Print Articles: Searching a Licensed Database

For many research projects, useful sources are print articles from your library's periodical collection, including scholarly journals, public affairs magazines, newspapers or newsmagazines, and niche magazines related to your research area. Some of these articles are available free on the World Wide Web, but most of them are not. Rather, they may be located physically in your library's periodical collection (or in that of another library and available through interlibrary loan) or located electronically in vast databases leased by your library.

What Is a Licensed Database?

Electronic databases of periodical sources are produced by for-profit companies that index articles in thousands of periodicals and construct engines that can search the database by author, title, subject, keyword, date, genre, and other characteristics. In most cases the database contains an abstract of each article, and in many cases it contains the complete text of the article that you can download and print. These databases are referred to by several different generic names: "licensed databases" (our preferred term), "general databases," or "subscription services." Because access to these databases is restricted to fee-paying customers, they can't be searched through Web engines like Yahoo! or Google. Most university libraries allow students to access these databases from a remote computer by using a password. You can therefore use the Internet to connect your computer to licensed databases as well as to the World Wide Web (see Figure 16.1).

Although the methods of accessing licensed databases vary from institution to institution, we can offer some widely applicable guidelines. Most likely your library has online one or more of the following databases:

- *EBSCOhost:* Includes citations and abstracts from journals in most disciplines as well as many full-text articles from over three thousand journals; its *Academic Search Elite* function covers material published as long ago as the early 1980s.

- *UMI ProQuest Direct:* Gives access to the full text of articles from journals in a variety of subject areas; includes full-text articles from newspapers.

- *InfoTrac:* Is often called "Expanded Academic Index," and is similar to EBSCOhost and UMI ProQuest in its coverage of interdisciplinary subjects.

- *FirstSearch Databases:* Incorporates multiple specialized databases in many subject areas, including WorldCat, which contains records of books, periodicals, and multimedia formats from libraries worldwide.

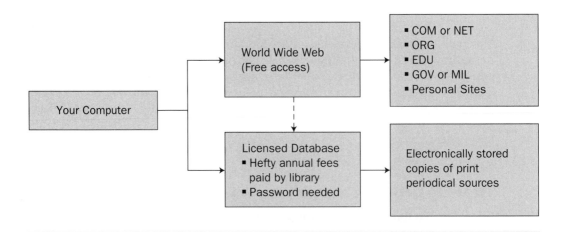

FIGURE 16.1   *Licensed database versus free-access portions of Internet*

- *LexisNexis Academic Universe:* Is primarily a full-text database covering current events, business, and financial news; includes company profiles and legal, medical, and reference information.

Generally, one of these database is the "default database" chosen by your library for most article searches. Your reference librarian will be able to direct you to the most useful licensed database for your purpose.

Keyword Searching

To use an online database, you need to be adept at keyword searching. When you type a word or phrase into a search box, the computer will find sources that contain the same words or phrases. If you want the computer to search for a phrase, put it in quotation marks. Thus if you type *"street people"* using quotation marks, the computer will search for those two words occurring together. If you type in *street people* without quotation marks, the computer will look for the word *street* and the word *people* occurring in the same document but not necessarily together. Use your imagination to try a number of related terms. If you are researching gendered toys and you get too many hits using the keyword *toys*, try *gender toys, Barbie, G.I. Joe, girl toys, boy toys, toys psychology*, and so forth. You can increase the flexibility of your searches by using Boolean terms to expand, narrow, or limit your search (see Table 16.3 for an explanation of Boolean searches).

TABLE 16.3   *Boolean search commands*

Command and Function	Research Example	What to Type	Search Result
X OR Y (Expands your search)	You are researching Barbie dolls and decide to include G.I. Joe figures.	"Barbie doll" OR "GI Joe"	Articles that contain either phrase
X AND Y (Narrows your search)	You are researching the psychological effects of Barbie dolls and are getting too many hits under *Barbie dolls.*	"Barbie dolls" AND psychology	Articles that include both the phrase "Barbie dolls" and the word *psychology*
X NOT Y (Limits your search)	You are researching girls' toys and are tired of reading about Barbie dolls. You want to look at other popular girls' toys.	"girl toys" NOT Barbie	Articles that include the phrase "girl toys" but exclude *Barbie*

Illustration of a Database Search

As an illustration of a database search, we'll draw again on Megan's process as she researched the effect of Navy sonar on whales. Using the database EBSCOhost, Meg entered the keywords *Navy sonar* AND *whales*, which revealed the six articles shown in Figure 16.2. As this Results list shows, EBSCOhost carries

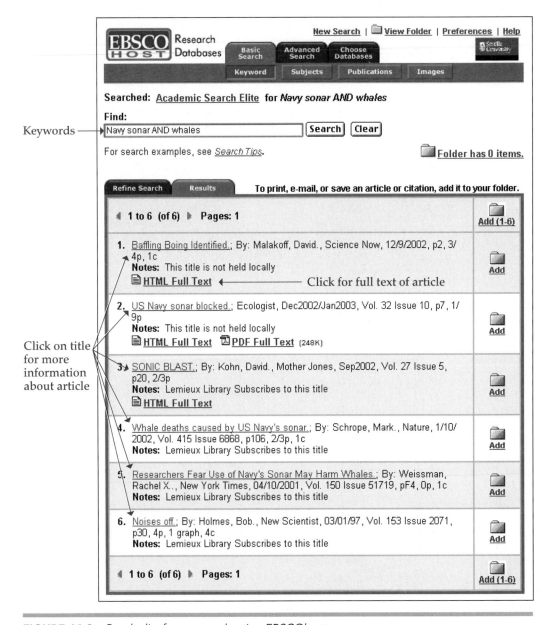

FIGURE 16.2 *Results list from a search using EBSCOhost*

the full text for the first three records: "Baffling Boing Identified," "US Navy Sonar Blocked," and "Sonic Blast." The results list also notes that the Lemieux Library (the name of her college's library) subscribes to all the listed periodicals except for *Science Now* (Record 1) and *Ecologist* (Record 2). Thus Megan had access to all six articles, either from her college's periodical collection or from the on-line database. Because she wanted to decide whether the *New Scientist* article (Record 6) was worth tracking down, she clicked on its title "Noises Off," which revealed the screen shown in Figure 16.3. This screen provides an abstract of the article, indicates that it is four pages long, and includes a graph and four color photographs or drawings.

After you've identified articles you'd like to read, locate physically all those available in your library's periodical collection. (This way you won't lose important contextual cues for reading them rhetorically.) For those unavailable in your library, print them from the database, if possible, or order them from interlibrary loan.

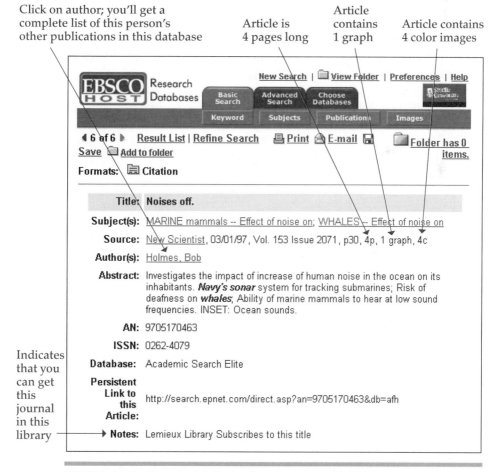

FIGURE 16.3   *Sample full display for an article on EBSCOhost*

Finding Cyberspace Sources: Searching the World Wide Web

Another valuable resource is the World Wide Web. In this section we begin by explaining in more detail the logic of the Internet—the difference between restricted portions of the Internet, such as licensed databases, and the amorphous, ever changing, "free-access" portion, commonly called the "World Wide Web" (see again Figure 16.1). We then offer suggestions for searching the Web.

The Logic of the Internet

To understand the logic of Web search engines, you need to know that the Internet is divided into restricted sections open only to those with special access rights and a "free-access" section. Web engines such as Yahoo! or Google search only the free-access portion of the Internet. When you type keywords into a Web search engine, it searches for matches in material made available on the Web by all the users of the world's network of computers—government agencies, corporations, advocacy groups, information services, individuals with their own Web sites, and many others.

The following example will quickly show you the difference between a licensed database search and a Web search. When Megan entered the keywords *Navy sonar* AND *whales* into EBSCOhost, she received six "hits"—the titles of six articles on this subject appearing in print periodicals. In contrast, when she entered the same keywords into the Web search engine Yahoo!, she received 5,180 hits; when she tried the search engine Google, she got even more—6,220. The Web search engines are picking up, in addition to print articles that someone may have posted on the Web, all the references to Navy sonar and whales that may appear in advocacy Web sites, government publications, newspapers, chat rooms, course syllabi posted by professors, student papers posted on the Web, and so forth.

For Class Discussion

Figure 16.4 shows the first screen of hits for the keywords *Navy sonar* and *whales* retrieved by the search engine Yahoo! Working in small groups or as a whole class, compare these items with those retrieved from the equivalent search using the licensed database EBSCOhost (Figure 16.2).

1. Explain in your own words why the results for the Web search are different from those of the licensed database search.

2. What do you suspect would be the bias or angle of vision for the first record under the Yahoo! search—"NRDC: Spread of Active Sonar Threatens Whales. . ."?

3. What do you suspect would be the bias or angle of vision of the *Mother Jones* article and the *New Scientist* article identified in the EBSCOhost

search? How could looking at the actual magazines in your college library help you determine the bias?

Using Web Search Engines

Although the hits you receive from a Web search frequently include useless, shoddy, trivial, or irrelevant material, the Web's resources for researchers are

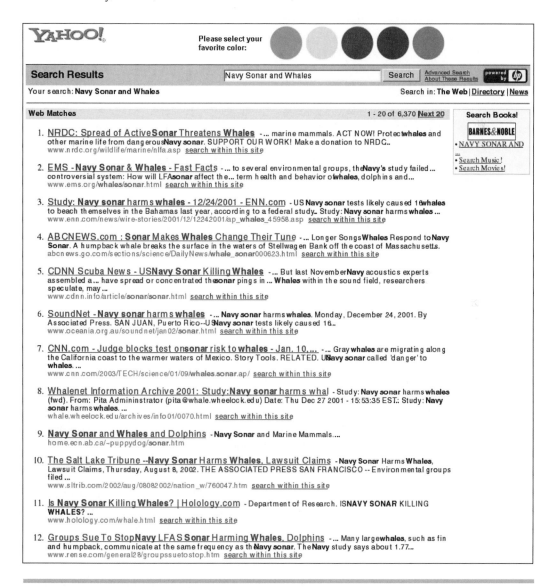

FIGURE 16.4   *First screen of hits from Yahoo!*

breathtaking. At your fingertips you have access to government documents and statistics, legislative and corporate white papers, court cases, persuasive appeals of advocacy groups, consumer information—the list is almost endless.

The World Wide Web can be searched by a variety of engines that collect and categorize individual Web files and search them for keywords. Most of these engines will find not only text files but also graphic, audio, and video files. Some look through the titles of files, whereas others scan the entire text of documents. Different engines search the Web in different ways, so it is important that you try a variety of search engines when you look for information. Although the Web is evolving rapidly, some of the best search engines are fairly stable. For starters, you might try Google (http://www.google.com), Yahoo! (http://yahoo.com), or AltaVista (http://www.altavista.com). Again, if you are in doubt, your reference librarian can help you choose the most productive search engine for your needs.

Determining Where You Are on the Web

As you browse the Web looking for resources, clicking from link to link, try to figure out what site you are actually in at any given moment. This information is crucial, both for properly documenting a Web source and for reading the source rhetorically.

To know where you are on the Web, begin by recognizing the codes contained in a site's URL (uniform resource locator). The generic structure of a typical URL looks like this:

http://www.servername.domain/directory/subdirectory/filename.filetype

Here is a specific example:

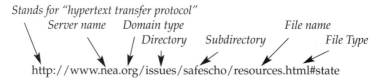

The file named "resources" is linked through a series of directories and subdirectories to the home page of the National Education Association (www.nea.org).

Often, when you click on a link in one site, you will be sent to a totally different site. To determine the home page of this new site, simply note the root URL immediately following the "www."* To view the home page directly, delete the codes to the right of the initial home page URL in your computer's location window and

---

*Not all URLs begin with "www" after the first set of double slashes. Our description doesn't include variations from the most typical URL types. You can generally find the home page of any site by eliminating all codes to the right of the first slash mark following the initial set of double slashes.

hit Enter. You will then be linked directly to the site's home page. As you will see later in this chapter and in Chapter 17, being able to examine a site's home page helps you read the site rhetorically and document it properly.

Reading Your Sources Rhetorically

Even when you have a research question that interests you, it's easy to feel overwhelmed when you return from a library with a stack of books and magazine or journal articles. How do you begin reading all this material? There is no one right answer to this question. At times you need to read slowly with analytical closeness, as we discussed in Chapter 2. At other times you can skim a source, looking only for its gist or for a needed piece of information.

Reading with Your Own Goals in Mind

How you read a source depends to a certain extent on where you are in the research process. Early in the process, when you are in the thesis-seeking, exploratory stage, your goal is to achieve a basic understanding about your research problem. You need to become aware of different points of view, learn what is unknown or controversial about your research question, see what values or assumptions are in conflict, and build up your store of background knowledge.

Given these goals, at the early stages of research you should select, where possible, easy-to-read, overview kinds of sources to get you into the conversation. In some cases, even an encyclopedia or specialized reference work can be a good start for getting general background.

As you get deeper into your research, your questions become more focused, and the sources you read become more specialized. Once you formulate a thesis and plan a structure for your paper, you can determine more clearly the sources you need and read them with purpose and direction.

Reading with Rhetorical Awareness

To read your sources rhetorically, you should keep two basic questions in mind: (1) What was the source author's purpose in writing this piece? And (2) What might be my purpose in using this piece? Table 16.4 sums up the kinds of questions a rhetorical reader typically considers.

This chart reinforces a point we've made throughout this text: All writing is produced from an angle of vision that privileges some ways of seeing and filters out other ways. You should guard against reading your sources as if they present hard, undisputed facts or universal truths. For example, if one of your sources says that "Saint-John's-wort [a herb] has been shown to be an effective treatment for depression," some of your readers might accept that statement as fact; but many wouldn't. Skeptical readers would want to know who the author is, where his views have been published, and what he uses for evidence. Let's say the author is someone named

---

TABLE 16.4   *Questions asked by rhetorical readers*

What was the source author's purpose in writing this piece?	What might be my purpose in using this piece in my own argument?

■ Who is this author? What are his or her credentials and affiliations?
■ What audience was this person addressing?
■ What is the genre of this piece? (If you downloaded the piece from the World Wide Web, did it originally appear in print?)
■ If this piece appeared in print, what is the reputation and bias of the journal, magazine, or press? Was the piece peer reviewed?
■ If this piece appeared only on the Web, who or what organization sponsors the Web site (check the home page)? What is the reputation and bias of the sponsor?
■ What is the author's thesis or purpose?
■ How does this author try to change his or her audience's view?
■ What is this writer's angle of vision or bias?
■ What is omitted or censored from this text?
■ How reliable and credible is this author?
■ What facts, data, and other evidence does this author use and what are the sources of these data?
■ What are this author's underlying values, assumptions, and beliefs?
	■ How has this piece influenced or complicated my own thinking?
	■ How does this piece relate to my research question?
	■ How will my own intended audience react to this author?
	■ How might I use this piece in my own argument?
	  ■ Is it an opposing view that I might summarize?
	  ■ Is it an alternative point of view that I might compare to other points of view?
	■ Does it have facts and data that I might use?
	■ Would a summary of all or part of this argument support or oppose one or more of my own points?
	■ Could I use this author for testimony? (If so, how should I indicate this author's credentials?)
	■ If I use this source, will I need to acknowledge the author's bias and angle of vision?

Samuel Jones. Skeptical readers would ask whether Jones is relying on published research, and if so, whether the studies have been peer reviewed in reputable, scholarly journals and whether the research has been replicated by other scientists. They would also want to know whether Jones has financial connections to companies that produce herbal remedies and supplements. Rather than settling the question about Saint-John's-wort as a treatment for depression, a quotation from Jones might open up a heated controversy about medical research.

Reading rhetorically is thus a way of thinking critically about your sources. It influences the way you take notes, evaluate sources, and shape your argument.

Taking Effective Notes

Taking good research notes serves two functions: First, it encourages you to read actively because you must summarize your sources' arguments, record usable information, and extract short quotations. Second, taking notes encourages you to do exploratory thinking—to write down ideas as they occur to you, to analyze sources as you read them, and to join your sources in conversation.

There are many ways to take notes, but we can offer several techniques that have worked especially well for other writers. First of all, you can try using a double-entry journal. Divide a page in half, entering your informational notes on one side and your exploratory writing on the other. Another system is to record notes on index cards or in a computer file and then write out your exploratory thinking in a separate research journal. Still another method is to record informational notes on your computer in a regular font and then to use a boldfaced font for exploratory writing. Your objective here is to create a visual way to distinguish your informational notes from your exploratory thinking.

A common practice of beginning researchers—one that experienced researchers almost never use—is *not* taking notes as they read and *not* doing any exploratory writing. We've seen students photocopy a dozen or more articles, but then write nothing as they read (sometimes they highlight passages with a marker), planning to rely later on memory to navigate through the sources. This practice reduces your ability to synthesize your sources and create your argument. When you begin drafting your paper, you'll have no notes to refer to, no record of your thinking-in-progress. Your only recourse is to revisit all your sources, thumbing through them one at a time—a practice that leads to passive cutting and pasting.

To make your notes purposeful, you need to imagine how a given source might be used in your research paper. Table 16.5 shows how notes are a function of your purpose.

TABLE 16.5   *Note taking according to purpose*

How Source Might Be Used in Your Paper	Notes to Take
Background information about research problem or issue	Summarize the information; record specific data.
Part of a section reviewing different points of view on your question	Summarize the source's argument; note its bias and perspective. In exploratory notes, jot down ideas on how and why different sources disagree.
As an opposing view that you must summarize and respond to	Summarize the argument fully and fairly. In exploratory notes, speculate about why you disagree with the source and whether you can refute the argument, concede to it, or compromise with it.
As data, information, or testimony to be used as evidence to support your thesis	Record the data or information; summarize or paraphrase the supporting argument with occasional quotations of key phrases; directly quote short passages for supporting testimony; note the credentials of the writer or person quoted. In exploratory notes, record new ideas as they occur to you.
As data, information, or testimony that counters your position or raises doubts about your thesis	Take notes on counterevidence. In exploratory notes, speculate on how you might respond to the counterevidence.

When you use a source's exact words, be meticulous in copying them exactly and marking the quoted passage with prominent quotation marks. If you record information without directly quoting it, be sure that you restate it completely in your own words to avoid later problems with plagiarism. Next, check that you have all the bibliographic information you may need for a citation including the page numbers for each entry in your notes. (Citing page numbers for articles downloaded from the Web or a licensed database is problematic—see Chapter 17, pp. 413–414.)

Evaluating Sources

When you read sources for your research project, you need to evaluate them as you go along. As you read each potential source, ask yourself questions about the author's angle of vision, degree of advocacy, reliability, and credibility.

Angle of Vision

By "angle of vision," we mean the way that a piece of writing gets shaped by the underlying values, assumptions, and beliefs of the author so that the text reflects a certain perspective, worldview, or belief system. The angle of vision is revealed by internal factors such as the author's word choice (especially notice the connotations of words), selection and omission of details, overt statements, figurative language, and grammatical emphasis; and by external factors such as the politics of the author, the genre of the source, the politics of the publisher, and so forth. When reading a source, see whether you can detect underlying assumptions or beliefs that suggest a writer's values or political views: Is this writer conservative or liberal? Predisposed toward traditional "family values" or new family structures? Toward technology or toward the simple life? Toward free markets or social controls on the economy? Toward business interests or labor? Toward the environment or jobs? Toward order or freedom?

You can also get useful clues about a writer's angle of vision by looking at external data. What are the writer's credentials? Is the writer affiliated with an advocacy group or known for a certain ideology? (If you know nothing about an author who seems important to your research, try typing the author's name into a Web search engine. You might discover useful information about the author's other publications or about the writer's reputation in various fields.) Also pay attention to publishing data. Where was this source originally published? What is the reputation and editorial slant of the publication in which the source appears? For example, editorial slants of magazines can range from very liberal to very conservative. Likewise, publications affiliated with advocacy organizations (the Sierra Club, the National Rifle Association) will have a clear editorial bias.* Table 16.6 shows our own assessment of the political biases of various popular magazines and media commentators.

---

*If you are uncertain about the editorial bias of a particular magazine or newspaper, consult the *Gale Directory of Publications and Broadcast Media* or *Magazines for Libraries*, which, among other things, identify the intended audience and political biases of a wide range of magazines and newspapers.

TABLE 16.6 *Political bias of media**

Far Left	Left Liberal	Left Center	Right Center	Right Conservative	Far Right
Media					
People's World The Guardian	The Nation Mother Jones The Progressive Utne Reader Washington Monthly	Village Voice LA Times NY Times Atlantic Newsweek Harper's PBS NPR	Time Washington Post New Republic CBS NBC ABC	U.S. News and World Report Reader's Digest The Wall Street Journal American Spectator National Review	New American Plain Truth Washington Times
Commentators					
Alexander Cockburn Edward Said Noam Chomsky Susan Sontag	Gore Vidal Barbara Ehrenreich Jesse Jackson Molly Ivins Ralph Nader Paul Krugman Bob Herbert Katha Pollitt	Michael Kinsley Anthony Lewis Bill Moyers Ted Koppel Ellen Goodman Mark Shields Jonathan Alter Anna Quindlen	David Broder William Safire	George Will Charles Krauthammer John Leo William Buckley Milton Friedman Thomas Sowell Paul Gigot Mona Charen Michelle Malkin	Rush Limbaugh Pat Buchanan Pat Robertson Phyllis Schlafly Paul Harvey Ann Coulter

*Our ideas in this table are adapted from Donald Lazere, "Teaching the Political Conflicts: A Rhetorical Schema," *College Composition and Communication* 43 (May 1992), 194–213.

Degree of Advocacy

By "degree of advocacy" we mean the extent to which an author unabashedly takes a persuasive stance on a contested position as opposed to adopting a more neutral, objective, or exploratory stance. When a writer has an ax to grind, you need to weigh carefully the writer's selection of evidence, interpretation of data, and fairness to opposing views. Although objectivity is itself an "angle of vision" and no one can be completely neutral, it is always useful to seek out authors who offer a balanced assessment of the evidence. Evidence from a more detached and neutral writer may be more trusted by your readers than the arguments of a committed advocate. For example, if you want to persuade corporate executives on the dangers of global warming, evidence from scholarly journals may be more persuasive than evidence from an environmentalist Web site or from a freelance writer in a leftist popular magazine like *Mother Jones*.

Reliability

"Reliability" refers to the accuracy of factual data in a source as determined by external validation. If you check a writer's "facts" against other sources, do you find that the facts are correct? Does the writer distort facts, take them out of context, or otherwise use them unreasonably? In some controversies, key data are highly disputed—for example, the number of homeless people in the United States, the frequency of date rape, or the risk factors for many diseases. A reliable writer acknowledges these controversies and doesn't treat disputed data as fact. Furthermore, if you check out the sources used by a reliable writer, they'll reveal accurate and careful research—respected primary sources rather than hearsay or secondhand reports.

Credibility

"Credibility" is similar to "reliability" but is based on internal rather than external factors. It refers to the reader's trust in the writer's honesty, goodwill, and trustworthiness and is apparent in the writer's tone, reasonableness, fairness in summarizing opposing views, and respect for different perspectives (what we have called "*ethos*"). Audiences differ in how much credibility they will grant to certain authors. Nevertheless a writer can achieve a reputation for credibility, even among bitter political opponents, by applying to issues a sense of moral courage, integrity, and consistency of principle.

Understanding the Rhetoric of Web Sites

In the previous section we focused on reading sources rhetorically by asking questions about a source's angle of vision, degree of advocacy, reliability, and credibility. In this section we turn to the skills of effectively evaluating and using Web sources by understanding the special rhetoric of Web sites.

The Web as a Unique Rhetorical Environment

Although many Web sites are highly professional and expensive to produce, the Web is also a great vehicle for democracy, giving voice to the otherwise voiceless. Anyone with a cause and a rudimentary knowledge of Web page design can create a Web site. Before the invention of the Web, people with a message had to stand on street corners passing out fliers or put money into newsletters or advocacy advertisements. The Web, in contrast, is cheap. The result is a rhetorical medium that differs in significant ways from print.

Analyzing the Purpose of a Site and Your Own Research Purpose

When you conduct research on the Web, your first question should be, Who placed this piece on the Web and why? You can begin answering this question by analyzing the site's home page, where you will often find navigational buttons linking to "Mission," "About Us," or other identifying information about the site's sponsors. You can also get hints about the site's purpose by asking, What kind of Web site is it? As we explained earlier, different kinds of Web sites have different purposes, often revealed by the domain identifier following the server name (.com, .net, .org, .gov, .mil). As you evaluate the Web site, also consider your own purpose for using it. For instance, are you trying to get an initial understanding of various points of view on an issue, or are you looking for reliable information? An advocacy site may be an excellent place for researching a point of view but a doubtful source of data and evidence for your own argument.

Sorting Sites by Domain Type

One powerful research strategy for reading Web sites rhetorically is to use the "advanced search" feature of a search engine to sort sites by domain type. As an example, consider again Megan's research dilemma when she plugged *Navy sonar* and *whales* into Google and received 6,220 "hits." How could she begin to navigate through such a huge number? Using Google's "advanced search" feature, Megan first sorted through her hits by selecting only .com sites (2,790 hits). These, she discovered, were primarily the sites of newspapers, news services, and tourist sites catering to "whale watching"—a billion-dollar business, she discovered from one source. These sites tended to repeat the same news stories and offer superficial coverage. She next looked at .org sites (1,400 hits). These were primarily the sites of environmental advocacy groups—organizations such as the National Resources Defense Council, the Sierra Club, the Humane Society, the League for Coastal Protection, the Cetacean Society International, the Ocean Futures Society, and so forth—all dedicated to protecting marine life. These advocacy sites were strongly pro-whale; in their arguments against Navy sonar they either discounted or ignored issues of national security. Next she looked at .edu sites (449 hits), which were primarily references to course descriptions and syllabi that included this controversy as a source of study. She didn't find these helpful. Finally, she sorted by .gov (348 hits) and .mil (138 hits). The .gov sites revealed documents on whales and sonar submitted to congressional hearings; it also revealed the sites of two key government agencies involved in the sonar dispute: the National Marine Fisheries Service and the National Oceanic and Atmospheric Administration. The .mil sites gave access to white papers and other documents provided by the Navy to justify its use of low-frequency sonar.

This overview of the territory helped Megan understand the angle of vision or bias of different sources. The .org sites focused on protecting marine life. In contrast, the .mil and the .gov sites helped her understand the national security issue. In the middle, trying to balance the competing demands of the environment, national security, and preservation of commerce, were the sites of government agencies not directly connected to the military. All of these sites provided valuable information and most them included links to scientific and research studies.

Evaluating a Web Site

Given this overview of the territory, Megan still had to decide which specific sites to use for her research. One of the most challenging parts of using the Web is determining whether a site offers gold or glitter. Sometimes the case may not be clear-cut. How do you sort out reliable, worthwhile sites from unreliable ones? We offer the following criteria developed by scholars and librarians as points to consider when you are using Web sites.

Criterion 1: Authority

- Is the author or sponsor of the Web site clearly identified?
- Does the site identify the occupation, position, education, experience, and credentials of the site's authors?
- Does the introductory material reveal the author's or sponsor's motivation for publishing this information on the Web?
- Does the site provide contact information for the author or sponsor such as an e-mail or organization address?

Criterion 2: Objectivity or Clear Disclosure of Advocacy

- Is the site's purpose (to inform, explain, or persuade) clear?
- Is the site explicit about declaring its author's or sponsor's point of view?
- Does the site indicate whether authors are affiliated with a specific organization, institution, or association?
- Does the site indicate whether it is directed toward a specific audience?

Criterion 3: Coverage

- Are the topics covered by the site clear?
- Does the site exhibit suitable depth and comprehensiveness for its purpose?
- Is sufficient evidence provided to support the ideas and opinions presented?

Criterion 4: Accuracy

- Are the sources of information stated? Can you tell whether this information is original or taken from someplace else?
- Does the information appear to be accurate? Can you verify this information by comparing this source with other sources in the field?

Criterion 5: Currency

- Are dates included in the Web site?
- Do the dates apply to the material itself or to its placement on the Web? Is the site regularly revised and updated?
- Is the information current, or at least still relevant, for the site's purpose?

To illustrate how these criteria can help you evaluate a site, consider how they could be applied to the article "Spread of Active Sonar Threatens Whales" found on the site of the National Resources Defense Council. The first screen of this article is shown in Figure 16.5. The site is clearly from an advocacy group, as indicated by the boxed text on the right side urging readers to "ACT NOW!" and "SUPPORT OUR WORK!" The article is four pages long and gives a detailed overview of the history of Navy sonar and its negative impact on whales and other marine mammals. However no author is identified. Is the article trustworthy and reliable or is it from a fringe environmental group apt to suppress or distort evidence? Using the criteria for evaluating Web sites, Megan was able to identify the strengths and weaknesses of this site in light of her research purpose.

The site does very well against the criteria "authority" and "clear disclosure of advocacy." Megan located the home page of the site, clicked on "About Us," and discovered that the National Resources Defense Council has been around for more than thirty years and established its first Web site in 1995. It is a large national organization with three regional offices, puts out numerous publications, and does extensive lobbying on environmental issues. The "About Us" section states:

> NRDC uses law, science, and the support of more than 500,000 members nationwide to protect the planet's wildlife and wild places and to ensure a safe and healthy environment for all living things. . . . We work to foster the fundamental right of all people to have a voice in decisions that affect their environment. We seek to break down the pattern of disproportionate environmental burdens borne by people of color and others who face social or economic inequities. Ultimately, NRDC strives to help create a new way of life for humankind, one that can be sustained indefinitely without fouling or depleting the resources that support all life on Earth.

The site provides contact information, the addresses of regional and national offices, and lists of phone numbers and e-mail addresses.

In terms of coverage (criteria 3), the site is unusually broad and deep. It covers hundreds of different environmental issues and has fun features for children as well as in-depth technical articles written for specialists. Megan also determined that the site was accurate (criteria 4). Technical articles had bibliographies, and references to factual data throughout the site had notes about sources. She discovered that information on this site corroborated well with references to the same data from other sites. Finally, the site was current (criteria 5). The home page has a "tip of the day," updated daily, and items within the site have clear indications of dates. This is an active, ongoing site.

Megan concluded that the site was an excellent source for both arguments and data from a pro-environmental perspective. She could use the site to understand potential dangers of Navy sonar to whales and other marine life. However, the site was not helpful for understanding the Navy's reasons for needing low-frequency sonar or for understanding the role of this sonar in the war against terrorism.

NATURAL RESOURCES DEFENSE COUNCIL

Wildlife & Fish
Animals & Birds
Fish
• Whales & Marine
Animals

In Brief
In Depth
Related Links
Habitat
Preservation

○ Clean Air &
Energy

○ Global Warming

○ Clean Water &
Oceans

◎ Wildlife & Fish

○ Parks, Forests &
Wildlands

○ Toxic Chemicals
& Health

○ Nuclear Weapons
& Waste

○ Cities &
Green Living

○ Environmental
Legislation

Magazine
Reference/Links
Publications
Fun Features
Subscribe
Media Center
En Español
Site Map
Contact Us

Wildlife & Fish: Whales & Marine Animals: In Brief: News
✉ **Email This Article**

Spread of Active Sonar Threatens Whales

The U.S. Navy wants to flood the world's oceans and coastal waters with sonar technology that deafens -- and kills -- whales and other marine mammals.

Around the globe, nations are testing and beginning to deploy "active sonar" technology, which uses extremely loud sound to detect submarines. The problem? Active sonar can injure and even kill marine mammals. It has been conclusively linked to the deaths of seven whales in the Bahamas in March 2000, and is thought to have caused a 1996 mass stranding of beaked whales on the west coast of Greece.

ACT NOW!
Protect whales and other marine life from dangerous Navy sonar.

SUPPORT OUR WORK!
Make a donation to NRDC.

The U.S. Navy has led the push toward use of active sonar. In full knowledge of the disastrous effects that active sonar's intense noise may have on whale populations all over the world, the Navy has also conducted testing in complete secrecy and has consistently evaded and violated environmental law.

In July 2002, despite strong concerns from many leading scientists, the Bush administration issued a long-sought permit allowing the Navy to use the biggest gun in its active-sonar arsenal, the SURTASS LFA system, in as much as 75 percent of the world's oceans. (NRDC has filed a lawsuit to stop deployment of the system.) In addition, the Navy is attempting to expand its active-sonar program into U.S. coastal waters, and wants to do so without conducting the environmental analysis required by law.

The Bahamas Whale Deaths

In March 2000, four different species of whales and dolphins were stranded on beaches in the Bahamas after a U.S. Navy battle group used active sonar in the area. Despite efforts to save the whales, seven of them died. The Navy initially denied that active sonar was to blame, but its own investigation later found hemorrhaging around the dead whales' eyes and ears, indicating severe acoustic trauma. The government's study of the incident established with virtual certainty that the strandings in the Bahamas had been caused by mid-frequency active sonar used by Navy ships passing through the area. Since the

Of the 13 beaked whales that stranded in the Bahamas in March 2000 after exposure to active sonar, seven died, including this one.
Center for Whale Research

incident, the area's population of beaked whales has disappeared, leading researchers to conclude that they abandoned their habitat or died at sea. Scientists are concerned that, under the right circumstances, even the transient use of high-intensity active sonar can have a severe impact on populations of marine mammals.

FIGURE 16.5 *First screen from article on Web site*

Conclusion

Our discussion of the rhetoric of Web sites concludes this chapter's introduction to college-level research. We have talked about the need to establish a good research question, to understand the key differences among different kinds of sources, to use purposeful strategies for searching libraries, databases, and Web sites, to use your rhetorical knowledge when you read and evaluate sources, and to understand the rhetoric of Web sites. In the next chapter we focus on how to integrate research sources into your own prose and how to cite and document them appropriately.

17 Using, Citing, and Documenting Sources

The previous chapter helped you pose a good research question and begin unlocking some of the resources of your library and the Internet. This chapter teaches you how to use sources in your own argument—how to incorporate them into your own prose through summary, paraphrase, or quotation; how to cite them using attributive tags and in-text citations; and how to document them using the style and format of the Modern Language Association or the American Psychological Association.

Using Sources for Your Own Purposes

To illustrate the purposeful use of sources, we will use the following short argument from the Web site of the American Council on Science and Health—a conservative organization of doctors and scientists devoted to providing scientific information on health issues and to exposing health fads and myths. Please read the argument carefully in preparation for the discussions that follow.

IS VEGETARIANISM HEALTHIER THAN NONVEGETARIANISM?

Many people become vegetarians because they believe, in error, that vegetarianism is uniquely conducive to good health. The findings of several large epidemiologic studies indeed suggest that the death and chronic-disease rates of vegetarians—primarily vegetarians who consume dairy products or both dairy products and eggs—are lower than those of meat eaters. . . .

The health of vegetarians may be better than that of nonvegetarians partly because of nondietary factors: Many vegetarians are health-conscious. They exercise regularly, maintain a desirable body weight, and abstain from smoking. Although most epidemiologists have attempted to take such factors into account in their analyses, it is possible that they did not adequately control their studies for nondietary effects.

People who are vegetarians by choice may differ from the general population in other ways relevant to health. For example, in Western countries most vegetarians are more affluent than nonvegetarians and thus have better living conditions and more access to medical care.

An authoritative review of vegetarianism and chronic diseases classified the evidence for various alleged health benefits of vegetarianism:

- The evidence is "strong" that vegetarians have (a) a lower risk of becoming alcoholic, constipated, or obese and (b) a lower risk of developing lung cancer.
- The evidence is "good" that vegetarians have a lower risk of developing adult-onset diabetes mellitus, coronary artery disease, hypertension, and gallstones.
- The evidence is "fair to poor" that vegetarianism decreases risk of breast cancer, colon cancer, diverticular disease, kidney-stone formation, osteoporosis, and tooth decay.

For some of the diseases mentioned above, the practice of vegetarianism itself probably is the main protective factor. For example, the low incidence of constipation among vegetarians is almost certainly due to their high intakes of fiber-rich foods. For other conditions, nondietary factors may be more important than diet. For example, the low incidence of lung cancer among vegetarians is attributable primarily to their extremely low rate of cigarette smoking. Diet is but one of many risk factors for most chronic diseases.

What we want to show you is that the way you use this article depends on your own research question and purpose. Sometimes you may decide to summarize a source completely—particularly if the source represents an opposing or alternative view that you intend to address. (See Chapter 2 for a detailed explanation of summary writing; see also Chapter 8, pp. 144–145, for the difference between a fair summary and an unfair summary or "strawman.") At other times you may choose to use only parts of a source. To illustrate how your rhetorical purpose governs your use of a source, we show you three different hypothetical examples:

- *Writer 1, arguing for an alternative treatment for alcoholism:* On some occasions, you will draw details from a source for use in a different context.

    Another approach to fighting alcoholism is through naturopathy, holistic medicine, and vegetarianism. Vegetarians generally have better health than the rest of the population and particularly have, according to the American Council on Science and Health, "a lower risk for becoming alcoholic." * This lower risk has been borne out by other studies showing that the benefits of the holistic health movement are particularly strong for persons with addictive tendencies. . . .[goes on to other arguments and sources]

---

*If the writer had found this quotation in a print source such as a book or magazine, the page number would be placed in parentheses immediately after the quotation, as explained on page 394 later in this chapter. Because the writer found this passage in a Web site, no page citation is possible. In a research paper, readers would find full information about the source in the bibliography at the end. In this case, the author would be listed as "American Council on Science and Health" indicated in the attributive tag preceding the quotation.

■ *Writer 2, arguing for the value of vegetarianism:* Sometimes you can use part of a source for direct support of your own claim. In this case, a summary of relevant parts of the argument can be used as evidence.

> Not only will a vegetarian diet help stop cruelty to animals, but it is also good for your health. According to the American Council on Science and Health, vegetarians have longer life expectancy than nonvegetarians and suffer from fewer chronic diseases. The Council summarizes evidence from the scientific literature strongly showing that vegetarians have reduced risk of lung cancer, obesity, constipation, and alcoholism. They also cite good evidence that they have a reduced risk of adult-onset diabetes, high blood pressure, gallstones, or hardening of the arteries. Although the evidence isn't nearly as strong, vegetarianism may also lower the risk of certain cancers, kidney stones, loss of bone density, and tooth decay.

■ *Writer 3, arguing for a skeptical view of vegetarianism:* Here Writer 3 uses portions of the article consciously excluded by Writer 2.

> The link between vegetarianism and death rates is a classic instance of correlation rather than causation. While it is true that vegetarians have a longer life expectancy than nonvegetarians and suffer from fewer chronic diseases, the American Council on Science and Health has shown that the causes can mostly be explained by factors other than diet. As the Council suggests, vegetarians are apt to be more health conscious than nonvegetarians and thus get more exercise, stay slender, and avoid smoking. The Council points out that vegetarians also tend to be wealthier than nonvegetarians and see their doctors more regularly. In short, they live longer because they take better care of themselves, not because they avoid meat.

For Class Discussion

Each of the hypothetical writers uses this short argument in different ways for different purposes. Working individually or in groups, respond to the following questions; be prepared to elaborate on and defend your answers.

1. How does each writer use the original article differently and why?
2. If you were the author of the article from the American Council on Science and Health, would you think that your article was used fairly and responsibly in each instance?
3. Suppose your goal were simply to summarize the argument from the American Council on Science and Health. Write a brief summary of the argument and then explain how your summary is different from the partial summaries used by Writers 2 and 3.

Creating Rhetorically Effective Attributive Tags

In the previous examples we used attributive tags to signal to readers which ideas are the writer's own and which ideas are being taken from another source, in this case the article from the American Council on Science and Health. Attributive tags can also be used rhetorically to shape your reader's response to a source.

Using Attributive Tags to Separate Your Ideas from Your Source's

Attributive tags are phrases such as "according to the American Council on Science and Health . . . ," "Smith claims that . . . ," or "the author continues. . . ." Such phrases signal to the reader that the material immediately following the tag is from the cited source. Sometimes writers indicate a source by citing it in parentheses at the end of the borrowed material—a particularly common practice in the social sciences. The more preferred practice when writing to general audiences is to indicate a source with attributive tags. Parentheses after a quotation or at the end of the borrowed material are then used only to indicate page numbers from a print text. The use of attributive tags is generally clearer and often more rhetorically powerful.

> LESS PREFERRED: INDICATING SOURCE THROUGH PARENTHETICAL CITATION
>
> Vegetarians are apt to be more health conscious than nonvegetarians (American Council on Science and Health).*
>
> MORE PREFERRED: INDICATING SOURCE THROUGH ATTRIBUTIVE TAG
>
> As the American Council on Science and Health has shown, vegetarians are apt to be more health-conscious than nonvegetarians.

Creating Attributive Tags to Shape Reader Response

When you introduce a source for the first time, you can use an attributive tag not only to introduce the source but also to shape your readers' attitude toward the source. For example, if you wanted your reader to respect the expertise of a source, you might say "according to noted chemist Marjorie Casper. . . ." If you wanted your reader to discount Casper's views, you might say "according to Marjorie Casper, an industrial chemist on the payroll of a major corporate polluter . . . ."

When you compose an initial tag, you can add to it any combination of the following kinds of information, depending on your purpose, your audience's values, and your sense of what the audience already knows or doesn't know about the source:

---

*This parenthetical citation is in MLA form. If this had been a print source rather than a Web source, page numbers would also have been given as follows: (American Council on Science and Health 43). APA form also indicates the date of the source: (American Council on Science and Health, 2002). We explain MLA and APA styles for citing and documenting sources later in this chapter.

Add to Attributive Tag	Example
Author's credentials or relevant specialty (enhances credibility)	Civil engineer David Rockwood, a noted authority on stream flow in rivers,
Author's lack of credentials (decreases credibility)	City council member Dilbert Weasel, a local politician with no expertise in international affairs,
Author's political or social views	Left-wing columnist Alexander Cockburn [has negative feeling]; Alexander Cockburn, a longtime champion of labor [has positive feeling],
Title of source if it provides context	In her book *Fasting Girls: The History of Anorexia Nervosa*, Joan Jacobs Brumberg shows that [establishes credentials for comments on eating disorders]
Publisher of source if it adds prestige or otherwise shapes audience response	Dr. Carl Patrona, in an article published in the prestigious *New England Journal of Medicine*,
Historical or cultural information about a source that provides context or background	In his 1960s book popularizing the hippie movement, Charles Reich claims that
Indication of source's purpose or angle of vision	Feminist author Naomi Wolfe, writing a blistering attack on the beauty industry, argues that

Our point here is that you can use attributive tags rhetorically to help your readers understand the significance and context of a source when you first introduce it and to guide your readers' attitudes toward the source.

Working Sources Into Your Own Prose

As a research writer, you need to incorporate sources gracefully into your own prose. One option is simply to draw factual data from a source. More complex options occur when you choose to summarize the whole or part of an argument, paraphrase a portion of an argument, or quote directly from the source. Let's look at these last three options in more detail.

Summarizing

Writing a summary of your source's argument (either of the whole argument or of a relevant section) is an appropriate strategy when the source represents an opposing or alternative view or when it supports or advances one of your own points. Summaries can be as short as a single sentence or as long as a paragraph. (See Chapter 2, pp. 27–30.)

Paraphrasing

Unlike a summary, which is a condensation of a source's whole argument, a paraphrase translates a short passage from a source into the writer's own words. You often paraphrase when you want to use specific information from a brief passage in the source and don't want to interrupt the flow of your own voice with a needless quotation. Of course, you must still acknowledge the source through an attributive tag or parenthetical citation. When you paraphrase, be careful to avoid the original writer's grammatical structure and syntax. If you mirror the original sentence structure while replacing occasional words with synonyms, you are *plagiarizing* rather than paraphrasing. (See pp. 392–393 for an explanation of plagiarism.) Here is an acceptable paraphrase of a short passage from the vegetarian article:

Original

- The evidence is "strong" that vegetarians have (a) a lower risk of becoming alcoholic, constipated, or obese and (b) a lower risk of developing lung cancer.
- The evidence is "good" that vegetarians have a lower risk of developing adult-onset diabetes mellitus, coronary artery disease, hypertension, and gallstones.

Paraphrase

The Council summarizes strong evidence from the scientific literature showing that vegetarians have reduced risk of lung cancer, obesity, constipation, and alcoholism. They also cite good evidence that they have a reduced risk of adult-onset diabetes, high blood pressure, gallstones, or hardening of the arteries.

[Note that to avoid plagiarism the writer has changed the sentence structure substantially. However, the writer still acknowledges the original source with the attributive tag "The Council summarizes."]

Quoting

Occasionally, you will wish to quote an author's words directly. Avoid quoting too much because the effect, from your reader's perspective, is to move from an argument to a sequence of cut-and-pasted quotations. Quote only when doing so strengthens your argument. Here are some occasions when a direct quotation is appropriate:

- When the quotation comes from a respected authority and, in a pithy way, supports one of your points. (Your use of the quotation is like expert testimony in a trial.)
- When you are summarizing an opposing or alternative view and want to use brief quotations to show you have listened carefully and accurately.

- When you want to give readers the flavor of a source's voice, particularly if the language is striking or memorable.
- When you want to analyze the writer's choice of words or metaphors. (You would first quote the passage and then begin your analysis.)

When you quote, you must be meticulous in copying the passage *exactly* including punctuation. When the quoted material takes up more than four lines in your paper, use the block quotation method by indenting the quoted material ten spaces (one inch). When using the block method, do not use quotation marks because the block indentation itself signals a quotation.

When you insert quotations into your own sentences, how you punctuate depends on whether the inserted quotation is a complete sentence or a part of a sentence.

Inserted Quotation When Quotation Is Complete Sentence

Example: According to the American Council on Science and Health, "Many people become vegetarians because they believe, in error, that vegetarianism is uniquely conducive to good health."

Explanation

- Because the quotation is a complete sentence, it starts with a capital letter and is separated from the introductory phrase by a comma.
- If the inserted quotation were taken from a print source, the page number would be indicated in parentheses between the ending quotation mark and the ending punctuation: ". . . conducive to good health" (43).

Inserted Quotation When Quotation Is Not a Complete Sentence

Example: The American Council on Science and Health argues that the cause of vegetarians' longer life may be "nondietary factors." The Council claims that vegetarians are more "health-conscious" than meat eaters and that they "exercise regularly, maintain a desirable body weight, and abstain from smoking."

Explanation

- Because the material quoted is not a complete sentence, it is worked into the grammar of the writer's own sentence.
- No comma introduces the quotation; commas should be used to fit the grammatical structure of the writer's own sentence.
- If the inserted quotation were taken from a print source, the page number would be indicated in parentheses between the ending quotation mark and the period.

Use Brackets to Indicate Changes in a Quotation

Example: The American Council on Science and Health hypothesizes that vegetarians maintain better health by "exercis[ing] regularly, maintain[ing] a desirable body weight, and abstain[ing] from smoking."

Example: According to the American Council on Science and Health, "They [vegetarians] exercise regularly, maintain a desirable body weight, and abstain from smoking."

Explanation

- In the first example, brackets indicate where the grammar of the original passage has been modified to fit the grammar of the writer's own sentence.

- In the second example, the word "vegetarians" has been added inside brackets to explain what "they" refers to.

Use Ellipses to Indicate Omissions from a Quotation

The ellipsis, which consists of three spaced periods, indicates words omitted from the original. When an omission occurs at the end of a sentence, include a fourth period to mark the end of the sentence.

Example: According to the American Council on Science and Health, people who are vegetarians by choice may differ . . . from the general population. For example, in Western countries most vegetarians are more affluent than nonvegetarians. . . .

If you wish to insert a parenthetical citation into the last sentence, insert a space before the first period and place the parentheses in front of the last period, which marks the end of the sentence.

Example: For example, in Western countries most vegetarians are more affluent than nonvegetarians . . . (43).

Use Double and Single Quotation Marks to Indicate a Quotation within a Quotation

Example: According to the American Council on Science and Health, "The evidence is 'strong' that vegetarians have (a) a lower risk of becoming alcoholic, constipated, or obese and (b) a lower risk of developing lung cancer."

Explanation

- The original passage has quotation marks around "strong." To indicate those marks within the quotation, the writer has changed the original double marks to single marks.

Avoiding Plagiarism

Plagiarism, a form of academic cheating, is always a serious academic offense. You can plagiarize in one of two ways: (1) by borrowing another person's ideas without indicating the borrowing with attributive tags in the text and a proper citation or (2) by borrowing another person's language without putting the borrowed language in quotation marks or using a block indentation. The first kind of plagiarism is usually outright cheating; the writer usually knows he is stealing material and tries to disguise it.

The second kind of plagiarism, however, often begins in a hazy never-never land between paraphrasing and copying. We refer to it in our classes as "lazy cheating" and still consider it a serious offense, like stealing from your neighbor's vegetable garden because you are too lazy to do your own planting, weeding, and harvesting. Anyone who appreciates how hard it is to write and revise even a short passage will appreciate why it is wrong to take someone else's language ready-made. Thus, in our classes, we would fail a paper that included the following passage. (Let's call the writer Writer 4.)

> The link between vegetarianism and death rates is a classic instance of correlation rather than causation. While it is true that vegetarians have a longer life expectancy than nonvegetarians and suffer from fewer chronic diseases, the American Council on Science and Health has shown that the health of vegetarians may be better than that of nonvegetarians partly because of nondietary factors. Many vegetarians are very conscious of their health. They exercise regularly, keep a desirable body weight, and abstain from smoking. The Council points out that in Western countries most vegetarians are more affluent than nonvegetarians and thus have better living conditions and more access to medical care. In short, they live longer because they take better care of themselves, not because they avoid meat.

For Class Discussion

Do you think it was fair to flunk Writer 4's essay? He claimed he wasn't cheating because he used attributive tags to indicate his source throughout this passage, and he listed the American Council on Science and Health article accurately in his "Works Cited" list (bibliography) at the end of his paper. Before answering, compare Writer 4's passage with the original article on pages 384–385; also compare the passage with Writer 3's passage on page 386. What justification is there for giving a high grade to Writer 3 and a failing grade to Writer 4?

The best way to avoid plagiarism is to be especially careful at the note-taking stage. If you copy from your source, copy exactly, word for word, and put quotation marks around the copied material or otherwise indicate that it is not your own wording. If you paraphrase or summarize material, be sure that you don't borrow any of the original wording. Also be sure to change the grammatical structure of the original. Lazy note taking, in which you follow the arrangement and grammatical structure of the original passage and merely substitute occasional synonyms, leads directly to plagiarism.

Also remember that you cannot borrow another writer's ideas without citing them. If you summarize or paraphrase another writer's thinking about a subject, you should indicate in your notes that the ideas are not your own and be sure to record all the information you need for a citation. If you do exploratory reflection to accompany your notes, then the distinction between other writers' ideas and your own should be easy to recognize when it's time to incorporate the source material into your paper.

Understanding Parenthetical Citation Systems with Bibliographies

Not too many years ago, most academic disciplines used footnotes or endnotes to document sources. Today, however, both the MLA (Modern Language Association) system, used primarily in the humanities, and the APA (American Psychological Association) system, used primarily in the social sciences, use parenthetical citations instead of footnotes or endnotes.* Before we examine the details of MLA and APA styles, we want to explain the logic of parenthetical citation systems with concluding bibliographies.

In both the MLA and APA systems, the writer places a complete bibliography at the end of the paper. In the MLA system this bibliography is called "Works Cited." In the APA system it is called "References." The bibliography is arranged alphabetically by author or by title (if an author is not named). The key to the system's logic is this:

- Every source in the bibliography must be mentioned in the body of the paper.
- Conversely, every source mentioned in the body of the paper must be listed in the bibliography.
- There must be a one-to-one correspondence between the first word in each bibliographic entry (usually, but not always, an author's last name) and the name used to identify the source in the body of the paper.

Suppose a reader sees this phrase in your paper: "According to Debra Goldstein." The reader should be able to turn to your bibliography and find an alphabetized entry beginning with "Goldstein, Debra." Similarly, suppose that in looking over your

---

*Our discussion of MLA style is based on Joseph Gibaldi, *MLA Handbook for Writers of Research Papers,* 6th ed. (New York: Modern Language Association of America, 2003). Our discussion of APA style is based on the *Publication Manual of the American Psychological Association,* 5th ed. (Washington, DC: American Psychological Association, 2001).

bibliography, your reader sees an article by "Guillen, Manuel." This means that the name "Guillen" has to occur in your paper in one of two ways:

- As an attributive tag: "Economics professor Manuel Guillen argues that. . . ."
- As a parenthetical citation, often following a quotation: ". . . changes in fiscal policy" (Guillen 43).

Understanding MLA Style

From this point on, we separate our discussions of the MLA and APA systems. We begin with the MLA system because it is the one most commonly used in writing courses. We then explain the APA system.

The MLA Method of In-Text Citation

To cite sources in your text using the MLA system, place the author's last name and the page reference in parentheses immediately after the material being cited. If an attributive tag already identifies the author, give only the page number in parentheses. Once you have cited the author and it is clear that the same author's material is being used, you need cite only the page references in parentheses. The following examples show parenthetical documentation with and without an attributive tag. Note that the citation precedes the period. If you are citing a quotation, the parenthetical citation follows the quotation mark but precedes the final period.

> The Spanish tried to reduce the status of Filipina women who had been able to do business, get divorced, and sometimes become village chiefs (Karnow 41).
>
> According to Karnow, the Spanish tried to reduce the status of Filipina women who had been able to do business, get divorced, and sometimes become village chiefs (41).
>
> "And, to this day," Karnow continues, "women play a decisive role in Filipino families" (41).

A reader who wishes to look up the source will find the bibliographic information in the Works Cited section by looking for the entry under "Karnow." If more than one work by Karnow was used in the paper, the writer would include in the in-text citation an abbreviated title of the book or article following Karnow's name.

> (Karnow, "In Our Image" 41)

Special Case 1: Citing from an Indirect Source   Occasionally you may wish to use a quotation that you have seen cited in one of your sources. You read Jones, who has a nice quotation from Smith, and you want to use Smith's quotation. What do you do? Whenever possible, find the quotation in its original source and cite that source. But if the original source is not available, cite the source indirectly by using the terms "qtd. in"; and list only the indirect source in your "Works Cited" list. In the following example, the writer wishes to quote a Buddhist monk, Thich Nhat Hanh, who has written a book entitled *Living Buddha, Living Christ.* However, the writer is unable to locate the actual book and instead has to quote from a review of the book by newspaper critic Lee Moriwaki. Here is how he would make the in-text citation:

> A Buddhist monk, Thich Nhat Hanh, stresses the importance of inner peace: "If we can learn ways to touch the peace, joy, and happiness that are already there, we will become healthy and strong, and a resource for others" (qtd. in Moriwaki C4).

The "Works Cited" list will have an entry for "Moriwaki" but not for "Thich Nhat Hanh."

Special Case 2: Citing Page Numbers for Downloaded Material   There is no satisfactory solution to the problem of citing page numbers for sources retrieved electronically from a database or the Web. Because different computers and printers will format the same source in different ways, the page numbers on a printout won't be consistent from user to user. Sometimes, a down-loaded article will indicate page numbers from the original print source, in which case you can cite page numbers in the ordinary way. At other times down-loaded material will have numbered paragraphs, in which case you can cite the paragraph number (preceded by *par.*) or numbers (preceded by *pars.*): (Jones, pars. 22–24). Most typically, however, downloaded sources will indicate neither page nor paragraph numbers. In such cases, MLA says to omit page references from the parenthetical citation. They assume that researchers can locate the source on a computer and then use a search engine to find a specific quotation or passage.

MLA Format for the "Works Cited" List

In the MLA system, you place a complete bibliography, titled "Works Cited," at the end of the paper. The list includes all the sources that you mention in your paper. However, it does not include works you read but did not use. Entries in the Works Cited list are arranged alphabetically by author, or by title if there is no author.

If you have more than one entry by the same author, begin the second and subsequent entries by typing three hyphens followed by a period rather than the author's name. Begin the list on a new sheet of paper with the words "Works Cited" centered one inch from the top of the page. Entries should use a "hanging indentation" so that the first line is flush with the left margin and succeeding lines indented one-half inch or five spaces. For an example of how to format a "Works Cited" page in MLA style, see the last page of Mark Bonicillo's researched argument (p. 350).

The remaining pages in this section show examples of MLA formats for different kinds of sources. We begin with a "Quick Reference Guide" for the most common citations. We then explain these citations in more depth and give the most frequently encountered variations and source types.

MLA Quick Reference Guide for the Most Common Citations

Table 17.1 provides MLA models for the most common kinds of citations. This table will help you distinguish the forest from the trees when you try to cite sources. All

TABLE 17.1   *Quick reference guide for MLA citations*

Kind of Source	Basic Citation Model	Index for Variations
Print Sources When You Have Used the Original Print Version		
Book	Tannen, Deborah. <u>The Argument Culture: Moving From Debate to Dialogue</u>. New York: Random, 1998.	One author, 398 Two or more authors, 398 Second, later, or revised edition, 398 Republished book, 398 Multivolume work, 398 Articles in reference works, 398 Translation, 399 Corporate author, 399 Anonymous author, 399
Article in anthology with an editor	Shamoon, Linda. "International E-mail Debate." <u>Electronic Communication Across the Curriculum</u>. Ed. Donna Reiss, Dickie Self, and Art Young. Urbana: NCTE, 1998. 151–61.	Citing the editor, 399 Citing an individual article, 399
Article in scholarly journal	Pollay, Richard W., Jung S. Lee, and David Carter-Whitney. "Separate, but Not Equal: Racial Segmentation in Cigarette Advertising." <u>Journal of Advertising</u> 21.1 (1992): 45–57.	Scholarly journal that numbers pages continuously, 400 Scholarly journal that restarts page numbering with each issue, 400
Article in magazine or newspaper	Beam, Alex. "The Mad Poets Society." <u>Atlantic Monthly</u> July–Aug. 2001: 96–103. Lemonick, Michael D. "Teens Before Their Time." <u>Time</u> 30 Oct. 2000: 66–74.	Magazine article with named author, 400 Anonymous magazine article, 400 Review of book, film, or performance, 400
	Cauvin, Henri E. "Political Climate Complicates Food Shortage in Zimbabwe." <u>New York Times</u> 18 July 2001, natl. ed.: A13.	Newspaper article, 401 Newspaper editorial, 401 Letter to the editor, 401
Print Sources That You Have Downloaded from a Database or the Web		
Article downloaded from database	Barr, Bob. "Liberal Media Adored Gun-Control Marchers." <u>Insight on the News</u> 5 June 2000: 44. <u>Research Library Complete</u>. ProQuest. Lemieux Lib., Seattle U. 15 Aug. 2001 <http://proquest.umi.com>.	Print article downloaded from licensed database, 401
Article downloaded from Web	Goodman, Ellen. "The Big Hole in Health Debate." <u>Boston Globe</u> 24 June 2001: D7. <u>Boston Globe Online</u> 18 July 2001 <http://www.boston.com/dailyglobe2/175/oped/The_big_hole_in_health_debate+.shtml>.	Article or book available online or from an information service, 401 Print article downloaded from Web, 402

(continued)

Kind of Source	Basic Citation Model	Index for Variations
Web Sources That Haven't Appeared in Print		
Home page (use for citing an entire Web site)	Menstuff: The National Men's Resource. 2003. National Men's Resource Center. 12 Mar. 2003 <http://www.menstuff.org/frameindex.html>.	Whole Web site, 402
Authored document within a Web site	Tobin, Sally. "Getting the Word Out on the Human Genome Project: A Course for Physicians." Stanford University Center for Biomedical Ethics 2000. 18 July 2001 <http://scbe.stanford.edu/research/current_programs.html#genomics>.	Authored document within a Web site, 402 Document without identified author within a Web site, 403
Anonymous document within a Web site	"Ouch! Body Piercing." Menstuff: The National Men's Resource. 1 Feb. 2001. National Men's Resource Center. 17 July 2001 <http://www.menstuff.org/issues/byissue/tattoo.html>.	Article from a scholarly e-journal, 403
Other		E-book, 403 Online reference database, 403 E-mail, 403 Bulletin board or newsgroup postings, 403
Miscellaneous Sources		
Interview	Van der Peet, Rob. Personal interview. 24 June 2001.	Interview, 404
Lecture, address, or speech	Jancoski, Loretta. "I Believe in God, and She's a Salmon." University Congregational United Church of Christ, Seattle. 30 Oct. 2001.	Lecture, speech, conference presentation, 404
Other		Television or radio program, 404 Film, 404 Sound recording, 404 Cartoon or advertisement, 404 Government publications, 404

the major categories of sources are displayed on this table. For further explanation of these citations, along with instructions on citing variations and sources not listed in the Quick Reference Guide, see the page indicated in the third column.

MLA Citations

Books

General Format for Books

Author. <u>Title</u>. City of Publication: Publisher, year of publication.

One Author

Brumberg, Joan J. <u>The Body Project: An Intimate History of American Girls</u>. New York: Vintage, 1997.

Two or More Authors

Dombrowski, Daniel A., and Robert J. Deltete. <u>A Brief, Liberal, Catholic Defense of Abortion</u>. Urbana: U of Illinois P, 2000.

Belenky, Mary, et al. <u>Women's Ways of Knowing: The Development of Self, Voice, and Mind</u>. New York: Basic, 1986.

If there are four or more authors, you have the choice of listing all the authors in the order in which they appear on the title page or using "et al." (meaning "and others") to replace all but the first author.

Second, Later, or Revised Edition

Montagu, Ashley. <u>Touching: The Human Significance of the Skin</u>. 3rd ed. New York: Perennial, 1986.

Republished Book (For Example, a Paperback Published after the Original Hardback Edition or a Modern Edition of an Older Work)

Hill, Christopher. <u>The World Turned Upside Down: Radical Ideas During the English Revolution</u>. 1972. London: Penguin, 1991.

Wollstonecraft, Mary. <u>The Vindication of the Rights of Woman, with Strictures on Political and Moral Subjects</u>. 1792. Rutland: Tuttle, 1995.

Multivolume Work

Churchill, Winston S. <u>A History of the English-Speaking Peoples</u>. 4 vols. New York: Dodd, 1956–58.

Churchill, Winston S. <u>The Great Democracies</u>. New York: Dodd, 1957. Vol. 4 of <u>A History of the English-Speaking Peoples</u>. 4 vols. 1956–58.

Use the first method when you cite the whole work; use the second method when you cite one specific volume of the work.

Article in Familiar Reference Work

"Mau Mau." <u>The New Encyclopedia Britannica</u>. 15th ed. 2002.

Article in Less Familiar Reference Work

Ling, Trevor O. "Buddhism in Burma." <u>Dictionary of Comparative Religion</u>. Ed. S. G. F. Brandon. New York: Scribner's, 1970.

Translation

De Beauvoir, Simone. <u>The Second Sex</u>. Trans. H. M. Parshley. New York: Bantam,
    1961.

Corporate Author (a Commission, Committee, or Other Group)

American Red Cross. <u>Standard First Aid</u>. St. Louis: Mosby Lifeline, 1993.

Anonymous Author

<u>The New Yorker Cartoon Album: 1975–1985</u>. New York: Penguin, 1987.
    [Alphabetize under "n."]

Edited Anthologies

Citing the Editor

O'Connell, David F., and Charles N. Alexander, ed. <u>Self Recovery: Treating
    Addictions Using Transcendental Meditation and Maharishi Ayur-Veda</u>. New
    York: Haworth, 1994.

Citing an Individual Article

Royer, Ann. "The Role of the Transcendental Meditation Technique in Promoting
    Smoking Cessation: A Longitudinal Study." <u>Self Recovery: Treating Addictions
    Using Transcendental Meditation and Maharishi Ayur-Veda</u>. Ed. David F.
    O'Connell and Charles N. Alexander. New York: Haworth, 1994. 221–39.

In these examples, O'Connell and Alexander are the editors of the anthology. Ann
Royer is the author of the article on smoking cessation. When you cite an individual article, the inclusive page numbers for the article come at the end of the citation.

Articles in Scholarly Journals Accessed in Print

When citing scholarly journals, you need to determine how the journal numbers
its pages. Typically, separate issues of a journal are published four times per year.
The library then binds the four separate issues into one "annual volume." Some
journals restart the page numbering with each issue, which means that during
the year there would be four instances of, say, page 31. Other journals number the
pages consecutively throughout the year. In such a case, the fall issue might begin
with page 253 rather than page 1. When pages are numbered sequentially
throughout the year, you need to include only the volume number in the volume
slot (for example, "25"). When page numbering starts over with each issue, you
need to include in the volume slot both the volume and the issue number, separated by a period (for example, "25.3").

General Format for Scholarly Journals

Author. "Article Title." <u>Journal Title</u> volume number.issue number (year): page
  numbers.

Scholarly Journal That Numbers Pages Continuously

Barton, Ellen L. "Evidentials, Argumentation, and Epistemological Stance." <u>College
  English</u> 55 (1993): 745–69.

Scholarly Journal That Restarts Page Numbering with Each Issue

Pollay, Richard W., Jung S. Lee, and David Carter-Whitney. "Separate, but Not
  Equal: Racial Segmentation in Cigarette Advertising." <u>Journal of
  Advertising</u> 21.1 (1992): 45–57.

Articles in Magazines and Newspapers Accessed in Print

Magazine and newspaper articles are easy to cite. If no author is identified, begin
the entry with the title or headline. Distinguish between news stories and editorials by putting the word "Editorial" after the title. If a magazine comes out weekly
or biweekly, include the complete date (27 Sept. 1998). If it comes out monthly,
then state the month only (Sept. 1998).

General Format for Magazines and Newspapers

Author. "Article Title." <u>Magazine Title</u> [day] Month year: page numbers.

Note: If the article continues in another part of the magazine or newspaper,
add "+" to indicate the nonsequential pages.

Magazine Article with Named Author

Snyder, Rachel L. "A Daughter of Cambodia Remembers: Loung Ung's Journey."
  <u>Ms</u> Aug.–Sept. 2001: 62–67.
Hall, Stephen S. "Prescription for Profit." <u>New York Times Magazine</u> 11 Mar. 2001:
  40–45+.

Anonymous Magazine Article

"Daddy, Daddy." <u>New Republic</u> 30 July 2001: 2–13.

Review of Book, Film, or Performance

Schwarz, Benjamin. "A Bit of Bunting: A New History of the British Empire
  Elevates Expediency to Principle." Rev. of <u>Ornamentalism: How the British Saw
  Their Empire</u>, by David Cannadine. <u>Atlantic Monthly</u> Nov. 2001: 126–35.

Kaufman, Stanley. "Polishing a Gem." Rev. of <u>The Blue Angel</u>, dir. Josef von
    Sternberg. <u>New Republic</u> 30 July 2001: 28–29.

Lahr, John. "Nobody's Darling: Fascism and the Drama of Human Connection in
    Ashes to Ashes." Rev. of <u>Ashes to Ashes</u>, by Harold Pinter. The Roundabout
    Theater Co. Gramercy Theater, New York. <u>New Yorker</u> 22 Feb. 1999: 182–83.

Newspaper Article

Henriques, Diana B. "Hero's Fall Teaches Wall Street a Lesson." <u>Seattle Times</u>
    27 Sept. 1998: A1+.

Newspaper Editorial

"Dr. Frankenstein on the Hill." Editorial. <u>New York Times</u> 18 May 2002, natl. ed.:A22.

Letter to the Editor of a Magazine or Newspaper

Tomsovic, Kevin. Letter. <u>New Yorker</u> 13 July 1998: 7.

Print Articles or Books Downloaded from a Database or the Web

Citations in this category begin with complete print information, followed by the
electronic information.

Print Article Downloaded from Licensed Database

Portner, Jessica. "Girl's Slaying Elicits Calls for Metal Detectors." <u>Education Week</u>
    14 Mar. 2000: 3. <u>Academic Search Elite</u>. EBSCO Publishing. Lemieux Lib.,
    Seattle U. 17 July 2001 <http://www.epnet.com/>.

Begin with the original print information; then cite the database used (underlined),
the name of the database company if different, the name and location of the library
leasing the service, your date of access, and the URL home page of the service.

Article or Book Available Online or on Microfiche from an Information Service

These services, such as ERIC (Educational Resources Information Center) or NTIS
(National Technical Information Service), provide material to your library on
microfiche or online with indexes on CD-ROM or online. Much of the material
from these services has not been published in major journals or magazines.

Eddy, P. A. <u>The Effects of Foreign Language Study in High School on Verbal Ability</u>
    <u>as Measured by the Scholastic Aptitude Test—Verbal</u>. Washington: Center for
    Applied Linguistics, 1981. ERIC ED 196 312.

The ERIC code at the end tells researchers that this work is available on
microfiche.

Print Article Downloaded from Web

Kane, Joe. "Arrested Development." <u>Outside Online</u> May 2001: 5 pp. 17 Nov. 2001

    <http://www.outsidemag.com/magazine/200105/200105molokai1.html>.

If the online magazine indicates the page numbers of the original print source, cite them after the date of publication; if not, indicate the number of pages in the on-line version followed by "pp."

Web Sources and Other Internet Sources

Although the Web is a rapidly evolving and often unstable medium, the principle that governs electronic citations is the same as that for print sources: Give enough information so that the reader can find the source you used. Also give the date you accessed the source, since Web sites are frequently updated, altered, or dropped.

General Format for a Web Source

Author of Document. "Title of Document." <u>Title of Web Site</u>. Date of document or

    last update of Web site. Length of document, if known. Name of institution or

    organization sponsoring the site if not already stated. Date you accessed the

    site <URL of the specific document enclosed in angle brackets>.

Rice, Condoleezza. "Press Briefing." <u>White House</u>. 24 Feb. 2003. 14 Mar. 2003

    <http://www.whitehouse.gov/news/releases/2003/02/20030224-14.html>.

[In this example the sponsoring organization (the White House) is already stated in the Web site title and so can be omitted. Also, the Web site doesn't state the length of the document, so that information is omitted.]

Three Ways to Show Web Location

In MLA style, the preferred way to show Web location is to copy exactly the source's URL. Sometimes, however, the URL is so long that readers would have difficulty keyboarding it accurately into their own computers. An alternative is to describe the path of mouse clicks from a specified homepage to the desired source. For example, the Sierra Club Web site contains a press release by Annie Strickler entitled "Refuge Centennial: Much to Celebrate, Much Left to Protect." Its URL is unwieldy: http://lists.sierraclub.org/SCRIPTS/WA.EXE?A2= ind0303&L=ce-scnews-releases&D=1&T=O&H=1&0=D&F=&S=&P=1204. Instead of the URL, you could specify the "path" as follows:

    <http://www.sierraclub.org>. Path: My Backyard; Wyoming; Refuge Centennial

    Fri. 14 Mar. 2003.

[**Explanation:** From the homepage of sierraclub.org, click on "My Backyard"; then click on "Wyoming"; then click on "Refuge Centennial Fri. 14 Mar. 2003"]

A second alternative is to provide the URL for a search box.

> <http://www.sierraclub.org/chaptersearch.asp>.

[Explanation: Go to this Web site and in the search box type in "Annie Stickler" (the author) or "Refuge Centennial" (key words from title).]

Whole Web Site

MyNRA. 2003. National Rifle Association. 14 Mar. 2003

> <http://www.mynra.org>.

Authored Document within a Web Site

Lithwick, Dahlia. "Creche Test Dummies: Nativity Scenes on Public Lands Are

> Illegal, Rules the Supreme Court. Except When They're Not." Slate 21 Dec.
>
> 2001. 22 Dec. 2001 <http://slate.msn.com/?id=2060070>.

In this case, the first date indicates when the article was posted on the Web. The second date indicates the researcher's date of accessing the article.

Document without an Identified Author within a Web Site

"Palestine Liberation Front (PLF)." International Policy Institute for Counter-

> Terrorism. 13 Mar. 2003. The Interdisciplinary Center, Herzliya, Israel. 14 Mar.
>
> 2003 <http://www.ict.org.il/inter_ter/orgdet.cfm?orgid=29>.

Article from a Scholarly E-journal

Welch, John R., and Ramon Riley. "Reclaiming Land and Spirit in the Western Apache

> Homeland." American Indian Quarterly 25 (2001): 5–14. 19 Dec. 2001
>
> <http://muse.jhu.edu/journals/american_indian_quarterly/v025/25.
>
> 1welch.pdf>.

E-book

Austen, Jane. Lady Susan. 1871. Ed. Henry Churchyard. Jane Austen Information

> Page. 15 Mar. 2003 <http://www.pemberley.com/janeinfo/ladysusn.html>.

Article in Online Reference Database

"Cosmology." Columbia Encyclopedia. 6th ed. 2002. Bartleby.com: Great Books

> Online. 15 Mar. 2003 <http://bartleby.com/65/co/cosmolog.html>.

E-mail

Daffinrud, Sue. "Scoring Guide for Class Participation." E-mail to the author. 12 Dec.

> 2001.

Bulletin Board or Newsgroup Postings

Dermody, Tony. "Re: Can We Have It All or Was It a Lie?" Online posting. 19 Dec.
     2001. Google newsgroup soc.feminism. 22 Dec. 2001 <http://groups.
     google.com/groups?hl=en&selm=n7os1us9ue4k8th1vtvlbepgtbun2booqk
     %404ax.com>.

For a bulletin board, newsgroup, or chat room posting, follow this format: Author
name. "Title of Posting." Online posting. Date of posting. Name of forum. Date of
access <URL>.

Miscellaneous Sources

Television or Radio Program

"Lie Like a Rug." <u>NYPD Blue</u>. Dir. Steven Bochco and David Milch. ABC. KOMO,
     Seattle. 6 Nov. 2001.

Film

<u>Shakespeare in Love</u>. Dir. John Madden. Perf. Joseph Fiennes and Gwyneth
     Paltrow. Screenplay by Marc Norman and Tom Stoppard. Universal Miramax,
     1998.

Sound Recording

Dylan, Bob. "Rainy Day Woman." <u>Bob Dylan MTV Unplugged</u>. Columbia, 1995.

For sound recordings begin the entry with what your paper emphasizes—for example, the artist's name, composer's name, or conductor's name—and adjust the
elements accordingly.

Cartoon, Comic Strip, or Advertisement

Trudeau, Garry. "Doonesbury." Comic strip. <u>Seattle Times</u> 19 Nov. 2001: B4.
Banana Republic. Advertisement. <u>Details</u> Oct. 2001: 37.

Interview

Castellucci, Marion. Personal interview. 7 Oct. 2001.

Lecture, Speech, or Conference Presentation

Sharples, Mike. "Authors of the Future." Conference of European Teachers of
     Academic Writing. U of Groningen. Groningen, Neth. 20 June 2001.

Government Publications   Government publications are often difficult to cite
because there are so many varieties. In general, follow these guidelines:

- Usually cite as author the government agency that produced the document. Begin with the highest level and then branch down to the specific agency:

  United States. Dept. of Justice. FBI
  Idaho. Dept. of Motor Vehicles

- Follow this with the title of the document, underlined.
- If a specific person is clearly identified as the author, you may begin the citation with that person's name, or you may list the author (preceded by the word "By") after the title of the document.
- Follow standard procedures for citing publication information for print sources or retrieval information for Web sources.

United States. Dept. of Justice. FBI. <u>The School Shooter: A Threat Assessment</u>

    <u>Perspective</u>. By Mary O'Toole. 2000. 16 Aug. 2001 <http://www.fbi.gov/

    publications/school/school2.pdf>.

Formatting an Academic Paper in MLA Style

An example research paper in MLA style is shown on pages 344–350. Here are the distinctive formatting features of MLA papers.

- Double-space throughout including block quotations and the Works Cited list.
- Use one-inch margins top and bottom, left and right. Indent one-half inch or five spaces from the left margin at the beginning of each paragraph.
- Number pages consecutively throughout the manuscript including the Works Cited list, which begins on a new page. Page numbers go in the upper right-hand corner, flush with the right margin, and one-half inch from the top of the page. The page number should be preceded by your last name. The text begins one inch from the top of the page.
- Do *not* create a separate title page. Type your name, professor's name, course number, and date in the upper left-hand corner of your paper (all double-spaced), beginning one inch from the top of the page; then double-space and type your title, centered, without underlines or any distinctive fonts (capitalize the first word and important words only); then double-space and begin your text.
- Start a new page for the Works Cited list. Type "Works Cited" centered, one inch from the top of the page in the same font as the rest of the paper; do not enclose it in quotation marks. Use hanging indentation for each entry longer than one line, of five spaces or one-half inch, formatted according to the example on page 350.

Student Example of an MLA-Style Research Paper

As an illustration of a student research paper written in MLA style, see Mark Bonicillo's proposal argument on pages 344–350.

Understanding APA Style

In many respects, the APA style and the MLA style are similar and the basic logic is the same. However, the APA style has a few distinguishing features:

- APA style emphasizes dates of books and articles and de-emphasizes the names of authors. Therefore the date of publication appears in parenthetical citations and is the second item mentioned in each entry in the "References" list (the name of the bibliography at the end of a paper).

- Only published or retrievable documents are included in the "References" list. Personal correspondence, e-mail messages, interviews, and lectures or speeches are referenced in text citations only.

- APA style uses fewer abbreviations and spells out the complete names of university presses. It uses an ampersand (&) instead of the word *and* for items in a series in the reference list and in text citations.

- APA style uses italics rather than underlines for titles and capitalizes only the first word of titles and subtitles of books and articles. It doesn't place titles of articles in quotation marks.

- APA style uses only an initial for authors' or editors' first names in the "References" citations.

- APA style has a distinctive format for title pages and frequently includes an "abstract" of the paper immediately following the title page.

- Page numbers are placed at the top right-hand margin and are preceded by a "running head" (a short version of the title).

- APA uses block indentation for quotations when they are longer than forty words. Quotations shorter than forty words are worked into your own text using quotation marks as in the MLA system.

APA Method of In-Text Citation

To cite sources in the APA system, you follow procedures very similar to those in the MLA system. When you make an in-text citation in APA style, you place inside the parentheses the author's last name and the year of the source as well as the page number if a particular passage or table is cited. The elements in the citation are separated by commas and a "p." or "pp." precedes the page number(s). If a source has more than one author, use an ampersand (&) to join their names. When the author is mentioned in an attributive tag, you include only the date (and page if applicable). The following examples show parenthetical documentation with and without attributive tags according to APA style.

> The Spanish tried to reduce the status of women who had been able to do business, get divorced, and sometimes become village chiefs (Karnow, 1989, p. 41).

According to Karnow (1989, p. 41), the Spanish tried to reduce the status of women who had been able to do business, get divorced, and sometimes become village chiefs.

Just as with MLA style, readers of APA style look for sources in the list of references at the end of the paper if they wish to find full bibliographic information. In the APA system, this bibliographic list is titled "References" and includes only the sources cited in the body of the paper. If your sources include two works by the same author published in the same year, place an "a" after the date for the first work and a "b" after the date for the second, ordering the works alphabetically by title in the References list. If Karnow had published two different works in 1989, your in-text citation would look like this:

(Karnow, 1989a, p. 41)

or

(Karnow, 1989b, p. 41)

APA style also makes provisions for quoting or using data from an indirect source. Use the same procedures as for MLA style (see the example on pp. 394–395), but in your parenthetical citation use "as cited in" rather than the MLA's "qtd. in." Here is the APA equivalent of the example on page 395:

A Buddhist monk, Thich Nhat Hanh, stresses the importance of inner peace: "If we can learn ways to touch the peace, joy, and happiness that are already there, we will become healthy and strong, and a resource for others" (as cited in Moriwaki, 1995, p. C4).

APA Format for the "References" List

Like the MLA system, the APA system includes a complete bibliography, called "References," at the end of the paper. Entries are listed alphabetically, with a similar kind of hanging indentation to that used in MLA style. If you list more than one item for an author, repeat the author's name each time and arrange the items in chronological order beginning with the earliest. If two works appeared in the same year, arrange them alphabetically, adding an "a" and a "b" after the year for purposes of in-text citation. Here is a hypothetical illustration:

Smith, R. (1995). *Body image in Western cultures, 1750–present.* London: Bonanza Press.

Smith, R. (1999a). *Body image in non-Western cultures.* London: Bonanza Press.

Smith, R. (1999b). Eating disorders reconsidered. *Journal of Appetite Studies, 45,* 295–300.

APA Quick Reference Guide for the Most Common Citations

Table 17.2 provides examples in APA style for the most common kinds of citations to be placed in a "References" list at the end of the paper. It also provides, in the third column, an index to other kinds of APA citations explained in the text.

TABLE 17.2   *Quick reference guide for APA citations*

Kind of Source	Basic Citation Model	Index for Variations
Print Sources When You Have Used the Original Print Version		
Book	Tannen, D. (1998). *The argument culture: Moving from debate to dialogue.* New York: Random House.	One author, 409 Two or more authors, 410 Second, later, or revised edition, 410 Republished book, 410 Multivolume work, 410 Article in reference work, 410 Translation, 411 Corporate author, 411 Anonymous author, 411
Article in anthology with an editor	Shamoon, L. (1998). International e-mail debate. In D. Reiss, D. Self, & A. Young (Eds.), *Electronic communication across the curriculum* (pp. 151–161). Urbana, IL: National Council of Teachers of English.	Citing the editor, 411 Citing an individual article, 411
Article in scholarly journal	Pollay, R. W., Lee, J. S., & Carter-Whitney, D. (1992). Separate, but not equal: Racial segmentation in cigarette advertising. *Journal of Advertising, 21* (1), 45–57.	Scholarly journal that numbers pages continuously, 411 Scholarly journal that restarts page numbering with each issue, 412
Article in magazine or newspaper	Beam, A. (2001, July–August). The mad poets society. *Atlantic Monthly, 288,* 96–103. Lemonick, M. D. (2000, October 30). Teens before their time. *Time, 156,* 66–74. Cauvin, H. E. (2001, July 18). Political climate complicates food shortage in Zimbabwe. *The New York Times,* p. A13.	Magazine article with named author, 412 Anonymous magazine article, 412 Review of book or film, 412 Newspaper article, 412 Newspaper editorial, 412 Letter to the editor, 412
Print Sources That You Have Downloaded from a Database or the Web		
Article downloaded from database	Barr, B. (2000, June 5). Liberal media adored gun-control marchers. *Insight on the News,* 44. Retrieved August 15, 2001, from ProQuest database.	Print article downloaded from licensed database, 413
Article downloaded from Web	Goodman, E. (2001, June 24). The big hole in health debate. *Boston Globe Online,* p. D7. Retrieved July 18, 2001, from http://www.boston.com/dailyglobe2/175/oped/The_big_hole_in_health_debate+.shtml	Article or book available online or from an information service, 413 Print article downloaded from the Web, 413

(continued)

Kind of Source	Basic Citation Model	Index for Variations
Web Sources That Haven't Appeared in Print		
Authored document within a Web site	Tobin, S. (2000). Getting the word out on the human genome project: A course for physicians. Retrieved July 18, 2001, from Stanford University, Center for Biomedical Ethics Web site: http://scbe.stanford.edu/research/current_programs. html#genomics	Authored document within a Web site, 413 Document without an identified author within a Web site, 413
Document with corporate or unnamed author within a Web site	National Men's Resource Center. (2001, February 1). *Ouch! Body piercing.* Retrieved July 17, 2001, from http://www.menstuff.org/issues/byissue/tattoo.html	Article from scholarly e-journal, 413
Other		E-book, 414 Online reference database, 414 Bulletin board or newsgroup posting, 414
Miscellaneous Sources		
Interview, personal communication	Van der Peet (personal communication, June 24, 2001) stated that. . . [In-text citation only; not included in References]	E-mail, interviews, and personal correspondence 414
Lecture, address, or speech	According to Jancoski (speech to University Congregational United Church of Christ, Seattle, October 30, 2001), salmon . . . [In-text citation only; not included in References; further details about speech can be included in text]	Unpublished paper presented at a meeting, 415
Other		Television program, 414 Film, 414 Sound recording, 414 Government publications, 415

APA Citations

Books

One Author

Brumberg, J. J. (1997). *The body project: An intimate history of American girls.* New York: Vintage.

Two or More Authors

Dombrowski, D. A., & Deltete, R. J. (2000). *A brief, liberal, Catholic defense of abortion.* Urbana: University of Illinois Press.

Belenky, M., Clinchy, B. M., Goldberger, N. R., & Tarule, J. M. (1986). *Women's ways of knowing: The development of self, voice, and mind.* New York: Basic Books.

APA style uses "et al." only for books with more than six authors.

Second, Later, or Revised Edition

Montagu, A. (1986). *Touching: The human significance of the skin* (3rd ed.). New York: Perennial Press.

Republished Book (For Example, a Paperback Published after the Original Hardback Edition or a Modern Edition of an Older Work)

Hill, C. (1991). *The world turned upside down: Radical ideas during the English revolution.* London: Penguin. (Original work published 1972)

The in-text citation should read: (Hill, 1972/1991).

Wollstonecraft, M. (1995). *The vindication of the rights of woman, with strictures on political and moral subjects.* Rutland, VT: Tuttle. (Original work published 1792)

The in-text citation should read: (Wollstonecraft, 1792/1995).

Multivolume Work

Churchill, W. S. (1956–1958). *A history of the English-speaking peoples* (Vols. 1–4). New York: Dodd, Mead.

Citation for all the volumes together. The in-text citation should read: (Churchill, 1956–1958).

Churchill, W. S. (1957). *A history of the English-speaking peoples: Vol. 4. The great democracies.* New York: Dodd, Mead.

Citation for a specific volume. The in-text citation should read: (Churchill, 1957).

Article in Reference Work

Ling, T. O. (1970). Buddhism in Burma. In S. G. F. Brandon (Ed.), *Dictionary of comparative religion.* New York: Scribner's.

Translation

De Beauvoir, S. (1961). *The second sex* (H. M. Parshley, Trans.). New York: Bantam
     Books. (Original work published 1949)

The in-text citation should read: (De Beauvoir, 1949/1961).

Corporate Author (a Commission, Committee, or Other Group)

American Red Cross. (1993). *Standard first aid.* St. Louis, MO: Mosby Lifeline.

Anonymous Author

The New Yorker cartoon album: 1975–1985. (1987). New York: Penguin Books.

The in-text citation should be a shortened version of the title as follows: (*New
Yorker cartoon album,* 1987).

Edited Anthologies

Citing the Editor

O'Connell, D. F., & Alexander, C. N. (Eds.). (1994). *Self recovery: Treating addictions
     using transcendental meditation and Maharishi Ayur-Veda.* New York: Haworth
     Press.

Citing an Individual Article

Royer, A. (1994). The role of the transcendental meditation technique in promoting
     smoking cessation: A longitudinal study. In D. F. O'Connell & C. N. Alexander
     (Eds.), *Self recovery: Treating addictions using transcendental meditation and
     Maharishi Ayur-Veda* (pp. 221–239). New York: Haworth Press.

The pattern is as follows: Author of article. (Year of publication). Title of article. In
Name of editor (Ed.), *Title of anthology* (pp. inclusive page numbers of article).
Place of publication: Name of press.

Articles in Scholarly Journals Accessed in Print

Scholarly Journal That Numbers Pages Continuously

Barton, E. L. (1993). Evidentials, argumentation, and epistemological stance.
     College English, 55, 745–769.

The pattern is as follows: Author. (Year of publication). Article title. *Name of
Journal, volume number,* inclusive page numbers. Note that the volume number is
italicized along with the title of the journal.

Scholarly Journal That Restarts Page Numbering with Each Issue

Pollay, R. W., Lee, J. S., & Carter-Whitney, D. (1992). Separate, but not equal: Racial segmentation in cigarette advertising. *Journal of Advertising, 21*(1), 45–57.

The citation includes the issue number in parentheses as well as the volume number. Note that the issue number and the parentheses are *not* italicized.

Articles in Magazines and Newspapers Accessed in Print

Magazine Article with Named Author

Snyder, R. L. (2001, August–September). A daughter of Cambodia remembers: Loung Ung's journey. *Ms.,* 12, 62–67.

Hall, S. S. (2001, March 11). Prescription for profit. *New York Times Magazine,* 40–45, 59, 91–92, 100.

The pattern is as follows: Author. (Year, Month [Day]). Title of article. *Name of Magazine, volume number [if stated in magazine],* inclusive pages. If page numbers are discontinuous, identify every page.

Anonymous Magazine Article

Daddy, daddy. (2001, July 30). *New Republic, 225,* 12–13.

Review of Book or Film

Schwarz, B. (2001, November). A bit of bunting: A new history of the British empire elevates expediency to principle [Review of the book *Ornamentalism: How the British saw their empire*]. *Atlantic Monthly, 288,* 126–135.

Kaufman, S. (2001, July 30). Polishing a gem [Review of the motion picture *The blue angel*]. *New Republic, 225,* 28–29.

Newspaper Article

Henriques, D. B. (1998, September 27). Hero's fall teaches Wall Street a lesson. *Seattle Times,* pp. A1, A24.

Newspaper Editorial

Dr. Frankenstein on the hill [Editorial]. (2002, May 18). *The New York Times,* p. A22.

Letter to the Editor of a Magazine or Newspaper

Tomsovic, K. (1998, July 13). Culture clash [Letter to the editor]. *New Yorker,* p. 7.

Print Articles or Books Downloaded from a Database or the Web

Print Article Downloaded from Licensed Database

Portner, J. (2000, March 14). Girl's slaying elicits calls for metal detectors. *Education Week*, 8. Retrieved July 17, 2001, from EBSCO Academic Search Elite database.

Article or Book Available Online or on Microfiche from an Information Service

These services, such as ERIC (Educational Resources Information Center) or NTIS (National Technical Information Service), provide material to your library on microfiche or online with indexes on CD-ROM or online.

Eddy, P. A. (1981). *The effects of foreign language study in high school on verbal ability as measured by the Scholastic Aptitude Test—verbal*. Washington, DC: Center for Applied Linguistics. (ERIC Document Reproduction Service No. ED 196 312)

Print Article Downloaded from the Web

Kane, J. (2001, May). Arrested development. *Outside Online*. Retrieved November 17, 2001, from http://www.outsidemag.com/magazine/200105/200105molokai1.html

Web Sources and Other Electronically Retrieved Sources

Authored Document within a Web Site

Lithwick, D. (2001, December 21). Creche test dummies: Nativity scenes on public lands are illegal, rules the Supreme Court. Except when they're not. *Slate*. Retrieved December 22, 2001, from http://slate.msn.com/?id=2060070

Document without an Identified Author within a Web Site

The Interdisciplinary Center, Herzliya. (n.d.). Palestine Liberation Front (PLF). Retrieved December 21, 2001, from http://www.ict.org.il/inter_ter/orgdet.cfm?orgid=29

Choose for the author slot the name of the organization that produced the document, if identified. If not, use the home page name of the Web site. The abbreviation "n.d." stands for "no date."

Article from a Scholarly E-journal

Welch, J. R., & Riley, R. (2001). Reclaiming land and spirit in the western Apache homeland. *American Indian Quarterly, 25*, 5–14. Retrieved December 19, 2001, from http://muse.jhu.edu/journals/american_indian_quarterly/v025/25.1welch.pdf

E-book

Hoffman, F. W. (1981). *The literature of rock: 1954–1978.* Retrieved December 19,
     2001, from http://www.netlibrary.com/ebook_info.asl?product_id=24355

The *Publication Manual of the American Psychological Association,* 5th ed., has no
example of an E-book. We followed the manual's advice about how to proceed
when an unusual case arises.

Online Reference Database

Uses and ethics of cloning. (1997). *Encyclopedia Britannica online.* (Year in Review
     1997). Retrieved December 22, 2001, from http://www.eb.com:180/bol/
     topic?eu=124355&sctn=1

The *Publication Manual of the American Psychological Association,* 5th ed., has no example of an online reference database. We followed the manual's advice about
how to proceed when an unusual case arises.

E-mail, Interviews, and Personal Correspondence   APA guidelines limit the
"References" list to publishable or retrievable information. Cite personal correspondence in the body of your text, but not in the References list: "Daffinrud
(personal communication, December 12, 2001) claims that. . . ."

Bulletin Board or Newsgroup Posting

Dermody, T. (2001, December 19). Re: Can we have it all or was it a lie? Message
     posted to soc.feminism group http://groups.google.com/groups?hl=
     en&selm=n7os1us9ue4k8th1vtvlbepgtbun2booqk%404ax.com

Miscellaneous Sources

Television Program

Bochco, S., & Milch, D. (Directors). (2001, November 6). Lie like a rug [Television
     series episode]. In *NYPD blue.* New York: American Broadcasting Company.

Film

Madden, J. (Director). (1998). *Shakespeare in love* [Motion picture]. United States:
     Universal Miramax.

Sound Recording

Dwarf Music. (1966). Rainy day woman [Recorded by B. Dylan]. On *Bob Dylan MTV
     unplugged* [CD]. New York: Columbia. (1995)

Follow this format: Writer of song or copyright holder. (Date of copyright). Title of song [Recorded by artist if different from writer]. On *Title of album* [Medium such as CD, record, or cassette]. Location: Label. (Date of album if different from date of song)

Unpublished Paper Presented at a Meeting

Sharples, M. (2001, June 20). *Authors of the future.* Keynote address presented at Conference of European Teachers of Academic Writing, Groningen, the Netherlands.

Government Publications

O'Toole, M. (2000). *The school shooter: A threat assessment perspective.* Washington, DC: U.S. Federal Bureau of Investigation. Retrieved August 16, 2001, from http://www.fbi.gov/publications/school/school2.pdf

Conclusion

This chapter has shown you how to use sources purposively, how to help readers separate your ideas from those of sources through the use of rhetorically effective attributive tags, and how to work sources into your own writing through summarizing, paraphrasing, and quoting. It has also defined plagiarism and showed you how to avoid it. The last half of the chapter has shown you the nuts and bolts of citing and documenting sources in both the MLA and APA styles. It has explained the logic of parenthetical citation systems, showing you how to match sources cited in your text with those in your concluding bibliography. It has also shown you the documentation formats for a wide range of sources in both MLA and APA styles.

Student Example of an APA-Style Research Paper

We conclude with a sample of a successful effort: Megan Matthews' researched argument on Navy sonar and whales. She uses the APA system for citing and documenting her sources.

Sounding the Alarm:

Navy Sonar and the Survival of Whales

Megan Matthews

English 260

November 1, 2002

Sounding the Alarm:

Navy Sonar and the Survival of Whales

Imagine that you are forced to live in an apartment next to a city freeway   1
with a constant roar of engines and tires against concrete. Cars cruise by on
the surface streets with bass systems so powerful that your windows shake
and your ears hurt. You tolerate the din day after day, but you and your friends
have to shout to be heard. What if you had no alternative place to live?

This scenario is, of course, preposterous. We can move to find the coveted   2
sound of silence. For whales, dolphins, and sea turtles, however, noise is
becoming an inescapable catastrophe that threatens far more than their
aesthetic sensibilities. The incessant rumbling of cargo ships, the loud
explosions of undersea mineral explorations, and the annoying cacophony of
the blasting devices used by fisheries have turned Jacques Cousteau's world of
silence into an underwater freeway. Now, however, a new and more dangerous
source of sound has been approved for use in the oceans—the United States
Navy's Low Frequency Active Sonar System (LFA sonar), which will track
enemy submarines. The Navy claims that the technology is needed to ensure
national security, since it detects submarines at greater distances than
previous sonar systems. However, the potential damage to marine life and to
the long-term health of the oceans themselves outweighs the Navy's
questionable claims about national security. The U. S. Congress should cut
funds for further deployment of LFA sonar.

Since the mid-1980s, the Navy has developed and tested LFA sonar   3
systems. LFA is *active* because it does more than just listen for nearby
submarines, like our older systems. With LFA, 18 acoustic transmitters the size
of bathtubs act like giant woofer speakers suspended beneath the ship on
cables. The speakers emit bursts of sound every 6 to 100 seconds. These bursts
can be as powerful as 215 decibels, a sound level equivalent to standing one
meter away from a departing commercial jet (National Marine Fisheries Service
[MNFS], 2002a, p. 3). The Navy prefers low-frequency sonar because low-
frequency waves travel farther than high-frequency waves, which is why the
bumping bass of a car stereo reverberates after the car spins around a street
corner. In this case, the sonar's sound waves reflect off objects from hundreds
of miles away and alert the ship's crew to the presence of submarines. In its

Environmental Impact Statement, the Navy explains that it needs LFA sonar because modern submarines are quieter than clunky Cold War versions. Their ability to run quietly makes the new subs virtually undetectable until they are close by, leaving the Navy only minutes to respond to a potential submarine threat (Department of the Navy [DON], 2001, p. ES-2) After studying possible solutions, the Navy believes LFA sonar is the only system capable of providing reliable and dependable long-range detection of quieter, harder-to-find submarines (DON, 2001, p. ES-2). Unfortunately, the far-traveling waves that bounce off enemy submarines also can pierce the inner ears of whales and dolphins.

4   To its credit, the Navy has acted to protect marine mammals and other sea life. The Navy studied existing research reports on the levels of sounds that can cause hearing damage to marine mammals and concluded that protecting whales and dolphins from levels above 180 dB would prevent any harm to their hearing and behavior. Based on these studies, the National Oceanic and Atmospheric Administration's National Marine Fisheries Service determined that the Navy's employment of LFA sonar at levels below 180 dB would have no more than a negligible impact on marine mammal species and stocks (National Oceanic and Atmospheric Administration [NOAA], 2002). The Navy therefore plans to use a maximum volume of 180 dB when marine mammals are nearby. As an initial protective measure, the sonar will not be allowed to operate above 180 dB if it is within 12 nautical miles of coastlines and islands to ensure that coastal stocks of marine mammals and sea turtles will be relatively unaffected by LFA sonar (NMFS, 2002b). This measure protects critically endangered species, like northern right whales, who feed in coastal areas. The Navy also plans to avoid damaging whale hearing and behavior by trying to prevent animals from swimming near the ships. The Navy wants to detect animals that wander within 1 kilometer of the vessel, where they might be exposed to sounds of 180 dB or more. The protective monitoring systems will rely on humans and technology to protect sea animals. Sailors who have been trained to detect and identify marine mammals and sea turtles will stand on deck to look for whales and dolphins (Schregardus, 2002, p. 48149). Underwater microphones will also listen for sounds that whales and dolphins make. Finally, the Navy has developed a second active sonar system

called the High Frequency Marine Mammal Monitoring Sonar. It will locate and monitor animals who enter the 180 dB area and will run before and during the LFA sonar transmissions. If whales, dolphins, or sea turtles are observed, the crew will turn off the LFA system until the animals move away.

These efforts to protect sea life are commendable, but current marine   5
research shows that LFA sonar poses a much higher risk to marine mammals than the Navy acknowledges. The conclusions drawn by the Navy about potential hearing damage to marine mammals are open to serious doubt, and their measures to protect the sea environment are inadequate.

To begin, biologists generally agree that hearing is the primary sense of   6
marine mammals. No one knows precisely what functions hearing performs, but it is likely that whales depend on sound to avoid predators, to communicate across great distances between pods and prospective mates, and to establish mother-calf bonds. According to a detailed study by the National Resources Defense Council (Jasny, 1999), significant noise interference could threaten individual mammals or entire populations if biologically important behaviors like these are disrupted. Furthermore, like the members of a rock band, whales and dolphins may experience hearing loss after repeated exposure to sounds at the same frequency. In 1996, two sperm whales residing in a heavily trafficked area of the Canary Islands made no apparent efforts to avoid a collision with a cargo ship and were killed. Autopsies revealed damage to their inner ears, which some environmental scientists believe could have been caused by repeated exposure to the sounds of cargo ships (Jasny, 1999). The Navy's tests of different kinds of sonar systems are also suspected to have caused 16 Cuvier's beaked whales to beach and die in the Bahamas. The Navy had been testing midrange active sonar in the area; autopsies of four whales revealed extensive bleeding in the inner ears and around the brain. The conclusions of the Navy and Fisheries Service interim and final reports named the sonar tests as the most likely cause of the beachings (DON and NMFS, 2001). Although the type of sonar was midrange, rather than low-frequency, the link still implies that whales can be harmed or even killed by sonar—and that the effects can be unanticipated. Beachings also occurred after naval sonar exercises in Greece and the Canary Islands. In Greece, sonar is the likely culprit; scientists cannot establish the cause of death, however, because the

initial examination of the bodies was not thorough (Jasny, 1999). Finally, according to Jasny, the long-term effects of noise pollution may not be limited to hearing; noise pollution can increase stress levels, which lead to shorter life spans and lower birth rates—effects that humans may not notice for decades. One ping from a low-frequency system may only *harass* whales, to use the term commonly encountered in Navy or Fisheries Service discussions of low frequency sonar, but if whales are exposed to LFA sound waves repeatedly, the effects may be long-lasting and even irreversible.

7   The importance of hearing to marine mammals means that the effect of LFA sonar on the sea environment needs to be extensively studied. Unfortunately, the studies used by the Navy to demonstrate that LFA sonar poses little threat to marine life are scant, scientifically flawed, and inconclusive. No one actually knows how loud or frequent sounds need to be to cause permanent or temporary hearing loss to whales and sea turtles. Most studies have focused on captive species like seals and some dolphins; the data is extrapolated to estimate the hearing capacities of other species. The Navy uses the findings of several scientific workshops that studied the range where serious hearing problems could occur. Based upon these conclusions, as well as the Navy's own examinations of marine mammal inner ear models and extrapolation from human results, the Navy believes that protecting marine mammals from levels above 180 dB will be sufficient (DON, 2001, p. 14). Yet the Navy itself admits, in its own environmental impact statement, that data regarding underwater hearing capabilities of marine mammals are rare and limited to smaller species that can be studied in laboratories (DON, 2001, p. 11). The Navy has tried to dispel fears that mammals are physically and behaviorally harmed by LFA sonar by releasing the results of three separate tests Navy scientists conducted on baleen whale populations in California and Hawaii; these studies concluded that most whales did not alter any observable aspect of their behavior for more than "a few tens of minutes" (DON, 2001, p. 16). Nevertheless, three tests on baleen whales is hardly adequate to conclude that other species of whales, as well as other marine mammals, would react in the same way as the baleen whale. Moreover, none of these studies examined the long-term effects of repeated exposures, nor were whales exposed to sounds above 155 dB, even though the estimated LFA safety level is 180 dB. One has difficulty understanding how the Navy can set 180 dB as their safety

threshold when their own tests did not monitor whales at this level. Moreover, some scientists claim that *less intense* sounds can be harmful. Dr. Marsh Green, the President of the Ocean Mammal Institute and an animal behavior specialist, claims that "a significant body of research show[s] that whales avoid underwater sounds starting at 110 to 120 decibels" (Knickerbocker, 2001). If the scientific community continues to debate this issue, it seems unlikely that the Navy could have indisputable evidence that the sonar will not harm whales.

Clearly the Navy's claim that LFA sonar will not hurt marine mammals and other sea life will not survive close scrutiny. Of even greater concern is the dangerous precedent that the U.S. Navy will set if it deploys LFA sonar on its surface ships. There is a strong possibility that other nations might develop LFA sonar systems in order to keep up with the United States. The nuclear weapons race of the past proves that military powers constantly compete with each other to be prepared for armed conflicts. This often results in a frantic struggle to develop the same technologies worldwide with no regard for environmental and social effects. Already, according to Jasny (1999), NATO countries are investigating their own use of similar LFA systems. If additional countries deploy the technology, whales and dolphins will face much greater risks of meeting sonar systems in open water. In addition, the world's governments have not discussed treaties that would require nations to turn off sonar systems in arctic waters, which the Navy currently plans to do. Whales, dolphins, and sea turtles will have no permanent safe havens if other militaries choose to run their systems worldwide.

The Navy justifies developing LFA sonar for the sake of national security; in light of the September 11, 2001, terrorist attacks, this claim almost guarantees unquestioned public support. Even so, in the age of terrorism, do enemy submarines present significant threats? A confusing array of Navy documents makes it nearly impossible for the general public to find out the facts about potential danger from submarines. The Navy argues that 224 diesel-electric submarines are operated by nonallied nations but never explains who these nations are or how much of a threat they actually pose (Schregardus, 2002, p. 48146). This long-standing anxiety about submarines feels like part of the old Cold War mentality when the nation to fear was the Soviet Union. Perhaps now we should be more concerned about cargo ships than submarines. A large percentage of freight containers are never inspected at our ports, and these seem to be easier targets for terrorists than our Navy ships. Finally, the most recent attack on a Navy ship, the USS *Cole*, came from another boat, not a submarine. The number of terrorists who have sophisticated submarine technology must be smaller than the number who can place a small bomb on a small boat, train, car, or cargo ship.

10   Moreover long-term national security also depends on healthy oceans. Millions of people incorporate fish into their diet, and oceans provide materials for countless human products. Any changes to the balance of marine life could degrade the entire ecosystem. If the health of the oceans is damaged by LFA sonar, it will be only a matter of time before humans feel the effects. Our national environmental security, which never receives much attention in the media, should be as important to the United States as our military readiness. The proposed widespread use of LFA sonar on the Navy's surface ships opens up a range of questions about the long-term effects of our underwater activities. When combined with other sources of human noise pollution, LFA sonar poses dangerous threats to marine life. According to Dr. Sylvia Earle, former Chief Scientist at the National Oceanic & Atmospheric Administration, undersea noise pollution is like the death of a thousand cuts (as cited in Jasny, 1999, executive summary, first sidebar). Each time we turn up the volume in the oceans, we make it more difficult for marine animals to communicate with each other. We may even diminish their hearing capacities, endangering their abilities to migrate safely and to avoid countless ships that crisscross their routes. Until more is known about the long-term effects of LFA sonar, the Navy should delay operation of LFA sonar voluntarily. If it does not do so, the U.S. Congress should cut off further funding. The debate over LFA sonar cannot be defined as a simple environment-versus-government battle. It is a discussion about whether or not environmental security and ocean health matter to humans. At its core, it is a debate about our futures.

Sounding the Alarm   8

References

Department of the Navy. (2001). *Executive summary: Final overseas environmental impact statement and environmental impact statement for Surveillance Towed Array Sensor System Low Frequency Active (SURTASS LFA) Sonar.* Retrieved October 5, 2002, from http://www.surtass-lfa-eis.com/docs/ EXSUM%20FEIS%201–15.pdf

Department of the Navy and National Marine Fisheries Service. (2001, December 20). *Joint interim report: Bahamas marine mammal stranding event of 15–16 March 2000.* Retrieved October 15, 2002, from http://www.nmfs.noaa.gov/prot_res/overview/ Interim_Bahamas_Report.pdf

Jasny, Michael. (1999, March). *Sounding the depths: Supertankers, sonar, and the rise of undersea noise.* Retrieved October 15, 2002, from the National Resources Defense Council Web site: http://www.nrdc.org/wildlife/marine/sound/sdinx.asp

Knickerbocker, Brad. (2001, August 20). US Navy plans for loud sonar raises fears for whales. *Christian Science Monitor.* Retrieved October 20, 2002, from http://news. nationalgeographic.com/news/2001/08/0815_wirenavyboom.html

National Marine Fisheries Service. (2002a). *Biological opinion on proposed employment of Surveillance Towed Array Sensor System Low Frequency Active Sonar.* Retrieved October 8, 2002, from http://www.nmfs.noaa.gov/prot_res/readingrm/ESAsec7/7pr_ surtass-2020529.pdf

National Marine Fisheries Service. (2002b). *Final determination and rulemaking on the harassment of marine mammals incidental to Navy operations of Surveillance Towed Array Sensor System Low Frequency Active (SURTASS LFA) Sonar.* Retrieved October 5, 2002, from http://www.nmfs.noaa.gov/prot_res/readingrm/MMSURTASS/ LFAexecsummary.PDF

National Oceanic and Atmospheric Administration. (2002, July 15). *Strong protection measures for marine mammals tied to operation of Low Frequency Sonar* (NOAA news release 2002–90). Retrieved October 15, 2002, from http://www. publicaffairs.noaa.gov/releases2002/july02/noaa02090.html

Schregardus, D. R. (2002, July 16). *Record of decision for Surveillance Towed Array Sensor System Low Frequency Active (SURTASS LFA) Sonar,* Fed Reg 67 (141), pp. 48145–48154 (July 23, 2002). Retrieved October 12, 2002, from http:// www.surtass-lfa-eis.com/docs/LFA%20EIS%20ROD.pdf

Appendix One

Informal Fallacies

In this appendix, we look at ways of testing the legitimacy of an argument. Sometimes, there are fatal logical flaws hiding in the heart of a perfectly respectable-looking argument, and if we miss them, we may find ourselves vainly defending the indefensible. Take, for example, the following cases. Do they seem persuasive to you?

Creationism must be a science because hundreds of scientists believe in it.

I am opposed to a multicultural curriculum because it will lead to ethnic separatism similar to what is happening in eastern Europe.

Smoking must cause cancer because a higher percentage of smokers get cancer than do nonsmokers.

Smoking doesn't cause cancer because my grandfather smoked two packs per day for fifty years and died in his sleep at age ninety.

An abnormal percentage of veterans who were marched to ground zero during atomic tests in Nevada died of leukemia and lung cancer. Surely their deaths were caused by the inhalation of radioactive isotopes.

The Problem of Conclusiveness in an Argument

Although it may distress us to think so, none of the arguments listed above is conclusive. But that doesn't mean they're false, either. So what are they? Well, they are, to various degrees, "persuasive" or "unpersuasive." The problem is that some people will mistake arguments such as those above for "conclusive" or airtight arguments. A person may rest an entire argument on them and then fall right through the holes that observant logicians open in them. Although few people will mistake an airtight case for a fallacious one, lots of people mistake logically unsound arguments for airtight cases. So let's see how to avoid falling into specious reasoning.

Some arguments are flawed because they fail to observe certain formal logical rules. In constructing syllogisms, for example, there are certain formal laws that must be followed if we are to have a valid syllogism. The following argument is beyond doubt invalid and inconclusive:

No Greeks are bald.

No Lithuanians are Greek.

Therefore, all Lithuanians are bald.

But to say the argument is invalid isn't to say that its conclusion is necessarily untrue. Perhaps all Lithuanians really are bald. The point is, if the conclusion were true, it would be by coincidence, not design, because the argument is invalid. All invalid arguments are inconclusive. And, by the same token, a perfectly valid syllogism may be untrue. Just because the premises follow the formal laws of logic doesn't mean that what they say is true. For a syllogistic argument to be absolutely conclusive, its form must be valid and its premises must be true. A perfectly conclusive argument would therefore yield a noncontroversial truth—a statement that no one would dispute.

This is a long way around to reach one point: The reason we argue about issues is that none of the arguments on any side of an issue is absolutely conclusive; there is always room to doubt the argument, to develop a counterargument. We can only create more or less persuasive arguments, never conclusive ones.

We have examined some of these problems already. In Chapter 12 on causal arguments we discussed the problem of correlation versus causation. We know, for example, that smoking and cancer are correlated but that further arguments are needed in order to increase the conclusiveness of the claim that smoking *causes* cancer.

In this appendix we explore the problem of conclusiveness in various kinds of arguments. In particular, we use the *informal fallacies* of logic to explain how inconclusive arguments can fool us into thinking they are conclusive.

An Overview of Informal Fallacies

The study of informal fallacies remains the murkiest of all logical endeavors. It's murky because informal fallacies are as unsystematic as formal fallacies are rigid and systematized. Whereas formal fallacies of logic have the force of laws, informal fallacies have little more than explanatory power. Informal fallacies are quirky; they identify classes of less conclusive arguments that recur with some frequency, but they do not contain formal flaws that make their conclusions illegitimate no matter what the terms may say. Informal fallacies require us to look at the meaning of the terms to determine how much we should trust or distrust the conclusion. The most common mistake one can make with informal fallacies is to assume that they have the force of laws like formal fallacies. They don't. In evaluating arguments with informal fallacies, we usually find that arguments are "more or less" fallacious, and determining the degree of fallaciousness is a matter of judgment.

Knowledge of informal fallacies is most useful when we run across arguments that we "know" are wrong, but we can't quite say why. They just don't "sound right." They look reasonable enough, but they remain unacceptable to us. Informal fallacies are a sort of compendium of symptoms for arguments flawed in this way. We must be careful, however, to make sure that the particular case before us "fits" the descriptors for the fallacy that seems to explain its problem. It's much easier, for example, to find informal fallacies in a hostile argument than in a friendly one simply because we are more likely to expand the limits of the fallacy to make the disputed case fit.

Not everyone agrees about what to include under the heading "informal fallacies." In selecting the following set of fallacies, we left out far more candidates than we included. Since Aristotle first developed his list of thirteen *elenchi* (refutations) down to the present day, literally dozens of different systems of informal fallacy have been put forward. Although there is a good deal of overlap among these lists, the terms are invariably different, and the definition of fallacy itself shifts from age to age. In selecting the following set of fallacies, we left out a number of other candidates. We chose the following because they seemed to us to be the most commonly encountered.

In arranging the fallacies, we have, for convenience, put them into three categories derived from classical rhetoric: *pathos*, *ethos*, and *logos*. Fallacies of *pathos* rest on a flawed relationship between what is argued and the audience for the argument. Fallacies of *ethos* rest on a flawed relationship between the argument and the character of those involved in the argument. Fallacies of *logos* rest on flaws in the relationship among statements of an argument.

Fallacies of *Pathos*

Argument to the People (Appealing to Stirring Symbols)   This is perhaps the most generic example of a *pathos* fallacy. Argument to the people appeals to the fundamental beliefs, biases, and prejudices of the audience in order to sway opinion through a feeling of solidarity among those of the group. For example, when a politician says, "My fellow Americans, I stand here, draped in this flag from head to foot, to indicate my fundamental dedication to the values and principles of these sovereign United States," he's redirecting to his own person our allegiance to nationalistic values by linking himself with the prime symbol of those values, the flag. The linkage is not rational, it's associative. It's also extremely powerful—which is why arguments to the people crop up so frequently.

Appeal to Ignorance (Presenting Evidence the Audience Can't Examine)
Those who commit this fallacy present assumptions, assertions, or evidence that the audience is incapable of judging or examining. If, for example, a critic were to praise the novel *Clarissa* for its dullness on the grounds that this dullness was the intentional effect of the author, we would be unable to respond because we have no idea what was in the author's mind when he created the work.

Appeal to Irrational Premises (Appealing to Reasons That May Have No Basis in Logic)   This mode of short-circuiting reason may take one of three forms:

1. Appeal to common practice. (It's all right to do X because everyone else does it.)

2. Appeal to traditional wisdom. (It's all right because we've always done it this way.)

3. Appeal to popularity—the bandwagon appeal. (It's all right because lots of people like it.)

In all three cases, we've moved from saying something is popular, common, or persistent to saying it is right, good, or necessary. You have a better chance of rocketing across the Grand Canyon on a motorcycle than you have of going from "is" to "ought" on a *because* clause. Some examples of this fallacy would include (1) "Of course I borrowed money from the company slush fund. Everyone on this floor has done the same in the last eighteen months"; (2) "We've got to require everyone to read *Hamlet* because we've always required everyone to read it"; and (3) "You should buy a Ford Escort because it's the best-selling car in the world."

Provincialism (Appealing to the Belief That the Known Is Always Better Than the Unknown)   Here is an example from the 1960s: "You can't sell small cars in America. In American culture, automobiles symbolize prestige and personal freedom. Those cramped little Japanese tin boxes will never win the hearts of American consumers." Although we may inevitably feel more comfortable with familiar things, ideas, and beliefs, we are not necessarily better off for sticking with them.

Red Herring (Shifting the Audience's Attention from a Crucial Issue to an Irrelevant One)   A good example of a red herring showed up in a statement by Secretary of State James Baker that was reported in the November 10, 1990, *New York Times*. In response to a question about the appropriateness of using American soldiers to defend wealthy, insulated (and by implication, corrupt) Kuwaiti royalty, Baker told an anecdote about an isolated encounter he had with four Kuwaitis who had suffered; he then made a lengthy statement on America's interests in the Persian Gulf. Although no one would argue that America is unaffected by events in the Middle East, the question of why others with even greater interests at stake had not contributed more troops and resources went unanswered.

Fallacies of *Ethos*

Appeal to False Authority (Appealing to the Authority of a Popular Person Rather Than a Knowledgeable One)   Appeals to false authority involve relying on testimony given by a person incompetent in the field from which the claims under question emerge. Most commercial advertisements are based on this fallacy. Cultural heroes are paid generously to associate themselves with a product without demonstrating any real expertise in evaluating that product. In at least one case, consumers who fell victim to such a fallacy made a legal case out of it. People bilked out of their life savings by a Michigan mortgage company sued the actors who represented the company on TV. Are people fooled by such appeals to false authority entitled to recover assets lost as a result?

The court answered no. The judge ruled that people gullible enough to believe that George Hamilton's capped-tooth smile and mahogany tan qualify him as a real estate consultant deserve what they get. Their advice to consumers? "Buyers beware," because even though sellers can't legally lie, they can legally use fallacious arguments—all the more reason to know your fallacies.

Keep in mind, however, that occasionally the distinction between a false authority fallacy and an appeal to legitimate authority can blur. Suppose that Tiger Woods were to praise a particular company's golf club. Because he is an expert on golf, it is possible that Woods actually speaks from authority and that the golf club he praises is superior. But it might also be that he is being paid to advertise the golf club and is endorsing a brand that is no better than its competitors'. The only way we could make even a partial determination of Woods's motives would be if he presented an *ad rem* ("to the thing") argument showing us scientifically why the golf club in question is superior. In short, appeals to authority are legitimate when the authority knows the field and when her motive is to inform others rather than profit herself.

Appeal to the Person/*Ad Hominem* (Attacking the Character of the Arguer Rather Than the Argument Itself)   Literally, *ad hominem* means "to the man" or "to the person." Any argument that focuses on the character of the person making the argument rather than the quality of the reasoning qualifies as an *ad hominem* argument. Ideally, arguments are supposed to be *ad rem*, or "to the thing," that is, addressed to the specifics of the case itself. Thus an *ad rem* critique of a politician would focus on her voting record, the consistency and cogency of her public statements, her responsiveness to constituents, and so forth. An *ad hominem* argument would shift attention from her record to irrelevant features of her personality or personal life. Perhaps an *ad hominem* argument would suggest that she had a less than stellar undergraduate academic record.

But not all *ad hominem* arguments are *ad hominem* fallacies. It's not always fallacious to address your argument to the arguer. There are indeed times when the credibility of the person making an opposing argument is at issue. Lawyers, for example, when questioning expert witnesses who give damaging testimony, will often make an issue of their credibility, and rightfully so. And certainly it's not that clear, for instance, that an all-male research team of social scientists would observe and interpret data in the same way as a mixed-gender research group. An *ad hominem* attack on an opponent's argument is not fallacious so long as (1) personal authority is what gives the opposing argument much of its weight, and (2) the critique of the person's credibility is fairly presented.

An interesting example of an *ad hominem* argument occurred in the 1980s in the context of the Star Wars antiballistic missile system debate. Many important physicists around the country signed a statement in which they declared their opposition to Star Wars research. Another group of physicists supportive of that research condemned them on the grounds that none of the protesting physicists stood to get any Star Wars research funds anyway. This attack shifted attention away from the reasons given by the protesting physicists for their convictions and put it instead on the physicists' motives. To some extent, of course, credibility is an issue here, because many of the key issues raised in the debate required some degree of expertise to resolve. Hence, the charges meet the first test for nonfallacious reasoning directed to the arguer.

But we must also ask ourselves if the charges being made are fair. If you'll recall from earlier discussions of fairness, we said that fairness requires similar treatment of similar classes of things. Applying this rule to this situation, we can simply reverse the charge being levied against the anti–Star Wars group and say of its supporters: "Because you stand to gain a good deal of research money from this project, we can't take your support of the Star Wars initiatives seriously." The Star Wars supporters would thus become victims of their own logic. *Ad hominem* attacks are often of this nature: The charges are perfectly reversible—for example, "Of course you support abortion; all your friends are feminists." "Of course you oppose abortion; you've been a Catholic all your life." *Ad hominem* debates resemble nothing so much as mental quick-draw contests. Whoever shoots first wins because the first accuser puts the burden of proof on the opposition.

It's important to see here that an *ad hominem* argument, even if not fallacious, can never be definitive. Like analogies, they are simply suggestive; they raise doubts and focus our attention. Catholic writers can produce reasonable arguments against abortion, and feminists can produce reasonable ones for it. *Ad hominem* attacks don't allow us to discount arguments; but they do alert us to possible biases, possible ways the reasoned arguments themselves are vulnerable.

Several subcategories of *ad hominem* argument that are almost never persuasive include

1. Name-calling (referring to a disputant by unsavory names)
2. Appeal to prejudice (applying ethnic, racial, gender, or religious slurs to an opponent)
3. Guilt by association (linking the opposition to extremely unpopular groups or causes)

Name-calling is found far more often in transcripts of oral encounters than in books or essays. In the heat of the moment, speakers are more likely to lapse into verbal abuse than are writers who have time to contemplate their words. The *Congressional Record* is a rich source for name-calling. Here, for example, one finds a duly elected representative referring to another duly elected representative as "a pimp for the Eastern establishment environmentalists." One of the biggest problems with such a charge is that it's unlikely to beget much in the way of reasoned response. It's far easier to respond in kind than it is to persuade people rationally that one is not a jackass of *that* particular sort.

When name-calling is "elevated" to include slighting reference to the opponent's religion, gender, race, or ethnic background, we have encountered an appeal to prejudice. When it involves lumping an opponent with unsavory, terminally dumb, or extremely unpopular causes and characters, it constitutes guilt by association.

Straw Man (Greatly Oversimplifying an Opponent's Argument to Make It Easier to Refute or Ridicule)   Although typically less inflammatory than the preceding sorts of *ethos* fallacies, the straw man fallacy changes the character of the opposition in order to suit the arguer's own needs. In committing a straw man fallacy, you basically make up the argument you *wish* your opponents had made and attribute it to them because it's so much easier to refute than the argument they actually made. Some political debates consist almost entirely of straw man exchanges such as: "You may think that levying confiscatory taxes on homeless people's cardboard dwellings is the surest way out of recession, but I don't." Or: "While my opponent would like to empty our prisons of serial killers and coddle kidnappers, I hold to the sacred principles of compensatory justice."

Fallacies of *Logos*

Logos fallacies comprise flaws in the relationships among the statements of an argument. Thus, to borrow momentarily from the language of the Toulmin schema discussed earlier, you can think of *logos* fallacies as breakdowns between arguments' warrants and their claims, between their warrants and their backing, or between their claims and their reasons and grounds.

Begging the Question (Supporting a Claim with a Reason That Is Really a Restatement of the Claim in Different Words)   Question begging is probably the most obvious example of a *logos* fallacy in that it involves stating a claim as though it warranted itself. For example, the statement "Abortion is murder because it involves the intentional killing of an unborn human being" is tantamount to saying "Abortion is murder because it's murder." The warrant "If something is the intentional killing of a human life, it is murder" simply repeats the claim; murder is *by definition* the intentional killing of another human being. Logically, the statement is akin to a statement like "That fellow is fat because he's considerably overweight." The crucial issue in the abortion debate is whether a fetus is a human being in the legal sense. This crucial issue is avoided in the argument that begins by assuming that the fetus is a legal human being. That argument goes in an endless circle from claim to warrant and back again.

Or consider the following argument: "How can you say Minnie Minoso belongs in the Hall of Fame? He's been eligible for over a decade, and the Selection Committee turned him down every year. If he belonged in the Hall of Fame, the Committee would already have chosen him." Because the point at issue is whether the Hall of Fame Selection Committee *should* elect Minnie Minoso (it should, we think), the use of the committee's vote as proof of the contention that it should not elect him is wholly circular and begs the question.

In distinguishing valid reasoning from fallacious examples of question begging, some philosophers say that a question has been begged when the premises of an argument are at least as uncertain as the claim. In such cases, we are not making any movement from some known general principle toward some new particular conclusion; we are simply asserting an uncertain premise in order to give the appearance of certainty to a shaky claim.

To illustrate the preceding observation, consider the controversy that arose in the late 1980s over whether to impose economic sanctions against South Africa in order to pressure the South Africans into changing their racial policies. One argument against economic sanctions went like this: "We should not approve economic sanctions against South Africa (claim) because economic sanctions will hurt blacks as much as whites" (premise or stated reason). The claim ("We should not impose economic sanctions") is only as certain as the premise from which it was derived ("because blacks will suffer as much as whites"), but many people argued that that premise was extremely uncertain. They thought that whites would suffer the most under sanctions and that blacks would ultimately benefit. The question would no longer be begged if the person included a documented defense of the premise. But without such a defense, the arguer's claim is grounded on a shaky premise that sounds more certain than it is.

Complex Question (Confronting the Opponent with a Question That Will Put Her in a Bad Light No Matter How She Responds)   A complex question is one that requires, in legal terms, a self-incriminating response. For example, the question "When did you stop abusing alcohol?" requires the admission of alcohol abuse. Hence the claim that a person has abused alcohol is silently turned into an assumption.

False Dilemma/Either–Or (Oversimplifying a Complex Issue So That Only Two Choices Appear Possible)   A good extended analysis of this fallacy is found in sociologist Kai Erikson's analysis of President Truman's decision to drop the A-bomb on Hiroshima. His analysis suggests that the Truman administration prematurely reduced numerous options to just two: Either drop the bomb on a major city, or sustain unacceptable losses in a land invasion of Japan. Erikson, however, shows there were other alternatives. Typically, we encounter false dilemma arguments when people are trying to justify a questionable action by creating a false sense of necessity, forcing us to choose between two options, one of which is clearly unacceptable. Hence, when someone orders us to "Do it my way or hit the highway" or to "Love it or leave it," it's probably in response to some criticism we made about the "way" we're supposed to do it or the "it" we're supposed to love.

But of course not all dilemmas are false. People who reject all binary oppositions (that is, thinking in terms of pairs of opposites) are themselves guilty of a false dilemma. There are times when we might determine through a rational process of elimination that only two possible choices exist. Deciding whether a dilemma is truly a dilemma or only an evasion of complexity often requires a difficult judgment. Although we should initially suspect any attempt to convert a complex problem into an either/or choice, we may legitimately arrive at such a choice through thoughtful deliberation.

Equivocation (Using to Your Advantage at Least Two Different Definitions of the Same Term in the Same Argument)   For example, if we're told that people can't "flourish" unless they are culturally literate, we must know which of the several possible senses of *flourish* are being used before we can test the persuasiveness of the claim. If by *flourishing* the author means acquiring great wealth, we'll look at a different set of grounds than if *flourishing* is synonymous with moral probity, recognition in a profession, or simple contentment. To the extent that we're not told what it means to flourish, the relationship between the claim and the grounds and between the claim and the warrant remains ambiguous and unassailable.

Confusing Correlation for Cause/*Post Hoc, Ergo Propter Hoc* (After This, Therefore Because of This) (Assuming That Event X Causes Event Y Because Event X Preceded Event Y)   Here are two examples in which this fallacy may be at work:

> Cramming for a test really helps. Last week I crammed for a psychology test and I got an A on it.
>
> I am allergic to the sound of a lawn mower because every time I mow the lawn I start to sneeze.

We've already discussed this fallacy in Chapter 12, particularly in our discussion of the difference between correlation and causation. This fallacy occurs when a sequential relationship is mistaken for a causal relationship. To be sure, when two events occur frequently in conjunction with each other in a particular sequence, we've got a good case for a causal relationship. But until we can show how one causes the other, we cannot be certain that a causal relationship is occurring. The conjunction may simply be a matter of chance, or it may be attributable to some as-yet-unrecognized other factor. For example, your A on the psych test may be caused by something other than your cramming. Maybe the exam was easier, or perhaps you were luckier or more mentally alert.

Just when an erroneous causal argument becomes an example of the *post hoc* fallacy, however, is not cut-and-dried. Many reasonable arguments of causality later turn out to have been mistaken. We are guilty of the *post hoc* fallacy only when our claim of causality seems naively arrived at, without reflection or consideration of alternative hypotheses. Thus in our lawn mower argument, it is probably not the sound that creates the speaker's sneezing but all the pollen stirred up by the spinning blades.

We arrived at this more likely argument by applying a tool known as Occam's Razor—the principle that "What can be explained on fewer principles is explained needlessly by more," or "Between two hypotheses, both of which will account for a given fact, prefer the simpler." If we posit that sound is the cause of our sneezing, all sorts of intermediate causes are going to have to be fetched from afar to make the explanation persuasive. But the blades stirring up the pollen will cause the sneezing more directly. So, until science connects lawn mower noises to human eardrums to sneezing, the simpler explanation is preferred.

Slippery Slope   The slippery slope fallacy is based on the fear that once we take a first step in a direction we don't like, we will have to keep going.

> We don't dare send weapons to eastern Europe. If we do so, we will next send in military advisers, then a special forces battalion, and then large numbers of troops. Finally, we will be in all-out war.
>
> Look, Blotnik, no one feels worse about your need for open-heart surgery than I do. But I still can't let you turn this paper in late. If I were to let you do it, then I'd have to let everyone turn in papers late.

We run into slippery slope arguments all the time, especially when person A opposes person B's proposal. Those opposed to a particular proposal will often foresee an inevitable and catastrophic chain of events that would follow from taking a first, apparently harmless step. In other words, once we put a foot on that slippery slope, we're doomed to slide right out of sight. Often, such arguments are fallacious insofar as what is seen as an inevitable effect is in fact dependent on some intervening cause or chain of causes to bring it about. Will smoking cigarettes lead inevitably to heroin addiction? Overwhelming statistical evidence would suggest that it doesn't. A slippery slope argument, however, would lovingly trace a teenager's inevitable descent from a clandestine puff on the schoolground through the smoking of various controlled substances to a degenerate end in some Needle Park somewhere. The power of the slippery slope argument lies as much as anything in its compelling narrative structure. It pulls us along irresistibly from one plausible event to the next, making us forget that it's a long jump from plausibility to necessity.

One other common place to find slippery slope arguments is in confrontations between individuals and bureaucracies or other systems of rules and laws. Whenever individuals ask to have some sort of exception made for them, they risk the slippery slope reply. "Sorry, Mr. Jones, if we rush your order, then we will have to rush everyone else's order also."

The problem, of course, is that not every slippery slope argument is an instance of the slippery slope fallacy. We all know that some slopes are slippery and that we sometimes have to draw the line, saying, "To here, but no farther." And it is true also that making exceptions to rules is dangerous; the exceptions soon get established as regular procedures. The slippery slope becomes a fallacy, however, when we forget that some slopes don't *have* to be slippery unless we let them be slippery. Often we do better to imagine a staircase with stopping places all along the way. The assumption that we have no control over our descent once we take the first step makes us unnecessarily rigid.

Hasty Generalization (Making a Broad Generalization on the Basis of Too Little Evidence)   Typically, a hasty generalization occurs when someone reaches a conclusion on the basis of insufficient evidence. But what constitutes "sufficient" evidence? No generalization arrived at through empirical evidence would meet a logician's strict standard of certainty. And generally acceptable standards of proof in any given field are difficult to determine.

The Food and Drug Administration (FDA), for example, generally proceeds very cautiously before certifying a drug as "safe." However, whenever doubts arise about the safety of an FDA-approved drug, critics accuse the FDA of having made a hasty generalization. At the same time, patients eager to have access to a new drug and manufacturers eager to sell a new product may lobby the FDA to "quit dragging its feet" and get the drug to market. Hence, the point at which a hasty generalization about drug safety passes over into the realm of a prudent generalization is nearly always uncertain and contested.

A couple of variants of hasty generalization that deserve mention are

1. Pars pro toto/*Mistaking the part for the whole (assuming that what is true for a part will be true for the whole). Pars pro toto* arguments often appear in the critiques of the status quo. If, say, individuals wanted to get rid of the National Endowment for the Arts, they might focus on several controversial grants they've made over the past few years and use them as justification for wiping out all NEA programs.

2. *Suppressed evidence (withholding contradictory or unsupportive evidence so that only favorable evidence is presented to an audience).* The flip side of *pars pro toto* is suppressed evidence. If the administrator of the NEA were to go before Congress seeking more money and conveniently forgot about those controversial grants, he would be suppressing damaging but relevant evidence.

Faulty Analogy (Claiming That Because X Resembles Y in One Regard, X Will Resemble Y in All Regards)   Faulty analogies occur whenever a relationship of resemblance is turned into a relationship of identity. For example, the psychologist Carl Rogers uses a questionable analogy in his argument that political leaders should make use of discoveries about human communication derived from research in the social sciences. "During the war when a test-tube solution was found to the problem of synthetic rubber, millions of dollars and an army of talent was turned loose on the problem of using that finding. [. . .] But in the social science realm, if a way is found of facilitating communication and mutual understanding in small groups, there is no guarantee that the finding will be utilized."

Although Rogers is undoubtedly right that we need to listen more carefully to social scientists, his analogy between the movement from scientific discovery to product development and the movement from insights into small-group functioning to political change is strained. The laws of cause and effect at work in a test tube are much more reliable and generalizable than the laws of cause and effect observed in small human groups. Whereas lab results can be readily replicated in different times and places, small-group dynamics are altered by a whole host of factors, including the cultural background, gender, and age of participants. The warrant that licenses you to move from grounds to claim in the realm of science runs up against a statute of limitation when it tries to include the realm of social science.

Non Sequitur (Making a Claim That Doesn't Follow Logically from the Premises, or Supporting a Claim with Irrelevant Premises)   The *non sequitur* fallacy (literally, "it does not follow") is a miscellaneous category that includes any claim that doesn't follow logically from its premises or that is supported with irrelevant premises. In effect, any fallacy is a kind of *non sequitur* because what makes all fallacies fallacious is the absence of a logical connection between claim and premises. But in practice the term *non sequitur* tends to be restricted to problems like the following:

> *A completely illogical leap:*   "Our university has one of the best faculties in the United States because a Nobel Prize winner used to teach here." (How does the fact that a Nobel Prize winner used to teach at our university make its present faculty one of the best in the United States?)
>
> *A clear gap in the chain of reasoning:*   "People who wear nose rings are disgusting. There ought to be a law against wearing nose rings in public." (This is a *non sequitur* unless the arguer is willing to state and defend the missing premise: "There ought to be a law against anything that I find disgusting.")
>
> *Use of irrelevant reasons to support a claim:*   "I should not receive a C in this course because I have received B's or A's in all my other courses (here is my transcript for evidence) and because I worked exceptionally hard in this course (here is my log of hours worked)." (Even though the arguer has solid evidence to support each premise, the premises themselves are irrelevant to the claim. Course grades should be based on actual performance in the class, not on performance in other classes or on amount of effort devoted to the material.)

For Class Discussion

Working individually or in small groups, determine the potential persuasiveness of each argument. If the arguments are nonpersuasive because of one or more of the fallacies discussed in this appendix, identify the fallacies and explain how they render the argument nonpersuasive.

1. a. All wars are not wrong. The people who say so are cowards.

   b. Either we legalize marijuana or we watch a steady increase in the number of our citizens who break the law.

c. The Bible is true because it is the inspired word of God.

d. Mandatory registration of handguns will eventually lead to the confiscation of hunting rifles.

e. All these tornadoes started happening right after they tested the A-bombs. The A-bomb testing has changed our weather.

f. Most other progressive nations have adopted a program of government-provided health care. Therefore, it is time the United States abandoned its outdated practice of private medicine.

g. The number of Hollywood movie stars who support liberal policies convinces me that liberalism is the best policy. After all, they are rich and will not benefit from better social services.

h. Society has an obligation to provide housing for the homeless because people without adequate shelter have a right to the resources of the community.

i. I have observed the way the two renters in our neighborhood take care of their rental houses and have compared that to the way homeowners take care of their houses. I have concluded that people who own their own homes take better care of them than those who rent. [This argument goes on to provide detailed evidence about the house-caring practices of the two renters and of the homeowners in the neighborhood.]

j. Since the universe couldn't have been created out of nothing, it must have been created by a divine being.

2. Consider the following statements. Note places where you think the logic is flawed. If you were asked by writers or speakers to respond to their statements, what advice would you give to those who wrote or said them to rescue them from charges of fallaciousness? What would each of these speakers/writers have to show, in addition to what's given, to render the statement cogent and persuasive?

a. "America has had the luxury throughout its history of not having its national existence directly threatened by a foreign enemy. Yet we have gone to war. Why?

"The United States of America is not a piece of dirt stretching mainly from the Atlantic to the Pacific. More than anything else, America is a set of principles, and the historical fact is that those principles have not only served us well, but have also become a magnet for the rest of the world, a large chunk of which decided to change course last year.

"Those principles are not mere aesthetic ideas. Those principles are in fact the distillation of 10,000 years of human social evolution. We have settled on them not because they are pretty; we settled on them because they are the only things that work. If you have trouble believing that, ask a Pole." (novelist Tom Clancy)

b. "What particularly irritated Mr. Young [Republican congressman from Alaska] was the fact that the measure [to prohibit logging in Alaska's

Tongass National Forest] was initiated by . . . Robert Mrazek, a Democrat from Long Island. 'Bob Mrazek never saw a tree in his entire life until he went to Alaska' said Mr. Young." (*New York Times,* November 10, 1990)

c. "When Senator Tim Wirth . . . was in Brazil earlier this year on behalf of an effort to save the tropical rain forest of the Amazon basin, the first thing Brazilian President Jose Sarney asked him was, 'What about the Tongass?'" (*New York Times,* November 10, 1990)

Appendix Two

The Writing Community
Working in Groups

In Chapter 1 we stressed that today truth is typically seen as a product of discussion and persuasion by members of a given community. Instead of seeing "truth" as grounded in some absolute and timeless realm such as Plato's forms or the unchanging laws of logic, many modern thinkers assert that truth is the product of a consensus among a group of knowledgeable peers. Our own belief in the special importance of argumentation in contemporary life follows from our assumption that truth arises out of discussion and debate rather than dogma or pure reason.

In this appendix, we extend that assumption to the classroom itself. We introduce you to a mode of learning often called *collaborative learning*. It involves a combination of learning from an instructor, learning independently, and learning from peers. Mostly it involves a certain spirit—the same sort of inquiring attitude that's required of a good arguer.

From Conflict to Consensus: How to Get the Most Out of the Writing Community

Behind the notion of the writing community lies the notion that thinking and writing are social acts. At first, this notion may contradict certain widely accepted stereotypes of writers and thinkers as solitary souls who retreat to cork-lined studies where they conjure great thoughts and works. But although we agree that every writer at some point in the process requires solitude, we would point out that most writers and thinkers also require periods of talk and social interchange before they retreat to solitude. Poets, novelists, scientists, philosophers, and technological innovators tend to belong to communities of peers with whom they share their ideas, theories, and work. In this section, we try to provide you with some practical advice on how to get the most out of these sorts of communities in developing your writing skills.

Avoiding Bad Habits of Group Behavior

Over the years, most of us have developed certain bad habits that get in the way of efficient group work. Although we use groups all the time to study and accomplish demanding tasks, we tend to do so spontaneously and unreflectively without asking why some groups work and others don't. Many of us, for example, have worked on committees that just didn't get the job done and wasted our time, or else got the job done because one or two tyrannical people dominated the group. Just a couple of bad committee experiences can give us a healthy skepticism about the utility of groups in general. "A committee," according to some people, "is a sort of centipede. It has too many legs, no brain, and moves very slowly."

At their worst, this is indeed how groups function. In particular, they have a tendency to fail in two opposite directions, failures that can be avoided only by conscious effort. Groups can lapse into "clonethink" and produce a safe, superficial consensus whereby everyone agrees with the first opinion expressed in order to avoid conflict or to get on to something more interesting. At the other extreme is a phenomenon we'll call "egothink." In egothink, all members of the group go their own way and produce a collection of minority views that have nothing to do with each other and would be impossible to act on. Clonethinkers view their task as conformity to a norm; egothinkers see their task as safeguarding the autonomy of individual group members. Both fail to take other people and other ideas seriously.

Successful groups avoid both extremes and achieve unity out of diversity. This means that any successful community of learners must be willing to endure creative conflict. Creative conflict results from an initial agreement to disagree respectfully with each other and to focus that disagreement on ideas, not people. For this reason, we say that the relationship among the members of a learning community is not so much interpersonal or impersonal as *transpersonal*, or "beyond the personal." Each member is personally committed to the development of ideas and does whatever is necessary to achieve that development.

The Value of Group Work for Writers

Because we are basically social animals, we find it natural, pleasurable even, to deal with problems in groups. Proof of this fact can be found on any given morning in any given student union in the country. Around the room you will find many students working in groups. Math, engineering, and business majors will be solving problems together, comparing solutions and their ways of arriving at solutions. Others will be comparing their class notes and testing their understanding of concepts and terms by explaining them to each other and comparing their explanations. To be sure, their discussions will occasionally drift off the topic to encompass pressing social issues such as what they're going to do next weekend, or why they like or dislike the class they're working on, but much of the work of college students seems to get done in convivial conversation over morning coffee or late-night popcorn. Why not ease into the rigors of writing in a similar fashion?

A second major advantage of working on writing in a group is that it provides a real and immediate audience for people's work. Too often, when students write in a school setting, they get caught up in the writing-for-teacher racket, which may distort their notion of audience. Argumentative writing is best aimed either at opponents or at a neutral "jury" that will be weighing both sides of a controversy. A group of peers gives you a better sense of a real-world audience "out there" than does a single teacher.

There's danger, of course, in having several audiences consider your writing. Your peer audience may well respond differently to your writing than your instructor. You may feel misled if you are praised for something by a peer and then criticized for the same thing by your instructor. These things can and will happen, no matter how much time you spend developing universally accepted criteria for writing. Grades are not facts but judgments, and all judgments involve uncertainty. Students who are still learning the criteria for making judgments will sometimes apply those criteria differently than an instructor who has been working with them for years. But you should know too that two or more instructors might give you conflicting advice, just as two or more doctors might give you different advice on what to do about the torn ligaments in your knee. In our view, the risks of misunderstanding are more than made up for by gains in understanding of the writing process, an understanding that comes from working in writing communities where everyone functions both as a writer and as a writing critic.

A third advantage to working in writing communities is closely related to the second advantage. The act of sharing your writing with other people helps you get beyond the bounds of egocentrism that limit all writers. By egocentrism, we don't mean pride or stuck-upness; we mean the failure to consider the needs of your readers. Unless you share your writing with another person, your audience is always a "mythical group," a fiction or a theory that exists only in your head. You must always try to anticipate the problems others will have in reading your work. But until others actually read it and share their reactions to it with you, you can never be fully sure you have understood your audience's point of view. Until another reads your writing critically, you can't be sure you aren't talking to yourself.

Forming Writing Communities: Skills and Roles

Given that there are advantages to working in groups, just how do we go about forming writing communities in the classroom? We first have to decide how big to make the groups. From our experience, the best groups consist of either five to seven people or simply two people. Groups of three or four tend to polarize and become divisive, and larger groups tend to be unmanageable. Because working in five- to seven-person groups is quite different from working in pairs, we discuss each of these different-size groups in turn.

Working in Groups of Five to Seven People

The trick to successful group work is to consider the maximum number of viewpoints and concerns without losing focus. Because these two basic goals frequently conflict, you need some mechanisms for monitoring your progress. In particular, it's important that each group member is assigned to perform those tasks necessary to effective group functioning. (Some teachers assign roles to individual students, shifting the roles from day to day. Other teachers let the groups themselves determine the roles of individuals.) That is, the group must recognize that it has two objectives at all times: the stated objectives of a given task and the objective of making the group work well. It is very easy to get so involved with the given task that you overlook the second objective, generally known as "group maintenance."

The first role is group leader. We hesitate to call persons who fill this role "leaders" because we tend sometimes to think of leaders as know-it-alls who take charge and order people about. In classroom group work, however, being a group leader is a role you play, not a fixed part of your identity. The leader, above all else, keeps the group focused on agreed-on ends and protects the right of every group member to be heard. It's an important function, and group members should share the responsibility from task to task. Here is a list of things for the leader to do during a group discussion:

1. Ensure that everyone understands and agrees on the objectives of any given task and on what sort of final product is expected of the group (for example, a list of criteria, a brief written statement, or an oral response to a question).

2. Ask that the group set an agenda for completing the task, and have some sense of how much time the group will spend at each stage. (Your instructor should always make clear what time limits you have to operate within and when he or she expects your task to be completed. If a time limit isn't specified, you should request a reasonable estimate.)

3. Look for signs of getting off the track, and ask individual group members to clarify how their statements relate to agreed-on objectives.

4. Actively solicit everyone's contributions, and take care that all viewpoints are listened to and that the group does not rush to incomplete judgment.

5. Try to determine when the task has been adequately accomplished.

In performing each of these functions, the leader must be concerned to turn criticisms and observations into questions. Instead of saying to one silent and bored-looking member of the group, "Hey, Gormley, you haven't said diddly-squat here so far; say something relevant or take a hike," the leader might ask, "Irwin, do you agree with what Beth just said about this paper being disorganized?" Remember, every action in nature is met with an equal and opposite reaction—commands tend to be met with resistance, questions with answers.

A second crucial role for well-functioning groups is that of recorder. The recorder's function is to provide the group with a record of their deliberations so they can measure their progress. It is particularly important that the recorder write down the agenda and the solution to the problem in precise form. Because the recorder must summarize the deliberations fairly precisely, he must ask for clarifications. In doing this, he ensures that group members don't fall into the "ya know?" syndrome (a subset of clonethink) in which people assent to statements that are in fact cloudy to them. (Ya know?) At the completion of the task, the recorder should also ask whether there are any significant remaining disagreements or unanswered questions. Finally, the recorder is responsible for reporting the group's solutions to the class as a whole.*

If these two roles are conscientiously filled, the group should be able to identify and solve problems that temporarily keep it from functioning effectively. Maybe you are thinking that this sounds dumb. Whenever you've been in a group, everyone has known whether there were problems without leaders or recorders. Too often, however, a troubled group may sense that there is a problem without being perfectly clear about the nature of the problem or the solution. Let's say you are in a group with Elwood Lunt Jr., who is very opinionated and dominates the discussions. (For a sample of Elwood's cognitive style, see his essay "Good Writing and Computers for Today's Modern American Youth of America," in Task 1 on pp. 446–447.) Group members may represent their problem privately to themselves with a statement such as "Lunt's such a jerk nobody can work with him. He talks constantly and none of the rest of us can get a word in." The group may devote all of its energies to punishing Lunt with ridicule or silence rather than trying to solve the problem. Although this may make you feel better for a short time, Lunt is unlikely to get any better, and the group is unlikely to get much done.

If Lunt is indeed bogging the group down by airing his opinions at great length, it is the leader's job to limit his dominance without excluding him. Because group members all realize that it is the group leader's role to handle such problems, the leader has a sort of license that allows her or him to deal directly with Lunt. Moreover, the leader also has the explicit responsibility to do so, so that each member is not forced to sit, silently seething and waiting for someone to do something.

The leader might control Lunt in one of several ways: (1) by keeping to the agenda ("Thanks, Elwood, hate to interrupt, but we're a bit behind schedule and we haven't heard from everyone on this point yet. Jack, shall we move on to you?"); (2) by simply asking Lunt to demonstrate how his remarks are relevant to the topic at hand. ("That's real interesting, Elwood, that you got to see Nelly in his last performance, but can you tell us how you see that relating to Melissa's point

---

*There is a debate among experts who study small-group communications about whether the roles of leader and recorder can be collapsed into one job. Your group may need to experiment until it discovers the structure that works best for bringing out the most productive discussions.

about national I. D. cards?"); or (3) by introducing more formal procedures such as asking group members to raise their hands and be called on by the chair. These procedures might not satisfy your blood lust, your secret desire to stuff Lunt into a Dumpster; however, they are more likely to let the group get its work done and perhaps, just maybe, to help Lunt become a better listener and participant.

The rest of the group members, though they have no formally defined roles, have an equally important obligation to participate fully. To ensure full participation, group members can do several things. They can make sure that they know all the other group members by their first names and speak to them in a friendly manner. They can practice listening procedures wherein they try not to dissent or disagree without first charitably summarizing the view with which they are taking issue. Most importantly, they can bring to the group as much information and as many alternative points of view as they can muster. The primary intellectual strength of group work is the ability to generate a more complex view of a subject. But this more complex view cannot emerge unless all individuals contribute their perspectives.

One collaborative task for writers that requires no elaborate procedures or any role-playing is reading your essays aloud within the group. A good rule for this procedure is that no one responds to any one essay until all have been read. This is often an effective last step before handing in any essay. It's a chance to share the fruits of your labor with others and to hear finished essays that you may have seen in the draft stages. Hearing everyone else's final draft can also help you get a clearer perspective on how your own work is progressing. Listening to the essays read can both reassure you that your work is on a par with other people's and challenge you to write up to the level of the best student writing in your group.

Many of you may find this process a bit frightening at first. But the cause of your fright is precisely the source of the activity's value. In reading your work aloud, you are taking responsibility for that work in a special way. Writing specialist Kenneth Bruffee, whose work on collaborative learning introduced us to many of the ideas in this chapter, likens the reading of papers aloud to reciting a vow, of saying "I do" in a marriage ceremony. You are taking public responsibility for your words, and there's no turning back. The word has become deed. If you aren't at least a little nervous about reading an essay aloud, you probably haven't invested much in your words. Knowing that you will take public responsibility for your words is an incentive to make that investment—a more real and immediate incentive than a grade.

Working in Pairs

Working in pairs is another effective form of community learning. In our classes we use pairs at both the early-draft and the late-draft stages of writing. At the early-draft stage, it serves the very practical purpose of clarifying a student's ideas and sense of direction at the beginning of a new writing project. The interaction best takes place in the form of pair interviews. When you first sit down to interview each other, each of you should have done a fair amount of exploratory writing and thinking about what you want to say in your essay and how you're going to say it. Here is a checklist of questions you can use to guide your interview:

1. "What is your issue?" Your goal here is to help the writer focus an issue by formulating a question that clearly has alternative answers.

2. "What is your position on the issue, and what are alternative positions?" After you have helped your interviewee formulate the issue question, help her clarify this issue by stating her own position and show how that position differs from opposing ones. Your interviewee might say, for example, that "many of my friends are opposed to building more nuclear power plants, but I think we need to build more of them."

3. "Can you walk me through your argument step by step?" Once you know your interviewee's issue question and intended position, you can best help her by having her walk you through her argument talking out loud. You can ask prompting questions such as "What are you going to say first?" "What next?" and so on. At this stage your interviewee will probably still be struggling to discover the best way to support the point. You can best help by brainstorming along with her, both of you taking notes on your ideas. Often at this stage you can begin making a schematic plan for the essay and formulating supporting reasons as *because* clauses. Along the way give your interviewee any information or ideas you have on the issue. It is particularly helpful at this stage if you can provide counterarguments and opposing views.

The interview strategy is useful before writers begin their rough drafts. After the first drafts have been written, there are a number of different ways of using pairs to evaluate drafts. One practice that we've found helpful is simply to have writers write a one-paragraph summary of their own drafts and of their partner's. In comparing summaries, writers can often discover which, if any, of their essential ideas are simply not getting across. If a major idea is not in the reader's summary, writer and reader need to decide whether it's due to a careless reading or to problems within the draft. The nice thing about this method is that the criticism is given indirectly and hence isn't as threatening to either party. At other times, your instructor might also devise a checklist of features for you to consider, based on the criteria you have established for the assignment.

For Class Discussion

1. As a group, consider the following quotation and then respond to the questions that follow: "In most college classrooms there is a reluctance to assume leadership. The norm for college students is to defer to someone else, to refuse to accept the position even if it is offered. There is actually a

competition in humility and the most humble person usually ends up as the leader."*

   a. Do you think this statement is true?

   b. On what evidence do you base your judgment of its truthfulness?

   c. As a group, prepare an opening sentence for a paragraph that would report your group's reaction to this quotation.

2. Read the following statements about group interaction and decide as a group whether these statements are true or false.

   a. Women are less self-assertive and less competitive in groups than are men.

   b. There is a slight tendency for physically superior individuals to become leaders in a group.

   c. Leaders are usually more intelligent than nonleaders.

   d. Females conform to majority opinion more than males in reaching group decisions.

   e. An unconventional group member inhibits group functioning.

   f. An anxious group member inhibits group functioning.

   g. Group members with more power are usually better liked than low-power group members.

   h. Groups usually produce more and better solutions to problems than do individuals working alone.

With the assistance of the group, the recorder should write a four- to five-sentence description of the process your group used to reach agreement on the true-false statements. Was there discussion? Disagreement? Did you vote? Did every person give an opinion on each question? Were there any difficulties?

A Several-Days' Group Project: Defining "Good Argumentative Writing"

The problem we want you to address in this sequence of tasks is how to define and identify "good argumentative writing." This is a particularly crucial problem for developing writers insofar as you can't begin to measure your growth as a writer until you have some notion of what you're aiming for. To be sure, it's no easy task defining good argumentative writing. In order for even experienced teachers to reach agreement on this subject, some preliminary discussions and no small amount of compromise are necessary. By the end of this task you will most certainly not have reached a universally acceptable description of good argumentative writing. (Such a description doesn't exist.) But you will have begun a dialogue with

---

*Gerald Philips, Douglas Pederson, and Julia Wood, *Group Discussion: A Practical Guide to Participant Leadership* (Boston: Houghton Mifflin, 1979).

each other and your instructor on the subject. Moreover, you will have developed a vocabulary for sharing your views on writing with each other.

For this exercise, we give you a sequence of four tasks, some homework, and other in-class group tasks. Please do the tasks in sequence.

Task 1 (Homework): Preparing for the Group Discussion   Freewrite for five minutes on the question "What is good argumentative writing?" After finishing your freewrite, read fictional student Lunt's argument that follows and, based on the principles that Lunt seems to break, develop a tentative list of criteria for good argumentative writing.

Explanation   Before you come together with a group of people to advance your understanding and knowledge collectively, you first need to explore your own thoughts on the matter. Too often, groups collapse not because the members lack goodwill but because they lack preparation. To discharge your responsibility as a good group member, you must therefore begin by doing your homework. By using a freewriting exercise, you focus your thinking on the topic, explore what you already know or feel about it, and begin framing questions and problems.

To help you establish a standard for good argumentative writing, we've produced a model of bad arguing by a fictional student, one Elwood P. Lunt Jr. If you can figure out what's bad about Lunt's argument, then you can formulate the principles of good argument that he violates. Of course, no student of our acquaintance has ever written anything as bad as Lunt's essay. That's the virtue of this contrived piece. It's an easy target. In going over it critically, you may well find that Lunt violates principles of good writing you hadn't thought of in your freewrite. (We tried to ensure that he violated as many as possible.) Thus you should be sure to go back and modify your ideas from your freewrite accordingly.

A couple of important points to keep in mind here as you prepare to critique another person's work: (1) Remember the principle of charity. Try to look past the muddied prose to a point or intention that might be lurking in the background. Your critique should speak as much as possible to Lunt's failure to realize this intent. (2) Direct your critique to the prose, not the writer. Don't settle for "He just doesn't make sense" or "He's a dimwit." Ask yourself why he doesn't make sense and point to particular places where he doesn't make sense. In sum, give Lunt the same sort of reading you would like to get: compassionate and specific.

Good Writing and Computers for Today's Modern American Youth of America

(A partial fulfillment of writing an argument in the course in which I am attending)

1   In todays modern fast paced world computers make living a piece of cake. You can do a lot with computers which in former times took a lot of time and doing a lot

of work. Learning to fly airplanes, for example. But there are no such things as a free lunch. People who think computers will do all the work for you need to go to Russia and take a look around, that's the place for people who think they can be replaced by computers. The precious computer which people think is the dawn of a new civilization but which is in all reality a pig in a poke makes you into a number but can't even add right! So don't buy computers for two reasons.

The first reason you shouldn't buy a computer is writing. So what makes people think that they won't have to write just because they have a computer on his desk. "Garbage in and garbage out one philosopher said." Do you want to sound like garbage? I don't. That's why modern American fast paced youth must conquer this affair with computers and writing by ourselves is the answer to our dreams and not just by using a computer for that aforementioned writing. A computer won't make you think better and that's the problem because people think a computer will do your thinking for you. No way, Jose. 2

Another thing is grammar. My Dad Elwood P. Lunt Sr. hit the nail on the head; when he said bad grammar can make you sound like a jerk. Right on Dad. He would be so upset to think of all the jerks out there who wasted their money on a computer so that the computer could write for them. But do computers know grammar? So get on the bandwagon and write good and get rich with computers. Which can make you write right. You think any computer could catch the errors I just made? Oh, sure you do. Jerk. And according to our handbook on writing writing takes intelligence which computers don't have. Now I'm not against computers. I am just saying that computers have there place. 3

In conclusion there are two reasons why you shouldn't buy a computer. But if you want to buy one that is all right as long as you understand that it isn't as smart as you think. 4

Task 2 (In-Class Group Work): Developing a Master List of Criteria As a group, reach a consensus on at least six or seven major problems with Lunt's argumentative essay. Then use that list to prepare a parallel list of criteria for a good written argument. Please have your list ready in thirty minutes.

Explanation Your goal for this task is to reach consensus about what's wrong with Lunt's argument. As opposed to a "majority decision," in which more people agree than disagree, a "consensus" entails a solution that is generally acceptable to all members of the group. In deciding what is the matter with Lunt's essay, you should be able to reach consensus also on the criteria for a good argument. After each group has completed its list, recorders should report each group's consensus to the class as a whole. Your instructor will facilitate a discussion leading to the class's "master list" of criteria.

Task 3 (Homework): Applying Criteria to Student Essays At home, consider the following five samples of student writing. (This time they're real examples.) Rank the essays "1" through "5," with 1 being the best and 5 the worst. Once you've done this, develop a brief rationale for your ranking. This rationale should force you to decide which criteria you rank highest and which lowest. For example, does "quality of reasons" rank higher than "organization and development"? Does "colorful, descriptive style" rank high or low in your ranking system?

Explanation   The following essays were written as short arguments developing two or three reasons in support of a claim. Students had studied the argumentative concepts in Chapters 1–6 but had not yet studied refutation strategies. Although the students were familiar with classical argument structure, this introductory assignment asked them to support a claim/thesis with only two or three reasons. Summarizing and responding to opposing views was optional.

Bloody Ice

1   It is March in Alaska. The ocean-side environment is full of life and death. Man and animal share this domain but not in peace. The surrounding iceflows, instead of being cold and white, are steaming from the remains of gutted carcasses and stained red. The men are hunters and the animals are barely six weeks old. A slaughter has just taken place. Thousands of baby Harp seals lie dead on the ice and thousands more of adult mothers lay groaning over the death of their babies. Every year a total limit of 180,000 seals set by the U.S. Seal Protection Act is filled in a terrifying bloodbath. But Alaska with its limit of 30,000 is not alone. Canadians who hunt seals off the coast of Northern Newfoundland and Quebec are allowed 150,000 seals. The Norwegians are allowed 20,000 and native Eskimos of Canada and Greenland are allowed 10,000 seals per year. Although this act appears heartless and cruel, the men who hunt have done this for 200 years as a tradition for survival. They make many good arguments supporting their traditions. They feel the seals are in no immediate danger of extinction. Also seal furs can be used to line boots and gloves or merely traded for money and turned into robes or fur coats. Sometimes the meat is even used for food in the off hunting months when money is scarce. But are these valid justifications for the unmerciful killings? No, the present limit on Harp seal killings should be better regulated because the continued hunting of the seals will lead to eventual extinction and because the method of slaughter is so cruel and inhumane.

2   The Harp seal killing should be better regulated first because eventual extinction is inevitable. According to *Oceans* magazine, before the limit of 180,000 seals was established in 1950, the number of seals had dwindled from 3,300,000 to 1,250,000. Without these limitations hundreds of thousands were killed within weeks of birth. Now, even with this allotment, the seals are being killed off at an almost greater rate than they can remultiply. Adult female seals give birth once every year but due to pollution, disease, predation, whelping success, and malnutrition they are already slowly dying on their own without being hunted. Eighty percent of the seals slaughtered are pups and the remaining twenty percent are adult seals and even sometimes mothers who try attacking the hunters after seeing their babies killed. The hunters, according to the Seal Protection Act, have this right.

Second, I feel the killing should be better regulated because of the inhumane
method used. In order to protect the fur value of the seals, guns are not used.
Instead, the sealers use metal clubs to bludgeon the seal to death. Almost immediately after being delivered a direct blow, the seals are gutted open and skinned.
Although at this stage of life the seal's skull is very fragile, sometimes the seals are
not killed by the blows but merely stunned; thus hundreds are skinned alive. Still
others are caught in nets and drowned, which, according to *America* magazine, the
Canadian government continues to deny. But the worst of the methods used is when
a hunter gets tired of swinging his club and uses the heel of his boot to kick the
seal's skull in. Better regulation is the only way to solve this problem because other
attempts seem futile. For example, volunteers who have traveled to hunting sites
trying to dye the seals to ruin their fur value have been caught and fined heavily.

The plight of the Harp seals has been long and controversial. With the
Canadian hunters feeling they have the right to kill the seals because it has been
their industry for over two centuries, and on the other hand with humane organizations fearing extinction and strongly opposing the method of slaughter, a compromise must be met among both sides. As I see it, the solution to the problem is simple. Since the Canadians do occasionally use the whole seal and have been sealing
for so long they could be allowed to continue but at a more heavily regulated rate.
Instead of filling the limit of 180,000 every year and letting the numbers of seals decrease, Canadians could learn to ranch the seals as Montanans do cattle or sheep.
The United States has also offered to help them begin farming their land for a new
livelihood. The land is adequate for crops and would provide work all year round instead of only once a month every year. As a result of farming, the number of seals
killed would be drastically cut down because Canadians would not be so dependent
on the seal industry as before. This would in turn lead back to the ranching aspect
of sealing and allow the numbers to grow back and keeping the tradition alive for
future generations and one more of nature's creatures to enjoy.

RSS Should Not Provide Dorm Room Carpets

Tricia, a University student, came home exhausted from her work-study job.
She took a blueberry pie from the refrigerator to satisfy her hunger and a tall
glass of milk to quench her thirst. While trying to get comfortable on her bed, she
tipped her snack over onto the floor. She cleaned the mess, but the blueberry and
milk stains on her brand new carpet could not be removed. She didn't realize that
maintaining a clean carpet would be difficult and costly. Tricia bought her own
carpet. Some students living in dorm rooms want carpeted rooms provided for
them at the expense of the University. They insist that since they pay to live on
campus, the rooms should reflect a comfortable home atmosphere. However,
Resident Student Services (RSS) should not be required to furnish the carpet

because other students do not want carpets. Furthermore, carpeting all the rooms totals into a very expensive project. And lastly, RSS should not have to provide the carpet because many students show lack of respect and responsibility for school property.

2   Although RSS considers the carpeting of all rooms a strong possibility, students like Tricia oppose the idea. They feel the students should buy their own carpets. Others claim the permanent carpeting would make dorm life more comfortable. The carpet will act as insulation and as a sound proofing system. These are valid arguments, but they should not be the basis for changing the entire residence hall structure. Those students with "cold feet" can purchase house footwear, which cost less than carpet. Unfortunately carpeting doesn't muffle all the noise; therefore, some students will be disturbed. Reasonable quietness should be a matter of respect for other students' privacy and comfort. Those opposed to the idea reason out the fact that students constantly change rooms or move out. The next person may not want carpet. Also, if RSS carpets the rooms, the students will lose the privilege they have of painting their rooms any color. Paint stains cannot be removed. Some students can't afford to replace the carpet. Still another factor, carpet color may not please everyone. RSS would provide a neutral color like brown or gray. With tile floors, the students can choose and purchase their own carpets to match their taste.

3   Finally, another reason not to have carpet exists in the fact that the project can be expensive due to material costs, installation cost, and the maintenance cost caused mainly by the irresponsibility of many students. According to Rick Jones, Asst. Director of Housing Services, the cost will be $300 per room for the carpet and installation. RSS would also have to purchase more vacuum cleaners for the students' use. RSS will incur more expense in order to maintain the vacuums. Also, he claims that many accidents resulting from shaving cream fights, food fights, beverage parties, and smoking may damage the carpet permanently. With floor tiles, accidents such as food spills can be cleaned up easier than carpet. The student's behavior plays an important role in deciding against carpeting. Many students don't follow the rules of maintaining their rooms. They drill holes into the walls, break mirrors, beds, and closet doors, and leave their food trays all over the floor. How could they be trusted to take care of school carpet when they violate the current rules? Many students feel they have the "right" to do as they please. This irresponsible and disrespectful behavior reflects their future attitude about carpet care.

4   In conclusion, the university may be able to afford to supply the carpets in each room, but maintaining them would be difficult. If the students want carpets, they should pay and care for the carpets themselves. Hopefully, they will be more cautious and value it more. They should take the initiative to fundraise or find other financial means of providing this "luxury." They should not rely on the school to provide unnecessary room fixtures such as carpets. Also, they must remember that if RSS provides the carpet and they don't pay for the damages, they and future students will endure the consequences. What will happen???? Room rates will skyrocket!!!!!

Sterling Hall Dorm Food

The quality of Sterling Hall dorm food does not meet the standard needed to   1
justify the high prices University students pay. As I watched a tall, medium-built
University student pick up his Mexican burrito from the counter it didn't surprise me
to see him turn up his nose. Johnny, our typical University student, waited five minutes before he managed to make it through the line. After he received his bill of $4.50
he turned his back to the cash register and walked away displeased with his meal.

As our neatly groomed University student placed his ValiDine eating card back   2
into his Giorgio wallet, he thought back to the balance left on his account. Johnny
had $24 left on his account and six more weeks left of school. He had been eating
the cheapest meals he could and still receive a balanced meal, but the money just
seemed to disappear. No student, not even a thrifty boy like Johnny, could possibly
afford to live healthfully according to the University meal plan system.

Johnny then sat down at a dirty table to find his burrito only half way cooked.   3
Thinking back to the long-haired cook who served him the burrito, he bit into the
burrito and noticed a long hair dangling from his lips. He realized the cook's lack of
preparation when preparing his burrito.

Since the food costs so much, yet the quality of the food remains low, University   4
students do not get the quality they deserve. From the information stated I can conclude that using the ValiDine service system University students would be jeopardizing their health and wasting their hard-earned money. University students deserve something more than what they have now.

ROTC Courses Should Not Get College Credit

One of the most lucrative scholarships a student can receive is a four-year ROTC   1
scholarship that pays tuition and books along with a living allowance. It was such a
scholarship that allowed me to attend an expensive liberal arts college and to pursue
the kind of well rounded education that matters to me. Of course, I am obligated to
spend four years on active duty—an obligation that I accept and look forward to.
What I am disappointed in, however, is the necessity to enroll in Military Science
classes. Strong ROTC advocates argue that Military Science classes are essential
because they produce good citizens, teach leadership skills, and provide practical
experience for young cadets. Maybe so. But we could get the same benefits without
having to take these courses for credit. Colleges should make ROTC training an
extracurricular activity, not a series of academic courses taken for academic credit.

First of all, ROTC courses, unlike other college courses, do not stress inquiry and   2
true questioning. The ROTC program has as its objective the preparation of future

officers committed to the ideals and structure of the military. The structure of the military is based upon obediently following the orders of military superiors. Whereas all my other teachers stress critical thinking and doing independent analysis, my ROTC instructors avoid political or social questions saying it is the job of civilian leaders to debate policies and the job of the military to carry them out. We don't even debate what role the military should play in our country. My uncle, who was an ROTC cadet during the Vietnam war, remembers that not only did ROTC classes never discuss the ethics of the war but that cadets were not allowed to protest the war outside of their ROTC courses. This same obedience is demanded in my own ROTC courses, where we are not able to question administration policies and examine openly the complexity of the situation in Iraq and Kuwait.

3   A second reason that Army ROTC courses do not deserve academic credit is that the classes are not academically strenuous, thus giving cadets a higher GPA and an unfair advantage over their peers. Much of what a cadet does for academic credit involves nonacademic activities such as physical training for an hour three days a week so that at least some of a cadet's grade is based on physical activity, not mental activity. In conducting an informal survey of 10 upper-classmen, I found out that none of them has ever gotten anything lower than an A in a Military Science class and they do not know of anyone who got anything lower than an A. One third-year cadet stated that "the classes are basic. A monkey coming out of the zoo could get college credit for a Military Science class." He went on to say that most of the information given in his current class is a brush-up to 8th grade U.S. history. In contrast, a typical liberal arts college class requires much thought, questioning, and analysis. The ROTC Military Science class is taught on the basis of "regurgitated knowledge," meaning that once you are given a piece of information you are required to know it and reproduce it at any time without thought or question. A good example is in my class Basic Officership. Our first assignment is to memorize and recite in front of the class the Preamble to the Constitution of the United States. The purpose of doing so doesn't seem to be to understand or analyze the constitution because we never talk about that. In fact, I don't know what the purpose is. I just do it because I am told to. Because the "A" is so easy to get in my ROTC class, I spend all my time studying for my other classes. I am a step ahead of my peers in the competition for a high GPA, even though I am not getting as good an education.

4   Finally, having to take ROTC classes means that I can't take other liberal arts courses which would be more valuable. One of the main purposes for ROTC is to give potential officers a liberal education. Many cadets have the credentials to get into an armed forces academy, but they chose ROTC programs because they could combine military training with a well-rounded curriculum. Unfortunately, by taking Military Science classes each quarter, cadets find that their electives are all but eaten up by the time they are seniors. If ROTC classes were valuable in themselves, I wouldn't complain. But they aren't, and they keep me from taking upper division electives in philosophy, literature, and the humanities.

5   All of these reasons lead me to believe that Army ROTC cadets are getting shortchanged when they enroll for Military Science classes. Because cadets receive

a lucrative scholarship, they should have to take the required military science courses. But these courses should be treated as extracurricular activities, like a work-study job or like athletics. Just as a student on a full-ride athletic scholarship does not receive academic credit for football practices and games, so should a student on a full-ride ROTC scholarship have to participate in the military education program without getting academic credit. By treating ROTC courses as a type of extracurricular activity like athletics, students can take more elective credits that will expand their minds, better enabling them to have the knowledge to make moral decisions and to enjoy their world more fully.

Legalization of Prostitution

Prostitution . . . It is the world's oldest profession. It is by definition the act of offering or soliciting sex for payment. It is, to some, evil. Yet the fact is it exists.   1

Arguments are not necessary to prove the existence of prostitution. Rather, the argument arises when trying to prove something must be done to reduce the problems of this profession. The problems which exist are in the area of crime, of health, and of environment. Crime rates are soaring, diseases are spreading wildly, and the environment on the streets is rapidly decaying. Still, it has been generally conceded that these problems cannot be suppressed. However, they can be reduced. Prostitution should be legalized because it would reduce the wave of epidemics, decrease high crime rates, provide good revenue by treating it like other businesses, and get girls off the streets where sexual crimes often occur.   2

Of course, there are those who would oppose the legalization of prostitution stating that it is one of the main causes for the spread of venereal diseases. Many argue that it is interrelated with drug-trafficking and other organized crimes. And probably the most controversial is the moral aspect of the subject; it is morally wrong, and legalizing it would be enforcing, or even justifying, such an existence.   3

These points propose good arguments, but I shall counter each point and explain the benefits and advantages of legalizing prostitution. In the case of prostitution being the main cause for the spread of epidemics, I disagree. By legalizing it, houses would be set up which would solve the problem of girls working on the streets and being victims of sexual crimes. It would also provide regular health checks, as is successfully done in Nevada, Germany, and other parts of the U.S. and Europe, which will therefore cut down on diseases spreading unknowingly.   4

As for the increase of organized crime if prostitution is legalized, I disagree again. Firstly, by treating it like businesses, then that would make good state revenue. Secondly, like all businesses have regulations, so shall these houses. That would put closer and better control in policing the profession, which is presently a problem. Obviously, if the business of prostitution is more closely supervised, that would decrease the crime rates.   5

6   Now, I come to one of the most arguable aspects of legalizing prostitution: the moral issue. Is it morally wrong to legalize prostitution? That is up to the individual. To determine whether anything is "right or wrong" in our society is nearly impossible to do since there are various opinions. If a person were to say that prostitution is the root of all evil, that will not make it go away. It exists. Society must begin to realize that fear or denial will not make the "ugliness" disappear. It still exists.

7   Prostitution can no longer go ignored because of our societal attitudes. Legalizing it is beneficial to our society, and I feel in time people may begin to form an accepting attitude. It would be the beginning of a more open-minded view of what is reality. Prostitution . . . it is the world's oldest profession. It exists. It is a reality.

Task 4 (In-Class Group Work): Reaching Consensus on Ranking of Essays
Working again in small groups, reach consensus on your ranking of the five essays. Groups should report both their rankings and their justification for the rankings based on the criteria established in Task 2 or as currently modified by your group.

Explanation   You are now to reach consensus on how you rank the papers and why you rank them the way you do. Feel free to change the criteria you established earlier if they seem to need modification. Be careful in your discussions to distinguish between evaluation of the writer's written product and your own personal position on the writer's issue. In other words, there is a crucial difference between saying, "I don't like Pete's essay because I disagree with his ideas," and "I don't like Pete's essay because he didn't provide adequate support for his ideas." As each group reports back the results of its deliberations to the class as a whole, the instructor will highlight discrepancies among the groups' decisions and collate the criteria as they emerge. If the instructor disagrees with the class consensus or wants to add items to the criteria, he or she might choose to make these things known now. By the end of this stage, everyone should have a list of criteria for good argumentative writing established by the class.

A Classroom Debate

In this exercise, you have an opportunity to engage in a variant of a formal debate. Although debates of this nature don't always lead to truth for its own sake, they are excellent forums for the development of analytical and organizational skills. The format for the debate is as follows.

First Hour   Groups will identify and reach consensus on "the most serious impediment to learning at this institution." Participants should have come to class prepared with their own individual lists of at least three problems. Once the class has reached consensus on the single most serious impediment to learning on your campus, your instructor will write it out as a formal statement. This statement constitutes the preliminary topic, which will eventually result in a proposition for your debate.

The instructor will then divide the class into an equal number of Affirmative and Negative teams (three to five members per team). Homework for all the Affirmative team members is to identify proposals for solving the problem identified by the class. Negative team members, meanwhile, will concentrate on reasons that the problem is not particularly serious and/or that the problem is "in the nature of things" and simply not solvable by any sort of proposal.

Second Hour   At the beginning of the period, the instructor will pair up each Affirmative team with a Negative team. The teams will be opponents during the actual debate, and there will be as many debates as there are paired teams. Each Affirmative team will now work on choosing the best proposal for solving the problem, while the Negative team pools its resources and builds its case against the seriousness and solvability of the problem. At the end of the period, each Affirmative team will share its proposal with its corresponding Negative team. The actual topic for each of the debates is now set: "Resolved: Our campus should institute Z (the Affirmative team's proposal) in order to solve problem X (the class's original problem statement)."

Homework for the next class is for each team to conduct research (interviewing students, gathering personal examples, polling students, finding data or expert testimony from the library, and so forth) to support its case. Each Affirmative team's research will be aimed at showing that the problem is serious and that the solution is workable. Each Negative team will try to show that the proposal won't work or that the problem isn't worth solving.

Third Hour   At this point each Affirmative team and each Negative team will select two speakers to represent their sides. During this hour each team will pool its ideas and resources to help the speakers make the best possible cases. Each team should prepare an outline for a speech supporting its side of the debate. Team members should then anticipate the arguments of the opposition and prepare a rebuttal.

Fourth (and Fifth) Hour(s)   The actual debates. (There will be as many debates as there are paired Affirmative and Negative teams.) Each team will present two speakers. Each speaker is limited to five minutes. The order of speaking is as follows:

FIRST AFFIRMATIVE: Presents best case for the proposal

FIRST NEGATIVE: Presents best case against the proposal

SECOND NEGATIVE: Rebuts argument of First Affirmative

SECOND AFFIRMATIVE: Rebuts argument of First Negative

Those team members who do not speak will be designated observers. Their task is to take notes on the debate, paying special attention to the quality of support for each argument and to those parts of the argument that are not rebutted by the opposition. By the next class period (fifth or sixth), they will have prepared a brief, informal analysis titled "Why Our Side Won the Debate."

Fifth or Sixth Hour   The observers will report to the class on their perceptions of the debates by using their prepared analysis as the basis of the discussion. The instructor will attempt to synthesize the main points of the debates and the most telling arguments for either side. At this point, your instructor may ask each of you to write an argument on the debate topic, allowing you to argue for or against any of the proposals presented.

An Anthology
of Arguments

This political cartoon, sympathizing with youth, explores two current social issues that have generated many civic arguments: the generation gap and the causes of teen violence.

Source: John Branch/San Antonio Express-News.

An Overview of the Anthology

Part Five, an anthology of engaging verbal and visual arguments addressing twelve important social issues, will let you put into practice your new skills of reading and analyzing arguments, conducting inquiry, and joining an argumentative conversation. As we discussed in Chapter 3, writers of arguments come from all walks of life and produce arguments from multiple social contexts within many communities in society. They may be ordinary citizens, members of advocacy groups or lobbyists, media commentators, professional staff writers for magazines and newspapers, scholars and academics, or other kinds of stakeholders within workplaces, neighborhoods, or civic or cultural organizations. Motivated by some occasion, these stakeholders write to an audience for a purpose within a genre, their rhetorical situations influencing their decisions about content, structure, and style.

We chose the articles in this anthology to show this rich variety of argumentative occasions, the multisided nature of argument, and the complexity of issues. The arguments you encounter here represent distinctly divergent angles of vision, different ways of conceptualizing controversies, and different argumentative strategies to influence readers' views and to win over decision makers. Passionate in their own ways, these stakeholders also differ in their commitment to persuasion versus truth-seeking, thereby creating differences in style, tone, and treatment of alternative views. In addition, faced with different rhetorical contexts and purposes, these writers create arguments in many genres: short opinion-editorials, academic arguments grounded in research, advocacy Web sites, congressional speeches, white papers to set forth the views and policy proposals of organizations, and a rich array of visual arguments, from public affairs advocacy ads, to poster arguments and fliers, to political cartoons and commercial advertisements.

To help you understand the cultural context for each set of readings, we have provided brief introductions to each unit, headnotes for each article, and a concluding set of discussion questions that urge you to see the complexity of the issue and the consequences of different claims. The introductions to each unit sketch key points of background, provide context, and suggest the cultural significance of the issue. The headnotes to each article give original publication data, identify the genre of the piece, and, in most cases, briefly identify the writer and the political perspective.* We encourage you to continue this contextualizing process by using the guide questions we provide in the next section. Finally, we encourage you to consider the class discussion questions at the end of each unit to help you appreciate the multisided views of stakeholders and to acknowledge the consequences, strengths, and limitations of different claims.

As you read through the arguments in this anthology, note how current topical issues (such as whether the federal government should require labeling of genetically engineered food) touch on broad, enduring questions about cultural value such as the rights of consumers versus the rights of corporations. No matter what

---

*For full citation information, see the Credits at the back of the book.

the specific issue is, certain recurring patterns of concern keep cropping up, such as principles versus consequences, spiritual values versus material values, rights of individuals versus rights of society, duties to self versus duties to others, short-range consequences versus long-range consequences, or tradition versus change. One advantage of an anthology of arguments is that in reading through them you can see for yourself how frequently these large issues recur in different guises.

In creating this anthology, we had in mind two main ways you might approach these readings. First, we invite you to enter these argumentative conversations yourself. After listening to and responsibly weighing the alternative views, you will face the responsibility of synthesizing various perspectives to create your own argument for a new context. Often you will need to do more research in order to clarify your views and take a stand. By eliciting your questions and enlarging your perspective—the process of dissent and synthesis at the heart of argument—the arguments in this anthology can challenge you to speak out on your own on these controversies.

A second way to approach these arguments—and one that can be combined with the first way—is to examine these articles for their wide variety of argumentative strategies to see how they can expand your repertoire as an arguer. In studying these arguments, you should ask questions like these: What works or doesn't work to make this argument persuasive? Why might a given argument be effective for its intended audience but not for some other audience? What can this argument teach me about presenting a positive *ethos*, about treating opposing views, about successful uses of evidence, or about appealing to *pathos*? Learning more about your options can empower you as a writer of arguments.

Guide Questions for the Analysis and Evaluation of Arguments

To help you develop skills at analyzing and evaluating arguments, we provide in this section three handy checklists of guide questions. These questions summarize the key principles of argument we have covered throughout the text.

List 1: Questions for Analyzing and Evaluating a Conversation

Whenever you read two or more arguments addressing the same issue, we recommend that you follow the principles of reading described in Chapter 2.

1. What does each argument say? (Reading as a believer, be able to summarize each argument, stating its main claim and supporting reasons in a single sentence if possible.)
2. How can each argument be doubted? (Reading as a doubter, search for weaknesses in the argument, think about what is left out, and articulate important questions that you would like to raise if you could talk to the author.)
3. How have the rhetorical context and genre shaped each argument?

4. Why do the disputants disagree? (Do they disagree about the facts of the case? Do they differ in the selection or interpretation of the facts or other data they use for evidence? Do they disagree about values, assumptions, and beliefs?)

5. Which arguments appear to be stronger? (Which arguments seem most persuasive to you? Before you could take a stand on the issue yourself, what further questions would you need to have answered? Which of your own assumptions, values, and beliefs would you have to examine further and clarify?)

List 2: Questions for Analyzing and Evaluating an Individual Argument

The previous questions ask you to examine arguments in the context of the conversations to which they belong. This next set of questions asks you to look closely at a single argument, examining in detail its structure, its argumentative strategies, and its rhetorical force.

1. What is the writer's purpose and audience?
   - Who are the intended readers? What are their values and beliefs?
   - How does the writer hope to change the intended readers' views on the issue?
   - What was the occasion for writing? What motivated the writer to produce this piece?

2. What genre is the piece?
   - Where was this piece published?
   - How does the genre of the piece—or its place of publication—influence its content, point of view, or style?
   - How can certain features of the text be explained by genre?

3. What seems to be the writer's perspective, bias, or angle of vision?
   - What does the text reveal about the author's values and beliefs?
   - What does the author omit?
   - How committed is the author to his or her claim?
   - What views does the author oppose? Why?

4. Does the argument have a strong logical core?
   - What is the writer's claim? Where is it explicitly stated or where is it implied?
   - What are the main reasons in support of the claim? Are the reasons audience-based?

5. How effective is the writer's use of evidence?
   - Is the evidence relevant, sufficient, and appropriately up-to-date?
   - Does the evidence come from reputable sources?
   - What kind of evidence is used?

- How is the argument reasonably supported and developed? Are there any obvious flaws or fallacies in the argument?

6. How effective is the writer at making ethical appeals?
   - What *ethos* does the writer project?
   - How does the writer try to seem credible and trustworthy to the intended audience?

7. How effective is the writer at creating pathetic appeals?
   - How effective is the writer at using audience-based reasons?
   - How effective is the writer's use of concrete language, word choice, examples, and analogies for giving the argument emotional presence?

8. How could the writer's argument be refuted?
   - Can the writer's reasons and grounds be called into question?
   - Can the writer's warrants and backing be called into question?

9. If used, how effective are the author's use of images, graphics, or other visuals?
   - Why did the author choose or design these particular images, graphics, or visuals?
   - How do font sizes and styles, the layout of images and text, and the use of color contribute to the effectiveness of the visual?
   - How does the composition of images—such as setting, props, clothing, poses of characters, and so forth—contribute to the effectiveness of the visual?
   - How are graphics used to tell a particular story with numbers? Why does the author focus on this particular story rather than another story?

List 3: Questions for Responding to a Reading and Forming Your Own Views

This final set of questions is designed to help you speak back to a text in order to form your own views.

1. Which of the author's points do you agree with?
2. What new insights has the reading given you?
3. Which of the author's points do you disagree with?
4. What gaps or omissions do you see in the text? What has the author overlooked?
5. What questions or problems does the text raise for you? How has it troubled you or expanded your views?
6. In terms of your own evolving views on this issue, how useful is this reading? How might you use it in your own argument?

ENVIRONMENTAL FRIENDLINESS VERSUS MARKET FREEDOM: THE CASE OF THE SPORT-UTILITY VEHICLE

With grand and mighty names like "Expedition," "Trailblazer," "Pathfinder," "Jeep Liberty," and "Denali," sport-utility vehicles are appearing in greater numbers on American roads, particularly urban streets. What social, political, economic, and cultural forces have made these large, expensive, and fuel-inefficient SUVs the vehicle of choice for more and more Americans? And how have SUVs become the focus of such intense public controversy?

Sport-utility vehicles gained sales prominence when car manufacturers responded to the federal government's 1975 regulations on fuel economy—known as CAFE (Corporate Average Fuel Economy—currently set at an average of 20.7 mpg for trucks and 27.5 mpg for cars)—by welding SUV bodies onto truck frames and marketing SUVs as light trucks. With this new category of vehicles, car manufacturers tapped into Americans' imagination and desire for space, physical security on the road, and options for an outdoor recreational lifestyle.

These basic facts, however, only begin to account for the complex phenomenon of SUV popularity, which in turn raises a host of interwoven issues. Environmentalists point to SUVs as gas guzzlers that contribute to global warming, while political economists worry about SUVs' contributing to our country's dependence on foreign oil. Meanwhile, proponents of the automotive industry state that car manufacturers produce what consumers want (and SUVs are enormously popular). The auto manufacturers are supported by advocates of consumer freedom who protest any regulatory efforts that might take away consumers' right to choose vehicles that fulfill their needs, perceived or real. So, what should we do about SUVs and the problems they bring and symbolize?

The readings and visual arguments in this unit as well as the ad for the Saturn VUE in Color Plate G explore these diverse perspectives on sport-utility vehicles.

Driving Global Warming

Bill McKibben

Bill McKibben, former staff writer for the New Yorker *and author of* The End of Nature *(1998), is a well-known environmental writer whose articles have appeared in* In These Times, *the* Utne Reader, Science & Spirit Magazine, *and other liberal magazines. This argument, which appeared in* The Christian Century *in 2001, casts owning and driving SUVs as a moral issue.*

Up until some point in the 1960s, people of a certain class routinely belonged to 1
segregated country clubs without giving it much thought—it was "normal." And
then, in the space of a few years, those memberships became immoral. As a society,
we'd crossed some threshold where the benefits—a good place to play golf, a nice
pool for the kids, business contacts, a sense of status and belonging—had to be
weighed against the recognition that racial discrimination was evil.

Belonging to Farflung Acres CC wasn't the same as bombing black churches 2
(perfectly sweet and decent people did it), and quitting wasn't going to change the
economic or social patterns of the whole society, but it had become an inescapable
symbol. Either you cared enough about the issue of race to make a stand or you did-
n't. If you thought we were all made in God's image, and that Jesus had died to save
us all, it was the least you could do.

For the past decade, buying a sport utility vehicle—an Explorer, a Navigator, a 3
CRV, a Suburban, a Rover, and so on down the list—has seemed perfectly normal.
Most people of a certain station did it. If you went to a grocery store in suburban
Boston, you would think that reaching it required crossing flooded rivers and
climbing untracked canyons. In any given parking lot, every other vehicle has four-
wheel drive, 18 inches of clearance, step-up bumpers. They come with a lot of
other features: leather seats, surround sound, comfort, status. Maybe even some
sense of connection with nature, for they've been advertised as a way to commune
with creation.

But now we've come to another of those threshold moments. In January, after 4
five years of exhaustive scientific study, the International Panel on Climate Change
announced the consensus of the world's leading experts: If we keep burning fossil
fuels at anything like our present rate, the planet will warm four or five degrees,
and perhaps as much as 11 degrees, before the century is out. Those temperatures
would top anything we've seen for hundreds of millions of years.

Already we can guess the effects. The decade we've just come through was the 5
warmest on record in human history: It saw record incidences of floods and drought
(both of which you'd expect with higher temperatures). Arctic ice, we now know,
has thinned 40 percent in the last 40 years. Sea level is rising steadily.

And what has the SUV to do with all of this? Well, it is mostly a machine for 6
burning gasoline. Say you switched from a normal car to a big sport "ute" and
drove it for one year. The extra energy you use would be the equivalent of leaving
the door to the fridge open for six years, or your bathroom light on for three
decades. Twenty percent of America's carbon dioxide emissions come from
automobiles.

Even as we've begun to improve efficiency in factories and power plants, our 7
cars and trucks have grown bigger and more wasteful: average fuel efficiency actually declined in the 1990s, even as engineers came up with one technology after another that could have saved gas. That's a big reason why Americans now produce
12 percent more CO2, the main global warming gas, than they did when Bill Clinton
took office.

If you drive an SUV, then you're "driving" global warming, even more than the 8
rest of us.

9   In Bangladesh people spent three months of 1998 living in the thigh-deep water that covered two-thirds of the nation. The inundation came because the Bay of Bengal was some inches higher than normal (as climate changes, sea level rises because warm water takes up more space). That high-water blocked the drainage of the normal summer floods, turning the nation into a vast lake. No one can say exactly how much higher that water was because of our recent fondness for semi-military transport in the suburbs. Maybe an inch, who knows?

10   But the connection is clear. If you care about the people in this world living closest to the margins, then you need to do everything in your power to slow the rate at which the planet warms, for they are the most vulnerable. I was naked and you did not clothe me. I was hungry and you drowned me with your Ford Explorer.

11   Here's more: Coral reefs the world over are dying as warmer sea water bleaches them to death—by some estimates, this whole amazing ecosystem, this whole lovely corner of God's brain, may be extinct by mid-century. In the far north, scientists recently found that polar bears were 20 percent scrawnier than they'd been just a few years before. As pack ice disappears, they can't hunt the seals that form the basis of their diet.

12   And on and on—according to many experts, the extinction spasm caused by climate change and other environmental degradation in this century will equal or surpass those caused by crashing asteroids in geological times. But this time it's us doing the crashing.

13   If we care about creation, if we understand the blooming earth as an exhibit of what pleases God, then we've got to do what we can to slow these massive changes. "Where were you when I set the boundaries of the oceans, and told the proud waves here you shall come and no further?" God asks Job. We can either spit in the old geezer's face and tell him we're in charge of sea level from here on out, or we can throttle back, learn to live a little differently.

14   Not so differently. Giving up SUVs is not exactly a return to the Stone Age. After all, we didn't have them a decade ago, when people with large families transported themselves in considerably more fuel-efficient minivans or station wagons. The only reason we have them now is that the car companies make immense profits from them. Ford's lucky to clear a grand selling you an Escort, but there's $10,000 clear profit in an Explorer.

15   Save for a very few special circumstances, we don't need them—nine in 10 SUVs never even leave the pavement. Where I live, in the Adirondack Mountains of New York, we have snow and ice six months of the year, bad roads and steep mountains. But we don't have many SUVs because no one has the money to buy one. Somehow we still get around.

16   Sometimes people cite safety as their cause for buying a behemoth. They reason that they need them because everyone else has them or because in an accident the other car will suffer more (a position that would probably not pass the test with many Christian ethicists). But even that's a flawed argument. It's true, says *The New York Times,* that in a collision an SUV is twice as likely as a car to kill the other driver. But because the things roll over so easily, overall "their occupants have roughly the same chance as car occupants of dying in a crash."

The big car companies are starting to sense that their franchise for mayhem is   17
running out. Last fall, after fuel prices soared and exploding tires killed dozens, the
big car companies said that half a decade from now they would try to increase their
fuel efficiency by 25 percent. Which is actually a nice start, but also sort of like the
country club board of directors saying, "Wait five years and we'll find a few token
blacks." Twenty-five percent better than 13 miles per hour is still a sick joke.
Already Toyota and Honda have hybrid vehicles on the lot that can get 50, 60, 70
miles to the gallon. And we don't have five or 10 or 15 years to wait.

No, the time has come to make the case in the strongest terms. Not to harass   18
those who already own SUVs—in a way, they're the biggest victims, since they get
to live in the same warmer world as the rest of us, but have each sent 40 grand to
Detroit to boot. But it's time to urge everyone we know to stop buying them. Time to
pass petitions around church pews collecting pledges not to buy the things in the
future. Time to organize your friends and neighbors to picket outside the auto dealerships, reminding buyers to ask about gas mileage, steering them away from the
monster trucks.

Time, in short, to say that this is a moral issue every bit as compelling as the civil   19
rights movement of a generation ago, and every bit as demanding of our commitment
and our sacrifice. It's not a technical question: It's about desire, status, power, willingness to change, openness to the rest of creation. It can't be left to the experts—the
experts have had it for a decade now, and we're pouring ever more carbon into the
atmosphere. It's time for all of us to take it on, as uncomfortable as that may be.

Calling it a moral issue does not mean we need to moralize. Every American is   20
implicated in the environmental crisis—there are plenty of other indulgences we
could point at in our own lives, from living in oversize houses to boarding jets on a
whim. But there's no symbol much clearer in our time than SUVs. Stop driving
global warming. If we can't do even that, we're unlikely ever to do much.

The American Dream: Why Environmentalists Attack the SUV

John Bragg

*John Bragg is a policy analyst for the Center for the Moral Defense of Capitalism
and a teacher of world history. This article was posted on May 31, 2001, on the
online* Capitalism Magazine, *a publication that takes a libertarian perspective,
giving priority to individual choice.*

The SUV is under attack. Greens say they use too much gas, threaten air qual-   1
ity and contribute pell-mell to the desecration of the environment. So why would
anyone build these horrible engines of death? They build them because SUVs have
advantages in safety, cargo space and power that Americans demand.

2   The large cars from Detroit's heyday have been abolished by environmental regulations of the 1970s. In 1975, Federal fuel efficiency mandates forced car manufacturers to smaller and lighter designs until 1983, when Chrysler adapted the first minivan. Unlike the once popular station wagon, the minivan fell under the lower "light truck and van" fuel efficiency regulations, a loophole which allowed companies to build larger, heavier, safer vehicles without falling under the "gas-guzzler" tax. The SUV, which became popular in the late 80s enjoyed a similar exemption. The minivan and the SUV gave America the powerful, spacious vehicles that they had demanded before the regulations—they were our reply to Washington's attempts to force everyone into smaller cars.

3   Yet today there is no symbol of consumption hated more than the SUV. There is a history behind this hatred: The people attacking SUVs are the same people who have spent the past thirty years attacking cars and hailing Al Gore's call ten years ago to abolish the internal-combustion engine. SUVs are attacked because they are today's foremost examples of what a car is.

4   The chief virtue of the automobile is the personal *independence* it gives the owner—a car can go anywhere roads go and some places they don't, with a speed unimaginable in the pre-automobile era. Its secondary virtue is protection—from the elements and from collision. In both a car and an SUV, passengers are protected by the vehicle's structure from the wind and rain. But in a collision, the SUV simply provides more protection than a smaller car does. Larger cars better protect the people in them—that's why your father wanted you to get a huge, boxy old car when you were sixteen instead of a little Mustang—so that you would live through your first accident. Protection is a big advantage.

5   So why then do the greens oppose safer cars? They oppose big cars for the same reason that they oppose big houses, new highways, new power plants, or basically any wealth-creating or wealth-enjoying endeavor. Wealth means that someone has changed their environment and *improved* it for human use. Most people want their environment arranged for their benefit—air-conditioned in summer, heated in winter, ventilated, bug-free and clean. In fact, it is man's ability to adapt his environment to his own desires that sets him apart from other animals and has allowed him to prosper.

6   The environmentalists respond that nature is intrinsically valuable, not for anything it does or can do but simply because it is. Since people disturb nature, people as such are a problem. Moderate environmentalists say that this is a straw man, that they do not hate people, they just want to protect endangered species and have clean air, water and food. Endangered species are valuable because, well, they are endangered—nature put them there. Intrinsic value.

7   Clean air and water benefit people. But if the moderate environmentalists really wanted people to benefit, then they would support the SUV. The SUV is an example of people using the best technology available to enhance their lives. Environmentalists attack America's SUVs because Americans like them—Americans like technology and we like the power over our surroundings.

8   It's appropriate then that the car is the greatest modern symbol of American freedom. If you don't agree, ask any teenager counting the days until his license. He won't need to ask for a ride to his job, to the mall, to school, to a friend's, to anywhere. Even

if he has to ask for Mom's keys, he's driving himself—a step towards independence. If he buys his own car, he has his first piece of meaningful property—it has a price, it has economic utility, it has a limited lifespan, there are operating costs, and it must be used with respect for others or there will be consequences.

Cars are such a symbol of Americanism that the Soviets in the 1930s had to 9 cancel propaganda showings of John Steinbeck's "Grapes of Wrath" because Soviet audiences were furious to find that even destitute Americans had pickups to migrate in. Contrary to the environmentalists, cars are a powerful symbol of what makes America the greatest, and the freest, country in the world.

Better Gas Mileage, Greater Security
Robert F. Kennedy, Jr.

This op-ed piece appeared in the New York Times *on November 24, 2001. Robert F. Kennedy, Jr., a lawyer for the Natural Resources Defense Council, president of the Waterkeeper Alliance, and a spokesman for democratic environmental views, champions higher Corporate Average Fuel Economy standards (CAFE) as he broadens the SUV issue to include national economic policy and questions of national security.*

It has become clear to most Americans that maintaining our national security will 1 require reducing our dependence on foreign oil. But Republicans are using the current crisis to push through a reckless energy agenda, including drilling in the Arctic National Wildlife Refuge, that will not improve America's security. Even the conservative Cato Institute has called President Bush's claim that Arctic oil would reduce gas prices or American dependency on foreign oil "not just nonsense, but nonsense on stills."

There is a clear and pragmatic way to reduce our dependency fast. Since 40 per- 2 cent of the oil used by America fuels light trucks and cars, an increase in corporate average fuel economy standards—called CAFE—could have a dramatic impact.

In the late 1970's, President Jimmy Carter implemented CAFE standards to com- 3 bat an oil shortage driven by policies of the Organization of Petroleum Exporting Countries. The standards raised fuel efficiency in American cars by 7.6 miles a gallon over six years, causing oil imports from the Persian Gulf to fall by 87 percent. Our economy grew by 27 percent during that period. Detroit, predictably, figured out how to build more fuel-efficient cars largely without reductions in size, comfort or power.

The CAFE standards worked so well that they produced an oil glut by 1986. 4 That's when the Reagan administration intervened to rescue America's domestic oil industry from gasoline price collapse. Ronald Reagan's rollback of CAFE standards caused America, in that year, to double oil imports from the Persian Gulf nations and to burn more oil than is in the Arctic National Wildlife Refuge.

According to a recent report by Amory Lovins of the Rocky Mountain institute, if 5 the United States had continued to conserve oil at the rate it did in the period from 1976 to 1985, it would no longer have needed Persian Gulf oil after 1985. Had we continued this wise course, we might not have had to fight the Persian Gulf war, and we would have insulated ourselves from price shocks in the international oil market. Fuel efficiency is a sound national energy policy, economic policy and foreign policy all wrapped into one. Every increase of one mile per gallon in auto fuel efficiency yields more oil than is in two Arctic National Wildlife Refuges. An improvement right now of 2.7 miles per gallon would eliminate our need for all Persian Gulf oil!

6   Yet the Republican Congress in 1995 made it illegal for the Environmental Protection Agency even to study higher CAFE standards. The result is that America now has the worst energy efficiency in 20 years.

7   If Congress is serious about ensuring our national security it should immediately pass legislation to raise fuel economy standards to 40 miles a gallon by 2012 and 55 by 2020. This would give automakers ample time to adjust their production. In the meantime, Congress should close the sport utility vehicle loophole by holding S.U.V.'s and minivans to the fuel economy standards for cars; automakers have the technology now to achieve this. Along with the other benefits, higher fuel economy standards could bring increased demand for efficient cars, leading to an increase in motor-vehicle-related jobs. We can also substantially cut gasoline consumption by requiring tire manufacturers to sell replacement tires that are as friction-free as tires on new cars.

8   We missed a huge opportunity in the 1980's and 1990's to increase our fuel efficiency. If overall energy conservation options available in 1989 were implemented today, each year we would save 54 times the oil that would have been used from the Arctic that year, at a fraction of the price of drilling there.

9   Mr. Bush's Energy Security Act will actually make us more dependent on foreign oil, and it will place our hopes for national energy security in an insecure pipeline that could even become a terrorist target. There is no reason to wait 10 years for Arctic oil to come on line when a small investment in conservation would quickly reduce American demand for oil.

Gas and Gasbags . . . or, the Open Road and Its Enemies

Henry Payne and Diane Katz

This article appeared in the March 25, 2002, issue of the conservative news commentary magazine the National Review. *Henry Payne, an editorial cartoonist for the* Detroit News *and a freelance writer, and Diane Katz, director of science, environment, and technology policy at the Mackinac Center for Public Policy in Michigan, identify problems with raising CAFE standards and with alternative fuel sources such as hydrogen fuel cells.*

1   Any crisis in the Middle East inevitably prompts Washington to scapegoat the automobile as a threat to national security. The dust had barely settled on lower Manhattan last fall before calls went forth—from pundits and pols across the spectrum—to relinquish our "gas-guzzlers" in the name of energy independence.

But just as the Cassandras will dominate media coverage of energy, so will 2
Middle Eastern oil continue to fuel America's vehicles for the foreseeable future.
Simple economics, geography, and consumer choice all demand it.

Since Sept. 11, Washington has mobilized to end our "dangerous addiction" to 3
foreign energy sources. Sens. John Kerry and John McCain are proposing dramatic
increases in federal fuel-economy standards. The energy package crafted by majority leader Tom Daschle advocates "biodiesels," and the Natural Resources Defense
Council is insisting that we could cut gasoline consumption by 50 percent over ten
years—if only the feds would mandate what and where we drove.

Even the "oil men" in the Bush administration have advocated doling out mil- 4
lions in research subsidies for hydrogen fuel cells that supposedly would replace
the internal-combustion engine. The project, Energy Secretary Spencer Abraham
announced in January, is "rooted in President Bush's call to reduce American
reliance on foreign oil."

In fact, the price of oil has declined since Sept. 11, as it consistently has for 5
decades, and with producers scattered all over the world, no single nation or region
can stop the flow.

But supporters of a comprehensive energy policy seem undeterred by these re- 6
alities. "Logic," Robert Samuelson writes in the *Washington Post*, "is no defense
against instability. We need to make it harder for [Middle Easterners] to use the oil
weapon and take steps to protect ourselves if it is used. Even if we avoid trouble
now, the threat will remain."

Past efforts to attain a petroleum-free utopia, however, have largely failed. For 7
example, despite three decades of federal fuel-economy standards, oil imports as a
share of U.S. consumption have risen from 35 to 59 percent.

A market-based solution, such as a gas tax, is the most obvious approach to 8
cutting consumption, but even environmentalists concede that proposing one would
spell political suicide. Moreover, gas taxes are an expensive solution and come with
no guarantee of energy independence. The European Union, for example, taxes gas
up to $4 per gallon—and still imports over half its oil.

So instead of enraging consumers at the pump, Washington has largely relied 9
on backdoor taxes.

The regulatory regime known as CAFE (Corporate Average Fuel Economy) was 10
hatched in the wake of the oilprice shocks of the early 1970s, when sedans still
made up most of the nation's fleet. Instead of the redesigned smaller, lighter, and
less powerful vehicles, however, consumers flocked to minivans, small trucks, and
sport utility vehicles, which are held to a lower CAFE standard (20.7 mpg versus
the 27.5 mpg required for cars).

Today, both passenger cars and light trucks are more efficient than ever, having 11
improved 114 percent and 56 percent, respectively, since 1974. But gasoline is so
cheap, despite continuing Middle Eastern crises, that on average Americans are driving twice as many miles as in years past.

A recent study by H. Sterling Burnett of the National Center for Policy Analysis 12
found that raising CAFE standards by 40 percent—as Kerry and others recommend—would not "reduce future U.S. dependence on foreign oil." CAFE's only function is to keep regulators busy calculating elaborate formulas for determining

compliance in which manufacturers then look for loopholes. (CAFE requires that a manufacturer's trucks meet an average standard of 20.7 mpg. Thus DaimlerChrysler AG, for example, designates its popular PT Cruiser as a "truck" in order to offset the low mpg of its large SUVs, such as the Dodge Durango.)

13   Worse, stricter CAFE standards would surely undermine the very economic security that proponents vow to protect. The profits of U.S. automakers—and tens of thousands of UAW jobs—depend on sales of SUVs and light trucks. According to an analysis by Andrew N. Kleit, a professor at Pennsylvania State University, the Kerry CAFE proposal would reduce the profits of General Motors by $3.8 billion, of Ford by $3.4 billion, and of DaimlerChrysler by $2 billion. Foreign manufacturers, which largely specialize in smaller vehicles, would see a profit increase of $4.4 billion.

14   Evidently hoping to shield automakers from a CAFE assault—and to win PR points for expanded domestic drilling—the Bush administration has embraced the latest alternative-fuel fad: the hydrogen fuel cell.

15   The Bush plan replaces the Partnership for a New Generation of Vehicles, Al Gore's vain attempt to produce an affordable, emissions-free family sedan capable of 80 mpg by 2004. Over eight years, Washington pumped more than $1.5 billion into the program—in addition to the $1.5 billion sunk into it by the Big Three. In its annual review of the project last August, the National Research Council judged the super-car goals to be inherently "unrealistic."

16   The Bush plan has drawn broad political support. Former Clinton chief of staff John Podesta cheers, "The next step is hydrogen-powered fuel-cell vehicles. But the only way to get these vehicles out of the lab and onto the road is with incentives and requirements aimed at producing 100,000 vehicles by 2010, 2.5 million by 2020."

17   But the 100-year dominance of conventional internal-combustion engines over alternatives is no accident. A quick primer on the complexities of hydrogen power helps explain why.

18   Hydrogen's status as the new darling of the sustainable-energy movement is understandable. Its promise lies first in its performance: Unlike ethanol, it supplies more energy per pound than gasoline. When used to power an automobile, its only emission is water—making it especially attractive to an industry already under pressure from clean-air and global-warming rules. And hydrogen is one of the most plentiful elements on the planet.

19   The trouble is, hydrogen always comes married to another element—as in methane gas or water.

20   Most fuel-cell technology today relies on hydrogen extracted from methane, in a process that emits large quantities of greenhouse gases. And as *Car and Driver* magazine's technical analyst, Patrick Bedard, explains, domestic sources of methane are "[t]oo limited to serve any significant demand for automobiles." A study by the Argonne National Laboratory concluded that the U.S. would have to look to foreign sources—primarily in Russia and Iran, and in other Middle East nations.

21   Goodbye, oil dependence. Hello, methane dependence.

22   Given these hurdles, attention is turning instead to electrolysis—the extraction of hydrogen from water, which is readily obtainable along America's ample coasts. Electrolysis is, however, the most energy-intensive process of any fuel alternative;

studies differ on whether it would consume more carbon-based fuels than the use of hydrogen would save. What is certain, points out Stanford University professor John McCarthy, is that "the advantage of hydrogen, if you have to burn carbon fuels (coal, oil, or gas) to manufacture it, would be negligible."

In other words, McCarthy explains, the unspoken truth about hydrogen is that "it is a synonym for nuclear power."   23

Leading researchers in the field—including David Scott of the University of Victoria in Canada, Cesare Marchetti of the International Institute for Applied Systems Analysis, and Jesse Ausubel of Rockefeller University—say that the only way to produce liquid hydrogen in the mass quantities needed for transportation is with a major investment in nuclear power. Says Scott: "[A]pplying the most elementary numeracy, nuclear fission is the only realistic option."   24

Ironically, many of the political voices now embracing hydrogen fuel are the same ones that have prevented the construction of a single new U.S. nuclear plant in 25 years. Ausubel has written in *The Industrial Physicist* magazine that "understanding how to use nuclear power, and its acceptance, will take a century or more."   25

For now, the answer is still gasoline. Compared with the technical barriers to developing alternative fuels, there already exist numerous market mechanisms to mitigate potential oil shortages. As suggested by Donald Losman, a National Defense University economist, these include: stockpiling, futures contracts, diversifying the supplier base, and relaxing the restrictions that currently mandate some 13 different fuel blends in 30 cities. Dramatic improvements in fuel efficiency also could be achieved if Washington allowed automakers to market diesel-powered vehicles. In Germany, for example, Volkswagen mass markets the 80-mpg Lupo, which is powered by a direct-injection diesel engine. But that's anathema to American greens who insist—without evidence—that diesel's particulate emissions are dangerous to public health.   26

All fuels require trade-offs, of course. But politically correct, misguided energy schemes will not make America more independent. Gasoline remains by far the best deal we have.   27

Gimme an SUV—ASAP: Teenagers Are the Next Big Market for Sport-Utility Vehicles— and the Consequences Could Be Deadly

Keith Bradsher

Keith Bradsher is the author of High and Mighty—SUVs: The World's Most Dangerous Vehicles and How They Got That Way *(2002). This article appeared in the September 28, 2002, edition of the* National Post.

Sitting at the wheel of her family's bright red Chevrolet Suburban sport-utility vehicle in a high school parking lot on a bright autumn afternoon in 1999, April   1 reached over to the front passenger seat and grabbed a plastic tiara. Brandishing it out the window, she explained how she had just been chosen as one of five home-coming princesses at her high school in a wealthy Los Angeles suburb partly be-cause of the popularity she enjoyed by driving the biggest vehicle of any student.

2   "I love big trucks because they just look cool and have big tires," she said. "Everybody knows me as the girl who drives the big red truck."

3   She never needed its four-wheel drive, but the vehicle's high ground clearance had given her the confidence to take occasional shortcuts across medians and lawns. "I'll go behind the bushes and along the railroad tracks," she explained. "I drive it to school every day—I feel safe, I feel like I'm the queen of the road be-cause I'm up high and can see everything for miles." April said she was 5-foot-6, but felt much taller in the SUV. Her father had jacked up the Suburban's suspension by six inches.

4   "Up here, I'm probably 6-foot-10," she said, staying in the driver's seat. "I love it, it just makes me feel powerful—if someone disses me, I can tailgate the crap out of them."

5   But as she kept talking, April confessed that the size of her vehicle also fright-ened her. Her voice fell somewhat and her initial bubbly enthusiasm ebbed as she began talking about her concerns of ending another person's life in a crash. These fears had grown ever since she had recently struck her neighbour's parked Chevrolet Astro van.

6   "I'm worried about if I might kill someone—I hit my neighbour's truck and lifted it up, and I barely hit it," she said. "That's one of my biggest fears, I might kill someone."

7   It is an appropriate fear, and one that unfortunately seems to dissuade few par-ents from allowing their children to drive SUVs. Of the students who drove their own vehicles to the high school that day in Whittier, Calif., at least a quarter seemed to be in sport utilities. By contrast, I couldn't help noticing there were no SUVs in the section of the parking lot reserved for the teachers, who probably earned less than many of their students' parents.

8   There are lines of sport-utility vehicles parked these days outside the affluent fraternities and sororities at the University of Michigan and other big universities across the United States. High school parking lots are beginning to look the same way. Young people are the next big market for SUVs, especially used SUVs, with alarming consequences for traffic safety. With more than half of U.S. SUVs less than five years old, and with very few SUVs more than 12 years old, their drivers until now have tended to be their first owners—responsible, middle-aged people. Many of the initial owners have been married people who drive in the daytime and early evening, when crashes are less frequent per million miles travelled than late at night.

9   Automakers' difficulties in keeping up with demand for new SUVs have kept the prices of used SUVs unusually high.

10   But the high prices for used models have also discouraged their purchase by young people and by hard-core drunk drivers, who tend to buy the oldest, cheapest vehicles on the market.

There are still very few SUVs in the vast pool of older vehicles, but there will be   11
far more over the coming decades. Indeed, SUVs built now may be especially likely
to stay on the roads for a long time, and to keep inflicting heavy damage on cars
and rolling over at an alarming rate through those years, too. Detroit's SUVs fare
better than its cars in reliability surveys by groups such as *Consumer Reports*, possibly because SUVs are of simple, heavy-duty construction and have had a lot of
money and managerial attention devoted to them. Even an SUV that has been in a
fatal collision, killing a car occupant and injuring its own occupants, can sometimes
be in fairly good driving condition, requiring repairs only to the surface metal and
passenger compartment, but not to the heavy steel underbody, according to police
investigators of crashes. The only thing scarier than a drunk or teenager at the
wheel of a shiny, new full-size SUV will be a drunk or teenager at the wheel of a 15-
year-old full-size SUV with failing brakes. And the more than 20 million SUVs that
have already been built with too little regard for stability and the safety of other
road users will be roaming the roads for a very long time.

Automakers do not try to attract drunks to SUVs, but they do market SUVs to   12
young people, both as a way to sell them new SUVs and as a way to keep demand
strong and prices high for used SUVs. This is a bad idea, although the safety implications have not yet received much attention. The teenaged SUV driver incident that has drawn the most attention so far has not even involved a person as
the victim, but a dog. On Jan. 2, 2002, U.S. President Bill Clinton's dog, Buddy,
ran into the street in Chappaqua, N.Y., while chasing a contractor's truck and was
struck and killed by a high school student driving an SUV. The police ruled the ca-
nine death an accident and did not bring charges. But the case highlighted that
SUVs have begun to catch on among the segment of the population with the worst
driving record.

This trend is ominous for three reasons. An unusually large proportion of the   13
American population is in its teens and early 20s, and their ranks are growing daily
for demographic reasons. Tastes in automobiles tend to form in the early teens and
often last for life. Yet no age group is less suited to drive SUVs than people in their
teens and early 20s.

Researchers for various automakers and their consulting firms have consis-   14
tently found that today's young people love the feeling of power of SUVs, and are
more likely than people in any other age bracket to prefer SUVs to cars. Indeed, influential market researchers such as Jim Bulin, the long-time Ford strategist, say
affection for SUVs varies inversely with age.

Men and women who grew up in the Depression or the Second World War very   15
seldom buy sport utilities. Baby Boomers are deeply split in their attitudes toward
SUVs, with some preferring cars and minivans while others have embraced four-
wheel drive vehicles. Drivers in their 20s and early 30s like SUVs but have had surprisingly little influence on the auto market because their numbers are limited and
because they have not yet reached their peak earning years.

Teenagers and college students, though, love SUVs with an extraordinary una-   16
nimity. (Automakers conduct focus groups with teens as young as 13 with their
parents' permission.)

17   According to GM, 90% of teens interviewed in 1999 said they preferred SUVs to any other class of vehicles. That is an alarming figure given that SUVs are still only about 17% of the market.

18   Automotive preferences seem to be a lot like tastes in music: They form early, often in rebellion against parents' tastes, and they last for life. Baby Boomers who came of age in the 1960s have never shaken their love of groups like the Beatles, the Grateful Dead and Rolling Stones. Some of their younger brothers and sisters retain an incomprehensible love of disco music from the 1970s.

19   Similarly, men and women who lusted after big cars in the 1930s and 1940s are still buying large cars today. People seem to form their strongest, most enduring attachments to music and to automobiles between the ages of 12 and 15, Ford officials say. The disheartening implication of all this is that people who have entered the auto market since the mid-1980s may go on buying SUVs for life.

20   Auto market researchers have taken notice of young people's interest in SUVs. "It's surprising, the appeal in younger generations," said Ed Molchany, the Ford brand manager for Explorers. "All of our SUVs are very strong with Generation Y, it's a very popular brand and imagery."

21   Ford's youth strategy did not get started until late 1997. Through the early and mid-1990s, the Ford factories in St. Louis and Louisville that assembled Explorers could not come close to meeting demand, so they mostly built bigger Explorers with four doors. The four-door models had larger profit margins than two-door models. Ford was building 430,000 Explorers a year, but only 30,000 to 50,000 a year had only two doors.

22   But the market for four-door, mid-sized sport-utility vehicles had changed by the end of 1997. Chrysler had introduced the four-door Dodge Durango and Mercedes had come out with its four-door M-Class, partly relieving the shortage that had kept Explorer factories working around the clock. A flood of foreign sport-utility vehicles was coming on the market, both truck-based and car-based. Ford itself had introduced the larger Ford Expedition in 1996, and many well-heeled families began choosing Expeditions instead of Explorers.

23   So Ford introduced a "Sport" options package for the two-door Explorer, with spiffier wheels and other details calculated to attract buyers in their 20s and even younger. It was an instant success. "There was this younger group, more singles, more females," said Douglas W. Scott, Ford's group marketing manager for all sport-utility vehicles, and Molchany's predecessor as the marketing manager just for Explorers. "It was a younger buyer really interested in the look."

24   The new version was so popular that Ford later labelled it a different model, the Explorer Sport. To go with it, Ford created an Explorer Sport Trac, which has an open, four-foot pickup truck bed in the back. Both were virtually identical to the Explorer beneath the sheet metal, and continued to be made on the same assembly lines. Annual production of two-door versions zoomed to 100,000 a year, as Ford sold fewer four-door models and more two-door models.

25   With these inexpensive Explorer variants, Ford has succeeded in lowering sharply the overall average age of Explorer buyers. "I'm working really hard to target youth," said Drew Cook, a Ford marketing manager for the Sport Trac and

Ranger small pickups. Compared to Ranger pickups, he said, "The Sport Trac is positioned a little bit earlier, firmly entrenched among Gen Xers."

This is particularly important in Detroit. The bane of the domestic industry is 26 that its models are mostly popular with older Americans who may soon buy their last car, as younger Americans have gravitated toward European and Asian models. The average age for buyers of Buick cars is nearly 70, near the end of their auto-purchasing years. Buyers of Explorer Sport and Sport Trac may be coming back to dealerships for as many as 15 additional vehicles over their lifetimes. "It's a lot of folks just out of college," Scott said.

But the goal is only partly to sell more vehicles now. Ford also wants to con- 27 vince people at as early an age as possible to become interested in Explorers, in the hope they will buy more Explorers of various sizes and configurations throughout their adult lives.

"We want to bring people in younger than ever before, and that's driving the 28 product offering," Molchany said Toward that goal, Ford has used direct-mail campaigns, tapping commercially available databases of prosperous households with young residents, said James G. O'Connor, the president of the Ford brand division. Ford has also provided promotional vehicles of the Explorer, Explorer Sport and Explorer Sport Trac for sports events that cater to younger television viewers.

Ford has not been alone in promoting SUVs to younger buyers. Executives at 29 other automakers say the fastest growth in SUVs at the expense of cars over the next decade will come in models that will cost less than US$20,000 and be affordable for young people.

"The next inroads we really see in trucks are really here." said Paul Ballew, 30 GM's top market researcher, while adding that Ford was ahead of GM in this area. "A large part of Ford's youth strategy is to leverage their truck strength."

Chrysler ran an extensive radio and television advertising campaign in the sum- 31 mer of 1996 aimed at persuading parents and grandparents to buy the small, inexpensive Jeep Wrangler for their children and grandchildren. Chrysler's market research had found that while many teenagers and early twentysomethings loved the Wrangler, they could not afford it and were buying cheap used vehicles instead. But Chrysler noticed that their elders could afford the Wrangler. So Chrysler ditched its previous, long-standing ad campaign, a macho series of television ads that featured Wranglers in fights with bulls and other adventures that nervous parents and grandparents might not want Junior to try.

Instead, Chrysler began running ads in which a clean-cut young man sat near a 32 clean-cut young woman at a campfire on a beautiful mountainside while a Jeep Wrangler sat parked nearby in the gathering dusk. The message, Chrysler marketing officials said, was that buying a Wrangler was a good way for parents and grandparents to help young people visit the pristine wilderness. There was no suggestion of sex in the ads to frighten the elders—the young men and women in these ads were not sitting too close together. There were not even any tents in sight, so perhaps the youngsters were supposed to drive back down the apparently roadless mountainside in the dark. Radio ads for the Wrangler were even more carefully tailored to parents, with one ad featuring a young woman who goes for a drive with her mother and has a cheerful chat about the young woman's boyfriend, whom the mother likes.

33   Whether the campaign worked is hard to judge. Statistics on teen ownership of vehicles are highly unreliable, because vehicles are often registered in the names of the teens' parents. There are no publicly available statistics at all on how teens pay for their vehicles. But whatever the reason, the Wrangler has sold well over the last five years, as have other small sport-utility vehicles, which tend to draw young drivers.

34   Teens and people in their early 20s may love SUVs, but should they be driving them? A wealth of recent research says parents who really care about the safety of their sons or daughters should not allow them to drive a sport-utility vehicle, and should discourage children from riding in SUVs driven by friends.

35   The death rate for young people in auto accidents has been extraordinary even without the recent rise of SUVs. A third of all death of Americans from ages 15 to 24, about 10,000 deaths a year, occur in motor vehicle accidents. That roughly equals all deaths in this age group from all diseases, and exceeds the number of deaths in this age bracket from homicides and suicides combined.

36   Surprisingly little work has been done on exactly how young people die in crashes. The existing research does show, however, that young people die disproportionately in single-vehicle crashes, apparently because of their inexperience, rather than perishing in collisions with other vehicles. And many of these single-vehicle crashes involve rollovers—the kind of crashes to which SUVs are especially vulnerable, accounting for three-fifths of all deaths in SUVs. Since rollovers appear to be the biggest single cause of paralysis, and since people paralyzed in their teen years lose more years of mobility than those paralyzed later in life, allowing a teen to drive an SUV can be an especially sad mistake.

37   The Insurance Institute for Highway Safety has issued a press release warning parents against allowing young drivers behind the wheel of SUVs: "Don't let your teen drive an unstable vehicle. Sport-utility vehicles, especially the smaller ones, are inherently less stable than cars because of their higher centres of gravity. Abrupt steering manoeuvres—the kind that can occur when teens are fooling around or overcorrecting a driver error—can cause rollovers in these less stable vehicles. A more stable car would, at worst, skid or spin out."

38   Indeed, even auto industry safety officials are wary of recommending SUVs for young people. Helen Petrauskas, the long-time Ford vice-president for safety and environment, said at a retirement lunch with reporters at Henry Ford's Fairlane Estate in the spring of 2001 that she had insisted her own daughter drive a Ford Tempo when she was learning to drive. Petrauskas even insisted that her daughter not choose an exciting colour, like red. Parents should choose cars that look like they would not be very interesting to drive, she suggested.

39   Sue Cischke, her successor, said at the same event that for teens, "probably a mid-sized sedan is good advice—what their image is, and what they want to do, is often different from what their parents want."

40   A few celebrities have taken an interest in what will happen as the next generation of SUV drivers takes over. The most prominent is Paul Newman, an actor who is also a racecar driver and understands the value of nimble steering and excellent brakes.

"In 1973, everybody's running around buying Volkswagen diesels," Newman   41
said in 1999. "And now they're buying Expeditions. And this is the thing that I don't
understand about the government. As this fad grew, why didn't they insist on certain bumper heights? I mean, it's criminal," Newman said.

"And when an Expedition is eight years old and it goes down to 7,000 bucks,   42
there'll be a lot of kids buying them and, unfortunately, it's the younger generation
that's responsible for a lot of accidents. So you put a 17-year-old kid behind a 5,500-
pound car and have them run into your blue-haired lady driving her Tercel Toyota.
You know, it's going to be mayhem."

CAFE Belongs in the Graveyard with Its Victims: We Can Increase Fuel Economy without Costing Lives

Tom Randall

*This March 2002 policy argument appeared on the Web site of the National
Center for Public Policy Research, which identifies itself as a "non-partisan con-
servative/freemarket foundation" (from the home page of its Web site). Tom
Randall directs Environmental and Regulatory Affairs for this organization.*

The Senate, laughably called the world's greatest deliberative body, recently   1
found itself locked in another absurd debate, spurred on by two men whose primary
motivation seems to be their desire for George W. Bush's job—Senators John
McCain (R-AZ) and John Kerry (D-MA).

The Johns and a handful of their colleagues got together to propose that corpo-   2
rate average fuel economy (CAFE) standards be raised from the current 27.5 miles
per gallon for cars and 20.7 mpg for light trucks to 36 mpg for both.[1]

The Johns are not stupid, so they had to know full well that such an increase is   3
not possible without eliminating sports utility vehicles, the transportation of choice
for many, including Moms who haul bevies of kids to their various games, parties
and outings of all sorts. It is a choice Moms make because the current CAFE standards eliminated the large family sedans and station wagons that used to serve
such purposes.[2]

The Johns also know that current CAFE standards have cost thousands of lives   4
because average vehicle weights had to be dramatically decreased to meet them. In
fact, nearly as many lives have been lost to CAFE as to the Vietnam War. We know
the Johns know this because the National Highway Transportation Safety
Administration (NHTSA) told them so.[3]

The Johns also know that their proposed large, across-the-board increase in   5
CAFE standards would cause additional deaths if implemented. They know this because the National Research Council told them, ". . . any increase in CAFE as

currently structured could produce additional road casualties, unless it is specifically targeted at the largest, heaviest light trucks. If an increase in fuel economy is
effected by a system that encourages either downweighting or the production and
sale of more small cars, some additional traffic fatalities would be expected."[4]

6   Interestingly, the Johns must also have known, as the Sierra Club's Dan Becker
told *Environment and Energy News,* that their measure had virtually no chance of
passing into laws.[5]

7   And it didn't.

8   However, since both John McCain and John Kerry have presidential aspirations,
and undoubtedly see environmentalists such as Becker essential to their success,
the Senate engaged itself in an absurd debate.

9   On the winning side was a group led by Senator Carl Levin (D-MI) and
Christopher "Kit" Bond (R-MO). Their amendment, which was approved, simply
leaves it up to the NHTSA to develop mileage standards and dates for implementation.[6] This seemingly harmless "do nothing" approach might have some chance of
passage. However, it may in the end be as disastrous as the Kerry-McCain proposal
would have been.

10   It was just such vague "leave it up to the bureaucrats" legislation that turned
the U.S. Environmental Protection Agency (EPA) into the 800-pound, answerable-
to-no-one regulatory gorilla that it is today.

11   Fortunately, there is a third way to go providing the Johns and other politicians
care as much about the safety and well-being of their constituents as they do about
preening for the presidency.

12   Stop government from reducing fuel efficiency. Here's how: Allow expanded use
of diesel engines.

13   Nearly every European automaker makes diesel versions of the gasoline-
powered cars they send to the U.S. They get incredible mileage with great performance. Volkswagen's Golf, Jetta and New Beetle, powered by their new unit-injector
turbo diesel engines, are running all over Europe getting 47/55 mpg. These engines
and others like them could be built to power just about any size vehicle with dramatically improved fuel economy.[7]

14   But not in the U.S.

15   The EPA doesn't like diesels because they emit fine particulate matter that the
agency says aren't good for us—though they don't seem to be hurting the greener-
than-thou Europeans.

16   And quit this business about wanting Americans to drive alternative fuel and
"dual-fuel" cars. The Department of Energy and EPA's own figures show they get,
pound-for-pound, about one-fourth to one-third fewer miles per gallon than gasoline-
powered vehicles.[8]

17   If, in the end you still want lighter vehicles, and want them to be safe, stand
aside. Industry experts say amazing new technology is on the way . . . without government help. It hold outs the promise of making cars both lighter, which increases
fuel economy, yet safer.[9]

18   The Johns and their ilk are not the solution. They contribute to the problem.
That's no way to run for President.

Footnotes

1. Gretchen Randall, "Fuel Efficiency Standards: What to Do Next," National Policy Analysis #393, The National Center for Public Policy Research, Washington, DC, February 2002, available online at http://www.nationalcenter.org/NPA393.html.
2. *Ibid.*
3. *Ibid.*
4. "Effectiveness and Impact of Corporate Average Fuel Economy (CAFE) Standards," National Research Council, Washington, DC, 2002.
5. Colin Sullivan, Suzanne Struglinski and Natalie M. Henry, "Energy Policy, Trading Reform Could Dominate Debate," Greenwire, March 13, 2001, downloaded from http://www.eenews.net/Greenwire/Backissues/031102gw.htm on March 12, 2002, paid subscription required for access.
6. *Ibid.*
7. Interview with Robert Brooks, Wards Engine and Vehicle Technology Update, March 13, 2002.
8. "Model Year 2002 Fuel Economy Guide," U.S. Department of Energy and Environmental Protection Agency, Washington, DC, DOE/SS-0250.
9. Interview with Robert Brooks.

Floor Statement on Boehlert-Markey CAFE Amendment

Congressman Sherwood Boehlert (R-NY)

This congressional speech, delivered August 1, 2001, and posted on the Web site of the U.S. House of Representatives, enters the debate over CAFE standards and over other solutions to the fuel inefficiency of SUVs.

Mr. Chairman:

1 I think that virtually every Member of this body agrees that we need to raise the fuel economy of passenger vehicles. It's frankly a "non-brainer." Raising fuel economy saves consumers money, makes us less dependent on foreign sources of oil, and helps protect the environment without cramping our lifestyles one bit. That's why even this bill, which is so tepid about conservation, includes a small increase in fuel economy standards. There's just no persuasive argument against raising standards; it's the simplest, most basic conservation step available to us.

2 The question, though, is whether we're going just to *appear* to take this step or whether we're going to do it for real. The language in the bill is about keeping up appearances; the Boehlert-Markey amendment is about actually saving oil. In fact, as the chart behind me makes clear, our amendment would save more oil than would be produced from drilling in ANWR under even the most optimistic scenarios. And those figures come from the non-partisan Congressional Research Service.

3 Now, the proponents of H.R. 4 will say that they're not just keeping up appearances. They claim to save 5 billion gallons of oil over five years. That's a big number, but it's not a lot of oil in a nation that burns more than 350 million gallons of oil

as gasoline on our highways each and every day. That's why we usually measure oil in barrels—because gallons are too small a unit to bother contemplating.

4   But the proponents will say, but 5 billion is, too, a lot; it's like parking next year's production of SUVs for two years. But guess what, during the second year and the year after that, and the year after that, ad infinitum, a whole new fleet of gas-guzzling SUVs will hit the highways, and they're not going to be metaphorically parked.

5   The nation is importing more than half its oil but the proponents of H.R. 4 have done nothing more on CAFE than put their fingers in the dike. The CAFE provision in the bill will have no long-range impact on the nation's demand for oil. The CAFE language in the bill is a distraction, not a solution.

6   Now, that might be okay if we didn't have the technological wherewithal to build safe, affordable, American cars and SUVs that meet a higher standard. But we do have that capability. In fact, we could reach CAFE standards far higher than the ones we're proposing in this amendment. But we're taking a truly moderate approach.

7   The Boehlert-Markey amendment would, after five years, include cars, SUVs and light trucks in a single fleet that would have to meet a 27.5 mile per gallon average—the level cars must meet today. That gives the automakers the flexibility to decide if they want to make cars more fuel efficient or SUVs more fuel efficient, or some combination of both.

8   Our amendment also creates additional, new incentives for the ethanol industry because we would provide credits to cars that actually run on ethanol, not to cars that could use ethanol, but don't. So we give the automakers incentives to see that ethanol does become a commonly available fuel.

9   In short, the standard we propose is flexible, it's fair; it's moderate, and it's feasible.

10   You can tell that because our opponents have hit new rhetorical heights in arguing against the amendment. But luckily we have the latest science on our side.

11   I refer my colleagues to the report of the National Academy of Sciences that was released this Monday. Here's what the Academy panel concluded:

12   First, the Academy says that having separate standards for cars and SUVs makes no sense. You can refer to pages ES-4 and 5-10 for confirmation.

13   Second, the Academy says that raising fuel economy standards will be a net savings for consumers. Look at page 4-7 to check that out.

14   Third, the Academy says that raising fuel economy standards won't hurt American workers, and they base this on the real experience of the past few decades. That's on page 2-16.

15   Fourth, the Academy says that raising fuel economy is perfectly feasible, even with currently available technology, and even for higher standards than we're proposing. That's on page ES-5. And the page of "Automotive News" that is on the easel behind me illustrates the technology that auto companies already have to meet our standard.

16   Fifth, and most important of all, the Academy says fuel economy can be achieved (and I quote) "without degradation of safety." Again, "without degradation of safety," so let's put that bogeyman behind us. That's on page 4-26.

17   Now, the opponents may say that the auto companies disagree. No surprise there; it's easier to just keep making gas guzzling cars, just like it was easier to keep making cars without seat belts, cars without air bags and cars without

pollution control equipment—all advances that the auto industry now touts even though it vehemently opposed each one initially. This case is no different.

Just look at the credibility of the auto industry. Here's what a top Ford executive said about safety standards in 1971: "The shoulder harnesses, the headrests are complete wastes of money . . . and you can see that safety has really killed all of our business." 18

Here's what GM said about pollution control in 1972: "It is conceivable that complete stoppage of the entire production could occur, with the obvious tremendous loss to the company." And I could go on and on with examples like this. 19

We should be used to these scare tactics now, and we should be wise to them. Let's not believe the folks who told us that seat belts would destroy the auto industry when they say they fear for our safety if we raise CAFE standards. 20

So I'm going to listen instead to the National Academy of Sciences. We've got the evidence we need to raise CAFE standards; we just need the will—the will to give the public what it wants. The public wants better fuel economy—if for no other reason than to save some money. And what the Academy report demonstrates is that we can give them that fuel economy without depriving anyone (including me) of our SUVs, without compromising safety, without threatening jobs. 21

We're sacrificing nothing if we pass this amendment; we're sacrificing our independence, our environment and our consumers, if we reject it. 22

Support the Boehlert-Markey-Shays-Waxman amendment. 23

Notice of Violation: Mock Ticket

StayFreeMagazine.Org

This prank ticket appeared on the advocacy Web site of StayFreeMagazine.org, one of the radical environmental activist organizations protesting SUVs' effect on the environment. Sites such as "StayFreeMagazine," "I Don't Care about the Air," and "I'm Changing the Environment! Ask Me How!" use barbed humor to convey their views.

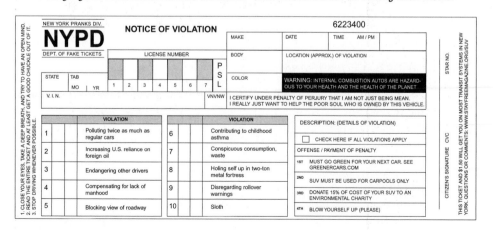

"Cancelled"
Henry Payne

This political cartoon by Henry Payne appeared in the Detroit News *on September 13, 2002.*

"THE GREEN WAS PUTTING US IN THE RED."

Source: HENRY PAYNE reprinted by permission of United Feature Syndicate, Inc.

Ford on Risk
Bill Wasserman

This political cartoon by Bill Wasserman appeared in the Boston Globe.

SUV and Miata

Horsey

This political cartoon by Horsey was posted on "I Don't Care About the Air," an advocacy Web site devoted to disseminating information and views about the damage SUVs are doing to the environment.

Courtesy of David Horsey/Seattle Post-Intelligencer.

For Class Discussion

1. The following exercise will help you sort out the multiple-issue questions and varied views on SUVs discussed in this unit's readings. Working individually or in groups, sketch out core arguments representing the following perspectives:

   ■ the environmental case against SUVs;
   ■ the automotive manufacturing position in support of SUVs;
   ■ consumers' arguments for buying SUVs;
   ■ the libertarian free-market perspective against raising CAFE standards;
   ■ the political argument rejecting increases in CAFE standards as a viable plan;
   ■ the pro-government intervention position on gasoline usage, fuel supply, and economic policy;
   ■ the arguments for and against the safety of SUVs.

   What other stakeholders or angles of vision are involved in this network of issues?

2. Find two-current magazine SUV ads that differ in their appeal to consumers. Examining the interplay of visual and textual elements in the ads, reconstruct the particular target audience for each ad and analyze the specific features and imaginative appeals that each ad emphasizes.

3. Working individually or in groups, analyze the argument implicit or explicit in several of the political cartoons on SUVs in this unit. What dimension of the SUV controversy does each cartoon choose to portray? Which cartoon do you think is most effective at conveying its point and why?

4. Choose one of the arguments for closer analysis, applying the second set of guide questions on pages 460–461.

OPTIONAL WRITING ASSIGNMENT   Imagine a scenario in which one of your best friends strongly disagrees with you about the ethics of buying and driving SUVs. If you would like to buy an SUV, your friend—a vehement environmentalist—thinks you should buy a car with fuel economy. If you yourself are opposed to SUVs, your friend is avidly saving to purchase an SUV. Using Rebekah Taylor's Rogerian argument as a model (Chapter 8, pp. 158–160), write a letter that seeks to open your friend's mind to a possible change in views. As Rebekah does, begin by articulating your understanding of your friend's position. Then, perhaps drawing on the reasons and evidence raised in the readings in this unit and any other readings on SUVs, present your own position. Finally, identifying a few common points that you and your friend can agree on, call for some change in your friend's views.

BIOTECHNOLOGY, ORGANIC FOOD, AND THE ETHICS OF FOOD PRODUCTION

Have you eaten any tomatoes, soybeans, potatoes, sugar beets, papaya, canola, or cantaloupe lately? If you have, chances are that you have eaten genetically modified foods, some of which have been on the market since 1994. Not too long ago, these issues were the province of health food fanatics or of scientists whose work might be reported in the back pages of newspapers. Now, however, the genetic engineering of foods and its controversial alternative, organic food, regularly dominate the covers of big news commentary magazines like *Time* and *Newsweek*. In addition, they are the focus of numerous advocacy Web sites.

Pervaded by much uncertainty, confusion, fear, and optimism, the multiple controversies surrounding biotechnology and food and organic food also involve numerous stakeholders. Proponents of genetic engineering point to its potential to increase crop yield, reduce the need for pesticides and herbicides (and thereby reduce the impact of these chemicals on the environment), lower production costs, add nutritional content to foods, and grow crops in formerly unsuitable conditions. Skeptics and opponents, however, consider genetically engineered foods highly experimental, even mutant, and object to the unleashing of new genetic material into the environment, to the rapid commercialization of products that may have unforeseen long-term consequences, and to food growers' and producers' lack of accountability to consumers concerning the ingredients of the food they are buying. Finally, lawmakers, policymakers, businesses, scientists, and public interest groups also argue about the driving forces behind the push for biotech foods, about the control of patents, and about international policy.

The readings and visual arguments in this unit, as well as those in Chapter 2 and on the Part One opening page, introduce you to a range of arguments representing these multiple controversies and exemplifying different angles of vision.

Organic Food Seasoned with Fear
Steven Milloy

Steven Milloy is the author of Junk Science Judo: Self-Defense against Health Scares & Scams *(2001) and is an adjunct scholar with the Cato Institute, a conservative public policy research foundation committed to "the traditional American principles of limited government, individual liberty, free markets and peace" (from "About Cato" on its Web site). This July 7, 2001, policy argument appeared on the Cato Institute's Web site.*

Organic foods are an official, "USDA-approved" scam. The U.S. Department of   1
Agriculture, not long ago, issued regulations defining what foods may be labeled
"organic."

The regulations provide that fruits, vegetables and meat and dairy products   2
may not be labeled as "organic" if they are produced with the use of pesticides, irradiation, genetic engineering, growth hormones, or sewage sludge.

Foods that meet the USDA criteria may carry the "USDA Organic." [label]   3

"Let me be clear about one other thing. The organic label is a marketing tool.   4
It is not a statement about food safety. Nor is 'organic' a value judgment about
nutrition or quality," said Agriculture Secretary Dan Glickman, in announcing the
new rules.

Glickman's disclaimer is amply supported by scientific evidence and our experi-   5
ence with non-organic or "conventional" foods.

No data indicate legally applied pesticides have caused even one health prob-   6
lem despite more than 50 years of use on agricultural crops—a fact that has even
been acknowledged by leading pesticide critic Dr. Phil Landrigan of the Mount Sinai
School of Medicine.

By killing dangerous foodborne pathogens such as E.coli and listeria, irradia-   7
tion reduces the risk of food poisoning. Biotech foods approved for human consumption are evaluated for safety before they are allowed to be marketed. Meat and dairy
products produced from cows supplemented with growth hormones are physically
indistinguishable from meat and dairy products from unsupplemented cows.

Foods grown with treated sewage sludge may seem unsavory, but is organic   8
food grown with cow manure any more appealing? In any event, food grown in
treated sewage sludge isn't a safety problem.

Despite Glickman's disclaimer, the rule is intended to do just what he says it isn't.   9
About one-half of the public already believes that organic foods are healthier, safer
and better for the environment, according to opinion surveys. The USDA label only
serves to validate and encourage these beliefs. The label doesn't carry Glickman's
disclaimer.

That's why the organic foods industry and its henchmen are so pleased about   10
the new U.S.-government-sanctioned myth. Many activists make livings promoting
fear campaigns around safe food while at the same time having personal financial
interests in alternative, organic products that benefit from those fear campaigns.

Glickman announced the new rules at a recently opened Fresh Fields super-   11
market in Washington, D.C. Fresh Fields is owned by Whole Foods Market Inc., an
organic foods business that pushed for the labeling requirement and markets itself
by scaring the public about conventional foods.

Greenpeace just entered the organic foods business, announcing it will license   12
a line of 12 organic products in Brazil.

After years of spreading fear about biotechnology, Lord Peter Melchett quit as   13
head of Greenpeace U.K. to join Iceland Foods, a major U.K. organic grocer that
supports Greenpeace. The U.K. Advertising Standards Authority censured Iceland
Foods in May for a supermarket brochure that spread fear about biotech foods, even
alleging that biotech foods were linked with deaths.

14   The Greenpeace-organic foods industry cabal operates in the U.S., too. Greenpeace's U.S. and U.K. operations share the same public relations outfit, Fenton Communications—the firm credited with starting the 1989 hysteria over alar in apples. Fenton represents organic foods businesses, such as ice cream manufacturer Ben & Jerry's Homemade Inc., working to scare consumers about dairy products from cows treated with recombinant bovine growth hormone.

15   Mark Ritchie, a key organizer of anti-biotech and anti-conventional agriculture activist campaigns through the Institute for Agriculture Trade Policy, Genetically Engineered Food Alert, Crop Choice Coalition and biotech activist Listserv, also runs a for-profit organic coffee company whose sales increase with each new food scare.

16   Craig Winters, an activist demanding labels on biotechnology-produced foods, also is a lobbyist and marketing consultant to the organic food industry. Winters has publicly stated his goal is to achieve a ban on biotechnology crops through labels. His list of organic and natural products financial ties is easily found at his web site, yet few challenge his motives.

17   The president and members of the board of directors of Genetic-ID, the firm now famous for helping Friends of the Earth discover that some taco shells contained unapproved—but safe—biotech corn, also run a wide range of organic and natural products and services companies.

18   They belong to a quasi-religious cult that promotes organic agriculture and a political movement, the Natural Law Party. The NLP platform promotes organic methods and attacks biotechnology. Each food scare they help promote with clients such as Friends of the Earth and Greenpeace increases the case flow into their various other interests.

19   Where does this cash come from? Consumers who are suckered into buying organic.

20   Organic foods cost an average of 57 percent more than conventional foods, according to *Consumer Reports.* These higher costs could amount to $4,000 annually for a family of four, according to the USDA.

21   Organic foods should be labeled. "Rip-off."

Ten Reasons Why Biotechnology Will Not Ensure Food Security, Protect the Environment, and Reduce Poverty in the Developing World

Miguel A. Altieri and Peter Rosset

This scholarly policy argument first appeared in the academic journal AgBioForum *in 1999 and subsequently was posted on the Web site for that publication. Miguel A. Altieri and Peter Rosset are affiliated with the University of California at Berkeley and Food First Institute for Food and Development Policy.*

Advocates of biotechnology affirm that the application of genetic engineering to develop transgenic crops will increase world agricultural productivity, enhance food security, and move agriculture away from a dependence on chemical inputs helping to reduce environmental problems. This paper challenges such assertions by first demystifying the Malthusian view that hunger is due to a gap between food production and human population growth. Second, we expose the fact that current bio-engineered crops are not designed to increase yields or for poor small farmers, so that they may not benefit from them. In addition, transgenic crops pose serious environmental risks, continuously underplayed by the biotechnology industry. Finally, it is concluded that there are many other agro-ecological alternatives that can solve the agricultural problems that biotechnology aims at solving, but in a much more socially equitable manner and in a more environmentally harmonious way.
Key Words: biotechnology; transgenic crops; developing countries; Malthusian view; environmental risks.

Biotechnology companies often claim that genetically modified organisms (GMOs)—specifically, genetically altered seeds—are essential scientific breakthroughs needed to feed the world, protect the environment, and reduce poverty in developing countries. The Consultative Group on International Agricultural Research (CGIAR) and its constellation of international centers around the world charged with research to enhance food security in the developing world echo this view, which rests on two critical assumptions. The first is that hunger is due to a gap between food production and human population density or growth rate. The second is that genetic engineering is the only or best way to increase agricultural production and, thus, meet future food needs. [1]

Our objective is to challenge the notion of biotechnology as a magic bullet solution to all of agriculture's ills, by clarifying misconceptions concerning these underlying assumptions. [2]

1. There is no relationship between the prevalence of hunger in a given country and its population. For every densely populated and hungry nation like Bangladesh or Haiti, there is a sparsely populated and hungry nation like Brazil and Indonesia. The world today produces more food per inhabitant than ever before. Enough food is available to provide 4.3 pounds for every person every day: 2.5 pounds of grain, beans and nuts, about a pound of meat, milk and eggs and another of fruits and vegetables. The real causes of hunger are poverty, inequality and lack of access to food and land. Too many people are too poor to buy the food that is available (but often poorly distributed) or lack the land and resources to grow it themselves (*Lappe, Collins & Rosset, 1998*).

2. Most innovations in agricultural biotechnology have been profit-driven rather than need-driven. The real thrust of the genetic engineering industry is not to make third world agriculture more productive, but rather to generate profits (*Busch et al., 1990*). This is illustrated by reviewing the principle technologies on the market today: (1) herbicide resistant crops, such as Monsanto's "Roundup Ready" soybeans, seeds that are tolerant to Monsanto's herbicide Roundup, and (2) "Bt" (*Bacillus thuringiensis*) crops which are

engineered to produce their own insecticide. In the first instance, the goal is to win a greater herbicide market-share for a proprietary product and, in the second, to boost seed sales at the cost of damaging the usefulness of a key pest management product (the *Bacillus thuringiensis* based microbial insecticide) relied upon by many farmers, including most organic farmers, as a powerful alternative to insecticides. These technologies respond to the need of biotechnology companies to intensify farmers' dependence upon seeds protected by so-called "intellectual property rights" which conflict directly with the age-old rights of farmers to reproduce, share or store seeds (*Hobbelink, 1991*). Whenever possible corporations will require farmers to buy a company's brand of inputs and will forbid farmers from keeping or selling seed. By controlling germplasm from seed to sale, and by forcing farmers to pay inflated prices for seed-chemical packages, companies are determined to extract the most profit from their investment (*Krimsky & Wrubel, 1996*).

3. The integration of the seed and chemical industries appears destined to accelerate increases in per acre expenditures for seeds plus chemicals, delivering significantly lower returns to growers. Companies developing herbicide tolerant crops are trying to shift as much per acre cost as possible from the herbicide onto the seed via seed costs and technology charges. Increasingly price reductions for herbicides will be limited to growers purchasing technology packages. In Illinois, the adoption of herbicide resistant crops makes for the most expensive soybean seed-plus-weed management system in modern history—between $40.00 and $60.00 per acre depending on fee rates, weed pressure, and so on. Three years ago, the average seed-plus-weed control costs on Illinois farms was $26 per acre, and represented 23% of variable costs; today they represent 35–40% (*Benbrook, 1999*). Many farmers are willing to pay for the simplicity and robustness of the new weed management system, but such advantages may be short-lived as ecological problems arise.

4. Recent experimental trials have shown that genetically engineered seeds do not increase the yield of crops. A recent study by the United States Department of Agriculture (USDA) Economic Research Service shows that in 1998 yields were not significantly different in engineered versus non-engineered crops in 12 of 18 crop/region combinations. In the six crop/region combinations where Bt crops or herbicide tolerant crops (HTCs) fared better, they exhibited increased yields between 5–30%. Glyphosphate tolerant cotton showed no significant yield increase in either region where it was surveyed. This was confirmed in another study examining more than 8,000 field trials, where it was found that Roundup Ready soybean seeds produced fewer bushels of soybeans than similar conventionally bred varieties (*USDA, 1999*).

5. Many scientists claim that the ingestion of genetically engineered food is harmless. Recent evidence, however, shows that there are potential risks of eating such foods as the new proteins produced in such foods could: (1) act themselves as allergens or toxins; (2) alter the metabolism of the food producing plant or animal, causing it to produce new allergens or toxins; or (3) reduce its nutritional quality or value. In the case of (3), herbicide resistant soybeans can contain less isoflavones, an important phytoestrogen present in soybeans, believed to protect women from a number of cancers. At present, developing countries are importing soybean and corn from the United States, Argentina, and Brazil. Genetically

engineered foods are beginning to flood the markets in the importing countries, yet no one can predict all their health effects on consumers, who are unaware that they are eating such food. Because genetically engineered food remains unlabeled, consumers cannot discriminate between genetically engineered (GE) and non-GE food, and should serious health problems arise, it will be extremely difficult to trace them to their source. Lack of labeling also helps to shield the corporations that could be potentially responsible from liability (*Lappe & Bailey, 1998*).

6. Transgenic plants which produce their own insecticides closely follow the pesticide paradigm, which is itself rapidly failing due to pest resistance to insecticides. Instead of the failed "one pest-one chemical" model, genetic engineering emphasizes a "one pest-one gene" approach, shown over and over again in laboratory trials to fail, as pest species rapidly adapt and develop resistance to the insecticide present in the plant (*Alstad & Andow, 1995*). Not only will the new varieties fail over the short-to-medium term, despite so-called voluntary resistance management schemes (*Mallet & Porter, 1992*), but in the process may render useless the natural Bt-pesticide which is relied upon by organic farmers and others desiring to reduce chemical dependence. Bt crops violate the basic and widely accepted principle of integrated pest management (IPM), which is that reliance on any single pest management technology tends to trigger shifts in pest species or the evolution of resistance through one or more mechanisms (*NRC, 1996*). In general, the greater the selection pressure across time and space, the quicker and more profound the pests' evolutionary response. An obvious reason for adopting this principle is that it reduces pest exposure to pesticides, retarding the evolution of resistance. But when the product is engineered into the plant itself, pest exposure leaps from minimal and occasional to massive and continuous exposure, dramatically accelerating resistance (*Gould, 1994*). *Bacillus thuringiensis* will rapidly become useless, both as a feature of the new seeds and as an old standby sprayed when needed by farmers that want out of the pesticide treadmill (*Pimentel et al., 1989*).

7. The global fight for market share is leading companies to massively deploy transgenic crops around the world (more than 30 million hectares in 1998) without proper advance testing of short-or long-term impacts on human health and ecosystems. In the United States, private sector pressure led the White House to decree "no substantial difference" between altered and normal seeds, thus evading normal Food and Drug Administration (FDA) and Environmental Protection Agency (EPA) testing. Confidential documents made public in an on-going class action lawsuit have revealed that the FDA's own scientists do not agree with this determination. One reason is that many scientists are concerned that the large scale use of transgenic crops poses a series of environmental risks that threaten the sustainability of agriculture (*Goldberg, 1992; Paoletti & Pimentel, 1996; Snow & Moran, 1997; Rissler & Mellon, 1996; Kendall et al., 1997; Royal Society, 1998*). These risk areas are as follows:

- The trend to create broad international markets for single products is simplifying cropping systems and creating genetic uniformity in rural landscapes. History has shown that a huge area planted to a single crop variety is very vulnerable to new matching strains of pathogens or insect pests. Furthermore, the widespread use of homogeneous transgenic varieties will unavoidably lead to "genetic erosion," as the local varieties used by thousands of farmers in the developing world are replaced by the new seeds (*Robinson, 1996*).

- The use of herbicide resistant crops undermines the possibilities of crop diversification, thus, reducing agrobiodiversity in time and space (*Altieri, 1994*).

- The potential transfer through gene flow of genes from herbicide resistant crops to wild or semidomesticated relatives can lead to the creation of superweeds (*Lutman, 1999*).

- There is potential for herbicide resistant varieties to become serious weeds in other crops (*Duke, 1996; Holt & Le Baron, 1990*).

- Massive use of Bt crops affects non-target organisms and ecological processes. Recent evidence shows that the Bt toxin can affect beneficial insect predators that feed on insect pests present on Bt crops (*Hilbeck et al., 1998*). In addition, windblown pollen from Bt crops, found on natural vegetation surrounding transgenic fields, can kill non-target insects such as the monarch butterfly (*Losey et al., 1999*). Moreover, Bt toxin present in crop foliage plowed under after harvest can adhere to soil colloids for up to 3 months, negatively affecting the soil invertebrate populations that break down organic matter and play other ecological roles (*Donnegan et al., 1995; Palm et al., 1996*).

- There is potential for vector recombination to generate new virulent strains of viruses, especially in transgenic plants engineered for viral resistance with viral genes. In plants containing coat protein genes, there is a possibility that such genes will be taken up by unrelated viruses infecting the plant. In such situations, the foreign gene changes the coat structure of the viruses and may confer properties, such as changed method of transmission between plants. The second potential risk is that recombination between RNA virus and a viral RNA inside the transgenic crop could produce a new pathogen leading to more severe disease problems. Some researchers have shown that recombination occurs in transgenic plants and that under certain conditions it produces a new viral strain with altered host range (*Steinbrecher, 1996*).

3   Ecological theory predicts that the large-scale landscape homogenization with transgenic crops will exacerbate the ecological problems already associated with monoculture agriculture. Unquestioned expansion of this technology into developing countries may not be wise or desirable. There is strength in the agricultural diversity of many of these countries, and it should not be inhibited or reduced by extensive monoculture, especially when consequences of doing so result in serious social and environmental problems (*Altieri, 1996*).

4   Although the ecological risks issue has received some discussion in government, international, and scientific circles, discussions have often been pursued from a narrow perspective that has downplayed the seriousness of the risks (*Kendall et al., 1997; Royal Society, 1998*). In fact, methods for risk assessment of transgenic crops are not well developed (*Kjellsson & Simonsen, 1994*) and there is justifiable concern that current field biosafety tests tell little about potential environmental

risks associated with commercial-scale production of transgenic crops. A main concern is that international pressures to gain markets and profits is resulting in companies releasing transgenic crops too fast, without proper consideration for the long-term impacts on people or the ecosystem.

8. There are many unanswered ecological questions regarding the impact of transgenic crops. Many environmental groups have argued for the creation of suitable regulation to mediate the testing and release of transgenic crops to offset environmental risks and demand a much better assessment and understanding of ecological issues associated with genetic engineering. This is crucial, as many results emerging from the environmental performance of released transgenic crops suggest that in the development of resistant crops not only is there a need to test direct effects on the target insect or weed, but the indirect effects on the plant. Plant growth, nutrient content, metabolic changes, and effects on the soil and non-target organisms should all be examined. Unfortunately, funds for research on environmental risk assessment are very limited. For example, the USDA spends only 1% of the funds allocated to biotechnology research on risk assessment, about $1–2 million per year. Given the current level of deployment of genetically engineered plants, such resources are not enough to even discover the "tip of the iceberg." It is a tragedy-in-the-making that so many millions of hectares have been planted without proper biosafety standards. Worldwide such acreage expanded considerably in 1998 with transgenic cotton reaching 6.3 million acres, transgenic corn reaching 20.8 million acres, and transgenic soybean 36.3 million acres. This expansion has been helped along by marketing and distribution agreements entered into by corporations and marketers (i.e., Ciba Seeds with Growmark and Mycogen Plant Sciences with Cargill), and in the absence of regulations in many developing countries. Genetic pollution, unlike oil spills, cannot be controlled by throwing a boom around it.

9. As the private sector has exerted more and more dominance in advancing new biotechnologies, the public sector has had to invest a growing share of its scarce resources in enhancing biotechnological capacities in public institutions, including the CGIAR, and in evaluating and responding to the challenges posed by incorporating private sector technologies into existing farming systems. Such funds would be much better used to expand support for ecologically based agricultural research, as all the biological problems that biotechnology aims at can be solved using agroecological approaches. The dramatic effects of rotations and intercropping on crop health and productivity, as well as of the use of biological control agents on pest regulation have been confirmed repeatedly by scientific research. The problem is that research at public institutions increasingly reflects the interests of private funders at the expense of public good research, such as biological control, organic production systems and general agroecological techniques. Civil society must request for more research on alternatives to biotechnology by universities and other public organizations (*Krimsky & Wrubel, 1996*). There is also an urgent need to challenge the patent system and intellectual property rights intrinsic to the World Trade Organization (WTO) which not only provide multinational corporations with the right to seize and patent genetic resources, but will also accelerate the rate at which market forces already encourage monocultural cropping with genetically uniform transgenic varieties. Based on history and ecological theory, it is not difficult to predict the negative impacts of such environmental simplification on the health of modern agriculture (*Altieri, 1996*).

10. Much of the needed food can be produced by small farmers located throughout the world using agroecological technologies (*Uphoff & Altieri, 1999*). In fact, new rural development approaches and low-input technologies spearheaded by farmers and non-governmental organizations (NGOs) around the world are already making a significant contribution to food security at the household, national, and regional levels in Africa, Asia and Latin America (*Pretty, 1995*). Yield increases are being achieved by using technological approaches, based on agroecological principles that emphasize diversity, synergy, recycling and integration; and social processes that emphasize community participation and empowerment (*Rosset, 1999*). When such features are optimized, yield enhancement and stability of production are achieved, as well as a series of ecological services such as conservation of biodiversity, soil and water restoration and conservation, improved natural pest regulation mechanisms, and so on (*Altieri et al., 1998*). These results are a breakthrough for achieving food security and environmental preservation in the developing world, but their potential and further spread depends on investments, policies, institutional support, and attitude changes on the part of policy makers and the scientific community; especially the CGIAR who should devote much of its efforts to the 320 million poor farmers living in marginal environments. Failure to promote such people-centered agricultural research and development due to the diversion of funds and expertise towards biotechnology will forego an historical opportunity to raise agricultural productivity in economically viable, environmentally benign, and socially uplifting ways.

References

Alstad, D. N., and Andow, D. A. (1995). Managing the evolution of insect resistance to transgenic plants. *Science, 268*, 1894–1896.

Altieri, M. A. (1994). *Biodiversity and pest management in agroecosystems.* New York: Haworth Press.

Altieri, M. A. (1996). *Agroecology: The science of sustainable agriculture.* Boulder, CO: Westview Press.

Altieri, M. A., Rosset, P., and Thrupp, L. A. (1998). *The potential of agroecology to combat hunger in the developing world* (2020 Brief No.55). Washington, DC: International Food Policy Research Institute.

Benbrook, C. (1999). *World food system challenges and opportunities: GMOs, biodiversity and lessons from America's heartland.* Unpublished manuscript.

Busch, L., Lacey, W. B., Burkhardt, J., and Lacey, L. (1990). *Plants, power and profit.* Oxford, England: Basil Blackwell.

Casper, R., and Landsmann, J. (1992). The biosafety results of field tests of genetically modified plants and microorganisms. P. K. Landers (Ed.), *Proceedings of the Second International Symposium Goslar,* pp. 89–97, Germany.

Donnegan, K. K., Palm, C. J., Fieland, V. J., Porteous, L. A., Ganis, L. M., Scheller, D. L., and Seidler, R. J. (1995). Changes in levels, species, and DNA fingerprints of soil microorganisms associated with cotton expressing the Bacillus thuringiensis var. Kurstaki endotoxin. *Applied Soil Ecology, 2,* 111–124.

Duke, S. O. (1996). *Herbicide resistant crops: Agricultural, environmental, economic, regulatory, and technical aspects.* Boca Raton: Lewis Publishers.

Goldberg, R. J. (1992). Environmental concerns with the development of herbicide-tolerant plants. *Weed Technology, 6,* 647–652.

Gould, F. (1994). Potential and problems with high-dose strategies for pesticidal engineered crops. *Biocontrol Science and Technology, 4,* 451–461.

Hilbeck, A., Baumgartner, M., Fried, P. M., and Bigler, F. (1998). Effects of transgenic Bacillus thuringiensis corn fed prey on mortality and development time of immature Chrysoperla carnea Neuroptera: Chrysopidae. *Environmental Entomology, 27*, 460–487.

Hobbelink, H. (1991). *Biotechnology and the future of world agriculture.* London: Zed Books, Ltd.

Holt, J. S., and Le Baron, H. M. (1990). Significance and distribution of herbicide resistance. *Weed Technology, 4*, 141–149.

James, C. (1997). *Global status of transgenic crops in 1997* (ISAAA Briefs No. 5.). Ithaca, NY: International Service for the Acquisition of Agri-Biotech Application (ISAAA). Available on the World Wide Web: *http://www.isaaa.org/frbrief5.htm*

Kendall, H. W., Beachy, R., Eismer, T., Gould, F., Herdt, R., Ravon, P. H., Schell, J., and Swaminathan, M. S. (1997). *Bioengineering of crops* (Report of the World Bank Panel on Transgenic Crops, pp.1–30). Washington, DC: World Bank.

Kennedy, G. G., and Whalon, M. E. (1995). Managing pest resistance to Bacillus thuringiensis endotoxins: Constraints and incentives to implementation. *Journal of Economic Entomology, 88*, 454–460.

Kjellsson, G., and Simonsen, V. (1994). *Methods for risk assessment of transgenic plants.* Basil, Germany: Birkhauser Verlag.

Krimsky, S., and Wrubel, R. P. (1996). Agricultural biotechnology and the environment: Science, policy and social issues. Urbana, IL: University of Illinois Press.

Lappe, F. M., Collins, J., and Rosset, P. (1998). *World hunger: Twelve myths.* New York: Grove Press.

Lappe, M., and Bailey, B. (1998). *Against the grain: Biotechnology and the corporate takeover of food.* Monroe, ME: Common Courage Press.

Liu, Y. B., Tabashnik, B. E., Dennehy, T. J., Patin, A. L., and Bartlett A. C. (1999). Development time and resistance to Bt crops. *Nature, 400*, 519.

Losey, J. J. E., Rayor, L. S., and Carter, M. E. (1999). Transgenic pollen harms monarch larvae. *Nature, 399*, 214.

Lutman, P. J. W. (1999). (Ed.). Gene flow and agriculture: Relevance for transgenic crops. *British Crop Protection Council Symposium Proceedings, 72*, 43–64.

Mallet, J., and Porter, P. (1992). Preventing insect adaptations to insect resistant crops: Are seed mixtures or refugia the best strategy? *Proceedings of the Royal Society of London Series B Biology Science, 250*, 165–169.

National Research Council (NRC). (1996). *Ecologically based pest management.* Washington, DC: National Academy of Sciences.

Palm, C. J., Schaller, D. L., Donegan, K. K., and Seidler, R. J. (1996). Persistence in soil of transgenic plant produced bacillus thuringiensis var. kustaki-endotoxin. *Canadian Journal of Microbiology, 42*, 1258–1262.

Paoletti, M. G., and Pimentel, D. (1996). Genetic engineering in agriculture and the environment: Assessing risks and benefits. *BioScience, 46*, 665–671.

Pimentel, D., Hunter, M. S., LaGro, J. A., Efroymson, R. A., Landers, J. C., Mervis, F. T., McCarthy, C. A., and Boyd, A. E. (1989). Benefits and risks of genetic engineering in agriculture. *BioScience, 39*, 606–614.

Pretty, J. (1995). Regenerating agriculture: Policies and practices for sustainability and self-reliance. London: Earthscan.

Rissler, J., and Mellon, M. (1996). *The ecological risks of engineered crops.* Cambridge, MA: MIT Press.

Robinson, R. A. (1996). Return to resistance: Breeding crops to reduce pesticide resistance. Davis, CA: AgAccess.

Rosset, P. (1999). *The multiple functions and benefits of small farm agriculture in the context of global trade negotiations* (IFDP Food First Policy Brief No. 4). Washington, DC: Institute for Food and Development Policy.

Royal Society. (1998, February). Genetically modified plants for food use. *Statement 2/98.* London: Royal Society.

Snow, A. A., and Moran, P. (1997). Commercialization of transgenic plants: Potential ecological risks. *BioScience, 47,* 86–96.

Steinbrecher, R. A. (1996). From green to gene revolution: The environmental risks of genetically engineered crops. *The Ecologist, 26,* 273–282.

United States Department of Agriculture (USDA). (1999). *Genetically engineered crops for pest management.* Washington, DC: USDA Economic Research Service.

Uphoff, N., and Altieri, M. A. (1999). *Alternatives to conventional modern agriculture for meeting world food needs in the next century* (Report of a Bellagio Conference). Ithaca, NY: Cornell International Institute for Food, Agriculture and Development.

Executive Summary:
Biotechnology and Food
American Council on Science and Health

The American Council on Science and Health is an independent, nonprofit organization composed of physicians, scientists, and policy advisers concerned about issues relating to public health and the environment. This executive summary, posted on the Council's Web site, provides an overview of the organization's position on biotechnology, which is developed in detail in its larger publication Biotechnology and Food. *(An executive summary is a brief statement, often outlining main points in bulleted form, of an organization's policy on a controversial issue. For more information, readers are directed to the organization's full-length publication.)*

1   **Modern biotechnology** greatly benefits the quality and quantity of food, human and animal health, and the environment. Unfortunately, misinformation and misunderstandings about biotechnology in the popular media make it difficult for consumers to make informed assessments. This booklet explains the facts behind genetic modification (GM) and explores some of the issues surrounding the increasingly contentious debate over its use in food production.

2   **Traditional biotechnology** has given us almost all of our foods, from corn and beef to bread and wine. In the 1970s, modern biotechnology (i.e., genetic modification, genetic engineering, recombinant DNA or rDNA, gene splicing, etc.) started giving us lifesaving drugs such as Humulin (human insulin). In the past several years, the same technology has been applied to enhance agriculture and food production. Gene modification is a natural event. Many of our traditional foods are products of natural mutations or genetic recombinations. Nature is constantly mutating genes and even moving them from one species to another. With biotechnology, humans can direct genetic changes to benefit human endeavors.

3   **Agricultural scientists** have already produced GM crops with:

- herbicide resistance, allowing farmers to use fewer chemicals and obtain weed-free crops;

- insect resistance to control insect pests feeding on the crops, while leaving non-pest insects alone;

- disease resistance to limit crop losses from epidemics;
- delayed ripening fruits that maintain their freshness longer;
- healthier vegetable oils, with lower saturated fat content.

New products under development include:

AGRICULTURAL

- Crops tolerant of environmental stresses such as drought, flooding, soil salinity, and frost;
- Crops with greater protection from insects, diseases and weeds.

Consumer-oriented

More consumer-oriented GM products will appear on our shelves, including

- Nutritionally enhanced foods;
- Lower calorie sugar (fructans) from GM sugar beets;
- Foods from which naturally occurring allergenic and antinutritional compounds have been eliminated.

ANIMAL HUSBANDRY

- GM medicines and vaccines can be delivered to animals via their feed, saving the expense of sick animals and veterinary bills;
- Quick-growing game fish;
- Important and valuable chemicals might be produced in GM goats' milk, where they can be readily separated and purified.

OTHER PRODUCTS

- Biomaterials such as biodegradable plastics made from GM plant starch;
- GM plants to make diesel fuel;
- Cotton and linen modified to increase quality and durability;
- Textiles and fabrics with built in dyes.

Assistance to developing nations

Rice, the major food staple throughout the developing world, has been nutritionally enhanced for increased iron and beta-carotene (provitamin A) content and increased yields. Cassava, another major food staple, can be protected from viral and other diseases through biotechnology. Inexpensive vitamins, minerals, medicines, and vaccines may soon be delivered to the ill and malnourished via GM fruit.

Public concerns over the safety of GM remain an issue of debate. However, most scientists conversant with GM technology are supporters; they know GM products are not inherently hazardous. Three hundred million North American consumers have been eating several dozen GM foods grown on hundreds of millions of acres since 1994, with no documented adverse effects.

Some widespread myths and misconceptions, which may cause consumer concern, include:

- GM potatoes being toxic to rats;
- GM soy becoming allergenic;
- GM corn killing butterflies.

All of these are readily refuted by the facts in each case.

FDA regulations already require answers to crucial safety questions:

- Does the food contain genes from known allergenic sources?
- Does it contain genes from toxic sources?
- Are the concentrations of natural toxic substances increased?
- Is the fat, cholesterol or other nutrient content changed?
- Does the food contain a substance that is new to the food supply?

Like all foods, GM foods bear labels if they carry allergens or toxins, or if they are substantially altered in nutritional composition, so consumers will be able to identify such foods.

Conclusion

Current regulatory scrutiny, plus the excellent track record of GM food safety, gives us confidence that GM foods are rigorously scrutinized and that the technology is safe. Consumers and farmers can expect a wide variety of beneficial new products in the not-too-distant future to augment those currently on the market.

Why Voluntary Labeling of Genetically Engineered Foods Won't Help Consumers

Center for Food Safety

This researched article was written by the Center for Food Safety, an environmental and public health organization, and was posted on the organization's Web site on December 21, 2000. Using clear headings and endnotes, this policy argument sets forth the consumer protection position on the marketing of genetically engineered food.

1   A significant percentage of processed food purchased today contains some genetically engineered food products. As a result, each day the majority of the American public eats genetically engineered foods without their knowledge. Currently, consumers have no way of knowing what foods are genetically engineered because the Food and Drug Administration (FDA) does not require labeling

of these products. The FDA's refusal to mandate labeling requirements for such foods has created significant trade tensions between the United States and its trading partners.[1] The position has also been met with significant public resistance. Recent revelations that a potentially allergenic genetically engineered corn variety has made its way illegally into hundreds of food products have made the American public more adamant for mandatory labeling.[2]

On May 3, 2000, the FDA announced that it would release guidelines for voluntary efforts to label genetically engineered food products as containing or not containing genetically engineered ingredients.[3] While the announcement was an effort to quell growing consumer concern on this issue, the voluntary labeling proposal will actually have a negative effect on consumers' ability to make informed purchasing decisions concerning genetically engineered foods. 2

As a food policy voluntary labeling for genetically engineered foods is inadequate to protect consumers' right-to-know, to ensure adequate safety oversight of our food supply, and may actually inhibit information on genetically engineered foods from reaching consumers. The Center for Food Safety believes that mandatory labeling of all genetically engineered foods and ingredients is necessary to ensure consumers' right-to-know and to embrace a thorough regulatory system to protect the public's health and welfare. As proposed, the FDA voluntary labeling guidelines will serve the interests of a few biotechnology companies at the expense of the rest of the food industry and millions of consumers. 3

WHY IS VOLUNTARY LABELING OF GENETICALLY ENGINEERED FOOD INADEQUATE?

1. **Voluntary Labeling Is Contrary to Consumer Demands for Mandatory Labeling.**   FDA's new guidance rejects the mandatory labeling of GE foods, a policy overwhelmingly preferred by the majority of Americans. Opinion polls consistently show that more than 90% of Americans strongly support the labeling of genetically engineered foods.[4] Failure to institute mandatory labeling regulations undercuts clear public sentiment for a right-to-know about genetically engineered foods.

2. **Voluntary Labels Prevent Food Allergenic Consumers From Consistent Safety Information.**   Of course, the first step with any food is safety testing. Should a food be hazardous or adulterated it is generally not allowed on supermarket shelves. If a food is generally recognized as safe but has material physical changes which are not evident in the food's appearance, food labeling is required. For example, a consumer cannot tell just from its appearance that a genetically engineered tomato has (a) flounder genes; (b) a bacterial vector; (c) a cauliflower mosaic virus promoter; and (d) an antibiotic marker system in it (real example). A consumer may be allergic to fish, taking antibiotics, and not eager to consume plant viruses. They should have the right to choose to avoid such a food and thereby avoid an allergic reaction, the rendering of their antibiotic ineffective, and the possible allergic or toxic reaction to a new virus in their food. The only way they can choose to avoid these risks is by full and mandatory labeling.

3. **Voluntary Labeling Prevents Post-Market Surveillance Traceability & Food Producer Liability.**   Genetic engineering of foods can increase natural toxin levels in food, create new toxins, transfer allergens into new foods, alter nutritional value and possibly create other potential health hazards. A food safety system that adequately works to prevent such foods from

causing health impacts requires both pre-market and post-market oversight. In the case of genetically engineered foods, the FDA has repeatedly stressed that should a hazardous genetically engineered food come onto the market it will be able to remove that product from the market. Such a system of post-market surveillance and enforcement, however, makes mandatory labeling of all genetically engineered foods critical. Mandatory labeling not only provides consumers with marketplace choice, but it is essential for the traceability of genetically engineered food products throughout the food supply. Health concerns arising from a commercially sold genetically engineered food will only be traceable with labels.

Additionally, labels ensuring traceability of products through the food supply also ensure that producers of genetically engineered foods will be held accountable for the foods they bring to market. Without mandatory labeling, should a genetically engineered food prove to be dangerous it will be hard for an injured consumer to prove "causation" of injury from such a food. By relying entirely on a voluntary labeling scheme, FDA is in effect protecting genetically engineered food producers from potential legal liability.

4. **Voluntary Labeling Unfairly Reverses The Burden Onto Producers Who Do Not Use GMOs.**   As a policy voluntary "GMO Free" labeling inappropriately reverses the burden onto producers and manufacturers who have opted not to expose consumers to the potential health risks associated with GE foods. Thus, companies not engaging in behavior that poses risks to consumers are expected to take on the cost of labeling and testing in a voluntary "GMO Free" labeling scenario. Simply put, many of the companies that could use a "GMO Free" label will choose not to take on this voluntary burden. The scope of products bearing a "GMO Free" label will likely be very narrow and voluntary "GMO Free" labeling will not provide consumers with a real choice or the ability to avoid GE foods. Ultimately, consumers concerned about issues posed by GE foods, such as allergenicity and food sensitivity, will have only an extremely limited range of products by which to address their health concerns.

5. **Food Companies Already Have A Constitutional Right To Label "GMO Free."**   FDA's pronouncement in favor of voluntary labeling is a redundancy. Companies already have a commercial free speech right (as long as it is a truthful claim) to label their foods GE-free. Use of a "GMO Free" lable by food producers should be protected from state or federal attempts to ban such labeling in that such government action would be an unconstitutional burden on free speech. Corporations have a free speech right to inform their customers that their products and ingredients meet exacting standards. This protection is derived from the U.S. Constitution's First Amendment. The First Amendment provides in pertinent part that "Congress shall make no law . . . abridging the freedom of speech." U.S. Const. Amend. I. (The First Amendment applies to the states through the Fourteenth Amendment. U.S. Const. Amend. XIV.) The "commercial speech" doctrine is an outgrowth of the freedom of speech issue. In 1976, the Supreme Court decided that certain speech involving commercial transactions merited protection under the First Amendment.[5] In protecting commercial free speech the Supreme Court has stated:

> The particular consumer's interest in the free flow of consumer information . . . may be as keen, if not keener by far, than his interest in the day's most urgent political debate . . . . The free flow of commercial information is indispensable . . . to proper allocation of resources in a free enterprise system . . . [and] to the formation of intelligent options as to how that system ought to be regulated or altered.[6]

The current atmosphere is especially conducive to the use of "GMO Free" labeling claims. Recent Supreme Court decisions have further bolstered the "commercial speech" doctrine and, as a result, extended constitutional protection to "GMO Free" label users.[7] As a result, use and adoption of truthful "GMO Free" labeling claims clearly should fall within the spirit and reasoning of prior Supreme Court commercial speech rulings.[8]

To the extent the Federal government burdens voluntary "GMO Free" labeling with additional conditions or contextual requirements it will be limiting food companies' constitutional right to inform the consumer. This may place legal hurdles in front of the few companies that are making product claims concerning their "GMO Free" nature by forcing them to challenge the constitutionality of FDA's actions.[9]

6. **Past Experience Suggests FDA's Voluntary Labeling Guidance Will Reduce Consumers' Access to Labeling Information About Genetic Engineering: The Case of Bovine Growth Hormone (rBGH).**   The food labeling issues surrounding dairy products derived from cows treated with genetically engineered Bovine Growth Hormone (rBGH) provide a case study as to why voluntary "GMO Free" labeling is unlikely to provide consumers widespread marketplace access to GMO-free labeled foods.

After the FDA's approval of the genetically engineered hormone, numerous small dairies and food producers began using "rBGH Free" labels. Monsanto, the manufacturer of rBGH, complained to the FDA that such labeling was misleading because the milk from rBGH cows was the same as milk from untreated cows (a point of contention still today). The FDA responded and announced that it would "allow" dairy products to be labeled "rBGH Free," but then released non-binding voluntary labeling guidelines suggesting that such "rBGH Free" labels would not be misleading so long as they contained a contextual disclaimer. [10] The FDA guidelines even stated that the "rBGH Free" guidelines were non-binding and that they did *not* create a legal right on anyone.[11]

Nonetheless, as soon as the guidance was published Monsanto sued two small dairies that were labeling milk and dairy products as "rBGH Free" without the FDA contextual disclaimer.[12] Monsanto claimed that without the disclaimer the dairies were impugning the safety of milk and rBGH. Monsanto was likely headed for losses in both the cases; however, their considerable war chest and reputation led to settlements with the two small dairies. While Monsanto may not have won legally, they achieved victory in the big battle because the lawsuits chilled the atmosphere for any small dairy engaged in voluntary labeling. Even several larger food producers such as Ben & Jerry's, Stoneyfield Farm and Whole Foods battled for years with the state of Illinois and the City of Chicago over their "rBGH Free" labeling claims.[13]

It is easy to envision a similar situation will unfold as a result of the FDA's voluntary labeling guidance. Ultimately, this will result in few companies moving forward with "GMO Free" labeling claims and consumers will still not be provided a choice on whether to consume genetically engineered foods or not.

Endnotes

1. Currently, the European Union, Japan, Korea, Australia, New Zealand and other countries have adopted (or are in the process of adopting) mandatory labeling regulations for genetically engineered foods.
2. *See*, e.g., Andrew Pollack, "Aventis Gives up License to Sell Bioengineered Corn," *New York Times*, Friday, October 13, 2000.

3. White House, Office of the Press Secretary, "Clinton Administration Agencies Announce Food and Agricultural Biotechnology Initiatives: Strengthening Science-based Regulation and Consumer Access to Information," May 3, 2000, at 3.

4. Hansen, Dr. Michael, & Halloran, J. "Why We Need Labeling of Genetically Engineered Food." Consumer International, Consumer Policy Institute, April 1998, *http://www.consumersunion.org/food/whywenny798.htm* (December 20, 2000); "Compilation and Analysis of Public Opinion Polls on Genetically Engineered Foods," Center for Food Safety, August 24, 2000, *http://www.centerforfoodsafety.org/facts&issues/polls.html.*

5. *Virginia State Board of Pharmacy v. Virginia Citizens Consumer Council,* 425 U.S. 758, 48 L. Ed. 2d. 346, 96 S.Ct. 1817 (1976).

6. *Id.* at 763–765.

7. *See, Rubin v. Coors Brewing Co.,* 514 US 476, 131 L.Ed. 2d 532, 115 S.Ct. 1585 (1995). (Federal regulations banning beer labels from displaying alcohol content violated the First Amendment. The Court found that Coors' disclosure of "truthful, verifiable, and non-misleading factual information about alcohol content on its beer label" was provided First Amendment protection.)

8. Any government effort to restrict commercial free speech must pass scrutiny of the four part test established in *Central Hudson Gas & Elec. Corp. v. Public Serv. Cmn. of New York,* 447 U.S. 557, 566, 65 L.Ed. 2d 341, 100 S.Ct. 2343 (1980). Central Hudson's four part test asks (1) whether the speech issue concerns lawful activity and is not misleading and (2) whether the asserted governmental interest is substantial; and, if so, (3) whether the regulation directly advances the governmental interest asserted and (4) whether it is not more extensive than is necessary to serve that interst. In this analysis the Government bears the burden of identifying a substantial interest and justifying challenged restrictions. *Edenfield v. Fane,* 507 U.S. 761, 770, 123 L.Ed. 2d 543, 113 S.Ct. 1972 (1993).

9. Examples include Whole Foods 365 Expeller Pressed Canola Oil claiming "the plants we use for our 365 Canola Oil are grown from seed that is not genetically altered"; Kettle Foods, Inc. Kettle Crisps "We make every effort to use non-gmo ingredients"; and Van's International Foods Inc. Organic Waffles claiming "Non-GMO Canola Oil."

10. FDA, "Interim Guidance of the Voluntary Labeling of Milk and Milk Products from Cows That Have Not Been Treated with Recombinant Bovine Somatotropin." 59 Fed. Reg. 6279 (Febuary 10, 1994). The guidance recommended that any rBGH free label should include the statement "No significant difference has been shown between milk derived from rbST (rBGH) treated cows and non-rbST (non-rBGH) cows."

11. *Id.* The FDA stated, "This document does not bind FDA or any State, and it does not create or confer any rights, privileges, benefits, or immunities for or on any persons."

12. *See, Monsanto v. Swiss Valley Farms Co.,* Docket No. 94C-1013 (N.D. Ill. 1994); *Monsanto v. Pure Milk Co.,* Docket No. W94-CA-051 (W.D. Tex. 1994).

13. *See generally, Ben & Jerry's Homemade, Inc v. Lumpkin,* 1996 U.S. Dist. LEXIS 12469 (N.D. Ill. 1996).

Invoking the Lessons of Edison in the Great "Frankenfoods" Dispute

John Bissell

This article by public relations, crisis management, and marketing expert John Bissell appeared in the summer 2000 edition of Public Relations Strategist, *a publication of the Public Relations Society of America. Bissell is principal and group management director of Publicis Dialog.*

PICTURE THIS SCENARIO

A group of scientists develops a revolutionary technology that promises to en-   1
hance the standard of living for people around the globe. The technology offers
tremendous environmental benefits and is reportedly safer than the technologies it
would displace. But some groups stand to lose out if the new technology is adopted,
and they undertake a masterful PR campaign portraying the technology as unsafe,
even deadly. As a result, adoption of the new technology is delayed for years, and
its developers are driven to financial ruin.

Anyone following the debate over genetically-modified foods will recognize that   2
this scenario is being played out right now in the media. For all the promise that
food biotechnology apparently offers, the life science companies that have invested
billions in researching and developing modified crops are watching their stock
prices plummet and their corporate brands suffer.

ENHANCED PRODUCTS ARE SAFE

Good science indicates that genetically enhanced products are safe. In addition,   3
so-called "biotech" crops can reduce the need for pesticides and herbicides, and more
food can be grown on less land, reducing global hunger. How, then, have anti-biotech
Forces so successfully persuaded their audiences to the contrary and been able to
portray these enhanced crops as "Frankenfoods" developed by reckless scientists?

What strategies and tactics have activists employed to raise doubts and fears   4
about the benefits of genetic engineering? Biotechnology advocates might take a
lesson from an earlier time, when opposing forces fought over the future of a now-
ubiquitous technology—alternating current, the delivery system of electricity now
used worldwide.

THOMAS EDISON AS PR SCHOLAR

Nikola Tesla was a brilliant scientist who harnessed the power of alternating   5
current (AC) in the 1880s. As he and his financial backers attempted to commer-
cialize their AC technology, they found themselves face-to-face with a formidable
foe: Thomas Alva Edison.

Today, Edison is known as the grandfatherly inventor of the light bulb and the   6
phonograph, and as the Wizard of Menlo Park. But in the 1880s, he showed that he
was also a powerful PR practitioner. Edison had built his business at that time
around the direct current (DC) method of delivering electricity and knew that his
own business would suffer huge losses if the public came to accept Tesla's AC system as safer and more economical.

While Tesla worked to perfect his AC technology, Edison began a national cam-   7
paign to demonstrate that AC was unproven and potentially deadly. He orchestrated
public electrocutions of small animals using AC (though either AC or DC could have
been used to the same effect). Edison had earlier been asked to develop a high-
voltage device to be used for executing criminals. He had refused on humanitarian
grounds, but now accepted the challenge on the condition that the device would be
powered with AC.

8   Edison helped design the electric chair, which was put to the test in the first high-profile public execution in 1890. This event drew national and international media attention, and Edison had made his point: Why would U.S. consumers want this deadly force unleashed in their living rooms?

9   At the same time that he fought to postpone the adoption of AC, Edison recognized its superiority and eventually helped to bring the technology to market. By that time Tesla had been driven out of the business and eventually died in near obscurity.

EDISON'S FORMULA FOR SUCCESS

10   Edison's campaign succeeded because he recognized three fundamental truths about the American public:

- Most people are not technically-minded and are ambivalent about technology.
- People respond readily to powerful graphic symbols and demonstrations.
- People respond readily to compelling emotional appeals, particularly those that relate to the safety of their children and families.

11   These are the same truths that anti-biotech forces are taking advantage of in their current "Frankenfoods" campaign.

12   The simple fact is that most people do not understand the science and engineering behind the technologies they use. Comparisons may be made between the beginning of the 20th century and that of the 21st century. Edison's audience did not understand electrical current any better than 21st century consumers understand the double helix of DNA.

FOCUS ON EFFECTS

13   Moreover, the majority of consumers are largely disinterested in having detailed knowledge about what lies behind or within new technologies. What people do understand and appreciate, however, is the spectrum of benefits, or conversely, of threats, that a given technology represents. Edison's campaign did not rely on the consumer's ability to grasp the workings of the electron, but, instead, painted a very clear and simple picture of the effects of the technology.

14   Similarly, anti-biotech groups have not focused on how foods are genetically modified, but rather, the negative effects of the unknown technology.

15   In addition, people have a fear of, and ambivalence toward, new technology that forces them out of their comfort zone. With tried-and-true technology, who needs something different? The adverse feeling people have toward change is used by the anti-biotech movement to further their cause with people who don't understand the nuances of the technology.

16   Because he knew that most people are not technically minded, Edison recognized that his audience needed to visualize the invisible force of electricity. This led him to the highly effective tactic of public electrocutions.

ELECTRIC CHAIR TO BAMBI

Anti-biotech groups have adopted a far less grisly, but just as effective, tactic, seizing on an icon provided by a Cornell University study. Research conducted at Cornell questioned the impact of genetically modified corn crops on monarch butterfly larvae. Despite the fact that even the research team cautioned against over-interpreting the study, anti-biotech activists quickly and effectively adopted the monarch as an icon in their communication efforts. Children dressed as colorful and vulnerable monarchs have appeared at street demonstrations and media events across the nation, with predictable impact when they fall to the ground, poisoned by a menacing ear of Bt corn. The "Bambi" of the insect world is being persuasively portrayed as an innocent creature potentially threatened by technology run amok. Just as Edison's electric chair provided a graphic demonstration of an invisible technology, the monarch provides a visual anchor for the compaign against food biotechnology, which is equally invisible. [17]

Edison knew that consumers would immediately resist a technology they considered unsafe. By tapping into human emotion—the safety of family, loved ones and property—he successfully derailed Tesla's AC technology for several years. [18]

Anti-biotech activists are making a similar emotional appeal by focusing on human health and environmental issues. Are scientists playing God? Do we risk environmental catastrophe? Are we ushering in a dangerous Brave New World? These questions are posed by activists in the food biotech debate, and are consistently accompanied by graphic visual images designed to raise suspicion and cause fear. [19]

ANTI-BIOTECHERS ARE GAINING

An integrated communications campaign combining media relations and well-placed advertising has put antifood biotech messages squarely before a national public. So far, they have hit their mark and have begun to shape public perception. National surveys indicate that consumers are less confident about the safety of genetically enhanced foods and about the impact of food biotechnology on the environment than they were early in 1999. Manufacturers, food processors and even some farmers have responded. [20]

Global food brands such as Heinz, Gerber and FritoLay have dropped biotech ingredients from some of their product offerings. [21]

Farmers are being pressured by activist groups to revert to nonbiotech seed. [22]

The federal government and other policy-making bodies have responded to public outcry as well. Attendance at last year's Food and Drug Administration public hearings on the subject wildly surpassed organizers' expectations. Several bills have been proposed at the state-and-federal levels, calling for special labeling of biotech foods. [23]

Life sciences companies, for the most part, have missed the opportunity to counter the growing doubts. In response to the emotional appeals of anti-biotech groups, the technology companies have responded with largely technical answers. Substantial time and resources have been spent trying to explain the safety, methodologies and review processes that go into developing and marketing biotech crops. But most of this effort is wasted on an audience that is not technically minded enough to care about or understand scientific arguments. [24]

REVERSING THE DAMAGE

25   Proponents of food biotechnology can benefit from Edison's approach, just as the opposition has. Strong, science-based facts are certainly important, but direct benefit statements and powerful emotional appeals are required for a pro-biotech campaign to be effective.

26   Anti-biotech images of Bt-stricken monarch butterflies and a human ear growing on a mouse's back have already touched consumers on an emotional level. Food biotech advocates must identify and incorporate equally compelling, emotional messages and images that communicate the human and environmental benefits of biotechnology. This is all the more important because the technology providers are in a defensive position. Public perceptions relative to food biotechnology are well on their way to being formed, and reversing opinion is always more difficult than shaping it in the first place.

27   In assessing the anti-food biotech campaign, Edison versus Tesla is an ideal case study, not only for its communication lessons, but also for what may be learned from its outcome. Although Edison's campaign was effective in the short-term, Tesla's AC technology ultimately triumphed and is the electrical standard today.

28   The success, to date, of the anti-biotech campaign can be similarly reversed, but only if advocates of food biotechnology fully (and immediately) participate in the debate. Only a united front that encompasses scientists, agricultural producers, food manufacturers, bio-ethicists, government regulators, industry experts and consumers can shape and direct the dialogue on the promising, but maligned, arena of food biotechnology.

Science Good, Nature Bad:
The Biotech Dogma
Kristina Canizares

This article, exposing the limitations of the science-versus-nature thinking that dominates the public controversy over biotech foods, was posted on the Alternet.org Web site on June 26, 2001. Alternet.org is connected to the Independent Media Institute, a nonprofit organization devoted to "strengthening and supporting independent and alternative journalism" (from its "About Us" statement).

1   Caesar had his soothsayer, King Tut had his high priest, and Napoleon had the Pope. But now we are enlightened. Now we have Science.

2   In this modern era, the role of trusted advisor has fallen to scientists. Science has finally triumphed over Nature through meticulous research, objectivity and ethics. If something has been "scientifically proven," it is gospel—irrefutable in a court of law—and if it can't be proven then it is little more than witchcraft and rumor.

3   We feel safe in the hands of experts, but our faith in Science can actually obfuscate the facts necessary to make informed policy decisions. Nowhere is this more readily apparent than in the current debate over biotechnology.

This week in San Diego, Science is facing off against Nature across a formidable barricade of concrete, barbed wire, and police in riot gear. Representing Science is the Biotechnology Industry Organization (BIO), host of BIO 2001—a convention of the biotech industry's best and brightest. In the ring for Nature is the multiorganizational crew of Biodevastation 2001, a gathering of biotechnology opponents showcasing heavy-hitters like international activist Vandana Shiva and populist writer Jim Hightower. 4

This event is only the most recent in a long series of confrontations between those who purport that biotechnology and genomics are humanity's path to salvation, and those who believe that these new technologies are dangerous, unnecessary and will actually serve to increase human misery and environmental destruction. It is a very complicated debate, one mired in economic justice, food safety, ecology and genetics, issues of which politicians, the media, the general public and even some of the debaters themselves may have a fleeting grasp at best. Therefore, the whole stew has been boiled down to a simple standoff between logical, provable Science and the emotional, spiritual Nature. 5

Hugh Gusterson, an anthropologist at MIT who studies scientists, looks at the way the scientific community is polarized by biotech's Science vs. Nature divide. The pro-biotech movement accuses opponents of being against Science, while anti-biotech activists charge the industry of violating the laws of Nature, or playing God. The implications belie the truth: that both sides have their share of scientists as well as environmentalists and humanitarians. Respected scientists have spoken out about the dangers of genetically modified organisms (GMOs) while some environmentalists have lauded the new crops as a way to reduce pesticide use and malnutrition among the poor. 6

Gusterson says that, ultimately, the concepts of Science and Nature are destroyed and the real issues—genetically modified plants and animals, cloning, stem cell research—are lost in a sea of rhetoric. Our inability to move beyond this false dichotomy ensures that we will remain incapable of making informed and intelligent decisions regarding the proper dispatch of these new technologies. 7

This puts the biotechnology choir at a distinct advantage. The biotech business, with its $25 million public relations budget, has claimed sole dominion over Science. In fighting a modern day Crusade, that's equivalent to having God on your side. After all, since Science is the new Gospel, those who oppose it are members of the anachronistic, backwards Nature cult—Luddites and Gaia-worshippers. 8

Carl B. Feldenbaum, BIO president, exalted in the industry's scientific achievements, comparing the work of geneticists to the Koran, the Torah or the Gospels. He repeatedly implied that protestors are a handful of religious zealots—"Jehovah's Witnesses" and "devout Buddhists"—who protest out of a "fear of the unknown" and a "primal" relationship with their food and their bodies. 9

Biotech's ability to propagate the Science vs. Nature divide has made them extremely powerful. Says Gusterson, "Science is so powerful because we believe that scientists stand for the truth, and there can only be one truth. We think that good scientists must agree." 10

But scientists rarely agree, especially in regards to a newly discovered phenomenon or technology. Trevor Pinch of Cornell's Science and Technology Department 11 has written about what he calls Experimenter's Regress. This is the tendency of scientists conducting experiments in a relatively new realm to get radically different results, even with repetition. This occurs because scientific experiments do not replicate the natural world, and are affected by the experimenter's biases. The Experimenter's Regress is often resolved over time, with many different experiments by a range of scientists, as is happening with the global warming debate.

12   Of course, the scientific methodology has been designed to safeguard against bias as much as possible, but it requires diligence. "It is a big responsibility to be a scientist; you have to follow a lot of rules," says Dr. Sharon Long, a biologist at Stanford and a member of the National Academy of Sciences. She says that a scientist must constantly fight to achieve objectivity in their experiments. "You have to bend over backward not to fool yourself, and you are always the easiest one to fool."

13   Because of the difficulties involved in maintaining a clean, objective experiment, scientists with contradictory findings tend to create a fervor of scrutiny. Dr. Long says that, rather than shy away from controversy, scientists work their whole lives to be in the spotlight with some new and groundbreaking discovery. "People who are afraid of making a splash don't go into science," says Long.

14   Yet there are very few dissenting voices speaking out against biotechnology. In policy and in media, the scientific community continues to appear as a united front, with respected papers such as the *New York Times* and the *Boston Globe* printing that GMOs have been scientifically proven to be safe. The public is lulled into a false security, buying the idea that all responsible scientists are in agreement and the only objections come from a bunch of nuts on the streets dressed as tomatoes and ears of corn. Where are those scientists, involved in responsible research, who disagree?

15   Certainly, part of the problem is financial. Dr. Long, who has worked in genomics, admits that this field is highly susceptible to monetary influences because of the massive overhead in equipment and materials. "Genomics has a very high threshold," says Long, "Unless you have a large amount of money you can do nothing."

16   Gusterson concurrs: "For any scientist who wants a good job and a nice home with mortgage payments, he's not going to choose the Union of Concerned Scientists."

17   The biotechnology companies offer highly competitive salaries and state-of-the-art equipment, tempting to a promising geneticist. Once the scientist joins the company, Gusterson says, "Corporations like Monsanto have ways of quashing desent," be it dismissal or lack of promotion. Financial concerns create a serious conflict of interest for many scientists who may find potential problems with genetic technologies.

18   However, there are a number of researchers with independent funding who have explored the darker side of genetic engineering. Reputable journals have published studies on the potential for genetic contamination, allergic reactions, and ecological disruption, and the National Academy of Sciences and the Union of Concerned Scientists have both been exploring these possibilities. But because the biotech industry has managed to monopolize Science, these scientists have not received the same attention and respect as their pro-biotech counterparts. Instead, many have experienced a significant backlash.

Gusterson has found that such backlashes are common throughout the scientific world; scientists who speak out against the common wisdom are often subjected to scrutiny. "If you dare to criticize the status quo you really have to know your stuff, but if you are in favor of the status quo you can do really shoddy work."   19

Dissenting scientists are attacked by the biotech industry and by other scientists who have bought into the new technology. The most dramatic and well-publicized example occurred at the Rowett Research Institute in Scotland in 1998, where a respected scientist, Dr. Arpad Pusztai, found that a diet of GM potatoes damaged the intestinal tract of rats. Dr. Pusztai lost his position at the Institute and was widely attacked and discredited, despite the fact that a notable British journal, the *Lancet,* published his study. Dr. Pusztai was subjected to a wide range of accusations, many of them completely groundless, and he is still struggling to regain his standing in the scientific community.   20

One year later, in Germany, Dr. Hans-Hinrich Kaatz found evidence that a gene inserted into oilseed rape crops had jumped species into the bacteria that live in the intestines of honey bees. The implications of the study are that new breeds of virulent bacteria could result from exposure to GMO crops, yet Dr. Kaatz has remained very reserved about his findings. In a May 2000 interview with *The Guardian,* Dr. Kaatz admitted that he did not want to speak too much about his research because of Dr. Pusztai's experiences.   21

Even more moderate researchers like John Losey, an entomologist at Cornell, have experienced pressure because of their research. Losey conducted experiements in 1998 and 1999 which found that pollen from genetically modified corn may harm monarch butterflies. Losey is not anti-GMO, believing that, for some GM crops, the benefits may outweigh the risks. He admitted that his study was only the first step and did not conclusively prove that the results would reoccur in the field. Yet Losey also experienced a backlash.   22

"There were some people who had a knee-jerk reaction—don't rock the boat— they didn't want anything that would point to even a potential problem," said Losey. Fortunately, Losey is not easily discouraged and has continued his work, but he can imagine that some scientists would veer away from such controversial research.   23

Gusterson claims that scientists are warned, directly or indirectly, not to step outside of the biotech doctrine. Those that have crossed the line pay a price—they are excommunicated from the church of Science, accused of sloppy research and thrown into the rabble with all of the other Nature heathens.   24

Obviously there is a pressing need for more independently funded, peer-reviewed studies, but it is everybody's responsibility to ensure that these studies are received without a reactionary hysteria. "All scientific research deserves scrutiny," says Long, "but it deserves to be attacked based on whether or not it followed the rules, not on whether or not it is convenient to one's viewpoint."   25

Just as we wisely separated church and state, so must we ensure that Science, for all its wonders, does not become dogma.   26

"We won't make progress until we stop expecting scientists to agree on everything," says Gusterson. "That enables scientists to abuse the trust we naively give to science. All of us have to be more sophisticated: scientists and non-scientists, activists and non-activists."   27

Lessen the Fear of Genetically Engineered Crops

Gregory A. Jaffe

This middle-ground policy argument appeared in the Christian Science Monitor *on August 8, 2001. Gregory A. Jaffe is codirector for the Project on Biotechnology for the Center for Science in the Public Interest.*

1   Protesters carrying signs stating "Biocide is Homicide" and shouting concerns about the risks of eating genetically engineered foods recently demonstrated outside the biotechnology industry's annual convention. Inside the convention center, the industry extolled the safety of genetically engineered foods and the benefits of future crops like "golden rice."

2   Neither corporate hyperbole nor radical slogans do much to inform the public. What is needed is the shaping of sensible measures to ensure that genetically engineered foods are safe. The first few engineered crops are already providing remarkable benefits. Cotton modified to kill insects has greatly diminished farmers' use of toxic insecticides, thereby reducing costs, increasing yields, and, presumably, reducing harm to nontarget species. Likewise, biotech soybeans facilitate no-till farming, which reduces soil erosion and water pollution.

3   Despite such benefits, agricultural biotechnology is under siege for reasons good and bad. Activists have burned fields and bombed labs. Farmers will not plant genetically engineered sweet corn, sugar beets, and apples, for fear of consumer rejection. And countries in Europe and Asia refuse to import US-grown genetically engineered crops. Some countries now require labeling of foods containing engineered ingredients. Those requirements have spurred food processors, who want to avoid negative-sounding labels, to eliminate bioengineered ingredients.

4   Buffeted by the polarized debate, many Americans oppose biotech foods, in part because farmers and seed companies get the benefits while consumers bear the risk. If anti-genetically engineered sentiment increases, US farmers may be forced to forgo the advantages of engineered crops. And most public and private investment in agricultural biotechnology would dry up.

5   To reap the benefits of agricultural biotechnology, minimize the risks, and boost public confidence, the US must upgrade its flawed regulatory system. Currently, the Food and Drug Administration (FDA) does not formally approve any genetically engineered crops as safe to eat. Instead, it reviews safety data provided voluntarily by seed companies. That consultation process, which the FDA admits is "not a comprehensive scientific review of the data," culminates with the FDA stating only that it has "no further questions . . . at this time." Although no health problems with genetically engineered crops have been detected, that industry-driven process is weak insurance. The recent FDA proposal requiring a formal notification before marketing a biotech food is an improvement.

All biotech foods should go through a mandatory approval process with specific 6 testing and data requirements. The National Academy of Sciences should be commissioned to recommend a precise method of assessment.

Genetically engineered crops also raise environmental concerns. They could 7 lead to pesticide-resistant insects and weeds and might contaminate plants that are close relatives of the crops. To safeguard our ecosystem, the current laws need fixing. Congress should close regulatory gaps to ensure that all future applications of biotechnology, ranging from fast-growing fish to corn plants that produce industrial chemicals, receive thorough environmental reviews. Also, the Environmental Protection Agency must enforce restrictions it has imposed on bioengineered crops to help prevent emergence of insecticide-resistant pests.

Although strong regulations would minimize environmental and safety risks, 8 nothing would boost public confidence more than engineered products that benefit consumers. No beneficial products currently exist.

Worldwide acceptance of biotechnology will only occur when other countries 9 reap benefits from this technology. Instead of spending millions of dollars on feel-good advertising campaigns, the biotech industry should train developing-country scientists and fund research in those countries. Companies—and universities—should donate patented crops and processes to developing countries. Agricultural biotechnology is not a panacea for all agricultural problems here or abroad, nor is it free from risk. But, with adequate safeguards, it could provide tremendous benefits for an ever-populous, pesticide-drenched, and water-deficient globe.

Food Industry Should Modify Its Stance on Altered Food
Froma Harrop

This op-ed piece by nationally syndicated columnist Froma Harrop appeared in newspapers across the United States in November 2002. The immediate context for Harrop's argument was an Oregon referendum—defeated by voters at the polls—to require labeling of genetically modified foods. The presence of the referendum on the Oregon ballot stimulated a corporate advertising blitz by the major growers of genetically modified foods, who outspent their opponents 25 to 1.

My primitive response to genetically modified foods is to ask, "What's wrong 1 with the grub of the last 250,000 years?" Mucking around with genetic material to create new kinds of fruits, vegetables and animals seems somehow unnecessary. Cows have produced pretty good milk over the millennia using their cow genes. So why insert rat genes into a perfectly acceptable cow?

Call me old-fashioned, but given a choice between a traditional tomato and a 2 tomato carrying fish DNA, I will select the former.

3   Are these genetically modified organisms (GMOs) safe to eat? I don't know. But regardless of the science, I remain an anchor in the stream of progress. I do not want GMOs on my plate for moral, ethical, emotional, religious, aesthetic, sentimental and other reasons I haven't thought of yet.

4   Monsanto, I'm obviously not your customer. But I'd like to make a deal with you and the other food/biotech companies pushing all this gene splicing. Let me decide whether or not to buy genetically engineered foods at the store. Don't force me onto a farm in the woods where I must sit guard over my organic vegetable patch with a shotgun and a crazed look on my face. In other words, stop fighting proposals to label foods for GMO content.

5   The biotech-food-industrial complex opposes such labeling for sound business reasons: The world is full of people like me. Polls consistently show Americans objecting to genetically manipulated food by solid majorities. Some 93 percent of the respondents to a poll conducted for ABCNEWS.com wanted mandatory labeling of bio-engineered products.

6   That's why the complex pounced on a potentially path-clearing referendum in Oregon that would have required labels. Monsanto joined Kraft, Unilever and other opponents to outspend supporters 25-to-1. The proposal was soundly defeated following ludicrous claims that a labeling law would cost the average Oregon family $550 a year. (Similar laws in Europe, Japan and Australia have not noticeably raised the price of food.)

7   Actually, the U.S. trade representative will soon decide whether to drag Europe before the World Trade Organization over its restrictions on importing genetically modified corn and soybeans. Right now, 34 percent of corn and 75 percent of soybeans in America are grown from genetically manipulated seed.

8   With Europeans already inflamed by U.S. environmental policies, this seems a swell time for the Bush administration to bully them over their food supply, Europe's No. 1 cultural issue. Prince Charles is going around the kingdom condemning genetically engineered food as something that "takes mankind into realms that belong to God and God alone."

9   The Bush administration and Monsanto like each other a great deal, which is why we can't trust our government to give us the straight story on GMOs. Of course, they will never conquer dine-o-saurs like me. But if they want to win over folks concerned only about how GMOs might affect health and the environment, they're going about it the wrong way.

10   A U.S. Food and Drug Administration confident about the safety of these products would not have weighed in so loudly against the Oregon labeling proposal. And what possessed the administration to name Monsanto's former Washington lobbyist for GMOs as second in command at the Environmental Protection Agency?

11   Over at the National Academy of Sciences, a panel sung the praises of federal efforts to regulate genetically engineered foods. It turned out that six of the 12 panel members had ties to the biotech industry.

12   The complex showers the public with rather impressive claims for GMOs. GMO farmers can up food production for a hungry world. GMO crops reduce pesticide use. GMO cows (the ones with rat genes) produce milk that's better for the heart. Hey, they may be right in some cases.

All this matters not to me. Others may forge ahead with new culinary traditions. 13
I won't chow down on GMOs and I will echo Prince Charles' call for "strong and sustained pressure from consumers to ensure that they keep the right not to eat them."

Our farmers produce beautiful and abundant food without putting moth genes 14
into catfish. Why mess with success?

What Is the FDA Trying to Feed Us?
Sustainusa.org

Using the "piranhaberry" as its main image, Sustainusa.org, a "non-profit organization that promotes a healthy, sustainable environment through innovative communication strategies" (from its Web page), launched a "Keep Nature Natural" campaign against Monsanto and other biotechnology companies. This striking image appeared on the campaign's fliers, posters, postcards, and magazine ads.

The Ethics of Eating
Rich Heffern

This article by opinion editor Rich Heffern appeared in the May 24, 2002, edition of the National Catholic Reporter, *a news commentary newspaper with a Catholic perspective.*

1   A walk through the local supermarket means navigating past the spectacle of the produce department. The Garden of Eden probably didn't look as good.

2   There all the radishes are lined up with their ends pointing out, the spinach leaves sparkle with fresh water droplets. Every variety from avocados to melons, rhubarb to zucchini gleams in the fluorescent light, free of blemish. Tall stacks of tomatoes and bins of crisp lettuce are available in the darkest days of winter. Kiwi fruits from southern latitudes near Antarctica show up in Muskogee, Okla., and Duluth, Minn. Just beyond the produce is the meat counter, stocked with every cut and variety of fish, fowl and beef. Prices are reasonable. Supermarkets are clean, well stocked and some of them are open 24 hours a day, 365 days a year.

3   This dazzling, mouth-watering scene in today's supermarkets is the result of practices, policies and habits that evolved over two or three generations. Food was once produced almost entirely on small family farms and brought into town and city one small truck at a time to packing houses and canneries, or markets and mom-and-pop stores in every neighborhood. The connections between farmer and consumer were fairly direct, with little processing between harvesting and eating.

4   Now it's different. There is much more variety in the offerings. It's more convenient, freeing us for quality time. Once common food deficiency diseases, like pellagra and rickets, are rare now. Many drudgery-filled jobs have been eliminated. We in North America probably eat better, with more variety, thrice-daily with snacks in between, than any people at any time in history.

5   Yet there are concerns. Our stomachs are full, but paradoxically we are still hungry—and a little scared.

6   The hunger is for the aesthetic value of real food, the satisfaction of eating together, the assurance that what we're putting into our mouths is both life-sustaining and safe. Our fears are about the hidden costs of "cheap" food, one of which is a widespread and continuing loss of small family farms in the United States.

7   This ongoing crisis for family farms, wrote Bishop Raymond Burke of LaCrosse, Wis., "is quickly leading to the last days of a system of farming that has contributed greatly to the building of our nation's cultural, economic, social and enviornmental fabric. The loss of these farms would be a tremendous loss for us as a nation and a people."

8   And we yearn for those missing spiritual connections our table once provided us almost automatically, as we prayed together over our plates, then

talked over the day ahead or behind as our stomachs filled. The Catholic bishops of the United States have probably written as much about our food system in their pastoral letters as they have any other subject. "Food, its production and consumption are at the very heart of the Catholic faith," said Holy Cross Br. Dave Andrews, executive director of the National Catholic Rural Life Conference. "And spirituality will play a central role in digging us out of the mess we've made of our food system."

Ben Kjelshus, national food activist and cofounder of the Midwest-based Food   9 Circles Networking Project, told *NCR*, "Since we all depend on food to live, its production and delivery system lives at the very heart of our health, our economy and our local community. Today many feel that our food system is environmentally and socially destructive, unsustainable, inhumane and unjust.

"Conventional agriculture has become dependent on petrochemicals and a   10 reliance on processes," said Kjelshus, that are "destroying the environment in ways almost too numerous to count: soil erosion, poisonous runoff in our streams and groundwater, the creation of pesticide-resistant insects, and the list goes on and on."

The food system has become highly centralized as well, according to Kjelshus.   11 Every aspect of it is now dominated by a small handful of corporations that control both production and retailing, and keep prices paid for raw commodities low. "Small family farms, once a bedrock of both our culture and agriculture, have found it impossible to compete," he said. Rural communities that once experienced self-sufficiency have been either destroyed or drawn into a state of complete dependency.

"It's estimated," Kjelshus said, "that while only 9 cents of every food dollar   12 goes to farmers, 10 cents now goes to Philip Morris and 6 cents to ConAgra."

"Such a system has given consumers abundant food that is perceived as low-   13 cost," Mary Hendrickson, professor of rural sociology at the University of Missouri, Columbia, told *NCR*, "but it hasn't worked for everyone. This system has also contributed to the loss of smaller farms and the rural communities they supported, and to major problems with food safety and security."

Many in the United States and Europe are raising questions about how our food   14 is produced and by whom.

According to a Roper Starch Worldwide survey released last year, 40 percent of   15 Americans said organic meat and produce, food that is produced in a more earth-friendly and socially just way, will be a bigger part of their diet within one year, and 63 percent buy organic foods and beverages at least sometimes. That was a 10 percent jump from the year before.

Eight of every 10 adults understand that organic products must be grown with-   16 out the use of added hormones or synthetic pesticides or fertilizers, according to the study. The study also points out that even those who do not buy organic products regularly reject the idea that organic products are just a gimmick. That's a large and growing market.

"Buying organic though is not enough," added Kjelshus. "In order to preserve fam-   17 ily farms and insure real food safety and quality, a regional food system is absolutely necessary, too. Nothing can substitute for that close connection between consumers and growers. If you want your food to be free of poisons, antibiotics and alien genes, if you want it fresh and produced at the lowest possible ecological cost, then it must be local."

18   Food issues bring together the environmentalist, the farmer, the chef, the gourmet and the social worker—all of us really, since we all eat. Concerns about the food system seem to cluster around six areas, with considerable overlap.

ENVIRONMENTAL EFFECTS

19   Food in the United States travels an average of 1,300 miles from the farm to the market shelf. Almost every state in the United States buys 90 percent of its food from someplace else. It's estimated that 10 calories of fossil fuel energy are used to produce, process and deliver one calorie of food energy. Such a far-flung and energy-intensive system has a bad effect on the environment. The practices of industrial agriculture in this country include widespread use of pesticide, herbicide and chemical fertilizer and resulting ground water pollution, together with loss of topsoil caused by cultivating practices.

20   The huge amounts of chicken and pork used in fast food outlets like McDonald's and Kentucky Fried Chicken mainly come today from large factory farms. What are now called Confined Animal Feeding Operations (CAFOs) have become a national issue.

21   According to Br. Dave Andrews, a new hog plant will produce more animal waste than the animal and human waste created by the city of Los Angeles; 1,600 dairies in the Central Valley of California produce more waste than a city of 21 million people. "The annual production of 600 million chickens on the Delmarva Peninsula near Washington, D.C., generates as much nitrogen as a city of almost 500,000 people," he told *NCR*. "This waste too often is not dealt with properly, with dire results for local wildlife, for the land and water."

22   Industrial meat factories discharge the waste from millions of hogs along with toxic disinfectants, antibiotics, pesticides and other poisons untreated to the environment. Hog factory odors make life unbearable for residents of adjacent communities. Spills from vast feces lagoons have aggravated fish kills involving billions of fish and poisoned soil, rivers, aquifers and public waterways. By saving money through illegal disposal practices, hog factories have artificially lowered their costs of production, driving hundreds of thousands of American family farmers off their land, according to the Water-keeper Alliance, a watch-dog group recently founded by Robert F. Kennedy, Jr.

23   There is also increasing concern about the growing use of genetic engineering in agriculture and the products made from these techniques, the so-called "Frankenfoods." Alarm centers on the consequent loss of biodiversity in crops, disturbance of ecological balance, and the introduction of artificially induced characteristics and inevitable side effects that will be passed on to subsequent generations and to other related organisms.

FOOD QUALITY AND TASTE

That tomato on the supermarket shelf, critics say, tastes as bland and lifeless   24
as cardboard, a pale ghost, vaguely reminiscent of tomato essence. These tomatoes
are actually green varieties, picked early to survive the long plane trip, then exposed to ethylene gas, which turns them red.

A ripe, homegrown tomato, on the other hand, is tangible proof that God is   25
great and good. A chicken produced in a factory farm is tasteless and rubbery compared to one that is raised in a free-range environment and fed quality organic feed.

The way we produce our food, critics say, now is more akin to mining than to   26
farming. Alice Waters, owner of Chez Panisse restaurant in Berkeley, Calif., recently named as the "mother of modern American cooking," hints at a spiritual connection, putting it this way:

> Farming isn't manufacturing: It's a continuing relationship with nature that has to be com-
> plete on both sides to work. People claim to know that plants are living things, but the sys-
> tem of food production, distribution and consumption we have known for the last 40 years
> has attempted to deny that they are. If our food has lacked flavor—if, in aesthetic terms, it
> has been dead—that may be because it was treated as dead even while it was being grown.
> And perhaps we have tolerated such food—and the way its production has affected our soci-
> ety and environment—because our senses, our hearts and our minds have been in some
> sense deadened, too.

FOOD SAFETY

A recent government-sponsored poll showed that 88 percent of women and 79   27
percent of men in the United States are concerned about food safety. If it's not E-coli
in beef or salmonella in chicken, then it's contaminated raspberries from Guatemala.
The "mad cow disease" outbreaks in Europe make many consumers nervous.

The chemical spraying used in raising vegetables and chemical additives in-   28
volved in their processing are serious concerns as well. Residues soak into the
produce on the grocery shelf. Cancers and other serious ailments have been linked
to these contaminants.

Some 30 percent of the U.S. dairy herd is now fed genetically engineered bovine   29
growth hormones (BGH) to stimulate milk production. The U.S. Food and Drug
Administration admits that these injections increase sickness and resultant antibiotic use in dairy cows. Consumers Union, publisher of *Consumer Reports* magazine,
reports that "because of increased udder infections, it is more likely that milk from
treated cows will be of lower quality—containing more pus and bacteria—than
milk from untreated cows." Milk from BGH-injected cows is more likely to contain
dangerous residues of the more than 80 different drugs, many of them antibiotics,
used to treat sick cows.

Intensive confinement of animals in large numbers causes disease. As a result,   30
confined animals receive regular large doses of penicillin and other antibiotics. These

drugs enable large-scale livestock operations, but their wide use also promotes the development of reservoirs of antibiotic-resistant bacteria. The greater the opportunity these bacteria have for exposure to antibiotics, the greater the threat to humans and our ability to fight off such bacteria.

31   The Union of Concerned Scientists has pointed at the growing specter of antibiotic resistant disease due to the overuse and misuse of these drugs. Although this includes antibiotics in human medicine and consumer products, the union has raised questions about antimicrobial use in agriculture.

32   Another recent practice in the food industry is to bombard food with large amounts of radiation, the equivalent of 33 million to 233 million chest X-rays. The aim is to kill bacteria in the food and to lengthen shelf life. In the United States, irradiation is approved for beef, pork, poultry, shell eggs, fruits, vegetables, flour, seeds, herbs and spices. Companies that produce over 75 percent of the United States' 9 billion pounds per year of ground beef and approximately 50 percent of the nearly 35 billion pounds per year of poultry have signed agreements to use irradiation technology, according to Public Citizen. "Rather than cleaning up the filthy conditions at corporate farms and industrial slaughterhouses," the group states, "the meat industry and its allies in government would rather rely on food irradiation to prevent food-borne illness."

33   The only way to know how much of their products are irradiated now is to query the company. Most irradiated meat is going to restaurants and other service outlets and is not labeled to the consumer. Long-term health effects of consuming irradiated food are unknown; irradiation reduces the antioxidant vitamins in vegetables.

SOCIAL JUSTICE

34   The foreign-grown and winter tomatoes and fruit raised in California and Arizona often come from producers whose laborers receive few benefits and work daily in an environment saturated with harmful pesticides, fungicides and other chemicals.

35   We love our chicken and turkey dinners. The poultry production and processing industry has grown exponentially in the last 10 years. Tyson Foods, the largest poultry company, produced more than 7.2 billion pounds of chicken in 1999, utilizing 66 processing plants and 7,402 contract poultry growers in the Midwest and South.

36   In November of 2000, 41 Catholic bishops in the South issued a pastoral letter on these factories, the so-called "Poultry Pastoral." In the letter they documented the frenetic pace of chicken processing—90 carcasses a minute whiz past a worker's station. With one bathroom break per shift and a short lunch they must keep up without complaining or get fired. Short-term they face careless knife accidents. Long-term it is repetitive motion disabilities. The average $6 an hour wage forces them to take a second job to maintain their families. Meanwhile, in local supermarkets, chicken quarters frequently sell for only 59 cents a pound.

37   Work in these processing plants has been called the most dangerous job in America.

Two years ago, Tyson, the largest poultry producer, violated child labor laws by allowing a 15-year-old immigrant to work illegally at one of its plants. The minor died, and a 14-year-old was seriously injured, according to Raul Yzaguirre, president of the National Council of La Raza, the nation's largest Hispanic civil-rights organization. Government officials fined Tyson. **38**

Last March 90 Florida farm workers and their supporters began a 15-city cross-country tour to call for the end of sweatshop labor in the fields. The group hopes this tour will educate the country about the wretched poverty and dangerous working conditions farm workers endure while a multi-billion dollar fast-food industry profits. Romeo Ramirez, a Florida tomato picker, said in an interview: "We as farm workers are tired of subsidizing Taco Bell's profits with our poverty." He points out that his local union, the Coalition of Immokalee Workers, discovered that Taco Bell was the primary purchaser of the tomatoes picked by workers in southwest Florida. The predominantly Mexican, Haitian and Guatemalan workers earn about $6,600 a year, with no overtime pay, health insurance, vacation, sick pay or pension. They are exposed to pesticides and long hours in the hot sun. The union's response was to launch the "Boycott the Bell" campaign. Students at Duke University and Notre Dame have successfully prevented the establishment of Taco Bell outlets on campus. **39**

CRUELTY TO ANIMALS

Not long ago, an element of the view on a drive in the country past small farms was a few pigs rooting in the leaf litter behind the barns for fallen acorns. In the last 10 years over half of the family farms raising pigs have been put out of business. Enabled by drugs, which allow animals to be confined in large numbers, and encouraged by federal tax breaks favoring big-scale farming, industrial pig factory farms now dominate the pork industry. **40**

Pigs are intelligent, sensitive and clean animals. But those unfortunate enough to be born on a large factory farm face a life of confinement and cruelty, according to the Humane Farming Association. After impregnation, a factory farm sow is locked in a narrow metal gestation crate, 24 inches wide and long enough so that she can move forward and backward only a few inches. By conveyer belt, she is fed at one end of the crate and her feces collected at the other. **41**

Deprived of all exercise and opportunity to meet her behavioral needs, she lives in a constant state of distress. A sow locked in a factory farm crate often is found frantically and repeatedly biting the metal bars. "Hundreds of thousands of sows are held captive in these desolate pig prisons," said the Humane Farming Association. **42**

After giving birth, the piglets are prematurely (at three weeks) separated from the mother, who is again impregnated and sent back to the gestation crate. This cycle is repeated over and over until the sow's "productivity" wanes, and she is sent to slaughter. **43**

Such practices are slowly being extended to poultry and beef production. While pork production uses isolation of the animals into cages, poultry production involves intensive crowding together to the extent that stress-induced cannibalism occurs. **44**

45   If a private citizen confined a dog or cat in conditions such as those that prevail at factory farms, that person would be pilloried in the local paper and hauled into court.

FOOD MONOPOLIES

46   Food processors and suppliers have become ever more concentrated in recent years. Four firms control over 80 percent of fed cattle processing and almost 60 percent of hog processing. In grain trade, large firms like Cargill, Archer Daniels Midland, the self-styled "supermarket to the world," and ConAgra dominate. In supermarkets, Kroger, Albertson's, Safeway, Winn-Dixie and Wal-Mart control most stores.

47   Big tobacco companies, flush with cash from cigarette sales and battered by anti-smoking sentiment, have been buying up smaller food processing concerns. R.J. Reynolds owns Nabisco. Phillip Morris recently bought up General Foods and Kraft. Phillip Morris is now the world's largest consumer products company.

48   Not only have agribusiness firms become concentrated monopolies, but many industries have experienced rapid vertical integration (where a firm controls its own suppliers and processors). Smithfield Foods, the largest pork packer in the United States, bought the largest hog producer, Murphy Family Farms, in 2000. Smithfield now owns nearly 700,000 sows. Such concentrations raise concerns about uncompetitive and unfair trade practice. Small farmers possess much less bargaining power in such a system.

49   A *Time* magazine article, part of a 1998 series on corporate welfare that won its authors, journalists Donald L. Bartlett and James B. Steele, a Pulitzer Prize, identified Seaboard Corporation, a huge international meat production/processing company based outside Kansas City, Mo., as the 1998 poster child for corporate welfare. Their feature, "The empire of pigs," was subtitled "A little-known company is a master at milking governments for welfare." The article details how Seaboard "plays the welfare game, maximizing the benefits to itself, often to the detriment of those who provide them." The authors point out early on that the Seaboard story is a "vivid reminder to cities and towns everywhere about the potential long-term liabilities they may one day face" by using public funds to support big agribusiness plants. "Wherever Seaboard is," they write, "there is a government throwing money at it."

50   The big food producers have moved to discourage such criticism. International trade bureaucrats in cooperation with transnational corporations attempted last year to get rid of what they call "ecolabeling," which allows product manufacturers to identify their products as beneficial or less harmful to health and the environment. Their effort was beaten back by environmental groups.

51   Fourteen states now carry so-called food disparagement laws, which make it possible for food producers to sue anyone spreading false and damaging information about such supermarket perennials as hamburger and cantaloupe. The laws grew out of the disputed Alar chemical scare around apples in the late 1980s. The laws' supporters claim the laws are needed to protect against baseless, wrong or unjustified claims about food dangers that threaten the livelihood of ranchers and farmers. Critics say these laws are dangerous steps beyond existing libel protections. In 1999, a group of Texas ranchers sued Oprah Winfrey and one of the guests

on her TV show, after a discussion about beef products in connection with the "mad cow disease" scare. Winfrey, after learning about the dangers associated with this disease, stated she would never eat a burger again. The grounds cited in the class action suit were "lambasting the American cattle industry" and placing "unfounded and unwarranted fear in the beef consumer's mind." Winfrey won the suit after spending nearly 1 million dollars in legal fees. A chill descended over the food debate that persists even now.

On the other end of the debate, a massive, unprecedented consumer backlash in 52 1998 over the U.S. Department of Agriculture's first proposed regulations on standards for the organic food industry shook up that agency, forcing it to back off on plans to degrade organic standards and allow biotech and corporate agribusiness to take over the rapidly growing organic food market. U.S. organic food sales this year will likely reach $12 billion—a sizable bite of the $350 billion total annual sales of the nation's supermarkets. At current growth rates, organic production will constitute 10 percent of American agriculture by the year 2010.

VOTE WITH YOUR FORK

In this ongoing, heated debate, supporters of the present food system lash back 53 at critics with accusations of food snobbery. We are feeding the world, they say, and creating jobs. Organic is a fad and, what's more, a luxury not available to the poor.

"When farmers are permitted to plant and raise whatever they wish whenever 54 they wish, for the market, not for government, then our food supply is secure and prices low," wrote Stephen Moore of the Cato Institute.

The Catholic church has weighed in on the debate. Catholic bishops around the 55 world and in the United States have issued pastoral letters and statements on various aspects of food issues. Last year the Catholic bishops' conference of South Africa called for a nationwide five-year freeze on genetic engineering and patenting in crop and food production. In 1999 the bishops of Minesota issued a statement pointing out moral and ethical implications of the rural crisis in their area.

The so-called "Poultry Pastoral" written by the bishops of the South called for in- 56 creased awareness of the dangers workers face in poultry processing plants. The bishops wrote, "Somebody's paying the price, not only for bigness but for cheap food."

A statement by the bishops of North Dakota on the crisis in rural life invoked 57 Catholic social teaching and called for a more just and environmentally conscious agricultural system. In 2001 the bishops of the Columbia River region of the Pacific Northwest issued a pastoral letter on the ethics, economics and ecology of the region. Kansas bishops last year went as a body to the state capital in Topeka to lobby on behalf of small farmers in their state.

In 1999, Cardinal Roger Mahony of Los Angeles, chairperson of the Domestic 58 Policy Committee of the U.S. Conference of Catholic Bishops, with Bishop Raymond Burke of La Crosse, Wis., wrote Sen. Richard Lugar, chair of the Senate Agriculture Committee, to express concern about the plight of U.S. farm families. They asked Lugar to hold hearings on the state of the family farm, addressing the long-term sustainability of the food system.

59   Br. Dave Andrews points out that the bishops of Appalachia first wrote a farm pastoral letter in 1975. "It changed the way the American church did pastoral summits," he told *NCR.* "Those bishops listened to people, consulted social scientists and ag specialists, did the social analysis, then wrote. Soon after that came both the Peace and the Economic Pastoral letters. To me, it was a sign of a newly emerging consciousness about these matters. And it started first on the farm, with food issues."

60   No one realistically expects us to go back to the old ways completely, digging up our backyards and planting corn and potatoes. "Yet better choices can be made," said Andrews. "Vote with your fork! What kind of people do we want to become? Your fork is a lever with which you can change the world. Making choices about food can get us there. Our current campaign is titled 'Eating is a moral act.' "

61   Eating, of course, is not just a moral act, it's a spiritual act, according to Andrews. "Our Catholic liturgy is centered on food images: fruit of the vine, work of human hands, living water that will nourish us forever. Even heaven is presented as a banquet. Food is at the center and heart of Christianity. If we lose touch with good food and become a nation of grazers and fast food gulpers, we lose much of that vital religious sense.

62   "We bought the system one bite at a time," said Andrews, "and we can sure change it back one bite at a time." Andrews and others are urging us to consider that the real bottleneck in changing the way we produce and consume food is the spiritual dilemma.

63   "If we no longer believe that the Earth is sacred," writes Gary Paul Nabhan, "or that we are blessed by the bounty around us or that we have a caretaking responsibility given to us by the Creator . . . then it does not really matter to most folks how much ecological and cultural damage is done by the way we eat."

For Class Discussion

1. The readings in this unit reveal a complex network of issues related to the genetic engineering of food and organic food. These issues can be grouped under headings such as "business and profit issues," "consumer safety and health issues," "environmental issues," "international relations issues," "ethical issues," and many others. Working in small groups or as a whole class, identify ten or more specific issue questions connected to the genetic engineering of food and organic food. For example, a specific issue question related to the environment might be "Do genetically modified soybeans really reduce the amount of pesticides or herbicides used in production of a crop?" What other issue questions arise in the readings in this unit?

2. Some of the disagreement about biotech food and organic food involves the concept of "natural." When is a food natural as opposed to unnatural or artificial? Do the terms "natural" and "unnatural" have a scientific

meaning or a cultural meaning? In written or visual arguments, how do antibiotech advocates portray biotech food as "unnatural"? How have supporters of biotech foods attempted to answer the accusations of using unnatural means?

3. A number of the arguments in this unit offer suggestions for regulating and managing the potential of genetically engineered food. Which proposals for legal and economic responses seem the most reasonable and promising to you and why? If you were to synthesize ideas from several sources to create your own position, what would your position be?

4. Choose one of the arguments for closer analysis, applying the second set of guide questions on pages 460–461.

OPTIONAL WRITING ASSIGNMENT   Many of the advocacy Web sites on all sides of the genetic engineering of food controversy elicit consumer feedback, suggesting that we tell our lawmakers and also our local supermarkets what we think about the labeling and selling of genetically engineered foods. Write a letter to (a) one of your state representatives in Congress or (b) the CEO of the supermarket where you or your family regularly buy groceries, urging him or her to adopt your position on biotech or organic foods. If you are writing to your legislator, you might argue for more rigorous, systematic, and extensive testing of genetically modified products, for a moratorium on the sale of genetically modified foods, or for government support of genetic engineering of foods. If you are writing to the CEO of your favorite supermarket chain, you might argue that the supermarket change its buying practices, provide more consumer information about sources of food, or lobby for or against the labeling of genetically modified ingredients in food products.

RESPONSES TO TERRORISM: PUBLIC SAFETY, CIVIL LIBERTIES, AND WAR

After September 11, 2001, the United States faced a military enemy without a country, without a clear political agenda, and without the goal of winning land that typically characterizes wars between competing armies. Within weeks after the September 11 tragedy, President Bush and his cabinet of advisers began formulating plans for combating terrorism. These plans included the initial overthrow of the Taliban government in Afghanistan and the passing of the USA PATRIOT (an acronym for "Uniting and Strengthening America by Providing Appropriate Tools Required to Intercept and Obstruct Terrorism") Act, which gave broad new policing powers to the federal government for gathering evidence on suspected terrorists and for making arrests. As the war on terrorism unfolded, a national conversation on terrorism took place on the Internet, in the newspapers and talk shows, in Congress, and in the courts. The same conversations took place worldwide as nations tried to decide the extent to which they aligned themselves with U.S. tactics and goals. Among the questions debated were these: How effective is the U.S. plan for fighting terrorism? To what extent has the war on terrorism made the United States a violator of human rights? Is racial profiling justified in the war against terrorism? To what extent are the American people willing to alter their normal behaviors to increase their safety and security?

We begin this unit with controversies over the USA PATRIOT Act including the arrest of "suspected terrorists" within the United States and the treatment of "enemy combatants" in Guantánamo Bay. We next look at disputes about racial profiling. We conclude with a series of arguments about particular strategies and tactics the United States should take in fighting terrorism. The readings in this unit connect also to our examination of "The United States as Superpower" later in this anthology (pp. 725–757), where the readings focus on U.S. foreign policy in a world where American military might makes the United States the world's sole superpower.

Testimony to the Senate Committee on the Judiciary

John Ashcroft

In this speech before the Senate Judiciary Committee, delivered on December 6, 2001, Attorney General John Ashcroft outlines the Bush administration's initial response to terrorism following September 11, 2001. Here he praises and justifies the procedures legalized by the USA PATRIOT Act.

Mr. Chairman, Senator Hatch, members of the Judiciary Committee, thank you [1] for this opportunity to testify today. It is a pleasure to be back in the United States Senate.

On the morning of September 11, as the United States came under attack, I was [2] in an airplane with several members of the Justice Department en route to Milwaukee, in the skies over the Great Lakes. By the time we could return to Washington, thousands of people had been murdered at the World Trade Center. One hundred eighty-nine were dead at the Pentagon. Forty-four had crashed to the ground in Pennsylvania. From that moment, at the command of the President of the United States, I began to mobilize the resources of the Department of Justice toward one single, overarching and overriding objective: to save innocent lives from further acts of terrorism.

America's campaign to save innocent lives from terrorists is now 87 days old. It [3] has brought me back to this committee to report to you in accordance with Congress's oversight role. I welcome this opportunity to clarify for you and the American people how the Justice Department is working to protect American lives while preserving American liberties.

Since those first terrible hours of September 11, America has faced a choice [4] that is as stark as the images that linger of that morning. One option is to call September 11 a fluke, to believe it could never happen again, and to live in a dream world that requires us to do nothing differently. The other option is to fight back, to summon all our strength and all our resources and devote ourselves to better ways to identify, disrupt and dismantle terrorist networks.

Under the leadership of President Bush, America has made the choice to fight [5] terrorism—not just for ourselves but for all civilized people. Since September 11, through dozens of warnings to law enforcement, a deliberate campaign of terrorist disruption, tighter security around potential targets, and a preventative campaign of arrest and detention of lawbreakers, America has grown stronger—and safer— in the face of terrorism.

Thanks to the vigilance of law enforcement and the patience of the American [6] people, we have not suffered another major terrorist attack. Still, we cannot—we must not—allow ourselves to grow complacent. The reasons are apparent to me each morning. My day begins with a review of the threats to Americans and American interests that were received in the previous 24 hours. If ever there were proof of the existence of evil in the world, it is in the pages of these reports. They are a chilling daily chronicle of hatred of America by fanatics who seek to extinguish freedom, enslave women, corrupt education and to kill Americans wherever and whenever they can.

The terrorist enemy that threatens civilization today is unlike any we have ever [7] known. It slaughters thousands of innocents—a crime of war and a crime against humanity. It seeks weapons of mass destruction and threatens their use against America. No one should doubt the intent, nor the depth, of its consuming, destructive hatred.

Terrorist operatives infiltrate our communities—plotting, planning and waiting to [8] kill again. They enjoy the benefits of our free society even as they commit themselves to our destruction. They exploit our openness—not randomly or haphazardly—but by deliberate, premeditated design.

9   This is a seized al Qaeda training manual—a "how-to" guide for terrorists—that instructs enemy operatives in the art of killing in a free society. Prosecutors first made this manual public in the trial of the al Qaeda terrorists who bombed U.S. embassies in Africa. We are posting several al Qaeda lessons from this manual on our website today so Americans can know our enemy.

10   In this manual, al Qaeda terrorists are told how to use America's freedom as a weapon against us. They are instructed to use the benefits of a free press—newspapers, magazines and broadcasts—to stalk and kill their victims. They are instructed to exploit our judicial process for the success of their operations. Captured terrorists are taught to anticipate a series of questions from authorities and, in each response, to lie—to lie about who they are, to lie about what they are doing and to lie about who they know in order for the operation to achieve its objective. Imprisoned terrorists are instructed to concoct stories of torture and mistreatment at the hands of our officials. They are directed to take advantage of any contact with the outside world to, quote, "communicate with brothers outside prison and exchange information that may be helpful to them in their work. The importance of mastering the art of hiding messages is self-evident here."

11   Mr. Chairman and members of the committee, we are at war with an enemy who abuses individual rights as it abuses jet airliners: as weapons with which to kill Americans. We have responded by redefining the mission of the Department of Justice. Defending our nation and its citizens against terrorist attacks is now our first and overriding priority.

12   We have launched the largest, most comprehensive criminal investigation in world history to identify the killers of September 11 and to prevent further terrorist attacks. Four thousand FBI agents are engaged with their international counterparts in an unprecedented worldwide effort to detect, disrupt and dismantle terrorist organizations.

13   We have created a national task force at the FBI to centralize control and information sharing in our investigation. This task force has investigated hundreds of thousands of leads, conducted over 500 searches, interviewed thousands of witnesses and obtained numerous court-authorized surveillance orders. Our prosecutors and agents have collected information and evidence from countries throughout Europe and the Middle East.

14   Immediately following the September 11 attacks, the Bureau of Prisons acted swiftly to intensify security precautions in connection with all al Qaeda and other terrorist inmates, increasing perimeter security at a number of key facilities.

15   We have sought and received additional tools from Congress. Already, we have begun to utilize many of these tools. Within hours of passage of the USA PATRIOT Act, we made use of its provisions to begin enhanced information sharing between the law-enforcement and intelligence communities. We have used the provisions allowing nationwide search warrants for e-mail and subpoenas for payment information. And we have used the Act to place those who access the Internet through cable companies on the same footing as everyone else.

Just yesterday, at my request, the State Department designated 39 entities as 16 terrorist organizations pursuant to the USA PATRIOT Act.

We have waged a deliberate campaign of arrest and detention to remove sus- 17 pected terrorists who violate the law from our streets. Currently, we have brought criminal charges against 110 individuals, of whom 60 are in federal custody. The INS has detained 563 individuals on immigration violations.

We have investigated more than 250 incidents of retaliatory violence and 18 threats against Arab Americans, Muslim Americans, Sikh Americans and South Asian Americans.

Since September 11, the Customs Service and Border Patrol have been at their 19 highest state of alert. All vehicles and persons entering the country are subjected to the highest level of scrutiny. Working with the State Department, we have imposed new screening requirements on certain applicants for non-immigrant visas. At the direction of the President, we have created a Foreign Terrorist Tracking Task Force to ensure that we do everything we can to prevent terrorists from entering the country, and to locate and remove those who already have.

We have prosecuted to the fullest extent of the law individuals who waste pre- 20 cious law enforcement resources through anthrax hoaxes.

We have offered non-citizens willing to come forward with valuable information 21 a chance to live in this country and one day become citizens.

We have forged new cooperative agreements with Canada to protect our com- 22 mon borders and the economic prosperity they sustain.

We have embarked on a wartime reorganization of the Department of Justice. 23 We are transferring resources and personnel to the field offices where citizens are served and protected. The INS is being restructured to better perform its service and border security responsibilities. Under Director Bob Mueller, the FBI is under- going an historic reorganization to put the prevention of terrorism at the center of its law enforcement and national security efforts.

Outside Washington, we are forging new relationships of cooperation with state 24 and local law enforcement.

We have created 93 Anti-Terrorism Task Forces—one in each U.S. Attorney's 25 district—to integrate the communications and activities of local, state and federal law enforcement.

In all these ways and more, the Department of Justice has sought to prevent 26 terrorism with reason, careful balance and excruciating attention to detail. Some of our critics, I regret to say, have shown less affection for detail. Their bold declara- tions of so-called fact have quickly dissolved, upon inspection, into vague conjec- ture. Charges of "kangaroo courts" and "shredding the Constitution" give new meaning to the term "the fog of war."

Since lives and liberties depend upon clarity, not obfuscation, and reason, not hy- 27 perbole, let me take this opportunity today to be clear: Each action taken by the Department of Justice, as well as the war crimes commissions considered by the President and the Department of Defense, is carefully drawn to target a narrow class of individuals—terrorists. Our legal powers are targeted at terrorists. Our investiga- tion is focused on terrorists. Our prevention strategy targets the terrorist threat.

28   Since 1983, the United States' government has defined terrorists as those who perpetrate premeditated, politically motivated violence against noncombatant targets. My message to America this morning, then, is this: If you fit this definition of a terrorist, fear the United States, for you will lose your liberty.

29   We need honest, reasoned debate; not fearmongering. To those who pit Americans against immigrants, and citizens against non-citizens; to those who scare peace-loving people with phantoms of lost liberty; my message is this: Your tactics only aid terrorists—for they erode our national unity and diminish our resolve. They give ammunition to America's enemies, and pause to America's friends. They encourage people of good will to remain silent in the face of evil.

30   Our efforts have been carefully crafted to avoid infringing on constitutional rights while saving American lives. We have engaged in a deliberate campaign of arrest and detention of law breakers. All persons being detained have the right to contact their lawyers and their families. Out of respect for their privacy, and concern for saving lives, we will not publicize the names of those detained.

31   We have the authority to monitor the conversations of 16 of the 158,000 federal inmates and their attorneys because we suspect that these communications are facilitating acts of terrorism. Each prisoner has been told in advance his conversations will be monitored. None of the information that is protected by attorney-client privilege may be used for prosecution. Information will only be used to stop impending terrorist acts and save American lives.

32   We have asked a very limited number of individuals—visitors to our country holding passports from countries with active Al Qaeda operations—to speak voluntarily to law enforcement. We are forcing them to do nothing. We are merely asking them to do the right thing: to willingly disclose information they may have of terrorist threats to the lives and safety of all people in the United States.

33   Throughout all our activities since September 11, we have kept Congress informed of our continuing efforts to protect the American people. Beginning with a classified briefing by Director Mueller and me on the very evening of September 11, the Justice Department has briefed members of the House, the Senate and their staffs on more than 100 occasions.

34   We have worked with Congress in the belief and recognition that no single branch of government alone can stop terrorism. We have consulted with members out of respect for the separation of powers that is the basis of our system of government. However, Congress' power of oversight is not without limits. The Constitution specifically delegates to the President the authority to "take care that the laws are faithfully executed." And perhaps most importantly, the Constitution vests the President with the extraordinary and sole authority as Commander-in-Chief to lead our nation in times of war.

35   Mr. Chairman and members of the committee, not long ago I had the privilege of sitting where you now sit. I have the greatest reverence and respect for the constitutional responsibilities you shoulder. I will continue to consult with Congress so that you may fulfill your constitutional responsibilities. In some areas, however, I cannot and will not consult you.

The advice I give to the President, whether in his role as Commander-in-Chief or in any other capacity, is privileged and confidential. I cannot and will not divulge the contents, the context, or even the existence of such advice to anyone—including Congress—unless the President instructs me to do so. I cannot and will not divulge information, nor do I believe that anyone here would wish me to divulge information, that will damage the national security of the United States, the safety of its citizens or our efforts to ensure the same in an ongoing investigation.   36

As Attorney General, it is my responsibility—at the direction of the President—to exercise those core executive powers the Constitution so designates. The law enforcement initiatives undertaken by the Department of Justice, those individuals we arrest, detain or seek to interview, fall under these core executive powers. In addition, the President's authority to establish war-crimes commissions arises out of his power as Commander-in-Chief. For centuries, Congress has recognized this authority and the Supreme Court has never held that any Congress may limit it.   37

In accordance with over two hundred years of historical and legal precedent, the executive branch is now exercising its core Constitutional powers in the interest of saving the lives of Americans. I trust that Congress will respect the proper limits of Executive Branch consultation that I am duty-bound to uphold. I trust, as well, that Congress will respect this President's authority to wage war on terrorism and defend our nation and its citizens with all the power vested in him by the Constitution and entrusted to him by the American people.   38

Thank you.   39

The Ashcroft Raids

David Cole

David Cole is a professor at Georgetown University Law Center and an attorney for the Center for Constitutional Rights. This article, sharply critical of human rights violations under the USA PATRIOT Act, appeared in Amnesty Now, *a publication of the human rights watchdog organization Amnesty International. We obtained this article from the Amnesty International USA Web site in November 2002.*

In 1919, a series of politically motivated bombing attempts culminated in an explosion at the Washington home of Attorney General A. Mitchell Palmer. The federal government responded by rounding up thousands of suspected subversive immigrants across the country. They were held in unconscionable conditions, interrogated incommunicado, and in some cases tortured. In the end, more than 500 were deported, not for the bombing, but for their political associations. The "Palmer   1

Raids" were led in part by a young J. Edgar Hoover, then head of the Justice Department's Alien Radical division. Eventually criticism of the raids brought the nation's first Red Scare to what appeared to be an end.

2   The government's current investigation of the terrorist attacks of September 11 does not yet appear to match the excesses of the Palmer Raids. But the government has been so secretive about the detentions this time around that it is difficult to be sure. We don't even know how many people have been detained.

3   In early November, less than two months into the investigation, the Justice Department said the number was 1,147. But as criticism mounted over the scope of the roundup, the Justice Department responded by simply stopping its practice of announcing the running tally. Thus, there has been no public accounting of the total number detained since November 5. And since the total was just about all the information the Justice Department was willing to share, the detentions remain shrouded in unprecedented secrecy.

4   What we do know, however, suggests that we may be repeating some of the mistakes of the past. As in the Palmer Raids, the government seems to have dispensed with developing probable cause before arresting individuals, and instead has used pretexts—usually of routine immigration violations—as justification for detaining hundreds of people about whom it has only the faintest suspicion. As in 1919, the government seems to be proceeding not on grounds of individual culpability, but of guilt by association. And as in the Palmer Raids, it has targeted almost exclusively immigrants, a group that by definition has no voice in the political process. As of February, despite the thousand-plus arrests, only one person had been charged with involvement in the 9/11 violence: Zaccarias Moussaoui. And he was picked up three weeks before the attacks. Justice officials claim that 10 or twelve detainees may be linked to Al Qaeda, but that leaves hundreds unaccounted for.

5   They fall into four categories. More than 725 have been held for alleged immigration status violations; about 120 for federal crimes unrelated to September 11; an undisclosed number for state criminal charges; and a similarly undisclosed but assertedly small number as federal material witnesses, purportedly to preserve their testimony for a criminal proceeding. The Justice Department has been especially closed-mouthed about the largest group of detainees, the more than 725 people held on immigration charges. It refuses even to name them and has ordered them tried in secret, with proceedings closed to the public, the press, legal observers, and even family members. On orders from Attorney General Ashcroft, Chief Immigration Judge Michael Creppy has instructed immigration judges not to list the cases on the public docket, and to refuse to confirm or deny that they even exist. Not even during the Palmer Raids did the U.S. engage in such a wholesale practice of secret detentions and trials.

6   But facts that have become public—in part from a Freedom of Information Act (FOIA) lawsuit filed by Amnesty International and the Center for National Security Studies, as well as investigations by enterprising journalists—indicate that nearly all the detainees are from Arab and largely Muslim population countries, and that most have little or no connection to the events of September 11.

The fact that the government has cast its net so widely—when it admits that   7
only a handful are even thought to be connected to Al Qaeda—is a reflection of how
lacking the government's intelligence was. Indeed, it seems fair to say that the
breadth of the government's sweep is inversely proportional to the shallowness of
its intelligence. It is swinging in the dark.

GUILTY UNTIL PROVEN INNOCENT

With the exception of Zaccarias Moussaoui and perhaps the material witnesses,   8
all the detainees are being held on "pretextual" charges. The real reason for their
incarceration is not that they worked without authorization or took too few academic credits, for example. Rather, the government used these excuses to detain them
because it thinks they just might have valuable information, because it suspects
them but lacks sufficient evidence to make a charge, or simply because the FBI is
not yet convinced that they are innocent.

Consider, for example, Ali Maqtari. A Yemeni citizen, Maqtari was picked up on   9
September 15 when he accompanied his U.S. citizen wife to Fort Campbell,
Kentucky, where she was reporting for Army basic training. Agents interrogated
him for more than 12 hours and accused him of involvement with terrorists.
Maqtari took and passed a lie detector test, but was detained on the highly technical charge that he had been in the country illegally for ten days while changing his
status from tourist to permanent resident. The government never offered any evidence linking him to terrorism or to crime of any kind. It merely submitted a boiler-
plate affidavit from an FBI agent arguing that Maqtari should be detained because
the investigation of terrorism is a "mosaic," and therefore, seemingly innocent facts
might at some future time turn out to indicate culpability. Two months later,
Maqtari was released without charges.

Another man, Osama Elfar, was detained on September 24, apparently be-   10
cause he was Egyptian, attended a Florida flight school, and worked as a mechanic
for a small airline in St. Louis. He agreed to leave the country, but as of November,
he was still detained. Hady Hassan Omar, also an Egyptian, spent two months in
jail because he made plane reservations on a Kinko's computer around the same
time as one of the hijackers. He was released without charges on November 23.

These and other cases suggest that the Justice Department policy has been to   11
lock up first, ask questions later, and to presume that an alien is dangerous until
the FBI has a chance to assure itself that he or she is not. Thus, government documents disclosed in the December FOIA lawsuit showed that of 725 people held
on immigration charges, more than 300 had been determined to be of no interest
to the investigation. Yet until individuals are "cleared," they are detained, even
when the government has no legitimate basis for detention. The *New York Times*
reported that as of February 18, for example, the Justice Department was blocking the departures of 87 foreign citizens who had either agreed to leave or had
been ordered deported. The government was continuing to hold them simply because it had not yet satisfied itself that they were innocent, even though they
were charged with no crimes.

CHANGING LAW TO FIT FEARS

12   Many of those detained were initially held without charges for several weeks. Shortly after September 11, the Immigration and Naturalization Service unilaterally amended a regulation governing detention without charges. The preexisting regulation had required the INS to file charges within 24 hours of detaining an alien. Under the new regulation, detention without charges is permissible for 48 hours, and for an unspecified "reasonable" period beyond that in times of emergency. Documents disclosed through the FOIA lawsuit show that many of the detainees were held for more than two weeks without any charges whatsoever.

13   Defenders of the administration often respond that the detainees violated immigration laws, and therefore deserve to be thrown in jail. But while an allegation of an immigration violation, if proven, may justify deportation, it does not in itself justify detention.

14   Before September 11, the INS could detain an alien charged with a deportable offense as a preventive matter, but only if it could show an immigration judge that the alien posed a threat to national security or a risk of flight. Under a new regulation issued October 29, however, even if the immigration judge rules that there is no basis for detention, INS prosecutors can keep the alien locked up simply by filing an appeal of the release order. Appeals of immigration custody decisions routinely take months, and often more than a year, to decide. And the prosecutor need not make any showing that the INS's appeal is likely to succeed.

15   None of these measures would pass muster if applied to citizens. Citizens are entitled to a public trial. They may be subjected to "preventive detention," but only if charged in a public proceeding and brought before an independent judge within 48 hours for a probable cause hearing. The requirement for a "speedy trial" means that unless a citizen agrees to an extension, preventive detention is limited to a matter of weeks. And if a judge rules that a citizen should be released on bail pending trial, the prosecutor cannot keep him in jail simply by filing an appeal.

16   In other words, the government has imposed on aliens widespread human rights deprivations that citizens would not tolerate. Yet, the Supreme Court has repeatedly stated that the due process clause applies to all persons, aliens and citizens alike.

THE LAST REFUGE OF SCOUNDRELS

17   It is likely to get still worse. An as yet unused provision in the USA Patriot Act, passed within six weeks of September 11, gives the attorney general unilateral authority to detain aliens on his say-so, without a hearing and without any opportunity for the alien to respond to the charges. The attorney general may detain any immigrant whom he certifies as a "suspected terrorist."

18   While "suspected terrorist" might sound like a class that ought to be locked up, the Patriot Act defines that class so broadly that it includes people who have never engaged in or supported a violent act in their lives, but are merely "associated" with disfavored groups. It also includes virtually every immigrant who has used or threatened to use a weapon, even in a barroom brawl, domestic dispute, or in other

routine settings having nothing whatsoever to do with terrorism as it is commonly understood. Such aliens can be held without charges for seven days, and in some circumstances can be held indefinitely, even if they cannot be deported because they have a legal right to remain in the U.S.

One reason the Patriot Act provision has not yet been invoked may be that it raises a multitude of serious constitutional concerns. The Supreme Court has never permitted preventive detention absent a finding of dangerousness or flight risk, yet this provision would authorize just that. [19]

Just last year, the Supreme Court interpreted another immigration law not to authorize indefinite detention because to do so would violate due process. In the criminal setting, the Court has limited detention without charges to 48 hours. And the INS is likely to argue that the Patriot Act standard for detention is less than probable cause, yet the Court has always required at least probable cause to arrest a person. [20]

The horror of September 11 has undoubtedly affected us all. Few things are more important than bringing the surviving perpetrators to justice and ensuring that such an attack never happens again. But precisely because the terrorists violated every rule of human decency, it is critical that in responding to the terrorist threat, we hold fast to the rule of law. Dragnet sweeps and secret detentions fail that test. They did under the Palmer Raids and still do today. [21]

Legally, What Are the Detainees?

Mary Jacoby

Mary Jacoby is a staff writer for the St. Petersburg Times *in Florida. This article, which explores the legal status of "detainees" at Guantánamo Bay Naval Base, appeared in the* St. Petersburg Times *on January 23, 2002.*

Are the al-Qaida and Taliban detainees at Guantánamo Bay Naval Base prisoners of war or are they what the U.S. government has called "unlawful combatants"? [1]

Although Defense Secretary Donald Rumsfeld insist the captives will be treated humanely either way, the distinction makes a difference. [2]

Under the 1949 Geneva Convention Relative to the Treatment of Prisoners of War, the United States cannot try prisoners of war simply for waging war against the country. But the united States could put "unlawful combatants" on trial for terrorist conspiracy to kill its citizens, human rights experts said. [3]

The experts, however, see a legal difference between the Taliban and al-Qaida fighters as they might be defined by the Geneva Convention. [4]

The Taliban fighters were part of the Afghan military, or "regular armed forces who profess allegiance to a government," as the convention states. Such captured fighters are defined as prisoners of war under the convention. [5]

6   The mostly Arab al-Qaida fighters would fall under the convention's category of "members of other militias and members of other volunteer corps . . . belonging to a Party to the conflict." However, a captured fighter in this class would have to meet further criteria to be considered a prisoner of war under the convention, including having borne arms openly and followed the laws and customs of war.

7   And this is what al-Qaida almost certainly did not do on Sept. 11, experts say.

8   "Clearly, you can make the case that al-Qaida did not abide by the laws of war. They completely flouted the laws of war. They engaged in massive attacks to kill civilians." said Tom Malinowski, Washington advocacy director for Human Rights Watch.

9   International treaties require the United States to resolve the prisoners' status through a judicial body; the U.S. military's own rules require a three-judge military panel to take up the question. Human rights advocates are urging the administration to do so.

10   "We think if they held those hearings and looked at the facts, the most likely determination would be that the Taliban prisoners are POWs while the al-Qaida prisoners are not," Malinowski said.

11   As to Tuesday, 158 detainees had been taken to Guantánamo, and more are expected.

12   Hurst Hannum, professor of international law at the Fletcher School of Law and Diplomacy at Tufts University, said he suspects the Bush administration hasn't resolved the prisoners' status because it doesn't know what it wants to do with them yet.

13   Any POWs will have to be released when a war is declared over, unless they are charged with engaging in specific hostile acts against the United States. But a prisoner thus charged would then be entitled to a fair trial, in either a civilian or military court: any venue in which regular U.S. citizens or military personnel would be tried.

14   But the United States would then have the difficult task of finding witnesses to make the charges stick.

15   "They've never used the word 'crime,' because if they use the word 'crime,' they have to use the word 'trial.' If they use the word 'trial,' they have to use the word 'fair,' " said Hannum, who is also co-director of the Center for Human Rights and Conflict Resolution at the Fletcher School.

16   Regardless of the prisoners' status, the Geneva Conventions require the United States to treat all detainees at the naval base in Cuba humanely, the experts say. And that means no torture, abuse or public mockery.

17   Rumsfeld, responding to an uproar in Britain over allegations of inhumane treatment of the prisoners, said Tuesday: "They are being treated humanely."

18   He added: "I have seen in headlines and articles words like 'torture' and one thing or another, which is utter nonsense. . . . We are giving them the treatment that is appropriate under the Geneva Convention."

19   Rumsfeld said his understanding of the legal reasoning behind the decision not to declare the detainees prisoners of war is that, "One of the higher purposes of the Geneva Conventions was to distinguish between legitimate combatants and unlawful combatants.

20   "The reason for doing that was they (drafters of the conventions) felt that a higher standard should be . . . given to people who in fact wore uniforms, who in fact were fighting on behalf of a legitimate government, who did carry their weapons openly."

Both Malinowski and Hannum agree that al-Qaida fighters are unlikely to qual- 21
ify for prisoner-of-war status. But they urge the United States to resolve the question through a panel of military judges or risk losing international support for the war on terrorism.

They also say the United States will have less moral leverage with enemy coun- 22
tries that in the future may take U.S. forces prisoner if it does not scrupulously follow the rules now. "We want to make sure our forces get 100 percent protection of the Geneva Conventions as well," Malinowski said.

The Geneva Conventions are four treaties that govern the treatment of sick or 23
wounded military personnel and civilians during wartime. Their goal is to prevent atrocities and to further humanitarian aid.

The first Geneva Convention in 1864 recognized the need for volunteers from 24
different countries to care for wartime wounded and said any such organization should be identified by a red cross on a white background. That's how the International Red Cross came into being.

The United States ratified the first convention in 1882 after a lobbying cam- 25
paign by American Red Cross founder Clara Barton and abolitionist Frederick Douglass, among others.

The conventions have been revised several times since then, including in 1949, 26
when 52 governments agreed upon the four Geneva Conventions still in force today. Both the United States and Afghanistan have ratified the conventions.

The term "unlawful combatants" is not found in the conventions. Rather, it is 27
from a 1942 U.S. Supreme Court decision upholding military tribunals for German saboteurs who were captured in America.

That decision said spies and saboteurs are not entitled to POW protections be- 28
cause they have violated the law of war, the same argument the administration is using against captured al-Qaida fighters.

In part, the confusion surrounding the status of the Guantánamo detainees is 29
the natural result of applying a 53-year-old treaty to a changed and modern world.

"One problem is, when the Geneva Conventions were drafted there was an as- 30
sumption you're either in the army or not," Hannum said. "I don't think when they were drafted they foresaw this never-never land of guerrillas and terrorists."

Guantánamo Prisoners Getting
What They Deserve
Charles Krauthammer

Syndicated columnist Charles Krauthammer, noted for his defense of conservative positions, argues that Guantánamo prisoners should not be considered "prisoners of war" protected by the Geneva Conventions. This op-ed piece appeared in newspapers throughout the United States in late January 2002.

1   Guantánamo is hopping and the jackals are howling. Sweden, Germany, Switzerland, the Netherlands—stalwart allies who held America's coat during the war in Afghanistan—are complaining that the Guantánamo prisoners are not accorded POW rights under the Geneva Conventions.

2   Amnesty International is shocked that we are using shackles. The U.N. high commissioner for human rights, Mary Robinson, is disturbed that the United States might be violating the International Covenant on Civil and Political Rights. (Yes, the same Mary Robinson who, in the name of famine relief, made the idiotic demand for a cessation of U.S. bombing five days after it began—a demand that would have resulted in untold Afghan deaths in a famine now ended by the American victory.)

3   The British tabloids are apoplectic, achieving full-throated silliness when the *Mail on Sunday* managed an allusion to slavery: "Each man is handcuffed and wears leg irons, a term that survives from slave-trading days."

4   Thanks for the etymology. No thanks for the advice. We should treat these complaints with the contempt they deserve.

5   The critical issue in the treatment of these captured fighters is whether, under international law, they are prisoners of war or "unlawful combatants."

6   An Iraqi soldier captured in Kuwait is a prisoner of war entitled to the protections of the Geneva Conventions. An al-Qaida fighter captured anywhere is not. By self-definition, al-Qaida members are "unlawful combatants," meaning people who fight outside the recognized rules of war.

7   Among the distinguishing characteristics of unlawful combatants are these: They deliberately attack civilians, and they deliberately infiltrate among civilians by not wearing an insignia or uniform.

8   Al-Qaida openly practices both. In 1996, Osama bin Laden issued "A Declaration of War Against the Americans." Note: not "against the United States." Unlike, say, Nazi Germany and Japan, al-Qaida declared war not on the state but on the people. In 1998, bin Laden declared that "to kill the Americans and their allies—civilians and military—is an individual duty for every Muslim."

9   Osama said it. And on Sept. 11, al-Qaida did it. And they did it the way terrorists do: out of uniform, by means of infiltration and concealment.

10   You join al-Qaida, you join an outlaw army. You explicitly violate—and thus forfeit the protection of—the Geneva Conventions. Indeed, denying such murderers POW rights vindicates the Geneva Conventions, and encourages others to adhere to them, by reserving their protections for those who observe their strictures.

11   The jackals are wrong on the law. They also deeply misunderstand the purpose of the capture of these prisoners. It is not to "bring them to justice" as we would domestic bank robbers, but to prosecute an ongoing war by finding out what they know about how al-Qaida works and what future massacres it is planning.

12   We need information, or more innocent civilians will die. Information obtained as a result of the Afghan war has already thwarted planned attacks on Americans in Singapore and Yemen and exposed sleeper agents throughout the world.

13   POWs are required to give only their name, rank, serial number and date of birth. Granting the Guantánamo prisoners POW status is thus militarily ridiculous. If they have information, we need to get it. There is a war on.

This fact, too, seems to have escaped the critics. They deem the prisoners 14 POWs of the Afghan war. But then, the Taliban having fallen and the war winding down, these men would have to be released, as are POWs at the end of "active hostilities," as ordinary Iraqi soldiers were released with the end of the Gulf War.

This is lunacy. The war is not against Afghanistan. It is against al-Qaida. And 15 the war is ongoing until al-Qaida either recants or surrenders or disbands or is destroyed. Until then, these prisoners are not the detritus of a leftover war. They are active combatants, and unlawful ones.

Reacting to this, Chris Patten, the European Union external affairs commis- 16 sioner, is concerned that the United States is "losing the moral high ground."

Too bad. Right now, what is of supreme importance to Americans is not the 17 moral high ground of salon opinion but the strategic high ground of military intelligence—the advantage we gain in combating terror with the knowledge we glean from these prisoners.

The world loves us, bleeding and suffering nobly, at the moral high ground of 18 Ground Zero. To which we say: No thank you. Our paramount national duty today is to prevent another Sept. 11, not to glory in the moral high ground—the moral vanity—of the victimhood we earned Sept. 11.

The New Face of Racial Profiling: How Terrorism Affects the Debate

Sherry F. Colb

Sherry F. Colb is a professor at Rutgers Law School and a columnist for FindLaw, a comprehensive Web resource for legal information and services. In this analytical piece, Colb explores how the war on terrorism might alter civic debates about racial profiling. Colb's article was posted on the FindLaw Web site on October 10, 2001.

One need not be Nostradamus to see law enforcement changes in our future. 1 Following the mass murders of September 11th, police at the national and local level have properly begun the process of developing strategies for detecting and apprehending terrorists.

Unlike ordinary criminal activity, terrorism cannot be addressed primarily by 2 "solving" acts of terrorism after the fact. Punishing offenders, though desirable from a retributive perspective, will not stop most future acts of terrorism. The prospect of a prison term or a lethal injection is unlikely to deter any aspiring suicide bomber.

As a result, discovering terrorist missions at the inchoate stage, prior to harm, 3 becomes a matter of great urgency. Among the many issues that may accordingly emerge is whether police, in the fight against terrorism, will be allowed to engage in racial profiling. The issue is hardly a new one, but a number of considerations may alter the terms of the debate.

DEFINING RACIAL PROFILING: USING RACE AS A FACTOR

4   As a first step, it is useful to define "racial profiling," because people use the term to mean different things. When I refer to "racial profiling," I mean the law enforcement practice of taking the race of a potential suspect into account in deciding whether to initiate investigation of that suspect.

5   One need not consider race to the exclusion of all other factors to be engaged in racial profiling. Rather, a "profile" will often contain a variety of factors: If one or more of them is race, then we have a racial profile.

6   The most familiar instance of racial profiling is what some have dubbed "Driving While Black" (or "DWB"). This kind of profiling involves police stopping motorists on the pretext that they have committed a traffic violation—often a minor one.

7   Although a traffic violation might be the objective foundation for the stop, the actual reason might include the race of the suspect. Police sometimes assume that African-American drivers are more likely than white drivers to be transporting illicit drugs. This assumption appears to trigger a large number of roadside stops.

8   Once a police officer has stopped an African-American suspect pursuant to a profile, the officer may ask the suspect for consent to search the vehicle. For reasons I explored in an earlier column, suspects generally consent to these searches, even when they have drugs secreted within their vehicles.

9   In other words, "DWB" profile stops—in conjunction with consent searches that occur in their wake—provide an opportunity for police to look for narcotics in the absence of probable cause.

PROFILING DENIES EQUAL PROTECTION BY TARGETING IMMUTABLE CHARACTERISTICS

10   Those of us who oppose "DWB" profiling have articulated a number of independent reasons for that opposition. One reason, common to any official instance of racial stereotyping, is that it denies affected African-Americans the equal protection of the laws guaranteed every person by the Fourteenth Amendment.

11   It is unfair, in other words, to visit disproportionate burdens upon one segment of the population, defined by its racial characteristics. In part, this is because race is immutable and therefore cannot be altered to avoid unwanted disparate treatment.

12   On this score, any new law enforcement initiative involving terrorist profiling that rests on ethnic or racial characteristics would meet with the same objections as "DWB" profiling.

IN DRUG-DEALING, STATISTICS DEFY PREJUDICES

13   A second reason so many people object to "DWB" profiling is that it rests on inaccurate factual assumptions about criminal conduct. Specifically, when police disproportionately stop African-Americans on the highway, they operate on the basis

of myths about the distribution of drug-related activities among various sectors of the population. Police officers might expect to find a stash of drugs when they search an African-American's vehicle. Yet in fact, they are no more likely to do so than they are to turn up drugs in a white person's car.

Many thus see "DWB" racial profiling as objectionable in part because it is use- 14
less in waging the "war on drugs." Disproportionately pulling over African-American drivers in large numbers does not in fact further the law enforcement interest in apprehending drug criminals. "DWB" therefore represents an arbitrary exercise of power that needlessly intrudes upon cherished liberty and privacy.

WHAT IF THERE WERE A TRUE RACIAL DISPARITY?

What does it mean, precisely, to say that "DWB" profiling is ineffective and ar- 15
bitrary? It cannot mean only that innocent African-Americans suffer undeserved intrusions when such policies are in effect. They do suffer these intrusions, of course, but that would be true even if racial profiling were based on statistically significant disparities in criminal behavior.

Say, for example, that one out of four white drivers was transporting illicit sub- 16
stances in the trunk of his car, while only one out of fifty African-American drivers was similarly transporting. If this were true, then race alone would provide a very potent means of distinguishing drug couriers from the rest of the driving population.

Under this racial disparity scenario, however, it would still be the case that 17
75% of white drivers stopped purely on the basis of race would be innocent and thus undeserving of police attention. This is an inevitable feature of conducting searches on less than perfect information: even legitimately based suspicion will often fall on innocents. Indeed, that cost is an inherent part of searches and seizures that take place on the authority of "probable cause" or "reasonable suspicion" rather than, for example, "guilt beyond a reasonable doubt" or a "preponderance of the evidence."

WILL RACIAL OR ETHNIC PROFILING OF TERRORISTS BE EFFECTIVE?

At this point, we are not in a position to judge accurately whether terrorist pro- 18
filing that includes a racial or ethnic factor will be "effective" at preserving safety in the United States.

We do know that most American citizens and residents of all racial groups are 19
innocent of terrorist activity and feel frightened by the events of September 11th. Therefore, stopping or otherwise intruding upon the privacy and liberty of people in a given group will certainly harm countless individuals who have done nothing to deserve such intrusions. This truth, however, will not entirely satisfy those who wish to consider the efficacy question.

Unlike the drug trade, in which very large numbers of people—of every race— 20
are involved, there is reason to think that relatively few individuals here are engaged in planning terrorist attacks on the United States. Therefore, *any* criteria police use to identify or "profile" terrorists, whether or not those criteria rely on suspect classifications such as race, ethnicity, or national origin, will yield many

more false positives than they will disclose true conspiring murderers. In other words, an overwhelming number of "suspects" will prove to be innocent, no matter what combination of factors is used to focus in on them.

21   It may turn out, moreover, that even though most people in any one ethnic group are innocent, the guilty nonetheless fall disproportionately within one group. Of course, it was also possible, before the data were in, that African-Americans would turn out to be disproportionately represented in the drug trade. It was a contingent fact—not an a priori truth—that they were not. It could accordingly turn out that in the case of terrorism, a particular segment of the population is in fact disproportionately represented among offenders. If the empirical reality is ultimately different for terrorism than it has been for drugs, then that difference could persuade some opponents of "DWB" profiling to support ethnic terrorism profiling.

THE URGENT INTEREST IN STOPPING TERRORISM

22   Yet another factor might lead some opponents of "DWB" to distinguish terrorism profiling. That factor is the urgency of the government interest that is at stake.

23   Large numbers of people apparently continue to support the "war on drugs," its utter failure (which I discussed in a prior column) notwithstanding. Yet even its most ardent supporters would probably admit that the prospect of drug distribution is not as threatening to this nation as the prospect of terrorism on American soil.

24   Though drug dealers are often violent, for example, their violence generally results from the unavailability of legal avenues for enforcing their contracts. Many individual drug transactions entail no violence at all. One could imagine a regime in which, once legal, the drug business could be entirely peaceful.

25   Terrorism, by contrast, does not lend itself to a similar legalization logic. There is no plausible argument that if only terrorism were legalized, it could be regulated and accordingly rendered nonviolent in nature. Terrorism is inherently violent and intolerable.

WHY THE INTENSE INTEREST MIGHT MATTER TO THE DEBATE

26   Why would anyone consider the interest in stopping terrorism relevant to the propriety of racial profiling? It would, of course, be irrelevant if profiling were to prove as ineffective in the war on terrorism as it has been in the war on drugs. And this is a distinct possibility. It may also be that terrorists from now on will consciously choose people falling outside of any profiled groups to carry out their atrocious objectives.

27   If, however, racial profiling turns out to be an effective way of narrowing down lists of potential suspects, then the compelling nature of the government interest could strike many people as highly relevant. Indeed, the constitutional test of when racial classifications are legally permissible is the "compelling interest test," in which courts scrutinize such classifications for whether their employment is narrowly tailored to achieve a compelling governmental interest.

28   If an effective terrorist profile were to emerge, and that profile included race among factors giving rise to suspicion, its efficacy could lead some opponents of "DWB" profiling to embrace its legality.

PAST, PRESENT, AND FUTURE PROFILING

The notion of using race to determine someone's likely willingness to slaughter 29
Americans is, of course, not entirely new.

The United States Supreme Court, in one of its most despised opinions, 30
Korematsu v. United States, upheld the internment of Japanese Americans after
Japan's attack on Pearl Harbor in 1941. Anyone of Japanese descent residing on the
pacific coast of the United States was presumed to be a traitor and accordingly
placed in what were essentially prisoner-of-war camps.

Very few people today defend this nation's treatment of Japanese Americans. In 31
part, this is because there appeared to have been no credible grounds—other than
pure racial animus and fear—for directing suspicion at the U.S. population subject
to internment.

But in part, condemnation of *Korematsu* may also stem from the belief that a de- 32
nial of equality on the basis of race is simply wrong, no matter how effective it
might be in realizing important objectives. And the objective defended in
Korematsu—winning World War II and defeating the Nazis—was theoretically no
less compelling than the present need to protect the country from terrorism.

Whatever this nation decides, future generations may judge us as harshly as 33
we now judge the supporters of internment during World War II. We must therefore
consider our nation's past, present, and future in facing the difficult challenge of
profiling in an age of terrorism.

Profiling Terrorists
Roger Clegg

*In the previous article, law professor Sherry F. Colb analyzes conflicting legal
and ethical issues involved in the use of racial profiling to seek suspected terrorists. In this argument posted on September 18, 2001, on the conservative Web
site* National Review Online, *Roger Clegg argues that racial profiling is justified in a war on terrorism. Roger Clegg is a contributing editor of* National
Review Online *and general counsel for the Center for Equal Opportunity, a
think tank that supports "colorblind public policies and seeks to block the expansion of racial preferences and to prevent their use in employment, education, and
voting" (from their Web site).*

A few news stories over the last week have reported on the fear of some people 1
that the government will use "racial profiling" in trying to identify terrorists. To
which there are two responses. First, it is not at all clear that what will be used really is racial profiling. And, second, so what?

2   If you are mugged by a six-foot-two-inch, black male wearing a red sweatshirt, it is not "racial profiling" for the police to be on the lookout for people who meet that description, even though one element in it is racial. The classic case of racial profiling is, instead, when the police decide to stop cars being driven by young black males, not because they have the description of a specific suspect, but because they know that statistically drugs are more likely to be smuggled by young black males than, say, old Asian females.

3   But there are other circumstances that fall in between these two extremes. Suppose, for instance, that you are looking for members of a particular drug cartel, who are engaged in particular acts of smuggling, and you know that they will all be Colombian nationals, but you don't have specific names or descriptions that go beyond that. Is it "racial profiling" to look harder at dark-eyed, dark-haired, darker-skin whites, and give shorter shrift to Asians, blacks, and folks with blond or red hair?

4   Enough hypotheticals. Suppose that you have already identified several members of a terrorist ring and want to find the rest. The ones you have identified so far meet a particular profile: Middle Eastern descent. Moslem. Several are trained pilots. Male. Young or middle-aged. Booked on transcontinental flights. Any problem with assuming that there is a good chance that the remaining members of the ring are likely to meet this profile, too?

5   This is a lot closer to the specific-description extreme of the spectrum than the statistically speaking end of the spectrum. Which means that this really isn't properly characterized as racial profiling at all. This doesn't mean you ignore everyone who doesn't meet the profile or shoot to kill anyone with black hair. But you look harder at those who fit the description.

6   But the other response is, so what if it *is* racial profiling? No on believes that the government should never, under any circumstances, consider race in its actions.

7   Suppose a prison has just suffered a race riot. Would it be barred from temporarily segregating prisoners? Of course not, as several of the justices noted—with none disagreeing—in one Supreme Court case. In an earlier decision, another justice wrote that the Constitution is not a suicide pact. Just so, and thus one would not expect it to bar the government from doing what is necessary to defend the ordered liberty of our society.

8   Racial classifications are allowed if they are "narrowly tailored" to a "compelling governmental interest," according to the Supreme Court's case law. If stopping terrorism is not a compelling interest, then nothing is. And in some circumstances there will be no way to safeguard this interest without taking the ethnicity of suspects into account. Such discrimination should be as limited and temporary as possible, but it is preferable to allowing mass murder, as all three branches of government would surely conclude.

9   And I doubt that few people would complain about it. My boss, a Latina, suspects that she is often assumed to be Middle Eastern when she travels on international flights, and that in Europe she is therefore more often stopped by security guards. She has no problem with that. And why should she—why should anyone—if the alternative is to diminish, however slightly, the chances of catching the next terrorist?

Racial Profiling and the War on Terrorism
American Civil Liberties Union

In this one-page poster argument, the American Civil Liberties Union (ACLU) expresses its opposition to racial profiling as a means of fighting terrorism. The ACLU is a liberal organization devoted to protecting civil liberties through defense of the Bill of Rights, particularly the first amendment guaranteeing freedom of speech. We obtained this poster from the Web site of the ACLU of Northern California.

Racial Profiling and the War on Terrorism

Have you been a victim of racial profiling?

If so, don't accept it: Report it today.
Call the ACLU Hotline: (415) 621-2493 ext.357

Since the tragic events of September 11th we have all become more concerned about our safety. Unfortunately, some law enforcement agencies have dramatically escalated racial profiling practices under the misguided belief that race discrimination will make us safer.

The ACLU wants to hear from you if you have been targeted on the basis of your race or ethnicity for:

 ➢ Detention
 ➢ Interrogation
 ➢ Search or arrest at an airport, bus depot, train station, or in your car.

Racial profiling is not the way to fight terrorism. Singling out people based on their race is discriminatory, counterproductive and inconsistent with American values.

Don't accept it: Report your complaint to the ACLU
today!
(415) 621-2493 ext. 357

AMERICAN CIVIL LIBERTIES UNION

What Would Mohammed [Atta] Do? An Interview with Michelle Malkin

Kathryn Jean Lopez

In this interview with journalist and Fox News analyst Michelle Malkin, author of Invasion: How America Still Welcomes Terrorists, Criminals, and Other Foreign Menaces to Our Shores, *Malkin argues that we need extensive "immigration reform" to cut down entrance of foreigners into the United States. Malkin, a second-generation Filipina born of immigrant parents, is a nationally syndicated conservative columnist. The interviewer, Kathryn Jean Lopez, is an associate editor of* National Review Online, *where this interview appeared on September 18, 2002.*

1   **Kathryn Jean Lopez:** Overall, how would you grade "immigration reform" since September 11, 2001?

2   **Michelle Malkin:** A big, fat "F." The United States is one of the few industrialized countries in the world that has not tightened immigration and entrance policies in response to the Sept. 11 attacks. Temporary visas for Middle Eastern students, tourists, and businessmen remain plentiful; immigrant visas continue to be given away at random or for the right price; the borders remain porous; the welcome mat for illegal aliens is expanding; and the deportation system is in shambles.

3   Despite strong public support for stronger controls, officials in both major parties continue to be paralyzed by political correctness and bureaucratic sclerosis. They have yet to come to grips with the reality of homicidal America-haters lurking at our doorstep—evildoers whose *modus operandi* is to infiltrate our country, then kill us. Our leaders have failed in one of their most basic constitutional responsibilities: to provide for the common defense.

4   **Lopez:** In what areas have there actually been practical improvements in the past year?

5   **Malkin:** Information-sharing between the Immigration and Naturalization Service and State Department improved after the attacks. Operation Tarmac weeded hundreds of illegal aliens out of high-security clearance jobs at airports nationwide. The Visa Express program disappeared this summer after relentless criticism by *National Review.* New, but temporary, scrutiny for young, male visa applicants from Middle Eastern countries was introduced. Congress sprinkled a few hundred more border-patrol agents on the frontlines. Immigration officers also received a few more boats, cameras, night goggles, and pepperball guns. The Social Security Administration began cracking down on illegal alien workers with bogus identification.

6   **Lopez:** What are the easiest ways for a terrorist to get into the U.S. undetected?

7   **Malkin:** The easiest way to enter is on a tourist, business, or student visa, just as the Sept. 11 hijackers did—without a comprehensive tracking system in place,

there are no consequences for overstaying. The State Department has issued more than 120,000 such visas to Middle Easterners since the Sept. 11 attacks.

Terrorists who can't get in through the front door (i.e., with a visa) need not 8 worry: There are plenty of ways they can enter the country through the back door (i.e., illegally).

Lopez: We hear outrageous stories about breast milk being questioned at the 9 airports and the like, but what is most outrageous is in some of the more mundane routines—like visas still not being checked. You write about security personnel being pressured to not check visas or check terror-watch lists in the interest of getting the lines moving, even now. How widespread is that?

Malkin: *Invasion* documents how immigration inspectors at several large inter- 10 national airports across the country are rushed and overburdened. The airport pressure cooker has its roots in a 1990 amendment to the Immigration and Nationality Act, which required INS officers to process foreign visitors arriving at air or sea ports of entry "within 45 minutes of their presentation for inspection." But the workforce has not kept pace with the onslaught of visitors—and national security is the sacrificial lamb. At the nation's busiest international airports, the time limit gives inspectors as little as 20 to 30 seconds to spend on each passenger's paperwork. That leaves little time to interview foreign visitors about their travel plans, a practice that is common in other countries.

The Enhanced Border Security and Visa Reform Act of 2002 included a provi- 11 sion repealing the 45-minute inspection limit, but added a little-noticed clause requiring the INS to staff ports of entry with the "goal of providing immigration services . . . within 45 minutes of a passenger's presentation for inspection." In other words: No relief from the speed demons.

Lopez: How is New York City, of all places on earth, a safe haven for terrorists— 12 still?

Malkin: New York City's sanctuary policy for illegal immigrants was created in 13 1989 by Mayor Ed Koch and upheld by every mayor succeeding him. When Congress enacted immigration-reform laws that forbade local governments from barring employees from cooperating with the INS, Mayor Rudy Giuliani filed suit against the feds in 1997. He was rebuffed by two lower courts, which ruled that the sanctuary order amounted to special treatment for illegal aliens and was nothing more than an unlawful effort to flaunt federal enforcement efforts against illegal aliens. In January 2000, the Supreme Court rejected his appeal, but Giuliani vowed to ignore the law. The Twin Towers are gone and Giuliani is out of office, but the city's policy of safe harbors for illegal immigrants stands.

The reason the September 11 attacks didn't prompt reconsideration of New 14 York City's sanctuary policy is that all of the hijackers entered the country legally. So people do not see a connection between interior enforcement and national security. Look past Sept. 11, and the link becomes clearer: Illegal aliens participated in the first attack on the World Trade Center, the Los Angeles Millennium bombing plot, and the New York subway bombing plot. Moreover, three of the September 11 hijackers were here illegally at the time of their attacks and several others obtained fraudulent ID cards with the assistance of an illegal alien. Clearly, illegal-friendly policies—not only sanctuary laws, but also driver's licenses, banking privileges, and college-tuition breaks—make it easier for terrorists to blend in and carry out their nefarious plans.

15   **Lopez:** How should the INS be dealt with?

16   **Malkin:** The INS bureaucracy is a cesspool of elbow-rubbers, string-pullers, chest-puffers and cover-uppers who care more about protecting their backsides than upholding the law. The current director of the agency, James Ziglar, freely admitted after Sept. 11 that "People who say I don't have any experience in the area are absolutely right," and assured illegal aliens that it is "not practical or reasonable" to deport them.

17   Americans deserve an INS that is committed to enforcing immigration laws. Ensure that all officials in immigration-related positions, including Ziglar's replacement, have no qualms about shoring up border security. Publish an annual list of INS officials convicted of misconduct, and remove them from sensitive positions. Strengthen federal whistleblower protections. Reward agency truth-tellers with plum management positions in their field of expertise. Demote or fire the supervisors who retaliate against them.

18   **Lopez:** If you were advising the president, in the interest of national security, what would you advise him—overall, and first—to do to deal with the immigration/porous-border problem?

19   **Malkin:** I would advise President Bush to stop pandering to pro-illegal alien ethnic groups and start treating immigration as a national-security issue. I would advise him to view immigration-related issues through the cold eyes of a terrorist killer like Mohammed Atta. I would advise him to ask at every turn: "What would Mohammed do?" How would he exploit our entry points, evade detection, and blend into the American mainstream? Then I would urge him to push for policies, like a moratorium on nonimmigrant visas to Middle Easterners, that will make it harder for the next Mohammed Atta to infiltrate our country. If the policy of preemption makes sense abroad, why not at home? There will be howling protestations from the usual suspects—Arab-American lobbyists, immigration lawyers, Saudi Arabian diplomats, the *Wall Street Journal* editorial page—but this is not the time to give in to abettors of terrorism.

20   **Lopez:** Why is immigration so untouchable, even after what happened last September 11?

21   **Malkin:** Our elected officials are unwilling to reform immigration because a conglomerate of interest groups stand in the way. The travel and tourism industries oppose efforts to eliminate dangerous visa-less travel programs. Education administrators, who reap $12 billion per year from foreign students, oppose common-sense efforts to track foreign students; multinational corporations oppose efforts to increase scrutiny of trucks crossing our borders or ships entering our ports; and alien rights' lawyers and ethnic lobby groups oppose efforts to beef up interior enforcement.

22   A book published in 1965 by economist Mancur Olson called *The Logic of Collective Action* argued that small, well-organized groups with strong feelings about an issue can defeat large, poorly organized groups, allowing narrow interests

to trump the national interest. This insight explains why the obstructionists have won time and time again even though most Americans favor immigration controls.

Lopez: What's the worst thing you learned while working on *Invasion*?   23

Malkin: That it will take another terrorist attack before our leaders start fix-   24
ing our broken immigration system.

All-American Osamas

Nicholas D. Kristof

This New York Times *op-ed piece (June 7, 2002) reminds readers that many terrorists are not foreign-born Muslims but white, ultra-right-wing American extremists. Kristof is a Pulitzer prize-winning columnist for the* New York Times.

We Americans have conjured so specific a vision of terrorists—swarthy, glow-   1
ering Muslims mumbling fanatically about Allah—that we're missing the threat from home-grown nuts, people like David Burgert.

Mr. Burgert, a 38-year-old who last made a living renting out snowmobiles here   2
in this spectacularly beautiful nook of northwestern Montana, had a terror plan that made Osama bin Laden's look rinky-dink. Not content merely to kill a few thousand people, Mr. Burgert's nine-member militia was planning a violent revolution and civil war to overthrow the entire United States government.

The plan, according to Sheriff James Dupont, was for the militia to use its ma-   3
chine guns, pipe bombs and 30,000 rounds of ammunition to assassinate 26 local officials (including Mr. Dupont), and then wipe out the National Guard when it arrived. After the panicked authorities sent in NATO troops, true American patriots would rise up, a ferocious war would ensue, and the U.S. would end up back in the hands of white Christians.

"The good thing is that most of the people who would do it are so stupid that   4
they would kill themselves first," said Sheriff Dupont, who runs the law here in rugged Flathead County, which is bigger than all of Connecticut and has lots more grizzly bears.

But the litany of domestic militia plots, failed ones, is still sobering. In   5
Michigan, militia members planned to bomb two federal buildings. Missourians planned to attack American military bases, starting with Fort Hood, Tex., on a day it opened to tens of thousands of visitors. California militia members planned to blow up a propane storage facility. Most unnerving, a Florida militia plotted to destroy a nuclear power plant.

If these were Muslims who were forming militias and exchanging tips for mak-   6
ing nerve gas, then we'd toss them in prison in an instant. But we're distracted by our own stereotypes, searching for Muslim terrorists in the Philippine jungle and

the Detroit suburbs and forgetting that there are blond, blue-eyed mad bombers as well. We're making precisely the mistake that the Saudis did a few years ago: dismissing familiar violent fanatics as kooks.

7   In fact, militia members and Al Qaeda members are remarkably similar. Both are galvanized by religious extremism (America's militias overlap with the Christian Identity movement, which preaches that Jews are the children of Satan and that people of color are sub-human), both see the United States government as utterly evil, and both are empowered by the information revolution that enables them to create networks, recruit disciples and trade recipes for bio- and chemical weapons.

8   It would be a mistake to put one's faith in the militias' being eternally incompetent. Jessica Stern of Harvard has written an essay about an anti-government activist named James Dalton Bell, who earned a degree in chemistry from M.I.T. and is unquestionably brilliant. By age 14, he says, "I was studying the isomerization of benzyl thiocyanate to the isocyanate."

9   Weren't we all? But Mr. Bell, who is now in jail, is also believed by the authorities to have manufactured sarin, a nerve gas, in his basement. He led a chemical attack against an I.R.S. office and wrote an Internet book called "Assassination Politics," which outlines a very clever scheme to pay for contract killings of federal officials with digital cash in a way that preserves anonymity at both ends. There is also evidence that Mr. Bell talked "hypothetically" of poisoning a city's water supply.

10   The things you learn in Montana: According to militia members here, the World Trade Center attacks were a plot by the Feds to declare an emergency and abolish the Bill of Rights; the Columbine school shootings were a federal test of new mind-control technology; a map on a Kix cereal box shows the occupation zones Americans will be herded into after the United Nations takes over.

11   Another thing you learn here is how to deal with grizzlies. Don't be so focused on a distant moose that you ignore the bear behind you. And if it charges, stand your ground until it's 10 feet away, then shoot pepper spray into its eyes, and—very quickly—step aside.

12   Right now, I'm afraid that the Bush administration is so focused on the distant moose that we're oblivious to the local grizzlies like Dave Burgert creeping up on us.

For Class Discussion

1. One of the chief disputes in this unit concerns the extent to which the United States is abusing human rights in its war against terrorism. Concerning human rights, where do writers in this unit disagree about the facts of the case? Where do they disagree about basic beliefs, values, and underlying assumptions?

2. Working in small groups or as a whole class, and drawing on the readings in this unit and on your own personal experiences and critical thinking,

create core arguments (reasons and possible kinds of evidence) for each of the following claims:

a. The USA PATRIOT Act has/has not led to excesses of police powers that violate American civil rights guaranteed by the U.S. Constitution and the courts.

b. The United States is/is not violating the Geneva Conventions and other international accords on human rights in its treatment of "detainees" at Guantánamo Bay.

c. Racial profiling is/is not justified in the war against terrorism.

d. In its war on terrorism, the United States should/should not reform immigration laws to make it harder for foreigners to enter the United States.

3. As a class consider this dilemma: Americans, as members of a free and open society, traditionally value individualism, privacy, freedom of movement, open access to government information, acceptance of diversity and multiculturalism, welcoming of immigrants (as symbolized by the Statue of Liberty), constitutional protections against unlawful arrest, and constitutional guarantees of free speech, free association, and freedom from governmental invasions of privacy. To what extent are you willing to exchange some of these freedoms for more safety and security against terrorism? How much are you willing to put your tax money into a new Department of Homeland Security as opposed, say, to universal medical coverage or better schools?

4. Choose one of the readings in this unit and analyze it carefully using the List 2 Guide questions on pages 460–461.

OPTIONAL WRITING ASSIGNMENT   From this unit, choose an argument on the U.S. response to terrorism with which you particularly disagree. Then write your own argument in which you summarize fairly the views you oppose, respond to those views, and then present your own perspective supported with reasons and evidence. Unless your instructor provides more specific directions, choose the audience and genre that most fit your rhetorical context

---

HIP-HOP, FILM, AND RACIAL IDENTITY

While some people think of music and film purely as sources of pleasure and entertainment, others, including cultural critics, acknowledge that music and films also significantly shape our perceptions of social reality. In this unit, we open up the subject of hip-hop music and film as popular art forms that raise controversial issues about culture and race. For instance, is white culture usurping hip-hop, a quintessential art form that grew out of urban black culture? Will hip-hop music, which has been a dominant influence on African American youth in the last twenty years, in the words of black writer Raquel Cepeda, "*stay* obsessed with living the ghetto-fabulous life,"[1] increasingly sell out to commercialism, or become a unifying force of black political consciousness? In a similar vein, what role have recent popular films starring black actors played in addressing problems of racism? And what role do African Americans and whites think that these films should play?

We hope that the articles in this unit, which we believe are interesting in themselves, will suggest new ways of thinking about popular culture.

Money, Power, Elect: Where's the Hip-Hop Agenda?

Raquel Cepeda

This article from a 2000 issue of Essence *magazine leans toward the inquiry, truth-seeking end of the argument spectrum as it argues for hip-hop's potential cultural and political power for African Americans. Raquel Cepeda is editor-in-chief of sayshe.com, a Web site focused on multiculturalism, women, and urban culture.*

1   Hip-hop culture has given my generation its tag line, if not its very identity: For more than 20 years, rap—hip-hop's sometimes furious, sometimes laid-back, rhythmic spoken-word expression—has provided a mesmerizing sound track for the lives of many young African-American and Latino people. Spawned from humble beginnings in New York City's South Bronx, hip-hop style spread like wildfire, while rap rocked our neighborhood block parties, turntables and boom boxes, and then White suburban headphones all over the country. Eventually rap would generate a $1.3 billion industry in the United States, exclusive of its still-growing global influences.

2   But consider how rap music, back at the end of the catastrophic Reagan administration, was also identified as *the* platform to educate *and* entertain the nation on

---

[1]Raquel Cepeda, "Money, Power, Elect: Where's the Hip-Hop Agenda?" *Essence* Aug. 2000, 118.

the realties of what was going on socially and politically in Black and Latino America. Only a decade ago, rapper KRS-One and his crew BDP (Boogie Down Productions) proclaimed in the title track to their 1990 album *Edutainment:* "Every time a Black man speaks up, KA-POW!/See people concentrate on the leader. . . ." Other groups such as Public Enemy, Brand Nubian, Poor Righteous Teachers and even such West Coast pioneers as Compton, California's gangsta-rappers N.W.A (Niggas With Attitude) penned tracks that depicted and responded to the political agendas brewing in their communities—namely, racial profiling, police brutality, the state of public education and the prison system, Black-on-Black crime and predatory drug peddling and abuse.

Compare that to the music that dominates the top of the charts today: Rap is   3
now a sample-heavy, benjamin-raking, crudely individualistic pop-culture phenomenon that is very far from its earlier countercultural and activist impulses. "There's no spiritual content to the majority of records being made today," says cultural critic Nelson George, 42, author of *Hip-Hop America.* Icons like Jay-Z, Puffy and Lil' Kim now compare themselves to high-profile White celebrity entrepreneurs like Donald Trump, Donatella Versace and Martha Stewart. Ironically, traditional Black community leaders like the Reverend Jesse L. Jackson, Sr., NAACP president and CEO Kweisi Mfume, and even the Reverend Al Sharpton have been far less successful at appealing politically to these hip-hop megastars and the young people who follow them than folks like Trump and *Playboy* monarch Hugh Hefner have been in *partying* with them.

Meanwhile, today's post–civil-rights hip-hop civilian masses seem politically in-   4
ert. Just as the rise of gangsta rap overwhelmed message rap, hip-hop's social energies have also been redirected by commercial success and corporate marketing. The popular mind, seduced by the ethic of getting paid, became preoccupied with rap's shiny, platinum-dipped dreams. Mogul Sean "Puffy" Combs almost single-handedly steered the sound of rap music into mainstream pop. Predictably, other popular hip-hop artists have followed suit.

Foxy Brown and Lil' Kim, in particular, enjoy new status as glam celebrity   5
spokespeople-for-hire, successfully marketing luxury goods. But the media power this trend represents is rarely put to use for the benefit of our communities. "The so-called Black celebrities are created by companies to be advertisements for what companies promote." observes Public Enemy's Chuck D. "These celebrities lose focus and think it's all about them; that's individual instead of collective thought."

But now, as we face the first national election season of the new century, will   6
the hip-hop generation *stay* obsessed with living the ghetto-fabulons life? Will we remain unorganized and politically unresponsive to racism and police brutality, bad schools, economic gaps and other persistent problems in our communities? After all, this generation, however flaccid its political muscle may seem to be is heir to the Black Power era. We have witnessed two Republican administrations, the 1992 Los Angeles riots, the 1999 murder of our immigrant brother Amadou Diallo and most recently, California's passing of Proposition 21, which disproportionately criminalizes urban youth. So why haven't we been galvanized into an articulate and

activist political movement by such events? Could the star power in merchandising and marketing, for example, ever be used successfully as a coalescing political force to get out our vote?

7   In fact, with the possible exceptions of Lauryn Hill and Queen Latifah, few platinum-level artists have ever considered moving beyond conscious rhetoric and rhyme to organize our people. Many ask, why even expect a celebrity to take a particular political stand? The answer is simple: There's a long-standing tradition in our communities that unites the arts and activism (Paul Robeson is a historic example, as are Ossie Davis, Ruby Dee and Harry Belafonte). But cultural commentators agree that while our rap celebrities have an enormous influence on urban-youth culture, there's little interest in transferring it to politics. "What hip-hop has done is taken the strategies of grass-roots organizing and used it to sell records and images," explains Nelson George. "The same kind of kids who used to canvass a neighborhood door-to-door to get people registered to vote now give parties."

8   A similar observation comes from another older "hip-hop head." Bill Stephney, 38, president of StepSun Music, board member of the National Urban League and founder of New York City's Families Organized for Liberty and Action (FOLA): "As Vernon Reid [musician and Black Rock Coalition founder] once said, the nineties were just the sixties turned upside down," recalls Stephney. "During the sixties, you had a generation of Black folks who were socially active and politically conscious. We wanted to change the world, but we really didn't have an idea, beyond the romance of revolution, how we were going to finance or set up any economic systems for Black and Latino people to survive. By the nineties, you have the kids of the sixties generation, who know how to make money, but who don't have the sociopolitical orientation their predecessors had. Imagine, if you will, having the social and political heart of Fannie Lou Hamer, Rosa Parks, Medgar Evers and Dr. King combined with the financial brains of Puffy."

9   Still, there *are* activist forces stirring within the twenty-first–century hip-hop community. I'm not talking about well-publicized, star-sponsored operations like Puffy's Daddy's House (which finances camps and other activities for inner-city youth) and Lauryn Hill's Refugee Project (which also works with at-risk urban youth); even these operations have been criticized—perhaps unjustly—for being vanity charity activities, not really informed by an overall social or political strategy. No, I'm talking about a largely unnoticed grass-roots hip-hop movement that is persistently making its way through urban neighborhoods all over the country. Most of this so-called hip-hop activism began in New York, just as rap did, but it has also cropped up among youths in Los Angeles, San Francisco, Washington, D.C., Atlanta and cyberspace, according to Angela Ards, a senior associate editor at *Ms.* magazine. Ards investigated hip-hop activism last year as a fellow at the Nation Institute (the independent nonprofit organization dedicated to protecting First Amendment freedoms and affiliated with *The Nation* magazine).

10   These local groups identify with hip-hop expression but tap into the energies of performers who are less well known than our stars. One example: Last year Mos Def and Talib Kweli—Brooklyn-based rappers–entrepreneurs who record individually and together as the duo Black Star—rescued a local landmark Black bookstore from

going out of business by buying it. Black Star is also known for spearheading anti–police brutality campaigns in the hip-hop industry, and other conscious artists like Common, OutKast and dead prez have joined them in representing and working with the urban neighborhoods they came from.

Such activity certainly deserves more recognition and support from the hip-hop nation's everyday citizens. Although many of our young adults seem to have little interest, or aspiration to participate, in politics or activism, a strident few, whom you will meet below, show that the hip-hop generation has untapped potential to become a serious political force. The question is, how do we pump up the volume?   11

VOTER REGISTRATION AND PARTICIPATION

In this election year, young Black people are at best skeptical about the political mainstream, and a few hardworking Black political organizers are trying to change that. Donna Frisby-Greenwood, former executive director of Rock the Vote (a nonpartisan, nonprofit organization dedicated to motivating young people to participate in the political process) and a political organizer who has worked with urban youth for more than a decade, points out that in the last Presidential election only about half the 8,928,000 eligible Black voters 18–34 registered to vote, and only 3.5 million of them—or about 72 percent—voted. (By comparison, about 68 percent of the 10,932,000 eligible Black voters 34–65 registered, and nearly 84 percent of them voted.) At Rock the Vote, Frisby-Greenwood organized the Hip-Hop Coalition for Political Power to reach out to the young Black voter. Artists like Public Enemy's Chuck D, Queen Latifah, LL Cool J and The Roots took an active role in the effort. Of the more than 500,000 voters Rock the Vote registered in 1996, at least 150,000 were registered through the efforts of the now-defunct Coalition.   12

Today, Frisby-Greenwood, 35, lives and works in Philadelphia and cochairs the Black Youth Vote (BYV) Coalition—part of the National Coalition on Black Civic Participation, Inc., in Washington, D.C.—with BET talk-show host Tavis Smiley, 34, and Chuck D, 39. "We are now registering voters on-line, in the streets and on college campuses," says Frisby-Greenwood. "We've planned summer workshops to train young people to organize, educate and register voters in Pennsylvania, North Carolina, Alabama, Florida, D.C., Los Angeles, Ohio, Georgia, Texas and California."   13

The BYV works with an advisory committee of 21–to–40-year-old leaders, including author and syndicated columnist Farai Chideya, 31; activists Conrad Muhammad, 35, and Ras Baraka, 31; and journalists Angela Ards, 31, and Kevin Powell, 34. "One of the things we emphasize in the BYV manifesto is awakening the sleeping giant of the hip-hop generation," says Chideya. "Black youths are such a force—I mean, we run American pop culture." Hoping to motivate at least 10 percent of young Black people between 18 and 29 to participate in the 2000 political process, BYV has been training local coordinators around the country. (For further information, see www.bigvote.com.)   14

These education and registration efforts are certainly needed, according to my sample of attitudes. "*Politics* is a dangerous word," says Black Star's Kweli, 24,   15 "because what it means to me is just a bunch of lies and rhetoric, not anything concrete." Still, Kweli, like many of his contemporaries, is motivated to do *something* about the issues that Black youths encounter every day in their own lives: police brutality and racial profiling, gun control, education and welfare reform, Black-on-Black crime and the racially slanted prison system, to name a few. But he feels neither elected politicians nor candidates speak to these issues directly in a language that makes sense to hip-hop youths. In fact, Black youths simply don't respond to politicians, including Black ones who, for the most part, have also made only token attempts to reach out to them.

16   One Black leader who insists that responsible Blacks in positions of authority can't give up on politically apathetic young people is Congresswoman Maxine Waters (D–CA). "I've tried to make the connection between rappers, young people and the Congressional Black Caucus," says Waters. "My main agenda is to connect to the hip-hop generation—more than to actual rappers—and close the communication gap between them and older adults." Freedom of speech and censorship issues have split the generations in Black communities. Some White politicians gleefully supported longtime Black political activist C. Delores Tucker in her 1996 campaign against gangsta rap, says Waters, "because they didn't like rap *or* young Black people." She also recalls the highly publicized congressional hearings, headed by then-Senator Carol Moseley Braun (D–IL): "I had to literally read lyrics from Snoop Dogg's records to show that all the words were not simply vulgar curse words. They were oftentimes deeply meaningful in describing young people's experiences, and they connected to many others who felt left outside of the system."

17   For the past few years at the annual Congressional Black Caucus Week in Washington, D.C., Waters has sponsored and moderated a workshop called Young, Gifted and Black, in which young people and rappers are given a platform before lawmakers to define themselves and their issues. But a surprising number of Black politicians have essentially thrown up their hands. Congressman Jesse L. Jackson, Jr. (D–IL), himself a member of the hip-hop generation at age 35, points out that he didn't see any rappers in Decatur, Illinois, "when my father was fighting to get six young African-Americans back in school." (The young Black men, who got into a fisfight at a local high-school football game in September 1999, were expelled because of the school district's zero-tolerance policy on school violence, which the young men argue has been disproportionately applied to Decatur's Black students.) When Congressman Jackson was pressed to detail the extent of Rev. Jackson's previous outreach efforts to the hip-hop community, he replied, "They probably wouldn't have shown up. I ain't blaming them. I'm just simply saying people are busy."

18   True. "Most rappers who say they're spokesmen for the generation generally are spokesmen only as it relates to social and cultural trends," says Conrad Muhammad, former minister of the Nation of Islam's Mosque No. 7 in Harlem and founder of A Movement for CHHANGE (Conscious Hip-Hop Activism Necessary for Global Empowerment), a national organization aimed at educating urban youth about the political process and registering young people to vote. CHHANGE aims to put 1 million Black young people on the rolls this November (call [718] 237-0064),

and Muhammad has also targeted several popular rappers to groom as candidates for local political office. Although he reports "opening the minds" of rappers like Fat Joe, DJ Kool Here and Vinnie and Treach of Naughty by Nature, no actual campaigns have moved beyond the talking stage.

Similarly, in a 1998 *Essence* cover story, Sean "Puffy" Combs himself expressed [19] interest in political activism and maybe even running for office. So far he has committed, along with LL Cool J, Mary J. Blige and Rosie Perez, to appear in public-service announcements for Rap the Vote 2000. A joint project of rap mogul Russell Simmons's new Web site, 360HipHop.com, and Rock the Vote, Rap the Vote 2000 aims to get 850,000 new young voters to the polls this year under the slogan "Register. Vote. Represent."

POLICE BRUTALITY AND RACIAL PROFILING

The death of the 22-year-old West African immigrant Amadou Diallo—an un- [20] armed man shot 41 times by four New York Police Department officers who were later acquitted of all charges—forced the ever-present issue of police brutality and racial profiling to the top of urban America's political agenda. The Hip-Hop for Respect Foundation (HHFRF) project was one activist response from the community of hip-hop artists. "Most of the people that got killed by police this year and in the past have probably been some of your fans" wrote rapper Mos Def, 26, in an open letter to the rap-music industry. "We are the senators and the congressmen of our communities. We come from communities that don't have anybody to speak for them and that's why they love us." As fund-raisers for the foundation, which supports activist groups that effectively deal with police brutality issues, Mos Def and Talib Kweli went on to organize the recording session for the maxisingle "One for Love, Pt. 1," which also features Common, Rah Digga, Pharoahe Monch, Pos (from De La Soul) and others.

But the acquittal of the four officers charged with the Diallo shooting elicited [21] strong statements from the hip-hop elite, like Russell Simmons (largely covered in the Black press and rap-music magazines), and, more important, thrust thousands of young protesters from a mix of races into the streets of Manhattan and the Bronx neighborhood where the killing took place. Some marchers replaced the slogans of yesteryear with a popular chorus from a Nas track: "I wanna talk to the mayor, to the governor and the muthaf—king President/I wanna talk to the FBI and the CIA and the muthaf—king congressmen." Here hip-hoppers took their music back to the streets to make a pointed political statement.

JUVENILE JUSTICE AND PROPOSITION 21

Another grassroots organization spawned by the hip-hop generation is San [22] Francisco's Third Eye Movement. This collective of 40 members became a major force in making the antigang–crime-prevention initiative Proposition 21 a center-piece debate in California's elections last spring. A campaign spearheaded by former Republican governor Pete Wilson put Prop 21 on the ballot. The measure gives police the right to make arrests under a number of questionable charges that disproportionately target young people of color. It's possible for a young woman and two of her friends, dressed similarly, to be classified as a gang and therefore arrested. "If I happen to be on the basketball court playing ball with somebody, and that person leaves and commits a crime, the doors are open for me to be put in jail under conspiracy charges because of my association," says Davey D. 35. a community-affairs director and on-air radio personality at 106 KMEL in Oakland. Prop 21 also allows courts to try juveniles as adults for felonies. as well as permit police surveillance and phone taps without a court order.

23   Jasmin de la Rosa, 24, coordinator and founder of Third Eye, organized school walkouts, free concerts, rallies and sit-ins to protest the initiative. But Prop 21 was ultimately passed last March in the statewide count, although it was defeated in several districts, including San Francisco and Oakland, where young protesters were active. More than 170 hip-hop heads were arrested after more than 500 people staged a sit-in at the San Francisco Hilton because they believed a Hilton family member pumped money into the "Yes on Prop 21" campaign. Here hip-hop aficionados customized a chant from an old-school rap song: "Hotel, motel and the Hilton, say what/If you fund the war on youth, you ain't gonna win." Bay Area rappers, including Digital Underground, Boots, Money B. and Sugar T., joined the anti–Prop 21 rallies. But the biggest impact was at the grass-roots level, according to De la Rosa. "The cultural events and hip-hop parties—getting young people to organize those events was very effective in calling them to action," she says. "The people who organize the shows get skills in political organizing."

24   Davey D, who is also the Web master for the popular Internet site Davey D's Hip-Hop Corner (www.daveyd.com), concludes: "The best way to bring people under one umbrella is for them to engage in politics on a local level first."

SCHOOLS, NOT JAILS

25   How can we cultivate strong leadership when the prison-industrial complex has an obscene percentage of our generation on lockdown? If you are imprisoned for a felony, depending on the state, your voting rights may be revoked for life. Marc Maurer, expert analyst and author of *Race to Incarcerate* (New Press), points out that three out of every ten Black males and one in six Latinos born today can expect to do time in prison if current trends continue. African-Americans make up half the prison population, with an increasing number of drug arrests made among nonviolent offenders. Maurer also argues that the $40-billion prison-industrial complex has encroached on funds for higher education.

26   There is also the concern that the educational system teaches young people a racially slanted, warped history of themselves and their place in society. "Next on Third Eye's agenda." says De la Rosa, "is exploring educational reform and reinforcing the allies we've made with teachers, principals and prison activists. We're studying how to frame these issues to have the most statewide appeal." (See its Web site, www.thirdeyemovement.org.)

Is the hip-hop generation going to do something effective to coalesce around 27
these issues? The outlook is still uncertain. "Artists, whether we accept it or not,
are more representative of their labels than they are of a community," says Angela
Ards. But she adds, "The sixties generation saw power as a political thing, and our
generation has come to understand that power is also economic. Mainstream artists
could be using their capital to finance grass-roots movements."

But Bill Stephney puts it another way: "To think that the NAACP, the Urban 28
League and other civil-rights organizations emerged in environments that, particularly for Black people, had nowhere near the level of capital finance and marketing
the hip-hop generation has." In the final analysis, Stephney says, "It's never from
the top down, anyway. It's always from the bottom up. That's the great thing about
'street' and 'neighborhood Black culture'—it grows like a beautiful flower, from the
ground up." So it must be with the hip-hop agenda.

The White Boy Shuffle

Yvonne Bynoe

This article, from the intellectual publication Doula: The Journal of Rap Music
and Hip Hop Culture, *was posted on the Web site of Urban Think Tank Inc.
This company is dedicated to critical analysis of hip-hop, to representing black
Americans' important concerns, and to speaking from the hip-hop generation's
perspective. Yvonne Bynoe, founder of the company, its Web site, and its literary
magazine, is a businesswoman and cultural commentator. Her article addresses
this issue: Many whites enjoy hip-hop music and purchase it in great quantities.
Does that mean that hip-hop music is building racial understanding or are superficial cultural appropriations subtly reinforcing racism?*

For many who may still not know, rap music continues to outsell other gen- 1
res of American music. Since Americans of African descent comprise about 12%
percent of the nation's population, this means that the vast majority of documented rap music buyers are white teenagers. Although white rapper Eminem
has struck platinum with his sophomore album *The Marshall Mathers LP*, and
artists like Kid Rock and the group Limp Bizkit pepper their rock music with
rap, the genre itself is still heavily influenced by the "Black" and Latino youth.
For idealists, white kids buying rap music represents a level of racial understanding and acceptance unknown to their parents. However for realists, this
phenomenon is nothing more than the re-emergence of the White Negro. True
cross-racial engagement necessitates meaningful interaction and buying a CD or
dressing "hip-hop" is not a substitute.

Norman Mailer coined the term "White Negro" in his 1957 essay of the same 2
name when he stated,

> So there was a new breed of adventurers. . . who drifted out at night looking for action with a black man's code to fit their facts. The hipster has absorbed the existentialist synapses of the Negro, and for all practical purposes could be considered a White Negro.

3   Critics of the day aptly pointed out that hipsters adhered to an idea of "black" which itself was based on racial stereotypes. Ned Polsky wrote,

> Even in the world of the hipster, the Negro remains essentially what Ralph Ellison called him—an invisible man. The White Negro accepts the real Negro not as a human being in his totality but as the bringer of a highly specified and restricted 'cultural dowry,' to use Mailer's phrase. In doing so he creates an inverted form of the nigger in his place.

4   In effect the White Negro can only enjoy African-American culture (and exploit it financially) as long as the African-American is deemed by society as different, strange or exotic. The co-opting of African-American characteristics is an act of rebellion against mainstream values. Therefore if African-Americans ever become regarded as an integral part of mainstream society, they would lose the primitive allure that the White Negro attempts to emulate.

5   Billy Wimsatt, a "hip-hop" journalist and activist, who was profiled recently in the *New York Times'* series on race, is indicative of the updated White Negro hipster. Wimsatt is a white boy who doggedly claims an affinity towards "Black" people and an allegiance to hip-hop culture. Wimsatt was looking to escape from the arid confines of his predominately white private school and his upper middle class existence and found his release in rap music and hip-hop culture. Having had little or no interaction with poor (or even middle class) Blacks heretofore, he nevertheless romanticized the pathology of ghetto life and submerged himself into the Black world of "hip-hop." Soon thereafter Wimsatt asked his parents to transfer him to a largely Black public school. According to the *Times* article, Wimsatt "increasingly disconnected from a white culture that he equated with false desires." At the Black public school, Wimsatt noticed that the "cool" kids wore fat sneaker laces, gold jewelry and did graffiti. Soon thereafter, like a bad cliché, Wimsatt began break dancing on the streets and tagging trains with "black and Latino" friends using the street moniker "Upski."

6   For Wimsatt and other White Negroes, Blackness is really more of a projection of their beliefs about "Black" people rather than a true understanding about the humanity of African-Americans. The appeal of rap music and hip-hop culture to the new White Negroes has little to do with African-Americans or their culture. The major interest of these white teenagers is living on the edge. For whites brought up in suburbia or in affluent, homogenous urban neighborhoods, the biggest, nastiest, lustiest, most uninhibited edge they can find in their nearly all white experience is dressing "black," talking "black," walking "black" even as their "black" is a distorted MTV version.

7   Although Wimsatt has attempted to enlighten other whites about Black people and race relations, it has been within the context of his own unrealized prejudices, ignorance and class privilege. Wimsatt's white girlfriend reportedly witnesses

changes in his speech and mannerisms depending on whether the person whom Wimsatt is speaking with is Black or white; with Blacks Wimsatt talks "Black" and/or adopts "Black" mannerisms. These affectations show that Wimsatt primarily identifies "Black" with a particular set of lower socio-economic characteristics i.e., Ebonics, the pimp walk and flashy clothes; at best it is a one-dimensional view of an entire race. Based on Wimsatt's definition of Blackness, he would have little in common with an educated, well-spoken, middle class African-American, since he or she would not conform to his racial precepts. While claiming "he felt Black in every respect but skin color," Wimsatt, the white man, still ruminates about his fear about meeting a "shabbily dressed Black man on the street" and whether or not African-Americans are less intelligent than whites. This self-proclaimed champion for racial equality by his own account did not act when he discovered that he had been paid twice as much as an African-American friend at the same speaking engagement. Wimsatt chose neither to tell the friend of the disparity in fees nor to confront the school that had booked them both. At best Wimsatt is a confused white boy searching for an identity, at worst he is an opportunist. Like Samuel Carter in Wallace Thurman's roman à clef, *Infants of the Spring*, Wimsatt may be using his whiteness among "Blacks" to further his own self-serving agenda. Samuel Carter was intent on becoming a martyr for a radical movement and took up the "Black cause" when he was not advancing quickly enough with the white ones.

> He entered the lists to an arena in which his mediocrity was overlooked because he had assumed the role of a belligerent latter-day abolitionist. He became a white hope, battling for the cause of the American Negro. . . . As a reward for all his vigorous crusading, Samuel soon found himself vociferously acclaimed by Negroes. . . . And what made his role eminently satisfying was the vilification and abuse visited upon him by certain cliques of his fellow whites. At last Samuel had become a martyr.

Billy Wimsatt, the earnest activist for Black justice, the writer of anti-white diatribes at Oberlin College, the proponent for the preservation of a "Black" dominance in rap music and hip-hop culture and the spokesperson for racial harmony unfortunately sounds remarkably like Samuel Carter. 8

In this country's ongoing dialogue about racial equality, the White Negro is just as reactionary as the bigot is. While the bigot openly espouses the inherent inferiority of "Blacks," the White Negro cloaks his biases with noblesse oblige, aiding but not empowering the underclass. The danger of the White Negro is that he is almost indistinguishable from the progressive white person. The true difference however is that the former pays lip service to change but in reality reinforces the status quo, the latter however actually works towards substantive systemic change. The mindset of the White Negro becomes evident when the White Negro extols aberrational social behavior as "authentically" Black, rather than encouraging self-examination, education and community advancement. Case in point was the film *Black and White*, released earlier this year by middle aged, white director James Tobak. Tobak supposedly sought to explore the fascination among affluent white teenagers for hip-hop culture and by extension, the lure of Black sexuality. The film *Black and White* 9 is essentially a conceptual melange of the movies *Kids* and *Jungle Fever,* mixed with the essay "The White Negro.

10   *Black and White* opens with a graphic ménage à trois scene set in Central Park between a Black male and two white girls. The initial shot focuses too long on the gropes, grinds and flushed pink flesh; a rap song that alludes slyly to "daddy's little girl" accompanies these images. Standing guard over the trio is a second, armed Black man. The sum total of Black men in this film is reduced to sexuality and violence. Moreover despite Tobak's avant-garde pretenses, his White Negro tendencies are revealed by his real take on rap music and hip-hop sub-culture. Tobak justifies his use of criminality and violence in his film by saying. "You can't make a movie about hip-hop without dealing with murder." This ignorant statement presupposes that hip-hop is just another Black pathology rather than a vibrant, albeit controversial cultural expression. This movie was hailed by older Black intellectuals like Stanley Crouch and Henry Louis Gates, as realistic and creative, however these critics have no involvement with rap music and know little about the hip-hop aesthete, therefore they were not credible commentators. Hence, this "innovative, ground-breaking film" amounted to little more than a regurgitation of the same old racial stereotypes. Unsurprisingly, the film was a sensation in white circles, but made no impact at all on the hip-hop demographic. It is perfectly valid for a white artist to explore the exploitation and commodification of Black men, by using rap music and hip-hop culture, unless the artist is perpetrating the exact dominate culture myths; that was the case with the film *Black and White.*

11   The White Negro can be reformed if he or she is willing to acknowledge how little he or she really knows about Black people and their lives. From a point of unfamiliarity, the white person opens him- or herself up to actually learning about people of color, rather than rehashing pat generalizations or imbuing "Black" life with starry-eyed sentimentality. The problem with the White Negro is that he or she is already an expert on Blacks, leaving him or her no room to receive additional (or conflicting) information about them. Furthermore, the While Negro insists on speaking to all African-Americans with slang or Ebonics, while the truly progressive white person will approach African-Americans in the same manner and voice that he or she uses with anyone else; for this person "Blackness" is not automatically equated with jive talking hipness.

12   The "Hip-Hop Nation," a term once reserved for African-American and Latino youth, has been expanded to include all races and ethnicities. While the gesture may be both politic and profitable, it negates the protest and social commentary that is the basis for rap music and hip-hop culture. Rap music and hip-hop culture developed in great part to address the feelings of being disenfranchised experienced by Afro-Caribbeans, Afro-Americans and Latinos in America. While whites and other ethnic groups are not exempt from experiencing problems and disillusionment, people of African extraction and Latinos by and large continue to occupy the lower rungs of the socio-economic ladder, comprise the majority of the prison population and confront racial discrimination that impacts employment, housing and educational opportunities. While many whites were offended

with the late 1980s slogan "It's a Black Thing, You Wouldn't Understand" that proliferated on Black college campuses, to a great extent it is true. While Americans of African descent and Latinos must be familiar with the customs, history and values of white Americans in order to succeed in this country, the converse is not true. White Americans can do extremely well in America with little or no interaction with or knowledge of people of color. By reducing the "Hip-Hop Nation" to a modern day version of Kumbaya, White Negroes are never forced to look beyond the "Black" style and language that they have adapted to explore the existences of African-Americans as real people. Moreover when their youth fades, White Negroes ultimately shed their "hip-hop" personas and assume their places in white society, with their biases about African-Americans as "different" largely intact.

Whites and some African-Americans mistakenly believe that deep racial 13 chasms can be eliminated solely through music. Unfortunately African-American culture cannot be taught in a two-minute music video or at the door of Phat Farm, FUBU, Mecca, or Karl Kani. As rap artist KRS-One says, "We've got white boys calling themselves niggers" and in this twisted admiration, white boys are simply seeing Black men as mythologized bodies, overflowing with sexual prowess and privy to a secret code of insider rhythms. Rap music alone does not force white youth to explore the reasons and circumstances behind a rap artist's choice of lyrical content, clothing or demeanor—they simply emulate it because it is "Black" and therefore dangerous and hip. Like their predecessors, these new White Negroes are still objectifying African-Americans to fulfill their own emotional needs and these fantasies about primitives continue to rationalize why these exotics warrant different, if not inferior treatment from whites. The racial divide will be bridged when white people can begin to see Blacks as real, complex human beings, rather than as vehicles to express their own sexual and social rebellion.

Denzel Washington Plays a Bad Guy, and That's Good

Leonard Pitts, Jr.

This op-ed piece, which appeared in the Seattle Times *in fall 2001, takes a stand on the conflicted African American responses to the film* Training Day, *which won Denzel Washington the Academy Award for Best Actor. Leonard Pitts, Jr., is a widely published African American syndicated columnist for the* Miami Herald.

You probably shouldn't read this column.   1

At least, not if you haven't yet seen the new Denzel Washington movie, *Training* 2 *Day.* I'll be giving away a major plot point. So if you want to preserve the element of surprise, turn back now.

3   You see, one spends a good part of the movie trying to figure out whether Washington's character, an LAPD narcotics detective named Alonzo Harris, is a committed cop or a cop who needs to be committed. Is he, in other words, a good cop whose unorthodox and even illegal methods are necessary to the dirty task at hand, or is he just a swaggering bully whose moral compass slipped down the sewer a long time ago?

4   The answer—last chance to turn back, folks—is the latter. Alonzo is downright evil. He's also, as near as I can tell, Washington's first truly malevolent role and the actor tears into it with the unadulterated joy of a starving man into prime rib. He makes Alonzo an utterly convincing villain.

5   For some people, that's a problem.

6   I saw *Training Day* at a preview screening at a convention for black journalists in August. Afterward, there was a question-and-answer session with director Antoine Fuqua. The gist of it: How could Fuqua, who is black, make a movie that offered such a "negative" portrayal of a black man? One woman pronounced herself disturbed at seeing Washington cast as a villain.

7   I felt the director's pain. Hey, if Antoine Fuqua or anybody else made a movie that cast aspersions on black men, I'd be the first to raise a ruckus. But *Training Day* doesn't indict black men, plural. It indicts a black man, singular. It's a measure of black folks' hypersensitivity to insult that some of us don't see the difference.

8   That hypersensitivity, of course, has firm roots in reality. Hollywood has historically depicted blacks in the crudest, most insulting terms. We were either desexed or oversexed, book dumb or street smart, lazy or, well, lazy. We were congenitally criminal, born ballplayers and unable to enter a room without dancing. And it was tacitly understood that if you'd met one, you'd met them all.

9   It's a depiction that hasn't changed nearly enough.

10   Which makes it a tricky thing to be conscientious, black and in the public eye. You must forever balance your aspirations and tastes, your very individuality, against that historical backdrop, against the understanding that your behavior—if it appears to corroborate stereotypes—will invariably be generalized to the group. You have to understand that you represent something larger than yourself.

11   It can be an ennobling burden, but it's a burden nevertheless. Consider Sidney Poitier, the first—and for years, the only—major African-American film star to enjoy wide popularity with white audiences. Because of that distinction he became, in effect, less an actor than an ambassador. And though Poitier did it well and though it was necessary, it's still sobering to think of what that must have cost him in terms of personal prerogative—if only his right as an actor to choose roles solely on the basis of whether they interested him. It's worth noting that, over the course of 52 years in cinema, Poitier has virtually never played the bad guy.

12   Robert DeNiro gets to play the bad guy. Jack Nicholson, too. But Sidney Poitier couldn't.

13   Worse, if an auditorium full of black folk is to be believed, Denzel Washington can't, either. That's the troubling part, the idea that arguably the biggest African-American film star of the millennium would be constrained by the same concerns that bedeviled his counterpart 35 years ago. I mean, Washington has played cops, coaches and military men. He's been Malcolm X, Hurricane Carter, and he's even been an angel. Yet, he can't be a bad guy?

I'm not naive. I understand that, to some degree a black actor still owes certain 14 things to black people. But, that said, the '60s are over. So maybe it's time we talked a little about the things all black people owe one another—and the things they don't.

If Sidney Poitier's life means anything, it means Denzel Washington ought to be 15 allowed to play a scoundrel. It means he has that right, he has that freedom.

Wasn't that the idea all along?   16

The False Promise of Being First
Ellis Cose

In this Newsweek *editorial following the 2002 Academy Awards, Ellis Cose challenges the idea that winning awards and fame in films really breaks down racial barriers. Ellis Cose is an eminent African American author, editor, and columnist who has held prominent positions with the* New York Daily News, *the* Chicago Sun-Times, *and* Newsweek. *He is author of eight books, among them* The Rage of a Privileged Class *(1994) and* Color-Blind: Seeing Beyond Race in a Race-Obsessed World *(1997).*

"For 40 years, I've been chasing Sidney." That was Denzel Washington's way of 1 noting the nearly four-decade drought endured by black leading men between Sidney Poitier's best-acting Oscar and his own. Yet Washington's wait is nothing compared with that of Clifton R. Wharton Jr.: it took America 96 years to make him the second African-American to head a big, predominantly white university.

The first was Patrick Healy, the son of a mixed-race slave and the Irish immi- 2 grant who bought her and made her his wife (or some approximation thereof in an age when miscegenation was illegal). Healy earned a Ph.D. in Belgium and became president of Georgetown University in 1874. When Wharton assumed the presidency of Michigan State University in 1970, the press made much the same fuss over him that was made last week over Washington. "Local and national reporters scrambled to cover me . . . ," Wharton recalls, "and the broader significance of a Negro who had breached the walls of another barrier."

But what, in fact, *is* the larger significance of Wharton's becoming the first African- 3 American in the 20th century to run such a place? Or of Washington's becoming the second black man in this century to get a best-actor Oscar? Or of Halle Berry's becoming the first black woman ever to win the world's top acting prize? What, in the scheme of things, does such trailblazing represent, especially if the trail has to be blazed all over again 39 or 96 years later? Berry's dramatic, tearful acceptance speech tried to put it in perspective. She dedicated her award, her moment, to "every nameless, faceless woman of color that now has a chance because this door tonight has been opened."

As I sat watching Berry, I found myself thinking of Marlee Matlin, whose pow- 4 erful performance as Sarah in *Children of a Lesser God* garnered the best-actress Oscar in 1987. In a scene every bit as touching—if not as hysterical—as Berry's,

Matlin signed "I love you" to the audience. As Matlin became the first deaf person so honored, there was the poignant sense of a closed door's being opened. No doubt, a barrier *was* broken. For Matlin has gone on to have a career unlike any deaf actress before her. But there hasn't exactly been a parade of deaf actresses claiming Academy Awards. Nor has there been an explosion of starring roles for the hearing impaired. How different will things be with Berry?

5   Perhaps that is not the point. Whether or not people follow trailblazers' paths, they can still draw pride and inspiration from their accomplishments—a point made by I. King Jordan, the first deaf president of Gallaudet University, the Washington-based institution serving the deaf.

6   "I am continually amazed how my achievement has raised the ambitions, the levels of self-expectation, of deaf people, especially deaf children," Jordan says. "And the fact is, since 1988, the number of deaf Ph.D.s, lawyers, stockbrokers, entrepreneurs and other professionals has increased dramatically. Our successful struggle showed that it's far more important to focus on the many things deaf people can do, not on the one thing they cannot."

7   Fair enough. We can all applaud when some deserving soul becomes the first of his or her kind to achieve a worthy goal. As Wharton put it, "breakthroughs are important." He should know, since his résumé is a catalog of firsts: first black to head a large university system (the State University of New York); first to head a major foundation (as chair of the Rockefeller Foundation); first to lead a huge company (when he became CEO of Teachers Insurance and Annuity Association, College Retirement Equities Fund, in 1987). But as Wharton readily acknowledges, being first is only a small part of the battle: "It's great to be one, but I'd like to see more twos, threes, fours and fives."

8   Indeed, uncelebrated though they may be, the fours and fives are a lot more important than the ones. For though the firsts may be glittering paragons of individual accomplishment, they are, by definition, also onlys. Time alone will resolve the question of whether they are more than that, whether they merit the weight we tend to give them—whether they, in other words, bring us any closer to the day when firsts become irrelevant because recognition of ability, wherever it resides, has finally become routine.

Save the Labels for the Category of Achievement

Ron Aiken

In this letter to the editor of the Seattle Times *commenting on Denzel Washington's Oscar at the 2002 Academy Awards, Ron Aiken urges Americans to forget about race and focus on artistic merit.*

Did anybody in the media listen to Denzel Washington when asked by a re- 1
porter backstage at the Oscars if he ever envisioned a time when it would not be
news that an African American received an Oscar? He replied with two questions:
Are you with the news media? If so, how about starting right now?

His point was absolutely on the mark. As long as the media continue to identify 2
newsworthy people by their race or religion, the perception of differences and prejudices will continue. Meanwhile, the day following the Oscars, The *Times* runs major
stories about the race of the best actor and actress ("Black and Gold: Academy
gives top acting Oscars to African Americans," *Times,* March 25). Obviously, The
Times feels this is important, so I would like to suggest follow-up stories with the
following "firsts":

- Skinny, balding, red-headed former childhood actor receives first Oscar for Best
  Director.
- Middle-aged, slightly overweight white guy receives first Oscar for musical score.
- Drop-dead-gorgeous 30-something brunette with no cleavage receives first Best
  Supporting Actress Oscar.
- Left-wing liberal superstar awards honorary Oscar to Robert Redford.

Of course these examples are ridiculous, but no more than the emphasis the me- 3
dia continue to place on the race of the winners. Here's a novel concept. How about
emphasizing the winners' artistic accomplishments? Forget about their race, religion,
age or politics and concentrate on what it was the artists did to earn their award.

Monster's Mask

Steven Mitchell

In this letter to the editor, also from the Seattle Times, *and also responding to
the 2002 Oscars, Steven Mitchell argues that the 2002 Academy Awards actually reinforced racism by celebrating Denzel Washington and Halle Berry playing
roles that disturbed and misrepresented the black community.*

Black Americans who are proud that two black actors finally won Academy 1
Awards for their performances last year desperately need de-programming. I was
outraged that the awards were given for movies that demean blacks, rather than for
movies that blacks can be proud of.

Training Day is offensive to blacks on many different levels. Depictions of a 2
rogue black cop defy the statistics, the probability, and the reality of police brutality
in this nation. White cops "go rogue" far more often than black cops, all things being equal, simply because there are more of them, as evidenced by the death of

Amadou Diallo, the sodomization of Abner Louima, the assassination of the just-elected black sheriff in the South. Seattle blacks do not have to look beyond their local community to see the reality that white cops kill black men for sport.

3   In contrast, Denzel Washington's portrayal of civil rights activist "Malcolm X" was both riveting and unforgettable. It was not even nominated.

4   Halle Berry's *Monster's Ball* and Hattie McDaniels' *Gone with the Wind* have much in common when examining Hollywood's penchant for black actors and actresses who play subservient roles to their white counterparts. Not because the prison population in this country is overwhelmingly black. Not because the death penalty is not applied equally among the races, but disproportionately given more often to blacks. It is because it is not possible for a woman to be more subservient to a man than for her to sleep with the man who killed her husband. It is the *Birth of a Nation* all over again.

5   This year's awards were actually a backhanded slap in the face to black Americans and the black movie-going public in an attempt to recognize blacks' contribution to the bottom line of theatres, while giving white audiences the satisfaction of seeing blacks in roles they cannot respect.

For Class Discussion

1. Several of the articles in this unit speculate about the enthusiastic white response to hip-hop music; some of these articles equate white appropriation of hip-hop music and culture with stealing. What reasons do these articles give for hip-hop's popularity with white listeners and for the increasing popularity of white rap artists? Which reasons seem the most convincing to you? What reasons of your own explain this phenomenon?

2. Although hip-hop music and films are meant to be entertaining, the underlying theory of many arguments in this unit is that these art forms convey serious social and political messages about racial identity and race relations. Working individually or in groups, choose one or more articles from this unit that persuade you that art forms can have a real-world impact. How do hip-hop artists or films about race shape your vision of the world (for instance, of social class, urban life, ethnic groups) and affect your actions? Can you recall a film, a song, or a rap artist or actor that profoundly influenced your view of society?

3. Some cultural critics assert that commercial success has diminished the cultural force and even creative energy of hip-hop music. How do the arguments in this unit support or contest this point? According to these articles, have other forces also negatively affected hip-hop music?

4. Some articles also suggest that rap artists and actors value individual success over responsibility to their art or their racial group. Working individually or in groups, list the reasons in favor of individual artistic and commercial freedom and then those in favor of social and racial responsibility.

OPTIONAL WRITING ASSIGNMENT   Write an op-ed piece for your university or local newspaper in which you respond to one of the arguments in this unit, either by agreeing with the writer and taking the ideas further or in a new direction, or by disagreeing with the writer. You can write from your own experiences: your personal preferences for and knowledge of contemporary popular music; your movie-going background; your ethnic or regional background. (For an example of how a white female student wrote about rap music from her own experience, see Tiffany Anderson's evaluation argument in Chapter 14, pp. 310–313.)

GENDER AND TECHNOLOGY IN ADVERTISING

In 1979, Erving Goffman, an influential sociologist, theoretician, and author of the book *Gender Advertisements*, argued that advertisements often depict women in frivolous, childlike, sexual, or silly poses that would be considered unacceptable and unbecoming for men. The effect of these depictions is to make women decorative and irrelevant, removed from serious power and serious attention. Even in advertisements that seem to depict women in a positive light, Goffman found that subtle details—such as body position, gesture, and setting—undermined women's power and independence and reinforced women's subordination. Although styles of advertising have changed, some cultural critics continue to find images of women in advertising problematic.

In this unit, we direct your attention to one of the biggest new areas of consumer goods—business technology and computers. How do advertisers market products related to office equipment, computers, information technology, and communication? Is there a difference between the way men and women are portrayed in the advertisements for these products? Are women depicted positively as serious professionals and competent users, or do these ads subtly undermine women's power and importance, as Goffman observed in earlier advertising? To help you with your examination of the persuasiveness of these ads, you may want to refer to the principles for using type, layout, and color and the questions for analyzing a photograph or drawing discussed in Chapter 9, "Conducting Visual Arguments."

This is Automatic Xerography
Haloid Xerox

This ad for Haloid Xerox proclaims the speed, capabilities, and low cost of an early generation of copy machines. What features of the images and the composition of this ad suggest the business world of the 1950s?

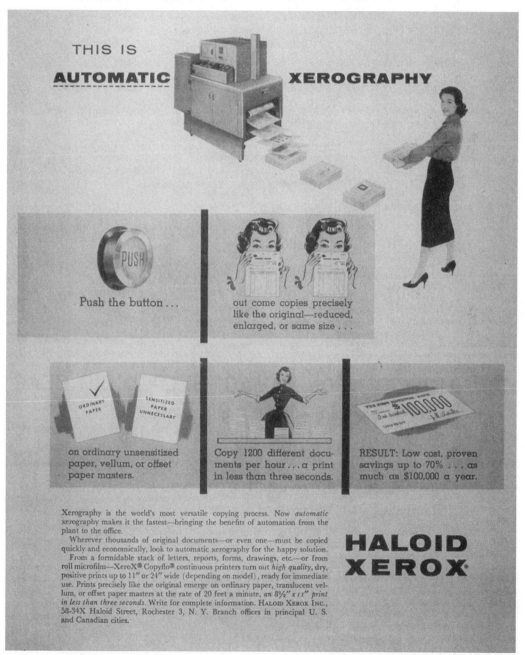

Like Magellan, Grady Has Pioneered a Global Network and Maria Hates Computers

FedEx Express

Part of a larger campaign that is currently popular and that has been appearing in magazines like Newsweek, *the next two ads strike a personal note while they seek to inspire complete confidence in the product. What are the narrative strategies they use to appeal to a range of people?*

Like Magellan,
Grady has pioneered
a global network.

Unlike Magellan, Grady has
access to key information
about international shipping.

Like Magellan, Grady is
proving pretty darn popular
with the headhunters.

©2002 FedEx.

Even globetrotting pioneers need an inside scoop. Psssst. Check out **FedEx Global Trade Manager,**™ powerful web-based tools that help you ship confidently all over the planet. Get important trade and embargo updates. Estimate duties and taxes. Download important customs forms and documents. Suddenly, the whole world seems to want you. Just try not to get a big head. Seeking safe passage around the world?
Don't worry. There's a FedEx for that.™

fedex.com

Express

So you're not exactly a digital mastermind, right? Not a problem. With **fedex.com**, your computer skills need hardly apply. Track packages. Prepare shipping labels and access critical shipping info. Store up to 1000 addresses and check account specific rate quotes. All with the greatest of ease. See? That wasn't so hard. Looking to simplify your shipping? **Don't worry. There's a FedEx for that.**[SM]

fedex.com

Try a MIT's Magazine of Innovation
Technology Review Digital Subscription
Technology Review

This ad for a digital subscription to Technology Review *features a man dressed casually and working on his laptop, most likely reading his digital subscription. How does this ad convey self-confidence and competence with technology?*

This ad for Siemens, a company producing state-of-the-art business communication systems, appeared in Fortune *magazine on October 28, 2002. Like many effective ads featuring the latest technology for business, this one plays with the idea of redefining work spaces. What is the dominant impression the image of the woman in this ad projects?*

For Class Discussion

1. Working individually or in groups, compare the following points in each of the ads: descriptions of the product; settings (room or scene) and the colors and objects in this scene; position, clothing, and appearance of the model in the ad; and the explicit or implicit relationship between the model and his/her use of the product. For help in examining the details of each ad, you might refer to the principles of visual design and points for analyzing images in Chapter 9, pages 166–172.

2. Commercial ads, like full-text arguments, make appeals to *logos, ethos,* and *pathos.* Choose several of the ads in this unit and compare the verbal-visual textual strategies they use to convey their argument, portray the company or product's reliability and quality, and tap the emotions and imagination of readers/viewers. (The core of the argument in each case will be some variant of "X product is excellent or superior and you should buy it because . . .). What role particularly does *pathos* play in each ad?

3. Rank these ads according to the degree of technological competence and business status/professionalism that they ascribe to the person featured in the ad. Which person in which ad comes across as most knowledgeable about his/her work and most competent with the technological equipment? Which seems least? Do any of these ads exemplify Goffman's theory that ads often subtly undermine women's status and power?

4. Scholars and organizations like the American Association of University Women Educational Foundation claim to have discovered a gender gap regarding technology—that is, that boys and men are assumed to be, and often are, more comfortable with digital technologies than girls and women and that the percentage of men holding high-tech jobs far exceeds that of women. Do you think the ads in this unit validate these claims? Additionally, do you think these ads help perpetuate the technology gap? On your own, find several ads for business equipment and computer technology in business and news commentary magazines, and determine whether they reinforce these claims or counter them.

OPTIONAL WRITING ASSIGNMENT   The AAUW's Commission on Technology, Gender, and Teacher Education concluded in its study *Tech-Savvy: Educating Girls in the New Computer Age* (2000) (see www.aauw.org) that girls' lack of interest in computer technology may derive in part from computer games and software that either ignore girls' interests (by featuring violent, "high-kill" elements) or fall into the category of "pink software" (by featuring games exclusively and stereotypically for girls). Research on your own the kinds of computer software or computer games marketed specifically for girls. (You might use the keywords "girls," "technology," and "computer games" with your favorite search engine to find sites like Mattel, Girl Tech, and Her Interactive.) What gender images do the games produced by these companies convey? To what extent do these games develop critical thinking, technical skills, and interest in computer technology? To what extent do they encourage action and independence versus superficiality and passivity? After analyzing a site or a specific computer game, write an evaluation argument intended for a popular family magazine in which you argue that this site or specific game is or is not helpful in encouraging girls' competence and engagement with technology.

MARRIAGE AND FAMILY IN THE NEW MILLENNIUM

You can get a quick overview of the central issues of this unit by looking at two Web sites: the National Marriage Project (http://marriage.rutgers.edu) and the Alternatives to Marriage Project (http://www.unmarried.org). The National Marriage Project, headed by sociologists David Popenoe and Barbara Defoe Whitehead, is a research organization housed at Rutgers University. According to its Web site, its mission is "to strengthen the institution of marriage" through research and analysis aimed at influencing public policy. In contrast, the Alternatives to Marriage Project, founded in 1998 by Marshall Miller and Dorian Solot in response to the National Marriage Project, celebrates a variety of social arrangements that fall outside the pattern of traditional marriage and family. The "About Us" link on their Web site says that the Alternatives to Marriage Project, although supportive of those who choose to marry, "advocates for equality and fairness of unmarried people, including people who choose not to marry, cannot marry, or live together before marriage."

At issue, then, is what vision we should project for marriage and family in the new millennium. The Bush administration, influenced by the National Marriage Project as well as by conservative think tanks such as the Heritage Foundation, has instituted federal policies to discourage cohabitation and premarital sex and to encourage traditional families as foundations of a stable society. Social conservatives also tend to oppose gay marriage, gay adoption, and reproductive technologies that blur the genetic boundaries of traditional parenthood. Social liberals, on the other hand, raise numerous objections to the conservative view. Meanwhile, many young persons today are avoiding or delaying marriage (see the discussion and tables in Chapter 9, pp. 189–193).

The readings in this unit will help you join this national conversation as well as think through your own views of marriage and family.

Restoring a Culture of Marriage: Good News for Policymakers from the Fragile Families Survey

Patrick Fagan and Jennifer Garrett

This white paper from the Heritage Foundation provides an overview of the Bush administration's social policies for promoting marriage. It also shows how sociological research conducted by universities, as well as by public or private think tanks, can enter the public arena to influence government policy. Patrick Fagan is a research fellow in family and cultural issues at the Heritage Foundation. Jennifer Garrett, who holds a masters degree in public administration and policy, is a research associate in domestic and economic policy at the Heritage Foundation. This white paper was posted on the foundation's Web site on June 13, 2002.

President George W. Bush has taken the first bold step in reshaping federal pol-   1
icy to address the root cause of many of society's ills: the breakdown of the married, two-parent family. Specifically, he has requested nearly $300 million a year in the reauthorization of the Temporary Assistance for Needy Families (TANF) Act for efforts that promote marriage.

Though critics of the proposal claim that most single parents do not have   2
strong desires or the wherewithal to marry, most of their assertions are to a large extent unfounded. As recently released data from an ongoing longitudinal survey of new parents show, a majority of unwed mothers and fathers not only have a strong desire to marry, but also believe the chances are good that they will. What these new parents need is more encouragement and preparation to realize their hopes.

The first round of data from the Fragile Families and Child Wellbeing Study[1]—   3
a four-year project of Princeton University's Center for Research on Child Wellbeing and Columbia University's Social Indicators Survey Center—already shows the promising potential for federal-state efforts to reduce out-of-wedlock births, especially among the poor. For example, according to the survey:[2]

- Contrary to public opinion, the overwhelming majority of children born out of wedlock have parents who are living together or who are romantically involved or seeing each other on a regular basis; they are not born to single mothers with absentee fathers.

- Moreover, a majority of unwed mothers say they are interested in marrying the father and believe they have a 50 percent chance of doing so, and an even greater percentage of these fathers believe their chances to be the same.

Thus, there exists within fragile families a very large group of parents who are   4
likely to participate in programs that would prepare them for marriage.

Members of Congress should study these survey data carefully in considering the   5
President's request for marriage-related funding in the reauthorization of TANF. As the authors of the preliminary national report on the findings suggest, policymakers could use the data to "design programs that encourage—rather than undermine—the efforts of new parents to raise healthy children, maintain self-sufficiency, and make productive contributions to their communities."[3] By funding initiatives that educate people on the benefits of marriage and encourage unwed parents to acquire the skills for stable marriages, Congress can jump start the process of rebuilding a culture of marriage in America and improving the prospects for millions of America's most fragile families.

WHAT THE FRAGILE FAMILIES SURVEY SHOWS

The Fragile Families and Child Wellbeing Study is designed to provide longi-   6
tudinal data on the conditions and capabilities of new unmarried parents and the

consequences of these factors on their children's well-being.[4] The survey, which follows a cohort of newborn children over the first four years of life, finished conducting the baseline interviews on a nationally representative sample of almost 5,000 mothers and 4,000 fathers in 20 cities—including a group of married parents in each city for comparison—by the fall of 2000.[5]

7   As the Fragile Families Study Web site explains, the survey's findings can address three primary issues of great interest today: out-of-wedlock childbearing, welfare reform, and the role of fathers in a child's well-being.[6] As many studies point out, many children who are born out of wedlock and spend some time on welfare with little support from their fathers experience behavioral problems and do poorly in school. Clearly, policymakers have reason to examine not only the causes of family breakdown that impose such heavy costs on children and society, but also the very policies they enact that actually undermine the formation of two-parent families.

KEY FINDINGS ON MARRIAGE AND COMMITMENT

8   One of the most significant findings in the preliminary report on the first follow-up interviews is that many of the unwed parents of the children in the study are committed to each other.[7] Specifically:

- 83 percent of unwed mothers reported being romantically involved with the father at the time of their child's birth and are either cohabiting (50 percent) or seeing each other frequently each week (33 percent).[8]
- 73 percent of unmarried mothers and 88 percent of the fathers of their children believed they had a 50-50 chance of marrying each other.[9]
- 64 percent of the unmarried mothers and 73 percent of the fathers agreed or strongly agreed that marriage is better for children.[10]
- 84 percent of the unmarried mothers and 93 percent of the fathers said they put the father's name on the child's birth certificate.[11]
- 79 percent of the unmarried mothers and 89 percent of the fathers said the child would use the father's surname.[12]
- 93 percent of the unwed mothers reported that they wanted the father involved in raising their child.[13] Furthermore, all of the cohabiting fathers and 96 percent of fathers romantically attached to the mothers but not living with them said they intended to stay involved with their child.[14]
- A majority of the unmarried mothers (65 percent) identified "showing love and affection to the child" as the most important quality the father could offer the child. Nearly half of the fathers ranked this quality first (49 percent), and only 12 percent of these couples said that providing financial support was the most important contribution the father could make to the child.[15]

9   The pattern of positive attitudes toward marriage that emerges for these parents is encouraging. The majority intended to marry and believed marriage is important for the welfare of their child. Of particular interest, and contrary to common rhetoric,

is the fact that fathers were even more likely to report a positive outlook on marriage than the mothers were.

KEY FINDINGS ON DOMESTIC VIOLENCE

There is good news in these initial data on the incidence of domestic violence in fragile families, which also suggests that these unmarried parents are more likely to marry:

- Only 5 percent of unmarried mothers said that the child's father was violent, and only 6.7 percent said that the fathers had drug or alcohol problems.[16]
- The rate of reported abuse was lowest among those who intended to marry and who did not cohabit (1.6 percent).[17]
- The rate of abuse was the same among parents cohabiting with an intention of marrying (2.2 percent) as among those parents in the control group who did marry (2.3 percent).[18]
- The rate of abuse is more than four times higher among those who cohabit and do not intend to marry or who think it is unlikely they will marry (9.3 percent) than among those who cohabit and intend to marry (2.2 percent).[19]
- Among romantically involved ("visiting") couples who do not intend to marry and who do not live together, the rate of abuse is more than four times higher (7.4 percent) than among those who are romantically involved and intend to marry (1.6 percent).[20] There is no significant difference between the rates for cohabitors and visitors with plans to marry and married parents.

KEY FINDINGS ON EMPLOYMENT, EARNINGS, AND EDUCATION

There is also good news in the data with regard to the earnings potential of fragile families—a factor that could contribute to a decision to marry. For example:

- 66 percent of the fathers and 63 percent of the unwed mothers had a high school education or more.[21]
- 98 percent of the fathers had worked in the previous year, and 72 percent had worked in the week prior to the survey.[22]
- The fathers who were living with the baby's mother earned on average $3,000 more per year than the romantically involved fathers who were not living with the baby's mother.[23]

THE POTENTIAL FOR MARRIAGE

Based on various reports of the Fragile Families survey data posted on the study's Web site, it is possible to summarize factors that indicate which unwed parents would be more likely to marry. These factors include the following:

- The unwed parents intend to marry and either live together or are romantically involved.

- The father's last name is on the child's birth certificate.
- Both parents want the father to remain involved with his child.
- Both parents believe the father's most important contribution is to show the child his affection.
- Both the father and mother have completed high school.
- The father is working.

13   The more these factors are present in a couple, the more likely it is that they will be good candidates for marriage preparation or support programs. The number of those who are clearly not good marriage prospects—couples with fathers who are abusive to their mates or who use drugs—is actually relatively small.

ARE EXPECTATIONS TOO HIGH?

14   Although the majority of unmarried parents surveyed for the Fragile Families Study believe that marriage is most advantageous for their children, various researchers report that their expectations for marriage frequently are not borne out by what actually occurs. For example, while 46 percent of mothers interviewed before their child's birth intended to marry the father, only about 24 percent did. And whereas only 28 percent of mothers had intended to cohabit with the father after the child's birth, 35 percent actually did.[24]

15   These findings should be seen not as discouraging, but as confirming the need to address the impact of federal and state policies so that they provide encouragement and skills training rather than act as a hindrance to the poor who want to marry. The President's proposals would help to fill this need.

LESSONS FROM WELFARE REFORM

16   Social policy matters. Perhaps the best example of how bad social policy encourages the kinds of behaviors it is meant to eliminate is the old system of welfare that Congress wisely reformed in 1996. Following the success of Wisconsin's reforms that tied welfare benefits to work, Temporary Assistance for Needy Families funding allowed the states to focus on those people on the rolls who were most likely to find and hold a job. In Wisconsin, this approach had quickly reduced caseloads by about one-third;[25] after that initial success, Wisconsin was able to focus resources on those who needed more help to move from dependency to work.

17   A similar approach makes sense for restoring a culture of marriage among unwed parents in fragile families, most of whom are likely to be receiving some government benefits. As the findings from the Fragile Families Study demonstrate, it is possible to identify which unwed parents are most marriageable in order to focus resources on programs that would help them acquire the skills and support they need for a successful marriage.[26]

THE PRESIDENT'S PROPOSALS

Because he recognizes the benefits of stable unions for parents, children, and the nation, President Bush hopes to make rebuilding a culture of marriage a focus of national policy. His current initiative requests nearly $300 million in federal and state TANF money to target state-level programs that promote marriage and marriage skills, particularly among fragile families. [18]

The initial findings of the Fragile Families Survey indicate that not only do most unwed mothers have a strong desire to marry the father of their child, but they believe they have a fair chance of doing so.[27] The President's proposals would provide the encouragement many of these parents need. It specifically requests funds for:[28] [19]

- Public advertising campaigns on the value of marriage and the skills that increase marital stability and health.
- High school education on the value of marriage, relationship skills, and budgeting.
- Marriage and relationship skills programs that include parenting skills, financial management, conflict resolution, and job and career advancement for non-married pregnant women and non-married expectant fathers.
- Premarital education and marriage skills training for engaged couples and couples interested in marriage.
- Marriage enhancement and marriage skills training programs for married couples.
- Divorce reduction programs that teach relationship skills.
- Marriage mentoring programs that use married couples as role models and mentors in at-risk communities.
- Programs to reduce the disincentives to marriage in means-tested aid programs if offered in conjunction with any activity described above.

President Bush's proposal also would enable the U.S. Department of Health and Human Services, as well as the states, local governments, and private organizations, to better understand how public policy can promote families in which children's well-being is secure. [20]

HOW CONGRESS CAN HELP

The findings of the Fragile Families Survey shatter the myths that most unwed mothers and fathers are uninvolved and that most unwed fathers do not care about their children's well-being. More important, the data show that the majority of these unmarried parents are romantically involved, are interested in marriage, consider their chances of getting married good, and agree that a two-parent married family is better for their child than a single-parent family. [21]

Congress clearly has an opportunity, in reauthorization of the Temporary Assistance for Needy Families Act, to use this research to fund programs that support marriage. The need for such action is further indicated by a May 6 Opinion [22]

Research Corporation poll, which found that Americans overwhelmingly believe that out-of-wedlock births harm children, families, and communities.[29]

To jump start the process of rebuilding fragile families, Congress should:

- **Approve** the President's request for $300 million per year in TANF funding for initiatives that encourage and support marriage.
- **Disregard** the straw-man objection that the President's proposal would lead to an increase in domestic violence. The Fragile Families findings indicate that the incidence of domestic violence is minimal among unwed parents who intend to marry.
- **Seek** to reduce the penalties on marriage that remain in means-tested federal welfare programs. These include penalties in the Earned Income Tax Credit (EITC) and on the receipt of food stamps and public housing and other programs that reduce benefits according to household income, thereby discouraging couples from marrying.[30]

CONCLUSION

23   Members of Congress should recognize from the wealth of social science research that the most effective way to reduce child poverty and increase child well-being is to increase the number of stable two-parent married families. The findings of the Princeton University and Columbia University Fragile Families and Child Wellbeing Study show that many unwed mothers have high expectations for the future of their children and their own chances of marrying their child's father. The findings show that a majority of unwed fathers want to be involved in their child's life and also have hopes for marriage.

24   It is time for Congress to implement policies and programs that would help such couples make a permanent commitment to each other and their children, and begin reaping the emotional, health, educational, social, and economic benefits of marriage. In reauthorizing the TANF Act, Congress should include the $300 million per year for marriage-based programs that meet the President's standards.

Notes

1. The Fragile Families Survey and the reports based on it and cited here can be found at the Center for Research on Child Wellbeing Web site, http://crcw.princeton.edu/fragilefamilies/index.htm. The term "fragile families" underscores the fact that unmarried parents and their children are at greater risk for poverty and behavioral problems than are two-parent married families. The survey follows newborns and their parents over four years. Data reported here reflect baseline interviews on these children and their parents that were completed by the fall of 2000.

2. See Sara McLanahan, Irwin Garfinkel, Nancy E. Reichman, Julien Teitler, Marcia Carlson, and Christina Norland Audigier, The Fragile Families and Child Wellbeing Study Baseline Report: The National Report, Center for Research on Child Wellbeing, August 2001, reporting their "preliminary national estimates," Table 2. Cited hereafter as National Report.

3. Ibid.

4. Ibid., Table 1. For additional information on this subject, see also Robert Rector, Kirk A. Johnson, Ph.D., and Patrick F. Fagan, "The Effects of Marriage on Child Poverty," Heritage Foundation Center for Data Analysis Report No. CDA02-04. April 15, 2002, at www.heritage.org/library/cda/cda02-04.html.

5. Baseline interviews for the Fragile Families and Child Wellbeing Study have been conducted in 75 hospitals in 20 cities across the United States: Austin, Corpus Christi, and San Antonio, Texas; Baltimore, Maryland; Boston, Massachusetts; Chicago, Illinois; Detroit, Michigan; Indianapolis, Indiana; Jacksonville, Florida; Milwaukee, Wisconsin; Nashville, Tennessee; Newark, New Jersey; New York, New York; Norfolk and Richmond, Virginia; Oakland and San Jose, California; Philadelphia and Pittsburgh, Pennsylvania; and Toledo, Ohio.

6. See Fragile Families Survey, "Study Design," at http://crcw.princeton.edu/fragilefamilies/index.htm.

7. See McLanahan et al., National Report, p. 3. The authors report the survey findings for interviews of 2,670 unmarried couples in 16 cities.

8. Ibid., Table 2. The findings reflect the level of cohabiting depending on who was being interviewed: mothers alone, mothers in the company of the fathers, or fathers alone.

9. Ibid.

10. Ibid.

11. Ibid., Table 3.

12. Ibid.

13. Bendheim-Thoman Center for Research on Child Wellbeing and Social Indicators Survey Center, "Dispelling Myths about Unmarried Fathers," Fragile Families Research Brief No. 1, May 2000.

14. Bendheim-Thoman Center for Research on Child Wellbeing and Social Indicators Survey Center, "Father Involvement, Maternal Health Behavior and Infant Health," Fragile Families Research Brief No. 5, January 2001.

15. McLanahan et al., National Report, Table 4.

16. Bendheim-Thoman Center for Research on Child Wellbeing and Social Indicators Survey Center, "Dispelling Myths about Unmarried Fathers."

17. Cynthia Osborne, "A New Look at Unmarried Families: Diversity in Human Capital, Attitudes and Relationship Quality," Center for Research on Child Wellbeing Working Paper No. 02-02-FF, April 2002, Table 4, p. 25. Cited with permission. "Abuse" here includes both physical and emotional abuse. Later studies intend to separate these data.

18. Ibid. These data are similar to findings from the 1999 National Crime Victimization Survey, in which women with children under 12 years of age experienced domestic violence at a rate of 3.8 per 1,000, compared with 32.9 per 1,000 for their never-married peers. See Patrick F. Fagan and Kirk Johnson, Ph.D., "Marriage: The Safest Place for Women and Children," Heritage Foundation Backgrounder No. 1535, April 10, 2002, at http://www.heritage.org/library/backgrounder/bg1535.html.

19. Osborne, "A New Look at Unmarried Families."

20. Ibid.

21. McLanahan et al., National Report, Table 1.

22. Ibid.

23. Bendheim-Thoman Center for Research on Child Wellbeing and Social Indicators Survey Center, "Unwed Fathers, the Underground Economy and Child Support Policy," Center for Research on Child Wellbeing Fragile Families Research Brief No. 3, January 2001.

24. Ronald B. Mincey and Allen T. Dupree, "Can the Next Step in Welfare Reform Achieve PRWORA's Fourth Goal? Family Formation in Fragile Families," Center for Research on Child Wellbeing Working Paper No. 00-23-FF, December 2000.

25. Robert E. Rector and Sarah E. Youssef, "The Determinants of Welfare Caseload Decline," Heritage Foundation Center for Data Analysis Report No. CDA99-04, May 11, 1999, at http://www.heritage.org/library/cda/cda99-04.html.

26. Recent reports that the welfare reforms have discouraged marriage do not tell the whole story. See, for example, Nina Bernstein, "Strict Limits on Welfare Benefits Discourage Marriage, Studies Say," *The New York Times* (regional edition), June 3, 2002. It should be noted that the studies reported by the article did not take into account the effects of the stringent penalties in current means-tested programs that couples face if they marry while on welfare.

27. McLanahan et al., National Report, Table 2.

28. As described in H.R. 4737, Section 103, Promotion of Family Formation and Healthy Marriage. The bill, which was passed by the House, was referred to the Senate on May 16, 2002; see http://thomas.loc.gov/cgi-bin/query/D?c107:3:./temp/~c107qCks1C:e18472.

29. As reported in Maggie Gallagher, "Marriage Polls and Pols," at http://www.townhall.com/columnists/maggiegallagher/mg20020515.shtml.

30. See C. Eugene Steuerle, Senior Fellow, Urban Institute, testimony before the Subcommittee on Human Resources, Committee on Ways and Means, U.S. House of Representatives, 107th Cong., 1st Sess., May 22, 2001, at http://waysandmeans.house.gov/humres/107cong/5-22-01/5-22steu.htm.

Statement Regarding Hearing on Welfare and Marriage Issues

Alternatives to Marriage Project

This white paper from the Alternatives to Marriage Project was submitted to the House Committee on Ways and Means, Subcommittee on Human Resources, held May 22, 2001. The purpose of the white paper is to oppose the Bush administration's proposal to use Temporary Assistance to Needy Families (TANF) funds to promote marriage and discourage "illegitimacy."

1   As a national organization for unmarried people, we believe that the use of Temporary Assistance to Needy Families (TANF) funds to promote marriage and discourage "illegitimacy" is not in the best interests of Americans who live in poverty.

2   One family form is marriage, and we agree that marriage should be supported. We believe, however that a marriage-promoting agenda does real damage in a nation whose strength is rooted in diversity and tolerance. We believe that the well-being of children is critical to our nation's future, and that to that end, all families should be valued and all committed relationships supported. We do not believe it is possible for public policy to promote marriage without simultaneously stigmatizing people who are divorced, withholding resources from single parents, shaming unmarried couples, and ignoring the needs of gay, lesbian, and bisexual people for whom marriage is not an option. Such policies disadvantage the children growing up in such families, and deepen social inequality.

The American family is indeed in profound transition. Although divorce rates 3 have receded from their 1981 peak, marriage is not gaining ground. Between 1990 and 2000, the number of families maintained by women without legally married partners in the home increased three times faster than did married-couple families. "Cohabitation is the fastest-growing living arrangement in modern society," observes Johns Hopkins sociologist Andrew Cherlin. It is far from a childless state: scholars Larry Bumpass and Hsien Hen Lu of the University of Wisconsin note that, "a large share of children born to supposedly 'single' mothers today are born into two-parent households." These mothers are legally single, but are living and parenting together with an unmarried partner.

Although much of the testimony delivered at your subcommittee meeting paints 4 a bleak portrait of these families, in reality there are millions of happy, healthy, unmarried families whose members are neither "illegitimate" nor a threat to the social fiber of our country. The notion that somehow compelling them to marry as a social cure-all is simplistic and unrealistic. Longer lifespans, the economic independence of women, and later ages at marriage have all contributed to reducing the importance of marriage in everyday life. This is true in nearly every industrial nation, not just the United States.

"Under these circumstances, putting all our eggs in the leaky basket of a cam- 5 paign to reinstitutionalize marriage is a risky strategy and may even backfire," writes family historian Stephanie Coontz in *Newsday* (5/27/01, page B8). Abundant research shows that the children of teen moms who marry the father after birth often do worse than those whose marital status remains unchanged, probably because the basis for the marriage is not a sound one. Researchers overwhelmingly agree that high-conflict marriages can do more damage to children than divorce. Promoting marriage is an appealing quick fix that ignores the deep complexity of family quality and process, which turn out to be far more important to children's well-being than family form.

The real question here is what do real-world American families need in order to 6 thrive? We believe that the first item on the agenda should be to reduce the economic stresses that contribute far more than any other factor to family instability. Consider the Minnesota Family Investment Program (MFIP), which allowed parents on welfare to continue to collect benefits as long as their earnings did not go over 40% of the poverty threshold, or about $18,200 for a family of three. An unexpected outcome of the pilot program was that MFIP clients were more likely to get and remain married than people enrolled in the standard welfare system. One place to start is with the minimum-wage, currently averaging $5.15 per hour, or $10,712 per year. According to the Department of Labor, if minimum wage had kept up with inflation over the last thirty years, it would be $7.80 an hour today. We encourage the Ways and Means Committee to promote an hourly wage or annual income that enables an individual to meet his or her family's basic needs.

Helping adults become gainfully employed is another legitimate way to foster 7 stable two-parent households. Not surprisingly, women are three times as likely to want to marry the father of their child if he holds a job. Job-training programs, affordable quality child care, health care, transportation and paid parental leave are all crucial ingredients of a stable family life. Higher drop-out rates and more health problems among children are the negative effects of poverty, not marital status.

8   In addition to a living wage and basic benefits, we believe that other laws and policies should be available to the full range of American families. These include domestic partner benefits, family and medical leave, hospital visitation rights, and survivors' benefits. Like public assistance, health care and benefits should not be contingent on one's relationship status, marital status, or sexual orientation. Although such policy changes will take time to effect, they are essential if TANF block grant requirements are to address the heart of economic and social injustice.

9   Given today's diversity of family forms, it is morally problematic and logistically difficult to restrict social and economic support to families headed by married couples. It ignores the forces of history and the complex reality of American family life, and it penalizes those who most need the assistance of fair and enlightened government policies.

10   Ultimately, diverting welfare money to programs that promote marriage denies basic services to millions of American children. Programs to promote marriage disregard the fact that marriage is not always the best choice, and may actually do harm, especially to women who are experiencing domestic violence. We hope the committee shares our support of principles that work toward creating healthy, loving relationships and families for all people, married and unmarried.

11   *The Alternatives to Marriage Project (www.unmarried.org) is a national organization for unmarried people, including people who choose not to marry, cannot marry, or live together before marriage. We work for greater understanding and acceptance of unmarried people.*

Here Comes the Groom: A (Conservative) Case for Gay Marriage

Andrew Sullivan

Andrew Sullivan is the former editor of the New Republic, *a centrist intellectual magazine, and a pioneering writer on gay rights. Holding a doctorate in political science from Harvard, Sullivan is a prolific political commentator who appears regularly on* Nightline, CBS Evening News, *National Public Radio's* Fresh Air, *and* Larry King Live. *As a practicing Catholic whose writing has a strong conservative following, Sullivan here presents an argument for gay marriage. This article, which appeared in the* New Republic *in August 1989, helped initiate the national conversation on gay marriage.**

---

*For an additional argument on same-sex marriage—one addressed to a gay rather than straight audience— see student writer Sam Isaacson's essay on pages 307–310.

Last month in New York, a court ruled that a gay lover had the right to stay in   1
his deceased partner's rent-control apartment because the lover qualified as a member of the deceased's family. The ruling deftly annoyed almost everybody. Conservatives saw judicial activism in favor of gay rent control: three reasons to be appalled. Chastened liberals (such as the *New York Times* editorial page), while endorsing the recognition of gay relationship, also worried about the abuse of already stretched entitlements that the ruling threatened. What neither side quite contemplated is that they both might be right, and that the way to tackle the issue of unconventional relationships in conventional society is to try something both more radical and more conservative than putting courts in the business of deciding what is and is not a family. That alternative is the legalization of civil gay marriage.

The New York rent-control case did not go anywhere near that far, which is the   2
problem. The rent-control regulations merely stipulated that a "family" member had the right to remain in the apartment. The judge ruled that to all intents and purposes a gay lover is part of his lover's family, inasmuch as a "family" merely means an interwoven social life, emotional commitment, and some level of financial interdependence.

It's a principle now well established around the country. Several cities have   3
"domestic partnership" laws, which allow relationships that do not fit into the category of heterosexual marriage to be registered with the city and qualify for benefits that up till now have been reserved for straight married couples. San Francisco, Berkeley, Madison, and Los Angeles all have legislation, as does the politically correct Washington, D.C., suburb, Takoma Park. In these cities, a variety of interpersonal arrangements qualify for health insurance, bereavement leave, insurance, annuity and pension rights, housing rights (such as rent-control apartments), adoption and inheritance rights. Eventually, according to gay lobby groups, the aim is to include federal income tax and veterans' benefits as well. A recent case even involved the right to use a family member's accumulated frequent-flier points. Gays are not the only beneficiaries; heterosexual "live-togethers" also qualify.

There's an argument, of course, that the current legal advantages extended to   4
married people unfairly discriminate against people who've shaped their lives in less conventional arrangements. But it doesn't take a genius to see that enshrining in the law a vague principle like "domestic partnership" is an invitation to qualify at little personal cost for a vast array of entitlements otherwise kept crudely under control.

To be sure, potential DPs have to prove financial interdependence, shared living   5
arrangements, and a commitment to mutual caring. But they don't need to have a sexual relationship or even closely mirror old-style marriage. In principle, an elderly woman and her live-in nurse could qualify. A couple of uneuphemistically confirmed bachelors could be DPs. So could two close college students, a pair of seminarians, or a couple of frat buddies. Left as it is, the concept of domestic partnership could open a Pandora's box of litigation and subjective judicial decision-making about who qualifies. You either are or are not married; it's not a complex question. Whether you are in a "domestic partnership" is not so clear.

More important, the concept of domestic partnership chips away at the prestige   6
of traditional relationships and undermines the priority we give them. This priority

is not necessarily a product of heterosexism. Consider heterosexual couples. Society has good reason to extend legal advantages to heterosexuals who choose the formal sanction of marriage over simply living together. They make a deeper commitment to one another and to society; in exchange, society extends certain benefits to them. Marriage provides an anchor, if an arbitrary and weak one, in the chaos of sex and relationships to which we are all prone. It provides a mechanism for emotional stability, economic security, and the healthy rearing of the next generation. We rig the law in its favor not because we disparage all forms of relationship other than the nuclear family, but because we recognize that not to promote marriage would be to ask too much of human virtue. In the context of the weakened family's effect upon the poor, it might also invite social disintegration. One of the worst products of the New Right's "family values" campaign is that its extremism and hatred of diversity has disguised this more measured and more convincing case for the importance of the marital bond.

7   The concept of domestic partnership ignores these concerns, indeed directly attacks them. This is a pity, since one of its most important objectives—providing some civil recognition for gay relationships—is a noble cause and one completely compatible with the defense of the family. But the decision to go about it is not to undermine straight marriage; it is to legalize old-style marriage for gays.

8   The gay movement has ducked this issue primarily out of fear of division. Much of the gay leadership clings to notions of gay life as essentially outsider, anti-bourgeois, radical. Marriage, for them, is co-optation into straight society. For the Stonewall generation, it is hard to see how this vision of conflict will ever fundamentally change. But for many other gays—my guess, a majority—while they don't deny the importance of rebellion 20 years ago and are grateful for what was done, there's now the sense of a new opportunity. A need to rebel has quietly ceded to a desire to belong. To be gay and to be bourgeois no longer seems such an absurd proposition. Certainly, since AIDS, to be gay and to be responsible has become a necessity.

9   Gay marriage squares several circles at the heart of the domestic partnership debate. Unlike domestic partnership, it allows for recognition of gay relationships, while casting no aspersions on traditional marriage. It merely asks that gays be allowed to join in. Unlike domestic partnership, it doesn't open up avenues for heterosexuals to get benefits without the responsibilities of marriage, or a nightmare of definitional litigation. And unlike domestic partnership, it harnesses to an already established social convention the yearnings for stability and acceptance among a fast-maturing gay community.

10   Gay marriage also places more responsibilities upon gays: it says for the first time that gay relationships are not better or worse than straight relationships, and that the same is expected of them. And it's clear and dignified. There's a legal benefit to a clear, common symbol of commitment. There's also a personal benefit. One of the ironies of domestic partnership is that it's not only more complicated than marriage, it's more demanding, requiring an elaborate statement of intent to qualify. It amounts to a substantial invasion of privacy. Why, after all, should gays be required to prove commitment before they get married in a way we would never dream of asking of straights?

Legalizing gay marriage would offer homosexuals the same deal society now offers heterosexuals: general social approval and specific legal advantages in exchange for a deeper and harder-to-extract-yourself-from commitment to another human being. Like straight marriage, it would foster social cohesion, emotional security, and economic prudence. Since there's no reason gays should not be allowed to adopt or be foster parents, it could also help nurture children. And its introduction would not be some sort of radical break with social custom. As it has become more acceptable for gay people to acknowledge their loves publicly, more and more have committed themselves to one another for life in full view of their families and their friends. A law institutionalizing gay marriage would merely reinforce a healthy social trend. It would also, in the wake of AIDS, qualify as a genuine public health measure. Those conservatives who deplore promiscuity among some homosexuals should be among the first to support it. Burke could have written a powerful case for it.

The argument that gay marriage would subtly undermine the unique legitimacy of straight marriage is based upon a fallacy. For heterosexuals, straight marriage would remain the most significant—and only legal—social bond. Gay marriage could only delegitimize straight marriage if it were a real alternative to it, and this is clearly not true. To put it bluntly, there's precious little evidence that straights could be persuaded by any law to have sex with—let alone marry—someone of their own sex. The only possible effect of this sort would be to persuade gay men and women who force themselves into heterosexual marriage (often at appalling cost to themselves and their families) to find a focus for their family instincts in a more personally positive environment. But this is clearly a plus, not a minus: gay marriage could both avoid a lot of tortured families and create the possibility for many happier ones. It is not, in short, a denial of family values. It's an extension of them.

Of course, some would claim that any legal recognition of homosexuality is a de facto attack upon heterosexuality. But even the most hardened conservatives recognize that gays are a permanent minority and aren't likely to go away. Since persecution is not an option in a civilized society, why not coax gays into traditional values rather than rail incoherently against them?

There's a less elaborate argument for gay marriage: it's good for gays. It provides role models for young gay people who, after the exhilaration of coming out, can easily lapse into short-term relationships and insecurity with no tangible goal in sight. My own guess is that most gays would embrace such a goal with as much (if not more) commitment as straights. Even in our society as it is, many lesbian relationships are virtual textbook cases of monogamous commitment. Legal gay marriage could also help bridge the gulf often found between gays and their parents. It could bring the essence of gay life—a gay couple—into the heart of the traditional straight family in a way the family can most understand and the gay offspring can most easily acknowledge. It could do as much to heal the gay-straight rift as any amount of gay rights legislation.

If these argumets sound socially conservative, that's no accident. It's one of the richest ironies of our society's blind spot toward gays that essentially conservative social goals should have the appearance of being so radical. But gay marriage is not a radical step. It avoids the mess of domestic partnership; it is humane; it is conservative in the best sense of the word. It's also practical. Given the fact that we already allow legal gay relationships, what possible social goal is advanced by framing the law to encourage those relationships to be unfaithful, undeveloped, and insecure?

Gay Marriage, an Oxymoron

Lisa Schiffren

This op-ed piece appeared in the New York Times *on March 23, 1996, at a time when the Hawaiian Supreme Court was considering whether to legalize gay marriage in Hawaii. Lisa Schiffren is a freelance journalist who writes regularly for the conservative magazine* American Spectator. *During the Reagan administration, she was a speechwriter for former Vice President Dan Quayle.*

1   As study after study and victim after victim testify to the social devastation of the sexual revolution, easy divorce and out-of-wedlock motherhood, marriage is fashionable again. And parenthood has transformed many baby boomers into advocates of bourgeois norms.

2   Indeed, we have come so far that the surprise issue of the political season is whether homosexual "marriage" should be legalized. The Hawaii courts will likely rule that gay marriage is legal, and other states will be required to accept those marriages as valid.

3   Considering what a momentous change this would be—a radical redefinition of society's most fundamental institution—there has been almost no real debate. This is because the premise is unimaginable to many, and the forces of political correctness have descended on the discussion, raising the cost of opposition. But one may feel the same affection for one's homosexual friends and relatives as for any other, and be genuinely pleased for the happiness they derive from relationships, while opposing gay marriage for principled reasons.

4   "Same-sex marriage" is inherently incompatible with our culture's understanding of the institution. Marriage is essentially a lifelong compact between a man and woman committed to sexual exclusivity and the creation and nurture of offspring. For most Americans, the marital union—as distinguished from other sexual relationships and legal and economic partnerships—is imbued with an aspect of holiness. Though many of us are uncomfortable using religious language to discuss social and political issues, Judeo-Christian morality informs our view of family life.

5   Though it is not polite to mention it, what the Judeo-Christian tradition has to say about homosexual unions could not be clearer. In a diverse, open society such as ours, tolerance of homosexuality is a necessity. But for many, its practice depends on a trick of cognitive dissonance that allows people to believe in the Judeo-Christian

moral order while accepting, often with genuine regard, the different lives of homosexual acquaintances. That is why, though homosexuals may believe that they are merely seeking a small expansion of the definition of marriage, the majority of Americans perceive this change as a radical deconstruction of the institution.

Some make the conservative argument that making marriage a civil right will bring stabillity, an end to promiscuity and a sense of fairness to gay men and women. But they miss the point. Society cares about stability in heterosexual unions because it is critical for raising healthy children and transmitting the values that are the basis of our culture. 6

Whether homosexual relationships endure is of little concern to society. That is also true of most childless marriages, harsh as it is to say. Society has wisely chosen not to differentiate between marriages, because it would require meddling into the motives and desires of everyone who applies for a license. 7

In traditional marriage, the tie that really binds for life is shared responsibility for the children. (A small fraction of gay couples may choose to raise children together, but such children are offspring of one partner and an outside contributor.) What will keep gay marriages together when individuals tire of each other? 8

Similarly, the argument that legal marriage will check promiscuity by gay males raises the question of how a "piece of paper" will do what the threat of AIDS has not. Lesbians seem to have little problem with monogamy, or the rest of what constitutes "domestication," despite the absence of official status. 9

Finally, there is the so-called fairness argument. The Government gives tax benefits, inheritance rights and employee benefits only to the married. Again, these financial benefits exist to help couples raise children. Tax reform is an effective way to remove distinctions among earners. 10

If the American people are interested in a radical experiment with same-sex marriages, then subjecting it to the political process is the right route. For a court in Hawaii to assume that it has the power to radically redefine marriage is a stunning abuse of power. To present homosexual marriage as a fait accompli, without national debate, is a serious political error. A society struggling to recover from 30 years of weakened norms and broken families is not likely to respond gently to having an institution central to most people's lives altered. 11

Affidavit of Steven K. Lofton

Steven K. Lofton

In May 1999, the American Civil Liberties Union filed a class action lawsuit to overturn Florida's ban on gay adoptions. One of the plaintiffs in this case was Steven K. Lofton, a gay man who with his partner has raised three HIV-positive foster children since infancy. (A fourth foster child died of AIDS.) In 1998, Lofton, his partner, and their foster children moved to Oregon, but the children remained wards of the state of Florida. One of them, "John Doe," became available for adoption in 1994. (By legal convention, minor children are often named anonymously in custody cases.) Lofton's application to adopt John Doe was rejected by the state. The case reached a national audience when it was publicized by Rosie O'Donnell (see the Web site on the case: http://www.lethimstay.com). This reading is Lofton's affidavit to the U. S. District Court in Florida.

UNITED STATES DISTRICT COURT
SOUTHERN DISTRICT OF FLORIDA

Case No: 99-10058-CIV-KING
Magistrate Judge O'Sullivan

STEVEN LOFTON, et al.,

Plaintiffs,

vs.

KATHLEEN A. KEARNEY, et al.,

Defendants.

AFFIDAVIT OF STEVEN K. LOFTON

I, Steven K. Lofton, state the following under penalty of perjury:

1. I am 44 years old and a registered nurse by training.

2. My partner is Roger Croteau. Roger, who is 46 years old, has been a registered nurse for 17 years and currently works in the pediatric immunology unit at a children's hospital. We have lived together in a committed relationship for 18 years.

3. In 1988, when Roger and I still lived in Florida, we began to care for HIV-positive children. I was licensed as a foster parent by the Department of Children and Families ("DCF"). Four Florida children have been in long-term foster care with me.

4. Frank joined our family in August 1988 when he was 8 months old. He is now nearly 14.

5. Tracy came home in September 1988 when she was one year old. She will turn 14 this month.

6. Ginger joined us in the Spring of 1989 when she was 6 months old. She died of AIDS in 1995 at age 6.

7. John Doe was the last Florida child to join our family. He came home in July 1991 when he was 2 months old. While he had tested positive for HIV shortly after birth, he seroreverted as a young child and remains HIV-negative. He is now 10 years old and a healthy, active young boy.

8. In 1998, Roger and I decided to move our family to Oregon in order to be closer to my parents, who are getting older, and because we felt that Portland is a good environment in which to raise children.

9. Shortly after we arrived in Oregon, I was contacted by a caseworker from Oregon's Services for Children and Families. I was asked if I would take care of two brothers, then aged 5 and 2, who have AIDS. I was told the children had no one else to take care of them. I agreed and Wayne and Ernie came home in February 1999. They are now 8 and 5.

10. John Doe became free for adoption in 1994. At that time, I applied to adopt him. Frank and Tracy are not free for adoption, and Wayne and Ernie are under the supervision of Oregon. Since it is only John who is at issue in this case, I will focus the remainder of this affidavit on him.

11. John is my son. I am committed to caring for him and providing for all his needs. I have been his parent in every way. For example, every day, I wake him up in the morning and help him get dressed and ready to go to school; I help him with his homework when he comes home from school; we have a family dinner together every night, cooked by Roger; and we spend our evenings engaged in a variety of family activities. I take care of John when he is sick. I make sure all his vaccinations are up to date. I am a parent volunteer in John's class once a week and an active P.T.S.A. member. I try to expand his horizons by taking him on trips. I encourage him to pursue the positive, healthy activities that he enjoys, such as swim team and drama. I provide a child-friendly home. I include John's friends in our family, inviting them over for dinner and having them join us on family outings to the beach or park. Roger and I teach John household responsibilities such as yard work, car maintenance and cooking. I discipline him appropriately when he misbehaves. I hug and comfort him when he is upset. I teach him manners, respect and other values that I consider important. I make sure he is safe. He calls me "Dad."

12. John is also close with Roger and with his brothers and sister.

13. My family is the only one that John has ever known.

14. Attached as Exhibit 1 are some family photos that were taken over the years.

15. Attached as Exhibit 2 is Ginger's Book, which is a book about our family.

16. I have long understood that John would be my son and stay with me forever. DCF has fostered this belief.

17. DCF has acknowledged that John's placement with me was permanent. Citizen Review Panel Reports, copies of which are sent to me, have stated that John's placement with me was a "permanent placement plan." *See* Citizen Review Panel Report dated September 13, 1995, attached hereto as Exh. 3. *See also* December 11, 1996, Citizen Review Panel Report ("DCF must submit a new plan for custody on a permanent basis with foster parent with legal guardianship or a permanent agreement in lieu of case plan."), attached hereto as Exh. 4; and July 21, 1999, Citizen Review Panel Report ("Panel commends foster father for providing a permanent home to [John]."), attached hereto as Exh. 5.

18. DCF did not recruit other adoptive families for John so that he could remain with me. *See* July 10, 1996, Addendum to Citizen Review Panel Report (HRS reports that it "will not seek another adoptive family as [it] intends to pursue permanency for [John] with his foster father."), attached hereto as Exh. 6.

19. DCF gave me permission to relocate to Oregon with John, finding that it was in his "manifest best interest" to go with me. *See* Order granting permission to relocate, attached hereto as Exh. 7; *see also* June 2, 1998, Interstate Compact memo to Oregon, copy attached hereto as Exh. 8.

20. DCF corresponded with me about alternatives for John to be able to achieve legal permanency with me. *See, e.g.,* June 30, 1998, letter from Ali to Lofton discussing guardianship, attached hereto as Exh. 9. In May 2000, John's permanency goal was changed to "long-term foster care." *See* July 19, 1999, Judicial Review ("the goal of adoption will change to long-term foster care pending change in Florida statute"), attached hereto as Exh. 10; *see also* April 17, 2001, Citizen Review Panel Report (noting that goal had been changed to long-term foster care so that Doe could continue to reside with Lofton). DCF wrote a letter to me advising that the goal was changed to long-term foster care "in order to allow you to keep [John] on a long-term/permanent basis until you are allowed to adopt." Copy attached hereto as Exh. 11.

21. John is eager to be adopted. For the last couple of years, he has been asking me when his adoption will be complete. It's important to him to be adopted. I want him to have the emotional security that comes with being adopted.

22. On June 21, 2001, I received a shocking phone call from a DCF caseworker, advising me that John's permanency goal had been changed from long-term foster care to adoption, and that she was recruiting other adoptive families for John. She asked if I knew anyone who might be interested in adopting him.

23. I am deeply concerned that DCF will remove John from his family. This family is the only one he has ever known. It is unthinkable that DCF would even consider taking him away. I can't even imagine how being separated from his parents and brothers and sister would affect him.

24. I love John deeply and want to protect him. But I cannot protect him unless I can adopt him.

I declare under penalty of perjury that the foregoing is true and correct.

Steven K. Lofton

Technical Report: Coparent or Second-Parent Adoption by Same-Sex Parents

Ellen C. Perrin

This technical report, produced through a study of the research literature by a committee of the American Academy of Pediatrics, was published in the scholarly journal Pediatrics *in February 2002. Ellen C. Perrin, M.D., is a professor of pediatrics at Tufts New England Medical Center in Boston.*

ABSTRACT. A growing body of scientific literature demonstrates that children who grow up with 1 or 2 gay and/or lesbian parents fare as well in emotional, cognitive, social, and sexual functioning as do children whose parents are heterosexual. Children's optimal development seems to be influenced more by the nature of the relationships and interactions within the family unit than by the particular structural form it takes.

Accurate statistics regarding the number of parents who are gay or lesbian are impossible to obtain. The secrecy resulting from the stigma still associated with homosexuality has hampered even basic epidemiologic research. A broad estimate is that between 1 and 9 million children in the United States have at least 1 parent who is lesbian or gay. (n1)

Most individuals who have a lesbian and/or gay parent were conceived in the context of a heterosexual relationship. When a parent (or both parents) in a heterosexual couple "comes out" as lesbian or gay, some parents divorce and others continue to live as a couple. If they do decide to live separately, either parent may be the residential parent or children may live part-time in each home. Gay or lesbian parents may remain single or they may have same-sex partners who may or may not develop stepparenting relationships with the children. These families closely resemble stepfamilies formed after heterosexual couples divorce, and many of their parenting concerns and adjustments are similar. An additional concern for these parents is that pervasively heterosexist legal precedents have resulted in denial of custody and restriction of visitation rights to many gay and lesbian parents.

Increasing social acceptance of diversity in sexual orientation has allowed more gay men and lesbians to come out before forming intimate relationships or becoming parents. Lesbian and gay adults choose to become parents for many of the same reasons heterosexual adults do. The desire for children is a basic human instinct and satisfies many people's wish to leave a mark on history or perpetuate their family's story. In addition, children may satisfy people's desire to provide and accept love and nurturing from others and may provide some assurance of care and support during their older years.

Many of the same concerns that exist for heterosexual couples when they consider having children also face lesbians and gay men. All parents have concerns about time, finances, and the responsibilities of parenthood. They worry about how children will affect their relationship as a couple, their own and their children's health, and their ability to manage their new parenting role in addition to their other adult roles. Lesbians and gay men undertaking parenthood face additional challenges, including deciding whether to conceive or adopt a child, obtaining donor sperm or arranging for a surrogate mother (if conceiving), finding an accepting adoption agency (if adopting), making legally binding arrangements regarding parental relationships, creating a substantive role for the nonbiologic or nonadoptive parent, and confronting emotional pain and restrictions imposed by heterosexism and discriminatory regulations.

Despite these challenges, lesbians and gay men increasingly are becoming parents on their own or in the context of an established same-sex relationship. Most lesbians who conceive a child do so using alternative insemination techniques with a donor's sperm. The woman or women may choose to become pregnant using sperm from a completely anonymous donor, from a donor who has agreed to be identifiable when the child becomes an adult, or from a fully known donor (e.g., a friend or a relative of the nonconceiving partner). Lesbians also can become parents by fostering or adopting children, as can gay men. These opportunities are increasingly available in most states and in many other countries, although they are still limited by legal statutes in some places.

6   A growing number of gay men have chosen to become fathers through the assistance of a surrogate mother who bears their child. Others have made agreements to be coparents with a single woman (lesbian or heterosexual) or a lesbian couple. (n2–n4) Still other men make arrangements to participate as sperm donors in the conception of a child (commonly with a lesbian couple), agreeing to have variable levels of involvement with the child but without taking on the responsibilites of parenting.

7   When a lesbian or a gay man becomes a parent through alternative insemination, surrogacy, or adoption, the biologic or adoptive parent is recognized within the legal system as having full and more or less absolute parental rights. Although the biologic or adoptive parent's partner may function as a coparent, he or she has no formal legal rights with respect to the child. Most state laws do not allow for adoption or guardianship by an unmarried partner unless the parental rights of the first parent are terminated. An attorney can prepare medical consent forms and nomination-of-guardian forms for the care of the child in the event of the legal parent's death or incapacity. These documents, however, do not have the force of an adoption or legal guardianship, and there is no guarantee that a court will uphold them. Some states recently have passed legislation that allows coparents to adopt their partner's children. Other states have allowed their judicial systems to determine eligibility for formal adoption by the coparent on a case-by-case basis. Coparent (or second-parent) adoption has important psychologic and legal benefits.

8   Historically, gay men and lesbians have been prevented from becoming foster parents or adopting children and have been denied custody and rights of visitation of their children in the event of divorce on the grounds that they would not be effective parents. Legal justifications and social beliefs have presumed that their children would experience stigmatization, poor peer relationships, subsequent behavioral and emotional problems, and abnormal psychosexual development. During the past 20 years, many investigators have tried to determine whether there is any empiric support for these assumptions.

RESEARCH EVIDENCE

9   The focus of research has been on 4 main topic areas. Investigators have concentrated on describing the attitudes and behaviors of gay and lesbian parents and the psychosexual development, social experience, and emotional status of their children.

Parenting Attitudes and Behavior, Personality, and Adjustment of Parents

10   Stereotypes and laws that maintain discriminatory practices are based on the assumption that lesbian mothers and gay fathers are different from heterosexual parents in ways that are important to their children's well-being. Empirical evidence reveals in contrast that gay fathers have substantial evidence of nurturance

and investment in their paternal role and no differences from heterosexual fathers in providing appropriate recreation, encouraging autonomy, (n5) or dealing with general problems of parenting. (n6) Compared with heterosexual fathers, gay fathers have been described to adhere to stricter disciplinary guidelines, to place greater emphasis on guidance and the development of cognitive skills, and to be more involved in their children's activities. (n7) Overall, there are more similarities than differences in the parenting styles and attitudes of gay and nongay fathers.

Similarly, few differences have been found in the research from the last 2 decades comparing lesbian and heterosexual mothers' self-esteem, psychologic adjustment, and attitudes toward child rearing. (n8, n9) Lesbian mothers fall within the range of normal psychologic functioning on interviews and psychologic assessments and report scores on standardized measures of self-esteem, anxiety, depression, and parenting stress indistinguishable from those reported by heterosexual mothers. (n10)   11

Lesbian mothers strongly endorse child-centered attitudes and commitment to their maternal roles (n11–n13) and have been shown to be more concerned with providing male role models for their children than are divorced heterosexual mothers. (n6, n14) Lesbian and heterosexual mothers describe themselves similarly in marital and maternal interests, current lifestyles, and child-rearing practices. (n14) They report similar role conflicts, social support networks, and coping strategies. (n15, n16)   12

Children's Gender Identity and Sexual Orientation

The gender identity of preadolescent children raised by lesbian mothers has been found consistently to be in line with their biologic sex. None of the more than 300 children studied to date have shown evidence of gender identity confusion, wished to be the other sex, or consistently engaged in cross-gender behavior. No differences have been found in the toy, game, activity, dress, or friendship preferences of boys or girls who had lesbian mothers, compared with those who had heterosexual mothers.   13

No differences have been found in the gender identity, social roles, or sexual orientation of adults who had a divorced homosexual parent (or parents), compared with those who had divorced heterosexual parents. (n17–n19) Similar proportions of young adults who had homosexual parents and those who had heterosexual parents have reported feelings of attraction toward someone of the same sex.(n20) Compared with young adults who had heterosexual mothers, men and women who had lesbian mothers were slightly more likely to consider the possibility of having a same-sex partner, and more of them had been involved in at least a brief relationship with someone of the same sex,(n10) but in each group similar proportions of adult men and women identified themselves as homosexual.

Children's Emotional and Social Development

Because most children whose parents are gay or lesbian have experienced the divorce of their biologic parents, their subsequent psychologic development has to be understood in that context. Whether they are subsequently raised by 1 or 2 separated parents and whether a stepparent has joined either of the biologic parents are important factors for children but are rarely addressed in research assessing outcomes for children who have a lesbian or gay parent.   14

15   The considerable research literature that has accumulated addressing this issue has generally revealed that children of divorced lesbian mothers grow up in ways that are very similar to children of divorced heterosexual mothers. Several studies comparing children who have a lesbian mother with children who have a heterosexual mother have failed to document any differences between such groups on personality measures, measures of peer group relationships, self-esteem, behavioral difficulties, academic success, or warmth and quality of family relationships. (n9, n11, n15, n16, n20, n21) Children's self-esteem has been shown to be higher among adolescents whose mothers (of any sexual orientation) were in a new partnered relationship after divorce, compared with those whose mothers remained single, and among those who found out at a younger age that their parent was homosexual, compared with those who found out when they were older. (n22)

16   Prevalent heterosexism and stigmatization might lead to teasing and embarrassment for children about their parent's sexual orientation or their family constellation and restrict their ability to form and maintain friendships. Adult children of divorced lesbian mothers have recalled more teasing by peers during childhood than have adult children of divorced heterosexual parents. (n23) Nevertheless, children seem to cope rather well with the challenge of understanding and describing their families to peers and teachers.

17   Children born to and raised by lesbian couples also seem to develop normally in every way. Ratings by their mothers and teachers have demonstrated children's social competence and the prevalence of behavioral difficulties to be comparable with population norms. (n8, n24) In fact, growing up with parents who are lesbian or gay may confer some advantages to children. They have been described as more tolerant of diversity and more nurturing toward younger children than children whose parents are heterosexual. (n25, n26)

18   In 1 study, children of heterosexual parents saw themselves as being somewhat more aggressive than did children of lesbians, and they were seen by parents and teachers as more bossy, negative, and domineering. Children of lesbian parents saw themselves as more lovable and were seen by parents and teachers as more affectionate, responsive, and protective of younger children, compared with children of heterosexual parents. (n25, n27) In a more recent investigation, children of lesbian parents reported their self-esteem to be similar to that of children of heterosexual parents and saw themselves as similar in aggressiveness and sociability. (n15)

19   Recent investigations have attempted to discern factors that promote optimal well-being of children who have lesbian parents. The adjustment of children who have 2 mothers seems to be related to their parents' satisfaction with their relationship and specifically with the division of responsibility they have worked out with regard to child care and household chores. (n28) Children with lesbian parents who reported greater relationship satisfaction, more egalitarian division of household and paid labor, (n29) and more regular contact with grandparents and other relatives (n30) were rated by parents and teachers to be better adjusted and to have fewer behavioral problems.

20   Children in all family constellations have been described by parents and teachers to have more behavioral problems when parents report more personal distress and

more dysfunctional parent-child interactions. In contrast, children are rated as better adjusted when their parents report greater relationship satisfaction, higher levels of love, and lower interparental conflict regardless of their parents' sexual orientation. Children apparently are more powerfully influenced by family processes and relationships than by family structure.

SUMMARY

The small and nonrepresentative samples studied and the relatively young age [21] of most of the children suggest some reserve. However, the weight of evidence gathered during several decades using diverse samples and methodologies is persuasive in demonstrating that there is no systematic difference between gay and nongay parents in emotional health, parenting skills, and attitudes toward parenting. No data have pointed to any risk to children as a result of growing up in a family with 1 or more gay parents. Some among the vast variety of family forms, histories, and relationships may prove more conducive to healthy psychosexual and emotional development than others.

Research exploring the diversity of parental relationships among gay and les- [22] bian parents is just beginning. Children whose parents divorce (regardless of sexual orientation) are better adjusted when their parents have high self-esteem, maintain a responsible and amicable relationship, and are currently living with a partner.(n22, n31) Children living with divorced lesbian mothers have better outcomes when they learn about their mother's homosexuality at a younger age, when their fathers and other important adults accept their mother's lesbian identity, and perhaps when they have contact with other children of lesbians and gay men.(n22, n24) Parents and children have better outcomes when the daunting tasks of parenting are shared, and children seem to benefit from arrangements in which lesbian parents divide child care and other household tasks in an egalitarian manner(n28) as well as when conflict between partners is low. Although gay and lesbian parents may not, despite their best efforts, be able to protect their children fully from the effects of stigmatization and discrimination, parents' sexual orientation is not a variable that, in itself, predicts their ability to provide a home environment that supports children's development.

References

(n1.) Laumann FO. National Health and Social Life Survey. Chicago, IL: University of Chicago and National Opinion Research Center; 1995

(n2.) Barret RL, Robinson BE. Gay Fathers. Lexington, MA: Lexington Books; 1990

(n3.) Bigner JJ, Bozett FW. Parenting by gay fathers. In: Bozett FW, Sussman MB, eds. Homosexuality and Family Relations. New York, NY: Harrington Park Press; 1990:155–175

(n4.) Patterson CJ, Chan RW. Gay fathers and their children. In: Cabaj RP, Stein TS, eds. Textbook of Homosexuality and Mental Health. Washington, DC: American Psychiatric Press; 1996:371–393

(n5.) Turner PH, Scadden L, Harris MB. Parenting in gay and lesbian families. J Gay Lesbian Psychother. 1990;1:55–66 (n6.) Harris MB, Turner PH. Gay and lesbian parents. J Homosex. 1985;12:101–113

(n7.) Bigner JJ, Jacobsen RB. Adult responses to child behavior and attitudes toward fathering: gay and nongay fathers. J Homosex. 1992;23:99–112

(n8.) Flaks DK, Ficher I, Masterpasqua F, Joseph G. Lesbians choosing motherhood: a comparative study of lesbian and heterosexual parents and their children. Dev Psychol. 1995;31:105–114

(n9.) Green R, Mandel JB, Hotvedt ME, Gray J, Smith L. Lesbian mothers and their children: a comparison with solo parent heterosexual mothers and their children. Arch Sex Behav. 1986;15:167–184

(n10.) Golombok S, Tasker F, Murray C. Children raised in fatherless families from infancy: family relationships and the socioemotional development of children of lesbian and single heterosexual mothers. J Child Psychol Psychiatry. 1997;38:783–791

(n11.) Golombok S, Spencer A, Rutter M. Children in lesbian and single-parent households: psychosexual and psychiatric appraisal. J Child Psychol Psychiatry. 1983;24:551–572

(n12.) Kirkpatrick M. Clinical implications of lesbian mother studies. J Homosex. 1987;14:201–211

(n13.) Miller J, Jacobsen R, Bigner J. The child's home environment for lesbian vs heterosexual mothers: a neglected area of research. J Homosex. 1981;7:49–56

(n14.) Kirkpatrick M, Smith C, Roy R. Lesbian mothers and their children: a comparative survey. Am J Orthopsychiatry. 1981;51:545–551

(n15.) Patterson CJ. Children of lesbian and gay parents. Adv Clin Child Psychol. 1997;19:235–282

(n16.) Patterson CJ. Children of the lesbian baby boom: behavioral adjustment, self-concepts, and sex role identity. In: Greene B, Herek GM, eds. Lesbian and Gay Psychology: Theory, Research, and Clinical Applications. Thousand Oaks, CA: Sage Publications; 1994:156–175

(n17.) Bailey JM, Bobrow D, Wolfe M, Mikach S. Sexual orientation of adult sons of gay fathers. Dev Psychol. 1995;31:124–129

(n18.) Gottman JS. Children of gay and lesbian parents. Marriage Fam Rev. 1989;14:177–196

(n19.) Patterson CJ. Children of lesbian and gay parents. Child Dev. 1992;63:1025–1042

(n20.) Tasker FL, Golombok S. Growing Up in a Lesbian Family: Effects on Child Development. New York, NY: Guilford Press; 1997

(n21.) Allen M, Burrell N. Comparing the impact of homosexual and heterosexual parents on children: meta-analysis of existing research. J Homosex. 1996;32:19–35

(n22.) Huggins SL. A comparative study of self-esteem of adolescent children of divorced lesbian mothers and divorced heterosexual mothers. J Homosex. 1989;18:123–135

(n23.) Tasker F, Golombok S. Adults raised as children in lesbian families. Am J Orthopsychiatry. 1995;65:203–215

(n24.) Patterson CJ. The family lives of children born to lesbian mothers. In: Patterson CJ, D'Augelli AR, eds. Lesbian, Gay, and Bisexual Identities in Families: Psychological Perspectives. New York, NY: Oxford University Press; 1998:154–176

(n25.) Steckel A. Psychosocial development of children of lesbian mothers. In: Bozett FW, ed. Gay and Lesbian Parents. New York, NY: Praeger; 1987:75–85

(n26.) Stacey J, Biblarz TJ. (How) Does the sexual orientation of parents matter? Am Sociol Rev. 2001;66:159–183

(n27.) Tasker F. Children in lesbian-led families: a review. Clin Child Psychol Psychiatry. 1999;4:153–166

(n28.) Patterson CJ. Families of the lesbian baby boom: parents' division of labor and children's adjustment. Dev Psychol. 1995;31:115–123 (n29.) Chan RW, Brooks RC, Raboy B, Patterson CJ. Division of labor among lesbian and heterosexual parents: associations with children's adjustment. J Fam Psychol. 1998;12:402–419

(n30.) Patterson CJ, Hurt S, Mason CD. Families of the lesbian baby boom: children's contact with grandparents and other adults. Am J Orthopsychiatry. 1998;68:390–399

(n31.) Emery RE. Interparental conflict and the children of discord and divorce. Psychol Bull. 1982;92:310–330

Egg Heads

Kathryn Jean Lopez

From a socially conservative perspective, the traditional family is threatened not only by gay marriage and gay adoption but also by modern reproductive technology involving sperm and egg donors, surrogate mothers, and the eugenic prospect of seeking and valuing only the "perfect child." In this article, which appeared in National Review *on September 1, 1998, Kathryn Jean Lopez, an associate editor for* National Review Online, *makes a case against egg donors.*

Filling the waiting room to capacity and spilling over into a nearby conference room, a group of young women listen closely and follow the instructions: Complete the forms and return them, with the clipboard, to the receptionist. It's all just as in any medical office. Then they move downstairs, where the doctor briefs them. "Everything will be pretty much normal," she explains. "Women complain of skin irritation in the local area of injection and bloating. You also might be a little emotional. But, basically, it's really bad PMS."

This is not just another medical office. On a steamy night in July, these girls in their twenties are attending an orientation session for potential egg donors at a New Jersey fertility clinic specializing in in-vitro fertilization. Within the walls of IVF New Jersey and at least two hundred other clinics throughout the United States, young women answer the call to give "the gift of life" to infertile couples. Egg donation is a quickly expanding industry, changing the way we look at the family, young women's bodies, and human life itself.

It is not a pleasant way to make money. Unlike sperm donation, which is over in less than an hour, egg donation takes the donor some 56 hours and includes a battery of tests, ultrasound, self-administered injections, and retrieval. Once a donor is accepted into a program, she is given hormones to stimulate the ovaries, changing the number of eggs matured from the usual one per month up to as many as fifty. A doctor then surgically removes the eggs from the donor's ovary and fertilizes them with the designated sperm.

Although most programs require potential donors to undergo a series of medical tests and counseling, there is little indication that most of the young women know what they are getting themselves into. They risk bleeding, infection, and scarring. When too many eggs are matured in one cycle, it can damage the ovaries and leave the donor with weeks of abdominal pain. (At worst, complications may leave her dead.) Longer term, the possibility of early menopause raises the prospect of future regret. There is also evidence of a connection between the fertility drugs used in the process and ovarian cancer.

5   But it's good money—and getting better. New York's Brooklyn IVF raised its "donor compensation" from $2,500 to $5,000 per cycle earlier this year in order to keep pace with St. Barnabas Medical Center in nearby Livingston, New Jersey. It's a bidding war. "It's obvious why we had to do it," says Susan Lobel, Brooklyn IVF's assistant director. Most New York–area IVF programs have followed suit.

6   Some infertile couples and independent brokers are offering even more for "reproductive material." The International Fertility Center in Indianapolis, Indiana, for instance, places ads in the *Daily Princetonian* offering Princeton girls as much as $35,000 per cycle. The National Fertility Registry, which, like many egg brokerages, features an online catalogue for couples to browse in, advertises $35,000 to $50,000 for Ivy League eggs. While donors are normally paid a flat fee per cycle, there have been reports of higher payments to donors who produce more eggs.

7   College girls are the perfect donors. Younger eggs are likelier to be healthy, and the girls themselves frequently need money—college girls have long been susceptible to classified ads offering to pay them for acting as guinea pigs in medical research. One 1998 graduate of the University of Colorado set up her own Web site to market her eggs. She had watched a television show on egg donation and figured it "seemed like a good thing to do"—especially since she had spent her money during the past year to help secure a country-music record deal. "Egg donation would help me with my school and music expenses while helping an infertile couple with a family." Classified ads scattered throughout cyberspace feature similar offers.

8   The market for "reproductive material" has been developing for a long time. It was twenty years ago this summer that the first test-tube baby, Louise Brown, was born. By 1995, when the latest tally was taken by the Centers for Disease Control, 15 percent of mothers in this country had made use of some form of assisted-reproduction technology in conceiving their children. (More recently, women past menopause have begun to make use of this technology.) In 1991 the American Society for Reproductive Medicine was aware of 63 IVF programs offering egg donation. That number had jumped to 189 by 1995 (the latest year for which numbers are available).

9   Defenders argue that it's only right that women are "compensated" for the inconvenience of egg donation. Brooklyn IVF's Dr. Lobel argues, "If it is unethical to accept payment for loving your neighbor, then we'll have to stop paying babysitters." As long as donors know the risks, says Mark McGee of the University of Pennsylvania's Center for Bioethics, this transaction is only "a slightly macabre version of adoption."

10   Not everyone is enthusiastic about the "progress." Egg donation "represents another rather large step into turning procreation into manufacturing," says the University of Chicago's Leon Kass. "It's the dehumanization of procreation." And as in manufacturing, there is quality control. "People don't want to say the word any

more, but there is a strong eugencis issue inherent in the notion that you can have the best eggs your money can buy," observes sociology professor Barbara Katz Rothman of the City University of New York.

The demand side of the market comes mostly from career-minded babyboomers, the frontierswomen of feminism, who thought they could "have it all." Indeed they *can* have it all—with a little help from some younger eggs. (Ironically, feminists are also among its strongest critics; *The Nation's* Katha Pollitt has pointed out that in egg donation and surrogacy, once you remove the "delusion that they are making babies for other women," all you have left is "reproductive prostitution.") 11

Unfortunately, the future looks bright for the egg market. Earlier this year, a woman in Atlanta gave birth to twins after she was implanted with frozen donor eggs. The same technology has also been successful in Italy. This is just what the egg market needed, since it avoids the necessity of coordinating donors' cycles with recipients' cycles. Soon, not only will infertile couples be able to choose from a wider variety of donor offerings, but in some cases donors won't even be needed. Young women will be able to freeze their own eggs and have them thawed and fertilized once they are ready for the intrusion of children in their lives. 12

There are human ovaries sitting in a freezer in Fairfax, Virginia. The Genetics and IVF Institute offers to cut out and remove young women's ovaries and cryopreserve the egg-containing tissue for future implantation. Although the technology was originally designed to give the hope of fertility to young women undergoing treatment for cancer, it is now starting to attract the healthy. "Women can wait to have children until they are well established in their careers and getting a little bored, sometime in their forties or fifties," explains Professor Rothman. "Basically, motherhood is being reduced to a good leisure-time activity." 13

Early this summer, headlines were made in Britain, where the payment of egg donors is forbidden, when an infertile couple traveled to a California clinic where the woman could be inseminated with an experimental hybrid egg. The egg was a combination of the recipient's and a donor's eggs. The clinic in question gets its eggs from a Beverly Hills brokerage, the Center for Surrogate Parenting and Egg Donation, run by Karen Synesiou and Bill Handel, a radio shock-jock in Los Angeles. Miss Synesiou recently told the London *Sunday Times* that she is "interested in redefining the family. That's why I came to work here." 14

The redefinition is already well under way. Consider the case of Jaycee Buzzanca. After John and Luanne Buzzanca had tried for years to have a child, an embryo was created for them, using sperm and an egg from anonymous donors, and implanted in a surrogate mother. In March 1995, one month before the baby was born, John filed for divorce. Luanne wanted child support from John, but he refused—after all, he's not the father. Luanne argued that John *is* Jaycee's father legally. At this point the surrogate mother, who had agreed to carry a baby for a stable two-parent household, decided to sue for custody. 15

Jaycee was dubbed "Nobody's Child" by the media when a California judge ruled that John was not the legal father nor Luanne the legal mother (neither one was genetically related to Jaycee, and Luanne had not even borne her). Enter Erin Davidson, the egg donor, who claims the egg was used without her permission. Not 16 to be left out, the sperm donor jumped into the ring, saying that his sperm was used without his permission, a claim he later dropped. In March of this year, an appeals court gave Luanne custody and decided that John is the legal father, making him responsible for child support. By contracting for a medical procedure resulting in the birth of a child, the court ruled, a couple incurs "the legal status of parenthood." (John lost an appeal in May.) For Jaycee's first three years on earth, these people have been wrangling over who her parents are.

17   In another case, William Kane left his girlfriend, Deborah Hect, 15 vials of sperm before he killed himself in a Las Vegas hotel in 1991. His two adult children (represented by their mother, his ex-wife) contested Miss Hect's claim of ownership. A settlement agreement on Kane's will was eventually reached, giving his children 80 per cent of his estate and Miss Hect 20 per cent. Hence she was allowed three vials of his sperm. When she did not succeed in conceiving on the first two tries, she filed a petition for the other 12 vials. She won, and the judge who ruled in her favor wrote, "Neither this court nor the decedent's adult children possess reason or right to prevent Hect from implementing decedent's pre-eminent interest in realizing his 'fundamental right' to procreate with the woman of his choice." One day, donors may not even have to have lived. Researchers are experimenting with using aborted female fetuses as a source of donor eggs.

18   And the market continues to zip along. For overseas couples looking for donor eggs, Bill Handel has the scenario worked out. The couple would mail him frozen sperm of their choice (presumably from the recipient husband); his clinic would use it to fertilize donor eggs, chosen from its catalogue of offerings, and reply back within a month with a frozen embryo ready for implantation. (Although the sperm does not yet arrive by mail, Handel has sent out embryos to at least one hundred international customers.) As for the young women at the New Jersey clinic, they are visibly upset by one aspect of the egg-donation process: they can't have sexual intercourse for several weeks after the retrieval. For making babies, of course, it's already obsolete.

Who Needs a Husband?

Hila Colman

In this op-ed piece that appeared in the New York Times *on July 17, 2002, Hila Colman, a widow after 40 years of happy marriage, explains why she doesn't want another husband—unlike the typical older widower, who really wants a wife. Hila Colman is a writer of adolescent fiction.*

1   When I was a girl, a long time ago, nice girls (and weren't we all?) wanted to get married. We were primed and indoctrinated by our mothers on how best to attract and capture a suitable young man into marital bliss for a happy life forever after. It worked. For better, and as often for worse, we got married.

But what I see now among my friends and peers in their 70's, 80's and 90's is a 2
strange reversal in the man-woman thing. From where I sit (I claim no statistics to
back me up), the roles have been switched: older widows do not want another marriage
while older widowers do, often fervently. This is not to say that an older woman does
not want a man in her life. Of course we do, I do. But not a husband 24 hours a day.

The reasons to me are quite obvious. I had a good marriage, I loved my husband 3
dearly for over 40 years. I was devastated when I lost him. But by now I have built
a life of living alone. It was not easy; it was hard work and took an emotional toll,
but I found it had its perks. My widow friends know them, too: we are not responsible for another person's comfort, we come and go as we please, eat when and what
we like, we are not vulnerable to someone else's moods. As one friend put it bluntly:
"I never want to do laundry for a man again."

What we dream about, my friends and I, is to meet a man with whom we can 4
have a relationship—not an affair or a marriage. You could call it a commitment,
two consenting adults who can share the same pleasures: dinner and a movie, a
concert, ball games, trips—whatever—but each being in his and her own digs.

But the men in our age group seem to want something quite different. They 5
want a wife. They want what they had before, a woman in the house to do all the
things that a wife is supposed to do—which is, to wrap it up under one big label, To
Take Care of Them.

Of course it's the fault of my own generation. We grew up when a wife catered to 6
her husband. But if we old ladies can take care of ourselves, why can't the old men?

Surely men, who have been running the world for so long, can learn to adapt to 7
managing a household for one and can have an intimate relationship with a woman
(albeit a faithful one) without the sanction of a license.

Companionship is always the best part of any marriage. So why not go for that 8
and leave out the cumber-some baggage that two older people carry from their previous lives?

For Class Discussion

1. Analyze and evaluate the differences among the writers in this unit concerning issues of traditional versus alternative families, single parenthood,
   same-sex marriage, and reproductive technology. How do you account for
   these differences? Do the writers disagree about the facts of the case?
   About definitions? About values, beliefs, and underlying assumptions?

2. The tables and graphics in Chapter 9 (pp. 190–195) show that young people
   are delaying marriage until later in life. What is your explanation for such
   delay? Working in small groups or as a whole class, make a bulleted list of
   reasons why the age of first marriage has risen so dramatically since 1960.

3. Working in small groups or as a whole class, make a bulleted list of reasons
   for and against getting married.

4. Imagine a case in which an infertile couple enters into contract with a surrogate mother to bear a child using another couple's frozen zygote.

Imagine further that the original couple divorces (as in the Buzzanca case) but that all three women in the case decide they want custody of the baby. What criteria would you use to decide whether the genetic mother, the gestational mother, or the woman whose "intent" led to the surrogate pregnancy should have custody of the child?

OPTIONAL WRITING ASSIGNMENT   As the junior staffer for Senator Murk, you've been asked to help the Senator determine an appropriate position on one of the following issues: (1) The Bush administration's plan to use welfare dollars for programs to promote marriage and discourage cohabitation and premarital intercourse; (2) same-sex marriage or gay adoption; (3) a bill making it illegal to pay egg donors (except for medical expenses). Write a white paper for Senator Murk arguing for the position you think the Senator should take.

GLOBALIZATION, WORLD MARKETS, AND THE CARNIVAL AGAINST CAPITALISM

When the World Trade Organization (WTO), created in 1995, began holding international conferences on open markets and free trade, the delegates often faced massive street protests opposing globalization and multinational corporations. The WTO states on its Web site that it is "the only international organization dealing with global rules of trade between nations." Its function is "to insure that trade flows as smoothly, predictably and freely as possible." However, this identity and function have been vehemently challenged. Protesters against the WTO include environmentalists (sometimes dressed as sea turtles, dolphins, and whales), advocates for poor people in third-world countries including opponents of sweatshops, and proponents worldwide of reduced consumption, local markets, and simple living. Often identified under the colorful label "the Carnival Against Capitalism" (see the poster on p. 609), street demonstrators represent a worldwide movement of people committed to undoing the dangers—real or perceived—of unfettered capitalism. Meanwhile, many economists, political scientists, and other scholars—as well as business leaders and politicians—argue that globalization will eventually lift third-world people out of poverty and create a better, more sustainable world.

In this unit you will encounter various perspectives on globalization. What should be our attitude toward international trade and free-market capitalism? How can we best help the world's poor break the cycle of poverty? Is there a connection between globalization and environmental threats such as global warming? Which poses the larger threat: American corporations or American consumers? These are some of the interconnected issues examined in the arguments that follow.

"I'd Like a Tall Decaf Non-Fat Mocha Latte"

Gary Clement

Internationally acclaimed cartoonist Gary Clement lives in Toronto, Canada, and is the daily political cartoonist for the National Post. *His cartoons have appeared in many magazines, including the* New Yorker, *the* New York Times Book Review, Toronto Life, Owl, Canadian Living, *and* Chickadee. *We found this cartoon in the* New York Times *on July 7, 2002.*

Source: Gary Clement, CARTOONIST & WRITERS SYNDICATE/cartoonweb.com

Carnival Against Capitalism

This poster, created for September 2000 rallies in New Zealand against the World Trade Organization, the International Monetary Fund, and the World Bank, recruited people for demonstrations against local banks "as embodying the same basic principles of profit, foreign control, and disregard for local communities as the World Bank and IMF conglomerates." We found this image, as well as the story of the protest, on the Web site of Scoop, *a New Zealand Internet news service that specializes in "raw and fast" news "without a spin put on it by journalists."*

Join the Carnival!

12 noon, Tuesday 26 September

Evolutionaries

Thomas L. Friedman

Thomas L. Friedman is the foreign affairs columnist for the New York Times, *a position he has held since 1995. He has won three Pulitzer prizes and is the author of the highly acclaimed book* The Lexus and the Olive Tree: Understanding Globalization *(Farrar, Strauss, and Giroux, 2000). Friedman's understanding of globalization is summarized on a Web site devoted to the book: "Globalization is not just a phenomenon and not just a passing trend. It is the international system that replaced the Cold War system. Globalization is the integration of capital, technology, and information across national borders, in a way that is creating a single global market and, to some degree, a global village."[1] "Evolutionaries" appeared as an op-ed piece in the* New York Times *on July 20, 2001.*

1   Throughout history, successful social protest movements have had one thing in common—a clear, simple message and objective. Whether it was the women's rights movement or the anti-Vietnam-War movement, the mere uttering of the name immediately conjured up who the protesters were and what their objective was.

2   The striking thing about the protesters at gatherings from the Seattle W. T. O. meeting in 1999 to this week's Genoa G-8 summit is that they tend to be called just "the protesters" or "the anti-globalization protesters," which in neither case conjures up much of anything. To be against globalization is to be against so many things—from cell phones to trade to Big Macs—that it connotes nothing. Which is why the anti-globalization protests have produced noise but nothing that has improved anyone's life.

3   What is intriguing about the Genoa summit, though, is that many of the serious activist groups that have participated in past protests have come to recognize that breaking McDonald's windows or just saying "no" does not a protest movement make.

4   They have come to recognize that if they have any hope of harvesting the attention they have drawn to the problems of globalization they have to decide exactly what they are protesting against, because the protesters actually fall into two broad categories: those who think the issue is *whether we globalize* and want to stop globalization in its tracks, and those who understand, as I would argue, that globalization is largely driven by technology—from the Internet to satellites to cell phones to PC's—which is shrinking the world from a size medium to a size small, whether we like it or not, and therefore the issue is *how we globalize*.

5   Up to now, these two groups have been mixed together: Anarchists and leftover Marxists who are simply looking for ways to undermine capitalism in a new guise and protectionist unions exploiting well-meaning college students to stop free trade

---

[1] http://www.lexusandtheolivetree.com/aboutbook.htm

are thrown together in the streets with environmentalists who believe trade, growth and green can go together; anti-poverty groups that understand that globalization, properly managed, can be the poor's best ladder out of misery; and serious social welfare groups that have useful ideas about debt relief and labor standards in a globalizing world.

Because the *whether we globalize* groups tend to be more noisy and violent, they have increasingly drowned out the *how we globalize* groups. In doing so they have created the misimpression that "the people" believe that globalization is all bad and can never work for the poor, when, in fact, it has both empowering and enriching features and disempowering and impoverishing features, and it all depends on how you manage it. If you think globalization is all good or all bad, you don't get it. 6

Fortunately, many of the serious *how we globalize* groups and government leaders are no longer willing to cede the moral high ground to the most idiotic *whether we globalize* groups, and what you've seen around Genoa is, for the first time, a split between the two. 7

Some serious groups, such as Friends of the Earth, Christian Aid, Jubilee 2000 and Oxfam, have been distancing themselves from violent protests and insisting on codes of conduct. "The political space around big international meetings has been hijacked by those who want to commit violence," Justin Forsyth, policy director of Oxfam, told *The Financial Times*. "It is counterproductive. They are taking the spotlight off those who want positive change." Prime Minister Tony Blair of Britain said people had been "far too apologetic" toward the violent protesters: "If the public knew their views, they'd disagree with them." And President Bush rightly declared: "Those who protest free trade seek to deny [the poor] their best hope for escaping poverty." 8

This split between the *whether we globalize* forces and the *how we globalize* forces is an important strategic moment that should be nurtured—not for its own sake but to actually make some progress. The serious protesters have made their point that it matters how we globalize, but they can make a difference only if they design solutions in partnership with big businesses and governments. The moment is ripe for a world leader who can bring them together. 9

The End of Globalization? Multinational Corporations Are More Vulnerable Than You Think

Michael Shuman

Michael Shuman is an attorney who focuses on creating local markets to fight globalization. He is the director of the Village Foundation's Institute for Economic Empowerment and Entrepreneurship and the author of numerous books including Going Local: Creating Self-Reliant Communities in a Global

Age (Routledge, 2000). This article appeared in Utne Reader—*a liberal/ progressive magazine that reprints articles from a variety of alternative presses—in July/August 2002.*

1   Globalization, argues *New York Times* columnist Tom Friedman, is "making it possible for . . . corporations to reach farther, faster, cheaper, and deeper around the world" and is fostering "a flowering of both wealth and technological innovation the likes of which the world has never before seen." To David Korten, a former Ford Foundation official and now a prominent globalization critic, it is "market tyranny . . . extending its reach across the planet like a cancer, colonizing ever more of the planet's living spaces, destroying livelihoods, displacing people, rendering democratic institutions impotent, and feeding on life in an insatiable quest for money." The careful listener to this by-now-familiar debate can actually discern a striking point of agreement: Both sides assume, one with euphoria and the other with fear, that global-scale business is the wave of the future. Yet there's mounting evidence that multinational firms may be *less* capable of delivering competitive products than national or local firms.

2   AT&T stunned financial analysts in October 2000 when it announced that it was carving itself up into four, more versatile, companies. In May 2001, British Telecom unveiled a plan to spin off its wholesale arm, part of its wireless business, and numerous assets in Asia. Other self-initiated split-ups and slim-downs seem likely to follow. These developments are important reminders of a point all but forgotten in the globalization debate: Scale matters.

3   Any first-year economics student learns that firms can lower average costs by expanding, *but only up to a point.* Beyond that point (according to the law of diminishing returns to scale), complexities, breakdowns, and inefficiencies begin to drive average costs back up. The collapse of massive state-owned enterprises in the old Soviet Union and the bankruptcies of Chrysler and New York City are notable reminders of a lesson we should have absorbed from the dinosaur: Bigger is not always better.

4   A telling example in economic life is commercial banking. Despite all the headlines about mergers, researchers at the Federal Reserve in Minneapolis have concluded that "after banks reach a fairly modest size [about $100 million in assets], there is no cost advantage to further expansion. Some evidence even suggests diseconomies of scale for very large banks." The Financial Markets Center, a financial research and education organization, has found that, compared to banks with far-flung portfolios, those that concentrate lending in a geographic region were typically twice as profitable and wind up with fewer bad loans. While the press has diligently reported national and global mergers, it has largely ignored the recent proliferation of community banks, credit unions, and microloan funds.

5   Banking, it turns out, is not the only exception to the rules of globalization. Five factors are playing a significant role in shrinking the economies of scale for a wide range of industries.

1. First, it turns out that global-scale industry is surprisingly inefficient at distribution. In 1910, for every dollar Americans spent for food, 50 cents went to farmers and 50 cents to marketers and providers of inputs like seeds, energy, and fertilizer; now 9 cents goes to

farmers, 24 cents to input providers, and 67 cents to marketers. The marketers' 67 cents are largely unrelated to the end product that consumers really want. They're wasted on packaging, refrigeration, spoilage, advertising, trucking, supermarket fees, and middlemen.

When farmers can link more directly with nearby consumers, they can cut out these inefficiencies. This explains the spread of community-supported agriculture (CSA), pioneered initially in Japan and then Switzerland, now growing by leaps and bounds across North America. It works like this: A farmer is supported by 60 or 70 households, each of which pays a fee to receive a weekly supply of vegetables. More than 600 community-supported agricultural or horticultural operations now operate in 42 states, with 100,000 members.

2. A second factor exacerbating the inefficiency of global-scale distribution is the rising cost of shipping. In the past two years the per-barrel price of oil has quadrupled. And with expected increases in global population and per capita consumption, the U. S. Energy Information Administration projects that demand for oil worldwide will grow by 20 million barrels a day, a third more than current consumption levels. Improving technologies for petroleum recovery may ease upward pressures on oil prices a bit. But political pressures, including attempts to levy "green taxes" and political instability in oil regions like the Middle East and Central Asia could drive up prices. Until other fuels are substituted for oil, global shipping probably will become more expensive.

3. A third challenge facing global businesses is the difficulty of managing information. Conservative economist Friedrich Hayek once argued convincingly against state socialism by noting that knowledge is too complex, too subjective, and too dependent on particular circumstances of time and place for even the best-intentioned national-scale bureaucracies to grasp it. The exact same problem afflicts multinational corporations.

In principle, a global producer can wield its resources to produce different products for different local tastes. But in practice, a local producer is better situated to intuit, design, manufacture flexibly, and deliver just-in-time products. Consumers can better communicate their needs to local producers, either directly or through local retailers. General Foods probably will never be able to convince New Yorkers to replace their locally baked bagels with Minnesota-made generics. Microbrewers have flourished throughout the United States and the United Kingdom because each of them caters to highly specialized tastes. The desires of Bay Area food shoppers wanting more varieties of locally grown fruits and vegetables have expanded the region's agricultural economy by 61 percent over the past decade, which translates into $915 million of additional agricultural income in the local economy each year.

4. A fourth trend is the transformation of the U. S. economy from manufacturing goods to providing services. The main reason for this shift, according to MIT's Paul Krugman and Harvard's Robert Lawrence, is that technological advances have brought down the prices of many manufactured goods. As Americans spend less to acquire the same refrigerators and toasters, they spend more on services. These changes, Krugman argues in *Pop Internationalism* (MIT Press, 1997), are moving the U. S. economy inexorably toward what he calls localization: "A steadily rising share of the workforce produces services that are sold only within that same metropolitan area." For most services—whether it is health care, teaching, legal representation, accounting, or massage—consumers demand a personal, trusting relationship.

5. A fifth difficulty facing large-scale business is the information revolution. Global corporations are still amassing huge networks of factories, technology centers, and experts at a time when profitability is increasingly uncoupled from size. Small companies can now fit what used to be busy departments overseeing accounting, management, taxes, communications, and publications neatly onto a desktop computer. The Internet has given even home-based businesses the ability to compete against established, large-scale players in practically everything, including books and CDs, stocks and bonds, airline travel, and hotel rooms.

Even for industries like automobiles, where large economies of scale still make sense, the communications revolution is making it possible for small firms to achieve the same advantages through collaborations and partnerships. In northern Italy, locally owned firms involved in flexible manufacturing networks have become world-class exporters of high-tech products like robotic arms. A network typically forms temporarily to create a specific project for a well-defined niche market. Once the project is complete, the network disbands. Following successful models in Europe, more than 50 flexible manufacturing networks have been set up in the United States.

6   These five trends do not mean that all goods and services can be produced cost-effectively in every community. (The economics of any company or industry depend on how the new diseconomies of large scale balance against the old economies of scale.) At a minimum, however, they suggest that much of the hype from globalization's fans—and its enemies too—is overblown. If smaller businesses wind up being the most efficient producers and suppliers of many goods and services to nearby markets, then neither the utopian nor the nightmare scenarios of globalization will come to pass. Indeed, global trade may simply become a relatively minor part of most economies, as it is for ours right now (exports are responsible for less than 10 percent of our national income)—provided, of course, that politicians resist the temptation to bail out global businesses doomed by inappropriate scale.

7   The next wave of economic development—local, national, and global—may turn not on the rise or fall of any grand concepts like globalization, but on the slow, steady creation of appropriately scaled businesses. As the poet Wendell Berry once remarked, "The real work of planet-saving will be small, humble, and humbling. . . . Its jobs will be too many to count, too many to report, too many to be publicly noticed or rewarded, too small to make anyone rich or famous."

Open Societies Do Better

Mike Moore

Mike Moore, a former Prime Minister of New Zealand, is the Director-General of the World Trade Organization. His reputation for being a dynamic supporter of free trade and an ardent believer in the benefits of globalization makes him a primary

*spokesperson for the WTO. This argument is a speech delivered at an international
conference of military chaplains. The frequent religious references in this speech reveal his understanding of his audience.*

Thank you for the invitation to speak and share some thoughts.   1

The millennium subject is globalization. I wish that word had never been in-   2
vented. The word conjures up a vision of an uncaring, unrepresentative future where
ordinary people, Parliaments, cultures and Nations lose their character, power and
sovereignty. In the absence of an "ism" to hate and to march against, globalism has
become the target. Globalization is a process, an idea not an ideology. But every
great lie has within a germ of truth. There is injustice, the world is unequal and we
are faced with unequalled opportunity and challenges. These must be answered.

I speak to you today as Director-General of the World Trade Organization or as   3
so much of my correspondence accuses, The World Terrorist Organization.

I sought the job as Director-General of the World Trade Organization because I be-   4
lieved, and still do, that open societies do better. Where peoples and nations enjoy each
other's culture and music, ideas and commerce they do better. Open societies always
tend to have better human, environmental, and labour rights. Those nations that trade,
enjoy each other's company and companies have better results. That is the lesson of
history. In Europe you have two visions: one a united Europe, a Union where people do
respect each other and see the benefits of exchange; and then the tribal hatred that is
the Balkans, the mirror opposite. I believe that we are all brothers and sisters, born in
the image of God, thus created equal. We are equal, but not the same. Trade and business is only one aspect of the interchanges and the civilising effect of cooperation.
Moreover, trade and increasing interdependence among nations is nothing new.
Neither is the exchange of ideas and the movement of peoples across borders.

Indeed, one of the first multinational institutions was the Church. Faith knows   5
no boundaries. Faith has withstood nationalism, persecution, empires and ideologies. It is eternal.

There will be no lasting peace unless there is peace and co-existence between   6
religions. There have been those who predicted the death of history, that there will
be one global community. This is not so. Yet there is so much in common among religions and faiths that should make this task easier. All the great religions and
great civilizations have at their heart, a core message of human unity. Can I quote
from Hans Küng's book *A Global Ethic for Global Politics and Economics* where he
writes of the Golden Rule of Humanity?

What I mean by this can be demonstrated relatively simply by means of that Golden Rule of
humanity which we find in all the great religious and ethical traditions. Here are some of its
formulations:

- Confucius (C.551–486 BCE): "What you yourself do not want, do not do to another person" (Analects 15.23).
- Rabbi Hillel (60 BC–10CE): "Do not do to others what you would not want them to do to
you" (Shabbat 31a).

- Jesus of Nazareth: "Whatever you want people to do to you, do also to them" (Matt. 7.12; Luke 6.31).

- Islam: "None of you is a believer as long as he does not wish his brother what he wishes himself" (Forty Hadith of an-Nawawi, 13).

- Jainism: "Human beings should be indifferent to worldly things and treat all creatures in the world as they would want to be treated themselves" (Sutrakritanga I, II, 33).

- Buddhism: "A state which is not pleasant or enjoyable for me will also not be so for him; and how can I impose on another a state which is not pleasant or enjoyable for me?" (Samyutta Nikaya V, 353, 35–342, 2).

- Hinduism: "One should not behave towards others in a way which is unpleasant for oneself: that is the essence of morality" (Mahabharata XIII, 114, 8).

7   No one thinks globalization can be stopped or should be. But there are dangers and fears that need to be addressed. Celebrating a non-result in Seattle is as useful as suggesting Europe ought not to enlarge or China engage.

8   There is anxiety because there is unfairness, not everyone is getting a fair opportunity. Alas they never have, this has been true of the other great economic and social upheavals. As we shifted from hunter-gatherers to an agricultural, feudal and then industrial society, we are now moving into a post-industrial society, the information age. Now as then these great upheavals cause social dislocations. Be they Kings or Popes in the past or politicians now, leaders are blamed for not preserving the present. Yesterday always looks better.

9   In a speech celebrating the 50th anniversary of the United Nations Pope John Paul II put it most eloquently:

> On the threshold of a new millennium we are witnessing an extraordinary global acceleration of that quest for freedom which is one of the great dynamics of human history. This phenomenon is not limited to any one part of the world; nor is it the expression of any single culture. Men and woman throughout the world, even when threatened with violence, have taken the risk of freedom, asking to be given a place in social, political, and economic life which is commensurate with their dignity as free human beings. This universal longing for freedom is truly one of the distinguishing marks of our time.

10   Any great change in history causes resentment and breeds fear and causes anxiety. You could mount a case, indeed some of our critics do, that the motorcar is lethal, pollutes, kills and divides communities. But it's not about banning the motorcar, we cannot uninvent the combustion engine! It's about road rules, road rage and better managing and sharing more equally the costs and advantages.

11   This is also true of the impact of globalization, technological change and the WTO and its sister organizations.

12   Now that the dust has started to settle after the turmoil of Seattle, perhaps we should revisit what the multilateral trading system means to us and to the people of the 135 other countries who are part of the WTO, and Governments representing some 1.5 billion people who want to join. Perhaps they did not dominate the headlines, as did the 30,000 outside protesting, but aren't their concerns important too?

We ought to get back to core principles and values, restate our case. We all re- 13
alize that no nation can now enjoy clean water, air, manage an airline, even organize
a tax system or hope to contain or cure AIDS or cancer without the cooperation of
others. Thus we must seek democratic internationalism and cooperation if we are
to prosper and enjoy balanced development on our crowded planet.

When the Berlin well came down, when Nelson Mandela was freed, and when 14
freedom has flourished elsewhere, the world celebrated. We celebrated the universal values of political and economic freedom. No one shouted, cursed and swore
about the evils of globalization or common values then.

Every mother with a sick child wants the best the world has to offer from sci- 15
ence, no one wants the old technology when they go to the dentist. They don't complain then about global or universal values.

And yet, at a time when the world is more integrated than ever, where technol- 16
ogy brings us all within reach of each other and offers unprecedented opportunities
for communication, increased cooperation and solidarity, there is a growing sense
of unease at the impact of this globalized world on people's lives.

I have some empathy with some of those who protest in the streets of Seattle, 17
New Delhi or Auckland about change and the WTO. People around the world are
right when they say they want a safer, cleaner, more healthy planet. They are correct
when they call for an end to poverty, more social justice, better living standards. But
they are wrong to blame the WTO for all the world's problems. They are especially
wrong when they say we are not a democratic house. We are owned by Governments
who represent hundreds of millions of voters. The Indian Ambassador is appointed
by his Government, his government is answerable to Parliament. Parliament and
congresses and governments must ratify our agreements. That's how it should be.
How do we manage? History tells us democracy and freedom is not just a moral
imperative. It makes better economic sense. Gets the best results.

There is a perceived loss of identity and ownership given the new economic age. 18
A democratic deficit. Our mission must be to ensure that people and Parliaments
own us, that the people are the masters of globalization and not the servants. Thus
the active understanding, engagement and ownership of the great institutions like
the WTO by Sovereign Governments and its people is necessary if we are to have any
moral authority. That's how it is. That's how it should be. The challenge to policymakers is how we can achieve this. I have some ideas and will be working with the
Heads of other institutions, Ministers and Ambassadors to help correct this democratic deficit. That deficit is so deep that almost one quarter of the Members of the
WTO cannot afford representation in Geneva. We have organized the first ever seminars for non-resident Ambassadors. We are working on some creative ways of advancing and facilitating their involvement; thus ownership.

The new century poses enormous challenges. Within 25 years over 3 billion 19
people will be added to the global population. Urban populations will treble over the
next 30 years. By the year 2020, two-thirds of Africa's population will live in cities.
Over the next 30 years food production will have to double. The World Bank reports
that 2 billion people will suffer from chronic water shortages within 30 years. Half
the world's population lives on under US$2 per day.

20   Who is brave enough to say that our political structures, that the international institutions you own such as the WTO, the UN, the IMF, the World Bank, are equipped to serve the people and their Governments to meet these challenges?

21   Clichés about coherence between the institutions must become a working reality. We must adapt and be bold enough to look at ourselves and how we can collectively do a better job.

22   To me it's a simple proposition. The first half of this century was marked by force and coercion. Our new century ought to be one marked by persuasion and cooperation. Of States settling their differences through that great equaliser, the law. Of a binding disputes mechanism, to settle differences, of engagement and interdependence.

23   I come from a small country. I see interdependence, and treaties and the great global institutions as guarantors of our sovereignty and safety. I recall a splendid comment of Julius Nyerere, of Tanzania, who claimed that as each village's wealth once depended on its neighbour's ability to purchase, this is now true of nations. Our parents learnt from the great depression, made deeper and more lethal by rising trade barriers from which came the twin tyrannies of our age, fascism and Marxism, thus war; hot and cold. Economists and historians have costed the hot wars. We know of the casualties. We are still carrying the cost of the cold war. Our global institutions do not yet reflect the new reality born of the post cold war era and the post industrial age where knowledge not coal is king.

24   Still, our parents had a profound and compelling vision, because they saw economic and political integration as assisting in uniting nations and promoting development and peace.

25   They created an international architecture which included the UN, IMF, World Bank, and the GATT, now the WTO, to achieve that peaceful purpose and noble vision. In the main it's worked. Far from perfect. But the world would be a less safe place without them. The WTO is NOT the GATT. We now have more countries in the much criticized "green rooms" than we had as original members. We endure a culture in Geneva based on an old organization of 30 Members when we now have over 130. And 20-plus more want to join.

26   That's why we must change how the WTO operates, we are driven by our Members, owned by them. So I will be calling Member Governments for advice, even giving some, to increase transparency and efficiency, to ensure that national governments and their parliaments must have a greater involvement and ownership.

27   This century offers us the opportunity to achieve much. The last 50 years have seen Empires shrink, democracy rise, freedoms grow, and living standards lift in most continents and countries. Not all. I'm full of confidence because I have an abiding, unshakeable confidence in the people who, given freedom, will do the right thing by their families and nations. Too much is at stake for us to falter, be timid or to fail.

28   As we address the issues of managing globalization, we could do a lot worse than heeding the words of the great Mahatma Gandhi who warned of the SEVEN deadly sins in today's world:

- Wealth without work
- Enjoyment without conscience

- Knowledge without character
- Business without morality
- Science without humanity
- Religion without sacrifice and
- Politics without principles.

The Neoliberal World Order: The View from the Highlands of Guatemala
John D. Abell

John D. Abell is a professor of economics at Randolph-Macon Woman's College. Committed to economic policies that would help the poor in Guatemala and other Latin American countries, Abell doubts whether the benefits of globalization, as imagined by the "neoliberal world order," will ever trickle down to the world's poor. This article originally appeared in the NA-CLA (North American Congress on Latin America) Report on the Americas in August 1999.

From the perspective of poor rural Guatemalans, the current global crisis has little to do with interest rates or budget deficits. It has everything to do with the fact that policies aimed at the developing world are far removed from the needs and realities of the majority of the world's peoples. 1

It had been a productive morning so far. The family I was helping had picked close to 200 pounds of red, ripe coffee beans and we were relaxing around a cooking fire where the women had prepared a feast of beans, tortillas and avocado. Life seemed peaceful for the moment. Bellies were full. Beautiful Lake Atitlan, the jewel of Guatemala, was glistening in the distance. The only serious issue that remained this day was the matter of getting a couple of 100-pound sacks of coffee two miles down the side of the Toliman volcano to the coffee-processing plant where they would be weighed and scrutinized for leaves and stems prior to the payout. 2

Our discussion at lunch ranged from coffee prices to politics, focusing especially on the recent Peace Accords. Yes, everyone agreed, life had improved since the cessation of hostilities in December 1996, if only because the Guatemalan military was no longer dragging their sons off the streets and soccer fields to fight in the counterinsurgency war against the Guatemalan National Revolutionary Unity (URNG). Also, sleep came a lot easier knowing that the chances of a visit in the middle of the night from a paramilitary death squad were significantly reduced if not entirely eliminated. 3

4   Had any of the benefits of the Accords on the economy or judicial reform trickled down their way? Beyond a basic recognition that the Accords had left land-holding patterns untouched, they were not aware of many details. Their lives had remained essentially unchanged, they told me, living from day to day, eagerly awaiting the coffee harvest in hopes that it would be profitable enough this year to allow them to keep their kids in school and to pay their medical bills.

5   I asked if they were aware of the global economic crisis that had engulfed Asia, Russia and Brazil, and if they were concerned that Guatemala might be next. Don Ramon, the patriarch of the family, patiently explained to me that during his entire lifetime, and that of his father—indeed, he said, for nearly 500 years—Guatemala had been going through an essentially permanent economic crisis. How, he asked, could a country possibly have a healthy economy when most of its people go to bed hungry each night, and when they do not have land or any control over their lives? How could the latest problems from Asia or wherever make their lives any worse?

6   I was thinking about this lesson in real-world economics the next day when I stumbled on an issue of *Newsweek* devoted to the global financial crisis.[1] One of the broad themes running through all the stories was that while calm was returning to financial markets, economic recovery in the developing world was slow in coming. Indeed, there is abundant evidence that poverty and suffering is widespread. In the arctic regions of Russia, for example, people whose life savings vaporized in the early days of the ruble crisis faced starvation during one of the worst winters on record. In Jakarta, fathers who were once gainfully employed have now joined their families in the garbage dumps scrounging for their next meal. For many people, life—which was never very easy—has become precarious and desperate.

7   Many are beginning to blame the global financial system itself for such outcomes.[2] With countries like Malaysia setting a "dangerous" example by establishing restrictions on the movement of foreign capital, there is genuine fear in the establishment that some serious backsliding may be in the offing among those countries that had so eagerly embraced the neoliberal agenda. This may help to explain why Klaus Schwab, president of the World Economic Forum, selected "Responsible Globality" as the theme of this year's conference in Davos, Switzerland. Globalization is not going away anytime soon, says Schwab. The key, therefore, for lifting people out of poverty, is an improved infrastructure—"procedural, legal and institutional mechanisms"—to help harness the global revolution. "The new dividing line between richness and poverty," he suggests, "is not between the haves and have-nots, but between the knows and don't knows. The best way to help the poor is to enable them to take advantage of a global knowledge-economy."[3]

8   Don Ramon's eyes would probably glaze over if I told him that there was a fellow by the name of Klaus Schwab who was of the opinion that it did not matter that he was a have-not, and that he could improve his life if he would just take advantage of the "global knowledge-economy." If Don Ramon could speak with Mr. Schwab, he would surely tell him that his knowledge of the coffee business is just fine, and that what he needs is not a fancy Internet hookup or a Web page, but rather a higher price for his coffee and more land on which to grow it.

Each of the 100-pound sacks (referred to as a quintal) that Don Ramon's sons   9
carried down the mountain that day only brought the family approximately $14.
They only have half an acre of coffee and, because of the age of the trees, will be
lucky to harvest a total of 2,500 pounds this year. If they can avoid the thieves
who prey on small producers—lying in wait to take a family's harvest at gun
point—they will earn an extra $360, a nice supplement to Don Ramon's weekly
income of $17, but still not yet within striking distance of Guatemala's average
annual income of $1,500.

Another way to think about the Ramon family's precarious position in the   10
global economic order is to suppose that with a bit of luck some of their coffee
ended up in the inventory of an upscale U.S. coffee shop. For every $4 cup of
cafe latte sold, Don Ramon would receive about $0.02—less than 1%. Coffee
processors and exporters, transportation companies, advertising agencies, roasters,
retailers and other intermediaries would take the remaining 99%.

In spite of all that, Don Ramon is one of the lucky ones. Most people have no   11
hope of owning their own land. In Guatemala, just 2% of the population owns 80%
of the land. Not coincidentally, three-quarters of Guatemalans live in poverty, with
nearly 60% of the population unable to meet minimal nutritional needs. Eighty-five
percent of children under age five experience malnourishment to some degree, and
stunted growth affects up to 95% of non-Spanish speaking children in some regions
of the country.[4]

Don Ramon is luckier still because of his steady $17 per week job as a bee   12
keeper. For many highlands residents, however, not only is land an impossible
dream, but work itself has become scarce. Many highlands families survived for
generations as residential employees of the giant coffee plantations, a throwback to
the days of the colonial encomienda, or royal land commissions, where the indigenous were expelled from their own lands and, through a variety of forced-labor
laws, made to work on the estates. The Constitution ostensibly protects modern
plantation workers by obligating owners to provide workers with housing, clean
water, a minimum wage (currently $2.80 per day), schooling and health care—not a
bad deal, on paper. In reality, many of those services are not provided, including
payment of the minimum wage. More often than not, a daily wage of only $2.10–
$2.60 is paid. Guatemala's own Ministry of Labor estimates that there is only 15%
compliance with payment of the minimum wage in rural areas.[5] Since workers are
generally poorly educated, not aware of their legal rights, and with no local authority to whom they can turn, owners can operate with impunity. Nevertheless, there is
some limited degree of security for the families in this arrangement, no matter how
inequitable.

A trend begun on the coastal sugar plantations in the 1980s, which is gaining   13
more and more acceptance on the coffee estates of the highlands, is to use seasonal
or sometimes daily contract laborers instead of permanent employees. For the owners, efficiencies—i.e., cost-savings from not having to provide year-round wages
and benefits—far outweigh the uncertainties associated with having to hire and supervise temporary workers. There is also a secondary financial benefit that comes
from releasing hundreds of families into the labor market. Their presence in the

contract labor force helps to put further downward pressure on an already dis-
tressed labor market, allowing the owner to pay wages far below the legal minimum. For the families, on the other hand, who have been kicked out of the only
homes they have ever known for generation upon generation, life takes a turn for
the worse. They have little choice but to join the ranks of the seasonal work force.
Their wages, which were never totally adequate in the first place, get cut in half or
more since seasonal work is just that—seasonal. Plus, without land, there is no
means to grow one's own food. Housing, medical care and schooling become additional complicated financial matters.

14   With at most six months of work at the subminimum wages of approximately
$2.30 a day, feeding and caring for a typical highlands family of six is nearly impos-
sible. All hopes will be pinned on a bountiful coffee harvest. The months of January
and February are the peak months and entire families will head up the mountain-
sides at daybreak to pick coffee for the owner. They are paid by the pound, and with
all hands working feverishly they may pick 300 pounds a day. At a pay scale aver-
aging $0.023 per pound, the family may bring home approximately $6.90 every day
during this peak period. It is imperative that these two months go well for the families because nearly 70% of their annual income is earned at this time. The yields
are so much lower in the month before and the month after that only 25–30 pounds
per day, or $0.62 per day, can be counted on.

15   With some luck, the father and possibly an older son may get hired for an extra
couple of months for weeding, pruning or planting on one of the plantations.
Additional work could conceivably be found on one of the coastal sugar plantations,
though the harvest season tends to overlap with that of coffee. At any rate, the family's income for the season will be in the vicinity of about $715, an amount that will
cover only about a third of the required minimal daily caloric intake of a basic corn
and beans diet.[6] In addition, housing, medical care, school and clothing will take as
much as a third out of this already strained family budget. Income-earning opportunities during the rainy season for families like the Ramons are limited. The occasional odd job—shining shoes, selling prepared foods in the market, or for the
desperate, begging or prostitution—brings only a modicum of financial relief. It is
not hard to see where the high statistics on malnutrition come from when so many
families face similar circumstances. It is also easy to see why a plot of one's own
land is so critical for survival.

16   To my knowledge, former U.S. Treasury Secretary Robert Rubin, the architect
of U.S. neoliberal economic policies during the 1990s, and his former deputy and
now successor, Lawrence Summers, never invited Don Ramon or any of the rest of
the world's poor campesinos to any of their free-market strategy sessions. Nor have
I seen any accounts of their visits to the countryside to share a meal and a discussion with the Don Ramons of the world for whom the benefits of trickle-down economics are slow to arrive.

17   Indeed, the current global crisis has little to do with the fact that Secretary Rubin
has not gotten interest rates or exchange rates right, or that the various countries'
budget deficits are too high, or some other statistical imbalance. It has a lot to do with
the fact that policies aimed at the developing world are far removed from the needs

and realities of the majority of the world's peoples. Such policies, implemented by the rich and powerful, assume a textbook world in which producers and consumers operate at arm's length, negotiating until a price and quantity are determined that clear the market and benefit both parties to the transaction. Overlooked are the more realistic scenarios whereby Don Ramon and other small producers receive take-it-or-leave-it prices from agribusiness concerns that control the world's markets.

A survey done by the Association for the Development of San Lucas Toliman, a highlands community in the heart of the coffee-growing region, indicated that small coffee producers need to receive a price of $28.50 per 100 pounds in order to cover their production costs and to put an adequate diet on the table. But the reality is that market prices have not been that high in years.[7] You can be sure that if there is a glut of coffee on world markets—and if the powerful coffee merchants have their way, there will always be a glut—prices will fall for Don Ramon and his family. On the other hand, cafe latte prices will hold firmly, or possibly rise a bit at the fashionable coffee houses.

U.S. Treasury policies, which draw upon free-trade concepts first espoused by the British economist David Ricardo over 200 years ago, are supposed to work like this: Guatemala should produce those products in which it has a comparative advantage, such as coffee, sugar and bananas. The United States, its largest trading partner, should do likewise, focusing on goods like sport utility vehicles (SUVs), computers and information services. Then, by trading freely with one another, their respective national incomes will be higher than if each country attempted to be self-sufficient in the production of all goods.

So how much coffee would a landowner in Guatemala have to produce to be able to afford to purchase the latest $50,000 SUV? At an average wholesale price for top-end, gourmet coffee of $100 per 100-pound sacks, the landowner would need to produce 250,000 pounds of coffee beans.[8] This would entail the use of approximately 50 acres of land.[9] The landowner would have to employ approximately 21 workers during a four-month harvest season and pay them approximately $0.23 per hour.[10] This would add up to a collective wage bill of about $5,700, or 11% percent of the cost of the SUV. If the plantation in this example happened to be among the country's largest, it might be in the vicinity of 600 acres, enabling the owner to buy a fleet of nearly 12 SUVs per year.[11]

On the other hand, suppose that one of the boss's workers also wanted to purchase a vehicle. If he were somehow able to save every single cent of his paycheck it would take him 18 years to accumulate enough money to buy a $5,000 used car. To buy an SUV he would have to share the purchase with each of his 21 co-workers and they would each have to save the entirety of their paychecks for nine years.

Such free-trade policies will be deemed successful as long as they can continue to generate 20% returns year in, year out, in the U.S. financial markets. But how long can this continue? The investment guru Peter Lynch emphasizes in his television commercials for Fidelity Investments that there is nothing magical about successful stock-market investing. Good portfolio performance results from doing one's homework, from carefully scrutinizing those companies that have strong profit potential. What is not mentioned, however, is how those profits come about, and especially how critical the connection is to the developing world.

23   Profits, of course, arise when sales revenues exceed the costs of production. Don Ramon might be amazed to realize just how vital he is to the amassing of global corporate profits—he figures critically in both variables in the profit equation (revenues and costs). To the coffee merchants, his family's 2,500 pounds of coffee sold at $14 represents just another cost of doing business. The more small growers like him there are around the world, the more coffee is produced. And with more coffee comes lower production costs for the coffee multinationals. The lower coffee prices are, however, the less food Dona Ramon can afford to buy for her family's meals. But that is not the concern of the coffee companies.

24   The Ramon family is also critical to the revenue side of the equation. Here is how that connection works. The United States produces many more goods than it is capable of consuming domestically. In certain industries such as agriculture, this imbalance is quite significant. For example, wheat production exceeds domestic consumption by as much as 50% in a given year, corn by 25%. In order for corporations to provide investors with healthy annual returns, not only do they need to hold the line on costs, but they also need to find overseas outlets for their surpluses. To follow our example, this entails finding markets for as much as 50,000,000 metric tons of wheat and corn per year.[12] Exports, therefore, represent an increasingly large share of gross domestic product (GDP), having grown from less than 6% to nearly 15% of GDP in the past ten years. Also, developing countries have become increasingly more important as destinations for U.S. surpluses during this period, increasing their share of U.S. exports from 35% to 45%.[13] In countries like Guatemala, the well-to-do have been consuming imports from the United States for years. It is people like Don Ramon and his highlands neighbors who are being called upon more and more these days to do their share.

25   We have created a system that generates enormous profits for a select few who sell products like soft drinks, snacks and cigarettes to the masses around the world. The glitch occurs when the masses can no longer afford to buy these things. When this happens, the system begins to grind to a halt. In other words, the system is sustainable only as long as the masses are actually able to participate in it—that is, when they are paid a living wage. And the system has limited sustainability when the people who actually have enough disposable income to buy these consumer goods number less than 10% in most countries of the developing world.

26   For the moment, thanks to aggressive advertising—as well as high sugar and nicotine content—Don Ramon and the remaining 90% in Guatemala who are among the have-nots are obediently consuming soft drinks, snacks and cigarettes like there is no tomorrow, much to the detriment of their health and well-being. It is not an uncommon sight to see a family that cannot afford to send its kids to school or buy them shoes spending their hard-earned quetzales on Coca-Cola, Chiclets, Doritos or Marlboro cigarettes. However, it seems unlikely that the means exist for the Ramons and their neighbors to increase their purchases of these products year after year so that the companies that peddle these products can continue to expand. Amazingly though, stock market investors continue to place their bets that somehow the multinationals will continue to reach more people throughout the world with their advertising, or convince those already in their grasp to big deeper into their pockets to buy even more.

Herein lies a core capitalist contradiction. With the goal of increasing global profits, corporations are searching all over the world for new customers like Don Ramon, promising them unlimited happiness if they would just buy their products. The corporations' hope, on the other hand, is that someone else will pay these customers a high enough wage so that they can afford the products. So far, no one appears willing to do so. 27

Like the global corporations, Guatemala's oligarchy also faces a contradiction. In its effort to maintain power, prestige and wealth, it refuses to treat the indigenous and campesino poor of its country humanely—to share the richness of the land. Without land, the poor are forced to work as seasonal laborers or to assemble clothes in the maquiladoras for wages that cannot put food on the table, much less buy consumer goods or luxury items. Guatemala's producers thus have no choice but to become ever more dependent on export sales. What they find, though, is that the oligarchy in nearly every other developing country is doing the same thing, from Brazil to Indonesia to Russia. Prices around the world fall as a result of the collective attempt to run trade surpluses. The people who have to tighten their belts as a result are not the landowners—they do not want to give up their SUVs and their country clubs—but rather the Don Ramons of the world. 28

Notes

1. *Newsweek International*, February 1, 1999.
2. See, for example, the four-part *New York Times* series "Global Contagion," February 15–18, 1999.
3. *Newsweek International*, February 1, 1999, p. 56.
4. *Bread for the World: Hunger 1990* (Washington, D.C.: Bread for the World Institute on Hunger and Development, 1990).
5. Tom Barry, *Inside Guatemala* (Albuquerque: Inter-Hemispheric Education Resource Center, 1992), p. 97.
6. At current market prices for corn ($0.11 per pound) and beans ($0.54 per pound), it would take $5.20 per day to provide a family of six with the minimal daily required calories (2,900—men, 2,340–women, 1,485–children) based on figures from the National Academy of Sciences. An annual income of $715 per year covers about 38% of the cost of the basic diet.
7. In an effort to address poverty in the area, the Association pays small coffee growers who meet exacting quality standards the above-market price of $28.50 per 100-pound sack. For more on this effort and other sustainable projects of the community, see John Abell, "Peace in Guatemala? The Story of San Lucas Toliman," in J. Brauer and W. G. Gissy, eds., *Economics of Conflict Resolution and Peace* (Brookfield: Ashgate Publishing Co., 1997), pp. 150–178.
8. This assumes a ratio of five-to-one raw bean to wholesale (what is known as green coffee).
9. This assumes a yield of approximately 5,000 pounds per acre.
10. This assumes each worker can pick on average 100 pounds per day. The actual day-to-day yield will depend, of course, on the stage in the harvest.
11. Barry, *Inside Guatemala*, p. 104. The exact average is 582.
12. Agricultural data from: U.S. Department of Agriculture, USDA Economic Research Service, an online data service.
13. Guatemala has gone from essentially being self-sufficient in the production of corn, importing only a negligible amount in the 1960s, to importing 25% of its domestic needs in the 1990s from the United States and other countries. Cheap U.S. wheat has swamped the domestic wheat industry such that nearly 100% of all wheat consumed domestically is imported.

Let Them Sweat

Nicholas D. Kristof

Nicholas D. Kristof is a columnist for the liberal newspaper the New York Times. *He and his wife, Sheryl WuDunn, won a 1990 Pulitzer prize for their joint coverage of the Tiananmen Square democracy movement in China. "Let Them Sweat" appeared as an op-ed piece in the* New York Times *on June 25, 2002, and immediately generated much angry rebuttal. Usually writing from a liberal perspective, Kristof surprised many readers with his support of sweatshops.*

1   When the G-8 leaders[1] meet this week, cowering in a Canadian mountain resort beyond the reach of organized anarchists, here's a way for them to bolster terror-infested third world countries like Pakistan.

2   They should start an international campaign to promote imports from sweatshops, perhaps with bold labels depicting an unrecognizable flag and the words "Proudly Made in a Third World Sweatshop!"

3   The Gentle Reader will think I've been smoking Pakistani opium. But the fact is that sweatshops are the only hope of kids like Ahmed Zia, a 14-year-old boy here in Attock, a gritty center for carpet weaving.

4   Ahmed, who dropped out of school in the second grade, earns $2 a day hunched over the loom, laboring over a rug that will adorn some American's living room. It is a pittance, but the American campaign against sweatshops could make his life much more wretched by inadvertently encouraging mechanization that could cost him his job.

5   "Carpet-making is much better than farm work," Ahmed said, mulling alternatives if he loses his job as hundreds of others have over the last year. "This makes much more money and is more comfortable."

6   Indeed, talk to third world factory workers and the whole idea of "sweatshops" seems a misnomer. It is farmers and brick-makers who really sweat under the broiling sun, while sweatshop workers merely glow.

7   The third world is already battered by heartless conservatives in the West who peddle arms and cigarettes or who (like the Bushies) block $34 million desperately needed for maternal and infant health by the United Nations Population Fund. So it's catastrophic for muddle-minded liberals to join in and cudgel impoverished workers for whom a sweatshop job is the first step on life's escalator.

8   By this point, I've offended every possible reader. But before you spurn a shirt made by someone like 8-year-old Kamis Saboor, an Afghan refugee whose father is dead and who is the sole breadwinner in the family, answer this question: How does shunning sweatshop products help Kamis? All the alternatives for him are worse.

---

[1]The G-8 (Group of 8) is an informal group of eight countries: Canada, France, Germany, Italy, Japan, Russia, the United Kingdom, and the United States. Each year, G-8 leaders and representatives from the European Union meet to discuss broad economic and foreign policies. Often G-8 meetings are closely allied with the World Trade Organization.

"I dream of a job in a factory," said Noroz Khan, who lives on a garbage dump   9
and spends his days searching for metal that he can sell to recyclers. He earns
about $1.40 a day, and children earn just 30 cents a day for scrounging barefoot in
the filth—a few feet away from us, birds were pecking at the bloated carcass of a
cow, its feet in the air.

Of course, Western anti-sweatshop activists mean well and aim only for   10
improved conditions and a "living wage." But the reality is that the bad publicity
becomes one more headache for companies considering operating in international
hellholes (where the only lure is wages so low that it would be embarrassing if journalists started asking questions about them), and so manufacturers opt to mecha-
nize their operations and operate in somewhat more developed countries.

For example, Nike has 35 contract factories in Taiwan, 49 in South Korea, only   11
3 in Pakistan and none at all in Afghanistan—if it did, critics would immediately
fulminate about low wages, glue vapors, the mistreatment of women.

But the losers are the Afghans, and especially Afghan women. The country is   12
full of starving widows who can find no jobs. If Nike hired them at 10 cents an hour
to fill all-female sweatshops, they and their country would be hugely better off.

Nike used to have two contract factories in impoverished Cambodia, among the   13
neediest countries in the world. Then there was an outcry after BBC reported that
three girls in one factory were under 15 years old. So Nike fled controversy by ceas-
ing production in Cambodia.

The result was that some of the 2,000 Cambodians (90 percent of them young   14
women) who worked in those factories faced layoffs. Some who lost their jobs probably were ensnared in Cambodia's huge sex slave industry—which leaves many
girls dead of AIDS by the end of their teenage years.

The G-8 leaders will never dare, of course, begin a pro-sweatshop campaign.   15
But at a summit that will discuss how to bring stability and economic growth to
some of the world's poorest nations, it would be a start if Westerners who denounce
sweatshops would think less of feel-good measures for themselves and more about
how any of this helps people like Ahmed and Kamis.

Nicholas D. Kristof: Columnist Endorses Slave Labor for Children

Chris Anderson

This letter to the editor appeared in the Seattle Post Intelligencer *on July 7, 2002. It disagrees with Kristof's op-ed piece "Let Them Sweat" (pp. 626–627).*

Nicholas D. Kristof says in his June 28 column that Third World sweatshops are   1
not entirely bad because they "are the only hope of such kids as Ahmed Zia, a 14-
year-old in Attock, a gritty center for carpet weaving."

2.   The fact that Kristof is endorsing child slave labor (he writes, "Zia earns $2 a day, hunched over the loom, laboring over a rug that will adorn some American's living room" and that "8-year-old Kamis Saboor, an Afghan refugee . . . is the sole breadwinner in the family . . .") is disgusting enough.

3   The fact that American corporations are becoming filthy rich through this child labor exploitation makes me want to vomit. The possibility that Zia would be worse off without that job is a cop-out, it's like saying before the Civil War that blacks in the South would be worse off it they were freed. The fact that many blacks may have been worse off does not give justification to the doctrine of slavery.

4   If the World Bank and the International Monetary Fund were to endorse their original agenda, which was to help out Third World countries; and if world trade laws were designed to promote democracy, labor rights, stringent health and safety regulations, child labor laws and environmental protection—then I might be more amenable to Krisof's argument—except for the fact that it's stealing jobs from American workers. As it is, the World Bank and the IMF work in conjunction with major corporations to push world trade laws that exploit Third World labor for private profits, which include virtual slavery for such children as Ahmed Zia and Kamis Saboor.

Pennies an Hour, and No Way Up
Tom Hayden and Charles Kernaghan

Tom Hayden, a former California state senator, was a prominent civil rights and antiwar activist in the sixties. In the seventies, with his then-wife Jane Fonda, he became a leader in the environmental and anti–nuclear war movements. He is the author of nine books, including The Lost Gospel of the Earth, The Whole World Was Watching, *and* Irish Hunger. *Charles Kernaghan is the director of the National Labor Committee, an independent, nonprofit human rights organization focused on the protection of worker rights. This argument appeared as a guest op-ed piece in the* New York Times *on July 6, 2002, in response to Kristof's "Let Them Sweat."*

1   In last week's meeting in Canada, the Group of Eight industrial nations grappled with the question of how to better economic conditions in poor nations. One powerful means would be to improve the conditions of workers in sweatshops. Two billion people in the world make less than two American dollars a day. As voters and consumers of sweatshop products, Americans can make a difference in ending the miserable conditions under which these people work.

2   Some argue that sweatshops are simply a step up a ladder toward the next generation's success: the garment worker at her loom is carrying out some objective law of development, or the young girl making toys for our children is breaking out of male-dominated feudalism. This line of thinking recalls the mythic rise of our immigrant ancestors to the middle class and beyond.

But the real story of those white ethnic ancestors was hardly a smooth ride up the escalator. Life in New York was better than oppression abroad, but people worked 16 hours a day for paltry wages, lived in cellars with raw sewage, died of starvation and fever and were crowded into tenements. Their misery shocked reformers like Jacob Riis and Charles Dickens. They fought their way out—marched for economic justice, built unions, voted and finally forced the Gilded Age to become the New Deal.

Today young, mostly female workers in Bangladesh, a Muslim country that is the fourth-largest garment producer for the United States market, are paid an average of 1.6 cents for each baseball cap with a Harvard logo that they sew. The caps retail at the Harvard bookstore for $17, which means the garment workers, who often are younger than the Harvard students, are being paid a tenth of 1 percent of the cap's price in the market. Also in Bangladesh, women receive 5 cents for each $17.99 Disney shirt they sew. Wages like these are not enough to climb the ladder with.

There are similar conditions in China. Three million young Chinese women working for wages as low as 12 cents an hour make 80 percent of the sporting goods and toys sold in the United States each year. Companies like Mattel spend 30 times more to advertise a toy than they pay the workers in China to make it.

Each year Americans buy 924 million garments and other textile items made in Bangladesh and $23.5 billion worth of toys and sporting goods from China. Don't we have the consumer and political power to pressure our corporations to end sweatshop wages paid to the people who make these goods? These workers are not demanding stock options and Jazzercise studios. Women in Bangladesh say they could care for their children if their wages rose to 34 cents an hour, two-tenths of 1 percent of the retail price of the Harvard hat.

Some economists argue that even the most exploited and impoverished workers are better off than those who are unemployed or trapped in slave labor. But that argument is not about offering anyone a ladder up, but about which ring of Dante's inferno people in developing nations are consigned to. We don't want Disney, Mattel, WalMart or other major American companies to leave the developing world. We simply want to end the race to the bottom in which companies force countries to compete in offering the lowest wages for their people's labor. There should be a floor beneath which no one has to live.

Our elected officials should end their subservience to corporate donors and begin asking some big questions: Aren't we entitled to know the addresses of corporate sweatshops in developing countries so they can be open to monitoring by local advocates? Why should our tax dollars subsidize government purchases from companies that operate sweatshops?

Under our customs laws, we ban imports made with inmate and indentured labor, so why not extend the ban to include those made with sweatshop and child labor? And if we insist on enforcement of laws against pirate labels and CD's, why not protect 16-year-olds who make CD's for American companies? We should be helping these workers elbow and push their way up from squalor just as American progressives once helped our immigrant forebears.

From Cherry Garcia to Sweatshop Reform

Danielle Stein (student)

Danielle Stein is an editorial writer for the Cornell Daily Sun. *According to its Web page, the* Cornell Daily Sun *was founded in 1880 and is the second oldest college newspaper in the United States. It "always has been completely independent from Cornell University" and is "entirely student-run." This student-written op-ed piece appeared in the* Cornell Daily Sun *on April 10, 2002.*

1   Thank goodness for Ben and Jerry. They are the men who have brought us Chubby Hubby, Cherry Garcia, and Festivus (a tasty new flavor named in honor of George Costanza's made-up family holiday). They have given us chocolate-covered pretzels in our ice cream and have made us feel good about consuming a pint chock full of brownies and cookie dough merely by labeling it "Frozen Yogurt." They've given us counterculture references for flavor names and quirkly commercials filmed in Vermont. And now they're giving us fashion.

2   Well actually, only Ben (he does have a last name—Cohen) gets credits for this one. The ice cream king, who has long been involved in social activism, has combined his politics and his entrepreneurial talents in a clothing line called SweatX. The company's goal is to create clothing while giving workers quality of life— paying them $8.50 per hour (much more than the average sweatshop factory employee receives) plus benefits, a pension, and profit sharing as well as top-of-the-line equipment and a pleasant environment in which to work. SweatX is out to prove that it's possible to be successful while still treating employees well. And in Los Angeles, a hotbed of sweatshops where workers are regularly paid less than minimum wage for long hours in unsafe conditions, this is a crucial message.

3   This new clothing firm, which will produce casual clothing like T-shirts and sweatpants, is perhaps the most hopeful step in the fight against sweatshop labor. Because there are many concerned people out there—myself included—who might deplore the way most of our clothing is produced, but who have few apparel alternatives. For instance, I know that Nike is a glaring example of abhorrent labor practices, so I avoid their products. But I don't have the statistics on most of the other clothing lines out there, and I would believe that many of the companies I do patronize are paying South American workers 15 cents per hour to make my cable-knit sweater. And for the average consumer who does not spend her life as a labor activist, it is difficult to avoid the products of all offending companies.

4   But SweatX gives us an entirely new angle from which to wage this battle. Instead of asking consumers to stop buying from companies with less-than-perfect labor policies, it invites us to support one that passes the test. Instead of making activism require a decrease in consumerism (which is an unsuccessful tactic in our consumer-driven society), it allows us to make a statement and simultaneously get

cool stuff! Throwing a little support in SweatX's direction contributes to its success, and the financial success of a garment business that practices humane treatment of workers would serve as proof to the industry that its trespasses are inexcusable. And if the industry loses its justification—that it needs cheap labor to profit—sweatshops are on the way out.

SweatX seeks to market its clothing in sports shops and college bookstores, 5 drawing on the recent increase in anti-sweatshop activism on campuses across the country (as is evident here at Cornell). But the director of the California Fashion Association, Ilse Metchek, was quoted in the *LA Times* expressing her skepticism that students would support the project. "Students protest. They yell and scream. But when push comes to shove, they go to Wal-Mart and buy clothing made in Saipan."

It's time to prove people like Metchek wrong. Many of us may not have enough 6 willpower or alternatives to shun big clothing labels like Nike, but this does not mean we won't rally around causes we support, especially if they require little effort (often a prerequisite for college student participation) and result in cute additions to our wardrobes. Ben Cohen and his colleagues have created something that has both innovation and integrity, and they deserve our support.

Ben Cohen's SweatX has the potential to revolutionize labor practices in the 7 garment industry. If successful, it could become the prototype for other companies who could no longer claim they can't turn profits without exploiting workers. But it's a new project and has yet to prove itself. As its success would mean progress for labor practices, its failure would mean regression. Support of this endeavor—in the form of consumerism, publicity, whatever—by college students is essential. It could make worker's rights the flavor of the future.

Heart of Cheapness

Paul Krugman

The occasion for this op-ed piece was a joint tour by Paul O'Neill, Secretary of the Treasury, and Bono, the lead singer for U2. Bono, a star-quality activist in the fight against African poverty and AIDS, described his awakening to these issues in a speech delivered to the African Development Bank Group in May 2002. "Seventeen years ago, I came to Ethiopia on a wave of tears and compassion . . . flowing from the rich countries to the poor, from soccer stadiums taken over by musicians to refugee camps taken over by the starving war weary people of Ethiopia. . . . We discovered what you here today already knew. That a lot of the problems facing the developing world are structural . . . deeply embedded in a dysfunctional relationship with the developed world that's been so wrong for so long."[1] In this op-ed piece, which appeared in the New York Times *on May 31,*

2002, Paul Krugman uses Bono's crusade to question America's spending priorities. Krugman is a liberal New York Times *columnist and an economics professor at Princeton.*

1   Poor Bono. He got stuck in a moment, and he couldn't get out of it.

2   In one of the oddest enterprises in the history of development economics, Bono—the lead singer for the rock band U2—has been touring Africa with Paul O'Neill, secretary of the treasury. For a while, the latent tensions between the two men were masked by Bono's courtesy; but on Monday he lost his cool.

3   The pair were visiting a village in Uganda, where a new well yielding clean water has radically improved the villagers' health. Mr. O'Neill's conclusion from this, as from the other development projects he saw, was that big improvements in people's lives don't require much money—and therefore that no big increase in foreign aid is required. By the way, the United States currently spends 0.11 percent of G.D.P. on foreign aid; Canada and major European countries are about three times as generous. The Bush administration's proposed "Millennium Fund" will increase our aid share, but only to 0.13 percent.

4   Bono was furious, declaring that the projects demonstrated just the opposite, that the well was "an example of why we need big money for development. And it is absolutely not an example of why we don't. And if the secretary can't see that, we're going to have to get him a pair of glasses and a new set of ears."

5   Maybe the easiest way to refute Mr. O'Neill is to recall last year's proposal by the World Health Organization, which wants to provide poor countries with such basic items as antibiotics and insecticide-treated mosquito nets. If the U.S. had backed the proposed program, which the W.H.O. estimated would save eight million lives each year, America's contribution would have been about $10 billion annually—a dime a day per American, but nonetheless a doubling of our current spending on foreign aid Saving lives—even African lives—costs money.

6   But is Mr. O'Neill really blind and deaf to Africa's needs? Probably not. He is caught between a rock star and a hard place: he wants to show concern about global poverty, but Washington has other priorities.

7   A striking demonstration of those priorities is the contrast between the Bush administration's curt dismissal of the W.H.O. proposal and the bipartisan drive to make permanent the recent repeal of the estate tax. What's notable about that drive is that opponents of the estate tax didn't even try to make a trickle-down argument, to assert that reducing taxes on wealthy heirs is good for all of us. Instead, they made an emotional appeal—they wanted us to feel the pain of those who pay the "death tax." And the sob stories worked; Congress brushed aside proposals to retain the tax, even proposals that would raise the exemption—the share of any estate that is free from tax—to $5 million.

8   Let's do the math here. An estate tax with an exemption of $5 million would affect only a handful of very wealthy families: in 1999 only 3,300 estates had a

---

[1]http://www.afdb.org/knowledge/speeches2001/statement-bono-am2002e.htm, retrieved on Oct. 31, 2002.

taxable value of more than $5 million. The average value of those estates was $16 million. If the excess over $5 million were taxed at pre-2001 rates, the average taxed family would be left with $10 million—which doesn't sound like hardship to me—and the government would collect $20 billion in revenue each year. But no; the whole tax must go.

So here are our priorities. Faced with a proposal that would save the lives of   9
eight million people every year, many of them children, we balk at the cost. But when asked to give up revenue equal to twice that cost, in order to allow each of 3,300 lucky families to collect its full $16 million inheritance rather than a mere $10 million, we don't hesitate. Leave no heir behind!

Which brings us back to the Bono-O'Neill tour. The rock star must have hoped   10
that top American officials are ignorant rather than callous—that they just don't realize what conditions are like in poor countries, and how foreign aid can make a difference. By showing Mr. O'Neill the realities of poverty and the benefits aid can bring, Bono hoped to find and kindle the spark of compassion that surely must lurk in the hearts of those who claim to be compassionate conservatives.

But he still hasn't found what he's looking for.   11

Aldo Leopold's Land Ethic: Is It Only Half a Loaf?

Douglas W. MacCleery

Douglas W. MacCleery is a professional forester who has worked in natural resource management and policy for his entire career. This article appeared in the scholarly Journal of Forestry *in October 2000. Its immediate occasion is MacCleery's pondering of a dilemma: Americans want to preserve national forests, but they also want to live in big houses made of wood. We have placed this article in this unit because it focuses on consumers rather than corporations and reveals a complex interconnection of issues. (We could just as easily have placed this article in the unit on SUVs, on corporate ethics, or even on the ethics of food production.)*

Over the past two decades there has been a substantial shift in the manage-   1
ment emphasis of public, particularly federal, lands in the United States. That shift has been to a substantially increased emphasis on managing these lands for biodiversity protection and amenity values, with a corresponding reduction in commodity outputs. Over the past decade, timber harvest on national forest lands has dropped by 70 percent, oil and gas leasing by about 40 percent, and livestock grazing by at least 10 percent.

Terms like "ecosystem management," an "ecological approach to manage-   2
ment," and, more recently, "ecological sustainability" have been used to describe

this change in the management emphasis on public lands. Many have referred to it as a significant "paradigm shift." Recently, a Committee of Scientists report proposed that the national forests be managed for "ecological sustainability," where primary management emphasis is to be placed on "what is left" out on the land, rather than "what is removed" (Committee of Scientists 1999). Commodity outputs, if they are produced, would be subservient to managing national forests for primarily a biodiversity protection objective. Significantly, some committee members bottomed this recommendation in part on "ethical and moral" grounds.

3   Many have attributed the move to ecosystem management or ecological sustainability to a belated recognition and adoption of Aldo Leopold's "land ethic"—the idea that management of land has, or should have, an ethical content. One sign that Leopold's ideas have finally struck a chord with the larger society is that conservation issues are increasingly being taken up as causes by American churches.

4   While a mission shift on US public lands is occurring in response to changing public preferences, that same public is making no corresponding shift in its commodity consumption habits. The "dirty little secret" about the management shift on US public lands is that, in the face of stable or increasing per capita consumption in the United States, the effect has been to shift the burden and impacts of that consumption to ecosystems somewhere else—for example, to private lands in this country or to lands in other countries.

5   Between 1987 and 1997, federal timber harvest dropped 70 percent, from about 13 billion to 4 billion board feet (bbf) annually (this 9 bbf reduction is "log scale," which translates into about a 15 bbf reduction in lumber that could have been processed from it—or about one-third of US annual softwood lumber production). A significant effect of this reduction, in the face of continuing high levels of US per capita wood consumption, has been to transfer harvest to private forest ecosystems in the United States and to forest ecosystems in Canada. For example:

- Since 1990, US softwood lumber imports from Canada rose from 12 to 18 bbf, increasing from 27 to 36 percent of US softwood lumber consumption. Much of the increase in Canadian lumber imports has come from the native old-growth boreal forests. In Quebec alone, the export of lumber to the United States has tripled since 1990. The increased harvesting of the boreal forests in Quebec has become a public issue there.
- Harvesting on private lands in the southern United States also increased after the reduction of federal timber in the West. Today, the harvest of softwood timber in the southeastern United States exceeds the rate of growth for the first time in at least 50 years. Increased harvesting of fiber by chip mills in the Southeast has become a public issue regionally.

6   The US public consumes more resources today than at any time in its history and also consumes more resources per capita than almost any other nation. Since the first Earth Day in 1970, the size of the average family in the United States has dropped by 16 percent, while the size of the average new single-family house has increased by 48 percent.

The US conservation community and the media have given scant attention to 7
the "ecological transfer effects" of the mission shift on US public lands. Any ethical
or moral foundation for ecological sustainability is weak indeed unless there is a
corresponding focus on the consumption side of the natural resource equation.
Without such a connection, ecological sustainability on public lands is subject to
challenge as just a sophisticated form of NIMBYism ("not in my back yard") rather
than a true paradigm shift.

A cynic might assert that one of the reasons for the belated adoption of Aldo 8
Leopold's land ethic is that it has become relatively easy and painless for most of us
to do so. When Leopold was a young man forming his ideas, more than 40 percent of
the US population lived on farms. An additional 20 percent lived in rural areas and
were closely associated with the management of land. Today, less than 2 percent of
us are farmers and most of us, even those living in rural areas, are disconnected
from any direct role in the management of land. Adopting a land ethic is easy for
most of us today because it imposes onto someone else the primary burden to act.

Even though few of us are resource producers anymore, we all remain resource 9
consumers. This is one area we all can act on that could have a positive effect on resource use, demand, and management. If one accepts the extension of ethics to the
management of land, it would seem to be a relatively minor leap of logic to accept
the idea that one's consumption choices—which also affect land—have an ethical
content as well. Yet few of us connect our resource consumption to what must be
done to the land to make it possible. While many of us espouse the land ethic, our
operating motto in the marketplace seems to be "shop 'til you drop" or "whoever
dies with the most toys wins."

The disjunct between people as consumers and the land is reflected in rising dis- 10
cord and alienation between producers and consumers. Loggers, ranchers, fishermen,
miners, and other resource producers have at times been subject to scorn and ridicule
by the very society that benefits from the products they produce. What is absent from
much environmental discourse in the United States today is a recognition that urban-
ized society is no less dependent on the products of forest and field than were the sub-
sistence farmers of America's past. This is clearly reflected in the language used in
such discourse. Rural communities traditionally engaged in producing timber and
other natural resources for urban consumers are commonly referred to as natural resource–"dependent" communities. Seldom are the other resource-dependent communities like Boulder, Denver, Detroit, or Boston ever referred to as such.

One of the relatively little known periods of Aldo Leopold's career are the years 11
he spent at the Forest Service's Forest Products Lab at Madison, Wisconsin. While
there, he spoke of the need for responsible consumption. In 1928 Leopold wrote:

> The American public for many years has been abusing the wasteful lumberman. A public
> which lives in wooden houses should be careful about throwing stones at lumbermen, even
> wasteful ones, until it has learned how its own arbitrary demands as to kinds and qualities of
> lumber, help cause the waste which it decries. . . . The long and the short of the matter is
> that forest conservation depends in part on intelligent consumption, as well as intelligent
> production of lumber. (p. 276–77)

12   If management of land has an ethical content, why does consumption not have a corresponding one? Is there a need for a "personal consumption ethic" to go along with Leopold's land ethic? In his wonderful land ethic chapter in *A Sand County Almanac,* Leopold wrote that, as evidence that no land ethic existed, a "farmer who clears the woods off a 75 percent slope, turns his cows into the clearing, and dumps its rainfall, rocks, and soil into the community creek, is still (if otherwise decent) a respected member of society" (Leopold 1949, p. 209).

13   To take off on that theme and make it more contemporary, the evidence that no personal consumption ethic exists today is that a suburban dweller with a small family who lives in a 4,000-square-foot home, owns three or four cars, commutes to work alone in a gas-guzzling sport utility vehicle (even though public transportation is available), and otherwise leads a highly resource-consumptive lifestyle is still (if otherwise decent) a respected member of society. Indeed, his or her social status in the community may even be enhanced by virtue of that consumption.

14   Ecosystem management or ecological sustainability on public lands will have weak or nonexistent ethical credentials and certainly will never be a truly holistic approach to resource management until the consumption side of the equation becomes an integral part of the solution, rather than an afterthought as it is today. Belated adoption of Leopold's land ethic was relatively easy. The true test of whether a paradigm shift has really occurred in the United States will be whether society begins to see personal consumption choices as having an ethical and environmental content as well—and then acts on them accordingly.

Literature Cited

Committee of Scientists. 1999. *Sustaining the people's lands: Recommendations for stewardship of the national forests and grasslands into the next century:* Washington, DC: US Department of Agriculture.
Leopold, A. 1928. The homebuilder conserves. *American Forests* May: 276–78.
———. 1949. *A Sand County almanac and sketches here and there.* New York: Oxford University Press.

For Class Discussion

1. Visit your campus bookstore and look at the labels of T-shirts and sweatshirts bearing your college or university logo. Who manufactures these garments? Where were they assembled? Try to ascertain whether your college or university has been involved in any discussion of sweatshop issues.

2. Suppose you wanted your college or university to take a stand on sweatshops. Based on the readings in this unit, what course of action would you recommend? What further research would you need to do?

3. The World Trade Organization (WTO), as we have seen, is an international organization that mediates trade disputes among its member organizations and tries to promote a tariff-free exchange of goods and labor across borders. Because its mission is to reduce restrictions on free trade, it typically

rules against countries whose trade practices try to protect domestic industries or local labor. Based on the readings in this unit and on any further research you might be assigned to do, what are the arguments for and against free trade?

4. When the World Trade Organization held a conference in Seattle in early December 1999, thousands of protesters disrupted the meetings. Equivalent protests have occurred at subsequent WTO or G-8 meetings around the world. Defenders of the WTO, who support free trade, praise multinational corporations for creating jobs in third-world countries and bringing technological advances to all nations. To what extent would the writers of the readings in this unit share the WTO's views about the benefits of multinational corporations? Imagine a panel discussion that included the writers of the readings in this section but also included Don Ramon from John D. Abell's "The Neoliberal World Order: The View from the Highlands of Guatemala"; a Carnival Against Capitalism protester like the one on the poster on page 609; Ahmid Zia, the 14-year-old Pakistani boy in Nicholas D. Kristof's "Let Them Sweat"; and Bono from U2. You might also choose to include in your imagined panel discussion a U.S. senator or representative from your home state.

   a. What points of view would emerge from this panel discussion?

   b. What position on free trade would you want the president of the United States to have (or your senator or representative)?

5. Choose one of the readings in this unit and analyze it carefully using the List 2 Guide questions on pages 460–461.

OPTIONAL WRITING ASSIGNMENT: Imagine that the editorial staff of your college or university newspaper is doing a series of articles on either (a) sweatshops, in response to the disclosure that your campus buys its college-logo apparel from a manufacturer that uses overseas assembly plants or (b) the World Trade Organization, in response to recent campus demonstrations promoted by the Carnival Against Capitalism. Write an op-ed piece for your campus newspaper persuading some campus constituency to accept your views on one of these issues.

INTERNET CENSORSHIP: HATE SITES, PORNOGRAPHY, AND SPAM

Along with the substantial benefits brought by the Internet—particularly its vast resources for information, opinion, and communication—the Internet has created new concerns about freedom and censorship. Many arguments about the Internet are highly technical pieces written for specialists in computer science or information technology—for example, discussions of encryption programs to protect privacy or the technical features of filtering devices to block out pornography or hate sites. In contrast, the issues examined in this unit are of broad public interest: Should children be protected from hate sites and pornography? Should e-mail hate speech, stalker messages, or death threats be protected as free speech? What can be done about spam and other junk e-mail? Parents, particularly, need to make decisions about their children's use of the Internet, and citizens in general need to decide how broadly they wish to interpret the Constitution's protection of free speech. Should libraries, for example, be required to block out pornography sites? Should free speech protection be extended to spam or to vicious hate sites? The readings in this unit will introduce you to these public conversations about Internet freedom.

Cracking Down on E-Mail Harassment
Brooke A. Masters

In the following news analysis piece published in the Washington Post *in November 1998, staff writer Brooke A. Masters narrates examples of e-mail harassment and raises the civil liberties question of whether these cases represent protected free speech or criminal stalking in cyberspace. Near the end of the article, she mentions the widely publicized Richard Machado case. On September 20, 1996, student Richard Machado, on academic probation for low grades, sent obscenity-laced emails to 59 Asian students at the University of California at Irvine threatening to hunt them down individually and kill him. Machado became the first person convicted of e-mail hate crime in the United States.*

1   The e-mails started coming in April. Every day, James Gress's electronic mailbox at the Pentagon was clogged with 50 or more unwanted communications, including offers for pornography and subscriptions to online magazines such as "Workstation Tip of the Day" and "WebShoppers Hot Products Daily."

2   Gress, an official with the Defense Information Systems Agency, had no idea who was signing him up for all these services, but it had become all but impossible for him to identify the legitimate e-mails that he received for work.

So he complained to the Defense Criminal Investigative Service's new computer crimes unit. It tracked the subscriptions to a former underling, Trung Ngo, who apparently was still angry about a 1995 performance evaluation that rated him "Highly Successful" rather than "Outstanding," according to court documents.

As the online population has soared to an estimated 80 million users, the real-world crimes of harassment and stalking have moved into cyberspace, causing annoyance and outright fear for victims and headaches for law enforcement officials.

The mechanics of the Internet—mailing services and free e-mail accounts that make it possible to send vast numbers of anonymous messages with one keystroke—make it a fertile field for those seeking to frighten or intimidate, analysts said. A single user can send the same file to hundreds of people in far less time than it would take to telephone or write them.

At the same time, many police agencies are reluctant or ill equipped to deal with the problem because it is still so new and because it is often unclear when online misbehavior crosses the legal line from annoying to criminal. Many states are rushing to adapt their penal codes; in Maryland, a law making it a misdemeanor to send e-mail "with the intent to harass" went into effect Oct. 1.

About 30 percent of the 47,000 complaints reported so far this year to the Web Police, an international group that attempts to address online crime, involved harassing or threatening e-mail, said founder Peter Hampton. Last year, the group received fewer than 13,000 complaints.

Victims report everything from e-mail "bombs" that flood them with hundreds of messages to outright extortion and death threats, law enforcement agencies said. In a variation on the old "for a good time call Sally" prank, a 30-year-old Alexandria woman discovered that her name and phone number had been posted on matchmaking and sexual Web sites, leading other Internet users to send her suggestive or obscene messages.

Academics and others who study cyberspace say it is not clear whether e-mail has simply become another venue for crimes that would occur anyway or whether the electronic medium exacerbates the problem by making it easier to stalk and harass.

"The architecture of cyberspace might make it more common because you can do it all from your chair . . . without going to the trouble of tracking [a victim] down, going to their house and leaving a note," said Jonathan Zittrain, executive director of Harvard University's Berkman Center for Internet and Society. "It's easier to do and easier to do anonymously."

Last year, a Northern Virginia couple found themselves on the receiving end of several forms of harassment when they banned a Florida man from their online chat room on professional wrestling. First, the man, Emmett Gulley, of West Melbourne, kept trying to get back on to the chat room, posting insulting and threatening messages before they could throw him off. Then, he branched out.

"My husband has a Web page on the Net, and it has a guest book, and he started signing it, saying he was going to come after us and kill us," said the woman, 38, who asked not to be identified because authorities think Gulley never learned the Fredericksburg area couple's real names. "We tried calling the police, and they were clueless. It went on and on, and finally he started threatening my children."

13   Gulley also e-mailed them profanity-laced audio files containing more threats and telephoned and e-mailed threats to several other members of the chat room, according to court papers. He pleaded guilty two weeks ago to transmitting threats in interstate commerce and faces up to five years in prison when he is sentenced in U.S. District Court in Orlando in January. His lawyer declined to comment.

14   The chat room couple got results, they said, because they decided to call the FBI, which took their problem seriously. Special Agent John Mesisca said his Washington-based squad will get involved when the threats are interstate and make explicit reference to doing bodily harm. The Washington Field Office, which covers the District and Northern Virginia, opens about six e-mail threat cases each month, he said.

15   Most victims have a harder time getting help from law enforcement, online advocacy groups say.

16   "Usually, state and local law enforcement will . . . throw their hands up in the air unless you can show them off-line harassment," said Parry Aftab, executive director of Cyber Angels, the online offshoot of the Guardian Angels.

17   That's what happened to former Crofton resident Jayne Hitchcock.

18   In 1996 and 1997, Hitchcock was receiving several hundred e-mails at a time, and fake e-mails and postings to online groups were being sent out under her name.

19   When the writer complained to Anne Arundel County police, they "said there was no law that covered that. And the FBI said that unless there was a death threat against me there was nothing they could do," she said.

20   Eventually, the harassment escalated. Hitchcock, 39, who since has moved to New England, started receiving lewd phone calls after her name and phone number were posted to sexually oriented sites.

21   "If there had been a law, it never would have escalated, and I wouldn't have felt my life was in danger," she said. Hitchcock has filed a civil suit against the people she believes are behind the harassment.

22   Hitchcock was one of those urging Maryland legislators to adopt the new state law. In all, 17 states now have laws against online stalking or harassment, up from fewer than a half-dozen 18 months ago, said Nancy Savitt, a New Jersey-based lawyer who specializes in cyberspace issues. Neither Virginia nor the District has specific laws on e-mail harassment or stalking.

23   Some law enforcement agencies are also using existing laws against stalking and telephone harassment to go after those who abuse e-mail.

24   In the Pentagon e-mail case, Ngo, 32, pleaded guilty last month to "repeated telecommunications harassment." He could go to prison when he is sentenced in January in U.S. District Court in Alexandria because Congress recently beefed up the maximum penalties from six months to two years in prison.

25   His attorney, John Bevis, said Ngo is "a nice guy who had no idea of the laws that govern these situations."

Similarly, Gulley was prosecuted under a law that often is used for telephone threats, lawyers said. "A lot of electronic mail, they use the telephone wires, so we just adapt the law," Mesisca said.   26

In a California case, an e-mail harasser was charged under a federal civil rights law. This year, a federal jury convicted Richard J. Machado, a former student at the University of California at Irvine, in connection with a 1996 e-mail he sent to 59 mostly Asian students. The anonymous message, signed "Asian Hater," said, "I personally will . . . find and kill every one of you personally." Machado already had served a year in jail while awaiting trial and was sentenced to probation.   27

Legal analysts say they expect to see more criminal cases involving online harassment and stalking. However, criminalizing e-mail could raise civil liberties concerns. Overt threats to do harm clearly are not protected by the First Amendment, but some legal analysts worry that in the rush to make Internet users feel safe, lawmakers may trample on free speech by banning "lewd" communications or other e-mail that isn't clearly harmful.   28

"You can be crude, you can be rude, you can be nasty," said Stephen Brock, a Philadelphia lawyer who has handled several civil cases involving e-mail. "It's not a federal crime to be a jerk."   29

Hate Speech Conviction Outlaws Email

Kenneth Lake

Journalist Kenneth Lake, publishing on the Web site of Internet Freedom, a British advocacy group "opposed to all forms of censorship and content regulation on the Net" (from its home page), outlines the dangers to free speech posed by the Machado decision in the United States. This Web opinion piece was posted on February 13, 1998.

"I personally will make it my life career to find and kill every one of you personally" signed Asian Hater.   1

The words of an email message that is to have serious consequences for Internet freedom. They were written by Richard Machado, a Los Angeles man who was convicted last Tuesday (10/2/98) of sending racist death threats to 59 Asian students.   2

The email accused Asians for all the crimes on campus, and suggested that Machado would personally "find," "hunt down" and "kill" them if they did not leave the University of California at Irvine. The email was sent from a campus computer and signed "Asian Hater." Machado, a newly naturalised US citizen from El Salvador, was originally charged with 10 counts of civil rights violations. In November, however, a mis-trial was declared after the jury deadlocked and a re-trial was ordered by judge Alice Marie Stolter for the 27th January 1998. For this Machado was to be charged   3 with only two counts: sending the threat based on the recipients' race or ethnicity and "interfering" with their right to attend the University.

4   The case sets a precedent because it puts email on an equal legal footing with telephone calls and postal mail, and introduces the legal category of hate crimes to the online world.

5   Barry Steinhardt, associate director of the American Civil Liberties Union (ACLU), commented that whilst non-specific comments are protected as free speech, a specific threat against an individual is not. Professor Eugene Velokn of the ACLU School of Law added "if you threaten somebody's life in a way that a typical listener will think you're serious, that's constitutionally unprotected." In contrast, Mr Machado's defence attorney has argued that the federal law being used to prosecute his client is in effect criminalising email. However the director of San Francisco's public defenders office has stated that the Internet has no special immunities or special privileges because speech occurs on it.

6   Machado is surely a crackpot racist but his conviction has serious consequences for free speech generally. For some time there has been an authoritarian shift in the focus of criminal law from deed to word to thought. It is clear in this case that part of the rationale for the charge was the fact that Machado's threat was racially motivated. This is also the reasoning behind Jack Straw's introduction of an offence of racially motivated violence in the UK. But the determination of criminal liability essentially concentrates upon an act and whether the defendant intentionally, recklessly or knowingly committed it. A murder may be motivated by anger, misogyny, political conviction or mercy, but all the court wants to know, in order to convict, is whether there was a murder and whether it was committed intentionally by the defendant.

7   In Machado's case the only "act" was the sending of a threatening email. The criminalisation of email indicates the continuing expansion of the category of mental crime. In the UK in 1936 the Public Order Act banned "threatening, abusive or insulting words or behaviour" which "might provoke a breach of the peace." In 1986 "breach of the peace" was replaced by "harassment, alarm or distress." In 1997 the Protection from Harassment Act created a further offence of "a course of conduct" (including speech) amounting to harassment of another. The trajectory is to make words as well as deeds much more susceptible to prosecution.

8   It is difficult to see how Machado could have actually intended to carry out his threat to assassinate 59 students. It is far more likely that Machado's racist comments, like much speech among news groups and mailing lists, were simply an idle threat. Any experienced user will know that abusive messages and flames are commonplace on the Net.

9   The conviction of Machado means that not only will we have to watch what we say on the Net, but also with the criminalisation of motive we will have to watch why we think it. Before now it had never been a crime to hate anyone. Now it seems that there is an ever expanding category of thoughts that could put you in the clink.

10   For those who value free expression it is worth remembering that sticks and stones may break your bones but emails will never hurt you.

Internet's Hate Sites Can Be Hidden, but They Can't Be Ignored
Lawrence J. Magid

A serious dilemma for educators and parents is the problem of hate sites. Here Lawrence J. Magid, writing for the Web site of the Online Safety Project, gives his own views on how to approach hate sites. Lawrence J. Magid is a syndicated columnist, broadcaster, and author of numerous articles about online safety. In 1999 he and his colleagues were called "high tech heroes" by Time *magazine for work in developing online strategies for finding missing children. This article was published on safeteens.com on July 19, 1999.*

1   When I agreed to write a column about hate sites on the Internet, I knew that it would be an unsettling experience. But I had no idea just how disturbing it would be.

2   When I researched this topic about three years ago, I found some pretty unsavory sites. But this time I found a lot more, and some, frankly, were nauseating.

3   One was operated by the Church of the Creator, the group that 21-year-old Benjamin Smith was part of until shortly before he embarked on a killing spree in the Midwest that ended when he took his own life. That site was bad enough, but there are hundreds more like it. The Los Angeles-based Simon Wiesenthal Center (http://www.wiesenthal.org), which tracks hate sites, identified more than 1,400 "problematic" Web sites as of March—twice as many as it found the year before. Even that number may be conservative. Rabbi Abraham Cooper, the center's associate dean, estimates that there may be as many as 2,100.

4   I'm not going to go into vivid detail about what I found after looking at about 20 of these sites, but even I was shocked—and I have pretty thick skin. I expected to find Web sites that ridicule African Americans, Jews, gays, immigrants and others, but some took it a few steps further by combining bigotry with articles about guns, bombs and other implements of violence.

5   Others were designed deliberately to shock, with displays of swastikas, burning crosses and nooses. One site mixes hate with stories and photographs that celebrate sex and violence in the most extreme way imaginable.

6   What's most disturbing about these sites is that they're very easy to find. Unlike most pornography sites, the people who run hate sites don't usually put up even a feeble effort to keep out children. On the contrary, some overtly invite children and teens to participate. The Church of the Creator Web site had a children's section complete with puzzles and a coloring book. Another site has a "kids page" that is reportedly maintained by a 10-year-old. Many have music graphics and rhetoric designed to appeal to teens.

7   What can we do about this? We can't ban hate sites because it's impossible to take away the 1st Amendment rights of bigots without jeopardizing the free speech rights of the rest of us. Some people argue that we should place limits on free

speech, but even if we could agree on where to draw the line, many of the subtler and seemingly reasonable sites would slip through. In fact, some of the most dangerous sites don't even look like hate sites. They contain what appear to be reasonable—albeit misguided—scientific and historical arguments that, if believed, could lead young people and others to conclude that target groups really are inherently inferior or dangerous.

8   I don't think the government can or should do anything to ban these groups from the Internet, but there are things that individuals and groups can do to shield or inoculate children from them.

9   One option for parents is to install a filtering program that blocks sites advocating hate or violence. Most of the programs designed to keep kids away from pornography can also be configured to keep them out of known hate sites. The Anti-Defamation League (http://www.adl.org) has teamed up with the Learning Company to produce a special version of CyberPatrol called the ADL HateFilter, which blocks hate sites and "encourages parents to teach their children about the nature of bigotry and the hatemongers who promote it." The program, which runs on Windows, costs $29.95. A seven-day free trial version can be downloaded from ADL's Web site.

10   With or without filters, it's important for parents to talk with their kids about hate sites and bigotry in general. David Lehr, Pacific Southwest regional director of the Anti-Defamation League, recommends that parents "sit with your kids and point out the logical inconsistencies and danger of hate." He suggests that you "use these sites as teachable moments."

11   Rabbi Cooper agrees. Because kids are more Net-savvy in many cases than grown-ups, they may actually be more likely to know about hate sites than their parents. "Ask the kids to take a half-hour to show you the stuff," he suggests. "It's a good point of departure to sit down with your child to talk about these issues." You also can use this time to talk about music and other media that celebrate violence or degrade women, gays, minorities and others.

12   I agree with Lehr and Cooper. But even if you are 100% successful in inoculating your own kids from the influence of these sites, a lot more work has to be done. Not all parents will bother teaching their kids about the dangers of hate, and some even encourage it. Even those of us who believe we can help keep our kids from becoming bigots can't necessarily prevent them from becoming victims of bigotry.

13   After spending three days wallowing in other people's racist, sexist, homophobic, anti-Semitic, anti-Catholic and anti-immigrant propaganda, I've come to the conclusion that the only way to drown out this type of hate speech is through a massive education campaign that encourages our society—especially our youth—to think critically and question anyone who blames their problems on people who look, act, speak or think differently. Web sites operated by ADL and the Wiesenthal Center are a good starting point for ideas.

14   This is one area in which we all have responsibility for everyone's children. Schools, religious organizations, civic groups, the media and political leaders of all persuasions—and even computer columnists—have a moral obligation to teach tolerance.

It's Time to Tackle Cyberporn

John Carr

John Carr is an Internet consultant to NCH, one of Great Britain's largest advocacy organizations for children. He is also a member of the British government's Internet Task Force on Child Safety. In this argument, published in the February 2, 1998, issue of New Statesmen, *Carr challenges the anticensorship position of those who champion complete freedom of the Net.*

The Great Internet Freedom Debate is rolling forward. At issue is the balance to be struck between "free speech" and the ability of families, employers, schools or other organisations to protect themselves against the receipt of material that is unwanted, illegal or both. The responsibility for striking the balance and providing mechanisms to enforce it—is, however, increasingly seen not as a job for governments, legislatures or police forces, but for private citizens and the private companies that own and run the Internet industry.

There is a tenacious cyber-myth that the Internet is a vast, anarchic forum, beyond the reach of any government or authority, uncontrolled and uncontrollable. The reality is that for all parts of the Internet there are several potential points of control, and for the typical UK cybernaut one of them has been in operation for a while. So this debate is not about whether some sacred principle of non-regulation or freedom from censorship should be breached: that point was passed some time ago. Now we are discussing practical questions of degree: the ways in which intervention or regulation might occur; the level at which a censorship option might be feasible or appropriate.

If you link up to the Internet with any of the big UK-based Internet service providers (ISPs), such as AOL, MSN, Compuserve, Poptel or LineOne, you already do not enjoy full and unrestricted access to the superhighway. Even Demon, the ISP that represents the liberal wing in this debate, does not allow its subscribers to access everything that is "out there." Most of what is kept from you is illegal material, principally child pornography. There are ways of circumventing the barriers, but you have to know first that you are being "deprived"; second, how to get around the obstacles; and third, you have to find an unrestricted source that will let you in. The last bit in particular is not easy.

It is only in the past two years that the ISPs operating in Britain have chosen to restrict what they provide as part of their standard service. They have done so as a result of a combination of threats from police and the last government, administrative convenience and their own sense of civic responsibility (all foreign-owned ISPs come within the jurisdiction of UK courts for their operation in this country).

The UK Internet industry also established the Internet Watch Foundation (IWF), on whose policy board I sit as an unpaid member. The IWF runs a hotline facility, which allows people who find potentially illegal material on the Internet to report it. Once a report is verified two things will happen: if the material is housed on a server owned by a British-based ISP it will be removed forthwith and the police will be notified. The deal between the industry, the IWF and police, however, is that, whereas possession of certain types of illegal material is normally a crime, if the material is removed promptly the policy will not prosecute the service provider.

6   The IWF's remit covers all illegal material on all parts of the Net, but it has prioritised child pornography, which is principally exchanged through newsgroups, occasionally is found on Web sites, and increasingly is being spread and procured through chat rooms.

7   Similar hotlines are springing up all over the world and the EU recently announced its intention to support their development as part of an ambitious package of measures aimed at making the Internet a safer, more congenial place.

8   However, the IWF and the police are powerless to do anything about a huge body of material which, though not illegal, is highly offensive to some (hardcore pornography, for instance) or else dangerous or undesirable (say, information about bomb-making). It is not simply a matter of overprotecting the frail or faint-hearted: anyone may by accident or through curiosity stumble on unwanted matter. Debate is now focused on what might be done about this type of material: in the US it is a topic of urgent public concern.

9   There is no legal basis for banning these categories; neither will the newsagents' answer to printed pornography work: the physical barrier a "top shelf" policy offers to children and customers who don't want to stand and stare at porn mags simply cannot be replicated on the Net.

10   Instead the buzz phrase is "ratings systems," a concept akin to film or video classification, although necessarily rather more complex. A ratings system is an agreed set of criteria for describing material to be published on the Internet. The originator or publisher of the material provides the rating, which appears as a label attached to the article or site, giving a brief standardised description of its content. As the system is based on self-assessment, there may eventually need to be a set of sanctions for migrating and methods for policing, but these are not yet in place. The idea is that the ratings labels are picked up and read by filtering programmes that work with your browser. The user will have told the filtering programme what to allow through and what to block. Those who do not want any material filtered will still be able to set that option on their computer.

11   There is no jurisprudentially savvy software available on the market that would filter out only illegal material. You have to describe categories or types of material you do not want to see. Thus if you do not want to access anything with violent images or bad language, you could programme accordingly; alternatively you might find "PG"-type levels acceptable.

12   It is easy to foresee the emergence of third-party ratings systems; so for instance if you are a devout Catholic, you might put your trust in "Vatican Net," a subscription service which, if it is ever formed, will only allow material through that would not trouble the Pontiff. Different ratings levels can also be set for different users of the same computer or network, allowing parents to set different access levels for their children than for themselves.

There is already one type of ratings system in widespread use, built into   13
Internet Explorer. That system was established and is managed by RSACi
(Recreational Software Advisory Council on the Internet), a not-for-profit body
linked to the Massachusetts Institute of Technology. However, the current RSACi
criteria are too narrowly American and their system is too crude. The UK's IWF has
been trying to work out a better alternative and will shortly be consulting on its proposals, with a view to co-operating eventually with RSACi and other interests in the
formulation of a global system. Some day a Baptist minister in the US Bible Belt, a
liberal atheist in Amsterdam and a party official in Peking should all be able to use
the same means to decide whether or not their nine year olds can visit this or that
Web site or newsgroup.

Not everyone welcomes the prospect, however. There is vocal opposition to the   14
development of ratings systems, most forcibly expressed by the American Civil
Liberties Union (ACLU) in its paper "Fahrenheit 451.2:—Is Cyberspace Burning?"
In ratings systems the cyber-libertarians see not enhanced consumer choice but
new tools being fashioned to allow authoritarian interests to "lock out" unpopular
views, or otherwise to control the content of the Internet by requiring all ISPs, for
example, to run it on their servers. They fear that minority opinions or tastes will be
excluded.

These anxieties about illiberal abuse of the Internet through ratings and similar   15
technologies are, I believe, at best misplaced and at worst paranoid, reckless or
self-serving. The days are over when the Internet was the private preserve of academics and computer geeks. Now that its trajectory is to become an integral part of
our living-room mass media (with a projected 200 million users worldwide by
2001), the rules simply have to change.

If we do nothing to curb some of the more rampant excesses, the Internet as   16
we know it will cease to exist in the not-too-distant future. It will be replaced by
(at least) two Internets: one which is safe, homogenised, dull, highly commer-
cialised and accessible by subscription only, and another which will be for the poor:
free and wild, but most definitely a place to go only at your own risk.

The anti-censorship lobby has had an early but significant victory in this   17
battle. In 1996 the US government tried to legislate against offensive Internet material. The Communications Decency Act (CDA) was fatally undermined during its
passage through Congress when the religious right sought to widen its ambit. The
ACLU sued and in June last year the Supreme Court struck down the relevant provisions as being contrary to the first amendment protection of free speech.

Its strategy in tatters, in July the White House reiterated its intention to make   18
the Internet "family-friendly," but stressed that it would look to the industry to take
the initiative. Self-regulation was the new approach, but with the clear warning that
inaction would lead to renewed legislative efforts. As Al Gore said at the time,
"Hands off does not mean indifference."

In December the US Internet industry gathered in Washington, DC, to deliver   19
its response. Many in the industry fully share their government's aims. Steve Case,
president of AOL, declared: "Let's face it, many of us are parents and we want to
work in an industry we can feel proud of."

20   All the major ISPs announced they were supporting ratings systems. The owners of some of the bigger Internet search services—Yahoo, Lycos and Excite—said they were considering in future allowing into their directories only material that had been rated. The ISPs also announced that they are going to amend their standard terms of contract to allow them to withdraw service from anyone found misusing their Internet connection by, for instance, soliciting or offering child pornography.

21   The conference also announced other initiatives being researched, notably to place greater requirements on distributors of hardcore porn not to sell to underage viewers; to make it easier to identify visitors to chat rooms; and to try to end the practice of anonymous e-mailing.

22   Disney and Time Warner announced they are establishing "whitelisting services": Internet subscription services that give you access not to the whole of the Net but only to the parts they have vetted. For "Vatican Net" read "Donald Duck Net." We are soon likely to see an explosion of similar whitelists here, especially aimed at the schools audience. BT's "Campus World" already exists and is being marketed as a safe haven.

23   Janet Reno, the US Attorney General, told the Washington conference that last year alone there were roughly 200 convictions for child pornography and other forms of paedophile activity where the Internet played a major part. She did not tell us how many arrests there had been, how many cases were awaiting trial or how many perpetrators escaped prosecution on technical grounds. The UK's IWF, in its first, underpublicised year of operation, received more than a thousand complaints, of which 300-plus were adjudged to contain illegal material, the great bulk of them relating to child pornography.

24   The Internet is far from a stable or mature technology. Advances are made almost daily, some of which can have profound and immediate consequences for the medium. It serves no one's interests to pretend we are on the brink of some last-ditch defence of democracy and free speech when we engage in this debate. Instead we should all recognise that almost all of us are looking, in good faith, for new answers to the new problems thrown up by the new technology.

25   In doing so I trust we will all give at least equal weight to the right of a child to grow up unmolested by paedophiles as we do to the rights of the rugged cyberfrontiersmen who pose as defenders of liberty in a medium that almost no one had even heard of six years ago.

Anti-Censorship Advocate Locks Horns with Anti-Pornography Filterers

Associated Press

This Associated Press news story, published on June 22, 2002, recounts the crusade of Internet activist Bennett Haselton, who developed free downloads to help minors unlock the filtering programs installed on their computers by parents. He is the founder of Peacefire.org, a site created in August 1996 "to represent the interests of people under 18 in the debate over freedom of speech on the Internet" (from Peacefire's "About Us" link).

Internet activist Bennett Haselton has made a name for himself by helping minors disable filtering programs designed to block Web sites that their parents deem offensive or pornographic. 1

His Peacefire.org site offers free downloads and details methods for circumventing filtering software that critics say also inevitably blocks out a range of useful, even beneficial, Internet content. 2

Yet while Haselton's crusade, launched six years ago while he was a college student, has made him a hero among some Web-savvy minors, he's something of a supervillain to filtering advocates. 3

"He's being totally irresponsible," said Marc Kanter, marketing director for Santa Barbara, Calif.-based Solid Oak Software, which makes the CYBERsitter program. 4

"When he started Peacefire, he was a kid himself," Kanter said. "Basically he was enticing minors into his beliefs and activities, which was to undermine parents' rights. As an adult now, he should know better than that." 5

Haselton, a 23-year-old who simultaneously earned a bachelor's and master's degree in mathematics from Vanderbilt University in Nashville, Tenn., says his objection to Net censorship is not born so much of passion as logic. 6

The criteria used by filter program designers is too arbitrary, he says. 7

Besides, children should be able to view whatever Web page they like, Haselton asserts: "I think intellectual development is one of the fundamental human rights and it's also a right that people under 18 have." 8

Haselton was heartened by a federal appeals court decision last month that struck down the Children's Internet Protection Act, ruling that public libraries cannot be forced to install filtering software in order to receive federal funding. 9

But many who share Haselton's opposition to filtering consider his position extreme. 10

"I'm not of the opinion that parents don't have any say where children should go" on the Internet, said Chris Hunter, a University of Pennsylvania researcher who testified on behalf of librarians at the trial. 11

Haselton's line of thinking "that parents shouldn't have a right to monitor their children's access," Hunter worries, "lends fuel to the other side saying that we're somehow uncaring about the issue." 12

Haselton, who works from a cramped one-bedroom apartment in Seattle's eastern suburbs, was raised as a U.S. citizen in Copenhagen, Denmark, where his mother taught music to diplomats' children and others. 13

After graduating from Vanderbilt at age 20, he went west to work for Microsoft. But he left in January 2000, frustrated that he was writing code rather than tracking bugs for the software giant. 14

In addition to running Peacefire, Haselton now does battle with purveyors of Internet spam and works to ferret out security flaws on the Internet. 15

16   He made about $15,000 in bounty from Netscape last year for discovering flaws in the company's browser software. And last month he gained notoriety for finding flaws with Anonymizer.com, a popular Internet privacy service that lets Web surfers visit sites anonymously.

17   "That was pretty sophisticated," Anonymizer President Lance Cottrell said. "The fact that he was able to find it is testimony to what a clever fellow he is."

18   Haselton also has won 10 of 14 small-claims cases and thousands of dollars in judgments against senders of e-mail spam—though he has yet to collect a cent. Washington is one of about two dozen states with anti-spam laws.

19   On a recent weekday, virtually every square foot of floor space in Haselton's apartment was covered by stacks of programming books, floppy disks, empty boxes, dirty clothes and an upended office chair. Four computers dominated a corner table, where Haselton probes for vulnerabilities in filtering programs.

20   Haselton says that while he intends to keep sniffing out bugs for bounty, he hopes to focus more of his energy on Peacefire's crusade.

21   "This is something that practically nobody else is working on, and only a couple of people in the world actually know as much about the blocking software issue," he said.

Taking On Junk E-Mail

New York Times

This editorial from the New York Times, *published on September 13, 2002, argues that junk e-mail—often called spam—overloads e-mail servers and reduces worker productivity.*

1   It will come as no surprise to anyone with an e-mail account that the scourge of spam has reached near-intolerable levels. One new study estimates that this year 7.3 billion e-mail messages will be sent each day, and spam—bulk, commercial e-mail—will make up nearly one-third of it. Increasingly, opponents of spam are using federal and state law to fight back. This growing movement is worthwhile, and deserves support from Congress, federal agencies, state legislatures and the courts.

2   Spam is popular with direct marketers for obvious reasons. Junk mail requires U.S. postage, but junk e-mail can be sent almost without cost. Computer time is cheap, and CD's containing millions of e-mail addresses sell online for about $150. For recipients, however, spam is far from free. Businesses report that unwanted e-mail is significantly reducing worker productivity and overloading computer-system capacity. Individuals are spending countless hours, both at the office and at home, sifting through their e-mail queues to weed out spam. Since this is an imperfect science, e-mail users often lose important, non-junk e-mail in the process.

This month the Telecommunications Research and Action Center and other   3
consumer groups petitioned the Federal Trade Commission to prohibit e-mail that
disguises its commercial intent by using a phony subject line or by misrepresenting
the sender. They are also asking the agency to require spammers to offer recipients
a way to "unsubscribe"—to get themselves removed from a spammers' list—and to
make it illegal to ignore such requests. These proposed rules fall squarely within
the F.T.C.'s mandate and deserve prompt action.

Other promising anti-spam efforts are under way at the state level. California,   4
for example, now requires spammers to include, at the start of the subject header
on every piece of junk e-mail, the abbreviation "ADV"—for advertisement. This
makes it reasonably easy for recipients not to open—or better yet, to set their
e-mail filters to keep out—unwanted spam. Morrison & Foerster, a large San
Francisco law firm, is suing one commercial e-mailer that it says is flouting the law.
Washington state, another leader in the anti-spam cause, has a law on its books
making it illegal to use misleading subject headers. The state attorney general is
using that law to sue spammers who use subject lines like "Payment Past Due" to
trick recipients into opening spam.

Yet spam has some powerful backers. Trade associations representing bulk   5
e-mailers have so far succeeded in blocking anti-spam bills in Congress, and they
can be counted on to lobby the F.T.C. not to act. Civil liberties groups have, unfortunately, too often come to the defense of spam on free-speech grounds. Spam is commercial speech, and as such entitled to a lower level of protection than other
speech. The regulations adopted so far by the states, and those now pending at the
F.T.C., fall well within what is constitutionally permissible.

According to one projection, spam will increase more than fivefold over the   6
next four years. At that rate, some experts fear, it could so swamp e-mail systems
that e-mail will become virtually unusable. By requiring bulk e-mailers to label
spam honestly, and by making it easy for recipients to filter it or choose not to receive it, the government can go a long way toward preserving e-mail for more
important uses.

An Approach to Spam

Jim Conway

*Efforts to create stringent antispamming laws have been opposed by the Direct
Marketing Association (DMA), which represents the interests of e-mail marketers. The official position of the DMA is that only some e-mail advertising is
spam. The DMA has lobbied for an "opt-out" system, whereby receivers of an unwanted e-mail advertisement can remove their names from the marketer's mailing
list, rather than an "opt-in" system, whereby Internet users can ask to have their
names placed on an advertiser's mailing list. In this letter to the editor of the*

New York Times, *published on September 16, 2002, Jim Conway, vice president for government relations of the Direct Marketing Association, explains the DMA's approach to spam.*

1   The Direct Marketing Association was the first group to require that e-mail solicitations include an opt-out address, disclosure of the marketer's identity and a clear, honest subject line. Our guidelines even require marketers to provide a physical address for consumers to seek redress.

2   "Taking On Junk E-Mail" (editorial, Sept. 13) lauds consumer groups and derides marketers, but does not mention that the solutions proposed by consumer groups could have been lifted directly from documents that were posted on the Direct Marketing Association's own Web site.

3   The association promulgated guidelines that its members are required to follow. Our industry, as much as anyone with Internet access these days, is materially hurt by the proliferation of unsolicited, untargeted and nearly ubiquitous, truly junk e-mail.

The Constitution Does Not Protect Spamming
Adam Cohen

This op-ed piece appeared in the New York Times *on May 12, 2002. Writer Adam Cohen challenges the contention that the First Amendment protects commercial speech and thus makes unconstitutional any attempts to censor or restrict spam.*

1   There's a new television commercial that pulls viewers in with a flurry of poignant phrases: "I love you" . . . "I felt the baby move" . . . "It's benign." The voice-over is a salute to free speech. "All words are created equal," it says. "The power to use them is our right as humans." Has the First Amendment gone out and gotten itself an advertising strategy? Not quite. The ad is for a phone company. The freedom it celebrates is in a calling plan that says "local and long distance calls are unlimited." Not exactly what James Madison had in mind when he gave the First Amendment top billing in the Bill of Rights.

2   Conflating the right to call for the overthrow of tyranny with the right to call at bargain rates seems harmless enough. But it is emblematic of a troubling trend in constitutional law: the erasing of the line between commercial and noncommercial speech. A campaign is under way, led primarily by conservatives like Supreme Court Justice Clarence Thomas, to make advertising the equal of political advocacy. If it succeeds, which a Supreme Court decision last month seems to make more

likely, it could become more difficult for the government to protect people from being harmed, in small ways and large, by corporations.

Commercial speech was once given no First Amendment protection at all. In 1942, the owner of a former Navy submarine docked in the East River was told that he could not hand out fliers advertising his boat as a tourist attraction because they littered the streets. He sued, citing his free speech rights, and the Supreme Court threw out the case, saying the Constitution does not protect "purely commercial advertising."

Over time, the court wisely backed away from that absolutist approach. It created a new category of commercial speech, which has been protected, but less than other speech. The court has held that the government can punish false or misleading claims about a product in a way that it cannot go after politicians or journalists for saying things that are untrue.

In commercial speech cases, courts balance the value of the speech against the government's interest in regulating it. Applying that test, the Supreme Court held that the speech rights of lawyers were not violated when a state disciplined them for misleading advertising.

Lately, however, corporations and their supporters, on the Supreme Court and off, have taken to calling the commercial speech doctrine a "contrived distinction," and they have been urging that advertising be accorded the same protection as political speech. At the same time, judges sympathetic to that point of view have been applying the current test in an increasingly aggressive manner to strike down worthy government regulations. Last month, for example, a court struck down a federal law banning junk faxes and affirmed the right of a company called American Blast Fax to continue to blast away.

If other courts push corporate free speech to this illogical limit, laws against spam e-mail may suffer the same fate, as judges elevate the right to send e-mail ads for get-rich-quick schemes and Internet pornography sites to a constitutional imperative.

More troubling, courts have been increasingly willing to overturn, on First Amendment grounds, laws aimed at protecting public health.

Last month, by a 5-to-4 vote, the Supreme Court struck down a federal law barring pharmacies from advertising "mixed to order" drugs, pharmaceuticals that have not gone through the usual safety screening. The largely conservative majority was more concerned about pharmacies' right to market these products than the government's interest in protecting the public from drugs that, as the dissenters noted, "can, for some patients, mean infection, serious side effects or even death."

In his dissenting opinion, Justice Stephen Breyer, writing for four members of the court, suggested that the majority's reasoning could return the country to the dark days of the early 20th century, when the Supreme Court routinely overturned important health and safety laws as a violation of the due process rights of corporations. In the Lochner era—named for *New York v. Lochner,* a case striking down a maximum-hours law for bakers—the courts threw out laws limiting the hours employees could be made to work, minimum wage laws and laws barring companies from making workers promise not to join a union as a condition of employment.

11   The Lochner era is in some ways a distant mirror of our own times. The Supreme Court's aggressive championing of corporations then is finding more and more parallels in the antiregulation decisions of today's court. What the Lochner-era justices did with their wildly expansive reading of the due process clause, today's court may wind up doing through an expansive reading of the First Amendment.

12   Commercial speech obviously has value, and the courts have been right to protect it when the government's interests in restricting it are minimal or the law being challenged is truly excessive in scope. The restrictions on commercial speech most offensive to the First Amendment are those that actually aim at speech, at stopping companies from contributing information and opinions to the marketplace of ideas.

13   But in most of the recent commercial speech cases, the government was curbing advertising in an effort to prevent physical harm. When laws protecting the public from floods of junk faxes, dangerous drugs and other corporate mischief collide with companies' desire to market products, the Supreme Court should continue to use its sensible balancing test, and it should be more willing to find that the balance tips in favor of the people.

China's Cyberspace Censorship
New York Times

Whereas the previous readings in this unit have focused on Internet censorship in a free and open society, we conclude this unit with a New York Times *editorial focusing on political censorship of the Internet in China. This editorial appeared on September 20, 2002.*

1   Type "Jiang Zemin" into the Internet search engine Google, and one of the first things to appear is a Web site that is sharply critical of the Chinese president, with topic headings like "Exposing the Crimes of Jiang Zemin." China's leaders, who are not keen on critiques of the ruling order, recently responded by blocking access to Google, and then by unblocking it but reining in the scope of its searches. In doing so, China is stifling the free dissemination of ideas within its borders and hurting its prospects for building a modern economy. China's leaders should reconsider.

2   The Internet has been on a roll in China. About 46 million Chinese are now online, and in a nation that has long censored its media, the Internet has been a powerful force for free information and modernization. Chinese Web surfers have

recently been allowed access to leading Western news media sites, including those of *The New York Times* and CNN. The Google search engine has been particularly popular in China because it allows searches of the World Wide Web using Chinese characters.

Lately, however, China has been cracking down. Upset that Google was bringing Chinese Web surfers to sites operated by Falun Gong, an outlawed religious group, and other critics of the government, the Chinese government blocked it. Chinese Internet users who went to www.google.com found that they were automatically redirected to search engines that are registered with the Chinese government and whose contents are censored. In recent days, China has unblocked Google but is using firewalls and a variety of other technological approaches to prevent Web surfers from using the search engine to access Web sites with banned material. 3

By cracking down on search engines, China is not only suppressing free speech—it is ultimately hurting itself. It has been trying to increase private investment and to encourage young Chinese who have been educated in the West to return to start new businesses. Blocking the free flow of information cuts the lifeblood of modern entrepreneurship. If China wants to compete in the global market, as it says it does, it cannot afford to limit its people to a government-filtered version of cyberspace. 4

For Class Discussion

1. Much of the disagreement over censorship on the Internet concerns who should be responsible for filtering out unwanted or dangerous material. Imagine a panel discussion with the following persons represented on the panel: Kenneth Lake, John Carr, Lawrence Magid, Bennett Haselton (featured in the Associated Press story on pp. 648–650), a parent of a third grader just becoming skilled at navigating the Internet, and a librarian. The discussion topic is this: Should the federal government mandate that libraries install filtering devices to block out pornography and hate sites from library computers? Assign different students in the class to role-play the views of each of the panelists.

2. The Direct Marketing Association, which represents the interests of e-mail advertisers, argues that a complete ban on e-mail advertising would be an unconstitutional denial of free speech. This association wants to distinguish between "legitimate and responsible" e-mail advertising and the truly "junk advertising" that we normally call spam. In your use of e-mail, what experiences have you had with spam? How would you define the difference between spam and more responsible e-mail advertising? Do you think spam should be made illegal? Should all e-mail advertising be illegal?

3. In the trial of Richard Machado, defense lawyers argued that a hate message sent to 59 different Asian-Americans is much less a personal threat than would be a single message sent to one person. They also argued that obscenity-laced hate messages are quite common when somebody gets "flamed" in a chat room. In other words, they argued that a hate message is a genre of Internet discourse that carries less physical threat than would, say, a handwritten death threat attached to a brick and thrown through a window. Do you agree? Should Machado have been sentenced to a year in prison?

4. Choose one of the readings in this unit and analyze it carefully using the List 2 Guide questions on pages 460–461.

OPTIONAL WRITING ASSIGNMENT   Find a current piece of legislation concerning some aspect of Internet censorship—either a proposed law or regulation, a piece of legislation in committee, a law or regulation being challenged in court, or a recently passed law or regulation that is still controversial. Write a public argument presenting your view of this law or regulation. Your argument might be a guest op-ed piece for a newspaper, a white paper for a legislator, or a piece for an advocacy Web site.

TROUBLED TEENS AND VIOLENCE

Two boys walk into their large suburban high school and gun down their schoolmates and teachers. A young teen pours gasoline on his friend and sets him on fire after seeing MTV's version of this act. A headline screams that a kid has shot his parents. As the anxiety level of the American public rises, cultural critics, journalists, news commentators, lawyers, psychologists, doctors, social scientists, and politicians cast about for social and psychological insights into these behaviors. Among the many causes proposed are violent television programs, movies, and video games; antisocial rap and rock music; teens' increasing use of antidepressants; changes in family patterns such as more single-parent homes, higher poverty rates, and more latchkey kids; availability of guns; the media's glorification of violence; and parental neglect or abuse. Controversies also swirl about the most effective ways to prevent and respond to teen violence, including whether violent teens should be treated as adult criminals by the criminal justice system.

Because these questions are far-ranging and complex, the readings in this unit touch on only some of these issues. However, we hope these readings will inspire you to think in a more complex way about the causes of teen violence and to pursue possible solutions.

Teenage Terrorism

Riki Anne Wilchins

In this op-ed piece from a fall 2002 issue of the gay and lesbian news commentary magazine The Advocate, *Riki Anne Wilchins argues that gender violence and bullying are a serious social problem in American schools today. Wilchins is a columnist for* The Advocate, *an author, a prominent speaker and leader in the gay community, and the executive director of GenderPAC (Gender Public Advocacy Coalition), an organization devoted to racial and gender equality.*

As another school year is getting under way, I want to propose a lesson plan   1
for teachers and administrators. It deals with three stories of gender stereotyping against four teenagers. It's also about the five victims who were lost in the wake of those stereotypes. Too often we shrug off stereotypes and name-calling as just another part of growing up. But these stories prove that this can't be further from the truth.

First there is the story of 13-year-old Aaron Vays, which was told in the August   2
4 Sunday magazine of *The New York Times.* Aaron, who is straight, moved with his parents from his native Russia to Rockland County, N.Y., so he could better pursue a career in figure skating, a sport at which he is reportedly very, very good.

3   But once his schoolmates learned that Aaron figure-skated, they filled his days with taunts and teasing that soon turned into punches, tripping, and finally group beatings. Instead of disciplining the bullies, school officials transferred Aaron to another school.

4   That didn't help much, of course. Aaron was soon spotted practicing his jumps at the local rink by boys on the ice hockey team. They told him that only sissies, girls, communists, and fags figure-skated. Shortly thereafter, a group of schoolmates beat Aaron so badly that he was hospitalized.

5   Then there is the story of Charles "Andy" Williams, which reminds us that there are victims on both sides of stereotypes. Williams was sentenced August 15 to 50 years in prison for a March 2001 school shooting in Santee, Calif., that left two of his schoolmates dead.

6   Williams told authorities after the shooting that he was frequently taunted as "wimp" and "bitch" by classmates. While he said he didn't know exactly what sparked his outburst, there is little doubt that it was connected to the frequent intimidation he suffered at school.

7   Finally, let's look at the story of two transgendered girls, Ukea Davis, 18, and Stephanie Thomas, 19. Both had dropped out of their Washington, D.C., high school because, in large part, of the regular harassment they suffered at the hands of classmates. Nevertheless, they were working to secure full-time jobs and looked forward to promising futures.

8   All that changed early August 12, when they were sitting quietly in Thomas's car. Someone pulled up alongside them and fired a hail of bullets into the car, killing the girls instantly. Police report that both girls suffered more than 10 bullet wounds each to the head, neck, and shoulders.

9   The level of violence, they say, is consistent with a hate crime, and Thomas's mother says she's certain it was someone from their neighborhood—someone who knew and teased her daughter and then murdered both girls.

10   There is a common thread connecting all these tragedies, and it is the constant threat of gender violence that haunts and hunts our kids at school. According to a study published by ABC News, 86% of teens report there is bullying and taunting at school. As we focus on the war against terror in the Middle East, we also must recognize the enduring war of terror against schoolchildren here at home.

11   This is a war against boys who are gentle or shy or who "throw like girls." It's a war against tomboy girls who are too aggressive or too "dykey." It's a war with real combatants and real casualties, like Aaron, Ukea, Stephanie, the students who lost their lives in Santee, and, yes, even Charles Williams.

12   We need to stop this war, not only to save these teens and others like them but so that all children—gay and straight, white and black, feminist and transgendered—can learn in schools in which they are safe, valued, and respected.

13   I'm reminded of a story an Atlanta mother just told me. She'd just bought her 11-year-old son a padlock for his locker, one of those cool new ones in bright, shiny metallic colors. He took one look at it and said, "Mom—magenta and lime! The guys would kill me for that. What were you thinking?" What, indeed.

Supremacy Crimes
Gloria Steinem

Gloria Steinem is a feminist, a politician, and a consulting editor for Ms. *magazine. In this article from a 1999 issue of* Ms., *Steinem argues that teen violence
must be examined within a social frame that includes gender and race.*

You've seen the ocean of television coverage, you've read the headlines: "How 1
to Spot a Troubled Kid," "Twisted Teens," "When Teens Fall Apart."

After the slaughter in Colorado that inspired those phrases, dozens of copycat 2
threats were reported in the same generalized way: "Junior high students charged
with conspiracy to kill students and teachers" (in Texas); "Five honor students
overheard planning a June graduation bombing" (in New York); "More than 100
minor threats reported statewide" (in Pennsylvania). In response, the White House
held an emergency strategy session titled "Children, Violence, and Responsibility."
Nonetheless, another attack was soon reported: "Youth with 2 Guns Shoots 6 at
Georgia School."

I don't know about you, but I've been talking back to the television set, waiting for 3
someone to tell us the obvious: it's not "youth," "our children," or "our teens." It's our
sons—and "our" can usually be read as "white," "middle class," and "heterosexual."

We know that hate crimes, violent and otherwise, are overwhelmingly com- 4
mitted by white men who are apparently straight. The same is true for an even
higher percentage of impersonal, resentment-driven, mass killings like those in
Colorado; the sort committed for no economic or rational gain except the need to
say, "I'm superior because I can kill." Think of Charles Starkweather, who reported feeling powerful and serene after murdering ten women and men in the
1950s; or the shooter who climbed the University of Texas Tower in 1966, raining
down death to gain celebrity. Think of the engineering student at the University of
Montreal who resented females' ability to study that subject, and so shot to death
14 women students in 1989, while saying "I'm against feminism." Think of nearly
all those who have killed impersonally in the workplace, the post office,
McDonald's.

White males—usually intelligent, middle class, and heterosexual, or trying 5
desperately to appear so—also account for virtually all the serial, sexually motivated, sadistic killings, those characterized by stalking, imprisoning, torturing, and
"owning" victims in death. Think of Edmund Kemper, who began by killing animals,
then murdered his grandparents, yet was released to sexually torture and dismem-
ber college students and other young women until he himself decided he "didn't
want to kill *all* the coeds in the world." Or David Berkowitz, the Son of Sam, who
murdered *some* women in order to feel in control of *all* women. Or consider Ted
Bundy, the charming, snobbish young would be lawyer who tortured and murdered
as many as 40 women, usually beautiful students who were symbols of the

economic class he longed to join. As for John Wayne Gacy, he was obsessed with maintaining the public mask of masculinity, and so hid his homosexuality by killing and burying men and boys with whom he had sex.

6   These "senseless" killings begin to seem less mysterious when you consider that they were committed disproportionately by white, non-poor males, the group most likely to become hooked on the drug of superiority. It's a drug pushed by a male-dominant culture that presents dominance as a natural right; a racist hierarchy that falsely elevates whiteness; a materialist society that equates superiority with possessions, and a homophobic one that empowers only one form of sexuality.

7   As Elliot Leyton reports in *Hunting Humans: The Rise of the Modern Multiple Murderer,* these killers see their behavior as "an appropriate—even 'manly'—response to the frustrations and disappointments that are a normal part of life." In other words, it's not their life experiences that are the problem, it's the impossible expectation of dominance to which they've become addicted.

8   This is not about blame. This is about causation. If anything, ending the massive cultural cover-up of supremacy crimes should make heroes out of boys and men who reject violence, especially those who reject the notion of superiority altogether. Even if one believes in a biogenetic component of male aggression, the very existence of gentle men proves that socialization can override it.

9   Nor is this about attributing such crimes to a single cause. Addiction to the drug of supremacy is not their only root, just the deepest and most ignored one. Additional reasons why this country has such a high rate of violence include the plentiful guns that make killing seem as unreal as a video game; male violence in the media that desensitizes viewers in much the same way that combat killers are desensitized in training; affluence that allows maximum access to violence-as-entertainment; a national history of genocide and slavery; the romanticizing of frontier violence and organized crime; not to mention extremes of wealth and poverty and the illusion that both are deserved.

10   But it is truly remarkable, given the relative reasons for anger at injustice in this country, that white, non-poor men have a near-monopoly on multiple killings of strangers, whether serial and sadistic or mass and random. How can we ignore this obvious fact? Others may kill to improve their own condition—in self-defense, or for money or drugs; to eliminate enemies; to declare turf in drive-by shootings; even for a jacket or a pair of sneakers—but white males addicted to supremacy kill even when it worsens their condition or ends in suicide.

11   Men of color and females are capable of serial and mass killing, and commit just enough to prove it. Think of Colin Ferguson, the crazed black man on the Long Island Railroad, or Wayne Williams, the young black man in Atlanta who kidnapped and killed black boys, apparently to conceal his homosexuality. Think of Aileen Carol Wuornos, the white prostitute in Florida who killed abusive johns "in self-defense," or Waneta Hoyt, the upstate New York woman who strangled her five infant children between 1965 and 1971, disguising their cause of death as sudden infant death syndrome. Such crimes are rare enough to leave a haunting refrain of disbelief as evoked in Pat Parker's poem "jonestown": "Black folks do not/Black folks do not/Black folks do not commit suicide." And yet they did.

Nonetheless, the proportion of serial killings that are not committed by white males is about the same as the proportion of anorexics who are not female. Yet we discuss the gender, race, and class components of anorexia, but not the role of the same factors in producing epidemics among the powerful. 12

The reasons are buried deep in the culture, so invisible that only by reversing our assumptions can we reveal them. 13

Suppose, for instance, that young black males—or any other men of color—had carried out the slaughter in Colorado. Would the media reports be so willing to describe the murderers as "our children"? Would there be so little discussion about the boys' race? Would experts be calling the motive a mystery, or condemning the high school cliques for making those young men feel like "outsiders"? Would there be the same empathy for parents who gave the murderers luxurious homes, expensive cars, even rescued them from brushes with the law? Would there be as much attention to generalized causes, such as the dangers of violent video games and recipes for bombs on the Internet? 14

As for victims, if racial identities had been reversed, would racism remain so little discussed? In fact, the killers themselves said they were targeting blacks and athletes. They used a racial epithet, shot a black male student in the head, and then laughed over the fact that they could see his brain. What if *that* had been reversed? 15

What if these two young murderers, who were called "fags" by some of the jocks at Columbine High School, actually had been gay? Would they have got the same sympathy for being gay-baited? What if they had been lovers? Would we hear as little about their sexuality as we now do, even though only their own homophobia could have given the word "fag" such power to humiliate them? 16

Take one more leap of the imagination: suppose these killings had been planned and executed by young women—of any race, sexuality, or class. Would the media still be so disinterested in the role played by gender-conditioning? Would journalists assume that female murderers had suffered from being shut out of access to power in high school, so much so that they were pushed beyond their limits? What if dozens, even hundreds, of young women around the country had made imitative threats—as young men have done—expressing admiration for a well-planned massacre and promising to do the same? Would we be discussing their youth more than their gender, as is the case so far with these male killers? 17

I think we begin to see that our national self-examination is ignoring something fundamental, precisely because it's like the air we breathe: the white male factor, the middle-class and heterosexual one, and the promise of superiority it carries. Yet this denial is self-defeating—to say the least. We will never reduce the number of violent Americans, from bullies to killers, without challenging the assumptions on which masculinity is based: that males are superior to females, that they must find a place in a male hierarchy, and that the ability to dominate *someone* is so important that even a mere insult can justify lethal revenge. There are plenty of studies to support this view. As Dr. James Gilligan concluded in *Violence: Reflections on a National Epidemic,* "If humanity is to evolve beyond the propensity toward violence . . . then it can only do so by recognizing the extent to which the patriarchal code of honor and shame generates and obligates male violence." 18

19   I think the way out can only be found through a deeper reversal: just as we as a society have begun to raise our daughters more like our sons—more like whole people—we must begin to raise our sons more like our daughters—that is, to value empathy as well as hierarchy; to measure success by other people's welfare as well as their own.

20   But first, we have to admit and name the truth about supremacy crimes.

Sex, Drugs, Rock 'n' Roll Revisited
Victor C. Strasburger

Victor C. Strasburger is an M.D., Professor of Pediatrics, and Chief of the Division of Adolescent Medicine at the University of New Mexico School of Medicine in Albuquerque. This editorial appeared in a column featuring controversial issues in the medical journal Clinical Pediatrics *in 2000. In this piece, Strasburger asks his generation to contemplate the differences between contemporary American society and the 1960s and to take more responsibility for teen problems.*

1   The White House Conference on "Sex, Drugs, and Rock 'n' Roll" held in early May 2000 brings to mind images of another conference that should be held soon. How about inviting a bunch of baby boomers to the White House to take a hard look at today's teenagers? After all, we were the original rock 'n' roll generation, the quintessential teenagers. Shouldn't the President be asking us what we think about growing up today (although he obviously has had his own experience with "sex, drugs, and rock 'n' roll")? Weren't we the first to question authority, to picket and be tear-gassed, to go on the Pill, to tune in, turn on, and drop out? I think we would have some pretty insightful things to say about today's teenagers.

2   For instance, school violence. When we went to school, the worst that could happen to us was a fist-fight, and even that was a rare event. Yes, juvenile violence has actually decreased in the late 1990s,[1] but now we have a very new and real phenomenon of mass schoolyard shootings. What would we baby boomers say about that? Well, for one thing, we didn't have guns when we grew up. The National Rifle Association didn't own Congress back then, nor were the media as graphically violent as they are today. For another, we liked and respected our school and our teachers, and our schools were relatively well funded. One political cartoonist recently suggested that we should add an extra $100 billion to the Federal education budget and hold a bake sale for new F-16 fighter planes, instead of the other way around.

3   And drugs, take drugs. We certainly did! What would we say about drugs, other than desperately hoping that our kids don't ask us what we used in the 1960s?

I think we would say that we're going about it all wrong. Marijuana and cocaine are dangerous drugs, yes, but they are not killing teenagers. Tobacco and alcohol are. According to the most recent data, 31% of 12th-graders have engaged in binge drinking within 2 weeks of being surveyed, and nearly 35% smoked cigarettes within the past month.[2] We would ask the President why there are no antialcohol ads and so very few antismoking ads on TV, why so many Hollywood stars smoke and drink on screen,[3] and why Congress took $30 million in payoffs last year to avoid having to pass any meaningful tobacco reform legislation. Why do school boards across the country continue to use DARE as their drug prevention program when it doesn't work?[4] In fact, we baby boomers have developed many programs that do work, programs that can cut drug use to 25% of expected levels.[5] These programs teach kids peer resistance skills and media literacy, but they cost money and require more of a commitment from local school boards than a phone call to the local police department.

So we try to scare kids away from drugs now, just as our parents did when we   4
were growing up. We try to scare them away from sex, too, and with HIV and AIDS, it's a lot easier than it used to be! Yet nearly 40 studies show that comprehensive sex education makes kids smarter about sex but doesn't increase their rates of sexual activity.[6] And giving kids access to birth control doesn't make them sexually active earlier. Sadly, abstinence-only sex education programs can only delay the onset of sex for a few months,[6] yet we allow the Federal government to spend $59 million a year on them. "Just say no"? Try telling that to Madison Avenue and Hollywood, with their rampant images of teen sex.

Speaking of media, we were the first media generation, too. But our media   5
were gentler and kinder. No Schwarzeneggers or Stallones, just Miss Nancy and Captain Kangaroo. No MTV, just *Howdy Doody*. Ain't modern civilization grand? We have evolved the art of storytelling to such an exquisite degree that American society is now completely enriched and nourished by the media it consumes. Today's teenagers see 10,000 acts of violence, 14,000 sexual references, and 2,000 beer commercials, all in an average year of TV-viewing.[7] But, of course, we know that it has no impact on them; that's why we adults allow such things to be shown to our kids.

Which brings me to my final point. Teenagers today are good kids,[8] just as we   6
were back then. Society has changed, not teenagers. It has become more materialistic, more violent. And who controls society now but us baby boomers? We said we would change the world. "Open it up or shut it down; power to the people," right? What have we accomplished, really? My old friend and mentor, Dr. Michael Rothenberg, used to wonder if there isn't a conspiracy against children and teenagers in this country. We know so much about how to protect them from violence, from drugs, from early sexual activity, yet we do so little. I can't help thinking that he's right. So if I were to attend the baby boomer White House Conference on Adolescence, here's what I would say: "I'm sorry. My generation thought it had all the answers. Obviously, we didn't. We apologize. We should have done better." Final answer.

References

1. Forum on Child and Family Statistics: America's Children: Key National Indicators of Child Well-Being, 1999. Washington, DC: United States Government Printing Office; Publication no. 0650000, 1248-1, 1999.
2. Johnston LD, Bachman JG, O'Malley PM. Drug trends in 1999 among American teens are mixed. Press release, December 17, 1999. Ann Arbor, MI: Institute for Social Research.
3. Roberts DF, Christenson PG. "Here's Looking at You, Kid": Alcohol, Drugs, and Tobacco in Entertainment Media. Menlo Park, CA: Henry J. Kaiser Family Foundation; 2000.
4. Kolata G. Experts are at odds on how best to tackle rise in teenagers' drug use. The New York Times, September 18, 1996, p. B7.
5. Schinke SP, Botvin GJ. Life skills training: a prevention program that works. Contents Pediatr 1999; 16:108–117.
6. Kirby D. Sexuality and sex education at home and school. Adolesc Med: State of the Art Rev. 1999; 10:195–209.
7. Strasburger VC, Donnerstein E. Children, adolescents, and the media in the 21st century. Adolesc Med: State of the Art Rev. 2000; 11:51–68.
8. Offer D, Ostrov E, Howard KI. Adolescence: what is normal? AmJ Dis Child. 1988; 143:731–738.

Debunking the 10 Worst Myths about America's Teens

Mike Males

In this piece from a 2001 issue of Teacher Librarian, *Mike Males seeks to change adult misperceptions of teens by reconceptualizing teen problems as adult problems. Mike Males is a sociology instructor at the University of California at Santa Cruz, a senior researcher at the Justice Policy Institute in San Francisco, and a columnist for* Youth Today *(www.youthtoday.org), an online advocacy organization for young people.*

1   Teenagers. If that word calls to mind gangs of young criminals and irresponsible pregnant girls, think again.

2   Adolescents behave like the adult society that raises them. They did not land on a meteorite. We raised them. They share our values. They act like us. When we criticize their behaviors, we are really engaging in devastating self-criticism without a mirror. If teenagers behave like the adult society that raises them, their evil is the same as ours, and it is not curable by aiming increasingly absurd, cosmetic panaceas at the young.

MYTH #1

3   Teenagers are uniquely violent and crime-prone.

4   Facts: Youths have slightly higher arrest rates than adults for public violence. But arrest figures substantially overstate youth violence. Police are over-inclined to arrest juveniles, especially minorities, therefore youths are arrested in much higher

proportion than the volume of crimes they commit. In terms of crime volume, youths and adults contribute roughly equal rates for their respective populations.

MYTH #2

The worst danger to youth is "children killing children." 5

Facts: Children are not the main killers of children: 90 percent of the children 6 under age 12, and 60 percent of the teens age 12–17, killed in this country are killed by adults. Unlike adults, youths are uniquely unlikely to be killed by persons within five years of their age.

MYTH #3

Youth violent crime is skyrocketing, while adult violence is declining. 7

Facts: According to FBI statistics, from 1980 to 1994, youth violent crime arrests 8 rose by 65 percent. But violent crime arrests among adults ages 30–49—the age group parenting teenagers—rose by an identical rate (66 percent), a fact which has received no attention. Most of the increase in violent crime among adults in their 30s and 40s appears to be domestic, reflecting the 300 percent increase in substantiated cases of household violence against children in the last 15 years.

MYTH #4

Teenagers are innately prone to reckless behavior and are stimulated to violence primarily 9 by media image, impulsiveness, and gun availability.

Facts: It is the United States that has the violence problem—our senior citizens 10 are three times more likely to kill somebody than a European teenager. The U.S. black teen murder rate is a dozen times higher than the European white teen murder level. But when poverty is factored out, we have the European pattern. In societies with low poverty rates, violence peaks not in teen years, but at low levels around age 30.

MYTH #5

Today's schools are cauldrons of drugs and violence. 11

Facts: Murder in schools is extremely rare. A student would have to attend 12 school every day for 1.5 million years to run an even risk of being murdered. During 1992–94, 60 murders were committed at schools in the U.S. Meanwhile, 4,000 to 6,000 children and youths were killed at home by their parents or caretakers.

MYTH #6

Teen-age birth rates are out of control due to teen-age immaturity, lack of information on 13 sex, lack of values, and "children having children."

Facts: Teenage birth trends and rates are identical to those of the adults around 14 them. The same factors that influence adult birth rates also influence teens. The biggest factor is poverty—six of seven teen mothers were poor before they got pregnant. The effect of poverty is to increase stress and to make events occur earlier in life (sex, parenthood, death). Three quarters of babies born to teenagers are fathered by adult men.

MYTH #7

15   Teenagers are the most at-risk for AIDS and members of the fastest growing group for HIV infection.

16   Facts: Teens rank third by age group when HIV infection was acquired. Nearly all HIV transmission is from adult partners or exploiters. Even among low-income youths, HIV infection rates are virtually zero among heterosexual teens with no risk factors. Yet among runaways, prostitutes, and those youth who engage in "survival sex" to get food, shelter, or money, HIV rates run as high as 17 percent.

MYTH #8

17   Teenagers are high risk for suicide.

18   Facts: Teens are very low risk for suicide. Suicide rates for high-school-age youths are half those of adults. Most of the supposed "tripling" in youth suicide since the 1950s appears to result from more accurate coroner certification of teens' deaths: "suicides" rose as "accidents" fell. Self-reports of suicide attempts or plans are found predominantly among females with histories of sexual abuse.

MYTH #9

19   Teenagers are the group most at-risk of drug abuse and are suffering skyrocketing rates.

20   Facts: Teenagers are the least at-risk of drug abuse and, until recently, experienced plummeting drug problems. What is being hyped is mainly an increase of a few percentage points in self-reported, occasional marijuana use by adolescents—exactly the drug style longitudinal studies have found that poses the least risk of future drug problems. Very few teens use harder drugs or indulge frequently. Meanwhile, an explosion to record levels of middle-aged drug abuse is being ignored—even though parental drug abuse is now linked to more than half of all foster placements for child abuse and neglect.

MYTH #10

21   Teenagers smoke because of immaturity, peer pressure, and tobacco ads.

22   Facts: Youths from homes where parents smoke are three times more likely to smoke than others. Teens from social groups with high proportions of adults who smoke, such as blue-collar and poorer white populations, are about three times more likely to smoke than higher-income groups. Teenagers display the largest decline and the lowest rates of smoking over the past 25 years. But the evidence

that tobacco ads influence brand choice among the fraction of teens who smoke is compelling. The evidence that tobacco ads lure teens to smoke who would not otherwise is virtually non-existent.

WHAT CAN WE DO ABOUT THESE "MYTHS"?

What I suggest is a two-part framework for analyzing and presenting research on youths and proposals to address their issues. First, the concept of "teenage" problems should be de-emphasized in most cases. There is really no such thing as "teenage sex," "teenage violence," "teenage drinking," or "teenage smoking." These are simply reflections of adult behaviors and often occur with adults whose practice of them is not condemned. Second, research should be rechanneled away from analyzing "teenage" behaviors in isolation and should instead examine under what contexts adolescents act like the adults around them—that is, the vast majority of behaviors—with a particular emphasis on the variable of poverty. For these, prevention measures would be aimed more or less uniformly at all age groups.   23

It is crucial that American institutions turn away from the destructive attack on youths and adopt a more integrated approach which recognizes that adult and teen behaviors are interconnected and that our fate is a shared one.   24

Children in a Violent World
A Metaphysical Perspective
James Garbarino

James Garbarino is the director of the Family Life Development Center and a professor of human development and family studies at Cornell University. He has written widely on children and class, poverty, and violence. This article, which originally appeared in the July 1998 issue of Family and Conciliation Courts Review, *explains how children are sucked into cycles of violence and proposes steps toward spiritual and psychological healing.*

For the past twenty-five years, I have sought to understand the meaning of violence in the lives of children, youths, and families. This has taken me to many of the world's war zones—to Mozambique, to Nicaragua, to Cambodia, to Kuwait, to Croatia, to Iraq, and to the streets of America's inner cities (cf. Garbarino, Kostelny, and Dubrow 1991; Garbarino et al. 1992). Out of these experiences have come the beginnings of an understanding of what it means to live in a violent world, what it means for a child's development and for the life course to come.   1

For me, commentary on war zones at home and abroad begins and ends with personal reflection. A few years ago, while watching the news in Chicago, a local   2 news story made a personal connection with me. The report concerned a teenager who had been shot because he had angered a group of his male peers. This act of violence caused me to recapture a memory from my own adolescence because of an instructive parallel in my own life with this boy who had been shot. When I was a teenager some thirty-five years ago in the New York metropolitan area, I wrote a regular column for my high school newspaper. One week, I wrote a column in which I made fun of the fraternities in my high school. As a result, I elicited the anger of some of the most aggressive teenagers in my high school. A couple of nights later, a car pulled up in front of my house, and the angry teenagers in the car dumped garbage on the lawn of my house as an act of revenge and intimidation.

3   In today's language, you could say I was a victim of a "drive-by littering." What I had seen on the television news in Chicago a few years ago was a boy who had done much the same thing that I did thirty years earlier (i.e., make his peers angry with him), but who had experienced something far more serious than I almost three decades earlier. When his peers responded in anger, the result was not a drive-by littering, but a drive-by shooting. For me, this juxtaposition captured something very disturbing about changes in American society.

4   Over the thirty plus years that intervened between the drive-by littering and the drive-by shooting, the social environment had changed such that the consequences of peer conflict had changed, as part of a broader change in the "terms of engagement" for adolescents in general. And the direction of that change was negative; now, you could get killed for behavior that a generation ago might only expose you to frightening experiences with limited long-term risks (I lived to recall the story of the drive-by littering at my thirtieth high school reunion). Out of that insight came the concept of "social toxicity," the idea that just as the quality of the physical environment can become so negative that it is justifiably called "toxic," the same thing can happen in the social environment.

5   The concept of social toxicity refers to the idea that there can be cultural and social poisons abroad in a society that shorten life and that bring about a deterioration of well-being, and that these poisons include and interact with violence (Garbarino 1995). With physical toxicity, we know that there are individual and group differences in vulnerability. For example, if there is an air pollution problem in a city, we would worry first and most about old people with emphysema or children with asthma. I believe that this is an analogy to what we see among children and youths in the social environment: there is a kind of psychological asthma that some children and youths have that makes them particularly vulnerable to whatever social toxins are in their environment.

6   I thought of this when I went to visit a day-treatment program for emotionally disturbed children in Chicago, a program that had been in operation for over twenty-five years. By all accounts this program once worked, but it now no longer does because these children, these highly vulnerable children, these psychologically asthmatic children, now bring with them into the school a level of aggression and nastiness and violence that overwhelms the program. We need to understand that these psychologically asthmatic kids exist in every society. They exist particularly when home has become empty or hostile. These children whose homes are

empty and hostile are likely to become socially and psychologically asthmatic and show us the worst that is going in society.

We know, for example, from research in the United States, that all children are affected by watching violent television but children who are otherwise at risk because of psychological or emotional vulnerability are the ones who are most affected (National Research Council 1993). We ourselves have done research in the Middle East that demonstrates that Palestinian children involved in the Intifada are most affected by political violence when their homes are abusive or neglectful (Garbarino and Kostelny 1996).

I think that there is a natural merging of the interests of those among us who have a primary focus on family with those of us who are concerned principally with community because those who fall victim to violence and social toxicity within the community are particularly those who have been hurt or neglected at home. And, more than even that, we have come to understand in child development research that the presence or absence of any single risk factor tells us very little about the outcome for a child. Rather, it is the accumulation of risk factors (Sameroff et al. 1987). This emerges over and over again in research when it is designed to reveal it. It may be accurate to say that runaways and drug addicts and sexually abused children come from all strata of society, but it is not to the point because the point is that victimization, when coupled with other risk factors, is what really does the damage.

One of the things I have learned from time spent talking with children and adults in war zones at home and abroad is that there are three dark secrets that children learn, three dark secrets that children learn from exposure to violent trauma. The first of these I call "Snowden's secret," and it refers to a book by Joseph Heller, *Catch-22* (1961). During the course of war-time combat on an American airplane, a character comes to understand what happens to human bodies when they are exposed to human violence. He witnesses the effect of shrapnel on the human body, in the form of another crew member, Snowden. Snowden's secret is that the human body, which appears strong and tough, is really just a fragile bag filled with gooey stuff and lumps. This knowledge is itself traumatic; it changes you forever, as anyone who has worked in an emergency room or visited with victims of war comes to understand. This is one of the dark secrets that children have to contend with. How do you rebuild your understanding of human life once you have learned Snowden's secret up close and personal?

A second dark secret that children learn I call "Dantrell's secret." The reference here is to a little boy in Chicago, seven-year-old Dantrell Davis, who was walked to school by his mother one day in a dangerous neighborhood. When they got to school, there were policemen on either corner, and there were teachers standing on the front steps of the school. But when his mother let go of his hand and he walked the last seventy-five feet from her hand to the teacher's hand, he was shot in the back of the head and killed. What do other children learn from his death? What other children learned from his death is that adults cannot protect you. And this is one of the darkest secrets of all that violent trauma can teach, that you as a child are alone. And if children understand that they are alone, they naturally turn to each other and to themselves to replace the adults gone missing in action. So a nine-year-old boy living in a dangerous area, when I asked him what it would take to make him feel safer, told me "if I had a gun of my own." A boy in Michigan said to me, "If I join a gang I am 50 percent safe; if I don't join a gang I am zero percent safe."

11   Adults don't enter into the equation. As we think about violence, we also have to think about the messages of strength and competence that we as adults send children and youths. The issue is our capacity and willingness to protect them. This is why a program like Mad Dads (begun in Omaha, Nebraska) makes sense. Mad Dads is a program in which adult men go out on the streets of their community with green jackets on to send a physical message that says to children, "We the adults of your community are in charge, not fifteen-year-olds with guns." This brave foolish act is essential to address the damage done by Dantrell's secret.

12   A third dark secret that children learn I call "Milgram's secret" from research conducted by psychologist Stanley Milgram many years ago on what he called the Eichmann Effect. In Milgram's study, normal people were put in a situation in which they were encouraged to behave barbarously, violently—to inflict horrible pain on a defenseless victim. They did it. When it comes to violence, "anything is possible." That is the secret unlocked by Milgram's research, the secret that victims and perpetrators share. None of us is immune from finding the wrong situation. Any of us can commit acts of atrocity. Children in Mozambique learned the secret when they saw their parents beheaded and then cooked in a pot. Children in Gautemala learned the secret when they saw their villages burned and their neighbors executed.

13   We made a film some years ago at Cornell called *I Still Can't Say It* about a child abuse prevention program. In the course of the film, one of the teachers discloses that she herself was a victim of abuse as a child. And she illustrates Milgram's secret. She says, "When I was a little girl my mama used to beat me. One day the police were called and they came to my house and they interviewed me and they said is your mama beating you. And I said no and they went away." Now thirty years later she looks into the camera and she says, "Later that day my mama came home and she said to me, 'Why didn't you tell the police that I beat you?' And I looked her in the eye and I said, 'cause you could kill me.'" Because you could kill me. As a child, she understood Milgram's secret, that when it comes to violence, anything is possible.

14   As I mediate upon these secrets and how to understand them, I am constantly drawn to the fact that there are at least three voices that we can use to make sense of violence in human experiences, three voices to help us understand and to develop efforts to prevent and to treat and to intervene. The first voice is the voice of social science. It is the voice of statistics, of empirical research, of epidemiology. It focuses on the social toxicity of images of viciousness in the life of children and asks us to understand posttraumatic stress disorder as Robert Pynoos (Pynoos and Nader 1988) has led us to understand it. It asks us to understand what Bruce Perry and his colleagues (1995) has been finding in his research on the impact of violence, trauma, and deprivation on brain development and the eventual impact of that damage on the very ability to

think and reason morally. It is really about the psychological wounds of violent trauma, and we have come to understand it pretty well. We have come to understand that experiencing the psychological wounds of violent trauma creates risk for future development, and, by the same token, we have come to understand that this knowledge can lead to programs. For example, Kellam and his colleagues (1994) developed a program called "The Good Behavior Game" that demonstrates its ability to reduce aggressive behavior in children starting at age six and continuing to a later age. In our own work, we have developed a book for children called *Let's Talk about Living in a World with Violence* (Garbarino 1993), and recently our research has shown that it too can reduce aggressive behavior in young children (Bolger et al. 1997). This emphasis on young children is important, because one of the conclusions of various longitudinal studies (e.g., National Research Council 1993) is that by age eight, patterns of aggression and violence become so well established, crystallized, and stabilized that without intervention they begin to predict onto adulthood. So we have to act early in this social science voice to understand the early origins of violence and to intervene to prevent it from continuing.

15 But this is not the only voice for understanding and intervening. There is a second, deeper voice that Bert Cohler (1991) at the University of Chicago calls "Human Studies." What he means is that there is an individual narrative account, a life story, a life history that each of us tells. And this act of making sense of life experience is a very important influence in the outcome of that experience. In fact, Cohler goes so far as to say it is not the experience of bad things early in life that predicts later difficulties but the quality of the story one can tell about that life, the making sense of it. Bessel Van der Kolk (1994), a psychiatrist working in Boston, has found that if children who are exposed to violent trauma early in life cannot make sense of it, they are in for a lifetime of difficulty. He finds, for example, that among his patients who have experienced violent trauma before the age of five when he asks the question, "Have you given up all hope of finding meaning in your life?" 75 percent answer "Yes."

16 This is what I would call the philosophical wound of violent trauma. The threat that it poses, the injury that it produces, is to our sense of meaningfulness. The social toxicity that perpetuates this is the shallow materialistic culture in which more and more people around the world live—what is now being called "affluenza."

17 I think traumatized American children are particularly at risk in this regard because of the shallowness of the culture around them, culture that we are exporting to the world with growing rapidity. The fact that there is nothing more to life than shopping and material acquisition is linked to nihilism in a culture that has no depth. And without any depth, where can children and youths at risk draw a compelling life story? But even these human studies, these narrative accounts, are not the whole story and not the only voice that we can use to understand what living in a world of violence means to children and youths.

18 There is a third voice, a voice I would call "soul-searching." This is the voice that begins from the fact that we are not best understood as animals with complicated brains but we humans are first and foremost to be understood as spiritual

beings having a physical experience in the world. Once this is recognized, we see that the third wound of violent trauma is not so much an injury but a spiritual challenge. The spiritual challenge of violent trauma is that it diverts us from the path of enlightenment (Garbarino and Bedard 1997). It diverts us from the path of being fully in touch with our nature as spiritual beings.

19   Violent trauma tends to divert us from this path to a series of dead ends. For example, it may divert us to the quest for revenge which is fundamentally against the human spirit. Some cultures contain the proverb, "If you begin a journey of revenge start by digging two graves; one for your enemy and one for yourself." That is a very spiritual message which I think is grounded in psychological realities. For inspiration, for intervention, for a basis for soul-searching, we can look to something like Joe Marshall's book *Street Soldier* (1996) in which he recognizes that without this spiritual depth to an intervention program with violently traumatized children, there is very little hope of their recovery because they have experienced the psychological wounds, the philosophical wounds, and the unmet spiritual challenge of trauma.

20   Here, too, American culture and increasingly world culture is toxic for the victims of violent trauma. Increasingly, the Western view of the world predominates. What is at the heart of that worldview? Our Native American colleagues from the earliest days of their contacts with Euro-American culture were very cognizant of the puzzling facts that European Americans thought of the world as being dead, that the trees were simply standing wood, that the animals were simply walking flesh. They were puzzled and often disturbed and depressed by this deadness in the way we looked at the world, when they saw the world as alive, with spirits everywhere.

21   I think particularly now we need to understand the aliveness of the entire universe, the spiritual unity of all of existence because indeed we are spiritual beings. I see this now particularly as I interview boys who are incarcerated in a maximum security institution because of murder and other acts of severe violence. It is a peculiar kind of maximum security institution, because unlike most of them, the boys are safe. This is unusual for a maximum security facility. But this one functions so well, the boys feel safe usually for the first time in their life. So, on the one hand, they are safe, but on the other hand, they are immobilized so that their energy cannot be diverted into guns or drugs or girls or cars or jewelry or gold or money. So they are immobilized. They are safe and immobilized. They need to be in a place like this that encourages reflection and discipline, without the "temptations" of the socially toxic environments from which they come (and to which most will return eventually). I think the model for such a setting is not the power-oriented "boot camp," which has garnered so much attention recently, but rather the reflection-oriented "monastery," where the vows of "obedience, chastity, and poverty" are coupled with mediation, reflection, study, and soul-nourishing work. This is what the most traumatized violent youths need, because all that is left for them is to go inward to their deepest core and upward, to make touch with the grandest spiritual realities that they can discover and as a result grow in wisdom in ways that were previously unavailable to them.

22   I would like to close by reminding each of us that whatever our religious allegiance or cultural traditions, we share a common spiritual ancestry and a common

spiritual aspiration. Therefore, we can find common ground in dealing with violence-related trauma. Each and every day, each of us as professionals and advocates should take a moment to meditate and to reflect on how well we are prepared for the spiritual journey that it will take to transform the world, because as Mahatma Gandhi said, "You must be the change you wish to see in the world." Our professional training teaches us to think and act, but the foundation for that thinking and action must be a solid spiritual and metaphysical base. Breathe and reflect, then think and act.

References

Bolger, K., C. Collins, J. Darcy, and J. Garbarino. 1997. *Evaluation of a violence prevention program.* Ithaca, NY: Family Life Development Center, Cornell University.

Cohler, B. 1991. The life story and the study of resilience and response to adversity. *Journal of Narrative and Life History 1:* 169–200.

Garbarino, J. 1993. *Let's talk about living in a world with violence.* Chicago, IL: Erikson Institute for Advanced Study in Child Development.

————. 1995. *Raising children in a socially toxic environment.* San Francisco: Jossey-Bass.

Garbarino, J., and C. Bedard. 1997. The spiritual challenges to children facing violent trauma. *Childhood 3:* 467–478.

Garbarino, J., N. Dubrow, K. Kostelny, and C. Pardo. 1992. *Children in danger: Coping with the consequences of community violence.* San Francisco: Jossey-Bass.

Garbarino, J., and K. Kostelny. 1996. The effects of political violence on Palestinian children: An accumulation of risk model. *Child Development 67:* 33–45.

Garbarino, J., K. Kostelny, and N. Dubrow. 1991. *No place to be a child: Growing up in a war zone.* New York: Lexington Books.

Heller, J. 1961. *Catch-22.* New York: Simon and Schuster.

Kellam, S. G., G. W. Rebok, N. Lalongo, and L. S. Mayer. 1994. The course and malleability of aggressive behavior from early first grade into middle school: Results of a developmental epidemiology-based preventive trial. *Journal of Child Psychology and Psychiatry and Allied Disciplines 35:* 259–81.

Marshall, J. 1996. *Street soldier.* New York: Delacorte.

National Research Council. 1993. *Understanding and preventing violence.* Washington, DC: National Academy Press.

Perry, B., R. Pollard, T. Blakley, W. Baker, and D. Vigilante. 1995. Childhood trauma, the neurobiology of adaptation, and "use-dependent" development of the brain: How "states" become traits. *Infant Mental Health Journal 16:* 271–91.

Pynoos, R., and K. Nader. 1988. Psychological first aid and treatment approach to children exposed to community violence: Research implications. *Journal of Traumatic Stress 1:* 445–73.

Sameroff, A., R. Seifer, R. Barocas, M. Zax, and S. Greenspan. 1987. Intelligence quotient scores of 4-year-old children: Socio-environmental risk factors. *Pediatrics 79:* 343–50.

Van der Kolk, B. 1994, October. *Meaning and trauma.* Presentation to the Rochester Symposium on Developmental Psychopathology, University of Rochester, Rochester, NY.

For Class Discussion

1. On the subject of teens and violence, part of the search for causes is an effort to grasp what the problem is. Although the "Bureau of Justice Statistics Indicators of School Crime and Safety, 2002" reports that crimes

in schools are continuing to decline and the percentage of students who stated that they were victimized in school has diminished in the last six years (www.ojp.usdoj.gov), the articles in this unit claim that there is a real problem with teens and violence. How do these articles make the case that, despite what statistics say, American society should be concerned about teens and violence?

2. Most of the articles in this unit also go beyond identifying a problem to arguing for causes. After reading these articles, working individually or in a group, list what you see as the different major causal explanations for teens' violent acts, both the notorious school shootings and individual violent crimes. Which argument do you think is most successful at avoiding oversimplified causal reasoning?

3. Some of the articles in this unit move from arguing for ways to think about teen problems to proposing new ways to tackle the problems, in particular, problems with violence. Which of the readings in this unit do you think offers the most helpful and persuasive road to solutions?

4. The political cartoon presented as the Part Opener on page 457 suggests that there is a gap in experience and understanding between adults and teens. Which of the readings in this unit does this political cartoon particularly agree with? What other political cartoons can you find that support these readings or offer an alternative view?

5. Choose one of the readings in this unit and analyze it carefully using the List 2 Guide questions on pages 460–461.

OPTIONAL WRITING ASSIGNMENT   After doing some research on your own to investigate the plans and programs that schools, communities, counties, and government organizations are using to prevent youth crime and violence, write a brief policy proposal in which you recommend a particular plan to prevent youth violence and keep children safe. You might direct your proposal toward city council members, school administrators, teachers, business leaders, or parents in your home town or city. For instance, you might choose to recommend a way to curb a violent behavior such as bullying, or you might focus on mechanisms for reporting all violent threats or on a plan for after-school and weekend programs for kids. In your search for constructive preventive measures, you might find the following organizations helpful: the Center for the Study and Prevention of Violence (University of Colorado at Boulder), the U.S. Department of Justice, the American Academy of Adolescent Psychiatry, the American Psychiatric Association, and the Centers for Disease Control and Prevention.

THE CULTURAL DEBATE ON STEM CELL RESEARCH AND CLONING

To many people, the word cloning conjures up the image of Dolly, the cloned sheep—a being that is an exact genetic copy of another being. Scientists call the process of producing a cloned creature "reproductive cloning." In experiments with animals, reproductive cloning has been successful in only a small percentage of attempts, and it often results in cloned creatures with various kinds of abnormalities. Although scientists have cloned mice, sheep, cows, and some other animals, no cases of human reproductive cloning have been reported. With few exceptions, the general public, ethicists, and scientists are opposed to human reproductive cloning.

Another kind of cloning, linked to the production of stem cells for possible use in genetic therapies to fight certain diseases, is called "therapeutic cloning." Therapeutic cloning (also called "nuclear transplantation") refers to the process of taking a single cell from a human donor (for example, a skin cell from a person suffering from a disease that might be cured through stem cell therapy), removing the nucleus, which contains the individual's genetic blueprint, and merging it with an egg cell that has had its own nucleus removed. Through an electrochemical process, the egg cell begins to grow, replicating the exact genetic structure of the donor nucleus. After about five days of growth, the resulting embryo is harvested for its stem cells, which match the genetic structure of the donor. These stem cells can then be stimulated to grow into different types of tissues that could be used to treat diabetes, Alzheimer's, Parkinson's, cystic fibrosis, and other diseases. Because the stem cells are harvested from a cloned embryo, they can be inserted into the donor with a much lower chance of rejection than if the stem cells had been harvested from a noncloned embryo (such as an embryo left over from a couple seeking in vitro fertilization for infertility).

The scientific community, politicians, and the public at large are divided on the ethics of this process and on the need for government regulation of it. As you will see from the readings in this unit, persons are divided on whether it is ethical to kill an embryo to harvest its stem cells, no matter whether the embryo is cloned or frozen in a fertility clinic's laboratories. They are also divided on the ethics of cloning itself and on the use of genetic engineering to fight diseases. On August 9, 2001, President Bush delivered a policy statement, announcing that the U.S. government would permit therapeutic stem cell research; Bush's proviso was that this experimentation must be limited to the existing stock of embryos left over from reproductive technology procedures and current research projects. He did not directly address therapeutic cloning, but since all kinds of cloning depend on the use of a donor egg, he presumably opposed it. Following up Bush's declaration, the U.S. House of Representatives passed a bill prohibiting the creation of cloned human embryos for stem cell research. As this book went to press, an anticloning bill sponsored by Senator Sam Brownback, a Republican from Kansas, was in committee in the Senate.

The cloning and stem cell research issue is explosive for many reasons: It entails many definitional issues that have rhetorical power and religious implications (Does a cloned "embryo" have the same status as an embryo created by the union of an egg and sperm? Does it have to be inside a woman's body to be considered a living human?). It also touches on other weighty, moral issues (Are human embryos commercial property to be exploited for financial gain? Will cloning and stem cell research lead to eugenics and "designer babies"?). It profoundly affects certain groups of people such as sufferers from diseases that might be cured through therapeutic cloning research, scientists seeking new knowledge, or medical research companies seeking new patents and avenues of profit. From the perspective of the voting public, it also continues to generate political proposals (Should the United States ban therapeutic cloning completely, establish a moratorium, or legalize open research?).

The readings in this unit probe these questions as they plunge you into the network of issues intertwined with cloning and stem cell research.

It's Worth Copying Canada's Model for Cloning Legislation

Richard Hayes

In this op-ed piece published in the Seattle Times *on June 3, 2002, Richard Hayes, executive director of the nonprofit Center for Genetics and Society in Oakland, California, proposes a compromise course as a way out of currently stalled conflicts between the many groups for and against scientific experimentation on human genetic materials. This article provides a good overview of issues related to cloning.*

1   Cloning and the new technologies of human genetic modification are among the most powerful and consequential technologies ever developed. If used wisely they offer new ways to prevent and cure disease, but if abused they could usher in an era of high-tech eugenics that would alter the nature of human life and society forever.

2   Two constituencies dominate the current debate over cloning and genetic modification: anti-abortion conservatives and biomedical scientists. Not surprisingly, most conservatives want restrictions on these technologies and most scientists don't.

3   Given this lineup, it's tempting to assume that the current debate is the latest extension of the abortion and embryo research wars. But this is not the case.

Many pro-choice feminists worry about a new eugenics that would commodify and   4
industrialize the process of child-bearing. Environmentalists fear that genetically altered humans would have few qualms about genetically altering the rest of the natural
world. Human-rights and civil-rights advocates worry that new eugenic technologies
would throw fuel on the flames of racial and ethnic hatred. Disability-rights leaders
know that a society obsessed with genetic perfection could regard the disabled as mistakes that should have been prevented. Peace and justice activists fear brutal international conflict as countries race to create genetically superior populations.

For these and other traditionally liberal constituencies, concern over the new   5
technologies of cloning and genetic manipulation is motivated not by beliefs concerning the moment that human life begins but by the profound dangers to human
relationships and society that these technologies pose, if misused.

These concerns are not fanciful.   6

Technologies that would allow creation of "designer babies" and full-term hu-   7
man clones are close to becoming practicable. Rogue scientists brag about covert
efforts underway to create cloned children. Other scientists declare, often with
barely disguised delight, that the routine production of human clones and genetically altered children is "inevitable," regardless of the wishes of society as a whole.

Current efforts by the U.S. Congress to pass legislation banning human cloning   8
appear unlikely to succeed, as religious conservatives and the biotech industry fight
each other to a stalemate. Although both sides support bans on creating cloned
children, conservatives also want immediate, permanent bans on the use of cloning
techniques that might have research applications, while the biotech industry resists
any meaningful regulation whatsoever.

It's been suggested as a compromise that Congress enact a ban on creating   9
cloned children while imposing a moratorium, rather than a permanent ban, on research cloning. During a moratorium the many proposed alternatives to the use of
clonal embryos for research could be explored. A moratorium would also allow time
to establish structures of regulation for any cloning technologies we might decide
should be permitted. Unfortunately, neither side has yet been willing to make the
first public move towards pragmatic compromises of this sort.

To break this deadlock we need a broader range of constituencies considering   10
the full implications of cloning and other new genetic technologies, and helping decide which applications should be allowed and which should not.

Fortunately, a model for how this might be done is close at hand. In 1990   11
Canada established a Royal Commission on the New Reproductive Technologies,
which over a period of several years conducted numerous hearings, workshops, surveys and other activities. Over 40,000 Canadians were involved.

The commission's final report represented a broad consensus and provided the   12
basis for federal legislation now before the Canadian Parliament.

This legislation addresses all the major issues: reproductive and research   13
cloning, genetic screening, animal-human genetic chimeras, inheritable genetic
modification, sex selection and more. Importantly, it ensures that laboratories, clinics and private firms doing controversial genetic research be licensed and subject to
monitoring and inspection.

14   The United States should take the Canadian experience to heart. A broad and informed debate is essential if we are to realize the best and avoid the worst that the new genetic technologies have to offer. We cannot afford to do less on a matter of such consequence. The future of our common humanity is at stake.

Of Clones and Clowns
Robert A. Weinberg

This article from the June 2002 Atlantic Monthly *exemplifies an argument that is both intellectual and popular (without scholarly documentation) intended for an educated but not scientifically trained audience. Robert A. Weinberg is a professor of biology at the Massachusetts Institute of Technology, winner of the prestigious National Medal of Science (1997), and a member of the Whitehead Institute for Biomedical Research. He is the author of several books on cancer research. In this argument, he exposes the media's distorting role in confusing serious science with sensational bogus science and shows the intersections and conflicts between peer-reviewed scientific research and commercial biotech industry science.*

1   Biologists have been rather silent on the subject of human cloning. Some others would accuse us, as they have with predictable regularity in the recent past, of insensitivity to the societal consequences of our research. If not insensitivity, then moral obtuseness, and if not that, then arrogance—an accusation that can never be disproved.

2   The truth is that most of us have remained quiet for quite another reason. Most of us regard reproductive cloning—a procedure used to produce an entire new organism from one cell of an adult—as a technology riddled with problems. Why should we waste time agonizing about something that is far removed from practical utility, and may forever remain so?

3   The nature and magnitude of the problems were suggested by the Scottish scientist Ian Wilmut's initial report, five years ago, on the cloning of Dolly the sheep. Dolly represented one success among 277 attempts to produce a viable, healthy newborn. Most attempts at cloning other animal species—to date cloning has succeeded with sheep, mice, cattle, goats, cats, and pigs—have not fared much better.

4   Even the successes come with problems. The placentas of cloned fetuses are routinely two or three times larger than normal. The offspring are usually larger than normal as well. Several months after birth one group of cloned mice weighed 72 percent more than mice created through normal reproduction. In many species cloned fetuses must be delivered by cesarean section because of their size. This abnormality, the reasons for which no one understands, is so common that it now has its own name—Large Offspring Syndrome. Dolly (who was of normal size at birth) was briefly overweight in her young years and suffers from early-onset arthritis of unknown cause. Two recent reports indicate that cloned mice suffer early-onset obesity and early death.

Arguably the most successful reproductive-cloning experiment was reported last year by Advanced Cell Technology, a small biotech company in Worcester, Massachusetts. Working with cows, ACT produced 496 embryos by injecting nuclei from adult cells into eggs that had been stripped of their own nuclei. Implanting the embryos into the uteruses of cows led to 110 established pregnancies, thirty of which went to term. Five of the newborns died shortly after birth, and a sixth died several months later. The twenty-four surviving calves developed into cows that were healthy by all criteria examined. But most, if not all, had enlarged placentas, and as newborns some of them suffered from the respiratory distress typical of Large Offspring Syndrome.

The success rate of the procedure, roughly five percent, was much higher than the rates achieved with other mammalian species, and the experiment was considered a great success. Some of the cows have grown up, been artificially inseminated, and given birth to normal offspring. Whether they are affected by any of the symptoms associated with Large Offspring Syndrome later in life is not apparent from the published data. No matter: for $20,000 ACT will clone your favorite cow.

Imagine the application of this technology to human beings. Suppose that 100 adult nuclei are obtained, each of which is injected into a human egg whose own nucleus has been removed. Imagine then that only five of the 100 embryos thus created result in well-formed, viable newborns; the other ninety-five spontaneously abort at various stages of development or, if cloning experiments with mammals other than cows are any guide, yield grossly malformed babies. The five viable babies have a reasonable likelihood of suffering from Large Offspring Syndrome. How they will develop, physically and cognitively, is anyone's guess. It seems unlikely that even the richest and most egomaniacal among us, intent on re-creating themselves exactly, will swarm to this technology.

Biological systems are extraordinarily complex, and there are myriad ways in which experiments can go awry or their results can be misinterpreted. Still, perhaps 95 percent of what biologists read in this year's research journals will be considered valid (if perhaps not very interesting) a century from now. Much of scientists' trust in the existing knowledge base derives from the system constructed over the past century to validate new research findings and the conclusions derived from them. Research journals impose quality controls to ensure that scientific observations and conclusions are solid and credible. They sift the scientific wheat from the chaff.

The system works like this: A biologist sends a manuscript describing his experiment to a journal. The editor of the journal recruits several experts, who remain anonymous to the researcher, to vet the manuscript. A month or two later the researcher receives a thumbs-up, a thumbs-down, or a request for revisions and more data. The system works reasonably well, which is why many of us invest large amounts of time in serving as the anonymous reviewers of one another's work. Without such rigorously imposed quality control, our subfields of research would rapidly descend into chaos, because no publicly announced result would carry the imprimatur of having been critiqued by experts.

10   We participate in the peer-review process not only to create a sound edifice of ideas and results for ourselves; we do it for the outside world as well—for all those who are unfamiliar with the arcane details of our field. Without the trial-by-fire of peer review, how can journalists and the public possibly know which discoveries are credible, which are nothing more than acts of self-promotion by ambitious researchers, and which smack of the delusional?

11   The hype about cloning has made a shambles of this system, creating something of a circus. Many of us have the queasy feeling that our carefully constructed world of science is under seige. The clowns—those who think that making money, lots of it, is more important than doing serious science—have invaded our sanctuary.

12   The cloning circus opened soon after Wilmut, a careful and well-respected scientist, reported his success with Dolly. First in the ring was Richard Seed, an elderly Chicago physicist, who in late 1997 announced his intention of cloning a human being within two years. Soon members of an international religious cult, the Raëlians (followers of Claude Vorilhon, a French-born mystic who says that he was given the name Raël by four-foot-high extraterrestrials, and who preaches that human beings were originally created by these aliens), revealed an even more grandiose vision of human cloning. To the Raëlians, biomedical science is a sacrament to be used for achieving immortality: their ultimate goal is to use cloning to create empty shells into which people's souls can be transferred. As a sideline, the Raëlian-affiliated company Clonaid hopes to offer its services to couples who would like to create a child through reproductive cloning for $200,000 per child.

13   Neither Seed nor the Raëlians made any pretense of subjecting their plans to review by knowledgeable scientists; they went straight to the popular press. Still, this wasn't so bad. Few science journalists took them seriously (although they did oblige them with extensive coverage). Biologists were also unmoved. Wasn't it obvious that Seed and the Raëlians were unqualified to undertake even the beginnings of the series of technical steps required for reproductive cloning? Why dignify them with a response?

14   The next wave of would-be cloners likewise went straight to the mainstream press—but they were not so easily dismissed. In March of last year, at a widely covered press conference in Rome, an Italian and a U.S. physician announced plans to undertake human reproductive cloning outside the United States. The Italian member of the team was Severino Antinori, a gynecologist notorious for having used donor eggs and *in vitro* fertilization to make a sixty-two-year-old woman pregnant in 1994. Now he was moving on. Why, he asked, did the desires of infertile couples (he claimed to have 600 on a waiting list) not outweigh the concerns about human cloning? He repeatedly shouted down reporters and visiting researchers who had the temerity to voice questions about the biological and ethical problems associated with reproductive cloning.

15   The American member of the team was Panayiotis Zavos, a reproductive physiologist and an *in vitro* fertilization expert at the Andrology Institute of America, in Lexington, Kentucky. "The genie is out of the bottle," he told reporters. "Dolly is here, and we are next." Antinori and Zavos announced their intention of starting a human cloning project in an undisclosed Mediterranean country. Next up was Avi Ben-Abraham, an Israeli-American biotechnologist with thwarted political ambitions (he

ran unsuccessfully for the Knesset) and no reputable scientific credentials, who attempted to attach himself to the project. Ben-Abraham hinted that the work would be done either in Israel or in an Arab country, because "the climate is more [receptive to human cloning research] within Judaism and Islam." He told the German magazine *Der Spiegel*, "We were all created by the Almighty, but now we will become the creators."

Both Antinori and Zavos glossed over the large gap between expertise with   16
established infertility procedures and the technical skills required for reproductive cloning. Confronted with the prospect of high rates of aborted or malformed cloned embryos, they claimed to be able to weed out any defective embryos at an early stage of gestation. "We have a great deal of knowledge," Zavos announced to the press. "We can grade embryos. We can do genetic screening. We can do [genetic] quality control." This was possible, he said, because of highly sensitive diagnostic tests that can determine whether or not development is proceeding normally.

The fact is that no such tests exist; they have eluded even the most expert biolo-   17
gists in the field, and there is no hope that they will be devised anytime soon—if ever. No one knows how to determine with precision whether the repertoire of genes expressed at various stages of embryonic development is being "read" properly in each cell type within an embryo. Without such information, no one can know whether the developmental program is proceeding normally in the womb. (The prenatal tests currently done for Down syndrome and several other genetic disorders can detect only a few of the thousands of things that can go wrong during embryonic development.)

Rudolf Jaenisch, a colleague of mine with extensive experience in mouse repro-   18
ductive cloning, was sufficiently exercised to say to a reporter at the *Chicago Tribune*, "[Zavos and Antinori] will produce clones, and most of these will die in utero. . . . Those will be the lucky ones. Many of those that survive will have [obvious or more subtle] abnormalities." The rest of us biologists remained quiet. To us, Antinori, Zavos, and Ben-Abraham were so clearly inept that comment seemed gratuitous. In this instance we have, as on other occasions, misjudged the situation: many people seem to take these three and their plans very seriously indeed. And, in fact, this past April, Antinori claimed, somewhat dubiously, that a woman under his care was eight weeks pregnant with a cloned embryo.

In the meantime, the biotechnology industry, led by ACT, has been moving   19
ahead aggressively with human cloning, but of a different sort. The young companies in this sector have sensed, probably correctly, the enormous potential of therapeutic (rather than reproductive) cloning as a strategy for treating a host of common human degenerative diseases.

The initial steps of therapeutic cloning are identical to those of reproductive   20
cloning: cells are prepared from an adult tissue, their nuclei are extracted, and each nucleus is introduced into a human egg, which is allowed to develop. However, in therapeutic cloning embryonic development is halted at a very early stage—when the embryo is a blastocyst, consisting of perhaps 150 cells—and the inner cells are harvested and cultured. These cells, often termed embryonic stem cells, are still very primitive and thus have retained the ability to develop into any type of cell in the body (except those of the placenta).

21   Mouse and human embryonic stem cells can be propagated in a petri dish and induced to form precursors of blood-forming cells, or of the insulin-producing cells of the pancreas, or of cardiac muscle or nerve tissue. These precursor cells (tissue-specific stem cells) might then be introduced into a tissue that has grown weak from the loss of too many of its differentiated worker cells. When the ranks of the workers are replenished, the course of disease may be dramatically reversed. At least, that is the current theory. In recent months one version of the technique has been successfully applied to mice.

22   Therapeutic cloning has the potential to revolutionize the treatment of a number of currently untreatable degenerative diseases, but it is only a potential. Considerable research will be required to determine the technology's possibilities and limitations for treating human patients.

23   Some worry that therapeutic-cloning research will never get off the ground in this country. Its proponents—and there are many among the community of biomedical researchers—fear that the two very different kinds of cloning, therapeutic and reproductive, have merged in the public's mind. Three leaders of the community wrote a broadside early this year in *Science,* titled "Please Don't Call It Cloning!" Call therapeutic cloning anything else—call it "nuclear transplantation," or "stem cell research." The scientific community has finally awakened to the damage that the clowns have done.

24   This is where the newest acts of the circus begin. President George Bush and many pro-life activists are in one ring. A number of disease-specific advocacy groups that view therapeutic cloning as the only real prospect for treating long-resistant maladies are in another. In a third ring are several biotech companies that are flogging their wares, often in ways that make many biologists shudder.

25   Yielding to pressure from religious conservatives, Bush announced last August that no new human embryonic stem cells could be produced from early human embryos that had been created during the course of research sponsored by the federal government; any research on the potential applications of human embryonic stem cells, he said, would have to be conducted with the existing repertoire of sixty-odd lines. The number of available, usable cell lines actually appears to be closer to a dozen or two. And like all biological reagents, these cells tend to deteriorate with time in culture; new ones will have to be derived if research is to continue. What if experiments with the existing embryonic-stem-cell lines show enormous promise? Such an outcome would produce an almost irresistible pressure to move ahead with the derivation of new embryonic stem cells and to rapidly expand this avenue of research.

26   How will we learn whether human embryonic stem cells are truly useful for new types of therapy? This question brings us directly to another pitfall: much of the research on human embryonic stem cells is already being conducted by biotech companies, rather than in universities. Bush's edict will only exacerbate this situation. (In the 1970s a federal decision effectively banning government funding of *in vitro* fertilization had a similar effect, driving such research into private clinics.)

27   Evaluating the science coming from the labs of the biotech industry is often tricky. Those who run these companies are generally motivated more by a need to

please stock analysts and venture capitalists than to convince scientific peers. For many biotech companies the peer-review process conducted by scientific journals is simply an inconvenient, time-wasting impediment. So some of the companies routinely bypass peer review and go straight to the mainstream press. Science journalists, always eager for scoops, don't necessarily feel compelled to consult experts about the credibility of industry press releases. And when experts are consulted about the contents of a press release, they are often hampered by spotty descriptions of the claimed breakthrough and thus limited to mumbling platitudes.

ACT, the company that conducted the successful cow-cloning experiment and has now taken the lead in researching human therapeutic cloning, has danced back and forth between publishing in respectable peer-reviewed journals and going directly to the popular press—and recently tried to find a middle ground. Last fall, with vast ambitions, ACT reported that it had conducted the first successful human-cloning experiment. In truth, however, embryonic development went only as far as six cells—far short of the 150-cell blastocyst that represents the first essential step of therapeutic cloning. Wishing to cloak its work in scientific respectability, ACT reported these results in a fledgling electronic research journal named *e-biomed: The Journal of Regenerative Medicine.* Perhaps ACT felt especially welcome in a journal that, according to its editor in chief, William A. Haseltine, a widely known biotech tycoon, "is prepared to publish work of a more preliminary nature." It may also have been encouraged by Haseltine's stance toward cloning, as revealed in his remarks when the journal was founded. "As we understand the body's repair process at the genetic level, we will be able to advance the goal of maintaining our bodies in normal function, perhaps perpetually," he said. 28

Electronic publishing is still in its infancy, and the publication of ACT's research report will do little to enhance its reputation. By the usual standards of scientific achievement, the experiments ACT published would be considered abject failures. Knowledgeable readers of the report were unable to tell whether the clump of six cells represented the beginning of a human embryo or simply an unformed aggregate of dying cells. 29

One prominent member of the *e-biomed* editorial board, a specialist in the type of embryology used in cloning, asked Haseltine how the ACT manuscript had been vetted before its publication. Haseltine assured his board member that the paper had been seen by two competent reviewers, but he refused to provide more details. The board member promptly resigned. Two others on the editorial board, also respected embryologists, soon followed suit. (Among the scientists left on the board are two representatives of ACT—indeed, both were authors of the paper.) Mary Ann Liebert, the publisher of the journal, interpreted this exodus as a sign that "clearly some noses were out of joint." The entire publication process subverted the potentially adversarial but necessary dynamic between journal-based peer review and the research scientist. 30

No one yet knows precisely how to make therapeutic cloning work, or which of its many claimed potential applications will pan out and which will not. And an 31 obstacle other than experimental problems confronts those pushing therapeutic cloning. In the wake of the cloning revolution a second revolution has taken place—quieter but no less consequential. It, too, concerns tissue-specific stem cells—but ones found in the tissues of adults. These adult stem cells may one day prove to be at least as useful as those generated by therapeutic cloning.

32   Many of our tissues are continually jettisoning old, worn-out cells and replacing them with freshly minted ones. The process depends on a cadre of stem cells residing in each type of tissue and specific to that type of tissue. When an adult stem cell divides, one of its two daughters becomes a precursor of a specialized worker cell, able to help replenish the pool of worker cells that may have been damaged through injury or long-term use. The other remains a stem cell like its mother, thus ensuring that the population of stem cells in the tissue is never depleted.

33   Until two years ago the dogma among biologists was that stem cells in the bone marrow spawned only blood, those in the liver spawned only hepatocytes, and those in the brain spawned only neurons—in other words, each of our tissues had only its own cadre of stem cells for upkeep. Once again we appear to have been wrong. There is mounting evidence that the body contains some rather unspecialized stem cells, which wander around ready to help many sorts of tissue regenerate their worker cells.

34   Whether these newly discovered, multi-talented adult stem cells present a viable alternative to therapeutic cloning remains to be proved. Many of the claims about their capabilities have yet to be subjected to rigorous testing. Perhaps not surprisingly, some of these claims have also reached the public without careful vetting by peers. Senator Sam Brownback, of Kansas, an ardent foe of all kinds of cloning, has based much of his case in favor of adult stem cells (and against therapeutic cloning) on these essentially unsubstantiated scientific claims. Adult stem cells provide a convenient escape hatch for Brownback. Their use placates religious conservatives, who are against all cloning, while throwing a bone to groups lobbying for new stem-cell-based therapies to treat degenerative diseases.

35   Brownback would have biologists shut down therapeutic-cloning research and focus their energies exclusively on adult stem-cell research. But no one can know at present which of those two strategies is more likely to work. It will take a decade or more to find out. Many biologists are understandably reluctant to set aside therapeutic-cloning research in the meantime; they argue that the two technologies should be explored simultaneously.

36   Precisely this issue was debated recently by advisory committees in the United States and Germany. The U.S. committee was convened by Bruce Alberts, the president of the National Academy of Sciences and a highly accomplished cell biologist and scientific educator. Quite naturally, it included a number of experts who are actively involved in exploring the advantages and disadvantages of stem-cell therapies. The committee, which announced its findings in January, concluded that therapeutic cloning should be explored in parallel with alternative strategies.

37   For their trouble, the scientists were accused of financial self-interest by Steven Milloy of Fox News, who said, "Enron and Arthur Andersen have nothing over the National Academy of Sciences when it comes to deceiving the public. . . .

Enter Bruce Alberts, the Wizard of Oz–like president of the NAS. . . . On his own initiative, Alberts put together a special panel, stacked with embryonic-stem-cell research proponents and researchers already on the taxpayer dole. . . . Breast-feeding off taxpayers is as natural to the NAS panel members as breathing."

The German committee, which reached a similar conclusion, was assembled by   38
Ernst-Ludwig Winnacker, the head of his country's national science foundation. Winnacker and his colleagues were labeled "cannibals" by the Cardinal of Cologne. Remarks like the ones from Steven Milloy and the cardinal seem calculated to make public service at the interface between science and society as unappealing as possible.

President Bush, apparently anticipating the NAS panel's conclusion, has ap-   39
pointed an advisory committee all but guaranteed to produce a report much more to his liking. Its chairman, Leon Kass, has gone on record as being against all forms of cloning. (Earlier in his career Kass helped to launch an attack on *in vitro* fertilization.)

Meanwhile, a coalition of a hundred people and organizations recently sent a   40
letter to Congress expressing their opposition to therapeutic cloning—among them Friends of the Earth, Greenpeace, the Sierra Club, the head of the National Latina Health Organization, and the perennial naysayer Jeremy Rifkin. "The problem with therapeutic cloning," Rifkin has said, "is that it introduces commercial eugenics from the get-go." Powerful words indeed. Few of those galvanized by Rifkin would know that therapeutic cloning has nothing whatsoever to do with eugenics.

Usually progress in biology is held back by experimental difficulties, inadequate   41
instruments, poorly planned research protocols, inadequate funding, or plain sloppiness. But in this case the future of research may have little connection with these factors or with the scientific pros and cons being debated earnestly by members of the research community. The other, more public debates will surely be the decisive ones.

The clashes about human therapeutic cloning that have taken place in the media   42
and in Congress are invariably built around weighty moral and ethical principles. But none of us needs a degree in bioethics to find the bottom line in the arguments. They all ultimately converge on a single question: When does human life begin? Some say it is when sperm and egg meet, others when the embryo implants in the womb, others when the fetus quickens, and yet others when the fetus can survive outside the womb. This is a question that we scientists are neither more nor less equipped to decide than the average man or woman in the street, than a senator from Kansas or a cardinal in Cologne. (Because Dolly and the other cloned animals show that a complete embryo can be produced from a single adult cell, some biologists have proposed, tongue in cheek, that a human life exists in each one of our cells.) Take your pick of the possible answers and erect your own moral scaffolding above your choice.

In the end, politics will settle the debate in this country about whether human   43
therapeutic cloning is allowed to proceed. If the decision is yes, then we will continue to lead the world in a crucial, cutting-edge area of biomedical research. If it is no, U.S. biologists will need to undertake hegiras to laboratories in Australia, Japan, Israel, and certain countries in Europe—an outcome that would leave American science greatly diminished.

What Human Genetic Modification Means for Women
Judith Levine

This article, originally published in the July–August 2002 edition of World Watch, *explores the potentially dangerous connections between human genetic modification and eugenics and argues that such experimentation is especially relevant to women and children. The WorldWatch Institute describes itself as "a nonprofit public policy research organization dedicated to informing policymakers and the public about emerging global problems and trends and the complex links between the world economy and its environmental support system" (from the "About WorldWatch" link on its Web site). Judith Levine, a well-known journalist on women's topics, has written for* Ms., New York Woman, *and* Salon, *and has recently published the book* Harmful to Minors: The Perils of Protecting Children from Sex *(2002).*

1   Seduced by the medical promises of genetic science or fearful of losing reproductive autonomy, many feminists have been slow to oppose human genetic engineering. But GE is a threat to women, and in the broadest sense a feminist issue. Here's why. If anyone should be wary of medical techniques to "improve" ordinary reproduction—as GE purports to do—it's women. History is full of such "progress," and its grave results. When limbless babies were born to mothers who took thalidomide, the drug was recalled. But the deadly results of another "pregnancy-enhancing" drug, DES, showed up only years later, as cancer in the daughters of DES mothers. The high-estrogen Pill was tested first on uninformed Puerto Rican mothers, some of whom may have died from it.

2   Today's fertility industry takes in $4 billion a year, even though in-vitro fertilization (IVF) succeeds in only 3 of 10 cases. Virtually unregulated and highly competitive, these fertility doctors often undertake experimental treatments. Recently, the Institute for Reproductive Medicine and Science at New Jersey's St. Barnabas Medical Center announced the success of a new fertility "therapy" called cytoplasmic transfer, in which some of the cellular material outside the nucleus of one woman's egg is transferred into the egg of another woman who is having difficulty sustaining embryo survival. The transferred cytoplasm contains mitochondria (organelles that produce energy for the cell), which have a small number of their own genes. So the embryo produced with cytoplasmic transfer can end up with two genetic mothers. This mixing, called "mitochondrial heteroplasmy," can cause life-threatening symptoms that don't show up until later in life. When the Public Broadcasting Service's *Nova* enthusiastically reported on the procedure, complete with footage of its cute outcome, Katy, it mentioned no risks.

3   Didn't these patients give informed consent? Yes and no. Most read warnings and signed their names. But with genetic therapies there's no such thing as

"informed," says Judy Norsigian of the Boston Women's Health Collective, "because the risks can't be known." Adds biologist Ruth Hubbard, the deadliness of DES was discovered "only because it showed itself in an otherwise very rare condition. If the effects [of human genetic engineering] are delayed, and if they are not associated with a particularly unusual pathology, it could take quite a long time to find out." Or indeed, "we might never know."

"PERFECTING" HUMAN GENETIC MODIFICATION WOULD REQUIRE EXPERIMENTATION ON WOMEN AND CHILDREN.

Scottish biologist Ian Wilmut, the "father" of the famously first-cloned sheep Dolly, provided these statistics in 2001: Of the 31,007 sheep, mice, pig, and other mammal eggs that had undergone somatic cell nuclear transfer (cloning), 9,391 viable embryos resulted. From those embryos came 267 live-born offspring. In these animals, *The New York Times* reported, "random errors" were ubiquitous—including fatal heart and lung defects, malfunctioning immune systems, and grotesque obesity. In all, "fewer than 3 percent of all cloning efforts succeed." Dolly may be a victim of accelerated aging, another problem in cloned animals. In January, it was reported that she has arthritis, at the unusually early age of five and a half. Mothers of clones are endangered too, since their bodies have trouble supporting the abnormally large fetuses that cloning often produces.   4

It's likely that scientists will get better at cloning animals, and at the more complex procedures required to produce inheritable genetic alterations. Then, as health activists quip, if it works on a mouse, they will try it on a woman. The problem, warns Stuart Newman, a cell biologist at New York Medical College in Valhalla, is that if it works on a mouse, it is likely not to work on a woman: "Every species presents a new set of problems." How might the process be perfected in humans? In clinical trials?   5

"The degree of risk to be taken should never exceed that determined by the humanitarian importance of the problem to be solved by the experiment," reads the Nuremburg Code, drawn up after World War II to forbid future torturous experiments of the sort Nazi "scientists" inflicted on concentration-camp inmates. What is the humanitarian importance of creating a faster 100-meter sprinter? Or even curing a disease with genetic engineering when other options are still untried? The science to find "safe" means of human GE, says Newman, would constitute "an entirely experimental enterprise with little justification." In other words, "We can't get there from here."   6

WE ARE NOT OUR GENES.

When the Human Genome Project finished its map of our DNA, its press releases called it the "blueprint" of humanity, the very Book of Life. The newspapers had already been filling up with reports of the discovery of a "gene for" breast cancer, and a "gene for" gayness. Many people had begun to believe our genes determine who we become.   7

This line of thinking should sound familiar to women. Not long ago, we were told that hormones, not sexism, explained why there has never been a U.S. female   8 president (she might start a nuclear war in a fit of PMS). A decade after that came the notion that gender is "hard-wired" into the brain. Not incidentally, these claims were made just when social movements were proving Simone de Beauvoir's adage that women are not born but made. Now the old determinism is raising its ugly head once again, with genetics. As "non-traditional" families finally bring legitimacy to social parenting, proponents of inheritable genetic modification tell us not only that we can pre-determine the natures of our children, but that cloning is the only means by which gays and lesbians can become real parents. "Real" parental ties, they imply, are biological, genetic.

9   "Genetic determinism" is not biologically accurate. "It is very unlikely that a simple and directly causal link between genes and most common diseases will ever be found," writes Richard Horton, editor of the British medical journal *The Lancet*. If this is true of disease, it is even more true of musicality, optimism, or sexual orientation. The more complex a trait, the less useful genetics are to explain it. Hubbard writes, "The lens of genetics really is one of the narrowest foci to define our biology, not to mention what our social being is about."

GENETIC MODIFICATION IS NOT A REPRODUCTIVE "CHOICE."

10   For feminists, one of the most galling aspects of the debate about human genetic manipulation is the way its proponents have hijacked the language of "choice" to sell its products. IVF clinics and biotech research shouldn't be regulated, say the companies that run them, because that would impinge on "choice" (for the paying customers, if not for their unsuspecting offspring). The Book of Life is becoming a "catalogue" of "consumer eugenics," says sociologist Barbara Katz Rothman.

11   Some ethicists, too, have posited a reproductive "right" to prenatal baby design. People decide whether or not to reproduce based on an expected "package of experiences," wrote John Robertson, an influential bioethicist, in 1998. "Since the makeup of the packet will determine whether or not they reproduce . . . some right to choose characteristics, either by negative exclusion or positive selection, should follow as well." Already, selective abortion is widely accepted after prenatal genetic screening uncovers an "anomaly." Although some (notably disability rights activists) critique such "negative eugenics," many people accept this practice for serious medical conditions. In any case, selecting from among a small number of embryos is a far cry from rearranging the DNA of a future child to achieve some preferred traits.

12   What feminists mean by "choice"—the ability to control fertility with safe and legal birth control and abortion—is far more concrete. It confers existential equality on the female half of the human race, which is why women worldwide have sought it for centuries. But genetic engineering designs in inequality: it will artificially confer heritable advantages only on those who can afford to buy them. Performed prenatally, moreover, it affects the new person without that person's prior consent and possibly to her physical or emotional detriment. "Ending an unwanted pregnancy is apples, and mucking around with genes is oranges," says Marcy Darnovsky of the Center for Genetics and Society. "We support abortion rights because we support a right to not have a child—or to have one. But we don't

support a woman's right to do anything to that child once it's alive, like abuse it or kill it." Ironically, as Lisa Handwerker of the National Women's Health Network has pointed out, anti-choice, anti-GE forces share with GE's proponents an obsessive focus on the embryo as an independent entity, while they both virtually ignore the pregnant woman and the child she may bear.

BANS ON DANGEROUS GENETIC TECHNOLOGIES
DO NOT GIVE FETUSES "RIGHTS."

Some choice advocates fear that any perceived concern about embryos will cede territory to anti-abortionists, who want full legal protection of embryos and fetuses. U.S. Congressman Henry Waxman reflected this confusion when he said at a Congressional hearing, "I do not believe that the Congress should prohibit potentially life-saving research on genetic cell replication because it accords a cell—a special cell, but only a cell—the same rights and protections as a person." 13

But pro-choice opponents of cloning do not propose to give cells rights. Rather, we worry that cloned embryos might be implanted by unscrupulous fertility entrepreneurs into desperate women, where they'll grow into cloned humans. And from cloning, it is not a big step to designing children. 14

For legal, political, and philosophical reasons, University of Chicago medical ethicist Mary Mahowald proposes clarifying the pro-choice position. "It does feminist support for abortion no good to confuse life with personhood," she told me. "We can admit that the embryo is life and therefore afford it respect—the respect, for instance, of not exchanging its genes with those of another cell. But respecting life is not the same as granting rights. Rights are reserved for living persons." 15

INDIVIDUAL FREEDOM MUST BE BALANCED WITH SOCIAL JUSTICE.

"We're against bans," said a member of a coalition of mainstream reproductive-rights groups, explaining why the coalition was reluctant to join a campaign against human cloning. This reaction is not surprising in the United States, where defense of personal freedom can often trump the public interest. 16

Women's liberation means more than personal freedom, though. Rooted in the Left, feminism is a critique of all kinds of domination and therefore a vision of an egalitarian world—racially and economically, as well as sexually. 17

In the case of species-altering procedures, social justice must prevail over individual "choice." Arguing for an international ban on reproductive cloning and regulation of related research, Patricia Baird, chair of Canada's Royal Commission on New Reproductive Technologies, put it this way: "The framework of individual autonomy and reproductive choice is dangerously incomplete, because it leaves out the effects on others and on social systems, and the effects on the child and future generations." The good news is that good public policy protects individuals too. Baird offered the example of overfishing, which might benefit the fisherman in the short run but deplete the fishery for everyone, including that fisherman, in the long run. Regulation sustains his and his children's livelihoods. "We all have a stake in the kind of community we live in," Baird said. 18

FEMINISTS CAN WORK ALONGSIDE ANTI-ABORTION CONSERVATIVES AGAINST SPECIES-ALTERING PROCEDURES.

19   "We are repelled by the prospect of cloning human beings . . . because we intuit and we feel, immediately and without argument, the violation of things that we rightfully hold dear," wrote Leon Kass, conservative social critic and chair of President Bush's committee to investigate stem-cell research.

20   Not every feminist holds dear what Kass holds dear: the "sanctity" of the family based in God-given, "natural" forms of reproduction. Still, Kass sat beside Judy Norsigian and Stuart Newman to testify before the U.S. Congress against cloning.

21   The genetic engineering debate has made strange bedfellows. But it has also rearranged the political definitions that made those bedfellows strangers. "Social conservatives believe [genetic engineering] is playing God and therefore unethical, while anti-biotech activists [of the Left] see it as the first step into a brave new world divided by biological castes," writes social critic Jeremy Rifkin. "Both oppose the emergence of a commercial eugenics civilization." Others suggest that the new political landscape divides differently, between libertarians and communitarians. Whether of the Left or the Right, the former would support an individual right to choose just about any intervention on one's own body or one's offspring, whereas the latter esteem public health and social equality and would reject those interventions, including GE, that endanger them.

22   Choice activists may at first be surprised when they find that their anti-cloning and anti-eugenics sentiments are shared by opponents of reproductive rights. But passionate arguments for the same position from historically sworn enemies can only make a legislator, or any citizen, listen up. Feminists need sacrifice no part of the defense of women's reproductive autonomy when we champion health and social justice for the future human community.

Human Cloning

Senator Sam Brownback

This brief policy statement posted on Senator Brownback's Web site presents his thinking behind the Human Cloning Prohibition Act (S. 1899), the bill he introduced to the Senate that would ban all research on human embryos.

1   Like many other Americans, I believe that efforts to create human beings by cloning mark a new and decisive step toward turning human reproduction into a manufacturing process in which children are made in laboratories to preordained specifications.

2   Creating cloned live-born children begins by creating cloned human embryos, a process which some also propose as a way to create embryos for research or as sources of cells and tissues for possible treatment of other humans.

3   The prospect of creating new human life solely to be exploited and destroyed in this way has been condemned on moral grounds by many as displaying a profound

disrespect for life. Moreover, recent scientific advances indicate that there are fruitful and morally unproblematic alternatives to this approach. There is no need for this technology to ever be used with humans, whether for reproductive purposes or for destructive research purposes.

The United States House of Representatives has already voted to ban all human   4
cloning, and the Senate will take up the issue in the coming Spring. The legislation before our Congress explicitly bans the creation of embryos through cloning techniques, and it imposes civil and criminal penalties on anyone who attempts to create a human clone through the process of human somatic cell nuclear transfer. Additionally, it is significant to note that such legislation has enjoyed support from both sides of our political spectrum.

Open Letter to U.S. Senators on Human Cloning and Eugenic Engineering
Center for Genetics and Society

The Center for Genetics and Society in Oakland, California, describes itself as a nonprofit public affairs organization devoted to promoting socially responsible use of new technologies related to human genetic modification and reproduction. This letter to the U.S. Senate, dated March 19, 2002, and calling for a moratorium on therapeutic cloning, was signed by over fifty scientists, professors, journalists and authors, public health officials, directors and CEOs, doctors, lawyers, nurses, and environmentalists.

Senate Majority Leader Tom Daschle
Senate Minority Leader Trent Lott
Members of the Senate
cc: President George W. Bush
Members of the House of Representatives

March 19, 2002

Dear Senators,

The United States Senate will soon be considering legislation on human   1
cloning. Your decisions will have profound implications for the future of humanity.

The new technologies of human genetic engineering are among the most   2
consequential technologies ever developed. If used wisely they hold great promise for preventing and treating disease, but if misused they could lead to a future more horrific than any we might imagine.

These technologies are being developed at a frenzied pace. The general pub   3
lic has had little real opportunity to understand and consider their full implications. There are few significant controls over their use.

4   These conditions leave us vulnerable to being pushed into a new era of eugenic engineering, one in which people quite literally become manufactured artifacts. The implications for individual integrity and autonomy, for family and community life, for social and economic justice and indeed for world peace are chilling. Once humans begin cloning and genetically engineering their children for desired traits we will have crossed a threshold of no return.

5   Given the rapid pace of development, the enormous stakes, the lack of societal controls and the fact that informed public debate has barely begun, what is the responsible course of legislative action at this time?

6   With regard to human cloning, we believe the answer is straightforward.

7   First and obviously, the United States should ban the creation of full-term human clones ("reproductive cloning"). There is no unmet need that requires the creation of genetic duplicates of existing people. Surveys show that 90% of Americans support bans on reproductive cloning. Nearly thirty countries worldwide have already agreed to such bans. The United States should do likewise without delay.

8   Second, the United States should enact a moratorium on the creation of clonal human embryos for research purposes (often prematurely called "therapeutic cloning"). The widespread creation of clonal embryos would increase the risk that a human clone would be born, and would further open the door to eugenic procedures. Fortunately, important research on embryonic stem cells does not yet require the use of clonal embryos. A moratorium would allow time for alternatives to research cloning to be investigated, for policy makers and the public to make informed judgments, and for regulatory structures to be established to oversee applications that society might decide are acceptable. A moratorium on research cloning is a middle ground between the two positions of an immediate permanent ban and an unconstrained green light.

9   We strongly urge as well that the United States join with other countries, under the auspices of the United Nations, to work towards an international convention that would ban dangerous applications of the new genetic technologies, while encouraging the many applications judged to contribute to the improvement of human well-being.

10   We are long-time advocates for human rights, the environment, and social justice. We are strong supporters of women's health and reproductive rights, disability rights, and biomedical research. We believe in the inherent equality and human dignity of all people. We want to help ensure that our descendants live in a world in which these values are sustained and nurtured.

11   We believe that a ban on reproductive cloning and a moratorium on the creation of clonal embryos are the policies most consistent with the values and commitments we share. We strongly urge you to support legislation that would enact such policies into law.

Sincerely,

Signed by over fifty scientists, professors, journalists, authors, public health officals, directors, CEOs, doctors, lawyers, and nurses.

Letter to Senator Tom Daschle Opposing a Moratorium on Nuclear Transplantation
American Society for Cell Biology

While most advocates on all sides object to human reproductive cloning, thera-
peutic cloning (also called "nuclear transplantation") is more controversial:
Should it be banned and criminalized, be put on investigative hold through a
moratorium, or be legalized but carefully regulated? This letter from the
American Society for Cell Biology, an organization of 10,000 biomedical
researchers from the United States and around the world, was written in
response to Senator Sam Brownback's proposal to ban all nuclear transplanta-
tion. It calls for legalization and regulation of nuclear transplantation.

June 12, 2002
The Honorable Tom Daschle
Majority Leader
United States Senate
509 Hart Senate Office Building
Washington, DC 20510

Dear Senator Daschle:

1   The American Society for Cell Biology represents over 10,000 basic biomedical researchers across the United States and throughout the world.

2   The Senate will soon begin debate on legislation by Senator Sam Brownback (R-KS) that, if signed into law, would place severe criminal and civil penalties on both human reproductive cloning and nuclear transplantation to obtain stem cells. In addition, the bill would place identical penalties on the importation into the United States of cures and treatments developed using this technology. No responsible scientist supports the cloning of a human being. But S. 1899 goes far beyond the prohibition of cloning a human being: it outlaws and criminalizes promising biomedical research.

3   Furthermore, we believe that supporters of the Brownback bill base their endorsement on misleading claims by the bill's proponents. While opponents of nuclear transplantation claim that the research will lead to the establishment of "egg farms," scientific researchers, including Nobel Laureates, understand that a critical element of this research is that it will allow science to move beyond the necessity for egg cells. It is hoped that information learned from nuclear transplantation will eventually apply to somatic cells. The goal is to produce genetically matched embryonic stem cells from an individual's own cells.

4   In his bill, Senator Brownback establishes severe civil and criminal sanctions for what has been described by Nobel Laureate and former National Institutes of Health Director Harold Varmus as an "incredibly promising avenue" of research.

5   One alternative to the Brownback bill that has been suggested is the implementation of a legislatively enforced moratorium on nuclear transplantation research. Some versions of the moratorium are only six months long while others are as long as five years. While well-intentioned, a moratorium, regardless of the length of time, is not a satisfactory alternative to the Brownback bill. It raises the specter of prolonged discussion and political machinations, perhaps stalling research on nuclear transplantation indefinitely. More important, it also sends a signal to the American research community, both present and future, that the United States Senate no longer wishes the United States to be the world leader in scientific research that it has been up to this time. In all likelihood, such a freeze on the scientific process in the United States will lead to an exodus from the United States of current investigators and cause the next generation of American scientists to pick other career options.

6   It is no exaggeration to say that a legislative moratorium would have a disastrous impact on the American biomedical community for as long as a generation.

7   The Senate should, instead, unite around legislation that would prohibit reproductive cloning while allowing research on nuclear transplantation to progress under suitable regulation and oversight.

Sincerely,

Paul Berg, Ph.D.
Chair, Public Policy Committee
The American Society for Cell Biology
Cahill Professor of Cancer Research and Biochemistry, Emeritus
Director, Beckman Center for Molecular & Genetic Medicine, Emeritus
Stanford University School of Medicine
Nobel Prize in Chemistry, 1980

The President's Narrow Morality

New York Times

This editorial representing the liberal views of the New York Times *appeared in the April 11, 2002, edition of the newspaper. From the* Times' *liberal perspective, the forty Nobel prize winners promoting a moderate course of regulated research have a better case than President Bush with his all—or in this instance, nothing—approach.*

1   President Bush and 40 Nobel Prize winners went head to head yesterday on the controversial issue of human cloning. The president, in a speech, said a promising area of cloning research should be banned as unethical. But from our perspective the Nobelists, who released a letter, held the higher moral ground in focusing on the great promise of cloning for curing intractable diseases.

The warring views on cloning were intended to frame the debate as the Senate   2
prepares to vote in coming weeks on what sort of ban to impose on the cloning of
human embryos. Mr. Bush, siding with social and religious conservatives, wants to
ban all human cloning for any purpose. The Nobelists, and this page as well, would
ban reproductive cloning to produce human babies but would allow cloning of embryonic cell clusters for research and therapeutic purposes. The nub of the dispute
is whether very early embryos are human life that should not be destroyed, or
primitive clusters of cells (no bigger than a pinhead) that have not yet developed
human attributes and are thus fit subjects for research on therapies that could
benefit all of humanity.

Mr. Bush argued that cloning, even for research purposes, is wrong because it   3
involves the creation of embryos that are then destroyed to derive stem cells for
potential treatments. Anything less than a total ban on cloning would be unethical,
he proclaimed, because "no human life should be exploited or extinguished for the
benefit of another." That effectively defined the cell clusters as human life and declared them sacrosanct. Mr. Bush also contended that it would be difficult to
enforce a ban on reproductive cloning while allowing research cloning, and he
called the presumed benefits of research cloning "highly speculative."

Our own guess is that the 40 Nobel laureates, whose letter was released yes-   4
terday by the American Society for Cell Biology, have a better grasp of the science.
They argued that a ban on research and therapeutic cloning "would impede
progress on some of the most debilitating diseases known to man." Those ailments
include Parkinson's, Alzheimer's, diabetes, cardiovascular diseases, spinal cord
injuries and various cancers and neurological diseases, among others. Research
cloning may help scientists develop embryonic stem cell treatments that would not
be rejected by a patient's own body, the Nobelists said. A ban on this important
science, they warned, would send a strong signal to young researchers that "unfettered and responsible scientific investigation is not welcome in the United States."

What was most disturbing about Mr. Bush's remarks was their black-and-   5
white, even apocalyptic tone. It was unfair and irresponsible for him to imply that
those who wish to pursue therapeutic cloning that could benefit millions of suffering humans are traveling "without an ethical compass into a world we could live to
regret." The real regret would come if we fail to pursue some of the most promising
medical research spawned by modern biotechnology.

Hatch Makes the Case for Regenerative Medicine

Senator Orrin G. Hatch

*In this press conference speech delivered April 30, 2002, Orrin G. Hatch,
Republican senator from Utah and a staunch Mormon, argues in favor of therapeutic cloning from a moral, religious, pro-life, pro-family position. We obtained
this speech from Hatch's Web site.*

1   In the weeks ahead, the United States Senate will debate an issue that is of extreme importance to millions of Americans suffering from disease. The challenge before Congress is twofold. We must craft a law to make sure that human beings are not cloned. At the same time, we must not stand in the way of scientific advances that hold the promise of treatments and cures for literally millions of Americans.

2   At the outset, I just want to read one letter I received from my constituents—the parents of Cody Anderson in West Jordan, Utah. This sums it up far better than I can:

Dear Senator Hatch,

We would first like to thank you for carefully studying stem cell research and coming out in favor of it last year. We appreciate your taking the correct moral stand on this very important issue. We now need you to again lead the way on another important issue, the cloning of human cells for research to cure the diseases such as diabetes. Let us just share a little of our story of why this is so important to our family.

I would first like to start by telling you how I became familiar with diabetes. My father was diabetic from the age of seven years old and by the time I was four years old he had lost his sight. He never saw my youngest brother. As we grew up we always knew that our father was different but we learned to live with the disease. We slowly watched more complications take shape because of the disease. He eventually lost function of his kidneys and was on kidney dialysis for 10 years. He eventually lost his left leg below the knee, had two toes amputated from the right foot because of poor circulation, had a colostomy, had his left eye removed to relieve pain and pressure and in total had 28 surgeries just to keep him alive, all because of the devastating effects of the diabetes. Finally on April 29, 1991, his heart just stopped and he died at the age of 47. The cause of death: diabetes.

I am now married and have three children of my own and my worst fears came true on June 9, 2000, when my youngest son Cody was diagnosed with diabetes at the age of 2. The same disease that I watched slowly take my father away from me at such a young age. Cody has to have his blood sugars tested at least 6–10 times daily. He is on an insulin pump and has to have his site changed 3 to 4 times a week. We have to know every bite of food that he eats and how many carbohydrates each bite has so we can figure the correct amount of insulin to give him. Every day is different depending on his activities for the day. A growth spurt can throw everything off for days at a time. Something as simple as the common cold can have devastating effects on his blood sugars. The stomach flu is also something extremely difficult to deal with as well.

Not only does diabetes affect Cody's life but it affects the lives of our entire family. My husband and I have to work opposite schedules just because we don't have anyone close by that can watch Cody. Anytime Cody goes to a friend's house for playgroup we need to be where they can reach us at all times because they don't understand the simple basics of taking care of a diabetic child.

With your leadership on this issue, we can help people understand that cloning human tissue for research has nothing to do with making carbon "copies of people" or creating life. It is about saving human lives and easing the pain and suffering of children like Cody.

Sincerely,

The Anderson Family

As a father of six, and a grandfather of 20, when I read that letter, it really   3
tugged at my heartstrings. It pointed out so clearly the challenge before us: to help
families like the Andersons, without sanctioning human cloning, which is anathema
to us all.

And so, I am pleased today to join with my colleagues to announce agreement   4
on legislation which we hope will do just that: prevent human beings from being
cloned, but promote—with appropriate safeguards—the new science of regenerative medicine.

This is not a position that I reached easily. Indeed, my decision came after   5
countless hours of study, reflection and prayer. I consulted as broadly as I could on
this issue, talking with Americans from all walks of life, scientific experts from
across the country, religious leaders and ethicists. I did all I could to make sure I
understood as completely as possible all the issues at stake.

I met with proponents of this research, such as Dr. Irv Weissman, who is with   6
us today, and with opponents, such as Dr. Leon Kass, the Chairman of the
President's Bioethics Commission. And I have great respect for the sincerity and
decency of those who disagree with me.

After considerable time, thought and prayer, I believed I knew enough to   7
make an informed decision on this issue. My study took me back to the books of
the Old Testament and forward to the latest issues of the *New England Journal of
Medicine.*

Once I identified and weighed what I considered to be the relevant factors, the   8
decision itself was not a close call.

The first part of the legislation was easy. There is near-universal agreement   9
that attempts to clone a baby should be stopped at all costs. This would directly interfere with God's sacred plan for human reproduction by a man and woman within
the bounds of marriage. Accordingly, our bill will criminalize any attempt to clone a
human being.

The second part was the more difficult.   10

In addition to banning human cloning, our bill advances the field of regenera-   11
tive medicine by explicitly authorizing—with appropriate safeguards—somatic cell
nuclear transfer or nuclear transplantation.

Let me be clear. It was only after my colleagues agreed to include these safe-   12
guards that I agreed to cosponsor the measure. It may be that we need further clarification of these safeguards, and I intend to work with my colleagues to make any
necessary changes as the bill moves forward. But, on balance, this is a bill that I
can support, and I will support given its enormous importance.

We have with us today many distinguished scientists who can explain nuclear   13
transplantation far better than I. The import of what they will say is that the
process of somatic cell transfer can be used as a potential source of stem cells that
are extremely useful in regenerative medicine research.

One of the goals of regenerative medicine is to learn how these undifferentiated   14
stem cells develop into the over 200 specialized cells and tissues that comprise the
human body. This knowledge could hold the key to understanding much about human health and disease and may yield new diagnostic tests and treatments to help
all the Cody Andersons of the world.

15   That is what this bill will do—promise to help the 100 million Americans who are struggling with the day-to-day challenges of currently incurable diseases. We are talking about cancer, heart disease, diabetes, AIDS, Alzheimer's, ALS, Parkinson's, multiple sclerosis and so many other diseases. We are talking about our grandmothers and grandfathers, our mothers and fathers, our children and our grandchildren. We are talking about the people with whom we work and worship, our friends in the neighborhood and our colleagues at work. We are talking about each of us here in the room today.

16   During this debate you will hear some question whether we really need to conduct the type of research our bill authorizes. Others will try to paint the measure as pro-embryo destruction. Each of us must search our own soul to come to grips with such fundamental questions as when life begins.

17   We will ask our colleagues and the public to listen carefully to what leading experts in science believe. For example, a group of 40 American Nobel Prize winners have written to Congress to ask us to support this research. I will also make available today copies of a few of the compelling letters I have received from Intel CEO Andy Grove and the Director of the prestigious Huntsman Cancer Institute, Stephen Prescott. We should listen to them and to the clerical leaders and patient advocates who are with us today.

18   I come to this issue with a strong pro-life, pro-family record. But I also strongly believe that a critical part of being pro-life is to support measures that help the living.

19   Some, including many in the Right to Life community, oppose this research on the grounds that the new cell created in the laboratory becomes a new human life at the moment it is electronically activated. That is a view I respect, but with which I do not agree. At the core of my support for regenerative medicine research is my belief that human life requires and begins in a mother's nurturing womb.

20   As I considered the ethical appropriateness of nuclear transplantation in regenerative medicine research, two facts stood out:

- The egg, with its nucleus removed, is never fertilized with sperm;
- The resulting unfertilized, electrically activated embryo will not be implanted into a woman's womb so there is no chance of a birth. I should add that our bill would prevent implantation into any type of artificial womb that may one day be developed.

21   The absence of a fertilized egg coupled with a legal prohibition against implantation leads me to conclude that this research can be conducted, with appropriate safeguards, in an ethically proper fashion.

22   Should we continue other forms of stem cell research, such as adult stem cell research? Absolutely. I hope that adult stem cell research lives up to its promise. But should we cut off the promising avenue that embryonic stem cell research holds out? The answer to me is clear: no.

23   Americans deserve the best treatments available. To ban human somatic cell nuclear transfer research would be a tragic mistake. It could force Americans to

travel abroad to seek the latest treatments. Prohibiting this research in our country could also drive many of our young, talented scientists overseas. As we have done so often in biomedical research, it is in the interest of our nation to lead the way in this new field and to help set the ethical and moral standards for the rest of the world.

Before I close, I want to recognize all the cosponsors of this important legislation. Senator Specter and our colleague, the Chairman of the Labor-HHS Appropriations Subcommittee, Tom Harkin, have held 14 hearings that have centered on the unprecedented promise of stem cell research. I am also pleased to have worked with Senators Feinstein and Kennedy in developing the legislation that is being introduced today. Along with Senator Specter, they provided leadership in this area by sponsoring earlier legislation that we build upon today. 24

I am particularly pleased that Senator Zell Miller joins us in this effort because he brings the level-headed, pragmatic approach that we will need in this debate. I also want to pay special recognition to Senators Brownback and Landrieu; while my conclusion ultimately differs with theirs, I respect their position and their work to bring this crucial issue to the forefront of public debate. Let us remember, we all have the same goal: we want to do what we believe in our hearts is the right thing to do. We just disagree. 25

Regenerative medicine is pro-life and pro-family; it enhances, not diminishes, human life. If encouraged to flourish, it can improve the lives of millions of Americans and could lead to new scientific frontiers not now in sight. I urge my colleagues in the Senate and the American public to support this bill that opposes human cloning but promotes regenerative medicine using nuclear transplantation. Thank you. 26

Stem Cell Simplicities
Mona Charen

Nationally syndicated columnist Mona Charen is one of the nation's most prolific conservative writers. During the Reagan administration, she was a speechwriter for Nancy Reagan and later for Republican presidential hopeful Jack Kemp. She has also been an editor for the conservative policy magazine National Review. *Her weekly syndicated column is published in more than 200 newspapers around the United States. This op-ed piece on stem cell research appeared in the online magazine* Jewish World Review *on July 6, 2001.*

Let's use the bodies of condemned criminals for medical research! We could donate the eyes and heart of a Timothy McVeigh-type to some worthy medical experiment, and the lungs and livers of other murderers for similar purposes. Well, after all, the bodies are only going to be buried anyway, at least this way some good will come of them. 1

2   Why do you squirm? Probably for the same reason that no one stood in line to receive "fresh" organs from Dr. Jack Kevorkian when he offered them.

3   We flinch from using the organs from condemned people for several reasons, but the most important is our well-grounded fear that using the organs of executed criminals might introduce temptations to the administration of capital punishment that would be immoral. If the state takes someone's life, it should be for one reason only—to exact punishment for a heinous crime. Imagine if judges and juries were also considering how many lives could be saved by making available fresh hearts, lungs, kidneys and so on?

4   And yet, in the debate over stem cell research, we are constantly reminded that these embryos are going to be "discarded" anyway. Well, that only shows how much work we have to do in sensitizing people to the sanctity of life.

5   Human embryos should never be "discarded." There are other options, like reducing the numbers of embryos that are created in the first place, or embryo adoption. But this is a secondary question. The heart of the matter is this: Is an embryo an entity that deserves special respect?

6   *Newsweek* magazine's cover story on the matter emphatically answers that question in the negative. Over a picture of a fuzzy ball of cells the cover proclaims "There's Hope for Alzheimer's, Heart Disease, Parkinson's and Diabetes. But Will Bush Cut Off the Money?"

7   Inside, one researcher thunders, "Anyone who would ban research on embryonic stem cells will be responsible for the harm done to real, alive, postnatal, sentient human beings who might be helped by this research."

8   Emphasis on *might*. It may be that the miracle cures confidently predicted for Parkinson's, diabetes and such will come to pass, but some caution is certainly in order. Recall that just a few years ago, medical and media circles were abuzz with hopes for the implantation of fetal brain cells into patients with Parkinson's. Then too, as Neil Munro reminds us in the *National Journal*, *The Washington Post* urged a president named Bush to lift federal bans on such research since it offered "the best hope for progress on curing such diseases as Parkinson's."

9   The federal ban was not lifted, but some scientists went ahead with the procedure anyway. The results were noted (very quietly) just a couple of months ago. The *New York Times* reported that the experimental treatment was a failure, and that some patients suffered side effects described as "absolutely devastating . . . tragic, catastrophic."

10   While results from stem cells may be better, one never hears a scientist asked: What is the marginal benefit of embryonic stem cells versus those found in umbilical cord blood, or those found in adults? Are we five years, or three, or one year away from achieving the same results with less morally comprised tissue?

11   To extract a stem cell from an embryo is to kill it. Now, Utah Sen. Orrin Hatch argues that an embryo in a fertility clinic freezer does not have the same status as a baby in a mother's womb.

12   A thought experiment: Suppose a burglar with a grudge against a couple went to her fertility clinic and methodically smashed the vials containing their frozen embryos. Would their damages be only the value of the broken glass?

It is difficult for people with limited imaginations to see an embryo as a human   13
being. They don't look like us. But that is the stupendous miracle of life. Each of us
begins as a dot of information smaller than the period at the end of this sentence.
We are dust—and yet with the magic of DNA and with time, we become people. And
those little clumps of cells, which even *Newsweek* agrees are "a world of potential,"
cannot ethically be sacrificed—no matter what the hoped-for gain.

A New Look, an Old Battle
Anna Quindlen

*The range of perspectives on therapeutic stem cell research is evident in the dif-
ferences between the previous argument by Mona Charen and this one by Anna
Quindlen, a contributing editor to* Newsweek, *a novelist, and a Pulitzer prize-
winning journalist. Quindlen's argument appeared as a "Last Word" editorial in*
Newsweek *on April 9, 2001.*

Public personification has always been the struggle on both sides of the abor-   1
tion battle lines. That is why the people outside clinics on Saturday mornings
carry signs with photographs of infants rather than of zygotes, why they wear
lapel pins fashioned in the image of tiny feet and shout, "Don't kill your baby,"
rather than, more accurately, "Don't destroy your embryo." Those who support the
legal right to an abortion have always been somewhat at a loss in the face of all
this. From time to time women have come forward to speak about their decision to
have an abortion, but when they are prominent, it seems a bit like grandstanding,
and when they are not, it seems a terrible invasion of privacy when privacy is the
point in the first place. Easier to marshal the act of presumptive ventriloquism
practiced by the opponents, pretending to speak for those unborn unknown to
them by circumstance or story.

But the battle of personification will assume a different and more sympathetic   2
visage in the years to come. Perhaps the change in the weather was best illustrated
when conservative Sen. Strom Thurmond invoked his own daughter to explain a position opposed by the anti-abortion forces. The senator's daughter has diabetes. The
actor Michael J. Fox has Parkinson's disease. Christopher Reeve is in a wheelchair
because of a spinal-cord injury, Ronald Reagan is locked in his own devolving mind
by Alzheimer's. In the faces of the publicly and personally beloved lies enormous
danger for the life-begins-at-conception lobby.

The catalytic issue is research on stem cells. These are versatile building   3
blocks that may be coaxed into becoming any other cell type, they could therefore
hold the key to endless mysteries of human biology, as well as someday help
provide a cure for ailments as diverse as diabetes, Parkinson's, spinal-cord degen-
eration and Alzheimer's. By some estimates, more than 100 million Americans

have diseases that scientists suspect could be affected by research on stem cells. Scientists hope that the astonishing potential of this research will persuade the federal government to help fund it and allow the National Institutes of Health to help oversee it. This is not political, researchers insist. It is about science, not abortion.

4   And they are correct. Stem-cell research is typically done by using frozen embryos left over from in vitro fertilization. If these embryos were placed in the womb, they might eventually implant, become a fetus, then a child. Unused, they are the earliest undifferentiated collection of cells made by the joining of the egg and sperm, no larger than the period at the end of this sentence. One of the oft-used slogans of the anti-abortion movement is "abortion stops a beating heart." There is no heart in this pre-implantation embryo, but there are stem cells that, in the hands of scientists, might lead to extraordinary work affecting everything from cancer to heart disease.

5   All of which leaves the anti-abortion movement trying desperately to hold its hard line, and failing. Judie Brown of the American Life League can refer to these embryos as "the tiniest person," and the National Right to Life organization can publish papers that refer to stem-cell research as the "destruction of life." But ordinary people with family members losing their mobility or their grasp on reality will be able to be more thoughtful and reasonable about the issues involved.

6   The anti-abortion activists know this, because they have already seen the defections. Some senators have abandoned them to support fetal-tissue research, less promising than stem-cell work but still with significant potential for treating various ailments. Elected officials who had voted against abortion rights found themselves able to support procedures that used tissue from aborted fetuses; perhaps they were men who had fathers with heart disease, who had mothers with arthritis and whose hearts resonated with the possibilities for alleviating pain and prolonging life. Senator Thurmond was one, Senator McCain another. Former senator Connie Mack of Florida recently sent a letter to the president, who must decide the future role of the federal government in this area, describing himself "as a conservative pro-life now former member" of Congress, and adding that there "were those of us identified as such who supported embryonic stem-cell research."

7   When a recent test of fetal tissue in patients with Parkinson's had disastrous side effects, the National Right to Life Web site ran an almost gloating report: "horrific," "rips to shreds," "media cheerleaders," "defy description." The tone is a reflection of fear. It's the fear that the use of fetal tissue to produce cures for debilitating ailments might somehow launder the process of terminating a pregnancy, a positive result from what many people still see as a negative act. And it's the fear that thinking—really thinking—about the use of the earliest embryo for life-saving research might bring a certain long-overdue relativism to discussions of abortion across the board.

8   The majority of Americans have always been able to apply that relativism to these issues. They are more likely to accept early abortions than later ones. They are more tolerant of a single abortion under exigent circumstances than multiple

abortions. Some who disapprove of abortion in theory have discovered that they can accept it in fact if a daughter or a girlfriend is pregnant.

And some who believe that life begins at conception may look into the vacant eyes of an adored parent with Alzheimer's or picture a paralyzed child walking again, and take a closer look at what an embryo really is, at what stem-cell research really does, and then consider the true cost of a cure. That is what Senator Thurmond obviously did when he looked at his daughter and broke ranks with the true believers. It may be an oversimplification to say that real live loved ones trump the imagined unborn, that a cluster of undifferentiated cells due to be discarded anyway is a small price to pay for the health and welfare of millions. Or perhaps it is only a simple commonsensical truth.

For Class Discussion

1. Many of the articles in this unit incorporate causal arguments to speculate about the potential consequences of different courses of action on cloning and stem cell research. Working individually or in groups, choose several of the views represented in this unit and sketch out the causal arguments that the writers use to support their claims. You might choose from among the following views or any others that you think of. What makes each instance of causal reasoning persuasive or weak?

   - Scientists in favor of therapeutic cloning
   - Public policymakers in favor of therapeutic cloning
   - Scientists in favor of a moratorium on therapeutic cloning
   - Spokespeople for conservative religious views against all cloning and stem cell research
   - Spokespeople for conservative religious views in favor of regulated therapeutic cloning and stem cell research
   - Nonreligious spokespeople against therapeutic cloning

2. One of the major rhetorical problems with a subject like cloning and stem cell research is the need to translate scientific ideas into terms that the general public can understand. In rhetorical language, we would say that this is an issue of finding audience-based reasons and presenting evidence that will be meaningful to a nonscientifically trained audience. Which of the arguments in this unit do you find particularly successful at making this scientific subject clear to readers? How do they work?

3. Where and how in the articles in this unit do arguers on these issues bring in the personal human element or other appeals to *pathos*?

4. According to some of the readings in this unit, where does the therapeutic cloning controversy intersect with abortion, reproductive technology (medical technology used to overcome infertility problems), and eugenics?

5. Choose one of the readings in this unit and analyze it carefully using the List 2 Guide questions on pages 460–461.

OPTIONAL WRITING ASSIGNMENT   Some of the readings in this unit reject quick closure and call for more informed public debate on therapeutic cloning and stem cell research. A number of the readings are written in the letter genre as direct messages to decision makers. After considering the multiple angles of vision reflected in these readings, write a letter to a U.S. senator from your state in which you speak for yourself or your family. Make a case for the way you would like your senator to vote on this controversial issue. What laws and regulations would you like your politician to support and why?

CRIMINAL JUSTICE AND POSTPARTUM PSYCHOSIS: THE CASE OF ANDREA YATES

On June 20, 2001, Andrea Yates, a stay-at-home mom in Houston, Texas, filled the family bathtub with water and systematically drowned her five children, varying in age from a six-month-old daughter to a seven-year-old son. The state of Texas charged Yates with premeditated first-degree murder and called for the death penalty. Yates's attorneys mounted an insanity defense based on a diagnosis of postpartum psychosis. On March 15, 2002, nine months after the event, a jury rejected the insanity plea, found Yates guilty of first-degree murder, and sentenced her to life imprisonment. The horror of this event shocked the nation, initiating a national conversation about criminal justice, the insanity defense, and the anxieties of middle-class, suburban motherhood.

In the readings in this unit, you will discover the complexity of the Yates case with its numerous intertwined issues. Among the questions examined in these readings are the following: How can a state draw the line between sanity and insanity? In borderline cases should society opt for punishment (prison) or for hospitalization and release upon recovery? Is postpartum psychosis a real disease? What are the causes of postpartum psychosis? When does postpartum depression become postpartum psychosis and then a legally defined instance of insanity? Should the criteria for insanity be applied more leniently to women than to men? To what extent was Yates's husband, Rusty, culpable in causing her depression and failing to prevent the tragedy? What social structures and practices contribute to postpartum depression and to mental stress on mothers? What social measures might be useful in preventing future cases of mothers going off the deep end?

Following two photos at the start of this unit is an overview article on postpartum psychosis by a practicing psychiatrist. We then move to a series of arguments by social and political commentators to reveal the wide range of perspectives on this complex and troubling issue.

Media Photographs of Andrea Yates

The following photographs of Yates regularly appeared in media discussions of her case. The first is a Yates family photograph, taken sometime in 2000 before the birth of their daughter, Mary. The second is a widely circulated photograph of Andrea Yates taken sometime after her arrest. You might explore the kinds of "arguments" made by these photographs. How do they influence your understanding of and feelings toward Yates? You might note that when the prosecuting attorney made his final speech to the jury, he used individual pictures of each Yates child rather than the family photograph. Why?

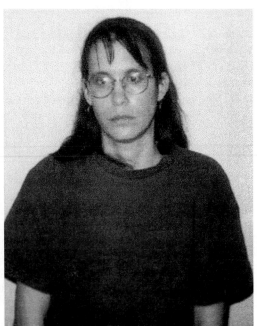

Mommy Undearest
Sally Satel

Sally Satel is a practicing psychiatrist and a fellow at the American Enterprise Institute, an influential conservative think tank. This article, which was written in the first few days after the June 20 killings, appeared in the online webzine Slate *on July 4, 2001.*

1   On the morning of June 20, Andrea Yates, a suburban Houston mother, killed her five children, drowning them one by one in the bathtub. "I killed my children," she confessed in a calm voice to the investigating policeman who arrived at her home.

2   Yates represents nature's aberration as a mother, but also a rather textbook example of postpartum psychosis. Or so it seems from the details provided in the media. Yates allegedly had been contemplating the murders for a few months and said she did it because the children were "damaged."

3   For years, it seems, Rusty Yates knew his wife was depressed, at times even "unrecognizable" as the Andrea he knew. She became deeply despondent after each child was born, he says, although she made no threats to harm her brood. In 1999, however, after the birth of her fourth child, Andrea Yates attempted suicide

twice—first with pills and later by cutting her throat. Yates' symptoms lifted after she was put under medical care and given antidepressants. Soon, Andrea had Mary, the couple's first girl.

A few months later, Andrea Yates' father died, and this sent her deeper into despair, according to her husband. Her darkness must have mutated into psychosis because her doctor gave her Haldol—an antipsychotic that treats symptoms like hallucinations, delusions, paranoia, and deeply confused thinking. For some reason, her doctor discontinued Haldol a week or so before the murders. Was this pivotal in the murders? As an antipsychotic, Haldol may have checked her impulses, or it may have softened the delusional ideas she had about herself and her children.

What is postpartum illness? The American Psychiatric Association, which referees this sort of thing for the profession with its *Diagnostic and Statistical Manual,* first recognized "post-partum psychosis" in 1968 (code 294.4 Psychosis Associated With Childbirth). The entry was removed shortly thereafter, not because postpartum psychosis wasn't real, but because clinicians disagreed over the proper classification of the condition. Postpartum illnesses returned in the 1994 edition of *DSM* as variants of depression and psychosis, not as a unique diagnosis.

Our culture uses the terms "postpartum depression," "postpartum illness," and "postpartum psychosis" interchangeably to describe the so-called baby blues—a transitory period of sadness, irritability, and anxiety that arrives within a week of childbirth. It affects over half of all new mothers in some form. According to the literature, about 10 percent to 15 percent of mothers suffer more substantial depression, marked by a sense of hopelessness, diminished interest, and an inability to experience pleasure. Those women have trouble concentrating and sleeping, lose interest in food, and occasionally contemplate suicide. They might imagine harming their babies or feel guilty about being bad or underserving mothers. The feelings start within a month of delivery and can last months, even a year. Before the advent of psychiatric medications, a handful of mothers remained ill for years, according to medical reports from the first half of the century.

Only about one in 1,000 postpartum cases progresses to the point of severe depression (immobilization, intense suicidal preoccupations) or develops a psychotic dimension to the depression, as seems to have been the case with Yates. A tiny fraction of all women giving birth—maybe 0.1 percent—become psychotic without first experiencing depression. When psychotic, the mother may think her baby is evil, that he must be destroyed to save humanity, or she may "hear" God telling her to kill him. Or she may think she's saving the baby by sending him from this hell-on-earth to heaven. Yates told police her children were "damaged," but it's likely that more florid delusions beset her.

The average mother is not at risk for severe postpartum illness. Most vulnerable are those who have endured episodes of significant depression or are bipolar (manic-depressive) and have already experienced depression or psychosis following childbirth. Yates' history of depressions put her at very high risk with this latest baby.

Postpartum psychosis was first used as an insanity defense in an American courtroom in the 1980s, though doctors have recognized it for thousands of years. Around 500 B.C., Hippocrates described the emotional turmoil of women in the third book of his treatise *Epidemics,* calling it "puerperal fever"(the puerperium referring to the period surrounding birth), and theorized that suppressed vaginal discharge in the days following birth were transported to the brain where they incited "agitation, delirium and attacks of mania." The 11th-century gynecologist Trotula of Salerno speculated "if the womb is too moist, the brain is filled with water," and this manifests as depression. The British medical journal the *Lancet* describes a case of postpartum psychosis in an 1846 article:

> For eight long months the patient was almost constantly excited by night and by day, talking incessantly, often swearing, untiringly active, running about the wards . . . and riding the rocking horses like one possessed . . . [o]ften mistaking persons and becoming very violent. She unfortunately began to mistake Mrs. Bowden for someone of whom she was jealous and made some rather desperate attacks on her.

10   The condition's neurobiology has not been defined, but modern researchers widely presume that hormonal shifts initiate, if not sustain, the disease process. In the 1960s, researchers treated women with long-acting estrogen immediately after delivery and were able to suppress most symptoms of "maternity" blues. Abnormalities in thyroid and pituitary function have also been implicated. Today, SSRI (selective serotonin reuptake inhibitor) antidepressants such as Prozac and Paxil are the most common treatment.

11   Not surprisingly, psychological factors help determine vulnerability. Mothers who didn't want to get pregnant experience greater risk for milder forms of postpartum illness than those who wanted their babies. The birth of a premature infant or difficult labor also enhances risk, as does a mother's feeling that she is not getting adequate emotional and material support. Mothers report the baby blues more often in the United States than in other countires, but the condition cuts across cultures.

12   Edward H. Hagen, an anthropologist at the University of California at Santa Barbara, offers a sociobiological theory of postpartum depression. He argues that diminished maternal investment in the offspring could be adaptive under conditions of insufficient intimacy and resources. Writes Hagen, "Because human infants require enormous amounts of investment, ancestral mothers needed to carefully assess both the availability of support from the father and family members and infant viability before committing to several years of nursing and childcare."

13   What distinguishes the baby blues from something more malignant? Families should be on the lookout for distress that doesn't disappear after a week or so, as well as symptoms that interfere with caretaking, such as sluggishness, sadness, uncontrollable crying, hopelessness, a sense of doom, poor concentration, confusion, and memory loss. Other markers include obsessive checking on the infant or an irrational fear on the mother's part that she might harm the baby or herself.

14   We should, however, resist the modern tendency to label all emotional discomfort—shyness in adults, for example—as sicknesses requiring medication. Postpartum doldrums are natural, whether their underlying causes be hormonal or psychological. For most mothers most of the time, the best remedies are helpful mates, supportive families and friends, and time.

Maternal Madness . . . or Sheer Iniquity? Mothers Who Kill

John Derbyshire

This article appeared in the conservative magazine National Review *on October 1, 2001. John Derbyshire is a novelist and contributing editor to* National Review.

MACBETH: How does your patient, doctor?
DOCTOR: Not so sick, my lord, As she is troubled with thick-coming fancies
That keep her from her rest.

Was Andrea Pia Yates sick when, on the morning of June 20, shortly after her   1
husband left for work, she drowned her five children in the family bathtub? Respectable members of the medical profession certainly think so. Mrs. Yates had been on prescription antidepressants and antipsychotic drugs (which are much stronger), and had been hospitalized twice for depression since her fifth child was born, six months before the killings.

If she was sick, it is at any rate plain that the treatment she was getting did not   2
heal her. Under the care of her doctors, paid for by the health-insurance plan that came with her husband's government job (he is a computer engineer for NASA), she killed her five children. There is to be a hearing to determine her fitness to stand trial. So: Is the lady sick, or just very wicked?

Before proceeding, let me tell you a true story. Several years ago, on a pleasant   3
summer afternoon, I was sitting in the garden of a house I owned in London, when I saw a tortoise. I should explain that tortoises are given to children as pets in England, or at least they used to be—I think there are now strict controls on the tortoise market. It was never a good idea, as tortoises lack most of the characteristics that make animals interesting to children: They are not cuddly, playful, winsome, fierce, or noisy. Furthermore, they require much more careful attention than most children are willing to bestow on them. Perhaps there had been something in the newspapers along these lines; I cannot remember. At any rate, there I was in the garden when I saw this tortoise making his patient way across the lawn. A small hole had been drilled in the edge of his shell, so that he could be tethered—a usual procedure. Tortoises are slow, but dogged, and will wander away if not constrained. I suppose this one had broken free from his tether in some other garden, or been left untethered.

Now, I was feeling rather sorry for myself at the time—relationship problem.   4
I suppose I was depressed. Watching that tortoise make his painstaking way across the lawn, some strange variant of the Sympathetic Fallacy kicked in. He was

unwanted; he had been bought as a gift for children who had then lost interest in him. Perhaps they had let him wander off deliberately. My heart went out to this fellow mortal, who obviously had no future—surely a tortoise could not survive in London. For his own sake, I decided to put him out of his misery. I picked him up, took him in to the kitchen, filled a bowl with water, and held him under it to drown him. I held him there for a long time, several minutes, waiting for him to expire. It is, I learned, rather difficult to know when a tortoise has given up the ghost. He was quite agitated when I first put him underwater, but soon became inert. A thick milky white fluid came out of his back end. His mouth, however, continued to make very small movements.

5   Quite suddenly I came to my senses. What on earth was I doing? I lifted him out of the bowl and stared at him in horror. I had tried to kill a tortoise! For no good reason at all! As I stared, he blinked at me. I took him back out to the garden and set him down. After a brief moment to reorient himself, he took off across the lawn exactly as if nothing had happened, and disappeared into a neighboring garden.

6   I relate this trivial and rather embarrassing episode to establish some kind of credentials for talking about Altruistic Filicide.

7   What Mrs. Yates did was filicide—the killing of one's own children. It is not a particularly rare crime. Of the 1,500 or so children who are killed each year in the U.S. by acts of violence directed at them, around 30 percent die at the hands of a parent. You may recall the 1994 case of Susan Smith, who strapped her two young sons into their car seats and then rolled the car into a lake. Even Mrs. Yates's modus operandi was not unprecedented: Back in 1965, 38-year-old Maggie Young of Honolulu (Mrs. Yates was 36) drowned her own five children in their bathtub and laid them out on a bed in exactly the Yates fashion, while her husband was away from home. Even worse was the case of Constance Fisher of Maine, who drowned her first three children—bathtub again—in 1954. After five years as a psychiatric patient in Augusta State Hospital, Fisher was declared "cured" and returned home. She then had three more children, all of whom she drowned in 1967.

8   The classic study on this subject, carried out over 30 years ago by forensic psychiatrist Dr. Phillip J. Resnick, places filicides into five categories: accidental (for example, someone kills a child by shaking him too vigorously), altruistic (killing a child from pity, "for his own good"), acutely psychotic (under the influence of hallucinogens or delirium), unwanted child (as in the case of Susan Smith, who believed the man she loved would not take her if she came burdened with children), and revenge against a partner (Medea). Now, Mrs. Yates's explanation of her actions was: "I am a bad mother and they were hopelessly damaged." To judge from that statement, she killed her children out of misplaced altruism. She felt about them the way I felt about that tortoise, the way Jude the Obscure's son felt about his siblings: that they had no hope of a happy life, and so would be better off in the next world. Her general state of mind must have been something drastically worse than mere low spirits, but I believe I have got at least the hint of an insight into her thought processes.

Mrs. Yates was, of course, mistaken. Her children were healthy and well adjusted, their life chances better than average. She herself, so far as anyone—including her husband—had been able to see, was a loving and conscientious mother, in spite of being prone to savage attacks of postpartum depression. Still, I think it is wrong to see the crime in terms of the intolerable frustrations of child-raising—the explanation that motivates all the celebrities and support groups that have come out in her defense. Rosie O'Donnell declared that she felt "overwhelming empathy" for Mrs. Yates. Katie Couric told viewers of her TV show where to send contributions to Mrs. Yates's legal-defense fund. Anna Quindlen chipped in with a rant against "the insidious cult of motherhood." A branch of the National Organization for Women has put together an Andrea Pia Yates Support Coalition, pulling in the ACLU and various antideath-penalty groups. 9

I believe that what all these people really have in mind is to establish "awareness" (as they would say) of another Victim Sickness. It is now a firm principle of victimology that members of designated victim groups are especially susceptible to certain diseases, brought on by the stress of their subjection to the oppressive white male heterosexual patriarchy. Some of these diseases are behavioral aberrations caused by that stress: Homosexuals would settle down into stable, AIDS-risk-free unions if they were not driven into promiscuity by the insults and cruelty of the breeder majority; black people are forced into crime and drug addiction, as well as hypertension, by white racism. And now Ms. Quindlen's "insidious cult of motherhood" is dragging women down into psychopathy and filicide. 10

I don't think we should buy this. The challenges, confusions, and hormonal changes of new motherhood sometimes cause massive unhappiness; but then, so do many other life events—broken love, the death of a partner, financial ruin, physical disability, and so on. I don't see how it helps to label these miseries "sickness," especially when it is plain that we have not much idea how to "cure" them. Further, the medicalization of these life problems, the notion that they have their origins in some infectious agent or organic malfunction (for neither of which is there any evidence), kicks out yet more props from under our system of ethics. Either we are responsible agents, even in the midst of the direst unhappiness, or we are not. If we are not, then the foundations of our social ethics, and in particular of our legal system, are reduced to mud. 11

With a great effort of imagination I think I can see what was in Mrs. Yates's mind when she drowned her children. I can't forgive her for it, though: Tout comprendre is not tout pardonner, and never should be. Mrs. Yates did a monstrously wicked thing, and ought to be punished for it. State prosecutors have asked for the death penalty. I hope they make their case. I hope Mrs. Yates will be executed, and soon. 12

MACBETH: Cure her of that. Canst thou not minister to a mind diseased,

Pluck from the memory a rooted sorrow,

Raze out the written troubles of the brain . . . ?

DOCTOR: Therein the patient must minister to himself.

Andrea Yates Wasn't Responsible for Her Crime

Charles Krauthammer

Syndicated columnist Charles Krauthammer wrote this op-ed piece in March 2002, after the guilty verdict was reached by the jury in the Yates case. Before becoming a political commentator, Krauthammer was a practicing psychiatrist.

1   I would have acquitted Andrea Yates.

2   It is not an easy call. But to be guilty, one needs to have free will. How free is the will of someone who is seriously psychotic?

3   Let's start with the easy cases. Just having a mental illness cannot be grounds for acquittal. The illness may not be active when you carry out a crime. Or it may not be relevant to the crime. Just having a diagnosis—and in recent decades they have proliferated ridiculously—does not give you legal carte blanche.

4   So you need mental illness plus. Plus what? Texas law says, plus the inability to distinguish right from wrong.

5   The easy case here is the guy who is hallucinating and takes an ax to a skull thinking it is a pumpkin. You cannot possibly find this person guilty. He literally knows not what he does.

6   That does not mean he walks free. Anybody that crazy is obviously a danger to the community. He needs to be controlled, confined and supervised for as long as it takes until society is sure that he will not again mistake a head for a pumpkin.

7   The hard case occurs when the murderer seems to know what he is doing. In one sense, Andrea Yates obviously knew what she was doing when she drowned each of her five children slowly, horribly, deliberately. The jury found her guilty, concluding that her actions that day—waiting until her husband had left home, calling the cops immediately after she had killed her children—demonstrated that she knew the killings were wrong.

8   It is a plausible line of argument, but I would argue differently. She clearly knew that what she did was illegal. And prohibited. And would cause her to be punished. But in the grip of a fantastic psychosis, she actually thought it was right. She thought she was saving her children from a worse fate, in this world and the next.

9   That is her story, and I do not believe it is a post hoc rationalization. It is simply too common in cases of maternal infanticide resulting from postpartum depression. The psychotic thinking is quite stereotypical: The mother feels some terrible satanic evil enveloping her and her children. She feels compelled—often ordered by voices or other hallucinatory forces—to "save" the children from that overwhelming evil by killing them.

10   Andrea Yates fits the classic pattern. Since the birth of her firstborn, Yates long had visions of a knife and blood and child-murder. She twice tried to commit suicide, and had told a psychologist, "I had a fear I would hurt somebody. I thought it better to end my own life and prevent it."

Said Dr. Eileen Starbranch, the psychiatrist who treated one of her depressions, "She would rank among the five sickest—and most difficult to get out of psychosis—people that I've ever treated."   11

And while her psychosis could often be controlled by medications, her doctor had stopped her antipsychotics just weeks before the killings. Even the prosecution psychiatrist admitted that the day after the killings, she was "grossly psychotic," telling the country jail psychiatrist that voices had told her to kill her children.   12

This is not to say that any criminal can rationalize his crime as being for some higher good. This extenuation only applies in the case of severe mental derangement. Andrea Yates was clearly mentally deranged, not as proved by the murders—that would make the murders self-acquitting—but as demonstrated by her non-criminal behavior: self-injury, severe withdrawal, bizarre behavior, occasional catatonia, delusion, hallucinations.   13

As a former psychiatrist, I found the film *A Beautiful Mind* brilliant in rendering to people who have never seen psychosis how compelling hallucinations can be. The movie substituted visual hallucinations (which are rare) for auditory hallucinations (which are far more common but less vivid on screen), but the idea is the same: These visions and voices are so powerful that they can be irresistible.   14

Andrea Yates' mental illness is now masked by the Haldol she should have been taking at the time of the murders. I find it hard to see how she can be deemed by society to be truly responsible for her crime.   15

This is not a matter of sympathy. I have infinitely more sympathy for the five innocents who died so terribly. This is a matter of justice. Guilt presupposes free will. Did Andrea Yates really have it?   16

Punishment That Fits

Michelle Cottle

Writing for The New Republic Online, *a Web supplement to the centrist political commentary magazine* The New Republic, *Michelle Cottle entered this national conversation on February 22, 2002, just at the opening of the Yates trial. Cottle positions herself against the liberal views of Yates's defenders and yet resists the assumption that lifetime imprisonment or the death penalty is the best way to achieve social justice. Michelle Cottle is a senior editor at* The New Republic.

On Monday, prosecutors with the Harris County, Texas, district attorney's office presented opening arguments in the trial of Andrea Pia Yates, the mother who drowned her five children in the bathtub last June. Yates is pleading not guilty by reason of insanity. Her lawyers claim she was in the grips of postpartum psychosis, a severe form of postpartum depression that brought with it voices and visions and catatonia. As always, Texas is seeking the death penalty.   1

2   The case has produced predictable protests from all the predictable places. Feminists and advocates for the mentally ill are saddened, shocked, and disturbed by the state's "inhumane" insistence on pushing for the death penalty. "Just as Andrea Yates' crime shocked the nation, Texas' desire to put to death a person who may be mentally ill should shock the nation's conscience," Kim Gandy, president of the National Organization of Women, said in a September 6 press release. On the other side, conservative commentators, including Mona Charen, Laura Ingraham, and the folks at the Independent Women's Forum have blown a gasket over what they see as the rush by liberal groups to transform a murderer into a martyr. On a recent episode of CNN's *The Point,* host Laura Ingraham scolded Mark Hardwick, president of the National Alliance for the Mentally Ill: "I just think, Mark, a lot of people are tired of the, 'I'm a victim, you're a victim, we're all victims together.'" Charen has written that expressions of empathy for Yates are part of liberals' on-going war against "domesticity" and "full-time motherhood."

3   With the cloud of self-righteousness growing thick enough to choke a goat, I would like to propose a perfectly sensible, relatively humane alternative that absolutely no one is talking about; Sterilize the defendant.

4   Yeah, yeah, yeah. Utter the dreaded "s" word and people reflexively wince and cross their legs a little tighter. Then they launch into a high-minded disquisition on the grim history of sterilization—usually speaking slowly and carefully, as if the mere mention of the subject is physically painful. But if we can seriously contemplate gassing Andrea Yates (revoking her constitutionally protected right to life, as the lawyers might say) or locking her in jail forever (ditto her right to liberty), we should damn well give her the option (see, no one is suggesting anything mandatory) of relinquishing instead a small piece of her "pursuit of happiness." Temporary institutionalization coupled with a tubal ligation may not be the defendant's dream sentence, but it damn sure beats the alternatives.

5   Disagree? Well, let's review the grizzly details. On the morning of June 20, shortly after her husband, Rusty, left for work, Andrea Yates drew a bath in which she submerged her two-year-old son, Luke, until he was dead. She then did the same to her three-year-old son, Paul, her five-year-old son, John, and her six-month-old daughter, Mary. As Mary lay dying, seven-year-old Noah came into the bathroom and asked, "What's wrong with Mary?" The little boy then began running through the house in terror. Yates chased after her oldest son and forced him shrieking and struggling into the tub with his sister. Police examiners say bruises on Noah's shoulders and neck indicated a struggle. Some of the other children had injuries to the backs of their heads, presumably from banging against the bottom of the tub.

6   Long before the trial began, the blame game was in full bloom. Yates's husband went on *60 Minutes* to blame the medical community for not adequately treating his wife. The defense team is blaming not only Andrea's doctors but also her husband, who they say exacerbated his wife's illness by pushing for more kids and insisting that Andrea home-school the older children. Andrea has repeatedly blamed herself for being a bad mother (hard to argue with that), while feminists and mental health advocates blame society for ignoring the scourge of postpartum depression.

There is truth to all these accusations but not total truth. And, as the case   7
stands now, there is virtually no chance that justice will be served. Yates is, by all
accounts, a very sick woman. She has been in and out of treatment and on and off
medication for postpartum depression for years. After the birth of her fourth child
in 1999, Yates twice attempted suicide—once with pills, once with a steak knife.
Compounding the problem, her husband seems to be an absolute cretin who, despite Andrea's obvious problems, kept pressuring her to churn out babies. In
1999, after Andrea's suicide attempts, he told her psychiatrist that he wanted to
get her off medication and pregnant again, according to medical records. After
the fourth child was born, Rusty (and presumably Andrea) also decided that a
preacher's advice to "live a Spartan life" meant that they should move the whole
family into a converted Greyhound bus. Spending all day, every day with four kids
in a living space all of 350 square feet large probably did wonders for Andrea's
mental state. Not that it excuses what she did, of course. But if you have any
qualms about executing the mentally ill, this case should give you the willies. It
should also make you wonder whether there isn't a way to charge dear Rusty
with reckless endangerment.

That said, all this babble about how Yates needs treatment not punishment is   8
equally nauseating. One tenderhearted *Dallas Morning News* columnist noted that
in Great Britain women cannot even be charged for murdering their children
within a year of childbirth. "[W]hat postpartum depression is is an illness of the
brain. Just like epilepsy. But we don't put people in prison for that. Or execute
them." While the sentiment may be well-intentioned, the analogy is crap. The
Yateses were well aware that Andrea had a serious, potentially life-threatening
condition, even if they previously assumed the life most in danger was Andrea's.
Still, despite warnings from Andrea's doctor, the couple continued to engage in
the behavior most likely to trigger Andrea's psychosis—namely, having more babies. This suggests that neither Andrea nor the pathetic Rusty has the sense God
gave a grapefruit—either because of a neurochemical imbalance, self-indulgent
stupidity, or some tragic combination of both. As such, even if you firmly believe
that Yates is hopelessly, helplessly ill and should not be punished for what she
did, the state has an overwhelming responsibility to ensure that this tragedy does
not happen again. The only way to do that is to see to it that Andrea Yates never
has another child.

Before the trial began, the DA offered to reduce its request to life imprisonment   9
if Yates would change her plea to guilty. The defense declined. They are banking on
their ability to convince the jury that only someone truly mentally ill would do what
Yates did to her own children.

But no matter how unhinged Yates may have been when she so efficiently dis-   10
patched the kids, the law is not on her side. According to *USA Today*, the insanity
defense is used in one-quarter of 1 percent of felonies, and even then works only a
third of the time. The law has a very precise legal definition of "insane." Yates's defense team must convince jurors that their client was not simply mentally ill at the

time of her crime but had so lost her grip on reality that she did not know it was wrong to methodically murder her children. Her case will not be helped by the fact that, promptly after drowning her fifth victim, Yates phoned 911 and asked police to come over. She then called her husband home from work. And during Yates's competency hearings last fall, a psychologist with the Harris County Mental Retardation Authority testified that the defendant told him that she had contemplated killing her kids for months and made her final decision the night before she filled their final bath. These factors are unlikely to sit well with the jurors in Texas, which, lest we forget, is by far the most capital-punishment-happy state in the union.

11   For the moment, though, let's assume that Yates is acquitted. Although neither the defense nor the prosecution is allowed to inform jurors of the consequences of an acquittal, Yates would most likely be remanded to an institution until she is deemed fit to reenter society. Assuming that Yates doesn't get pregnant while in said institution—again triggering her postpartum psychosis—it's entirely possible that she could some day be pronounced healthy and released. At that point, what if she decided to try motherhood again? After all, she and her husband have disregarded medical warnings (not to mention common sense) in the past. Even after her suicide attempts, Andrea resisted taking medication for her psychosis and didn't bother to show up for outpatient treatment. So even if a judge ordered Yates not to become pregnant, what if—oops—something happens by accident? Would the court force an abortion? Would they throw a pregnant woman in jail? Would they take her baby away from her? How is that in the best interest of any hypothetical child Yates might someday decide she needs? Or maybe we're supposed to trust the healthcare system to keep an eye on her, as it so effectively did after her fifth child was born and she sank into a black hole of psychosis.

12   Bottom line: If there is any circumstance under which Andrea Yates is allowed to live outside the confines of a prison or institution, the state must make certain that she will never again be able to conceive a child. Norplant or Depo-provera shots could be a less-icky option. But here again, what happens if Yates "forgets" to show up for a shot and "accidentally" gets herself impregnated? How many times have we heard about someone who forgot to show up for his court-ordered meds or to meet with his parole officer, and the case simply slipped through the cracks? And once the publicity from this case fades, how many dollars and man-hours will Texas waste keeping tabs on some middle-class white woman who probably won't hurt anybody else again anyway? More to the point, if the goal is (and it clearly should be) to guarantee that, wherever she goes and whatever she does, Andrea Yates never has another child, why pretend otherwise? Forcing her to repeatedly get shots or implants might make us feel better—as though we weren't *really* taking away her right to conceive. But such a plan is still riskier and less practical than sterilization.

13   Of course, given the choice, Yates might still prefer to take her chances with the death penalty. Fine. But we should at least present her with the option. It's not only in her best interest—it's in ours, too.

Playing God on No Sleep
Anna Quindlen

Although all commentators expressed horror at Yates's deed, many writers ex-
pressed varying degrees of sympathy and understanding for Yates herself. In this
article, written for Newsweek *(July 2, 2001) in a special edition that featured*
the Andrea Yates case on the cover, Anna Quindlen discusses the silent pressures
on mothers that make real motherhood different from the Hallmark-card image.
Anna Quindlen is a contributing editor to Newsweek, *a novelist, and a Pulitzer*
prize-winning journalist.

Isn't motherhood grand? Do you want the real answer or the official Hallmark-card version?

So a woman walks into a pediatrician's office. She's tired, she's hot and she's   1
been up all night throwing sheets into the washer because the smaller of her two
boys has projectile vomiting so severe it looks like a special effect from "The
Exorcist." Oh, and she's nauseated, too, because since she already has two kids under the age of 5 it made perfect sense to have another, and she's four months pregnant. In the doctor's waiting room, which sounds like a cross between an orchestra
tuning loudly and a 747 taking off, there is a cross-stitched sampler on the wall. It
says GOD COULD NOT BE EVERYWHERE SO HE MADE MOTHERS.

This is not a joke, and that is not the punch line. Or maybe it is. The woman   2
was me, the sampler real, and the sentiments it evoked were unforgettable: in-
credulity, disgust and that out-of-body feeling that is the corollary of sleep deprivation and adrenaline rush, with a soupçon of shoulder barf thrown in. I kept reliving
this moment, and others like it, as I read with horrified fascination the story of
Andrea Yates, a onetime nurse suffering from postpartum depression who apparently spent a recent morning drowning her five children in the bathtub. There is a
part of my mind that imagines the baby, her starfish hands pink beneath the water,
or the biggest boy fighting back, all wiry arms and legs, and then veers sharply
away, aghast, appalled.

But there's another part of my mind, the part that remembers the end of a   3
day in which the milk spilled phone rang one cried another hit a fever rose the
medicine gone the car sputtered another cried the cable out *Sesame Street* gone
all cried stomach upset full diaper no more diapers Mommy I want water Mommy
my throat hurts Mommy I don't feel good. Every mother I've asked about the
Yates case has the same reaction. She's appalled; she's aghast. And then she gets
this look. And the look says that at some forbidden level she understands.
The looks says that there are two very different kinds of horror here. There is the
unimaginable idea of the killings. And than there is, the entirely imaginable idea
of going quietly bonkers in the house with five kids under the age of 7.

4   The insidious cult of motherhood is summed up by the psychic weight of the sampler on that doctor's wall. We are meant to be all things to small people, surrounded by bromides and soppy verse and smiling strangers who talk about how lucky we are. And we *are* lucky. My children have been the making of me as a human being, which does not mean they have not sometimes been an overwhelming and mind-boggling responsibility. That last is the love that dare not speak its name, the love that is fraught with fear and fatigue and inevitable resentment. But between the women who cannot have children and sometimes stare at our double strollers grief-stricken, and the grandmothers who make raising eight or 10 sound like a snap and insist we micromanage and overanalyze, there is no leave to talk about the dark side of being a surrogate deity, omniscient and out of milk all at the same time.

5   The weight was not always so heavy. Once the responsibility was spread around extended families, even entire towns. The sociologist Jessie Bernard has this to say: "The way we institutionalize motherhood in our society—assigning sole responsibility for child care to the mother, cutting her off from the easy help of others in an isolated household, requiring round-the-clock tender, loving care, and making such care her exclusive activity—is not only new and unique, but not even a good way for either women or—if we accept as a criterion the amount of maternal warmth shown—for children. It may, in fact, be the worst."

6   It has gotten no better since those words were written 25 years ago. Worse, perhaps, with all the competing messages about what women should do and be and feel at this particular moment in time. Women not working outside their homes feel compelled to make their job inside it seem both weighty and joyful; women who work outside their homes for pay feel no freedom to be ambivalent because of the sub rosa sense that they are cutting parenting corners. All of us are caught up in a conspiracy in which we are both the conspirators and the victims of the plot. In the face of all this "M is for the million things she gave me" mythology it becomes difficult to admit that occasionally you lock yourself in the bathroom just to be alone.

7   The great motherhood friendships are the ones in which women can admit this quietly to one another, over cups of tea at a table sticky with spilt apple juice and littered with markers without tops. But most of the time we keep quiet and smile. So that when someone is depressed after having a baby, when everyone is telling her that it's the happiest damn time of her life, there's no space to admit what she's really feeling. So that when someone does something as horrifying as what Andrea Yates did, there is no room for even a little bit of understanding. Yap yap yap, the world says. How could anyone do that to her children?

8   Well, yes. But I'm imagining myself with five children under the age of 7, all alone after Dad goes off to work. And they're bouncing off the walls in that way little boys do, except for the baby, who needs to be fed. And fed. And fed again. And changed. The milk gets spilled. The phone rings. Mommy, can I have juice? Mommy, can I have lunch? Mommy, can I go out back? Mommy, can I come in? And I add to all that depression, mental illness, whatever was happening in that house. I'm not making excuses for Andrea Yates. I love my children more than life itself. But just because you love people doesn't mean that taking care of them day in and day out isn't often hard, and sometimes even horrible. If God made mothers because he

couldn't be everywhere, maybe he could have met us halfway and eradicated vomiting, and colic too, and the hideous sugarcoating of what we are and what we do that leads to false cheer, easy lies and maybe sometimes something much, much worse, almost unimaginable. But not quite.

Yates Should Be Treated Like Any Other Murderer

Peter Renn (Student)

This student-written op-ed piece, by University of Texas student Peter Renn, appeared in the Daily Texan *on August 31, 2001. The* Daily Texan *is the student newspaper for the University of Texas.*

1   Women get away with murder literally. For all the discrimination that women may suffer in other parts of society, the criminal justice system is one place in which it can pay to have two X chromosomes, especially if you've just committed premeditated first-degree murder.

2   In those rare instances that prosecutors pursue the death penalty against a woman, as Harris County recently revealed it would seek for Andrea Yates, a mother who killed all five of her children, it is most often due to the unusually heinous nature of the crime. But, even then, every last mitigating factor, psychological defense and character witness testimony is exhausted before the guillotine goes down.

3   The reluctance to execute a woman has been well documented across history. According to the Death Penalty Information Center, approximately 20,000 confirmed executions have occurred in America since the early 1600s; women comprise only 3 percent of that figure. Similarly, since the Supreme Court reinstated capital punishment in 1976, the percentage of women put to death compared to men remains below 1 percent. Texas, by the way, ranks fourth in the number of women sentenced to death since 1973 though probably a more telling sign of our death penalty zeal than progressive attitudes about gender equality.

4   Certainly, men are the overwhelming perpetrators of capital murder, but this alone fails to explain the gender bias. Ohio Northern University law school Dean Victor Streib reports that while women account for approximately one out of eight murder arrests, only one out of every 52 death sentences handed down go to women. Further, only one out of 72 death row inmates is a woman, and that ratio grows even smaller for actual executions. The conclusion, according to a report by Streib, is that "women are unlikely to be arrested for murder, extremely unlikely to be sentenced to death and almost never executed."

5   This glaring inequality grows out of sexism, the kind that hides under the name of chivalry. It is the kind that treats women as the weaker sex, warranting special protection. It is also the kind that cannot bear to see women as anything beyond

those childhood visions of "sugar and spice and everything nice," and certainly not as criminals guilty of offenses punishable by death. A sweet Southern belle strapped in the chair? Banish the thought.

6   It is the "ism" in the capital punishment debate that hardly anyone pays attention to. The ACLU's briefing paper on the death penalty doesn't spare a word on the topic. And feminists, in particular, have been conspicuously silent. It seems that they only prefer equality when it works to their benefit. And so patriarchy lives.

7   The system absolves women of moral culpability and legal responsibility. When a man commits murder, he is a criminal; when a woman commits murder, she is a victim. The culprits are many, ranging from physical abuse to mental illness and insanity.

8   None of this is meant to dispute the legitimacy of psychological disorders, which in some cases may disproportionately affect women. But people automatically presume an external cause for women's criminal behavior and rush to find evidence confirming their beliefs. This predisposition "lumps women in with the retarded and children by implying they can't control their own actions," Streib commented in *Human Rights* magazine.

9   The speculation surrounding Andrea Yates is proof enough of the gender bias, given that the details of the case have been effectively suppressed by a gag order. Yet, even with such limited information, nearly every amateur criminal profile spewed forth by columnists across the country posited Yates' alleged modus operandi as external in nature. Susan Resnick of *Salon.com* magazine blamed it on postpartum depression: "They can't help it that their brain is diseased . . . They're just sick, sick people. People to be pitied."

10   Kathleen Parker of the *Orlando Sentinel* points the finger to the husband: "The woman was out of her mind, and no one, notably her husband, bothered to notice. [He] bears some moral, if not legal, responsibility . . . " But these are mere hypotheses, indicative perhaps of what we want to believe.

11   And they may actually turn out to be true or completely false. But that's not the issue. The issue is that there exists a systemic bias in the criminal justice system, not only based on race or socioeconomic status, but also on gender. The solution to this bias won't be found in getting "tough on crime" (or "tough on women"). But it is revealing in itself that what we find good enough for a man isn't good enough for a woman.

Questioning the Motives of Home-Schooling Parents

Froma Harrop

In this op-ed piece, Froma Harrop shifts the focus of the Andrea Yates conversation to the subject of home schooling. Froma Harrop is a nationally syndicated columnist who writes for the Providence Journal *in Providence, Rhode Island. We found this article in the* Seattle Times *on June 28, 2001.*

America's most famous home-schooling parents at the moment are Andrea 1
Yates and JoAnn McGuckin. Yates allegedly drowned her five children in a Houston
suburb. McGuckin was arrested and charged with child neglect in Idaho. Her six
kids barricaded themselves in the family's hovel when child-care workers came to
remove them.

The intention here is not to smear the parents who instruct 1.5 million mostly 2
normal children at home. But a social phenomenon that isolates children from the
outside world deserves closer inspection.

The home-schooling movement runs an active propaganda machine. It portrays 3
its followers in the most flattering terms—as bulwarks against the moral decay
found in public, and presumably private, schools. Although now associated with
conservative groups, modern home-schooling got its start among left-wing dropouts
in the '60s.

Home-schooled students do tend to score above average on standardized tests. 4
The most likely reason, however, is that most of the parents are themselves upper
income and well educated. Students from those backgrounds also do well in traditional schools.

Advocates of home-schooling have become a vocal lobbying force in 5
Washington, D.C. Children taught at home may be socially isolated, but the parents
have loads of interaction. Membership in the anti-public-education brigade provides
much comradeship.

The mouthpiece for the movement, the Home School Legal Defense Association 6
(*www.hslda.org*), posts articles on its Web site with headlines like, "The Clinging
Tentacles of Public Education." Trashing the motivations of professional teachers
provides much sport.

Perhaps the time has come to question the motives of some home-schooling 7
parents. Are the parents protecting their children from a cesspool of bad values in
the outside world? Or are the parents just people who can't get along with others?
Are they "taking charge" of their children's education. Or are they taking their children captive?

Yates and McGuckin are, of course, extreme cases and probably demented. But 8
a movement that insists on parents' rights to do as they wish with their children
gives cover for the unstable, for narcissists and for child-abusers.

In West Akron, Ohio, reporters would interview Thomas Lavery on how he suc- 9
cessfully schooled his five children in their home. The kids all had top grades and
fine manners. They recalled how their father loved to strut before the media.

Eventually, however, the police came for Lavery and charged him with nine 10
counts of child endangerment. According to his children, Lavery smashed a daughter over the head with a soda can after she did poorly in a basketball game. Any
child who wet a bed would spend the night alone, locked in the garage.

A child who spilled milk had to drop on his or her knees and lick it up from the 11
floor. And in an especially creepy attempt to establish himself as master, Lavery
would order his children to damn the name of God.

The best way to maintain the sanctity of a family madhouse is to keep the in- 12
mates inside. Allowing children to move about in the world could jeopardize the deal.

13   In some cases, it might also prevent tragedy. Suppose one of Andrea Yates' children had gone to a school and told a teacher of the mother's spiraling mental state. The teacher could have called a child-welfare officer and five little lives might have been saved.

14   Putting the horror stories aside, there's something sad about home-schooled children. During the New Hampshire presidential primary race, I attended an event directed at high-school and college students. The students were a lively bunch, circulating around the giant room, debating and arguing. Except for my table.

15   About four young people and middle-aged woman were just sitting there. The teenagers were clearly intelligent and well behaved. I tried to chat, but they seemed wary of talking with strangers. The woman proudly informed me that they were her children and home-schooled.

16   The Home School Legal Defense Association condemns government interference in any parent's vision of how a child might be educated. The group's chairman, Michael Farris, says things like, "We just want to say to the government: We are doing a good job, so leave us alone."

17   Could that be where JoAnn McGuckin found her twisted sense of grievance? "Those are my kids," she said as Idaho removed her children from their filthy home. "The state needs to mind its own business."

Andrea Yates: New Moms and Our Misplaced Priorities

Lynne K. Varner

Lynne K. Varner, an editorial columnist for the Seattle Times, *here links the case of Andrea Yates to the lack of social supports for mothers, including mental health services. She particularly focuses on inadequate mental health services in the state of Washington—hence her references to Olympia, the state capital, and other regional cities. A graduate of the University of Maryland, Varner is the Western regional director for the National Association of Black Journalists.*

1   Andrea Yates shouldn't have been alone all those months in a prison cell, nor all of those weeks in a courtroom full of accusers and the curious. Her husband should have been sitting next to her facing charges of cluelessness.

2   At every step in this woman's isolated, psychotic-soaked life, Russell Yates was there promoting his twisted men-rule-and-women-submit vision. The legal system didn't serve this woman much better. If our criminal-justice system sees punishment as part deterrence, someone please explain how jailing a psychotic woman for killing her children while in the grips of her illness will deter other psychotic women.

I'm not launching the free-Andrea Yates movement here. This woman commit-   3
ted a most unspeakable crime when she drowned her five children one by one. I also
vehemently disagree with the parade of women's groups who argued this case
should not have reached the criminal courts. I don't see how you get beyond five
murdered children without a stop in the criminal-justice system. No way should
Andrea Yates escape responsibility for her actions.

But let's target some of that answerability toward the mental-health-care sys-   4
tem and its paltry assistance to women facing post-partum illnesses. Yates will go
down in history as a child murderer, true, but she should also be remembered as a
prime example of how the misplaced priorities of government spending leave new
mothers on their own.

Before adjourning last week, lawmakers in Olympia restored funding for public-   5
health nurses and programs for new mothers that had originally been cut.

If not for the last-minute save, funding would have disappeared for public-   6
health nurses who visit new moms at home; same for grants that help families at
risk for abusing or neglecting their children. Money would have also disappeared
for the alternative-response system, a network of resources designed for neglect
complaints or those not severe enough to trigger an investigation by the
Department of Social and Health Services.

The trickle-down effect of all this budget-cutting might have hurt King County's   7
Maternity Support Services where low-income pregnant women receive psychosocial treatment before having their babies, and afterwards receive 60 days of postpartum home visits and other care.

"There is an extensive network of (mental-health provisions for new moms) but   8
it is limited" by a lack of funding, says Rep. Ruth Kagi, D-Lake Forest Park.
Legislators saved the programs this time but they'll be vulnerable next time.
Despite research showing that pre-natal and post-partum care saves $4 for every $1
spent on criminal justice and special education, it is still difficult to convince budget
hawks that prevention is cost effective.

An investment in mental-health services for new moms would be expensive but   9
worth it.

"Short-term pain for long-term gain," says Rep. Mary Lou Dickerson, D-Ballard.   10

In addition to beefing up mental-health services targeting new moms, state leg-   11
islatures nationwide should consider creating legal provisions guiding prosecutors
confronting women who harm their children soon after childbirth. In Great Britain,
post-partum illness is automatically considered a mitigating factor when a woman
kills her child less than a year after birth. This extra step often means the difference between a murder charge and one of manslaughter. And it also allows prosecutors to choose a medical or criminal approach to crimes committed by post-partum women.

These steps are critical. As we saw with the Yates case, women and their fami-   12
lies are not always the best advocates for themselves. Yates' husband and family
seemed unable to grasp the gravity of a woman literally pulling out chunks of her
hair and spending hours staring vacantly at the television. Women suffering from
mental illness are hard-pressed to seek the help they need.

13   This is where government kicks in, to help all of the women touched by post-partum depression navigate that rocky road between the blues and infanticide. It requires refocusing state priorities and budgets. But this is where we should concentrate our energy.

14   There is no need to worry that greater recognition of post-partum illnesses will allow women to get away with murder. Yates hasn't gotten away with murder. As her emotional numbness wears off, she'll be in a special kind of hell no prison can replicate.

15   Now let's turn our attention and resources to the not-yet-Andrea Yateses, those moms suffering from depression and other post-partum illnesses in the silent shame of their homes.

For Class Discussion

1. Drawing on arguments made in the readings for this unit and on your own reasoning and knowledge, summarize the core arguments for each of the following claims:

   ■ Andrea Yates was not legally insane when she drowned her five children.
   ■ Andrea Yates was legally insane when she drowned her five children.

2. When the verdict of guilty was declared by the jury, Andrea Yates's husband, Russell Yates, was quoted as saying: "I believe in Andrea. . . . She's the kindest, sweetest, gentlest, most caring person I've ever met. And she's a victim here, not only of the medical community but of the justice system" (*Seattle Times*, March 16, 2002). Working in small groups or as a whole class, explore the arguments for and against Russell Yates's assertion.

3. On its Web site, the American Psychological Association provides an overview of the insanity defense, explaining how definitions vary from state to state. In advance of class, read this brief report at http://www.psych.org/public_info/insanity.cfm. Then find out the definition of "legally insane" in your own state. Might the outcome of the Andrea Yates trial have been different if she were tried under the laws of your state rather than Texas's?

OPTIONAL WRITING ASSIGNMENT   Another famous "insanity defense" trial was that of John Hinckley, who tried to assassinate President Ronald Reagan to impress the actress Jodie Foster. Hinckley, unlike Andrea Yates, was acquitted of the attempted murder charge and placed in a mental institution. Research the John Hinckley case and then write a comparative analysis of the Hinckley and Yates trials, attempting to answer the following question: Why did the jury accept the insanity defense plea of John Hinckley but reject it for Andrea Yates?

THE UNITED STATES AS SUPERPOWER

The concept of "superpower" arose during the Cold War when there were two superpowers—the United States and the Soviet Union. These two nations, restrained from nuclear war by the policy of MAD (mutual assured destruction), coexisted from 1945 through the early 1990s when the Soviet Union collapsed. During the Cold War, the United States used its military might in regional conflicts to ward off communist aggressors (North Korea) or communist revolutionary insurgents (Vietnam). When the Soviet Union collapsed, many Americans hoped that U.S. military spending might be reduced and converted into either tax cuts or domestic programs such as health care, education, and environmental projects. However, despite some reductions in military spending, military preparedness remained a high priority—often for regional police actions (Gulf War during the administration of the first President Bush) or for peacekeeping missions (Balkans, Kosovo under the Clinton administration).

After September 11, 2001, the "war on terrorism" again accelerated military spending, first, for the war against the Taliban in Afghanistan, and then for the war against Iraq. This flexing of military muscle has sparked an international controversy over the U.S. role as the world's sole superpower. With unquestioned military supremacy, how should the United States position itself against other nations? Should the United States seek to remain the world's sole superpower? If so, what kind of superpower should the United States be? To what extent should the United States bind itself by signing treaties or by relinquishing some of its sovereignty to the United Nations or a world court? Should the United States act unilaterally to protect its own interests or seek international agreements and cooperation?

The Bush administration's apparent answers to these questions touched off intense debate, as you will see in the readings that follow. President Bush, propelled by his vision of "moral clarity" in the wake of the September 11 attacks, began a series of policies and actions that moved the United States toward unilateralism. The Justice Department suspended the civil rights of persons suspected of ties to terrorism, in apparent violation of international agreements on human rights. The Bush administration withdrew from a Cold War antiballistic missile treaty with Russia in order to proceed with a missile defense system. It also announced its intention not to abide by a nuclear nonproliferation treaty in order to plan possible use of tactical nuclear weapons in its war on terrorism. At a graduation speech at West Point, President Bush proclaimed the policy of "preemptive strike," through which he justified an attack on Saddam Hussein for reasons other than immediate self-defense. During this same period, opposition to the Bush administration's policies arose both within the United States and throughout the world.

The readings in this unit will enable you to see the beliefs and values in conflict in this debate and to understand the general lines of reasoning of disputants who confront the fact of America's military strength and its worldwide political, cultural, and economic hegemony.

President Bush Delivers Graduation Speech at West Point

George W. Bush

Widely regarded as one of his most important speeches, President Bush's gradu-
ation address to the United States Military Academy at West Point on June 1,
2002, was the occasion for announcing the Bush administration's policy of
preemptive first strikes and providing a supporting rationale for this doctrine.
(We omit the first minutes of his speech, where President Bush establishes
rapport with the cadets, tells some in-jokes about West Point versus other
military academies, and sets the stage for the serious remarks to follow.)

1   . . . Every West Point class is commissioned to the Armed Forces. Some West Point classes are also commissioned by history, to take part in a great new calling for their country. Speaking here to the class of 1942—six months after Pearl Harbor—General Marshall said, "We're determined that before the sun sets on this terrible struggle, our flag will be recognized throughout the world as a symbol of freedom on the one hand, and of overwhelming power on the other." (Applause.)

2   Officers graduating that year helped fulfill that mission, defeating Japan and Germany, and then reconstructing those nations as allies. West Point graduates of the 1940s saw the rise of a deadly new challenge—the challenge of imperial communism—and opposed it from Korea to Berlin, to Vietnam, and in the Cold War, from beginning to end. And as the sun set on their struggle, many of those West Point officers lived to see a world transformed.

3   History has also issued its call to your generation. In your last year, America was attacked by a ruthless and resourceful enemy. You graduate from this Academy in a time of war, taking your place in an American military that is powerful and is honorable. Our war on terror is only begun, but in Afghanistan it was begun well. (Applause.)

4   I am proud of the men and women who have fought on my orders. America is profoundly grateful for all who serve the cause of freedom, and for all who have given their lives in its defense. This nation respects and trusts our military, and we are confident in your victories to come. (Applause.)

5   This war will take many turns we cannot predict. Yet I am certain of this: Wherever we carry it, the American flag will stand not only for our power, but for freedom. (Applause.) Our nation's cause has always been larger than our nation's defense. We fight, as we always fight, for a just peace—a peace that favors human liberty. We will defend the peace against threats from terrorists and tyrants. We will preserve the peace by building good relations among the great powers. And we will extend the peace by encouraging free and open societies on every continent.

6   Building this just peace is America's opportunity, and America's duty. From this day forward, it is your challenge, as well, and we will meet this challenge together.

(Applause.) You will wear the uniform of a great and unique country. America has no empire to extend or utopia to establish. We wish for others only what we wish for ourselves—safety from violence, the rewards of liberty, and the hope for a better life.

In defending the peace, we face a threat with no precedent. Enemies in the past 7 needed great armies and great industrial capabilities to endanger the American people and our nation. The attacks of September the 11th required a few hundred thousand dollars in the hands of a few dozen evil and deluded men. All of the chaos and suffering they caused came at much less than the cost of a single tank. The dangers have not passed. This government and the American people are on watch, we are ready, because we know the terrorists have more money and more men and more plans.

The gravest danger to freedom lies at the perilous crossroads of radicalism and 8 technology. When the spread of chemical and biological and nuclear weapons, along with ballistic missile technology—when that occurs, even weak states and small groups could attain a catastrophic power to strike great nations. Our enemies have declared this very intention, and have been caught seeking these terrible weapons. They want the capability to blackmail us, or to harm us, or to harm our friends—and we will oppose them with all our power. (Applause.)

For much of the last century, America's defense relied on the Cold War doc- 9 trines of deterrence and containment. In some cases, those strategies still apply. But new threats also require new thinking. Deterrence—the promise of massive retaliation against nations—means nothing against shadowy terrorist networks with no nation or citizens to defend. Containment is not possible when unbalanced dictators with weapons of mass destruction can deliver those weapons on missiles or secretly provide them to terrorist allies.

We cannot defend America and our friends by hoping for the best. We cannot 10 put our faith in the word of tyrants, who solemnly sign non-proliferation treaties, and then systemically break them. If we wait for threats to fully materialize, we will have waited too long. (Applause.)

Homeland defense and missile defense are part of stronger security, and they're 11 essential priorities for America. Yet the war on terror will not be won on the defensive. We must take the battle to the enemy, disrupt his plans, and confront the worst threats before they emerge. (Applause.) In the world we have entered, the only path to safety is the path of action. And this nation will act. (Applause.)

Our security will require the best intelligence, to reveal threats hidden in caves 12 and growing in laboratories. Our security will require modernizing domestic agencies such as the FBI, so they're prepared to act, and act quickly, against danger. Our security will require transforming the military you will lead—a military that must be ready to strike at a moment's notice in any dark corner of the world. And our security will require all Americans to be forward-looking and resolute, to be ready for preemptive action when necessary to defend our liberty and to defend our lives. (Applause.)

The work ahead is difficult. The choices we will face are complex. We must un- 13 cover terror cells in 60 or more countries, using every tool of finance, intelligence and law enforcement. Along with our friends and allies, we must oppose proliferation and confront regimes that sponsor terror, as each case requires. Some nations need military training to fight terror, and we'll provide it. Other nations oppose terror, but tolerate the hatred that leads to terror—and that must change. (Applause.) We will send diplomats where they are needed, and we will send you, our soldiers, where you're needed. (Applause.)

14   All nations that decide for aggression and terror will pay a price. We will not leave the safety of America and the peace of the planet at the mercy of a few mad terrorists and tyrants. (Applause.) We will lift this dark threat from our country and from the world.

15   Because the war on terror will require resolve and patience, it will also require firm moral purpose. In this way our struggle is similar to the Cold War. Now, as then, our enemies are totalitarians, holding a creed of power with no place for human dignity. Now, as then, they seek to impose a joyless conformity, to control every life and all of life.

16   America confronted imperial communism in many different ways—diplomatic, economic, and military. Yet moral clarity was essential to our victory in the Cold War. When leaders like John F. Kennedy and Ronald Reagan refused to gloss over the brutality of tyrants, they gave hope to prisoners and dissidents and exiles, and rallied free nations to a great cause.

17   Some worry that it is somehow undiplomatic or impolite to speak the language of right and wrong. I disagree. (Applause.) Different circumstances require different methods, but not different moralities. (Applause.) Moral truth is the same in every culture, in every time, and in every place. Targeting innocent civilians for murder is always and everywhere wrong. (Applause.) Brutality against women is always and everywhere wrong. (Applause.) There can be no neutrality between justice and cruelty, between the innocent and the guilty. We are in a conflict between good and evil, and America will call evil by its name. (Applause.) By confronting evil and lawless regimes, we do not create a problem, we reveal a problem. And we will lead the world in opposing it. (Applause.)

18   As we defend the peace, we also have an historic opportunity to preserve the peace. We have our best chance since the rise of the nation state in the 17th century to build a world where the great powers compete in peace instead of prepare for war. The history of the last century, in particular, was dominated by a series of destructive national rivalries that left battlefields and graveyards across the Earth. Germany fought France, the Axis fought the Allies, and then the East fought the West, in proxy wars and tense standoffs, against a backdrop of nuclear Armageddon.

19   Competition between great nations is inevitable, but armed conflict in our world is not. More and more, civilized nations find ourselves on the same side—united by common dangers of terrorist violence and chaos. America has, and intends to keep, military strengths beyond challenge—(applause)—thereby, making the destabilizing arms races of other eras pointless, and limiting rivalries to trade and other pursuits of peace.

20   Today the great powers are also increasingly united by common values, instead of divided by conflicting ideologies. The United States, Japan and our Pacific

friends, and now all of Europe, share a deep commitment to human freedom, embodied in strong alliances such as NATO. And the tide of liberty is rising in many other nations.

Generations of West Point officers planned and practiced for battles with Soviet Russia. I've just returned from a new Russia, now a country reaching toward democracy, and our partner in the war against terror. (Applause.) Even in China, leaders are discovering that economic freedom is the only lasting source of national wealth. In time, they will find that social and political freedom is the only true source of national greatness. (Applause.)

When the great powers share common values, we are better able to confront serious regional conflicts together, better able to cooperate in preventing the spread of violence or economic chaos. In the past, great power rivals took sides in difficult regional problems, making divisions deeper and more complicated. Today, from the Middle East to South Asia, we are gathering broad international coalitions to increase the pressure for peace. We must build strong and great power relations when times are good; to help manage crisis when times are bad. America needs partners to preserve the peace, and we will work with every nation that shares this noble goal. (Applause.)

And finally, America stands for more than the absence of war. We have a great opportunity to extend a just peace, by replacing poverty, repression, and resentment around the world with hope of a better day. Through most of history, poverty was persistent, inescapable, and almost universal. In the last few decades, we've seen nations from Chile to South Korea build modern economies and freer societies, lifting millions of people out of despair and want. And there's no mystery to this achievement.

The 20th century ended with a single surviving model of human progress, based on non-negotiable demands of human dignity, the rule of law, limits on the power of the state, respect for women and private property and free speech and equal justice and religious tolerance. America cannot impose this vision—yet we can support and reward governments that make the right choices for their own people. In our development aid, in our diplomatic efforts, in our international broadcasting, and in our educational assistance, the United States will promote moderation and tolerance and human rights. And we will defend the peace that makes all progress possible.

When it comes to the common rights and needs of men and women, there is no clash of civilizations. The requirements of freedom apply fully to Africa and Latin America and the entire Islamic world. The peoples of the Islamic nations want and deserve the same freedoms and opportunities as people in every nation. And their governments should listen to their hopes. (Applause.)

A truly strong nation will permit legal avenues of dissent for all groups that pursue their aspirations without violence. An advancing nation will pursue economic reform, to unleash the great enterpreneurial energy of its people. A thriving nation will respect the rights of women, because no society can prosper while denying opportunity to half its citizens. Mothers and fathers and children across the Islamic world, and all the world, share the same fears and aspirations. In poverty, they struggle. In tyranny, they suffer. And as we saw in Afghanistan, in liberation they celebrate. (Applause.)

27   America has a greater objective than controlling threats and containing resentment. We will work for a just and peaceful world beyond the war on terror.

28   The bicentennial class of West Point now enters this drama. With all in the United States Army, you will stand between your fellow citizens and grave danger. You will help establish a peace that allows millions around the world to live in liberty and to grow in prosperity. You will face times of calm, and times of crisis. And every test will find you prepared—because you're the men and women of West Point. (Applause.) You leave here marked by the character of this Academy, carrying with you the highest ideals of our nation.

29   Toward the end of his life, Dwight Eisenhower recalled the first day he stood on the plain at West Point. "The feeling came over me," he said, "that the expression 'the United States of America' would now and henceforth mean something different than it had ever before. From here on, it would be the nation I would be serving, not myself."

30   Today, your last day at West Point, you begin a life of service in a career unlike any other. You've answered a calling to hardship and purpose, to risk and honor. At the end of every day you will know that you have faithfully done your duty. May you always bring to that duty the high standards of this great American institution. May you always be worthy of the long gray line that stretches two centuries behind you.

31   On behalf of the nation, I congratulate each one of you for the commission you've earned and for the credit you bring to the United States of America. May God bless you all. (Applause.)

The New Bush Doctrine
Richard Falk

This article, which directly critiques Bush's graduation speech at West Point, appeared in the liberal political commentary magazine Nation *on July 15, 2002. Richard Falk is an emeritus professor of international law and policy at Princeton University and chairs the Nuclear Age Peace Foundation.*

1   President Bush's June graduation address to the cadets at West Point has attracted attention mainly because it is the fullest articulation, so far, of the new strategic doctrine of pre-emption. The radical idea being touted by the White House and Pentagon is that the United States has the right to use military force against any state that is seen as hostile or makes moves to acquire weapons of mass destruction—nuclear, biological or chemical. The obvious initial test case for pre-emption is Iraq, whose government the United States is continually threatening to overthrow, either on the model of the displacement of the Taliban in Afghanistan or by some other

method. Washington's war plans have evidently not been finalized, and whether the intimations of war—despite the numerous objections voiced by neighboring governments and European allies—are to be taken literally is still unclear.

What is certain, and scary, is the new approach to the use of international force 2 beneath the banner of counterterrorism and in the domestic climate of fervent nationalism that has existed since September 11. This new approach repudiates the core idea of the United Nations Charter (reinforced by decisions of the World Court in The Hague), which prohibits any use of international force that is not undertaken in self-defense after the occurrence of an armed attack across an international boundary or pursuant to a decision by the UN Security Council. When Iraq conquered and annexed Kuwait in 1990, Kuwait was legally entitled to act in self-defense to recover its territorial sovereignty even without any UN authorization. And the United States and others were able to join Kuwait in bolstering its prospects, thereby acting in what international lawyers call collective self-defense.

Back in 1956, when the American commitment to this Charter effort to limit the 3 discretion of states to the extent possible was still strong, the US government surprised its allies and adversaries by opposing the Suez war of Britain, France and Israel because it was a nondefensive use of force against Egypt, despite the provocations associated at the time with Nasser's anti-Israeli, anti-Western militancy. This legal commitment had evolved by stages in the period after World War I, and when the surviving leaders of Germany and Japan were prosecuted for war crimes, "crimes against the peace" were declared to be even worse than atrocities committed in the course of the war. The task of the Charter was to give this concept as clear limits as possible.

Pre-emption, in contrast, validates striking first—not in a crisis, as was done 4 by Israel with plausible, if not entirely convincing, justification in the 1967 war, when enemy Arab troops were massing on its borders after dismissing the UN war-preventing presence, but on the basis of shadowy intentions, alleged potential links to terrorist groups, supposed plans and projects to acquire weapons of mass destruction, and anticipations of possible future dangers. It is a doctrine without limits, without accountability to the UN or international law, without any dependence on a collective judgment of responsible governments and, what is worse, without any convincing demonstration of practical necessity.

It is true that the reality of the mega-terrorist challenge requires some rethink- 5 ing of the relevance of rules and restraints based on conflict in a world of territorial states. The most radical aspects of the Al Qaeda challenge are a result of its non-territorial, concealed organizational reality as a multistate network. Modern geopolitics was framed to cope with conflict, and relations among sovereign states; the capacity of a network with modest resources to attack and wage a devastating type of war against the most powerful state does require acknowledgment that postmodern geopolitics needs a different structure of security.

Postmodernity refers here to preoccupations that can no longer be reduced to 6 territorial dimensions. This contrasts with "modernity," born internationally in 1648 at the Peace of Westphalia with the emergence of the secular sovereign state, and a world politics that could be understood by reference to territorial ambitions and defense. For Osama bin Laden, the focus has been on nonterritorial empowerment via mega-terrorism, with the vision of an Islamic umma replacing the modern, Western-inspired structure of distinct sovereign states. For George W. Bush, the emphasis has been on carrying the retaliatory war to the networked enemy concealed in some sixty countries, and on declaring war against all those nonstate forces around the world.

7   To respond to the threat of mega-terrorism does require some stretching of international law to accommodate the reasonable security needs of sovereign states. Prior cross-border military reactions to transnational terrorism over the years by the United States, India, Israel and others were generally tolerated by the UN and international public opinion because they seemed proportionate and necessary in relation to the threats posed, and the use of force relied upon was in its essence reactive, not anticipatory. International law was bent to serve these practical imperatives of security, but not broken. But the Bush doctrine of pre-emption goes much further, encroaching on highly dangerous terrain. It claims a right to abandon rules of restraint and of law patiently developed over the course of centuries, rules governing the use of force in relation to territorial states, not networks.

8   To propose abandoning the core legal restraint on international force in relations among states is to misread the challenge of September 11. It permits states to use force nondefensively against their enemies, thereby creating a terrible precedent. There is every reason to think that containment and deterrence remain effective ways to approach a state that threatens unwarranted expansion. There is no evidence to suggest that Iraq cannot be deterred, and its pattern of behavior in relation to its war against Iran in the 1980s, as well as its conquest and annexation of Kuwait in 1990, were based on a rational calculation of gains that, when proved incorrect, led to a reversal of policy. Brutal and oppressive as the regime in Iraq is, it was accepted until 1990 as a geopolitical ally of sorts. As a state, it acts and behaves normally, that is, by weighing benefits and costs. It is surrounded and threatened by superior force, and any attempt to lash out at neighbors or others would almost certainly result in its immediate and total destruction. There is no reason whatsoever to think that deterrence and containment would not succeed, even should Baghdad manage to acquire biological, chemical or nuclear weapons. Deterrence and containment succeeded in relation to the Soviet Union for more than four decades, under far more demanding circumstances.

9   What is at stake with pre-emption, as tied to the "axis of evil" imagery, is more hidden and sinister. What is feared in Washington, I think, is not aggressive moves by these countries but their acquisition of weapons of mass destruction that might give them a deterrent capability with respect to the United States and other nations. Since the end of the cold war the United States has enjoyed the luxury of being undeterred in world politics. It is this circumstance that makes Bush's "unilateralism" particularly disturbing to other countries, and it must be understood in relation to the moves of the Pentagon, contained in a report leaked last December, to increase US reliance on nuclear weapons {a variety of strategic circumstances}. At West Point, Bush declared with moral fervor that "our enemies . . . have been caught seeking these terrible weapons." It never occurs to our leaders that these

weapons are no less terrible when in the hands of the United States, especially when their use is explicitly contemplated as a sensible policy option. There is every reason for others to fear that when the United States is undeterred it will again become subject to "the Hiroshima temptation," in which it might threaten and use such weapons in the absence of any prospect of retaliation.

Bush goes further, combining empire with utopia, reminding his West Point audience that "the twentieth century ended with a single surviving model of human progress based on nonnegotiable demands of human dignity, the rule of law, limits on the power of the state, respect for women and private property, and free speech and equal justice and religious tolerance." The clear intention is to suggest that America is the embodiment of this model. And while Bush does concede that "America cannot impose this vision," he does propose that it "can support and reward governments that make the right choices for their own people," and presumably punish those that don't. Not only does the United States claim the right to global dominance but it also professes to have the final answers for societal well-being, seeming to forget its homeless, its crowded and expanding prisons, its urban blight and countless other domestic reminders that ours may not be the best of all possible worlds, and especially not for all possible peoples. 10

This vision of postmodern geopolitics is underwritten by a now-familiar strong message of evangelical moralism. Bush notes that "some worry that it is somehow undiplomatic or impolite to speak the language of right and wrong. I disagree," and adds that "moral truth is the same in every culture, in every time, and in every place." Such moral absolutism is then applied to the current global realities. Bush insists that "we are in a conflict between good and evil, and America will call evil by its name. By confronting evil and lawless regimes, we do not create a problem, we reveal a problem. And we will lead the world in opposing it." Aside from occupying the moral high ground, which exempts America from self-criticism or from addressing the grievances others have with respect to our policies, such sentiments imply a repudiation of dialogue and negotiation. As there can be no acceptable compromise with the forces of evil, there can be no reasonable restraint on the forces of good. We may lament fundamentalism in the Islamic world and decry the fulminations of Osama bin Laden, but what about our own? 11

In contemplating this geopolitical vision for the future, one wonders what happened to candidate Bush's rhetoric about the importance of "humility" in defining America's role in the world. Of course, he was then trying to downsize the humanitarian diplomacy attributed (mostly wrongly) to Clinton/Gore, but the contrast in tone and substance is still striking. One wonders whether the heady atmosphere of the Oval Office has fed these geopolitical dreams, or whether our President, well-known for his lack of foreign policy knowledge, has been manipulated into a crusading mode by bureaucratic hawks who seized the opportunity so tragically provided by September 11. 12

Many influential Americans share this dream of a borderless global empire but adopt less forthright language. For instance, the respected military commentator Eliot Cohen, writing in a recent issue of *Foreign Affairs,* suggests that "in the twenty-first century, characterized like the European Middle Ages by a universal 13 (if problematic) high culture with a universal language, the U.S. military plays an extraordinary and inimitable role. It has become, whether Americans or others like it or not, the ultimate guarantor of international order." To make such an assertion without apology or justification is to say, in effect, that the imperial role of the United States is no longer in doubt, or even subject to useful debate. To acknowledge that it makes no difference whether Americans or others support this destiny is to reveal the fallen condition of democracy and the irrelevance of international public opinion. Along similar lines of presupposition, Stephen Biddle, in the same issue of *Foreign Affairs,* observes in relation to the problems of the Balkans, and specifically Kosovo, that "Americans do well in crusades," but then he cites Cohen and Andrew Bacevich to the effect that "they are not suited . . . to the dirty work of imperial policing to secure second- or third-tier interest." Such an outlook makes the fact of an American global empire a foregone conclusion.

14   But pre-emption and double standards were not the only troubling features of this postmodern geopolitical outlook outlined in the West Point speech. There is first of all the issue of global dominance, a project to transform the world order from its current assemblage of sovereign states in the direction of a postmodern (that is, nonterritorial) global empire administered from Washington. Bush misleadingly assured the graduating cadets that "America has no empire to extend or utopia to establish," and then went on to describe precisely such undertakings. The President mentioned that past rivalries among states arose because of their efforts to compete with one another, but insisted that the future will be different because of American military superiority: "America has, and intends to keep, military strengths beyond challenge, thereby making the destabilizing arms races of other eras pointless, and limiting rivalries to trade and other pursuits of peace." The ambition here is breathtaking and imperial—nothing less than to remind all states that the era of self-help security is essentially over, that America is the global gendarme, and that other states should devote their energies to economic and peaceful pursuits, leaving overall security in Washington's hands. One can only wonder at the reaction of foreign ministries around the world, say in Paris or Beijing, when confronted by this language, which dramatically diminishes traditional sovereign rights, as well as by the reinforcing moves to scrap the ABM treaty, to build a missile defense shield and to plan for the weaponization of space.

15   Whether it is Bush at West Point, or the more sedate writings of the foreign policy elite writing for each other, or for that matter intelligent and progressive criticism, useful analysis must proceed from the postmodern realization that we are addressing a menacing nonstate adversary concealed in a network that is simultaneously everywhere and nowhere. These new circumstances definitely call for new thinking that adapts international law and global security in an effective and constructive manner. But the adjustments called for by Bush do not meet the specific challenge of mega-terrorism, and they unleash a variety of dangerous forces. What is needed is new thinking that sees the United States as part of a global community that is seeking appropriate ways to restore security and confidence, but builds on existing frameworks of legal restraints and works toward a more robust UN, while not claiming for itself an imperial role to make up the rules of world politics as it

goes along. Given the bipartisan gridlock that has gripped the country since September 11, positive forms of new thinking will almost certainly come, if they come, from pressures exerted by the citizenry outside the Beltway. We as citizens have never faced a more urgent duty.

Our "Next Manifest Destiny"
John J. Miller

At the end of the previous article, Richard Falk noted the Bush administration's desire "to build a missile defense shield and to plan for the weaponization of space" (p. 734). In this article, which appeared in the conservative magazine National Review, *John J. Miller presents the conservative argument in favor of military control of space—in Miller's words, "to use space for projecting American power around the globe." John J. Miller is the national political reporter for* National Review *magazine and the author of* The Unmaking of Americans: How Multiculturalism Has Undermined the Assimilation Ethic *(The Free Press, 1998).*

On the morning of September 13, 1985, Air Force Major Doug Pearson 1 smashed through the sound barrier in his F-15. Pointed almost directly upward more than seven miles above the Pacific Ocean, he tapped a little red button on the side of his control stick, and released a missile strapped to the belly of his plane. The missile blazed out of sight, leaving the earth's atmosphere quickly and reaching a speed of 13,000 miles per second. Pearson wondered if it would hit anything.

The mission was classified, so Pearson had developed a code with the folks 2 back at Edwards Air Force Base: The radioman would tell him to level off at a certain altitude if his missile struck its target, an obsolete scientific probe orbiting 345 miles over Hawaii. As it happened, the code wasn't necessary. When Pearson checked in a few minutes after firing, he could hear cheering in the background from the control room.

It was the one time an American pilot had ever destroyed an object in outer 3 space. People still talk about Pearson as the country's first "space ace." He remains its only space ace. A few weeks after the satellite was destroyed, Congress banned further tests. "We had hoped to conduct more," recalls Pearson, now a general. "But politics were what they were, and the nation decided to go another way."

Space is the next great frontier of military innovation, but for 17 years the na- 4 tion has gone another way. It has squandered a remarkable opportunity that may not be available much longer. Rather than move rapidly to build on the success of Pearson and many others involved in the military use of space, the United States has refused to develop technologies that will be essential to national security in the 21st century, from anti-satellite (ASAT) missiles like Pearson's to space-based lasers that can destroy ICBMs right after they've left their launch pads.

5   Democrats ridiculed Ronald Reagan's Strategic Defense Initiative as "Star Wars," and not much has changed: Rep. Dennis Kucinich, Democrat of Ohio, recently introduced the Space Preservation Act of 2002, which would ban weapons from space "for the benefit of all humankind." The language of his bill is so broad that it would effectively reinstate the now-defunct Anti-Ballistic Missile Treaty. It would also block construction of the limited missile-defense system now underway at Fort Greely in Alaska, as well as a sea-based system whose development the Pentagon says it may now accelerate.

6   That's because ABMs that intercept their targets above the atmosphere—all of them, basically—may reasonably be deemed weapons in space. (ICBMs are weapons in space, too, but they don't engage anything until their warheads dive back into the earth.) With the ABM Treaty at last finding its deserved place on the ash heap of history, however, we now have an unprecedented occasion to rethink U.S. military strategy in space. What the country needs is an aggressive commitment to achieving space control—a kind of Monroe Doctrine for the heavens, opening them to the peaceful purposes of commerce and science but closing them to anything that threatens American national security. The United States today is the undisputed leader in space technology, but the gap between our capabilities and those of potential adversaries won't remain so wide forever. The time for bold action is now.

OLD HAT, NEW HAT

7   The military space age arguably began during the Second World War, when 1,400 German V-2 rockets rained down on England. The V-2s did not do an enormous amount of physical damage, but they did terrify the public and highlight the revolutionary potential of space weapons. "The significance of this demonstration of German skill and ingenuity lies in the fact that it makes complete nonsense out of strategic frontiers, mountains, and river barriers," said CBS newsman Edward R. Murrow from London.

8   The Pentagon began to exploit the vast emptiness of space soon after. Military satellites have been in orbit for more than 40 years. In this sense, the militarization of space is old hat. Today, in fact, the armed services rely on space so much that they simply couldn't function as they currently do without access to it. Satellites facilitate communications, monitor enemy activity, and detect missile launches. Their surveillance capabilities are astounding: The KH-11 supposedly can spot objects six inches in size from hundreds of miles up. These functions were critical to the success of American campaigns against Iraq and Serbia in the 1990s, and they are essential to operations in Afghanistan.

9   Even seemingly mundane uses of space have military value. The Global Positioning System is well known to civilian navigators, but it was designed for military navigational purposes, such as helping cruise missiles locate their targets and special-ops units find their rally points. On June 6, 1944, General Eisenhower surely would have appreciated a weather forecast of the type we now routinely get from satellites via local TV and radio broadcasts. On September 11, 2001, it was

the space-enabled transmission of cell-phone signals and instant news that helped Todd Beamer and the other passengers of United Flight 93 prevent an already catastrophic day from turning even worse.

These are all examples of "force enhancement," to use Pentagon parlance. By 10 generating and channeling information, space-based assets help earthbound soldiers, sailors, and pilots improve their performance. Yet the United States will also need tools of "force application"—weapons that act against adversaries directly in and from space, for both offensive and defensive purposes. What our country requires, in short, is the weaponization outer space.

This already would have occurred in at least limited form, but for the mulish 11 opposition of arms-control liberals. Reagan's SDI routinely struggled for funding in the 1980s and early 1990s, and then went on life support during the Clinton administration. The budget for ground-based ABMs was slashed by nearly 80 percent in Clinton's first year—defense contractors even had their system-development bids returned to them unopened. The Brilliant Pebbles program, an outgrowth of SDI that would have placed a swarm of maneuverable interceptors in orbit, was eliminated completely. "These actions effectively destroyed the nation's space-based missile-defense options for the following decade," says Henry Cooper, who ran the Strategic Defense Initiative Organization at the Pentagon during the first Bush administration.

The budgets of other programs, such as the ASAT technology tested by 12 Pearson in 1985, were essentially trimmed to death. In 1990, Democrats in Congress forbade ASAT laser testing (the Republican majority let the ban lapse in 1995). The Army worked on ground-based ASAT missiles through the 1990s, and by 1997 its tests were starting to show real promise. The next year, however, Clinton had a test of his own to run—the line-item veto, since ruled unconstitutional by the Supreme Court—and he used it against the Army program, "We could have had something online," says Steven Lambakis of the National Institute for Public Policy. "Now we'd be forced to cobble together an emergency response if we really needed to knock out a satellite."

The United States soon will have at least a residual ASAT capability—any 13 national missile-defense system that can shoot down ICBMs also can obliterate satellites. What we don't have, however, is a growing architecture of space-based weapons along the lines of what Reagan began to describe in his visionary SDI speech in 1983. This May, Senate Democrats passed big cuts to ground-based missile defense, which is humdrum compared with space-based lasers and the like—and the White House has not yet beaten back even this challenge.

UP IN THE BLUE

The wrangling over weapons and budgets stems from a fundamental confusion 14 over what space is and how we should use it. From the standpoint of physics, space begins about 60 miles above sea level, which is roughly the minimum height a satellite must attain to achieve orbit. In this sense, space is just another medium, much like land, water, and air, with its own special rules of operation. For military purposes, however, space is more: It's the ultimate high ground, a flank from above whose importance, for those able to gain access to it, may represent the critical difference in future conflicts.

15   For arms-control fanatics, however, space is a kind of sanctuary, and putting weapons in it poses an unconscionable threa. U.N. secretary general Kofi Annan has called for ensuring "that outer space remains weapons-free." Theresa Hitchens of the Center for Defense Information warns of threats to "global stability" and "the potential for starting a damaging and destabilizing space race." With space, there's always the sense that weapons violate some pristine nature. This is clearly one of the sentiments behind the Kucinich bill. Yet it is exactly wrong—there should be weapons way up there because then there will be fewer of them right down here.

16   Space power is now in its infancy, just as air power was when the First World War erupted in 1914. Back then, military planes initially were used to observe enemy positions. There was an informal camaraderie among pilots; Germans and French would even wave when they flew by each other. Yet it wasn't long before the reality of war took hold and they began shooting. The skies were not to be a safe haven.

17   The lesson for space is that some country inevitably will move to seize control of it, no matter how much money the United States sinks into feel-good projects like the International Space Station. Americans have been caught napping before, as when the Soviet Union shocked the world with Sputnik in 1957. In truth, the United States could have beaten the Soviets to space but for a deliberate slow-down strategy that was meant to foster sunny relations with the world's other superpower.

18   The United States is the world's frontrunner in space, with about 110 military satellites in operation, compared with about 40 for Russia and 20 for the rest of the world. Yet a leadership role in space is not the same as dominance, and the United States today lacks the ability to defend its assets against rudimentary ASAT technology or to deny other countries their own weapons in space. No country appears to be particularly close to putting weapons in orbit, though the Chinese are expected to launch their first astronaut in the next year or two and they're working hard to upgrade their military space capabilities. "It would be a mistake to underestimate the rapidity with which other states are beginning to use space-based systems to enhance their security," says the just-released annual report of the Stockholm International Peace Research Institute. At a U.N. disarmament conference two years ago, Chinese officials called for a treaty to keep weapons out of space—a possible sign that what they really want is some time to play catch-up.

19   The private sector also requires a secure space environment. When the Galaxy IV satellite failed in 1998, paging services shut down, affecting an estimated 44 million customers. Banks and credit-card companies also were affected, along with a few television and radio stations. Saddam Hussein may lack the rocket power to lob a nuclear warhead halfway around the world, but he could mount one on top of a

Scud and fire it straight upward. A nuclear explosion in low orbit could disable scores of satellites and wreak havoc on modem economies everywhere—an example of space-age terrorism.

Plenty of people inside the government already recognize how much the United   20
States relies on space. There's a U.S. Space Command headquartered in Colorado Springs, and each branch of the military is to some extent involved in space power. In 1999, secretary of defense William Cohen called space power "as important to the nation as land, sea, and air power." His successor, Donald Rumsfeld, chaired a commission on space and national security right before joining the Bush administration. The panel's report, issued last year, warned of a "Space Pearl Harbor" if the country doesn't develop "new military capabilities."

While Cohen's rhetoric was fine, his boss, Bill Clinton, didn't seem to agree   21
with it. Rumsfeld is friendly to the notion of space power, but President Bush so far hasn't talked much about it. When Bush gave his missile-defense speech at the National Defense University a year ago, he spoke of land-, sea-, and air-based defenses—but made no mention of space. "A lot of us noticed that," says one Air Force officer.

The Rumsfeld commission also emphasized defense: how to protect American   22
satellites from foreign enemies. It had almost nothing to say about offense: how to use space for projecting American power around the globe. The commission was a creature of consensus, so this does not necessarily represent Rumsfeld's own thinking. And defense certainly is important. Military satellites are tempting targets because they're so crucial to the United States in so many ways. They are protected by their remoteness, but not much else. Their frail bodies and predictable flight paths are a skeet shoot compared with hitting speedy ICBMs, an ability that the United States is just starting to master. They're also vulnerable to jamming and hacking. Hardening their exteriors, providing them with some maneuverability, and having launch-on-demand replacements available are all key ingredients to national security. Yet defense doesn't win wars. In the future, the mere act of protecting these assets won't be enough to preserve American military superiority in space.

ASTRO POLITICS

In addition to an assortment of high-tech hardware, the United States could use   23
an Alfred Thayer Mahan for the 21st century. In 1890, Mahan was a captain in the Navy when the first edition of his book *The Influence of Sea Power on World History* was published. Today it ranks among the classic texts of military theory. Mahan argued that nations achieve greatness only if they dominate the seas and their various geographic "pressure points," holding up the example of the British Royal Navy. One of Mahan's early readers was a young man named Theodore Roosevelt, who began to apply these ideas while working in the Department of the Navy during the 1890s, and later as president. Mahanian principles shook the country loose from its traditional strategy of coastal defense and underwrote a period of national

dynamism, which included the annexation of Hawaii, victory in the Spanish-American War, and the construction of the Panama Canal.

24   No writer has clearly become the Mahan of space, though one candidate is Everett C. Dolman, a professor at the Air Force's School of Advanced Airpower Studies, in Alabama. Dolman's new book *Astropolitik* offers a grand strategy that would have the United States "endeavor at once to seize military control of low-Earth orbit" and impose "a police blockade of all current spaceports, monitoring and controlling all traffic both in and out." Dolman identifies low-Earth orbit as a chokepoint in the sense of Mahan—anybody who wants access to space must pass through it. "The United States should grab this vital territory now, when there's no real competition for it," Dolman tells me. "Once we're there, we can make sure the entry cost for anybody else wanting to achieve space control is too high. Whoever takes space will dominate Earth."

25   Dolman would benefit from a political benefactor. Mahan enjoyed the patronage of Roosevelt, who took a scholar's ideas and turned them into policies. Space has a number of advocates within the military bureaucracy, mostly among its younger members. It does not have a political champion, with the possible exception of Sen. Bob Smith, a New Hampshire Republican who has made the subject a personal passion. Smith calls space America's "next Manifest Destiny" and believes the Department of Defense should establish an independent Space Force to serve alongside the Army, Navy, and Air Force. Smith, however, may not stay in the Senate much longer, facing stiff political challenges at home.

26   With the right mix of intellectual firepower and political muscle, the United States could achieve what Dolman calls "hegemonic control" of space. The goal would be to make the heavens safe for capitalism and science while also protecting the national security of the United States. "Only those spacecraft that provide advance notice of their mission and flight plan would be permitted in space," writes Dolman. Anything else would be shot down.

27   That may sound like 21st-century imperialism, which, in essence, it would be. But is that so bad? Imagine that the United States currently maintained a battery of space-based lasers. India and Pakistan could inch toward nuclear war over Kashmir, only to be told that any attempt by either side to launch a missile would result in a boost-phase blast from outer space. Without taking sides, the United States would immediately defuse a tense situation and keep the skies above Bombay and Karachi free of mushroom clouds. Moreover, Israel would receive protection from Iran and Iraq, Taiwan from China, and Japan and South Korea from the mad dictator north of the DMZ. The United States would be covered as well, able not merely to deter aggression, but also to defend against it.

28   National security always has been an expensive proposition, and there is no getting around the enormous costs posed by a robust system of space-based weaponry. It would take a supreme act of national will to make it a reality. We've done it before: Winning the Cold War required laying out trillions of dollars, much of it on machines, missiles, and warheads that never saw live combat. Seizing control of space also would cost trillions, but it would lead to a world made immeasurably safer for America and what it values.

I Want You to Invade Iraq
TomPaine.com

The liberal organization TomPaine.com, named after the famous revolutionary thinker during the time of the American revolution, paid for this newspaper ad in a variety of American newspapers in early fall 2002.

Briefing #2: Preemptive Strikes and International Law
Jeff Guntzel

In an earlier article on page 740, John J. Miller imagines world peace resulting from America's "21st-century imperialism" based on the weaponization of space. This short "briefing paper," published on the Web site of Voices in the Wilderness on August 27, 2002, imagines the path to peace through international cooperation, treaty-building, and adherence to international law. Voices in the Wilderness, and its subgroup the Iraq Peace Team, is a humanitarian organization devoted to publicizing the suffering of the Iraqi people, especially children, caused by economic sanctions against Iraq following the 1990s Gulf War.

1   Addressing an enthusiastic crowd of West Point Military Academy graduates on June 1, 2002, George W. Bush declared, "Our security will require all Americans to be forward-looking and resolute, to be ready for preemptive action when necessary to defend our liberty and to defend our lives." The crowd roared.

2   Bush was thinking about Iraq that morning. He was not thinking about international law.

3   "The Bush administration's apparent resolve to wage war against Iraq, tempered for the moment by conservative critics . . . disregards the prohibitions on the use of force that are set forth in the UN Charter and accepted as binding rules of international law." Or so says Richard Falk, Professor Emeritus of International Law and Policy at Princeton University.[1]

4   Bush administration hawk Richard Perle disagrees. "I don't believe it does violate international law. We certainly have the right, not conferred, but acknowledged in the United Nations Charter, Article 51, to defend ourselves."[2]

5   It is true that Article 51 supports the "right of individual or collective self-defense if an armed attack occurs against a Member of the United Nations, until the Security Council has taken measures necessary to maintain international peace and security."[3] But Iraq has not attacked America, nor is there evidence that it intends to. There is no case for self-defense.

6   Again, Richard Falk: "Article 2 of the UN Charter states: 'All Members shall refrain in their international relations from the threat or use of force against the territorial integrity or political independence of any state, or in any other manner inconsistent with the Purposes of the United Nations.' "[4]

7   Among the United Nations' most important achievements has been the development of a body of international law. The United Nations Charter specifically calls on the United Nations to help in the settlement of international disputes by peaceful means.

8   Phyllis Bennis, a researcher at the Institute for Policy Studies and a longtime critic of Washington's misuse and outright disregard for the United Nations, wrote recently, "Some administration spokespeople are fond of a sound-bite that says 'the

UN Charter is not a suicide pact.' Others like to remind us that Iraq (and other nations) routinely violate the Charter. Both statements are true. But the United States has not been attacked by Iraq, and there is simply no evidence that Iraq is anywhere close to being able to carry out such an attack. The U.S. is the strongest international power—in terms of global military reach, economic, cultural, diplomatic and political power—that has ever existed throughout history. If the United States does not recognize the UN Charter and international law as the foundation of global society, how can we expect others to do so?"

"When it comes to policy on Iraq," Bennis says, "the U.S. has a history of sidelin-   9 ing the central role that should be played by the United Nations. This increasingly unilateralist trajectory is one of the main reasons for the growing international antagonism towards the U.S. By imposing its will on the Security Council—insisting on the continuation of economic sanctions when virtually every other country wants to lift them, announcing its intention to ignore the UN in deciding whether to go to war against Iraq—the U.S. isolates us from our allies, antagonizes our friends, and sets our nation apart from the international systems of laws that govern the rest of the world. This does not help, but rather undermines, our long-term security interests."[5]

Sources

1. *No War Against Iraq,* by Richard Falk and David Krieger
2. *Striking First, News Hour with Jim Lehrer,* July 1, 2002
3. *Charter of the United Nations,* Chapter VII, Article 51
4. *Charter of the United Nations,* Chapter I, Article 2, Paragraph 4
5. *Testimony Prepared for Hearings on Iraq Policy*, by Phyllis Bennis

The Moral Authority of the UN

Mona Charen

Despite the hopes of persons like Jeff Guntzel (previous reading), Mona Charen argues that the "the world does not and probably never will run on cooperation, peaceful dispute resolution, and friendship." One of the nation's most prolific conservative writers, Charen believes that America must assert its superpower status to create peace through power. This op-ed piece opposing the moral authority of the UN appeared in the online magazine Jewish World Review *on September 20, 2002, during the height of debate about possible war with Iraq.*

"What happens in the Security Council more closely resembles a mugging than either a political debate or an effort at problem-solving."

The United Nations is one of those institutions, like the Women's National   1 Basketball Association, that sails above its failures because it just seems to so many people like a good idea.

2   Despite its corruption, bias, indolence, and waste, the UN retains so much moral authority that former President Bush felt he had to appeal to the UN in order to get Democrats to authorize the Gulf War in 1991. And today, George W. Bush had to punch his ticket in Manhattan before being able to count on support from a number of U.S. allies abroad as well as the same Democrats in the U.S. Congress his father had to worry about. (It's worth pausing to note that the current President Bush struck just the right note at the UN, challenging the institution to enforce its own resolutions.)

3   The United Nations, like the League of Nations before it that crumbled at the first challenge from armed thugs, is an exercise in utopianism. It embodies the hope that the nations of the world can cooperate to eliminate scourges like dysentery and river blindness and settle their differences over polished conference tables rather than with machetes and M16s. The UN can boast some modest success in battling disease and poverty, but its record on peace and reconciliation is abysmal.

4   Though blue-helmeted UN peacekeeping forces have been deployed around the globe, they have proved highly vulnerable to political manipulation—in other words, they've been useless. In 1967, UN forces were summarily ejected from the Sinai desert—where they were theoretically keeping the peace between Egypt and Israel—when President Nasser waved them off with a flick of his wrist. In 1991, when the Croats counterattacked against the Serbs, the blue helmets were left standing impotently in the dust as tanks and APCs rolled through.

5   The fantasies of the UN's founders were limitless. Roosevelt's Secretary of State, Cordell Hull, imagined that the UN would rid the world of "spheres of influence, alliances, balance of power, or any of the other special arrangements through which, in the unhappy past, the nations strove to safeguard their security or to promote their interests."

6   It isn't the fault of the UN per se that the unrealistic hopes pinned on it have been punctured. The UN reflects its membership. Before the end of the Cold War, the great blocs that held sway there consisted of communists and a variety of other criminals, potentates, and presidents for life. In those days, the Commission on Human Rights was always looking into the situation in Puerto Rico and Tel Aviv, but never in Havana or Moscow. Even today, when more of the world's nations are free and democratic than ever before in history, China still holds a seat on the Security Council and the Arab nations still comprise the largest bloc vote. Israel has been condemned countless times (though Israel is not, as callers to talk radio and C-SPAN constantly assert, in violation of resolutions 242 and 338), but the Security Council has never once condemned Arab terrorists, far less the Chinese occupation of Tibet, the massacre in Rwanda, the Indonesian occupation of East Timor, Russian conduct in Chechnya, or Serbian acts in Bosnia.

7   And yet, most Americans and an overwhelming majority of Europeans believe that the moral imprimatur of the United Nations is necessary before any military action can be contemplated. When people tell pollsters what high regard they have for the UN, they are forgetting about the "Zionism is racism" resolution; the orgy of America and Israel-bashing at the Durban conference on racism; the instant pronouncements by UN personnel that Israel had committed an "atrocity" in Jenin

(only to be contradicted by the facts later), and so on. They are engaged in the same sort of utopianism that motivated the UN's founders.

But the world does not and probably never will run on cooperation, peaceful   8 dispute resolution, and friendship. Peace is maintained today as it always was, by armed force and balance of power. We are fortunate to live in a time—most unusual in human history—when the good guys also have the biggest guns. That is the source of our security and the world's hope, not the fond figment on the East River.

A Statement of Conscience
Not in Our Name Project

Dismayed by the strategies of the Bush administration in its war on terrorism, a group of activists met in New York City on March 23, 2002, to initiate the Not in Our Name Project. What follows is the text of a full-page newspaper ad appearing in major newspapers across the United States. In the actual ad, half the page is dominated by the names of prominent left-wing citizens who signed the statement, including Robert Altman, Edward Asner, Russell Banks, Barbara Ehrenreich, Barbara Kingsolver, Noam Chomsky, bell hooks, Edward Said, Pete Seeger, Art Spiegelman, Gloria Steinem, Kurt Vonnegut, Cornel West, Marisa Tomei, and many others.

Let it not be said that people in the United States did nothing when their govern-   1 ment declared a war without limit and instituted stark new measures of repression.

The signers of this statement call on the people of the U.S. to resist the policies   2 and overall political direction that have emerged since September 11, 2001, and which pose grave dangers to the people of the world.

We believe that peoples and nations have the right to determine their own   3 destiny, free from military coercion by great powers. We believe that all persons detained or prosecuted by the United States government should have the same rights of due process. We believe that questioning, criticism, and dissent must be valued and protected. We understand that such rights and values are always contested and must be fought for.

We believe that people of conscience must take responsibility for what their   4 own governments do—we must first of all oppose the injustice that is done in our own name. Thus we call on all Americans to RESIST the war and repression that has been loosed on the world by the Bush administration. It is unjust, immoral, and illegitimate. We choose to make common cause with the people of the world.

We too watched with shock the horrific events of September 11, 2001. We too   5 mourned the thousands of innocent dead and shook our heads at the terrible scenes of carnage—even as we recalled similar scenes in Baghdad, Panama City, and, a generation ago, Vietnam. We too joined the anguished questioning of millions of Americans who asked why such a thing could happen.

6   But the mourning had barely begun, when the highest leaders of the land unleashed a spirit of revenge. They put out a simplistic script of "good vs. evil" that was taken up by a pliant and intimidated media. They told us that asking why these terrible events had happened verged on treason. There was to be no debate. There were by definition no valid political or moral questions. The only possible answer was to be war abroad and repression at home.

7   In our name, the Bush administration, with near unanimity from Congress, not only attacked Afghanistan but arrogated to itself and its allies the right to rain down military force anywhere and anytime. The brutal repercussions have been felt from the Philippines to Palestine, where Israeli tanks and bulldozers have left a terrible trail of death and destruction. The government now openly prepares to wage all-out war on Iraq—a country which has no connection to the horror of September 11. What kind of world will this become if the U.S. government has a blank check to drop commandos, assassins, and bombs wherever it wants?

8   In our name, within the U.S., the government has created two classes of people: those to whom the basic rights of the U.S. legal system are at least promised, and those who now seem to have no rights at all. The government rounded up over 1,000 immigrants and detained them in secret and indefinitely. Hundreds have been deported and hundreds of others still languish today in prison. This smacks of the infamous concentration camps for Japanese-Americans in World War 2. For the first time in decades, immigration procedures single out certain nationalities for unequal treatment.

9   In our name, the government has brought down a pall of repression over society. The President's spokesperson warns people to "watch what they say." Dissident artists, intellectuals, and professors find their views distorted, attacked, and suppressed. The so-called Patriot Act—along with a host of similar measures on the state level—gives police sweeping new powers of search and seizure, supervised if at all by secret proceedings before secret courts.

10   In our name, the executive has steadily usurped the roles and functions of the other branches of government. Military tribunals with lax rules of evidence and no right to appeal to the regular courts are put in place by executive order. Groups are declared "terrorist" at the stroke of a presidential pen.

11   We must take the highest officers of the land seriously when they talk of a war that will last a generation and when they speak of a new domestic order. We are confronting a new openly imperial policy towards the world and a domestic policy that manufactures and manipulates fear to curtail rights.

12   There is a deadly trajectory to the events of the past months that must be seen for what it is and resisted. Too many times in history people have waited until it was too late to resist.

13   President Bush has declared: "you're either with us or against us." Here is our answer: We refuse to allow you to speak for all the American people. We will not give up our right to question. We will not hand over our consciences in return for a hollow promise of safety. We say NOT IN OUR NAME. We refuse to be party to

these wars and we repudiate any inference that they are being waged in our name or for our welfare. We extend a hand to those around the world suffering from these policies; we will show our solidarity in word and deed.

We who sign this statement call on all Americans to join together to rise to this 14 challenge. We applaud and support the questioning and protest now going on, even as we recognize the need for much, much more to actually stop this juggernaut. We draw inspiration from the Israeli reservists who, at great personal risk, declare "there IS a limit" and refuse to serve in the occupation of the West Bank and Gaza.

We also draw on the many examples of resistance and conscience from the past 15 of the United States: from those who fought slavery with rebellions and the underground railroad, to those who defied the Vietnam war by refusing orders, resisting the draft, and standing in solidarity with resisters.

Let us not allow the watching world today to despair of our silence and our failure to act. Instead, let the world hear our pledge: we will resist the machinery of war and repression and rally others to do everything possible to stop it.

The Progressive *Interview:* *Edward W. Said*

David Barsamian

One of the signers of the "Not in Our Name" newspaper ad (previous article) was Edward W. Said, an eminent American intellectual who is a professor of English at Columbia University. A Palestinian born in Jerusalem, Said came to the United States in the 1950s. He is a prominent spokesperson for the Palestinian cause and noted theorist who critiques the power dynamics of colonialism. The following conversation with Said is an interview conducted by David Barsamian, the director of Alternative Radio in Boulder, Colorado, for The Progressive *magazine (November 2001), whose mission, according to its Web site, is "to be a journalistic voice for peace and social justice at home and abroad."*

Q: The events of September 11 have bewildered and confused many 1 **Americans. What was your reaction?**

Edward W. Said: Speaking as a New Yorker, I found it a shocking and terrifying 2 event, particularly the scale of it. At bottom, it was an implacable desire to do harm to innocent people. It was aimed at symbols: the World Trade Center, the heart of American capitalism, and the Pentagon, the headquarters of the American military establishment. But it was not meant to be argued with. It wasn't part of any negotiation. No message was intended with it. It spoke for itself, which is unusual. It transcended the political and moved into the metaphysical. There was a kind of cosmic, demonic quality of mind at work here, which refused to have any interest in dialogue and political organization and persuasion. This was bloody-minded destruction for no other reason than to do it. Note that there was no claim for these attacks. There were no demands. There were no statements. It was a silent piece of terror. This was part of nothing. It was a leap into another realm—the realm of crazy abstractions and mythological generalities, involving people who have hijacked Islam for their own purposes. It's important not to fall into that trap and to try to respond with a metaphysical retaliation of some sort.

3   **Q: What should the U.S. do?**

4   **Said:** The just response to this terrible event should be to go immediately to the world community, the United Nations. The rule of international law should be marshaled, but it's probably too late because the United States has never done that; it's always gone it alone. To say that we're going to end countries or eradicate terrorism, and that it's a long war over many years, with many different instruments, suggests a much more complex and drawn-out conflict for which, I think, most Americans aren't prepared.

5   There isn't a clear goal in sight. Osama bin Laden's organization has spun out from him and is now probably independent of him. There will be others who will appear and reappear. This is why we need a much more precise, a much more defined, a much more patiently constructed campaign, as well as one that surveys not just the terrorists' presence but the root causes of terrorism, which are ascertainable.

6   **Q: What are those root causes?**

7   **Said:** They come out of a long dialectic of U.S. involvement in the affairs of the Islamic world, the oil-producing world, the Arab world, the Middle East—those areas that are considered to be essential to U.S. interests and security. And in this relentlessly unfolding series of interactions, the U.S. has played a very distinctive role, which most Americans have been either shielded from or simply unaware of.

8   In the Islamic world, the U.S. is seen in two quite different ways. One view recognizes what an extraordinary country the U.S. is. Every Arab or Muslim that I know is tremendously interested in the United States. Many of them send their children here for education. many of them come here for vacations. They do business here or get their training here.

9   The other view is of the official United States, the United States of armies and interventions. The United States that in 1953 overthrew the nationalist government of Mossadegh in Iran and brought back the shah. The United States that has been involved first in the Gulf War and then in the tremendously damaging sanctions against Iraqi civilians. The United States that is the supporter of Israel against the Palestinians.

10   If you live in the area, you see these things as part of a continuing drive for dominance, and with it a kind of obduracy, a stubborn opposition to the wishes and desires and aspirations of the people there. Most Arabs and Muslims feel that the United States hasn't really been paying much attention to their desires. They think it has been pursuing its policies for its own sake and not according to many of the principles that it claims are its own—democracy, self-determination, freedom of speech, freedom of assembly, international law. It's very hard, for example, to justify the thirty-four-year occupation of the West Bank and Gaza. It's very hard to justify 140 Israeli settlements and

roughly 400,000 settlers. These actions were taken with the support and financing of the United States. How can you say this is part of U.S. adherence to international law and U.N. resolutions? The result is a kind of schizophrenic picture of the United States.

Now we come to the really sad part. The Arab rulers are basically unpopular. 11 They are supported by the United States against the wishes of their people. In all of this rather heady mixture of violence and policies that are remarkably unpopular right down to the last iota, it's not hard for demagogues, especially people who claim to speak in the name of religion, in this case Islam, to raise a crusade against the United States and say that we must somehow bring America down.

Ironically, many of these people, including Osama bin Laden and the muja- 12 hedeen, were, in fact, nourished by the United States in the early eighties in its efforts to drive the Soviets out of Afghanistan. It was thought that to rally Islam against godless communism would be doing the Soviet Union a very bad turn indeed, and that, in fact, transpired. In 1985, a group of mujahedeen came to Washington and was greeted by President Reagan, who called them "freedom fighters."

These people, by the way, don't represent Islam in any formal sense. They're 13 not imams or sheiks. They are self-appointed warriors for Islam. Osama bin Laden, who is a Saudi, feels himself to be a patriot because the U.S. has forces in Saudi Arabia, which is sacred because it is the land of the prophet Mohammed. There is also this great sense of triumphalism, that just as we defeated the Soviet Union, we can do this. And out of this sense of desperation and pathological religion, there develops an all-encompassing drive to harm and hurt, without regard for the inno- cent and the uninvolved, which was the case in New York.

Now to understand this is, of course, not at all to condone it. And what terrifies 14 me is that we're entering a phase where if you start to speak about this as some- thing that can be understood historically—without any sympathy—you are going to be thought of as unpatriotic, and you are going to be forbidden. It's very dangerous. It is precisely incumbent on every citizen to quite understand the world we're living in and the history we are a part of and we are forming as a superpower.

Q: Some pundits and politicians seem to be echoing Kurtz in *Heart of* 15 ***Darkness* when he said, "Exterminate all the brutes."**

Said: In the first few days, I found it depressingly monochromatic. There's been 16 essentially the same analysis over and over again and very little allowance made for different views and interpretations and reflections.

What is quite worrisome is the absence of analysis and reflection. Take the word 17 "terrorism." It has become synonymous now with anti-Americanism, which, in turn, has become synonymous with being critical of the United States, which, in turn, has become synonymous with being unpatriotic. That's an unacceptable series of equations. The de- finition of terrorism has to be more precise, so that we are able to discriminate between, for example, what it is that the Palestinians are doing to fight the Israeli military occu- pation and terrorism of the sort that resulted in the World Trade Center bombing.

Q: What's the distinction you're drawing? 18

Said: Take a young man from Gaza living in the most horrendous conditions— 19 most of it imposed by Israel—who straps dynamite around himself and then throws himself into a crowd of Israelis. I've never condoned or agreed with it, but at least it is understandable as the desperate wish of a human being who feels himself being crowded out of life and all of his surroundings, who sees his fellow citizens, other Palestinians, his parents, sisters, and brothers, suffering, being injured, or being killed. He wants to do something, to strike back. That can be understood as the act of a truly desperate person trying to free himself from unjustly imposed conditions. It's not something I agree with, but at least you could understand it.

20   The people who perpetrated the terror of the World Trade Center and Pentagon bombings are something different because these people were obviously not desperate and poor refugee dwellers. They were middle class, educated enough to speak English, to be able to go to flight school, to come to America, to live in Florida.

21   **Q: In your introduction to the updated version of *Covering Islam: How the Media and The Experts Determine How We See The Rest of The World*, you say: "Malicious generalizations about Islam have become the last acceptable form of denigration of foreign culture in the West." Why is that?**

22   **Said:** The sense of Islam as a threatening Other—with Muslims depicted as fanatical, violent, lustful, irrational—develops during the colonial period in what I called Orientalism. The study of the Other has a lot to do with the control and dominance of Europe and the West generally in the Islamic world. And it has persisted because it's based very, very deeply in religious roots, where Islam is seen as a kind of competitor of Christianity.

23   If you look at the curricula of most universities and schools in this country, considering our long encounter with the Islamic world, there is very little there that you can get hold of that is really informative about Islam. If you look at the popular media, you'll see that the stereotype that begins with Rudolph Valentino in *The Sheik* has really remained and developed into the transnational villain of television and film and culture in general. It is very easy to make wild generalizations about Islam. All you have to do is read almost any issue of *The New Republic* and you'll see there the radical evil that's associated with Islam, the Arabs as having a depraved culture, and so forth. These are impossible generalizations to make in the United States about any other religious or ethnic group.

24   **Q: In a recent article in the *London Observer*, you say the U.S. drive for war uncannily resembles Captain Ahab in pursuit of Moby Dick. Tell me what you have in mind there.**

25   **Said:** Captain Ahab was a man possessed with an obsessional drive to pursue the white whale which had harmed him—which had torn his leg out—to the ends of the Earth, no matter what happened. In the final scene of the novel, Captain Ahab is being borne out to sea, wrapped around the white whale with the rope of his own harpoon and going obviously to his death. It was a scene of almost suicidal finality. Now, all the words that George Bush used in public during the early stages of the crisis—"wanted, dead or alive," "a crusade," etc.—suggest not so much an orderly and considered progress towards bringing the man to justice according to international norms, but rather something apocalyptic, something of the order of the criminal atrocity itself.

That will make matters a lot, lot worse, because there are always consequences. And it would seem to me that to give Osama bin Laden—who has been turned into Moby Dick, he's been made a symbol of all that's evil in the world—a kind of mythological proportion is really playing his game. I think we need to secularize the man. We need to bring him down to the realm of reality. Treat him as a criminal, as a man who is a demagogue, who has unlawfully unleashed violence against innocent people. Punish him accordingly, and don't bring down the world around him and ourselves.

Terrorism and the Intellectuals

Donald Kagan

Countering the liberal-leftist views of Edward Said is the conservative perspective of Donald Kagan. In this article, which appeared in the conservative scholarly journal The Intercollegiate Review *(spring 2002), Kagan critiques the "fashionable assaults on patriotism" characterized, as he claims, by the liberal intellectuals who hold sway in American universities. Two of the intellectuals that he cites specifically in this article—Katha Pollitt and Barbara Kingsolver—signed the "Not in Our Name" newspaper ad (pp. 745–747). Donald Kagan is Hillhouse Professor of Classics and History at Yale University.*

On September 11, members of an international terrorist movement attacked   1
two American cities, killing thousands of innocent American civilians and citizens of many other nations, and causing the destruction of billions of dollars in property. When they had recovered from the shock, most Americans reacted in the same two ways. They unequivocally supported their government's determination to prevent future attacks by capturing or killing the perpetrators, tearing up their organizations root and branch, and removing the leaderships of states that gave refuge to these people. They also expressed a new unity, an explicit patriotism and love of country not seen among us for a very long time.

That is not what we have seen and heard from the faculty of most elite universi-   2
ties in the United States—and certainly not from the majority of people designated as "intellectuals" who have spoken up in public. Their first concern has been to discuss the motives of the attackers, which are always seen as deep-rooted, underlying, and understandable when viewed with the required sympathy. We need, they say, to reflect on the deeper causes of this conflict with Osama bin Laden. They have urged us to consider the killers' anger and resentment, provoked by their poverty in a world dominated by American wealth, by their understandable hatred of American power and influence throughout the world, by their appropriate dismay at the alleged errors or wickedness of American policies, whether political, economic, military, or environmental. At Yale, we have been told that we must seek the "underlying causes" of these attacks; that "it is from the desperate, angry, and bereaved that these suicide pilots came"; that "offensive cultural messages" spread by the United States understandably provoke hatred, as they would in us if the roles were reversed.

3   These academics and intellectuals offer any and all explanations, so long as the explanation indicates that the attackers are really the victims, that the responsibility for September 11 really rests with the United States. What is most striking about such statements is their arrogance. They suggest that the enlightened commentator can penetrate the souls of the attackers and know their deepest motives. Yet strangely enough, their conclusions square with their own prejudices.

4   A far better guide might be the actual statements of the perpetrators, who have not been reluctant to reveal their motives. In February 1998, bin Laden published a declaration of holy war against America in which he said, "To kill Americans and their allies, both civil and military, is an individual duty of every Muslim who is able." His particular complaints included what he called the American "occupation" of Saudi Arabia, America's economic sanctions against the Iraqi regime of Saddam Hussein, and America's support for Israel, among other things. In countless statements, he and other terrorists have made it clear that the U.S. is "the great Satan," the enemy of all they hold dear. And what these terrorists hold dear includes the establishment of an extreme and reactionary Muslim fundamentalism in all currently Muslim lands, at least—which is a considerable portion of the globe. Such a regime would impose a totalitarian theocracy that would subjugate the mass of the people, especially women. They hate the U.S. not only because its power stands in the way of achieving their vision, but because our free, open, democratic, tolerant, liberal, and prosperous society is a powerful competitor for the allegiance of millions of Muslims around the world. No change of American policy, no retreat from the world, no repentance for past deeds or increase of national modesty can change these things. Only the destruction of America and its way of life will do, and Osama bin Laden makes no bones about this. In a videotaped statement after the attacks on New York and Washington he said:

> Here is America struck by God Almighty in one of its vital organs, so that its greatest buildings are destroyed, grace and gratitude to God. America has been filled with horror from north to south and east to west, and thanks be to God. God has blessed a group of vanguard Muslims, the forefront of Islam, to destroy America. May God bless them and allot them a supreme place in heaven. . . . As to America, I say to it and its people a few words: I swear to God that America will not live in peace before peace reigns in Palestine, and before all the army of infidels depart the land of Muhammad, peace be upon him.

5   I think this statement of the attackers' motives and intentions is more reliable than the guesses and explanations of America's intellectuals, laden as they are with their own agendas. Yet here at Yale, and elsewhere, we hear calls for "prayerful reflection . . . and repentance on our part," and we are urged to ask "whether we really have to be such a colossus, so engaged across the globe, and so sure that we have the best system and the best answers in this complicated . . . world of ours." One need not be a Western chauvinist to believe that most people around the world, Muslims included, would prefer our "system" and our "answers" to bin Laden's, if the choice were open to them. But most Muslims live under despotisms, and the choice is not open to them. Make no mistake about it: we are at war, a war waged against us by angry and determined men who will not let us escape, a war that will

be more difficult and longer than most of us understand. If America is defeated in this war or driven to a cowering withdrawal into isolationism, liberty's brightest light will go out, and a terrible darkness will descend on the whole world.

We must face the fact that Americans and our friends around the world are in great danger from people who make it plain that they are determined to kill us, to destroy our country and our way of life. Betraying our friends, retreating from the world, expressing our guilt, our shame, our repentance for anything and everything they claim we have done, will neither appease nor deter them. It is our very existence that arouses their hatred. In this war, we seek not vengeance but only safety—and the establishment of an order in the world that is secure against wanton violence and that allows people freely to choose the way of life that pleases them. 6

Even if the U.S. were not the prime target of this unholy war against modern civilization, America would need to take a leading role in defeating it, for America has been a beacon of liberty to the world since its creation, and especially in the twentieth century. The attacks on America have produced a wave of vilifications from intellectuals here and abroad, but I think it useful to quote an Englishman writing in the London *Sunday Times* who has a different view: "Let us ponder exactly what the Americans did in that most awful of all centuries, the twentieth. They saved Europe from barbarism in two world wars. After the Second World War they rebuilt the continent from the ashes. They confronted and peacefully defeated Soviet communism, the most murderous system ever devised by man. . . . America, primarily, ejected Iraq from Kuwait and stopped the slaughter in the Balkans while the Europeans dithered. . . ." 7

"People should think," David Halberstam writes from the blasted city of New York, "what the world would be like without the backdrop of American leadership with all its flaws over the past sixty years. Probably, I think, a bit like hell." It does not take an American to find some small virtue in a country that has helped save the world from Wilhelmine Germany's right-wing imperialism, Hitler's Nazi tyranny, Stalin's totalitarianism, and Japan's militaristic domination. Yet voices here and abroad from the world of leftist intellectual orthodoxy condemn and blame the U.S., as they have done for more than half a century. One Italian journalist wrote that "ninety percent of the Arab world believes that America got what it deserved." This, she says, is not an exaggeration but an understatement. On this side of the Atlantic, Susan Sontag tells us that the assaults on America are not an "attack on 'civilization' or 'humanity' or 'the free world' but an attack on the world's self-proclaimed superpower, undertaken as a consequence of specific American alliances and actions." Another writer announces, "Force will get us nowhere. It is reparations that are owing, not retribution." 8

None of this should be surprising, for such voices have been plentiful, and disastrous, throughout the last century, as was lamented by a wiser voice from an earlier era: 9

> The worst difficulties from which we suffer . . . come from within. They do not come from the cottages of the wage earners, they come from a peculiar type of brainy people always found in our country, who, if they add something to its culture, take much from its strength. Our diffi-

culties come from the mood of unwarrantable self-abasement into which we have been cast by a powerful section of our own intellectuals. . . . Nothing can save England if she will not save herself. If we lose faith in ourselves, in our capacity to guide and govern, if we lose our will to live, then indeed our story is told.

10   That statement was made by Winston Churchill in 1933, as he vainly tried to rally his country to rearm and resist Adolf Hitler before it was too late. The problems he encountered are with us again today, and not six years before the onset of violence but after we have already been attacked.

11   Some members of the same intelligentsia have also decried the new patriotism that has awakened after the assault on America. Katha Pollitt, writing in *The Nation,* wrote that her daughter "thinks we ought to fly an American flag out the window. Definitely not, I say: the flag stands for jingoism and vengeance and war." The novelist Barbara Kingsolver writes, "Patriotism threatens free speech with death. . . . The American flag stands for intimidation, censorship, violence, bigotry, sexism, homophobia, and shoving the Constitution through a paper-shredder."

12   Such ideas have a wide currency and should especially concern those of us who take some part in educating the young. The encouragement of patriotism is no longer a part of our public educational system, and the cost of that omission is now making itself felt. This would have alarmed and dismayed the founders of our country.

13   Thomas Jefferson, for example, believed that the most important goals of education were civic and moral. He urged that all students have a political education through the study of forms of government, political history, and foreign affairs. Such an education was meant to communicate the special virtues of representative democracy, the dangers that threatened it, and the responsibility of citizens under a republican constitution to esteem and protect their political order.

14   Since every citizen has natural rights and powers, every one of them must understand and esteem the institutions, laws, and traditions of his country if it is to succeed. Jefferson intended American education to elicit a necessary patriotism, and to add one humble voice to a great one, I agree. Democracy, of all political systems—because it depends on the participation of its citizens in their own government and because it depends on their own free will to risk their lives in its defense—stands in the greatest need of an education that inculcates patriotism.

15   I recognize that I have here said something shocking. For the first hundred and fifty years of American history such a statement would have been a commonplace, so widespread was its acceptance. But the last half-century has seen a sharp turn away from what had been the traditional attitude regarding the purposes and functions of education. Our schools have retreated from the idea of moral education—except for some attempts at what is called "values clarification," which is generally a cloak for moral relativism verging on a nihilism of the sort that asserts that whatever feels good is good.

16   Even more vigorously have the schools fled from the idea of encouraging patriotism. In the intellectual climate of our time, the very suggestion has brought contemptuous sneers or outrage, depending on the mood of the listener. There is no end of quoting Samuel Johnson's famous remark that "patriotism is the last refuge

of a scoundrel"—but no recollection of Boswell's accompanying explanation that "he did not mean a real and generous love for our country, but that pretended patriotism which so many, in all ages and countries, have made a cloak for self-interest."

Many have been the attacks on patriotism for intolerance, arrogance, and bellicosity, but to do so is unfairly to equate patriotism with its bloated distortion, chauvinism. Patriotism properly understood does not require us to hate, condemn, denigrate, or attack any other country, nor does it require us to admire our own country uncritically. Indeed, few countries have been subjected to as much criticism and questioning as our own. Most Americans would empathize with at least the second part of Winston Churchill's remark, "When I am abroad, I always make it a rule never to criticize or attack the government of my own country. I make up for lost time when I come home."

So distant are we from a proper understanding of patriotism that I sometimes hear people say, "It is silly to be patriotic. Why should I love, support, and defend a country just because, quite by chance, I happened to be born there?" In fact, there should be a presupposition in favor of patriotism, for human beings are not solitary creatures; rather, they require organized societies if they are to flourish or even survive. Just as an individual must have an appropriate love of himself if he is to perform well, an appropriate love of his family if he and it are to prosper, so, too, must he love his country if it is to survive. Neither family nor nation can flourish without love, support, and defense. Every individual who has benefited from those institutions serves his self-interest in defending them, but also has a moral responsibility to extend to them his support.

The fashionable assaults on patriotism, in the end, are failures of character. They are made by privileged individuals who enjoy the full benefits offered by the country they deride and detest—its opportunities, its freedom, its riches—but who lack the basic decency to pay their country the allegiance and respect that honor demands. Honor, of course, is often another object of their derision. For the rest of us, our own honor and our devotion to our nation's special virtues require us to respect and defend their freedom to be irresponsible and subversive of our safety. But nothing forbids us from pointing out the despicable nature of their behavior.

Free countries like our own have an even more powerful claim on the patriotism of their citizens than do others, and our country has an even greater need of it than most. Every country requires a high degree of cooperation and unity among its citizens if it is to achieve the internal harmony that every good society requires. Unity and cooperation must rest on something shared and valued in common. Most countries have relied on the common ancestry and traditions of their people as the basis of their unity, but the United States of America can rely on no such commonality. We are an enormously diverse and varied people, almost all immigrants or the descendants of immigrants. We come from every continent on the face of the earth, our forebears spoke, and many of us still speak, many different languages, and all the races and religions of the world are to be found among us. The great strengths provided by this diversity are matched by great dangers. We are always vulnerable to divisions among us that can be exploited to set one group against another and thus to destroy the unity that has enabled us to flourish.

21   We live in a time when civic devotion has been undermined and national unity is under attack. The individualism that is so crucial a part of our tradition is often used to destroy civic responsibility. The idea of a common American culture, enriched by the diverse elements that compose it but available equally to all, is under assault. Attempts are made to replace our common culture with narrower and politically divisive programs that are certain to set one group of Americans against another.

22   The answer to these problems and our only hope for the future must lie in education, which philosophers have rightly put at the center of the propagation of justice and the good society. We rightly look to education to solve the pressing current problems of our economic and technological competition with other nations, but we must not neglect the inescapable political and ethical effects of education. We in the academic community have too often engaged in *mis*education. If we encourage separatism, we will get separatism—and the terrible conflicts in society it will bring. If we encourage rampant individualism to trample on the need for a common citizenship, if we ignore civic education, the forging of a single people, the building up of a legitimate patriotism, then we will find ourselves a nation of selfish individuals, heedless of the needs of others. We will have the war of all against all, and we will have no common defense.

23   The civic sense America needs can come only from a common educational effort. In telling the story of the American political experience, we must insist on the honest search for truth. We must permit no comfortable self-deception or evasion, no seeking of scapegoats. But the story of this country's vision of a free, democratic republic and of its struggle to achieve it need not fear the most thorough examination. Our country's story can proudly stand comparison with that of any other land, and that story provides the basis for the civic devotion we so badly need.

24   In spite of the shock caused by the attacks on New York and Washington and the discovery of anthrax in the mail, I am not sure that we really understand how serious is the challenge that now faces us. We are only at the beginning of a long and deadly war that will inflict much loss and pain, one that will require sacrifice and steady determination during very dark hours to come. We must be powerfully armed, morally as well as materially, if we are to do what must be done. That will take courage and unity, and these must rest on a justified and informed patriotism, to sustain us through the worst times.

25   A verse by Edna St. Vincent Millay provides a clear answer to the question of why Americans should love their country:

> *Not for the flag*
> *Of any land because myself was born there*
> *Will I give up my life.*
> *But will I love that land where man is free,*
> *And that will I defend.*

26   Ours is such a land.

27   Up to now, I fear, too many American intellectuals and too many faculty members of our greatest universities have been a part of our country's problem. If we are

to overcome the dangers that face us, we will need them to become part of the solution. My hope is that the natural, admirable, vitally necessary patriotism that is now gaining strength and expression among the ordinary people of our land will help to educate those among us who feel intellectually superior to them. We will need that patriotism in the long, dangerous, and difficult struggle that lies before us.

For Class Discussion

1. Based on the readings in this unit and on your own knowledge and perspectives, sketch out the core arguments for and against each of the following positions:

   - The doctrine of preemptive strikes in the war on terrorism
   - Building a missile defense shield and weaponizing space
   - Using U.S. troops for peacekeeping or humanitarian reasons (for example, protecting ethnic Albanians in the Kosovo crisis) versus using troops only in situations directly related to national interests
   - Abiding by international law as determined by treaties and the United Nations

2. How would you describe the differences in underlying values, assumptions, and beliefs between the conservative perspectives of Bush, Miller, Krauthammer, and Kagan and the liberal perspectives of Falk, Guntzel, Said, and the signers of the "Not in Our Name" document?

3. This book went to press after the national debate over a possible war with Iraq and soon after the United States went to war. It is impossible for us to see the future, but you who are reading this text know what happened after March 2003. Looking back on these readings from your point in time, analyze the wisdom of the different perspectives.

4. Choose one of the readings in this unit and analyze it carefully using the List 2 Guide questions on pages 460–461.

OPTIONAL WRITING ASSIGNMENT Choose an issue related to the superpower controversy but rooted in your current political climate—a climate that we can't predict at this time. Enter the political conversation of your current time by writing an argument on some issue related to foreign policy, the war on terrorism, the war in Iraq, or U.S. status as a superpower. Depending on your current political situation, your motivating occasion, and your instructor's desires, you might write an op-ed piece for your college newspaper, a letter to a congressperson, an advocacy poster or newspaper ad, or a researched white paper to be sent to a policymaker.

Credits

Text

Page 5. Wilfred Owen, "Dulce et Decorum Est" from *The Complete Poems and Fragments of Wilfred Owen*, ed. Jon Stallworthy (New York: W. W. Norton, 1984).

Page 14. Sara Jean Green, excerpt from "Mosh Pits: It's Not All Fun, Music" from *The Seattle Times*, June 4, 2002, pp. A1, A9.

Page 15. Excerpt from "Homeless Hit the Streets to Protest Proposed Ban." Reprinted by permission of the Associated Press.

Page 17. Gordon F. Adams, "Petition to Waive the University Math Requirement." Reprinted with the permission of the author.

Page 24. Lisa Turner, "Playing with Our Food," *Better Nutrition*, Vol. 62, No. 6, June 2000, pp. 56–59. Copyright © 2000 Lisa Turner. Reprinted by permission of the author.

Page 40. "Biotech Labeling" from www.whybiotech.com. Courtesy of the Council for Biotechnology Information.

Page 126. David Langley, "'Half-Criminals' or Urban Athletes? A Plea for Fair Treatment of Skateboarders." Reprinted with the permission of the author.

Page 146. George C. Lodge and Jeffrey F. Rayport, "Knee-Deep and Rising: America's Recycling Crisis," *Harvard Business Review*, September–October 1991, p. 132.

Page 147. John Tierney, "Recycling Is Garbage," *New York Times Magazine*, June 30, 1996, p. 28.

Page 150. Marybeth Hamilton, from "First Place: A Healing School for Homeless Children." Reprinted with the permission of the author.

Page 153. Ellen Goodman, "Minneapolis Pornography Ordinance," from the *Boston Globe* (1985). Copyright © 1985 by the Boston Globe Company. Reprinted with the permission of The Washington Post Writers Group.

Page 158. Rebekah Taylor, "Letter to Jim." Reprinted with the permission of the author.

Page 231. Jack K. C. Chiang, "Letter to the Editor," The *Seattle Times*, March 24, 2002, p. B7. Copyright © 2002 Jack K.C. Chiang. Reprinted by permission.

Page 233. Kathy Sullivan, "Oncore, Obscenity, and the Liquor Control Board." Reprinted with the permission of the author.

Page 235. Charles Krauthammer, "This Isn't a 'Legal' Matter, This Is War," *The Seattle Times*, September 13, 2001, p. B6. Copyright 2001, The Washington Post Writers Group.

Page 238. Blaine Newnham, "Court Win for Martin Not a Defeat for Pro Sports," *The Seattle Times*, May 30, 2001, pp. D1, D4. Copyright © 2001 The Seattle Times. Used with permission.

Page 259. Daeha Ko, "The Monster That Is High School," *University of Washington Daily*, May 9, 1999. Copyright © 1999 by the *University of Washington Daily*. Reprinted with permission of the publisher.

Page 263. Richard Rothstein, "When Mothers on Welfare Go to Work," *New York Times*, June 5, 2002, p. A20. Copyright © 2002 New York Times Co., Inc. Used with permission.

Page 265. Holly M. Miller, "The Causes of Teen Sexual Behavior." Reprinted with the permission of the author.

Anthology

Images

Page 573. Courtesy of Siemens Corporation.

Page 609. Courtesy of Scoop.

Page 706. Left: CORBIS/SYGMA.

Page 706. Right: Phillippe Diederich/Getty Images.

Page 741. TomPaine.com is an online public interest journal, a project of the nonprofit Florence Fund.

Color Plates

COLOR PLATE A   Courtesy of Sustain USA.

COLOR PLATE B   Courtesy of the Council for Biotechnology Information.

COLOR PLATE E   Courtesy of Save the Children.

COLOR PLATE F   Courtesy of Earthjustice.

COLOR PLATE H   Courtesy of The Center for Consumer Freedom.

Index

Abell, John D., "Neoliberal World Order, The: The View from the Highlands of Guatemala," 619–25

Abstract, 27

Academic papers. *See* Research papers

Academics, as argument writers, 50–51

Accidental criterion, in Aristotelian definition, 219

Accommodation
of audience, 140–63
in Rogerian argument, 158

Ad hominem fallacy, 149, 428–30

Advertisements. *See also* Advocacy ads
analysis of visual argument in, 169–71
MLA style for, 404

Advocacy
groups as argument writers, 49–50
Web sites for, 35–36

Advocacy ads, 35
critiquing, 261–62, 351–53
design elements of, 169, 170, 173–74
one-page, 337
proposal arguments for, 325–26, 333
visual arguments in, 180–83

Advocacy posters, proposal arguments as, 325–26

"Affidavit of Steven K. Lofton" (Lofton), 591–94

Against Our Will: Men, Women, and Rape (excerpt) (Brownmiller), 285–88

Agreement, in Rogerian argument, 157

Aiken, Ron, "Save the Labels for the Category of Achievement," 564–65

"Aldo Leopold's Land Ethic: Is It Only Half a Loaf?" (MacCleery), 633–36

"All-American Osamas" (Kristof), 547–48

AltaVista, 372

Alternative views
seeking sources of, 46
synthesizing, 47–48

Altieri, Miguel A., "Ten Reasons Why Biotechnology Will Not Ensure Food Security, Protect the Environment and Reduce Poverty in the Developing World," 488–96

Amar, Akhil Reed, "Supreme Court's Unfree Speech, The," 350–51

Ambiguity, 45–46

"American Dream, The: Why Environmentalists Attack the SUV" (Bragg), 465–67

American Psychological Association. *See* APA (American Psychological Association) documentation system

Analogy
arguments by, 272–75
for causal argument, 251–52
extended, 273–74
faulty, 434
for pathos, 136
undeveloped, 273

Anderson, Chris, "Nicholas D. Kristof: Columnist Endorses Slave Labor for Children," 627–28

Anderson, Tiffany (student), "Woman's View of Hip-Hop, A," 310–14

"Andrea Yates: New Moms and Our Misplaced Priorities" (Varner), 722–24

"Andrea Yates Wasn't Responsible for Her Crime" (Krauthammer), 712–13

Angle of vision, evaluating sources and, 376

Anthologies
APA style for, 411
MLA style for, 399

"Anti-Censorship Advocate Locks Horns with Anti-Pornography Filterers" (Associated Press), 648–50

APA (American Psychological Association)
documentation system, 29, 384, 405–23
document conventions of, 168
quick reference guide for common citations, 407, 408–9
References list in, 393, 407
student research paper in, 415, 416–23

Appeal to false authority fallacy, 427–28

Appeal to ignorance fallacy, 426

Appeal to irrational premises fallacy, 427

Appeal to prejudice fallacy, 429
Appeal to stirring symbols
  fallacy, 426
Appeal to the person fallacy.
  See Ad hominem fallacy
"Approach to Spam, An"
  (Conway), 651–52
Arbeiter, Jean, "Iraq War
  Plans," 281–82
Argument. *See also* specific
  types
  causal, 241–68
  classical, 62–66
  committee model for, 15–20
  conclusiveness in, 424–25
  core of, 75–86
  defining features of, 7–12
  evidence in, 109–28
  explicit and implicit, 4–7
  frame of, 81–82, 92
  genres of, 33–36
  genuine vs. pseudo-, 79–80
  guide questions for analysis
    and evaluation of, 459–61
  introduction to, 3–21
  logical structure of, 76–108
  one-sided vs. multisided,
    140–41
  persuasion and, 11–12
  as process and product, 9–10
  pro-con debate and, 4
  quarrel vs., 3–4, 7–8
  reading, 22–48
  self-announcing structure of,
    84, 86
  shaping, 62–66
  Toulmin system for, 91–101
  truth and, 10–14
  unfolding structure of,
    84–85
  writing, 49–71
Argumentation, 77
Argument to the people
  fallacy, 426
Aristotelian definitions, 219–22
  rhetorical context and,
    221–22
Aristotle, 88, 91
  on appeal from *ethos*, 131

Articles
  APA style for, 411–13
  MLA style for, 399–402
Ashcroft, John, "Testimony to
  the Senate Committee on
  the Judiciary," 524–29
"Ashcroft Raids, The" (Cole),
  529–33
Assumptions, 8–9, 63
  disagreement about, 38–43
  shared, 79–80
  unstated, 89, 90
  warrant as unstated, 91–92
Attributive tags, for research,
  387–88
Audience
  accommodation of, 140–63
  claim types and, 206
  conceptualizing, 11–12
  credibility and, 132
  determining issue and
    information questions,
    77–78
  ethical appeal to, 75
  neutral or undecided,
    144–52
  resistant, 141–43, 152–63
  in rhetorical triangle, 75
  shaping argument for, 62–66
  supportive, 143–44
  Toulmin system and, 91–94
  writing community as, 440
Audience-based reasons, 63
  finding, 104–7
  power of, 101–8
Authority, questioning
  credibility of, 149

Backing
  evidence as, 109
  in Toulmin system, 92–93,
    96
Bar graphs, 191–92
Barsamian, David,
  "*Progressive, The,*
    Interview: Edward W.
    Said," 747–51
Battin, Margaret P., 161n

Because clauses, 89, 95
  brainstorming for pro and
    con, 60–61
  expressing reasons in, 82–84,
    86
Becker, Alton, 156n
Begging the question fallacy,
  430–31
Begley, Sharon, 251n
Beliefs
  disagreement about, 38–43
  pathos and, 132–37
Believers
  fanatical, 79
  reading as, 23–31
Believing, game of, 58–60
Bentham, Jeremy, 297
"Better Gas Mileage, Greater
  Security" (Kennedy),
  467–68
Bias, of sources, 376, 377
Bibliography
  parenthetical citations
    systems with, 393–94
  References as, 393
  Works Cited as, 393
Bissell, John, "Invoking the
  Lessons of Edison in the
  Great 'Frankenfoods'
  Dispute," 502–6
Blind writing, 56
Body (text) type, 167
Boehlert, Sherwood, "Floor
  Statement on
  Beohlert-Markey CAFE
  Amendment," 479–81
Bonicillo, Mark (student),
  public policy proposal by,
  343–49
Books, 360
  APA style for, 409–11
  MLA style for, 397–99,
    401–2
  online catalog for, 365
  scholarly vs. trade, 363–64
Boolean searches, 367
Booth, Wayne, 22
Brackets, for changes in
  quotations, 391

Bradsher, Keith, "Gimme an SUV—ASAP: Teenagers Are the Next Big Market for Sport-Utility Vehicles—and the Consequences Could Be Deadly," 471–77

Brainstorming
    for network of related issues, 61–62
    for pro and con *because* clauses, 60–61
    sources of evidence, 122–23

"Briefing #2: Preemptive Strikes and International Law" (Guntzel), 742–43

Brochures, 180

Brown, Catherine, 157n

Brownback, Sam, "Human Cloning," 690–91

Brownmiller, Susan, from *Against Our Will: Men, Women, and Rape*, 285–88

Bruffee, Kenneth, 443

Bush, George W., "President Bush Delivers Graduation Speech at West Point," 726–30

Business professionals, as argument writers, 50

Bynoe, Yvonne, "White Boy Shuffle, The," 557–61

"CAFE Belongs in the Graveyard with Its Victims: We Can Increase Fuel Economy Without Costing Lives" (Randall), 477–79

Calabresi, Steven G., "Supreme Court's Unfree Speech, The," 350–51

"Cancelled" (Payne), 482

Canizarees, Kristina, "Science Good, Nature Bad: The Biotech Dogma," 506–9

"Carnival Against Capitalism," 609

Carr, John, "It's Time to Tackle Cyberporn," 645–48

Cartoons, 183–86. *See also* Political cartoon

Catalog, online, 365

Categorical arguments, 208–13
    simple, 200–201, 210–13

Categorical evaluation argument
    conducting, 291–96
    criteria for, 292–94
    criteria-match structure of, 290–91

Category search, 328

Causal arguments, 241–68
    exploring ideas for, 255–56
    inductive methods for, 248–50
    methods for arguing causation, 246–52
    nature of, 242–44
    organizing, 256–57
    questioning and critiquing, 257–59
    terms used with, 252–54
    in Toulmin terms, 244–46
    writing of, 254–57

Causal induction, analogy or precedent for, 251–52

Causation, correlation and, 432

Cause/consequence arguments, 16, 201

"Causes of Teen Sexual Behavior, The" (Miller), 265–68

Cepeda, Raquel, "Money, Power, Elect: Where's the Hip-Hop Agenda?", 550–57

Charen, Mona
    "Moral Authority of the UN, The," 743–45
    "Stem Cell Simplicities," 699–701

Charts. *See also* Graphs
    pie charts, 192–93

Chat rooms, 36

Chiang, Jack K. C., "Why Not Taiwan?", 231–32

"Children in a Violent World" (Garbarino), 667–73

"China's Cyberspace Censorship" (New York Times), 654–55

Citation systems. *See also* APA (American Psychological Association) documentation system; MLA (Modern Language Association) documentation system
    parenthetical, 393–94
    for Web quotation, 385n

Citizens, as argument writers, 51

Claims, 89, 90, 92, 93, 95–97
    cause/consequence arguments, 201, 241–68
    as core of argument, 75–86
    definitional arguments, 201, 214–39
    evaluation arguments, 202–3, 289–317
    to focus argument, 204–7
    to generate ideas, 204–7
    identifying, 86
    justifying, 7–9
    to organize and develop arguments, 207
    proposal arguments, 203, 319–53
    resemblance arguments, 202, 269–88
    supported by reasons, 81–82
    types of, 199–200
    value of studying, 204–7

Claim-type strategy, for proposal arguments, 327–30, 334

Classical argument
    body of, 63
    design of, 64
    for neutral or undecided audience, 144–52
    as planning guide, 65–66
    structure of, 62–66

Classroom debate exercise, in writing community, 454–56

Clegg, Roger, "Profiling Terrorists," 541–42

Clement, Gary, "I'd Like a Tall Decaf Non-Fat Mocha Latte," 608

Clonethink, 439

Closed-form structure, 85n

Closed-response questions, 124

Cohen, Adam, "Constitution Does Not Protect Spamming, The," 652–54

Colb, Sherry F., "New Face of Racial Profiling, The: How Terrorism Affects the Debate," 537–41

Cole, David, "Ashcroft Raids, The," 529–33

Collaboration
  by writers, 443
  writing community and, 438–56

Colman, Hila, "Who Needs a Husband," 604–5

Color, as design element, 172

Comic strips, MLA style for, 404

Committee model for argument, 15–20

Common ground, in Rogerian argument, 157

Community, belonging to, 67

Complex question fallacy, 431

Conceding to opposing views, 152

Conclusiveness, in argument, 424–25

Concrete language, for pathos, 133

Confirmatio, 63

Conflict, 7–8
  in writing community, 438–40

Confusing correlation for cause fallacy, 432

Confutatio, 63

Connecting words, showing reason, 81

Connotations, for pathos, 136

Consensus, in writing community, 438–40

Consequences
  evaluating, 322
  predicting, 322

Consequences-based ethics argument, 297, 299–300, 307

Consequence search, 329

"Constitution Does Not Protect Spamming, The" (Cohen), 652–54

Constraints, in causal arguments, 253

Contested terms, in definitional argument, 222–26

Context
  for data, 119
  of information and issue questions, 77–78
  rhetorical, 36–37, 68, 111–22
  social, 75

Contrary evidence, 119
  subordinating, 120

Contributing causes, 253

Controversies
  for exploration in writing, 68
  over genetic engineering of food, 23–27

Conversation
  argumentative, 22
  oral and written as process, 9–10

Conway, Jim, "Approach to Spam, An," 651–52

Cook, Blanche Wiesen, 212n

Core argument, 88–89

Correctness, editing for, 55

Correlation
  causal hypotheses and, 249–50
  causation and, 432

Cose, Ellis, "False Promise of Being First, The," 563–64

Cost, in evaluation arguments, 302

Cost-benefit analysis, 322

Cottle, Michelle, "Punishment That Fits," 713–16

Counterexamples/countertestimony, 148

Court decisions, 35

"Court Win for Martin Not a Defeat for Pro Sports" (Newnham), 238–40

"Cracking Down on E-Mail Harassment" (Masters), 638–41

Credibility
  ethos and, 131–32
  of sources, 378

Criteria-match structure
  of categorical evaluations, 290–91
  of definitional arguments, 214–16

Cyberspace. See Web sites

Daeha Ko (student), "Monster That Is High School, The," 259–61

Data
  from interviews, 123–24
  persuasive use of, 109–11
  questioning, 149
  sources of, 112–16
  statistical, 114–15
  from surveys/questionnaires, 124
  on tables, 189–91

Database
  APA style for, 408, 409
  citing print articles or books downloaded from, 401
  keyword searching in, 367
  MLA style for, 396, 413, 414
  print articles in, 365–69

"Debunking the 10 Worst Myths about America's Teens" (Males), 664–67

Declaration of Independence, 15

Definitional arguments, 16, 201, 214

conceptual problems of definitions and, 217–19

criteria-match structure of, 214–16

defining contested term in, 222–26

kinds of definitions, 219–22

match part of, 226

organizing, 228

questioning and critiquing, 230–31

revising draft for, 229–30

rule of justice and, 217–18

writing, 227–30

Definitions

Aristotelian, 219–22

operational, 222

reportive, 222, 223–24

stipulative, 222–23, 224–26

Degree of advocacy, of sources, 377

Delayed thesis, for resistant audience, 153–56

"Denzel Washington Plays a Bad Guy, and That's Good" (Pitts), 561–63

Derbyshire, John, "Maternal Madness...or Sheer Iniquity? Mothers Who Kill," 709–11

Design elements

color as, 172

images and graphics as, 172

space or layout as, 168–69

type as, 166–68

Detail, 119

Devine, Robert S., 247

Dialogue, 16

Dictionaries

definitions and, 217

etymological, 223

specialized, 223

Disagreement

analyzing sources of, 37–45

about facts or their relevance, 38

productive use of, 45–48

about values, beliefs, or assumptions, 38–43

writing analysis of, 43–45

Display type, 167

Disputed definitions, 214

Documentation systems. *See* APA (American Psychological Association) documentation system; MLA (Modern Language Association) documentation system

Domain type, sorting Web sites by, 379

Double-entry journal, for note taking, 375

Doubting an argument

game of, 58–60

reading as a doubter, 31–32

suspending doubt, 30–31

Drafting, 53–55

first draft, 53–54

revising, 54–55, 229–30

Drawings, compositional features of, 174–79

"Driving Global Warming" (McKibben), 462–65

"Dulce et Decorum Est" (Owen), 5

Earlier meaning strategy, 223

EBSCOhost, 366, 370

Editing, for style, impact, and correctness, 55

Editorial. *See also* Newspapers

policy proposal as, 333

"Egg Heads" (Lopez), 601–4

Egocentrism, of writers, 440

Egothink, 439

"Eight Is Too Many: The Case Against Octuplets" (Emanuel), 315–18

Either-or fallacy, 431–32

Elbow, Peter, 58n

Electronic bulletin boards, 36

Ellipses, for omissions from quotation, 391

Emanuel, Ezekiel, "Eight Is Too Many: The Case Against Octuplets," 315–18

Emotional appeal, 75

pathos and, 132–37

of resemblance arguments, 270

visual arguments for, 137–39, 165–96

Empathetic listening, 23

Empirical measures, in evaluation arguments, 301–2

"End of Globalization, The? Multinational Corporations Are More Vulnerable Than You Think" (Shuman), 611–14

Enthymeme, 88–89, 95–97

Equivocation fallacy, 432

Ethical arguments, 296–300

conducting, 298–302

consequences-based ethics and, 297, 299–300, 307

critiquing, 306–7

ethical systems and, 297–98

principles-based ethics and, 298–99, 306–7

"Ethics of Eating, The" (Heffern), 514–22

Ethos, 75

credibility and, 131–32

fallacies of, 427–30

forecasting (withholding), 85–86

as persuasive appeal, 129–31

Etymology, 223

Evaluation

of sources, 376, 377

of Web sites, 380–81

Evaluation arguments, 16, 202–3, 289–317

common problems in, 300–302

conducting categorical, 291–96

criteria-match structure of, 290–91

Evaluation arguments *(contd.)*
  ethical arguments as, 296–300
  questioning and critiquing,
    305–6
  writing, 302–5
Evidence
  angle of vision and, 116–17
  effective use of, 109–28
  framing of, 116–17, 119–20,
    121
  gathering of, 122–24
  kinds of, 112–16
  rhetorical understanding of,
    111–22
"Evolutionaries" (Friedman),
  610–11
Examples
  casting doubt on, 149
  for pathos, 133–34
Exclusionary rule, 96
"Executive Summary:
    Biotechnology and Food"
    (American Council on
    Science and Health),
    496–98
Existential quantifiers, 252
Exordium, 62
Explication, 77
Explicit arguments, 4–7
  categorical arguments as,
    209
  narrative for, 135
Exploratory writing, 56–66,
    67–70
  areas of controversy for,
    68
  blind writing, 56
  brainstorming a network of
    related issues, 61–62
  brainstorming for pro and
    con *because* clauses, 60–61
  freewriting, 56
  idea mapping, 57–58
  playing the believing and
    doubting game, 58–60
  rehearsal and, 69–70
Exploring, for starting writing,
    53, 67–70
Extended analogy, 273–74

Facts
  differences between simple
    categorical claims and,
    210–11
  disagreement about, 38
  seeking sources of, 46–47
Fagan, Patrick, "Restoring a
    Culture of Marriage:
    Good News for
    Policymakers from the
    Fragile Families Survey,"
    576–84
Fairness, credibility and, 131–32
Falk, Richard, "New Bush
    Doctrine, The," 730–35
Fallacies. *See also* specific types
  ad hominem, 149, 428–30
  hasty generalization, 110,
    249
  informal, 425–35
  of oversimplified cause, 252
  *post hoc, ergo propter hoc
    fallacy,* 248–49, 432
False authority, appeal to,
    427–28
False dilemma/either-or
    fallacy, 431–32
"False Promise of Being First,
    The" (Cose), 563–64
Fanatics, pseudo-arguments
    by, 79
Faulty analogy fallacy, 434
"Figures," as graphics, 194
Films
  APA style for, 414
  MLA style for, 404
FirstSearch Database, 366
Fisher, John, 161n
Fliers, 180
"Floor Statement on Beohlert-
    Markey CAFE
    Amendment" (Boehlert),
    479–81
Fonts, as design element,
    167
"Food Industry Should
    Modify Its Stance on
    Altered Food" (Harrop),
    511–13

"Ford on Risk" (Wasserman),
    483
Forecasting, ethos and, 85–86
Formal setting, product in, 9
Framing
  of argument, 81–84, 92
  of evidence, 116–17, 119–20,
    121
Frankenstein (Shelley), 23
Freelance writers, as argument
    writers, 50
Freewriting, 56, 359
Friedman, Thomas L.,
    "Evolutionaries," 610–11
"From Cherry Garcia to
    Sweatshop Reform"
    (Stein), 630–31
Fulkerson, Richard, 110–11

Garbarino, James, "Children in
    a Violent World," 667–73
Garrett, Jennifer, "Restoring a
    Culture of Marriage: Good
    News for Policymakers
    from the Fragile Families
    Survey," 576–84
"Gas and Gasbags...or, the
    Open Road and Its
    Enemies" (Payne and
    Katz), 468–71
"Gay Marriage, an
    Oxymoron" (Schiffren),
    590–91
Generalization, 249
  hasty, 110
Genres of argument, 33–36
Genuine argument, vs.
    pseudo-argument, 79–80
Gibaldi, Joseph, 393n
"Gimme an SUV—ASAP:
    Teenagers Are the Next
    Big Market for Sport-
    Utility Vehicles—and the
    Consequences Could Be
    Deadly" (Bradsher),
    471–77
Goodman, Ellen, 153–55,
    241–42

Goods vs. bads, in evaluation arguments, 301
Google, 370, 372
Government officials, as argument writers, 50
Government publications
  APA style for, 414–15
  MLA style for, 404–5
Grammar checkers, 55
Grapes of Wrath (Steinbeck), 4
Graphics
  as design elements, 172
  designing, 194
  graphs as, 191–92
  incorporating into argument, 194–96
  numbering, labeling, and titling, 194–95
  referencing in text, 195–96
  tables as, 189–91
  as visual arguments, 189–94
Graphs, 191–94
  bar graphs, 191–92
  line graphs, 193–94
Grounds
  evidence as, 109
  in Toulmin system, 92–93, 95–97
Groups. *See also* Writing community
  bad habits of, 439
  size of, 440, 441–43
  value of group work for writers, 439–40
"Guantánamo Prisoners Getting What They Deserve" (Krauthammer), 535–37
Guest editorial, policy proposal as, 333
Guilt by association fallacy, 429
Guntzel, Jeff, "Briefing #2: Preemptive Strikes and International Law," 742–43

Harrop, Froma
  "Food Industry Should Modify Its Stance on Altered Food," 511–13

"Questioning the Motives of Home-Schooling Parents," 720–22
Hasty generalization fallacy, 110, 249, 434
Hatch, Orrin G., "Hatch Makes the Case for Regenerative Medicine," 695–99
"Hatch Makes the Case for Regenerative Medicine" (Hatch), 695–99
"Hate Speech Conviction Outlaws Email" (Lake), 641–43
Hayden, Tom, "Pennies an Hour, and No Way Up" (Hayden and Kernaghan), 628–29
Hayes, Richard, "It's Worth Copying Canada's Model for Cloning Legislation," 676–78
"Heart of Cheapness" (Krugman), 631–33
Heffern, Rich, "Ethics of Eating, The," 514–22
"Here Comes the Groom: A (Conservative) Case for Gay Marriage" (Sullivan), 586–90
Hillocks, George Jr., 224n
Hirsh, Peter, 162
Home page. *See* Web pages
Horsey, "SUV and Miata," 484
"Human Cloning" (Brownback), 690–91
Hume, David, 243
Humor, with resistant audience, 160–63
Hyperbole, 161
Hypertext, on Web pages, 186

Ideas
Idea mapping, 57–58
  for causal arguments, 255–56
  for definitional argument, 227–28

for evaluation arguments, 302–3
for proposal arguments, 334
for resemblance arguments, 278
"I'd Like a Tall Decaf Non-Fat Mocha Latte" (Clement), 608
Illustrations. *See* Images
Images. *See also* Visual argument
  as design elements, 172
  visual argument analyzed with, 176–79
Immediate/remote causes, 252–53
Impact, editing for, 55
Implicit arguments, 4–7
  categorical arguments as, 209
  narrative for, 135
Incomplete logic structure, 88–89
Independent redundancy, referencing convention as, 195–96
Inductive methods, for causal arguments, 248–50
Informal discussion, product in, 9
Informal fallacies, 425–35
Informal induction, 248–49
Information question, 77–78
InfoTrac, 366
Inquiry, in reading arguments, 22
Internet
  licensed database vs. free-access portions of, 365
  logic of, 370–71
"Internet's Hate Sites Can Be Hidden, but They Can't Be Ignored (Magid), 643–44
Internet sources
  APA style for, 409, 413–14, 400–8
  MLA style for, 396, 397, 402–3

Interviews
    APA style for, 409
    data from, 113, 123–24
    MLA style for, 397, 404
    in writing community,
        443–44
In-text citation
    in APA style, 406–7
    in MLA style, 394–95
Inventory of issues, 67–68
Investigation, disagreement
    used for, 45–48
"Invoking the Lessons of
    Edison in the Great
    'Frankenfoods' Dispute"
    (Bissell), 502–6
"Iraq War Plans" (Arbeiter),
    281–82
Isaacson, Sam (student),
    "Would Legalization of
    Gay Marriage Be Good
    for the Gay
    Community?", 307–10
Issue question, 77–78
"It's Time to Tackle
    Cyberporn" (Carr),
    645–48
"It's Worth Copying Canada's
    Model for Cloning
    Legislation" (Hayes),
    676–78
"I Want You to Invade Iraq"
    (TomPaine.com), 741

Jacoby, Mary, "Legally, What
    Are the Detainees?",
    533–35
Jaffe, Gregory A., "Lessen the
    Fear of Genetically
    Engineered Crops,"
    510–11
Jefferson, Thomas, 15
Johannessen, Larry R., 224n
Journals, 361, 363
    APA style for, 408, 411–12,
        413
    MLA style for, 399–402
    scholarly, 364

Judeo-Christian ethics, 298
Judges, as argument writers,
    50
Justification
    of claims, 7–9
    for enacting proposal,
        324–25

Kagan, Donald, "Terrorism and
    the Intellectuals," 751–57
Kahn, Elizabeth A., 224n
Kant, Immanuel, 298 , 299
Katz, Diane, "Gas and
    Gasbags...or, the Open
    Road and Its Enemies,"
    468–71
Kennedy, Robert F., Jr., "Better
    Gas Mileage, Greater
    Security," 467–68
Kernaghan, Charles, "Pennies
    an Hour, and No Way
    Up" (Hayden and
    Kernaghan), 628–29
Keyword searching, in online
    database, 367
Kilpatrick, James, 273
Knowledge, credibility and, 131
Krauthammer, Charles
    "Andrea Yates Wasn't
        Responsible for Her
        Crime," 712–13
    "Guantánamo Prisoners
        Getting What They
        Deserve," 535–37
    This Isn't a 'Legal' Matter,
        This Is War," 235–37
Kristof, Nicholas D.
    "All-American Osamas,"
        547–48
    "Let Them Sweat," 626–27
Krugman, Paul
    "Heart of Cheapness,"
        631–33
    "Long Haul, The," 282–84

La Basi, Phil, 161–62
Labels

controlling reader response
    through, 120
    for graphics, 194
Lake, Kenneth, "Hate Speech
    Conviction Outlaws
    Email," 641–43
"Law of inertia," conservatism
    and, 322
Lawyers, as argument writers,
    50
Layout, as design element,
    168–69
Leader, of group, 441
Learning communities, 439
Lectures, addresses, or
    speeches
    APA style for, 409
    MLA style for, 397, 404
Legal briefs, 35
"Legally, What Are the
    Detainees?" (Jacoby),
    533–35
Legislators, as argument
    writers, 50
Leo, John, 244
"Lessen the Fear of
    Genetically Engineered
    Crops" (Jaffe), 510–11
Letters to the editor, 33
"Letter to Senator Tom
    Daschle Opposing a
    Moratorium on Nuclear
    Transplantation"
    (American Society for Cell
    Biology), 693–94
"Let Them Sweat" (Kristof),
    626–27
Levine, Judith, "What Human
    Genetic Modification
    Means for Women,"
    686–90
LexisNexis Academic Universe,
    367
Licensed database, 365–69
"Like Magellan, Grady Has
    Pioneered a Global
    Network Maria Hates
    Computers" (FedEx
    Express), 570

Line graphs, 193–94
Listening
    empathetic, 23
    in Rogerian argument,
    157
Lobbyists, as argument
    writers, 49–50
Lodge, George C., 146
Lofton, Steven K., "Affidavit
    of Steven K. Lofton,"
    591–94
Logic
    because relationships and,
    82–84
    flawed, 425
    formal vs. real-world
    argument, 88
Logical appeal, 75
Logical structure of
    arguments, 76–86
    overview of, 87–90
    power of audience-based
    reasons and, 101–8
    Toulmin system for,
    91–101
Logos, 75, 129, 132
    fallacies of, 430–35
    as logical structure of
    arguments, 76–108
    overview of, 87–90
"Long Haul, The" (Krugman),
    282–84
Looping, to earlier writing
    stages, 55
Lopez, Kathryn Jean
    "Egg Heads," 601–4
    "What Would Mohammed
    [Atta] Do? An Interview
    with Michelle Malkin,"
    544–47

MacCleery, Douglas W., "Aldo
    Leopold's Land Ethic: Is It
    Only Half a Loaf?", 633–36
Magazines, 34, 361, 363
    APA style for, 412
    vs. journals, 364
    MLA style for, 400–401

Magid, Lawrence J.,
    "Internet's Hate Sites Can
    Be Hidden, but They
    Can't Be Ignored, 643–44
Males, Mike, "Debunking the
    10 Worst Myths about
    America's Teens," 664–67
Mapping, idea, 57–58
"Maria Hates Computers"
    (FedEx), 571
Martin, Casey, 237
Masters, Brooke A., "Cracking
    Down on E-Mail
    Harassment," 638–41
Match argument, 226
"Maternal Madness...or Sheer
    Iniquity? Mothers Who
    Kill" (Derbyshire), 709–11
Matthews, Megan (student),
    "Whales Need Silence,"
    280–81
McKibben, Bill, "Driving
    Global Warming," 462–65
Media commentators, as
    argument writers, 50
"Media Photographs of
    Andrea Yates," 705, 706
Message, 75
Metaphors, for pathos, 136
Mill, John Stuart, 248, 297
Miller, Holly M. (student),
    "Causes of Teen Sexual
    Behavior, The," 265–68
Miller, John J., "Our 'Next
    Manifest Destiny'", 735–40
Mitchell, Steven, "Monster's
    Mask," 565–66
Mitigating circumstances, in
    evaluation arguments, 301
MLA (Modern Language
    Association)
    documentation system,
    29–30, 384, 393, 394–405
    in-text citations, 394–95
    parenthetical citations in,
    114–15
    quick reference guide for most
    common citations, 395–97
    Works Cited list, 393, 395

Molloy, Steven, "Organic Food
    Seasoned With Fear,"
    486–88
"Mommy Undearest" (Satel),
    706–8
"Money, Power, Elect: Where's
    the Hip-Hop Agenda?"
    (Cepeda), 550–57
"Monster's Mask" (Mitchell),
    565–66
"Monster That Is High School,
    The" (Daeha Ko), 259–61
Moore, Mike, "Open Societies
    Do Better," 614–19
Moore, Ronald, 161n
MOOs, 36
Moral arguments. *See* Ethical
    arguments
"Moral Authority of the
    UN, The" (Charen),
    743–45
Moral tenets, 298
Multisided argument, 140–41

Name-calling, 429–30
Names, controlling reader
    response through, 120
Narratio, 62
Narrative
    implicit vs. explicit
    argument and, 135
    for pathos, 134–35
Necessary criterion, in
    Aristotelian definition,
    219–20
Necessary/sufficient causes,
    253–54
"Neoliberal World Order, The:
    The View from the
    Highlands of Guatemala"
    (Abell), 619–25
Neutral audience, 144–52
"New Bush Doctrine, The"
    (Falk), 730–35
"New Face of Racial Profiling,
    The: How Terrorism
    Affects the Debate"
    (Colb), 537–41

"New Look, an Old Battle, A"
(Quindlen), 701–3

Newnham, Blaine, 237
"Court Win for Martin Not
a Defeat for Pro Sports,"
238–40

Newspapers
APA style for, 412–13
editorials, 34
MLA style for, 400–401

Niche magazine articles, 34

"Nicholas D. Kristof:
Columnist Endorses Slave
Labor for Children"
(Anderson), 627–28

Non sequitur, 435

Note taking, 374–76
double-entry journal for, 375
for evidence, 124
plagiarism and, 392–93
purposeful, 375

"Notice of Violation: Mock
Ticket"
(StayFreeMagazine.Org),
481

Numbering, of graphics, 194

Occam's Razor, 432–33

"Of Clones and Clowns"
(Weinberg), 678–85

"Oncore, Obscenity, and the
Liquor Control Board"
(Sullivan), 233–35

One-sided argument,
140–41
as appeal to supportive
audience, 143–44

Online catalog, for books, 365

Online database, illustration of
search in, 368–69

Op-ed section, 10, 34

Open-form structure, 85n

"Open Letter to U.S. Senators
on Human Cloning and
Eugenic Engineering"
(Center for Genetics and
Society), 691–92

Open-response questions, 124

"Open Societies Do Better"
(Moore), 614–19

Operational definitions, 222

Opposing views
conceding to, 152
refuting, 145–48
summarizing, 144–45

Oral product, 9

Organizational white papers,
34–35

Original intentions strategy,
223

"Our 'Next Manifest Destiny'"
(Miller), 735–40

Oversimplified cause, fallacy
of, 252

Owen, Wilfred, 5

Paraphrasing
plagiarism and, 392
working into writing, 389

Parenthetical citations
with bibliographies, 393–94
in MLA style, 114–15

Parody, 162–63

Partitio, 62

Pathos, 75
beliefs, emotions, and,
132–37
concrete language for, 133
examples for, 133–34
fallacies of, 426–27
images for emotional
appeals, 137–39
narratives for, 134–35
as persuasive appeal, 129–31
words, metaphors,
analogies, and
connotations for, 136

Payne, Henry
"Cancelled," 482
"Gas and Gasbags...or, the
Open Road and Its
Enemies," 468–71

Pederson, Douglas, 445n

"Pennies an Hour, and No
Way Up" (Hayden and
Kernaghan), 628–29

Periodicals, 360–63, 363

Peroratio, 63

Perrin, Ellen C., "Technical
Report: Coparent or
Second-Parent Adoption
by Same-Sex Parents,"
594–601

Personal correspondence, 33

Personal experience, data
from, 112

Perspective, of photographs, 6

Persuasion, 10–12
audience for, 101, 102–3,
104–7
ethos, pathos, and, 129–31
evidence and, 109–11

Persuasive speeches, classical
argument and, 62

Philips, Gerald, 445n

Photographs. *See also* Visual
argument
compositional features of,
174–79
perspective of, 6

Pie charts, 192–93

Pike, Kenneth, 156n

Pitts, Leonard Jr., "Denzel
Washington Plays a Bad
Guy, and That's Good,"
561–63

Plagiarism, 389, 392–93

"Playing God on No Sleep"
(Quindlen), 717–19

Policy proposal, 320
as guest editorial, 333

Political candidates, as
argument writers, 50

Political cartoon, 184, 457
on education/testing, 314–15
by Horsey, 484
MLA style for, 404
by Van Assche, 284, 285

Posters, 180

Post hoc, ergo propter hoc fallacy,
248–49, 432

Practical proposals, 320

Precedent
arguments by, 275–77
for causal argument, 251–52

Precipitating/contributing
causes, 253
Précis, 27
Prejudice, appeal to, 429
Premise, 81
Presence, in proposal
arguments, 321, 323
"President Bush Delivers
Graduation Speech at
West Point" (Bush,
George W.), 726–30
"President's Narrow Morality,
The" (New York Times),
694–95
Principles-based ethics
argument, 298–99, 306–7
Print sources
APA style for, 408, 413
vs. cyberspace sources, 364
licensed database for,
365–69
MLA style for, 396, 401–2
overview of, 360–63
Pro and con *because* clauses,
brainstorming for, 60–61
Process, argument as, 9–10
Pro-con debate, 4
Product, argument as, 9–10
"Profiling Terrorists" (Clegg),
541–42
"Progressive, The, Interview:
Edward W. Said"
(Barsamian), 747–51
Proofreading, 55
Proposal argument, 16, 202,
203, 319–53
as advocacy posters or
advertisements, 325–26
claim-type strategy for,
327–30
developing, 323–25
justification in, 324–25
overcoming conservatism
with, 322
predicting future
consequences and, 322
presence and, 321, 323
proving that problem exists,
323–24

questioning and critiquing,
337–39
specifics of proposal and,
324
"stock issues" strategy for,
330–32
writing, 332–37
Proposals, 35
evaluating consequences
and, 322
policy, 320
practical, 320
Propositio, 62
Provincialism fallacy, 427
Pseudo-argument, vs. genuine
argument, 79–80
Public affairs advocacy
advertisements, 35,
180–83
Public affairs articles, 34
Public policy, proposal
argument for, 333
Punctuation. *See* specific
punctuation marks
"Punishment That Fits"
(Cottle), 713–16

Qualifier, in Toulmin system,
94, 96, 97
"Questioning the Motives of
Home-Schooling Parents"
(Harrop), 720–22
Questionnaires, data from,
113, 124
Questions, for analysis and
evaluation of arguments,
459–61
Quindlen, Anna
"New Look, an Old Battle,
A," 701–3
"Playing God on No Sleep,"
717–19
Quotation marks, for
quotation within a
quotation, 391
Quotations
brackets for changes in, 391
citation styles for, 389–91

inserted, 390
omissions from, 391
questioning accuracy or
context of, 149
within quotations, 391

"Racial Profiling and the War
on Terrorism" (American
Civil Liberties Union), 543
Radio programs, MLA style
for, 404
Randall, Tom, "CAFE Belongs
in the Graveyard with Its
Victims: We Can Increase
Fuel Economy Without
Costing Lives," 477–79
Rayport, Jeffrey F., 146
Reading, data from, 113–14
Reading arguments
genres of argument, 33–36
identifying claim in, 86
reading as a believer, 23–31
reading as a doubter, 31–32
rhetorical context and, 36–37
sources of disagreement in,
37–45
strategies for, 22–45
suspending doubt and,
30–31
Reality arguments, 202
Real-world arguments, 88
Reason(s), 92, 93
in *because* clauses, 82–84
as core of argument, 75–86
defined, 81
stated, 89, 90, 95–97
Reasonable arguments
claim and, 81–82
genuine vs. pseudo-
arguments and, 79–80
Rebuttal. *See also* Refutation
strategies for, 148–49
in Toulmin system, 94, 96–97
Recorder, as role in group, 442
Red herring fallacy, 427
References
in APA system, 393, 407
to graphics, 195–96

Reference works, specialized dictionaries as, 223
Refutation
  of opposing views, 145–48
  of simple categorical claims, 213
Rehearsal
  exploration and, 69–70
  for starting writing, 53
Relativism, truth and, 13–14
Reliability, of sources, 378
Remote causes, 252–53
Renn, Peter, "Yates Should Be Treated Like Any Other Murderer," 719–20
Repetition, 161
Reportive definition, 222, 223–24
Research
  data from, 113–14
  for starting writing, 53
Research papers
  in APA style, 415, 416–23
  in MLA style, 344–50, 405
  sources for, 357–83
Research question, formulating, 358–59
Resemblance arguments, 16, 202, 269–88
  by analogy, 272–75
  by precedence, 275–77
  Toulmin analysis of, 270–72
  writing, 278
Resemblance search, 329
Resistant audience
  delayed thesis for, 153–56
  humor with, 160–63
  Rogerian argument for, 156–60
"Restoring a Culture of Marriage: Good News for Policymakers from the Fragile Families Survey" (Fagan and Garrett), 576–84
Revision
  of draft for definitional argument, 229–30

of draft for evaluation argument, 304–5
of draft for proposal argument, 335–37
through multiple drafts, 54–55
Rhetoric
  Socrates and, 12–13
  of Web sites, 378–82
Rhetorical context, 36–37, 68
  Aristotelian definitions and, 221–22
Rhetorical reading, of sources, 373–74
Rhetorical triangle, 75, 76
Rhetorical understanding of evidence, 111–22
Riger, Stephanie, 220n
Right Action, 13
Rogerian argument, for resistant audience, 156–60
Rogers, Carl, 23, 156
  faulty analogy and, 434
Rosset, Peter, "Ten Reasons Why Biotechnology Will Not Ensure Food Security, Protect the Environment and Reduce Poverty in the Developing World," 488–96
Rothstein, Richard, 262
  "When Mothers on Welfare Go to Work," 263–64
Rowson, Martin, 183–84
Rule of justice, definitions and, 217–18

Sans serif type, 167
Satel, Sally, "Mommy Undearest," 706–8
Satire, 162–63
"Save the Labels for the Category of Achievement" (Aiken), 564–65
Schiffren, Lisa, "Gay Marriage, an Oxymoron," 590–91

Scholarly articles accessed in print
  APA style for, 411–12
  MLA style for, 399–402
Scholarly books, 363–64
Scholarly journals, 34
Scholars, as argument writers, 50–51
"Science Good, Nature Bad: The Biotech Dogma" (Canizares), 506–9
Scientific experimentation, causal hypotheses and, 249
Search engines, 370, 371–73
Selection, of evidence, 116–17
Self-announcing structure, 84–85, 86
Serif type, 167
Serra, Richard, 161
"Sex, Drugs, Rock 'n' Roll Revisited" (Strasburger), 662–64
Shaping arguments, 62–66
Shared assumptions, lack of, 79
Shelley, Mary, 23
Shuman, Michael, "End of Globalization, The? Multinational Corporations Are More Vulnerable Than You Think," 611–14
Silvers, Anita, 161n
Simple categorical arguments, 200–201, 210–13
Simple categorical claim
  difference from fact, 210–11
  refuting, 213
  supporting, 212–13
  wording of, 211–12
Skeptic, fanatical, 79
Slippery slope fallacy, 433
Small-group communication, 441–43
Social act, writing as, 438
Social context, of arguments, 75
Socrates, 12–13
Sontag, Susan, 270

Sophists, 12
Sound recordings
  APA style for, 414–15
  MLA style for, 404
Sources. *See also* APA
  (American Psychological
  Association)
  documentation system;
  MLA (Modern Language
  Association)
  documentation system
  bias of, 376, 377
  credibility of, 378
  for data, 111
  degree of advocacy of, 377
  differences in kinds of, 360–65
  evaluating, 376, 377
  finding and evaluating,
    357–83
  reliability of, 378
  rhetorical reading of, 373–74
  using for one's own
    purpose, 384–86
  working into one's own
    writing, 388–91
  on World Wide Web, 370–73
Space, as design element,
  168–69
"Spacious Corner Office,
  Redefined" (Siemens
  Corporation), 573
Speaker. *See* Writer/speaker
Specialized dictionaries, 223
Speeches, 9, 36
Sproule, J. Michael, 277n
Staff writers, as argument
  writers, 50
Standards, in evaluation
  arguments, 301
STAR criteria, 110–11
Starting point, 52–53, 67–70, 89
Stated reason, 89, 90, 95–97
"Statement of Conscience"
  (Not in Our Name
  Project), 745–47
"Statement Regarding Hearing
  on Welfare and Marriage
  Issues" (Alternatives to
  Marriage Project), 584–86

Statistical data, 114–15
  questioning, 149
Stein, Danielle, "From Cherry
  Garcia to Sweatshop
  Reform," 630–31
Steinbeck, John, 4
Steinem, Gloria, "Supremacy
  Crimes," 659–62
"Stem Cell Simplicities"
  (Charen), 699–701
Stempel, Vincent F., 209n
Stipulative definition, 222–23,
  224–26
Stirring symbols, appealing to,
  426
"Stock issues" strategy, for
  proposal argument,
  330–32, 334
Strasburger, Victor C., "Sex,
  Drugs, Rock 'n' Roll
  Revisited," 662–64
Straw man fallacy, 430
Style. *See also* specific style
  formats
  editing for, 55
Sufficient causes, 253–54
Sufficient criterion, in
  Aristotelian definition,
  220
Sullivan, Andrew, "Here
  Comes the Groom: A
  (Conservative) Case for
  Gay Marriage," 586–90
Sullivan, Kathy (student), 223
  "Oncore, Obscenity, and the
  Liquor Control Board,"
  233–35
Summarizing, working into
  writing, 388
Summary writing, 63
  of opposing views in
    classical argument, 144–45
  as reading to believe, 27–30
Summers, Dana, 184
Supportive audience, 143–44
Support strategy
  evidence in, 119
  Toulmin's schema for,
    98–101

"Supremacy Crimes"
  (Steinem), 659–62
"Supreme Court's Unfree
  Speech, The" (Amar and
  Calabresi), 350–51
Surveys, data from, 113, 124
"SUV and Miata" (Horsey), 484
Syllogism, valid, 425
Symbols, appealing to, 426
Synopsis, 27

Tables, 189–91
  as graphics, 194
"Taking On Junk E-Mail"
  (New York Times), 650–51
"Technical Report: Coparent
  or Second-Parent
  Adoption by Same-Sex
  Parents" (Perrin), 594–601
"Teenage Terrorism"
  (Wilchins), 657–58
Television programs
  APA style for, 414
  MLA style for, 404
Ten Commandments, 298
"Ten Reasons Why
  Biotechnology Will Not
  Ensure Food Security,
  Protect the Environment
  and Reduce Poverty in
  the Developing World"
  (Altieri and Rosset),
  488–96
Terminology. *See also* Toulmin
  system
  in causal arguments, 252–54
"Terrorism and the
  Intellectuals" (Kagan),
  751–57
"Testimony to the Senate
  Committee on the
  Judiciary" (Ashcroft),
  524–29
Thesis, revealing, 156
Thesis statement. *See also*
  Claims
  working, 83–84
Thinking, dialogue and, 16

"This is Automatic Xerography" (Haloid Xerox), 569
"This Isn't a 'Legal' Matter, This Is War" (Krauthammer), 235–37
Tierney, John, 146–48
Titles, for graphics, 194–95
Toulmin system, 91–101, 147
    for categorical evaluations, 290–91
    for causal arguments, 244–46
    for definitional argument, 215–16, 229
    for precedence arguments, 276–77
    for resemblance arguments, 270–72
    for strategy of support, 98–101
Trade books, 363–64
Truth
    problem of, 12–14
    seeking, 10–12
Truth arguments, 202
Truth of data, denial of, 148
"Try MIT's Magazine of Innovation Technology Review Digital Subscription" (Technology Review), 572
Type, as design element, 166–68

UMI ProQuest Direct, 366
Uncertainty, 45–46
Undecided audience, 144–52
Understatement, 161, 162
Undeveloped analogy, 273
Unfolding structure, 84–85
United Way advocacy ad, 261–62
Universal/existential quantifiers, 252
Universal Truth, 13
Unstated assumption, warrant as, 91–92

URL (uniform resource locator), 372
Utilitarianism, 297

Value-laden arguments, 153
Values
    determining and articulating, 47
    disagreement about, 38–43
    ethical arguments and, 296
    in evaluation and proposal arguments, 202
    selecting and framing data through, 120
    shared with audience, 105–6
Van Assche, Sven, 284, 285
Varner, Lynne K., "Andrea Yates: New Moms and Our Misplaced Priorities," 722–24
Verbal arguments, on Web pages, 186
Viewpoints
    of audience, 140
    audience resistance to your viewpoint, 141–43
    refuting opposing, 145–48
    summarizing opposing, 144–45
    writer's position between, 142–43
Visual argument, 5–6, 36
    analysis using type and spatial elements, 169–71
    analyzed with all design components, 173–74
    analyzed with images, 176–79
    compositional features of photographs and drawings, 174–79
    constructing one's own, 186–89
    controlling reader response through, 120
    design elements in, 166–74

for emotional appeal, 137–39, 165–96
genres of, 179–86
graphics as, 189–94

Walter, Carolyn Calhoun, 224n
Warrant, 63
    assumption as, 8n
    in Toulmin system, 91–92, 95–97
Wasserman, Bill, "Ford on Risk," 483
Web. See Web pages; World Wide Web
Web pages, 186
Web sites, 186, 362–63
    advocacy, 35–36
    APA style for print sources downloaded from database or, 408
    evaluating, 380–81
    MLA citations for nonprint Web sources, 396
    MLA citations for print sources from, 396
    purpose of, 378–79
    rhetoric of, 378–82
    sorting by domain type, 379
    as sources, 360–63, 364
Web sources
    APA style for, 413–14
    MLA style for, 395, 396, 402–3
Weinberg, Robert A., "Of Clones and Clowns," 678–85
"Whales Need Silence" (Matthews), 280–81
"What Human Genetic Modification Means for Women" (Levine), 686–90
"What Is the FDA Trying to Feed Us?" (Sustainusa.org), 513
"What Would Mohammed [Atta] Do? An Interview with Michelle Malkin" (Lopez), 544–47

"When Mothers on Welfare Go to Work" (Rothstein), 262, 263–64

"White Boy Shuffle, The" (Bynoe), 557–61

White papers. *See* Organizational white papers

"Who Needs a Husband" (Colman), 604–5

"Why Not Taiwan?" (Chiang), 231–32

"Why Voluntary Labeling of Genetically Engineered Foods Won't Help Consumers" (Center for Food Safety), 498–502

Wilchins, Riki Anne, "Teenage Terrorism," 657–58

Wilson, Laurel (student), proposal argument by, 339–43

Winkler, Karen, 280n

Wit, 161

"Woman's View of Hip-Hop, A" (Anderson), 310–14

Wood, Julia, 445n

Words, for pathos, 136

Working thesis statement, 83

Works Cited, in MLA system, 393

World Wide Web. *See also* Web sites
browsing, 372–73
logic of Internet and, 370–71
search engines for, 370, 371–73
sources on, 370–73
visual images on, 186

"Would Legalization of Gay Marriage Be Good for the Gay Community?" (Isaacson), 307–10

Writer, professional, 50

Writer-based reasons, 102–3

Writer/speaker, 75
credibility of, 75

Writing. *See also* Writing arguments
analysis of disagreement, 43–45
exploring, researching, rehearsing, and, 53
of first draft, 53–54
revising through multiple drafts, 54–55
as social act, 438
starting point for, 52–53
summary, 27–30
working sources into, 388–91

Writing arguments, 49–71. *See also* Writing
exploratory writing, 56–66
tips for improving, 52–55

Writing assignments
analyzing sources of disagreement, 70
on appealing to audience and accommodating audience views, 164
appeals to *ethos* and *pathos*, 164
argument summary, 70
causal argument, 254–57
classical argument, 125–26
definitional argument, 227–30
evaluation argument, 302–5
exploratory writing, 70–71

microtheme, 125

microtheme using quantitative graphic, 196

poster argument, 196

problem proposal, 71

proposal argument, 332–37

resemblance argument, 278

Writing community, 438–56
classroom debate exercise, 454–56
conflict to consensus in, 438–40
"good argumentative writing" defined by, 445–46
groups of five to seven people in, 441–43
skills and roles in, 440–44
value of group work for, 439–40
working in pairs in, 443–44

Written product, 10

www, use of, 372n. *See also* World Wide Web

Yahoo!, 370, 371, 372

"Yates Should Be Treated Like Any Other Murderer" (Renn), 719–20

Young, Richard, 156n

Zinn, Howard, 277, 279

READINGS AND VISUAL ARGUMENTS

Unless otherwise indicated, the readings or visual arguments appear in the Anthology.

PROFESSIONAL READINGS

Public Affairs or Trade Magazine Articles
Lisa Turner, "Playing with Our Food" (Ch. 2)

Ezekiel J. Emanuel, "Eight Is Too Many" (Ch. 14)

Bill McKibben, "Driving Global Warming"

Henry Payne and Diane Katz, "Gas and Gasbags..."

John Bissell, "Invoking the Lessons of Edison"

Rich Heffern, "The Ethics of Eating"

Raquel Cepeda, "Money, Power, Elect"

Andrew Sullivan, "Here Comes the Groom"

Kathryn Jean Lopez, "Egg Heads"

Robert A. Weinberg, "Of Clones and Clowns"

Judith Levine, "Human Genetic Modification and Women"

John Derbyshire, "Maternal Madness...or Sheer Iniquity?"

Michael Shuman, "The End of Globalization?"

John D. Abell, "The Neoliberal World Order"

John Carr, "It's Time to Tackle Cyberporn"

Gloria Steinem, "Supremacy Crimes"

Richard Falk, "The New Bush Doctrine"

John J. Miller, "Our 'Next Manifest Destiny'"

Articles in Web Magazines
John Bragg, "The American Dream"

Roger Clegg, "Profiling Terrorists"

Sally Satel, "Mommy Undearest"

Michelle Cottle, "Punishment That Fits"

Newspaper Op-Ed Arguments or Magazine Editorials
Ellen Goodman, "Minneapolis Pornography" (Ch. 8)

Charles Krauthammer, "This Isn't a Legal Matter" (Ch. 11)

Blaine Newnham, "Court Win for Martin" (Ch. 11)

Richard Rothstein, "When Mothers on Welfare" (Ch. 12)

Paul Klugman, "The Long Haul" (Ch. 13)

Akhil Reed Amar and Steven G. Calabresi, "The Supreme Court's Unfree Speech" (Ch. 15)

Robert F. Kennedy, Jr., "Better Gas Mileage, Greater Security"

Gregory Jaffe, "Fear of Genetically Engineered Crops"

Froma Harrop, "Food Industry Should Modify Its Stance"

Charles Krauthammer, "Guantánamo Prisoners"

Nicholas D. Kristof, "All-American Osamas"

Leonard Pitts, Jr., "Denzel Washington Plays a Bad Guy"

Lisa Schiffren, "Gay Marriage, an Oxymoron"

Hila Colman, "Who Needs a Husband?"

Ellis Cose, "The False Promise of Being First"

Richard Hayes, "It's Worth Copying Canada's Model"

Mona Charen, "Stem Cell Simplicities"

Anna Quindlen, "A New Look, an Old Battle"

Charles Krauthammer, "Andrea Yates Wasn't Responsible"

Anna Quindlen, "Playing God on No Sleep"

Froma Harrop, "Questioning Home-Schooling Parents"

Lynne K. Varner, "Andrea Yates"

Thomas L. Friedman, "Evolutionaries"

Nicholas D. Kristof, "Let Them Sweat"

Tom Hayden and Charles Kernaghan, "Pennies an Hour"

Paul Krugman, "Heart of Cheapness"

Adam Cohen, "Constitution Does Not Protect Spamming"

Riki Anne Wilchins, "Teenage Terrorism"

Mona Charen, "The Moral Authority of the UN"

Newspaper Editorials
New York Times, "Taking On Junk E-Mail"

New York Times, "China's Cyberspace Censorship"

New York Times, "The President's Narrow Morality"

Letters to the Editor
Jack K.C. Chiang, "Why Not Taiwan?" (Ch. 11)

Jean Arbeiter, "Iraq War Plans" (Ch. 13)

Ron Aiken, "Save the Labels"

Steven Mitchell, "Monster's Mask"

Chris Anderson, "Columnist Endorses Slave Labor"

Jim Conway, "Spam"

Newspaper Feature Articles or News Stories
Keith Bradsher, "Gimme an SUV—ASAP"

Mary Jacoby, "Legally, What Are the Detainees?"

Associated Press, "Anti-Censorship Advocate Locks Horns with Anti-Pornography Filterers"

White Papers or Position Papers on the Web
Council for Biotechnology Information, "Why Biotech Labeling Can Confuse Consumers" (Ch. 2)

Tom Randall, "CAFE Belongs in the Graveyard"

Steven Milloy, "Organic Food Seasoned with Fear"

American Council on Science and Health, "Executive Summary: Biotechnology and Food"

Center for Food Safety, "Why Voluntary Labeling of Genetically Engineered Foods Won't Help"

Kristina Canizares, "Science Good, Nature Bad"

David Cole, "The Ashcroft Raids"

Sherry F. Colb, "The New Face of Racial Profiling"

Senator Sam Brownback, "Human Cloning"

Patrick Fagan and Jennifer Garrett, "Restoring a Culture of Marriage"

Alternatives to Marriage Project, "Welfare and Marriage"

Brooke A. Masters, "Cracking Down on E-Mail Harassment"

Kenneth Lake, "Hate Speech Conviction"

Lawrence J. Magid, "Internet's Hate Sites"

Jeff Guntzel, "IPT Briefing #2"

Articles in Scholarly Journals
Miguel A. Altieri and Peter Rosset, "Ten Reasons Why Biotechnology Will Not Ensure Food Security..."

Yvonne Bynoe, "The White Boy Shuffle"

Ellen C. Perrin, "Adoption by Same-Sex Parents"

Douglas Maccleery, "Aldo Leopold's Land Ethic"